http://weber.u.washington.edu/~chill

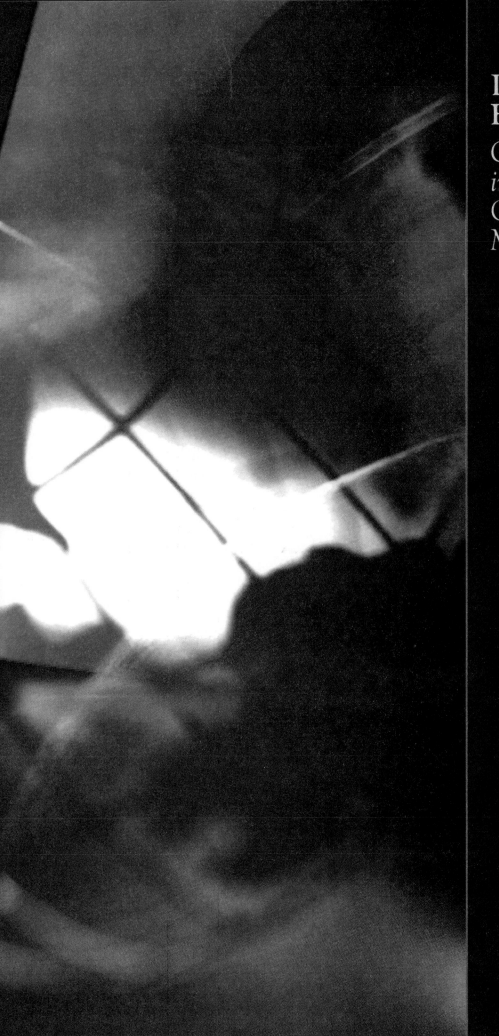

INTERNATIONAL BUSINESS

*Competing
in the
Global
Marketplace*

Irwin Titles in International Business and Economics

SECOND EDITION

INTERNATIONAL BUSINESS
Competing in the Global Marketplace

Charles W. L. Hill

Chicago • Bogotá • Boston • Buenos Aires • Caracas
London • Madrid • Mexico City • Sydney • Toronto

Irwin Book Team

Publisher: Rob Zwettler
Executive editor: Craig S. Beytien
Developmental editor: Jennifer R. Boxell
Marketing manager: Michael Campbell
Project editor: Paula M. Buschman
Production supervisor: Dina L. Genovese
Manager, Prepress Purchasing: Kimberly Meriwether David
Designer: Keith McPherson
Cover and part opening photographer: Jerry Burns
Coordinator, Graphics and Desktop Services: Keri Johnson
Compositor: Times Mirror Higher Education Group, Inc., Imaging Group
Typeface: 10.5/12 Goudy
Printer: Von Hoffmann Press, Inc.

**Times Mirror
Higher Education Group**

Library of Congress Cataloging-in-Publication Data

Hill, Charles W. L.
    International business : competing in the global marketplace /
Charles W. L. Hill. — 2nd ed.
        p.   cm.
    Includes index.
    ISBN 0–256–18876–9
    1. International business enterprises—Management.
2. Competition, International.   I. Title.
HD62.4.H55   1997
658'.049—dc20   96–12058

Printed in the United States of America
1 2 3 4 5 6 7 8 9 0 VH 3 2 1 0 9 8 7 6

For June Hill and Mike Hill,
my parents

ABOUT THE AUTHOR

Charles W. L. Hill is the Hughes M. Blake Professor of International Business at the School of Business, University of Washington. Professor Hill received his Ph.D. in industrial organization economics in 1983 from the University of Manchester's Institute of Science and Technology (UMIST) in Britain. In addition to the University of Washington, he has served on the faculties of UMIST, Texas A&M University, and Michigan State University.

Professor Hill has published over 40 articles in peer-reviewed academic journals. He has also published two college textbooks, one on strategic management and the other on international business. Professor Hill serves on the editorial boards of several academic journals and is currently consulting editor at the *Academy of Management Review*.

Professor Hill teaches in the MBA and executive MBA programs at the University of Washington and has received awards for teaching excellence in both programs. He has also taught on several customized executive programs.

PREFACE

International Business: Competing in the Global Marketplace is intended for the first international business course at either the undergraduate or the M.B.A. level. My goal in writing this book has been to set a new standard for international business textbooks: I have attempted to write a book that (1) is comprehensive and up-to-date, (2) goes beyond an uncritical presentation and shallow explanation of the body of knowledge, (3) maintains a tight, integrated flow between chapters, (4) focuses managerial implications, and (5) makes important theories accessible and interesting to students.

COMPREHENSIVE AND UP-TO-DATE

To be comprehensive, an international business textbook must:

- Explain how and why the world's countries differ.
- Present a thorough review of the economics and politics of international trade and investment.
- Explain the functions and form of the global monetary system.
- Examine the strategies and structures of international businesses.
- Assess the special roles of an international business's various functions.

This textbook does all these things. Too many other textbooks pay scant attention to the strategies and structures of international businesses and to the implications of international business for firms' various functions. This omission is a serious deficiency, because the students in these international business courses will soon be international managers, and they will be expected to understand the implications of international business for their organization's strategy, structure, and functions. This book pays close attention to these issues.

Comprehensiveness and relevance also require coverage of the major theories. Although many international business textbooks do a reasonable job of reviewing long-established theories (e.g., the theory of comparative advantage and Vernon's product life-cycle theory) they tend to ignore such important newer work as:

- The new trade theory and strategic trade policy.
- Michael Porter's theory of the competitive advantage of nations.
- Robert Reich's work on national competitive advantage.

- The new growth theory championed by Paul Romer and Gene Grossman.
- The work of Douglass North and others on national institutional structures and the protection of property rights.
- The market imperfections approach to foreign direct investment that has grown out of Ronald Coase and Oliver Williamson's work on transaction cost economics.
- Bartlett and Ghoshal's research on the transnational corporation.
- The writings of C. K. Prahalad and Gary Hamel on core competencies, global competition, and global strategic alliances.

The failure of many books to discus such work is a serious deficiency considering how influential these theories have become, not just in academic circles, but also in the world at large. A major proponent of strategic trade policy, Laura Tyson served for a time as chairperson of President Clinton's Council of Economic Advisors. Robert Reich served as Secretary of Labor in the Clinton administration. Ronald Coase won the 1992 Nobel Prize in economics, giving the market imperfections approach new respectability. Two years later, Douglass North won the Nobel Prize in economics for his work showing how a nation's economic history influences its contemporary institutions and property rights regime. The work of Bartlett, Ghoshal, Hamel, and Prahalad is having an important impact on business practices.

I have incorporated all relevant state-of-the-art work at the appropriate points in this book. For example, in Chapter 2, "National Differences in Political Economy," reference is made to the new growth theory and the work of North and others on national institutional structures and property rights. In Chapter 4, "International Trade Theory," in addition to such standard theories as the theory of comparative advantage and the Heckscher-Ohlin theory, there is detailed discussion of the new trade theory and Porter's theory of national competitive advantage. In Chapter 5, "The Political Economy of International Trade," the pros and cons of strategic trade policy are discussed. In Chapter 6, "Foreign Direct Investment," the market imperfections approach is reviewed. Chapters 12, 13, and 14, which deal with the strategy and structure of international business, draw extensively on the work of Bartlett, Ghoshal, Hamel, and Prahalad.

In addition to including leading edge theory, in light of the fast-changing nature of the international business environment, every effort is being made to ensure that the book is as up-to-date as possible when it goes to press. A significant amount has happened in the world since the first edition of this book was published in 1993. The Uruguay Round of GATT negotiations was successfully concluded and the World Trade Organization was established. The European Union moved forward with its post-1992 agenda to achieve a closer economic and monetary union, including plans to establish a common currency by the end of the decade. The North American Free Trade Agreement passed into law, and Chile indicated its desire to become the next member of the free trade area. The Asian Pacific Economic Cooperation forum (APEC) emerged as the kernel of a possible future Asia Pacific free trade area. The former Communist states of Eastern Europe and Asia continued on the road to economic and political reform. As they did, the euphoric mood that followed the collapse of communism in 1989 was slowly replaced with a growing sense of realism about the hard path ahead for many of these countries. The global money market continued its meteoric growth. By 1995 over $1 trillion per day was flowing across national borders. The size of such flows fueled concern about the ability of short-term speculative shifts in global capital markets to destabilize the world economy. These fears were fanned by the well-publicized financial problems of a number of organizations that traded derivatives through the global money market, such as Baring's Bank. The World Wide Web emerged from nowhere to become the backbone of an emerging global network for electronic commerce. The world continued to become more global. Several Asian Pacific economies, including most notably China, continued to grow their economies at a rapid rate. New multinationals continued to emerge from developing nations in addition to the world's established industrial powers. And increasingly, the globalization of the world economy impacted on a wide range of firms of all sizes, from the very large to the very small.

Reflecting this rapid pace change, in this edition of the book I have tried to ensure that all material and statistics are as up-to-date as possible as of 1996. However, being absolutely up-to-date is impossible since change is always with us. What is current today may well be outdated tomorrow. Accordingly, I have established a home page for this book on the World Wide Web. From this home page the reader can access regular updates of chapter material and reports on topical developments that are relevant to students of international business. The address for the home page is **http://weber.u.washington.edu/~chill.** I hope readers find this a useful addition to the support material for this book.

BEYOND UNCRITICAL PRESENTATION AND SHALLOW EXPLANATION

Many issues in international business are complex and thus necessitate considerations of pros and cons. To demonstrate this to students, I have adopted a critical approach that presents the arguments for and against economic theories, government policies, business strategies, organizational structures, and so on.

Related to this, I have attempted to explain the complexities of the many theories and phenomena unique to international business so the student might fully comprehend the statements of a theory or the reasons a phenomenon is the way it is. These theories and phenomena are typically explained in more depth in this book than they are in competing textbooks, the rationale being that a shallow explanation is little better than no explanation. In international business, a little knowledge is indeed a dangerous thing.

INTEGRATED PROGRESSION OF TOPICS

Many textbooks lack a tight, integrated flow of topics from chapter to chapter. In this book students are told in Chapter 1 how the book's topics are related to each other. Integration has been achieved by organizing the material so that each chapter builds on the material of the previous ones in a logical fashion.

Part One Chapter 1 provides an overview of the key issues to be addressed and explains the plan of the book.

Part Two Chapters 2 and 3 focus on national differences in political economy and culture. Most international business textbooks place this material at a later point, but I believe it is vital to discuss national differences first. After all, many of the central issues in international trade and investment, the global monetary system, international business strategy and structure, and international business operations arise out of national differences in political economy and culture. To fully understand these issues, students must first appreciate the differences in countries and cultures.

Part Three Chapters 4 through 8 investigate the political economy of international trade and investment. The purpose of this part is to describe and explain the trade and investment environment in which international business occurs.

Part Four Chapters 9 through 11 describe and explain the global monetary system, laying out in detail the monetary framework in which international business transactions are conducted.

Part Five In Chapters 12 through 14 attention shifts from the environment to the firm. Here the book examines the strategies and structures that firms adopt to compete effectively in the international business environment.

Part Six In Chapters 15 through 20 the focus narrows further to investigate business operations. These chapters explain how firms can perform their key functions—manufacturing, marketing, R&D, human resource management, accounting, and finance—in order to compete and succeed in the international business environment.

Throughout the book, the relationship of new material to topics discussed in earlier chapters is pointed out to the students to reinforce their understanding of how the material comprises an integrated whole.

FOCUS ON MANAGERIAL IMPLICATIONS

Many international business textbooks fail to discuss the implications of the various topics for the actual practice of international business. This does not serve the needs of business school students who will soon be practicing managers. Accordingly, the usefulness of this book's material in the practice of international business is discussed explicitly. In particular, at the end of each chapter in Parts Two, Three, and Four—where the focus is on the environment of international business, as opposed to particular firms—there is a section entitled *Implications for Business*. In this section, the managerial implications of the material discussed in the chapter are clearly explained. For example, Chapter 4, "International Trade Theory," ends with a detailed discussion of the various trade theories' implications for international business management.

In addition, each chapter begins with a case that illustrates the relevance of chapter material for the practice of international business. Chapter 2, "National Differences in Political Economy," for example, opens with a case that describes the problems General Electric has had trying to establish profitable operations in Hungary. As the case makes clear, these problems are rooted in the political economy of Hungary and in General Electric's initial failure to fully appreciate the impact that political economy has on business operations. I have also added a closing case to each chapter. These cases are also designed to illustrate the relevance of chapter material for the practice of international business. The closing case to Chapter 2, for example, describes how the political economy of Russia has adversely affected the operations of a General Motors dealership established by U.S. investors in Moscow. Each closing case is followed by a list of discussion questions, which facilitates the use of these cases as a vehicle for in-class case discussion and analysis. Another tool that I have used to focus on managerial implications are "Management Focus" boxes. There is at least one "Management Focus" in each chapter. Like the opening case, the purpose of these boxes is to illustrate the relevance of chapter material for the practice of international business. The

"Management Focus" in Chapter 2, for example, looks at Microsoft's battle against software piracy in China. This box fits in well with a section of the chapter that looks at the protection of intellectual property rights in different countries.

ACCESSIBLE AND INTERESTING

The international business arena is fascinating and exciting, and I have tried to communicate my enthusiasm for it to the student. Learning is easier and better if the subject matter is communicated in an interesting, informative, and accessible manner. One technique I have used to achieve this is weaving interesting anecdotes into the narrative of the text—stories that illustrate theory. The opening cases and focus boxes, of which there are two per chapter, are also used to make the theory being discussed in the text both accessible and interesting. The opening cases and boxed material are not free floating. I continually refer to and utilize opening cases and boxed material in the main body of the text. The idea, once more, is to show students real-world examples of the issues being discussed in the text.

Just how accessible and interesting this book actually is will be revealed by time and student feedback. I am confident, however, that this book is far more accessible to students than its competitors. For those of you who view such a bold claim with skepticism, I urge you to read the sections in Chapter 1 on the globalization of the world economy, the changing nature of international business, and how international business is different.

SUPPORT MATERIAL

Instructor's Manual and Test Bank
The Instructor's Manual, prepared by Duane Helleloid of the University of Washington, contains chapter overviews, teaching suggestions, lecture notes, video notes, and a test bank of multiple-choice, short-answer, and essay questions.

Computest
A computerized version of the test bank is available and allows the instructor to generate random tests and to add his or her own questions.

Teletest
Customized exam preparation is furnished by the publisher.

Transparency Package
A set of full-color transparencies contains key figures and maps from the book.

PowerPoint® Presentation Package
All maps, figures, and selected tables from the text are included in a PowerPoint® presentation package.

Videos
Six videotape segments bring the fast-changing world of international business into the classroom for students. Highlighting major sections of the book, these videos focus on such topics as international trade, entering foreign markets, and Coca-Cola's entry into Japan.

World Wide Web Home Page
This book has a home page on the World Wide Web. From this page you can access monthly updates of chapter material and commentary on topical issues. The page also contains links to a large number of other sites that students of international business might find useful and interesting. The address of the home page is **http://weber.u.washington.edu/~chill.**

World Atlas CD-Rom Package
The World Atlas Cd-Rom is an atlas, almanac, and world fact book that combines state-of-the-art maps of every country in the world with a database of international information. Ask your local representative for information on how to package the CD-Rom with this text.

ACKNOWLEDGMENTS

Numerous people deserve to be thanked for their assistance in preparing this book. First, thank you to all the people at Irwin who have worked with me on this project:

Craig Beytien, Executive Editor
Jennifer Boxell, Development Editor

Paula Buschman, Project Supervisor
Keith McPherson, Designer
Dina Genovese, Production Manager

Second, my thanks go to the reviewers, who provided good feedback that helped shape the book.

Suhail Abboushi, Duquesne University
Poul Andersen, The Aarhus School of Business
David Aviel, California State University
Thomas Bates, San Francisco State University
Thomas Becker, Florida Atlantic University
Dharma de Silva, Wichita State University
Gary Dicer, University of Tennessee
Robert Hopely, University of Massachusetts
C. Thomas Howard, University of Denver
Ben Kedia, Memphis State University
V. H. Kirpalani, Concordia University
Hermann Kopp, Norwegian School of Management
Jeffrey A. Krug, The University of Memphis
Morris Lamberson, University of Central Arkansas
Franz T. Lohrke, Louisiana State University
Kamlesh Mehta, St. Mary's University
Ron Meyer, Erasmus University
Hanne Norreklit, The Aarhus School of Business
Sam C. Okoroafo, University of Toledo
William Renforth, Florida International University
John Stanbury, Indiana University at Kokomo
Peter Wilamoski, Seattle University

Third, I would like to thank my M.B.A. research assistants, Maria Gonzalez and Maureen Kibelsted, for their assistance in preparing this manuscript. And last, but by no means least, I would like to thank my wife, Alexandra, and my daughters, Elizabeth, Charlotte, and Michelle, for their support and, indeed, for giving me the strength to write this book.

Charles W. L. Hill

BRIEF TABLE OF CONTENTS

BRIEF TABLE OF CONTENTS

CONTENTS

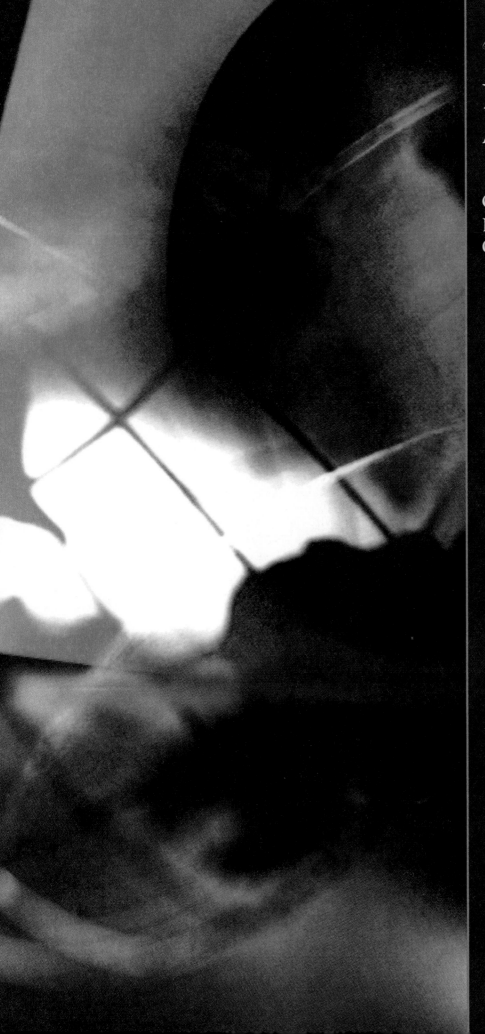

INTRODUCTION AND OVERVIEW

DEUTSCHE TELEKOM POSITIONS ITSELF FOR GLOBAL COMPETITION

Ten years ago most of the world's telecommunications service providers were state-owned corporations that had a monopoly position in their home market and were protected from both domestic and foreign competition by government-imposed regulatory barriers. Now telecommunications service providers around the globe are facing a brave new world characterized by rapidly changing technology, the growth of new telecommunications services such as wireless (cellular phones) and the Internet, the privatization of state-owned telecommunications monopolies, massive deregulation, the emergence of aggressive new competitors, and the decline of barriers to cross-border investment in the telecommunications industry.

Consider Deutsche Telekom (DT), Germany's state-owned telecommunication provider. Long accustomed to an easy life of minimal competition and regulated prices, DT is now facing the prospect of a host of new competitors. For DT the prime event ushering in this brave new world was a 1994 decision by the European Union, of which Germany is a member, to open the markets for telecommunications infrastructure and services in the EU's 15 member states after January 1, 1998. This will effectively end DT's long-standing monopoly. Several new competitors are already gearing up to enter the market. These include British Telecom, which has an alliance with Viag, a diversified German energy company that owns 4,000 km of fiber optic network. This fiber optic network will form the backbone of the BT/Viag system in Germany. Other likely competitors include Thyssen, the Ger-

man steel company, which has formed an alliance with Bell South of America; Veba, a German energy and chemicals group that has an alliance with the British telecommunications company Cable & Wireless; Daimler Benz, which is linked with Northern Telecom of Canada; and AT&T, the largest U.S. carrier, which is in talks with RWE, a large German electric utility that has itself linked with six other German utilities and plans to string fiber optic wires alongside the electric wires in its power transmission network. Many of these new competitors have already indicated they will offer wireless, Internet, and multimedia services in addition to traditional "wireline" telecommunications services.

To prepare Deutsche Telekom for this new competitive environment, the German government has already taken a number of steps, starting with the hiring of Ron Sommer as CEO in 1994. Sommer is a multilingual Israeli who formerly headed Sony's European operations. Hiring Sommer as CEO represents a decisive break with the past. The German government also started privatizing DT in 1996 with the sale of $6.2 billion worth of

shares to investors through offerings on the London, German, and New York stock markets.

Sommer faces a daunting task. Following deregulation and the arrival of new competitors, prices for telecommunication services are expected to plummet by at least half. To ensure that DT remains profitable, Sommer plans to boost employee productivity at DT by 50 percent. To do this he will have to reduce DT's bloated work force by 60,000 jobs, which amounts to about one quarter of DT's total employees. As might be expected, Sommer is encountering stiff resistance from labor unions, which have so far agreed to only 30,000 in job cuts through early retirements, and then only reluctantly.

Sommer has also started to position DT to become a multinational player in this rapidly globalizing industry. The cornerstone of his strategy is an alliance with France Telecom and Sprint, the third largest long-distance carrier in the United States. Deutsche Telekom and France Telecom had already agreed to jointly develop their international network business in December 1993. Under the terms of the expanded alliance, DT and France Telecom proposed to pay $4.2 billion for a 20 percent stake in Sprint. Although the alliance has to be approved by regulators in Europe and the United States, this now seems likely.

The initial target of this alliance, which is known as Phoenix, is the $30 billion market for global networks. This is the business of selling high-speed voice, data, and multimedia communications services to connect the offices and computers of far-flung multinational corporations. Between them Germany and France contain some 14 percent of the world's multinational corporations. A further 29 percent are located in the United States. Thus, in theory at least, the alliance has a potential market of 43 percent of the world's multinational corporations before it starts the harder task of trying to win business from multinationals based in other countries, such as Australia, Japan, and South Korea. Beyond the corporate market, many analysts see the ultimate goal of the alliance as being to help its members become the first truly global telecommunications companies, serving households and businesses in every country in the world.

However, DT, France Telecom, and Sprint are unlikely to have it all their own way. British Telecom and MCI, the second largest U.S. long-distance carrier, have a joint venture known as Concert. AT&T, the largest U.S. long-distance operator, has loose agreements with a number of operators including KDD of Japan and Singapore Telecom, a venture called "World Partners." AT&T has also linked up with Unisource, which is an alliance among the Swedish, Dutch, Italian, and Swiss carriers. Both Concert and the AT&T-led "World Partners/Unisource" ventures are targeting the same corporate market as the Phoenix venture between DT, France Telecom, and Sprint.

Sources: J. Flynn and C. Arnst, "Who'll Be the First Global Phone Company?" *Business Week,* March 27, 1995, pp. 176–80; A. Cane, "Competition Down the Line," *Financial Times,* January 19, 1995, p. 11; K. L. Miller and G. Edmondson, "The Toughest Job in Europe," *Business Week,* October 9, 1995, pp. 52–53; M. Lindeman and A. Cane, "Germany to Allow Strong Competition for Telecoms," *Financial Times,* March 27, 1995, pp. 1, 2.

INTRODUCTION

An **international business** is any firm that engages in international trade or investment. **International trade** occurs when a firm exports goods or services to consumers in another country. **International investment** occurs when a firm invests resources in business activities outside its home country. This book is about the issues confronting managers in an international business, whether that business is small or large. It is about the problems managers face when they try to export to another country or invest in another country. It is about policy issues related to a firm's strategy, organizational structure, manufacturing, materials management, marketing, R&D, human relations, finance, and accounting that arise in an international business. A central presumption of the book is that to understand these issues and problems, one must first understand the economic, political, and cultural environment within which international business occurs. One must understand how countries differ and what these differences imply for an international business. One must understand the political and economic context within which international trade and investment occur. And one must understand the nature of the world monetary system, including, and most important, the mechanisms governing currency exchange rates between countries. Accordingly, the first half of this book deals with the environmental context of international business, while the second half focuses explicitly on the issues and problems confronting managers in an international business.

One point that must be made immediately is that the international business environment is changing rapidly. This was one message contained in the opening case. There we saw how a combination of rapid technological change, privatization, deregulation, and falling barriers to cross-border investment are fundamentally changing the nature of the telecommunications industry. What was once an industry segmented into self-contained national markets, each dominated by a monopoly provider whose position was protected by regulations, is now becoming a much more competitive and global industry in which telecommunications providers are aggressively forming alliances, entering each other's markets, and competing head to head. The likely end result of this process will be a more competitive global marketplace in which only the most efficient telecommunication service providers survive. Ron Sommer, the CEO of Deutsche Telekom, the telecommunications firm profiled in the opening case, clearly understands this, which is why he is trying to cut the work force of Deutsche Telekom by over 25 percent.

What is occurring in the telecommunications industry is also occurring in a vast array of other industries. From automobiles to steel, from banking to insurance, and from airlines to shipping, the story is basically the same. We are living through an era of enormous transformation in the nature of competition. In industry after industry firms that once dominated their national markets, and were protected from foreign competition by barriers to trade and investment, are now finding themselves to be just another player in a larger and much more competitive global marketplace. Like Deutsche Telekom they are having to go through difficult changes to position themselves to survive.

In the next section we discuss the reasons for this change when we consider the globalization of the world economy. In subsequent chapters of the first half of the book, we elaborate on the nature and implications of the forces for change in the world economy. For now, note that changes in the international business environment are forcing many firms to think of the world as one vast market. At the same time, despite all the talk in the popular press about the globalization of world markets, the "global village," the "global factory," and "global products" (e.g., Coca-Cola, Levi's jeans, and Sony Walkmans), national differences still exist and have a profound effect on the way business is conducted in different nations. The tension between the need to view the world as a single market and the need to be responsive to differences between countries is fundamental in international business. As a theme, it will recur often throughout this book, particularly in the second half of the book when we look at issues pertaining to managing an international business.

The remainder of this chapter is divided into four sections. The first section discusses the forces for change in the world economy. The second section discusses the changing nature of international business. The third section outlines how international business differs from business in a purely domestic context. The fourth section provides an outline of the chapters that make up this book and explains how the topics in each chapter relate to an integrated whole.

❧ THE GLOBALIZATION OF THE WORLD ECONOMY

A popular feeling is that something fundamental is happening in the world economy. The term *global shift* has been coined by one author to capture the essence of the change.[1] We seem to be witnessing the globalization of markets and production. With regard to the *globalization of markets*, it has been argued that we are moving away from an economic system in which national markets are distinct entities, isolated from each other by trade barriers and barriers of distance, time, and culture, and toward a system in which national markets are merging into one huge global marketplace. According to this view, the tastes and preferences of consumers in different nations are beginning to converge on some global norm. Thus, in many industries it is no longer meaningful to talk about the "German market," "the American market," or the "Japanese market"; there is only the "global market." The global acceptance of Coca-Cola, Levi's jeans, Sony Walkmans, and McDonald's hamburgers exemplifies this trend.[2]

Companies such as Coca-Cola and McDonald's are more than just benefactors of this trend; they are also instrumental in facilitating it. By offering a standardized product worldwide, Coca-Cola and McDonald's are helping to *create* a global market. Nor does a company have to be the size of these two multinational giants to facilitate, and benefit from, the globalization of markets. For example, the "Management Focus" describes how a small British enterprise, Harry Ramsden's, a fish 'n' chip establishment with annual sales of £10 million ($16 million), is trying to capitalize on the Japanese love of high-fat foreign food.

Despite the global prevalence of Coca-Cola, Levi's blue jeans, McDonald's hamburgers, and (perhaps one day) Harry Ramsden's fish 'n' chips, it is important not to push too far the view that national markets are giving way to the global market. As we shall see in later chapters, very significant differences in consumer tastes and preferences between national markets still remain in many industries. These differences frequently require that marketing strategies and product features be customized to local conditions. Notwithstanding this, however, there is no doubt that there are more global markets today than at any previous period in history.

---

[1]P. Dicken, *Global Shift* (New York: Guilford Press, 1992).
[2]T. Levitt, "The Globalization of Markets," *Harvard Business Review*, May–June 1983, pp. 92–102.

Management Focus
Harry Ramsden's Plans to get the World Hooked on Fish and Chips

Deep-fried fish and chips is perennially popular food in England. Harry Ramsden's, whose first fish and chip shop was located in Guiseley, Yorkshire, has long been considered one of the premium fish and chip "shops" in England, and it is one of the few to open at multiple locations. In 1994 the company had eight branches in Britain, with four more scheduled for opening, and one in Dublin. Its busiest U.K. location, the resort town of Blackpool, generates annual sales of £1.5 million ($2.3 million). Harry Ramsden's managers, however, are not satisfied with this success, they want to turn Harry Ramsden's into a global enterprise.

To this end, in 1992 the company opened its first international operation in Hong Kong. According to finance director Richard Taylor, "We marketed the product as Britain's fast food, and it's proved extremely successful." Indeed, within two years the Hong Kong venture was already generating annual sales equivalent to its Blackpool operations. Moreover, while half of the initial clientele in Hong Kong were British expatriates, now more than 80 percent are ethnic Chinese. Harry Ramsden's seems to be well on the way to changing the tastes and preferences of Hong Kong Chinese.

Emboldened by this success, Harry Ramsden's has plans to open additional branches in Singapore and Melbourne, Australia, but its biggest target market is Japan. To get a feel for the market, in the spring of 1994 Harry Ramsden's set up a temporary store in Tokyo's Yoyagi Park. The shop, which served more than 500 portions of fish and chips covered in salt and vinegar, was an experiment to see whether the Japanese would take to the product. Despite the traditional aversion of Japanese consumers to greasy food, apparently they did. According to Katie Garritt, who cooked the fish and chips over the 12 days the shop was open: "Sometimes one member of the family would try it, and then all the others would buy portions." Now Harry Ramsden's is looking for a Japanese partner to establish a joint venture in Japan, and it hopes to open its first stores in 1995.

As for the future, according to Richard Taylor, "We want Harry Ramsden's to become a global brand. In the short term the greatest returns will be in the U.K. But it would be a mistake to saturate the U.K. and then turn to the rest of the world. We'd probably come a cropper when we internationalized. We need experience now."

Source: P. Abrahams, "Getting Hooked on Fish and Chips in Japan," *Financial Times*, May 17, 1994.

As for the *globalization of production*, individual firms are dispersing parts of their production process to various locations around the globe to take advantage of national differences in the cost and quality of production factors (e.g., labor, energy, land, capital). As a consequence, it is no longer always meaningful to talk about "American products," "German products," or "Japanese products." A few years ago Robert Reich, who is secretary of labor under U.S. President Bill Clinton, came up with a now famous example of how meaningless it can be to talk about national products.[3] Reich's example was the Pontiac Le Mans, which is commonly perceived as an "American product" because of its General Motors nameplate. However, Reich pointed out that based on a comparison of national differences in production costs, GM had dispersed many of the Le Mans production activities to other countries. As a result, of the $20,000 paid to GM for a Le Mans, Reich maintained:

- $6,000 went to South Korea, where the Le Mans was assembled.
- $3,500 went to Japan for advanced components (engines, transaxles, and electronics).

[3] R. B. Reich, *The Work of Nations* (New York: Alfred A. Knopf, 1991).

- $1,500 went to Germany, where the Le Mans was designed.
- $800 went to Taiwan, Singapore, and Japan for small components.
- $500 went to Great Britain for advertising and marketing services.
- About $100 went to Ireland for data processing services.
- The remaining $7,600 went to GM and to the lawyers, bankers, and insurance agents that GM uses in the United States.

So is the Le Mans an "American product"? According to Reich it is not; but neither is it a "Korean product," a "Japanese product," nor a "German product." Like an increasing number of the products we buy today, it is, in fact, a global product.

GM is hardly alone in establishing a global web of production activities. Building the Boeing Company's new commercial jet aircraft, the 777, involves 132,500 engineered parts that are produced around the world by 545 different suppliers. For example, eight Japanese suppliers make parts of the fuselage, doors, and wings; a supplier in Singapore makes the doors for the nose landing gear; and three suppliers in Italy manufacture wing flaps. Part of Boeing's rationale for outsourcing so much production to foreign suppliers is that these various suppliers are the best in the world at performing their particular activity. Therefore, the result of having foreign suppliers build specific parts is a better final product.[4]

Nor is the global dispersal of productive activities limited to giants like Boeing and GM. Many much smaller companies are also getting into the act. Consider Swan Optical, a U.S.-based manufacturer and distributor of eyewear. With sales revenues only in the $20 to $30 million range, Swan is hardly a giant, yet Swan manufactures its eyewear in low-cost factories in Hong Kong and China that it jointly owns with a Hong Kong-based partner. Swan also has a minority stake in eyewear design houses in Japan, France, and Italy. Swan has dispersed its manufacturing and design processes to different locations around the world to take advantage of the favorable skill base and cost structure found in foreign countries. Foreign investments in Hong Kong and then China have helped Swan to lower its cost structure, while investments in Japan, France, and Italy have helped it to produce designer eyewear for which it can charge a premium price. The critical point is that by dispersing its manufacturing and design activities in this manner, Swan has established a competitive advantage for itself in the global marketplace for eyewear, just as GM and Boeing have tried to do by dispersing some activities to other countries.[5]

Two factors seem to underlie the trend toward globalization of markets and production. The first is the decline in barriers to the free flow of goods, services, and capital that has occurred since the end of World War II. The second factor is the dramatic developments in communication, information, and transportation technologies in the same period.

Declining Trade and Investment Barriers

During the 1920s and 30s many nations erected formidable barriers to international trade and investment. Many of these barriers took the form of high tariffs on imports of manufactured goods. The typical aim of such tariffs was to protect domestic industries from foreign competition. One consequence, however, was "beggar thy neighbor" retaliatory trade policies; countries progressively raised trade barriers against each other. Ultimately, this depressed world demand and contributed to the Great Depression of the 1930s.

Having learned from this experience, after World War II, the advanced industrial nations of the West—under U.S. leadership—committed themselves to the goal of removing barriers to the free flow of goods, services, and capital between nations.[6] The goal of removing barriers to the free flow of goods was enshrined in the treaty known as the **General Agreement on Tariffs and Trade** (GATT). Under the umbrella of

[4]I. Metthee, "Playing a Large Part," *Seattle-Post Intelligencer*, April 9, 1994, p. 13.
[5]C. S. Tranger, "Enter the Mini-Multinational," *Northeast International Business*, March 1989, pp. 13–14.
[6]J. Bhagwati, *Protectionism* (Cambridge, MA: MIT Press, 1989).

	1913	1950	1990	2000*
France	21%	18%	5.9%	3.9%
Germany	20	26	5.9	3.9
Italy	18	25	5.9	3.9
Japan	30	—	5.3	3.9
Holland	5	11	5.9	3.9
Sweden	20	9	4.4	3.9
Britain	—	23	5.9	3.9
United States	44	14	4.8	3.9

*Rates for 2000 based on full implementation of Uruguay agreement.
Source: "Who Wants to Be a Giant?" The Economist, June 24, 1995, pp. 3–4.

GATT, there have been eight rounds of negotiations between member states, which now number over 120, designed to lower barriers to the free flow of goods and services. The most recent round of negotiations—known as the Uruguay Round—was completed in December 1993. The Uruguay Round further reduced trade barriers; extended GATT to cover services as well as manufactured goods; provided enhanced protection for patents, trademarks, and copyrights; and established a **World Trade Organization** to police the international trading system.[7]

Table 1.1 summarizes the impact of GATT agreements on average tariff rates for manufactured goods. As can be seen, average tariff rates have fallen significantly since 1950 and under the Uruguay agreement, they will approach 3.9 percent by 2000. In addition to falling trade barriers, many countries have also been progressively removing restrictions on capital inflows and outflows. During 1991 alone, for example, 34 countries, rich and poor, made 82 changes to their laws governing foreign direct investment. All but two of those changes made the laws less restrictive, thereby encouraging both outward investment by domestic firms and inward investment by foreign firms.[8]

These trends facilitate both the globalization of markets and the globalization of production. Increasingly, the lowering of trade barriers enables firms to view the world, rather than a single country, as their market. The lowering of trade barriers also enables firms to base individual production activities at the optimal location for that activity, serving the world market from that location. Thus a firm might design a product in one country, produce component parts in two other countries, assemble the product in yet another country, and then export the finished product around the world.

There is plenty of evidence that the lowering of trade barriers has facilitated the globalization of production. For example, over the last decade the volume of world trade grew faster than the volume of world output. Between 1980 and 1994, total world output grew by about 40 percent, while world trade grew by more than 70 percent (see Figure 1.1). These figures imply that more and more firms are doing what GM does with the Pontiac Le Mans and dispersing manufacturing, marketing, and design activities around the globe to the optimal location for each activity.

Consistent with this trend, the evidence suggests that foreign direct investment (FDI) is playing an increasing role in the global economy as firms ranging in size from General Motors to Harry Ramsden's increase their cross-border investments (see the "Management Focus"). Between 1985 and 1994 the total annual flow of FDI from all countries increased nearly fourfold to $204 billion, more than twice as fast as the growth rate in world trade.[9] The major investors have been U.S., Japanese, and Western European companies investing in Europe, Asia (particularly China), and the United States.[10] For example, Japanese auto companies have been investing rapidly in Asian, European, and U.S.-based auto assembly operations.

---

[7]F. Williams, "Trade Round Like This May Never Be Seen Again," *Financial Times*, April 15, 1994, p. 8.
[8]"Another World," *The Economist*, September 19, 1992, pp. 15–18.
[9]G. de Jonquieres, "Rocky Road to Liberalization," *Financial Times*, April 10, 1995, p. 15.
[10]United Nations, *World Investment Report*, 1994.

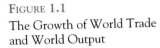

FIGURE 1.1
The Growth of World Trade
and World Output

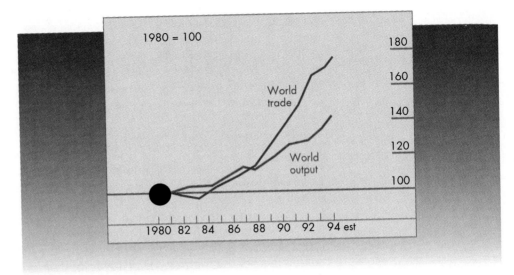

Source: F. Williams, "World Trade in Goods Jumps 9%," Financial Times, *April 4, 1995, p. 22.*

Finally, the globalization of markets and production and the resulting growth of world trade, foreign direct investment, and imports all imply that firms around the globe are finding their home markets under attack from foreign competitors. This is true in Japan, where Kodak has taken market share in the film industry away from Fuji in recent years; in the United States where Japanese automobile firms have taken market share away from GM, Ford, and Chrysler; and in Western Europe where the once-dominant Dutch company, Philips, has seen its market share in the consumer electronics industry taken by Japan's JVC, Matsushita, and Sony. The growing integration of the world economy into a single, huge marketplace is increasing the intensity of competition in a wide range of manufacturing and service industries.

Having said all of this, it would be a mistake to take declining trade barriers for granted. As we shall see in the following chapters, demands for "protection" from foreign competitors are still often heard in the United States and elsewhere. Although a return to the "beggar thy neighbor" trade policies of the 1920s and 30s is unlikely, it is not clear whether the political majority in the industrialized world favors further reductions in trade barriers. If trade barriers decline no further, at least for the time being, a temporary limit may have been reached in the globalization of both markets and production.

The Role of Technological Change

Whereas the lowering of trade barriers made globalization of markets and production a theoretical possibility, technological change made it a tangible reality. Since the end of World War II, there have been major advances in communications, information processing, and transportation technology including, most recently, the explosive emergence of the Internet and World Wide Web.

Microprocessors and telecommunications

Perhaps the single most important innovation has been development of the microprocessor, which enabled the explosive growth of high-power, low-cost computing, vastly increasing the amount of information that can be processed by individuals and firms. Moreover, the microprocessor underlies many recent advances in telecommunications technology. Over the last 30 years global communications have been revolutionized by developments in satellite, optical fiber, and wireless technology, and now the Internet and the World Wide Web. All these technologies rely on the microprocessor to encode, transmit, and decode the vast amount of information that flows along these electronic highways. Moreover, the cost of microprocessors continues to fall, while their power increases (a phenomenon known as **Moore's Law,** which predicts that the power of microprocessor technology doubles and its costs of production fall in half every 18 months).[11] As this happens, so the costs of global communications are plummeting, which is lowering the costs of coordinating and controlling a global organization. For example, between 1973 and 1993 the cost of a three-minute phone call from London to New York fell from $13.73 to $1.78.[12] Recent estimates suggest the cost of servicing a long-distance call will fall to 5 cents per minute by 2000, down from 20 cents per minute today.[13]

The Internet and World Wide Web

The phenomenal recent growth of the Internet and the associated World Wide Web (which utilizes the Internet to communicate between World Wide Web sites) is the latest expression of this development. In 1990 fewer than 1 million users were connected to the Internet. By mid-1995 the Internet had about 40 million users, connected more than 40,000 individual networks within organizations and almost 5 million host computers (this book also has its own World Wide Web site—the address is http://weber.u.washington.edu/~chill). By the year 2000 there may be well over 100 million users of the Internet. As of 1995 over half of all U.S. publicly traded companies with sales in excess of $1.5 billion had a presence on the Internet, and new commercial sites were being added at a rate of over 100 percent per annum.[14]

The Internet and World Wide Web (WWW) promise to develop into the information backbone of tomorrow's global economy. By the year 2000 it is likely that not only will voice, data, and real-time video communication such as videoconferencing be transmitted through the WWW, but also a vast array of commercial transactions may be executed via the WWW. Included in these will be many cross-border transactions. For example, an individual in India that wishes to purchase some software from Microsoft in the United States may be able to do this by going to Microsoft's home page on the web and purchasing the software using a credit card. The software will then be downloaded in a matter of minutes directly onto her computer via the Internet. More generally, across a whole range of markets the WWW holds the promise of being able to bring together buyers and sellers who are scattered around the globe.

For illustration, imagine a construction company in Brazil that wishes to purchase a bulldozer. Using a WWW search engine (for example, "yahoo"—the address is www.yahoo.com) the purchasing manager of the Brazilian firm may be able to quickly identify every firm in the world that manufactures bulldozers. He may find that firms in Japan, South Korea, Germany, Sweden, China, and the United States are all in this business. He will be able to quickly visit their WWW sites and download information on product specifications and prices. He may find two products he likes—one produced by a German firm and the other by a Chinese firm. He may then be able to talk directly to salespeople at these firms using a real-time videoconferencing link. On the basis of these discussions and the ensuing negotiations, all of which will be conducted via videoconferencing and all of which will occur in English (the probable business language of the 21st century) he may decide to purchase the bulldozer from the Chinese firm. The transaction may then be executed over the WWW—with both money and all the documents required for exporting from China to Brazil being transmitted over the Web.

This example is hardly far-fetched; the technology required for this to occur already exists and is being used by many organizations. The important point to understand is that the WWW will do two things; it will further lower the costs of global communications, and it will facilitate the creation of a truly global electronic marketplace for all kinds of goods and services, such as the software and bulldozers used

---

[11]Moore's Law is named after Intel founder Gorden Moore.

[12]A. Adonis, "Lines Open for the Global Village," *Financial Times,* September 17, 1994, p. 8.

[13]A. Cane, "Competition Down the Line," *Financial Times,* January 19, 1995, p. 11.

[14]P. Taylor, "Revenues of $10 Billion," *Financial Times,* June 15, 1995, p. 4.

FIGURE 1.2   The Shrinking Globe

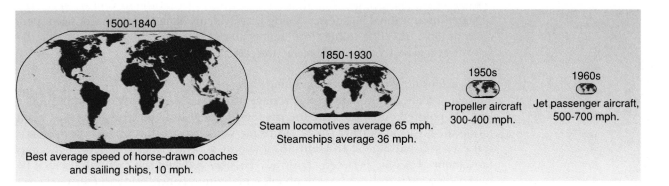

1500-1840

1850-1930

1950s
Propeller aircraft
300-400 mph.

1960s
Jet passenger aircraft,
500-700 mph.

Steam locomotives average 65 mph.
Steamships average 36 mph.

Best average speed of horse-drawn coaches
and sailing ships, 10 mph.

Source: P. Dicken, Global Shift *(New York: Guilford Press, 1992), p. 104.*

in the above examples. By doing these things, the WWW makes it much easier for firms of all sizes to enter the global marketplace.

Transportation technology

In addition to these developments, several major innovations in transportation technology have occurred since World War II. In economic terms, the most important are probably development of commercial jet aircraft and superfreighters and the introduction of containerization, which greatly simplifies transshipment from one mode of transport to another. Most significant is the advent of commercial jet travel, which by reducing the time needed to get from one location to another has effectively shrunk the globe (see Figure 1.2). As a consequence of jet travel, New York is now "closer" to Tokyo than it was to Philadelphia in the Colonial days.

Implications for the globalization of production

As a result of the technological innovations discussed above, the real costs of information processing and communication have fallen dramatically in the last two decades. This has made it possible for a firm to manage a globally dispersed production system. Indeed, a worldwide communications network has become essential for many international businesses. For example, Texas Instruments (TI), the U.S. electronics firm, has approximately 50 plants in 19 countries. A satellite-based communications system allows TI to coordinate, on a global scale, its production planning, cost accounting, financial planning, marketing, customer service, and personnel management. The system consists of more than 300 remote job-entry terminals, 8,000 inquiry terminals, and 140 mainframe computers. The system enables managers of TI's worldwide operations to send vast amounts of information to each other instantaneously and to effect tight coordination between the firm's different plants and activities.[15]

A similar example is that of another U.S. electronics firm, Hewlett-Packard, which uses satellite communications and information processing technologies to link its worldwide operations. Hewlett-Packard has new-product development teams composed of individuals based in different countries (e.g., Japan, the United States, Great Britain, and Germany). When developing new products, these individuals use videoconferencing technologies to meet on a weekly basis. They also communicate with each other daily via telephone, electronic mail, and fax. Communication technologies have enabled Hewlett-Packard to increase the integration of its globally dispersed operations and to reduce the time needed for developing new products.[16]

---

[15]Dicken, *Global Shift.*
[16]Interviews with Hewlett-Packard personnel by the author.

In addition to communications and information processing technology, the development of commercial jet aircraft has helped knit together the worldwide operations of many international businesses. Using jet travel, an American manager need spend a day at most traveling to her firm's European or Asian operations. This enables her to oversee a globally dispersed production system.

Implications for the globalization of markets

The same technological innovations have also facilitated the globalization of markets. As pointed out above, the Internet and WWW hold out the promise of facilitating the creation of truly global electronic marketplaces for products as diverse as software and bulldozers. In addition, low-cost jet travel has resulted in the mass movement of people between countries. This has reduced the cultural distance between countries and is bringing about some convergence of consumer tastes and preferences. At the same time, global communications networks and global media are creating a worldwide culture. U.S. television networks such as CNN, MTV, and HBO are now received in many countries around the world, and Hollywood films are shown the world over. In any society the media are primary conveyors of culture; as global media develop, we must expect the evolution of something akin to a global culture. A logical result of this evolution is the emergence of global markets for consumer products. The first signs that this is occurring are already apparent. It is now as easy to find a McDonald's restaurant in Tokyo as it is in New York, to buy a Sony Walkman in Rio as it is in Berlin, and to buy Levi's jeans in Paris as it is in San Francisco.

On the other hand, we must be careful not to overemphasize this trend. While modern communications and transport technologies are ushering in the "global village," very significant differences remain among countries in culture, consumer preferences, and the ways in which business is conducted. As we shall see in subsequent chapters, a firm that ignores these differences does so at its peril.

Implications for Management

The trend toward globalization of production and markets has several important implications for the manager of an international business. The manager of today's firm operates in an environment that offers more opportunities but one that is more complex and competitive than the one her predecessor faced a generation ago. Opportunities are greater because the movement toward free trade has opened many formerly protected national markets and because new technologies such as the WWW are helping to create global electronic marketplaces. Consequently, the potential for export, for making direct investments overseas, and for dispersing productive activities to the optimal locations around the globe are now all greater than ever. The environment is more complex because today's manager often must meet the challenges of doing business in countries with radically different cultures and of coordinating globally dispersed operations. The environment is more competitive because, in addition to domestic competitors, the modern manager must also deal with cost-efficient foreign competitors. It is these management issues that we will address throughout this book.

❧ THE CHANGING NATURE OF INTERNATIONAL BUSINESS

Hand in hand with the trends toward globalization of markets and of production, there has been a fairly dramatic change in the nature of international business over the last 30 years or so. As late as the 1960s, four stylized facts described much of international business. The first fact was U.S. dominance in the world economy and world trade picture. The second fact was U.S. dominance in the world foreign direct investment picture. Related to this, the third fact was the dominance of large, multinational U.S. firms on the international business scene. The fourth fact was that roughly half the globe—the centrally planned economies of the Communist world—

TABLE 1.2
The Changing Pattern of
World Output and Trade

Country	Share of World Output 1963	Share of World Output 1993	Share of World Exports 1993
United States	40.3%	25.6%	11.8%
Japan	5.5	15.9	9.5
Germany*	9.7	7.8	12.0
France	6.3	5.7	6.5
Great Britain	6.5	3.9	5.3
Italy	3.4	5.3	5.0
Canada	3	2.1	3.7

*1963 figure for Germany refers to the former West Germany.
Source: World Bank, World Development Report (New York: Oxford University Press, various issues).

was off-limits to Western international businesses. As will be explained below, all four of these stylized facts either have changed or are now changing rapidly.

The Changing World Output and World Trade Picture

In the early 1960s the United States was still by far the world's dominant industrial power. In 1963, for example, the United States accounted for 40.3 percent of world manufacturing output. By 1993 the United States accounted for only 25.6 percent (see Table 1.2). This decline in the U.S. position was not an absolute decline, since the U.S. economy grew at a relatively robust average annual rate of 2.8 percent in the 1963–93 time period. Rather, it was a relative decline, reflecting the faster economic growth of several other economies, most notably that of Japan. As can be seen in Table 1.2, in the 1963–93 time period, Japan's share of world manufacturing output increased from 5.5 percent to 15.9 percent. Other countries that markedly increased their share of world output included South Korea and Taiwan.

Reflecting the relative decline in U.S. dominance, by the end of the 1980s its position as the world's leading exporter was threatened. Over the last 30 years U.S. dominance in export markets has waned as Japan, Germany, and a number of newly industrialized countries such as South Korea and Taiwan have taken a larger share of world exports. During the 1960s the United States routinely accounted for 20 percent of world exports of manufactured goods. Table 1.2 also reports manufacturing exports as a percentage of the world total in 1993. As can be seen, the U.S. share of world exports of manufactured goods had slipped to 11.8 percent by 1993, slightly behind the 12 percent share enjoyed by Germany. Japan, with 9.5 percent of world exports, was also closing in on the United States.

Given the rapid economic growth rates now being experienced by countries such as China, Thailand, and Indonesia, further *relative* decline in the share of world output and world exports accounted for by the United States seems likely. By itself, however, this is not necessarily a bad thing. The relative decline of the United States reflects the growing industrialization of the world economy, as opposed to any absolute decline in the health of the U.S. economy.

If we look 20 years into the future, most forecasts now predict a rapid rise in the share of world output accounted for by developing nations such as China, India, Indonesia, Thailand, and South Korea, and a commensurate decline in the share enjoyed by rich industrialized countries such as Britain, Japan, and the United States. The World Bank, for example, forecasts that the world's developing nations will grow their economic output by 4.8 percent per annum between 1994 and 2003, while the rich industrialized states will enjoy an annual average growth rate of 2.7 percent per annum.[17] Moreover, the World Bank sees even higher growth rates being attained by the developing nations of East and South Asia. East Asia, which includes China and South Korea, is forecasted to increase economic output at an annual rate of 7.6 percent between 1994 and 2003, while the forecasted growth rate for South Asia, which includes India, is 5.3 percent per annum.

---

[17]Data reported in The Economist. See "War of the Worlds," The Economist, October 1, 1994, pp. 3–4.

FIGURE 1.3

The Changing Nature of
Global Output

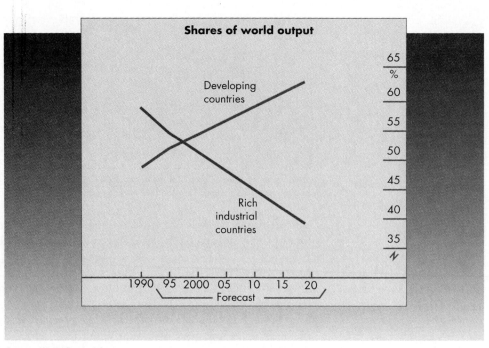

Source: World Bank data.

If these growth rates are attained and sustained over the next quarter of a century, then we will witness a dramatic shift in the economic geography of the world. World Bank forecasts suggest that by 2020 the Chinese economy could be 40 percent larger than that of the United States, while the economy of India will be larger than that of Germany. Figure 1.3 illustrates the likely share of world output enjoyed by today's rich industrialized and developing nations by 2020 if current World Bank forecasts hold true. Today's developing nations may account for over 60 percent of world economic activity by 2020, while today's rich nations, which currently account for over 55 percent of world economic activity, may account for only about 38 percent by 2020.[18] For international businesses the implications of this changing economic geography are clear; many of tomorrow's economic opportunities may be found in the developing nations of the world, and many of tomorrow's most capable competitors will probably also emerge from these regions.

The Changing Foreign Direct Investment Picture

Reflecting the dominance of the United States in the global economy, U.S. firms accounted for 66.3 percent of worldwide foreign direct investment flows in the 1960s. British firms were second, accounting for 10.5 percent, while Japanese firms were a distant eighth, with only 2 percent. The dominance of U.S. firms was so great that in Europe, books were written about the economic threat posed to Europe by U.S. corporations.[19] Several European governments, most notably that of France, talked of limiting inward investment by U.S. firms in their economies.

However, as the barriers to the free flow of goods, services, and capital fell, and as other countries increased their shares of world output, non-U.S. firms increasingly began to invest across national borders. The motivation for much of this foreign direct investment by non-U.S. firms was the desire to disperse production activities to optimal locations and to build a direct presence in major foreign markets. Thus, for example, during the 1970s and 80s European and Japanese firms began to shift labor-intensive manufacturing operations from their home markets to developing nations

[18]"War of the Worlds," *The Economist*, October 1, 1994, pp. 3–4.

[19]One of the classics being J. J. Servan-Schreiber, *The American Challenge* (New York: Atheneum, 1968).

FIGURE 1.4   The Changing Stock of Foreign Direct Investment (Percentage of World Total)

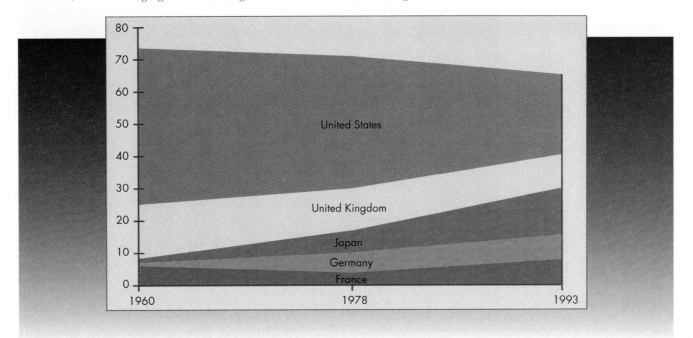

Source: United Nations, World Investment Report, *1994.*

where labor costs were lower. In addition many Japanese firms have invested in North America and Europe, often as a hedge against unfavorable currency movements and the possible imposition of trade barriers. For example, Toyota, the Japanese automobile company, rapidly increased its investment in automobile production facilities in the United States and Britain during the late 1980s and early 1990s. These investments were driven by Toyota's belief that an increasingly strong Japanese yen would price Japanese automobile exports out of foreign markets, and therefore production in the most important foreign markets, as opposed to exports from Japan, made sense. Toyota also undertook these investments to head off growing political pressures in the United States and Europe to restrict Japanese automobile exports into those markets.

One consequence of these developments is mapped out in Figure 1.4. Figure 1.4 shows how the stock of foreign direct investment accounted for by the world's five most important national sources of such investment—the United States, Britain, Japan, Germany, and France—changed between 1960 and 1993. (The **stock of foreign direct investment** refers to the total cumulative value of foreign investments.) As can be seen, the share of the total stock accounted for by U.S. firms declined substantially, while the shares accounted for by Japan and Germany increased markedly. There was also a slight decline in the share of the total stock of foreign direct investment accounted for by these five nations. This reflects a small but growing trend for firms from developing nations, such as South Korea, to invest outside of their borders (see the "Country Focus" on the emergence of South Korean multinationals).

Figure 1.5 illustrates another important trend; the increasing tendency for cross-border investments to be directed at developing rather than rich industrialized nations. Figure 1.5 details recent changes in the annual inflows of foreign direct investment (the **flow of foreign direct investment** refers to amounts invested across national borders each year). Figure 1.5 shows the rapid rise in the share of foreign direct investment inflows accounted for by developing countries, and the commensurate decline in the share of inflows directed at developing nations. Table 1.3 adds detail to this picture by listing the 10 largest recipients of foreign direct investment among developing nations during the 1988–92 period. As suggested by Table 1.3,

FIGURE 1.5

Changes in the Annual
Inflows of Foreign Direct
Investment

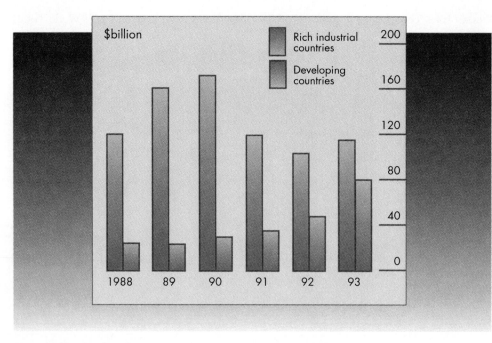

Source: United Nations, World Investment Report, *1994.*

TABLE 1.3

10 Largest Recipients of
Foreign Direct Investment
among Developing Nations,
1988–92

Country	1988–92 ($billion)
China	25.6
Singapore	21.7
Mexico	18.4
Malaysia	13.2
Argentina	10.6
Thailand	9.5
Hong Kong	7.9
Brazil	7.6
Taiwan	6.0
Indonesia	5.6

Source: United Nations data reported in The Economist, *October 1, 1994, p. 23.*

underlying the data presented in Figure 1.5 is the increasing trend for Western and Japanese businesses to invest in productive activities in newly industrializing developing economies such as China, Mexico, and India. Given the likely rapid increase in the share of world output accounted for by these developing nations (see Figure 1.3), and their more rapid growth rates, this shift in foreign direct investment inflows makes good sense. Clearly, many Western and Japanese international businesses are already positioning themselves to be active participants in those areas of the world that are expected to grow most rapidly over the next quarter of a century.

The Changing Nature of the Multinational Enterprise

Two trends are worth mentioning here. The first is the rise of non-U.S. multinationals, particularly Japanese multinationals. The second is the growth of mini-multinationals.

Non-U.S. multinationals

In the 1960s the widespread perception was that international business was dominated by large U.S. multinational corporations, and this was not far off the mark. With U.S. firms accounting for approximately two thirds of foreign direct investment during the 1960s, one would expect most multinationals to be U.S. enterprises. According to the data presented in Table 1.4, in 1973, 48.4 percent of the world's

TABLE 1.4

The National Composition of
the Largest Multinationals

	Of the Top 260 in 1973	Of the Top 500 in 1994
United States	126 (48.4%)	151 (30.2%)
Japan	9 (3.5%)	149 (29.8%)
Britain	49 (18.8%)	33 (6.6%)
France	19 (7.3%)	40 (8%)
Germany	21 (8.1%)	44 (8.8%)
Switzerland	8 (3.1%)	14 (2.8%)

Sources: Figures for 1973 from Hood and Young, The Economics of the Multinational Enterprise (New York: Longman, 1979). Figures for 1994 from "The Global 500," Fortune, August 7, 1995, pp. 130–31.

260 largest multinationals were U.S. firms. The second largest source country was Great Britain, with 18.8 percent of the largest multinationals. Japan accounted for only 3.5 percent of the world's largest multinationals at the time. The large number of U.S. multinationals reflected U.S. economic dominance in the three decades after World War II, while the large number of British multinationals reflected that country's industrial dominance in the early decades of the 20th century.

By 1994, however, things had shifted significantly. In that year U.S. firms accounted for 30.2 percent of the world's 500 largest multinationals, followed closely by Japan with 29.8 percent. Germany was a distant third with 8.8 percent. Although the two sets of figures in Table 1.4 are not strictly comparable (the 1973 figures are based on the largest 260 firms, whereas the 1994 figures are based on the largest 500 firms), they illustrate the trend. In particular, the globalization of the world economy, together with Japan's rise to the top rank of economic powers, has resulted in a relative decline in the dominance of U.S. (and, to a lesser extent, British) firms in the global marketplace.

Looking forward to the future, we can reasonably expect the growth of new multinational enterprises from the world's developing nations. Indeed, as the next "Country Focus" clearly demonstrates, there is already a strong tendency for South Korean firms to start investing outside their national borders. The South Koreans may soon be followed by firms from countries such as Mexico, China, Russia, and Brazil.

The rise of mini-multinationals

Another trend in international business has been the growth of medium-sized and small multinationals (mini-multinationals). When people think of international businesses they tend to think of firms like Exxon, General Motors, Ford, Fuji, Kodak, Matsushita, Procter & Gamble, Sony, and Unilever—large, complex multinational corporations with operations that span the globe. Although it is certainly true that most international trade and investment is still conducted by large firms, it is also true that many medium-sized and small businesses are increasingly involved in international trade and investment. We have already discussed two examples in this chapter: Swan Optical and Harry Ramsden's (see "Management Focus"). For another example, consider Lubricating Systems, Inc., of Kent, Washington. Lubricating Systems, which manufactures lubricating fluids for machine tools, employs 25 people and generates sales of $6.5 million. Hardly a large, complex multinational, yet more than $2 million of the company's sales are generated by exports to a score of countries from Japan to Israel and the United Arab Emirates. Moreover, Lubricating Systems is now setting up a joint venture with a German company to serve the European market.[20] As another example consider Lixi, Inc., a small U.S. manufacturer of industrial X-ray equipment; 70 percent of Lixi's $4.5 million in revenues came from exports to Japan.[21] Or take G. W. Barth, a manufacturer of cocoa-bean roasting machinery based in Ludwigsburg, Germany. Employing just 65 people, this small company has captured 70 percent of the global market for cocoa-bean roasting machines.[22] The point is, international business is conducted not just by large firms but also by medium-sized and small enterprises.

[20]R. A. Mosbacher, "Opening Up Export Doors for Smaller Firms," *Seattle Times*, July 24, 1991, p. A7.
[21]"Small Companies Learn How to Sell to the Japanese," *Seattle Times*, March 19, 1992.
[22]W. J. Holstein, "Why Johann Can Export but Johnny Can't," *Business Week*, November 4, 1991, pp. 64–65.

COUNTRY FOCUS
South Korea's New Multinationals

In the forefront of South Korea's emergence as a modern industrial economy over the last 25 years have been the diversified business groups known as the *chaebol*. Samsung, the largest of the *chaebol*, had 1994 revenues of $63 billion and is involved in a wide range of industries including electronics (it is the world's largest manufacturer of memory chips for computers), automobiles, shipbuilding, aerospace, and machinery. Samsung is closely followed in size by three other major *chaebol*, Hyundai, LG (formerly Lucky Goldstar), and Daewoo. Together with six smaller *chaebol*, these large diversified industrial groups collectively account for about one quarter of South Korea's gross national product.

Historically, South Korea's *chaebol* took advantage of low labor costs to export a wide range of goods to industrialized countries. In recent years, however, the costs of both land and labor in South Korea have risen sharply, effectively nullifying important sources of the *chaebol's* competitive advantage in the global economy. Indeed, a recent analysis of national competitiveness by the Swiss-based International Institute of Management Development (IMD) ranked South Korea 24th out of 41 developed and developing nations, just behind Thailand and Chile, and just ahead of Spain and Mexico (the three top countries were the United States, Singapore, and Japan).

Unlike Japanese enterprises, with which the South Koreans are so often compared, many of the *chaebol* suffer from relatively poor product quality and inferior product design. Thus, they have been unable to respond to higher costs by moving their exported products up market and raising prices. Rather, in an attempt to maintain their competitive position, the *chaebol* have responded to rising costs at home by expanding overseas, establishing factories in countries where direct labor costs are lower and employee productivity is higher than in South Korea. Daewoo, for example, has found that the average $1,300 monthly wage at its videocassette recorder plant in Kumi, South Korea, is now higher than the $1,200 it pays at a similar factory in Antrim, Northern Ireland, while the output per employee is 20 percent higher at the Irish plant.

The Changing World Order

Between 1989 and 1991 a series of remarkable democratic revolutions swept the Communist world. For reasons that are explored in more detail in Chapter 2, in country after country throughout Eastern Europe and eventually in the Soviet Union itself, Communist governments collapsed like the shells of rotten eggs. The Soviet Union is now history, having been replaced by 15 independent republics. Czechoslovakia has divided itself into two states, while Yugoslavia has dissolved into a bloody civil war among its five successor states.

Many of the former Communist nations of Europe and Asia seem to share a commitment to democratic politics and free market economics. If this continues, the opportunities for international businesses may be enormous. For the best part of half a century, these countries were essentially closed to Western international businesses. Now they present a host of export and investment opportunities. Just how this will play itself out over the next 10 to 20 years is difficult to say. The economies of most of the former Communist states are in very poor condition, and their continued commitment to democracy and free market economics cannot be taken for granted. Disturbing signs of growing unrest and totalitarian tendencies are seen in many Eastern European states. Thus the risks involved in doing business in such countries are very high, but then again, so may be the returns.

Another reason for foreign investment by the *chaebol* has been to acquire foreign-owned entities that have the quality, design, engineering know-how, or market presence that the *chaebol* lack. For example, in early 1995 Samsung acquired 40 percent of AST, one of the largest manufacturers of personal computers in the United States, for $378 million. Similarly, Hyundai Electronics Industries, a subsidiary of Hyundai, the second largest *chaebol*, recently acquired U.S. computer diskmaker, Maxtor, for $165 million and a semiconductor division of AT&T for $340 million. Daewoo, meanwhile, has been acquiring automobile plants in Eastern Europe, Vietnam, and Brazil, as part of its strategy to become a major supplier of automobiles to developing nations, and to use that low-cost base to export to the developed world.

A third rationale for foreign expansion by South Korea's *chaebol* has been to placate foreign governments who have expressed concerns about the rising tide of Korean imports into their economies. This has been particularly notable in Western Europe, where a succession of lawsuits have been filed with the European Commission claiming that Korean firms have been dumping products in the European market—selling them at a price below their cost of production—in an attempt to gain market share and drive European firms out of business. Korean firms are increasingly trying to sidestep such charges by setting up production facilities in Europe. For example, a recent complaint against Samsung and Hyundai by European manufacturers of earth-moving equipment triggered direct investments by both *chaebol* in facilities to manufacture the equipment in Europe.

Spurred on by such forces, foreign direct investment by South Korea's *chaebol* has accelerated rapidly in recent years. In 1985 South Korean firms invested a little over $300 million in foreign establishments. By 1990 the figure had risen to $1.5 billion and by 1994 the figure had risen to $3.5 billion. In total, since 1985 about 50 percent of this investment has been directed at other Asian countries, 30 percent at North America, and 15 percent at Europe. It seems unlikely that this trend will slow down anytime soon. Recent revisions in South Korea's foreign exchange regulations have made it easier for the *chaebol* to take money out of the country and invest it elsewhere, which has facilitated the migration of production out of Korea. Moreover, all of the big four *chaebol* have announced aggressive plans to invest in foreign productive capacity. Samsung plans to establish electronics facilities in China and Mexico; Hyundai plans to invest $4 billion in foreign automobile, telecommunications, and semiconductor facilities; Daewoo is investing heavily in automobile and electronics plants in developing nations; and LG has announced plans to set up petrochemical and electronics plants in developing countries. It seems highly probable, therefore, that the Korean multinational corporation is here to stay.

Sources: L. Nakarmi, "A Flying Leap Toward the 21st Century," *Business Week,* March 20, 1995, pp. 78–80; J. Burton, "Samsung Drives on towards Globalization," *Financial Times,* October 25, 1994, p. 21; and G. de Jonquieres and J. Burton, "Big Gamble on a European Thrust," *Financial Times,* October 2, 1995, p. 13.

In addition to these changes, more quiet revolutions have been occurring in China and Latin America. Their implications for international businesses may be just as profound as the collapse of communism in Eastern Europe. China suppressed its own prodemocracy movement in the bloody Tiananmen Square massacre of 1989. Despite this, China seems to be moving progressively toward evergreater free market reforms. The southern Chinese province of Guangong, where these reforms have been pushed the furthest, now has the fastest growing economy in the world.[23] If what is now occurring in southern China continues, and particularly if it spreads throughout the country, China may move from Third World to industrial superpower status even more rapidly than Japan did. If China's GDP per capita grows by an average of 6 percent to 7 percent, which is slower than the 8 percent growth rate achieved during the last decade, then by 2020 this nation of 1.2 billion people could boast an average income per capita of about $13,000, roughly equivalent to that of Spain today. The potential consequences for Western international business are enormous. On the one hand, with 1.2 billion people, China represents a huge and largely untapped market. Reflecting this, between

---

[23]P. Engardio and L. Curry, "The Fifth Tiger Is on China's Coast," *Business Week,* April 6, 1992, pp. 42–43.

1983 and 1994 annual foreign direct investment in China increased from less than $2 billion to over $20 billion. On the other hand, China's new firms are already proving to be very capable competitors, and they might take global market share away from Western and Japanese enterprises. Thus the changes in China are creating both opportunities and threats for established international businesses.

As for Latin America, here too both democracy and free market reforms seem to have taken hold. For decades most Latin American countries were ruled by dictators, many of whom seemed to view Western international businesses as instruments of imperialist domination. Accordingly, they restricted direct investment by foreign firms. In addition, the poorly managed economies of Latin America were characterized by low growth, high debt, and hyperinflation—all of which discouraged investment by international businesses. Now all this seems to be changing. Throughout most of Latin America, debt and inflation are down, governments are selling state-owned enterprises to private investors, foreign investment is welcomed, and the region's economies are growing rapidly. These changes have increased the attractiveness of Latin America, both as a market for exports and as a site for foreign direct investment. At the same time, given the long history of economic mismanagement in Latin America, there is no guarantee that these favorable trends will continue. As in the case of Eastern Europe, substantial opportunities are accompanied by substantial risks.

⚜ HOW INTERNATIONAL BUSINESS IS DIFFERENT

How do we justify a whole book on international business? The task of managing an international business differs from that of a purely domestic business in many ways. At the most fundamental level, the differences arise from the simple fact that countries are different. Countries differ in their cultures, political systems, economic systems, legal systems, and levels of economic development. Despite all the talk about the emerging global village, and despite the trends toward globalization of markets and production, as we shall see in this book, many of these differences are very profound and enduring.

Differences among countries require that an international business vary its practices country by country. Marketing a product in Brazil may require a different approach from marketing the product in Germany; managing U.S. workers might require different skills than managing Japanese workers; maintaining close relations with a particular level of government may be very important in Mexico and irrelevant in Great Britain; the business strategy pursued in Canada might not work in South Korea; and so on. Managers in an international business must not only be sensitive to these differences, but they must also adopt the appropriate policies and strategies for coping with them. Much of this book is devoted to explaining the sources of these differences and the methods for coping with them successfully.

A further way in which international business differs from domestic business is the greater complexity of managing an international business. In addition to the problems that arise from the differences between countries, a manager in an international business is confronted with a range of other issues that the manager in a domestic business never confronts. An international business must decide where in the world to site its production activities to minimize costs and to maximize value added. Then it must decide how best to coordinate and control its globally dispersed production activities (which, as we shall see later in the book, is not a trivial problem). An international business also must decide which foreign markets to enter and which to avoid. Moreover, it must choose the appropriate mode for entering a particular foreign country. Is it best to export its product to the foreign country? Should the firm allow a local firm to produce its product under license in that country? Should the firm enter into a joint venture with a local firm to produce its product in that country? Or should the firm set up a wholly owned subsidiary to serve the market in that country? As we shall see, the choice of entry mode is critical, because it has major implications for the long-term health of the firm.

Another way international business is different is that the conduct of business involves transactions across national borders. Because it is involved in international trade and investment, an international business must deal with government restrictions on international trade and investment. It must find ways to work within the limits imposed by specific governmental interventions in the international trade and investment system. As this book explains, despite the fact that many governments are nominally committed to free trade, their interventions to regulate cross-border trade and investment are actually substantial. International businesses must develop strategies and policies for dealing with this.

In addition, cross-border transactions also require that money be converted from the firm's home currency into a foreign currency and vice versa. Since currency exchange rates are not stable over time but vary in response to changing economic conditions, an international business must develop policies for dealing with exchange rate movements. A firm that adopts a wrong policy can lose large amounts of money, whereas a firm that adopts the right policy can actually increase the profitability of its international transactions.

In sum, international business is different from domestic business for at least four reasons: (1) countries are different, (2) the range of problems confronted by a manager in an international business is wider and the problems themselves more complex than those confronted by a manager in a domestic business, (3) an international business must find ways to work within the limits imposed by government intervention in the international trade and investment system, and (4) international transactions involve converting money into different currencies. In this book we examine all these issues in depth.

❧ ORGANIZATION OF THIS BOOK

The remainder of this book is divided into 19 chapters within five parts. Chapters 2 to 11 deal with the environmental context within which international transactions are conducted. Chapters 12 to 14 take a firm-level view of the strategy and structure of international business. Chapters 15 to 20, on business operations, examine how individual business functions are performed within an international business. Thus the book starts out looking at the environment; then it looks at the firm; and finally it looks at individual operations within a firm (see Figure 1.6). Put another way, the book begins by discussing the international business environment before examining specific strategies, structures, and operational policies that firms must adopt to survive and prosper in that environment.

The Environmental Context

Discussion of the environmental context of international business is further subdivided into three parts in this book; Part Two deals with country factors, Part Three deals with the global trade and investment environment, and Part Four looks at the global monetary system.

Country factors

As noted in the previous section, international business is different from domestic business because countries are different. Taking this as our cue, we start by discussing country factors. Chapter 2 looks at the foundations of national differences in political and economic systems. We discuss the different political, economic, and legal systems found in the world and outline the implications of these differences for an international business. Chapter 3 looks at the foundations of national differences in culture. We identify the various factors of a society that make up its culture (e.g., social structure, religion, language, education), identify how these differ from country to country, and explain the implications of these differences for the practice of international business.

FIGURE 1.6
The Structure of the Book

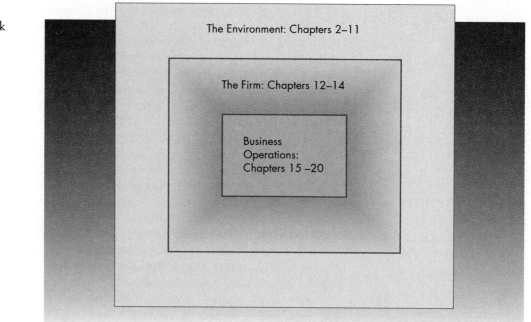

The global trade and investment environment

We begin this part in Chapter 4 by reviewing the economic theories of international trade. These theories form the basis of the intellectual case for free trade. As such, they are the driving force behind the General Agreement on Tariffs and Trade (GATT), which establishes the rules of the game for international trade. In Chapter 5 we move from theory to practice by looking closely at the political economy of international trade. Although the theory of international trade advocates unrestricted free trade, in practice, all countries use policies to restrict certain imports and to protect their producers in certain sectors. In Chapter 5 we review the various instruments of governmental trade policy that international businesses are likely to encounter. We also look at the international trade framework of the 1990s (including the current state of GATT), and we discuss the case for and against government regulation of international trade through trade policy.

In Chapter 6 we switch our attention to the economic theories of foreign direct investment (FDI). These theories outline the conditions under which it makes sense for a firm to establish operations in a foreign country, as opposed to exporting goods and services from its home country or licensing a foreign firm to produce its output. As such, the theories help to identify with some precision the conditions under which it is and is not profitable for a firm to engage in FDI. Chapter 7 looks at the political economy of foreign direct investment. Governments around the world have adopted a variety of postures toward FDI, ranging from—at one extreme—a free market view of *laissez-faire* toward it to—at the other extreme—a radical view that prohibits FDI under all circumstances. In this chapter we look at the political ideology that determines a government's attitudes toward FDI. We review the costs and benefits of FDI both to the host country (the country receiving FDI) and to the home country (the source country for FDI). We also look at the various policy instruments that governments adopt for regulating FDI.

Chapter 8 is the last chapter that deals explicitly with the global trade and investment environment. The focus of Chapter 8 is on regional economic integration—the emergence of regional trade blocks. The ultimate purpose of regional economic integration is to remove all barriers to the free flow of goods, services, and factors of production between countries within a region, thereby enabling member countries to realize the gains from trade that are discussed in detail in Chapter 4. The most comprehensive regional grouping in the world is the European Union (EU); however, even the EU falls far short of the theoretical ideal. Other regional groupings include the North American Free Trade Association (NAFTA) and regional groupings in Latin America and Asia. In Chapter 8 the case for regional economic integration is discussed. We take a close look at economic integration in the EU and review regional economic integration elsewhere.

The global monetary system

The last component of the environmental context of international business that we examine is the global monetary system. Different countries have different currencies. To engage in international trade and investment a firm must change its money from one currency into another. This process is complicated by the fact that exchange rates are not stable; they vary over time. Chapter 9 explains how money can be converted from one currency to another by using the foreign exchange market. The chapter also outlines the economic theories that explain how exchange rates are determined. Chapter 10 builds on Chapter 9 by taking a close look at the international monetary system, of which the foreign exchange market is just one part. The international monetary system plays a key role in the workings of the foreign exchange market. Chapter 11 looks at another component of the global monetary system, the global capital market. A striking development of the last 20 years has been the rapid growth of the global capital market. It is now possible for firms to raise funds not just from domestic investors, but also from foreign investors in foreign capital markets. In Chapter 11 we review the reasons for the growth of the global capital market and discuss the attractions of the market to international businesses.

The Firm

Chapters 12 to 14 deal with the strategy and structure of international business. Chapter 12 focuses on the strategy of international business. The chapter opens with a general discussion of the role of strategy—the purpose of which is to help a firm maximize its value added. Then we look at the different ways in which firms can profit from international expansion. Next, the pros and cons of various strategies pursued by international businesses are reviewed. The chapter also discusses how international businesses must respond to pressures for local responsiveness and for cost efficiency, and how these pressures can place conflicting demands on the firm.

Chapter 13 builds on Chapter 12 by looking at the structure of international business. A central theme is that a firm's structure must be matched to its strategy if the firm is to survive. We consider the basic dimensions of structure and control that firms must work with, focusing attention on the implications of the various dimensions of structure and control for an international business. We then pull all this material together in a synthesis that reviews the structures and controls that international businesses must operate with if they are to survive.

Chapter 14 focuses on the alternative entry modes for firms entering a foreign market—exporting, licensing, franchising, a joint venture with a local firm, and setting up a wholly owned subsidiary. We compare and contrast these entry modes, highlight the advantages and disadvantages of each, and identify factors that help determine the appropriate mode in a given situation. Chapter 14 also looks at the topic of global strategic alliances—alliances with actual or potential competitors. We discuss the pros and cons of strategic alliances and provide some steps firms can take to help make these alliances work.

Business Operations

The remaining six chapters of the book focus on business operations. Throughout these chapters, a deliberate attempt is made to relate the material to the material in the earlier chapters on the environment, the strategies, and the structure of international business.

Chapter 15 looks at exporting, importing, and countertrade. This is a nuts-and-bolts chapter. It explains how to identify export opportunities, how to finance exports and imports, and the types of public and private assistance available to help exporters. The chapter also deals with the issue of countertrade—the exchange of goods for goods; essentially a bartering arrangement. Countertrade is used when a firm trades with a country whose currency is not freely convertible into other currencies. We discuss the growth of countertrade, the types of countertrade, and the pros and cons of using countertrade.

Chapter 16 looks at manufacturing and materials management in an international business. The chapter opens with a discussion of the factors that determine the optimal global location for manufacturing facilities. For example, we try to identify the factors that might influence a U.S. firm's decision to manufacture component parts in Hong Kong, rather than Germany. The chapter then moves on to discuss the issue of make or buy decisions—that is, whether the firm will produce its own component parts or contract them out to independent suppliers. Make or buy decisions of international businesses are complicated by the volatile nature of the international political economy, exchange rate movements, temporal changes in relative factor costs, and the like. In this chapter we look at the arguments for making components internally, the arguments for contracting out component manufacturing to independent suppliers, and the inevitable trade-offs involved in these decisions. The chapter closes with a detailed discussion of how to coordinate a globally dispersed manufacturing and supply system. This final section is principally about the central role of materials management in an international business.

Chapter 17 looks at marketing and R&D in an international business. We begin by reviewing the debate on the globalization of markets. Then we look in turn at the four elements of the marketing mix—product attributes, distribution strategy, communication strategy, and pricing strategy. The marketing mix is the set of choices that determine a firm's offer to its target market(s). Firms often vary their marketing mix from country to country in light of differences in national culture, economic development, product standards, distribution channels, and so on. The chapter discusses how this is done. The chapter closes with a discussion of new-product development in an international business and of the implications of this for the organization of the firm's R&D function.

Chapter 18 looks at the human resource management (HRM) function. Staffing, management development, performance evaluation, and compensation activities are complicated in an international business by the profound differences between countries in labor markets, culture, legal systems, economic systems, and the like. We discuss the strategic role of HRM in an international business and then turn our attention to four major tasks of the function: staffing policy, management training and development, performance appraisal, and compensation policy. The chapter closes with a look at international labor relations and at the desirable relationship between a firm's labor relations and its strategy.

Chapter 19 focuses on accounting within the multinational firm. We look at how and why accounting standards differ from country to country and at the efforts now underway to harmonize accounting practices across countries. We discuss the rationale behind the practice of producing consolidated accounts for a multinational firm, and we look at the problems associated with currency translation. The chapter closes with a detailed look at several issues relating to the use of accounting-based control systems within an international business.

The final chapter, Chapter 20, is concerned with financial management in an international business. We explain how decisions about investments, financing, and money management in an international business are complicated by differences in currencies, tax regimes, levels of political and economic risk, and so on. We discuss how financial managers can consider all these factors when deciding where to invest the firm's scarce financial resources, how the firm's foreign investments can be financed, how the flow of funds within the firm can be managed, and how best to protect the firm from various political and economic risks it is exposed to (including foreign exchange risk) in the process.

❦ SUMMARY OF CHAPTER

The purpose of this chapter has been to set the scene for the rest of the book. We have looked at the globalization of the world economy, discussed the changing nature of international business, explained the differences between international business and domestic business, outlined the material to be discussed in the book, and shown how this material fits together in an integrated whole. These major points were made in the chapter:

1. Over the last two decades we have witnessed the globalization of markets and production.

2. The globalization of markets implies that national markets are merging into one huge marketplace. However, it is important not to push this view too far.

3. The globalization of production implies that firms are basing individual productive activities at the optimal world locations for the particular activities. As a consequence, it is increasingly irrelevant to talk about "American" products, "Japanese" products, or "German" products, since these are being replaced by "global" products.

4. Two factors seem to underlie the trend toward globalization: declining trade barriers and changes in communication, information, and transportation technologies.

5. Since the end of World War II there has been a significant lowering of barriers to the free flow of goods, services, and capital. More than anything else, this has facilitated the trend toward the globalization of production and has enabled firms to view the world as a single market.

6. As a consequence of the globalization of production and markets, in the last decade, world trade has grown faster than world output, foreign direct investment has surged, imports have penetrated more deeply into the world's industrial nations, and competitive pressures have increased in industry after industry.

7. The development of the microprocessor and related developments in communications and information processing technology have helped firms link their worldwide operations into sophisticated information networks. Jet air travel, by shrinking travel time, has also helped to link the worldwide operations of international businesses. These changes have enabled firms to achieve tight coordination of their worldwide operations and to view the world as a single market.

8. Over the last three decades a number of dramatic changes have occurred in the nature of international business. In the 1960s the U.S. economy was dominant in the world, U.S. firms accounted for most of the foreign direct investment in the world economy, U.S. firms dominated the list of large multinationals, and roughly half the world—the centrally planned economies of the Communist world—was closed to Western businesses.

9. By the end of the 1980s, the U.S. share of world output had been cut in half, with major shares of world output being accounted for by Western European and Southeast Asian economies. The U.S. share of worldwide foreign direct investment had also fallen, by about two-thirds. Moreover U.S. multinationals were now facing competition from a large number of Japanese and European multinationals. In addition, the emergence of mini-multinationals was noted.

10. The most dramatic environmental trend has been the collapse of Communist power in Eastern Europe, which has created enormous long-run opportunities for international businesses. In addition, the move toward free market economies in China and Latin America is creating opportunities (and threats) for Western international businesses.

11. International business is different from domestic business for at least four reasons: (*i*) because countries are different, (*ii*) because the range of problems confronted by a manager in an international business is wider and the problems themselves more complex than those confronted by a manager in a domestic business, (*iii*) because an international business must find ways to work within the limits imposed by governments' intervention in the international trade and investment system, and (*iv*) because international transactions involve converting money into different currencies.

12. This book begins by discussing the environmental context of international business and then moves on to discuss the strategies, structures, and operational policies that firms must adopt to survive and prosper in that environment.

❦ CRITICAL DISCUSSION QUESTIONS

1. Describe the shifts in the world economy over the last 30 years. What are the implications of these shifts for international businesses based in
   - Britain?
   - North America?
   - Hong Kong?

2. "The study of international business is fine if you are going to work in a large multinational enterprise, but it has no relevance for individuals who are going to work in small firms." Critically evaluate this statement.

3. How have changes in technology contributed to the globalization of markets and of production? Would the globalization of production and markets have been possible without these technological changes?

4. How might the Internet and the associated World Wide Web affect international business activity and the globalization of the world economy?

5. If current trends continue, China may emerge as the world's largest economy by 2020. Discuss the possible implications for such a development for

- The world trading system.
- The world monetary system.
- The business strategy of today's European and U.S.-based global corporations.

6. "Ultimately, the study of international business is no different from the study of domestic business. Thus there is no point in having a separate course on international business." Evaluate this statement.

CLOSING CASE   Kodak versus Fuji in 1995

Kodak started selling photographic equipment in Japan in 1889, and by the 1930s it had a dominant position in the Japanese market. Then came World War II and the subsequent occupation of Japan. In the aftermath of the war, U.S. occupation forces persuaded most U.S. companies, including Kodak, to leave Japan to give the war-torn local industry a chance to recover. Kodak reluctantly handed over the marketing of its products to Japanese distributors. Kodak was effectively priced out of the market by tariff barriers; over the next 35 years Fuji gained a 70 percent share of the market while Kodak saw its share slip to a miserable 5 percent. During this period Kodak limited much of its activities in Japan to the sale of technology. To quote Albert Sieg, who headed Kodak's Japanese operations from 1984 until the early 1990s, "Like most American companies (in the 1950s and 1960s) we were content to sell technology to the Japanese to make money. And we did. We sold technology to Fuji Photo Film and Konica and anybody that came to our door. That was the way we decided to make money in Japan. It was also a judgment—obviously not right—that we didn't need to worry about the Japanese as a competitor."

This situation persisted until the early 1980s when Fuji launched an aggressive export drive, attacking Kodak in the North American and European markets where for decades Kodak had enjoyed a lucrative dominance in color film. Fuji's onslaught squeezed Kodak's margins, took market share, and forced the company to slash costs. With their backs to the wall, Kodak's top executives admitted that their company faced a global challenge from Fuji that would only grow. Deciding that a good offense is the best defense, in 1984 Kodak set out to invade its rival's home market. Over the next six years, Kodak spent an estimated $500 million in Japan. At a time when Fuji was committed to heavy spending on promotion abroad, Kodak outspent Fuji in Japan by a ratio of more than 3 to 1. It erected mammoth $1 million neon signs as landmarks in many of Japan's big cities. It sponsored sumo wrestling, judo, and tennis tournaments, and even the Japanese team at the 1988 Seoul Olympics, a neat reversal of Fuji's 1984 coup when it won the race to become the official sponsor of the Los Angeles Olympics.

Kodak realized that to make any headway in Japan, it had to control its own distribution and marketing channels. Rather than go it alone, Kodak established a joint venture with its distributor, Nagase Sangyo, an Osaka-based trading company specializing in chemicals. Kodak also realized that it would not succeed in Japan unless it thought and acted just like a Japanese company. Today, apart from a small unit that liaises with Kodak's headquarters in Rochester, New York, all Kodak's employees in Japan are Japanese, complete with a Japanese boss and Japanese management. There are only 30 foreigners among Kodak's 4,500 employees in Japan. So thoroughly Japanese has Kodak become that it even has its own *keiretsu* (family of suppliers with cross-holdings in each other).

All this activity has bought success. Between 1984 and 1990, Kodak's sales in Japan soared sixfold to an estimated $1.3 billion. Kodak's share of sales to amateur photographers has grown by a steady 1 percent each year for the past six years. Kodak now has a 15 percent share of that market and may well overtake second-place Konica within the next few years. Kodak's success has been even more impressive in Tokyo, where it now has 35 percent of the amateur market. In addition, Kodak now has 85 percent of the market for medical X-ray film and photographic supplies to the graphic arts and publishing industries. Perhaps the most important effect of Kodak's Japanese thrust, however, is that Fuji's margins in Japan have been squeezed. Kodak has put Fuji on the defensive, forcing it to divert resources from overseas to defend itself at home. By 1990, some of Fuji's best executives had been pulled back to Tokyo.

All this success, however, was apparently not enough for Kodak. In May 1995 Kodak filed a petition with the U.S. Trade Office that accused the Japanese government and Fuji of "unfair trading practices." According to the petition, the Japanese government helped to create a "profit sanctuary" for Fuji in Japan by systematically denying Kodak access to Japanese distribution channels for consumer film and paper. In Japan, unlike in the United States, film manufacturers do not sell directly to retailers and photofinishers; in between stand distributors. Kodak claims Fuji has effectively shut Kodak products out of four distributors that have a 70 percent share of the photo distribution market. Fuji has an equity position in two of the distributors, gives large year-end rebates and cash payments to all four distributors as a reward for their loyalty to Fuji, and owns stakes in the banks that finance them. Kodak also claims that Fuji uses similar tactics to control 430 wholesale photofinishing labs in Japan to which it is the exclusive supplier. Moreover, Kodak's petition claims the Japanese government has actively encouraged these practices.

Fuji has not taken these charges lying down. In a 585-page document called "Rewriting History," Fuji states bluntly that

Kodak's charges are a clear case of the pot calling the kettle black. Fuji claims that Kodak has locked up chunks of the U.S. market through exclusive dealing arrangements with retailers won by up-front payments and rebates. Among other charges, Fuji's document claims Kodak has an exclusive agreement with Eckerd Corp., the fourth largest photo retailer in the United States, that Kodak paid rebates of $2.7 million per year to the Army and Air Force Exchange Services for an exclusive arrangement, and that Kodak offered Genovese Drug Stores Inc., a 144-store chain based in New York, $40,000 plus rebates if the company promised to carry no brand of film other than Kodak. Kodak has responded that while it does offer incentives, "Retailers are free to carry other brands if they wish. These relationships are completely voluntary."

This trade dispute may take several years to resolve. There are signs that the U.S. government is taking a go-slow approach to pushing Kodak's case while it works with the Japanese government on issues that it sees as more pressing, such as opening the Japanese market to imports of U.S. automobiles. In the meantime, Kodak has further intensified its war with Fuji. In August 1995 Kodak announced that under a co-branding agreement with a group of Japanese retailers, it will sell its film in Japan for half of the prevailing retail price.

In September 1995 Kodak began to sell film to Niho Ryutsu Sangyo Co., a group of Japanese retailers with about 800 sales outlets. The film will carry both the Kodak name and a Japanese name. Analysts doubt that Fuji will cut prices in Japan to meet Kodak's challenge, since that would decimate profits in its home market.

CASE DISCUSSION QUESTIONS

1. How might it be said that Kodak helped to create a competitor in Fuji Photo Film?

2. What was the critical catalyst that led Kodak to start taking the Japanese market seriously?

3. What have been the keys to Kodak's post-1984 success in Japan?

4. From the evidence given in the case, do you think Kodak's charges of unfair trading practices against Fuji are valid, or are they simply a case of the kettle calling the pot black?

Source: E. Norton, "Kodak to Slash Price for Film It Sells in Japan," The Wall Street Journal, August 24, 1995, p. A2; "The Revenge of Big Yellow," The Economist, November 10, 1990, pp. 77–78; D. P. Hamilton and V. Reitman, "Fuji Hoping to Derail U.S. Probe," The Wall Street Journal, August 1, 1995, p. A11; W. Bounds, "Fuji Accused by Kodak of Hogging Markets," The Wall Street Journal, July 31, 1995, p. A1; and S. Latham, "Kodak's Self-Inflicted Wounds," The Wall Street Journal, August 14, 1995, p. A10.

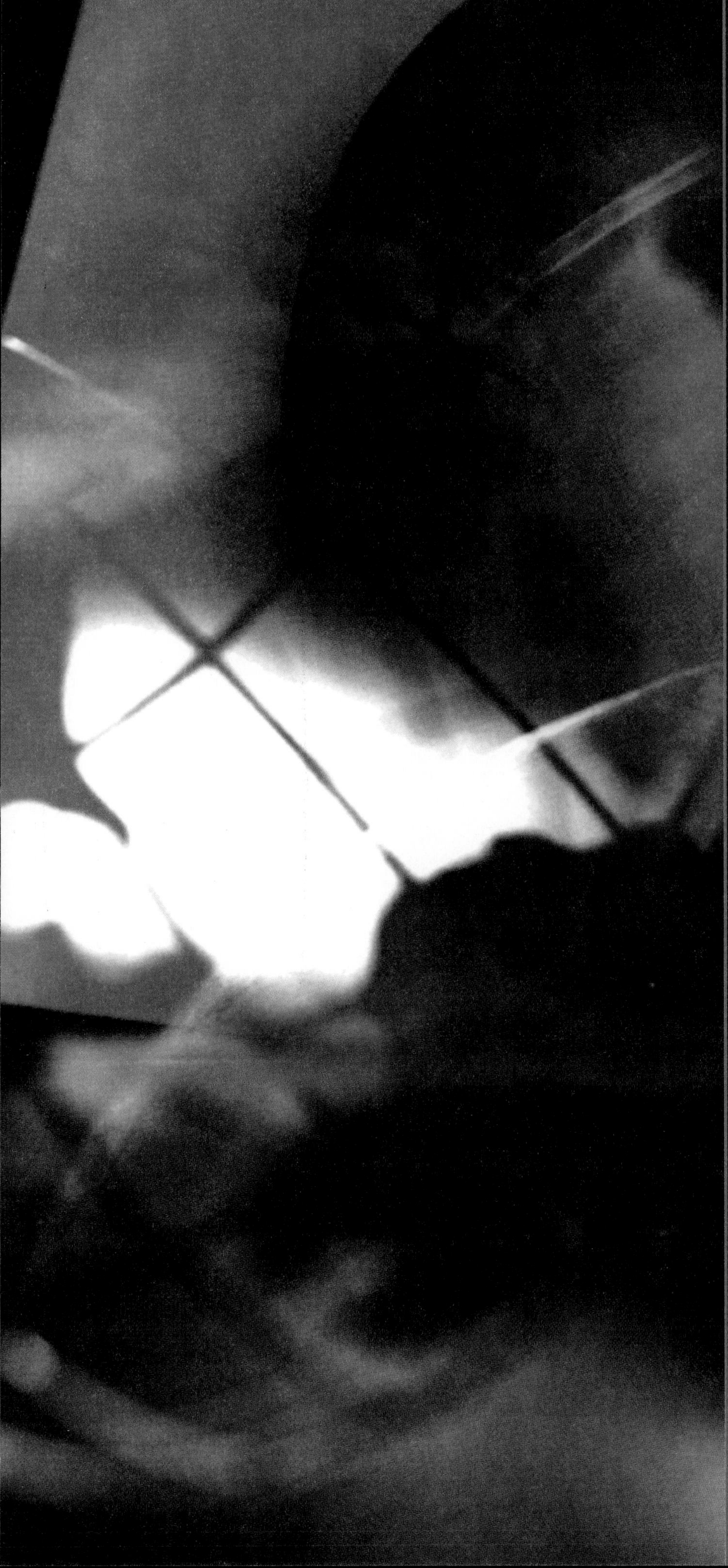

Part II

Country Factors

CHAPTER TWO

NATIONAL DIFFERENCES IN POLITICAL ECONOMY

GENERAL ELECTRIC STUMBLES IN HUNGARY

In the heady days of late 1989 when Communist regimes were disintegrating across Eastern Europe, General Electric Company (GE) launched a major expansion in Hungary with the $150 million acquisition of a 51 percent interest in Tungsram. A manufacturer of lighting products, Tungsram was widely regarded as one of Hungary's industrial gems. GE was attracted to Tungsram by Hungary's low wage rates and by the possibility of using the company to export lighting products to Western Europe. Moreover, like many other Western companies, GE believed that Hungary's shift from a totalitarian Communist country with a state-owned and planned economic system to a politically democratic country with a largely free market economic system would create enormous long-run business opportunities.

At the time, many observers believed General Electric would show other Western companies how to turn enterprises once run by Communist Party hacks into capitalist moneymakers. GE promptly transferred some of its best management talent to Tungsram and waited for the miracle to happen. It's still waiting! As losses mounted General Electric faced the reality of what happens when grand expectations collide with the grim realities of an embedded culture of waste, inefficiency, and indifference about customers and quality.

The American managers complained that the Hungarians were lackadaisical; the Hungarians thought the Americans pushy. The company's aggressive management system depends on communication between workers and managers; the old Communist system had forbidden this, and changing the attitudes at Tungsram proved difficult. The Americans wanted strong sales and marketing functions that would pamper customers; used to life in a centrally planned economy, the Hungarians believed these things took care of themselves. Hungarians expected GE to deliver Western style wages, but GE came to Hungary to take advantage of the country's low wage structure. In retrospect, GE managers admit they underestimated how long it would take to turn Tungsram around—and how much it would cost. As Charles Pipper, Tungsram's American general manager, says, "Human engineering was much more difficult than product engineering." GE now believes it has turned the corner. However, getting to this point has meant laying off half of Tungsram's 20,000 employees, including two out of every three managers. It has also meant an additional $400 million investment in new plant and equipment, and in retraining the employees and managers that remained.

Sources: J. Perlez, "GE Finds Tough Going in Hungary," *New York Times*, July 25, 1994, pp. C1, C3; and C. R. Whitney, "East Europe's Hard Path to New Day," *New York Times*, September 30, 1994, pp. A1, A4.

◆ INTRODUCTION

As noted in Chapter 1, international business is much more complicated than domestic business because countries differ in many ways. Different countries have different political, economic, and legal systems. Cultural practices can vary dramatically from country to country, as can the education and skill level of the population, while different countries are at different stages of economic development. All of these differences have major implications for the practice of international business. They have a profound impact on the benefits, costs, and risks associated with doing business in different countries, on the way in which operations in different countries should be managed, and on the strategy that international firms should pursue in different countries. The international manager that has no awareness of or appreciation for these differences is like a fool walking in front of a buffalo stampede—he is likely to get trampled very quickly. One of the principal functions of this chapter and the next is to develop an awareness of and appreciation for the significance of country differences in political systems, economic systems, legal systems, and national culture.

The opening case illustrates some problems created by country differences in political systems, economic systems, and culture. The culture of Hungarian society has been shaped by over 40 years of Communist rule. Although both the Communist government and the centrally planned economic system it fostered collapsed in 1989, its influence is still felt through its more enduring impact on attitudes to work, business efficiency, and customer service. Like many other Western companies, General Electric did not fully appreciate how enduring the impact of such attitudes would be, and how difficult they would make it to transform an enterprise like Tungsram into a Western-style business operation. Although General Electric's managers now feel they have turned an important corner at Tungsram, the economic cost to GE of getting to this point has been far higher than originally anticipated.

In this chapter we focus our attention on how the political, economic, and legal systems of countries differ. Collectively we refer to these systems as constituting the **political economy** of a country. The political, economic, and legal systems of a country are not independent of each other. As we shall see, they interact and influence each other, and in doing so they affect the level of economic well-being in a country. In addition to reviewing these systems, in this chapter we also explore how differences in political economy influence the benefits, costs, and risks associated with doing business in different countries, and how they impact management practice and strategy. In the next chapter we will look at how differences in culture influence the practice of international business. Bear in mind, however, that the political economy and culture of a nation are not independent of each other. Thus the opening case tells us that the political and economic institutions that existed in Hungary during 40 plus years of Communist rule have cast a long shadow over the culture that exists in Hungary today.

◆ POLITICAL SYSTEMS

The economic and legal systems of a country are often shaped by its political system.[1] As such, it is important that we understand the nature of different political systems before discussing the nature of different economic and legal systems. By **political system** we mean the system of government in a nation. Political systems can be assessed according to two *related* dimensions. The first is the degree to which they emphasize collectivism as opposed to individualism. The second dimension is the degree to which they are democratic or totalitarian. These dimensions are interrelated;

---

[1]Although, as we shall see, there is not a strict one-to-one correspondence between political systems and economic systems. A. O. Hirschman, "The On and Off Again Connection between Political and Economic Progress," *American Economic Review*, 84, no. 2 (1994), pp. 343–48.

systems that emphasize collectivism tend to be totalitarian while systems that place a high value on individualism tend to be democratic. However, there is a gray area in the middle. It is possible to have democratic societies that emphasize a mix of collectivism and individualism. Similarly, it is possible to have totalitarian societies that are not collectivist.

Collectivism and Individualism

The term **collectivism** refers to a system that stresses the primacy of collective goals over individual goals.[2] When collectivism is emphasized, the needs of society as a whole are generally viewed as being more important than individual freedoms. In such circumstances, an individual's right to do something may be restricted on the grounds that it runs counter to "the good of society" or to "the common good." Advocacy of collectivism can be traced to the ancient Greek philosopher Plato (427–347 BC), who in *The Republic* argued that individual rights should be sacrificed for the good of the majority and that property should be owned in common. In modern times the collectivist mantle has been picked up by socialists.

Socialism

Socialists trace their intellectual roots back to Karl Marx (1818–1883). Marx's basic argument is that in a capitalist society where individual freedoms are not restricted, the few benefit at the expense of the many. While successful capitalists are able to accumulate considerable wealth, Marx postulated that the wages earned by the majority of workers in a capitalist society will be forced down to subsistence levels. Marx argued that capitalists expropriate for their own use the value created by workers, while paying workers only subsistence wages in return. Put another way, according to Marx, the pay of workers does not reflect the full value of their labor. To correct this perceived wrong, Marx advocated state ownership of the basic means of production, distribution, and exchange (i.e., businesses). His logic being that if the state owned the means of production, the state could ensure that workers were fully compensated for their labor. Thus, the idea is to manage state-owned enterprise to benefit society as a whole, rather than individual capitalists.[3]

In the early 20th century, the socialist ideology split into two broad camps. On the one hand there were the **communists** who believed that socialism could be achieved only through violent revolution and totalitarian dictatorship. On the other hand there were the **social democrats** who committed themselves to achieving socialism by democratic means, and who turned their backs on violent revolution and dictatorship. Both versions of socialism have waxed and waned during the 20th century.

The communist version of socialism reached its high point in the late 1970s, when the majority of the world's population lived in communist states. The countries under communist rule at that time included the former Soviet Union; its Eastern European client nations (e.g., Poland, Czechoslovakia, Hungary); China; the South East Asian nations of Cambodia, Laos, and Vietnam; various African nations (e.g., Angola, Mozambique); and the Latin American nations of Cuba and Nicaragua. By the early 1990s, however, communism was in retreat worldwide. Most significantly, the Soviet Union had collapsed and had been replaced by a collection of 15 republics, most of which were at least nominally structured as democracies, while communism was swept out of Eastern Europe by the largely bloodless revolutions of 1989. Many feel it is now only a matter of time before communism collapses in China, the last major communist power left

---

[2]For a discussion of the roots of collectivism and individualism see H. W. Spiegel, *The Growth of Economic Thought* (Durham, NC: Duke University Press, 1991). An easily assessable discussion of collectivism and individualism can be found in M. Friedman and R. Friedman, *Free to Choose* (London: Penguin Books, 1980).

[3]For a classic summary of the tenets of Marxism details see A. Giddens, *Capitalism and Modern Social Theory* (Cambridge: Cambridge University Press, 1971).

Indeed, while China is still nominally a Communist state, and while substantial limits to individual political freedom exist, in the economic sphere at least the country has recently moved significantly away from strict adherence to communist ideology.[4]

Social democracy also seems to have passed its high water mark, although the ideology may prove to be more enduring than communism. Social democracy has had perhaps its greatest influence in a number of democratic Western nations including Australia, Britain, France, Germany, Norway, Spain, and Sweden, where Social Democratic parties have from time to time held political power. Other countries where social democracy has had an important influence include India and Brazil. Consistent with their Marxists roots, many social democratic governments have nationalized private companies in certain industries, transforming them into state-owned enterprises to be run for the "public good rather than private profit." In Britain, for example, by the end of the 1970s, state-owned companies had a monopoly in the telecommunications, electricity, gas, coal, railway, and shipbuilding industries, as well as substantial interests in the oil, airline, auto, and steel industries.

However, experience demonstrates that state ownership of the means of production often runs counter to the public interest. In many countries the performance of state-owned companies has been poor. Protected from significant competition by their monopoly position and guaranteed government financial support, many state-owned companies became increasingly inefficient. In the end, individuals found themselves having to pay for the luxury of state ownership through higher prices and higher taxes.

As a result, in a number of Western democracies, many Social Democratic parties were voted out of office in the late 1970s and early 1980s. They were succeeded by political parties, such as Britain's Conservative Party and Germany's Christian Democratic Party, that were more committed to free market economics. These parties have spent most of the last decade selling state-owned enterprises to private investors (a process referred to as **privatization**). Thus in Britain the Conservative government of Margaret Thatcher sold the state's interests in telecommunications, electricity, gas, shipbuilding, oil, airlines, autos, and steel to private investors. Moreover, even those Social Democratic parties that remain in power now seem to be committed to greater private ownership.

Individualism

Individualism is the opposite of collectivism. In a political sense, **individualism** refers to a philosophy that an individual should have freedom in his or her economic and political pursuits. In contrast to collectivism, individualism stresses that the interests of the individual should take precedence over the interests of the state. Like collectivism, however, individualism can be traced back to an ancient Greek philosopher, in this case Plato's disciple Aristotle (384–322 BC). In contrast to Plato, Aristotle argued that individual diversity and private ownership are desirable. In a passage that might have appeared in a speech by Margaret Thatcher or Ronald Reagan, he argued that private property is more highly productive than communal property and will thus make for progress. According to Aristotle, communal property receives little care, whereas property that is owned by an individual will receive the greatest care and therefore be most productive.

After sinking into oblivion for the best part of two millennia, individualism was reborn as an influential political philosophy in the Protestant trading nations of England and the Netherlands during the 16th century. The philosophy was refined

---

[4]For details see "A Survey of China," *The Economist*, March 18, 1995.

in the work of a number of British philosophers including David Hume (1711–1776), Adam Smith (1723–1790), and John Stuart Mill (1806–1873). The philosophy of individualism exercised a profound influence on those in the American colonies who sought independence from Britain. Indeed, individualism underlies the ideas expressed in the Declaration of Independence. In more recent years, the philosophy has been championed by several Nobel Prize-winning economists, including Milton Friedman, Fiedrich Hayek, and James Buchanan.

Individualism is built on two central tenets. The first is an emphasis on the importance of guaranteeing individual freedom and self-expression. As John Stuart Mill put it,

> The sole end for which mankind are warranted, individually or collectively, in interfering with the liberty of action of any of their number is self-protection . . . The only purpose for which power can be rightfully exercised over any member of a civilized community, against his will, is to prevent harm to others. His own good, either physical or moral, is not a sufficient warrant . . . The only part of the conduct of any one, for which he is amenable to society, is that which concerns others. In the part which merely concerns himself, his independence is, of right, absolute. Over himself, over his own body and mind, the individual is sovereign.[5]

The second tenet of individualism is that the welfare of society is best served by letting people pursue their own economic self-interest, as opposed to having some collective body (such as government) trying to dictate what is in society's best interest. Or as Adam Smith put it in a famous passage from *The Wealth of Nations,* an individual who intends his own gain is

> led by an invisible hand to promote an end which was no part of his intention. Nor is it always worse for the society that it was no part of it. By pursuing his own interest he frequently promotes that of the society more effectually than when he really intends to promote it. I have never known much good done by those who effect to trade for the public good.[6]

The central message of individualism, therefore, is that individual economic and political freedoms are the ground rules upon which a society should be based. This puts individualism in direct conflict with collectivism. Collectivism asserts the primacy of the collective over the individual, while individualism asserts just the opposite. This underlying ideological conflict has shaped much of the recent history of the world. The Cold War, for example, was essentially a war between collectivism, championed by the now defunct Soviet Union, and individualism, championed by the United States.

Individualism translates into an advocacy for democratic political systems and free market economics. Viewed this way, we can see that in the late 1980s and early 1990s, the waning of collectivism has been matched by the ascendancy of individualism. A wave of democratic ideals and free market economics is currently sweeping away socialism and communism worldwide. The changes of the last few years go beyond the revolutions in Eastern Europe and the former Soviet Union, to include a move toward greater individualism in Latin America and in some of the social democratic states of the West (e.g., Britain and Sweden). This is not to claim that individualism has finally won a long battle with collectivism; it has not. But as a guiding political philosophy, there is no doubt that individualism is on the ascendancy. This represents good news for international business, since the pro-business and pro-free trade values of individualism create a favorable environment within which international business can thrive.

---

[5]J. S. Mill, *On Liberty* (London: Longman's, 1865), p. 6.
[6]A. Smith, *The Wealth of Nations*, Vol. 1 (London: Penguin Books), p. 325.

Democracy and Totalitarianism

Democracy and totalitarianism are at different ends of a political dimension. **Democracy** refers to a political system in which government is by the people, exercised either directly or through elected representatives. **Totalitarianism** is a form of government in which one person or political party exercises absolute control over all spheres of human life, and opposing political parties are prohibited. The democratic–totalitarian dimension is not independent of the collectivism–individualism dimension. Democracy and individualism go hand in hand, as do the communist version of collectivism and totalitarianism. However, gray areas do exist; it is possible to have a democratic state where collective values predominate, and it is possible to have a totalitarian state that is hostile to collectivism and in which some degree of individualism—particularly in the economic sphere—is encouraged. For example, Chile in the 1980s was ruled by a totalitarian military dictatorship that encouraged economic freedom, but not political freedom.

Democracy

The pure form of democracy, as originally practiced by several city states in ancient Greece, is based on a belief that citizens should be directly involved in decision-making processes. In complex advanced societies with populations in the tens or hundreds of millions, this is impractical. Most modern democratic states practice what is commonly referred to as **representative democracy.** In a representative democracy, citizens periodically elect individuals to represent them. These elected representatives then form a government, whose function is to make decisions on behalf of the electorate. A representative democracy rests on the assumption that if elected representatives fail to perform this job adequately, they can and will be voted down at the next election.

To guarantee that elected representatives can be held accountable for their actions by the electorate, an ideal representative democracy has a number of safeguards that are typically enshrined in constitutional law. These include (1) an individual's right to freedom of expression, opinion, and organization; (2) a free media; (3) regular elections in which all eligible citizens are allowed to vote; (4) universal adult suffrage; (5) limited terms for elected representatives; (6) a fair court system that is independent from the political system; (7) a nonpolitical state bureaucracy; (8) a nonpolitical police force and armed service; and (9) a relatively free access to state information.[7]

Totalitarianism

A totalitarian country denies citizens all the constitutional guarantees on which representative democracies are built, such as an individual's right to freedom of expression and organization, a free media, and regular elections. In most totalitarian states, political repression is widespread and those who question the right of the rulers to rule find themselves imprisoned, or worse.

Map 2.1 reports data on the extent of totalitarianism in the world. This map charts political freedom in 1995 on a scale from 1 for the highest degree of political freedom to 7 for the lowest. Among the criteria for a high rating are recent free and fair elections, a parliament with effective power, a significant opposition, and recent shifts in power through election. Factors contributing to a low rating (i.e., to totalitarianism) include military or foreign control, the denial of self-determination to major population groups, a lack of decentralized political power, and an absence of democratic elections.

There are four major forms of totalitarianism in the world today. Until recently the most widespread was **communist totalitarianism.** As discussed earlier, communism is a version of collectivism that advocates socialism can be achieved only through totalitarian dictatorship. Communism, however, is in decline worldwide and

---

[7]R. Wesson, *Modern Government–Democracy and Authoritarianism*, 2nd ed. (Englewood Cliffs, NJ: Prentice Hall, 1990).

MAP 2.1 Political Freedom in 1994

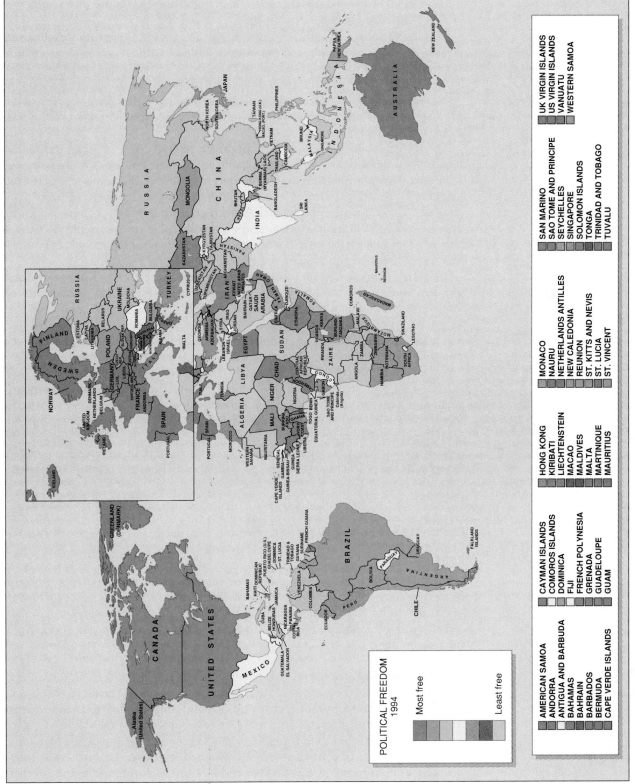

Source: Map data from Freedom Review 26, no. 1 (January–February 1995), pp. 15–17.

many of the old Communist dictatorships have collapsed since 1989. The major exceptions to this trend (so far) are China, Vietnam, Laos, North Korea, and Cuba, although in all of these states there are clear signs that the Communist party's monopoly on political power is under attack.

A second form of totalitarianism might be labeled **theocratic totalitarianism.** Theocratic totalitarianism is found in states where political power is monopolized by a party, group, or individual that governs according to religious principles. The most common form of theocratic totalitarianism is that based on Islam. It is exemplified by states such as Iran and Saudi Arabia. In these states freedom of political expression is restricted and so is freedom of religious expression. The laws of the state are based on Islamic principles.

A third form of totalitarianism might be referred to as **tribal totalitarianism.** Tribal totalitarianism is found principally in African countries such as Zimbabwe, Tanzania, Uganda, and Kenya. The borders of most African states reflect the administrative boundaries drawn by the old European colonial powers, rather than tribal realities. Consequently, the typical African country contains a number of different tribes. Tribal totalitarianism occurs when a political party that represents the interests of a particular tribe (and not always the majority tribe) monopolizes power. Such one-party states are found scattered throughout Africa.

A fourth major form of totalitarianism might be described as **right-wing totalitarianism.** Right-wing totalitarianism generally permits individual economic freedom but restricts individual political freedom on the grounds that it would lead to a rise of communism. One of the common features of most right-wing dictatorships is an overt hostility to socialist or communist ideas. Many right-wing totalitarian governments are backed by the military, and in some cases the government may be made up of military officers. Until the early 1980s, right-wing dictatorships, many of which were military dictatorships, were common throughout Latin America. They were also found in several Asian countries, particularly South Korea, Taiwan, Singapore, Indonesia, and the Philippines. Since the early 1980s, however, this form of government has been in retreat. The majority of Latin American countries are now genuine multiparty democracies, while significant political freedoms have been granted to the political opposition in South Korea, Taiwan, and the Philippines.

❧ ECONOMIC SYSTEMS

It should be clear from the previous section that there is a connection between political ideology and economic systems. In countries where individual goals are given primacy over collective goals, we are more likely to find free market economic systems. In contrast, in countries where collective goals are given preeminence, the state may have taken control over many enterprises, while markets in such countries are likely to be restricted rather than free. More specifically, we can identify three broad types of economic system—a market economy, a command economy, and a mixed economy.

Market Economy

In a pure **market economy,** the goods and services a country produces, and the quantity in which they are produced, is not planned by anyone. Rather, it is determined by the interaction of supply and demand and signaled to producers through the price system. If demand for a product exceeds supply, prices will rise, signaling producers to produce more. If supply exceeds demand, prices will fall, signaling producers to produce less. In this system consumers are sovereign. It is the purchasing patterns of consumers, as signaled to producers through the mechanism of the price system, that determines what is produced and in what quantity.

For a market to work in this manner, there must be no restrictions on supply. A restriction on supply occurs when a market is monopolized by a single firm. In such circumstances, rather than increasing output in response to increased demand, a monopolist might restrict output and let prices rise. This allows the monopolist to take a greater profit margin on each unit it sells. Although this is good for the monopolist, it is bad for the consumer, who has to pay higher prices. Moreover, it is probably bad for the welfare of society. Since, by definition, a monopolist has no competitors, it has no incentive to search for ways to lower its production costs. Rather, it can simply pass on cost increases to consumers in the form of higher prices. The net result is that the monopolist is likely to become increasingly inefficient, producing high-priced, low-quality goods, while society suffers as a consequence.

Given the dangers inherent in monopoly, the role of government in a market economy is to encourage vigorous competition among producers. Governments do this by outlawing monopolies and restrictive business practices designed to monopolize a market (antitrust laws serve this function in the United States). Private ownership also encourages vigorous competition and economic efficiency. Private ownership ensures that entrepreneurs have a right to the profits that are generated by their own efforts. This gives entrepreneurs an incentive to search for better ways of serving consumer needs; whether that be through introducing new products, by developing more efficient production processes, by providing better marketing and aftersales service, or simply through managing their businesses more efficiently than their competitors. In turn, the constant improvement in product and process that results from such an incentive has been argued to have a major positive impact on economic growth and development.[8]

Command Economy

In a pure **command economy,** the goods and services that a country produces, the quantity in which they are produced, and the prices at which they are sold, are all *planned* by the government. Consistent with the collectivist ideology, the objective of a command economy is for government to allocate resources for "the good of society." In addition, in a *pure* command economy, all businesses are state owned; the government can then direct them to make investments that are in the best interests of the nation as a whole, rather than in the interests of private individuals.

Command economies are typically found in communist countries where collectivist goals are given priority over individual goals. However, much government planning, mixed with some state ownership, has also been undertaken in a number of democratic nations by socialist-inclined governments. France and India, in particular, have both experimented with extensive government planning and state ownership, although in both countries government planning has recently fallen into disfavor.

While the objective of a command economy is to mobilize economic resources for the public good, in practice just the opposite seems to have occurred. In a command economy, state-owned enterprises have little incentive to control costs and be efficient, since they cannot go out of business. Moreover, the abolition of private ownership means there is no incentive for individuals to look for better ways of serving consumer needs; hence there is a general absence of dynamism and innovation in command economies. Instead of growing and becoming more prosperous, they tend to be characterized by economic stagnation.

Mixed Economy

In between market economies and command economies can be found mixed economies. In a mixed economy, certain sectors of the economy are left to private ownership and free market mechanisms, while in other sectors there is significant state ownership and government planning. Mixed economies are relatively common among the states of Western Europe; although they are becoming less so. Britain, France, Italy, and Sweden can all be classified as mixed economies. In these countries the government intervenes in those sectors where it believes private ownership is not in the best interests of society. For example, Britain and Sweden both

---

[8]For a detailed but accessible elaboration of this argument, see M. Friedman and R. Friedman, *Free to Choose* (London: Penguin Books, 1980). Also see P. M. Romer, "The Origins of Endogenous Growth," *Journal of Economic Perspectives* 8, no. 1 (1994), pp. 2–32.

have extensive state-owned health systems that provide free universal health care to all citizens (actually it's not really free since it is paid for through higher taxes). In both countries it is felt that government has a moral obligation to provide for the health of its citizens. One consequence is that private ownership of health care operations is very restricted in both countries.

In mixed economies governments also tend to take into state ownership troubled firms whose continued operation is felt to be vital to national interests. The French automobile company Renault was until recently state owned. The government took over the company when it ran into serious financial problems. The French government reasoned that the social costs of the unemployment that might result if Renault collapsed were unacceptable, so it nationalized the company to save it from bankruptcy. Of course, Renault's competitors weren't exactly thrilled by this move, since they had to compete with a company whose costs were subsidized by the state.

◈ LEGAL SYSTEMS

The **legal system** of a country refers to the system of rules, or laws, that regulate behavior, along with the processes by which the laws of a country are enforced and through which redress for grievances is obtained. The legal system of a country is of immense importance to international business. A country's laws regulate business practice, define the manner in which business transactions are to be executed, and set down the rights and obligations of those involved in business transactions. The legal environments of different countries can and do differ in significant ways. As we shall see, differences in legal systems can have an important impact on the attractiveness of a country as an investment site and/or market.

Like the economic system of a country, the legal system is influenced by the prevailing political system. The government of a country defines the legal framework within which firms do business, and often the laws that regulate business are a reflection of the rulers' dominant political ideology. For example, collectivist-inclined totalitarian states tend to enact laws that severely restrict private enterprise, while the laws enacted by governments in democratic states where individualism is the dominant political philosophy tend to be pro-private enterprise and pro-consumer.

Here we do not attempt to give a full description of variations in legal systems. Rather, we will focus on three issues that illustrate how legal systems can vary among countries—and how such variations can affect international business. First, we look at the laws governing property rights with particular reference to patents, copyrights, and trademarks. Second, we look at laws covering product safety and product liability. Third, we look at country differences in contract law.

Property Rights

In a legal sense the term *property* refers to resources over which individuals or businesses hold legal title; that is, resources that they own. **Property rights** refer to the bundle of legal rights over the use to which a resource is put and over the use made of any income that may be derived from that resource.[9] Countries differ significantly in the extent to which their legal system protects property rights. Although almost all countries have laws on their books that protect property rights, in many countries these laws are not well enforced by the authorities and property rights are routinely violated. Property rights can be violated in two ways—through private actions and through public action.

Private action

Private action refers to theft, piracy, blackmail, and the like by private individuals or groups. While theft occurs in all countries, in some countries a weak legal system allows for a much higher level of criminal action than in others. An example much in

---

[9]D. North, *Institutions, Institutional Change, and Economic Performance* (Cambridge: Cambridge University Press, 1991).

the news of late is Russia where the chaotic legal system of the post-Communist era, coupled with a weak police force and judicial system, offers both domestic and foreign businesses scant protection from blackmail by the "Russian Mafia." Indeed, often successful business owners must pay "protection money" to the Mafia or face violent retribution, including bombings and assassinations (more than 500 business-people were murdered in 1994).[10]

Of course, Russia is not alone in having Mafia problems. The Mafia has a long history in the United States. Similarly, in Japan the local version of the Mafia, known as the *yakuza*, runs protection rackets, particularly in the food and entertainment industries.[11] However, there is an enormous difference between the large magnitude of such activity in Russia and its limited impact in Japan and the United States. This difference arises because the legal enforcement apparatus, such as the police and court system, is so weak in Russia. Many other countries have problems similar or even greater in magnitude than those currently being experienced by Russia. In Somalia during 1993–94, for example, the breakdown of law and order was so complete that even United Nations food relief convoys proceeding to famine areas under armed guard were held up by bandits.

Public action

Public action to violate property rights occurs when public officials, such as politicians and government bureaucrats, extort income or resources from property holders. This can be done through a number of mechanisms including implementing excessive taxation, requiring expensive licenses or permits from property holders, taking assets into state ownership without compensating the owners (as occurred to the assets of numerous U.S. firms in Iran after the 1979 Iranian revolution), or demanding bribes from businesses in return for the rights to operate in a country, industry, or location. For example, the government of the late Ferdinand Marcos in the Philippines was famous for demanding bribes from foreign businesses wishing to set up operations in that country.[12]

Another example of such activity surfaced in mid-February 1994 when the British *Sunday Times* ran an article that alleged a 1 billion sterling ($750m) sale of defense equipment by British companies to Malaysia was secured only after bribes had been paid to Malaysian government officials and after the British Overseas Development Administration (ODA) had agreed to approve a £234 million grant to the Malaysian government for a hydroelectric dam of (according to the *Sunday Times*) dubious economic value. The clear implication was that U.K. officials, in their enthusiasm to see British companies win a large defense contract, had yielded to pressures from "corrupt" Malaysian officials for bribes—both personal and in the form of the £234 million development grant.[13]

The Protection of Intellectual Property

Intellectual property refers to property, such as computer software, a screen play, a music score, or the chemical formula for a new drug, that is the product of intellectual activity. It is possible to establish ownership rights over intellectual property through patents, copyrights, and trademarks. A **patent** grants the inventor of a new product or process exclusive rights to the manufacture, use, or sale of that invention. **Copyrights** are the exclusive legal rights of authors, composers, playwrights, artists, and publishers to publish and dispose of their work as they see fit. **Trademarks** are designs and names, often officially registered, by which merchants or manufacturers designate and differentiate their products (e.g., Christian Dior clothes, McDonald's restaurants).

---

[10]P. Klebnikov, "Russia's Robber Barons," *Forbes*, November 21, 1994, pp. 74–84. C. Mellow, "Russia: Making Cash from Chaos," *Fortune*, April 17, 1995, pp. 145–51.

[11]K. Van Wolferen, *The Enigma of Japanese Power* (New York: Vintage Books, 1990), pp. 100–105.

[12]K. M. Murphy, A. Shleifer, and R. Vishny, "Why Is Rent Seeking So Costly to Growth," *American Economic Review* 83, no. 2 (1993), pp. 409–14.

[13]Keiran Cooke, "Honeypot of as Much as $4 billion down the Drain," *Financial Times*, February 26, 1994, p. 4.

The philosophy behind intellectual property laws is to reward the originator of a new invention, book, musical record, clothes design, restaurant chain, and the like, for his or her idea and effort. As such, they are a very important stimulus to innovation and creative work. They provide an incentive for people to search for novel ways of doing things and they reward creativity. Consider innovation in the pharmaceutical industry. A patent will grant the inventor of a new drug a 17-year monopoly for production of that drug. This gives pharmaceutical firms an incentive to undertake the expensive, difficult, and time consuming basic research required to generate new drugs (on average it costs $100 million in R&D and takes 12 years to get a new drug on the market). Without the guarantees provided by patents, it is unlikely that companies would commit themselves to extensive basic research.[14]

Protection of intellectual property rights differs greatly from country to country. While many countries have stringent intellectual property regulations on their books, the enforcement of these regulations has often been lax. This has tended to be the case even among some countries that have signed important international agreements to protect intellectual property, such as the **Paris Convention for the Protection of Industrial Property,** which 96 countries are party to. Weak enforcement encourages the piracy of intellectual property. China and Thailand have recently been among the worst offenders in Asia. For example, in China local bookstores commonly maintain a section that is off-limits to foreigners—it ostensibly is reserved for sensitive political literature but more often displays illegally copied textbooks. Pirated computer software is also widely available in China. Similarly, the streets of Bangkok, the capital of Thailand, are lined with stands selling pirated copies of Rolex watches, Levi blue jeans, videotapes, and computer software.

Estimates suggest Asian violations of intellectual property rights cost U.S. computer software companies $6 billion annually and U.S. pharmaceutical companies at least $500 million annually.[15] China emerges as the biggest single offender. According to the U.S. Department of Commerce, during 1994 some 98 percent of computer software in use in China was pirated, as were 90 percent of all CD music recordings. In total, the Department of Commerce estimates that business worth $3 billion to U.S. corporations is lost to piracy in China.[16]

International businesses have a number of possible responses to such violations. Firms can lobby their respective governments to push for international agreements to ensure that intellectual property rights are protected in law and that the law is enforced. An example of such lobbying is given in the next "Management Focus," which looks at how Microsoft prompted the U.S. government to start insisting that other countries abide by stricter intellectual property laws.

Partly as a result of such actions, international laws are currently being strengthened. As we shall see in Chapter 5, the most recent world trade agreement, which was signed in 1994 by 117 countries, for the first time extends the scope of the **General Agreement on Tariffs and Trade** (GATT) to cover intellectual property. Under the new agreement, as of 1995, a council of the newly created **World Trade Organization** (WTO) will oversee the enforcement of much stricter intellectual property regulations. These regulations oblige WTO members to grant and enforce patents lasting at least 20 years and copyrights lasting 50 years. Rich countries must comply with the rules within a year. Poor countries, in which such protection has generally been much weaker, have 5 years' grace, and the very poorest have 10 years.[17] (For further details, see Chapter 5.)

---

[14]Douglass North has argued that the correct specification of intellectual property rights is one of the factors that lowers the costs of doing business and, thereby, stimulates economic growth and development. See D. North, *Institutions, Institutional Change, and Economic Performance* (Cambridge: Cambridge University Press, 1991).

[15]M. Magnier, "U.S. Gains in Effort to Protect Intellectual Property in Asia," *Journal of Commerce,* February 3, 1992, pp. 1A, 3A.

[16]"Making War on China's Pirates," *The Economist,* February 11, 1995, pp. 33–34.

[17]"Trade Tripwires," *The Economist,* August 27, 1994, p. 61.

One problem with these new regulations, however, is that the world's biggest violator—China—is not yet a member of the WTO and is therefore not obliged to adhere to the agreement. However, after pressure from the U.S. government, which included the threat of substantial trade sanctions, in February 1995 the Chinese government agreed to enforce its existing intellectual property rights regulations (in China, as in many countries, the problem is not a lack of laws; the problem is that the existing laws are not enforced).

In addition to lobbying their governments, firms may want to stay out of countries where intellectual property laws are lax rather than risk having their ideas stolen by local entrepreneurs (such reasoning partly underlaid decisions by Coca-Cola and IBM to pull out of India in the early 1970s). Firms also need to be on the alert to ensure that pirated copies of their products produced in countries where intellectual property laws are lax do not turn up in their home market or in third countries. The U.S. computer software giant Microsoft, for example, recently discovered that pirated Microsoft software, produced illegally in Thailand, was being sold worldwide as the real thing (including in the United States). In addition, Microsoft has encountered significant problems with pirated software in China, the details of which are discussed in the "Management Focus."

Product Safety and Product Liability

Product safety laws set certain safety standards to which a product must adhere. Product liability involves holding a firm and its officers responsible when their product causes injury, death, or damage. Product liability can be much greater if a product does not conform to required safety standards. There are both civil and criminal product liability laws. Civil laws call for payment and money damages. Criminal liability laws result in fines or imprisonment. Both civil and criminal liability laws are probably more extensive in the United States than in any other country, although many other Western nations also have comprehensive liability laws. Liability laws are typically least extensive in less developed nations.

A U.S. boom in product liability suits and awards has resulted in a dramatic increase in the cost of liability insurance. In turn, many business executives argue that the high cost of liability insurance makes American businesses less competitive in the global marketplace. This view was supported by the Bush administration. Former Vice President Dan Quayle once argued that the United States has too many lawyers and that product liability awards are too large. According to Quayle, product liability insurance rates are typically much lower overseas, thereby giving foreign firms a competitive advantage. Quayle does have a point; tort costs amount to about 2.4 percent of U.S. GDP, three times as much as in any other industrialized country. So the costs of lawsuits does seem to put America at a competitive disadvantage.[18]

Aside from the competitiveness issue, country differences in product safety and liability laws raise an important ethical issue for firms doing business abroad. Specifically, when product safety laws are tougher in a firm's home country than in a foreign country, and/or when liability laws are more lax, should a firm doing business in that foreign country adhere to the more relaxed local standards, or should it follow the standards of its home country? While the ethical thing to do is to adhere to home country standards, firms have been known to take advantage of lax safety and liability laws to do business in a manner that would not be allowed at home.

---

[18]"A Survey of the Legal Profession," *The Economist*, July 18, 1992, pp. 1–18.

MANAGEMENT FOCUS
Microsoft Battles Software Piracy in China

Microsoft, the world's biggest personal computer software company, developed MS-DOS and then Windows, the operating system and graphical user interface that now reside on over 90 percent of the world's personal computers. In addition, Microsoft has a slew of best-selling applications software, including its word processing program (Microsoft Word), spreadsheet program (Excel), and presentation program (Power Point). An integral part of Microsoft's international strategy has been expansion into mainland China, where there were an estimated 2.2 million personal computers in use in 1994, a number that is expected to grow by at least 1 million per year through the rest of the decade. Moreover, with a population of 1.5 billion, China represents a potentially huge market for Microsoft.

Microsoft's initial goal is to build Chinese sales from nothing in 1994 to $100 million by 2000. However, the company has to overcome a very serious obstacle before it can achieve this goal—software piracy. Over 95 percent of the software used in China in 1995 was pirated. Microsoft is a prime target of this activity. Most Microsoft products used in China are illegal copies made and then sold with no payment being made to Microsoft. For example, Microsoft executives in China recently came across a pirated CD-ROM set containing nearly every top-selling program that Microsoft had ever written. China's government is believed to be one of the worst offenders. Microsoft's lawyers complain that Beijing doesn't yet budget for software purchases, forcing its cash-strapped bureaucracy to find cheap software solutions. Thus, Microsoft claims, much of the government ends up using pirated software.

To make matters worse, China is becoming a mass exporter of counterfeit software. Microsoft executives don't have to go far to see the problem. Just a few blocks from the company's Hong Kong office a tiny shop offers CD-ROMs, each crammed with dozens of computer programs that collectively are worth about $20,000. The asking price of the CD-ROM is about 500 Hong Kong dollars, or $52! In further evidence of the problem, Hong Kong customs recently seized a shipment of

Contract Law

A contract is a document that specifies the conditions under which an exchange is to occur and details the rights and obligations of the parties to a contract. Many business transactions are regulated by some form of contract. Contract law is the body of law that governs contract enforcement. The parties to an agreement normally resort to contract law when one party believes the other has violated either the letter or the spirit of an agreement.

Contract law can differ significantly across countries, and as such it affects the kind of contracts that an international business will want to use to safeguard its position should a contract dispute arise. The main differences can be traced to variations in legal tradition. The two main legal traditions found in the world today are the **common law system** and the **civil law system.**

The common law system evolved in England over hundreds of years. It is now found in most of Britain's former colonies, including the United States. Common law is based on tradition, precedent, and custom. When law courts interpret common law, they do so with regard to these characteristics.

Civil law is based on a very detailed set of laws that are organized into codes. Among other things, these codes define the laws that govern business transactions. When law courts interpret civil law, they do so with regard to these codes. Over 80 countries, including Germany, France, Japan, and Russia, operate with a civil law

2,200 such disks on route from China to Belgium.

Microsoft officials are quick to point out the problem arises because the Chinese judicial authorities do not enforce their own laws. Microsoft found this out in 1993 when it first tried to use China's judicial system to sue software pirates. Microsoft pressed officials in China's southern province of Guangdong to raid a manufacturer that was producing counterfeit holograms that Microsoft used to authenticate its software manuals. The Chinese authorities prosecuted the counterfeit manufacturer, acknowledged that a copyright violation had occurred, but awarded Microsoft only $2,600 and fined the pirate company $3,000! Microsoft is appealing the verdict and is requesting $20 million in damages.

Another Microsoft response to the problem has been to reduce the price on its software in order to compete with pirated versions. In October 1994 Microsoft reduced the price on its Chinese software by as much as 200 percent. However, this action may have little impact, for the programs are still priced at $100 to $200, compared to a price of about $20 for an illegal copy of the same software.

Yet another tactic adopted by the company has been to lobby the U.S. government to pressure the Chinese authorities to start enforcing their own laws. As part of its lobbying effort, Microsoft has engaged in its own version of "guerrilla warfare," digging through trash bins, paying locals to spy, even posing as money-grubbing businessmen to collect evidence of piracy that is then passed on to U.S. trade officials.

The tactic has worked because the US government currently has some leverage over China. China wishes to join the new World Trade Organization and views U.S. support as crucial. The United States has said it will not support Chinese membership unless China starts enforcing its intellectual property laws. This demand was backed up by a threat to impose tariffs of $1.08 billion on Chinese exports unless China agreed to stricter enforcement. After a tense period during which both countries were at loggerheads, the Chinese acquiesced to U.S. demands in February 1995.

The Chinese government agreed to start enforcing its own intellectual property rights laws, to crack down on factories that the United States identified as pirating U.S. goods, to respect U.S. trademarks including Microsoft's, and to instruct Chinese government ministries to stop using pirated software.

Whether this agreement will make a difference remains to be seen. Microsoft, however, is taking no chances. Recently the company announced it would work with the Chinese Ministry of Electronics to develop a Chinese version of the Windows 95 operating system. Microsoft's logic is that the best way to stop the Chinese government from using pirated software is to go into business with it. Once the Chinese have a stake in maximizing sales of legitimate Microsoft products, the company reckons they will also have a strong incentive to crack down on sales of counterfeit software.

Sources: S. Bilello, "U.S. Wages War on China's Pirates," *Newsday*, February 7, 1995, p. A41; C. S. Smith, "Microsoft May Get Help in China from its Uncle Sam," *The Wall Street Journal*, November 21, 1994, p. B4; "Making War on China's Pirates," *The Economist*, February 11, 1995, pp. 33–34; and interviews with Microsoft officials.

system. Since common law tends to be relatively ill-specified, contracts drafted under a common law framework tend to be very detailed with all contingencies spelled out. In civil law systems, however, contracts tend to be much shorter and less specific, since many of the issues typically covered in a common law contract are already covered in a civil code.

❧ THE DETERMINANTS OF ECONOMIC DEVELOPMENT

One reason for looking at the different political, economic, and legal systems in the world is that collectively these different systems can have a profound impact on the level of a country's economic development, and hence on the attractiveness of a country as a possible market and/or production location for a firm. Here we look first at how countries differ in their level of development. Then we look at how political economy affects economic progress.

Differences in Economic Development

Countries have dramatically different levels of economic development. One of the most common measures of economic development is a country's gross national product (GNP) per head of population. GNP is often regarded as a yardstick for the economic activity of a country; it measures the total value of the goods and services produced annually. Map 2.2 summarizes the GNP per head in 1993. As can be seen, countries such as Japan, Sweden, Switzerland, and the United States are among the richest on this measure, while the large countries of China and India are among the poorest. Japan, for example, had a 1993 GNP per head of $28,190, whereas China achieved only $470, and India $310. The world's poorest country, Mozambique, had a GNP per head of only $60, while the world's richest, Switzerland, came in at $36,080.[19]

However, GNP per capita figures can be misleading because they don't consider differences in the cost of living. For example, although the 1993 GNP per head in Switzerland at $36,080 exceeded that of the United States, which was $23,240, the higher cost of living in Switzerland meant American citizens could actually afford more goods and services than Swiss citizens. To account for differences in the cost of living, the United Nations has calculated a purchasing power parity index (PPP). This adjusts GNP per capita for the cost of living. This index allows for a more direct comparison of living standards in different countries. The index is set equal to 100 for the country in which PPP is the highest (the United States). The PPP index for a selection of countries is summarized in Figure 2.1.

As can be seen, there are striking differences among the standards of living in different countries. Figure 2.1 suggests that the average Indian citizen can afford to consume only 5 percent of the goods and services consumed by the average U.S. citizen. Given this, one might conclude that despite having a population of close to 900 million, India is unlikely to be a very lucrative market for the consumer products produced by many Western international businesses. However, this is not quite the correct conclusion to draw, for India has a fairly wealthy middle class, despite its large number of very poor people.

A problem with the data presented in both Map 2.2 and Figure 2.1 is that they give a static picture of development. They tell us, for example, that China is much poorer than the United States, but they do not tell us if China is closing the gap. To assess this, we have to look at the economic growth rates achieved by different countries. Figure 2.2 summarizes the rate of growth in Gross Domestic Product (GDP) achieved by a number of countries between 1985 and 1993. This tells us that although countries such as China and India are currently very poor, their economies are growing more rapidly than those of many of the advanced nations of the West. Thus, in time they may become advanced nations themselves and huge markets for the products of international businesses. Given their future potential, it may well be good advice for international businesses to get a foothold in these markets now. Even though their current contribution to an international firm's revenues might be small, their future contributions could be much larger. One might also note, however, that Figure 2.2 tells us that the economies of the former Communist states of Russia and Hungary have shrunk substantially over the 1985–93 time period.

A number of other indicators can also be used to assess the level of a country's economic development and its likely future growth rate. These include literacy rates, the number of people per doctor, infant mortality rates, life expectancy, calorie (food) consumption per capita, car ownership per 1,000 people, and education spending as a percentage of GDP. In an attempt to assess the impact of such factors on the quality of life in a country, the United Nations has developed a **human development index.**

This index is based on three measures—life expectancy, literacy rates, and whether average incomes, based on PPP estimates, are sufficient to meet the basic needs (adequate food, shelter, and health care). The human development index is scaled from 0 to 100. Countries scoring less than 50 are classified has having low human development (the quality of life is poor); those scoring from 50 to 80 are

---

[19]The Economist, *Pocket World in Figures* (London: Penguin Books, 1995).

✤ Map 2.2 1993 GDP per Capita

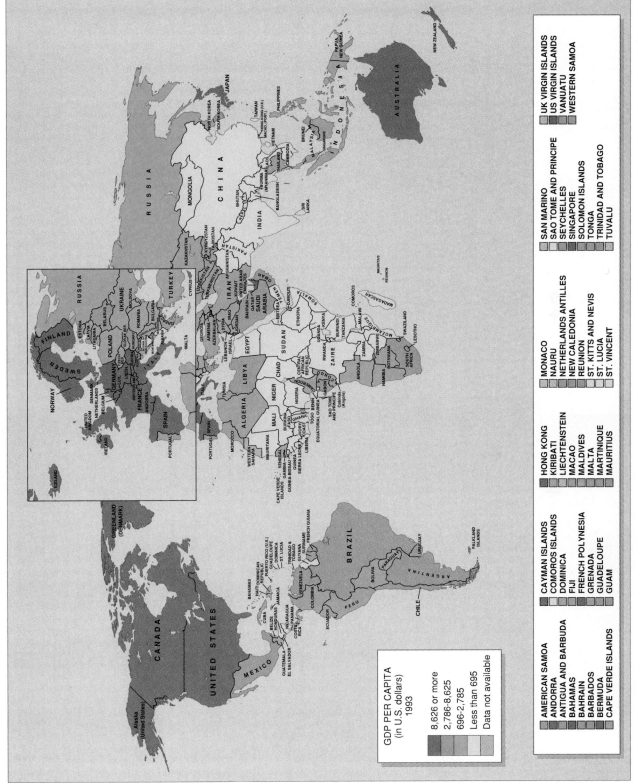

GDP PER CAPITA
(in U.S. dollars)
1993

- 8,626 or more
- 2,786-8,625
- 696-2,785
- Less than 695
- Data not available

AMERICAN SAMOA
ANDORRA
ANTIGUA AND BARBUDA
BAHAMAS
BAHRAIN
BARBADOS
BERMUDA
CAPE VERDE ISLANDS

CAYMAN ISLANDS
COMOROS ISLANDS
DOMINICA
FIJI
FRENCH POLYNESIA
GRENADA
GUADELOUPE
GUAM

HONG KONG
KIRIBATI
LIECHTENSTEIN
MACAO
MALDIVES
MALTA
MARTINIQUE
MAURITIUS

MONACO
NAURU
NETHERLANDS ANTILLES
NEW CALEDONIA
REUNION
ST. KITTS AND NEVIS
ST. LUCIA
ST. VINCENT

SAN MARINO
SAO TOME AND PRINCIPE
SEYCHELLES
SINGAPORE
SOLOMON ISLANDS
TONGA
TRINIDAD AND TOBAGO
TUVALU

UK VIRGIN ISLANDS
US VIRGIN ISLANDS
VANUATU
WESTERN SAMOA

Source: Map data from World Bank, World Development Report, 1994.

FIGURE 2.1
PPP Index for Selected Countries

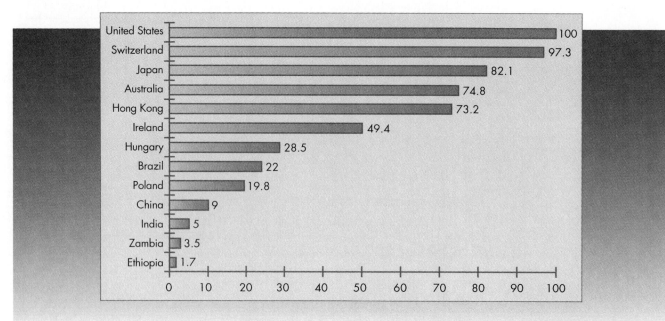

Source: United Nations

FIGURE 2.2
Average Annual Percentage Change in Real GDP for Select Countries, 1985–93

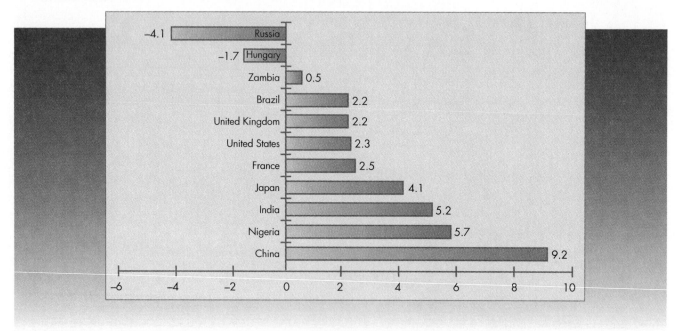

classified as having medium human development, while those countries that score above 80 are classified as having high human development. Figure 2.3 summarizes the scores a select group of countries received on this index in 1993. Also given in Figure 2.3 are population figures and annual population growth rates.

The disturbing fact revealed by Figure 2.3 is that some of the world's poorest countries, as measured by the human development index, are not only heavily populated, but also have rapidly expanding populations. (For example, if India's

FIGURE 2.3
Human Development Index
and Population Statistics

Country	Human Development Index	Population (millions)	Annual Percentage Population Growth Rate
Japan	98	124.3	0.4%
United States	98	255.4	0.9
Canada	98	27.9	1.4
Great Britain	96	57.7	0.3
Germany	96	80.5	0.6
Hungary	89	10.2	−0.6
Mexico	81	85.0	1.8
Malaysia	79	18.6	2.5
Brazil	73	153.8	1.8
Thailand	72	58.0	1.7
China	57	1,166.1	1.5
Indonesia	52	185.3	1.8
India	31	883.5	2.1
Pakistan	31	119.3	3.1
Nigeria	25	101.9	2.9
Bangladesh	19	112.8	2.2

Sources: The Economist, Pocket World in Figures *(London: Penguin Books, 1994); and World Bank,* World Development Report, *1994.*

population growth rate of 2.1 percent is maintained, the country's population will double in just over 34 years). Thus, their situation may deteriorate rather than improve over the next few decades. If this occurs, the implications for the rest of the world could be profound and may include widespread famine and war. In such circumstances, the underdevelopment of the Third World may hold back the continuing economic growth of the world's advanced industrialized nations.

Political Economy and Economic Progress

What is the relationship between political economy and economic progress? This question has been the subject of a vigorous debate among academics and policy makers for some time. Despite the long debate, this remains a question for which it is not possible to give an unambiguous answer. However, it is possible to untangle the main threads of the academic arguments and make a few broad generalizations as to the nature of the relationship between political economy and economic progress.

Innovation is the engine of growth

There is general agreement that innovation is the engine of long-run economic growth.[20] Those who make this argument define **innovation** broadly to include not just new products, but also new process, new organizations, new management practices, and new strategies. Thus, Toys R Us's strategy of establishing large warehouse type toy stores and then engaging in heavy advertising and price discounting to sell the merchandise can be classified as an innovation because Toys R Us was the first company to pursue this particular strategy. So one can conclude that if a country's economy is to sustain long-run economic growth, the business environment within that country must be conducive to the production of innovations.

Innovation requires a market economy

This leads logically to a further question. What is required for the business environment of a country to be conducive to innovation? One factor highlighted by those who have considered this issue is the advantages of a market economy in this regard.[21] It has been argued that a market economy creates greater incentives for innovation than either a planned or mixed economy. In a market economy any

---

[20]G. M. Grossman and E. Helpman, "Endogenous Innovation in the Theory of Growth," *Journal of Economic Perspectives* 8, no. 1 (1994), pp. 23–44. P. M. Romer, "The Origins of Endogenous Growth," *Journal of Economic Perspectives* 8, no. 1 (1994), pp. 3–22.
[21]F. A. Hayek, *The Fatal Conceit: Errors of Socialism* (Chicago: University of Chicago Press, 1989).

individual who has an innovative idea is free to try to make money out of that idea by starting a business (by engaging in entrepreneurial activity). Similarly, existing businesses are free to improve their operations through innovation. To the extent that they are successful, both individual entrepreneurs and established businesses can reap rewards in the form of high profits. Thus, in market economies there are enormous incentives to develop innovations.

In contrast, in a planned economy the state owns all means of production. Consequently there is no opportunity for entrepreneurial individuals to try to develop valuable new innovations, since it is the state, rather than the individual, that captures all the gains. The lack of incentives for innovation was probably a main factor in the economic stagnation of so many former Communist states. A similar stagnation phenomenon occurred in many mixed economies in those economic sectors where the state had a monopoly (such as health care and telecommunications in Britain). In turn, this stagnation provided the impetus for the widespread privatization of state-owned enterprises that started in many mixed economies during the mid-1980s and that is still going on today. (**Privatization** refers to the process of selling state-owned enterprises to private investors.)

Innovation requires strong property rights
Strong legal protection of property rights is another factor that is required for a business environment to be conducive to innovation and economic growth.[22] Both individuals and businesses must be given the opportunity to profit from innovative ideas. Without strong property rights protection, businesses and individuals run the risk that the profits from their innovative efforts will be expropriated, either by criminal elements or by the state itself. The state can expropriate the profits from innovation through legal means such as excessive taxation or through illegal means such as demands from state bureaucrats for kickbacks in return for granting an individual or firm a license to do business in a certain area. According to the Nobel Prize-winning economist Douglass North, throughout history many governments have displayed a marked tendency to engage in such behavior. Inadequately enforcing property rights reduces the incentives for innovation and entrepreneurial activity—since the profits from such activity are "stolen"—and, hence, reduces the rate of economic growth.

The required political system
There is a great deal of debate as to the kind of political system that best achieves a functioning market economy where there is strong protection for property rights.[23] We in the West tend to associate a representative democracy with a market economic system, strong property rights protection, and economic progress. Building on this, we tend to argue that democracy is good for growth.[24] However, there are examples of totalitarian regimes that have fostered a market economy and strong property rights protection and where economic growth has been rapid. The examples include four of the fastest growing economies of the last 30 years—South Korea, Taiwan, Singapore, and Hong Kong—all of which have grown faster than the Western democracies. All these economies had one thing in common for at least the first period of their economic take-off—undemocratic governments! At the same time, there are examples of countries with stable democratic governments, such as India, where economic growth has remained very sluggish for long periods (although things are now changing in India).

---

[22]D. C. North, *Institutions, Institutional Change and Economic Performance* (Cambridge: Cambridge University Press, 1990). See also K. M. Murphy, A. Scheifer, and R. Vishny, "Why Is Rent Seeking So Costly to Growth?" *American Economic Review* 83, no. 2 (1993), pp. 409–14.

[23]A. O. Hirschman, "The On-and-Off Connection between Political and Economic Progress," *American Economic Review* 84, no. 2 (1994), pp. 343–48. A. Przeworski and F. Limongi, "Political Regimes and Economic Growth," *Journal of Economic Perspectives* 7, no. 3 (1993), pp. 51–59.

[24]As an example, see "Why Voting Is Good for You," *The Economist*, August 27, 1994, pp. 15–17.

Commenting on this issue in 1992, Lee Kuan Yew, Singapore's leader for many years, told an audience, "I do not believe that democracy necessarily leads to development. I believe that a country needs to develop discipline more than democracy. The exuberance of democracy leads to undisciplined and disorderly conduct which is inimical to development."[25] Others have argued that many of the current problems in Eastern Europe and the states of the former Soviet Union resulted because democracy arrived before economic reform, making it more difficult for elected governments to introduce the painful policies that were needed to promote rapid economic growth. It has become something of a cliché to argue that Russia got its political and economic reforms the wrong way round—unlike China, which maintains a totalitarian government but has moved rapidly toward a market economy.

However, those who argue for the value of a totalitarian regime miss an important point—if dictators made countries rich, then much of Africa, Asia, and Latin America should have been growing rapidly for the last 40 years, and this has not been the case. Only a certain kind of totalitarian regime is capable of promoting economic growth. It must be a dictatorship that is committed to a free market system and strong protection of property rights. Moreover, there is no guarantee that a dictatorship will continue to pursue such progressive policies. Dictators are rarely so benevolent; many are tempted to use the apparatus of the state to further their own private ends, in which case property rights are often violated and economic growth stalls. Given this, it seems likely that democratic regimes are far more conducive to long-term economic growth than a dictatorship, even one of the benevolent kind. Only in a well-functioning mature democracy are property rights truly secure.[26]

Economic progress begets democracy

While it is possible to argue that democracy is not a necessary precondition for establishment of a free market economy in which property rights are protected, it seems evident that subsequent economic growth leads to establishment of a democratic regime. Several of the fastest growing Asian economies have recently adopted more democratic governments, including South Korea, Taiwan, and Hong Kong. Thus, while democracy may not always be the cause of initial economic progress, it seems to be one of the consequences of that progress.

A strong belief that economic progress leads to the adoption of a democratic regime underlies the fairly permissive attitude that many Western governments have adopted toward human rights in China. Although China has a totalitarian government in which human rights are abused, many Western countries have been hesitant to criticize the country too much for fear that this might negatively affect the country's march toward a free market system. The belief is that once China has a free market system, democracy will follow. Whether this optimistic vision comes to pass remains to be seen. Nevertheless, such a vision was an important factor in the U.S. government's 1994 decision to grant China most favored nation trading status (which makes it easier for Chinese firms to sell products in the United States) despite reports of widespread human rights abuses in China.

❧ STATES IN TRANSITION

Since the late 1980s there have been major changes in the political economy of many of the world's nation states. Two trends have been evident. First, during the late 1980s and early 1990s, a wave of democratic revolutions swept the world. In country after country totalitarian governments collapsed, to be replaced by democratically elected governments that were typically more committed to free market

---

[25]Ibid.

[26]For details of this argument, see M. Olson, "Dictatorship, Democracy, and Development," *American Political Science Review*, September 1993.

FIGURE 2.4
Changing Political Economy, 1985–95

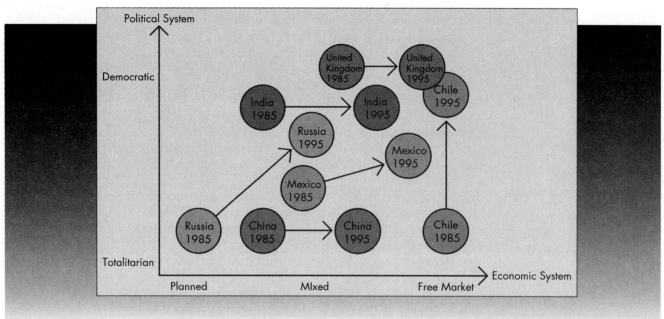

capitalism than their predecessors had been. The change was most dramatic in Eastern Europe, where the collapse of communism brought an end to the Cold War and led to the breakup of the Soviet Union, but similar changes were occurring throughout the world during the same period. Much of Asia, Latin America, and Africa experienced a marked shift toward greater democracy. Second, there has been a strong move away from centrally planned and mixed economies and toward a free market economic model.

Figure 2.4 illustrates some shifts in political economy that occurred during the 1985–95 time period. While changes were widespread and while there was a general shift toward democratic political institutions and a free market system, there was a major difference in the degree of change from country to country. Russia has undergone a particularly marked change, with major shifts in both its political and economic systems. The same is true of most other Eastern European states in the post-Communist era (e.g., the Czech Republic, Poland, Hungary). In contrast, countries such as India and the United Kingdom, which already had democratic political institutions and a mixed economy in place, have undergone a less dramatic shift toward a more free market system. Below we briefly review some of these changes and their implications for business.

Eastern Europe and the Former Soviet Union

Following the end of World War II, Soviet-backed Communist governments took power in eight Eastern European states—Poland, Czechoslovakia, East Germany, Hungary, Romania, Bulgaria, Albania, and Yugoslavia. This set the scene for 40 years of ideological conflict between the Communist bloc, dominated by the Soviet Union, and the democratic West.

The conflict began to thaw in 1985 when Mikhail Gorbachev became general secretary of the Soviet Communist party and began his program of *perestroika.* By that time the gulf between the vibrant and wealthy economies of the West and the stagnant economies of the Communist East had become so immense that even the most hard-line Communist ideologue had to have noticed. With the tacit support of Gorbachev, several of the Communist regimes of Eastern Europe began to loosen their repressive economic and political systems in an attempt to revive their stalled economies. What they discovered, however, was that once the genie of freedom had been let out of the bottle, it could not easily be put back. During 1989 a domino effect occurred as Communist government after Communist government fell.

The biggest change took place in 1991 in the Soviet Union itself. By 1991 the Soviet Union had already moved significantly down the road toward political freedom—but not economic freedom. Faced with the breakup of the country into quasi-independent and democratically inclined states, the old Communist hard-liners attempted to remove Mikhail Gorbachev from power. The coup d'état attempt collapsed when it became apparent that much of the military was not going to back the coup plotters. The end result was that the Communist party was outlawed and the reform movement gained strength. On January 1, 1992, the Union of Soviet Socialist Republics passed into history, to be replaced by 15 independent republics, 11 of which elected to remain associated as a Commonwealth of Independent States.

The post-Communist history of this region has not been easy. The move toward greater political and economic freedom has often been accompanied by economic and political chaos.[27] Most of these countries began to liberalize their economies in the heady days of the early 1990s. They dismantled decades of price controls, allowed widespread private ownership of businesses, and permitted much greater competition. Most also planned to sell state-owned enterprises to private investors. However, given the vast number of such enterprises and how inefficient many were, and hence how unappealing to private investors, most privatization efforts moved forward only slowly. In this new environment many inefficient state-owned enterprises found that without a guaranteed market they could not survive. The newly democratic governments often continued to support these loss-making enterprises in an attempt to stave off massive unemployment. The resulting subsidies to state-owned enterprises led to ballooning budget deficits that were typically financed by printing money. The tendency of governments in these countries to print money, along with the lack of price controls, also often led to hyperinflation. In 1993 the inflation rate was 21 percent in Hungary, 38 percent in Poland, 841 percent in Russia, and a staggering 10,000 percent in the Ukraine.[28]

Another consequence of the shift toward a market economy was collapsing output as inefficient state-owned enterprises failed to find buyers for their goods. As Figure 2.5 illustrates, real gross domestic production (GDP) fell dramatically in many of post-Communist states in the 1990–94 time period. However, there are now signs that the corner has been turned in a number of countries. Poland, the Czech Republic, and Hungary now all boast growing economies and relatively low inflation. On the other hand, countries such as Russia and the Ukraine still find themselves grappling with major economic problems.

Western Europe

Although most of Western Europe has enjoyed stable democratic government for some time, here too there has been a major ideological shift in recent years. For most of the post-WW II period, social democratic ideology, with its emphasis on state involvement in certain sectors of the economy, was adhered to throughout Western Europe. In many Western European nations, basic industries such as telecommunications, energy production, airlines, and railroads were often state owned, while many other sectors of the economy faced heavy state regulation. Starting with Margaret Thatcher's Conservative government in Britain during the early 1980s, governments have moved progressively away from this mixed economy model. State industries have been **privatized** (sold to private investors) and restrictive regulations have been lifted, allowing for much greater competition in industries formally dominated by state-owned monopolies. For example, the privatization of British Telecom (BT) in the mid-1980s was followed by deregulation of the British telecommunications industry, which allowed other companies to compete head to head with the former state-owned company.

[27]M. Bleaney, "Economic Liberalization in Eastern Europe: Problems and Prospects," *The World Economy* 17, no. 4 (1994), pp. 497–507.
[28]M. Wolf and C. Freeland, "The Long Day's Journey to Market," *Financial Times*, March 7, 1995, p. 15.

FIGURE 2.5

Real Percentage GDP Growth, 1990–94, for Five Post-Communist States

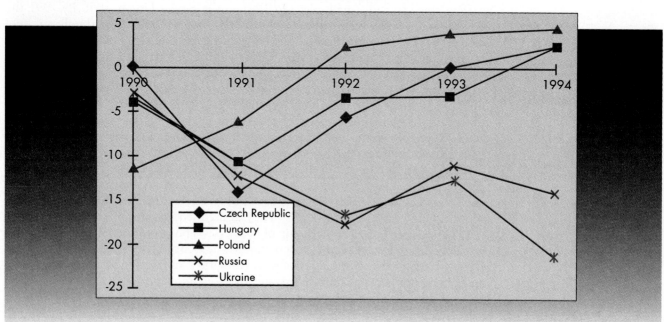

Source: M. Wolf and C. Freeland, "The Long Day's Journey to Market, Financial Times, March 7, 1995, p. 15.

The trend toward privatization and deregulation is still ongoing today. In France the government is currently implementing a program that calls for the privatization of 21 state-owned enterprises between 1994 and 2000, including some of France's most powerful industrial groups such as oil giant Elf-Aquitaine, Renault, and Union des Assurances de Paris, an insurance company. In Germany the government is pressing ahead slowly but steadily with its privatization plans, including Deutsche Telekom, the German telecommunications monopoly. In Italy there are plans to privatize 18 state-owned enterprises.[29]

Asia

During the 1980s and early 1990s significant changes were also taking place in Asia. A shift toward greater political democracy occurred in the Philippines, Thailand, Taiwan, and South Korea. In Vietnam the ruling Communist party removed many price controls and began to shift toward a market economy. In North Korea, still one of the most repressive of all Communist regimes, signs of a thaw in relations with its long-time capitalist enemy, South Korea, could be seen. In India, a democratic country since 1947, but one with a long history of government involvement in economic activity and a mixed economy, the government of P. V. Narasimha Rao embarked on an aggressive reform program aimed at moving the Indian economy sharply in the direction of the free market model. The "Country Focus" reviews these changes in detail.

Notwithstanding what is now occurring in India (see "Country Focus"), perhaps the most momentous changes in Asia are those taking place in China. In 1979 the Communist government of China started to shift the Chinese economy from a pure command economy to a mixed economy. The government began by permitting private ownership of farmland and allowing free markets for farm products. The growth rate of farmers' output quadrupled, from 2 percent a year from 1958 to 1978 to 8 percent a year from 1979 to 1984. In 1984 the reforms were extended to the cities. Private ownership was allowed in a number of industries; the number of products allocated through central planning was reduced from 250 to 20; and free markets were allowed to function in a wide range of industries.

[29]T. Jackson, "State-Run Groups Get Used to New Identity," *Financial Times*, January 24, 1994, pp. 13, 15.

Perhaps the most important reform at this time, however, was the creation of a number of special economic zones in which free markets were allowed to operate without any restrictions; private ownership was allowed; and foreign companies were permitted to invest. Three of the original four economic zones were set up in the southern province of Guangdong (next door to Hong Kong). Since then, Guangdong has become the fastest growing region in the world, with growth rates of over 20 percent per year during the late 1980s and early 1990s. Clearly, the shift toward free market economics, by creating incentives for entrepreneurial activity, is sending China down a road that has already been taken by many of its Asian neighbors, such as Japan, Taiwan, and South Korea.[30]

As with much of Eastern Europe, in 1989 China was also swept by a wave of protests in favor of greater political democracy. Unlike Eastern Europe, however, in China the democracy movement was violently suppressed by the brutal 1989 massacre in Tiananmen Square. This was initially accompanied by a scaling back of China's pro-market reforms. Fortunately, the reduction seems to have been temporary. China now seems to be back on the road to economic reform and many longtime observers feel that political reform will eventually follow.[31]

Latin America

In Latin America, too, a shift toward greater democracy and a greater commitment to free market economics occurred during the late 1980s and early 1990s. At the beginning of the 1980s, almost all the countries of Latin America were run by dictatorships, most of them of the military variety (although Communists held sway in Nicaragua and Cuba). By the early 1990s almost all the countries were run by democratic governments (although in 1992 Peru's democratically elected president suspended many democratic institutions, and in Cuba Communists still ruled).

Under their dictatorships, for decades Latin American countries erected high barriers to imports and foreign direct investment. The feeling was that allowing free trade and investment would result in Latin American economies becoming dominated by Western—and particularly U.S.—multinational firms. Thus, in the interest of preserving their "national sovereignty," many Latin countries severely restricted trade and investment. At the same time, socialist-inclined governments in several countries took major corporations into state ownership. However, these policies failed to deliver economic growth and seemed to have had the opposite effect.

The tide began to turn in Chile in the 1970s when that country, under the government of an unsavory military dictatorship, shifted sharply in the direction of a free market economy. The largest shift, however, occurred in 1989 when Mexico, then run by the civilian government of President Salinas, moved toward a more free market economy. Under Salinas the Mexican government privatized many state-owned enterprises, repealed many laws that limited foreign direct investment, cut import tariffs to world levels, and in 1994 brought Mexico into the North American Free Trade Agreement (NAFTA) with the United States and Canada (discussed in Chapter 8). Many other countries are now following Mexico's lead including, most notably, the two Latin American giants of Argentina and Brazil.

Africa

In Africa, too, there are signs of a shift toward more democratic modes of government and free market economics. Most African countries gained their independence from colonial powers, particularly Britain, France, and Portugal, in the 1950s and 1960s. Although there were originally high hopes that the newly independent nations of Africa would become Western-style democracies, this did not happen. Instead, most rapidly became one-party states ruled by authoritarian leaders. Moreover, most of these leaders adhered to socialist theories. One result was 30 years of economic mismanagement during which the African continent stagnated.

---

[30]D. Perkins, "Completing China's Move to the Market," *Journal of Economic Perspectives* 8, no. 2 (1994), pp. 23–46.
[31]"A Survey of China," *The Economist*, March 8, 1995.

COUNTRY FOCUS
The Changing Political Economy of India

After gaining independence from Britain in 1947, India adopted a democratic system of government. However, the economic system that developed in India was a mixed economy characterized by a heavy dose of state enterprise and planning. This system placed major constraints around the growth of the private sector. Private companies could expand only with government permission. Under this system, derisively dubbed the "License Raj," private companies often had to wait months for government approval of routine business activities, such as expanding production or hiring a new director. It could take years to get permission to diversify into a new product. Moreover, much of heavy industry, such as autos, chemicals, and steel production, was reserved for state-owned enterprises. The development of a healthy private sector was also stunted by the imposition of production quotas and high tariffs on imports. Access to foreign exchange was limited, investment by foreign firms was restricted, land use was strictly controlled, and prices were routinely managed by the government, as opposed to being determined by market forces.

By the early 1990s it was clear that after 40 years of near stagnation, this economic system was incapable of delivering the kind of dramatic economic progress that many Southeastern Asian nations had started to enjoy. By 1994 India had an economy that was smaller than Belgium's, despite having a population of 950 million. Its GDP per capita was a paltry $310; less than half the population could read; only 6 million had access to telephones; only 14 percent had access to clean sanitation; the World Bank estimated that some 40 percent of the world's desperately poor lived in India; and only 2.3 percent of the population had a household income in excess of $2,484.

In 1991 the lack of progress led the government of Prime Minister

Today both socialism and totalitarianism are in retreat across Africa. Since the late 1980s some 30 African countries have abandoned their experiments with socialism and moved toward a market economy. Similarly, democratic regimes are now gaining a foothold in Africa. During 1994 South Africa, Malawi, and Mozambique all held their first democratic elections. Nevertheless, even optimistic observers note that most African countries have a long way to go. During the 1970s and 1980s, the economies of most African states contracted sharply. According to a recent World Bank report, even if African countries now achieve a 3 percent annual growth rate in GDP, it will take 40 years before many return to the level they were at in the early 1970s!

The same report notes that foreign investors who might otherwise be attracted by Africa's cheap labor are deterred by the problems of doing business in countries where the rule of law is so weak that even simple contracts can be difficult to enforce, and where businesses that do persevere have to bribe many poorly paid bureaucrats who can otherwise make business impossible.[32] The great hope for Africa is that the continent's potential economic powers, which include Nigeria, Kenya, and South Africa, will get their act together and pull the rest of Africa along with them.

Implications

The geopolitical changes discussed above have several implications for international business. It would seem the ideological conflict between collectivism and individualism that so defined the 20th century is winding down. The democratic free market ideology

---

[32]"A Flicker of Light," *The Economist*, March 5, 1994, pp. 21–23; and "Continent of Hazard and Opportunity," *Financial Times*, February 7, 1994, p. 14.

P. V. Narasimha Rao to embark on an ambitious economic reform program. Much of the industrial licensing system was dismantled, and several areas once closed to the private sector were opened, including electricity generation, parts of the oil industry, steelmaking, air transport, and some areas of the telecommunications industry. Foreign investment, formerly allowed only grudgingly and subject to arbitrary ceilings, was suddenly welcomed. Approval is now automatic for foreign equity stakes of up to 51 percent in an Indian enterprise, and 100 percent foreign ownership is now allowed under certain circumstances. Raw materials and many industrial goods can now be freely imported, and the maximum tariff that can be levied on imports has been reduced from 400 percent to 65 percent. The top rate of income tax has also been reduced, and corporate tax has come down from 57.5 percent to 46 percent.

Judged by some measures, the response has been impressive. The economy has been expanding at an annual rate of just under 4 percent since 1992; exports have begun to grow at a respectable pace (they were up by 20 percent between 1993 and 1994); and corporate profits jumped 102 percent during 1994. Delivery trucks loaded with once-banned foreign products, such as Ruffles potato chips and Nestlé Crunch bars, rumble over India's potholed highways. Advertisements for AT&T's communications solutions can be seen on New Delhi streets, signs of an upcoming liberalization of the telecommunications industry. Moreover, foreign investment, which is a good indicator of perceptions about the health of the India economy, has surged from $150 million in 1991 to $700 million in 1994.

However, India is still some way from achieving the kind of free market economic system that can be found in the West. The reform process is being fought by many bureaucrats and politicians. Several Western companies now investing in India have painful memories of the 1970s when India nationalized the assets of foreign companies on terms that were tantamount to confiscation. Such memories are one reason companies such as IBM, Coca-Cola, and Mobil have kept their investment modest. Other foreign companies have made major investment commitments to India only after securing special guarantees. For example, AES Corporation, a power-generating company based in Virginia, recently concluded a deal to build power stations in India, but only after the Indian government agreed to guarantee that it would pay for power delivered to Indian electric utilities if the utilities defaulted.

Sources: S. Moshavi and P. Endarido, "India Shakes off Its Shackles," *Business Week*, January 30, 1995, pp. 48–49; "A Survey of India: The Tiger Steps Out," *The Economist*, January 21, 1995; J. F. Burns, "India Now Winning U.S. Investment," *New York Times*, February 3, 1995, pp. C1, C5.

of the West has won the Cold War and has never been more widespread than it is in the mid-1990s. Although command economies still remain and although totalitarian dictatorships can still be found around the world, for the time being at least, the tide is running in favor of democracy and free markets.

The implications for business are enormous. For the best part of 50 years, half the world was off-limits to Western businesses. Now all that is changing. Many of the national markets of Eastern Europe, Latin America, Africa, and Asia may still be undeveloped and impoverished, but they are potentially enormous. With a population of 1.2 billion, the Chinese market alone is potentially bigger than that of the United States, the European Community, and Japan combined! Similarly India, with its 930 million people, is a potentially huge future market. In Latin America there are another 400 million potential consumers. It is unlikely that China, Russia, Poland, or any of the other states now moving toward a free market system will attain the living standards of the West anytime soon. Nevertheless, the upside potential is so large that companies need to consider making inroads now.

However, just as the upside potential is large, so are the risks. Take the newly democratic states of Eastern Europe—they all profess a desire to move toward a free market economic system. Yet today, five years after the collapse of communism, not all appear to know what that means. After decades of central planning and tight control over prices, markets are poorly understood, profit is still too often a dirty word, and the laws required to regulate business transactions, which we take for granted in the West, are largely absent. Moreover, faced with economic chaos, there is no guarantee that democracy will thrive. Totalitarian dictatorships could return, although they are unlikely to be of the Communist variety. Put another way, while the long-term potential for economic gain from investment in the world's new market economies is large, the risks associated with any such investment are also substantial. It would be foolish to ignore these.

 IMPLICATIONS FOR BUSINESS

The implications for international business of the material discussed in this chapter falls into two broad categories. First, the political, economic, and legal environment of a country clearly influences the *attractiveness* of that country as a market and/or investment site. The benefits, costs, and risks associated with doing business in a country are in part a function of that country's political, economic, and legal systems. Second, the political, economic, and legal systems of a country can raise important *ethical issues* that have implications for the practice of international business. Here we consider each of these issues.

Attractiveness

The overall attractiveness of a country as a market and/or investment site depends on balancing the likely long-term benefits of doing business in that country against the likely costs and risks. Below we consider the determinants of benefits, costs, and risks.

Benefits

In the most general sense, the long-run monetary benefits of doing business in a country are a function of the size of a market, the present wealth (purchasing power) of consumers in that market, and the likely future wealth of consumers. While some markets are very large when measured by numbers of consumers (e.g., China and India), low living standards may imply limited purchasing power and, therefore, a relatively small market when measured in economic terms. While international businesses need to be aware of this distinction, they also need to keep in mind the likely future prospects of a country. In 1960, for example, South Korea was viewed as just another impoverished Third World nation. By 1988 it was the world's 18th largest economy, measured in terms of GDP. If present trends continue, by the year 2000 it will be one of the 10 largest economies in the world and the fourth largest trading nation after Japan, the United States, and Germany. International firms that recognized South Korea's potential in 1960 and began to do business in that country may have reaped greater benefits than those that wrote off South Korea as another Third World nation.

By identifying and investing early in a potential future economic star, international firms may be able to build brand loyalty and experience of business practices in that country. These will pay back substantial dividends if that country is subsequently able to achieve sustained high economic growth rates. In contrast, late entrants may find that they lack the brand loyalty and experience necessary to achieve a significant presence in the market. Put differently, in the language of business strategy, early entrants into potential future economic stars may be able to reap substantial **first mover advantages,** while late entrants may fall victim to **late mover disadvantages.**[33]

Two factors that are reasonably good predictors of a country's future economic prospects are its economic system and property rights regime. In this chapter we have seen that countries with free market economies in which property rights are well protected tend to achieve greater economic growth rates than command economies and/or economies where property rights are poorly protected. It follows that a country's economic system and property rights regime, when taken together with market size (in terms of population), probably constitute reasonably good indicators of the potential long-run benefits of doing business in a country.

Costs

The costs of doing business in a country are determined by a number of political, economic, and legal factors. With regard to political factors, the costs of doing business in a country can be increased by a need to pay off the politically powerful to be allowed by the government to do business in that country. As a general rule, the need to pay what are essentially bribes is greater in closed totalitarian states than in open democratic societies where politicians are held accountable by the electorate (although this is not a hard and fast distinction). Of course, whether a company should actually pay bribes in return for market access should be determined on the basis of the ethical implications of such action, which we discuss below.

With regard to economic factors, one of the most important variables is the sophistication of a country's economy. It may well be more costly to do business in relatively primitive or undeveloped economies because of the lack of infrastructure and supporting businesses. At the extreme, an international firm may have to provide its own infrastructure and supporting business, which obviously raises costs. For example, when McDonald's decided to open its first restaurant in Moscow, it found, much to its initial dismay, that in order to serve food and drink indistinguishable from that served in McDonald's restaurants elsewhere, it had to vertically integrate backward to supply its own needs. The quality of Russian grown-potatoes and meat was simply too poor. Thus, to protect the quality of its product, McDonald's set up its own dairy farms, cattle ranches, vegetable plots, and food-processing plants within Russia. This raised the costs of doing business in Russia relative to the costs in more sophisticated economies where quality inputs could be purchased on the open market.

As for legal factors, it can be more costly to do business in a country where local laws and regulations set strict standards with regard to product safety, safety in the workplace, environmental pollution, and the like (since adhering to such regulations is costly). It can also be more costly to do business in a country such as the United States, where the absence of a cap on damage awards has meant spiraling liability insurance rates. Moreover, it can be more costly to do business in a country that lacks well-established laws for regulating business practice (as is the case in many of the former Communist nations). In the absence of a well-developed body of business contract law, international firms may find that there is no satisfactory way to resolve contract disputes and, consequently, routinely face large losses from contract violations. Similarly, when local laws fail to adequately protect intellectual property, this can lead to the "theft" of an international business's intellectual property, with all that such action means in terms of lost income (see the "Management Focus" on Microsoft).

Risks

As with costs, the risks of doing business in a country are determined by a number of political, economic, and legal factors. On the political front, there is the issue of **political risk.** Political risk has been defined as *the likelihood that political forces will cause drastic changes in a country's business environment that adversely affect the profit and other goals of a particular business enterprise.*[34] So defined, political risk tends to be greater in countries experiencing social unrest and disorder, or in countries where the underlying nature of a society means the likelihood of social unrest occurring is high. Social unrest typically finds expression in strikes, demonstrations, terrorism, and perhaps violent conflict. Such unrest is more likely to be found in countries that contain more than one ethnic nationality, in countries where competing ideologies are battling for political control, and in countries where economic mismanagement has created high inflation and falling living standards (e.g., Russia in the early 1990s).

Social unrest can result in abrupt changes in government and government policy or, in some cases, in protracted civil strife. By its very nature, such strife tends to have negative economic implications, which may well affect the profit goals of business enterprises. For example, in the aftermath of the 1979 Islamic revolution in Iran, the Iranian assets of numerous U.S. companies were seized by the new Iranian government without compensation. Similarly, today the violent disintegration of the Yugoslavian federation into warring states, including Bosina, Croatia, and Serbia, has precipitated a collapse in the local economy and, consequently, a collapse in the profitability of investments in those countries.

---

[34]S. H. Robock, "Political Risk: Identification and Assessment," *Columbia Journal of World Business,* July/August 1971, pp. 6–20.

On the **economic front,** economic risks arise from economic mismanagement by the government of a country. Economic risks can be defined as *the likelihood that economic mismanagement will cause drastic changes in a country's business environment that adversely affect the profit and other goals of a particular business enterprise.* Of course, economic risks are not independent of political risk. Economic mismanagement may give rise to significant social unrest and hence political risk. Nevertheless, economic risks are worth emphasizing as a separate category, since there is not always a one-to-one relationship between economic mismanagement and social unrest. The most visible indicator of economic mismanagement tends to be a country's inflation rate.

On the legal front, risks arise when a country's legal system fails to provide adequate safeguards in the case of contract violations or to provide for the protection of property rights. When legal safeguards are weak, firms are more likely to break contracts and/or steal intellectual property if they perceive it as being in their interests to do so. Thus, **legal risks** might be defined as *the likelihood that a trading partner will opportunistically break a contract or expropriate property rights.* When legal risks in a country are high, an international business might be hesitant to enter into a long-term contract, or joint venture agreement, with a firm in that country.

For example, in the 1970s when the Indian government passed a law requiring all foreign investors to enter into joint ventures with Indian companies, U.S. companies such as IBM and Coca-Cola closed their investments in India. They did this because they believed the Indian legal system did not provide for adequate protection of intellectual property rights. Thus, a very real danger existed that the Indian partners of IBM and Coca-Cola might be able to expropriate the intellectual property of the American companies, which in the case of both IBM and Coca-Cola amounted to the core of their competitive advantage.

Overall attractiveness

The overall attractiveness of a country as a potential market and/or investment site for an international business depends on balancing the benefits, costs, and risks associated with doing business in that country. The costs and risks associated with doing business in a foreign country are typically lower in economically advanced and politically stable democratic nations, whereas they are greater in less developed and politically unstable nations. The calculus is complicated, however, by the fact that the potential *long-run* benefits bear little relationship to a nation's current stage of economic development or political stability. Rather, they are dependent on likely future economic growth rates.

In turn, among other things, economic growth appears to be a function of a free market system and a country's capacity for growth (which may be greater in less developed nations). This leads one to the conclusion that, other things being equal, the benefit, cost, risk trade-off is likely to be most favorable in the case of politically stable developing nations that have free market systems. It is likely to be least favorable in politically unstable developing nations that operate with a mixed or command economy.

Ethical Issues

Country differences give rise to some interesting and contentious ethical issues. One of the major ethical dilemmas facing firms from Western democracies is whether they should do business in totalitarian countries that routinely violate the human rights of their citizens (such as China). There are those who argue that investing in totalitarian countries provides comfort to dictators and can prop up repressive regimes. Without investment by Western firms, critics claim that many repressive regimes would collapse and be replaced by more democratically inclined governments. In recent years, firms that have invested in Chile, China, Iraq, and South Africa have all been the targets of such criticisms. Interestingly enough, the dismantling of the apartheid system in South Africa, which occurred in 1994, has been credited to economic sanctions by Western nations, including a lack of investment by Western firms. This, say those who argue against investment in totalitarian countries, is proof that investment boycotts work.

On the other hand, there are those who argue that investment by a Western firm, by raising the level of economic development of a totalitarian country, can help change it from within. They note that economic well-being and political freedoms often go hand in hand.

Thus, for example, when arguing against attempts to apply trade sanctions to China in the wake of the violent 1989 government crackdown on prodemocracy demonstrators, the Bush administration claimed that U.S. firms should continue to be allowed to invest in mainland China, since greater political freedoms would follow the resulting economic growth.

Since both positions have some merit, it is extremely difficult to arrive at a general statement of what firms should do. It is probably fair to say that unless mandated by government (as in the case of investment in South Africa), each firm must make its own judgments on a case-by-case basis about the ethical implications of investment in totalitarian states. The more repressive the regime, however, and the less amenable it seems to be to change, the greater the case for not investing.

A second interesting ethical issue is whether an international firm should adhere to the same standards of product safety, work safety, and environmental protection that are required in its home country. This is of particular concern to many firms based in Western nations, where product safety, worker safety, and environmental protection laws are among the toughest in the world.

Should Western firms investing in less developed countries adhere to tough Western standards, even though local laws don't require them to do so? Again there is no easy answer. While on the face of it the argument for adhering to Western standards might seem strong, on closer examination the issue becomes more complicated. What if adhering to Western standards would make the foreign investment unprofitable, thereby denying the foreign country much-needed jobs? What then is the ethical thing to do? To adhere to Western standards and not invest, thereby denying people jobs, or to adhere to local standards and invest, thereby providing jobs and income? As with many ethical dilemmas, there is no easy answer. Each case needs to be assessed on its own merits.

A final ethical issue concerns bribes. Should an international business pay bribes to government officials in order to gain market access to a foreign country? To most Westerners bribery seems to be a corrupt and morally repugnant way of doing business, so the answer might initially be no. However, in many parts of the world, the simple fact is that pay-offs to government officials are a part of life. Moreover, not investing if bribes are required ignores the fact that such investment can bring substantial benefits to the local populace in terms of income and jobs. Given this, from a purely ethical standpoint, perhaps the practice of giving bribes, although a little evil, is the price that must be paid to do a greater good (assuming the investment creates jobs where none existed before). Again, given the complexity of the issue, generalization is difficult. One thing seem certain, however; it is clearly unethical to offer bribes.

❧ SUMMARY OF CHAPTER

This chapter has reviewed how the political, economic, and legal systems of different countries vary. The potential benefits, costs, and risks of doing business in a country are a function of its political, economic, and legal systems. More specifically:

1. Political systems can be assessed according to two dimensions—the degree to which they emphasize collectivism as opposed to individualism and the degree to which they are democratic or totalitarian.

2. Collectivism is an ideology that views the needs of society as being more important than the needs of the individual. Collectivism translates into an advocacy for state intervention in economic activity and, in the case of communism, a totalitarian dictatorship.

3. Individualism is an ideology that is built on an emphasis on the primacy of individual's freedoms in the political, economic, and cultural realm. Individualism translates into an advocacy for democratic ideals and free market economics.

4. Democracy and totalitarianism are at different ends of a political spectrum. In a representative democracy, citizens periodically elect individuals to represent them and political freedoms are guaranteed by a constitution. In a totalitarian state, political power is monopolized by a party, group, or individual, and basic political freedoms are denied to citizens of the state.

5. There are three broad types of economic system—a market economy, a command economy, and a mixed economy. In a market economy prices are free of any controls and private ownership is predominant. In a command economy prices are set by central planners, productive assets are owned by the state, and private ownership is forbidden. A mixed economy has elements of both a market economy and a command economy.

6. Differences in the structure of law between countries can have important implications for the practice of international business. The degree to which property rights are protected can vary dramatically as can product safety and product liability legislation and the nature of contract law.

7. The rate of economic progress in a country seems to depend on the extent to which that country has a well-functioning market economy in which property rights are protected.

8. Many countries are now in a state of transition. There is a marked shift away from totalitarian governments and command or mixed economic systems and toward democratic political institutions and free market economic systems.

9. The attractiveness of a country as a market and/or investment site depends on balancing the likely long-run benefits of doing business in that country against the likely costs and risks.

10. The benefits of doing business in a country are a function of the size of the market (population), its present wealth (purchasing power), and its future growth prospects. By investing early in countries that are currently poor, but are growing rapidly, firms can gain first mover advantages that could pay back substantial dividends in the future.

11. The costs of doing business in a country tend to be greater in those countries where political payoffs are required to gain market access, where supporting infrastructure is lacking or underdeveloped, and where adhering to local laws and regulations is costly.

12. The risks of doing business in a country tend to be greater in countries that are politically unstable, subject to economic mismanagement, and equipped with a legal system that fails to provide adequate safeguards in the case of contract or property rights violations.

13. Country differences give rise to several ethical dilemmas, including should a firm do business in a repressive totalitarian state? should a firm conform to its home product, workplace, and environmental standards when they are not required by host country laws? and should a firm pay bribes to government officials to gain market access?

🦬 CRITICAL DISCUSSION QUESTIONS

1. Free market economies stimulate greater economic growth, whereas command economies stifle growth! Discuss.

2. A democratic political system is an essential condition for *sustained* economic progress. Discuss.

3. During the late 1980s and early 1990s, China was routinely cited by various international organizations such as Amnesty International and Freedom Watch for major human rights violations, including torture, beatings, imprisonment, and executions of political dissidents. Despite this, in 1991 China was the recipient of record levels of foreign direct investment, principally from firms based in democratic societies such as the United States, Japan, and Germany. Evaluate this trend from an ethical perspective. If you were the CEO of a firm that had the option of making a potentially very profitable investment in China, what would you do?

4. You are the CEO of a company that has to choose between making a $100 million investment in either Russia or the Czech Republic. Both investments promise the same long-run return, so your choice of which investment to make is driven by risk considerations. Assess the various risks of doing business in each of these nations. Which investment would you favor and why?

🦬 CLOSING CASE   Trinity Motors Struggles in Russia

Mark Thimming moved to Moscow in 1992 to run Trinity Motors, a General Motors dealership owned by private investors from Britain, Russia, and the United States. On Mark Thimming's office wall is a large map of Russia with about 40 major cities highlighted in orange. Ultimately, Thimming hopes to franchise dealerships in each of these cities. So far Trinity sells its North American-made Chevrolets, Pontiacs, and Cadillacs in Moscow, St. Petersburg, and Kiev—but it hasn't been easy going.

Several problems are hurting Trinity's efforts to expand in Russia. One problem is the cash-strapped Russian government has tried to raise funds by placing steep duties on all kinds of imports, including the cars Trinity brings in, and by raising taxes across the board. In 1992 duties and value-added taxes amounted to about 25 percent of the value of an imported car; today the figure is closer to 166 percent! The result, a Chevrolet Caprice that retails for $24,000 in the United States sells for about $58,000 in Moscow. It's hardly surprising then that Trinity's sales have fallen 50 percent from their early 1993 peak.

Russia's gangsterism, too, is taking its toll. One associate of Mark Thimming, Boris Berezovsky, who runs a major Russian car dealer, Logo VAZ, narrowly escaped a recent car bomb attack. Thimming won't travel without an armed guard, while his wife and children remain in the United States. Thimming has good reason to be worried; according to a 1994 report prepared for Russian President Boris Yeltsin, the Russian Mafia controlled 70 to 80 percent of all business and banking activity in 1994. Primarily, this control is exercised by demanding payment of protection money (the Mafia has a much higher collection rate than the official state tax authorities). But in an increasing number of cases, organized crime groups have a minority or even majority ownership stake in businesses.

Indeed, Mark Thimming fears that his main competitors in the car import business are Russian gangsters who pay bribes to state bureaucrats so they can import Western cars without paying the staggering import duties and taxes that are crippling Trinity Motors. Thimming estimates that around 80 percent of all cars imported into Moscow come via the black or gray markets. To make matters worse, frequently the GM cars imported into Russia by the Mafia aren't those designed for the market. They can't run on the leaded fuel used in Russia, for example, or they lack the special suspension systems required for Russia's rough roads. As a result, Thimming is concerned that GM buyers may get a negative attitude toward the company.

In an ironic twist, however, Thimming reckons that some of his best customers are themselves gangsters. The high retail prices dictated by the steep taxes and import duties mean that the successful members of the criminal underworld are among the few who have enough cash to purchase one of Trinity's imports. When requesting service on their GMs, he says, these people "have a tendency to go to their strong suit and show off their guns and ammunition." Trinity tries to cope with the problem by offering good service to all clients. As Mark Thimming's service department manager once told a Mafia member; "There is no use killing me, because no one else could service your car."

Despite all these problems Mark Thimming remains remarkably upbeat. He continues to see great long-run growth prospects in Russia. Trinity Motors is profitable, thanks to its service and parts department, which covers 80 percent of its expenses. Thimming figures the economy and legal system will have improved enough by 2000 to transform the country into a real growth opportunity for Western businesses. In the meantime Thimming is content to build Trinity's reputation for excellent products and service. Still, sales remain slack at under 1,000 per year, compared to the 5,000 plus per year that Thimming thinks should be attainable in Moscow alone.

CASE DISCUSSION QUESTIONS

1. What is the exact nature of the problems encountered by Trinity Motors in Russia? Specifically, are these problems due to deficiencies in Russia's political system, economic system, or legal system? What will it take to correct these problems?

2. Until the problems that Trinity is facing are corrected, how should Mark Thimming deal with them?

3. Does it make sense for Trinity to tough it out in Russia until the current problems are resolved?

4. How long do you think it will be before Russia resembles a stable Western democracy?

Sources: A. Ignatius, "GM Dealer Hits Rough Road in Russia," The Wall Street Journal, June 28, 1994, pp. A1, 15; and M. Goldman, "In Russia the Mafia Seizes the Commanding Heights of the Economy," Washington Post, February 12, 1995, p. C2.

CHAPTER THREE

DIFFERENCES IN CULTURE

"BUT WHERE ARE THE FRENCH?"—THE TRIALS AND TRIBULATIONS OF EURO-DISNEYLAND

Until 1992 the Walt Disney Company had experienced nothing but success in the theme park business. Its first park, Disneyland, opened in Anaheim, California, in 1955. Its theme song, "It's a Small World After All," promoted an idealized vision of America spiced with reassuring glimpses of exotic cultures all calculated to promote heartwarming feelings about living together as one happy family. There were dark tunnels and bumpy rides to scare the children a little but none of the terrors of the real world . . . The Disney characters that everyone knew from the cartoons and comic books were on hand to shepherd the guests and to direct them to the Micky Mouse watches and Little Mermaid records.

The Anaheim park was an instant success.

In the 1970s the triumph was repeated in Florida, and in 1983 Disney proved that the Japanese, too, have a real affinity for Mickey Mouse with the successful opening of Tokyo Disneyland. Having wooed the Japanese, in 1986 Disney executives turned their attention to France and, more specifically, to Paris, the self-proclaimed capital of European high culture and style. "Why did they pick France?" many asked. Good question; when word first got out that Disney wanted to build another international theme park, officials from more than 200 locations all over the world descended on Disney with pleas and cash inducements to work the Disney magic in their hometowns. But Paris was chosen because of demographics and subsidies. About 17 million Europeans live less than two hours' drive from Paris. Another 310 million can fly there in the same time or less. Moreover, the French government was so eager to attract Disney to Paris that it offered the company more than

$1 billion in various incentives, all in the expectation that the project would create 30,000 French jobs.

From the beginning cultural gaffes by Disney set the tone for the project. By late 1986 Disney was deep in negotiations with the French government. To the exasperation of the Disney team, headed by Joe Shapiro, the talks were taking far longer than expected. Jean-Rene Bernard, the chief French negotiator, said he was astonished when Mr. Shapiro, his patience ebbing, ran to the door of the room and in a very un-Gallic gesture, began kicking it repeatedly, shouting, "Get me something to break!"

There was also snipping from Parisian intellectuals who attacked the transplantation of Disney's dream world as an assault on French culture; "a cultural Chernobyl," one prominent intellectual called it. The minister of culture announced he would boycott the opening, proclaiming it to be an unwelcome symbol of American clichés and a consumer society. Unperturbed, Disney pushed ahead with the planned summer 1992 opening of the $5 billion park. Shortly after Euro-Disneyland opened, French farmers drove their tractors to the entrance and blocked it. This globally televised act of protest was aimed not at Disney but at the U.S. government, which had been demanding that French agricultural subsidies be cut. Still, it focused

world attention on the loveless marriage of Disneyland and Paris.

Then there were the operational errors. Disney's policy of serving no alcohol in the park, since reversed, caused astonishment in a country where a glass of wine for lunch is a given. Disney thought Monday would be a light day for visitors and Friday a heavy one and allocated staff accordingly; but the reality was the reverse. Another unpleasant surprise was the hotel breakfast debacle. "We were told that Europeans 'don't take breakfast,' so we downsized the restaurants," recalled one Disney executive. "And guess what? Everybody showed up for breakfast. We were trying to serve 2,500 breakfasts in a 350-seat restaurant at some of the hotels. The lines were horrendous. And they didn't just want croissants and coffee. They wanted bacon and eggs." Lunch turned out to be another problem. "Everybody wanted lunch at 12:30. The crowds were huge. Our smiling cast members had to calm down surly patrons and engage in some 'behavior modification' to teach them that they could eat lunch at 11 AM or 2 PM."

There were major staffing problems, too. Disney tried to use the same teamwork model with its staff that had worked so well in America and Japan, but it ran into trouble in France. Within the first nine weeks of Euro-Disneyland's operation, roughly 1,000 employees, 10 percent of the total, left. One former employee was a 22-year-old medical student from a nearby town who signed up for a weekend job. After two days of "brainwashing," as he called Disney's training, he left following a dispute with his supervisor over the timing of his lunch hour. Another former employee noted, "I don't think that they realized what Europeans were like . . . that we ask questions and don't think all the same way."

One of the biggest problems, however, was that Europeans didn't stay as long at the park as Disney expected. While Disney did succeed in getting close to 1 million visitors a year through the park gates, in line with its plans, most stayed only a day or two. Few stayed the four to five days that Disney had hoped for. It seems that most Europeans regard theme parks as places for day excursions. This was a big shock for Disney; the company had invested billions in building luxury hotels next to the park—hotels that the day-trippers didn't need

and that stood half empty most of the time. To make matters worse, the French didn't show up in the expected numbers. In 1994 only 40 percent of the park's visitors were French. One puzzled executive noted that many visitors were Americans living in Europe, or stranger still, Japanese on a European vacation! As a result,

by the end of 1994 Euro-Disneyland had cumulative losses of $2 billion.

*R. J. Barnet and J. Cavanagh, *Global Dreams* (New York: Touchstone Books, 1994), p. 33.

Sources: P. Gumble and R. Turner, "Mouse Trap: Fans Like Euro-Disney but Its Parent's Goofs Weigh the Park Down," *The Wall Street Journal*, March 10, 1994, p. A1; Barnet and Cavanagh, *Global Dreams*, pp. 33–34; J. Huey, "Eisner Explains Everything," *Fortune*, April 17, 1995, pp. 45–68; and R. Anthony, "Euro-Disney: The First 100 Days," *Harvard Business School Case # 9-693-013*.

🐾 INTRODUCTION

International business is different from domestic business because countries are different. In Chapter 2 we saw how national differences in political, economic, and legal systems influence the benefits, costs, and risks associated with doing business in different countries. In this chapter we will explore how differences in culture both across *and* within countries can impact the practice of international business.

Two themes run through this chapter. One theme is that cross-cultural literacy is required to successfully do business in a variety of countries. By cross-cultural literacy, we mean an understanding of how cultural differences both across and within nations can affect the way in which business is practiced. In these days of global communications, rapid transportation, and global markets, when the era of the global village seems just around the corner, it is easy to forget just how different various cultures really are. Deep cultural differences remain. The importance of cross-cultural literacy cannot be overemphasized. Without it, managers may make mistakes that put lucrative opportunities in jeopardy.

The opening case illustrates how a lack of cross-cultural literacy can affect a business venture. Walt Disney has been one of the most successful managers of theme parks in the world, but its Euro-Disney venture has yet to turn a profit. Although a lack of cultural literacy on the part of Disney's American managers hardly constitutes the whole explanation for this failure, it didn't help either. The tone was set early on by Joe Shapiro when he displayed his frustrations with the slow pace of negotiations by kicking down the door to the room in the expensive French hotel where Disney and French government officials were meeting. This inappropriate action was widely reported in the French press as an example of the "cowboy values" of Disney's managers.

Then there was Disney's underestimation of the negative press that would be created by the juxtaposition of Paris and Disney. Disney was focused on demographics and subsidies when choosing a location. As one observer put it, "I think as far as the (Disney) management is concerned, Euro-Disney just happens to be in the middle of Europe handy for a big population." Disney's management lost sight of the fact that Mickey Mouse and left-bank intellectuals do not mix well; and the French take their intellectuals seriously. The characterization of Euro-Disneyland as "a cultural Chernobyl" resonated not just with French intellectuals, but also with many middle-class French—the ones Disney wanted to attract to its expensive hotels. In retrospect, Paris was not the best location for this theme park; locating it there simply raised a red flag to France's influential intellectuals. Nor did it help that Disney's managers publicly characterized some criticisms as the "ravings of a small cultural elite." While the cultural elite in America may be easily dismissed, and often is, the French take their cultural elite more seriously and saw such criticisms as an attack on their national character.

Disney's managers also erred by making assumptions about European cultural habits that were based on simplistic characterizations, such as assuming Europeans didn't eat breakfast. Further, after having worked with the clean-cut and service-oriented staff in America and Japan, Disney was caught off-guard by the less enthusiastic and malleable character of many European employees. Nor did Disney's managers appreciate the different attitudes toward vacationing and theme parks that exist in Europe. Disney assumed Europeans would vacation like Americans and Japanese; that they would be happy to stay for several days at a theme park. But middle-class Europeans try to "get away from it all" on their vacations by going to the beach or the mountains, and Euro-Disneyland lacked that kind of appeal.

A second theme found in this chapter is that a relationship may exist between culture and the costs of doing business in a country or region. It can be argued that the culture of some countries (or regions) is supportive of the capitalist mode of production and lowers the costs of doing business there. To the extent that this is the case, cultural factors can help firms based in such countries achieve a competitive advantage in the world economy. For example, some observers have argued that cultural factors have helped to lower the costs of doing business in Japan.[1] In turn, this may have helped some Japanese businesses achieve a competitive advantage in the world economy.

By the same token cultural factors can sometimes raise the costs of doing business. For example, until recently firms found it difficult to achieve cooperation between management and labor in Britain, historically a culture that emphasized class conflict. Such conflict was reflected in a high level of industrial disputes. In turn, this raised the costs of doing business in Britain, relative to the costs of doing business in countries such as Switzerland, Norway, Germany, or Japan, where class conflict was historically less prevalent.

We open this chapter with a general discussion of what culture actually is. Then we focus on how differences in social structure, religion, language, and education influence the culture of a country. The implications for business will be highlighted throughout the chapter and summarized at the end.

❧ WHAT IS CULTURE?

Scholars have never been able to agree on a simple definition of culture. In the 1870s the anthropologist Edward Tylor defined culture as *that complex whole which includes knowledge, belief, art, morals, law, custom, and other capabilities acquired by man as a member of society.*[2] Since then hundreds of other definitions have been offered. Geert Hofstede, an expert on cross-cultural differences and management, defined culture as *the collective programming of the mind which distinguishes the members of one human group from another . . . Culture, in this sense, includes systems of values; and values are among the building blocks of culture.*[3] Another definition of culture comes from sociologists Zvi Namenwirth and Robert Weber who see culture as *a system of ideas* and argue that these ideas constitute *a design for living.*[4]

Here we follow both Hofstede and Namenwirth and Weber by viewing **culture** as *a system of values and norms that are shared among a group of people and that when taken together constitute a design for living.* By **values** we mean abstract *ideas* about what a group believes to be good, right, and desirable. Put differently, values are shared assumptions about how things ought to be.[5] By **norms** we mean the social rules and guidelines that prescribe appropriate behavior in particular situations. We shall use the term **society** to refer to a group of people who share a common set of values and norms.

Values and Norms

Values form the bedrock of a culture. They provide the context within which a society's norms are established and justified. They may include a society's attitudes toward such concepts as individual freedom, democracy, truth, justice, honesty, loyalty, social obligations, collective responsibility, the role of women, love, sex, marriage, and so on. Values are not just abstract concepts; they are invested with considerable

---

[1]See R. Dore, *Taking Japan Seriously* (Stanford, CA: Stanford University Press, 1987).

[2] E. B. Tylor, *Primitive Culture* (London: Murray, 1871).

[3] Geert Hofstede, *Culture's Consequences: International Differences in Work Related Values* (Beverly Hills, CA: Sage, 1984), p. 21.

[4] J. Z. Namenwirth and R. B. Weber, *Dynamics of Culture* (Boston: Allen & Unwin, 1987), p. 8.

[5]R. Mead, *International Management: Cross-Cultural Dimensions* (Oxford: Blackwell Business, 1994), p. 7.

emotional significance. People argue, fight, and even die over values such as freedom. Values may also often be reflected in the political and economic system of a society. As we saw in Chapter 2, democratic free market capitalism is a reflection of a philosophical value system that emphasizes individual freedom.

Norms are the social rules that govern the actions of people toward one another. Norms can be subdivided further into two major categories—folkways and mores. **Folkways** are the routine conventions of everyday life. Generally, folkways are actions of little *moral* significance. Rather, folkways are social conventions concerning things such as what constitutes the appropriate dress code in a particular situation, good social manners, eating with the correct utensils, neighborly behavior, and the like. While folkways define the way people are expected to behave, violation of folkways is ultimately not normally a serious matter. People who violate folkways may be thought of as eccentric or ill-mannered, but they are not usually considered to be evil or bad. In many countries foreigners may be initially excused for violating folkways.

A good example of folkways concerns attitudes toward time in different countries. In the United States people are very time conscious. Americans tend to arrive a few minutes early for business appointments. When invited for dinner to someone's home, it is considered polite to arrive on time or just a few minutes late. In other countries the concept of time can be very different. It is not necessarily a breach of etiquette to arrive a little late for a business appointment; indeed it might be considered more impolite to arrive early. As for dinner invitations, arriving on time for a dinner engagement can be very bad manners. In Britain, for example, when someone says, "Come for dinner at 7 PM," what they mean is "Come for dinner at 7:30 to 8 PM." The guest who arrives at 7 PM is likely to find an unprepared and embarrassed host. Similarly, when an Argentinean says, "Come for dinner anytime after 8 PM," what he means is "Don't come at 8 PM—it's far too early!"

Mores are norms that are seen as central to the functioning of a society and to its social life. They take on a much greater significance than folkways. Accordingly, the violation of mores can bring serious retribution. Mores include such factors as indictments against theft, adultery, incest, and cannibalism. In many societies certain mores have been enacted into law. Thus, all advanced societies have laws against theft, incest, and cannibalism. However, there are also many differences between cultures as to what is perceived as mores. In America, for example, drinking alcohol is widely accepted, whereas in Saudi Arabia the consumption of alcohol is viewed as violating important social mores and is punishable by imprisonment (as some Western citizens working in Saudi Arabia have found out).

Culture, Society, and the Nation-State

We have defined a society as a group of people that share a common set of values and norms; that is, people who are bound together by a common culture. However, there is *not* a strict one-to-one correspondence between a society and a nation-state. Nation-states are political creations. As such they may contain a single culture, but a nation-state may also contain several distinct cultures. For example, during the Gulf War the prevailing view presented to Western audiences was that Iraq was a homogenous Arab nation. But in the chaos that followed the war it became apparent that there are several different societies within Iraq, each with its own culture. In the north are the Kurds, who don't view themselves as Arabs and have their own distinct history and traditions. Then there are two Arab societies, the Shiites in the south and the Sunnis who populate the middle of the country and who rule Iraq (the terms *Shiites* and *Sunnis* refer to different sects within the religion of Islam). Moreover, among the southern Sunnis is another distinct society of 500,000 "Marsh Arabs" who live at the confluence of the Tigris and Euphrates rivers pursuing a way of life that dates back 5,000 years.[6]

To complicate things further, it is also possible to talk about culture at different levels. It is reasonable to talk about "American society" and "American culture," but we

---

[6]"Iraq: Down but Not Out," *The Economist*, April 8, 1995, pp. 21–23.

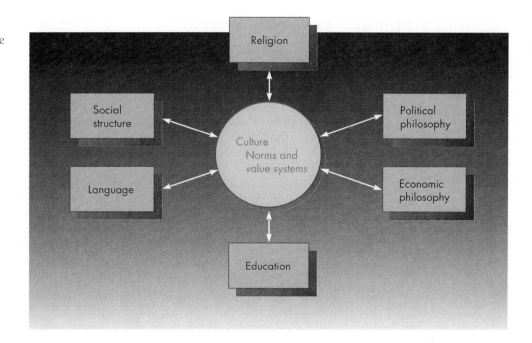

must recognize that at another level there are several societies within America, each with its own culture. One can talk about African-American culture, Cajun culture, Chinese-American culture, Hispanic culture, Indian culture, Irish-American culture, and Southern culture. The point is that the relationship between culture and country is often ambiguous. One cannot always characterize a country as having a single homogenous culture, and even when one can do this, one must also often recognize that the national culture is itself a mosaic of subcultures, many of which can be quite distinct.

The Determinants of Culture

The values and norms of a culture do not emerge from nowhere fully formed. They are the evolutionary product of a number of factors at work in a society. These factors include the prevailing political and economic philosophy, the social structure of a society, and the dominant religion, language, and education (see Figure 3.1). We discussed political and economic philosophy at length in Chapter 2. Such philosophy clearly influences the value systems of a society. For example, the values found in the former Soviet Union toward freedom, justice, and individual achievement were clearly different from the values found in the United States, precisely because each society operated according to a different political and economic philosophy. Below we will discuss the influence of social structure, religion, language, and education. Bear in mind that the chain of causation runs both ways. While factors such as social structure and religion clearly influence the values and norms of a society, the values and norms of a society can influence social structure and religion.

❧ SOCIAL STRUCTURE

A society's "social structure" refers to its basic social organization. Although there are many different aspects of social structure, two main dimensions stand out as being of particular importance when explaining differences among cultures. The first is the degree to which the basic unit of social organization is the individual, as opposed to the group. Western societies tend to emphasize the primacy of the individual, while groups tend to figure much larger in many other societies. The second dimension is the degree to which a society is stratified into classes or castes. Some societies are characterized by a high degree of social stratification and relatively low mobility between strata (e.g., Indian and to a lesser extent British), while other societies are characterized by a low degree of social stratification and high mobility between strata (e.g., American).

Individuals and Groups

A **group** is an association of two or more individuals who have a shared sense of identity and who interact with each other in structured ways on the basis of a common set of expectations about each other's behavior.[7] Human social life is group life. Individuals are involved in families, work groups, social groups, recreational groups, and so on. However, while groups are found in all societies, societies differ according to the degree to which the group is viewed as the primary means of social organization.[8] In some societies individual attributes and achievements are viewed as being more important than group membership, while in other societies just the reverse is true.

The individual

In Chapter 2 we discussed individualism as a political philosophy. However, individualism is more than just an abstract political philosophy. In many Western societies the individual is the basic building block of social organization. This is reflected not just in the political and economic organization of society, but also in the way in which people perceive themselves and relate to each other in social and business settings. In the value systems of many Western societies, for example, individual achievement is emphasized. The social standing of an individual is not so much a function of whom they work for, as of their individual performance in whatever work setting they choose for themselves.

The emphasis placed on individual performance in many Western societies has both beneficial and harmful aspects. For example, the United States voices an admiration of "rugged individualism" and entrepreneurship. One of the benefits of this is the high level of entrepreneurial activity in the United States and other Western societies. New products and new ways of doing business have repeatedly been created in the United States by entrepreneurial individuals (e.g., personal computers, photocopiers, computer software, biotechnology, supermarkets, and discount retail stores). One can argue that the dynamism of the U.S. economy owes much to the philosophy of individualism.

On the other hand, the philosophy of individualism also finds expression in a high degree of managerial mobility between companies, and this is not always good. While moving from company to company may be good for individual managers, who are trying to build impressive résumés, it is not necessarily a good thing for many American companies. The lack of loyalty and commitment to an individual company, and the tendency to move when a better offer comes along, can result in the creation of managers that have good general skills but lack the in-depth knowledge, experience, and network of interpersonal contacts that come from years of working within the same company. Company-specific experience, knowledge, and personal contacts are probably all good things, since they may increase the ability of a manager to perform his or her job effectively. A manager may draw on past experience, knowledge, and a network of contacts to find solutions to current problems. It follows that American companies may suffer if their managers lack these things.

Moreover, the emphasis on individualism may make it difficult to build teams within an organization to perform collective tasks. If individuals are always competing with each other, it may prove difficult for them to cooperate. A recent study of U.S. competitiveness by MIT concluded that U.S. firms are hurt in the global economy by a failure to achieve cooperation both within a company (e.g., between functions; between management and labor) and between companies (e.g., between a firm and its suppliers). Given the emphasis placed on individualism in the American value system, perhaps this failure is not surprising.[9] Put another way, the emphasis on individualism in the United States, while helping to create a dynamic entrepreneurial economy, may raise the costs of doing business due to its adverse impact on managerial mobility and cooperation.

---

[7]M. Thompson, R. Ellis, and A. Wildavsky, *Cultural Theory* (Boulder, CO: Westview Press, 1990).

[8]M. Douglas, "Cultural Bias," *In the Active Voice* (London: Routledge, 1982), pp. 183–254.

[9]M. L. Dertouzos, R. K. Lester, and R. M. Solow, *Made in America.* (Cambridge, MA: MIT Press, 1989).

There is one positive aspect of high managerial mobility. Moving from firm to firm exposes executives to different ways of doing business. The ability to compare different business practices helps U.S. executives to identify how good practices and techniques developed in one firm might be profitably applied to other firms.

The group

In contrast to the Western emphasis on the individual, in many other societies the group is the primary unit of social organization. In Japan, for example, the social status of an individual is determined as much by the standing of the group to which he or she belongs as by his or her individual performance.[10] In traditional Japanese society the group was the family or village to which an individual belonged. Today the group has frequently come to be associated with the work team or business organization to which an individual belongs. In a now classic study of Japanese society, Nakane has noted how this expresses itself in everyday life:

> When a Japanese faces the outside (confronts another person) and affixes some position to himself socially he is inclined to give precedence to institution over kind of occupation. Rather than saying, "I am a typesetter" or "I am a filing clerk," he is likely to say, "I am from B Publishing Group" or "I belong to S company."[11]

Nakane goes on to observe that the primacy of the group to which an individual belongs often evolves into a deeply emotional attachment in which identification with the group becomes all important in one's life. Put another way, one of the central values of Japanese culture is the importance attached to group membership. This may have beneficial implications for business firms.

Strong identification with the group is said to pressure for mutual self-help and collective action. If the worth of an individual is linked to the achievements of the group (e.g., firm), as Nakane maintains is the case in Japan, this creates a strong incentive for individual members of the group to work together for the common good. In other words, the lack of cooperation that the MIT study found in many American firms may not be a problem in Japanese firms. Some argue that the competitive advantage of Japanese enterprises in the global economy is based partly on their ability to achieve close cooperation between individuals within a company and between companies. Among other things, this finds expression in the widespread diffusion of self-managing work teams within Japanese organizations, the close cooperation between different functions within Japanese companies (e.g., between manufacturing, marketing, and R&D), and the cooperation between a company and its suppliers on issues such as design, quality control, and inventory reduction.[12] In all these cases, cooperation is driven by the need to improve the performance of the group (i.e., the business firm) to which individuals belong.

The primacy of the value of group identification in cultures such as Japan can also discourage managers and workers from moving from company to company. This is the case in Japan where lifetime employment in a particular company is the norm in certain sectors of the economy (estimates suggest between 20 and 40 percent of all Japanese employees have formal or informal lifetime employment guarantees). One result of the lifetime employment system is that managers and workers build up knowledge, experience, and a network of interpersonal business contacts. All these can help managers perform their jobs more effectively and assist them in achieving cooperation with others.

However, the primacy of the group is not always beneficial. Just as U.S. society is characterized by much dynamism and entrepreneurship, reflecting the primacy of values associated with individualism, there are those who argue that Japanese society is characterized by a corresponding lack of dynamism and entrepreneurship.

---

[10]C. Nakane, *Japanese Society* (Berkeley: University of California Press, 1970).

[11]Ibid.

[12]For details, see, M. Aoki, *Information, Incentives, and Bargaining in the Japanese Economy* (Cambridge: Cambridge University Press, 1988); and Dertouzos, Lester, and Solow, *Made in America*.

Although it is not clear how this will play itself out in the long run, it is possible that the United States will continue to create more new industries than Japan. Put another way, for cultural reasons the United States may continue to be more successful than Japan at pioneering radically new products and new ways of doing business.

Social Stratification

All societies are stratified on a hierarchical basis into social categories—that is, into **social strata.** These strata are typically defined on the basis of characteristics such as family background, occupation, and income. Individuals are born into a particular stratum. They become a member of the social category to which their parents belong. Individuals born into a stratum toward the top of the social hierarchy tend to have better *life chances* than individuals born toward the bottom of the hierarchy. They are likely to have a better education, better health, a better standard of living, and better work opportunities. Although all societies are stratified to some degree, societies differ from each other in two related ways that are of interest to us here. First, they differ from each other with regard to the degree of *mobility* between social strata, and second, they differ from each other with regard to the *significance* attached to social strata in business contexts.

Social mobility

The term **social mobility** refers to the extent to which individuals can move out of the stratum into which they are born. Social mobility varies significantly from society to society. The most rigid system of stratification is a caste system. A **caste system** is a *closed system of stratification* in which social position is determined by the family into which a person is born, and change in that position is usually not possible during an individual's lifetime (i.e., social mobility is very limited). Often a caste position carries with it a specific occupation. Members of one caste might be shoemakers, members of another caste might be butchers, and so on. These occupations are embedded in the caste and passed down through the family to succeeding generations.

Although the number of societies with caste systems has diminished rapidly during the 20th century, one major example still remains—India. India has four main castes and several thousand subcastes. Even though the caste system was officially abolished in 1949, two years after India became independent, the caste system is still a powerful force in rural Indian society where occupation and marital opportunities are still partly related to caste.

A **class system** is a less rigid form of social stratification in which social mobility is possible. A class system is a form of *open stratification* in which the position a person has by birth can be changed through achievements and/or luck. Individuals born into a class at the bottom of the hierarchy can work their way up, while individuals born into a class at the top of the hierarchy can slip down.

While many societies have class systems, social mobility within a class system varies from society to society. One of the better examples of a class society with relatively low mobility is Britain.[13] British society is divided into three main classes—the *upper class*, which is made up of individuals whose families have had wealth, prestige, and occasionally power for generations; the *middle class*, whose members are involved in professional, managerial, and clerical occupations; and the *working class*, whose members earn their living from manual occupations. The middle class is further subdivided into the *upper-middle class*, whose members are involved in important managerial occupations and the prestigious professions (e.g., lawyers, accountants, doctors), and the *lower-middle class*, whose members are involved in clerical work (e.g., bank tellers) and the less prestigious professions (e.g., schoolteachers).

---

[13]For an excellent historical treatment of the evolution of the English class system, see E. P. Thompson, *The Making of the English Working Class* (London: Vintage Books, 1966). See also, R. Miliband, *The State in Capitalist Society* (New York: Basic Books, 1969), especially chap. 2.

The British class system creates diverse life chances for members of different classes. The upper and upper-middle classes typically send their children to a select group of private schools, where they don't mix with lower-class children, and where they pick up many of the speech accents and social norms that mark them as being from the higher strata of society. These same private schools often have close ties with the most prestigious universities, such as Oxford and Cambridge. Until recently Oxford and Cambridge guaranteed to reserve a certain number of places for the graduates of these private schools. Having been to a prestigious university, the offspring of the upper and upper-middle classes then have an excellent chance of being offered a prestigious job in companies, banks, brokerage firms, and law firms that are themselves run by members of the upper and upper-middle classes.

In stark contrast, the members of the British working and lower-middle classes typically go to state schools. The majority of them leave school at 16, and those that go on to higher education find it more difficult to get accepted at the best universities. When they do, they will find that their lower-class accent and lack of social skills mark them as being from a lower social stratum. Unless they can change this, it will be more difficult for them to get access to the most prestigious jobs.

As a result, the class system in Britain tends to perpetuate itself, and mobility is limited. Although upward mobility is possible, it cannot normally be achieved in one generation. While an individual from a working-class background may reach an income level that is consistent with membership of the upper-middle class, he or she may not be accepted as such by others of that class due to accent and background. However, by sending his or her offspring to the "right kind of school," the individual can ensure that his or her children are accepted.

The class system in the United States is less extreme than in Britain and mobility is much greater. Like Britain, the United States has its own upper, middle, and working classes. However, in the United States class membership is determined principally by individual economic achievements, as opposed to background and schooling. Thus, individuals can, by their own economic achievement, move smoothly from the working class to the upper class in their own lifetime. Indeed, in American society successful individuals from humble origins are highly respected, whereas in British society such individuals are regarded as being *nouveau riche* and never quite accepted by their economic peers.

Significance

From a business perspective the stratification of a society is significant in so far as it affects the operation of business organization. In American society the high degree of social mobility and the emphasis on individualism limits the impact of class background on business operations. The same is true in Japan, where most people perceive themselves to be middle class. In a country such as Britain, however, the relative lack of class mobility and the striking differences between classes has resulted in the emergence of class consciousness. **Class consciousness** refers to a condition where people tend to perceive themselves in terms of their class background, and this shapes their relationships with members of other classes.

This is seen in British society in the traditional hostility between upper-middle-class managers and their working-class employees. Mutual antagonism and lack of respect has made it difficult to achieve cooperation between management and labor in many British companies. Historically British industry has been racked by a high level of strikes, many of which have been politically motivated and depicted as "class warfare" between the disadvantaged working classes and the advantaged middle and upper classes. Moreover, politics in Britain tends to follow class lines to a much greater degree than in the United States, with the Labor Party representing the interests of the working class, and the Conservative Party representing middle- and upper-class interests.

FIGURE 3.2
World's Major Religions
(millions of adherents)

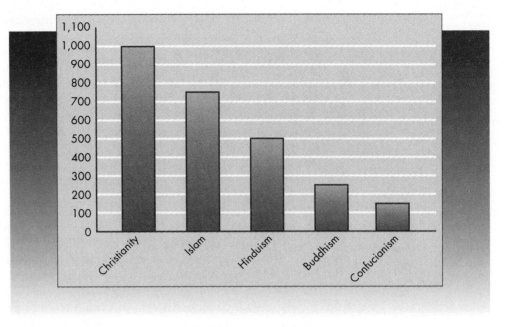

The antagonistic relationship between management and labor in countries such as Britain, and the resulting lack of cooperation and high level of industrial disruption, tends to raise the costs of production in Britain relative to the costs of production in countries such as the United States and Japan where the degree of class-based conflict is significantly lower. In turn, this has made it more difficult for companies based in Britain to establish a competitive advantage in the global economy. However, Britain is not the only society where class-based differences have resulted in industrial disruption and a lack of cooperation. Similar problems have emerged in Italy, Spain, Greece, and Australia, to name some other examples. Indeed, the level of industrial disruption has been significantly higher in all of these countries in recent years than in Britain.

❧ RELIGION

Religion may be defined as a system of shared beliefs and rituals that are concerned with the realm of the sacred.[14] The relationship between religion and society is subtle, complex, and profound. While there are thousands of different religions in the world today, five dominate—Christianity, Islam, Hinduism, Buddhism, and Confucianism (see Figure 3.2). We review each, focusing primarily on their business implications. Perhaps the most important business implication of religion centers on the extent to which different religions shape attitudes to work and entrepreneurship and the degree to which the religious ethics of a society affect the costs of doing business in a country.

Christianity

Christianity is the most widely practiced religion in the world. About 1 billion people, approximately 20 percent of the world's population, identify themselves as Christians. The vast majority of Christians live in Europe and the Americas, although their numbers are growing rapidly in Africa. Christianity grew out of Judaism. Like Judaism it is a monotheistic religion (monotheism is the belief in one god). A religious division in the 11th century led to establishment of two major Christian organizations—the Roman Catholic church and the Orthodox church. Today the Roman Catholic church accounts for over half of all Christians, most of

---

[14]N. Goodman, *An Introduction to Sociology* (New York: Harper Collins, 1991).

whom are found in Southern Europe and Latin America. The Orthodox church, while less influential, is still of major importance in several countries, such as Greece and Russia. In the 16th century the Reformation led to a further split with Rome; the result was the establishment of Protestantism. In turn, the nonconformist nature of Protestantism has facilitated the emergence of numerous denominations under the Protestant umbrella (e.g., Baptist, Methodist, Calvinist).

Economic implications of Christianity: the Protestant work ethic

Some sociologists have argued that of the two main branches of Christianity—Catholicism and Protestantism—the latter has the most important economic implications. In 1904 a German sociologist, Max Weber, made a connection between Protestant ethics and "the spirit of capitalism" that has since become famous.[15] Weber noted that capitalism emerged in Western Europe. Moreover, he noted that in Western Europe:

> Business leaders and owners of capital, as well as the higher grades of skilled labor, and even more the higher technically and commercially trained personnel of modern enterprises, are overwhelmingly Protestant.[16]

According to Weber, there was a relationship between Protestantism and the emergence of modern capitalism. Weber argued that Protestant ethics emphasize the importance of hard work and wealth creation (for the glory of God) and frugality (abstinence from worldly pleasures). According to Weber, this was just the kind of value system needed to facilitate the development of capitalism. Protestants worked hard and systematically to accumulate wealth. However, their ascetic beliefs suggested that rather than consume this wealth by indulging in worldly pleasures, they should reinvest it in the expansion of capitalist enterprises. Thus, the combination of hard work and the accumulation of capital that could be used to finance investment and expansion paved the way for the development of capitalism in Western Europe and, subsequently, in the United States. In contrast, Weber argued that the Catholic promise of salvation in the next world, rather than this world, did not foster the same kind of work ethic among members of the Catholic religion.

There is also another way in which Protestantism may have encouraged the development of capitalism. By breaking away from the hierarchical domination of religious and social life that characterized the Catholic church for much of its history, Protestantism gave individuals significantly more freedom to develop their own relationship with God. The right to freedom of form of worship was central to the nonconformist nature of early Protestantism. In turn, the emphasis on individual religious freedom may have paved the way for the subsequent emphasis on individual economic and political freedoms, and the development of individualism as an economic and political philosophy. As we saw in Chapter 2, such a philosophy forms the bedrock on which entrepreneurial free market capitalism is based.

Islam

With 750 million adherents, Islam is the second largest of the world's religions. Islam dates back to 610 AD when the Prophet Mohammed first began spreading the word. Adherents of Islam are referred to as Muslims. Muslims constitute a majority in over 35 countries and inhabit a nearly contiguous stretch of land from the northwest coast of Africa, through the Middle East, to the confines of China and Malaysia in the Far East.

Islam has roots in both Judaism and Christianity (Islam views Jesus Christ as one of God's prophets). Like Christianity and Judaism, Islam is a monotheistic religion

---

[15]M. Weber, *The Protestant Ethic and the Spirit of Capitalism* (New York: Scribner's Sons, 1958 (original 1904–1905). For an excellent review of Weber's work, see A. Giddens, *Capitalism and Modern Social Theory* (Cambridge: Cambridge University Press, 1971).

[16]Weber, *Protestant Ethic*, p. 35.

COUNTRY
FOCUS
Islamic Dissent
in Saudi Arabia

The desert kingdom of Saudi Arabia is a new nation. This state of 7 million was a loosely governed area inhabited by numerous Bedouin tribes until King Abdel-Aziz unified the country by conquest and intermarriage in 1935. His descendants—the House of Saudi—still rule what remains a monarchy with few democratic institutions. The majority of Saudis are Sunnis, although a Shiite minority lives on the eastern coast. Saudi Arabia has long been thought of as a close ally of the West. Western governments have gone out of their way to curry the favor of Saudi Arabia, a cynic might say because the country sits on top of more than a quarter of the world's oil reserves—oil that the West needs to keeps its industrial machinery humming. In the 1970s and early 1980s, high oil prices turned Saudi Arabia into one of the world's richest countries when measured by GDP per capita. This oil wealth supported a spending spree on basic infrastructure that gave the country all the trappings of a modern state. Nevertheless, traditional tribal values remained just below the surface.

The spending spree is now over. The high oil prices that sustained Saudi spending collapsed in 1985 and have yet to recover. Moreover, while Saudi Arabia was on the winning side in the Gulf War, the cost of financing the war drained the Saudi treasury. As a consequence, government spending has been declining sharply since 1991. In 1994 the Saudi government announced that it would cut spending by 20 percent.

The central principle of Islam is that there is no god but the one true omnipotent God. Other major principles of Islam include (1) honoring and respecting parents, (2) respecting the rights of others, (3) being generous but not a squanderer, (4) avoiding killing except for justifiable causes, (5) not committing adultery, (6) dealing justly and equitably with others, (7) being of pure heart and mind, (8) safeguarding the possessions of orphans, and (9) being humble and unpretentious.[17] There are obvious parallels here with many of the central principles of both Judaism and Christianity.

Islam is an all-embracing way of life governing the totality of a Muslim's being. As God's surrogate in this world, a Muslim is not a free agent but is circumscribed by religious principles—by a code of conduct for interpersonal relations—in his or her social and economic activities. Religion is paramount in all areas of life. The Muslim lives in a social structure that is shaped by Islamic values and norms of moral conduct. The ritual nature of everyday life in a Muslim country is perhaps one of the most striking things to a Western visitor. Among other things, Muslim ritual requires prayer five times a day (it is not unusual for business meetings to be put on hold while the Muslim participants engage in their daily prayer ritual), demands that women should be dressed in a certain manner and be subordinate to men, and forbids the consumption of either pig meat or alcohol.

Islamic fundamentalism

The past two decades have witnessed a surge in Islamic fundamentalism.[18] Although this rise of fundamentalism has no one cause, in part it is a response to the

---

[17]See S. M. Abbasi, K. W. Hollman, and J. H. Murrey, "Islamic Economics: Foundations and Practices," *International Journal of Social Economics* 16, no. 5 (1990), pp. 5–17; and R. H. Dekmejian, *Islam in Revolution: Fundamentalism in the Arab World* (Syracuse, NY: Syracuse University Press, 1995).

[18]R. H. Dekmejian, *Islam in Revolution.*

As oil revenues and government spending shrunk, the Saudis began to experience unemployment and social unrest. This has led Islamic fundamentalists to question the legitimacy of the rule of the House of Saudi. The irony of the current Saudi predicament is that the House of Saudi has always seen itself as the guardian of traditional Islamic values. The legitimacy of the royal family has been based in part on the backing of the *ulema,* an influential group of Islamic scholars. Moreover, the laws of Saudi Arabia have always been based on Islamic principles. Still, dissident members of the *ulema* have united with hard-line Islamic radicals—a group that includes preachers, professors, students, and marginalized city dwellers—to criticize the ruling family. These radicals tend to be xenophobic, anti-Western, anti-Shiite, and highly critical of the ruling family. Their opposition is based not just on economic problems, but it is also based on a perception that the House of Saudi has been corrupted by its wealth and has monopolized political power in the country. Moreover, there is lingering resentment among the radicals to the government's decision to allow 500,000 Western troops onto Saudi soil during the Gulf War. The fact that Saudi Arabia was on the winning side during the war apparently matters less to the fundamentalists than the "dishonor" associated with having to rely on outsiders, and Western ones at that, to protect Saudi sovereignty.

The sermons of radical preachers denounce a Judeo-Christian conspiracy against Islam and criticize Western values and lifestyles. In September 1994 one of the best-known radical preachers, Sheik Salman al-Audah, was asked by the government to sign a gag order. He refused, published the order, and was arrested. Hundreds of his followers were also arrested when they protested by taking to the streets of Buraida, a fundamentalist stronghold. Harassing, arresting, and sometimes torturing its fundamentalist opponents may prove to be a costly error. As the governments of Algeria and Egypt have recently discovered, fundamentalists seem to be able to draw strength from repression.

Source: "The Cracks in the Kingdom," *The Economist,* March 18, 1995, pp. 21–25.

social pressures created in traditional Islamic societies by the move toward modernization and by the influence of Western ideas, such as liberal democracy, materialism, equal rights for women, and of Western attitudes toward sex, marriage, and alcohol. In many Muslim countries modernization has been accompanied by a growing gap between a rich urban minority and an impoverished urban and rural majority. For the impoverished majority, modernization has offered little in the way of tangible economic progress, while threatening the traditional value system. Thus, for a Muslim who cherishes his traditions and feels that his identity is jeopardized by the encroachment of alien Western values, Islamic fundamentalism has become a cultural anchor.

Fundamentalists demand a rigid commitment to traditional religious beliefs and rituals. The result has been a marked increase in the use of symbolic gestures that confirm Islamic values. Women are once again wearing floor-length, long-sleeved dresses and covering their hair; religious studies have increased in universities; the publication of religious tracts has increased; more religious orations are heard in public.[19] Moreover, the sentiments of some fundamentalist groups are increasingly anti-Western. Rightly or wrongly, Western influence is blamed for a range of social ills, and the actions of many fundamentalists are directed against Western governments, cultural symbols, businesses, and even individuals.

In several Muslim countries fundamentalists have gained political power and have used this to try to make Islamic law (as set down in the Koran, the bible of Islam) the law of the land. The fundamentalists have been most successful in Iran, where a fundamentalist party has held power since 1979, but they also have a considerable and growing influence in many other countries, such as Algeria, Egypt, Pakistan, and Saudi Arabia. The above "Country Focus" profiles the rise of Islamic fundamentalism in Saudi Arabia.

---

[19]M. K. Nydell, *Understanding Arabs* (Yarmouth, ME: Intercultural Press, 1987).

Economic implications of Islam

Some quite explicit economic principles are set down in the Koran.[20] Many of the economic principles of Islam are pro-free enterprise. The Koran speaks approvingly of free enterprise and of earning *legitimate* profit through trade and commerce (the Prophet Mohammed was himself once a trader). Protection of the right to private property is also embedded within Islam, although Islam does assert that all property is a favor from Allah (God), who created and so owns everything. In this sense, those who hold property are regarded as trustees who are entitled to receive profits from it, rather than owners in the Western sense of the word. Moreover, those who hold property are admonished to use it in a righteous, socially beneficial, and prudent manner. This reflects Islam's concern with social justice.

Islam is critical of those who earn profit through the exploitation of others. In the Islamic view of the world, man is part of a collective in which the wealthy and successful have obligations to help the disadvantaged. Put simply, in Muslim countries it is fine to earn a profit, so long as that profit is justly earned and not based on the exploitation of others for one's own advantage. It also helps if those making profits undertake charitable acts to help the poor. Furthermore, Islam stresses the importance of living up to contractual obligations, of keeping one's word, and of abstaining from deception.

In general, fundamentalist critiques apart, Islamic countries are likely to be receptive to international businesses so long as those businesses behave in a manner that is consistent with Islamic ethics. Businesses that are perceived as making an unjust profit through the exploitation of others, by deception, or by breaking contractual obligations are unlikely to be welcomed in an Islamic state. In addition, in Islamic states where fundamentalism is on the rise, it is also likely that hostility to Western-owned businesses will be increasing.

One economic principle of Islam that has received particular attention is the prohibition of the payment or receipt of interest, which is considered usury. To the devout Muslim, acceptance of interest payments is seen as a very grave sin. Practitioners of the black art of usury are warned on the pain of hellfire to abstain; the giver and the taker are equally damned. This is not just a matter of theology; in several Islamic states it is also becoming a matter of law. In 1992, for example, Pakistan's Federal Shariat Court, the highest Islamic law-making body in the country, pronounced interest to be un-Islamic and therefore illegal and demanded that the government amend all financial laws accordingly.[21]

On the face of it, rigid adherence to this particular Islamic law could wreak havoc with a country's financial and banking system, raising the costs of doing business and scaring away international businesses and investors. To skirt the ban on interest, Islamic banks have been experimenting with a profit sharing system to replace interest on borrowed or loaned money. When an Islamic bank lends money to a business, rather than charging that business interest on the loan, it takes a share in the profits that are derived from the investment. Similarly, when a business (or individual) deposits money at an Islamic bank in a savings account, the deposit is treated as an equity investment in whatever activity the bank uses the capital for. Thus, the depositor receives a share in the profit from the bank's investment (as opposed to interest payments). Some Muslims claim this is a more efficient system than the Western banking system, since it encourages both long-term savings and long-term investment. However, there is no hard evidence of this, and many believe that an Islamic banking system is less efficient than a conventional Western banking system.

---

[20]The material in this section is based largely on Abbasi, Hollman, and Murrey, "Islamic Economics," pp. 5–17.
[21]"Islam's Interest," *The Economist*, January 18, 1992, pp. 33–34.

Hinduism

Hinduism has approximately 500 million adherents, most of whom are to be found in the Indian subcontinent. Hinduism began in the Indus Valley in India over 4,000 years ago, making it the world's oldest major religion. Unlike Christianity and Islam, its founding is not linked to a particular person. Nor does it have an officially sanctioned sacred book like the Bible or the Koran. Hindus believe there is a moral force in society that requires the acceptance of certain responsibilities, called *dharma*. Hindus believe in *reincarnation*, rebirth into a different body after death. Hindus also believe in *karma*, the spiritual progression of each person's soul. A person's karma is affected by the way he or she lives. The moral state of an individual's karma determines the challenges he or she will face in the next life. By perfecting the soul in each new life, Hindus believe that an individual can eventually achieve *nirvana*, a state of complete spiritual perfection that renders reincarnation no longer necessary. Many Hindus believe that the way to achieve nirvana is to lead a severe ascetic lifestyle of material and physical self-denial, devoting life to a spiritual rather than material quest.

Economic implications of Hinduism

Max Weber, who is known for expounding on the Protestant work ethic, also argued that whatever its spiritual merits, the ascetic principles embedded in Hinduism do not encourage the kind of entrepreneurial activity in pursuit of wealth creation that we find in Protestantism.[22] According to Weber, traditional Hindu values emphasize that individuals should not be judged by their material achievements, but by their spiritual achievements. Indeed, Hindus perceive the pursuit of material well-being as making nirvana more difficult to attain. Given the emphasis on a severe ascetic lifestyle, Weber thought that devout Hindus would be less likely to engage in entrepreneurial activity than devout Protestants.

Mahatma Gandhi, the famous Indian nationalist and spiritual leader, was certainly the embodiment of Hindu asceticism. It has been argued that the values of Hindu asceticism and self-reliance that Gandhi advocated had a negative impact on the economic development of postindependence India.[23] On the other hand, one must be careful not to read too much into Weber's arguments. Today there are millions of hardworking entrepreneurs in India where they form the economic backbone of a rapidly growing economy.

Hinduism also supports India's caste system. The concept of mobility between castes within an individual's lifetime makes no sense to Hindus. Hindus see mobility between castes as something that is achieved through spiritual progression and reincarnation. Individuals can be reborn into a higher caste in their next life if they achieve spiritual development in this life. In so far as the caste system limits the opportunities for otherwise able individuals to adopt positions of responsibility and influence in society, the economic consequences of this religious belief are bound to be negative. For example, within a business organization the most able individuals may find their route to the higher levels of the organization blocked simply because they come from a lower caste. By the same token, individuals may get promoted to higher positions within a firm as much because of their caste background as because of their ability.

Buddhism

Buddhism was founded in India in the sixth century BC by Siddhartha Gautama, an Indian prince who renounced his wealth to pursue an ascetic lifestyle and spiritual perfection. Siddhartha achieved nirvana, but decided to remain on earth to teach his followers how they too could achieve this state of spiritual enlightenment. Siddhartha became known as the Buddha (which means "the awakened one"). Today Buddhism has 250 million followers, most of whom are found in Central and

---

[22]For details of Weber's work and views, see Giddens, *Capitalism and Modern Social Theory*.

[23]See, for example, the views expressed in " A Survey of India: The Tiger Steps Out," *The Economist*, January 21, 1995.

Southeast Asia, China, Korea, and Japan. According to Buddhism, life is comprised of suffering. Misery is everywhere and originates in people's desires for pleasure. These desires can be curbed by systematically following the *Noble Eightfold Path,* which emphasizes right seeing, thinking, speech, action, living, effort, mindfulness, and meditation. Unlike Hinduism, Buddhism does not support the caste system. Nor does Buddhism advocate the kind of extreme ascetic behavior that is encouraged by Hinduism. Nevertheless, like Hindus, Buddhists stress the afterlife and spiritual achievement, rather than involvement in this world.

Because Buddhists, like Hindus, stress spiritual achievement, the emphasis on wealth creation that is embedded in Protestantism is not found in Buddhism. Thus, in Buddhist societies we do not see the same kind of cultural stress on entrepreneurial behavior that we see in the Protestant West. On the other hand, unlike Hinduism, the lack of support for the caste system and extreme ascetic behavior in Buddhism suggests that a Buddhist society may represent a more fertile ground for entrepreneurial activity than Hinduism.

Confucianism

Confucianism was founded in the fifth century BC by K'ung-Fu-tzu, more generally known as Confucius. For more than 2,000 years until the 1949 Communist revolution, Confucianism was the official religion of China. While religious observance has weakened in China since 1949, over 150 million people still follow the teachings of Confucius, principally in China, Korea, and Japan. Confucianism teaches the importance of attaining personal salvation through right action. Confucianism is built around a comprehensive ethical code that sets down guidelines for relationships with others. High moral and ethical conduct and loyalty to others are central to Confucianism. Unlike other religions, Confucianism is not concerned with the supernatural and has little to say about the concept of an afterlife. This has led many to argue that Confucianism is not a religion, but simply an ethical system. However, Confucianism is treated by many of its adherents as a religion.

Economic implications of Confucianism

Some people maintain that Confucianism may have economic implications as profound as those found in Protestantism, although they are of a different nature.[24] The basic thesis of those who take this position is that the influence of Confucian ethics on the cultures of Japan, South Korea, and Taiwan, by lowering the costs of doing business in those countries, may help explain their economic success. In this regard, three values that are central to the Confucian system of ethics are of particular interest—*loyalty, reciprocal obligations, and honesty.*

In Confucian thought, loyalty to one's superiors is regarded as a sacred duty—an absolute obligation that is necessary for religious salvation. In modern organizations based in Confucian cultures, the loyalty that binds employees to the heads of their organization can be seen as reducing the conflict between management and labor that we find in class-conscious societies such as Britain. Put another way, cooperation between management and labor can be achieved at a lower cost in a culture where the virtue of loyalty is emphasized in the value system.

However, loyalty to one's superiors, such as a worker's loyalty to management, is not blind loyalty in a Confucian culture. The concept of reciprocal obligations also comes into play. Confucian ethics stresses that superiors are obliged to reward the loyalty of their subordinates by bestowing blessings on them. If these "blessings" are not forthcoming, then neither will be the loyalty. In Japanese organizations this Confucian ethic exhibits itself in the concept of lifetime employment. The employees of a Japanese company are loyal to the leaders of the organization,

---

[24]See Dore, *Taking Japan Seriously;* and C. W. L. Hill, "Transaction Cost Economizing as a Source of Comparative Advantage: The Case of Japan," *Organization Science,* 6 (1995).

and in return the leaders bestow on them the "blessing" of lifetime employment. The business implications of this particular cultural practice have been touched on earlier in this chapter when we discussed the importance of group identification in Japanese society.

A third concept found in Confucian ethics is the importance attached to honesty in dealings with others. Confucian thinkers emphasize that although dishonest behavior may yield short-term benefits for the transgressor, in the long run dishonesty does not pay. The importance attached to honesty in dealings with others has major economic implications. In a society where companies can trust each other not to break contractual obligations, the costs of doing business are lowered. Expensive lawyers are not needed to resolve contract disputes. In addition, in a Confucian society there may be less hesitation to commit substantial resources to cooperative ventures than in a society where honesty is less pervasive. When companies adhere to Confucian ethics, they can trust each other not to violate the terms of cooperative agreements. Thus, the costs of achieving cooperation between companies may be lowered in societies like Japan (relative, that is, to societies like the United States where trust is less pervasive).

For example, it has been argued that the close ties between the automobile companies and their component part suppliers in Japan are facilitated by a combination of trust and reciprocal obligations. These close ties allow the auto companies and their suppliers to work together on a range of issues, including inventory reduction, quality control, and design. In turn, it is claimed that the competitive advantage of Japanese auto companies can in part be explained by such factors.[25]

❧ LANGUAGE

One of the most obvious ways in which countries differ is with regard to language. By language, we mean both the spoken and the unspoken means of communication. Language is one of the defining characteristics of a culture.

Spoken Language

Language obviously enables people to communicate with each other, but it does far more than this. The nature of a language also structures the way we perceive the world. The language of a society can direct its members' attention to certain features of the world. The classic illustration of this phenomenon is that whereas the English language has but one word for snow, the language of the Inuit (Eskimos) lacks a general term for it. Instead, because distinguishing different forms of snow is so important in the lives of the Inuit, they have 24 words that describe different types of snow (e.g., powder snow, falling snow, wet snow, drifting snow).[26]

Since language shapes the way people perceive the world, it also helps define culture. In countries with more than one language, one also often finds more than one culture. In Canada, for example, there is an English-speaking culture and a French-speaking culture. Tensions between the two run quite high, with a substantial proportion of the French-speaking minority demanding independence from a Canada "dominated by English speakers." The same phenomenon can be observed in many countries around the world. For example, Belgium is divided into Flemish and French speakers, and tensions between the two groups exist; in Spain a Basque-speaking minority with its own distinctive culture has been agitating for independence from the Spanish-speaking majority for decades; on the Mediterranean island of Cyprus the culturally diverse Greek- and Turkish-speaking populations of the island engaged in

---

[25]See Aoki, *Information, Incentives, and Bargaining*; and J. P. Womack, D. T. Jones, and D. Roos, *The Machine That Changed the World* (New York: Rawson Associates, 1990).

[26]This hypothesis dates back to two anthropologists, Edward Sapir and Benjamin Lee Whorf. See E. Sapir, "The Status of Linguistics as a Science," *Language* 5 (1929), pp. 207–14; and B. L. Whorf, *Language, Thought, and Reality* (Cambridge, MA: MIT Press, 1956).

FIGURE 3.3
Mother Tongues

Language	Percentage of World Population for Whom This Is a First Language
Chinese	20.0%
English	6.0
Hindi	4.5
Russian	3.5
Spanish	3.0
Portuguese	2.0
Japanese	2.0
Arabic	2.0
French	1.5
German	1.5
Other	54.0

Source: The Economist Atlas *(The Economist Books, 1991), p. 116.*

open conflict in the 1970s, and the island is now partitioned into two halves. While it does not necessarily follow that language differences create differences in culture and, therefore, separatist pressures, (e.g., witness the harmony in Switzerland, where four languages are spoken) there certainly seems to be a tendency in this direction.

Chinese is the "mother tongue" of the largest number of people, followed by English and Hindi, which is spoken in India (see Figure 3.3). However, the most widely spoken language in the world is English, followed by French, Spanish, and Chinese (many people speak English as a second language). It is increasingly the case that English is becoming the language of international business. When a Japanese and a German businessperson get together to do business, it is almost certain that they will communicate in English. However, while English is widely used, there are still considerable advantages to be derived from learning the local language. For one thing, most people prefer to converse in their own language, and being able to speak the local language can aid in building rapport, which may be very important for a business deal.

International businesses that do not understand the local language can make some major blunders through improper translation. For example, the Sunbeam Corporation used the English words for its "Mist-Stick" mist-producing hair curling iron when it entered the German market, only to discover after an expensive advertising campaign that *mist* means *excrement* in German. In another example General Motors was troubled by the lack of enthusiasm among Puerto Rican dealers for its newly introduced Chevrolet Nova. When literally translated into Spanish, *Nova* meant star. However, when spoken it sounded like "no va," which in Spanish means "it doesn't go." General Motors subsequently changed the name of the car to Caribe.[27]

Unspoken Language

Unspoken language refers to nonverbal communication. We all communicate with each other by a host of nonverbal cues. The raising of eyebrows, for example, is a sign of recognition in most cultures, while a smile is a sign of joy. Many nonverbal cues, however, are culturally bound. A failure to understand the nonverbal cues of another culture can lead to a failure of communication. For example, making a circle with the thumb and the forefinger is a friendly gesture in the United States, but it is a vulgar sexual invitation in Greece and Turkey. Similarly, while most Americans and Europeans use the "thumbs-up" gesture to indicate "it's all right," in Greece the gesture is obscene.

Another aspect of nonverbal communication is personal space, which is the comfortable amount of distance between you and someone you are talking to. In the United States, the customary distance from each other adopted by parties in a business discussion is five to eight feet. In Latin America it is three to five feet. Consequently, many North Americans unconsciously feel that Latin Americans are invading their personal space and can be seen backing away from them during a

---

[27]D. A. Ricks, *Big Business Blunders: Mistakes in Multinational Marketing* (Homewood, IL: Dow Jones-Irwin, 1983).

conversation. In turn, the Latin American may interpret such backing away as aloofness. The result can be a regrettable lack of rapport between two businesspeople from different cultures.

❧ EDUCATION

Formal education plays a key role in a society. Formal education is the medium through which individuals learn many of the language, conceptual, and mathematical skills that are indispensable in a modern society. Formal education also supplements the family's role in socializing the young into the values and norms of a society. Values and norms are taught both directly and indirectly. Schools generally teach basic facts about the social and political nature of a society. They also tend to focus on the fundamental obligations of citizenship. Cultural norms are also taught indirectly at school. Respect for others, obedience to authority, honesty, neatness, punctuality, and so on, are all part of the "hidden curriculum" of schools. The use of a grading system also teaches children the value of personal achievement and competition.[28]

From an international business perspective, perhaps one of the most important aspects of education is its role as a determinant of national competitive advantage.[29] The availability of a pool of skilled and educated human resources seems to be a major determinant of the likely economic success of a country. In turn, such a pool of skilled and educated people is the product of a good national education system. In analyzing the competitive success of Japan since 1945, for example, Michael Porter notes that after the war Japan had almost nothing except a pool of skilled and educated human resources:

> With a long tradition of respect for education that borders on reverence, Japan possessed a large pool of literate, educated, and increasingly skilled human resources . . . Japan has benefited from a large pool of trained engineers. Japanese universities graduate many more engineers per capita than in the United States . . . A first-rate primary and secondary education system in Japan operates based on high standards and emphasizes math and science. Primary and secondary education is highly competitive . . . Japanese education provides most students all over Japan with a sound education for later education and training. A Japanese high school graduate knows as much about math as most American college graduates.[30]

Porter's point is that Japan's excellent education system was an important factor explaining the country's postwar economic success. Not only is a good education system a determinant of national competitive advantage, but it is also an important factor guiding the location choices of international businesses. For example, it would make little sense to base production facilities that require highly skilled labor in a country where the education system was so poor that a skilled labor pool wasn't available, no matter how attractive the country might seem on other dimensions. On the other hand, it might make sense to base production operations that require only unskilled labor in such a country.

The general education level of a country is also a good index of the kind of products that might sell in a country and of the type of promotional material that should be used. For example, a country such as Pakistan where 73.8 percent of the population is illiterate is unlikely to be a very good market for popular books. Moreover, promotional materials containing written descriptions of mass-marketed products are unlikely to have an effect in a country where almost three-quarters of the population cannot read. It is far better to use pictorial promotions in such circumstances.

Maps 3.1 and 3.2 provide some important data on education worldwide. Map 3.1 shows the percentage of a country's GNP that is devoted to education. Map 3.2

[28] N. Goodman, *An Introduction to Sociology* (New York: Harper Collins, 1991).

[29] M. E. Porter, *The Competitive Advantage of Nations* (New York: Free Press, 1990).

[30] Ibid., pp. 395–97.

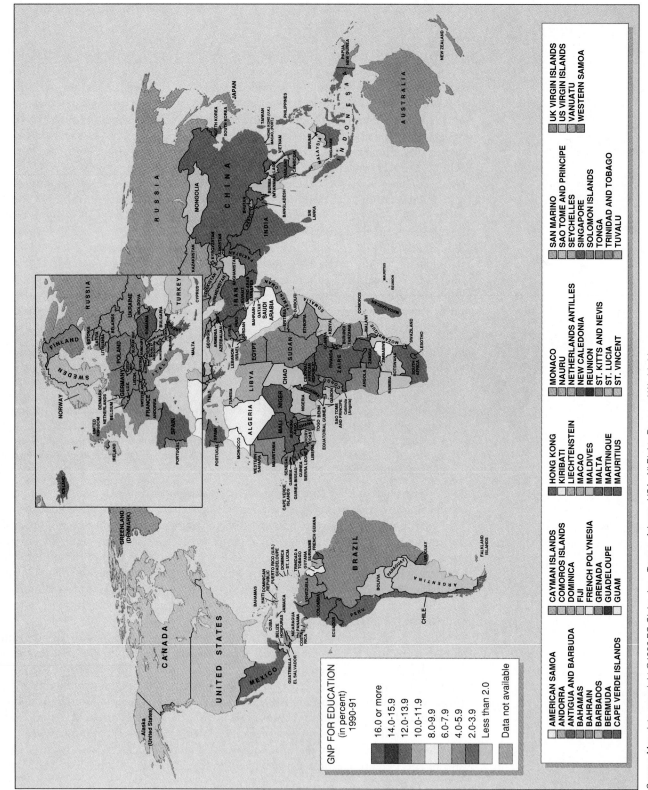

Map 3.1 Percentage of Gross National Product (GNP) Spent on Education

GNP FOR EDUCATION
(in percent)
1990-91

16.0 or more
14.0-15.9
12.0-13.9
10.0-11.9
8.0-9.9
6.0-7.9
4.0-5.9
2.0-3.9
Less than 2.0

Data not available

AMERICAN SAMOA
ANDORRA
ANTIGUA AND BARBUDA
BAHAMAS
BAHRAIN
BARBADOS
BERMUDA
CAPE VERDE ISLANDS

CAYMAN ISLANDS
COMOROS ISLANDS
DOMINICA
FIJI
FRENCH POLYNESIA
GRENADA
GUADELOUPE
GUAM

HONG KONG
KIRIBATI
LIECHTENSTEIN
MACAO
MALDIVES
MALTA
MARTINIQUE
MAURITIUS

MONACO
NAURU
NETHERLANDS ANTILLES
NEW CALEDONIA
REUNION
ST. KITTS AND NEVIS
ST. LUCIA
ST. VINCENT

SAN MARINO
SAO TOME AND PRINCIPE
SEYCHELLES
SINGAPORE
SOLOMON ISLANDS
TONGA
TRINIDAD AND TOBAGO
TUVALU

UK VIRGIN ISLANDS
US VIRGIN ISLANDS
VANUATU
WESTERN SAMOA

Source: Map data copyright ©1992 PC Globe, Inc., Tempe, Arizona, USA. All Rights Reserved Worldwide.

MAP 3.2 Percentage World Literacy Rates

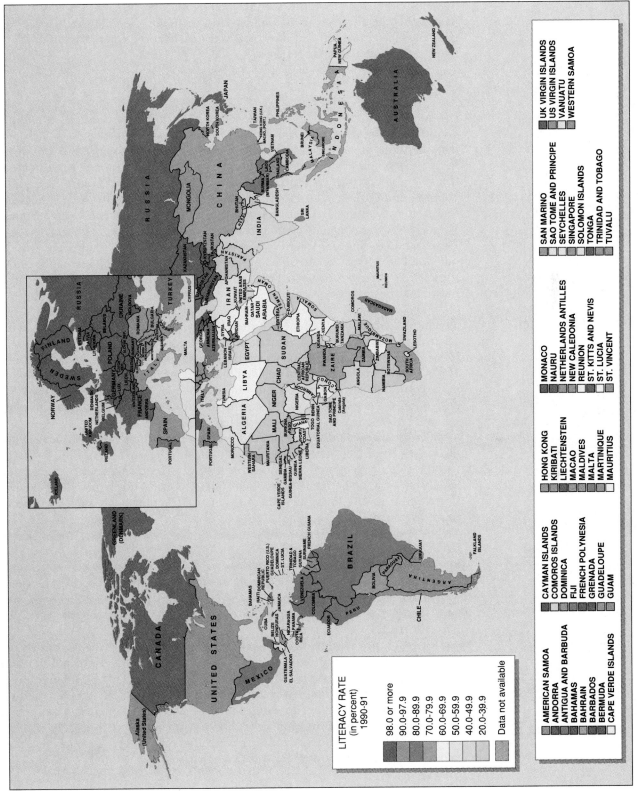

LITERACY RATE
(in percent)
1990-91

98.0 or more
90.0-97.9
80.0-89.9
70.0-79.9
60.0-69.9
50.0-59.9
40.0-49.9
20.0-39.9

Data not available

AMERICAN SAMOA
ANDORRA
ANTIGUA AND BARBUDA
BAHAMAS
BAHRAIN
BARBADOS
BERMUDA
CAPE VERDE ISLANDS

CAYMAN ISLANDS
COMOROS ISLANDS
DOMINICA
FIJI
FRENCH POLYNESIA
GRENADA
GUADELOUPE
GUAM

HONG KONG
KIRIBATI
LIECHTENSTEIN
MACAO
MALDIVES
MALTA
MARTINIQUE
MAURITIUS

MONACO
NAURU
NETHERLANDS ANTILLES
NEW CALEDONIA
REUNION
ST. KITTS AND NEVIS
ST. LUCIA
ST. VINCENT

SAN MARINO
SAO TOME AND PRINCIPE
SEYCHELLES
SINGAPORE
SOLOMON ISLANDS
TONGA
TRINIDAD AND TOBAGO
TUVALU

UK VIRGIN ISLANDS
US VIRGIN ISLANDS
VANUATU
WESTERN SAMOA

Source: Map data copyright ©1992 PC Globe, Inc., Tempe, Arizona, USA. All Rights Reserved Worldwide.

shows literacy rates. Although there is not a perfect one-to-one correspondence between the percentage of GNP devoted to education and the quality of education, the overall level of spending gives some indication of a country's commitment to education. Note that the United States spends more of its GNP on education than many other advanced industrialized nations, including Germany and Japan. Despite this, the *quality* of U.S. education is often argued to be inferior to that offered in many other industrialized countries.

❧ Culture and the Workplace

For an international business with operations in different countries a question of considerable importance is *how does a society's culture impact on the values found in the workplace?* The question matters because it points to the need to vary management process and practices to take different culturally determined work-related values into account. So, for example, if the United States and France have different cultures, and if these cultures result in different work-related values, it might make sense for an international business with operations in both the United States and France to vary its management process and practices. The opening case showed Disney tried to impose American work practices on French employees, who had a different set of work-related values. The result was employee resistance and high turnover, as those who objected to Disney's "brainwashing," as one former employee put it, left the company.

Hofstede's Model

The most famous study of how culture relates to values in the workplace was undertaken by Geert Hofstede.[31] As part of his job as a psychologist working for IBM, from 1967 to 1973 Hofstede collected data on employee attitudes and values for over 100,000 individuals. This data enabled him to compare dimensions of culture across 40 countries. Hofstede isolated four dimensions that he claimed summarized different cultures. These were power distance, uncertainty avoidance, individualism versus collectivism, and masculinity versus femininity.

Hofstede's **power distance** dimension focused on how a society deals with the fact that people are unequal in physical and intellectual capabilities. According to Hofstede, high power distance cultures were found in countries that let inequalities grow over time into inequalities of power and wealth. Low power distance cultures were found in societies that tried to play down such inequalities as much as possible.

The **individualism versus collectivism** dimension focused on the relationship between the individual and his or her fellows. In individualistic societies the ties between individuals were loose and individual achievement and freedom were highly valued. In societies where collectivism was emphasized, the ties between individuals were tight. In such societies people were born into collectives, such as extended families, and everyone was supposed to look after the interest of his or her collective.

Hofstede's **uncertainty avoidance** dimension measured the extent to which different cultures socialized their members into accepting ambiguous situations and tolerating uncertainty. Members of high uncertainty avoidance cultures placed a premium on job security, career patterns, retirement benefits, and so on. They also had a strong need for rules and regulations; the manager was expected to issue clear instructions, and subordinates' initiatives were tightly controlled. Lower uncertainty avoidance cultures were characterized by a greater readiness to take risks and less emotional resistance to change.

---

[31]G. Hofstede, "The Cultural Relativity of Organizational Practices and Theories," *Journal of International Business Studies,* Fall 1983, pp. 75–89.

FIGURE 3.4
Key to Countries and Regions
in Hofstede's Graphs

ARA	Arab countries (Egypt, Lebanon, Lybia, Kuwait, Iraq, Saudi-Arabia, U.A.E.)	JAM	Jamaica
		JPN	Japan
		KOR	South Korea
ARG	Argentina	MAL	Malaysia
AUL	Australia	MEX	Mexico
AUT	Austria	NET	Netherlands
BEL	Belgium	NOR	Norway
BRA	Brazil	NZL	New Zealand
CAN	Canada	PAK	Pakistan
CHL	Chile	PAN	Panama
COL	Colombia	PER	Peru
COS	Costa Rica	PHI	Philippines
DEN	Denmark	POR	Portugal
EAF	East Africa (Kenya, Ethiopia, Zambia)	SAF	South Africa
		SAL	Salvador
EOA	Equador	SIN	Singapore
FIN	Finland	SPA	Spain
FRA	France	SWE	Sweden
GBR	Great Britain	SWI	Switzerland
GER	Germany	TAI	Taiwan
GRE	Greece	THA	Thailand
GUA	Guatemala	TUR	Turkey
HOK	Hong Kong	URU	Uruguay
IDO	Indonesia	USA	United States
IND	India	VEN	Venezuela
IRA	Iran	WAF	West Africa (Nigeria, Ghana, Sierra Leone)
IRE	Ireland		
ISR	Israel	YUG	Yugoslavia
ITA	Italy		

Source: G. Hofstede, "The Cultural Relativity of Organizational Practices and Theories," Journal of International Business Studies 14 (Fall 1983), pp. 75–89.

Hofstede's **masculinity versus femininity** dimension looked at the relationship between gender and work roles. In masculine cultures sex roles were sharply differentiated and traditional "masculine values," such as achievement and the effective exercise of power, determined cultural ideals. In feminine cultures sex roles were less sharply distinguished, and little differentiation was made between men and women in the same job.

Hofstede created an index score for each of these four dimensions that ranged from 0 to 100 and scored high for high individualism, high power distance, high uncertainty avoidance, and high masculinity. He averaged the score for all employees from a given country and plotted the resulting score for each country on a series of graphs, two of which are shown in Figures 3.5 and 3.6 (the key to the countries and regions given in these figures is reported in Figure 3.4).

Figure 3.5 plots the power distance index against the individualism dimension (low individualism implies high collectivism). This graph tells us that advanced Western nations such as the United States, Canada, and Britain score high on the individualism scale and low on the power distance scale. At the other extreme are Latin American and Asian countries that emphasize collectivism over individualism and score high on the power distance scale.

Figure 3.6 plots the uncertainty avoidance index against the masculinity index. Again some countries stand out. Japan is highlighted as a country with a culture of strong uncertainty avoidance and high masculinity. This characterization fits the standard stereotype of Japan as a country that is male dominant and where uncertainty avoidance exhibits itself in the institution of lifetime employment. Sweden and Denmark stand out as countries that have both low uncertainty avoidance and low masculinity (high emphasis on "feminine" values).

FIGURE 3.5   Individualism and Power Distance

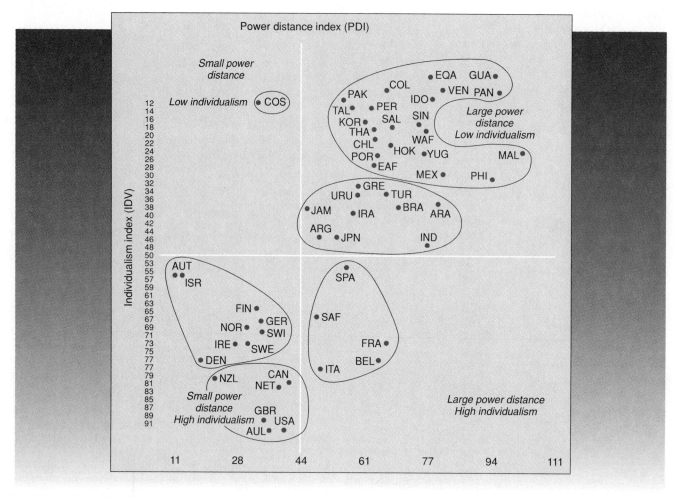

Source: G. Hofstede, "The Cultural Relativity of Organizational Practices and Theories," Journal of International Business Studies 14 (Fall 1983), pp. 75–89.

Evaluating Hofstede's Model

Hofstede's results are interesting for what they tell us in a general way about differences between cultures. Many of Hofstede's findings are consistent with some standard Western stereotypes about cultural differences. For example, finding Americans are more individualistic and egalitarian than the Japanese (they have a lower power distance), who in turn are more individualistic and egalitarian than Mexicans, might strike many people as having a reasonable amount of face validity. Similarly, many might agree that Latin countries, such as Italy, Columbia, and Mexico, place a higher emphasis on masculine value—they are machismo cultures—than the Nordic countries of Denmark, Finland, Norway, and Sweden.

However, one should be careful about reading too much into Hofstede's research. For all its fame, it is deficient in a number of important respects.[32] First, Hofstede assumes there is a one-to-one correspondence between culture and the nation-state, but as we saw earlier, many countries have more than one culture. Hofstede's results do not capture this distinction. Second, the research itself may have been culturally bound. The research team was composed of Europeans and Americans. The questions they asked of IBM employees, and the analysis they made of the answers, may well have been shaped by their own cultural biases and concerns. So it is perhaps not surprising that Hofstede's results confirm Western stereotypes, since it was Westerners who undertook the research! Third, Hofstede's informants worked not only within a

---

[32]For a more detailed critique, see R. Mead, *International Management: Cross-Cultural Dimensions* (Oxford: Blackwell, 1994), pp. 73–75.

Figure 3.6   Uncertainty Avoidance and Masculinity

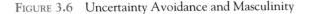

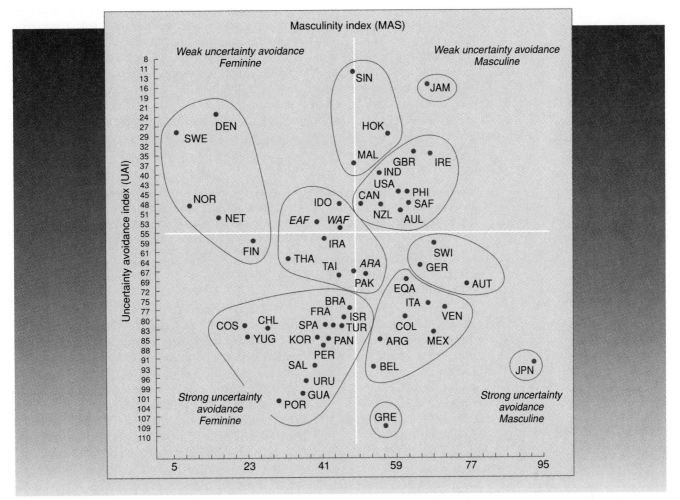

Source: G. Hofstede, *"The Cultural Relativity of Organizational Practices and Theories,"* Journal of International Business Studies *14 (Fall 1983), pp. 75–89.*

single industry, the computer industry, but also within a single company, IBM. At the time IBM was renowned for its own strong corporate culture and employee selection procedures. It is possible, therefore, that the values of IBM employees are different in important respects from the values that underlie the cultures from which those employees came. Moreover, certain social classes (such as unskilled manual workers) were excluded from Hofstede's sample. A final caution is that Hofstede's work is now beginning to look dated. Cultures do not stand still, they evolve over time, albeit slowly. What was a reasonable characterization in the 1960s and 1970s may not be so reasonable today.

Still, just as it should not be accepted without question, Hofstede's work still should not be dismissed lightly either. When all is said and done it does represent a reasonable starting point for managers trying to figure out how cultures differ and what that might mean for management practices. At the same time, it is no more than a starting point. Managers should use the results with caution, for they are not necessarily accurate.

❧ CULTURAL CHANGE

Culture is not a constant. It can and does evolve over time, although changes in value systems can be slow and painful for a society. In the 1960s, for example, American values toward the role of women, love, sex, and marriage underwent significant changes. Much of the social turmoil of that time reflected these changes. Similarly, today the value systems of many ex-Communist states, such as Russia, are undergoing significant changes as those countries move away from values that emphasize collectivism and toward those that emphasize individualism. Social turmoil is an inevitable outcome of this process.

In another example, some claim that a major cultural shift is now occurring in Japan, with a move toward much greater individualism.[33] The model Japanese office worker, or salary man, is pictured as being loyal to his boss and the organization to the point of giving up evenings, weekends, and vacations in order to serve the organization, which is the collective of which he is a member. However, a new generation of office workers does not seem to fit this model. It is claimed that an individual from the new generation:

> is more direct than the traditional Japanese. He acts more like a Westerner, a *gaijian*. He does not live for the company, and will move on if he gets the offer of a better job. He is not keen on overtime, especially if he has a date with a girl. He has his own plans for his free time, and they may not include drinking or playing golf with the boss.[34]

A more detailed example of the kind of changes now occurring in Japan is given in the "Management Focus," which looks at the impact of Japan's changing culture on the Hitachi Corporation.

The Hitachi example in the "Management Focus" points to two forces that may result in culture change—economic advancement and globalization. Several studies have suggested that both these forces may be important factors in societal change.[35] For example, there is evidence that economic progress is accompanied by a shift in values away from collectivism and toward individualism.[36] Thus, as Japan has become richer, so the cultural stress placed on collectivism has declined and greater individualism is being witnessed. If the Hitachi example is any guide, one reason for this shift may be that in richer societies there is less need for social and material support structures built on collectives, whether the collective is the extended family or the paternalistic company. People are better able to take care of their own needs. As a result, the importance attached to collectivism declines, while greater economic freedoms lead directly to an increase in opportunities for expressing individualism.

The culture of societies may also change as they become richer because economic progress affects a number of other factors, which in turn impact on culture. For example, increased urbanization and improvements in the quality and availability of education are both a function of economic progress, and both can lead to declining emphasis on the traditional values associated with poor rural societies.

As for globalization, here it can be argued that advances in transportation and communications technologies, the dramatic increase in trade in goods and services that we have witnessed since WWII, and the rise of global corporations such as Hitachi, Disney, Microsoft, and Levi Strauss, whose products and operations can be found around the globe, are creating the conditions for the merging of cultures.[37] With McDonald's in China, Levi's in India, Sony Walkmans in South Africa, and MTV everywhere helping to foster a ubiquitous youth culture, one can argue that the conditions for a reduction in cultural variation across societies have been created. At the same time, one must not ignore important countertrends, such as the shift toward Islamic fundamentalism in several Muslim countries, the separatist movement in Quebec, Canada, or the continuing ethnic

---

[33]Ibid., chap. 17.

[34]"Free, Young, and Japanese," *The Economist*, December 21, 1991.

[35]Namerwirth and Weber, *Dynamics of Culture*.

[36]G. Hofstede, "National Cultures in Four Dimensions," *International Studies of Management and Organization* 13, no. 1, pp. 46–74.

[37]Barnet and Cavanagh, *Global Dreams*.

Hitachi was founded in 1911 by Namihei Odaira, who named his company after the town in which it was based. By 1965 Hitachi was one of the giants of Japanese industry, with its sales accounting for over 1 percent of Japan's gross national product. In many ways, Hitachi was a typical Japanese company. New recruits were lectured on Odaira's reverence for *wa*, or harmony. Managers and workers, dressed in identical uniforms, were tirelessly punctual and trusted each other like brothers. Decision making was characterized by the consensus model, so typical of Japanese corporations, where managers consulted juniors exhaustively before making a decision. And the lifetime employment system was instituted at Hitachi.

According to old Hitachi hands, the harmony and togetherness owed as much to poverty as it did to anything else. Historically, many employees and their families were housed in company dormitories because they could afford nothing else. Younger employees slept two to a room, and all ate their meals communally in the company cafeteria. Because public facilities were few, everyone went to the company bathhouse. In the evenings employees saw the same colleagues in the same company bars. Their wives shopped at the company store. The company even provided a wedding hall and funeral parlor.

Today two forces are affecting Japan's culture—prosperity and globalization. Both are leading to changes at Hitachi. Over the last four decades Japan has become one of the world's richest countries. At Hitachi, prosperity means nobody sleeps two to a room in the company dormitory anymore. Since the 1960s employees have been moving "outside the fence," away from the company dormitories. Prosperity has brought more entertainment and leisure options. The company bathhouse has given way to private bathhouses. The choice between a French restaurant and an Indian restaurant divides one employee from the next. Hobbies are more diverse. There are cars, drinking, bonsai gardening, music bands; before it was only drinking in company bars. Employees spend more time with their families; the biological family is replacing the company family as the anchor of social life. Companies like Hitachi used to provide for all aspects of employees' lives. Now leisure is an opportunity for individualism, not a prop for workplace harmony.

Then there is globalization; like many other Japanese companies Hitachi is now a global enterprise with worldwide operations. Japanese society, too, has become more international in recent years. In this new environment, top management states bluntly that monoculture firms will not survive. In 1991 Hitachi set up a department to educate executives on other cultures. This department deliberately downplays the old notions of harmony and consensus decision making in its programs. Hitachi is also sending increasing numbers of its executives for prolonged postings overseas, and it is starting to bring foreign managers back to Japan. The foreign experience has encouraged senior managers to seek firmer leadership in Japan—to shift away from the old consensus decision-making model—and Hitachi's top executives have encouraged this trend.

Source: "The Long March from Harmony," *The Economist*, July 9, 1994, pp. 6–10.

strains and separatist movements in Russia. Such countertrends are in many ways a reaction to the pressures for cultural convergence that we have been discussing here. In an increasingly homogenous and materialistic world, some societies are trying to reemphasize their cultural roots and uniqueness.

IMPLICATIONS FOR BUSINESS

International business is different because countries and societies are different. In this chapter we have seen just how different societies can be. Societies differ because their culture is different. Their culture is different because of profound differences in social structure, religion, language, education, economic philosophy, and political philosophy. Two important implications for international business flow from these differences. The first is the need to develop cross-cultural literacy. There is a need to appreciate not only that cultural differences exist, but also to appreciate what such differences mean for the practice of international business. A second implication centers on the connection among culture, the costs of doing business in a country, and national competitive advantage. As has been alluded to throughout this chapter, there may be a link between culture and national competitive advantage. In this section, we will explore both of these issues in greater detail.

Cross-Cultural Literacy

One of the biggest dangers confronting a company that goes abroad for the first time is the danger of being ill-informed. International businesses that are ill-informed about the practices of another culture are unlikely to succeed. Doing business in a different culture requires adaptation to conform with the value systems and norms of that culture. Adaptation can embrace all aspects of an international firm's operations in a foreign country. The way in which deals are negotiated, the appropriate incentive pay systems for salespeople, the structure of the organization, the name of a product, the tenor of relations between management and labor, the manner in which the product is promoted, and so on, are all sensitive to cultural differences. As we saw in the Euro-Disney case that opened the chapter, what works in one culture might not work in another.

To combat the danger of being ill-informed, international businesses should consider employing local citizens to help them do business in a particular culture. They must also ensure that home country executives are cosmopolitan enough to understand how differences in culture affect the practice of international business. One way to build a cadre of cosmopolitan executives is to transfer executives overseas at regular intervals so they gain exposure to different cultures. This is the approach Hitachi is now taking as it transforms itself from a Japanese into a global company (see the "Management Focus" for details).

An international business must also be constantly on guard against the dangers of **ethnocentric behavior.** Ethnocentrism is a belief in the superiority of one's own ethnic group or culture. Hand in hand with ethnocentrism goes a disregard or contempt for the culture of other countries. Unfortunately ethnocentrism is prevalent; many Americans are guilty of it, as are many French people, Japanese people, British people, and so on. Ugly as it is, ethnocentrism happens to be a fact of life. It is one, however, that the international business must be on guard against.

Culture and Competitive Advantage

One theme in this chapter is the relationship between culture and national competitive advantage. Put simply, the value systems and norms of a country influence the costs of doing business in that country. The costs of doing business in a country influence the ability of firms based in that culture to establish a competitive advantage in the global marketplace. For example, we have seen how attitudes toward cooperation between management and labor, toward work, and toward the payment of interest are influenced by social structure and religion. It can be argued that the class-based conflict between workers and management that we find in British society, in so far as it leads to industrial disruption, raises the costs of doing business in that culture. This factor will tend to work against British firms, relative to, say Japanese firms, where the importance of group identification minimizes conflict between management and labor. Similarly, we have seen how the ascetic "other worldly" ethics of Hinduism may not be as supportive of capitalism as the ethics embedded in Protestantism and Confucianism. We have also alluded to the possibility that the constraints on a country's banking system contained in Islamic laws on interest payments may put enterprises based in Islamic countries at a competitive disadvantage. Islamic banking laws may raise the costs of doing business in countries where Islamic fundamentalism is transforming the legal system.

Japan presents us with an interesting example of how culture can influence competitive advantage. It can be argued that the culture of modern Japan lowers the costs of doing business in that country, relative to the costs of doing business in most Western nations. We have seen how the Japanese emphasis on group affiliation, loyalty, reciprocal obligations, honesty, and education all boost the competitiveness of Japanese companies. The emphasis on group affiliation and loyalty encourages individuals to identify strongly with the companies in which they work. In turn, this tends to foster an ethic of hard work and cooperation between management and labor "for the good of the company."

Similarly, the concepts of reciprocal obligations and honesty help foster an atmosphere of trust between companies and their suppliers. In turn, this encourages them to enter into long-term relationships with each other to work on factors such as inventory reduction, quality control, and joint design—all of which have been shown to improve the competitiveness of an organization. This level of cooperation has often been lacking in the West, where the relationship between a company and its suppliers tends to be a short-term one structured around competitive bidding, rather than one based on long-term mutual commitments.

In addition, the availability of a pool of highly skilled labor, and particularly engineers, has undoubtedly helped Japanese enterprises develop a number of cost-reducing process innovations that have boosted productivity.[38] Thus, cultural factors may help explain the competitive advantage enjoyed by many Japanese businesses in the global marketplace. Indeed, the rise of Japan as an economic superpower during the second half of the 20th century may be in part attributed to the economic consequences of its culture.

For international business, the connection between culture and competitive advantage is important for two reasons. First, the connection suggests which countries are liable to produce the most viable competitors. For example, it is likely that U.S enterprises are going to see a continued growth in aggressive cost-efficient competitors from those Pacific Rim nations where a combination of free market economics, Confucian ideology, group-oriented social structures, and advanced education systems can all be found (e.g., South Korea, Taiwan, Japan, and increasingly China).

Second, the connection between culture and competitive advantage has important implications for the choice of countries in which to locate production facilities and do business. Consider a hypothetical case when a company has to choose between two countries, A and B, for locating a production facility. Both countries are characterized by low labor costs and good access to world markets. Both countries are of roughly the same size (in terms of population) and currently both are at a similar stage of economic development. In country A the education system is undeveloped, the society is characterized by a marked stratification between the upper and lower classes, the dominant religion stresses the importance of reincarnation, and there are three major linguistic groups. In country B the education system is well developed, there is a lack of social stratification, group identification is a value that is stressed by the culture, the dominant religion stresses the virtue of hard work, and there is only one linguistic group. Which country makes the best investment site?

The answer is obvious; country B does. The culture of country B is supportive of the capitalist mode of production and social harmony, whereas the culture of country A is not. In country A conflict between management and labor, and between different language groups, can be expected to lead to social and industrial disruption, thereby raising the costs of doing business. The lack of a good education system and the dominance of a religion that stresses ascetic behavior as a way of achieving advancement in the next life can also be expected to work against the attainment of business goals.

The same kind of comparison could be made for an international business trying to decide which country to push its products in, A or B. Again, country B would be the logical choice, precisely because cultural factors suggest that in the long run, country B is the nation most likely to achieve the greatest level of economic growth. In comparison, the culture of country A may produce economic stagnation.

---

[38]See Aoki, *Information, Incentives, and Bargaining;* Dertouzos, Lester, and Solow, *Made in America;* and Porter, *The Competitive Advantage of Nations,* pp. 395–97.

❦ SUMMARY OF CHAPTER

We have looked at the nature of social culture and some implications for business practice. The following points have been made:

1. Culture is that complex whole that includes knowledge, belief, art, morals, law, custom, and other capabilities acquired by people as members of society.

2. Values and norms are the central components of a culture. Values are abstract ideas about what a society believes to be good, right, and desirable. Norms are social rules and guidelines that prescribe appropriate behavior in particular situations.

3. Values and norms are influenced by political and economic philosophy, social structure, religion, language, and education.

4. The social structure of a society refers to its basic social organization. There are two main dimensions along which social structures differ—the individual-group dimension and the stratification dimension.

5. In some societies the individual is the basic building block of social organization. In these societies individual achievements are emphasized above all else. In other societies the group is the basic building block of social organization. In these societies group membership and group achievements are emphasized.

6. All societies are stratified into different classes. Class-conscious societies are characterized by low social mobility and a high degree of stratification. Less class-conscious societies are characterized by high social mobility and a low degree of stratification.

7. Religion may be defined as a system of shared beliefs and rituals that are concerned with the realm of the sacred. The world's major religions are Christianity, Islam, Hinduism, Buddhism, and Confucianism. The value systems of different religions have different implications for business practice.

8. Language is one of the defining characteristics of a culture. It has both a spoken and an unspoken dimension. In countries with more than one spoken language, we tend to find more than one culture.

9. Formal education is the medium through which individuals learn skills and are socialized into the values and norms of a society. Education plays an important role in the determination of national competitive advantage.

10. Geert Hofstede studied how culture relates to values in the workplace. Hofstede isolated four dimensions that he claimed summarized different cultures—power distance, uncertainty avoidance, individualism versus collectivism, and masculinity versus femininity.

11. Culture is not a constant; it can and does evolve over time. Economic progress and globalization seem to be two important engines of cultural change.

12. One danger confronting a company that goes abroad for the first time is being ill-informed. To develop cross-cultural literacy international businesses need to employ host country nationals, build a cadre of cosmopolitan executives, and guard against the dangers of ethnocentric behavior.

13. The value systems and norms of a country can affect the costs of doing business in that country.

❦ CRITICAL DISCUSSION QUESTIONS

1. Outline why the culture of a country influences the costs of doing business in that country. Illustrate your answer with examples.

2. How do you think business practices in an Islamic country are likely to differ from business practices in the United States?

3. What are the implications for international business of the dominant religion of a country?

4. Choose two countries that appear to be culturally diverse. Compare the culture of those countries and then indicate how cultural differences influence (a) the costs of doing business in each country, (b) the likely future economic development of that country, and (c) business practices.

❧ CLOSING CASE   Cultural Differences at ABB

 Asea Brown Boveri (ABB) is a quintessential global enterprise. Formed out of the merger of two engineering companies, one Swiss and the other Swedish, ABB has worldwide revenues of over $35 billion, 250,000 employees, and activities in 140 countries. Percy Barnevik, the company's CEO, notes that ABB is a company with no geographical center, no national ax to grind:

> Are we a Swiss company? Our headquarters are in Zurich, but only 100 professionals work at headquarters . . . Are we a Swedish company? I'm the CEO, and I was born and educated in Sweden. But our headquarters is not in Sweden, and only two of the eight members of our board of directors are Swedes. Perhaps we are an American company. We report our financial results in U.S. dollars, and English is ABB's official language. We conduct all high-level meetings in English . . . My point is that ABB is none of these things—and all of these things. We are not homeless. We are a company with many homes.

In this company with many homes, Barnevik stresses the advantage of building a culturally diverse cadre of global managers. In particular, Barnevik believes that such a management group can improve the quality of managerial decision making. To quote:

> If you have 50 business areas and five managers on each business area team, that's 250 people from different parts of the world—people who meet regularly in different places, bring their national perspectives to bear on tough problems, and begin to understand how things are done elsewhere. I experience this every three weeks in our executive committee. When we sit together as Germans, Swiss, American, and Swedes, with many of us living, working, and traveling in different places, the insights can be remarkable.

Barnevik also stresses the need to acknowledge cultural differences without becoming paralyzed by them—to work with those differences. Again, Barnevik states the point clearly:

> We've done some surveys (at ABB) . . . and we find interesting differences in perception. For example, a Swede may think a Swiss is not completely frank and open, that he doesn't know exactly where he stands. That is a cultural phenomenon. Swiss culture shuns disagreement. A Swiss might say, "Let's come back to that point later, let me review it with my colleagues." A Swede would prefer to confront the issues directly. How do we undo hundreds of years of upbringing and education? We don't, and we shouldn't try to. But we do need to broaden understanding (of cultural differences).

Thus Barnevik's argument is that a culturally diverse set of managers can be a source of strength. According to Barnevik, managers should not try to eradicate these differences and establish a uniform managerial culture. Rather, they should seek to understand these cultural difference, to empathize with the views of people from different cultures, and to make accommodations for such differences.

CASE DISCUSSION QUESTIONS

1. How can ABB's culturally diverse management team be a source of competitive strength?

2. What barriers are likely to stand in the way of Percy Barnevik's attempt to make his culturally diverse management team a source of competitive strength?

3. What do you think Barnevik means by the need to acknowledge cultural differences without becoming paralyzed by them—to work with those differences? What does working with cultural differences at a global company such as ABB actually mean?

4. How can ABB increase the cross-cultural literacy of its management cadre?

Source: W. Taylor, "The Logic of Global Business: An Interview with ABB's Percy Barnevik," Harvard Business Review, March–April 1991, pp. 91–105.

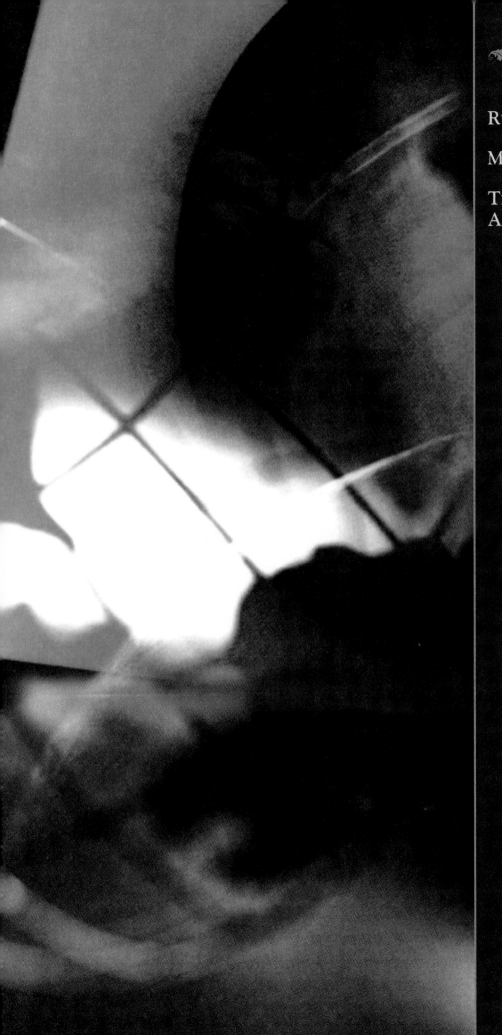

RUSSIAN PRIVATIZATION

⚜ INTRODUCTION

In the aftermath of the collapse of Soviet-style communism in Russia and the breakup of the Soviet Union, the Russian government has been trying to transform a centrally planned economy in which almost all productive assets were owned by the state into a vibrant market economy. A main tool in this task has been the privatization of state-owned enterprises. The great hope of Russian reformers is that putting state enterprises into private hands, and making them accountable to their new owners for their performance, will result in major efficiency gains and a more productive economy. This process began in 1991 and by mid-1995 Russia's private sector employed over 80 percent of the nation's nonagrarian work force, more than half of Russia's estimated 240,000 enterprises had been privatized, and some 40 million Russians owned shares in more than 15,000 mid- and large-scale enterprises. However, it was too early to say whether the privatization process had been a major success.

⚜ THE PRIVATIZATION PROCESS

The Russian privatization process officially began in mid-1991 when Russian President Boris Yeltsin signed a privatization law that created a state agency, the State Property Committee, known by its Russian initials GKI, to oversee the transfer of state assets into private hands. However, little happened until after the failed coup attempt in 1991 by a small and poorly organized group of pro-Soviet politicians and generals. Following the failed coup, and the subsequent breakup of the Soviet Union, Boris Yeltsin appointed a young politician from St. Petersburg, Anatoly Chubais, to head the GKI. Yeltsin gave Chubais free rein to devise a program for rapidly privatizing the Russian economy, and more importantly Yeltsin placed his then considerable political weight squarely behind the privatization process.

Chubais quickly assembled a team of like-minded people, all of them young and all of them willing to work all day, every day, until they had attained their goal. To help decide on a basic privatization strategy, Chubais and his team analyzed the privatization efforts then being carried out in a number of other countries, including the gradual case-by-case approach to privatization pursued in Poland and the rapid mass privatization approach adopted by the Czech Republic.

The approach chosen by the GKI team was strongly influenced by conditions prevailing in Russia at that time. In early 1992 the Russian economy was still centrally controlled by ministries or subministries, each running an industry. The GKI team realized these organizations might not easily or willingly give up their authority. Reporting to the ministries were legions of so called "red directors," the former Communist party apparatchiks spread across Russia who actually ran state enterprises on a day-to-day basis. As products of the old system, these individuals were likely to attempt to frustrate any reform effort that limited or deprived them of power.

The GKI team decided that tackling this network of entrenched bureaucrats would require more speed and scope than finesse. The process they devised was driven by three goals. The first was to move quickly to break up the old Soviet system before opposition could build, primarily by privatizing most state assets within two years. The second goal was to "divide and conquer" the potential opposition by splitting the red directors away from the ministries. The reformers aimed to entice the red directors into supporting the privatization program by offering them ownership stakes in the enterprises they were already managing for

Source: Charles W. L. Hill.

the state. The theory was that the industrial ministries, stripped of their assets, would then be left to wither. A third goal was to quickly create a broad base of property owners who would be opposed to reversing the changes.

For small enterprises and assets, such as shops, restaurants, and apartments, the reformers chose to leave details of the privatization effort to local authorities. The thinking at GKI was that such decentralization of responsibility would result in a more rapid and flexible approach to privatization. The most common approach was to auction small enterprises and assets for cash. Often the buyers were the workers themselves. The approach proved successful, and by 1995 over two-thirds of all small businesses in Russia had been privatized. These small businesses have become the foundation for a growing middle class, which the reformers hope will back further efforts to push the Russian economy toward a free market model.

For midsized and large enterprises, the GKI adopted a mass privatization strategy that utilized a voucher system. Modeled after the system used in the Czech Republic, the first step was for thousands of state enterprises to be transformed into "corporatized" companies with shareholdings, with some portion of their shares to be slated for auction. The Russian government then issued vouchers, available from October 1992 to January 1993. For a fee of 25 rubles (then about 10 cents), each Russian was eligible to receive one voucher. About 144 million vouchers were given out in this way, meaning that about 97 percent of the population took up the offer. Each voucher had a face value of 10,000 rubles (i.e., about $25). The voucher holder had three options: sell the voucher for cash (a lively market for vouchers soon developed); use the vouchers to bid at auctions for the shares in corporatized firms; or invest the vouchers in private mutual funds that would then purchase packets of shares.

To win over managers and workers of state enterprises, as well as local politicians, GKI allowed each state enterprise to choose from a menu of privatization plans. To varying degrees, the plans allotted packets of shares, and in many cases controlling stakes, to company insiders in exchange for cash or vouchers, or sometimes as straight giveaways. Another portion of the shares would be auctioned to voucher holders who were not company employees, and in many cases a third packet of shares was reserved for the state to sell later for cash or investment tenders—commitments to make substantial investments in companies in exchange for blocks of shares. When managers and workers could choose to keep a controlling interest in their privatized business, they usually did so.

One of the earliest large enterprises to be privatized under the voucher arrangement was the Bolshevik Biscuit Factory, Russia's largest cookie factory, which was auctioned off in December 1992. Roughly 80 percent of the company's shares were put up for auction and all were sold. More voucher auctions followed with another 17 companies being auctioned off during December 1992. Throughout 1993 and the first half of 1994 several hundred companies were privatized each month under the voucher program. For the grand finale in June 1994, when the vouchers were set to expire, stakes in 2,621 medium and large enterprises were auctioned. By the end of June 1994, 86 percent of Russia's industrial labor force was working in the private sector.

Since June 1994 Russia has moved to a less systematic and more cumbersome process of selling still more state-owned businesses, along with the remaining state stakes in many companies for investment tenders. Investment tenders allow large investors to put up the big money that is needed for restructuring companies in exchange for big stakes.

Alfa Kapital, a Moscow-based investment company that has 2 million shareholders and stakes in more than 60 companies, is typical of the new enterprises that are purchasing state-owned shareholdings in return for investment guarantees. Alexei Kalinin, Alfa Kapital's managing director of long-term investments, works to restructure and turn around companies in which Alfa holds ownership stakes. Before 1992 the directors of these companies answered to government ministers who were concerned with the enterprises' ability to meet centrally determined five-year plans. Now they answer to Alexei Kalinin, who cares about profit.

❧ EVALUATING THE PROCESS

Although Russia's privatization process achieved its primary goals of rapidly transforming state-owned enterprises into private entities, the process has had critics. One criticism is that the tilt toward giving shares to insiders—enterprise employees and workers—was far from ideal in Russia's economy. Many of these insiders were the same red directors who had presided over the poor management of the enterprises when they were state owned. Critics have suggested that the old Communist elite were among the largest gainers of the privatization program. Several studies in Russia have concluded that new owners and managers are more likely than old insiders to restructure a newly privatized company. GKI supporters counter that from a political standpoint, the approach was necessary to win support from managers and workers for the privatization process.

Another frequently voiced criticism is of the voucher system. The state gave away many valuable assets for virtually nothing. In many other countries the government first restructured state-owned enterprises to make them more efficient and then sold them to the highest bidder, often for considerable financial returns. In Russia, the state placed enterprises in private hands in exchange for 144 million 25 ruble (10 cent) vouchers, leaving their new owners to get on with the restructuring. This was a serious mistake on two counts, argue the critics. First, the state received no revenue from the privatization process, and second, many of the new private owners simply lacked the capital required to restructure their enterprises. However, GKI supporters contend that imperfect as the process was, it was the only way of rapidly shifting ownership of enterprises into private hands. Russia simply did not have the luxury of taking its time to turn around state enterprises and then selling them to the highest bidder.

Many newly privatized enterprises are finding it difficult to raise the investment funds they need from the capital market to restructure their operations and purchase new equipment. Consider the experience of Red October, a privatized Moscow-based candy company with an 80 percent market share in the local region. Red October went to the capital market in 1994 with a new share issue to raise funds to build a new factory. In an attempt to bring international investors into the offering, the new share issue was handled in part by a British investment company. Red October did raise $22 million. However, this was short of expectations, primarily because there was little interest among foreign investors in buying the shares of a Russian enterprise, albeit one with a dominant position in its local market.

GKI is facing similar problems in its attempt to sell remaining state-owned stakes for investment tenders. In the first nine months of 1995 GKI raised only $36 million from the sale of investment tenders, far short of the $2 billion target set for the whole of 1995. The poor showing is largely attributed to a lack of interest by foreign investors. The point was driven home in December 1995, when Stet, the Italian telephone company, pulled out of a deal to purchase a 25 percent stake in the Russian regional telephone holding company, Svyazinvest, for about $1.4 billion.

While the lack of interest by foreign investors may be in part due to the current poor state of the Russian economy, much seems to be attributed to the confusing state of Russian property laws and uncertainty as to the long-term direction of economic and political reform in the country. Russian property laws are highly ambiguous and have deterred many foreign investors. For example, Russia's emerging stock market went into a serious slump in late 1994 when many foreign investors discovered they could not be sure they owned the stock they had paid for. Company insiders could simply strike their names off the shareholder registers, most of which the companies themselves ran. As odd as it might seem, at the time there was no legal recourse to such action.

The decision by Stet to pull out of its planned investment in Svyazinvest also illustrates some of the problems Russia has in attracting foreign investors. Stet reportedly pulled out of the deal because it did not have a chance to perform due diligence on Svyazinvest and because of confusion over the legal status of many of Svyazinvest's operations. In particular Stet wanted the rights of the 85 regional telecommunications companies that form Svyazinvest to be clearly defined and was pressing for a clearer definition of the relationship between Svyazinvest and Rostelecom, Russia's dominant telephone company and Svyazinvest's future competitor. Apparently these definitions were not forthcoming from Russian authorities.

In a further development that may have influenced Stet's decision, in December 1995 the Communist party emerged as the big winner from parliamentary elections with close to 25 percent of the vote. Many Communist candidates had promised during the election campaign that they would revoke "unfair" privatizations, and while they claimed to be in favor of private ownership of businesses, they also claimed to be against the sale of land to the public. While the power of the Duma, Russia's parliament, is relatively limited compared to the power of the Russian president, many fear that the Communists will now be able to frustrate any attempts to improve Russia's tax code or property rights legislation to make the country more attractive to foreign investors. Moreover, there are growing fears that the Communists might do well in the 1996 presidential elections, which could bring Russia's economic reforms grinding to a halt.

DISCUSSION QUESTIONS

1. What are the strengths and weaknesses of the Russian privatization process? Could a better process have been devised?

2. Do you think the privatization of formerly state-owned enterprises is sufficient to induce foreign companies to invest in Russia? If not, what else needs to be put in place before Russia becomes an attractive location for inward investment?

3. What are the nature of the political and economic risks confronting foreign investors in the Russian economy in late 1995? Given the nature of these risks, and the existence of attractive investment opportunities elsewhere in the world, what approach do you think foreigners should adopt toward investing in Russia?

SOURCES

1. Allen, M. "How It Works: What Is Privatization Anyway?" *The Wall Street Journal,* October 2, 1995, p. R4.

2. Banerjee, N. "Major Investment in Russia Is Stymied." *The Wall Street Journal,* December 26, 1995.

3. Freeland, C. "Russia's Privatization: From Bang to Whimper." *Financial Times,* December 29, 1995, p. 2.

4. Guyon, J. "Russian Firms Face Fund-Raising Woes." *The Wall Street Journal,* April 17, 1995, p. B6.

5. Lane, D. "Communists Blamed as Telecom Deal Collapses." *Financial Times,* December 27, 1995, p. 1.

6. Liesman, S. "Russian Communists Are a New Breed." *The Wall Street Journal,* December 19, 1995.

7. Rosett, C., and Liesman, S. "Much Has Gone Wrong with Russia's Privatization Efforts; but Much Has Gone Right." *The Wall Street Journal,* October 2, 1995, p. R14.

8. "Special Report: Russia's Emerging Market. The Sale of the Century." *The Economist,* April 8, 1995, pp. 5–9.

MULTIGAMA

In 1946 Romania regained much of the territory it had lost earlier in World War II, but Bessarabias and Bukovina remained in the hands of the Soviet Union. The Soviet-backed regime, of which King Michael had served as figurehead since 1944, took over firm control. The Romanian government became the most Stalinist of all the regimes in Eastern Europe, which earned it a certain independence. Because the Soviet Union felt more secure with this "hard-line" regime, it withdrew its troops in 1958, much earlier than it did from other Eastern European countries. Thus the Romanian government enjoyed more independence than other Soviet bloc governments in their internal operations and in their contact and trade with the West. When the Soviet Union invaded Czechoslovakia in 1968, President Nicolae Ceauşescu's refusal to support the effort made him extremely popular with the Romanian people. It also made him popular with Western leaders; Ceauşescu was applauded as a champion of democratic reforms. Ceauşescu was actually increasing the internal control during the period, and Romania soon had a more centrally controlled economy than other countries in Eastern Europe except Albania.

Ceauşescu liked to do things on a grand scale. He ordered oil refineries built even though Romania had no oil for them to refine. He constructed massive steel mills that produced products in large quantity but of such low quality that there was little demand for them outside of Romania. He instituted a policy of economic self-sufficiency that resulted in a large central bureaucracy, firms of tremendous size, and production of thousands of products at costs that were prohibitive. In an effort to modernize the country, he destroyed thousands of beautiful old buildings, including whole villages. In most cases the architecture of the buildings that replaced them was nondescript at best. In other cases, wide empty roadways, leading to public buildings, replaced the old buildings. Agriculture was largely ignored during this period, and the living standard dropped as Ceauşescu attempted to reduce Romania's foreign debt.

In the late 1980s the economy started to collapse. A group in the Communist governmental hierarchy, prompted by a popular uprising, overthrew Ceauşescu. After the overthrow, Ion Iliescu, head of the National Salvation Front, was voted into power. Although Iliescu was nominally a Communist, his government quickly attempted to portray itself as an important force in the movement toward free markets. This led to the passage of Law Number 15, which provided that all of Romania's state-owned enterprises would be transformed into either joint-stock or limited-liability companies. It provided that Romanian citizens would receive, free of charge, nominal securities representing 30 percent of the nominal share capital of the newly created companies. The law also created the National Agency for Privatization. The Commercial Companies Privatization Law Number 58, enacted in August 1991, specified how this privatization should occur.

Private companies became legal, and small firms began to emerge immediately, especially in Bucharest. Private enterprise was seen initially in the retail sector, but eventually manufacturing firms began to appear in larger numbers. In some cases, such as restaurants, these firms charged much higher prices, but they were also generally perceived as providing better services or better products. By late winter of 1992, the privatization board had completed its initial evaluations on a series of small firms and had effectively privatized 50 *very* small state enterprises. The success with this initial series of privatizations gave the National Agency for Privatization confidence that it could move forward and meet the government's five-year timetable for privatization. In addition, it was meeting with more success interesting foreign firms in joint ventures with some of the larger state-owned enterprises.

❧ INTRODUCTION

Early in March 1992, Dan Banu left his job as the chief of the quality assurance department at Aversa, the largest pump manufacturer in Romania, to join his partners at Multigama on a full-time basis. Dan had joined Aversa in 1979 as a member of a team that designed pumps for the Romanian nuclear power plant being build at Cernavoda. The plant had been funded by a $400 million grant from the Canadian government. Dan and his colleagues' department handled designing, purchasing, and shipping of special pumps for this power plant. The first nuclear pumps were produced in 1984, and by 1987 they were producing pumps that were actually being used in the new plant.

The work group at Aversa was very unusual in that the engineers were in constant contact with the Canadians. At the time, contact between Romanians and Westerners was very restricted, but because this unit needed to be familiar with the ANSII Code requirements for nuclear plants, frequent foreign contact was required. There was some political surveillance of the employees in this unit, but because their conversations with the Canadians were highly technical, the political oversight officials concluded that the contacts did not constitute a political problem. However, the engineers valued these foreign contacts, which were forbidden for most Romanians, and they enjoyed their conversations, which often centered on subjects with little technical relevance.

It was during this time that Dan and his colleagues concluded that the ways things were done at Aversa were not optimal. They could see that the managerial practices lagged far behind those used in other countries, especially Canada. With the overthrow of Nicolae and Elena Ceaușescu in December 1989, the Aversa management was removed. Ion Iliescu, leader of the National Salvation Front, became the head of the interim government. After six weeks in office, Iliescu restored the jobs of the deposed managers as part of an effort to keep the electorate sufficiently happy to vote for him in the upcoming elections. To further enhance his party's chances in the election, he increased wages for workers and managers across the country, with no strings attached. At this point Dan and seven of his colleagues decided that Aversa could not be changed from within and that they must start their own business.

The first thing they needed was the 100,000 lei that the government required as a business license application fee.[1] They pulled together the money and got the license. However, they didn't have the manufacturing facilities or cash resources needed to produce pumps, so they entered into a business arrangement with a Syrian exchange student who was interested in selling bubble gum, curtains, and shoes. He sent them goods on consignment, which they would then sell. An empty house was used as a warehouse. The founding group of engineers appreciated this contact, because it provided them with some valuable managerial experience. At this time little commercial interest was being directed at Romania. As Dan Banu stated, "Only the Arab and Turkish people had the courage to come to Romania in 1990. They didn't have the best merchandise, but they were not afraid to come." They named the new firm *Syryus*.

The first shipment of consigned goods arrived in October 1990. Orders were solicited and received almost exclusively by telephone. Interestingly, all of the goods were sold to state-owned trade companies, which then resold them to individual consumers. The eight engineers remained at Aversa during this period and worked in the evenings and on weekends at the trading company.[2] As revenues increased, the engineers began to quit their jobs at Aversa so that they could work at Syryus full time. Dan Banu was the last of the founders to quit his job at Aversa, and by

---

[1]U.S. dollar = 197 lei in 1990 at the official bank exchange rate.

[2]The normal workweek in Romania was Monday through Saturday at this time.

the time he did, Syryus had evolved into a new firm, Multigama. After a time, the Syrian student had decided he wanted to do more than just consign goods. It was decided that he would return to Romania and enter into a joint venture with the engineers. This business relationship resulted in company expansion, and sales increased rapidly. This provided the entrepreneur-engineers the cash flow they needed to begin manufacturing pumps.

MULTIGAMA BEGINS

They began with the manufacture of small pumps designed specifically for small farms. The pump they built also proved ideal for smaller buildings, especially those in Bucharest, where the water pressure was notoriously low. In addition, hot water is produced centrally in Bucharest and then distributed to buildings. Additional pumps permit the users to enjoy a more effective distribution, especially if they are on upper floors or have multiple outlets for hot water.

Production runs were kept small in the beginning. The partners purchased 10 motors, some miscellaneous parts, and a total of 20 kg of raw materials. Once the pumps were produced, they were sold quickly, and all of the profit was reinvested. This reinvestment was necessary, because bank credit was not available. At this time Romanian banks required that loans be secured by assets worth at least 130 percent of the value of the loan. The banks had little expertise in evaluating assets, so they tended to be ultraconservative. The legislature was still discussing what to do about land titles, thus the banks were unwilling to accept land as collateral. Even if they had been willing, the existing law limited the rights of property transfer in 1990. After the government returned the land to the people it feared that farmers would be swindled out of their land by unscrupulous investors, so it prohibited land sales. In many cases the new owners did not have titles; they had pieces of paper that stated they would get title to the land in the future if it was decided that people could have title to the land. Although villagers were able to acquire 6 to 10 hectares, they did not get proper titles either. They received a piece of paper that stated they had acquired the right to acquire the land. Thus, during this period, new businesses were unlikely to look to banks as a source of funds, and there were no other institutional sources.

As the demand for their pumps began to increase, the firm was divided into two divisions, the trading company, *Syryus*, and the pump manufacturing company, *Multigama*. They attempted to find a location in Bucharest for their production facilities. They thought they could get the space they needed if they agreed to pay all the overhead and maintenance costs for an existing facility, since the decrease in demand for Romanian goods had left many firms with excess production space. However, government officials were reluctant to agree to this type of arrangement, and since the government still controlled all the larger firms, Multigama was unable to arrange for any work space in Bucharest. They spent from February to September of 1991 looking for suitable production space and fell far behind schedule. Without their own production facility, they were forced to have existing firms manufacture the components they needed.

A great contrast existed between state-owned firms and the newer private firms. Phrases such as a "warm place" and "an orphanage for older workers" were frequently used to describe the state enterprises. For instances, Don Banu felt that 2,500 employees could achieve the same output as the 5,000 Aversa employees. He felt that privatization might not be able to solve this problem, because social networks had been the source of new employees for many firms in Romania. This meant that many employees were related or close friends. Lacking established staffing and evaluation criteria, these friendships and family relationships might make professional human resource practices impossible.

❧ PRODUCTION BEGINS

For these reasons Multigama decided to find a private firm to do its manufacturing. In October 1991 they identified a small firm 100 kilometers from Bucharest that had been purchased by its employees. The firm was currently producing small car trailers, and it had the necessary equipment and employees to produce the small pumps required by Multigama. They entered into a manufacturing agreement with this firm.

The production arrangements were completed just in time for Multigama to attend the International Industrial Product Exhibit held in Bucharest in October 1991. Multigama rented the cheapest display space available. On the first day of the fair a pipe broke, and all water-using facilities, including restrooms, stopped working. Fair officials went to Aversa for help, but it could not do anything. At this point Multigama stepped in and provided one of its pumps. This earned the company a lot of free publicity at the fair, as well as the personal gratitude of those exhibiting and attending the fair. In addition, because theirs was one of the cheapest spaces at the fair, it was near a nonworking drinking fountain. This allowed them to attach one of their pumps to the nonworking fountain, which not only showed how well their pumps worked but also enhanced their space and attracted additional people to their area. This led to their first order for 10 pumps. At the time of the fair they had manufactured only five pumps, so this order was essential to their next production run, which was set at 30 pumps.

After the fair they began to advertise in newspapers, more to inform people that they had pumps than to sell them. Because of supply shortages, it was more important to advise people in Romania where they could find things than to generate new demand. A large number of newspapers had been founded after the overthrow of Nicolae and Elena Ceauşescu and the great amount of competition kept advertising costs low.

The initial batch of 30 pumps sold quickly. Gradually, production runs were increased to 300 to 500 pumps. Currently Multigama is manufacturing between 500 and 700 pumps each month. Newspaper advertising has been eliminated, because the partners believe their potential customers are aware of them. Management still views advertising as merely a way of informing predisposed buyers as to where they can purchase the goods they need. Also, Multigama is selling all of the pumps it is currently capable of manufacturing, which reduces its interest in advertising.

Product development has also expanded rapidly. The initial selection of three pumps has been expanded to five models, each of which comes in two or three sizes. Currently, the profit margins are lower and the turnaround is slower on the industrial (Multigama) side of the firm. However, management is more interested in this side of the business. It accounts for over 80 percent of the revenue, and management expects this percentage to increase in the future. They have more expertise in this side of the business, too. They have seen that it is easier to get a trading business started, and they expect margins to gradually fall in this area as more competitors emerge.

The organizational structure of Multigama has become more formal as the business has grown. The eight original partners form the General Owner Assembly, from which they elect a president. Once a month an administrative board, consisting of the owners and the president, reviews a report from the president. In addition, the president must prepare the general balance and financial report, which is due each March. This report is also required by the government. It is expected that as the government's privatization effort expands, additional financial reporting will be required, and this will impact the firm.

❧ DIVERSIFICATION

Multigama is planning to build a facility for both its own use and to provide rental income. They plan to have apartments on the upper floors and commercial space for their own administrative offices and to rent to other firms on the first floor. The rent will provide needed revenue, while offering them room for expansion as the firm grows. They have found a potential partner/investor, who wants to build a building in the center of Bucharest. The government paperwork has been completed, and a contractor has been hired. The building is expected to take one year to complete. To further test the feasibility of this idea, Multigama ran a newspaper advertisement to announce what they were doing. The response was encouraging; several businesses have already committed to rent some of the first-floor commercial space. They believe demand will be high because there is a housing shortage in Bucharest, and many of the commercial buildings started by Ceaușescu are of poor quality and will probably be demolished rather than completed.

Multigama is also considering the possibility of manufacturing food-processing equipment. They have been developing a relationship with a Lynnwood, Washington, firm headed by a Romanian expatriate. This potential partner has expertise in refrigeration, which Multigama lacks.

It has been very difficult to attract investors because Romania is not viewed as a good place to invest. The EEC, Canada, and the IMF have directed their investments toward energy generation, because there is currently a shortage of energy production capability in Romania. In addition, most foreign credits have been going to state-owned firms, and Romania's existing Communist government status has resulted in its not being considered for some foreign investment programs, especially those with government sponsorship.

However, the best employees have been gradually moving to private firms. In the old days, the large state firms were required to produce an item domestically, even if only one of the items was needed. With privatization, the larger state-owned firms have been left with labor forces geared to this type of response mode. The turn toward free market operations and privatization has led to much speculation about what form of commercial activity is most appropriate for Romania. Dan Banu feels that these factors will combine to produce an environment that is more conducive to investments in new private start-ups.

❧ THE FUTURE

Banu and his partners are doing a lot of thinking and planning. They are trying to determine where the best opportunities for profit exist and how to obtain the necessary cash, or investors, to exploit these opportunities. In addition, they are seeking ways to move from a purely domestic mode to one more focused on foreign trade. Labor costs are currently quite low in Romania, which will allow Multigama to price its product competitively, and their pumps seem ideal for use in many less developed countries. They are also concerned about their lack of managerial experience; all of the founders still consider themselves primarily engineers. The potential effects of privatization are unclear. They are aware that Aversa may find a powerful and efficient foreign partner, which could limit Multigama's potential for growth.

DISCUSSION QUESTIONS

1. As an executive of a multinational enterprise, would you to consider investing in Multigama? What would be the main issues to consider?
2. What about investing in Aversa? What are the advantages and disadvantages of investing in each?
3. Given the industries in which Romania had invested under the Communist regime, how likely are these industries to help lead Romania toward economic prosperity?

4. As an IMF or World Bank official, how would you target lending to assist in the development of Romania?

5. Given their success to date, and the opportunities they have, what advice would you give to Multigama's management?

THE CHINA STRATEGY: A TALE OF TWO FIRMS

Political patronage created the Taibao venture; but not only was it unable to ensure the ultimate success of the project, it appears to have contributed significantly to its failure. Our *guanxi* with the central leadership in China didn't automatically lead to cooperation at the local level and we paid heavy prices for that.

> Ray Schon, chairman
> Western Energy Inc.

The heart of our success lies at our willingness to work with local suppliers, ensure quality standards, and support a nationwide dealer network in China.

> John White, vice president,
> international operations
> American Copier Company

"I am sorry to hear about the tragedy of Mr. Arnold Tanner. We have been friends for years." In September 1990 on a plane to China, John White, vice president of international operations for American Copier Company (ACC), happened to sit next to Ray Schon, chairman of Western Energy Inc. (WEI) and they compared notes on their firms' experiences in China.

White was a good friend of Arnold Tanner, then chairman of WEI who had suddenly passed away a few weeks ago at the age of 85. Schon was Tanner's successor and one of his first priorities was to terminate a deal, the Taibao coal mine, which Tanner struck with the Chinese. The $700 million joint venture was plagued by a host of problems almost from the time the contract was signed in 1982. But the personal commitment of Tanner and China's supreme leader Deng Xiaoping, which elevated the venture into a symbol of China's "Open Door" policy, kept the project going while Tanner was still alive. Schon clearly lacked this political commitment and intended to withdraw from this unprofitable deal as part of the new restructuring program at WEI.

"Oh, really?" White was surprised to hear Schon talk about WEI's intended withdrawal from China. He was flying to China to visit with ACC Shanghai, to celebrate its third anniversary, and to review ACC's China strategy with the joint venture's resident managers. Formed in late 1987, the $30 million ACC Shanghai joint venture was already number one in China's expanding copier market and planned to capture even greater market share. Recalling his first trip to China in 1983, which was encouraged by his friend Tanner, White began to think of why ACC successfully stayed in China while WEI had to pull out.

❧ ARNOLD TANNER, WESTERN ENERGY INC. AND CHINA

Background

Primarily an oil company, Western Energy Inc. conducted business in more than 100 countries and employed more than 78,000 people worldwide. With annual sales around $10 billion in the 1980s and the early 1990s, WEI was among the top 10 major energy firms in the United States. WEI consisted of one of the world's largest petroleum (oil and gas) operations, a growing chemical business, a coal exploration

Source: Mike W. Peng of the University of Hawai'i at Manoa prepared this case as a basis for class discussion rather than to illustrate effective or ineffective management practice. The names of the companies have been disguised. © 1996 by Mike W. Peng.

TABLE 1

Five-Year Summary of
Selected Financial Data:
Western Energy Inc.

	1991	1990	1989	1988	1987
Operations (in $ millions)					
Revenues	$10,096	$11,509	$10,939	$10,351	$9,415
Operational income (loss)	$379	$(1,715)	$247	$295	$102
Net income (loss)	$460	$(1,695)	$293	$316	$220
Financial position (in $ millions)					
Total assets	$16,115	$18,619	$19,557	$19,533	$16,861
Total debt	$5,546	$7,425	$7,738	$7,227	$5,925
Stockholders' equity	$4,340	$4,114	$5,901	$6,218	$5,144
Per share data					
Earnings (loss) per share from operations	$1.25	$(5.89)	$0.89	$1.19	$0.39
Earnings (loss) per share	$1.52	$(5.82)	$1.06	$1.27	$0.96

business, and a nationwide retailing operation in the United States. Its strategy emphasized foreign production and the firm had production facilities in Argentina, Bolivia, Canada, Ecuador, Malaysia, Pakistan, the Philippines, Syria, and the U.K. North Sea as well as the United States when it entered China in 1980. (See Table 1 for a five-year summary of selected financial data for WIE.)

From 1962 to 1990, Arnold Tanner was first the CEO and then chairman of the San Francisco-based firm. Before becoming the CEO in 1962, he worked for WEI for 25 years in various capacities. His long years of service at WEI and his leadership role made an enormous impact on WEI. Tanner was well respected as a dynamic and charismatic leader in the industry. Moreover, Tanner's foresight on business opportunities led his firm to actively seek opportunities in the Eastern Bloc. His legendary achievements included striking one of the first deals between a Western businessman and the Soviets in the 1930s, supplying the Soviets during the Second World War, and trading with Eastern Europe since the détente in the 1970s. As a result, his name was also well recognized in many quarters of the Eastern Bloc. When China started its "Open Door" policy in 1979, China's political leaders naturally looked to Tanner for his initiatives.

Tanner responded to the Chinese inquiry with enthusiasm. His first visit to China was in 1979 and he later became a frequent flyer to Beijing. As always, he took a high-profile approach and befriended China's supreme leader Deng Xiaoping. In the early 1980s, China desperately needed to prove to a suspicious West that its "Open Door" policy was credible and that direct investment from abroad was genuinely welcome. Well respected both in the West and in the Eastern Bloc, Tanner became an ideal candidate to bridge the gap between China and the outside world. Of course Tanner didn't respond to the Chinese interest with goodwill only. WEI earnings were flat for the last few years in the late 1970s and Tanner was exploring new avenues in foreign exploration and production for growth of sales and earnings. Tanner sensed that if WEI penetrated China early, it might be able to capitalize on some first-mover advantages[1] like preempting rival Western firms in the acquisition of China's energy resources.

In short, China's new "Open Door" and its drive for modernization, Tanner's longtime interest in doing business with the Eastern Bloc, and WEI's desire to expand its global operations into a new market made WEI a pioneering American firm entering China.

---

[1]M. B. Lieberman and D. B. Montgomery, "First Mover Advantages: A Survey," *Strategic Management Journal* 9 (Summer Special Issue 1988), pp. 41–58.

Politics and the Taibao Coal Mine

Since the initiation of the "Open Door" policy in the late 1970s, developing the energy sector to support industrial development has become a priority goal of the Chinese government.[2] Among various energy resources, coal is the most important one to China as three quarters of the country's energy demand is met by coal. China's proven coal reserves exceed 900 billion tonnes, behind only the Soviet Union and the United States. Total estimated reserves, however, are in the neighborhood of 2 trillion tonnes; at current production levels it would take 2,000 years to exhaust the total supply.[3]

Despite the abundant coal supply, the lack of capital and technology to effectively exploit the coal in sufficient amounts to meet energy needs led to a national headache in the 1980s. In many parts of China factories had to shut down for one or two days a month due to energy shortages; at one point Shanghai had only two days' worth of coal reserves on hand for power generation. It is evident that without the development of its energy sector, China's goal of modernization would not be realized. Therefore, seeking foreign partners to help develop China's energy resources became an important part of the "Open Door" policy.

In 1980 China opened its premier coal mine—the Taibao coal mine in Shanxi Province of northern China—to international bidding and sought a foreign partner. One of the largest open-pit coal mines in the world, the Taibao mine became the largest energy project in China that was ever opened to foreign firms at that time. Eight Western firms participated in the bidding, including three from the United States, two from Germany, and one each from France, Japan, and the United Kingdom. Not surprisingly, Tanner's WEI beat all the competitors.

Politics were instrumental in this process and China's central leadership was heavily involved in this "pet project." Politically, China preferred having a major U.S. company as its partner as an unambiguous signal to American investors conveying the message that the "Open Door" policy was for real. Unlike European and Japanese companies that had been doing business with China for years, the United States virtually had no business with China until 1979, when the two countries normalized their diplomatic relations. Decades of hostility between the two countries made American investors especially suspicious at that time. However, China sensed that the United States possessed more advanced technologies and more abundant capital that China needs and that courting American investment would be of strategic importance to the "Open Door" policy.[4] Among the three American firms that entered the bidding, WEI was better respected and financially stronger. Moreover, Tanner's assiduous cultivation of developing *guanxi* (connections)[5] with Chinese leaders, especially Deng Xiaoping, and previous contacts throughout the Eastern Bloc played an important role in China's selection of WEI as its sole foreign partner.

The Economics of the Taibao Joint Venture

On winning the bid, Western Energy Inc. became the foreign partner in this 50-50 equity joint venture, which was incorporated as the Taibao Mine Group in China in 1982.[6] A 30-year, renewable joint-venture contract was signed. The Chinese partners included a consortium of Chinese organizations led by China National Coal Corp., the country's leading coal producer. The venture called for $700 million in capital endowment, with each side contributing $200 million and the remaining $300 million syndicated by 39 international banks (see Table 2). At full capacity, the mine should produce 12 million tonnes a year and employ 3,000 workers, 20 to 30 of which would be WEI expatriates.

---

[2]M. W. Peng, "Modeling China's Economic Reforms through an Organizational Approach: The Case of the M-Form Hypothesis," *Journal of Management Inquiry* (in press).

[3]J. P. Huang, "Fueling the Economy," *The China Business Review,* March–April 1991, p. 22.

[4]B. S. Chen, "Economic Development Strategy for China's Coastal Areas and U.S. Investment in China, "*Meiguo Yanjiu* (Journal of American Studies) 2, no. 3 (1988), pp. 7–25.

[5]See Appendix 1 for a description of *guanxi* in China.

[6]See Appendix 2 for a summary of China's Joint Venture Law.

Table 2
Partners and Finances of the
Taibao Mine Venture

United States (50% share)	China (50% share)
Western Energy Inc. (responsible for $200 million initial capital)	China National Coal Corp. China Coal Import/Export Corp. China International Trust & Investment Corp. Province of Shanxi (The Chinese partners were responsible for $200 million initial capital)
$300 million loan syndicated by 39 international banks (each side guarantees 50 percent of the loan)	

In the initial courtship during 1980–82, WEI responded to Chinese interest with a number of extravagant promises, ranging from the scale of the mine to Chinese workers' salaries to the amount of coal it could export. It agreed to export 75 percent of total output and to assume complete responsibilities of marketing the coal in the export market. Noted for their preference for "general principles" in the negotiations, the Chinese were serious about those promises and treated them as a foundation on which details could be worked out with WEI later.

However, after the joint-venture contract was signed and the feasibility study begun, the economics of the project had already become shaky in light of falling world coal prices. WEI was forced to hedge its earlier promises and began to pressure the Chinese side to grant it various concessions. For instance, WEI tried to make China Coal Import/Export Corp., one of the Chinese partners, buy WEI's share of export coal at prevailing international prices, thus retreating from its earlier promise to market the coal itself in the international market. The Chinese negotiators were surprised and intense arguments between the two sides occurred. On several occasions during the negotiations, disputes at the working level came close to derailing the project. But Tanner and the Chinese political leadership always intervened to enforce a solution. Numerous public ceremonies throughout the negotiation phase bound the prestige of Tanner and the Chinese leadership even more tightly to the consummation of the project. Eventually WEI won several concessions from the Chinese side in 1985, including shifting the responsibilities of export marketing to China Coal Import/Export Corp.

Operational Problems: Central versus Local *Guanxi*

The operational phase of the Taibao venture since 1986 improved to be even more problematic than the negotiation phase. Although getting the mine up and running was undeniably a major achievement, the project, as of September 1990, still wasn't certified as "complete" despite being operational for four years. In 1990, its best year in terms of production, it produced only three-quarters of its 12 million-tonne capacity and suffered a $31 million loss. Exports were probably less than half of the 8 to 9 million tonnes WEI originally anticipated.

Four sources of problems contributed to the venture's lackluster performance. First, continuing low world coal prices prevented the venture from earning the foreign exchange necessary to break even. Second, lower-then-expected coal quality, with high sulfur content in one seam and high ash content in another, further depressed the marketability of the coal produced at Taibao on the international market. Technical problems such as defective equipment and the worker's lack of training created the third source of problems. However, to WEI, the largest source of problems came from the lack of cooperation between WEI and its local partners, despite its influential *guanxi* with the central leadership.

Tanner was very skillful in cultivating *guanxi* with the central leadership in Beijing and was able to use his central *guanxi* influence to make his Chinese partners grant him concessions. However, WEI failed to develop close *guanxi* relations with local partners, which caused a lot of problems. Many WEI managers reported that disputes over production and marketing strategies have been common among partners. For instance, the Americans would like to decrease the production of high-sulfur coal, which could only be sold on the domestic market for local currency, and to increase the production of low-sulfur coal for the export market. However, the Chinese insisted that due to the depressed export market, producing a large amount of low-sulfur coal would result in large inventories, thus further hampering the venture's already bad cash flow situations. Instead of working together, both sides seemed to develop an appetite to blame each other for whatever problems occurred. On another occasion, WEI accused the China Coal Import/Export Corp. of failing to aggressively market the coal in the export market. In response, the Chinese managers pointed out the insincerity on WEI's part by retreating from its earlier promises and relinquishing the entire responsibilities of international marketing. Due to political pressure from China's central leadership, China Coal Import/Export Corp. reluctantly assumed the exporting functions for the Taibao venture in 1985. Now a depressed world market and the less-than-expected coal quality gave the reluctant Chinese partner as excuse for not living up to its promises. Many WEI officials believed that their Chinese partners deliberately exacerbated these problems despite the political pressures that forced them to make concessions to WEI in the first place.

Still More Politics

In June 1989 the Tiananmen Square incident in Beijing shocked the world. Foreign businesspeople were pulling out of China immediately following the incident and international investors led by the World Bank were hesitant to commit further funds to China. The Chinese leadership desperately needed to prove to the world that despite all the tragedies, China's 10-year-old "Open Door" policy would continue. As the government's credibility declined to a record low in recent history, a live example would be worth a thousand words. Once again, the Taibao venture played into the hands of the Chinese leadership. Despite internal disagreement at WEI, in late 1989 Arnold Tanner went back to China in a "business as usual" fashion to meet with the Chinese leaders, who promptly used this visit by an "old friend" as a photo opportunity to appease the West.

Inside WEI, as the company's financial situation worsened in the late 1980s with increasing debts, discussions of withdrawing from the Taibao venture were going on for a few years. In a manner similar to how Deng Xiaoping ruled China, Tanner dismissed such ideas and urged a "long-term" perspective. The Chinese leadership, on the other hand, had the strong desire to save its political face and to avoid the failure of a flagship project. Therefore, despite huge financial losses that depleted WEI's cash flow, the Taibao venture continued until Tanner's sudden death in August 1990.

Exit?

Within weeks of becoming WEI's new chairman, Ray Schon reassessed the company's overall strategic position and concluded, "The business climate of the 1990s is vastly different from that of the 1980s." To him the 1990s seemed to be defined by lack of liquidity in financial markets, recessionary pressure on global economics, and increasing volatility in energy prices and chronic instability in world markets. The year 1990 during which Arnold Tanner passed away left the company with a net lost of $1.7 billion (see Table 1). In response, Schon started a major restructuring and divestiture program aimed at "building on proven strengths and having the operational and financial flexibility to respond in a timely manner to unpredictable markets." Specifically, this program would sell unprofitable lines of business to reduce debt, which was running at $7.4 billion in 1990, and focus WEI's resources on those businesses in which it already excelled—oil and natural gas and chemicals.

	1991	1990	1989	1988	1987
Operations (in $ millions)					
Revenues	$12,869	$12,692	$11,720	$11,152	$10,438
Operational income	$454	$605	$653	$347	$542
Net income	$454	$243	$704	$388	$578
Financial position (in $ millions)					
Total assets	$31,658	$31,635	$30,088	$26,441	$22,450
Total debt	$9,886	$10,579	$10,754	$7,874	$5,722
Stockholders' equity	$5,140	$5,051	$5,035	$5,371	$5,105
Per share data					
Earnings per share from operations	$3.91	$5.51	$6.05	$3.09	$4.94
Earnings per share	$3.91	$1.66	$6.56	$3.49	$5.30

The corporate strategy changes decided the fate of the Taibao venture. In his announcement to start the restructuring program, Schon publicly announced his intention to withdraw WEI from the unprofitable project, which was Tanner's favorite project but never part of WEI's core business. To do that, WEI would have to write off $200 million in unprofitable investment but would be relieved of $150 million loan guarantees. At present, WEI would have two options: (1) to sell its share to its Chinese partners, or (2) to sell to another foreign investor. One way or the other, Ray Schon understood that his trip to China would be a stormy one.

"Political patronage created the Taibao," Schon told White on the plane, "but not only was it unable to ensure the ultimate success of the project, it appears to have contributed significantly to its failure. Contrary to our expectations, our *guanxi* connections with the central leadership didn't automatically lead to cooperation at the local level and we paid heavy prices for that. The business in the 1990s simply won't be the same as when Tanner was around; we can no longer afford to support such an unprofitable business."

❧ AMERICAN COPIER COMPANY IN SHANGHAI

Unlike Western Energy Inc.'s approach in China characterized by early entry, high profile, and central *guanxi*-developing, American Copier Company's China strategy was markedly different: It was cautious, low profile, and aimed at building cooperative relations with local partners. It took about four years (1983–87) of long negotiations for ACC to set up its Shanghai joint venture, but the project was apparently worth the wait. For ACC, China has proved a good match, offering both low-cost design and labor and a growing market for copier machines and products. Formed in late 1987, the $30 million ACC Shanghai became number one in China's growing copier market by 1989 and planned to capture even greater market share.

Choosing Joint Venturing in Shanghai

With annual sales in the neighborhood of $10 billion throughout the 1980s, ACC is a global company serving the worldwide document processing markets. (See Table 3 for a five-year summary of ACC's selected financial data.) Its activities encompassed developing, manufacturing, marketing, servicing, and financing a wide range of document processing product and service offerings. Its copiers, duplicators, production publishers, electronic printers, facsimile products, scanners, and computer products were marketed in over 130 countries. In addition to a worldwide network of dealers and distributors, ACC maintained research and development (R&D) facilities in Canada, Great Britain, Japan, and the United States. Moreover, before joint venturing with the Chinese, ACC already had substantial experience from its joint-venture operations in Australia, Brazil, Germany, Great Britain, India, and Japan.

TABLE 4

Partners and Finances of the
American Copier Company's
Shanghai Venture

United States (51% share)	China (49% share)
American Copier Co. (responsible for $15 million initial investment)	Shanghai Photo Industry Co. (holding 44% share and contributing plants and labor, assessed at $5 million)
	Bank of China (holding 5% share and responsible for $10 million investment)

When ACC entered China in the early 1980s through exporting, the copier market in China was dominated by Japanese makers, including Canon, Minolta, Ricoh, and Toshiba. Many of these companies had a longer history of serving the China market, but ACC was the only copier producer thus far to establish a joint venture in the country. Though it would take ACC significantly longer than its competitors (some of which signed technology transfer agreements with Chinese firms) to show a return on its $15 million investment, the company's dominant position in a restricted-size market undoubtedly reflected in part greater official support for the joint venture than for its competitors.

ACC's initial exporting to China in the early 1980s was considered moderately successful. In order to capture a larger share of the growing market, ACC initially considered a technology transfer agreement in 1983. But it soon decided to pursue a joint venture instead due to China's underdeveloped intellectual property protection regime. Numerous sites were considered for the venture, and all the local authorities who learned of ACC's interest courted ACC for its investment. ACC avoided being too involved with local Chinese politics and didn't provide vague promises or agree on "general principles" that the Chinese would like. Eventually ACC settled on Shanghai due to the large concentration of components suppliers and the skilled labor in the area.

ACC's Shanghai venture partners included Bank of China, which held 5 percent of the venture and provided $10 million for investment, and the Shanghai Photo Industry Co., which held 44 percent of the shares and contributed existing plants, equipment, and some personnel assessed at $5 million. ACC held the remaining 51 percent of the venture and invested $15 million (see Table 4). Signed in 1987, ACC Shanghai has a 30-year, renewable joint-venture contract and 10-year renewable technology license for production of desktop copiers and accessories and other copier products. The license gave ACC Shanghai the right to use the ACC's desktop office copier technology. ACC Shanghai was designed to produce low-end and mid-range copiers suitable for the Chinese market and was capable of switching to produce more advanced designs. At full capacity, which was expected to be reached in 1994, ACC Shanghai would be capable of producing 40,000 units annually and employ 900 workers. In September 1990 ACC Shanghai employed more then 600 people, six of which were expatriates.

Localizing Production

Despite the Chinese preference to have a high percentage of the venture's output be exported, the ACC negotiation team, led by John White, persuaded the Chinese that the models ACC would introduce to China would be mid-range to low-end ones suitable for China and the focus should be on the domestic market. In return ACC accepted a stipulation by the Chinese side that 70 percent of the venture's components would be sourced locally by the end of 1992. To date, ACC managers claimed the venture was on track to achieve this goal, though the process was difficult since none of the local suppliers initially had the technical expertise or equipment necessary to produce the quality components needed by ACC Shanghai.

To overcome these obstacles, ACC heavily engaged in what's called "vendor development" in the United States. ACC, through its Shanghai venture, either transferred technology or provided technical support to approximately 60 suppliers, mostly in Shanghai. Aside from training the supplies how to use the technology or equipment transferred, ACC also coached them in materials management and handling, as well as in accounting. Moreover, ACC Shanghai developed close working relations with the Shanghai Foreign Investment Commission, which provided funding to local companies to enable them to upgrade their plants and purchase the new technology.

ACC estimated that it spent several million dollars in training, support, and monitoring of Chinese suppliers to ensure consistent quality and delivery. Some of these development costs were charged to the suppliers, and the rest was absorbed by ACC Shanghai. While the training did pay off in improved quality of locally supplied components over the past few years, Chinese components still tended to be produced at above world market prices, thus forcing up the final cost of ACC Shanghai copiers. By company estimates, locally sourced components cost on average 10 to 20 percent more than imported ones.

Ensuring Quality

ACC was renowned throughout the world for its quality products. All components used by ACC Shanghai were subject to quality standards established by ACC. The parent company also instituted its corporate quality control culture in the venture to ensure the ACC Shanghai's output was on par with ACC products manufactured in other countries. ACC attempted to reinforce the concept of quality at all levels, not just in interaction with the end user. The company's "LUTI" system—learn, use, teach, and inspect—was ongoing, with each management level teaching it to the level below, as well as to new employees.

A customer satisfaction review board, which met on a monthly basis, was established by ACC Shanghai to ensure the reputation of its products. The board, composed of representatives from the venture's marketing, service, distribution, management, engineering, and quality control departments, examined complaints and conducted customer surveys to determine where improvement would be needed. The results from the first survey, conducted in 1989, one year after the first copier rolled off the production line, indicated 90 percent customer satisfaction with the venture's products. Further proof of ACC Shanghai's success in attaining high quality came from the Shanghai municipal government, which awarded the venture the Shanghai Quality Award in 1989 and 1990, and from the parent company, which awarded the venture an in-house quality award in 1990.

Capturing the Market

The first ACC Shanghai 2020 copier was produced in October 1988, little more than a year after the joint-venture contract was signed. A mid-range model, the 2020 didn't incorporate the latest technology, but its reliable, sturdy operation was very suitable for China.

To meet demand outside the Shanghai area for its copiers, ACC Shanghai—with help from its partner Shanghai Photo Industry Co.—established a nationwide distribution, sales, and service network in China. The network included over 100 dealers throughout China, all of whom were trained by ACC Shanghai. Three ACC representatives offices—in Beijing, Guangzhou, and Shanghai—provided additional dealer support in such areas as training, inventory, and advertising.

A vigorous advertising campaign was launched through television and newspaper media in China to increase the publicity of ACC Shanghai in 1987. Competing against Japanese brands like Canon, Minolta, Ricoh, and Toshiba, ACC Shanghai skillfully named its products *Shang Am* (*Hu Mei* in Mandarin Chinese pronunciation), which stands for "Shanghai Beauty."[7] American name brands usually carry a premium among Chinese customers and historically products from Shanghai are renowned for their high quality in China. Thus the eye-catching name "Shanghai

---

[7]"America" (*Mei Guo*), when pronounced in Mandarin Chinese, China's official language, stands for "beautiful country."

Beauty," which highlighted the combination of American technology and Shanghai production, created an attractive and trustworthy image among Chinese users. Moreover, despite the high components' cost, ACC Shanghai competitively priced its copiers to be within the range of Japanese offerings.

Vigorous quality standards, extensive dealer networks, and an aggressive and skillfully executed advertising campaign accompanied with reasonable prices led ACC Shanghai to become the number one copier seller in China. In 1989 ACC Shanghai gained 32 percent of the Chinese desktop copier market and around 45 percent by late 1990.

Problems

As expected, the China market was full of problems, some of which were anticipated. The original feasibility study proved to be overly optimistic in its assumptions of production costs and size of the copier market in China. "These miscalculations were perhaps unavoidable," John White said as he continued to share this experience with a frustrated Schon on the plane, "given the unforeseen nature of some of the factors that have affected ACC Shanghai's performance."

Besides high costs of locally sourced components, the devaluation of the Chinese *yuan* against the U.S. dollar in the mid-1980s resulted in higher costs of imported components to the venture. Perhaps more important, the introduction of government purchase controls as part of the government's austerity policy since 1988 led to a far smaller market than ACC had originally envisioned. To purchase a copier, a prospective buyer must first obtain permission from several government agencies. This market-restricting policy was further strengthened in the post-Tiananmen implementation of the government's austerity program. Such a system seriously inhibited market forces; ACC estimated the real market in China to be five times its present size.

Despite the government's austerity program since the late 1980s, the general policy of "Open Door" was to continue and the policy to support joint-venture companies was unchanged. Therefore, in this difficult situation, ACC's joint-venture strategy paid off since government agencies would be more likely to approve the purchase of a domestically produced, reasonably priced copier like "Shang Am" than to buy an imported model, even when the two models were of the same performance and price level. Thus ACC Shanghai was able to receive greater official support though it didn't deliberately cultivate *guanxi* with the government.

Problems unrelated to the macroeconomic environment also confronted ACC Shanghai. For instance, the paper feeders initially produced by the venture malfunctioned due to the poor quality of Chinese paper. The feeders were since redesigned by ACC Shanghai engineers to handle the low-grade paper used in most Chinese offices and were reportedly functioning well.

Future Prospects

In September 1990, ACC Shanghai was approaching its third year of operations and John White was going to review the parent company's China strategy with the joint venture's resident managers. He envisioned that in the immediate future, ACC Shanghai should focus on designing two new products—a low-end model for developing segments in the China market and a more sophisticated, high-end model for the upper-stream segments. ACC Shanghai engineers initially worked in conjunction with ACC corporate engineers to develop the prototypes for the two models, but total design responsibility was recently turned over to ACC Shanghai. The first model of the low-end copier, which was expected to become a major product line in China, was scheduled to enter the China market in 1992. According to a similar plan, small volumes of the high-end model should hit the market in 1993.

Looking several years ahead, with the existing 2020 mid-range model, ACC Shanghai would have three models each concentrating on the low-end, middle, and high-end segments of the China market. Whether other new product lines would be manufactured by ACC Shanghai was undetermined yet. "My inclination is to continue the three-model operations with ACC Shanghai for a few more years," White commented. "We have built up a vendor base there and have spent a long time training people in quality control and other areas. But starting a new product line is very taxing; I wouldn't let our joint ventures in India and Brazil, for example, even contemplate it. While there are advantages to keeping everything in one organization, it could be too much for a young venture like the one we have in Shanghai. I want to make sure that ACC Shanghai continues to operate on a sound financial footing. This venture is already ahead of where our first venture in Japan was at the equivalent time. Eventually, I'd like to see it become like ACC Japan or ACC UK, a stand-alone operation with its own product lines."

On the other hand, White also noted that whether ACC Shanghai could meet such lofty aspirations would depend on two factors. First, the market would have to expand, which would require the abolition or liberalization of the government purchase-control system. However, the Chinese government didn't seem to be willing to liberalize its stringent purchase-control policy and ACC found it had little influence on the government. To expand customer bases (and to project good corporate image), ACC Shanghai recently started a school program to give selected high schools in China a gift package consisting of copiers and accessories. Second, costs would have to come down, which would require further improvements in the local supplier network. Given existing good *guanxi* with the local suppliers built through years of cooperative working relations, ACC Shanghai felt confident it could overcome the components cost problems and bring the costs of locally sourced components on par with the international level in a few years.

⚓ EPILOGUE

As the plane landed in Shanghai, John White shook hands with Ray Schon, wished Schon good luck, and then stepped out of the plane. Though the future was still daunting, he was delighted with ACC Shanghai's past three years and had strong hopes that the Shanghai venture would turn out to be a successful one for his company.

After a two-hour stop, the plane continued its journey to Beijing. Schon, already exhausted, decided not to stop in Beijing to meet Tanner's "old friends" in the Chinese leadership; instead, he made up his mind to go directly to Shanxi to terminate the Taibao venture as soon as possible.

Appendix 1—The Importance of Guanxi *(Connections) in China*
Guanxi is the word that describes the intricate, pervasive network of personal relations that every Chinese cultivates with energy, subtlety, and imagination. It is a relationship between two people or organizations containing implicit mutual obligation, assurances, and understanding and governs Chinese attitudes toward long-term social and business relationship. If a *guanxi* relationship of trust and mutual benefits is established, an excellent foundation will be built to develop a future relationship. *Guanxi* ties may also be helpful in dealing with the Chinese bureaucracy as personal interpretations are often used in lieu of legal interpretations.

Though the use of *guanxi* networks has mushroomed during the reform in China since 1979,[8] *guanxi* has much stronger and deeper roots embedded in the Chinese society. Traditionally the strong value of family ties has placed an emphasis on getting things done through whom you know. One of the most important aspects of the *guanxi* network is that it is neither officially acknowledged nor written down. Members of *guanxi* networks highly value reciprocity, trust, and implicit understanding between the two parties involved (i.e., "I give you a favor now and I believe that you will return a favor to me in the future whenever I need it.") thus reducing the need to write everything down.

---

[8]See M. W. Peng, "Organizational Changes in Planned Economics in Transition: An Eclectic Model," *Advances in International Comparative Management* 9 (1994), pp. 223–51; and M. W. Peng and P. S. Heath, "The Growth of the Firm in Planned Economics in Transition: Institutions, Organizations and Strategic Choice," *Academy of Management Review* (in press).

Due to cultural differences and language barriers, visitors to China are not in a position to cultivate *guanxi* with the depth possible between two Chinese. Nevertheless, *guanxi* is an important aspect of social life in China and deserves attention so that good relations may be developed and things can get done. If a foreigner seeks to develop *guanxi* with the Chinese, then he or she should be pleased when being called by the Chinese as an "old friend." Among American dignitaries, Richard Nixon, Henry Kissinger, and Jimmy Carter enjoy the "old friend" status.

Appendix 2—Summary of the Law of the People's Republic of China on Joint Ventures Using Chinese and Foreign Investment (adopted in 1979 at the Second Session of the Fifth National People's Congress)

1. Foreign companies and individuals within the territory of the People's Republic of China (PRC) may incorporate themselves into joint ventures with Chinese companies or other Chinese entities with the objective of expanding international economic cooperation and technological exchange.

2. The Foreign Investment Commission must authorize joint ventures, and if approved, ventures are required to register with the General Administration for Industry and Commerce of the PRC, which will then issue a license within three months.

3. Joint ventures shall have limited liability and the foreign parties will contribute not less than 25 percent of the registered capital.

4. The participants will share profits, risks, and losses of the joint venture in proportion to their capital contributions.

5. The equity of each party may be capital goods, industrial property rights, cash, etc., in the ventures.

6. The contributors of technology or equipment run the risk of forfeiture or damages if the technology or equipment contributed is not truly advanced and appropriate for Chinese needs. If losses are caused by deception through the intentional provision of outdated equipment or technology, compensation must be paid for the losses.

7. Investments by the Chinese participants may include the right of use of a site but it shall not constitute a part of the investment as the joint venture shall pay the Chinese government for its use.

8. A joint venture will have a board of directors and the chairman of the board is to be appointed by the Chinese participants. The foreign parties may appoint two vice presidents. These do not necessarily have to be Chinese but must be approved by the partners of the joint venture.

9. A joint-venture agreement must stipulate procedures for the employment and discharge of the workers and staff members and comply with Chinese laws.

10. The net profit of a joint venture shall be distributed in proportion to the parties' respective investment shares after deductions for reserve funds. Bonuses and welfare funds for the workers and the expansion funds of the venture and the profit or losses shall be in accordance with the capital investment of the parties involved and be subject to the tax laws of PRC and expatriation.

11. Joint ventures must maintain open accounts in a bank approved by the Bank of China.

12. All foreign exchange transactions shall be in accordance with the foreign exchange regulations of the PRC.

13. Joint ventures may borrow funds directly from foreign banks. Appropriate insurance will be provided by Chinese insurance companies. A joint venture equipped with up-to-date technology by world standards may apply for a reduction of or an exemption from income tax for the first two or three profit-making years.

14. A joint venture is encouraged to market its products outside China through direct channels, its associated agencies, or Chinese foreign trade establishments. Its products may also be distributed in the Chinese market.

15. The contract period of a joint venture must be agreed on by both parties and may be extended subject to authorization by the Foreign Investment Commission.

16. Disputes that cannot be settled though consultation between partners may be settled through consultation or arbitration by a Chinese arbitral body or an arbitral body agreed on by the parties involved.

CHAPTER FOUR

INTERNATIONAL TRADE THEORY

THE GAINS FROM TRADE: GHANA AND SOUTH KOREA

In 1970 living standards in Ghana and South Korea were roughly comparable. Ghana's 1970 gross national product (GNP) per head was $250, and South Korea's was $260. By 1992 the situation had changed dramatically. South Korea had a GNP per capita of $6,790, while Ghana's was only $450, reflecting vastly different economic growth rates. Between 1968 and 1988 the average annual growth rate in Ghana's GNP was 1.5 percent; between 1980 and 1992 it was an anemic negative 0.1 percent. In contrast, South Korea achieved a rate of around 9 percent per annum between 1968 and 1992.

What explains the difference between Ghana and South Korea? There is no simple answer, but there are reasons for believing that the attitudes of both countries toward international trade provide part of the explanation. A study by the World Bank suggests that whereas the South Korean government has had a strong protrade bias, the actions of the Ghanaian government discouraged domestic producers from becoming involved in international trade.

Ghana was the first of Great Britain's West African colonies to become independent, doing so in 1957. Its first president, Kwame Nkrumah, influenced the rest of the continent with his theories of pan-African socialism. For Ghana this meant high tariffs on many imports, an import substitution policy aimed at fostering Ghanaian self-sufficiency in certain manufactured goods, and policies that discouraged Ghana's enterprises from exporting. The results were an unmitigated disaster that transformed one of Africa's most prosperous nations into one of the world's poorest.

As an illustration of how Ghana's antitrade policies destroyed the Ghanaian economy, consider the government's involvement in the cocoa trade. A combination of favorable climate, good soils, and ready access to world shipping routes has given Ghana an absolute advantage in cocoa production. It is one of the best places in the world to grow cocoa. As a consequence, Ghana was the world's largest producer and exporter of cocoa in 1957. Then the government of the newly independent nation created a state-controlled cocoa marketing board. The board was given the authority to fix prices for cocoa and was designated the sole buyer of all cocoa grown in Ghana. The board held down the prices it paid farmers for cocoa, while selling the cocoa it bought from them on the world market at world prices. Thus it might buy cocoa from farmers at 25 cents a pound and sell it on the world market for the world price of 50 cents a pound. In effect, the board was taxing exports by paying farmers considerably less for their cocoa than it was worth on the world market and putting the difference into government coffers. This money was used to fund the government policy of nationalization and industrialization.

One result of the cocoa policy was that between 1963 and 1979 the price paid by the cocoa marketing board to Ghana's farmers increased by a factor of 6, while the price of consumer goods in Ghana increased by a factor of 22, and while the price of cocoa in neighboring countries increased by a factor of 36! In real terms, the Ghanaian farmers were paid less every year for their cocoa by the cocoa marketing board, while the world price increased significantly.

Ghana's farmers responded by producing subsistence foodstuffs that could be sold within Ghana, and the country's production and exports of cocoa plummeted by more than one third in seven years. At the same time, the Ghanaian government's attempt to build an industrial base through state-run enterprises failed. The resulting drop in Ghana's export earnings plunged the country into recession, led to a decline in its foreign currency reserves, and severely limited its ability to pay for necessary imports.

In essence, the inward-oriented trade policy of the Ghanaian government resulted in a shift of that country's resources away from the profitable activity of growing cocoa—where it had an absolute advantage in the world economy—and toward growing subsistence foods and manufacturing, where it had no advantage. This inefficient use of the country's resources severely damaged the Ghanaian economy and held back the country's economic development.

In contrast, consider the trade policy adopted by the South Korean government. The World Bank has characterized the trade policy of South Korea as "strongly outward-oriented." Unlike in Ghana, the policies of the South Korean government emphasized low import barriers on manufactured goods (but not on agricultural goods) and the creation of incentives to encourage South Korean firms to export. Beginning in the late 1950s, the South Korean government progressively reduced import tariffs from an average of 60 percent of the price of an imported good to less than 20 percent in the mid-1980s. Moreover, on most nonagricultural goods, import tariffs were reduced to zero. In addition, the number of imported goods subjected to quotas was reduced from more than 90 percent in the late 1950s to zero by the early 1980s. Over the same period South Korea progressively reduced the subsidies given to South Korean exporters from an average of 80 percent of their sales price in the late 1950s to an average of less than 20 percent of their sales price in 1965, and down to zero in 1984. Put another way, with the exception of the agricultural sector (where a strong farm lobby maintained import controls), South Korea moved progressively toward a free trade stance.

South Korea's outward-looking orientation has been rewarded by a dramatic transformation of its economy. Initially, South Korea's resources shifted from agriculture to the manufacture of labor-intensive goods, especially textiles, clothing, and footwear. An abundant supply of cheap but well-educated labor helped form the basis of South Korea's comparative advantage in labor-intensive manufacturing. More recently, as labor costs have risen, the growth areas in the economy have been in the more capital-intensive manufacturing sectors, especially motor vehicles, aerospace, consumer electronics, and advanced materials. As a result of these developments, South Korea has gone through some dramatic changes. In the late 1950s 77 percent of the country's employment was in the agricultural sector; today the figure is less than 20 percent. Over the same period the percentage of its GNP accounted for by manufacturing increased from less than 10 percent to more than 30 percent, while the overall GNP grew at an annual rate of more than 9 percent.

Sources: "Poor Man's Burden: A Survey of the Third World," *The Economist,* September 23, 1989; World Bank, *World Development Report, 1944* (Oxford: Oxford University Press, 1944).

❧ INTRODUCTION

The opening case illustrates the gains that come from international trade. For a long time the economic policies of the Ghanaian government discouraged trade with other nations. The result was a shift in Ghana's resources away from productive uses (growing cocoa) and toward unproductive uses (subsistence agriculture). The economic policies of the South Korean government encouraged trade with other nations. The result was a shift in South Korea's resources away from uses where it had no comparative advantage in the world economy (agriculture) and toward more productive uses (labor-intensive manufacturing). As a direct result of their policies toward international trade, Ghana's economy declined while South Korea's grew.

This chapter has two goals that are related to the story of Ghana and South Korea. The first is to review a number of theories that explain why it is beneficial for a country to engage in international trade. The second goal is to explain the pattern of international trade that we observe in the world economy. We will be primarily concerned with explaining the pattern of exports and imports of products between countries. We will not be concerned with the pattern of foreign direct investment between countries; that is discussed in Chapter 7.

❧ AN OVERVIEW OF TRADE THEORY

Propagated in the 16th and 17th centuries, mercantilism advocated that countries should simultaneously encourage exports and discourage imports. Although mercantilism is an old and largely discredited doctrine, its echoes remain in modern political debate and in the trade policies of many countries.

Adam Smith's theory of absolute advantage, proposed in 1776, was the first to explain why unrestricted free trade is beneficial to a country. **Free trade** occurs when a government does not attempt to influence through quotas or duties what its citizens can buy from another country, or what they can produce and sell to another country. Smith argued that the invisible hand of the market mechanism, rather than government policy, should determine what a country imports and what it exports. Moreover, his arguments imply that such a *laissez-faire* stance toward trade was in the best interests of a country.

Building on Smith's work are two additional theories that we shall review. One is the theory of comparative advantage, advanced by the 19th century English economist David Ricardo. This theory is the intellectual basis of the modern argument for unrestricted free trade. In the 20th century Ricardo's work was refined by two Swedish economists, Eli Heckscher and Bertil Ohlin, whose theory is known as the Heckscher-Ohlin theory.

Benefits of Trade

The great strength of the theories of Smith, Ricardo, and Heckscher-Ohlin is that they identify with precision the specific benefits of international trade. Of course, common sense suggests that some international trade is beneficial. For example, nobody would suggest that Iceland should grow its own oranges. Iceland can benefit from trade by exchanging some products it can produce at a low cost (fish) for some products it cannot produce at all (oranges). By engaging in international trade, Icelanders are able to add oranges to their diet of fish.

The theories of Smith, Ricardo, and Heckscher-Ohlin go beyond this commonsense notion, however, to show why it is beneficial for a country to engage in international trade *even for products it is able to produce for itself*. This is a difficult concept for people to grasp. For example, many people in the United States believe that American consumers should buy products produced in the United States by American companies whenever possible to help save American jobs from foreign competition. The same kind of nationalistic sentiments can be observed in many other countries. However, the theories of Smith, Ricardo, and Heckscher-Ohlin tell us that a country's economy may gain if its citizens buy from other nations certain products that could be produced at home.

The gains arise because international trade allows a country to specialize in the manufacture and export of products that can be produced most efficiently in that country, while importing products that can be produced more efficiently in other countries. So it may make sense for the United States to specialize in the production and export of commercial jet aircraft, since the efficient production of commercial jet aircraft requires resources that are abundant in the United States, such as a highly skilled labor force and cutting-edge technological know-how. On the other hand, it may make sense for the United States to import textiles from India since the efficient production of textiles requires a relatively cheap labor force—and cheap labor is not abundant in the United States.

Of course, this economic argument is often difficult for segments of a country's population to accept. With their future threatened by imports, American textile companies and their employees have tried hard to persuade the U.S. government to limit the importation of textiles by demanding quotas and tariffs to restrict imports. Although such import controls may benefit particular groups, such as American textile businesses and their employees, the theories of Smith, Ricardo, and Heckscher-Ohlin suggest the economy as a whole is hurt by this kind of protectionist action.

Pattern of International Trade

The theories of Smith, Ricardo, and Heckscher-Ohlin also help to explain the pattern of international trade that we observe in the world economy. Some aspects of the pattern are easy to understand. Climate and natural resources explain why Ghana exports cocoa, Brazil exports coffee, and Saudi Arabia exports oil. But much of the observed pattern of international trade is more difficult to explain. For example, why does Japan export automobiles, consumer electronics, and machine tools? Why does Switzerland export chemicals, watches, and jewelry? David Ricardo's theory of comparative advantage offers an explanation in terms of international differences in labor productivity. The more sophisticated Heckscher-Ohlin theory emphasizes the interplay between the proportions in which the factors of production (such as land, labor, and capital) are available in different countries and the proportions in which they are needed for producing particular goods. This explanation rests on the assumption that different countries have different endowments of the various factors of production. Tests of this theory, however, suggest it is a less powerful explanation of real-world trade patterns than once thought.

One early response to the failure of the Heckscher-Ohlin theory to explain the observed pattern of international trade was the *product life-cycle theory*. Proposed by Raymond Vernon, this theory suggests that early in their life cycle, most new products are produced in and exported from the country in which they were developed.

As a new product becomes widely accepted internationally, however, production starts in other countries. As a result, the theory suggests, the product may ultimately be exported back to the country of its original innovation.

In a similar vein, during the 1980s economists such as Paul Krugman of MIT developed what has come to be known as the *new trade theory*. New trade theory stresses that in some cases countries specialize in the production and export of particular products not because of underlying differences in factor endowments, but because in certain industries the world market can support only a limited number of firms. (This is argued to be the case for the commercial aircraft industry.) In such industries, firms that enter the market first build a competitive advantage that is difficult to challenge. Thus the observed pattern of trade between nations may in part be due to the ability of firms within a given nation to capture first-mover advantages. Put another way, the United States predominates in the export of commercial jet aircraft because American firms such as Boeing were first-movers in the world market. Boeing built a competitive advantage that has subsequently been difficult for firms from countries with equally favorable factor endowments to challenge.

In a work related to the new trade theory, Michael Porter of Harvard Business School has recently developed a theory that attempts to explain why certain nations achieve international success in particular industries. We shall refer to this theory as the theory of national competitive advantage. Like the new trade theorists, in addition to factor endowments, Porter points out the importance of country factors such as domestic demand and domestic rivalry in explaining a nation's dominance in the production and export of particular products.

Trade Theory and Government Policy

Although all these theories agree that international trade is beneficial to a country, they lack agreement in their recommendations for government policy. Mercantilism makes a crude case for government involvement in promoting exports and limiting imports. The theories of Smith, Ricardo, and Heckscher-Ohlin form part of the case for unrestricted free trade. The argument for unrestricted free trade is that both import controls and export incentives (such as subsidies) are self-defeating and result in wasted resources. On the other hand, both the new trade theory and Porter's theory of national competitive advantage can be interpreted as justifying some limited and selective government intervention to support the development of certain export-oriented industries. We will discuss the pros and cons of this argument, known as strategic trade policy, as well as the pros and cons of the argument for unrestricted free trade, in Chapter 5.

❧ MERCANTILISM

The first theory of international trade emerged in England in the mid-16th century. Referred to as *mercantilism*, its principal assertion was that gold and silver were the mainstays of national wealth and essential to vigorous commerce. At that time, gold and silver were the currency of trade between countries; a country could earn gold and silver by exporting goods. By the same token, importing goods from other countries would result in an outflow of gold and silver to those countries. The main tenant of **mercantilism** was that it was in a country's best interests to maintain a trade surplus, to export more than it imported. By doing so, a country would accumulate gold and silver and, consequently, increase its national wealth and prestige. As the English mercantilist writer Thomas Mun put it in 1630:

> The ordinary means therefore to increase our wealth and treasure is by foreign trade, wherein we must ever observe this rule: to sell more to strangers yearly than we consume of theirs in value.[1]

---

[1] H. W. Spiegel, *The Growth of Economic Throught* (Durham, NC: Duke University Press, 1991).

Consistent with this belief, the mercantilist doctrine advocated government intervention to achieve a surplus in the balance of trade. The mercantilists saw no virtue in a large volume of trade per se. Rather, they recommended policies to maximize exports and minimize imports. In order to achieve this, imports were limited by tariffs and quotas, and exports were subsidized.

An inherent inconsistency in the mercantilist doctrine was pointed out by the classical economist David Hume in 1752. According to Hume, if England had a balance-of-trade surplus with France (it exported more than it imported), the resulting inflow of gold and silver would swell the domestic money supply and generate inflation in England. In France, however, the outflow of gold and silver would have the opposite effect. France's money supply would contract, and its prices would fall. This change in relative prices between France and England would encourage the French to buy fewer English goods (because they were becoming more expensive) and the English to buy more French goods (because they were becoming cheaper). The result would be a deterioration in the English balance of trade and an improvement in France's trade balance, until the English surplus was eliminated. Hence, according to Hume, in the long run no country could sustain a surplus on the balance of trade and so accumulate gold and silver as the mercantilists had envisaged.

Hume's critique apart, the flaw with mercantilism was that it viewed trade as a zero-sum game. (A **zero-sum game** is one in which a gain by one country results in a loss by another.) It was left to Adam Smith and David Ricardo to show the shortsightedness of this approach and to demonstrate that trade is a **positive-sum game,** that being a situation in which all countries can benefit, even if some benefit more than others. We shall discuss the views of Smith next. Before doing so, however, we must note that the mercantilist doctrine is by no means dead.[2] For example, Jarl Hagelstam, a director at the Finnish Ministry of Finance, has observed that in most trade negotiations:

> The approach of individual negotiating countries, both industrialized and developing, has been to press for trade liberalization in areas where their own comparative competitive advantages are the strongest, and to resist liberalization in areas where they are less competitive and fear that imports would replace domestic production.[3]

Hagelstam attributes this strategy by negotiating countries to a neo-mercantilist belief held by the politicians of many nations. This belief equates political power with economic power, and economic power with a balance-of-trade surplus. Thus the trade strategy of many nations is designed to simultaneously boost exports and limit imports. For example, as described in the next "Country Focus," many American politicians claim that Japan is a neo-mercantilist nation because its government, while publicly supporting free trade, simultaneously seeks to protect certain segments of its economy from more efficient foreign competition.

❧ ABSOLUTE ADVANTAGE

In his 1776 landmark book *The Wealth of Nations*, Adam Smith attacked the mercantilist assumption that trade is a zero-sum game. Smith argued that countries differ in their ability to produce goods efficiently. In his time, for example, by virtue of their superior manufacturing processes, the English were the world's most efficient manufacturers of textiles. On the other hand, due to the combination of favorable climate, good soils, and accumulated expertise, the French had the world's most efficient wine industry. Put another way, the English had an *absolute advantage* in the production of textiles, while the French had an *absolute advantage* in the production of wine. Thus a country has an **absolute advantage** in the production of a product when it is more efficient than any other country in producing it.

---

[2]G. de Jonquieres, "Mercantilists Are Treading on Thin Ice," *Financial Times*, July 3, 1994, p. 16.

[3]Jarl Hagelstam, "Mercantilism Still Influences Practical Trade Policy at the End of the Twentieth Century," *Journal of World Trade*, 1991, pp. 95–105.

COUNTRY
FOCUS
Is Japan a
Neo-Mercantilist
Nation?

In the international arena Japan has long been a strong supporter of free trade agreements. However, the U.S. government has repeatedly suggested that the approach taken by the Japanese is a cynical neo-mercantilist one. The Japanese, they say, are all to happy to sign international agreements that open foreign markets to the products of Japanese companies, but at the same time they protect their home market from foreign competition. As evidence, U.S. officials point to the large trade imbalance between America and Japan, which in 1994 ran at over $80 billion (meaning the United States imported $80 billion more of goods from Japan than it exported to Japan).

The U.S. government recently received support from an unlikely source—three Japanese economists.

In a study published in 1994 the three economists cited food products, cosmetics, and chemical production as areas where the Japanese government protected Japanese industry from more efficient foreign competition by a variety of import restrictions, such as quotas (limits) on the amounts of a product that can be imported into Japan. According to the economists, without barriers protecting these areas from foreign competition, imports would have more than doubled and prices in Japan would have fallen substantially. The study suggested that falling prices would have saved the average Japanese consumer about $890 per year in 1989. At the same time, however, there would have been a fall in Japanese production of more than 20 percent in certain areas including wheat,

According to Smith, countries should specialize in the production of goods for which they have an absolute advantage and then trade these goods for goods produced by other countries. In Smith's time this suggested the English should specialize in the production of textiles while the French should specialize in the production of wine. England could get all the wine it needed by selling its textiles to France and buying wine in exchange. Similarly, France could get all the textiles it needed by selling wine to England and buying textiles in exchange. Smith's basic argument, therefore, is that you should never produce goods at home that you can buy at a lower cost from other countries. Moreover, by specializing in the production of goods in which each has an absolute advantage, both countries benefit by engaging in trade.

To see why this is so, consider the effects of trade between Ghana and South Korea. The production of any good (output) requires resources (inputs) such as land, labor, and capital. Assume Ghana and South Korea both have the same amount of resources and these resources can be used to produce either rice or cocoa. Assume further that 200 units of resources are available in each country. Imagine that in Ghana it takes 10 resources to produce one ton of cocoa and 20 resources to produce one ton of rice. Thus Ghana could produce 20 tons of cocoa and no rice, 10 tons of rice and no cocoa, or some combination of rice and cocoa between these two extremes. The different combinations that Ghana could produce are represented by the line GG′ in Figure 4.1. This is referred to as Ghana's production possibility frontier (PPF). Similarly, imagine that in South Korea it takes 40 resources to produce one ton of cocoa and 10 resources to produce one ton of rice. Thus South Korea could produce 5 tons of cocoa and no rice, 20 tons of rice and no cocoa, or some combination in between these two extremes. The different combinations available to South Korea are represented by the line KK′ in Figure 4.1,

oilseeds, leaf tobacco, canned fruit and vegetables, and cosmetics. Trade liberalization would also have resulted in the loss of more than 180,000 Japanese jobs. It would seem, therefore, that Japan's government protects these areas from more efficient foreign competition in order to save jobs, even though the average Japanese consumer has to pay for this action through higher prices. Protection of the food products area in particular may be motivated by the fact that Japanese farmers, who benefit most from this protection, are a powerful political force within Japanese society.

The U.S. government claims that Japan also has taken a neo-mercantilist stance in the importation of automobiles and automobile parts. Japan is a major exporter of autos

and auto parts to the United States and Europe, but historically it has imported only 3 percent of its autos and 2 percent of its auto components. Other developed countries import between 22 percent and 78 percent of their autos and 16 to 60 percent of their auto parts. According to U.S. trade negotiators, the Japanese government limits imports into Japan by requiring stringent safety inspections on imports that are explicitly designed to raise the costs to foreigners trying to sell in Japan. For example, the U.S. Commerce Department claims the addition of front brush guards to a recreational vehicle, a safety feature required only in Japan, necessitates a complete reinspection that costs up to $3,000 per vehicle.

For its part the Japanese government rejects such charges. The

Japanese government argues that the main reason U.S. auto companies have not been successful in Japan is that they do not make cars that are suited to the Japanese market. They point out that while 80 percent of the autos sold in the Japanese market are under 2,000cc, no U.S. auto company sells cars in Japan in that range. They also point out that imported autos and auto parts are increasing their share of the Japanese market. Between 1990 and 1994, for example, the share of the Japanese market accounted for by imported cars increased from 5.1 percent to 8.1 percent.

Sources: Y. Sazanami, S. Urata, and H. Kawai, *Measuring the Costs of Protection in Japan* (Washington DC: Institute for International Economics, 1994), M. Nakamoto, "All Action and No Talk," *Financial Times*, March 17, 1995, p. 5; and N. Dunne, "U.S. Threatens WTO Complaint against Japan," *Financial Times*, March 29, 1995, p. 6.

FIGURE 4.1   The Theory of Absolute Advantage

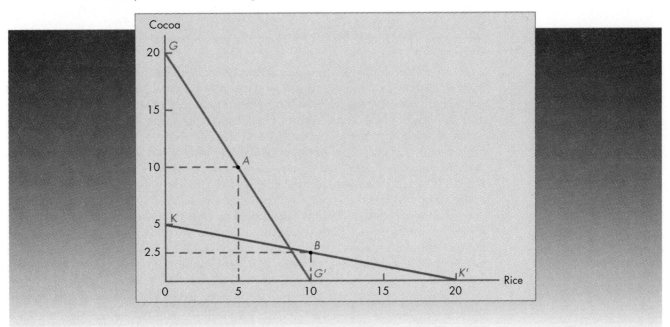

which is South Korea's PPF. Clearly, Ghana has an absolute advantage in the production of cocoa. (More resources are needed to produce a ton of cocoa in South Korea than in Ghana.) By the same token, South Korea has an absolute advantage in the production of rice.

TABLE: 4.1

Absolute Advantage and the Gains from Trade

| | Resources Required to Produce 1 Ton of Cocoa and Rice | |
	Cocoa	Rice
Ghana	10	20
South Korea	40	10
	Production and Consumption without Trade	
	Cocoa	Rice
Ghana	10.0	5.0
South Korea	2.5	10.0
Total production	12.5	15.0
	Production with Specialization	
	Cocoa	Rice
Ghana	20.0	0.0
South Korea	0.0	20.0
Total production	20.0	20.0
	Consumption after Ghana Trades 6 Tons of Cocoa for 6 Tons of South Korean Rice	
	Cocoa	Rice
Ghana	14.0	6.0
South Korea	6.0	14.0
	Increase in Consumption as a Result of Specialization and Trade	
	Cocoa	Rice
Ghana	4.0	1.0
South Korea	3.5	4.0

Now consider a situation in which neither country trades with any other. Each country devotes half its resources to the production of rice and half to the production of cocoa. Each country must also consume what it produces. Ghana would be able to produce 10 tons of cocoa and 5 tons of rice (point A in Figure 4.1), while South Korea would be able to produce 10 tons of rice and 2.5 tons of cocoa. Without trade, the combined production of both countries would be 12.5 tons of cocoa (10 tons in Ghana plus 2.5 tons in South Korea) and 15 tons of rice (5 tons in Ghana and 10 tons in South Korea). If each country were to specialize in producing the good for which it had an absolute advantage and then trade with the other for the good it lacks, Ghana could produce 20 tons of cocoa, and South Korea could produce 20 tons of rice. Thus, by specializing, the production of both goods could be increased. Production of cocoa would increase from 12.5 tons to 20 tons, while production of rice would increase from 15 tons to 20 tons. The increase in production that would result from specialization is therefore 7.5 tons of cocoa and 5 tons of rice. These figures are summarized in Table 4.1.

By engaging in trade and swapping one ton of cocoa for one ton of rice, producers in both countries could consume more of both cocoa and rice. Imagine that Ghana and South Korea swap cocoa and rice on a one-to-one basis; that is, the price of one ton of cocoa is equal to the price of one ton of rice. If Ghana decided to export 6 tons of cocoa to South Korea and import 6 tons of rice in return, its final consumption after trade would be 14 tons of cocoa and 6 tons of rice. This is 4 tons more cocoa than it could have consumed before specialization and trade, and 1 ton more rice. Similarly, South Korea's final consumption after trade would be 6 tons of cocoa

FIGURE 4.2   The Theory of Comparative Advantage

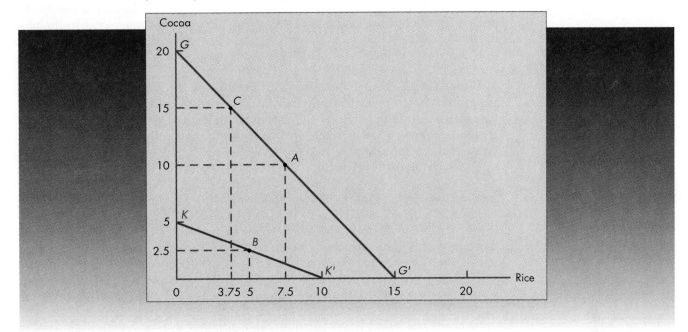

and 14 tons of rice. This is 3.5 tons more cocoa than it could have consumed before specialization and trade and 4 tons more rice. Thus, as a result of specialization and trade, output of both cocoa and rice would be increased, and consumers in both nations would be able to consume more. Thus we can see that trade is a positive-sum game; it produces net gains for all involved.

❧ COMPARATIVE ADVANTAGE

David Ricardo took Adam Smith's theory one step further by exploring what might happen when one country has an absolute advantage in the production of all goods.[4] Smith's theory of absolute advantage suggests that such a country might derive no benefits from international trade. In his 1817 book *Principles of Political Economy*, Ricardo showed that this was not the case. According to Ricardo's theory of **comparative advantage,** it makes sense for a country to specialize in the production of those goods that it produces most efficiently and to buy the goods that it produces less efficiently from other countries, even if it could produce them more efficiently itself.[5] While this may seem counterintuitive, the logic can be explained with a simple example.

Let us stay with the example of Ghana and South Korea that we used to explain Adam Smith's theory. This time assume Ghana is more efficient in the production of both cocoa and rice; that is, Ghana has an absolute advantage in the production of both products. In Ghana it takes 10 resources to produce one ton of cocoa and 13 1/3 resources to produce one ton of rice. Thus, given its 200 units of resources, Ghana can produce 20 tons of cocoa and no rice, 15 tons of rice and no cocoa, or any combination in between on its PPF (the line GG′ in Figure 4.2). In South Korea it takes 40 resources to produce one ton of cocoa and 20 resources to produce one ton of rice. Thus South Korea can produce 5 tons of cocoa and no rice, 10 tons of rice and no cocoa, or any combination on its PPF (the line KK′ in Figure 4.2). Again assume that without trade, each country uses half of its resources to produce rice and half to produce cocoa. Thus without trade, Ghana will produce 10 tons of cocoa and 7.5 tons of rice (point A in Figure 4.2), while South Korea will produce 2.5 tons of cocoa and 5 tons of rice (point B in Figure 4.2).

[4]S. Hollander, *The Economics of David Ricardo* (Buffalo, NY: The University of Toronto Press, 1979).

[5]D. Ricardo, *The Principles of Political Economy and Taxation* (Homewood, IL: Richard D. Irwin, 1967) (first published in 1817).

In light of Ghana's absolute advantage in the production of both goods, why should it trade with South Korea? Although Ghana has an absolute advantage in the production of both cocoa and rice, it has a comparative advantage only in the production of cocoa: Ghana can produce 4 times as much cocoa as South Korea, but only 1.5 times as much rice. Ghana is *comparatively* more efficient at producing cocoa than it is at producing rice.

Without trade the combined production of cocoa will be 12.5 tons (10 tons in Ghana and 2.5 in South Korea), and the combined production of rice will also be 12.5 tons (7.5 tons in Ghana and 5 tons in South Korea). Without trade each country must consume what it produces. By engaging in trade, the two countries can increase their combined production of rice and cocoa, and consumers in both nations can consume more of both goods.

The Gains from Trade

Imagine that Ghana exploits its comparative advantage in the production of cocoa to increase its output from 10 tons to 15 tons. This uses up 150 units of resources, leaving the remaining 50 units of resources to use in producing 3.75 tons of rice (point C in Figure 4.2). Meanwhile, South Korea specializes in the production of rice, producing 10 tons. The combined output of both cocoa and rice has now increased. Before specialization, the combined output was 12.5 tons of cocoa and 12.5 tons of rice. Now it is 15 tons of cocoa and 13.75 tons of rice (3.75 tons in Ghana and 10 tons in South Korea). The source of the increase in production is summarized in Table 4.2.

Not only is output higher, but also both countries can now benefit from trade. If Ghana and South Korea swap cocoa and rice on a one-to-one basis, with both countries choosing to exchange 4 tons of their export for 4 tons of the import, both countries are able to consume more cocoa and rice than they could before specialization and trade (see Table 4.2). Thus, if Ghana exchanges 4 tons of cocoa with South Korea for 4 tons of rice, it is still left with 11 tons of cocoa, which is 1 ton more than it had before trade. Moreover, the 4 tons of rice it gets from South Korea in exchange for its 4 tons of cocoa, when added to the 3.75 tons it now produces domestically, leaves it with a total of 7.75 tons of rice, which is .25 of a ton more than it had before trade. Similarly, after swapping 4 tons of rice with Ghana, South Korea still ends up with 6 tons of rice, which is more than it had before trade. In addition, the 4 tons of cocoa it receives in exchange is 1.5 tons more than it produced before trade. Thus, consumption of cocoa and rice can increase in both countries as a result of specialization and trade.

Generalizing from this example, the basic message of the theory of comparative advantage is that *potential world production is greater with unrestricted free trade than it is with restricted trade*. Moreover, Ricardo's theory suggests that consumers in all nations can consume more if there are no restrictions on trade. This occurs even in the case of countries that lack an absolute advantage in the production of any good. In other words, to an even greater degree than the theory of absolute advantage, the theory of comparative advantage suggests that trade is a positive-sum game in which all gain. As such, this theory provides a strong rationale for encouraging free trade. Indeed, so powerful is Ricardo's theory that it remains a major intellectual weapon for those who argue for free trade.

Qualifications and Assumptions

At this point one might object that the conclusion that free trade is universally beneficial is a rather bold one to draw from such a simple model. There are many unrealistic assumptions inherent in our simple model, including:

1. We have assumed a simple world in which there are only two countries and two goods. In the real world there are many countries and many goods.

2. We have assumed away transportation costs between countries.

3. We have assumed away differences in the prices of resources in different countries. We have said nothing about exchange rates and instead simply assumed that cocoa and rice could be swapped on a one-to-one basis.

TABLE 4.2

Comparative Advantage and the Gains from Trade

	Resources Required to Produce 1 Ton of Cocoa and Rice	
	Cocoa	Rice
Ghana	10	13.33
South Korea	40	20
	Production and Consumption without Trade	
	Cocoa	Rice
Ghana	10.0	7.5
South Korea	2.5	5.0
Total Production	12.5	12.5
	Production with Specialization	
	Cocoa	Rice
Ghana	15.0	3.75
South Korea	0.0	10.0
Total production	15.0	13.75
	Consumption after Ghana Trades 4 Tons of Cocoa for 4 Tons of South Korean Rice	
	Cocoa	Rice
Ghana	11.0	7.75
South Korea	4.0	6.0
	Increase in Consumption as a Result of Specialization and Trade	
	Cocoa	Rice
Ghana	1.0	0.25
South Korea	1.5	1.0

4. We have assumed that while resources can move freely from the production of one good to another within a country, they are not free to move internationally. In reality, some resources are somewhat internationally mobile. This is true of capital and, to a lesser extent, labor.

5. We have assumed constant returns to scale; that is, specialization by Ghana or South Korea has no effect on the amount of resources required to produce one ton of cocoa or rice. In reality, both diminishing and increasing returns to specialization exist. The amount of resources required to produce a good might decrease or increase as a nation specializes in production of that good.

6. We have assumed that each country has a fixed stock of resources and that free trade does not change the efficiency with which a country uses its resources. This static assumption makes no allowances for the dynamic changes in a country's stock of resources and in the efficiency with which the country uses its resources that might result from free trade.

7. We have assumed away the effects of trade on income distribution within a country.

Given these assumptions, the question arises as to whether the conclusion that free trade is mutually beneficial can be extended to the real world of many countries, many goods, positive transportation costs, volatile exchange rates, internationally mobile resources, nonconstant returns to specialization, and dynamic changes. Although a detailed extension of the theory of comparative advantage is beyond the scope of this book, economists have shown that the basic result derived from our simple model can be generalized to a world composed of many countries producing many different goods, in which case the above assumptions no longer hold.[6] Moreover, despite all its shortcomings, research suggests the basic proposition of the Ricardian model—that countries will export the goods they are most efficient at producing—is born out by the data.[7] However, once all the assumptions are dropped, the case for unrestricted free trade, while still positive, has been argued by some economists associated with the "new trade theory" to lose some of its strength.[8] We return to this issue later in this chapter and in the next.

Simple Extensions of the Ricardian Model

Let us explore the effect of relaxing two of the assumptions identified above in the simple comparative advantage model. Below we relax the assumption of constant returns to specialization and the static assumption that trade does not change a country's stock of resources or the efficiency with which it utilizes those resources.

Diminishing returns

The simple comparative advantage model developed in the preceding subsection assumes constant returns to specialization. By **constant returns to specialization** we mean that the units of resources required to produce a good (cocoa or rice) are assumed to remain constant no matter where one is on a country's production possibility frontier (PPF). Thus we assumed it always took Ghana 10 units of resources to produce one ton of cocoa. However, it is more realistic to assume diminishing returns to specialization. **Diminishing returns to specialization** occur when the more of a good a country produces, the greater the units of resources required to produce each additional unit. In the case of Ghana, for example, whereas 10 units of resources may be sufficient to increase output of cocoa from 12 tons to 13 tons, 11 units of resources may be needed to increase output of cocoa from 13 to 14 tons, 12 units of resources to increase output from 14 tons to 15 tons, and so on. Diminishing returns implies a convex PPF for Ghana (see Figure 4.3), rather than the straight line depicted in Figure 4.2.

There are two reasons it is more realistic to assume diminishing returns. First, not all resources are of the same quality. As a country tries to increase its output of a certain good, it is increasingly likely to draw upon more marginal resources whose productivity is not as great as those initially employed. The end result is that it requires ever more resources to produce an equal increase in output. For example, some land is more productive (fertile) than other land. As Ghana tries to expand its output of cocoa, it might have to utilize increasingly marginal land that is less fertile than the land it originally used. As yields per acre decline, Ghana must use more land to produce one ton of cocoa.

A second reason for diminishing returns is that different goods use resources in different proportions. For example, imagine that growing cocoa uses more land and less labor than growing rice, and that Ghana tries to transfer resources from rice production to cocoa production. The rice industry will release proportionately too much labor and too little land for efficient cocoa production. To absorb the additional resources of labor and land, the cocoa industry will have to shift toward more labor-intensive methods of production. The efficiency with which the cocoa industry uses labor will decline; returns will diminish.

The significance of diminishing returns is that it is not feasible for a country to specialize to the degree suggested by the simple Ricardian model outlined earlier. Diminishing returns to specialization suggest that the gains from specialization are likely to be exhausted before specialization is complete. In reality, most countries do

---

[6]For example, R. Dornbusch, S. Fischer, and P. Samuelson, "Comparative Advantage: Trade and Payments in a Ricardian Model with a Continuum of Goods," *American Economic Review* 67 (December 1977), pp. 823–39.

[7]B. Balassa, "An Empirical Demonstration of Classic Comparative Cost Theory," *Review of Economics and Statistics*, 1963, pp. 231–38.

[8]See P. R. Krugman, "Is Free Trade Passé?" *Journal of Economic Perspectives* 1 (Fall 1987), pp. 131–44.

Figure 4.3   Ghana's PPF under Diminishing Returns

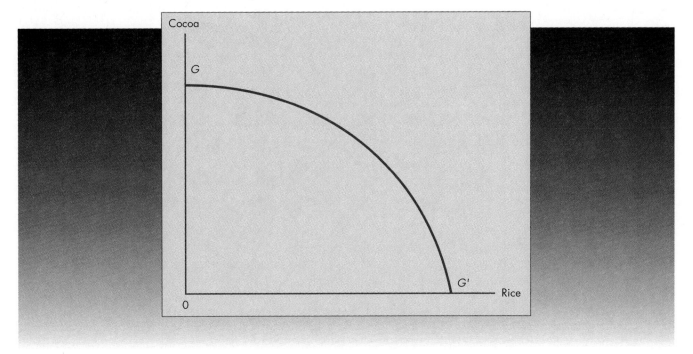

not specialize, but instead, produce a range of goods. However, the theory predicts that it is worthwhile to specialize until that point where the resulting gains from trade are outweighed by diminishing returns. Thus the basic conclusion that unrestricted free trade is beneficial still holds, although due to diminishing returns, the gains may not be as great as suggested in the constant returns case.

Dynamic effects and economic growth

Our simple comparative advantage model assumed that trade does not change a country's stock of resources or the efficiency with which it utilizes those resources. This static assumption makes no allowances for the dynamic changes that might result from trade. If we relax this assumption, it becomes apparent that opening an economy to trade is likely to generate dynamic gains.[9] These dynamic gains are of two sorts. First, free trade might increase a country's stock of resources as increased supplies of labor and capital from abroad become available for use within the country. This is occurring now in Eastern Europe; many Western businesses are investing large amounts of capital in the former Communist bloc countries.

Second, free trade might also increase the efficiency with which a country utilizes its resources. Gains in the efficiency of resource utilization could arise from a number of factors. For example, economies of large-scale production might become available as trade expands the size of the total market available to domestic firms. Trade might make better technology from abroad available to domestic firms. In turn, better technology can increase labor productivity or the productivity of land. (The so-called green revolution had just this effect on agricultural outputs in developing countries.) It is also possible that opening an economy to foreign competition might stimulate domestic producers to look for ways to increase the efficiency of their operations. Again, this phenomenon is arguably occurring currently in the once-protected markets of Eastern Europe, where many former state monopolies are having to increase efficiency to survive in the competitive world market.

---

[9]P. Samuelson, "The Gains from International Trade Once Again," *Economic Journal* 72 (1962), pp. 820–29.

FIGURE 4.4   The Influence of Free Trade on the PPF

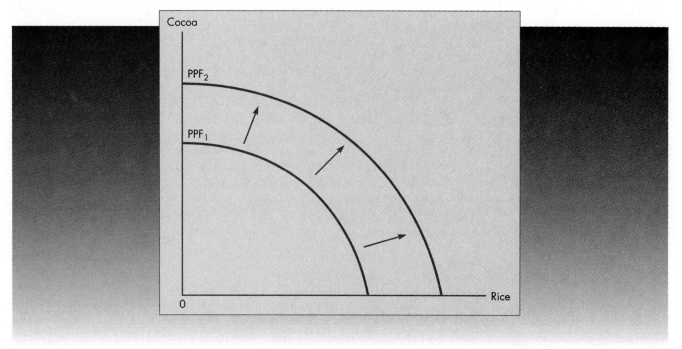

Dynamic gains in both the stock of a country's resources and the efficiency with which resources are utilized will cause a country's PPF to shift outward. This is illustrated in Figure 4.4, where the shift from PPF_1 to PPF_2 results from the dynamic gains that arise from free trade. As a consequence of this outward shift, the country in Figure 4.4 can produce more of both goods than it did before free trade. Put another way, the theory suggests that opening an economy to free trade not only results in static gains of the type discussed earlier, but also results in dynamic gains that stimulate economic growth. If this is so, the case for free trade becomes stronger. The World Bank has assembled evidence that suggests a free trade stance does have these kind of beneficial effects on economic growth.[10]

✺ HECKSCHER-OHLIN THEORY

Ricardo's theory stresses that comparative advantage arises from differences in productivity. Thus, whether Ghana is more efficient than South Korea in the production of cocoa depends on how productively it uses its resources. Ricardo himself stressed labor productivity and argued that differences in labor productivity between nations underlie the notion of comparative advantage. Swedish economists Eli Heckscher (in 1919) and Bertil Ohlin (in 1933) put forward a different explanation of comparative advantage. They argued that comparative advantage arises from differences in national factor endowments.[11] By factor endowments they meant the extent to which a country is endowed with such resources as land, labor, and capital. Different nations have different factor endowments, and different factor endowments explain differences in factor costs. The more abundant a factor, the lower its cost.

---

[10]For a summary see "The Gains from Trade," *The Economist*, September 23, 1989, pp. 25–26.

[11]B. Ohlin, *Interregional and International Trade* (Cambridge, MA: Harvard University Press, 1933). For a summary see R. W. Jones and J. P. Neary, "The Positive Theory of International Trade," in *Handbook of International Economics*, ed. R. W. Jones and P. B. Kenen (Amsterdam: North Holland, 1984).

The Heckscher-Ohlin theory predicts that countries will export those goods that make intensive use of those factors that are locally abundant, while importing goods that make intensive use of factors that are locally scarce. Thus the Heckscher-Ohlin theory attempts to explain the pattern of international trade that we observe in the world economy. Like Ricardo's theory, the Heckscher-Ohlin theory argues that free trade is beneficial. Unlike Ricardo's theory, however, the Heckscher-Ohlin theory argues that the pattern of international trade is determined by differences in factor endowments, rather than differences in productivity.

The Heckscher-Ohlin theory also has commonsense appeal. For example, the United States has long been a substantial exporter of agricultural goods, reflecting in part its unusual abundance of large tracts of arable land. In contrast, South Korea has excelled in the export of goods produced in labor-intensive manufacturing industries, such as textiles and footwear. This reflects South Korea's relative abundance of low-cost labor. The United States, which lacks abundant low-cost labor, has been a primary importer of these goods. Note that it is relative, not absolute, endowments that are important; a country may have larger absolute amounts of land and labor than another country, but be relatively abundant in one of them.

The Leontief Paradox

The Heckscher-Ohlin theory has been one of the most influential theoretical ideas in international economics. Most economists prefer the Heckscher-Ohlin theory to Ricardo's theory because it makes fewer simplifying assumptions. Not surprisingly then, it has been subjected to many empirical tests. Beginning with a famous study published in 1953 by Wassily Leontief (winner of the Nobel Prize in Economics in 1973), many of these tests have raised questions about the validity of the Heckscher-Ohlin theory.[12] Using the Heckscher-Ohlin theory, Leontief postulated that since the United States was relatively abundant in capital compared to other nations, the United States would be an exporter of capital-intensive goods and an importer of labor-intensive goods. To his surprise, however, he found that U.S. exports were less capital intensive than U.S. imports. Since this result was at variance with the predictions of the theory, it has become known as the Leontief paradox.

Why do we observe the Leontief paradox? No one is quite sure. One possible explanation is that the United States has a special advantage in producing new products or goods made with innovative technologies. Such products may well be less capital intensive than products whose technology has had time to mature and become suitable for mass production. Thus the United States may be exporting goods that heavily use skilled labor and innovative entrepreneurship, while importing heavy manufactures that use large amounts of capital. Some more recent empirical studies tend to confirm this.[13] However, recent tests of the Heckscher-Ohlin theory using data for a large number of countries tend to confirm the existence of the Leontief paradox.[14]

This leaves economists with a difficult dilemma. They prefer the Heckscher-Ohlin theory, but it is a relatively poor predictor of real-world international trade patterns. On the other hand, the theory they regard as being too limited, Ricardo's theory of comparative advantage, actually predicts trade patterns with greater accuracy. The best solution to this dilemma may be to return to the Ricardian idea that trade patterns are largely driven by international differences in productivity. Thus one might argue that the United States exports commercial aircraft and imports automobiles not because its factor endowments are especially suited to aircraft manufacture and not suited to automobile manufacture, but because the United States is more efficient at producing aircraft than automobiles.

---

[12]W. Leontief, "Domestic Production and Foreign Trade: The American Capital Position Re-Examined," *Proceedings of the American Philosophical Society* 97 (1953), pp. 331–49.

[13]R. M. Stern and K. Maskus, "Determinants of the Structure of U.S. Foreign Trade," *Journal of International Economics* 11 (1981), pp. 207–44.

[14]See H. P. Bowen, E. E. Leamer, and L. Sveikayskas, "Multicountry, Multifactor Tests of the Factor Abundance Theory," *American Economic Review* 77 (1987), pp. 791–809.

☙ THE PRODUCT LIFE-CYCLE THEORY

Raymond Vernon proposed the product life-cycle theory in the mid-1960s.[15] Vernon's theory was based on the observation that for most of the 20th century a very large proportion of the world's new products had been developed by U.S. firms and sold first in the U.S. market (e.g., mass-produced automobiles, televisions, instant cameras, photocopiers, personal computers, and semiconductor chips). To explain this, Vernon argued that the wealth and size of the U.S. market gave U.S. firms a strong incentive to develop new consumer products. In addition, the high cost of U.S. labor gave U.S. firms an incentive to develop cost-saving process innovations.

Just because a new product is developed by a U.S. firm and first sold in the U.S. market, it does not follow that the product must be produced in the United States. It could be produced abroad at some low-cost location and then exported back into the United States. However, Vernon argued that most new products were initially produced in the America. Apparently, the pioneering firms thought it was better to keep production facilities close to the market and to the firm's center of decision making, given the uncertainty and risks inherent in new-product introduction. Moreover, the demand for most new products tends to be based on nonprice factors. Consequently, firms can charge relatively high prices for new products, which obviates the need to look for low-cost production sites in other countries.

Vernon went on to argue that early in the life cycle of a typical new product, while demand is starting to grow rapidly in the United States, demand in other advanced countries is limited to high-income groups. The limited initial demand in other advanced countries does not make it worthwhile for firms in those countries to start producing the new product, but it does necessitate some exports from the United States to those countries.

Over time, however, demand for the new product starts to grow in other advanced countries (e.g., Great Britain, France, Germany, and Japan). As it does, it becomes worthwhile for foreign producers to begin producing for their home markets. In addition, U.S. firms might set up production facilities in those advanced countries where demand is growing. Consequently, production within other advanced countries begins to limit the potential for exports from the United States.

As the market in the United States and other advanced nations matures, the product becomes more standardized, and price becomes the main competitive weapon. As this occurs, cost considerations start to play a greater role in the competitive process. One result is that producers based in advanced countries where labor costs are lower than in the United States (e.g., Italy, Spain) might now be able to export to the United States.

If cost pressures become intense, the process might not stop there. The cycle by which the United States lost its advantage to other advanced countries might be repeated once more, as developing countries (e.g., South Korea and Thailand) begin to acquire a production advantage over advanced countries. Thus the locus of global production initially switches from the United States to other advanced nations, and then from those nations to developing countries.

Over time the United States switches from being an exporter of the product to an importer of the product as production becomes concentrated in lower-cost foreign locations. These dynamics are illustrated in Figure 4.5, which shows the growth of production and consumption over time in the United States, other advanced countries, and developing countries.

---

[15]R. Vernon, "International Investments and International Trade in the Product Life Cycle," *Quarterly Journal of Economics*, May 1966, pp. 190–207; and R. Vernon and L. T. Wells, *The Economic Environment of International Business*, 4th ed. (Englewood Cliffs, NJ: Prentice Hall, 1986).

FIGURE 4.5   The Product Life-Cycle Theory

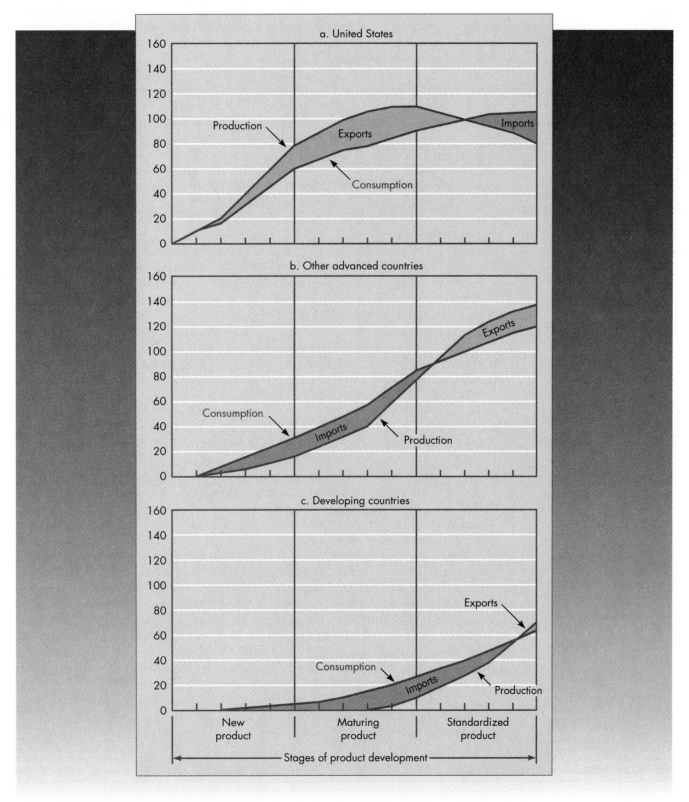

Source: Adapted from R. Vernon and L. T. Wells, The Economic Environment of International Business, 4th ed. (Englewood Cliffs, NJ: Prentice Hall, 1986).

Evaluating the Product Life-Cycle Theory

How well does the product life-cycle theory explain international trade patterns? Historically, it is quite accurate. Consider photocopiers; the product was first developed in the early 1960s by Xerox in the United States and sold initially to U.S. users. Originally Xerox exported photocopiers from the United States, primarily to Japan and the advanced countries of Western Europe. As demand began to grow in those countries, Xerox entered into joint ventures to set up production in Japan (Fuji-Xerox) and Great Britain (Rank-Xerox). In addition, once Xerox's patents on the photocopier process expired, other foreign competitors began to enter the market (e.g., Canon in Japan, Olivetti in Italy). As a consequence, exports from the United States declined, and U.S. users began to buy some of their photocopiers from lower-cost foreign sources, particularly from Japan. More recently, Japanese companies have found that their own country is too expensive a location to manufacture photocopiers, so they have begun to switch production to developing countries such as Singapore and Thailand. As a result, initially the United States and now several other advanced countries (e.g., Japan and Great Britain) have switched from being exporters of photocopiers to being importers. This evolution in the pattern of international trade in photocopiers is obviously consistent with the predictions of the product life-cycle theory. The product life-cycle theory clearly does go some way toward explaining the migration of mature industries out of the United States and into low-cost assembly locations.

However, the product life-cycle theory is not without weaknesses. Viewed from an Asian or European perspective, Vernon's argument that most new products are developed and introduced in the United States seems ethnocentric. Although it may be true that during the period of U.S. global dominance (1945–75) most new products were introduced in the United States, there have always been important exceptions. In recent years these exceptions appear to have become more common. Many new products are now first introduced in Japan (e.g., high-definition television or digital audiotapes). More importantly, with the increased globalization and integration of the world economy that we discussed in Chapter 1, a growing number of new products are now introduced simultaneously in the United States, Japan, and the advanced European nations (e.g., laptop computers, compact disks, and electronic cameras). This may be accompanied by globally dispersed production, with particular components of a new product being produced in those locations around the globe where the mix of factor costs and skills is most favorable (as predicted by the theory of comparative advantage).

Consider laptop computers, which were introduced simultaneously into a number of major national markets by Toshiba. Although various components for Toshiba laptop computers are manufactured in Japan (e.g., display screens, memory chips), other components are manufactured in Singapore and Taiwan, and still others (e.g., hard drives and microprocessors) are manufactured in the United States. All the components are shipped to Singapore for final assembly, and the completed product is then shipped to the major world markets (the United States, Western Europe, and Japan). The pattern of trade associated with this new product is both different from and more complex than the pattern predicted by Vernon's model. Trying to explain this pattern using the product life-cycle theory would be very difficult. Indeed, the theory of comparative advantage might better explain why certain components are produced in certain locations and why the final product is assembled in Singapore. In short, although Vernon's theory may be useful for explaining the pattern of international trade during the brief period of American global dominance, its relevance in the modern world is limited.

◆ THE NEW TRADE THEORY

The new trade theory began to emerge in the 1970s. At that time a number of economists were questioning the assumption of diminishing returns to specialization.[16]

---

[16]For a good summry of this literature, see E. Helpman and P. Krugman, *Market Structure and Foreign Trade: Increasing Returns, Imperfect Competition, and the International Economy* (Boston: MIT Press, 1985). Also see P. Krugman, "Does the New Trade Theory Require a New Trade Policy?" *World Economy* 15, no. 4 (1992), pp. 423–41.

They argued that in many industries, because of the presence of substantial economies of scale, there are increasing returns to specialization. As output expands with specialization, the ability to realize economies of scale increases and so the unit costs of production should decrease. Economies of scale are primarily derived by spreading fixed costs (such as the costs of developing a new product) over a larger output. Consider the commercial jet aircraft industry. The fixed costs of developing a new commercial jet airliner are astronomical. For example, Boeing spent an estimated $5 billion to develop its new 777. The company will have to sell at least 200 777s just to recoup these development costs and break even. Thus, due to the high fixed costs of developing a new jet aircraft, the economies of scale in this industry are substantial.

The new trade theorists further argue that due to the presence of substantial scale economies, in many industries world demand will support only a few firms. This is the case in the commercial jet aircraft industry; estimates suggest that, at most, world demand can profitably support only three major manufacturers. For example, the total world demand for 300-seater commercial jet aircraft similar to Boeing's 777 model will probably be only 1,500 aircraft over the 10 years between 1995 and 2005. If we assume that firms must sell at least 500 aircraft to get an acceptable return on their investment (which is reasonable, given the break-even point of 200 aircraft), we can see that, at most, the world market can profitably support only three firms!

The new trade theorists go on to argue that in those industries where the existence of substantial economies of scale imply that the world market will profitably support only a few firms, countries may export certain products simply because they have a firm that was an early entrant into that industry. Underpinning this argument is the notion of **first-mover advantages,** which are the economic and strategic advantages that accrue to early entrants into an industry.[17] Because they are able to gain economies of scale, the early entrants into an industry may get a lock on the world market that discourages subsequent entry. In other words, the ability of first movers to reap economies of scale creates a barrier to entry. In the commercial aircraft industry, for example, the fact that Boeing, Airbus, and McDonnell Douglas are already in the industry and have the benefits of economies of scale effectively discourages new entry.

This theory has profound implications. The theory suggests that a country may predominate in the export of a good simply because it was lucky enough to have one or more firms among the first to produce that good. This is at variance with the Heckscher-Ohlin theory, which suggests that a country will predominate in the export of a product when it is particularly well endowed with those factors used intensively in its manufacture. Thus the new trade theorists argue that the United States leads in exports of commercial jet aircraft not because it is better endowed with the factors of production required to manufacture aircraft, but because two of the first movers in the industry, Boeing and McDonnell Douglas, were U.S. firms. It should be noted, however, that the new trade theory is not at variance with the theory of comparative advantage. Since economies of scale result in an increase in the efficiency of resource utilization, and hence in productivity, the new trade theory identifies an important source of comparative advantage.

How useful is this theory in explaining trade patterns? It is perhaps too early to say; the theory is so new that little supporting empirical work has been done. Consistent with the theory, however, a recent study by Harvard business historian Alfred Chandler suggests that the existence of first-mover advantages is an important factor in explaining the dominance of firms from certain nations in certain industries.[18] Moreover, it is true that the number of firms is very limited in many global

[17]M. B. Lieberman and D. B. Montgomery, "First-Mover Advantages," *Strategic Management Journal* 9 (Summer 1988), pp. 41–58.

[18]A. D. Chandler. *Scale and Scope* (New York: Free Press, 1990).

industries. This is the case with the commercial aircraft industry, the chemical industry, the heavy construction-equipment industry, the heavy truck industry, the tire industry, the consumer electronics industry, and the jet engine industry, to name but a few examples.

Perhaps the most contentious implication of the new trade theory is the argument that it generates for government intervention and strategic trade policy.[19] New trade theorists stress the role of luck, entrepreneurship, and innovation in giving a firm first-mover advantages. According to this argument, the reason Boeing was the first mover in commercial jet aircraft manufacture—rather than firms like Great Britain's DeHavilland and Hawker Siddely, or Holland's Fokker, all of which could have been—was that Boeing was both lucky and innovative. One way Boeing was lucky is that DeHavilland shot itself in the foot when its Comet jet airliner, introduced two years earlier than Boeing's first jet airliner, the 707, was found to be full of serious technological flaws. Had DeHavilland not made some serious technological mistakes, Great Britain might now be the world's leading exporter of commercial jet aircraft!

Boeing's innovativeness was demonstrated by its independent development of the technological know-how required to build a commercial jet airliner. Several new trade theorists have pointed out, however, that Boeing's R&D was largely paid for by the U.S. government, that the 707 was in fact a spinoff from a government-funded military program. Herein lies a rationale for government intervention.

By the sophisticated and judicious use of subsidies, might not a government be able to increase the chances of its domestic firms becoming first movers in newly emerging industries, as the U.S. government apparently did with Boeing? If this is possible, and the new trade theory suggests it might be, then we have an economic rationale for a proactive trade policy that is at variance with the free trade prescriptions of the trade theories we have reviewed so far. We will consider the policy implications of this issue in Chapter 5.

🐾 NATIONAL COMPETITIVE ADVANTAGE: PORTER'S DIAMOND

In 1990 Michael Porter of Harvard Business School published the results of an intensive research effort that attempted to determine why some nations succeed and others fail in international competition.[20] Porter and his team looked at 100 industries in 10 nations. The book that contains the results of this work, *The Competitive Advantage of Nations,* seems destined to become an important contribution.

Like the work of the new trade theorists, Porter's work was driven by a feeling that the existing theories of international trade told only part of the story. For Porter, the essential task was to explain why a nation achieves international success in a particular industry. Why does Japan do so well in the automobile industry? Why does Switzerland excel in the production and export of precision instruments and pharmaceuticals? Why do Germany and the United States do so well in the chemical industry? These questions cannot be answered easily by the Heckscher-Ohlin theory, and the theory of comparative advantage offers only a partial explanation. The theory of comparative advantage would say that Switzerland excels in the production and export of precision instruments because it uses its resources very productively in these industries. Although this may be correct, this does not explain why Switzerland is more productive in this industry than Great Britain, Germany, or Spain. It is this puzzle that Porter tries to solve.

---

[19]Krugman, "Does the New Trade Theory Require a New Trade Policy?"

[20]M. E. Porter, *The Competitive Advantage of Nations* (New York: Free Press, 1990). For a good review of this book, see R. M. Grant, "Porter's Competitive Advantage of Nations: An Assessment," *Strategic Management Journal* 12 (1991), pp. 535–48.

FIGURE 4.6
Determinants of National
Competitive Advantage:
Porter's Diamond

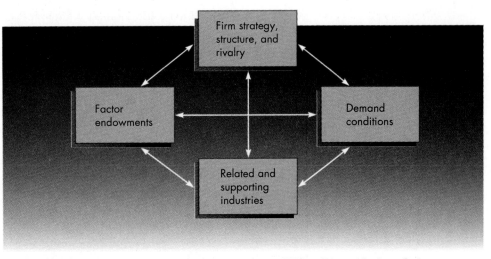

Source: Adapted from M. E. Porter, "The Competitive Advantage of Nations," Harvard Business Review,
March–April 1990, p. 77.

Porter's thesis is that four broad attributes of a nation shape the environment in which local firms compete, and these attributes promote or impede the creation of competitive advantage (see Figure 4.6). These attributes are

- *Factor endowments*—a nation's position in factors of production such as skilled labor or the infrastructure necessary to compete in a given industry.
- *Demand conditions*—the nature of home demand for the industry's product or service.
- *Related and supporting industries*—the presence or absence in a nation of supplier industries and related industries that are internationally competitive.
- *Firm strategy, structure, and rivalry*—the conditions in the nation governing how companies are created, organized, and managed and the nature of domestic rivalry.

Porter speaks of these four attributes as constituting *the diamond*. He argues that firms are most likely to succeed in industries or industry segments where the diamond is most favorable. He also argues that the diamond is a mutually reinforcing system. The effect of one attribute is contingent on the state of others. For example, Porter argues, favorable demand conditions will not result in competitive advantage unless the state of rivalry is sufficient to cause firms to respond to them.

Porter maintains that two additional variables can influence the national diamond in important ways—chance and government. Chance events, such as major innovations, create discontinuities that can unfreeze or reshape industry structure and provide the opportunity for one nation's firms to supplant another's. Government, by its choice of policies, can detract from or improve national advantage. For example, regulation can alter home demand conditions; antitrust policies can influence the intensity of rivalry within an industry; and government investments in education can change factor endowments.

Factor Endowments

We have seen that factor endowments lie at the center of the Heckscher-Ohlin theory. While Porter does not propose anything radically new, he does analyze the characteristics of factors of production in some detail. He recognizes hierarchies among factors, distinguishing between basic factors (e.g., natural resources, climate, location, and demographics) and advanced factors (e.g., communications infrastructure, sophisticated and skilled labor, research facilities, and technological know-how). He argues that advanced factors are the most significant for competitive advantage. Moreover, unlike basic factors (which are naturally endowed), advanced factors are a product of investment by individuals, companies, and governments. Thus government investments in basic and higher education, by improving the general skill and knowledge level of the population and by stimulating advanced research at higher education institutions, can upgrade a nation's advanced factors.

The relationship between advanced and basic factors is complex. Basic factors can provide an initial advantage that is subsequently reinforced and extended by investment in advanced factors. Conversely, disadvantages in basic factors can create pressures to invest in advanced factors. The most obvious example of this phenomenon is Japan, a country that lacks much in the way of arable land or mineral deposits and yet through investment has built a substantial endowment of advanced factors. In particular, Porter notes that Japan's large pool of engineers (reflecting a much higher number of engineering graduates per capita than almost any other nation) has been vital to Japan's success in many manufacturing industries.

Demand Conditions

Porter emphasizes the role home demand plays in providing the impetus for upgrading competitive advantage. Firms are typically most sensitive to the needs of their closest customers. Thus the characteristics of home demand are particularly important in shaping the attributes of domestically made products and in creating pressures for innovation and quality. Porter argues that a nation's firms gain competitive advantage if their domestic consumers are sophisticated and demanding. Sophisticated and demanding consumers pressure local firms to meet high standards of product quality and to produce innovative products. Porter notes that Japan's sophisticated and knowledgeable buyers of cameras helped stimulate the Japanese camera industry to improve product quality and to introduce innovative models. A similar example can be found in the cellular phone equipment industry, where sophisticated and demanding local customers in Scandinavia helped push Nokia of Finland and Ericsson of Sweden to invest in cellular phone technology long before demand for cellular phones took off in other developed nations. As a result, Nokia and Ericsson, together with Motorola, are today dominant players in the global cellular telephone equipment industry. The case of Nokia is reviewed in more depth in the next Management Focus.

Related and Supporting Industries

The third broad attribute of national advantage in an industry is the presence of suppliers or related industries that are internationally competitive. The benefits of investments in advanced factors of production by related and supporting industries can spill over into an industry, thereby helping it achieve a strong competitive position internationally. Swedish strength in fabricated steel products (e.g., ball bearings and cutting tools) has drawn on strengths in Sweden's specialty steel industry. Technological leadership in the U.S. semiconductor industry up until the mid-1980s provided the basis for U.S. success in personal computers and several other technically advanced electronic products. Similarly, Switzerland's success in pharmaceuticals is closely related to its previous international success in the technologically related dye industry.

One consequence of this process is that successful industries within a country tend to be grouped into clusters of related industries. This was one of the more pervasive findings of Porter's study. One such cluster is the German textile and apparel sector, which includes high-quality cotton, wool, synthetic fibers, sewing machine needles, and a wide range of textile machinery.

Firm Strategy, Structure, and Rivalry

The fourth broad attribute of national competitive advantage in Porter's model is the strategy, structure, and rivalry of firms within a nation. Porter makes two important points here. His first is that different nations are characterized by different "management ideologies," which either help them or do not help them to build national competitive advantage. For example, Porter notes the predominance of engineers on the top-management teams of German and Japanese firms. He attributes this to these firms' emphasis on improving manufacturing processes

and product design. In contrast, Porter notes a predominance of people with finance backgrounds on the top-management teams of many U.S. firms. He links
this to the lack of attention of many U.S. firms to improving manufacturing
processes and product design, particularly during the 1970s and 80s. He also argues that the dominance of finance has led to a corresponding overemphasis on
maximizing short-term financial returns. According to Porter, one consequence of
these different management ideologies has been a relative loss of U.S. competitiveness in those engineering-based industries where manufacturing processes and
product design issues are all-important (e.g., the automobile industry).

Porter's second point is that there is a strong association between vigorous domestic rivalry and the creation and persistence of competitive advantage in an industry.
Vigorous domestic rivalry induces firms to look for ways to improve efficiency, which
in turn makes them better international competitors. Domestic rivalry creates pressures to innovate, to improve quality, to reduce costs, and to invest in upgrading advanced factors. All of this helps to create world-class competitors. As an illustration
Porter cites the case of Japan:

> Nowhere is the role of domestic rivalry more evident than in Japan, where it is all-out
> warfare in which many companies fail to achieve profitability. With goals that stress
> market share, Japanese companies engage in a continuing struggle to outdo each other.
> Shares fluctuate markedly. The process is prominently covered in the business press.
> Elaborate rankings measure which companies are most popular with university graduates.
> The rate of new product and process development is breathtaking.[21]

A similar point about the stimulating effects of strong domestic competition can be
made with regard to Nokia's rise to global preeminence in the market for cellular
telephone equipment. For details, see the next "Management Focus."

**Evaluating Porter's
Theory**

In sum, Porter's argument is that the degree to which a nation is likely to achieve international success in a certain industry is a function of the combined impact of factor endowments, domestic demand conditions, related and supporting industries,
and domestic rivalry. He argues that the presence of all four components is usually
required for "this diamond" to positively impact competitive performance (although
there are some exceptions). Porter also contends that government can influence
each of the four components of the diamond either positively or negatively. Factor
endowments can be affected by subsidies, policies toward capital markets, policies
toward education, and the like. Government can shape domestic demand through
local product standards or with regulations that mandate or influence buyer needs.
Government policy can influence supporting and related industries through regulation and influence firm rivalry through such devices as capital market regulation, tax
policy, and antitrust laws.

If Porter is correct, we would expect his model to predict the pattern of international trade that we observe in the real world. Countries should be exporting
products from those industries where all four components of the diamond are favorable, while importing in those areas where the components are not favorable.
Is he correct? At this point we simply do not know. Porter's theory is so new it has
not yet been subjected to independent empirical testing. There is certainly much
about the theory that rings true, but the same can be said for the new trade theory, the theory of comparative advantage, and the Heckscher-Ohlin theory. In reality it may well be that each of these theories explains something about the pattern of international trade. After all, in many respects these theories complement
each other.

---

[21]Porter, *Competitive Advantage*, p. 121.

MANAGEMENT
FOCUS
The Rise of
Finland's Nokia

The cellular telephone equipment industry is one of the great growth stories of the 1990s. The number of cellular subscribers has been expanding rapidly. By the end of 1994 there were over 50 million cellular subscribers worldwide, up from under 10 million in 1990. Three firms currently dominate the global market for cellular equipment (e.g. cellular phones, base station equipment, digital switches)—Motorola, Nokia, and Ericsson. Of the three, the dramatic rise of Nokia has perhaps been the most surprising.

Nokia's roots are in Finland, not normally a country that jumps to mind when one talks about leading edge technology companies. In the 1980s Nokia was a rambling Finnish conglomerate with activities that embraced tire manufacturing, paper production, consumer electronics, and telecommunications equipment. Today it is a focused $10 billion telecommunications equipment

manufacturer with a global reach second only to that of Motorola and sales and earnings that are growing in excess of 30 percent per annum. How has this former conglomerate emerged to take a global leadership position in cellular equipment? Much of the answer lies in the history, geography, and political economy of Finland and its Nordic neighbors.

The story starts in 1981 when the Nordic nations got together to create the world's first international cellular telephone network. They had good reason to become pioneers; sparsely populated and inhospitably cold, it cost far too much to lay down a traditional wireline telephone service. Yet the same features make telecommunications all the more valuable there—people driving through the Arctic winter and owners of remote northern houses that need a telephone to summon help if things go wrong. As a result, Sweden, Norway, and Finland became the first nations in the world to take

IMPLICATIONS FOR BUSINESS

Why does all of this matter for business? There are at least three main implications of the material discussed in this chapter for international businesses: location implications, first-mover implications, and policy implications.

Location Implications

One way in which the material discussed in this chapter matters to an international business concerns the link between the theories of international trade and a firm's decision about where to locate its various productive activities. Underlying most of the theories is the notion that different countries have particular advantages in different productive activities. Thus, from a profit perspective, it makes sense for a firm to disperse its various productive activities to those countries where, according to the theory of international trade, they can be performed most efficiently. If design can be performed most efficiently in France, that is where design facilities should be located; if the manufacture of basic components can be performed most efficiently in Singapore, that is where they should be manufactured; and if final assembly can be performed most efficiently in China, that is where final assembly should be performed. The end result is a global web of productive activities, with different activities being performed in various locations around the globe depending on considerations of comparative advantage, factor endowments, and the like. If the firm does not do this, it may find itself at a competitive disadvantage relative to firms that do.

Consider the process of producing a laptop computer, a process with four major stages: (1) basic research and development of the product design, (2) manufacture of standard electronic components (e.g., memory chips), (3) manufacture of advanced components (e.g., flat-top color display screens and microprocessors), and (4) final assembly. Basic R&D and design require a pool of highly skilled and educated workers with good backgrounds in microelectronics. The two countries with a comparative advantage in basic microelectronics R&D and

cellular telecommunications seriously. They found, for example, that while it cost up to $800 per subscriber to bring a traditional wireline service to remote locations in the far north, the same locations could be linked by wireless cellular for only $500 per person. As a consequence, by 1994 12 percent of people in Scandinavia owned cellular phones, compared with less than 6 percent in the United States, the world's second most developed market.

Nokia, as a longtime telecommunications equipment supplier, was well positioned from the start to take advantage of this development, but other forces were also at work in Finland that helped Nokia develop its competitive edge. Unlike virtually every other developed nation, Finland has never had a national telephone monopoly. Instead, the country's telephone services have long been provided by about 50 or so autonomous local telephone companies, whose elected boards set prices by referendum (which naturally means low prices). This army of independent and cost conscious telephone service providers prevented Nokia from taking anything for granted in its home country. With typical Finnish pragmatism, the providers have been willing to buy from the lowest cost supplier, whether that was Nokia, Ericsson, Motorola, or someone else. This situation contrasted sharply with that prevailing in most developed nations until the late 1980s and early 1990s, where domestic telephone monopolies typically purchased equipment from a dominant local supplier, or made it themselves. Nokia responded to this competitive pressure by doing everything possible to drive down its manufacturing costs while still staying at the leading edge of cellular technology.

The consequences of these forces are clear. While Motorola remains the number one firm in cellular equipment, the once obscure Finnish firm, Nokia, is snapping at its heels. It is Nokia, not Motorola, that is the leader in digital cellular technology, which seems to be the wave of the future. In no small part Nokia has the lead because Scandinavia started switching to digital technology five years before the rest of the world. Moreover, spurred on by its cost conscious Finnish customers, Nokia now has the lowest cost structure of any cellular phone equipment manufacturer in the world; the result being that it is a more profitable enterprise than Motorola. Nokia's operating margins in 1994 were 17.7 percent, compared with 14.4 percent at Motorola.

Sources: "Lessons from the Frozen North," *The Economist,* October 8, 1994, pp. 76–77; and G. Edmondson, "Grabbing Markets from the Giants," *Business Week, Special Issue: 21st Century Capitalism,* 1995, p. 156.

design are Japan and the United States, so most producers of laptop computers locate their R&D facilities in one, or both, of these countries. (Apple, IBM, Motorola, Texas Instruments, Toshiba, and Sony all have major R&D facilities in both Japan and the United States.)

The manufacture of standard electronic components is a capital-intensive process requiring semiskilled labor, and cost pressures are intense. The best locations for such activities today are places such as Singapore, Taiwan, Malaysia, and South Korea. These countries have pools of relatively skilled, low-cost labor. Thus many producers of laptop computers have standard components, such as memory chips, produced at these locations.

The manufacture of advanced components such as microprocessors and display screens is a capital-intensive process requiring highly skilled labor, and cost pressures are less intense. Since cost pressures are not so intense at this stage, these components can be—and are—manufactured in countries with high labor costs that also have pools of highly skilled labor (primarily Japan and the United States).

Finally, assembly is a relatively labor-intensive process requiring only low-skilled labor, and cost pressures are intense. As a result, final assembly may be carried out in a country such as Mexico, which has an abundance of low-cost, low-skilled labor.

The end result is that when we look at a laptop computer produced by a U.S. manufacturer, we may find that it was designed in California, its standard components were produced in Taiwan and Singapore, its advanced components were produced in Japan and the United States, its final assembly occurred in Mexico, and the finished product was then sold in the United States or elsewhere in the world. By dispersing production activities to different locations around the globe, the U.S. manufacturer is taking advantage of the differences between countries identified by the various theories of international trade.

**First-Mover
Implications**

The new trade theory suggests the importance to firms of building and exploiting first-mover advantages. According to the new trade theory, firms that establish a first-mover advantage with regard to the production of a particular new product may subsequently dominate global trade in that product. This is particularly true in those industries where the global market can profitably support only a limited number of firms—such as the aerospace market—but early commitments also seem to be important in less concentrated industries such as the market for cellular telephone equipment (again, see the "Management Focus" on Nokia). For the individual firm, the clear message is that it pays to invest substantial financial resources in trying to build a first-mover, or early-mover, advantage, even if that means several years of substantial losses before a new venture becomes profitable. Although the precise details of how to achieve this are beyond the scope of this book, there is a vast literature on strategies for exploiting first-mover advantages.[22] It is often argued that in recent years Japanese firms, rather than their European or North American competitors, seem to have been prepared to undertake the vast investments and bear the years of losses required to build a first-mover advantage. This has certainly been true in the production of liquid crystal display (LCD) screens for laptop computers. While firms such as Toshiba and NEC invested heavily in this technology during the 1980s, many large European and American firms exited the market. As a result, today Japanese firms dominate global trade in LCD screens, even though the technology was invented in the United States.

Policy Implications

The theories of international trade also matter to international businesses because business firms are major players on the international trade scene. Business firms produce exports, and business firms import the products of other countries. Because of their pivotal role in international trade, business firms can and do exert a strong influence on government trade policy. By lobbying government, business firms can help promote free trade or they can promote trade restrictions. The message for business contained in the theories of international trade is that promoting free trade is generally in the best interests of their home country, although it may not always be in the best interest of an individual firm. Many firms recognize this and lobby for open markets.

For example, in 1991 when the U.S. government announced its intention to place a tariff on Japanese imports of liquid crystal display (LCD) screens, IBM and Apple Computer protested strongly. Both IBM and Apple pointed out that (1) Japan was the lowest-cost source of LCD screens, (2) they used these screens in their own laptop computers, and (3) the proposed tariff, by increasing the cost of LCD screens, would increase the cost of laptop computers produced by IBM and Apple, thus making them less competitive in the world market. In other words, the tariff, designed to protect U.S. firms, would be self-defeating. In response to these pressures, the U.S. government reversed its posture on this issue.

Unlike IBM and Apple, however, businesses do not always lobby for free trade. In the United States, for example, "voluntary" restrictions on imports on automobiles, machine tools, textiles, and steel are the result of direct pressure on the government by U.S. firms in these industries. The government has responded by getting foreign companies to agree to "voluntary" restrictions on their imports, using the implicit threat of more comprehensive formal trade barriers to get them to adhere to these agreements. As predicted by international trade theory, many of these agreements have been self-defeating. Take the voluntary restriction on machine tool imports agreed to in 1985 as an example. Due to limited import competition from more-efficient foreign suppliers, the prices of machine tools in the United States have risen to higher levels than would have prevailed under a free trade scenario. Since machine tools are used throughout the manufacturing industry, the result has been an increase in the cost of U.S. manufacturing in general and a corresponding loss in world market competitiveness. Moreover, shielded from international competition by import barriers, the U.S. machine tool industry has had no incentive to increase its efficiency. Consequently, it has lost many of its export markets to ever-more-efficient foreign competitors. Thus the U.S.

---

[22]Lieberman and Montgomery, "First-Mover Advantages."

machine tool industry is now smaller than it was in 1985. For anyone schooled in international trade theory, none of these events are surprising.[23]

Finally, Porter's theory of national competitive advantage also contains important policy implications. Porter's theory suggests it is in the best interest of business for a firm to invest in upgrading advanced factors of production; for example, to invest in better training for its employees and to increase its commitment to research and development. It is also in the best interests of business to lobby the government to adopt policies that have a favorable impact on each component of the national "diamond." Thus, according to Porter, businesses should urge government to increase its investment in education, infrastructure, and basic research (since all these enhance advanced factors) and to adopt policies that promote strong competition within domestic markets (since this makes firms stronger international competitors, according to Porter's findings).

❧ SUMMARY OF CHAPTER

This chapter has reviewed a number of theories that explain why it is beneficial for a country to engage in international trade and has explained the pattern of international trade that we observe in the world economy. We have seen how the theories of Smith, Ricardo, and Heckscher-Ohlin all make strong cases for unrestricted free trade. In contrast, the mercantilist doctrine and, to a lesser extent, the new trade theory can be interpreted to support government intervention to promote exports through subsidies and to limit imports through tariffs and quotas.

With regard to explaining the pattern of international trade, the second objective of this chapter, we have seen that with the exception of mercantilism, which is silent on this issue, the different theories offer largely complementary explanations. Although no one theory may explain the apparent pattern of international trade, taken together, the theory of comparative advantage, the Heckscher-Ohlin theory, the product life-cycle theory, the new trade theory, and Porter's theory of national competitive advantage do suggest which factors are important. Comparative advantage tells us that productivity differences are important; Heckscher-Ohlin tells us that factor endowments matter; the product life-cycle theory tells us that where a new product is introduced is important; the new trade theory tells us that increasing returns to specialization and first-mover advantages matter; and Porter tells us that all these factors may be important insofar as they impact on the four components of the national diamond.

The following points have been made in this chapter:

1. Mercantilists argued it was in a country's best interests to run a balance-of-trade surplus. They viewed trade as a zero-sum game, in which one country's gains cause losses for other countries.

2. The theory of absolute advantage suggests that countries differ in their ability to produce goods efficiently. The theory suggests that a country should specialize in producing goods in areas where it has an absolute advantage and import goods in areas where other countries have absolute advantages.

3. The theory of comparative advantage suggests it makes sense for a country to specialize in producing those goods that it can produce most efficiently, while buying goods that it can produce relatively less efficiently from other countries—even if that means buying goods from other countries that it could produce more efficiently itself.

4. The theory of comparative advantage suggests that unrestricted free trade brings about increased world production; that is, trade is a positive-sum game.

5. The theory of comparative advantage also suggests that opening a country to free trade stimulates economic growth, which in turn creates dynamic gains from trade.

6. The Heckscher-Ohlin theory argues that the pattern of international trade is determined by differences in factor endowments. It predicts that countries will export those goods that make intensive use of locally abundant factors and will import goods that make intensive use of factors that are locally scarce.

7. The product life-cycle theory suggests that trade patterns are influenced by where a new product is introduced. In an increasingly integrated global economy, the product life-cycle theory seems to be less predictive than it was between 1945 and 1975.

8. The new trade theory argues that in those industries where the existence of substantial economies of scale imply that the world market will profitably support only a few firms, countries may predominate in the export of certain products simply because they had a firm that was a first mover in that industry.

9. Some new trade theorists have promoted the idea of strategic trade policy. The argument is that government, by the sophisticated and judicious use of subsidies, might be able to increase the chances of domestic firms becoming first movers in newly emerging industries.

---

[23]C. A. Hamilton, "Building Better Machine Tools," *Journal of Commerce*, October 30, 1991, p. 8; and "Manufacturing Trouble," *The Economist*, October 12, 1991, p. 71.

10. Porter's theory of national competitive advantage suggests that the pattern of trade is influenced by four attributes of a nation: (*i*) factor endowments, (*ii*) domestic demand conditions, (*iii*) related and supporting industries, and (*iv*) firm strategy, structure, and rivalry.

11. Theories of international trade are important to an individual business firm primarily because they can help the firm decide where to locate its various production activities.

12. Firms involved in international trade can and do exert a strong influence on government policy toward trade. By lobbying government bodies, business firms can help promote free trade or they can promote trade restrictions.

❧ CRITICAL DISCUSSION QUESTIONS

1. Mercantilism is a bankrupt theory that has no place in the modern world. Discuss.

2. The "Country Focus" contained in this chapter reviews the arguments of those who suggest that Japan is a neo-mercantilist nation. Do you agree with this assessment? Can you think of cases in which your country has taken a neo-mercantilist stance to foreign competition?

3. Using the theory of comparative advantage to support your arguments, outline the case for free trade.

4. Using the new trade theory and Porter's theory of national competitive advantage, outline the case for government policies that would build national competitive advantage in a particular industry. What kind of policies would you recommend that the government adopt? Are these policies at variance with the basic free trade philosophy?

5. You are the CEO of a textile firm that designs and manufactures mass-market clothing products in the United States. Your manufacturing process is labor-intensive and does not require highly skilled employees. Currently you have design facilities in Paris and New York and manufacturing facilities in North Carolina. Drawing on the theory of international trade, decide whether these are optimal locations for these activities.

6. In general, policies designed to limit competition from low-cost foreign competitors do not help a country to achieve greater economic growth. Discuss this statement.

❧ CLOSING CASE   The Rise of the Italian Ceramic Tile Industry to Global Preeminence

By the early 1990s Italian firms were by far the world leaders in the production and export of ceramic roofing and flooring tiles, accounting for over 30 percent of world production and 60 percent of world exports. The rise to global preeminence of the Italian tile industry was based on the superior mechanical and aesthetic qualities of Italian tiles. Italian tile production was concentrated in the Emilia-Romagna region of northern Italy around the small town of Sassuolo. In the Sassuolo region hundreds of firms were involved in the ceramic tile industry and in various supporting industries such as the manufacture of glazes, enamels, and ceramic tile production equipment. As a result, Sassuolo boasted the greatest concentration in the world of firms in the ceramic tile and supporting industries.

The ceramic tile industry in Sassuolo grew out of the earthenware and crockery industry, which itself could be traced to the 13th century. Demand for ceramic tiles grew rapidly in Italy in the years immediately after World War II. Reconstruction after the war created a boom in the building industry. Demand for ceramic tiles grew substantially as a result of this boom. One reason for the high domestic demand was Italy's Mediterranean climate (ceramic floor tiles were cool to the touch in warm weather). There was also a tradition in Italy of using natural stone materials for flooring, as opposed to carpeting or wood. Because of this tradition, per capita tile consumption in Italy has long been the highest in the world. In 1987 it stood at 3.33 square meters per capita, followed by 2.55 in Spain, and 1.81 in Switzerland.

As a result of booming demand, the number of ceramic tile firms in the Sassuolo region grew rapidly during the 1950s and 1960s. In 1955 there were 14 tile firms in the region, by 1962 the figure had leapt to 102. In addition to booming demand, this rapid growth in the number of enterprises was spurred on by the low cost of setting up a ceramic tile business. Rivalry between firms in the Sassuolo region was intense. They had to compete vigorously against each other to get access to retail outlets. Retailers demanded high quality, low cost, and aesthetically pleasing tiles. Firms constantly sought to gain an edge against each other in technology, design, and distribution. Innovations were usually known within a matter of weeks and quickly copied by rivals. Firms seeking a leadership position, whether in technology or productive efficiency or design, had to constantly improve their processes and turn over their product line to stay ahead of rivals.

As the industry grew around Sassuolo, so process technicians from local tile companies left to start their own process equipment firms. Process equipment in tile making includes kilns for firing the tiles, presses for forming tiles, and glazing machines. By the mid-1980s over 120 firms in the Sassuolo area were making process equipment for ceramic tile companies. These equipment manufacturers competed fiercely for the business of tile manufacturers. In an attempt to gain business they devoted considerable effort to upgrading the quality of their production equipment and driving down their own manufacturing costs. One result of this competitive process among equipment suppliers in the Sassuolo region was the development of a number of important process innovations that significantly lowered the energy and labor costs of manufacturing ceramic tiles. Advances in kiln technology in particular soon made Sassuolo a leader not just in the tile industry but also in the supporting equipment industry.

By the 1970s the tile industry in Italy was beginning to mature. The long post-war boom in domestic demand was losing steam and excess capacity was beginning to develop among Italian tile firms. They responded to this problem by seeking international markets for their products, particularly in North America. In the international marketplace the Sassuolo firms found they had a competitive advantage over their nearest competitors, who were typically from Spain and Germany. This advantage was based on higher productivity, lower costs, better design, and the Italian reputation for style. As a consequence, by the early 1990s Italian firms enjoyed almost twice the global market share of their nearest competitors, the Spanish.

Case Discussion Questions

1. To what extent does the theory of comparative advantage explain the rise of Italian tile firms to global preeminence in the tile industry?

2. To what extent does the Heckscher-Ohlin theory explain the rise of Italian tile firms to global preeminence in the tile industry?

3. Use Michael Porter's diamond to analyze the rise to global preeminence of the Italian tile industry. What does this analysis tell you about how firms gain a competitive advantage in the world economy?

4. Which of the above theories—comparative advantage, Heckscher-Ohlin, or Porter's—gives the best explanation of the rise to global preeminence of the Italian tile industry? Why?

Source: This case is based on a case prepared by M. J. Enright and P. Tenti, "The Italian Ceramic Tile Industry," which is reported in M. E. Porter, The Competitive Advantage of Nations (New York: Free Press, 1990).

CHAPTER FIVE

THE POLITICAL ECONOMY OF INTERNATIONAL TRADE

ANATOMY OF A TRADE DISPUTE—THE U.S. PRIES OPEN JAPAN'S CELLULAR TELEPHONE MARKET

The United States and Japan boast one of the largest bilateral trading relationships in the world. It is also a trading relationship that many see as lopsided, with Japan exporting nearly $80 billion more in goods to the United States in 1993 than it imported from the United States. This unbalanced trading relationship has given rise to a trade dispute that continued into 1995. The trade dispute had its roots in a series of talks between Japan and the United States begun in mid–1993. The talks focused on Japan's trade imbalance with the United States, and steps that might be taken to open the Japanese market to more foreign goods and services. In particular, the Clinton administration felt that various administrative trade barriers worked to exclude foreign companies from competing effectively in Japan's automobile, construction, telecommunications, insurance, and medical equipment industries.

For months the U.S. side had been pushing the Japanese government to agree to set numerical targets for foreign imports. The model here was a 1991 agreement between Japan and the United States to increase foreign access to Japan's semiconductor market. That agreement contained an *expectation* that due to improved market access, by the end of 1992 foreign companies would be able to gain 20 percent of the Japanese market for semiconductors. The U.S. negotiators chose to view the 20 percent figure as a *target*—as opposed to an expectation—and when the 20 percent figure was reached they concluded that numerical targets work, much to the horror of the Japanese who had never seen the 20

percent figure as a target. The Japanese resisted the idea of numerical targets for what they saw as a very rational reason; Japan has a free market economy, and in a free market economy the government cannot tell consumers and companies how much of a foreign product to buy. To complicate matters, the government of Morihiro Hosokawa, which was then in power, was a fragile coalition government, and Hosokawa was under strong domestic pressure to stand up to the United States on the issue of numerical targets. The net result was that the Japanes`e refused to budge on numerical targets, and on February 11, 1994, the market access talks collapsed.

The American response was swift. On February 15 the United States government announced its intent to introduce formal trade sanctions against Japan for protecting its cellular telephone market. The United States stated that within 30 days it would produce a list of Japanese companies that would be punished with trade sanctions unless Japan opened its cellular telephone market. The cellular telephone market was chosen because it was relatively easy to make a case that administrative trade barriers had

made it difficult for Motorola Inc. to gain market share in Japan. Japan had agreed to open a big part of the cellular telephone market to Motorola in 1989. At that time the Japanese cellular phone service company, IDO, was building a mobile phone system using a rival technology developed by Nippon Telegraph and Telephone (NTT) to serve the highly populated Tokyo–Nagoya corridor. Under pressure from the Japanese government, IDO agreed to build a separate system using Motorola's technology. However, IDO could not easily afford to build two systems, so it concentrated on the one utilizing NTT technology. As a consequence, as of January 1994, it had 400 base stations for the NTT-compatible system compared with 110 for the Motorola system. This meant the NTT phones could be used in 94 percent of the area, compared with 61 percent for the Motorola phones. Given this disparity, it is hardly surprising that more than 310,000 customers have chosen NTT-compatible phones, and only 10,000 use the Motorola phones. According to the U.S. government, the resulting lack of sales violated the comparable market access that Japan promised in 1989.

According to many observers, the real agenda of the U.S. government when it announced its intent to introduce trade sanctions was to create as much uncertainty and anxiety in Japan as possible about Washington's next move. The belief was that uncertainty would drive up the value of the Japanese yen, thereby making Japan's exports more expensive and further hurting Japan's troubled exporting companies—companies that were already mired in their deepest recession since World War II. The net effect, it was hoped, would be to force the Japanese to come back to the bargaining table and make concessions on the key issue of numerical targets.

The U.S. government increased the pressure on Japan in early March 1994 when it revived a trade law known as "Super 301" that had lapsed in 1990. Super 301 allows individuals or the government to retaliate against "unjustifiable, unreasonable, or discriminatory traders abroad." While few believe that the United States will apply Super 301, they see the revival of this law as another step in the game of piling pressure on the Japanese in an attempt to bring them back to the bargaining table with concessions.

While there is still no sign that the Japanese are willing to give ground on the issue of numerical targets, they do seem willing to make some concessions in an attempt to avoid getting drawn into a trade war. To this extent, the U.S. tactics might be judged to be eliciting the desired response. On March 13, 1994, Japan announced it had brokered a deal between Motorola and IDO that would increase Motorola's access to the Japanese market. The deal called for IDO to bring forward its investment in a further 159 base stations for the Motorola phone system and complete that investment by autumn of 1995. IDO also agreed to reallocate some of its radio frequency used by NTT to Motorola. Further, the Japanese government agreed to monitor IDO's progress in achieving these goals and to provide IDO with low interest rate loans to help it make the accelerated investments.

On March 30, 1994, the Japanese government followed up the cellular phone deal with a package of market-opening measures intended to increase imports, reduce its trade surplus, boost the domestic economy, and open markets to foreign competition through deregulation. The main thrust of the package was to streamline or eliminate many of the bureaucratic procedures that have been used in the past to block foreign competition in certain sectors. The package, however, did not include the numerical targets that the U.S. side had been asking for.

Sources: Thomas Friedman, "U.S. Hoping to Use Fears of Trade War to Pressure Japan," *The New York Times,* February 16, 1994, pp. C1, C4; Michiyo Nakamoto, "Japan "Trapped" by Chip Import Deal," *Financial Times,* March 23, 1994, p. 4; and Emiko Terazono, "Japan Trade Package Yields to U.S. Demands on Imports," *Financial Times,* April 30, 1994, pp. 1, 4.

❧ INTRODUCTION

Our review of the classical trade theories of Smith, Ricardo, and Heckscher-Ohlin in Chapter 4 showed us that in a world without trade barriers, trade patterns will be determined by the relative productivity of different factors of production in different countries. Countries will specialize in the production of products that they can produce most efficiently, while importing products that they can produce less efficiently. Chapter 4 also laid out the intellectual case for free trade. Remember, **free trade** refers to a situation where a government does not attempt to restrict what its citizens can buy from another country or what they can sell to another country. As we saw in Chapter 4, the theories of Smith, Ricardo, and Heckscher-Ohlin predict that the consequences of free trade include both static economic gains (because free trade supports a higher level of domestic consumption and more efficient utilization of resources) and dynamic economic gains (because free trade stimulates economic growth and the creation of wealth).

In this chapter we look at the political reality of international trade. While many nations are nominally committed to free trade, in practice nations tend to adopt a neo-mercantilist stance, protecting their home market from foreign competition if possible, while simultaneously trying to gain access to the markets of others for their exports. These political realities are illustrated in the case that opens this chapter. The case describes how the lopsided trade imbalance between the United States and Japan has given rise to a long standing trade dispute between the two countries. In this dispute, the U.S. side claims the Japanese government is limiting foreign access to the Japanese market, while benefiting from America's low trade barriers. The Japanese government denies this is the case. Instead the Japanese claim the U.S. side is making unreasonable demands that cannot be enforced by a government in a country with a free market system. Thus, both sides are implicitly charging that the other is adopting a neo-mercantilist position. In truth, both sides may have a point, which is why resolution of this particular trade dispute has been so difficult. Nevertheless, despite denying the American charges, in 1994 the Japanese government felt pressured enough by the U.S. claims to make it easier for Motorola to compete in the Japanese market for cellular telephone equipment.

In this chapter we explore the political and economic reasons that governments have for intervening in international trade. When governments intervene, they typically do so by restricting imports of goods and services into their nation, while adopting policies that promote exports. Normally their motives for intervention are to protect domestic producers and jobs from foreign competition, while at the same time increasing the foreign market for the products of domestic producers. We start by describing the range of policy instruments that governments use to intervene in international trade. This is followed by a detailed review of the various political and economic motives that governments have for intervention. In the third section of this chapter, we consider how the case for free trade stands up in view of the various justifications given for government intervention in international trade. Then we look at the emergence of the modern international trading system, which is based on multinational agreements, particularly the General Agreement on Tariffs and Trade. Known as GATT, the **General Agreement on Tariffs and Trade** is an agreement among more than 120 countries, the purpose of which is to lower barriers to the free flow of goods and services between nations. The GATT has tried to promote free trade by limiting the ability of national governments to adopt policies that restrict imports into their nations. In the final section of this chapter we discuss the implications of this material for business practice.

❧ INSTRUMENTS OF TRADE POLICY

We review six main instruments of trade policy in this section: tariffs, subsidies, import quotas, voluntary export restraints, local content requirements, and administrative policies. Tariffs are the oldest and simplest instrument of trade policy. As we shall see later in this chapter, they are also the instrument that GATT has been most successful in limiting. But a fall in tariff barriers in recent decades has been accompanied by a rise in nontariff barriers such as subsidies, quotas, and voluntary export restraints.

Tariffs

A **tariff** is a tax levied on imports. The oldest form of trade policy, tariffs fall into two categories. **Specific tariffs** are levied as a fixed charge for each unit of a good imported (for example, $3 per barrel of oil). **Ad valorem tariffs** are levied as a proportion of the value of the imported good. An example of an ad valorem tariff is the 25 percent tariff the American government placed on imported light trucks (pickup trucks, four-wheel-drive vehicles, minivans) in the late 1980s.

A tariff raises the cost of imported products relative to domestic products. Thus the 25 percent tariff on light trucks imported into the United States increased the price of European and Japanese light truck imports relative to U.S.-produced light trucks. This tariff has afforded some protection for the market share of U.S. auto manufacturers (although a cynic might note that, in practice, all the tariff did was speed up the plans of European and Japanese automobile companies to build light trucks in the United States). While the principal objective of most tariffs is to protect domestic producers and employees against foreign competition, they also raise revenue for the government. Until the introduction of the income tax, for example, the U.S. government raised most of its revenues from tariffs.

The important thing to understand about a tariff is who suffers and who gains. The government gains, because the tariff increases government revenues. Domestic producers gain, because the tariff gives them some protection against foreign competitors by increasing the cost of imported foreign goods. Consumers lose since they must pay more for certain imports. Whether the gains to the government and domestic producers exceed the loss to consumers depends on various factors such as the amount of the tariff, the importance of the imported good to domestic consumers, the number of jobs saved in the protected industry, and so on.

Although detailed consideration of these issues is beyond the scope of this book, two conclusions can be derived from a more advanced analysis.[1] First, tariffs are unambiguously pro-producer and anti-consumer. While they protect producers from foreign competitors, this restriction of supply also raises domestic prices. Thus, as noted in Chapter 4, a recent study by Japanese economists calculated that in 1989 restrictions on imports of foodstuffs, cosmetics, and chemicals into Japan cost the average Japanese consumer about $890 per year in the form of higher prices.[2] The finding that import tariffs impose significant costs on domestic consumers in the form of higher prices has been the conclusion of almost all studies that have looked at this issue.[3] For another example, see the next "Country Focus," which looks at the cost to U.S. consumers of tariffs on imports into the United States.

A second point worth emphasizing is that tariffs reduce the overall efficiency of the world economy. They reduce efficiency because a protective tariff encourages domestic firms to produce products at home that, in theory, could be produced more efficiently abroad. The consequence is an inefficient utilization of resources. For example, tariffs on the importation of rice into South Korea have meant that the land of South Korean rice farmers has been used in an unproductive manner. It would make more sense for the South Koreans to purchase their rice from lower cost foreign producers and to utilize the land now employed in rice production in some other way, such as growing foodstuffs that cannot be produced more efficiently elsewhere, or for residential and industrial purposes.

Subsidies

A **subsidy** is a government payment to a domestic producer. Subsidies take many forms including cash grants, low-interest loans, tax breaks, and government equity participation in domestic firms. By lowering costs, subsidies help domestic producers in two ways: they help them compete against low-cost foreign imports and they help them gain export markets.

According to official national figures, government subsidies to industry in most industrialized countries during the late 1980s amounted to between 2 percent and 3.5 percent of the value of industrial output. (These figures exclude subsidies to agriculture and public services.) The average rate of subsidy in the United States was 0.5 percent; in Japan it was 1 percent; and in Europe it ranged from just below 2 percent in Great Britain and West Germany to as much as 6 to 7 percent in Sweden and Ireland.[4] These figures, however, almost certainly underestimate the true value of subsidies, since they are based only on cash grants and ignore other kinds of subsidies (e.g., equity participation or low-interest loans). A more detailed study of subsidies within the European Union (EU) was undertaken by the EU Commission. This study found that subsidies to manufacturing enterprises in 1990 ranged from a low of 2 percent of total valued added in Great Britain to a high of 14.6 percent in Greece. Among the four largest EU countries, Italy was the worst offender; its subsidies are three times those of Great Britain, twice those of Germany, and 1.5 times those of France.[5]

The main gains from subsidies accrue to domestic producers, whose international competitiveness is increased as a result of them. Advocates of strategic trade policy (which as you will recall from Chapter 4 is an outgrowth of the new trade theory) favor the use of subsidies to help domestic firms achieve a dominant position in those industries where economies of scale are important and the world market is not large enough to profitably support more than a few firms (e.g., aerospace, semiconductors). According to this argument, subsidies can help a firm achieve a first-mover

---

[1]For a detailed welfare analysis of the effect of a tariff, see P. R. Krugman and M. Obstfeld, *International Economics: Theory and Policy* (New York: Harper Collins, 1994), chap. 9.

[2]Y. Sazanami, S. Urata, and H. Kawai, *Measuring the Costs of Protection in Japan* (Washington, DC: Institute for International Economics, 1994).

[3]See J. Bhagwati, *Protectionism* (Cambridge, MA: MIT Press, 1988), and "Costs of Protection," *Journal of Commerce*, September 25, 1991, p. 8A.

[4]"From the Sublime to the Subsidy," *The Economist*, February 24, 1990, p. 71.

[5]"Aid Addicts," *The Economist*, August 8, 1992, p. 61.

COUNTRY FOCUS
The Costs of Protectionism in the United States

The United States likes to think of itself as a nation that is committed to unrestricted free trade. In their negotiations with trading partners, such as China, the European Union, and Japan, U.S. trade representatives can often be heard claiming that the U.S. economy is an open one with few import tariffs. However, while it is true that tariffs on the importation of goods into the United States are low when compared to those found in many other industrialized nations, they still exist. A recent study concluded that during the 1980s these tariffs cost U.S. consumers about $32 billion per year.

The study, by Gary Hufbauer and Kim Elliott of the Institute for International Economics, looked at the effect of import tariffs on economic activity in 21 industries with annual sales of $1 billion or more that the United States protected most heavily from foreign competition. The industries looked at included apparel, ceramic tiles, luggage, and sugar. In most of these industries import tariffs had originally been imposed to protect U.S. firms and employees from the effects of low-cost foreign competitors. The typical reasoning behind the tariffs was that without such protection, U.S. firms in these industries would go out of business and substantial unemployment would result. So the tariffs were presented as having positive effects for the U.S. economy, not to mention the U.S. Treasury, which benefited from the associated revenues.

What the study found, however, was that while these import tariffs saved about 200,000 jobs in the protected industries that would otherwise have been lost to foreign competition, they also cost American consumers about $32 billion per year in the form of higher prices. Even when the proceeds from the tariffs that accrued to the U.S. Treasury were added into the equation, the total cost to the nation of this protectionism still amounted to $10.2 billion per year, or over $50,000 per job saved.

Moreover, the two economists who undertook the study argued that these figures understated the true cost to the nation of the tariffs. They maintained that by making imports less competitive with American-made products, tariffs allowed domestic producers to charge more than they might otherwise because they did not have to compete with low-priced imports. By dampening competition, even a little, these tariffs removed an incentive for firms in the protected industries to become more efficient, thereby retarding economic progress. Further, the study's authors noted that if the tariffs had not been imposed, some of the $32 billion freed every year would undoubtedly have been spent on other goods and services, and that growth in these areas would have created additional jobs, thereby offsetting the loss of 200,000 jobs in the protected industries.

Sources: C. Hufbauer and K. A. Elliott, *Measuring the Costs of Protectionism in the United States* (Washington, DC: Institute for International Economics, 1993), and S. Nasar, "The High Costs of Protectionism," *New York Times*, November 12, 1993, pp. C1, C2.

advantage in an emerging industry (just as U.S. government subsidies, in the form of substantial R&D grants, allegedly helped Boeing). If this is achieved, further gains to the domestic economy arise from the employment and tax revenues that a major global company can generate.

On the other hand, subsidies must be paid for. Typically governments pay for subsidies by taxing individuals. Therefore, whether subsidies generate national benefits that exceed their national costs is debatable. Moreover, in practice many subsidies are not that successful at increasing the international competitiveness of domestic producers. Rather, they tend to protect the inefficient, rather than promote efficiency.

Import Quotas and Voluntary Export Restraints

An **import quota** is a direct restriction on the quantity of some good that may be imported into a country. The restriction is normally enforced by issuing import licenses to a group of individuals or firms. For example, the United States has a quota on imports of cheese. The only firms allowed to import cheese are certain trading companies, each of which is allocated the right to import a maximum number of pounds of cheese each year. In some cases the right to sell is given directly to the governments of exporting countries. This is the case for sugar and textile imports in the United States.

A variant on the import quota is the voluntary export restraint (VER). A **voluntary export restraint** is a quota on trade imposed by the exporting country, typically at the request of the importing country's government. One of the most famous examples is the limitation on auto exports to the United States enforced by Japanese automobile producers in 1981. A response to direct pressure from the U.S. government, this VER limited Japanese imports to no more than 1.68 million vehicles per year. The agreement was revised in 1984 to allow Japanese producers to import 1.85 million vehicles per year. In 1985 the agreement was allowed to lapse, but the Japanese government indicated its intentions at that time to continue to restrict exports to the United States to 1.85 million vehicles per year.[6]

Foreign producers agree to VERs because they fear that if they do not, far more damaging punitive tariffs or import quotas might follow. Agreeing to a VER, therefore, is seen as a way of making the best of a bad situation by appeasing protectionist pressures in a country.

As with tariffs and subsidies, both import quotas and VERs benefit domestic producers by limiting import competition. On the other hand, quotas do not benefit consumers. An import quota or VER always raises the domestic price of an imported good. When imports are limited to a low percentage of the market by a quota or VER, the effect is to bid the price up for that limited foreign supply. In the case of the automobile industry, for example, the VER increased the price for the limited supply of Japanese imports into the United States. As a result, according to a study by the U.S. Federal Trade Commission, the automobile industry VER cost U.S. consumers about $1 billion per year between 1981 and 1985. That $1 billion per year went to Japanese producers in the form of higher prices.[7]

Local Content Requirements

A **local content requirement** is a demand that some specific fraction of a good be produced domestically. The requirement can be expressed either in physical terms (e.g., 75 percent of component parts for this product must be produced locally) or in value terms (e.g., 75 percent of the value of this product must be produced locally). Local content regulations have been widely used by developing countries to shift their manufacturing base from the simple assembly of products whose parts are manufactured elsewhere into the local manufacture of component parts. More recently, the issue of local content has been raised by several developed countries. In the United States, for example, pressure is building to insist that 75 percent of the component parts that go into cars built in the United States by Japanese companies such as Toyota and Honda be manufactured in the United States. Both Toyota and Honda have reacted to such pressures by announcing their intention to buy more American-manufactured parts.

From the view of a domestic producer of component parts, local content regulations provide protection in the same way an import quota does: by limiting foreign competition. The aggregate economic effects are also the same; domestic producers benefit, but the restrictions on imports raise the prices of imported components. In

[6]R. W. Crandall, *Regulating the Automobile* (Washington, DC: Brookings Institute, 1986).

[7]Quoted in Krugman and Obstfeld, *International Economics*.

turn, higher prices for imported components are passed on to consumers of the final product in the form of higher final prices. So as with all trade policies, local content regulations tend to benefit producers and not consumers.

Administrative Policies

In addition to the formal instruments of trade policy, governments of all types sometimes use a range of informal or administrative policies to restrict imports and boost exports. **Administrative trade policies** are bureaucratic rules that are designed to make it difficult for imports to enter a country. Some would argue that the Japanese are the masters of this kind of trade barrier. In recent years Japan's formal tariff and nontariff barriers have been among the lowest in the world. However, critics charge that their informal administrative barriers to imports more than compensate for this. One example is that of tulip bulbs; the Netherlands exports tulip bulbs to almost every country in the world except Japan. Japanese customs inspectors insist on checking every tulip bulb by cutting it vertically down the middle, and even Japanese ingenuity cannot put them back together again! Another example concerns the U.S. express mail operator Federal Express. Federal Express has had a tough time expanding its global express services into Japan, primarily because Japanese customs inspectors insist on opening a large portion of express packages to check for pornography—a process that can delay an "express" package for days. Japan is not the only country that engages in such policies. France required that all imported videotape recorders arrive through a small customs entry point that was both remote and poorly staffed. The resulting delays kept Japanese VCRs out of the French market until a VER agreement was negotiated.[8] As with all instruments of trade policy, administrative instruments benefit producers and hurt consumers, who are denied access to possibly superior foreign products.

❧ THE CASE FOR GOVERNMENT INTERVENTION

Now that we have reviewed the various instruments of trade policy that governments can use, it is time to take a more detailed look at the case for government intervention in international trade. In general, there are two types of argument for government intervention—political and economic. Political arguments for intervention are concerned with protecting the interests of certain groups within a nation (normally producers), often at the expense of other groups (normally consumers). Economic arguments for intervention are typically concerned with boosting the overall wealth of a nation (to the benefit of all, both producers and consumers).

Political Arguments for Intervention

Political arguments for government intervention cover a range of issues including protecting jobs, protecting industries deemed important for national security, and retaliating to unfair foreign competition. Political arguments for government intervention are not always based on careful economic reasoning. Thus they tend to be relatively easy for economists to refute.

Protecting jobs and industries
Perhaps the most common political argument for government intervention is that it is necessary for protecting jobs and industries from foreign competition. The voluntary export restraints (VERs) that offered some protection to the U.S. automobile, machine tool, and steel industries during the 1980s were motivated by such considerations. Similarly, Japan's quotas on imports of rice are aimed at protecting jobs in that country's agricultural sector. The same motives underlay the establishment of the Common Agricultural Policy (CAP) by the European Union. The CAP was designed to protect the jobs of Europe's politically powerful farmers

---

[8]Bhagwati, *Protectionism*; and "Japan to Curb VCR Exports," *New York Times*, November 21, 1983, p. D5.

by restricting imports and guaranteeing prices. However, the higher prices that resulted from the CAP have cost Europe's consumers dearly. This is true of most attempts to protect jobs and industries through government intervention. As we saw earlier in the chapter, all that the VER in the automobile industry succeeded in doing was raising the price of Japanese imports, at a cost of $1 billion per year to U.S. consumers.

In addition to hurting consumers, trade controls may sometimes hurt the very producers they are intended to protect. In Chapter 4, for example, we noted how the VER agreement in the U.S. machine tool industry has been self-defeating. By limiting Japanese and Taiwanese machine tool imports, the VER raised the prices of machine tools purchased by U.S. manufacturers to levels above those prevailing in the world market. In turn, this raised the capital costs of the U.S. manufacturing industry in general, thereby decreasing its international competitiveness.

National security

Countries sometimes argue that it is necessary to protect certain industries because they are important for national security. Defense-related industries often get this kind of attention (e.g., aerospace, advanced electronics, semiconductors, etc.). Although not as common as it used to be, this argument is still made from time to time. Those in favor of protecting the U.S. semiconductor industry from foreign competition, for example, argue that semiconductors are now such important components of defense products that it would be dangerous to rely primarily on foreign producers for them. In 1986 this argument helped persuade the federal government to support Sematech, a consortium of 14 U.S. semiconductor companies that accounts for 90 percent of the U.S. industry's revenues. Sematech's mission is to conduct joint research into manufacturing techniques that can be parceled out to members. The U.S. government provides a $100 million per year subsidy to Sematech.

Retaliation

Some argue that governments should use the threat to intervene in trade policy as a bargaining tool to help open foreign markets and force trading partners to "play by the rules of the game." Successive U.S. governments have been among those that adopted this "get tough" approach. The opening case to this chapter illustrates how the U.S. government recently used the threat of imposing trade sanctions on Japanese imports, including punitive tariffs, to pry open the Japanese market for cellular telephone equipment. Similarly, the U.S. government also successfully used the same threat of punitive trade sanctions to get the Chinese government to enforce its intellectual property laws. As you will recall from Chapter 2, lax enforcement of these laws had given rise to massive copyright infringements in China that had been costing U.S. companies such as Microsoft hundreds of millions of dollars per year in lost sales revenues. After the United States threatened to impose 100 percent tariffs on a range of Chinese imports into the United States, and after harsh words between officials from the two countries, the Chinese backed down at the 11th hour and agreed to tighter enforcement of intellectual property regulations.[9]

If it works, such a politically motivated rationale for government intervention may liberalize trade and bring with it economic gains. It is a risky strategy, however; the country that is being pressured might not back down and instead might raise trade barriers of its own. This is exactly what the Chinese government threatened to do when pressured by the United States, although it ultimately did back down. If a government does not back down, however, the results could be higher trade barriers all around and an economic loss to all involved.

---

[9]N. Dunne and R. Waters, "U.S. Waves a Big Stick at Chinese Pirates," *Financial Times,* January 6, 1995, p. 4.

Economic Arguments for Intervention

With the development of the new trade theory and strategic trade policy (see Chapter 4), the economic arguments for government intervention have undergone something of a renaissance in recent years. Until the early 1980s, most economists saw little benefit in government intervention and strongly advocated a free trade policy. This position has changed somewhat with the development of strategic trade policy, although as we will see in the next section, there are still strong economic arguments for sticking to a free trade stance.

The infant industry argument

The infant industry argument is by far the oldest economic argument for government intervention. It was first proposed by Alexander Hamilton in 1792. According to this argument, many developing countries have a potential comparative advantage in manufacturing, but new manufacturing industries there cannot initially compete with well-established industries in developed countries. To allow manufacturing to get a toehold, the argument is that governments should temporarily support new industries (with tariffs, import quotas, and subsidies) until they have grown strong enough to meet international competition.

This argument has had substantial appeal for the governments of developing nations during the past 40 years. Moreover, the infant industry argument has been recognized as a legitimate reason for protectionism by the GATT. Nevertheless, many economists remain very critical of this argument. They make two main points. First, protection of manufacturing from foreign competition does no good unless the protection helps make the industry efficient. In case after case, however, protection seems to have done little more than foster the development of inefficient industries that have little hope of ever competing in the world market. Brazil, for example, built the world's 10th largest auto industry behind tariff barriers and quotas. Once those barriers were removed in the late 1980s, however, foreign imports soared and the industry was forced to face up to the fact that after 30 years of protection, the Brazilian industry was one of the world's most inefficient.[10]

Second, the infant industry argument relies on an assumption that firms are unable to make efficient long-term investments by borrowing money from the domestic or international capital market. Consequently, governments have been required to subsidize long-term investments. Given the development of global capital markets over the past 20 years, this assumption no longer looks as valid as it once did (see Chapter 11 for details). Today if a developing country really does have a potential comparative advantage in a manufacturing industry, firms in that country should be able to borrow money from the capital markets to finance the required investments. Moreover, given financial support, firms based in countries with a potential comparative advantage have an incentive to go through the necessary period of initial losses in order to make long-run gains without requiring government protection. This is what many Taiwanese and South Korean firms did in industries such as textiles, semiconductors, machine tools, steel, and shipping. Thus, given efficient global capital markets, the only industries that would require government protection would be those that are not worthwhile.

Strategic trade policy

The strategic trade policy argument has been proposed by the new trade theorists.[11] We reviewed the basic argument in Chapter 4 when we considered the new trade theory. To recap, the new trade theory argues that in industries where the

---

[10]Brazil's Auto Industry Struggles to Boost Global Competitiveness," *Journal of Commerce*, October 10, 1991, p. 6A.

[11]For reviews see J. A. Brander, "Rationales for Strategic Trade and Industrial Policy," in *Strategic Trade Policy and the New International Economics*, ed. P. R. Krugman (Cambridge, MA: MIT Press, 1986); P. R. Krugman, "Is Free Trade Passé?" *Journal of Economic Perspectives* 1 (1987), pp. 131–44; and P. R. Krugman, "Does the New Trade Theory Require a New Trade Policy?" *World Economy* 15, no. 4 (1992), pp. 423–41.

existence of substantial scale economies implies that the world market will profitably support only a few firms, countries may predominate in the export of certain products simply because they had firms that were able to capture first-mover advantages. The dominance of Boeing in the commercial aircraft industry is attributed to such factors.

Against this background, there are two components to the strategic trade policy argument. First, it is argued that by appropriate actions, a government can help raise national income if it can somehow ensure that the firm or firms to gain first-mover advantages in such an industry are domestic rather than foreign enterprises. Thus, according to the strategic trade policy argument, a government should use subsidies to support promising firms that are active in newly emerging industries. Advocates of this argument point out that the substantial R&D grants the U.S. government gave Boeing in the 1950s and 60s probably helped tilt the field of competition in the newly emerging market for jet passenger planes in Boeing's favor. (Boeing's 707 jet airliner was derived from a military plane.) Similar arguments are now made with regard to Japan's dominance in the production of liquid crystal display screens (used in laptop computers). Although these screens were invented in the United States, the Japanese government, in cooperation with major electronics companies, targeted this industry for research support in the late 1970s and early 80s. The result was that Japanese firms, not U.S. firms, subsequently captured the first-mover advantages in this market.

The second component of the strategic trade policy argument is that it might pay for a government to intervene in an industry if it helps domestic firms overcome the barriers to entry created by foreign firms that have already reaped first-mover advantages. This catch-up argument underlies government support of Airbus Industrie, Boeing's major competitor. Airbus is a consortium of four companies from Great Britain, France, Germany, and Spain formed in 1966. When it began production in the mid-1970s it had less than 5 percent of the world commercial aircraft market. By 1990 it had increased its share to over 30 percent and was beginning to threaten Boeing's dominance. How has Airbus achieved this feat? According to the U.S. government, the answer is a $13.5 billion subsidy from the governments of Great Britain, France, Germany, and Spain.[12] Without this subsidy, Airbus would have never been able to break into the world market. In another example, the rise to dominance of the Japanese semiconductor industry, despite the first-mover advantages enjoyed by U.S. firms, is attributed to intervention by the Japanese government. In this case the government did not subsidize the costs of domestic manufacturers. Rather, it protected the Japanese home market while pursuing policies that ensured Japanese companies got access to the necessary manufacturing and product know-how.

If these arguments are correct, they clearly suggest a rationale for government intervention in international trade. Specifically, governments should target technologies that may be important in the future and use subsidies to support development work aimed at commercializing those technologies. Furthermore, governments should provide export subsidies until the domestic firms have established first-mover advantages in the world market. Government support may also be justified if it can help domestic firms overcome the first-mover advantages enjoyed by foreign competitors and emerge as viable competitors in the world market (as in the Airbus and semiconductor examples). In this case, a combination of home-market protection and export-promoting subsidies may be called for.

---

[12]"Airbus and Boeing: The Jumbo War," *The Economist*, June 15, 1991, pp. 65–66.

❧ THE REVISED CASE FOR FREE TRADE

As we have just seen, the strategic trade policy arguments of the new trade theorists suggest an economic justification for government intervention in international trade. This justification challenges the rationale for unrestricted free trade found in the work of classic trade theorists such as Adam Smith and David Ricardo. In response to this challenge to economic orthodoxy, a number of economists—including some of those responsible for the development of the new trade theory, such as Paul Krugman of MIT—have been quick to point out that although strategic trade policy looks nice in theory, in practice it may be unworkable. This response to the strategic trade policy argument constitutes the revised case for free trade.[13]

Retaliation and Trade War

Krugman argues that strategic trade policy aimed at establishing domestic firms in a dominant position in a global industry are beggar-thy-neighbor policies that boost national income at the expense of other countries. A country that attempts to use such policies will probably provoke retaliation. In many cases, the resulting trade war between two or more interventionist governments will leave all countries involved worse off than if a hands-off approach had been adopted in the first place. If the U.S. government were to respond to the Airbus subsidy by increasing its own subsidies to Boeing, for example, the result might be that the subsidies would cancel each other out. In the process, both European and U.S. taxpayers would end up supporting an expensive and pointless trade war, and both Europe and the United States would be worse off.

Krugman may be right about the danger of a strategic trade policy leading to a trade war. The problem, however, is how to respond when one's competitors are already being supported by government subsidies; that is, how should Boeing and the United States respond to the subsidization of Airbus? According to Krugman, the answer is probably not to engage in retaliatory action, but to help establish rules of the game that minimize the use of trade-distorting subsidies in the first place. This, of course, is what the GATT seeks to do.

Domestic Politics

Governments do not always act in the national interest when they intervene in the economy. Instead they are influenced by politically important interest groups. The European Union's support for the common agricultural policy, which arose because of the political power of French and German farmers, is an example of this. The CAP benefited inefficient farmers and the politicians who relied on the farm vote, but no one else. Thus a further reason for not embracing strategic trade policy, according to Krugman, is that such a policy is almost certain to be captured by special-interest groups within the economy, which will distort it to their own ends. Krugman concludes that with regard to the United States:

> To ask the Commerce Department to ignore special-interest politics while formulating detailed policy for many industries is not realistic; to establish a blanket policy of free trade, with exceptions granted only under extreme pressure, may not be the optimal policy according to the theory but may be the best policy that the country is likely to get.[14]

❧ DEVELOPMENT OF THE WORLD TRADING SYSTEM

We have seen in this chapter and the previous one that there are strong economic arguments for supporting unrestricted free trade. While many governments have recognized the value of these arguments, they have been unwilling to unilaterally lower their trade barriers for fear that other nations might not follow suit. Consider the

---

[13]For details see Krugman, "Is Free Trade Passé?" and Brander, "Rationales."
[14]Krugman, "Is Free Trade Passé?"

problem that two neighboring countries, say France and Italy, face when considering whether to lower barriers to trade between them. In principle, the government of Italy might favor lowering trade barriers, but it might be unwilling to do so for fear that France would not do the same. Instead, they might fear that the French will take advantage of Italy's low barriers to enter the Italian market, while at the same time continuing to shut Italian products out of their market by high trade barriers. The French government might believe it faces exactly the same dilemma. The essence of the problem is a lack of trust between the governments of France and Italy. Both governments recognize that their respective nations will benefit from lower trade barriers between them, but neither government is willing to lower barriers for fear that the other might not follow.[15]

How is such a deadlock to be resolved? Both countries could negotiate a set of rules that would govern cross-border trade and lower trade barriers. But who is to monitor the governments to make sure they are playing by the trade rules and not cheating? And who is to impose sanctions on a government that cheats? These are difficult questions, but they have an answer; both governments could set up an independent body whose function is to act as a referee. This referee could monitor trade between the countries, make sure that no side cheats, and impose sanctions on a country if it does cheat.

While it might sound unlikely that any government would compromise its national sovereignty by submitting to such an arrangement, since World War II an international trading framework has evolved that has exactly these features. For its first 50 years this framework was known as the General Agreement on Tariffs and Trade (the GATT). Since 1995 it has been known as the World Trade Organization (WTO). Here we look at the evolution and workings of the GATT and the WTO. We begin, however, with a brief discussion of the pre-GATT history of world trade, since this helps set the scene.

From Smith to the Great Depression

As we saw in Chapter 4, the intellectual case for free trade goes back to the late 18th century and the work of Adam Smith and David Ricardo. Free trade as a government policy was first officially embraced by Great Britain in 1846, when the British Parliament repealed the Corn Laws. The Corn Laws placed a high tariff on imports of foreign corn. The objectives of the Corn Law tariff were to raise government revenues and to protect British corn producers. There had been annual motions in Parliament in favor of free trade since the 1820s when David Ricardo was a member of Parliament. However, agricultural protection was withdrawn only as a result of a protracted debate when the effects of a harvest failure in Britain were compounded by the imminent threat of famine in Ireland. Faced with considerable hardship and suffering among the populace, Parliament narrowly reversed its long-held position.

During the next 80 years or so, Great Britain, as one of the world's dominant trading powers, pushed the case for trade liberalization; but by and large the British government was a voice in the wilderness. Its policy of unilateral free trade was not reciprocated by its major trading partners. The only reason Britain was able to hold on to this policy for so long was that, as the world's largest exporting nation, it had far more to lose from a trade war than did any other country.

By the 1930s, however, the British attempt to stimulate free trade was buried under the economic rubble of the Great Depression. The Great Depression had roots in the failure of the world economy to mount a sustained economic recovery after the end of World War I in 1918. Things got worse in 1929 with the U.S. stock

---

[15]This dilemma is a variant of the famous Prisoner's Dilemma, which has become a classic metaphor for the difficulty of achieving cooperation between self-interested and mutually suspicious entities. For a good general introduction see A. Dixit and B. Nalebuff, *Thinking Strategically: The Competitive Edge in Business, Politics, and Everyday Life* (New York: W. W. Norton & Co., 1991).

market collapse and the subsequent run on the U.S. banking system. Economic problems were compounded in 1930 when the U.S. Congress passed the Smoot-Hawley tariff. Aimed at avoiding rising unemployment by protecting domestic industries and diverting consumer demand away from foreign products, the Smoot-Hawley tariff erected an enormous wall of tariff barriers. Almost every industry was rewarded with its "made to order" tariff. A particularly odd aspect of the Smoot-Hawley tariff-raising binge was that the United States was running a balance-of-payment surplus at the time and it was the world's largest creditor nation. In any event, the Smoot-Hawley tariff had a damaging effect on employment abroad. Other countries reacted to the U.S. action by raising their own tariff barriers. U.S. exports tumbled in response, and the world slid further into the Great Depression.[16]

1947–1979: GATT, Trade Liberalization, and Economic Growth

The economic damage caused by the beggar-thy-neighbor trade policies that the Smoot-Hawley Act ushered in exerted a profound influence on the economic institutions and ideology of the post–World War II world. The United States emerged from the war not only victorious but also economically dominant. After the debacle of the Great Depression, opinion in the U.S. Congress had swung strongly in favor of free trade. As a consequence, under U.S. leadership, the General Agreement on Tariffs and Trade (GATT) was established in 1947.

The GATT is a multilateral agreement whose objective is to liberalize trade by eliminating tariffs, subsidies, import quotas, and the like. Since its foundation in 1947, the GATT's membership has grown from 19 to more than 120 nations. The GATT did not attempt to liberalize trade restrictions in one fell swoop; that would have been impossible. Rather, tariff reduction has been spread over eight rounds. The latest, the Uruguay Round, was launched in 1986 and completed in December 1993. In these rounds mutual tariff reductions are negotiated among all members, who then commit themselves not to raise import tariffs above negotiated rates. GATT regulations were enforced by a mutual monitoring mechanism. If a country believed that one of its trading partners was violating a GATT regulation, it could ask the Geneva-based bureaucracy that administered the GATT to investigate. If GATT investigators found the complaints to be valid, member countries could be asked to pressure the offending party to change its policies. In general such pressure has always been sufficient to get an offending country to change its policies. If it were not, the offending country could in theory have been expelled from the GATT.

In its early years the GATT was by most measures very successful. In the United States, for example, the average tariff declined by nearly 92 percent over the 33 years spanning the Geneva Round of 1947 and the Tokyo Round of 1973–79 (see Figure 5.1). Consistent with the theoretical arguments first advanced by Ricardo and reviewed in Chapter 4, the move toward free trade under the GATT appeared to stimulate economic growth. From 1953 to 1963 world trade grew at an annual rate of 6.1 percent, and world income grew at an annual rate of 4.3 percent. Performance in the period 1963 to 1973 was even better; world trade grew at 8.9 percent per annum, and world income grew at 5.1 percent per annum.[17]

1980–1993: Disturbing Trends

During the 1980s and early 1990s, the world trading system erected by the GATT began to come under strain as protectionist pressures rose around the world. There were three main reasons for the rise in these pressures during the 1980s. First, Japan's economic success strained the world trading system. Japan was in ruins when the GATT was created. By the early 1980s, however, it had become the world's second largest economy and its largest exporter. Japan's success in such

---

[16]Note that the Smoot-Hawley tariff did not cause the Great Depression. However, the beggar-thy-neighbor trade policies that it ushered in certainly made things worse. See Bhagwati, *Protectionism.*

[17]Ibid.

FIGURE 5.1   Average Reductions in U.S. Tariff Rates, 1947–85

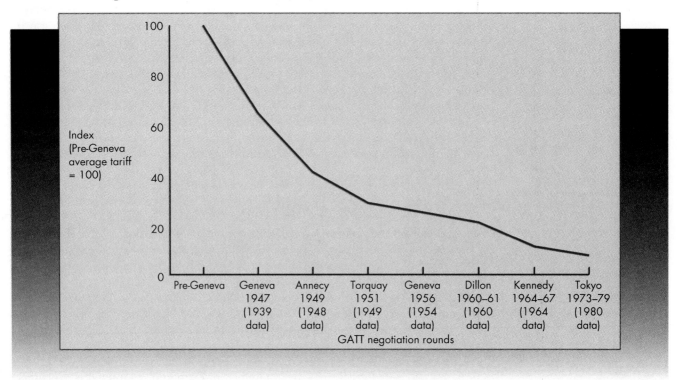

Note: Indexes are calculated from percentage reductions in average weighted tariff rates given in Finger, 1979 (Table 1, p. 425), World Bank, 1987 (Table 8.1, p. 136), and World Bank, World Development Report, Oxford University Press, 1994. Weighted average U.S. tariff rate after Tokyo Round was 4.6 percent (World Bank, 1987).

industries as automobiles and semiconductors by itself might have been enough to strain the world trading system. Things were made worse, however, by the widespread perception in the West that despite low tariff rates and subsidies, Japanese markets were closed to imports and foreign investment by administrative trade barriers.

Second, the world trading system was further strained by the persistent trade deficit in the world's largest economy, the United States. Although the deficit peaked in 1987 at over $170 billion, by the end of 1992 the annual rate was still running at about $80 billion. From a political perspective, the matter was worsened in 1992 by the $45 billion deficit in U.S. trade with Japan—a country perceived as not playing by the rules. The consequences of the U.S. deficit included painful adjustments in industries such as automobiles, machine tools, semiconductors, steel, and textiles, where domestic producers steadily lost market share to foreign competitors. The resulting unemployment gave rise to renewed protectionist pressures in the U.S. Congress.

A third reason for the trend toward greater protectionism was that many countries found ways to get around GATT regulations. Bilateral voluntary export restraints (VERs) circumvent GATT agreements, because neither the importing country nor the exporting country complains to the GATT bureaucracy in Geneva—and without a complaint, the GATT bureaucracy can do nothing. Exporting countries agreed to VERs to avoid far more damaging punitive tariffs. One of the best-known examples is the VER between Japan and the United States, under which Japanese producers promised to limit their auto imports into the United States as a way of defusing growing trade tensions. According to a World Bank study, 13 percent of the imports of industrialized countries in 1981 were subjected to nontariff trade barriers such as VERs. By 1986 this figure had increased to 16 percent. The most rapid rise was in the United States, where the value of imports affected by nontariff barriers (primarily VERs) increased by 23 percent between 1981 and 1986.[18]

---

[18]World Bank, *World Development Report* (New York: Oxford University Press, 1987).

The Uruguay Round and the World Trade Organization

Against the background of rising protectionist pressures, in 1986 GATT members embarked on their eighth round of negotiations to reduce tariffs, the Uruguay Round (so named because they occurred in Uruguay). This was the most difficult round of negotiations yet, primarily because it was also the most ambitious. Until now GATT rules had applied only to trade in manufactured goods and commodities. In the Uruguay Round member countries sought to extend GATT rules to cover trade in services. They also sought to write rules governing the protection of intellectual property, to reduce agricultural subsidies, and to strengthen the GATT's monitoring and enforcement mechanisms.

The Uruguay Round dragged on for seven years. For a time it looked as if an agreement might not be possible, raising fears that the world might slip into a trade war. The main impediment to an agreement was a long-standing dispute between the United States and the European Union on agricultural subsidies. An agreement had to be reached before December 16, 1993, which was when the "fast-track negotiating authority" granted to President Bill Clinton by the U.S. Congress would have expired. Had this authority expired, any agreement would have required approval by the U.S. Congress as a whole, rather than just the president, a much more difficult proposition. An 11th hour compromise on agricultural subsidies—which reduced the level of subsidies significantly, but not by as much as the United States had wanted—saved the day, and an agreement was reached on December 15, 1993. The agreement was signed by member-states at a meeting in Marrakech, Morocco, on April 15, 1994. It went into effect July 1, 1995.

The most important components of the Uruguay Round agreement are detailed in Table 5.1. The Uruguay Round agreement has the following effects: tariffs on industrial goods will be reduced by more than one-third; there will be a substantial reduction in agricultural subsidies; GATT fair trade and market access rules will be extended to cover a wide range of services; GATT rules will also now be extended to provide enhanced protection for patents, copyrights, and trademarks (intellectual property); barriers on trade in textiles will be significantly reduced over 10 years; GATT rules will in general be much clearer and stronger; and a World Trade Organization (WTO) will be created to implement the GATT agreement.

Services and intellectual property

In the long run the extension of GATT rules to cover services and intellectual property may be particularly significant. Until now GATT rules have applied only to industrial goods (i.e., manufactured goods and commodities). In 1992 world trade in services amounted to $900 billion out of a total of $3,580 billion. Extension of GATT rules to this important trading arena could significantly increase both the total share of world trade accounted for by services and the overall volume of world trade. Moreover, the extension of GATT rules to cover intellectual property will make it much easier for high-technology companies to do business in developing nations where intellectual property rules have historically been poorly enforced (see Chapter 2 for details). High-technology companies will now have a mechanism to force countries to prohibit the piracy of intellectual property.

The World Trade Organization

The clarification and strengthening of GATT rules and the creation of the World Trade Organization also hold out the promise of more effective policing and enforcement of GATT rules. Promoting trade should spur overall economic growth and development. The WTO will act as an umbrella organization that will encompass the GATT along with two new sister bodies; one on services and the other on intellectual property. The WTO will take over responsibility for arbitrating trade disputes and monitoring the trade policies of member countries. While the WTO will operate as GATT now does—on the basis of consensus—in dispute settlements, member countries will no longer be able to block adoption of arbitration reports. Arbitration panel reports on trade disputes between member countries will be automatically

Up to 1993	The 1993 Agreement	Main Impact
Industrial Tariffs		
Backbone of previous GATT rounds. Tariffs on industrial goods average 5% in industrialized countries; down from 40% in the late 1940s.	Rich countries will cut tariffs on industrial goods by more than one-third. Tariffs will be scrapped on over 40% of manufactured goods.	Easier access to world markets for exports of industrial goods. Lower prices for consumers.
Agriculture		
High farm subsidies and protected markets in U.S. and EC lead to overproduction and dumping.	Subsidies and other barriers to trade in agricultural products will be cut over six years. Subsidies cut by 20%. All import barriers will be converted to tariffs and cut by 36%.	Better market opportunities for efficient food producers. Lower prices for consumers. Restraint of farm subsidies war.
Services		
GATT rules do not extend to services. Many countries protect service industries from international competition.	GATT rules on fair trade principles extended to cover many services. Failure to reach agreement on financial services and telecommunications. Special talks will continue.	Increase in trade in services. Further liberalization of trade in services now seems likely.
Intellectual Property		
Standards of protection for patents, copyrights, and trademarks vary widely. Ineffective enforcement of national laws a growing source of trade friction.	Extensive agreements on patents, copyrights, and trademarks. International standards of protection and agreements for effective enforcement all established.	Increased protection and reduction of intellectual property piracy will benefit producers of intellectual property (e.g., computer software firms, performing artists). Will increase technology transfer.
Textiles		
Rich countries have restricted imports of textiles and clothing through bilateral quotas under Multi-Fiber Arrangement (MFA).	MFA quotas progressively dismantled over 10 years and tariffs reduced. Normal GATT rules will apply at end of 10 years.	Increased trade in textiles should benefit developing countries. Reduced prices for consumers worldwide.
GATT Rules		
GATT remains the same as when drafted in 1947, even though many more countries have entered the world trading community and trade patterns have shifted.	Many GATT rules revised and updated. They include codes on customs valuation and import licensing, customs unions and free trade areas, and rules dealing with waivers from GATT regulations.	Greater transparency, security, and predictability in trading policies.
World Trade Organization		
GATT originally envisioned as part of an International Trade Organization. ITO never ratified and GATT applied provisionally.	GATT becomes a permanent world trade body covering goods, services, and intellectual property with a common disputes procedure. WTO to implement results of Uruguay Round.	More effective advocacy and policing of the international trading system.

Source: "The GATT Deal," Financial Times, December 16, 1993, pp. 4–7.

adopted by the WTO unless there is a consensus to reject them. Countries that have been found by the arbitration panel to violate GATT rules may appeal to a permanent appellate body, but its verdict will be binding. If offenders then fail to comply with the recommendations of the arbitration panel, trading partners will have the right to compensation or, in the last resort, to impose (commensurate) trade sanctions. Every stage of the procedure will be subject to strict time limits. Thus the WTO will have something that the GATT never had—teeth.[19]

Implications of the Uruguay Round
Some general implications of the GATT deal are noted in Table 5.1. On balance, the world is better off with a GATT deal than without it. Without the deal the world might have slipped into increasingly dangerous trade wars, which might have triggered a recession. With a GATT deal concluded, the current world trading system looks secure, and there is a good possibility the world economy will now grow faster than would otherwise have been the case. Estimates as to the overall impact of the GATT agreement, however, are not that dramatic. Three studies undertaken in mid-1993 (before the agreement was finalized) estimated the deal will add between $213 billion and $274 billion in 1992 U.S. dollars to aggregate world income by 2002—or about 0.75 percent to 1 percent of gross global income by that time.[20]

Others argue that these figures underestimate the potential gain because they do not factor in the gains from the liberalization of trade in services, stronger trade rules, and greater business confidence. Considering such factors, the GATT agreement could cause global economic output to be as much as 8 percent higher than it would otherwise have been by 2002.[21] Whatever figure is closer to the truth, keep in mind what a successful GATT agreement helps avoid—the risk of a trade war that might reduce global economic growth and raise prices for consumers around the globe.

For individual firms, there emerge some clear winners—and some that have not done so well—in the GATT deal. Two big winners in the United States are Caterpillar Inc. and Deere & Co, both manufacturers of heavy construction equipment. The GATT deal eliminates import tariffs on the construction equipment and engines that these companies produce. Caterpillar estimates the deal will add $125 million to its annual sales of $10 billion and result in another 800 jobs at Caterpillar and a further 1,600 jobs at Caterpillar's suppliers. Other big winners include many small exporters around the world, who will find that they like the simplified import licensing rules and steps for harmonizing customs procedures contained in the GATT deal. These rules promise to simplify the procedures for exporting—procedures that raise exporting costs and are argued to deter many small firms from getting into the export business.

Not everyone is pleased with the deal. While pharmaceutical companies are pleased that tariffs on drugs will be phased out over the next few years, they expressed disappointment that it will take 10 years to phase in patent protection for their products (weak patent protection in many countries has led to local competitors violating patents and copying the successful drugs of multinational pharmaceutical firms). Among the disappointed were financial services companies, particularly big banks. They had hoped the GATT deal would eliminate many of the barriers

---

[19]Frances Williams, "WTO—New Name Heralds New Powers," *Financial Times*, December 16, 1993, p. 5; and Frances Williams, "Gatt's Successor to Be Given Real Clout," *Financial Times*, April 4, 1994, p. 6.

[20]The studies are OECD and the World Bank, *Trade Liberalization: The Global Economic Implications*, Paris and Washington, 1993; OECD, *Assessing the Effects of the Uruguay Round*, Paris, 1993; and GATT Secretariat, *Background Paper: The Uruguay Round*, Gatt, 1993.

[21]Martin Wolf, "Doing Good Despite Themselves," *Financial Times*, December 16, 1993, p. 15.

that prevent them from selling their financial services across borders, but a failure to reach agreement resulted in financial services being excluded from the deal to extend GATT rules to services. Also disappointed was the Hollywood film and television industry. Hollywood had hoped to use the GATT to break down European quotas that limit the amount of U.S. movies that can be broadcast on European TV, but opposition from the French government led to this part of the deal being dropped in a last minute compromise.[22]

The Future: Unresolved Issues

The 1994 GATT deal still leaves a lot to be done on the international trade front. Substantial trade barriers still remain in areas such as financial services and broadcast entertainment, although these seem likely to be reduced eventually. More significantly perhaps, there are still a whole range of issues that GATT, and now the WTO, have yet to deal with but increasingly will need to. Three of the most important areas for future development are in the areas of environmentalism, workers' rights, and foreign direct investment.[23]

High on the list of the WTO's future concerns will be the interaction of environmental and trade policies and the issue of how best to promote sustainable development and ecological well-being without resorting to protectionism. The WTO will have to find ways to deal with the increasingly vigorous claims by environmentalists that expanded international trade encourages companies to locate factories in areas where they are freer to pollute and degrade the environment.

Paralleling environmental concerns are concerns that free trade encourages firms to shift their production to countries with low labor rates where workers' rights are routinely violated. The United States has repeatedly and unsuccessfully pressed for discussion of common international standards on workers' rights, an idea strongly opposed by poorer nations who fear it is just another excuse for protectionism by the rich.

GATT regulations have never been extended to embrace foreign direct investment (investment by a firm based in one country in productive facilities in another country). Given the globalization of production that we are now witnessing, barriers to foreign direct investment seem antiquated, and yet they are still widespread (we will discuss these in detail in Chapter 7). Currently many countries limit investment by foreign companies in their economies (e.g., local content requirements, local ownership rules, and even outright prohibition). Extending GATT to embrace foreign direct investment might require countries to grant establishment rights to foreign companies.

❧ IMPLICATIONS FOR BUSINESS

What are the implications of all this for business practice? Why should the international manager care about the political economy of free trade? About the relative merits of arguments for free trade and protectionism? The first answer to these questions concerns the impact of trade barriers on a firm's strategy. The second concerns the role that business firms can play in promoting free trade and/or trade barriers.

Trade Barriers and Firm Strategy

To understand how trade barriers impact a firm's strategy, consider first the material we covered in Chapter 4. Drawing on the theories of international trade, we discussed how it may make sense for the firm to disperse its production activities to those countries where they can be performed most efficiently. It may make sense for a firm to design and engineer its product in one country, to manufacture components in another, to perform final assembly operations in yet another country, and then to export the finished product to the rest of the world.

---

[22]Brent Bowers, "For Small Firms, Big Gains Are Seen in the Fine Print," *The Wall Street Journal*, December 16, 1993, p. A12; and "U.S. Business Likes Trade Pact as a Whole: But Not Some Parts," *The Wall Street Journal*, December 16, 1993, pp.A3, A13.
[23]"A Disquieting New Agenda for Trade," *The Economist*, July 16, 1994, pp. 55–56; and Frances Williams, "Trade Round Like This May Never Be Seen Again," *Financial Times*, December 16, 1993, p. 7.

Clearly, trade barriers are a constraint on a firm's ability to disperse its productive activities in such a manner. Tariff barriers raise the costs of exporting products to a country (or of exporting partly finished products between countries). This may put the firm at a competitive disadvantage vis-à-vis indigenous competitors in that country. In response, the firm may then find it economical to locate production facilities in that country so it can compete on an even footing with indigenous competitors. Voluntary export restraints (VERs) also may limit a firm's ability to serve a country from foreign locations. Again, the response by the firm might be to set up production facilities in that country—even though it may result in higher production costs. Such reasoning was one factor behind the rapid expansion of Japanese automaking capacity in the United States during the 1980s. This followed establishment of a VER agreement between the United States and Japan that limited U.S. imports of Japanese automobiles. For details, see the next "Management Focus," which describes how Toyota responded to protectionist threats by opening car plants in the United States and Europe.

To conform with local content regulations, a firm may have to locate more production activities in a given market than it would otherwise. Again, from the firm's perspective, the consequence might be to raise costs above the level that could be achieved if each production activity was dispersed to the optimal location for that activity. Even when trade barriers do not exist, the firm may still want to locate some production activities in a given country to reduce the threat of trade barriers being imposed in the future.

All the above effects are likely to raise the firm's costs above the level that could be achieved in a world without trade barriers. The higher costs that result need not translate into a significant competitive disadvantage, however, if the countries imposing trade barriers do so to the imported products of all foreign firms. But when trade barriers are targeted at exports from a particular nation, firms based in that nation may be at a competitive disadvantage vis-à-vis the firms of other nations (VERs are targeted trade barriers). One strategy the firm may adopt to deal with such targeted trade barriers is to move production into the country imposing barriers. Another strategy is to move production to countries whose exports are not targeted by the specific trade barrier.

Policy Implications

As noted in Chapter 4, business firms are major players on the international trade scene. Because of their pivotal role in international trade, business firms can and do exert a strong influence on government policy toward trade. This influence can encourage protectionism, or it can encourage the government to support the GATT and push for open markets and freer trade among all nations. Moreover, government policies with regard to international trade can have a direct impact on business.

Consistent with strategic trade policy, examples can be found of government intervention in the form of tariffs, quotas, and subsidies helping firms and industries establish a competitive advantage in the world economy. In general, however, the arguments contained in this chapter suggest that a policy of government intervention has the three following drawbacks. Intervention can be self-defeating, because it tends to protect the inefficient rather than help firms become efficient global competitors. Intervention is dangerous because it might invite retaliation and trigger a trade war. Finally, intervention is unlikely to be well executed, given the opportunity for such a policy to be captured by special interest groups. Does this mean that business should simply encourage government to adopt a laissez-faire, free trade policy?

Most economists would probably argue that the best interests of international business are served by a free trade stance, but not a laissez-faire stance. It is probably in the best long-run interests of the business community to encourage the government to aggressively promote greater free trade by, for example, strengthening the WTO. In general, business probably has much more to gain from government efforts to open protected markets to imports and foreign direct investment than from government efforts to support certain domestic industries in a manner consistent with the recommendations of strategic trade policy.

MANAGEMENT
FOCUS
Toyota's Response
to Rising
Protectionist
Pressures in
Europe and the
United States

In many respects Toyota has been a victim of its own success. Until the 1960s Toyota was viewed as little more than an obscure Japanese automobile company. In 1950 Toyota produced a mere 11,700 vehicles. In 1970 it was producing 1.6 million vehicles, and by 1990 the figure had increased to 4.12 million. In the process, Toyota rose to become the third largest automobile company and the largest automobile exporter in the world. In the view of most analysts, Toyota's dramatic rise was due to the company's world-class manufacturing and design skills. These made Toyota not only the most productive automobile company in the world, but also the one that consistently produced the highest quality and best-designed automobiles.

For most of its history Toyota has exported automobiles to the world market from its plants in Japan. However, by the early 1980s political pressures and talk of local content regulations in the United States and Europe were forcing an initially reluctant Toyota to rethink its exporting strategy. Toyota had already agreed to "voluntary" export restraints with the United States in 1981. The consequence for Toyota was stagnant export growth between 1981 and 1984. Against this background, in the early 1980s Toyota began to think seriously about setting up manufacturing operations overseas.

Toyota's first overseas operation was a 50/50 joint venture with General Motors established in February 1983 under the name New United Motor Manufacturing Inc. (NUMMI). NUMMI, which is based in Fremont, California, began producing Chevrolet Nova cars for GM in December 1984. The maximum capacity of the Fremont plant is about 250,000 cars per year.

For Toyota, the joint venture provided a chance to find out whether it could build quality cars in the United States using American workers and American suppliers. It also provided Toyota with experience dealing with an American union (the United Auto Workers union) and with a means of circumventing voluntary import restrictions. By the fall of 1986 the NUMMI plant was running at full capacity and early indications were that the plant was achieving productivity and quality levels close to those achieved at Toyota's major Takaoka plant in Japan.

This conclusion is reinforced by a phenomenon we touched on in Chapter 1—the increasing integration of the world economy and internationalization of production that has occurred over the last two decades. We live in a world where many firms of all national origins increasingly depend on globally dispersed production systems for their competitive advantage. Such systems are the result of free trade. Free trade has brought great advantages to firms that have exploited it and to consumers who benefit from the resulting lower prices. Given the danger of retaliatory action, business firms that lobby their governments to engage in protectionism must realize that by doing so they may be denying themselves the opportunity to build a competitive advantage by constructing a globally dispersed production system. Moreover, by encouraging their governments to engage in protectionism, their own activities and sales overseas may be jeopardized if other governments retaliate. This is a nontrivial danger for U.S. firms, which, despite their perceived relative decline, still have enormous economic interests abroad. The United States, after all, is still the world's number one exporter.

Encouraged by its success at NUMMI, in December 1985 Toyota announced it would build an automobile manufacturing plant in Georgetown, Kentucky. The plant, which came on stream in May 1988, officially had the capacity to produce 200,000 Toyota Camrys a year. However, by early 1990 it was producing the equivalent of 220,000 cars per year. This success was followed by an announcement in December 1990 that Toyota would build a second plant in Georgetown with a capacity to produce a further 200,000 vehicles per year. The two plants and NUMMI now give Toyota the capacity to build 660,000 vehicles per year in North America.

In addition to its North American transplant operations, Toyota moved to set up production facilities in Europe in response to growing protectionist pressures. Toyota was also anticipating the 1992 lowering of trade barriers among the member-states of the European Union. In 1989 the company announced it would build a plant in England with the capacity to manufacture 200,000 cars per year by 1997. The clear implication was that after 1992, much of the output of this

plant would be exported to the rest of the EU. This decision prompted the French prime minister to describe Britain as "a Japanese aircraft carrier, sitting off the coast of Europe waiting to attack." Fearing that the EU would limit its expansion, Toyota joined other Japanese automobile companies in agreeing to keep their share of the European auto market to under 11 percent, at least until 2000.

Despite Toyota's apparent commitment to expand its U.S. and European assembly operations, it has not all been smooth sailing. A major problem has been building an overseas supplier network that is comparable to Toyota's Japanese network. For example, in a 1990 meeting of Toyota's North American suppliers' association, Toyota executives informed their North American suppliers that the defect ratio for parts produced by 75 North American and European suppliers was 100 times greater than the defect ratio for parts supplied by 147 Japanese suppliers. Moreover, Toyota executives pointed out that parts manufactured by North American and European suppliers tended to be significantly more

expensive than comparable parts manufactured in Japan.

Due to these problems, Toyota initially imported many parts from Japan for its European and U.S. assembly operations. However, the general increase in imports of automobile components from Japan only heightened trade tensions between the two countries. The high volume of such imports has become a major sticking point in trade negotiations between the United States and Japan. In an attempt to diffuse the situation, Toyota is striving to increase the local content of cars assembled in North America and Europe. The company's plan was for 70 percent of the value of Toyota cars assembled in Europe and the United States to be locally produced by January 1996, up from less than 40 percent in 1990. To achieve this, Toyota embarked on an aggressive supplier education drive in both Europe and the United States aimed at familiarizing its local suppliers with Japanese production methods.

Source: C. W. L. Hill, "The Toyota Corporation in 1994," in C. W. L. Hill and G. R. Jones, *Strategic Management: An Integrated Approach* (Boston: Houghton Mifflin, 1995).

✖ SUMMARY OF CHAPTER

The objective of this chapter was to describe how the reality of international trade deviates from the theoretical ideal of unrestricted free trade that we reviewed in Chapter 4. In this chapter we have reviewed the various instruments of trade policy, reviewed the political and economic arguments for government intervention in international trade, reexamined the economic case for free trade in light of the strategic trade policy argument, and looked at the evolution of the world trading framework. The main conclusion reached is that, while a policy of free trade may not always be the theoretically optimal policy (given the arguments of the new trade theorists), in practice it is probably the best policy for a government to pursue. In particular, the long-run interests of business and consumers may be best served by strengthening

international institutions such as the WTO and the GATT. Given the danger that isolated protectionism might escalate into a trade war, business probably has far more to gain from government efforts to open protected markets to imports and foreign direct investment (through the WTO) than from government efforts to protect domestic industries from foreign competition.

In this chapter the following points have been made:

1. Tariffs raise the cost of imported products. Gains accrue to the government (from revenues) and to producers (who are protected from foreign competitors). Consumers lose, since they must pay more for imports.

2. By lowering costs, subsidies help domestic producers to compete against low-cost foreign imports and to gain export markets. However, subsidies must be paid for by taxpayers. Moreover, they tend to be captured by special interests who use them to protect the inefficient.

3. An import quota is a direct restriction imposed by an importing country on the quantity of some good that may be imported. A voluntary export restraint (VER) is a quota on trade imposed from the exporting country's side. Both import quotas and VERs benefit domestic producers by limiting import competition, but they result in higher prices, which hurts consumers.

4. A local content requirement is a requirement that some specific fraction of a good be produced domestically. Local content requirements benefit the producers of component parts, but they raise prices of imported components, which hurts consumers.

5. An administrative policy is an informal instrument or bureaucratic rule that can be used to restrict imports and boost exports. Such policies benefit producers but hurt consumers, who are denied access to possibly superior foreign products.

6. There are two types of arguments for government intervention in international trade: political and economic. Political arguments for intervention are concerned with protecting the interests of certain groups, often at the expense of other groups. Economic arguments for intervention are about boosting the overall wealth of a nation.

7. The most common political argument for intervention is that it is necessary to protect jobs. However, political intervention often hurts consumers and it can be self-defeating.

8. Countries sometimes argue that it is important to protect certain industries for reasons of national security.

9. Some argue that government should use the threat to intervene in trade policy as a bargaining tool to open foreign markets. This can be a risky policy; if it fails the result can be higher trade barriers all around.

10. The infant industry argument for government intervention is that to let manufacturing get a toehold, governments should temporarily support new industries. In practice, however, governments often end up protecting the inefficient.

11. Strategic trade policy suggests that with subsidies, government can help domestic firms gain first-mover advantages in global industries where economies of scale are important. Government subsidies may also help domestic firms overcome barriers to entry into such industries.

12. The problems with strategic trade policy are twofold: such a policy may invite retaliation, in which case all will lose, and strategic trade policy may be captured by special-interest groups, which will distort it to their own ends.

13. The Smoot-Hawley tariff, introduced in 1930, erected an enormous wall of tariff barriers to U.S. imports. Other countries responded by adopting similar tariffs, and the world slid further into the Great Depression

14. The GATT was a product of the post-war free trade movement. The GATT was successful in lowering trade barriers on manufactured goods and commodities. The move toward greater free trade under the GATT appeared to stimulate economic growth.

15. The completion of the Uruguay Round of GATT talks and the establishment of the World Trade Organization has strengthened the world trading system by extending GATT rules to services, increasing protection for intellectual property, reducing agricultural subsidies, and enhancing monitoring and enforcement mechanisms.

16. Trade barriers constrain a firm's ability to disperse its various production activities to optimal locations around the globe. One response to trade barriers is to establish more production activities in the protected country.

17. Business may have more to gain from government efforts to open protected markets to imports and foreign direct investment, than from government efforts to protect domestic industries from foreign competition.

✎ CRITICAL DISCUSSION QUESTIONS

1. Do you think the U.S. government is correct to use a "get tough" approach in its trade negotiations with Japan (see opening case)? What are the risks of such an approach?

2. Whose interests should be the paramount concern of government trade policy—the interests of producers (businesses and their employees) or those of consumers?

3. Given the arguments relating to the new trade theory and strategic trade policy, what kind of trade policy should business be pressuring government to adopt?

4. You are an employee of a U.S. firm that produces personal computers in Thailand and then exports them to the United States and other countries for sale. The personal computers were originally produced in Thailand to take advantage of relatively low labor costs and a skilled work force. Other possible locations considered at the time were Malaysia and Hong Kong. The U.S. government decides to impose punitive 100 percent ad valorem tariffs on imports of computers from Thailand to punish the country for administrative trade barriers that restrict U.S. exports to Thailand. How should your firm respond? What does this tell you about the use of targeted trade barriers?

✎ CLOSING CASE Malaysia and Britain Enter into a Trade Dispute

In mid-February 1994 the British paper, the *Sunday Times* ran an article that alleged that a 1 billion sterling ($750m) sale of defense equipment by British companies to Malaysia was secured only after bribes had been paid to Malaysian government officials and after the British Overseas Development Administration (ODA) had agreed to approve a 234 million sterling grant to the Malaysian government for a hydroelectric dam of (according to the *Sunday Times*) dubious economic value. The clear implication was that U.K. officials, in their enthusiasm to see British companies win a large defense contract, had yielded to pressures from "corrupt" Malaysian officials for bribes—both personal and in the form of the 234 million sterling development grant.[24]

What happened next took everyone by surprise. The Malaysian government promptly announced a ban on the import of all British goods and services into Malaysia and demanded an apology from the British Government. Officially the ban applied only to government orders for British goods and services; the private sector was free to buy as it chose. However, British companies with experience in the region were nervous that the private sector would follow the government's lead in shunning British products. At stake was as much as 4 billion sterling in British exports and construction activities in Malaysia and a presence in one of the world's fastest growing developing economies (Malaysia's economic growth has averaged 8 percent per annum since 1989). In announcing the ban, Malaysia's prime minister, Dr. Mahathir Mohamad, noted that the British media portrays Malaysians as corrupt because "they are not British and not white" . . . and "we believe the foreign media must learn the fact that developing countries, including a country led by a brown Moslem, have the ability to manage their own affairs successfully."[25]

The British government responded by stating it could not tell the British press what and what not to publish, to which Dr. Mahathir replied there would be "no contracts for British press freedom to tell lies." At the same time the British government came under attack from members of Parliament in Britain, who suspected the government acted unethically and approved the ODA hydroelectric grant to help British companies win orders in Malaysia.

CASE DISCUSSION QUESTIONS

1. What does this case teach us about the relationship between politics and international trade?

2. You are the CEO of a British company that now faces the loss of a lucrative contract in Malaysia because of the dispute. What action should you take?

3. How do you think the British government should respond to the Malaysian action?

---

[24]Keiran Cooke, "Honeypot of as Much as 4 Billion Sterling down the Drain," *Financial Times*, February 26, 1994, p. 4.

[25]Keiran Cooke, "Arrogance of the West Riles a Maverick," *Financial Times*, February 26, 1994, p. 4; and Rober Peston, "Malaysia PM Says Die Is Cast over U.K. Ban," *Financial Times*, March 17, 1994, p. 1.

CHAPTER SIX

FOREIGN DIRECT INVESTMENT

ELECTROLUX INVESTS IN ASIA AND EASTERN EUROPE

With 1994 sales of over $13.5 billion, Electrolux is one of the world's largest manufacturers of household appliances (washing machines, dishwashers, refrigerators, vacuum cleaners, etc.). A Swedish company with a small home market, Electrolux has always had to look to other markets for its growth. As a result, by 1994 the company was generating over 85 percent of its sales outside Sweden. Most of this activity was in Western Europe, where Electrolux held a 25 percent share of the total market for household appliances in 1994, and in North America.

An early 1990s planning review at Electrolux concluded demand for household appliances was now mature in these regions. Since future growth would be limited to replacement demand and the growth in population, it would be unlikely to exceed 2 to 3 percent per annum. It was at this point that Leif Johansson, the CEO of Electrolux, decided the company was too dependent on these mature markets. He reasoned the company would have to expand aggressively into the emerging markets of Asia and Eastern Europe if it was to maintain its historic growth rate. The company estimated that demand for household appliances in these regions could grow at 20 percent per year for at least the next decade, and probably beyond. Accordingly, in 1994 he set an

ambitious goal for Electrolux; the company would have to double its sales in these emerging markets from the current $1.35 billion, or 10 percent of total 1994 sales, to $2.7 billion by 1997. As an additional goal he stated that Electrolux should become one of the top three suppliers of household goods in Southeast Asia by the year 2000.

In addition to the obvious growth potential, another consideration for Electrolux was that its main global competitors, General Electric and Whirlpool of the United States and Germany's Bosch-Siemans, had recently announced similar plans. Electrolux thought it had better move quickly, lest it be left out in the race to profit from these emerging markets.

Having committed itself to expansion, the next issue Electrolux had to grapple with was how to achieve its ambitious goals. A combination of cost considerations

and import barriers made direct exporting from its Western European and North American plants uneconomical. Instead, different approaches are being adopted for different regions and countries. Acquisitions of going concerns, greenfield developments, joint ventures, and enhanced marketing are all being considered. Electrolux says it is prepared to spend $200 million per year to increase its presence in these emerging markets.

Electrolux made its fist move into Eastern Europe in 1991 when it acquired Lehel, Hungary's largest manufacturer of household appliances. In addition, Electrolux has decided to establish 100 percent owned operating companies in Russia, Poland, and the Czech Republic. Each of these operating subsidiaries will be a greenfield development. In Asia there is a much greater need to adapt to local conditions. Regulations concerning foreign ownership in India and China, for example, virtually compel Electrolux to work through joint ventures with local partners. In China, the world's fastest growing market, the company already has joint ventures in compressors, vacuum cleaners, and water purification equipment, and it plans to spend $100 million to build another five manufacturing plants in the country by 1997. In Southeast Asia the emphasis is on the marketing of goods imported from China, rather than local production.

Source: C. Brown-Humes, "Electrolux Plugs into Households All over Asia," *Financial Times,* April 27, 1995, p. 15.

❧ INTRODUCTION

This chapter is concerned with foreign direct investment (FDI). **Foreign direct investment** occurs when a firm invests directly in facilities to produce and/or market a product in a foreign country. The 1991 purchase of Hungary's Lehel by Electrolux is an example of FDI, as is the company's decision to invest in joint ventures to manufacture products in China, and the company's investment in greenfield (new) 100 percent owned production facilities in Russia, Poland, and the Czech Republic (for details, see the opening case). The U.S. Department of Commerce has come up with a more precise definition of FDI. According to the department, FDI occurs whenever a U.S. citizen, organization, or affiliated group takes an interest of 10 percent or more in`a foreign business entity. Once a firm undertakes FDI it becomes a **multinational enterprise** (the meaning of multinational here being "more than one country").

There is an important distinction between FDI and **foreign portfolio investment** (FPI). Foreign portfolio investment is investment by individuals, firms, or public bodies (e.g., national and local governments) in foreign financial instruments (e.g., government bonds, foreign stocks). FPI does not involve taking a significant equity stake in a foreign business entity. FPI is determined by different factors than FDI and raises different issues. Accordingly, we do not consider FPI in this chapter, but we do discuss it in Chapter 11 in our review of the international capital market.

In Chapter 4 we considered several theories that sought to explain the pattern of trade between countries. These theories focus on why countries export some products and import others. But none of these theories addresses why a firm might decide to invest directly in production facilities in a foreign country, rather than exporting its domestic production to that country. In other words, the theories we reviewed in Chapter 4 do not explain the pattern of foreign direct investment between countries. The theories we examine in this chapter seek to do just this.

Our central objective will be to identify the economic rationale that underlies foreign direct investment. The first point that must be made is that firms often view exports and FDI as substitutes for each other. In the opening case, for example, we saw how Electrolux considered and then ruled out serving emerging markets by exports from Western Europe. Instead, the company decided to invest directly in production facilities in those markets. One question that this chapter attempts to answer is, *Under what conditions do firms such as Electrolux prefer FDI to exporting?* The opening case hints at some of the answers (e.g., trade barriers, access to markets, cost considerations). Here we will review various theories that attempt to provide a comprehensive explanation for this question.

This is not the only question these theories need to address. They also need to explain why it is preferable for a firm to engage in FDI rather than licensing. Licensing occurs when a domestic firm, the licensor, licenses the right to produce its product, to use its production processes, or to use its brand name or trademark to a foreign firm, the licensee. In return for giving the licensee these rights, the licensor collects a royalty fee on every unit the licensee sells. The great advantage claimed for licensing over FDI is that the licensor does not have to pay for opening a foreign market; the licensee does that. For example, one might ask why Electrolux acquired Lehel of Hungary, when it could have simply allowed Lehel to build Electrolux products under license and collected a royalty fee on each product that Lehel subsequently sold. Why did Electrolux prefer to bear the substantial risks and costs associated with purchasing Lehel, when in theory it could have earned a good return by licensing? The theories reviewed herein attempt to provide an answer to this puzzle.

The remainder of the chapter is structured as follows. First, we look at the importance of FDI in the world economy. Next we look at the theories that have been used to explain horizontal foreign direct investment. **Horizontal foreign direct investment** is FDI in the same industry in which a firm operates at home.

Inflows and Outflows of FDI, 1981–94 (Billions of Dollars)

	1981–85 Annual Average	1986–90 Annual Average	1990	1991	1992	1993	1994
Inward FDI							
Developed countries	37	130	176	121	102	109	117
Developing countries	13	25	31	39	51	80	80
Outward FDI							
Developed countries	47	163	222	185	174	181	192
Developing countries	1	6	10	7	10	12	12

1994 figures are estimates.

Sources: 1981–93 data from United Nations, World Investment Report, *1994; 1994 data from G. de Jonquieres, "Rocky Road to Liberalization,"* Financial Times, *April 10, 1995, p. 15.*

Electrolux's investments in Eastern Europe and Asia are examples of horizontal FDI. Having reviewed horizontal FDI, we move on to consider the theories that help to explain vertical foreign direct investment. **Vertical foreign direct investment** is FDI in an industry that provides inputs for a firm's domestic operations. Alternatively, it may be FDI in an industry abroad that sells the outputs of a firm's domestic operations. Finally, as always, we review the implications of these theories for business practice.

❦ FOREIGN DIRECT INVESTMENT IN THE WORLD ECONOMY

When discussing foreign direct investment, it is important to distinguish between the *flow* of FDI and the *stock* of FDI. The **flow of FDI** refers to the amount of FDI undertaken over a given time period (normally a year). The **stock of FDI** refers to the total accumulated value of foreign-owned assets at a given time. We also talk of **outflows of FDI,** meaning the flow of FDI out of a country, and **inflows of FDI,** meaning the flow of FDI into a country.

Several facts characterize foreign direct investment trends over the past 20 years. First, there has been a rapid increase in the total volume of FDI undertaken. Second, there has been a change in the importance of various countries as sources for FDI. In particular, there has been some decline in the *relative* importance of the United States as a source for FDI, while several other countries, most notably Japan, have increased their share of total FDI outflows. Third, there have been notable shifts in the direction of FDI. An increasing share of FDI seems to be directed at the developing nations of Asia and Eastern Europe. The United States has become a major recipient of FDI. Finally, there has been a notable increase in the amount of FDI undertaken by small and medium-sized enterprises. In this section we review and explain the reason for these various trends.

The Growth of FDI

Over the past 20 years there has been a marked increase in both the *flow* and *stock* of FDI in the world economy. The average yearly *outflow* of FDI from the larger industrialized (developed) countries increased from about $47 billion per annum during the 1981–85 period to $163 billion per annum during the 1986–90 period (see Table 6.1). In 1990 the outflow exceeded even this figure, reaching a record $222 billion. Although it subsequently fell back to $174 billion in 1992, it rose again to $192 billion in 1994. Not only did the flow of FDI accelerate during the

FIGURE **6.1**   The Growth of FDI, World Trade, and World Output

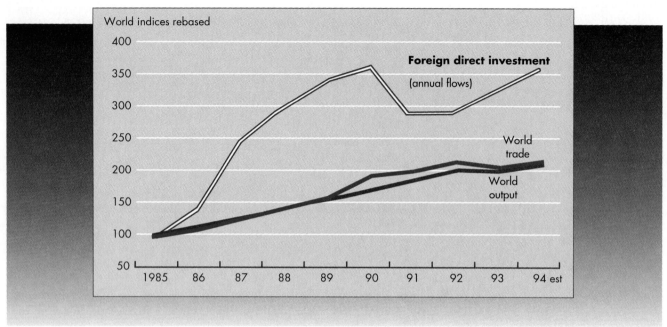

Source: UNCTAD (United Nations Committee for Trade and Development).

1980s, but it also accelerated faster than the growth in world trade. Indeed, between 1985 and 1994 the total flow of FDI from all countries increased fourfold to $204 billion, twice as fast as the growth in world trade, which itself has exceeded the growth in world output (see Figure 6.1).[1]

There are several reasons FDI is growing more rapidly than world trade and world output. For a start, despite the general decline in trade barriers that we have witnessed over the past 30 years, there is still some fear among business firms of protectionist pressures. To the extent that this is the case, business executives see FDI as a way of circumventing future trade barriers. Thus much of the investment in the United States undertaken by Japanese automobile companies during the 1980s and early 1990s was driven by a desire to reduce exports from Japan, thereby alleviating trade tensions between the two nations.

Second, much of the recent increase in FDI is being driven by the dramatic political and economic changes that have been occurring in many of the world's developing nations. The general shift toward democratic political institutions and free market economics that we discussed in Chapter 2 has encouraged FDI. Across much of Asia, Eastern Europe, and Latin America, increasing economic growth, economic deregulation, privatization programs that are open to foreign investors, and the removal of many restrictions on FDI have all made these countries more attractive to foreign investors. We saw in the opening case how Electrolux has responded to these trends by investing in Eastern Europe and Asia. The acquisition of Lehel of Hungary, for example, was the result of a privatization program that allowed foreign investors to purchase state-owned enterprises.

The globalization of the world economy, a phenomenon that we first discussed in Chapter 1, is also having a positive impact on the volume of FDI. Firms such as Electrolux now see the whole world as their market, and they are undertaking FDI in an attempt to make sure they have a significant presence in every region of the world. Moreover, for reasons that we shall explore later in this book, many firms now believe it is important to have production facilities based close to their major customers. This too is creating pressures for greater FDI.

---

[1]G. de Jonquieres, "Rocky Road to Liberalization," *Financial Times*, April 10, 1995, p. 15.

FIGURE **6.2**   Outflows of FDI from the Five Major Source Countries, 1981–93 (Billions of Dollars)

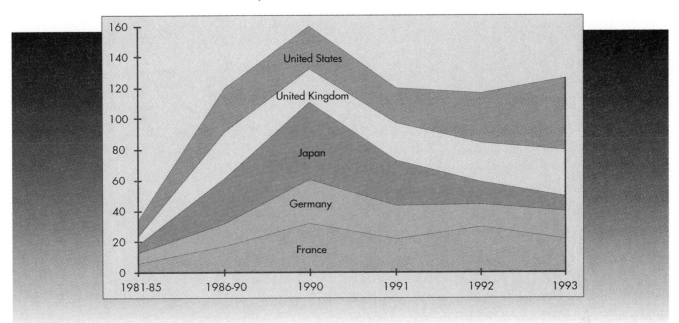

1981–85 and 1986–90 figures are annual averages.
Source: United Nations, World Investment Report, 1994.

Changes in the Source of FDI

Not only has the outflow of FDI been accelerating, but its composition has also been changing (see Figure 6.2). For most of the period after World War II, the United States was by far the largest source country for FDI. Even during the late 1970s the United States was still accounting for about 47 percent of all FDI *outflows* from industrialized countries, while the second-placed United Kingdom accounted for about 18 percent. U.S. firms so dominated the growth of FDI in the 1960s and 70s that the words *American* and *multinational* became almost synonymous. As a result, by 1980 178 of the world's largest 382 multinationals were U.S. firms, and 40 of them were British.[2] By 1990, how-ever, the U.S. share of total FDI outflows had slumped to 10.3 percent, pushing the United States into second place behind Japan, although the U.S. share increased again to reach close to 27 percent in 1993. This relative decline in the share of FDI outflows accounted for by the United States is to be expected. It is a reflection of the increasing number of countries joining the ranks of developed nations that are themselves becoming important sources for FDI. Despite its declining share, the United States is once again the largest source country for FDI, albeit by a smaller margin than in the 1960s and 1970s.

The big gainer over most of the past 20 years has been Japan. Japan's share of total FDI outflows increased from about 6 percent during the late 1970s to 21 percent in 1990. As Figure 6.3 demonstrates, one consequence of this was that Japan's share of the total *stock* of world FDI increased from 0.7 percent in 1960 to 13 percent in 1993, while the stock accounted for by the United States fell from 49.2 percent to 25.3 percent over the same period. Japan's increased share of FDI outflows has been one consequence of that country's rapid economic progress. However, reflecting Japan's severe economic re-cession in the early 1990s, Japanese FDI has slumped since 1990 and accounted for only 6 percent of total outflows in 1993. The low level of Japanese FDI continued into 1994, although most observers expect it to increase again once Japan's economy recovers from its current recession.[3] The other major source countries for FDI include Germany, France, and the United Kingdom. Among these countries, the total share of FDI stock accounted for by the United Kingdom has shrunk (see Figure 6.3), while that ac-counted for by France and Germany has grown.[4]

---

[2]M. Kidron and R. Segal, *The New State of the World Atlas* (New York: Simon & Schuster, 1987).
[3]E. S. Browning, "British Firms' Outlays in U.S. Top Japanese," *The Wall Street Journal*, October 28, 1994, p. 2.
[4]United Nations, *World Investment Report*, 1994.

FIGURE 6.3   The Changing Stock of FDI (Percentage of World Total)

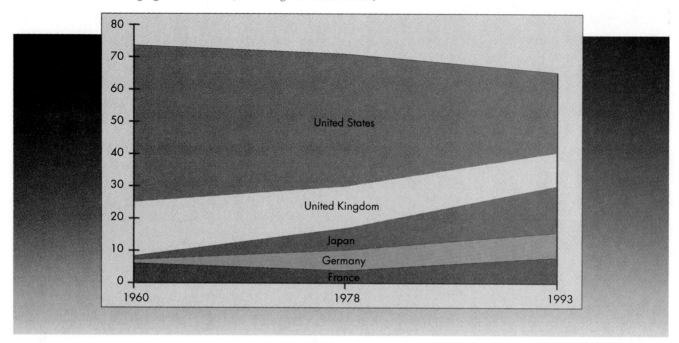

Source: United Nations, World Investment Report, *1994.*

Changes in the Recipients of FDI

With regard to *inflows* of FDI, two trends are worthy of note. First, as Table 6.1 reveals, there has been a surge of FDI into developing nations. From 1986 to 1990, developing nations were the recipients of about 16 percent of all FDI. By 1994 this figure had increased to 41 percent. We have already referred to many of the reasons for this development. They include the rapid economic progress of many of these developing nations and their adoption of economic liberalization policies, which have lowered barriers to FDI. An example is China, which in 1994 attracted $30 billion in foreign direct investment inflows, second only to the United States.[5] China's importance as a recipient of FDI is a result of economic liberalization policies, the country's rapid economic growth (which has averaged over 9 percent per annum since 1985), and the vast potential inherent in a country with a population of 1.2 billion. Another example of a developing country that has recently become a target for FDI is Vietnam, which is profiled in the next "Country Focus."

Another development worthy of comment in recent years has been the rise of FDI inflows into the United States. This is shown in Table 6.2, which plots the changes in the stock of FDI owned by U.S. firms abroad and by foreign firms in the United States from 1970 through 1993. As can be seen, in 1970 U.S. firms owned almost six times as many assets abroad as foreign firms owned in the United States. By 1994, however, the ratio was close to 6:5.

A widespread perception is that the majority of FDI inflows into the United States during the 1980s and early 90s were undertaken by Japanese corporations intent on buying America's industrial base.[6] In reality, however, the two leading investors in the United States for most of the 1970s and 80s were the British and the Dutch.[7] Although there was a surge in Japanese investment, it peaked in 1989 and has declined since. In the first half of 1994, for example, British companies invested more than $2 billion in the United States, while Japanese companies invested just $50.2 million.

---

[5]"The Taipan and the Dragon," *The Economist,* April 8, 1995, p. 62.
[6]For an example of this viewpoint, see M. Tolchin and S. Tolchin, *Buying into America* (New York: Times Books, 1988).
[7]"Foreign Investment in the U.S.," *New York Times,* July 17, 1990, p. D2.

Vietnam's Infant Auto Industry Attracts Substantial Foreign Direct Investment

After the fall of Saigon (now Ho Chi Minh City) to the Communist forces of North Vietnam in April 1975, Vietnam effectively closed its doors to foreign investors. However, the doors have opened again. Although the government of Vietnam is still officially Communist, in recent years it has pursued an economic liberalization policy that is similar in many respects to that adopted by another nominally Communist state, China. Market-based reforms have been introduced, price controls in many areas have been scrapped, restrictions on foreign direct investment have been loosened, and there is talk of privatizing state-owned enterprises.

Vietnam has a long way to go, however, before it attains the levels of other rapidly developing nations. At $210 per annum, its GDP per capita is one of the lowest in the world and much of the country's infrastructure remains in tatters, the result of war damage and poor upkeep. Still, with a population of over 70 million, economic growth in excess of 8 percent per annum during the first half of the 1990s, and a strategic location in the heart of Southeast Asia, Vietnam's long-run prospects are too bright for many foreign investors to ignore. The result has been a rapid rise in the amount of FDI into Vietnam, particularly in the automobile industry. By early 1995 Ford, Chrysler, Daimler-Benz, Toyota, Suzuki, and a consortium of Japanese and Indonesian interests known as VINDACO had all applied to the government for permission to set up production facilities in Vietnam. In total, the planned investment amounts to over $600 million, a large amount for a country as poor as Vietnam.

Typical of the planned investments is that of Daimler-Benz. The German company wants to build two production plants, one in the north and one in the south, for a total investment of $70 million. Both plants will come on stream around 2000. They will focus on producing trucks, buses, and some cars. The attraction of Vietnam to foreign investors such as Daimler-Benz is twofold. First, with economic growth expected to average a robust 8 to 10 percent per annum for the next decade, both the investors and the Vietnamese government believe that by 2000 incomes will be high enough to justify making and selling cars locally, first in Ho Chi Minh City in the south and then in the north. Daimler-Benz estimates that demand for commercial vehicles will reach 11,000 per annum by 2005.

A second reason for investing in Vietnam is that ultimately vehicle manufacturers hope to be able to export some of what they produce to other countries, particularly members of the Association of South East Asian Nations (ASEAN), an Asian trade bloc that Vietnam joined in July 1994. With low barriers to trade between ASEAN members a possibility in the future, and given its low labor costs, Vietnam could become an export base for the whole region.

However, this investment is not without its problems. The Vietnamese government is insisting that foreign investors in the auto industry ensure that 30 percent of all parts used in vehicles are made locally within 6 to 10 years of the establishment of an assembly plant. The decision on local content worries many foreign investors. Making auto parts is likely to be tough in a country where even the indigenous bicycle industry has difficulty surviving with outmoded technology. The foreign investors are working hard to persuade at least some of their component part suppliers to follow them to Vietnam. If successful, the result could be a further surge in inward FDI.

Source: "Crowded Road Leads to Vietnam Car Market," *Financial Times*, October 21, 1994, p. 5.

TABLE 6.2

The Changing Stock of FDI in the United States, 1970–93 (Millions of Dollars)

Year	Stock of U.S. FDI Abroad	Stock of Foreign FDI in the United States
1994	$612,109	$504,401
1993	559,733	464,110
1992	502,063	427,566
1991	450,196	407,577
1990	424,086	396,702
1989	372,419	368,924
1988	335,893	314,754
1987	314,307	263,394
1986	259,800	220,414
1985	230,250	184,615
1984	211,480	164,583
1983	207,203	137,061
1982	207,725	124,677
1981	228,348	108,714
1980	215,375	83,046
1979	187,858	54,462
1978	162,727	42,471
1977	145,990	34,595
1976	136,809	30,770
1975	124,050	27,662
1974	110,078	25,144
1973	101,313	20,556
1972	89,878	14,868
1971	82,760	13,914
1970	75,480	13,270

Source: U.S. Department of Commerce, Survey of Current Business, *various issues.*

Although the Japanese had the largest *stock* of FDI in the United States in 1993, with $96 billion out of a total stock of $445 billion, Britain was a close second with $95 billion.[8] Moreover, Britain regained its lead from Japan in 1994.

A number of factors lay behind the inflow of FDI into the United States during the 1980s and early 90s. For a start, as the largest and richest consumer market in the world, the United States was clearly attractive to foreign firms. Also the 1994 expansion of the North American Free Trade Agreement (NAFTA) to include Mexico may have promoted some inward investment from foreign firms eager to share in the gains created by an enlarged market (see Chapter 8 for details of NAFTA). In addition, from 1985 through 1995 the value of the dollar on the foreign exchange market fell quite rapidly. At the same time the value of the Japanese yen and the German mark rose. (For an explanation of this, see Chapter 9). This made it expensive for U.S. firms to purchase assets abroad and relatively cheap for Japanese and German firms to purchase U.S. assets.[9] To some extent this factor lay behind the decline in outward FDI by U.S. firms and the rise of direct investment in the United States by foreign firms.

The rise of FDI in the United States during the 1980s and early 1990s also seems to have been due to a belief on the part of foreign firms that they could manage U.S. workers and assets more efficiently than U.S. managers and investors could. Put another way, the perceived decline in the competitiveness of many firms during the 1970s and 80s may have been the reason for the rise of FDI by foreigners in the United States. On the face of it, some evidence suggests many foreigners have

---

[8]Browning, "British Firms' Outlays."

[9]R. E. Caves, "Japanese Investment in the U.S.: Lessons for the Economic Analysis of Foreign Investment," *The World Economy* 16 (1993), pp. 279–300.

judged correctly. For example, the success of Japanese-owned automobile assembly plants in the United States is largely due to Japanese managers' ability to utilize U.S. workers to make a higher quality car in less time than U.S.-owned automakers can.[10] The next "Management Focus" tells how another foreign firm, the British company Hanson PLC, has been able to utilize U.S. assets and workers more efficiently than U.S. managers do. If much FDI is driven by foreigners' belief that they can manage U.S. workers and assets more efficiently than U.S. managers can, the rise of FDI into the United States will come to a halt once U.S. managers succeed in managing workers and assets as efficiently as their foreign competitors do.

Is the growth of FDI into the United States good or bad for the U.S. economy? We discuss the impact of FDI on a host economy in detail in the next chapter, but for now, note that if one believes that foreigners are doing a better job of managing U.S. workers and assets than U.S. managers, the answer is that it is good. It can be argued that foreign know-how is helping to improve U.S. competitiveness as well as providing jobs and investment that otherwise would not be there. On the other hand, critics charge that the United States has a lot to lose and little to gain from the growth of FDI. Japanese FDI tends to be the main target of these critics. They argue that in exchange for a few lower-skilled, lower-paying jobs, U.S. companies are sacrificing their competitiveness to a Japanese strategy that keeps higher-valued, higher-paying jobs in Japan. The United States, they believe, will ultimately be left with "screwdriver" plants, where low-wage U.S. workers assemble Japanese products.[11] We will return to this issue in the next chapter when we review the pros and cons of FDI from the perspective of a host country in more detail.

FDI by Medium-Sized and Small Firms

FDI used to be associated almost exclusively with multibillion-dollar multinational corporations. Most people probably still think the two are synonymous. In practice, however, the globalization of world markets has been accompanied by the rapid growth of FDI by small and medium-sized firms. FDI by such firms has been driven by a need to stay close to major customers who have gone abroad. Although hard statistics detailing the growth of smaller multinationals are hard to come by, some examples will give a feel for what now seems to be occurring.

Consider first the experience of Molex, a Chicago-based company with worldwide sales of about $750 million in 1994. Molex makes some 2,500 varieties of connectors used in such applications as linking the wires in an automobile or in the circuit boards of computers and videorecorders. The company had little choice but to go abroad, because its customers began investing abroad in the early 1970s to take advantage of cheap labor. Molex, which in those days generated revenues of less than $20 million, had to go abroad to hold on to this business. Today the company's 46 factories in more than 20 countries employ 6,000 foreign workers.

For another example, consider Loctite, a U.S. manufacturer of industrial adhesives that in 1994 generated sales of over $450 million worldwide. Loctite has pushed hard overseas since its founding in the 1950s. Today the company does business in more than 80 countries and has factories in Ireland, Brazil, and Japan (where it dominates the industrial market). Of the 3,000 people in the company worldwide, two-thirds are employed outside North America.

As an even smaller example, consider Lubricating Systems, Inc., of Kent, Washington. In 1991 this manufacturer of lubricating fluids for machine tools employed 25 people and generated sales of $6.5 million, hardly an industrial giant. Yet more than $2 million of the company's total sales were generated by exports to a score of countries from Japan to Israel and the United Arab Emirates. Moreover, Lubricating Systems is now investing in a joint venture with a German company to serve

---

[10]See J. P. Womack, D. T. Jones, and D. Roos, *The Machine that Changed the World* (New York: Rawson Associates, 1990).

[11]R. B. Reich and E. D. Mankin, "Joint Ventures with Japan Give Away Our Future," *Harvard Business Review*, March–April 1986, pp. 78–90.

MANAGEMENT FOCUS
Hanson PLC's FDI in the United States

In 1973 Gordon White, cofounder of the British conglomerate Hanson Trust PLC, arrived in the United States to start the North American arm of Hanson Trust. Thirteen years later the company he set up, Hanson Industries, was ranked 97th among the Fortune 500 Industrials. Hanson Industries' achievement in joining the elite of U.S. companies capped a 22-year period during which Hanson Trust's pretax profits had grown at an average rate of 45 percent a year. This phenomenal growth was based on a carefully thought-out acquisition strategy. Between 1974 and 1990 Hanson Industries bought 12 U.S. corporations for a total purchase price of $4.96 billion. Among these acquisitions was the 1984 purchase of US Industries, a conglomerate with 33 operating divisions, for $532 million; the 1986 purchase of SCM Corporation, a typewriter and chemicals conglomerate, for $930 million; and the 1988 purchase of Kidde, a conglomerate with 108 operating divisions, for $1.7 billion.

The basis of the company's strategy has been to acquire businesses cheaply, often against the existing management's will, to liquidate surplus assets, and then to manage what is left in such a way as to increase earnings and generate cash for the next acquisition. When seeking companies to acquire, Hanson looks for fundamentally sound but poorly managed businesses based in mature, low-tech industries. It seems particularly interested in acquiring firms that historically have had good earnings but that are suffering a short-term setback due to poor management or adverse economic conditions.

Once Hanson acquires a company, it typically cuts costs by selling headquarters buildings and eliminating staff jobs or pushing them down into operations. Underperforming divisions in acquired companies are either turned around quickly or sold. The remaining divisions are given substantial operating autonomy but held accountable for their performance through a system of tight financial controls. Strong profit incentives encourage divisional executives to focus on the bottom line. Hanson's objective is to markedly improve the profitability of the companies it acquires.

These factors can produce remarkable results. For example, Hanson Industries paid $930 million for SCM in January 1986, after a bitterly contested takeover battle. By September 1986 it had sold a number of SCM subsidiaries for more than $1 billion. Hanson held onto the typewriter and chemicals businesses, which, in effect, cost nothing and earned record pretax profits of $165 million in 1987. Since 1987 the chemicals and typewriter businesses have shown further significant improvements in performance.

Consider Smith-Corona, SCM's typewriter business. Under Hanson, Smith-Corona reduced the number of parts in its leading products from 1,400 to 400 and the required time for assembly from 8 hours to 1.5 hours. In addition, employment was cut from 5,200 workers in 1985 to 3,100 by 1988. By such moves, Smith-Corona has established a cost advantage over its major Japanese competitors. As a consequence, by 1989 Smith-Corona had regained its hold on more than 50 percent of the U.S. typewriter market, after having seen its share sink to as low as 32 percent in 1986.

Sources: H. Lampert, "Britons on the Prowl," *New York Times Magazine*, November 29, 1987, pp. 22–24; and C. W. L. Hill, "Hanson PLC," in *Strategic Management: An Integrated Approach*, 3rd ed., ed. C. W. L. Hill and G. R. Jones (Boston: Houghton-Mifflin, 1995).

the European market.[12] The point is that although large firms still account for the lion's share of FDI, opportunities exist for medium-sized and small firms to profit from investing abroad.

❧ Horizontal Foreign Direct Investment

Horizontal FDI is FDI in the same industry abroad as a firm operates in at home. We need to understand why firms go to the trouble of acquiring or establishing operations abroad, when the alternatives of exporting and licensing are available to them. Why, for example, did Electrolux choose FDI in Hungary over exporting from its Western European plant or licensing a Hungarian automaker to build its appliances in Hungary? This puzzle is a very real one given that, other things being equal, FDI is expensive and risky compared to exporting or licensing.

FDI is expensive because a firm must bear the costs of establishing production facilities in a foreign country or of acquiring a foreign enterprise. FDI is risky because of the problems associated with doing business in a different culture where the "rules of the game" may be very different. Relative to firms native to the particular culture, there is a greater probability that a firm undertaking FDI in a foreign culture will make costly mistakes due to its ignorance. When a firm exports, it need not bear the costs of FDI, and the risks associated with selling abroad can be reduced by using a native sales agent. Similarly, when a firm licenses its know-how it need not bear the costs or risks of FDI, since these are borne by the native firm that licenses the know-how. So why do so many firms apparently prefer FDI over either exporting or licensing?

The quick answer is that other things are not equal! A number of factors can alter the relative attractiveness of exporting, licensing, and FDI. We will consider these factors: (1) transportation costs, (2) market imperfections, (3) following competitors, (4) the product life cycle, and (5) location-specific advantages.

Transportation Costs

When transportation costs are added to production costs, it becomes unprofitable to ship some products over a large distance. This is particularly true of products that have a low value-to-weight ratio and that can be produced in almost any location (e.g., cement, soft drinks, etc.). For such products, relative to either FDI or licensing, the attractiveness of exporting decreases. For products with a high value-to-weight ratio, however, transport costs are normally a very minor component of total landed cost (e.g., electronic components, personal computers, medical equipment, computer software, etc.). In such cases, transportation costs have little impact on the relative attractiveness of exporting, licensing, and FDI.

Market Imperfections (Internalization Theory)

Market imperfections provide a major explanation of why firms may prefer FDI to either exporting or licensing. **Market imperfections** are factors that inhibit markets from working perfectly. At this time, it is probably correct to say the market imperfections explanation of FDI is the one favored by most economists.[13] In the international business literature the market imperfections approach to FDI is typically referred to as **internalization theory.**

---

[12]A. Barret, "It's a Small (Business) World," *Business Week*, April 17, 1995, pp. 96–101; R. A. Mosbacher, "Opening Export Doors for Smaller Firms," *Seattle Times*, July 24, 1991, p. A7; and R. A. King, "You Don't Have to Be a Giant to Score Big Overseas," *Business Week*, April 13, 1987, pp. 62–63.

[13]For example, see S. H. Hymer, *The International Operations of National Firms: A Study of Direct Foreign Investment* (Cambridge, MA: MIT Press, 1976), A. M. Rugman, *Inside the Multinationals: The Economics of Internal Markets* (New York: Columbia University Press, 1981), D. J. Teece, "Multinational Enterprise, Internal Governance, and Industrial Organization," *American Economic Review* 75 (May 1983), pp. 233–38; and C. W. L. Hill and W. C. Kim, "Searching for a Dynamic Theory of the Multinational Enterprise: A Transaction Cost Model," *Strategic Management Journal* (special issue) 9 (1988), pp. 93–104.

With regard to horizontal FDI, market imperfections arise in two circumstances: when there are impediments to the free flow of products between nations, and when there are impediments to the sale of know-how. (Licensing is a mechanism for selling know-how.) Impediments to the free flow of products between nations decrease the profitability of exporting, relative to FDI and licensing. The existence of impediments to the sale of know-how increases the profitability of FDI relative to licensing. Thus the market imperfections explanation predicts that FDI will be preferred whenever there are impediments that make both exporting and the sale of know-how difficult and/or expensive. We will consider each situation in turn.

Impediments to exporting

Governments are the main source of impediments to the free flow of products between nations. By placing tariffs on imported goods, governments can increase the cost of exporting relative to FDI and licensing. Similarly, by limiting imports through quotas, governments increase the attractiveness of FDI and licensing. Thus, for example, the wave of FDI by Japanese auto companies in the United States during the 1980s was partly driven by protectionist threats from Congress and by quotas on the importation of Japanese cars. For Japanese auto companies, these factors have decreased the profitability of exporting and increased the profitability of FDI.

Impediments to the sale of know-how

The competitive advantage that many firms enjoy comes from their technological, marketing, or management know-how. Technological know-how can enable a company to build a better product; for example, Xerox's technological know-how enabled it to build the first photocopier, and Motorola's technological know-how has given it a competitive advantage in the global market for cellular telephone equipment (Motorola is currently number one in this rapidly growing market). Alternatively, technological know-how can enable a company to improve its production process vis-à-vis competitors; for example, many claim that Toyota's competitive advantage comes from its superior production system. Marketing know-how can enable a company to better position its products in the marketplace vis-à-vis competitors; the competitive advantage of such companies as Kellogg, H. J. Heinz, and Procter & Gamble seems to come from superior marketing know-how. Management know-how with regard to factors such as organizational structure, human relations, control systems, planning systems, and so on, can enable a company to manage its assets more efficiently than competitors; the competitive advantage of Hanson PLC, profiled in the "Management Focus" seems to derive from management know-how.

If we view know-how (expertise) as a competitive asset, it follows that the larger the market in which that asset is applied, the greater the profits that can be earned from the asset. Put simply, Motorola can earn greater returns on its know-how by selling its cellular telephone equipment worldwide than by selling it only in North America. However, this alone does not explain why Motorola undertakes FDI (which it does; the company has production locations around the world). For Motorola to favor FDI, two conditions must hold. First, transportation costs and/or impediments to exporting must rule out exporting as an option. Second, there must be some reason Motorola cannot sell its cellular know-how to foreign producers. Since licensing is the main mechanism by which firms sell their know-how, it follows that there must be some reason Motorola is not willing to license a foreign firm to manufacture and market its cellular telephone equipment. Other things being equal, licensing might look attractive to such a firm, since it would not have to bear the costs and risks associated with FDI yet it could still earn a good return from its know-how in the form of royalty fees.

According to economic theory (and depicted in Figure 6.4), there are three reasons the market does not always work well as a mechanism for selling know-how, or why licensing is not as attractive as it initially appears. First, *licensing may result in a firm's giving away its technological know-how to a potential foreign competitor.* For example, in the

FIGURE 6.4

Impediments to the Sale of Know-how

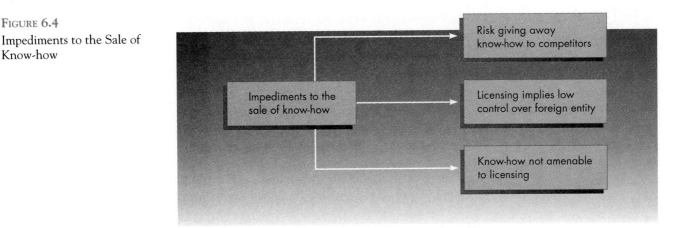

1960s RCA licensed its leading-edge color television technology to a number of Japanese companies, including Matsushita and Sony. At the time RCA saw licensing as a way to earn a good return from its technological know-how in the Japanese market without the costs and risks associated with FDI. However, Matsushita and Sony quickly assimilated RCA's technology and used it to enter the U.S. market to compete directly against RCA. As a result, RCA is now a minor player in its home market, while Matsushita and Sony have a much bigger market share.

Second, *licensing does not give a firm the tight control over manufacturing, marketing, and strategy in a foreign country that may be required to profitably exploit its advantage in know-how.* With licensing, control over manufacturing, marketing, and strategy is granted to a licensee in return for a royalty fee. However, for both strategic and operational reasons, a firm may want to retain control over these functions.

The rationale for wanting control over the strategy of a foreign entity is that a firm might want its foreign subsidiary to price and market very aggressively as a way of keeping a foreign competitor in check. Kodak is pursuing this strategy in Japan. The competitive attacks launched by Kodak's Japanese subsidiary are keeping its major global competitor, Fuji, busy defending its competitive position in Japan. Consequently, Fuji has had to pull back from its earlier strategy of attacking Kodak aggressively in the United States. Unlike a wholly owned subsidiary, a licensee would be unlikely to accept such an imposition, since the implication of such a strategy is that the licensee would be allowed to make only a low profit, or might have to take a loss.

The rationale for wanting control over the operations of a foreign entity is that the firm might wish to take advantage of differences in factor costs across countries, producing only part of its final product in a given country, while importing other parts from elsewhere where they can be produced at lower cost. Again a licensee would be unlikely to accept such an arrangement, since it would limit the licensee's autonomy. For these reasons, when tight control over a foreign entity is desirable, horizontal FDI is preferable to licensing.

Third, *a firm's know-how may not be amenable to licensing.* This is particularly true of management and marketing know-how. It is one thing to license a foreign firm to manufacture a particular product, but quite another to license the way a firm does business—how it manages its process and markets its products. For example, consider Toyota, a company whose competitive advantage in the global auto industry is acknowledged to come from its superior ability to manage the overall process of designing, engineering, manufacturing, and selling automobiles; that is, from its management and organizational know-how. Toyota is credited with pioneering the development of a new production process, known as lean production, that enables it to produce higher quality automobiles at a lower cost than its global rivals.[14] Although

[14]Womack, Jones, and Roos, *The Machine That Changed the World.*

Toyota has certain products that can be licensed, its real competitive advantage comes from its management and process know-how. These kinds of skills are difficult to articulate or codify; they certainly cannot be written in a simple licensing contract. They are organizationwide and they have been developed over the years. They are not embodied in any one individual, but instead are widely dispersed throughout the company. Put another way, Toyota's skills are embedded in its organizational culture, and culture is something that cannot be licensed. Thus as Toyota moves away from its traditional exporting strategy, it has increasingly pursued a strategy of FDI, rather than licensing foreign enterprises to produce its cars.

All of this suggests that when one or more of the following conditions holds, markets fail as a mechanism for selling know-how and FDI is more profitable than licensing: (1) when the firm has valuable know-how that cannot be adequately protected by a licensing contract, (2) when the firm needs tight control over a foreign entity to maximize its market share and earnings in that country, and (3) when a firm's skills and know-how are not amenable to licensing.

Following Competitors

Another theory used to explain FDI is based on the idea that firms follow their domestic competitors overseas. First expounded by F. T. Knickerbocker, this theory has been developed with regard to oligopolistic industries.[15] An **oligopoly** is an industry composed of a limited number of large firms (e.g., an industry in which four firms control 80 percent of a domestic market). A critical competitive feature of such industries is interdependence of the major players: What one firm does can have an immediate impact on the major competitors, forcing a response in kind. Thus if one firm in an oligopoly cuts prices, this can take market share away from its competitors, forcing them to respond with similar price cuts to retain their market share.

This kind of imitative behavior can take many forms in an oligopoly. One firm raises prices, the others follow; someone expands capacity, and the rivals imitate lest they be left in a disadvantageous position in the future. Building on this, Knickerbocker argued that the same kind of imitative behavior characterizes FDI. Consider an oligopoly in the United States in which three firms—A, B, and C—dominate the market. Firm A establishes a subsidiary in France. Firms B and C reflect that if this investment is successful, it may knock out their export business to France and give Firm A a first-mover advantage. Furthermore, Firm A might discover some competitive asset in France that it could repatriate to the United States to torment Firms B and C on their native soil. Given these possibilities, Firms B and C decide to follow Firm A and establish operations in France.

There is evidence that imitative behavior does lead to FDI. Most of the empirical studies that have been done relate to FDI by U.S. firms during the 1950s and 60s. In general these studies show that firms based in oligopolistic industries tended to imitate each other's FDI.[16] More recently, the same phenomenon has been observed with regard to Japanese firms.[17] For example, Toyota and Nissan responded to investments by Honda in the United States and Europe by undertaking their own FDI in the United States and Europe. Similarly, in the opening case we saw how Electrolux's expansion into Eastern Europe and Asia was in part being driven by the fact that its global competitors, such as Whirlpool and General Electric, were making similar moves.

Although Knickerbocker's theory explains imitative behavior by firms in an oligopolistic industry, it does not explain why the first firm in an oligopoly to undertake FDI decides to do so, rather than to export or license. In contrast, the market imperfections explanation addresses this phenomenon. Moreover, the imitative theory

---

[15]The argument is most often associated with F. T. Knickerbocker, *Oligopolistic Reaction and Multinational Enterprise* (Boston: Harvard Business School Press, 1973).

[16]R. E. Caves, *Multinational Enterprise and Economic Analysis* (Cambridge, UK: Cambridge University Press, 1982).

[17]Caves, "Japanese Investment in the U.S."

does not address the issue of whether FDI is more efficient than exporting or licensing for expanding abroad. Again the market imperfections approach does address the efficiency issue. For these reasons, most economists favor the market imperfections explanation for FDI, although most would agree that the imitative explanation tells part of the story.

The Product Life Cycle

We considered Raymond Vernon's product life-cycle theory in Chapter 4. What we did not dwell on, however, was Vernon's contention that his theory also explains FDI. Vernon argued that in many cases the establishment of facilities abroad to produce a product for consumption in that market, or for export to other markets, is often undertaken by the same firm or firms that first pioneered the product and introduced it in their home market. Thus Xerox introduced the photocopier into the U.S. market, and it was Xerox that originally set up production facilities in Japan (Fuji-Xerox) and Great Britain (Rank-Xerox) to serve those markets.

Vernon's view is that firms undertake FDI at particular stages in the life cycle of a product they have pioneered. They invest in other advanced countries when local demand in those countries grows large enough to support local production (as Xerox did). They subsequently shift production to developing countries when product standardization and market saturation give rise to price competition and cost pressures. Investment in developing countries, where labor costs are lower, is seen as the best way to reduce costs.

There is significant merit to Vernon's theory. Firms do invest in a foreign country when demand in that country will support local production, and they do invest in low-cost locations (e.g., developing countries) when cost pressures become intense.[18] What Vernon's theory fails to explain, however, is why it is profitable for a firm to undertake FDI at such times, rather than continuing to export from its home base, and rather than licensing a foreign firm to produce its product. Just because demand in a foreign country is large enough to support local production, it does not necessarily follow that local production is the most profitable option. It may still be more profitable to produce at home and export to that country (to realize the scale economies that arise from serving the global market from one location). Alternatively, it may be more profitable for the firm to license a foreign firm to produce its product for sale in that country. The product life-cycle theory ignores these options and simply argues that once a foreign market is large enough to support local production, FDI will occur. This limits its explanatory power and its usefulness to business (in that it fails to identify when it is profitable to invest abroad).

Location-Specific Advantages

The British economist John Dunning has argued that in addition to the various factors discussed above, location-specific advantages are also of considerable importance in explaining the nature and direction of FDI.[19] By **location-specific advantages,** Dunning means the advantages that arise from utilizing resource endowments or assets that are tied to a particular foreign location and that a firm finds valuable to combine with its own unique assets (such as the firm's technological, marketing, or management know-how). Dunning accepts the internalization argument that market failures make it difficult for a firm to license its own unique assets (know-how). Therefore, he argues that combining location-specific assets or resource endowments *and* the firm's own unique assets often requires FDI. That is, it requires the firm to establish production facilities where those foreign assets or resource endowments are located (Dunning refers to this argument as the **eclectic paradigm**).

---

[18]For the use of Vernon's theory to explain Japanese direct investment in the United States and Europe, see S. Thomsen, "Japanese Direct Investment in the European Community," *The World Economy* 16 (1993), pp. 301–15.

[19]J. H. Dunning, *Explaining International Production* (London: Unwin Hyman, 1988).

An obvious example of Dunning's arguments are natural resources, such as oil and other minerals, which are by their character specific to certain locations. Dunning suggests that to exploit such foreign resources a firm must undertake FDI. Clearly this explains the FDI undertaken by many of the world's oil companies, which have to invest where oil is located in order to combine their technological and managerial knowledge with this valuable location-specific resource. Another obvious example are valuable human resources, such as low-cost, high-skilled labor. The cost and skill of labor varies from country to country. Since labor is not internationally mobile, according to Dunning it makes sense for a firm to locate production facilities in those countries where the cost and skills of local labor are most suited to its particular production processes. For example, one reason Electrolux is building factories in China is that China has an abundant supply of low-cost but well-educated and skilled labor. Thus, other factors aside, China is a good location for producing household appliances both for the Chinese market and for export elsewhere.

However, Dunning's theory has implications that go beyond basic resources such as minerals and labor. Consider Silicon Valley, which is the world center for the computer and semi-conductor industry. Many of the world's major computer and semi-conductor companies, such as Apple Computer, Silicon Graphics, and Intel, are located close to each other in the Silicon Valley region of California. As a result, much of the cutting-edge research and product development in computers and semi-conductors occurs here. According to Dunning's arguments, there is knowledge being generated in Silicon Valley with regard to the design and manufacture of computers and semiconductors that is available nowhere else in the world. To be sure, as it is commercialized that knowledge diffuses throughout the world, but the leading edge of knowledge generation in the computer and semiconductor industries is to be found in Silicon Valley. In Dunning's language, this means that Silicon Valley has a *location specific advantage* in the generation of knowledge related to the computer and semiconductor industries. In part, this advantage comes from the sheer concentration of intellectual talent in this area, and in part it arises from a network of informal contacts that allows firms to benefit from each others' knowledge generation. Economists refer to such knowledge "spillovers" as **externalities,** and there is a well-established theory suggesting that firms can benefit from such externalities by locating close to their source.[20]

In so far as this is the case, it makes sense for foreign computer and semiconductor firms to invest in research and (perhaps) production facilities so they too can benefit from being where the knowledge is first generated. The belief being that externalities will allow firms based there to learn about and utilize valuable new knowledge before those based elsewhere, thereby giving them a competitive advantage in the global marketplace. If this argument is correct, one would expect to see significant evidence of FDI by European, Japanese, South Korean, and Taiwanese computer and semiconductor firms in the Silicon Valley region. And there does seem to be such evidence.[21] Dunning's theory, therefore, seems to be a useful addition to those outlined above, for it helps explain like no other how location factors affect the direction of FDI.

✍ VERTICAL FOREIGN DIRECT INVESTMENT

Vertical FDI takes two forms. First, there is backward vertical FDI into an industry abroad that provides inputs for a firm's domestic production processes. Historically most backward vertical FDI has been in extractive industries (e.g., oil extraction, bauxite mining, tin mining, copper mining). The objective has been to provide inputs into a firm's downstream operations (e.g., oil refining, aluminum smelting and

[20]P. Krugman, "Increasing Returns and Economic Geography," *Journal of Political Economy* 99, no. 3 (1991), pp. 483–99.

[21]J. H. Dunning and R. Narula, "Transpacific Foreign Direct Investment and the Investment Development Path," *South Carolina Essays in International Business*, (CIBER: University of South Carolina, May 1995).

fabrication, tin smelting and fabrication). Firms such as Royal Dutch Shell, British Petroleum (BP), RTZ, Consolidated Gold Field, and Alcoa are among the classic examples of such vertically integrated multinationals.

A second form of vertical FDI is forward vertical FDI. Forward vertical FDI is FDI into an industry abroad that sells the outputs of a firm's domestic production processes. Forward vertical FDI is less common than backward vertical FDI. For example, when Volkswagen first entered the U.S. market, rather than distribute its cars through independent U.S. dealers, at no small expense it acquired a large number of dealers.

With both horizontal and vertical FDI, the question that must be answered is why would a firm go to all the trouble and expense of setting up operations in a foreign country? Why, for example, did petroleum companies like BP and Royal Dutch Shell vertically integrate backward into oil production abroad? The location-specific advantages argument that we reviewed in the previous section helps explain the *direction* of such FDI, for vertically integrated multinationals in extractive industries invest where the raw materials are. However, this argument does not clarify why they did not simply import raw materials extracted by local producers? And why do companies such as Volkswagen believe it is necessary to acquire their own dealers in foreign markets, when in theory it might seem less costly to rely on foreign dealers? There are two basic answers to these kinds of questions. The first is a market power argument, and the second draws, once again, on the market imperfections approach.

Market Power

One aspect of the market power argument is that firms undertake vertical FDI to limit competition and strengthen their control over the market. The most common argument is that by vertically integrating backward to gain control over the source of raw material inputs, a firm can effectively shut new competitors out of an industry. Such a strategy involves FDI only because the raw material inputs are found abroad. An example occurred in the 1930s, when commercial smelting of aluminum was pioneered by North American firms like Alcoa and Alcan. Aluminum is derived by smelting bauxite. Although bauxite is a common mineral, the percentage of aluminum in bauxite is typically so low that it is not economical to mine and smelt. During the 1930s only one large-scale deposit of bauxite with an economical percentage of aluminum had been discovered, and it was on the Caribbean island of Trinidad. Alcoa and Alcan vertically integrated backward and acquired ownership of the deposit. This action created a barrier to entry into the aluminum industry. Potential competitors were deterred because they could not get access to high-grade bauxite; it was all owned by Alcoa and Alcan. Those that did enter the industry had to use lower-grade bauxite than Alcan and Alcoa, and found themselves at a cost disadvantage vis-à-vis these two companies. This situation persisted until the 1950s and 1960s, when new high-grade deposits were discovered in Australia and Indonesia.

However, despite the bauxite example, the opportunities for barring entry through vertical FDI seem far too limited to explain the incidence of vertical FDI among the world's multinationals. In most extractive industries, mineral deposits are not as concentrated as in the case of bauxite in the 1930s, and new deposits are constantly being discovered. Consequently, any attempt to monopolize all viable raw material deposits is bound to prove very expensive if not impossible.

Another strand of the market power explanation of vertical FDI sees such investment not as an attempt to build entry barriers, but as an attempt to circumvent the barriers established by firms already doing business in a country. This may explain Volkswagen's decision to establish its own dealer network when it entered the North American auto market. The market was then dominated by GM, Ford, and Chrysler. Each firm had its own network of independent dealers that carried their cars. Volkswagen thought the only way to get quick access to the U.S. market was to promote its cars through independent dealerships.

Market Imperfections

As in the case of horizontal FDI, a more general explanation of vertical FDI can be found in the market imperfections approach.[22] The market imperfections approach offers two explanations for vertical FDI. As with horizontal FDI, the first explanation revolves around the idea that there are impediments to the sale of know-how through the market mechanism. The second explanation is based on the idea that investments in specialized assets expose the investing firm to hazards that can be reduced only through vertical FDI.

Impediments to the sale of know-how
Consider the case of oil refining companies such as British Petroleum (BP) and Royal Dutch Shell. Historically these firms pursued backward vertical FDI in order to supply their British and Dutch oil refining facilities with crude oil. When this occurred in the early decades of this century, neither Great Britain nor the Netherlands had domestic oil supplies. Why did these firms pursue backward vertical FDI to provide oil inputs? Why did they not just import oil from firms in oil-rich countries such as Saudi Arabia and Kuwait?

The answer is that originally there were no Saudi Arabian or Kuwaiti firms with the technological expertise for finding and extracting oil. BP and Royal Dutch Shell had to develop this know-how themselves to get access to oil. This alone does not explain FDI, however, for once BP and Shell had developed the necessary know-how they could have licensed it to Saudi Arabian or Kuwaiti firms. However, as we saw in the case of horizontal FDI, licensing can be self-defeating as a mechanism for the sale of know-how. If the oil refining firms had licensed their prospecting and extraction know-how to Saudi Arabian or Kuwaiti firms, they would have risked giving away their technological know-how to those firms, creating future competitors in the process. Once they had the know-how, the Saudi and Kuwaiti firms might have gone prospecting for oil in other parts of the world, competing directly against BP and Royal Dutch Shell. Thus it made more sense for these firms to undertake backward vertical FDI and extract the oil themselves, instead of licensing their hard-earned technological expertise to local firms.

Generalizing from this example, the prediction is that backward vertical FDI will occur when a firm has the knowledge and the ability to extract raw materials in another country and there is no efficient producer in that country that can supply raw materials to the firm.

Investment in specialized assets
Another strand of the market imperfections argument predicts that vertical FDI will occur when a firm must undertake investments in specialized assets whose value is dependent on inputs provided by a foreign supplier. In this context a specialized asset is an asset designed to perform a specific task, and whose value is significantly reduced in its next-best use. Consider the case of an aluminum refinery, which is designed to refine bauxite ore and produce aluminum. There are several types of bauxite ore; the ores vary in content and chemical composition from deposit to deposit. Each type of ore requires a different type of refinery. Running one type of bauxite through a refinery designed for another type increases production costs by 20 percent to 100 percent.[23] Thus, the value of an investment in an aluminum refinery depends on the availability of the desired kind of bauxite ore.

Imagine that a U.S. aluminum company must decide whether to invest in an aluminum refinery designed to refine a certain type of ore. Assume further that this ore is available only through an Australian mining firm at a single bauxite mine. Using a

[22]J. F. Hennart, "Upstream Vertical Integration in the Aluminum and Tin Industries," *Journal of Economic Behavior and Organization* 9 (1988), pp. 281–99; and O. E. Williamson, *The Economic Institutions of Capitalism* (New York: Free Press, 1985).
[23]Hennart, "Upstream Vertical Integration."

different type of ore in the refinery would raise production costs by at least 20 percent. Therefore, the value of the U.S. company's investment is dependent on the price it must pay the Australian firm for this bauxite. Once the U.S. company has made the investment in a new refinery, there is nothing to stop the Australian firm from raising bauxite prices. And once it has made the investment, the U.S. firm is locked into its relationship with the Australian supplier. The Australian firm can increase bauxite prices, secure in the knowledge that so long as the increase in the total production costs of the U.S. firm is less than 20 percent, the U.S. firm will continue to buy from it. (It would become economical for the U.S. firm to buy from another supplier only if total production costs increased by more than 20 percent.)

But the U.S. firm can reduce the risk of the Australian firm opportunistically raising prices by buying it out. If the U.S. firm can buy the Australian firm, or its bauxite mine, it need no longer fear that bauxite prices will be increased after it has invested in the refinery. In other words it would make economic sense for the U.S. firm to engage in vertical FDI. These kinds of considerations have driven aluminum firms to pursue vertical FDI to such a degree that in 1976, 91 percent of the total volume of bauxite was transferred within vertically integrated firms.[24]

 ## IMPLICATIONS FOR BUSINESS

The implications of the theories of horizontal and vertical FDI for business practice are relatively straightforward. The location-specific advantages argument associated with John Dunning does help explain the *direction* of FDI, both with regard to horizontal and vertical FDI. However, the location-specific advantages argument does not explain *why* firms prefer FDI to licensing or to exporting.

From both an explanatory and a business perspective, perhaps the most useful theory is the market imperfections approach. With regard to horizontal FDI, this approach is useful because it identifies with some precision how the relative profitabilities of horizontal FDI, exporting, and licensing vary with circumstances. The theory suggests that exporting is preferable to licensing and horizontal FDI as long as transport costs are minor and tariff barriers are trivial. As transport costs and/or tariff barriers increase, exporting becomes unprofitable, and the choice is between horizontal FDI and licensing. Since horizontal FDI is more costly and more risky than licensing, other things being equal, the theory argues that licensing is preferable to horizontal FDI. Other things are seldom equal, however. Although licensing may work, it is not an attractive option when one or more of the following conditions exist: (*a*) the firm has valuable know-how that cannot be adequately protected by a licensing contract, (*b*) the firm needs tight control over a foreign entity to maximize its market share and earnings in that country, and (*c*) a firm's skills and know-how are not amenable to licensing. Figure 6.5 presents these considerations as a decision tree.

Firms for which licensing is not a good option tend to be clustered in three types of industries:

1. High-technology industries where protecting firm-specific expertise is of paramount importance and licensing is hazardous.
2. Global oligopolies, where competitive interdependence requires that multinational firms maintain tight control over foreign operations so they can launch coordinated attacks against their global competitors (as Kodak has done with Fuji).
3. Industries where intense cost pressures require that multinational firms maintain tight control over foreign operations so they can disperse manufacturing to locations around the globe where factor costs are most favorable in order to minimize costs.

Although empirical evidence is limited, the majority of the evidence seems to support these conjectures.[25]

---

[24]Ibid.

[25]See Caves, *Multinational Enterprise and Economic Analysis*.

FIGURE 6.5
A Decision Framework

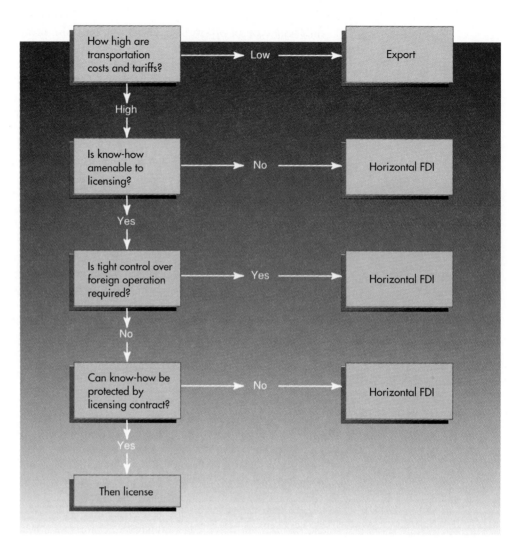

Firms for which licensing is a good option tend to be in industries whose conditions are opposite to those specified above. That is, licensing tends to be more common (and more profitable) in fragmented, low-technology industries in which globally dispersed manufacturing is not an option. A good example is the fast food industry. McDonald's has expanded globally by using a franchising strategy. Franchising is essentially the service-industry version of licensing—although it normally involves much longer-term commitments than licensing. With franchising, the firm licenses its brand name to a foreign firm in return for a percentage of the franchisee's profits. The franchising contract specifies the conditions that the franchisee must fulfill if it is to use the franchisor's brand name. Thus McDonald's allows foreign firms to use its brand name so long as they agree to run their restaurants on exactly the same lines as McDonald's restaurants elsewhere in the world. This strategy makes sense for McDonald's because (*a*) like many services, fast food cannot be exported, (*b*) franchising economizes the costs and risks associated with opening foreign markets, (*c*) unlike technological know-how, brand names are relatively easy to protect using a contract, (*d*) there is no compelling reason for McDonald's to have tight control over franchisees, and (*e*) McDonald's know-how, in terms of how to run a fast-food restaurant, is amenable to being specified in a written contract.

In contrast to the market imperfections approach, the product life-cycle theory and Knickerbocker's theory of horizontal FDI tend to be less useful from a business perspective. The problem with these two theories is that they are descriptive rather than analytical. They do a good job of describing the historical evolution of FDI by U.S. firms, but they do a relatively poor job of identifying the factors that influence the relative profitability of FDI, licensing, and exporting. The issue of licensing as an alternative to FDI is ignored by both these theories.

Finally, with regard to vertical FDI, both the market imperfections approach and the market power approach have some useful implications for business practice. The market power approach points out that vertical FDI may be a way of building barriers to entry into an industry. The strength of the market imperfections approach is that it points out the conditions under which vertical FDI might be preferable to the alternatives. Most importantly, the market imperfections approach points to the importance of investments in specialized assets and imperfections in the market for know-how as factors that increase the relative attractiveness of vertical FDI.

❧ Summary of Chapter

The objective of this chapter was to review theories that attempt to explain the pattern of FDI between countries. This objective takes on added importance in light of growing importance of FDI in the world economy. As we saw early in the chapter, the volume of FDI has grown more rapidly than the volume of world trade in recent years. We also noted that any theory seeking to explain FDI must explain why firms go to the trouble of acquiring or establishing operations abroad, when the alternatives of exporting and licensing are available to them.

We reviewed a number of theories that attempt to explain horizontal and vertical FDI. With regard to horizontal FDI, it was argued that the market imperfections and location-specific advantages approaches might have the greatest explanatory power, and therefore be most useful for business practice. This is not to belittle the explanations for horizontal FDI put forward by Vernon and Knickerbocker, since these theories also have value in explaining the pattern of FDI in the world economy. However, both theories seem dated now that the United States no longer dominates the flow of outward FDI. Moreover, both theories are weakened by their failure to explicitly consider the factors that drive the choice between exporting, licensing, and FDI. Finally, with regard to vertical FDI, it was argued that the market power and market imperfections approaches both have a certain amount of explanatory power.

More specifically, in this chapter the following points have been made:

1. Foreign direct investment occurs when a firm invests directly in facilities to produce a product in a foreign country. It also occurs when a firm buys an existing enterprise in a foreign country.

2. Horizontal FDI is FDI in the same industry abroad as a firm operates at home. Vertical FDI is FDI in an industry abroad that provides inputs into a firm's domestic operations.

3. Any theory seeking to explain FDI must explain why firms go to the trouble of acquiring or establishing operations abroad, when the alternatives of exporting and licensing are available to them.

4. Four factors seem to characterize FDI trends over the past 20 years: (*i*) there has been a rapid increase in the total volume of FDI undertaken; (*ii*) there has been some decline in the *relative* importance of the United States as a source of FDI, while several other countries, most notably Japan, have increased their share of total FDI outflows; (*iii*) an increasing share of FDI seems to be directed at the developing nations of Asia and Eastern Europe, while the United States has become a major recipient of FDI; and (*iv*) there has been a notable increase in the amount of FDI undertaken by small and medium-sized enterprises.

5. High transportation costs and/or tariffs imposed on imports help explain why many firms prefer horizontal FDI or licensing over exporting.

6. Impediments to the sale of know-how explain why firms prefer horizontal FDI to licensing. These impediments arise when: (*i*) a firm has valuable know-how that cannot be adequately protected by a licensing contract, (*ii*) a firm needs tight control over a foreign entity to maximize its market share and earnings in that country, and (*iii*) a firm's skills and know-how are not amenable to licensing.

7. Knickerbocker's theory suggests that much FDI is explained by imitative behavior by rival firms in an oligopolistic industry. However, this theory does not address the issue of whether FDI is more efficient than exporting or licensing for expanding abroad.

8. Vernon's product life-cycle theory suggests that firms undertake FDI at particular stages in the life cycle of products they have pioneered. However, Vernon's theory does not address the issue of whether FDI is more efficient than exporting or licensing for expanding abroad.

9. Dunning has argued that location-specific advantages are of considerable importance in explaining the nature and direction of FDI. According to Dunning, firms undertake FDI to exploit resource endowments or assets that are location-specific.

10. Backward vertical FDI may be explained as an attempt to create barriers to entry by gaining control over the source of material inputs into the downstream stage of a production process. Forward vertical FDI may be seen as an attempt to circumvent entry barriers and gain access to a national market.

11. The market imperfections approach suggests that vertical FDI is a way of reducing a firm's exposure to the risks that arise from investments in specialized assets.

12. From a business perspective, the most useful theory is probably the market imperfections approach, because it identifies with some precision how the relative profitabilities of horizontal FDI, exporting, and licensing vary with circumstances.

❦ CRITICAL DISCUSSION QUESTIONS

1. In recent years Japanese FDI in the United States has grown far more rapidly than U.S. FDI in Japan. Why do you think this is the case? What are the implications of this trend?

2. Compare these explanations of horizontal FDI: the market imperfections approach, Vernon's product life-cycle theory, and Knickerbocker's theory of FDI. Which theory do you think offers the best explanation of the historical pattern of horizontal FDI? Why?

3. Compare these explanations of vertical FDI: the market power approach and the market imperfections approach. Which theory do you think offers the better explanation of the historical pattern of vertical FDI? Why?

4. You are the international manager of a U.S. business that has just developed a revolutionary new personal computer that can perform the same functions as IBM and Apple computers and their clones but costs only half as much to manufacture. Your CEO has asked you to formulate a recommendation for how to expand into the Western European market. Your options are (*i*) to export from the United States, (*ii*) to license a European firm to manufacture and market the computer in Europe, and (*iii*) to set up a wholly owned subsidiary in Europe. Evaluate the pros and cons of each alternative and suggest a course of action to your CEO.

❦ CLOSING CASE   Honda in North America

One of the most dramatic trends during the 1980s was the surge in Japanese direct investment in the United States. Leading this trend were the Japanese automobile companies, particularly Honda, Mazda, Nissan, and Toyota. Collectively these companies invested $5.3 billion in North American-based automobile assembly plants between 1982 and 1991. The early leader in this trend was Honda, which by 1991 had invested $1.13 billion in three North American auto assembly plants—two major plants in central Ohio and a smaller one in Ontario, Canada. Honda has invested an additional $500 million in an engine plant in Ohio that supplies its Ohio assembly plants. The company has also established major R&D and engineering facilities at its Ohio plants and has purchased an existing automotive test center—adjacent to the assembly plants—from the state of Ohio for $31 million.

As a result of these investments, Honda now employs 10,000 workers in its central Ohio plants and pumps a payroll of $7.3 million per week into the local economy. Of the 854,879 cars that Honda sold in the United States during 1990, nearly two-thirds were built at its three North American assembly plants—the vast majority of them in Ohio. Moreover, Honda claims the domestic content of its American-built cars is 75 percent—meaning that three-fourths of the final cost of a car is accounted for by North American labor, components, and other costs. The remaining 25 percent of the cost is for imported parts.

Honda had considered establishing auto assembly operations in North America as early as 1974, but initially ruled out investment due to the high cost of North American labor. In 1977, Honda announced it had selected a site in the small town of Marysville, Ohio, for a motorcycle assembly plant. Motorcycle production would test the ground for the possible manufacture of automobiles. This experiment was deemed necessary because Honda's internal feasibility studies still predicted that high labor costs and poor productivity would make North American-based automobile production unprofitable. However, Honda quickly realized its assumptions about poor productivity of U.S. workers were unfounded, and in 1979 it announced plans to construct an automobile assembly plant adjacent to its Marysville motorcycle plant. In November 1982 the first U.S.-built Honda was assembled, and by 1984 the plant was producing 150,000 automobiles per year.

Throughout the 1980s Honda's direct investment in North America produced complementary investments by many of its Japanese suppliers of component parts. By 1989 at least 29 major Japanese supplier companies had established transplant manufacturing facilities in Ohio to supply Honda with component parts. In addition, 33 other Japanese firms had invested in the United States to supply Honda and several other Japanese and U.S. automobile manufacturers. Honda required many of these companies to build their plants close to its Ohio complex so they could introduce a just-in-time production system, in which parts are delivered to the assembly plants just as they are needed. This technique virtually eliminates the need to hold in-process inventories and is regarded as a major source of cost savings. In addition Honda wanted major suppliers close so they could conveniently collaborate on the design of major components and on techniques for reducing costs and boosting quality.

A number of concerns seem to underlie Honda's decision to invest in North America. First, it is widely assumed that many Japanese firms, including Honda, did this largely to circumvent the threat of protectionist trade legislation, which seemed very real following the rapid increase in Japanese automobile exports to North America during the 1970s and early 80s. The threat of protectionism—especially the 1981 voluntary restraint agreement under which Japanese companies agreed not to further increase their imports into the United States—may have accelerated Honda's late-1980s investments in Ohio. A second concern was probably the sharp rise in the value of the Japanese yen against the U.S. dollar during 1987. This dramatically increased the cost of exporting both finished automobiles and component parts from Japan to North America. This also may have accelerated Honda's investments in the late 1980s.

However, it is also necessary to consider Honda's investment in North America in the context of its long-term corporate strategy. As a latecomer to automobile production in Japan, Honda had always struggled to remain profitable in the intensely competitive Japanese auto industry. Against this background, Honda's establishment of North American assembly plants can be seen as part of a strategy designed to circumvent Toyota and Nissan and to make major inroads in the U.S. market ahead of its Japanese rivals.

Underlying this strategy was Honda's strong belief that products need to be customized to the requirements of local markets. To paraphrase Hideo Sugiura, the former chairman of Honda, there are subtle differences, from country to country and from region to region, in the way a product is used and what customers expect of it. If a corporation believes that simply because a product has succeeded in a certain market it will sell well throughout the world, it is most likely destined for large and expensive errors or even failure. To produce products that account for local differences in customer tastes and preferences, Sugiura claimed that a company needed to establish top-to-bottom engineering, design, and production facilities in each major market in which it competed. Thus in the late 1970s Honda decided to invest in North America. Its success can be judged by the fact that although it was only the fourth largest automobile manufacturer in Japan in 1990 (with 9.3 percent of the market, compared to Toyota's 32.5 percent), it was the second largest Japanese automobile manufacturer in the United States (with 6.14 percent of the market, compared to first-place Toyota's 7.6 percent).

CASE DISCUSSION QUESTIONS

1. Drawing on the market imperfections approach to FDI, explain why Honda chose to invest in production facilities in the United States, as opposed to contracting with an established U.S. auto company to produce its cars under licensing in the United States?

2. Which of the theories of FDI reviewed in this chapter best explain Honda's FDI into the United States?

3. Are there aspects of Honda's investment in the United States that are not explained by the theories of FDI reviewed in this chapter? What are these aspects and how would you explain them?

Sources: A. Mair, R. Florida, and M. Kenney, "The New Geography of Automobile Production: Japanese Transplants in North America," Economic Geography 64 (1988), pp. 352–73; H. Sugiura, "How Honda Localizes Its Global Strategy," Sloan Management Review, Fall 1990, pp. 77–82; S. Toy, N. Gross, and J. B. Treece, "The Americanization of Honda," Business Week, April 25, 1988, pp. 90–96; and P. Magnusson, J. B. Treece, and W. C. Symonds, "Honda: Is It an American Car?" Business Week, November 18, 1991, pp. 105–09.

CHAPTER SEVEN

THE POLITICAL ECONOMY OF FOREIGN DIRECT INVESTMENT

NISSAN IN THE UNITED KINGDOM

The Nissan Motor Company, Japan's second largest carmaker, first began to invest in the United Kingdom in 1984. The investment was originally driven in part by fear that rising protectionist pressures would make it increasingly difficult for Nissan to serve the European market by exports from Japan. Nissan's plan was to invest in a single country within the European Community (now the European Union) and serve other countries within the European market by exports from that base. After reviewing a number of locations in Europe, Nissan decided to build a production plant in Sunderland, in the northeast part of the United Kingdom. In part, Nissan selected the Sunderland location over alternatives in Spain and Belgium because of significant financial incentives, including major tax breaks, that were being offered by the British government. In addition, a combination of low wage rates and high employee productivity made the United Kingdom in general, and Sunderland in particular, an attractive location. The incentives offered to Nissan by the British government were thought by many other European governments to be far too generous, and they prompted the French president to characterize Britain as "a Japanese aircraft carrier sitting off the coast of Europe."

When the investment was announced many critics in Britain believed the plant would be nothing more than a "screwdriver plant" assembling cars from parts and components imported from Japan. Experience, however, has proved the critics wrong. When the plant was announced in 1984 the plan was to have 60 percent local (European Union) content by 1990. At the official opening ceremony in September 1986 the president of Nissan announced an acceleration of its U.K. manufacturing program, with local content rising to 60 percent by 1988. This goal was achieved, and subsequently local content has risen to comprise 80 percent of the value of cars rolling off the Sunderland assembly plant. The plant now uses 197 European suppliers accounting for an annual average expenditure of $1,300 million. Two-thirds of these suppliers are located in the United Kingdom, with other major component suppliers based in Germany, France, and Spain. Thirty suppliers are in the area immediately surrounding the Sunderland plant.

The Nissan plant has produced tangible benefits for the U.K. economy in terms of both exports and jobs. By 1994 Nissan was producing over 250,000 vehicles annually at the Sunderland plant. Over 80 percent of this output was exported to other countries, primarily the European Union nations of Germany, Italy, France, and Spain. In addition, the Nissan plant exported to over 30 other countries, including Japan. The plant is now Britain's largest car exporter. As a consequence of this export-led growth, employment at the Nissan plant has also grown. When it opened in 1986 the plant had 470 employees. By 1994 the number employed had risen to 4,250. Additional jobs have been created in supporting industries, including 3,000 in nearby component suppliers. Nissan estimates the total permanent employment generated in the northeast part of the United Kingdom from its Sunderland plant was 8,029 in 1994.

Sources: United Nations, *World Investment Report 1994*, pp. 196–97; Nissan Motor Manufacturing Company (United Kingdom) Ltd.; and "A Survey of the Car Industry," *The Economist*, October 17, 1992, pp. 13–15.

❦ INTRODUCTION

In Chapter 6 we looked at the phenomenon of foreign direct investment (FDI) and reviewed several theories that attempt to explain the economic rationale for FDI. But we did not discuss the role of governments in FDI. Through their choice of policies, governments can both encourage and restrict FDI. Host governments can encourage FDI by providing incentives for foreign firms to invest in their economies, and they can restrict FDI through a variety of laws and policies. In the opening case, for example, we saw how the British government actively encouraged Nissan to invest in Britain. The British government encouraged Nissan to invest because it believed, correctly as it turned out, that substantial employment benefits would follow.

The government of a source country for FDI (the home government) also can encourage or restrict FDI by domestic firms. In recent years, for example, the Japanese government has pressured many Japanese firms to undertake FDI. The Japanese government sees FDI as a substitute for exporting, and thus as a way of reducing Japan's politically embarrassing balance of payments surplus. In contrast, the U.S. government has, for political reasons, from time to time restricted FDI by domestic firms. In 1995, for example, in response to a belief that the Iranian government actively supports terrorist organizations, the Clinton administration prohibited U.S. firms from investing in or exporting to Iran.

Historically one of the most important determinants of a government's policy toward FDI has been its political ideology. Accordingly, this chapter opens with a discussion of how political ideology influences government policy. As we shall see, to a greater or lesser degree, the officials of many governments tend to be pragmatic nationalists who weigh the benefits and costs of FDI and tend to vary their stated policy on a case-by-case basis. Following the discussion of political ideology, we will turn our attention to a consideration of the benefits and costs of FDI. Then we will look at the various policies home and host governments adopt to encourage and/or restrict FDI. The chapter closes with a detailed discussion of the implications of government policy for the business firm. In this closing section we examine the factors that determine the relative bargaining strengths of a host government and a firm contemplating FDI. We will look at how the negotiations between firm and government are often played out in practice and at how firms can use this knowledge to their advantage.

❦ POLITICAL IDEOLOGY AND FOREIGN DIRECT INVESTMENT

Historically ideology toward FDI has ranged from a dogmatic radical stance that is hostile to all FDI at one extreme to an adherence to the noninterventionist principle of free market economics at the other. Between these two extremes is an approach that might be called pragmatic nationalism. The spectrum is shown in Figure 7.1, and we will review each of these approaches.

The Radical View

The radical view traces its roots back to Marxist political and economic theory. In a nutshell, radical writers argue that the multinational enterprise (MNE) is an instrument of imperialist domination. They see the MNE as a tool for exploiting host countries to the exclusive benefit of their capitalist-imperialist home countries. They argue that MNEs extract profits from the host country and take them to their home country, giving nothing of value to the host country in exchange. They note, for example, that key technology is tightly controlled by the MNE, and that important jobs in the foreign subsidiaries of MNEs go to home-country nationals rather than to citizens of the host country. Because of this, according to the radical view, FDI by the MNEs of advanced capitalist nations keeps the less developed countries of the world relatively backward and dependent on advanced capitalist nations for investment, jobs, and technology. Thus, according to the extreme version of this view, no country under any circumstances should permit foreign

FIGURE 7.1

The Spectrum of Political
Ideology toward FDI

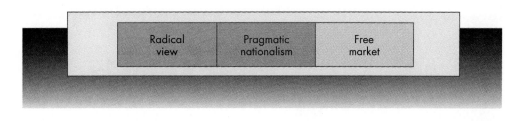

corporations to undertake FDI, since they can never be instruments of economic development, only of economic domination. Moreover, where MNEs already exist in a country, they should be immediately nationalized.[1]

From 1945 until the 1980s the radical view was very influential in the world economy. Until the collapse of communism between 1989 and 1991, the countries of Eastern Europe were largely opposed to any FDI. Similarly, Communist countries elsewhere, such as China, Cambodia, and Cuba, were all opposed in principle to FDI (although the Chinese started to allow FDI in mainland China in the 1970s). The radical position was also embraced by many socialist countries, particularly in Africa where one of the first actions of many newly independent states was to nationalize foreign-owned enterprises. The radical position was further embraced by countries whose political ideology was more nationalistic than socialistic. This was true in Iran and India, for example, both of which adopted tough policies restricting FDI and nationalized many foreign-owned enterprises. Iran is a particularly interesting case because its Islamic government, while rejecting Marxist theory, has essentially embraced the radical view that FDI by MNEs is an instrument of imperialism.

By the end of the 1980s, however, the radical position was in retreat almost everywhere. There seem to be three reasons for this:

1. The collapse of communism in Eastern Europe.
2. The generally abysmal economic performance of those countries that embraced the radical position, and a growing belief by many of these countries that, contrary to the radical position, FDI can be an important source of technology and jobs and can stimulate economic growth.
3. The strong economic performance of those developing countries that embraced capitalism rather than radical ideology (e.g., Singapore, Hong Kong, South Korea, and Taiwan).

The Free Market View   The free market view traces its roots to classical economics and the international trade theories of Adam Smith and David Ricardo (see Chapter 4). The intellectual case for this view has been strengthened by the market imperfections explanation of horizontal and vertical FDI that we reviewed in Chapter 6. The free market view argues that international production should be distributed among countries according to the theory of comparative advantage. That is, countries should specialize in the production of those goods and services that they can produce most efficiently. Within this framework, the MNE is seen as an instrument for dispersing the production of goods and services to those locations around the globe where they can be produced most efficiently. Viewed this way, FDI by the MNE is a way to increase the overall efficiency of the world economy.

Consider a well-publicized decision made by IBM in the mid-1980s to move assembly operations for many of its personal computers from the United States to Guadalajara in Mexico (the decision is profiled in the next "Management Focus"). IBM invested about $90 million in a state-of-the-art assembly facility with the capacity to produce 100,000 PCs per year, 75 percent of which were exported back to

---

[1]For elaboration see S. Hood and S. Young, *The Economics of the Multinational Enterprise* (London: Longman, 1979); and P. M. Sweezy and H. Magdoff, *The Dynamics of U.S. Capitalism* (New York: Monthly Review Press, 1972).

MANAGEMENT FOCUS
IBM's FDI in Mexico

In 1973 Mexico passed a law requiring foreign investors to agree to a minimum of 51 percent local ownership of any production facilities they establish in Mexico (the law was repealed as part of the 1994 North American Free Trade Agreement). The stated rationale for this law was Mexico's desire to reduce its economy's dependence on foreign-owned enterprises, thereby preserving its national sovereignty. However, as with many such laws, in practice the law was used as a bargaining chip by the Mexican government to extract concessions from foreign firms wishing to establish production facilities in Mexico. The government was often quite willing to waive the 51 percent ownership requirement if a foreign firm would make concessions that would benefit the Mexican economy.

A good illustration of how the process worked occurred in 1984 and 1985 when IBM tried to get permission to establish a facility to manufacture personal computers in Guadalajara, Mexico. IBM proposed to invest about $40 million in a state-of-the-art production facility with the capacity to produce 100,000 PCs per year, 75 percent of which would be exported (primarily to the United States). IBM's strategic objective was to take advantage of Mexico's low labor costs to reduce the costs of manufacturing PCs. Given the proprietary nature of the product and process technology involved in the design and manufacture of PCs, IBM wanted to maintain 100 percent ownership of the Guadalajara facility. IBM believed that if it

the United States.[2] According to the free market view, moves such as this increase the overall efficiency of resource utilization in the world economy. Mexico, due to its low labor costs, has a comparative advantage in the assembly of PCs. According to the free market view, by moving the production of PCs from the United States to Mexico, IBM frees up U.S. resources for use in activities in which the United States has a comparative advantage (e.g., the design of computer software, the manufacture of high value-added components such as microprocessors, or basic R&D). Moreover, U.S. consumers benefit because the PCs they want now cost less than they would if they were produced domestically. In addition Mexico gains from the technology, skills, and capital that IBM transfers with its FDI. Contrary to the radical view, the free market view stresses that such resource transfers benefit the host country and stimulate its economic growth. Thus the free market view argues that FDI is a benefit to both the source country and the host country.

The free market view has been embraced in principle by a number of advanced and developing nations, including the United States, Britain, Chile, Switzerland, Singapore, Hong Kong, the Netherlands, and Denmark. In addition, the free market view has been embraced by many of the former Communist countries of Eastern Europe, particularly Poland, the new Czech state, and Hungary, which currently are aggressively seeking foreign capital and investment.

In practice, however, no country has adopted the free market view in its pure form (just as no country has adopted the radical view in its pure form). Countries such as Britain and the United States are among the most open to FDI, but the governments of both countries have demonstrated a tendency to intervene. Britain does

---

[2]S. Weiss, "The Long Path to the IBM–Mexico Agreement: An Analysis of Microcomputer Investment Decisions," working paper no. 3, NYU School of Business, 1989.

entered into a joint venture with a Mexican firm to produce PCs, as required under Mexico's 1973 law, it would risk giving away valuable technology to a potential future competitor.

When presenting its case to the Mexican government, IBM stressed the benefits of the proposed investment for the Mexican economy. These included the creation of 80 direct jobs and 800 indirect ones, the transfer of high-technology job skills to Mexico, new direct investment of $7 million (the remaining $33 million required to finance the investment would be raised from the Mexican capital market), and exports of 75,000 personal computers per year. The Mexican government rejected the proposal on the grounds that IBM did

not propose to use sufficient local content in the plant and would thus be importing too many parts and materials.

IBM twice resubmitted its proposal. Maintaining its insistence on 100 percent ownership, with each proposal IBM increased its commitment to purchase local parts, increased the level of its direct investment, and raised its planned level of exports. The Mexican government agreed to the third proposal, which had in effect extracted significant concessions from IBM.

The final agreement required IBM to invest $91 million (up from $40 million). This money was distributed among expansion of the Guadalajara plant ($7 million), investment in local R&D ($35

million), development of local component-part suppliers ($20 million), expansion of its purchasing and distribution network ($13 million), contributions to a Mexican government-sponsored semiconductor technology center ($12 million), and various other minor investments. In addition, IBM agreed to achieve 82 percent local content by the fourth year of operation and to export 92 percent of the PCs produced in Mexico. In exchange the Mexican government waived its 51 percent local ownership requirement and allowed IBM to maintain 100 percent control.

Sources: J. Behrman and R. E. Grosse, *International Business and Government: Issues and Institutions* (Columbia, SC: University of South Carolina Press, 1990); and Weiss, "The Long Path to the IBM–Mexico Agreement."

so formally by reserving the right to block foreign takeovers of domestic firms if the takeovers are seen as "contrary to national security interests" or if they have the potential for "reducing competition." (In practice this right is rarely exercised.) U.S. controls on FDI are more limited still and largely informal. As noted earlier, for political reasons the United States will occasionally restrict U.S. firms from undertaking FDI in certain countries (e.g., Cuba and Iran). In addition, there are some limited restrictions on inward FDI. For example, foreigners are currently prohibited from purchasing more than 25 percent of any U.S. airline or from acquiring a controlling interest in a U.S. television broadcast network. Moreover, since 1989 the government has had the right to review foreign investment on the grounds of "national security." It is of note, however, that the rise of FDI into the United States in recent years has created pressures to pass stricter laws limiting it. In 1991, for example, there were 24 bills before Congress aimed at restricting FDI in the United States. Although none of these bills passed, the fact that so many were introduced indicates the mood in the Congress.

Pragmatic Nationalism

Most countries have adopted neither a radical policy nor a free market policy toward FDI, but instead a policy that can best be described as pragmatic nationalism. The pragmatic nationalist view is that FDI has both benefits and costs. FDI can benefit a host country by bringing capital, skills, technology, and jobs, but those benefits often come at a cost. When products resulting from an investment are produced by a foreign company rather than a domestic company, the profits from that investment go abroad. Many countries are also concerned that a foreign-owned manufacturing plant may import many components from its home country, which has negative implications for the host country's balance-of-payments position.

Recognizing this, countries adopting a pragmatic stance pursue policies designed to maximize the national benefits and minimize the national costs. According to

TABLE 7.1

Political Ideology towards FDI

Ideology	Characteristics	Host-Government Policy Implications
Radical	Marxist roots Views the MNE as an instrument of imperialist domination	Prohibit FDI Nationalize subsidiaries of foreign-owned MNEs
Free market	Classical economic roots (Smith) Views the MNE as an instrument for allocating production to most efficient locations	No restrictions on FDI
Pragmatic nationalism	Views FDI as having both benefits and costs	Restrict FDI where costs outweigh benefits Bargain for greater benefits and fewer costs Aggressively court beneficial FDI by offering incentives

this view, FDI should be allowed only if the benefits outweigh the costs. Mexico's demands that IBM meet a number of conditions before it be allowed to set up a 100 percent-owned subsidiary in Guadalajara provide a good example of such a pragmatic national policy (see "Management Focus"). By making such demands, Mexico was essentially trying to maximize the benefits and minimize the costs that IBM's investment might have for the Mexican economy.

Japan offers a more extreme version of pragmatic nationalism. Until the 1980s Japan's policy was probably one of the most restrictive among countries adopting a pragmatic nationalist stance. The Japanese believed that direct entry of foreign (especially U.S.) firms into the Japanese markets could be detrimental to the development and growth of their own industry and technology.[3] This belief led Japan to block the majority of applications by foreign firms to invest in Japan. However, there were always exceptions to this policy. Firms that had important technology often were permitted to undertake FDI if they insisted they would neither license their technology to a Japanese firm nor enter into a joint venture with a Japanese enterprise. IBM and Texas Instruments were among the firms that set up wholly owned subsidiaries in Japan by adopting this negotiating position. From the perspective of the Japanese government, the benefits of FDI in such cases—the stimulus these firms might impart to the Japanese economy—outweighed the perceived costs.

Another aspect of pragmatic nationalism is the tendency to aggressively court FDI seen to be in the national interest by, for example, offering subsidies to foreign MNEs in the form of tax breaks or grants. As we saw in the opening case, subsidies in the form of tax breaks were one factor that helped persuade Nissan to build an assembly plant in the United Kingdom, as opposed to another European Union nation such as Spain or Belgium. The countries of the European Union often seem to be competing with each other to attract U.S. and Japanese FDI by offering large tax breaks and subsidies. Among these countries, Britain has been the most successful at attracting Japanese investment in the automobile industry. In addition to Nissan, Toyota and Honda also now have major assembly plants in Britain. All three now use this country as their base for serving the rest of Europe—with obvious employment and balance-of-payments benefits for Britain.

Summary

The three main ideological positions with regard to FDI are summarized in Table 7.1. Recent years have seen a decline in the number of countries that adhere to a radical ideology. Moreover, although no countries have adopted a *pure* free market policy stance, an increasing number of countries are gravitating toward the free

---

[3]M. Itoh and K. Kiyono, "Foreign Trade and Direct Investment," in *Industrial Policy of Japan*, ed. R. Komiya, M. Okuno, and K. Suzumura (Tokyo: Academic Press, 1988).

market end of the spectrum and have liberalized their foreign investment regime. This includes many countries that only a few years ago were firmly in the radical camp (e.g., the former Communist countries of Eastern Europe and many of the socialist countries of Africa) and several countries that until recently could best be described as pragmatic nationalists with regard to FDI (e.g., Japan, South Korea, Italy, Spain, and most Latin American countries). One result has been the surge in the volume of FDI worldwide, which, as we noted in Chapter 6, has been growing twice as fast as the growth in world trade. Another result has been a dramatic increase in the volume of FDI directed at countries that have recently liberalized their FDI rules, such as China, India, and Vietnam.

❦ THE BENEFITS OF FDI TO HOST COUNTRIES

To a greater or lesser degree, most of the world's countries are now pragmatic nationalists with regard to FDI. For these countries, the main issue is to weigh the relative benefits against the cost of FDI. In this section we explore the three main benefits of FDI for a host country: resource-transfer effects, employment effects, and balance-of-payments effects. In the following section we will explore the costs of FDI to host countries. Economists who favor the free market view argue that the benefits of FDI to a host country so outweigh the costs that pragmatic nationalism is itself a misguided policy. According to the free market view, in a perfect world the best policy would be for all countries to forgo intervening in the investment decisions of MNEs.[4]

Resource-Transfer Effects

Foreign direct investment can make a positive contribution to a host economy by supplying capital, technology, and management resources that would otherwise not be available. If capital, technology, or management skills are scarce in a country, the provision of these skills by an MNE (through FDI) may boost that country's economic growth rate. The next "Country Focus" describes how the Venezuelan government has been encouraging FDI in its petroleum industry in an attempt to benefit from resource-transfer effects.

Capital

The basic argument with regard to capital is that many MNEs, by virtue of their large size and financial strength, have access to financial resources not available to host-country firms. These funds may be available from internal company sources, or, because of their reputation, large MNEs may find it easier to borrow money from capital markets than host-country firms would. This consideration was a factor in the Venezuelan government's decision to invite foreign oil companies to enter into joint ventures with PDVSA, the state-owned Venezuelan oil company, to develop Venezuela's oil industry (see "Country Focus").

Technology

As we saw in Chapter 2, the crucial role played by technological progress in economic growth is now widely accepted.[5] Technology is a catalyst that can stimulate economic development and industrialization. Technology can take two forms, both of which are valuable. It can be incorporated in a production process (e.g., the technology for discovering, extracting, and refining oil) or in a product (e.g., personal computers). However, many countries lack the research and development resources and skills required to develop their own indigenous product and process technology. This is particularly true of the world's less developed nations. Such countries must rely on advanced industrialized nations for much of the technology required to stimulate economic growth,

---

[4]Most of the material for this section is drawn from Hood and Young, *Economics of the Multinational Enterprise*.
[5]P. M. Romer, "The Origins of Endogenous Growth," *Journal of Economic Perspectives* 8, no. 1 (1994), pp. 3–22.

COUNTRY FOCUS
Foreign Direct Investment in Venezuela's Petroleum Industry

In 1993 Venezuela announced a plan to invest $45.5 billion in its petroleum industry over the next 10 years. The plan, as outlined by Gustavo Roosen, president of Venezuela's state-owned national oil company, Petroleos de Venezuela SA (PDVSA), assigns a key role to foreign investment in Venezuela's oil and gas sectors for the first time since the country nationalized all private oil companies in 1976. PDVSA ranks as one of the world's biggest oil companies; at the end of 1992 it had 63.3 billion barrels of crude oil reserves, one of the largest outside of the Middle East. A main thrust of the company's investment program is to develop a crude oil production potential of 4 million barrels per day by 2002, up 1.1 million barrels per day from the current capacity.

Of the $45.5 billion in projected capital spending, PDVSA plans to invest $29.1 billion (60 percent) of the total, while private companies, mainly foreign investors, will supply the remaining $19.4 billion. Groups such as Royal Dutch/Shell, Exxon, Conoco, Mitsubishi, and Total are already planning large joint-venture projects with PDVSA. PDVSA is turning to foreign investors for three reasons. First, it simply does not have the capital to undertake the investment alone. Second, the company recognizes that it lacks the technological resources and skills of many of the world's major oil companies, particularly in the areas of oil exploration, oil field development, and sophisticated refining. PDVSA realizes that if it wants to develop many of Venezuela's oil fields in a timely fashion, it has no alternative but to turn to these foreign companies. Third, PDVSA is hoping to use the joint ventures with foreign oil companies as a vehicle for learning about modern management techniques in the industry, which it can then use to improve the efficiency of its own operations.

The first FDI agreement was signed in 1992 with British Petroleum (BP). BP agreed to invest $60 million by 1995 to develop a marginal oil field that it would then be given the rights to for 20 years. Using a BP study, PDVSA has also identified sectors in eastern Venezuela with strong prospects for large discoveries of crude oil. PDVSA is now looking for foreign partners to develop these zones. If commercial quantities of oil are discovered, PDVSA will share future production with its partners. Furthermore, together with foreign investors such as Conoco and Total, PDVSA is investing in state-of-the-art refining facilities that can be used to convert heavy crude oil into a lighter weight, high-value crude oil for export. Finally, PDVSA, Shell, Exxon, and Mitsubishi have entered into a $5.6 billion joint venture to produce liquefied natural gas for export.

Sources: J. Mann, "A Little Help from Their Friends," *Financial Times*, November 10, 1993, p. 28; and "Venezuela: A Survey," *The Economist*, October 14, 1994.

and FDI can provide it. Before IBM's investment, for example, Mexico probably lacked the technological know-how required to develop its own personal computer industry. However, FDI and the associated technological transfer by MNEs such as IBM and Apple Computer have created a viable personal computer industry in Mexico and have probably had a beneficial effect on the economic well-being of Mexico as a whole. Similarly, as we saw in the "Country Focus" on Venezuela, a lack of relevant technological know-how with regard to the discovery, extraction, and refining of oil was one factor that underlay the Venezuelan government's decision to invite foreign oil companies into the country.

However, FDI is not the only way to access advanced technology. Another option is to license that technology from foreign MNEs. The Japanese government, in particular, has long favored this strategy. The belief of the Japanese government has been that technology is still ultimately controlled by the foreign MNE in the case of FDI. Consequently, it is difficult for indigenous Japanese firms to develop their own, possibly better, technology, since they are denied access to the basic technology. With this in mind, the Japanese government insisted that technology be transferred to Japan through licensing agreements, rather than through FDI.

The advantage of licensing is that in return for royalty payments, host-country firms are given direct access to valuable technology. The licensing option is generally less attractive to the MNE, however. By licensing its technology to foreign companies, an MNE risks creating a future competitor—as many U.S. firms have learned at great cost in Japan. Given this tension, the mode for transferring technology—licensing or FDI—can be a major negotiating point between an MNE and a host government. Whether the MNE gets its way depends on the relative bargaining powers of the MNE and the host government. In the case of Japan, for example, such was the bargaining power of IBM that it was able to get around Japan's preference for licensing arrangements and establish a wholly owned subsidiary in Japan.

Management

The foreign management skills provided through FDI may also produce important benefits for the host country. Particularly valuable may be the spin-off effects. Beneficial spin-off effects arise when local personnel who are trained to occupy managerial, financial, and technical posts in the subsidiary of a foreign MNE subsequently leave the firm and help to establish indigenous firms. Similar benefits may arise if the superior management skills of a foreign MNE stimulate local suppliers, distributors, and competitors to improve their own management skills.

The beneficial effects may be considerably reduced if most management and highly skilled jobs in the subsidiaries of foreign firms are reserved for home-country nationals. In such cases citizens of the host country do not receive the benefits of training by the MNE. This may limit the spin-off effect. The percentage of management and skilled jobs that go to citizens of the host country can be a major negotiating point between an MNE wishing to undertake FDI and a potential host government. In recent years most MNEs have responded to host-government pressures on this issue by agreeing to reserve a large proportion of management and highly skilled jobs for citizens of the host country.

Employment Effects

The beneficial employment effect claimed for FDI is that FDI brings jobs to a host country that would otherwise not be created there. As we saw in the opening case on Nissan in the United Kingdom, employment effects are both direct and indirect. Direct effects arise when a foreign MNE directly employs a number of host-country citizens. Indirect effects arise when jobs are created in local suppliers as a result of the investment and when jobs are created because of the increased spending in the local economy resulting from employees of the MNE. The indirect employment effects are often as large as, if not larger than, the direct effects. In the opening case for example, we saw that Nissan's investment in the United Kingdom created 4,250 direct jobs and at least another 4,000 jobs in support industries.

On the other hand, cynics note that not all the "new jobs" created by FDI represent net additions in employment. In the case of FDI by Japanese auto companies in the United States, for example, some argue that the jobs created by this investment have been more than offset by the jobs lost in U.S.-owned auto companies, which have lost market share to their Japanese competitors. As a consequence of such substitution effects, the net number of new jobs created by FDI may not be as great as initially claimed by an MNE. Not surprisingly, then, the issue of the likely net gain in employment may be a major negotiating point between an MNE wishing to undertake FDI and the host government.

Table 7.2
U.S. Balance of Payments
Accounts for 1993
(Millions of Dollars)

Current Account	Credits	Debits
Exports of goods, services, and income:	$755,533	
Merchandise	456,866	
Services	184,811	
Income receipts on investments	113,856	
Imports of goods, services, and income:		$–827,312
Merchandise		–589,441
Services		–127,961
Income payments on investments		–109,910
Unilateral transfers		–32,117
Balance of current account		$–103,896

Capital Account		
U.S. assets abroad (net):		$–147,989
U.S. official reserve assets		–1,379
Other U.S. government assets		–306
U.S. private assets		–147,898
Foreign assets in U.S.:	$230,698	
Foreign official assets	71,681	
Other foreign assets	159,017	
Balance on capital account	$82,709	
Statistical discrepancy	$21,187	

Source: U.S. Department of Commerce, Survey of Current Business, *June 1994, p. 86.*

Balance-of-Payments Effects

The effect of FDI on a country's balance-of-payments accounts is an important policy issue for most host governments. To understand this concern we must first familiarize ourselves with balance-of-payments accounting. Then we will examine the link between FDI and the balance-of-payments accounts.

Balance-of-payments accounts

A country's **balance-of-payments accounts** keep track of both its payments to and its receipts from other countries. A summary copy of the U.S. balance of payments accounts for 1993 is given in Table 7.2. Any transaction resulting in a payment to other countries is entered in the balance-of-payments accounts as a debit and given a negative (–) sign. Any transaction resulting in a receipt from other countries is entered as a credit and given a positive (+) sign.

Balance-of-payments accounts are divided into two main sections: the current account and the capital account. The **current account** records transactions that pertain to three categories, all of which can be seen in Table 7.2. The first category, *merchandise trade*, refers to the export or import of goods (e.g., autos, computers, chemicals). The second category is the export or import of *services* (e.g., intangible products such as banking and insurance services). The third category, *investment income*, refers to income from foreign investments and payments that have to be made to foreigners investing in a country. So, for example, if a U.S. citizen owns a share of a Finnish company and receives a dividend payment of $5, that payment shows up on the U.S. current account as the receipt of $5 of investment income.

A **current account deficit,** or **trade deficit** as it is often called, occurs when a country imports more goods, services, and income than it exports. A **current account surplus (trade surplus)** occurs when a country exports more goods, services, and income than it imports. In recent years the United States has run a persistent trade deficit. Table 7.2, for example, shows that in 1993 the current account deficit was $103,896 million.

The **capital account** records transactions that involve the purchase or sale of assets. Thus, when a Japanese firm purchases stock of a U.S. company, the transaction enters the U.S. balance of payments as a credit on the capital account. This is because capital is flowing into the country. When capital flows out of the United States, it enters the U.S. capital account as a debit.

A basic principle of balance-of-payments accounting is double-entry bookkeeping. Every international transaction automatically enters the balance of payments twice—once as a credit and once as a debit. As an explanation of why this is so, imagine that you purchase a car produced in Japan by Toyota for $12,000. Since your purchase represents a payment to another country for goods, it will enter the balance of payments as a debit on the current account. Toyota now has the $12,000 and must do something with it. If Toyota deposits the money at a U.S. bank, Toyota has purchased a U.S. asset—a bank deposit worth $12,000—and the transaction will show up as a $12,000 credit on the capital account. Alternatively, Toyota might deposit the cash in a Japanese bank in return for Japanese yen. Now the Japanese bank must decide what to do with the $12,000. Any action that it takes will ultimately result in a credit for the U.S. balance of payments. For example, if the bank lends the $12,000 to a Japanese firm that uses it to import personal computers from the United States, then the $12,000 must be credited to the U.S. balance-of-payments current account. Alternatively, the Japanese bank might use the $12,000 to purchase U.S. government bonds, in which case it will show up as a credit on the U.S. balance-of-payments capital account.

Thus any international transaction automatically gives rise to two offsetting entries in the balance of payments. Because of this, the current account balance and the capital account balance should always add up to zero. (In practice, this does not always occur due to the existence of *statistical discrepancies*, which need not concern us here.)

Governments normally are concerned when their country is running a deficit on the current account of their balance of payments (i.e., when there is a trade deficit).[6] When a country runs a current-account deficit, the money that flows to other countries is typically then used by those countries to purchase assets in the deficit country. Thus, when the United States runs a trade deficit with Japan, the Japanese use the money that they receive from U.S. consumers to purchase U.S. assets such as stocks, bonds, and the like. Put another way, a deficit on the current account is financed by selling assets to other countries; that is, by a surplus on the capital account. Thus, for example, the U.S. current-account deficit during the 1980s was financed by a steady sale of U.S. assets (stocks, bonds, real estate, and increasingly, whole corporations) to other countries. In effect, countries that run current-account deficits become net debtors.

What is wrong with this? The main problem is that debtor nations owe people money. As a result of financing its current-account deficit through asset sales, from now on the United States will be obliged to deliver a stream of interest payments to foreign bondholders, rents to foreign landowners, and dividends to foreign stockholders. Such payments to foreigners drain resources from a country and limit the amount of funds available for investment within the country. Since investment within a country is necessary to stimulate economic growth, a persistent current-account deficit can choke off a country's future economic growth.

FDI and the balance of payments

Given the concern about current-account deficits, the balance-of-payments effects of FDI can be an important consideration for a host government. From a balance-of-payments perspective, there are three potential consequences of FDI. First, when an MNE establishes a foreign subsidiary, the capital account of the host country benefits from the initial capital inflow. (A debit will be recorded in the capital account of the

---

[6]P. Krugman, *The Age of Diminished Expectations* (Cambridge, MA: MIT Press, 1990).

home country, since capital is flowing out of the home country.) However, this is a one-time-only effect. Set against this must be the outflow of earnings to the foreign parent company, which will be recorded as a debit on the current account of the host country.

Second, if the FDI is a substitute for imports of goods or services, the effect can be to improve the current account of the host country's balance of payments. Much of the FDI by Japanese automobile companies in the United States and United Kingdom, for example, can be seen as substituting for imports from Japan. Thus the current account of the U.S. balance of payments has improved somewhat, because many Japanese companies are now supplying the U.S. market from production facilities in the United States, as opposed to facilities in Japan. Insofar as this has reduced the need to finance a current-account deficit by asset sales to foreigners, the United States has clearly benefited from this.

A third potential benefit to the host country's balance-of-payments position arises when the MNE uses a foreign subsidiary to export goods and services to other countries. As outlined in the opening case, one of the benefits to Britain of Nissan's investment was that Nissan has subsequently exported up to 80 percent of the automobiles assembled at its Sunderland plant, which has had a commensurately favorable impact on the current account of Britain's balance of payments.

❧ THE COSTS OF FDI TO HOST COUNTRIES

Three costs of FDI concern host countries. They arise from possible adverse effects on competition within the host nation, adverse effects on the balance of payments, and the perceived loss of national sovereignty and autonomy.

Adverse Effects on Competition

Host governments sometimes worry that the subsidiaries of foreign MNEs operating in their country may have greater economic power than indigenous competitors because they may be part of a larger international organization than the indigenous firms. As such, the foreign MNE may be able to draw on funds generated elsewhere to subsidize its costs in the host market, which could drive indigenous companies out of business and allow the firm to monopolize the market. (Once the market was monopolized, the foreign MNE could raise prices above those that would prevail in competitive markets, with harmful effects on the economic welfare of the host nation.) This concern tends to be greater in countries that have few large firms of their own that are able to compete effectively with the subsidiaries of foreign MNEs (generally less developed countries). It tends to be a relatively minor concern in most advanced industrialized nations.

Another variant of the competition argument is related to the infant industry concern that we first discussed in Chapter 6. Import controls may be motivated by a desire to let a local industry develop to a stage where it is capable of competing in world markets. The same logic suggests FDI should be restricted. If a country with a potential comparative advantage in a particular industry allows FDI in that industry, indigenous firms may never have a chance to develop.

The above arguments are often used by inefficient indigenous competitors when lobbying their government to restrict direct investment by foreign MNEs. Although a host government may state publicly in such cases that its restrictions on inward FDI are designed to protect indigenous competitors from the market power of foreign MNEs, they may have been enacted to protect inefficient but politically powerful indigenous competitors from foreign competition.

Adverse Effects on the Balance of Payments

The possible adverse effects of FDI on a host country's balance-of-payments position have been hinted at earlier. There are two main areas of concern with regard to the balance of payments. First, as mentioned earlier, set against the initial capital inflow that comes with FDI must be the subsequent outflow of earnings from the foreign subsidiary to its parent company. Such outflows show up as a debit on the capital account. Some governments have responded to such outflows by restricting the amount of earnings that can be repatriated to a foreign subsidiary's home country.

A second concern arises when a foreign subsidiary imports a substantial number of its inputs from abroad, which results in a debit on the current account of the host country's balance of payments. One criticism leveled against Japanese-owned auto assembly operations in the United States, for example, is that they tend to import a large number of component parts from Japan. The favorable impact of this FDI on the current account of the U.S. balance-of-payments position may not be as great as initially supposed. The Japanese auto companies have responded to these criticisms by pledging to purchase 75 percent of their component parts from U.S.-based manufacturers (but not necessarily U.S.-owned manufacturers). In the case of Nissan's investment in the United Kingdom, Nissan responded to concerns about local content by pledging to increase the proportion of local content to 60 percent, and by subsequently raising it to over 80 percent.

National Sovereignty and Autonomy

Many host governments worry that FDI is accompanied by some loss of economic independence. The concern is that key decisions that can affect the host country's economy will be made by a foreign parent that has no real commitment to the host country, and over which the host country's government has no real control. Twenty years ago this concern was expressed by several European countries, which feared that FDI by U.S. MNEs was threatening their national sovereignty. Ironically, the same concerns are now surfacing in the United States with regard to European and Japanese FDI. The main fear seems to be that if foreigners own assets in the United States, they can somehow "hold the country to economic ransom." Twenty years ago when officials in the French government were making similar complaints about U.S. investments in France, many U.S. politicians dismissed the charge as silly. Now that the shoe is on the other foot, many U.S. politicians no longer think the notion is silly. However, most economists dismiss such concerns as groundless and irrational. Political scientist Robert Reich recently spoke of such concerns as the product of outmoded thinking, because they fail to account for the growing interdependence of the world economy.[7] In a world where firms from all advanced nations are increasingly investing in each other's markets, it is not possible for one country to hold another to "economic ransom" without hurting itself.

❧ THE BENEFITS AND COSTS OF FDI TO HOME COUNTRIES

Although the costs and benefits of FDI for a host country have received most attention, there are also costs and benefits to the home (or source) country that warrant study. Does the U.S. economy benefit or lose from investments by its firms in foreign markets? Does the Japanese economy lose or gain from Nissan's investment in the United Kingdom? Some would argue that FDI is not always in the home country's national interest and should be restricted. Others argue that the benefits far outweigh the costs, and that any restrictions would be contrary to national interests. To understand why people take these positions, let us look at the benefits and costs of FDI to the home (source) country.[8]

Benefits of FDI to the Home Country

The benefits of FDI to the home country arise from three sources. First, and perhaps most important, the capital account of the home country's balance of payments benefits from the inward flow of foreign earnings. Thus one benefit to Japan from Nissan's investment in the United Kingdom are the earnings that are subsequently

---

[7]Robert B. Reich, *The Work of Nations: Preparing Ourselves for the 21st Century* (New York: Alfred A. Knopf, 1991).

[8]For a recent review see John H. Dunning, "Re-evaluating the Benefits of Foreign Direct Investment," *Transnational Corporations* 3, no. 1 (February 1994), pp. 23–51.

repatriated to Japan. FDI can also have a beneficial impact on the current account of the home country's balance of payments if the foreign subsidiary creates demands for home-country exports of capital equipment, intermediate goods, complementary products, and the like.

Second, benefits to the home country from outward FDI arise from employment effects. As with the balance of payments, positive employment effects arise when the foreign subsidiary creates demand for home-country exports of capital equipment, intermediate goods, complementary products, and the like. Thus Nissan's investment in auto assembly operations in the United Kingdom has had a beneficial effect on both the Japanese balance-of-payments position and employment in Japan, because Nissan imports some component parts for its U.K.-based auto assembly operations directly from Japan.

Third, benefits arise when the home-country MNE learns valuable skills from its exposure to foreign markets that can be transferred back to the home country. This amounts to a reverse resource-transfer effect. Through its exposure to a foreign market, an MNE can learn about superior management techniques and superior product and process technologies. These resources can then be transferred back to the home country, with a commensurate beneficial effect on the home country's economic growth rate.[9] For example, by investing in Japanese automobile companies, General Motors, which owns part of Isuzu, and Ford, which owns part of Mazda, learn about those companies' management techniques and production processes. If GM and Ford are successful in transferring this know-how back to their U.S. operations, the result may be a net gain for the U.S. economy.

Costs of FDI to the Home Country

Against these benefits must be set the apparent costs of FDI for the home (source) country. The most important concerns center around the balance-of-payments and employment effects of outward FDI. The home country's balance of payments may suffer in three ways. First, the capital account of the balance of payments suffers from the initial capital outflow required to finance the FDI. This effect, however, is usually more than offset by the subsequent inflow of foreign earnings. Second, the current account of the balance of payments suffers if the purpose of the foreign investment is to serve the home market from a low-cost production location. This certainly was the case with IBM's investment in Mexico, the purpose of which was to build PCs for sale in the U.S. market (see "Management Focus"). Third, the current account of the balance of payments suffers if the FDI is a substitute for direct exports. Thus, insofar as Toyota's assembly operations in the United States are intended to substitute for direct exports from Japan, the current-account position of Japan will deteriorate.

With regard to employment effects, the most serious concerns arise when FDI is seen as a substitute for domestic production. This was the case with IBM's investment in Mexico and with Nissan's investment in the United Kingdom. One obvious result of such FDI is reduced home-country employment. If the labor market in the home country is already very tight, with little unemployment (as was the case in both Japan and the United States during the 1980s), this concern may not be that great. However, if the home country is suffering from unemployment, concern about the "export of jobs" may rise to the fore. For example, one objection frequently raised by U.S. labor leaders to the free trade pact between the United States, Mexico, and Canada (see the next chapter) is that the United States will lose hundreds of thousands of jobs as U.S. firms invest in Mexico to take advantage of cheaper labor and then export back to the U.S. market.[10]

---

[9]This idea has recently been articulated, although not quite in this form, by C. A. Bartlett and S. Ghoshal, *Managing across Borders: The Transnational Solution* (Boston: Harvard Business School Press, 1989).

[10]P. Magnusson, "The Mexico Pact: Worth the Price?" *Business Week*, May 27, 1991, pp. 32–35.

International Trade Theory and Offshore Production

When assessing the costs and benefits of FDI to the home country, we should remember the lessons of international trade theory (see Chapter 4). International trade theory tells us that home-country concerns about the negative economic effects of offshore production may be misplaced. The term *offshore production* refers to FDI undertaken to serve the home market, such as IBM's investment in Mexico to produce PCs for the U.S. market. Far from reducing home-country employment, such FDI may actually stimulate economic growth (and hence employment) in the home country by freeing home-country resources to concentrate on activities where the home country has a comparative advantage. In addition, home-country consumers benefit if the price of the particular product falls as a result of the FDI. Thus U.S. consumers arguably benefited from IBM's decision to produce personal computers in Mexico for export to the United States, primarily because IBM was able to reduce the price of its PCs as a result.

Also bear in mind that if a company such as IBM were prohibited from making such investments on the grounds of negative employment effects while its international competitors were able to reap the benefits of low-cost production locations, IBM would undoubtedly lose market share to its international competitors. Under such a scenario, the adverse long-run economic effects for the U.S. economy would probably far outweigh the relatively minor balance-of-payments and employment effects associated with offshore production.

❧ GOVERNMENT POLICY INSTRUMENTS AND FDI

We have now reviewed the costs and benefits of FDI from the perspective of both home country and host country. Before tackling the important issue of bargaining between the MNE and the host government, we need to discuss the policy instruments that governments use to regulate FDI activity by MNEs. Both home (source) countries and host countries have a range of policy instruments they can use. We will look at each in turn.

Home-Country Policies

By their choice of policies, home countries can both encourage and restrict FDI by local firms. We look at policies designed to encourage outward FDI first. These include foreign risk insurance, capital assistance, tax incentives, and political pressure. Then we will look at policies designed to restrict outward FDI.

Encouraging outward FDI

Many investor nations now have government-backed insurance programs to cover major types of foreign investment risk. The types of risks insurable through these programs include the risks of expropriation (nationalization), war losses, and the inability to transfer profits back home. Such programs are particularly useful in encouraging firms to undertake investments in politically unstable countries.[11] In addition several advanced countries also have special funds or banks that make government loans to firms wishing to invest in developing countries. As a further incentive to encourage domestic firms to undertake FDI, many countries have eliminated double taxation of foreign income (i.e., taxation of income in both the host country and the home country). Last, and perhaps most significant, a number of investor countries (particularly the United States) have used their political influence to persuade host countries to relax their restrictions on inbound FDI. For example, in response to direct U.S. pressure, Japan relaxed many of its formal restrictions on inward FDI in the early 1980s. Now, in response to further U.S. pressure, Japan is beginning to move toward relaxing its informal barriers to inward FDI. One of the most recent beneficiaries of this trend is Toys R Us, which, after five years of intensive lobbying by company and U.S. government officials, opened its first retail stores in Japan in December 1991.

---

[11]C. Johnston, "Political Risk Insurance," in *Assessing Corporate Political Risk*, ed. D. M. Raddock (Totowa, NJ: Rowan & Littlefield, 1986).

Restricting outward FDI

Virtually all investor countries, including the United States, have exercised some control over outward FDI from time to time. One of the most common policies has been to limit capital outflows out of concern for the country's balance of payments. From the early 1960s until 1979, for example, Britain had exchange-control regulations that effectively limited the amount of capital a firm could take out of the country. Although the main intent of such policies was to improve the British balance of payments, an important secondary intent was to make it more difficult for British firms to undertake FDI.

In addition, countries have occasionally manipulated tax rules to try to encourage their firms to invest at home. The objective behind such policies is to create jobs at home rather than in other nations. At one time these policies were also adopted by Britain. The British advanced corporation tax system taxed British companies' foreign earnings at a higher rate than their domestic earnings. This tax code created an incentive for British companies to invest at home.

Finally, countries sometimes prohibit national firms from investing in certain countries for political reasons. Such restrictions can be formal or informal. For example, formal U.S. rules have prohibited U.S. firms from investing in countries such as Cuba, Libya, and Iran, whose political ideology and actions are judged to be contrary to U.S. interests. Similarly, during the 1980s informal pressure was applied to dissuade U.S. firms from investing in South Africa. In this case the objective was to pressure South Africa to change its apartheid laws, which occurred during the early 1990s. Thus this policy was successful.

Host-Country Policies

Host countries adopt policies designed both to restrict and to encourage inward FDI. As noted earlier in this chapter, political ideology has determined the type and scope of these policies in the past. In the last decade of the 20th century, we seem to be moving quickly away from a situation where many countries adhered to some version of the radical stance and prohibited much FDI and toward a situation where a combination of free market objectives and pragmatic nationalism seems to be taking hold.

Encouraging inward FDI

It is increasingly common for governments to offer incentives to foreign firms to invest in their countries. Such incentives take many forms, but the most common are tax concessions, low-interest loans, and grants or subsidies. Incentives are motivated by a desire to gain from the resource-transfer and employment effects of FDI. They are also motivated by a desire to capture FDI away from other potential host countries. For example, as we saw in the opening case, the governments of Britain and Spain competed with each other on the size of the incentives they offered Nissan to invest in their respective countries. Britain won this competition, and the size of the tax concessions granted to Nissan was no small factor in the final decision. Not only do countries compete with each other to attract FDI; regions of countries do as well. In the United States, for example, state governments often compete with each other to attract FDI. In one case it has been estimated that in attempting to persuade Toyota to build its U.S. automobile assembly plants in Kentucky, rather than elsewhere in the United States, the state offered Toyota an incentive package worth $112 million. The package included tax breaks, new state spending on infrastructure, and low-interest loans.[12]

Restricting inward FDI

Host governments use a wide range of controls to restrict FDI in one way or another. The two most common, however, are ownership restraints and performance requirements. Ownership restraints can take several forms. In some countries

---

[12]Martin Tolchin and Susan Tolchin, *Buying into America: How Foreign Money Is Changing the Face of Our Nation* (New York: Times Books, 1988).

foreign companies are excluded from certain business fields. For example, they are excluded from tobacco and mining in Sweden and from the development of certain natural resources in Brazil, Finland, and Morocco. In other industries foreign ownership may be permitted, although there may be a requirement that a significant proportion of a subsidiary of a foreign MNE be owned by local investors. For example, foreign ownership is restricted to 25 percent or less of an airline in the United States.

The rationale underlying ownership restraints seems to be twofold. First, foreign firms are often excluded from certain sectors on the grounds of national security or competition. Particularly in less developed countries, the feeling seems to be that local firms might not be able to develop unless foreign competition is restricted by a combination of import tariffs and controls on FDI. This is really a variant of the infant industry argument we discussed in Chapter 5.

Second, ownership restraints seem to be based on a belief that local owners can help to maximize the resource-transfer and employment benefits of FDI for the host country. Consistent with this belief, until the early 1980s the Japanese government prohibited most FDI but was prepared to allow joint ventures between Japanese firms and foreign MNEs if the MNE had a particularly valuable technology. The Japanese government clearly believed such an arrangement would help speed the subsequent diffusion of the MNE's valuable technology throughout the Japanese economy.

As for performance requirements, these too can take several forms. Performance requirements are controls over the behavior of the local subsidiary of an MNE. In the "Management Focus," Mexico's insistence that IBM's PC subsidiary achieve 82 percent local content and export 92 percent of its output are performance requirements. The most common performance requirements are related to local content, exports, technology transfer, and local participation in top management. As with certain ownership restrictions, the logic underlying performance requirements is that such rules help to maximize the benefits and minimize the costs of FDI for the host country. Virtually all countries employ some form of performance requirement when it suits their objectives. However, performance requirements tend to be more common in less developed countries than in advanced industrialized nations. For example, one study found that some 30 percent of the affiliates of U.S. MNEs in less developed countries were subject to performance requirements, while only 6 percent of the affiliates in advanced countries were faced with such requirements.[13]

IMPLICATIONS FOR BUSINESS

A number of fairly obvious implications for business are inherent in the material discussed in this chapter. A host government's attitude toward FDI should be an important variable in decisions about where to locate foreign production facilities and where to make a foreign direct investment. Other things being equal, investing in countries that have permissive policies toward FDI is clearly preferable to investing in countries that restrict FDI.

Generally, however, the issue is not this straightforward. Despite the move toward a free market stance in recent years, many countries still have a rather pragmatic stance toward FDI. In such cases a firm considering FDI usually must negotiate the specific terms of the investment with the country's government. Such negotiations center on two broad issues. If the host government is trying to attract FDI, the central issue is likely to be the kind of incentives the host government is prepared to offer to the MNE and what the firm will commit in exchange. If the host government is uncertain about the benefits of FDI and might choose to restrict access, the central issue is likely to be the concessions the firm must make to be allowed to go forward with a proposed investment. Given this, in the remainder of this section we will focus our attention on the issue of negotiating with a host government.

---

[13]Behrman and Grosse, *International Business and Government*.

FIGURE 7.2
The Context of Negotiation—
the Four Cs

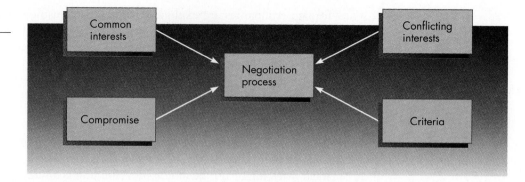

The Nature of Negotiation

The objective of any negotiation is to reach an agreement that benefits both parties. Negotiation is both an *art* and a *science*. The science of it requires systematically analyzing the relative bargaining strengths of each party and the different strategic options available to each party and assessing how the other party might respond to various bargaining ploys.[14] The art of negotiation incorporates "interpersonal skills, the ability to convince and be convinced, the ability to employ a basketful of bargaining ploys, and the wisdom to know when and how to use them."[15] In the context of international business, it might be added that the art of negotiation also includes understanding the influence of national norms, value systems, and culture on the approach and likely negotiating tactics of the other party as well as sensitivity to such factors in shaping a firm's approach to negotiations with a foreign government. For example, negotiating with the Japanese government for access is likely to be very different from negotiating with the British government. Consequently, it requires different interpersonal skills and bargaining ploys. We discussed the importance of national differences in society and culture in Chapter 3. It would be well to keep these differences in mind at this juncture.

The negotiation process has been characterized as occurring within the context of "the four Cs": common interests, conflicting interests, compromise, and criteria (see Figure 7.2).[16] In the IBM and Mexico example (see the "Management Focus") the common interest of both IBM and Mexico is in establishing a new enterprise in Mexico. Conflicting interests arise from such issues as the proportion of component parts that will be procured locally rather than imported, the total amount of investment, the total number of jobs to be created, and the proportion of output that will be exported. Compromise involves reaching a decision that brings benefits to both parties, even though neither will get all they want. IBM's criteria or objectives are to achieve satisfactory profits and to maintain 100 percent ownership. Mexico's criteria are to achieve satisfactory net benefits from the resource-transfer, employment, and balance-of-payments effects of the investment.

Bargaining Power

To a large degree, the outcome of any negotiated agreement depends on the relative bargaining power of both parties. Each side's bargaining power depends on three factors (see Table 7.3):

- The value each side places on what the other has to offer.
- The number of comparable alternatives available to each side.
- Each party's time horizon.

---

[14]For a good introduction, see M. H. Bazerman, *Negotiating Rationally* (New York: Free Press, 1991; and A. Dixit and B. Nalebuff, *Thinking Strategically: The Competitive Edge in Business, Politics, and Everyday Life* (New York: W. W. Norton, 1991).

[15]H. Raiffa, *The Art and Science of Negotiation* (Cambridge, MA: Harvard University Press, 1982).

[16]J. Fayerweather and A. Kapoor, *Strategy and Negotiation for the International Corporation* (Cambridge, MA: Ballinger, 1976).

TABLE 7.3
Determinants of Bargaining Power

	Bargaining Power of Firm	
	High	**Low**
Firm's time horizon	Long	Short
Comparable alternatives open to firm	Many	Few
Value placed by host government on investment	High	Low

From the perspective of a firm negotiating the terms of an investment with a host government, the firm's bargaining power is high when the host government places a high value on what the firm has to offer, many comparable alternatives are open to the firm, and the firm has a long time in which to complete the negotiations. The converse also holds. The firm's bargaining power is low when the host government places a low value on what the firm has to offer, few comparable alternatives are open to the firm, and the firm has a short time in which to complete the negotiations.

To see how this plays out in practice, consider again the case of IBM and Mexico in the "Management Focus." First, note that IBM was in a fairly strong bargaining position, primarily because Mexico was suffering from a flight of capital out of the country at the time (1985 and 1986), which made the government eager to attract new foreign investment. On the other hand, IBM's bargaining power was moderated somewhat by three things.

First, the size of the proposed investment was unlikely to have more than a marginal impact on the Mexican economy, so the economic value placed by Mexico on the investment was not that great.

Second, IBM was looking for a low-labor-cost, politically stable location close to the U.S. market. Mexico was obviously the most desirable location given these criteria. Greater distance and higher transportation costs made alternative low-labor-cost locations, such as Taiwan or Singapore, relatively less attractive, while other potential locations in Central America were ruled out by political instability.

Third, given the profusion of low-cost competitors moving into the U.S. personal computer market during the mid-1980s, IBM probably felt it needed to move quickly to establish its own low-cost production facilities. There was no compelling reason for Mexico to close a deal quickly.

Due to all these factors, the Mexican government also held a degree of bargaining power in the negotiations and thus was able to extract some concessions from IBM. On the other hand, IBM's basically strong position allowed it to insist that it maintain 100 percent ownership of its Mexican subsidiary. This represented a significant concession from the Mexican government; IBM was the first major company for which Mexico waived its prohibition of majority ownership.

In a similar case during the 1960s, by using its bargaining power IBM was one of the few firms able to get the Japanese government to waive the restriction on FDI that would allow it to establish a 100 percent-owned subsidiary in Japan. IBM was able to do this because it was the only major source of mainframe computer technology at that time, and numerous Japanese companies needed that technology for data processing. The lack of comparable alternatives available to the Japanese enabled IBM to pry open the Japanese market.

Similarly, during the 1980s Toyota extracted significant concessions from the state of Kentucky in the form of tax breaks, low-interest loans, and grants, and Honda received similar concessions from the state of Ohio, when both companies undertook investment in U.S.-based auto assembly operations. At that time both these states were suffering from high unemployment, and the proposed investments promised to have a substantial impact on employment. Moreover, both companies had a number of states from which to choose. Thus the high value placed by state governments on the proposed investment and the number of comparable alternatives open to each company considerably strengthened the bargaining power of both companies relative to that of the state governments.

✖ SUMMARY OF CHAPTER

The main objective of this chapter has been to examine the influence of governments on firms' decisions to invest in foreign countries. By their choice of policies, both host-country and home-country governments encourage and restrict FDI. A second objective has been to explore the factors that influence negotiations between a host-country government and a firm contemplating FDI. In particular, the following points have been made:

1. An important determinant of government policy toward FDI is political ideology. Political ideology ranges from a radical stance that is hostile to FDI to a noninterventionist, free market stance. Between the two extremes is an approach best described as pragmatic nationalism.

2. The radical view sees the MNE as an imperialist tool for exploiting host countries. According to this view, no country should allow FDI. Due to the collapse of communism, the radical view was in retreat everywhere by the end of the mid-1990s.

3. The free market view sees the MNE as an instrument for increasing the overall efficiency of resource utilization in the world economy. FDI can be viewed as a way of dispersing the production of goods and services to those locations around the globe where they can be produced most efficiently. This view is embraced in principle by a number of nations; in practice, however, most are pragmatic nationalists.

4. Pragmatic nationalism views FDI as having both benefits and costs. Countries adopting a pragmatic stance pursue policies designed to maximize the benefits and minimize the costs of FDI.

5. The benefits of FDI to a host country arise from resource-transfer effects, employment effects, and balance-of-payments effects.

6. FDI can make a positive contribution to a host economy by supplying capital, technology, and management resources that would otherwise not be available. Such resource transfers can stimulate the growth of the host economy.

7. Employment effects arise from the direct and indirect creation of jobs by FDI.

8. Balance-of-payments effects arise from the initial capital inflow to finance FDI, from import substitution effects, and from subsequent exports by the new enterprise.

9. The costs of FDI to a host country include adverse effects on competition and balance of payments and a perceived loss of national sovereignty.

10. Host governments are concerned that foreign MNEs may have greater economic power than indigenous companies and that they may be able to monopolize the market.

11. Adverse effects on the balance of payments arise from the outflow of a foreign subsidiary's earnings and from the import of inputs from abroad.

12. With regard to national sovereignty, the concern is that with FDI, key decisions that affect the host country will be made by a foreign parent that has no real commitment to the host country and that the host government will have no control over them.

13. The benefits of FDI to the home (source) country include improvement in the balance of payments as a result of the inward flow of foreign earnings, positive employment effects when the foreign subsidiary creates demand for home-country exports, and benefits from a reverse resource-transfer effect. A reverse resource-transfer effect arises when the foreign subsidiary learns valuable skills abroad that can be transferred back to the home country.

14. The costs of FDI to the home country include adverse balance-of-payments effects that arise from the initial capital outflow and from the export substitution effects of FDI. Costs also arise when FDI exports jobs abroad.

15. Home countries can adopt policies designed to both encourage and restrict FDI. Host countries try to attract FDI by offering incentives and try to restrict FDI by dictating ownership restraints and requiring that foreign MNEs meet specific performance requirements.

16. A firm considering FDI usually must negotiate the terms of the investment with the host government. The object of any negotiation is to reach an agreement that benefits both parties. Negotiation inevitably involves compromise.

17. The outcome of negotiation is typically determined by the relative bargaining powers of the foreign MNE and the host government. Bargaining power depends on the value each side places on what the other has to offer, the number of comparable alternatives available to each side, and each party's time horizon.

✖ CRITICAL DISCUSSION QUESTIONS

1. Explain how the political ideology of a host government might influence the process of negotiating access between the host government and a foreign MNE.

2. Under what circumstances is an MNE in a powerful negotiating position vis-à-vis a host government? What kind of concessions is a firm likely to win in such situations?

3. Under what circumstances is an MNE in a weak negotiating position vis-à-vis a host government? What kind of concessions is a host government likely to win in such situations?

4. Inward FDI is bad for the U.S. economy and should be subjected to stricter controls! Discuss.

5. U.S. firms should not be investing abroad when there is a need for investment to create jobs at home! Discuss.

❧ CLOSING CASE   Conoco's Russian Investment

Since the collapse of communism and the shift toward a market economy, senior officials of the Russian government have gone out of their way to encourage foreign companies to invest in Russia. Their rationale is fairly obvious—Russia is in desperate need of capital resources to upgrade its crumbling infrastructure, which is suffering from years of neglect and mismanagement under communism. The Russian oil and gas industry is an example.

Russia has the largest oil and gas reserves in the world, but increasingly it is finding it difficult to get these reserves out of the ground and to the international market. This is a major problem for a country that is as short of export earnings and foreign currency as Russia. Between 1990 and 1994 oil and gas production in Russia declined by 40 percent. The problems include leaking pipelines, aging oil wells, a lack of new drilling, and conflict between the various states of the former Soviet Union as to who actually owns much of the oil and gas infrastructure. According to estimates by the World Bank, Russia will need to spend between $40 billion and $50 billion per year just to maintain oil and gas production at its current (relatively low) levels. Boosting production to the levels achieved in the 1980s could require investments of $80 to $100 billion per year—money that Russia does not have!

Conoco, a subsidiary of Du Pont, is one foreign oil company that has invested in the Russian oil and gas industry. In 1991 Conoco participated in the first U.S.–Russian joint venture to develop a new oil field. The field is in the Arkhangel'sk region, north of the Arctic Circle and 1,000 miles northeast of Moscow. Conoco's joint-venture partner is the Russian geologic enterprise Arkhangelskgeologia, and the joint venture is called Polar Lights. One of Conoco's motives was to use the joint venture as a test case to learn whether the company could successfully do business in Russia.

To its surprise, Conoco has found that the Russian workers' technical skills are excellent. In most instances, Conoco officials also found that the physical infrastructure was in better condition than they had been led to believe. But they have encountered serious logistical, efficiency, and managerial shortcomings. Conoco's management believes these problems are short term and with proper training and tools Russian managers will improve rapidly.

The major problem encountered by Conoco so far has been the generally adverse political and legal climate toward foreign investment. Although Russian law currently allows Western joint ventures to export oil, in practice the ability to export has been significantly reduced as a result of the government's bureaucratic efforts to allocate export licenses. Conoco has not always been able to get export licenses or has been asked to pay unrealistically high prices for the right to export oil from Russia. Another problem concerns the lack of a defined tax code in Russia. Various taxes are being invented by different government entities, which often seem to be working at cross-purposes with each other. Conoco has calculated that if these taxes were actually imposed, they would exceed the total income that their investments would generate. To make matters worse, growing disillusionment with the reform process in Russia has led to calls from some quarters for the renationalization of newly privatized assets and for limiting foreign direct investment in key industries, such as oil and gas. Although the current Russian government has worked hard to play down the importance of such calls, there is no doubt they have spooked several foreign investors.

CASE DISCUSSION QUESTIONS

1. What are the benefits to the Russian economy from Conoco's investment?

2. What are the risks for Conoco in investing in Russia?

3. How can Conoco reduce these risks without significantly curtailing its investment in Russia?

Sources: C. S. Nicandros, "The Russian Investment Dilemma," Harvard Business Review, May–June 1994, p. 40; T. Carrington, "World Bank President Says Economists Were Too Optimistic on Soviet Block," The Wall Street Journal, October 14, 1994, p. 13; and R. Holman, "Russia to Lift Oil Restrictions," The Wall Street Journal, December 6, 1994, p. 24A.

Chapter Eight

Regional Economic Integration

TALES FROM THE NEW EUROPE

On January 1, 1993, the 12 member-states of the European Union implemented the Single European Act (the European Union, or EU, was expanded from 12 to 15 members on January 1, 1996). This act mandated the removal of all frontier controls between EU countries, thereby abolishing delays and reducing the resources required for complying with trade bureaucracy. The act was the logical culmination of the 35-year history of this trading bloc, which has progressively reduced barriers to the free flow of goods, services, and factors of production between its member-states. With the implementation of the Single European Act, the EU became a single market of 340 million consumers.

For some the creation of a single market has had a profound impact. Consider Bernard Cornille, a Frenchman who lives in the port of Calais just 20 miles across the English Channel from the British port of Dover. Cornille is an agent for a French manufacturer of cash machines. Before January 1, 1993, he made a decent income selling this equipment, enough to live well and employ three assistants. However, in the months after the implementation of the Single European Act, he watched demand for these products—and hence his income—plunge as less expensive equipment poured in from Spain and Italy. A desperate Cornille was forced to lay off his assistants and found himself looking for another source of income. He noted that British shoppers were beginning to flood into Calais via ferries to purchase alcohol and tobacco, which cost half as much in France as in Britain, and which the shoppers could now take home in unlimited amounts. So Cornille turned the garage behind his sales office into a wine cellar and distributed leaflets at the ferry dock with directions to his new "Cash & Carry Wine Store." Now his machine showroom is quiet, but he is making over $2,000 per week from the wine business, more than his previous income.

Barry Cotter has also seen his life take a turn for the better. A beer-bellied English truck driver, Barry Cotter speaks no foreign languages and jokes about "Cloggies" (the Dutch) and "Kermits"(as in "Frogs," or the French). Despite his provincialism Cotter can't say enough good things about the new Europe. This Englishman makes his living by driving for a German trucking company, primarily hauling chemicals between Spain and Italy. Before 1993 Cotter needed 70 forms to cross the frontier between Spain and France. It could take hours, even days, but now he speeds straight through without so much as a glance from the lone guard. With traditional delays vanishing across Europe, he can now cross the Continent in just three days, compared with five before 1993. "In this business time is money," he says, "and these days I've got a lot more of both."

Not everyone has had it as easy as Bernard Cornille and Barry Cotter. For many of Europe's companies, barriers of language, culture, and custom still remain daunting. Take Atag Holdings NV, a Dutch company whose main business is kitchen appliances. Atag thought it was well placed to benefit from the single market, but so far it has found it tough going. Atag's plant is just one mile from the German border and near the center of EU's population. The company thought it could cater to both the "potato" and "spaghetti" belts— marketers' terms for consumers in Southern and Northern Europe—by producing two main product lines and selling these standardized "Euro-products" to "Euro-consumers." Atag quickly discovered the "Euro-consumer" is a myth. Consumer preferences vary much more across nations than Atag had thought. Consider ceramic stove tops; Atag planned to market just 2 varieties throughout the EU, but has found it needs 11. Belgians, who cook in huge pots, require extra-large burners. Germans like oval pots and burners to fit. The French need small burners and very low temperatures for simmering sauces and broths. Germans like oven knobs on the top; the French want them on the front. Most Germans and French prefer black and white cookers; the British demand a vast range of different colors including peach, pigeon blue, and mint green. Despite these problems, foreign sales of Atag's kitchenware have increased from 4 percent of its total revenues in 1985 to 25 percent in 1994. But the company now has a much more realistic assessment of the benefits of a single market among a group of countries whose cultures and traditions still differ in deep and often profound ways. Atag now believes that its range of designs and product quality, rather than the magic bullet of a "Euro-product" designed for a "Euro-consumer," will keep the company competitive.

Sources: T. Horwitz, "Europe's Borders Fade," *The Wall Street Journal*, May 18, 1993, pp. A1, A12; "A Singular Market," *The Economist*, October 22, 1994, pp. 10–16; and "Something Dodgy in Europe's Single Market," *The Economist*, May 21, 1994, pp. 69–70.

❧ INTRODUCTION

One of the most notable trends in the global economy in recent years has been the accelerated movement toward regional economic integration. By **regional economic integration** we mean agreements between groups of countries in a geographic region to reduce, and ultimately remove, tariff and nontariff barriers to the free flow of goods, services, and factors of production between each other. Between 1990 and 1994 the GATT was notified of 33 regional agreements, compared with 11 in the previous decade.[1] Consistent with the predictions of international trade theory, and particularly the theory of comparative advantage (see Chapter 4), the belief has been that regional free trade zones will produce nontrivial gains from trade for all member-countries. Of course, as we saw in Chapter 5, the General Agreement on Tariffs and Trade (GATT) and its successor, the World Trade Organization (WTO), also seek to reduce trade barriers. However, with over 120 member-states the WTO has a worldwide perspective. By entering into regional agreements, groups of countries aim to reduce trade barriers more rapidly than can be achieved under the auspices of the WTO.

Nowhere has the movement toward regional economic integration been more successful than in Europe. As noted in the opening case, on January 1, 1993, the European Union (EU) effectively became a single market with 360 million consumers. Nor does the EU intend to stop here. The member-states of the EU are discussing plans for a single currency; they are moving toward a closer political union; and they are actively discussing further enlargement of the EU from the current 15 countries to ultimately include another 15 Eastern European states.

Similar moves toward region integration are being pursued elsewhere in the world. Canada, Mexico, and the United States have recently implemented the North American Free Trade Agreement (NAFTA). This promises to ultimately remove all barriers to the free flow of goods and services between the three countries. Argentina, Brazil, Paraguay, and Uruguay have now implemented a 1991 agreement to start reducing barriers to trade between themselves. Known as Mercosur, this free trade area is now widely viewed as the first step in a move toward the creation of a South American Free Trade Area (SAFTA). Somewhat further back, 18 Pacific Rim countries, including the NAFTA member states, Japan, and China, have been discussing the possible creation of a pan-Pacific free trade area under the auspices of the Asian Pacific Economic Cooperation forum (APEC). There are also active attempts at regional economic integration to be found in Central America, the Andean Region of South America, Southeast Asia, and parts of Africa.

As the opening case demonstrates, the move toward regional economic integration is not without some dislocation and economic pain. As described in the case, Bernard Cornille found his traditional line of work threatened by a flood of imports from Italy and Spain. His income fell and he had to lay off employees. At the same time, however, regional economic integration can create new opportunities. This was the case for Cornille, who took advantage of the opportunities created by the single market to establish a new wine merchant business. But even here, Cornille's gain was someone else's loss; in this case, wine merchants in Britain who have seen their business decline as a result of an increase in direct purchases from France by British consumers.

Although there are winners and losers in this kind of situation, in general, as predicted by the theory of comparative advantage (see Chapter 4), there should be a substantial net gain from regional free trade agreements such as that implemented by the EU. This argument, however, is of little help to those who suffer from regional free trade agreements, and as a result, many regional agreements have

---

[1] World Trade Organization, *Regionalism and the World Trading System* (Geneva: World Trade Organization, 1995).

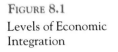

FIGURE 8.1
Levels of Economic
Integration

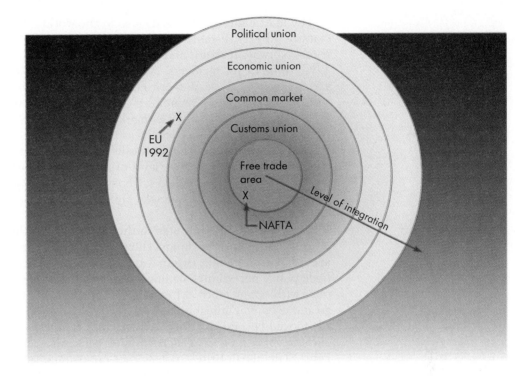

aroused substantial opposition from those whose interests are threatened. In addition, there are fears that the world is moving toward a situation in which regional trade blocs compete against each other. In this scenario of the future, free trade will exist within each bloc, but each bloc will protect its market from outside competition with high tariffs. The specter of the EU and NAFTA turning into "economic fortresses" that shut out foreign producers with high tariff barriers is particularly worrisome to those who believe in the value of unrestricted free trade. If such a scenario were to materialize, the resulting decline in trade between blocs could more than offset the gains from free trade within blocs.

With these issues in mind, the main objectives of this chapter are as follows: (1) to explore the economic and political debate surrounding regional economic integration, paying particular attention to the economic and political benefits and costs of integration; (2) to review progress toward regional economic integration around the world; and (3) to map the important implications of regional economic integration for the practice of international business. Before tackling these objectives, however, we first need to examine the levels of integration that are theoretically possible.

❧ LEVELS OF ECONOMIC INTEGRATION

Several levels of economic integration are possible in theory (see Figure 8.1). From least integrated to most integrated, they are a free trade area, a customs union, a common market, an economic union, and, finally, a full political union.

Free Trade Area

In a free trade area all barriers to the trade of goods and services among member-countries are removed. In the theoretically ideal free trade area, no discriminatory tariffs, quotas, subsidies, or administrative impediments are allowed to distort trade between member-countries. Each country, however, is allowed to determine its own trade policies with regard to nonmembers. Thus, for example, the tariffs placed on the products of nonmember countries may vary from member-country to member-country.

The most enduring free trade area in the world is the European Free Trade Association (EFTA). Established in January 1960, EFTA currently joins three countries—Norway, Iceland, and Switzerland—down from six in 1995 (on January 1, 1996, three EFTA members, Austria, Finland, and Sweden joined the EU). EFTA was founded by those Western European countries that initially decided not to be part of the European Community (the forerunner of the EU). Its original members included Austria, Britain, Denmark, Finland, and Sweden, all of whom are now members of the EU. The emphasis of EFTA has been on free trade in industrial goods. In the main, agriculture was left out of the arrangement, each member being allowed to determine its own level of support. Members were also free to determine the level of protection applied to goods coming from outside EFTA. Other free trade areas include the North American Free Trade Agreement (NAFTA).

Customs Union

The customs union is one step further along the road to full economic and political integration. A customs union eliminates trade barriers between member-countries and adopts a common external trade policy. Establishment of a common external trade policy necessitates significant administrative machinery to oversee trade relations with nonmembers. Most countries that enter into a customs union desire even greater economic integration down the road. The EU began as a customs union and has moved beyond this stage. Other customs unions around the world include the current version of the Andean Pact (between Bolivia, Colombia, Ecuador, and Peru). The aims of the Andean Pact are to establish free trade between member-countries and to impose a common tariff, of 5 to 20 percent, on products imported from outside.[2]

Common Market

Like a customs union, the theoretically ideal common market has no barriers to trade between member-countries and a common external trade policy. Unlike in a customs union, in a common market factors of production also are allowed to move freely between member-countries. Thus labor and capital are free to move, as there are no restrictions on immigration, emigration, or cross-border flows of capital between member-countries. Hence, a much closer union is envisaged in a common market than in a customs union. The EU is currently a common market, although its goal is full economic union. Other than the EU, no successful common market has been established, although several regional groupings have aspired to this goal. Establishing a common market demands a significant degree of harmony and cooperation on fiscal, monetary, and employment policies. Achieving this degree of cooperation has proven very difficult.

Economic Union

An economic union entails even closer economic integration and cooperation than a common market. Like the common market, an economic union involves the free flow of products and factors of production between member-countries and the adoption of a common external trade policy. Unlike a common market, a full economic union also requires a common currency, harmonization of the member-countries tax rates, and a common monetary and fiscal policy. Such a high degree of integration demands a coordinating bureaucracy and that member-countries sacrifice significant amounts of their national sovereignties to that bureaucracy. There are no true economic unions in the world today, but the EU aims to establish itself as one by the end of the century.

Political Union

The move toward economic union raises the issue of how to make a coordinating bureaucracy accountable to the citizens of member-nations. The answer is through political union. The EU is already on the road toward political union. The European

---

[2]The Andean Pact has been through a number of changes since its original inception. The latest version was established in 1991. See "Free-Trade Free for All," *The Economist*, January 4, 1991, p. 63.

Parliament, which is playing an ever more important role in the EU, has been directly elected by citizens of the EU countries since the late 1970s. In addition the Council of Ministers (the controlling, decision-making body of the EU) is composed of government ministers from each EU member-country. Canada and the United States provide examples of even closer degrees of political union; in each country independent states were effectively combined into a single nation. Ultimately, the EU may move toward a similar federal structure.

❧ THE CASE FOR REGIONAL INTEGRATION

The case for regional integration is both economic and political. The case for integration is typically not accepted by many groups within a country, which explains why most attempts to achieve regional economic integration have been contentious and halting. In this section we examine the economic and political cases for integration and two impediments to integration. In the next section we look at the case against integration.

The Economic Case for Integration

The economic case for regional integration is relatively straightforward. We saw in Chapter 4 how economic theories of international trade predict that unrestricted free trade will allow countries to specialize in the production of goods and services that they can produce most efficiently. The result is greater world production than would be possible with trade restrictions. We also saw in that chapter how opening a country to free trade stimulates economic growth in the country, which in turn creates dynamic gains from trade. Further, we saw in Chapter 6 how foreign direct investment (FDI) can transfer technological, marketing, and managerial know-how to host nations. Given the central role of knowledge in stimulating economic growth, opening a country to FDI also is likely to stimulate economic growth. In sum, economic theories suggest free trade and investment is a positive-sum game, in which all participating countries stand to gain.

Given this, the theoretical ideal is a total absence of barriers to the free flow of goods, services, and factors of production among nations. However, as we saw in Chapters 5 and 7, a case can be made for government intervention in international trade and FDI. Because many governments have accepted part or all of the case for intervention, unrestricted free trade and FDI have proved to be only an ideal. Although international institutions such as the GATT and WTO have been moving the world toward a free trade regime, success has been less than total. In a world of many nations and many political ideologies, it is very difficult to get all countries to agree to a common set of rules.

Against this background, regional economic integration can be seen as an attempt to achieve additional gains from the free flow of trade and investment between countries beyond those attainable under international agreements such as GATT and the WTO. Undoubtedly, it is easier to establish a free trade and investment regime among a limited number of adjacent countries than among the world community. Problems of coordination and policy harmonization are largely a function of the number of countries that seek agreement. The greater the number of countries involved, the greater the number of different perspectives that must be reconciled, and the harder it will be to reach agreement. Thus attempts at regional economic integration are motivated by a desire to exploit the gains from free trade and investment.

The Political Case for Integration

The political case for regional economic integration has also loomed large in most attempts to establish free trade areas, customs unions, and the like. By linking neighboring economies and making them increasingly dependent on each other, incentives are created for political cooperation between the neighboring states. In turn the potential for violent conflict between the states is reduced. By grouping their economies together, the countries can enhance their political weight in the world.

These considerations certainly underlay the establishment of the European Community (EC) in 1957. Europe had suffered two devastating wars in the first half of the century, both arising out of the unbridled ambitions of nation-states. Those who have sought a united Europe have always had at the forefront of their minds the desire to prevent another outbreak of war in Europe, to make it unthinkable. Many Europeans also believed that after World War II the European nation-states were no longer large enough to hold their own in world markets and world politics. The need for a united Europe to deal with the United States and the politically alien Soviet Union certainly loomed large in the minds of many of the EC's founders.[3]

Impediments to Integration

Despite the strong economic and political arguments for integration, it has never been easy to achieve or sustain. There are two main reasons for this. First, although economic integration benefits the majority, it has its costs. Although a nation as a whole may benefit significantly as a result of entering into a regional free trade agreement, certain groups may lose. Moving to a free trade regime inevitably involves some painful adjustments. For example, as a result of the 1994 establishment of NAFTA some Canadian and U.S. workers in such industries as textiles, which employ low-cost, low-skilled labor, will certainly lose their jobs as Canadian and U.S. firms move production to Mexico. The promise of significant net benefits to the Canadian and U.S. economies as a whole is little comfort to those who will lose as a result of the NAFTA. It is understandable then, that such groups were in the forefront of opposition to the NAFTA agreement and will continue to oppose any widening of the agreement.

A second impediment to integration arises from concerns over national sovereignty. For example, Mexico's concerns about maintaining control of its oil interests resulted in an agreement with Canada and the United States to exempt the Mexican oil industry from any liberalization of foreign investment regulations achieved under the NAFTA. More generally, concerns about national sovereignty arise because close economic integration demands that countries give up some degree of their control over such key policy issues as monetary policy, fiscal policy (e.g., tax policy), and trade policy. This has been a major stumbling block in the EU. To achieve full economic union, the EU is trying to reach agreement on a common currency to be controlled by a central EU bank. With most member-states agreeing in principle, Britain remains an important holdout. A politically important segment of public opinion in Britain opposes a common currency on the grounds that it would require relinquishing control of the country's monetary policy to the EU, which many British perceive as bureaucracy run by foreigners. In 1992 the British won the right to opt out of any single currency agreement.

❧ THE CASE AGAINST REGIONAL INTEGRATION

Although the tide has been running strongly in favor of regional free trade agreements in recent years, some economists have expressed concern that the benefits of regional integration have been oversold, while the costs have often been ignored.[4] They point out that the benefits of regional integration to the participants are determined by the extent of trade creation, as opposed to trade diversion. **Trade creation** occurs when high-cost domestic producers are replaced by low-cost producers within the free trade area. **Trade diversion** occurs when lower-cost external suppliers are replaced by higher-cost suppliers within the free trade area. A regional free trade agreement will benefit the world only if the amount of trade it creates exceeds the amount it diverts.

---

[3]D. Swann, *The Economics of the Common Market*, 6th ed. (London: Penguin Books, 1990).

[4]See J. Bhagwati, "Regionalism and Multilateralism: An Overview," Columbia University discussion paper 603, Department of Economics, Columbia University, New York; and Augusto de la Torre and Margaret Kelly, "Regional Trade Arrangements," occasional paper 93, Washington DC: International Monetary Fund, March 1992.

For example, suppose the United States and Mexico imposed tariffs on imports from all countries, and then they set up a free trade area, scrapping all trade barriers between them but maintaining tariffs on imports from the rest of the world. If the United States began to import textiles from Mexico, would this change be for the better? If the United States previously produced all its own textiles at a higher cost than Mexico, then the free trade agreement has shifted production to the cheaper source. According to the theory of comparative advantage, trade has been created within the regional grouping, and there would be no decrease in trade with the rest of the world. The change would be for the better. If, however, the United States previously imported textiles from South Korea, which produced them more cheaply than either Mexico or the United States, then trade has been diverted from a low-cost source—a change for the worse.

In theory, GATT and WTO rules should ensure that a free trade agreement does not result in trade diversion. These rules allow free trade areas to be formed only if the members set tariffs that are not higher or more restrictive to outsiders than the ones previously in effect. However, as we saw in Chapter 5, recent years have seen a proliferation of nontariff barriers not covered by the GATT and WTO (e.g., voluntary export restraints, VERs). As a result, fear is growing that regional trade blocs could emerge whose markets are protected from outside competition by high nontariff barriers. In such cases, the trade diversion effects might well outweigh the trade creation effects. The only way to guard against this possibility, according to those concerned about this potential, is to increase the scope of the WTO so it covers nontariff barriers to trade such as VERs. There is no sign that this will occur anytime soon, however, so the risk remains that regional economic integration will result in trade diversion.

❧ REGIONAL ECONOMIC INTEGRATION IN EUROPE

There are now two trade blocs in Europe; the European Union (EU) and the European Free Trade Association (EFTA). Of the two, the EU is by far the more significant, not just in terms of membership (the EU has 15 members, and EFTA has 3), but also in terms of economic and political influence in the world economy. Many now see the EU as an emerging economic and political superpower of the same order as the United States and Japan. Accordingly, we will concentrate our attention on the EU.[5]

Evolution of the European Union

The EU is the product of two political factors; first, the devastation of two world wars on Western Europe and the desire for a lasting peace, and second, the European nations' desire to hold their own on the world's political and economic stage. In addition many Europeans were aware of the potential economic benefits of closer economic integration of their countries.

The original forerunner of the EU, the European Coal and Steel Community, was formed in 1951 by Belgium, France, West Germany, Italy, Luxembourg, and the Netherlands. Its objective was to remove barriers to intragroup shipments of coal, iron, steel, and scrap metal. With the signing of the Treaty of Rome in 1957, the European Community (EC) was established. The name changed again in 1994 when the *European Community* became the *European Union* following the ratification of the Maastricht treaty (discussed later).

The Treaty of Rome provided for the creation of a common market. This is apparent in Article 3 of the treaty, which laid down the key objectives of the new community. Article 3 calls for the elimination of internal trade barriers and the creation of

[5]Sources for the material in this section: N. Colchester and D. Buchan, *Europower: The Essential Guide to Europe's Economic Transformation in 1992* (London: The Economist Books, 1990); and Swann, *Common Market*.

🐾 **MAP 8.1**
The European Union

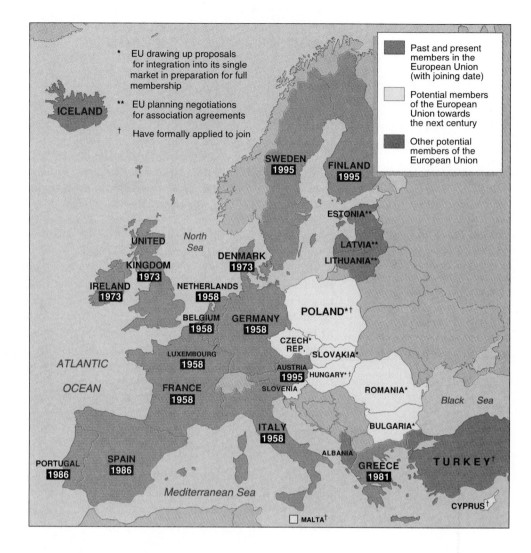

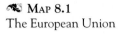

a common external tariff and requires member-states to abolish obstacles to the free movement of factors of production among the member-states. To facilitate the free movement of goods, services, and factors of production, the treaty provides for any necessary harmonization of the member-states' laws. Furthermore, the treaty committed the EC to establish common policies in agriculture and transportation.

The first enlargement of the community occurred in 1973, when Great Britain, Ireland, and Denmark joined. These three were followed in 1981 by Greece, in 1986 by Spain and Portugal, and in 1996 by Austria, Finland, and Sweden (see Map 8.1) bringing the total membership to 15 (East Germany became part of the EC after the reunification of Germany in 1990). With a population of 350 million and a GDP greater than that of the United States, these enlargements made the EU a potential global superpower.

Political Structure of the European Union

The economic policies of the EU are formulated and implemented by a complex and still-evolving political structure. The five main institutions in this structure are the European Council, the Council of Ministers, the European Commission, the European Parliament, and the Court of Justice.[6]

---

[6]D. Swann, *The Economics of the Common Market*, 6th ed. (London: Penguin Books, 1990); N. Colchester and D. Buchan, *Europower: The Essential Guide to Europe's Economic Transformation in 1992* (London: The Economist Books, 1990); "The European Union: A Survey," *The Economist*, October 22, 1994; and "The European Community: A Survey," *The Economist*, July 3, 1993.

The European Council

The European Council is composed of the heads of state of the EU's member nations and the president of the European Commission. Each head of state is normally accompanied by his or her foreign minister to these meetings. The European Council meets at least twice a year and as befits such an august body, it is the European Council that often resolves major policy issues and sets policy directions.

The European Commission

The European Commission is responsible for proposing EU legislation, implementing it, and monitoring compliance with EU laws by member-states. Headquartered in Brussels, Belgium, there are over 10,000 employees working for the Commission. The Commission is run by a group of 20 commissioners appointed by each member-country for four-year renewable terms. Most countries appoint only one commissioner, although the most populated states—Britain, France, Germany, Italy, and Spain—appoint two each. A president and six vice-presidents are chosen from among these commissioners for two-year renewable terms. Each commissioner is responsible for a portfolio that is typically concerned with a specific policy area. For example, there is a commissioner for agricultural policy and another for competition policy. Although they are appointed by their respective governments, commissioners are meant to act independently and in the best interests of the EU, as opposed to being advocates for a particular national interest.

The Commission has a monopoly in proposing European Union legislation. The Commission starts the legislative ball rolling by making a proposal that goes first to the Council of Ministers, and then to the European Parliament. The Council of Ministers cannot legislate without a Commission proposal in front of it. The Treaty of Rome gave the Commission this power in an attempt to limit national infighting by taking the right to propose legislation away from nationally elected political representatives, giving it to "independent" commissioners.

The Commission is also responsible for implementing aspects of EU law, although in practice much of this must of necessity be delegated to member-states. Another responsibility of the Commission is to monitor member-states to make sure they are complying with EU laws. In this policing role the Commission will normally ask a state to comply with any EU laws that are being broken. If this persuasion is not sufficient the Commission can refer a case to the Court of Justice.

The Council of Ministers

The Council of Ministers is the body where the interests of member states are represented. It is clearly the ultimate controlling authority within the EU since draft legislation from the Commission can become EU law only if the council agrees. The council is composed of one representative from the government of each member-state. The membership, however, varies depending on the topic being discussed. When agricultural issues are being discussed it will be the agriculture ministers from each state that attend council meetings, when transportation is being discussed it is transportation ministers, and so on. Before 1993 all council issues had to be decided by unanimous agreement. As can be imagined, this often led to marathon council sessions and a failure to make progress or reach any agreement on proposals submitted from the Commission. In an attempt to clear the resulting logjams, the Single European Act formalized the use of majority voting rules on issues "which have as their object the establishment and functioning of a single market." Most other issues, however, such as tax regulations and immigration policy, still require unanimity among council members if they are to become law.

The European Parliament

The European Parliament, which now has about 630 members, is directly elected by the population of the member-states. The parliament, which meets in Strasbourg,

France, is primarily a consultative rather than legislative body. It debates legislation proposed by the Commission and forwarded to it by the council. It can propose amendments to that legislation, which the Commission and ultimately the council are not obliged to take up, but often will. Recently the power of the parliament has been increasing, although by not as much as parliamentarians would like. The European Parliament now has the right to vote on the appointment of commissioners, as well as veto power over some laws (such as the EU budget and single-market legislation). One of the major debates now being waged in Europe is whether the council, or the parliament, should ultimately be the most powerful body in the EU. There is concern in Europe over the democratic accountability of the EU bureaucracy. Some think that the answer to this apparent democratic deficit lies in increasing the power of the parliament, while others think that true democratic legitimacy lies with elected governments, acting through the Council of Ministers.[7]

The Court of Justice

The Court of Justice, which is comprised of one judge from each country, is the supreme appeals court for EU law. Like commissioners, the judges are required to act as independent officials, rather than as representatives of national interests. The Commission or a member-country can bring other members to the court for failing to meet treaty obligations. Similarly, member-countries, companies, or institutions can bring the commission or council to the court for failure to act according to an EU treaty.

The Single European Act

Two revolutions occurred in Europe in the late 1980s. The first was the dramatic collapse of communism in Eastern Europe. The second revolution was much quieter, but its impact on Europe and the world may have been just as profound as the first. It was the adoption of the Single European Act by the member-nations of the EC in 1987. This act committed the EC countries to work toward the establishment of a single market by December 31, 1992.

The stimulus for the Single European Act

The Single European Act was born of a frustration among EC member-countries that the community was not living up to its promise. By the early 1980s it was clear that the EC had fallen short of its objectives of removing barriers to the free flow of trade and investment between member-countries and of harmonizing the wide range of technical and legal standards for doing business. At the end of 1982 the European Commission found itself inundated with 770 cases of intra-EC protectionism to investigate. In addition some 20 EC directives setting common technical standards for a variety of products ranging from cars to thermometers were deadlocked.

As far as many companies were concerned, the main problem with the EC was the disharmony of the member-countries' technical, legal, regulatory, and tax standards. The "rules of the game" differed substantially from country to country, which stalled the creation of a true single internal market.

Consider the European automobile industry. In the mid-1980s there was no single EC-wide automobile market analogous to the U.S. automobile market. Instead the EC market remained fragmented into 12 national markets. There were four main reasons for this:

- Different technical standards in different countries required cars to be customized to national requirements (e.g., the headlights and sidelights of cars sold in Great Britain must be wired in a significantly different way than those of cars sold in Italy, and the standards for car windscreens in France are very different from those in Germany).

---

[7]"The European Community: A Survey," *The Economist,* July 3, 1993.

- Different tax regimes in the countries created price differentials that would not be found in a single market.

- An agreement to allow automobile companies to sell cars through exclusive dealer networks allowed auto companies and their dealers to adapt their model ranges and prices on a country-by-country basis with little fear that these differences would be undermined by competing retailers.

- In violation of Article 3 of the Treaty of Rome, each country had adopted its own trade policy with regard to automobile imports (e.g., whereas Japanese imports were not restricted in Belgium, they were limited to 11 percent of the car market in Great Britain and to less than 2 percent in France and Italy). The net result of these divisions was substantial price differentials between countries. For example, in 1989 the prices of the same model of car were, on average, 31 percent higher in Great Britain and 11 percent higher in Germany than in Belgium.[8]

Numerous other administrative barriers to intra-EC trade and investment had become apparent by the mid-1980s. French buildings were uninsurable unless tiled with French-standard tiles. Government procurement policies often favored local companies. Local banking rules effectively inhibited the creation of a single EC banking industry. The French had persistently refused to abolish exchange controls, thereby limiting French companies' ability to invest in other EC countries and other EC countries companies' ability to repatriate profits to their home countries. Truck drivers traveling between EC countries had to carry some 35 documents for import-export declarations and community transit forms. Simply dealing with the paperwork could make a journey take three to five times longer than it would have needed to take, and the costs of the paperwork accounted for more than 3 percent of the value of the sales involved.[9]

In addition to the profusion of barriers to intra-EC trade, many member-countries were subsidizing national firms, thereby distorting competition. For example, in 1990 the French government decided to pump FFr 6 billion into Groupe Bull, a state-owned computer maker, and Thompson, a defense and electronics group. This brought protests from ICL, a British computer maker, on the grounds that such a subsidy would allow Groupe Bull to capture more of the EC computer market.[10]

Against this background, in the early 1980s many of the EC's prominent businesspeople mounted an energetic campaign to end the EC's economic divisions. Under the leadership of industrialists such as Wisse Dekker, CEO of the Dutch company Philips, the Roundtable of European Industrialists was established in 1983. Roundtable participants were chairmen, CEOs, and managing directors of large corporations with important manufacturing and technological commitments in the EC. Its principal objective was to foster the creation of a single market by encouraging the EC to harmonize the rules of the game and by encouraging the member-countries to remove their administrative barriers to trade within the EC. The roundtable members believed that a single EC market was absolutely essential if European firms were to be competitive with their U.S. and Asian rivals.

The EC responded to this stimulus by creating the Delors Commission. Under the chairmanship of Jacques Delors, the former French finance minister and president of the EC Commission, the commission produced a discussion paper in 1985. The discussion paper proposed that all impediments to the formation of a single market be eliminated by December 31, 1992. Two more years passed before the EC persuaded all member-countries to accept the proposals contained in the discussion paper. The result was the Single European Act, which was independently ratified by the parliaments of each member-country and became EC law in 1987.

[8]Colchester and Buchan, *Europower.*

[9]Nan Stone, "The Globalization of Europe: An Interview with Wisse Dekker," *Harvard Business Review*, May–June 1989, pp. 90–95.

[10]"The Aid Plague: Business in Europe, A Survey," *The Economist*, June 8, 1991, pp. 12–18.

The objectives of the act

The purpose of the Single European Act was to have a single market in place by December 31, 1992. The changes the act proposed included the following.[11]

1. **Frontier controls:** Removing all frontier controls between EC countries would abolish delays and reduce the resources required for complying with trade bureaucracy.

2. **Mutual recognition of standards:** To harmonize the product standards of different EC members would be a huge task. Germany alone has some 20,000 standards, France 8,000, and Great Britain 12,000. Instead, the EC will apply the principle of "mutual recognition," which is that a standard developed in one EC country should be accepted in another, provided it meets basic requirements in such matters as health and safety.

3. **Public procurement:** Opening procurement to nonnational suppliers should reduce costs directly by allowing lower-cost suppliers into national economies and indirectly by forcing national suppliers to compete.

4. **Financial services:** The EC's retail banking and insurance businesses were split into national markets. The act proposed lifting barriers to competition, which should drive down the costs of financial services, including borrowing, throughout the EC.

5. **Exchange controls:** All restrictions on foreign exchange transactions between member-countries were to be removed by the end of 1992.

6. **Freight transport:** Restrictions on cabotage—the right of foreign truckers to pick up and deliver goods within another member-state's borders—were to be abolished by the end of 1992. This could reduce the cost of haulage within the EC by 10 to 15 percent.

7. **Supply-side effects:** All those changes should lower the costs of doing business in the EC, but the single-market program is also expected to have more complicated supply-side effects. For example, the expanded market should give EC firms greater opportunities to exploit economies of scale. In addition, the increase in competitive intensity brought about by removing internal barriers to trade and investment should force EC firms to become more efficient.

In an attempt to signify the importance of the Single European Act, the European Community also decided to change its name to the European Union once the act went into effect.

Implications

The implications of the Single European Act are potentially enormous. We discuss the implications for business practice in more detail later in the chapter. For now it should be noted that, as long as the EU is successful in establishing a single market, the member-countries can expect significant gains from the free flow of trade and investment. These gains may be greater than those predicted by standard trade theory that accrue when regions specialize in producing those goods and services that they produce most efficiently. The lower costs of doing business implied by the Single European Act will benefit EU firms, as will the potential economies of scale inherent in serving a single market of 360 million consumers.

On the other hand, as a result of the Single European Act many EU firms are facing increased competitive pressure. Countries such as France and Italy have long used administrative trade barriers and subsidies to protect their home markets from

---

[11]"One Europe, One Economy," *The Economist*, November 30, 1991, pp. 53–54; "Market Failure: A Survey of Business in Europe," *The Economist*, June 8, 1991, pp. 6–10.

foreign competition. Removal of these barriers has increased competition, and some firms may go out of business. Ultimately, however, both consumers and EU firms will benefit from this. Consumers will benefit from the lower prices implied by a more competitive market. EU firms will benefit if the increased competitive pressure forces them to become more efficient, thereby transforming them into more effective international competitors capable of going head-to-head with U.S. and Asian rivals in the world marketplace.

On the other hand, the shift toward a single market has not been as rapid as many would like. Three years after the Single European Act became EU law, there have been a number of delays in applying the act to certain industries, often because countries have appealed to the Council of Ministers for "more time." The insurance industry, for example, was exempt until July 1994, and even now is moving only slowly toward a single market (see the "Regional Focus" for details). Investment services were not liberalized until January 1996, and there is no compulsion to liberalize basic telephone services until 1998 (and until 2003 in poorer countries such as Greece to protect local telephone companies from being "crushed" by the likes of Britain's BT or America's AT&T).[12] Moreover, as the opening case illustrated, many European countries have found their dreams of a single market dashed by the realities of deep and enduring cultural and language barriers between countries, which still separate many national markets, although not as effectively as formal barriers to trade once did. Still, the long-run prognosis remains very strong, and despite all the short-term setbacks the EU will probably have a reasonably well-functioning single market by the early years of the next century.

The Treaty of Maastricht and Its Aftermath

In December 1991 leaders of the 12 EC member-states met in Maastricht, the Netherlands, to discuss the next steps for the EC. The results of the Maastricht meeting surprised both Europe and the rest of the world. For months the countries of the EC had been fighting over a common currency. Although many economists believed a common currency was required to cement a closer economic union, a deadlock had been predicted. The British in particular had opposed any attempt to establish a common currency. Instead, the 12 members signed a treaty that not only committed them to adopting a common EC currency by January 1, 1999, but also paved the way for closer political cooperation and the possible creation of a European superstate.

The treaty lays down the main elements, if only in embryo, of a future European government: a single currency, a common foreign and defense policy, a common citizenship, and an EU parliament with teeth. It is now just a matter of waiting, some believe, for history to take its course and a "United States of Europe" to emerge. Of more immediate interest are the business implications of the plans to establish a single currency by 1999.

As with many of the provisions of the Single European Act, the move to a single currency should significantly lower the costs of doing business in the EU. The gains come from reduced exchange costs and reduced risk.[13] The EU has calculated that EU businesses convert roughly $8 trillion from one EU currency to another every year, which necessitates about $12 billion in exchange costs. A single currency would avoid these costs and help firms in other ways, as fewer resources would be required for accounting, treasury management, and the like. As for reduced risk, a single currency would reduce the risks that arise from currency fluctuations. The values of currencies fluctuate against each other continually. As we will see in Chapter 9, this introduces risks into international transactions. For example, if a British firm builds a factory in Greece, and the value of the Greek currency subsequently declines against the British pound, the value of the British firm's Greek assets will also

---

[12]"A Singular Market."

[13]"One Europe, One Economy," *The Economist*, November 30, 1991, pp. 53–54.

COUNTRY
FOCUS
The Creation of a
Single European
Insurance Market

In early 1994 a simple 10-year life insurance policy in Portugal cost three times more than the same policy in France, while automobile insurance for an experienced driver cost twice as much in Ireland as in Italy and four times as much as in Britain. But after July 1994 such price discrepancies began to fade as new rules freeing restrictions on cross-border trade in the European Union insurance market came into effect. These rules represent implementation of guidelines set down in the Single European Act, which became EU law January 1, 1993. It took 18 months to get to this point because many member-states pleaded for more time to adjust to the coming deregulation. Only 5 EU countries implemented all the new rules in July 1994, although 10 had done so by January 1995.

The new rules do two main things. First, they make genuine cross-border trade possible by allowing insurance companies to sell their products anywhere in the EU on the basis of regulations in their home state, the so-called single license. Second, insurers throughout the EU will be allowed to set their own rates for all classes of insurance policies. They will no longer need to submit policy wordings to local officials for approval, thus effectively dismantling the highly regulated protectionist regime behind which much of the industry has sheltered.

Although some countries, such as France and Belgium, liberalized their insurance regulations well in advance of July 1994, many other countries had not. In the countries that have been slowest to move toward a deregulated environment, the new EU rules will unleash a sharp increase in the intensity of competition. The overall effect will be to erode the

decline. A single currency would eliminate such risks. In turn, eliminating these risks would reduce the cost of capital. Interest rates would fall, and investment and output would increase as a consequence.

The drawback, for some, of a single currency is that national authorities would lose control over monetary policy. Thus it is crucial to ensure that the EU's monetary policy is well managed. The Maastricht Treaty calls for an independent EU central bank, similar to the U.S. Federal Reserve, with a clear mandate to manage monetary policy so as to ensure price stability. The British in particular are concerned about the effectiveness of such an arrangement and the implied loss of national sovereignty. Accordingly, Britain won the right from other members to stay out of the monetary union if it should so choose. Although this has pleased the elements of the British public that are hostile to the EU, if the British do opt out, London would probably cease being the financial capital of Europe.

Before becoming law the treaty had to be ratified by each member-state, and it was here that the treaty ran into problems. Danish voters initially rejected the treaty by a narrow margin; the British House of Commons refused to pass the treaty unless some modifications were made; French voters approved the treaty by the slimmest of margins; while in Germany the treaty was challenged on the grounds that it violated the German Constitution. Just as damaging to the vision of monetary and political union laid out in the Maastricht Treaty was the partial collapse of the European Monetary System in late 1992, which highlighted the difficulties of achieving monetary union (see Chapter 10 for details) and the failure of the 12 EU countries to agree on a common foreign policy position toward the political turmoil in the former Yugoslavia—a sign of the impediments that lie in the way of political union.

cartel-like arrangements through which large national companies, such as Allianz of Germany and Generali of Italy, have long dominated their local markets. Consumers should benefit from the resulting lower prices for insurance products.

However, despite the injection of greater competition, price differentials between countries are likely to stay in effect for some time for several reasons. First, the incidence of claims varies widely across the EU. For example, when setting prices motor insurers must consider varying degrees of road safety and different levels of court awards to accident victims across states. Second, the level of service offered by insurers, and expected by customers, varies from country to country, and this too can lead to price differentials. Belgium consumers, for example,

expect insurance brokers to drive to their homes at all hours of the day to settle claims. This drives up costs and hence prices. Third, variations in tax regimes across member-states will inhibit the development of a single market. The tax advantages of life insurance policies, for example, vary from country to country, and until tax regimes are harmonized (which is still some way off) these differences will be reflected in pricing differences. Finally, cultural factors will also inhibit cross-border trade. Most continental insurers market home, life, and motor insurance through networks of exclusive local agents, who enjoy long-term and loyal relationships with customers. Many customers are thus unlikely to switch insurers on the basis of price alone.

Notwithstanding all these factors, the new rules do open up the potential for insurance companies to

penetrate each other's national markets. However, given existing distribution arrangements this may require setting up operations in other EU countries, rather than simple cross-border selling. Control over retail outlets will be critical to successful market entry. Because of this, the volume of mergers and acquisitions in the European insurance industry has been growing by 20 percent per annum in recent years as European companies purchase each other. In one such example, Union des Assurances de Paris, France's largest insurance company, acquired Germany's Colonia Insurance for about $3.9 billion.

Sources: R. Lapper, "Hard Work to Be Free and Single," *Financial Times*, July 1, 1994, p. 19; "A Singular Market."

To deal with Danish and British objections to some items contained in the Maastricht agreement, the treaty was renegotiated to allow for greater flexibility in the timetable for economic and political union. Thus, although the goal of monetary union was set for 1999, both Britain and Denmark were allowed to temporarily opt out of any such union if they did not feel ready to participate. With this commitment in hand, the British House of Commons voted to approve the Maastricht Treaty, while Danish voters signaled their acceptance of the revised pact in a national referendum. The last impediment to ratification of the Maastricht Treaty was removed October 12, 1993, when Germany's Constitutional Court ruled that the treaty did not violate the German Constitution.

With all countries having finally agreed to the terms of the treaty, it went into force January 1, 1994. Skepticism remains, however, as to whether the timetable for closer economic and political union laid out in the treaty will be met. According to the treaty, to achieve monetary union by 1999 member-countries must achieve low inflation rates, a stable exchange rate, and limit public debt to 60 percent of a country's gross domestic product. No country at present meets all criteria and precious few seem likely to within the Maastricht timetable—in which case monetary union will not occur in 1999.

Enlargement of the European Union

The other big issue the EU must now grapple with is that of enlargement. After a bitter dispute between the existing 12 members, in March 1994 they agreed to enlarge the EU to include Austria, Finland, Sweden, and Norway. Most of the opposition to enlargement came from Britain, which worried that enlargement and a subsequent reduction in its voting power in the EU's top decision-making body, the Council of Ministers, would limit its ability to block EU developments that it did not like. Britain backed down in the face of strong opposition from other EU members and agreed to enlargement. Voters in the four countries went to the polls in late 1994. Austria, Finland, and Sweden all voted to join the EU, but Norway voted to stay out. Thus the EU of 12 became the EU of 15 on January 1, 1996. Next the EU must deal with membership applications from Hungary, Poland, the Czech Republic, Malta, Cyprus, and Turkey.[14]

Fortress Europe?

A main concern of the United States and Asian countries is that the EU will impose new barriers on imports from outside the EU. The fear is that the EU might increase external protection as weaker member-states attempt to offset their loss of protection against other EU countries by arguing for limitations on outside competition.

In theory, given the free market philosophy that underpins the Single European Act, this should not occur. In October 1988 the European Commission debated external trading policy and published a detailed statement of the EU's trading intentions in the post-1992 era.[15] The commission stressed the EU's interests in vigorous external trade. It noted that exports by EU countries to non-EU countries are equivalent to 20 percent of total world exports, as against 15 percent from the United States and 9 percent from Japan. These external exports are equivalent to 9 percent of its own GDP, compared to 6.7 percent for the United States and 9.7 percent for Japan. It is not in the EU's interests to adopt a protectionist stance, given the EU's reliance on external trade. The commission has also promised loyalty to GATT and now WTO rules on international trade. As for the types of trade not covered by the WTO, the EU states it will push for reciprocal access. The EU has stated that in certain cases it might replace individual national trade barriers with EU protection against imports, but it also has promised that the overall level of protection would not rise.

Despite such reassurances, there is no guarantee the EU will not adopt a protectionist stance toward external trade, and there are indications that this has occurred in two industries—agriculture and automobiles. In agriculture the EU has continued the Common Market Agricultural Policy, which limits many food imports. In autos the EU has reached an agreement with the Japanese to limit the Japanese market share of the EU auto market. Between 1993 and 1998 those countries that have quotas on Japanese car imports will lift them gradually until the end of 1998, when they are scheduled to be abolished. Meanwhile Japanese producers have committed themselves to voluntarily restraining sales so that by the end of the century they hold no more than 17 percent of the European market. After that all restrictions are to be abolished. These examples of protectionism, however, are not the norm, and in general the EU countries have adopted a liberal trade policy with regard to third parties, such as Japan and the United States. In a recently published report the WTO has stated that so far the growth of regional trade groups such as the EU has not impeded the growth of freer world trade, as some fear, and in fact may have helped to promote it.[16]

⬧ REGIONAL ECONOMIC INTEGRATION IN THE AMERICAS

No other attempt at regional economic integration comes close to the EU in its boldness or its potential implications for the world economy. But attempts at regional economic integration are on the rise in the Americas. The most significant is

---

[14]"From the Arctic to the Mediterranean," *The Economist*, March 5, 1994, pp. 52, 57; Lionel Barber, "More Does Not Mean Merrier," *Financial Times*, March 14, 1994, p. 13; and L. Barber, "Hopes of Wider Union Turn to Fear of No Union," *Financial Times*, December 9, 1994, p. 2.

[15]"What Are They Building? Survey of Europe's Internal Market," *The Economist*, July 8, 1989, pp. 5–7; and Colchester and Buchan, *Europower*.

[16]World Trade Organization, *Regionalism and the World Trading System*.

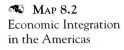

❧ MAP 8.2
Economic Integration
in the Americas

the North American Free Trade Agreement (NAFTA). In addition to NAFTA, several other trade blocs are in the offing in the Americas (see Map 8.2), the most significant of which appear to be the Andean Group and Mercosur.

The North American Free Trade Agreement

In 1988 the governments of the United States and Canada agreed to enter into a free trade agreement (FTA), which went into effect January 1, 1989. The goal of the FTA was to eliminate all tariffs on bilateral trade between Canada and the United States by 1998. This was followed in 1991 by talks among the United States, Canada, and Mexico aimed at establishing a North American Free Trade Agreement. The talks concluded in August 1992 with an agreement in principle to establish the free trade area.

For NAFTA to become a reality, each country had to ratify it. Both Canada and Mexico committed themselves to NAFTA by the fall of 1993, leaving only the U.S. government to signal its intention to go forward with the agreement. The Clinton administration had already committed itself to NAFTA, and passage by the U.S. Senate looked likely, but the agreement faced stiff opposition in the U.S. House of Representatives. The vote on NAFTA in the House of Representatives was scheduled for November 17, 1993. Until only hours before the vote the outcome was still in doubt, and then a last minute round of lobbying by President Clinton, which included numerous side deals to "buy" the support of wavering representatives, led to a late surge for NAFTA and the bill passed the House by a comfortable margin.

The NAFTA Agreement

NAFTA became law January 1, 1994.[17] The contents of the agreement include the following:

- NAFTA will mean abolition within 10 years of tariffs on 99 percent of the goods traded among Mexico, Canada, and the United States.
- NAFTA will remove most of the barriers on the cross-border flow of services, allowing financial institutions, for example, unrestricted access to the Mexican marketplace by 2000.
- NAFTA contains provisions to protect intellectual property rights.
- NAFTA removes most restrictions on foreign direct investment between the three member countries, although special treatment (protection) will be given to Mexican energy and railway industries, U.S. airline and radio communications industries, and Canadian culture.
- Under NAFTA each country is allowed to apply its own environmental standards, provided such standards have a scientific basis. Lowering of standards to lure investment is described as being inappropriate.
- NAFTA established two commissions with the power to impose fines and remove trade privileges when environmental standards or legislation involving health and safety, minimum wages, or child labor are ignored.

Arguments for NAFTA

Opinions remained divided as to the consequences of the NAFTA agreement. Proponents argue that NAFTA should be viewed as an opportunity to create an enlarged and more efficient productive base for the entire region. One likely short-term effect of NAFTA will be that many U.S. and Canadian firms will move some of their production to Mexico to take advantage of lower labor costs. In 1991 the average hourly labor costs in Mexico were $2.32, compared with $14.31 in the United States and $14.71 in Canada. Movement of production to Mexico is most likely to occur in low-skilled, labor-intensive manufacturing industries where Mexico might have a comparative advantage (e.g., textiles).

Many will benefit from such a trend. Mexico benefits because it gets much-needed investment and employment. The United States and Canada should benefit because the increased incomes of the Mexicans will allow them to import more U.S. and Canadian goods, thereby recycling demand and making up for the jobs lost in industries that moved production to Mexico. U.S. and Canadian consumers will benefit from the lower costs, and hence prices, of products produced in Mexico. In addition the international competitiveness of U.S. and Canadian firms that move production to Mexico to take advantage of lower labor costs will be enhanced, enabling them to better compete with Asian and European rivals.

Arguments against NAFTA

Those who opposed NAFTA claimed ratification would be followed by a mass exodus of jobs from the United States and Canada into Mexico as employers sought to profit from Mexico's lower wages and less strict environmental and labor laws. According to one extreme opponent, Ross Perot, up to 5.9 million U.S. jobs would be lost to Mexico after NAFTA. Most economists, however, dismiss these numbers as

---

[17]"What is NAFTA?" *Financial Times*, November 17, 1993, p. 6; and Susan Garland, "Sweet Victory," *Business Week*, November 29, 1993, pp. 30–31.

being absurd and alarmist. They point out that Mexico would have to run a bilateral trade surplus with the United States of close to $300 billion for job loss on such a scale to occur—and $300 billion is about the size of Mexico's present GDP. In other words, such a scenario is implausible.

More sober estimates of the impact of NAFTA range from a net creation of 170,000 jobs in the United States (due to increased Mexican demand for U.S. goods and services) and an increase of $15 billion per year to the U.S. and Mexican GDPs, to a net loss of 490,000 U.S. jobs. To put these numbers in perspective, employment in the U.S. economy is predicted to grow by 18 million over the next 10 years. As most economists repeatedly stress, in the grand scheme of things NAFTA will have a small impact on both Canada and the United States. It could hardly be any other way, since the Mexican economy is at present only 5 percent of the size of the U.S. economy. The country that is really taking the economic leap of faith by signing NAFTA is neither Canada nor the United States; it is Mexico. Falling trade barriers will now expose Mexican firms to highly efficient U.S. and Canadian competitors that, when compared to the average Mexican firm, have far greater capital resources, access to highly educated and skilled work forces, and much greater technological sophistication. The short-run outcome is bound to be painful economic restructuring and unemployment in Mexico. But if economic theory is any guide, in the long run there should be dynamic gains in the efficiency of Mexican firms as they adjust to the rigors of a more competitive marketplace. To the extent that this happens, Mexico's long-run rate of economic growth will accelerate, and Mexico might yet become a major market for Canadian and U.S. firms.[18]

Environmentalists have also voiced concerns about NAFTA. They point to the sludge in the Rio Grande River and the smog in the air over Mexico City and warn that Mexico could degrade clean air and toxic waste standards across the continent. Already, they claim, the lower Rio Grande is the most polluted river in the United States, increasing in chemical waste and sewage along its course from El Paso, Texas, to the Gulf of Mexico.

There is also continued opposition in Mexico to NAFTA from those who fear a loss of national sovereignty. Mexican critics argue that their entire country will be dominated by U.S. firms that will not really contribute to Mexico's economic growth, but instead will use Mexico as a low-cost assembly site, while keeping their high-paying, high-skilled jobs north of the border.

The early experience

The first year after NAFTA turned out to be a largely positive experience for all three countries. U.S. trade with Canada and Mexico expanded at about twice the rate of trade with non-NAFTA countries in the first nine months of 1994, compared with the same period in 1993. U.S. exports to Mexico grew by 22 percent, while Mexican exports to the U.S. grew by 23 percent. Anti-NAFTA campaigners had warned of doom for the U.S. auto industry, but exports of autos to Mexico from the United States increased by nearly 500 percent in the first nine months of 1993. The U.S. Commerce Department estimated the surge in exports to Mexico secured about 130,000 U.S. jobs, while only 13,000 people applied for aid under a program designed to help workers displaced by the movement of jobs to Mexico, suggesting that job losses from NAFTA had been small.[19]

However, the early euphoria over NAFTA was snuffed out in December 1994 when the Mexican economy was shaken by a financial crisis. Through 1993 and 1994 Mexico's trade deficit with the rest of the world had grown sharply, while Mexico's inflation rate had started to accelerate. This put increasing pressure on the

---

[18]"NAFTA: The Showdown," *The Economist*, November 13, 1993, pp. 23–36.

[19]"Happy Ever NAFTA?" *The Economist*, December 10, 1994, pp. 23–24; and Douglas Harbrecht, "What Has NAFTA Wrought? Plenty of Trade?" *Business Week*, November 21, 1994, pp. 48–49.

Mexican currency, the peso. Traders in the foreign exchange markets, betting there would be a large decline in the value of the peso against the dollar, began to sell pesos and buy dollars. As a result, in December 1994 the Mexican government was forced to devalue the peso by about 35 percent against the U.S. dollar. This effectively increased the cost of imports from the United States by 35 percent. The devaluation of the peso was followed quickly by a collapse in the value of the Mexican stock market, and the country suddenly and unexpectedly appeared to be in the midst of a major economic crisis. Shortly afterward, the Mexican government introduced an austerity program designed to rebuild confidence in the country's financial institutions and rein in growth and inflation. The program was backed by a $20 billion loan guarantee from the U.S. government.[20]

One result of this turmoil has been a sharp decline in Canadian and U.S. exports to Mexico. Many companies have also reduced or put on hold their plans for expansion into Mexico. The U.S. retailer, Wal-Mart, for example, delayed plans to open 24 stores in Mexico (for further details on Wal-Mart's post-NAFTA experience, see the "Management Focus"). As might be expected, critics of NAFTA seized on Mexico's financial crisis to crow that they had been right. But in reality, just as the celebrations of NAFTA's success were premature, so are claims of its sudden demise. It is far too early to reach a judgment on the success or failure of NAFTA. It will probably be at least 10 years before the true impact of NAFTA becomes apparent.

Enlargement

One big issue now confronting NAFTA is that of enlargement. After Congress approved NAFTA a number of other Latin American countries indicated their desire to eventually join NAFTA. Currently the governments of both Canada and the United States are adopting a wait-and-see attitude with regard to most countries. Getting NAFTA approved was such a bruising political experience that neither the Canadian nor U.S. governments have a desire to repeat the process soon. Nevertheless the Canadian, Mexican, and U.S. governments began earnest negotiations in May 1995 with Chile regarding that country's possible entry into NAFTA.

The Andean Pact

The Andean Pact was formed in 1969 when Bolivia, Chile, Ecuador, Colombia, and Peru signed the Cartagena Agreement. The Andean Pact was largely based on the EU model, but it has been far less successful at achieving its stated goals. The integration steps begun in 1969 included an internal tariff reduction program, the creation of a common external tariff, a transportation policy, a common industrial policy, and special concessions for the smallest members, Bolivia and Ecuador.

By the mid-1980s the Andean Pact had all but collapsed. The pact had failed to achieve any of its stated objectives. There was no tariff-free trade between member-countries, no common external tariff, and no harmonization of economic policies. The attempt to achieve cooperation between member-countries seems to have been substantially hindered by political and economic problems. The countries of the Andean Pact have had to deal with low economic growth, hyperinflation, high unemployment, political unrest, and crushing burdens of debt. All these problems have made it extremely difficult to achieve cooperation. In addition the dominant political ideology in many of the Andean countries during this period tended toward the radical/socialist end of the political spectrum. Since such an ideology is hostile to the free market economic principle on which the Andean Pact was based, progress toward closer integration could not be expected.

---

[20]P. B. Carroll and C. Torres, "Mexico Unveils Program of Harsh Fiscal Medicine," *The Wall Street Journal*, March 3, 1995, pp. A1, A6.

MANAGEMENT FOCUS
Wal-Mart's Expansion Plans in Mexico Run into Red Tape

Wal-Mart, a major U.S. discount retail chain, saw the January 1, 1994, implementation of NAFTA as a chance to expand its operations into Mexico. Only five years before, Mexican regulations severely limited any direct investment by foreign companies into its market. Now managers at Wal-Mart thought they had received a green light for investment. The company responded by launching an ambitious expansion program in Mexico that involved opening four Wal-Mart stores in 1994 and 10 warehouse style Sam's Clubs, with more to follow.

Reality struck home in the summer of 1994 when Mexican government inspectors made a surprise visit to Wal-Mart's new superstore in Mexico City. The green light was apparently wrapped in bureaucratic red tape. The inspectors found thousands of products they claimed were improperly labeled or lacking instructions in Spanish. The store was ordered shut for 72 hours while the oversights were corrected. This brush with what they see as overzealous inspectors has sobered Wal-Mart's managers. They note the 200,000-square-foot supercenter that was raided carries about 80,000 products. Each now has to be labeled in Spanish indicating the country of origin, content, instructions, and in some cases an import permit number. The inspectors charged that some 11,700 pieces of merchandise lacked such labels.

Wal-Mart's managers responded by pointing out that many of the targeted goods—some 40 percent or more—were purchased from a local Mexican distributor. The regulators insisted the retailer had ultimate responsibility for the labeling. Wal-Mart's managers see this kind of bureaucratic red tape as a deliberate attempt by government bureaucrats to raise their costs of doing business in Mexico, thereby frustrating their expansion plans.

To make matters worse, Mexico's financial crisis, which exploded unexpectedly in December 1994, effectively stalled Wal-Mart's ambitious expansion plans. Wal-Mart saw the dollar value of its Mexican assets and earnings plunge as the peso fell by more than 35 percent against the dollar. At the same time, the sharp drop in Mexican business and consumer confidence that followed the peso's free fall translated into a marked decline in sales at Wal-Mart stores in Mexico. The company responded by putting on hold plans to open 24 new stores in Mexico in 1995. Despite all the bureaucratic and currency problems Wal-Mart has experienced in Mexico, the company insists it will remain in Mexico for the long haul, and it is still optimistic about the long-run potential of the Mexican economy and the benefits of NAFTA.

Sources: G. Smith, "NAFTA: A Green Light for Red Tape," *Business Week*, July 25, 1994, p. 48; and A. DePalma, "Big Companies in Mexico among the Peso's Worst Victims," *New York Times*, January 30, 1995, p. D4.

The tide began to turn in the late 1980s when, after years of economic decline, the governments of Latin America began to adopt free market economic policies. In 1990 the heads of the five current members of the Andean Pact—Bolivia, Ecuador, Peru, Colombia, and Venezuela—met in the Galápagos Islands. The resulting Galápagos Declaration effectively relaunched the Andean Pact. The declaration's objectives included the establishment of a free trade area by 1992, a customs union by 1994, and a common market by 1995.

It remains to be seen how successful this attempt at integration will be. However, there are grounds for cautious optimism. For the first time the controlling political ideology of the Andean countries is at least consistent with the free market principles underlying a common market. In addition, since the Galapagos Declaration, internal tariff levels have been reduced by all five members, and a customs union with a common external tariff was established in mid 1994, six months behind schedule. But significant differences between member-countries still exist that may make harmonization of policies and close integration difficult. For example, Venezuela's GDP per person is four times that of Bolivia's, and Ecuador's tiny production-line industries can hardly compete with Colombia's and Venezuela's more advanced industries. Such differences are a recipe for disagreement and suggest that many of the adjustments required to achieve a true common market will be painful—even though the net benefits will probably outweigh the costs.[21]

❧ MERCOSUR

MERCOSUR originated in 1988 as a free trade pact between Brazil and Argentina. The modest reductions in tariffs and quotas accompanying this pact reportedly helped bring about an 80 percent increase in trade between the two countries in the late 1980s.[22] Encouraged by this success, the pact was expanded in March 1990 to include Paraguay and Uruguay. The aim of the MERCOSUR pact is to establish a full free trade area by the end of 1994 and a common market sometime later. The four countries of MERCOSUR have a combined population of 200 million. With a market of this size, MERCOSUR could have a significant impact on the economic growth rate of the four economies. On the other hand, it could just as easily fall victim to economic mismanagement in Brazil and Argentina. For the present, however, MERCOSUR appear to be functioning relatively well. The four member-states of MERCOSUR have now formally committed themselves to the establishment of a wider free trade area, the South American Free Trade Area (SAFTA). The aim here is to bring other South American countries into the agreement and to have internal free trade for not less than 80 percent of goods produced in the region by 2005.[23]

Other Latin American Trade Pacts

The countries of Central America are trying to revive their trade pact. In the early 1960s Costa Rica, El Salvador, Guatemala, Honduras, and Nicaragua attempted to set up a Central American common market. It collapsed in 1969 when war broke out between Honduras and El Salvador after a riot at a soccer match between teams from the two countries. Now the five countries are trying to revive their agreement, although no definite progress had been made by 1995.

A customs union was to have been created in 1991 between the English-speaking Caribbean countries under the auspices of the Caribbean Community. Referred to as CARICOM, it was established in 1973. However, it has repeatedly failed to progress toward economic integration. A formal commitment to economic and monetary union was adopted by CARICOM's member-states in 1984, but since then little progress has been made. In October 1991 the CARICOM governments failed, for the third consecutive time, to meet a deadline for establishing a common external tariff.

❧ REGIONAL ECONOMIC INTEGRATION ELSEWHERE

Outside of Western Europe and the Americas, there have been few significant attempts at regional economic integration. Although there are a number of groupings throughout Asia and Africa, few exist in anything other than name. Perhaps the most significant group outside of Europe and the Americas today is the

---

[21]"NAFTA Is Not Alone," *The Economist*, June 18, 1994, pp. 47–48; Sweeney, "First Latin American Customs Union Looms over Venezuela," *Journal of Commerce*, September 26, 1991, p. 5A; and "The Business of the American Hemisphere," *The Economist*, August 24, 1991, pp. 37–38.

[22]"Business of the American Hemisphere."

[23]"NAFTA Is Not Alone."

❧ MAP 8.3
Asia Pacific Economic Cooperation

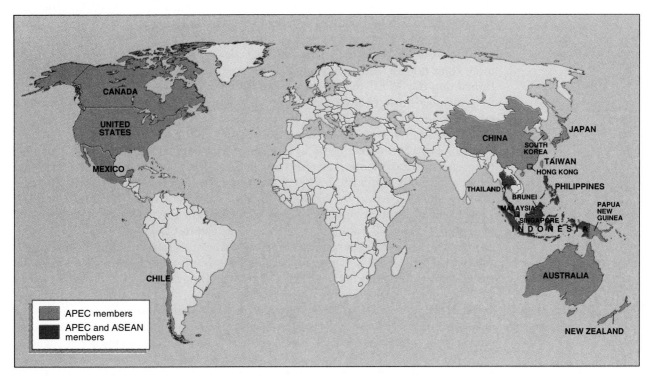

Association of Southeast Asian Nations (ASEAN). In addition, the Asian Pacific Economic Cooperation (APEC) forum has recently emerged as the kernel of a potential free trade region.

Association of Southeast Asian Nations

Formed in 1967, ASEAN currently includes Brunei, Indonesia, Malaysia, the Philippines, Singapore, and Thailand. The ASEAN countries are characterized by an abundance of natural resources (with the exception of the city-state of Singapore), large international trade sectors, and an emphasis on free market economic policies. Singapore and Thailand are two of Southeast Asia's most successful economies. Thus the potential exists for a vibrant free trade area.

The basic objectives of ASEAN are to foster freer trade between member-countries and to achieve some cooperation in their industrial policies. Progress has been very limited, however. For example, although some progress has been made in tariff reduction between ASEAN countries, only 5 percent of intra-ASEAN trade currently consists of goods whose tariffs have been reduced through ASEAN preferential trade arrangements.

Asia Pacific Economic Cooperation

Asia Pacific Economic Cooperation (APEC) was founded in 1990 at the suggestion of Australia. APEC currently has 18 member-states including such economic powerhouses as the United States, Japan, and China (see Map 8.3). Collectively the 18 member-states account for half of the world's GDP, 40 percent of world trade, and most of the growth in the world economy. The stated aim of APEC is to increase multilateral cooperation in view of the economic rise of the Pacific nations and the growing interdependence within the region. U.S. support for APEC was also based on the belief that it might prove a viable strategy for heading off any moves to create Asian groupings from which it would be excluded.

Interest in APEC was heightened considerably in November 1993 when for the first time the heads of APEC member-states met for a two-day conference in Seattle. Before the meeting debate centered around the likely future role of APEC. One view was that APEC should commit itself to the ultimate formation of a free trade area. Such a move would transform the Pacific Rim from a geographical expression into the world's largest free trade area. Another view was that APEC would produce no more than hot air and lots of photo opportunities for the leaders involved. As it turned out, the APEC meeting produced little more than some vague commitments from member-states to work closely together for greater economic integration and a general lowering of trade barriers. However, significantly, member-states did not rule out the possibility of closer economic cooperation in the future.[24]

The heads of state met again in November 1994 in Jakarta, Indonesia. This time they agreed to take more concrete steps and the joint statement at the end of the meeting formally committed APEC's industrialized members to remove their trade and investment barriers by 2010 and for developing economies to do so by 2020. They also called for a detailed blueprint charting how this might be achieved to be presented; this was discussed at the 1995 APEC summit held in Osaka, Japan.[25] Although few observers believe much progress toward this lofty goal will be made anytime soon, if the goal is eventually attained the result will be the formation of the world's largest free trade area. APEC is worth watching closely.

IMPLICATIONS FOR BUSINESS

Currently the most significant developments in regional economic integration are occurring in Europe and North America. Although some Latin American trade blocs may have greater economic significance in the future, as ultimately may APEC, at present the events in Europe and North America have far more profound and immediate implications for business practice. Accordingly, in this section we will concentrate on the business implications of the EU and NAFTA. Similar conclusions, however, could be drawn with regard to the creation of a single market anywhere in the world.

Opportunities

The creation of a single market offers significant opportunities as markets that were protected from foreign competition are opened. For example, in Europe before 1992 the large French and Italian markets were among the most protected. These markets are now much more open to foreign competition in the form of both exports and direct investment. Nonetheless, the specter of "Fortress Europe" suggests that to fully exploit such opportunities, it will pay non-EU firms to set up EU subsidiaries. Many major U.S. firms have long had subsidiaries in Europe. Those that do not would be well advised to consider establishing them now, lest they run the risk of being shut out of the EU by nontariff barriers. Non-EU firms rapidly increased their direct investment in the EU in anticipation of the creation of a single market. From 1985 to 1989, for example, approximately 37 percent of the FDI inflows into industrialized countries was directed at the EC. By 1991 this figure had risen to 66 percent.[26]

Additional opportunities arise from the inherent lower costs of doing business in a single market—as opposed to 15 national markets in the case of the EU or 3 national markets in the case of NAFTA. Free movement of goods across borders, harmonized product standards, and simplified tax regimes make it possible for firms based in the EU and the NAFTA countries to realize potentially enormous cost economies by centralizing production in those EU and NAFTA locations where the mix of factor costs and skills is optimal. At the extreme, rather than producing a product in each of the 15 EU countries or the 3 NAFTA countries, a firm may be able to serve the whole EU or North American market from a single location. This location must be chosen carefully, of course, with an eye on local factor costs and skills.

---

[24]"Aimless in Seattle," *The Economist*, November 13, 1993, pp. 35–36.
[25]Guy de Jonquieres, "Different Aims, Common Cause," *Financial Times*, November 18, 1995, p. 14.
[26]"World Economic Survey," *The Economist*, September 19, 1992, p. 17.

For example, in response to the challenges created by EU after 1992, the Minneapolis company 3M has been consolidating its European manufacturing and distribution facilities to take advantage of economies of scale. Thus a plant in Great Britain now produces 3M's printing products and a German factory its reflective traffic control materials for all of the EU. In each case 3M chose a location for centralized production after carefully considering the likely production costs in alternative locations within the EU. The ultimate goal of 3M is to dispense with national distinctions, directing R&D, manufacturing, distribution, and marketing for each product group from an EU headquarters.[27] Similarly, Unilever, one of Europe's largest companies, was busy rationalizing its production in advance of 1992 to attain scale economies. Unilever concentrated its production of dishwashing powder for the EU in one plant, toilet soap in another, and so on.[28]

Even after the removal of barriers to trade and investment, enduring differences between nations in culture and competitive practices often limit the ability of companies to realize cost economies by centralizing production in key locations and producing a standardized product for the single multicountry market. Thus, as we saw in the opening case, Atag, the Belgium-based producer of kitchenware, thought it would be able to realize cost economies by supplying just two types of cookers to consumers throughout the EU. The reality, however, was that consumers in different countries demanded different types of cookers. Atag was forced to respond by producing 11 different models, not 2. Similarly, the profile of the European insurance market (see the "Regional Focus") illustrated that the removal of barriers to trade and investment is by itself not enough to create a true single market. Cultural, historic, and institutional factors still get in the way. Dealing with these factors requires that insurance companies customize their pricing and selling practices on a country by country basis within the EU.

Threats

Just as the emergence of single markets in the EU and North America creates opportunities for business, so it also presents a number of threats. For one thing, the business environment within both groups will become more competitive. The lowering of barriers to trade and investment between countries is likely to lead to increased price competition throughout the EU and North America. For example, before 1992 a Volkswagen Golf cost 55 percent more in Great Britain than in Denmark and 29 percent more in Ireland than in Greece.[29] Such price differentials will vanish in a single market. This is a direct threat to any firm doing business in the EU or the NAFTA countries. To survive in the tougher single-market environment, firms must take advantage of the opportunities offered by the creation of a single market to rationalize their production and reduce their costs. Otherwise they will be severely disadvantaged.

A further threat to non-EU and/or non-North American firms arises from the likely long-term improvement in the competitive position of many European and North American firms. This is particularly relevant in the EU, where many firms are currently limited by a high cost structure in their ability to compete globally with North American and Asian firms. The creation of a single market and the resulting increased competition in the EU can be expected to result in serious attempts by many EU firms to reduce their cost structure by rationalizing production. This could transform many EU companies into efficient global competitors. The message for non-EU businesses is that they need to prepare for the emergence of more capable European competitors by reducing their own cost structures.

A final threat to non-EU and/or non-North American firms inherent in the creation of a single market has already been alluded to. This is the threat of being shut out of the single market by the creation of "Fortress Europe" or "Fortress North America." As noted earlier in the chapter, although the free trade philosophy underpinning the EU theoretically argues

---

[27]P. Davis, "A European Campaign: Local Companies Rush for a Share of EC Market While Barriers Are Down," *Minneapolis-St. Paul City Business*, January 8, 1990, p. 1.
[28]"The Business of Europe," *The Economist*, December 7, 1991, pp. 63–64.
[29]E. G. Friberg, "1992: Moves Europeans Are Making," *Harvard Business Review*, May–June 1989, pp. 85–89.

against the creation of any "fortress" in Europe, there are signs that the EU may raise barriers to imports and investment in certain areas, such as autos. Non-EU firms might be well advised, therefore, to set up their own EU operations as quickly as possible. This could also occur in the NAFTA countries, but it seems less likely.

☙ SUMMARY OF CHAPTER

Three main objectives have been pursued in this chapter. They were to examine the economic and political debate surrounding regional economic integration; to review the progress toward regional economic integration in Europe, the Americas, and elsewhere; and to distinguish the important implications of regional economic integration for the practice of international business. The following points have been made in the chapter.

1. A number of levels of economic integration are possible in theory. In order of increasing integration, they include a free trade area, a customs union, a common market, an economic union, and full political union.

2. In a free trade area, barriers to trade between member-countries are removed, but each country determines its own external trade policy. In a customs union, internal barriers to trade are removed and a common external trade policy is adopted. A common market is similar to a customs union, except that in a common market factors of production also are allowed to move freely between countries. An economic union involves even closer integration, including the establishment of a common currency and the harmonization of tax rates. A political union is the logical culmination of attempts to achieve ever-closer economic integration.

3. Regional economic integration is an attempt to achieve economic gains from the free flow of trade and investment between neighboring countries.

4. Integration is not easily achieved or sustained. Although integration brings benefits to the majority, it is never without costs for the minority. Concerns over national sovereignty often slow or stop integration attempts.

5. Regional integration will not increase economic welfare if the trade creation effects in the free trade area are outweighed by the trade diversion effects.

6. The Single European Act sought to create a true single market by abolishing administrative barriers to the free flow of trade and investment between EU countries.

7. The Treaty of Maastricht aims to take the EU even further along the road to economic union by establishing a common currency. The economic gains from a common currency come from reduced exchange costs and reduced risk associated with currency fluctuations.

8. Although no other attempt at regional economic integration comes close to the EU in terms of potential economic and political significance, various other attempts are being made in the world. The most notable include NAFTA in North America, the Andean Pact and MERCOSUR in Latin America, ASEAN in Southeast Asia, and (perhaps) APEC.

9. The creation of single markets in the EU and North America means many markets that were formerly protected from foreign competition are now more open. This creates major investment and export opportunities for firms within and outside these regions.

10. The free movement of goods across borders, the harmonization of product standards, and the simplification of tax regimes make it possible for firms based in the EU and North America to realize potentially enormous cost economies by centralizing production in those locations in the EU and NAFTA countries where the mix of factor costs and skills is optimal.

11. The lowering of barriers to trade and investment between countries will probably be followed by increased price competition throughout the EU and North America.

☙ CRITICAL DISCUSSION QUESTIONS

1. NAFTA is likely to produce net benefits for the U.S. economy. Discuss.

2. What are the economic and political arguments for regional economic integration? Given these arguments, why don't we see more integration in the world economy?

3. What is the effect of creation of a single market within the EU likely to be on competition within the EU? Why?

4. How should a U.S. firm that currently exports only to Western Europe respond to the creation of a single market?

5. How should a firm with self-sufficient production facilities in several EU countries respond to the creation of a single market? What are the constraints on its ability to respond in a manner that minimizes production costs?

❧ CLOSING CASE   Martin's Textiles

August 12, 1992, was a really bad day for John Martin. That was the day Canada, Mexico, and the United States announced an agreement in principle to the North American Free Trade Agreement (NAFTA). Under the plan, all tariffs between the three countries would be eliminated within the next 10 to 15 years, with most being cut in five years. What disturbed Martin most was the plan's provision that all tariffs on trade of textiles among the three countries are to be removed within 10 years. Under the proposed agreement, Mexico and Canada would also be allowed to ship a specific amount of clothing and textiles made from foreign materials to the United States each year, and this quota would rise slightly over the first five years of the agreement. "My God!" thought Martin. "Now I'm going to have to decide about moving my plants to Mexico."

Martin is the CEO of a New York-based textile company, Martin's Textiles. The company has been in the Martin family for four generations, having been founded by his great-grandfather in 1910. Today the company employs 1,500 people in three New York plants that produce cotton-based clothes, primarily underwear. All production employees are union members, and the company has a long history of good labor relations. The company has never had a labor dispute, and Martin, like his father, grandfather, and great-grandfather before him, regards the work force as part of the "Martin family." Martin prides himself not only on knowing many of the employees by name, but also on knowing a great deal about the family circumstances of many of the longtime employees.

Over the past 20 years the company has experienced increasingly tough competition, both from overseas and at home. The mid-1980s was particularly difficult. The strength of the dollar on the foreign exchange market during that period enabled Asian producers to enter the U.S. market with very low prices. Since then, although the dollar has weakened against many major currencies, the Asian producers have not raised their prices in response to the falling dollar. In a low-skilled, labor-intensive business such as clothing manufacture, costs are driven by wage rates and labor productivity. Not surprisingly, most of Martin's competitors in the northeastern United States responded to the intense cost competition by moving production south, first to states such as South Carolina and Mississippi, where nonunion labor could be hired for significantly less than in the unionized Northeast, and then to Mexico, where labor costs for textile workers were less than $2 per hour. In contrast, wage rates are $12.50 per hour at Martin's New York plant and $8 to $10 per hour at nonunion textile plants in the southeastern United States.

The last three years have been particularly tough at Martin's Textiles. The company has registered a small loss each year, and Martin knows the company cannot go on like this. His major customers, while praising the quality of Martin's products, have warned him that his prices are getting too high and they may not be able to continue to do business with him. His longtime banker has told him he must get his labor costs down. Martin agrees, but he knows of only one surefire way to do that, to move production south—way south, to Mexico. He has always been reluctant to do that, but now he seems to have little choice. He fears that in five years the U.S. market will be flooded with cheap imports from Asian, U.S., and Mexican companies, all producing in Mexico. It looks like the only way for Martin's Textiles to survive is to close the New York plants and move production to Mexico. All that would be left in the United States would be the sales force.

Martin's mind was spinning. How could something that throws good honest people out of work be good for the country? The politicians said it would be good for trade, good for economic growth, good for the three countries. Martin could not see it that way. What about Mary Morgan, who has worked for Martin's for 30 years. She is now 54 years old. How will she and others like her find another job? What about his moral obligation to his workers? What about the loyalty his workers have shown his family over the years? Is this a good way to repay it? How would he break the news to his employees, many of whom have worked for the company 10 to 20 years? And what about the Mexican workers? Could they be as loyal and productive as his present employees? From other U.S. textile companies that had set up production in Mexico he had heard stories of low productivity, poor workmanship, high turnover, and high absenteeism. Is this true? If so, how could he ever cope with that? Martin has always felt that the success of Martin's Textiles was partly due to the family atmosphere, which encourages worker loyalty, productivity, and attention to quality, an atmosphere that has been built up over four generations. How could he replicate that in Mexico with a bunch of foreign workers who speak a language he doesn't even understand?

CASE DISCUSSION QUESTIONS

1. What are the economic costs and benefits to Martin's Textiles of shifting production to Mexico?
2. What are the social costs and benefits to Martin's Textiles of shifting production to Mexico?
3. Are the economic and social costs and benefits of moving production to Mexico independent of each other?
4. What seems to be the most ethical action?
5. What would you do if you were John Martin?

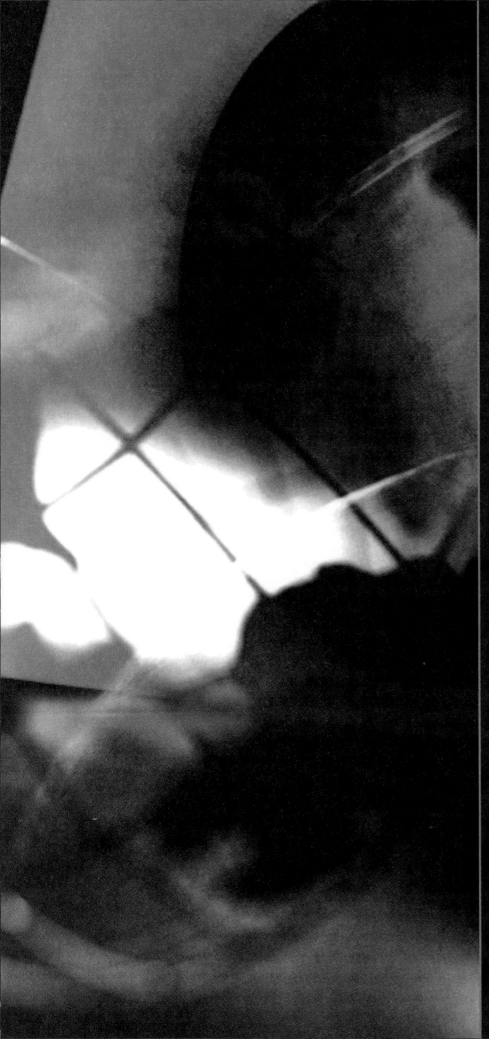

CASES

THE RISE (AND STALL)
OF THE JAPANESE
SEMICONDUCTOR
INDUSTRY

THE COMMERCIAL
AIRCRAFT INDUSTRY
IN 1995: AIRBUS
INDUSTRIE, BOEING, AND
MCDONNELL DOUGLAS

ACTIVE -MATRIX LIQUID
CRYSTAL DISPLAYS (A):
1990–91 TRADE DISPUT

ACTIVE -MATRIX LIQUID
CRYSTAL DISPLAYS (B):
1992–94

THE RISE (AND STALL) OF THE JAPANESE SEMICONDUCTOR INDUSTRY

The semiconductor industry was born with the invention of the transistor at Bell Telephone laboratories in 1947. The transistor was first commercialized in the 1950s by U.S. firms and it soon became a major component of electronic products. In the 1960s the transistor was replaced by the integrated circuit. Like the transistor, the integrated circuit was first developed and commercialized by U.S. firms. Today semiconductors are the main components of numerous electronic products including computers, photocopiers, and telecommunications equipment. In addition they are increasingly finding their way into a host of other products from automobiles to machine tools.

Semiconductors can be divided into several broad product groups, the most important of which are *memory devices* such as DRAMs (dynamic random access memory chips) and *logic chips,* such as the microprocessors and microcontrollers. The total world market for semiconductors, which stood at $35 billion in 1988, reached $91.5 billion in 1994 and is predicted to total $250 billion by the year 2000. Worldwide sales of memory devices totaled $32 billion in 1994, while sales of logic chips totaled $18.3 billion.

U.S. enterprises dominated the world market from the 1950s until the early 1980s. At the height of U.S. success in the mid-1970s U.S. firms held close to 70 percent of the world market. During the 1980s, however, the market share of U.S. firms plummeted, falling to 29 percent by 1990, while the share held by Japanese producers rose from 24 percent at the end of the 1970s to 49 percent by 1990. By the end of the 1980s the United States was a net importer of semiconductors, while 5 of the 10 largest semiconductor producers were Japanese. More significantly still, by 1988 Japanese firms had captured more than 80 percent of the world market for the most widely used integrated circuit in digital equipment, the DRAM, which was invented by Intel and once produced exclusively by U.S. firms. But as of 1988 there were only two U.S. firms in the DRAM market—Micron Technology and Texas Instruments, and Texas Instruments was manufacturing most of its DRAMs in Japan!

However, the late 1980s may have been something of a high-water mark in the global success of Japanese semiconductor firms. By the mid-1990s the U.S. industry was again gaining global market share. By 1994 U.S. manufacturers had increased their share of the world semiconductor market to 42 percent, while the share taken by Japanese firms stood at 41 percent, down almost ten percentage points from their high (see Figure 1). Foreign firms held 22.4 percent of the Japanese semiconductor market in 1994, up from about 14 percent in 1990. In this case we explore some of the reasons for the rise of Japan's semiconductor industry and for the apparent recent stalling of its growth in global market share.

❧ JAPAN'S INDUSTRIAL POLICY

Why were the Japanese so successful in the global semiconductor industry between the 1970s and late 1980s? One argument is that the industrial policy of the Japanese government was the driving force behind Japan's success in semiconductors. During the 1960s and 1970s the Japanese government, principally through the Ministry of International Trade and Industry (MITI), sought to build a competitive semiconductor industry by limiting foreign competition in the domestic market and acquiring foreign technology and know-how. The foreign investment laws created after World War II (ironically by the U.S. occupation government) required the Japanese government to review for approval all applications for foreign direct investment in Japan. MITI consistently rejected all applications by U.S. semiconductor firms to set

Source: Charles W. L. Hill.

Figure 1

Worldwide Semiconductor
Market Share 1994

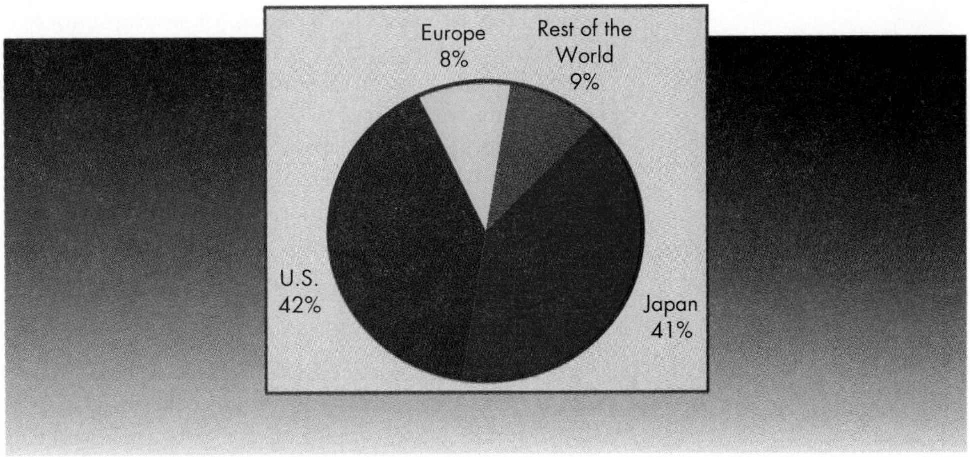

up wholly owned subsidiaries in Japan, to set up joint ventures in which the U.S. partner would have a majority stake, or to acquire equity in Japanese semiconductor firms. At the same time the government limited foreign import penetration of the Japanese market through a combination of high tariffs and restrictive quotas. Import penetration of the Japanese market was also limited by requirements that Japanese companies get permission from MITI before buying advanced integrated circuits from foreign companies. For example, until 1974, integrated circuits that contained more than 200 circuit elements could not be imported without special permission.

Because U.S. producers were denied direct access to the Japanese semiconductor market, they typically sought indirect access by licensing their product and process know-how to Japanese enterprises. This too was regulated closely by MITI. MITI's policy was to insist that if a foreign firm was going to license technology in Japan, that technology had to be licensed to all Japanese firms that requested access. In other words, U.S. firms were not able to discriminate between licensees. MITI also conditioned approval of certain deals on the willingness of the involved Japanese firms to diffuse their technological developments, through sublicensing agreements, to other Japanese firms. The net result of these policies was to encourage the rapid diffusion of advanced semiconductor product and process technology throughout the Japanese semiconductor industry.

U.S. firms went along with this policy because it was their only way to get access to the Japanese market. Initially licensing was a very lucrative arrangement for the U.S. firms involved. By the end of the 1960s Japanese semiconductor firms were reportedly paying at least 10 percent of their sales revenues as royalties to U.S. firms—2 percent to Western Electric, 4.5 percent to Fairchild, and 3.5 percent to Texas Instruments. The most notable long-run consequence, however, was a transfer of U.S. technological know-how to a number of emerging Japanese competitors. Shielded from foreign competition by import barriers and restrictions on foreign direct investment, and armed with state-of-the-art technological know-how, the Japanese firms had only each other to compete with for a share of the rapidly growing Japanese semiconductor market. Stimulated by MITI's insistence that technology be shared between all Japanese semiconductor firms, this competition was intense and based primarily on cost (since everyone had the same technology). The end result was that the firms that rose to the top in this tough environment, such as NEC, were by the mid-1970s more than capable of going head to head with U.S. semiconductor firms.

❧ Trade Agreements

By the mid-1980s the changing fortunes of the Japanese and U.S. semiconductor industries had given birth to a bitter trade dispute between the two countries. After incurring heavy losses, U.S. firms claimed they were facing unfair competition from

Japan. They accused the Japanese of selling semiconductors, and especially DRAMs, in the United States for less than their fair market value while simultaneously shutting U.S. firms out of the important and lucrative Japanese semiconductor market. The dispute was settled by a 1986 trade agreement between the United States and Japan. The agreement specified a fair market value for semiconductors. Japanese companies were not supposed to sell their semiconductors for less than this price outside Japan. The agreement also sought to increase foreign access to Japan's domestic semiconductor market. In a nonbinding side letter the Japanese government agreed to help ensure that foreign manufacturers gained more than 20 percent of the Japanese market by the end of 1991, a significant increase from the 8.6 percent share held in 1986.

Although the agreement did lead to an increase in prices for semiconductors in the United States, foreign producers were still not able to capture a major share of Japan's semiconductor market. By early 1991 when the 1986 agreement was close to expiration, the American Semiconductor Industry Association claimed that foreigners held only a 12 percent share of the Japanese market (in contrast, the Japanese claimed the foreign share was closer to 17 percent).

In June 1991 the United States and Japan signed a new five-year pact to replace the 1986 agreement. Unlike the previous agreement, this pact formally committed the Japanese to ensuring that foreign producers gained a 20 percent share of their semiconductor market by the end of 1992. In return the United States agreed to abolish the fair market value system created under the 1986 pact.

This new agreement was greeted with a mixed reception on both sides. While most U.S. semiconductor manufacturers approved of the agreement, some analysts and politicians argued that the government should not have abolished the fair market value system. House Majority Leader Richard Gephart, for example, criticized the agreement for its lack of specific commitments by Japan to widen its chip market to foreign sellers. Clyde Prestowitz, a former U.S. trade official who helped to craft the 1986 agreement, called the pact "a step backwards," primarily because it abolished the fair market value system. The Japanese, in contrast, expressed pleasure that the fair market value system had been removed, but many in Japanese industry criticized the formal commitment to a 20 percent foreign market share. For example, a senior official at Toshiba, one of Japan's largest semiconductor manufacturers, noted, "We believe that the agreement infringes the principles of free trade, which shouldn't be limited by an agreement of any kind." Similarly a senior official from the NEC Corporation made the following observation: "As you know, the semiconductor was invented in the U.S. and the U.S. was number one in the world for a long time in semiconductors. The U.S. might be a little complacent about what it has achieved. There has been a lack of effort."

Despite such misgivings, the pact seemed to deliver what it promised. The foreign share of the Japanese semiconductor market reached 20 percent in the fourth quarter of 1992. Although it fell back somewhat in the first half of 1993, foreign producers again gained share in the fourth quarter, pushing their total share for the year to 19.4 percent, up from an average of 16.7 percent for all of 1992. The performance of foreigners was even better in 1994 when they captured over 22 percent of the Japanese market. In the fourth quarter of 1994 foreign producers gained a record 23.7 percent market share. However, some analysts wondered whether the pact had that much to do with foreign success. They pointed out that the value of the Japanese yen had strengthened by about 40 percent against the U.S. dollar since 1991. With the yen this high, the terms of trade in the Japanese semiconductor market had swung sharply toward foreign producers, which now had a distinct cost advantage over their Japanese rivals.

Moreover, critics note that in the important DRAM market there has been only a limited U.S. resurgence (this was in contrast to the market for logic chips, where Intel and Motorola continue to dominate). While both Micron Technology and Texas Instruments, the only two U.S. DRAM manufacturers, have done extremely well during 1994 and 1995, much of the DRAM market share gain in Japan has been made by Korean firms, particularly Samsung. Samsung, which didn't even produce DRAMs in 1988, accounted for 12.7 percent of the world DRAM market in 1994, ahead of Japan's Hitachi Corp. and NEC, which accounted for 9.7 percent and 9.2 percent respectively. The Japanese share of the world DRAM market has been cut in half since 1988 as customers have switched to low-cost producers such as market leader Samsung and Micron Technology (which enjoyed a 4.5 percent market share in 1994). As of 1995 this process shows no sign of slowing. One 1995 estimate suggests that South Korean firms are reinvesting 30 percent to 55 percent of their semiconductor revenues back in new plants and equipment, the Americans are reinvesting 22 percent, while the Japanese are reinvesting only 15 percent. Furthermore, a number of Taiwanese firms have announced aggressive plans to expand their presence in the DRAM business. In the face of this rapid investment in capacity by non-Japanese firms—and the apparent reluctance of Japanese firms to invest—it will be very difficult for the Japanese producers to hold onto their current 37 percent share of the global DRAM market.

CASE DISCUSSION QUESTIONS

1. What factors account for the rise of Japan's semiconductor manufacturers during the 1970s and 1980s?

2. Does the rise of Japanese semiconductor companies during the 1970s and 1980s indicate that government industrial policy can play an important role in facilitating national competitiveness in industries targeted by that policy?

3. What explains the relative decline of Japanese semiconductor firms since 1988? Can it be attributed to the 1991 semiconductor pact, or to other economic factors?

4. What are the implications of your answer to Question 3 for national trade policy?

REFERENCES

Borrus, M.; L. A. Tyson; and J. Zysman. "Creating Advantage: How Government Policies Created Trade in the Semiconductor Industry." In *Strategic Trade Policy and the New International Economics*, ed. P. Krugman. Cambridge, MA: MIT Press, 1986.

Chao, J., and D. Hamilton. "Bad Times Are Just a Memory for DRAM Chip Makers." *The Wall Street Journal*, August 28, 1995, p. B4.

Darlin, D. "South Korean Chip Firms Play Catch-Up." *The Wall Street Journal*, July 29, 1991, p. A5.

Davis, B. "Chip Report Eases U.S.-Japan Conflict." *The Wall Street Journal*, March 21, 1994, p. A2.

Dertouzos, M. L.; R. K. Lester; and R. M. Solow. *Made in America*. Cambridge, MA: MIT Press, 1989.

Schlesinger, J. "As U.S. Firms Hail Semiconductor Pact, Some Japan Concerns Have Reservations." *The Wall Street Journal*, June 6, 1991, p. A14.

Standard & Poors Industry Surveys. "Electronics." August 3, 1995.

Yamamura, K. "Caveat Emptor: The Industrial Policy of Japan." In *Strategic Trade Policy and the New International Economics*, ed. P. Krugman. Cambridge, MA: MIT Press, 1986.

THE COMMERCIAL AIRCRAFT INDUSTRY IN 1995: AIRBUS INDUSTRIE, BOEING, AND McDONNELL DOUGLAS

For years the commercial aircraft industry has been an American success story. Until 1980 U.S. manufacturers held a virtual monopoly. Even today, despite the rise of the Europe-based Airbus Industrie, two U.S. firms, Boeing and McDonnell Douglas, account for over two-thirds of world market share. The industry is routinely the largest net contributor to the U.S. balance of trade, and Boeing, the dominant manufacturer in the industry, is the largest U.S. exporter. In the late 1980s and early 90s, the U.S. industry regularly ran a substantial positive trade balance with the rest of the world of $12 to $15 billion per year. The impact of the industry on U.S. employment is also enormous. Boeing directly employs around 100,000 people in the Seattle area and indirectly probably supports another 300,000 in subcontractors and through its payroll.

In recent years, however, U.S. dominance has been threatened by the rise of Airbus Industrie, a consortium of four European aircraft manufacturers—one British (20.0 percent ownership stake), one French (37.9 percent ownership), one German (37.9 percent ownership), and one Spanish (4.2 percent ownership). Founded in 1970, Airbus was initially a marginal competitor and was regarded as unlikely to challenge U.S. dominance. Since 1981, however, Airbus has confounded its critics and emerged as the world's second-largest aircraft manufacturer. By the late 1980s and early 1990s Airbus's share of aircraft orders in any one year stood between 20 percent and 30 percent, up from 14 percent in 1981. In 1994 Airbus achieved something of a coup, capturing a bigger share of orders than Boeing for the first time in history (Airbus garnered 121 orders against Boeing's 122). However, most analysts point out that this was an aberration, given the extremely low level of aircraft orders that year. In the first nine months of 1995, Boeing captured over 70 percent of all new aircraft orders, leaving Airbus with less than a 25 percent share. Nevertheless Airbus has set its sights on gaining a 50 percent share of all new orders for commercial jet aircraft of more than 100 seats by 2000.

Many in the United States responded to the success of Airbus by crying foul, claiming that Airbus is heavily subsidized by the governments of Great Britain, France, Germany, and Spain. Airbus has responded in kind, pointing out that both Boeing and McDonnell Douglas have benefited for years from hidden U.S. government subsidies. In this case we examine the debate between the two sides in this trade dispute. First, however, let us look at the competitive structure of the commercial aircraft industry.

❧ INDUSTRY COMPETITIVE STRUCTURE

The commercial aircraft industry has a unique set of characteristics.

1. The costs of developing a new airliner are enormous. For example, Boeing spent a reported $5 billion developing and tooling its 777 wide-bodied jetliner that was introduced in 1994. The projected development costs for a new 600-800 seat super jumbo jet that is currently being considered by both Boeing and Airbus are reckoned to be in the $10 to $15 billion range.

2. Given such enormous development costs, a company must capture a significant share of world demand to break even. In the case of the 777, for example, Boeing will have to sell more than 200 aircraft to break even, a figure that represents about 15 percent of predicted industry sales for this class of aircraft between 1994 and 2004. Given this, it can take 10 to 14 years of

Source: Charles W. L. Hill.

production for an aircraft to reach its break-even point—and this is on top of the 5 to 6 years of negative cash flows during development. By late 1995 Boeing had already amassed over 200 firm orders for the 777.

3. Worldwide consensus is that a significant "experience curve" exists in aircraft production. Due to learning effects, on average, unit cost falls by about 20 percent with each doubling of accumulated output. Companies that fail to move along the experience curve face a significant unit-cost disadvantage. A company that achieves only half of the market share required to break even will suffer a 20 percent unit-cost disadvantage.

4. Demand for aircraft is highly volatile. This fact makes long-run planning difficult and raises the risks involved in producing aircraft. The commercial airline business is prone to boom-and-bust cycles. During the early 1990s many major airlines experienced financial trouble. Pan Am, Continental, Eastern, Braniff, and TWA were all either in Chapter 11 or had recently folded. Many other airlines were losing money. In response airlines slowed their ordering of new aircraft, pushed back delivery dates for aircraft already on firm order, and decided not to convert their options on future aircraft deliveries to firm orders. Thus, although both Boeing and Airbus had entered the 1990s with record orders, the troubles in the airline business spread to them. The low point was reached in 1994 when 260 large (100-seat plus) commercial jet aircraft were ordered worldwide. However, 1995 witnessed a significant recovery with close to 500 aircraft orders. The 1995 total, however, is still some way down from the peak of the last order boom in the late 1980s when over 1,000 new large commercial jets were being ordered every year.

The combination of high development costs, break-even levels that constitute a significant percentage of world demand, substantial experience curve effects, and volatile demand makes for an industry that can support only a few major players. Analysts seem to agree that the large jet commercial aircraft market can profitably support only two, or possibly three, major producers.

In 1995 there were only three major producers in the industry. Boeing was dominant, followed by Airbus, and McDonnell Douglas came in a distant third. Both Boeing and Airbus produce a family of commercial aircraft (see Figure 1), while McDonnell Douglas's current offering is limited to just three planes, the MD-80, the MD-95, and the MD-11. Of the three companies, only Boeing is currently generating a profit from its commercial aircraft operations. In 1994 Boeing had profits of $856 million on sales of $21.92 billion. Although Airbus does not publish its accounts, most analysts believe the consortium is currently losing money. Certainly the two largest partners in Airbus—the French and Germans—are known to be losing money on their commercial aircraft operations, so it seems highly probable that the whole consortium is in the red. McDonnell Douglas is also currently losing money on its commercial aircraft operations, and the company's long-term survival in the commercial aircraft business is now being questioned.

❧ THE TRADE DISPUTE

In the late 1980s and early 1990s both Boeing and McDonnell Douglas argued that Airbus had an unfair competitive advantage due to the level of subsidy it received from the governments of Great Britain, France, Germany, and Spain. They argued that the subsidies allowed Airbus to set unrealistically low prices, to offer concessions and attractive financing terms to airlines, to write off development costs, and to use state-owned airlines to obtain orders. In making these claims, Boeing and McDonnell Douglas had the support of the U.S. government. According to a study by the Department of Commerce, Airbus received more than $13.5 billion in government subsidies between 1970 and 1990 ($25.9 billion if

FIGURE 1

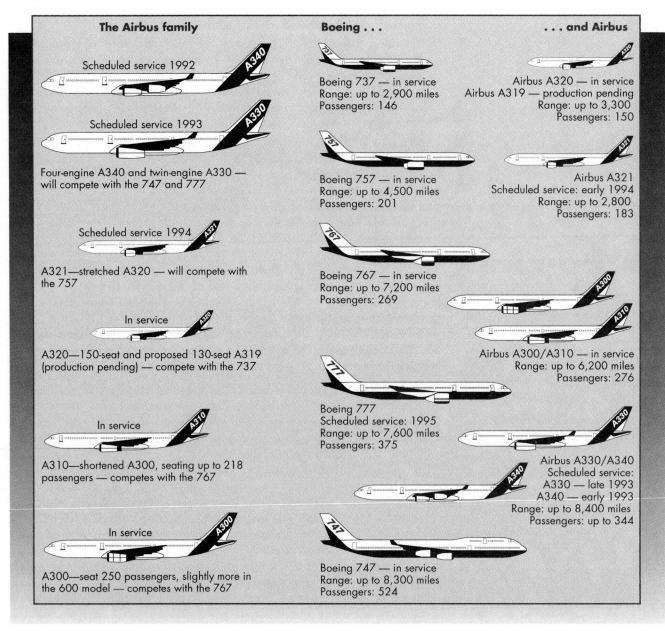

Source: Adapted from a chart designed by Sheila Raymond from data supplied by Boeing Commercial Airplane Group. Range and passenger data based on two-class configuration.

commercial interest rates are applied). Most of these subsidies were in the form of loans at below-market interest rates and tax breaks. The subsidies financed research and development and provided attractive financing terms for Airbus's customers. For most of its customers, Airbus is believed to have financed 80 percent of the cost of aircraft for 8 to 10 years at an annual interest rate of approximately 7 percent. In contrast, the U.S. Export-Import Bank required 20 percent down payments from Boeing and McDonnell Douglas customers, financed only 40 percent of the cost of an aircraft directly, and guaranteed the financing of the remaining 40 percent by private banks at an average interest rate of 8.4 percent to 8.5 percent for a period of 10 years.

Airbus's response to these charges was to point out that its success is not due to subsidies at all but to a good product and a good strategy. Most observers agree that Airbus's aircraft incorporate state-of-the-art technology, particularly in materials applications, systems for flight control and safety, and aerodynamics. Airbus gained ground initially by targeting market segments not served by new aircraft or not served at all. Thus Airbus has taken the initiative in targeting two segments of the market with wide-bodied twin-engined aircraft, then in developing a new generation of aircraft for the 150-seat market, and most recently in going after the market below the 747 for a 250-to-300-seat airliner with its A330 and A340 models (to which Boeing's 777 is a belated but apparently successful competitive response).

Airbus also argued that both Boeing and McDonnell Douglas have benefited from U.S. government aid for a long time and that the aid it has received has merely leveled the playing field. In the United States, planes were built under government contract during World War I, and the construction of mail planes was subsidized between the world wars. Almost all production was subsidized during World War II, and subsidies continued at a high level after the war. The Boeing 707, for example, is a derivative of a military transport program that was subsidized by the U.S. government. Boeing's subsidized programs include the B-17, B-29, B-47, B-52, and K-135, just to name a few. Its nonairline programs have included the Minuteman missile, Apollo-Saturn, and space station programs.

A 1991 European Commission study attempted to estimate the amount of subsidies currently received by the U.S. industry. The study contends that Boeing and McDonnell Douglas received $18 billion to $22 billion in indirect government aid between 1976 and 1990. The report claims that commercial aircraft operations benefited through Defense Department contracts by as much as $6.34 billion during the 1976–90 period. In addition, the report claims NASA has pumped at least $8 billion into commercial aircraft production over the same period, and that tax exemptions have given an additional $1.7 billion to Boeing and $1.4 billion to McDonnell Douglas.

Boeing rejected the claims of the European Commission report. The company pointed out that the report's assumption that Boeing receives direct government grants in the form of an additional 5 percent for commercial work with every military or space contract it receives was false. Moreover, the company argued that during the 1980s only 3 percent of Boeing's R&D spending has come from Department of Defense funding and only 4 percent from NASA funding. Boeing also argued that since the four companies in the Airbus consortium do twice as much military and space work as Boeing, they must receive much larger indirect subsidies.

❧ THE 1992 AGREEMENT

In mid-1992 the United States and the four European governments involved agreed to a pact that seemed likely to end the long-standing dispute. The 1992 pact, which was negotiated by the European Union on behalf of the four member-states, limited direct European government subsidies to each Airbus partner to 33 percent of new development costs and specified that future subsidies must be repaid with interest. The agreement also limited indirect subsidies, such as military research that has applications to commercial aircraft, to 5 percent of development costs for commercial aircraft. Although Airbus officials say the controversy has been resolved, Boeing officials say they will be competing for years against subsidized products.

❧ AFTERMATH

In February 1993 it looked as if the trade dispute was about to reemerge. The newly elected President Clinton repeatedly blasted the European Union for allowing subsidies of Airbus to continue, blamed job losses in the U.S. aerospace industry on the subsidies, and called for the EU to renegotiate the 1992 deal.

To the surprise of the administration, however, this renewed attack on Airbus subsidies was greeted with conspicuous silence from the U.S. industry itself. Many analysts theorized this was because a renewed dispute could prompt damaging retaliation from Europe. For one thing, Airbus equips its aircraft with engines made by two U.S. companies—Pratt & Whitney and General Electric, and with avionics made by U.S. companies. In addition many state-owned airlines in Europe purchase aircraft from Boeing and McDonnell Douglas. Many in the U.S. industry apparently felt that this lucrative business would be put at risk if the government reopened the trade dispute so soon after the 1992 agreement.

A similar cool response from the U.S. industry greeted attempts by two U.S. senators, Danforth and Baucus, to reopen the trade dispute with Airbus. In early 1993 Danforth and Baucus cosponsored legislation requiring the U.S. government to launch a trade case against Airbus on charges of unfair subsidies. They also sponsored a bill to create an aerospace industry consortium called Aerotech that would finance aerospace research, with half of the funds coming from industry and half from the U.S. government. Vice President Al Gore called the establishment of Aerotech "an administration priority," but a Boeing spokesman said the company was "very guarded about Aerotech" because it could violate the 1992 accord. Both the Danforth/Baucus bills died in the committee stage of hearings, and the Clinton administration quietly dropped all talk of reopening the trade dispute.

In signs that the long-standing dispute may still reemerge, however, in February 1994 the French government said it would pump 2 billion francs, about $341 million, into the state-owned aerospace group and Airbus member, Aerospatial. A spokesman for Aerospatial stated that part of the new state funds would be used to reduce the company's debt, which stood at about $2.2 billion. The rest would be invested across the range of the company's activities to help it prepare for privatization, which was expected to occur within the next few years. The French economic and defense minister, Edmond Alphandery, stated, "This decision by the state will allow Aerospatial to benefit fully from a gradual recovery in aerospace markets, notably through new projects like the Airbus A330 and A340." A spokesman for Boeing commented, "Any infusion of state aid must conform with the 1992 agreement."

CASE DISCUSSION QUESTIONS

1. Do you believe Airbus could have become a viable competitor without subsidies?
2. Why do you think the four European governments agreed to subsidize the establishment of Airbus?
3. Is Airbus's position with regard to the dispute over subsidies reasonable?
4. Given the 1992 agreement, what additional action (if any) should the U.S. government take with respect to Airbus?
5. Why do you think the U.S. industry reacted with caution to attempts by U.S. politicians to reopen the trade dispute in 1993?

SOURCES

1. Cohen, R. "France Pledges Subsidy to Aerospace Group." *New York Times*, February 3, 1994, p. 5.
2. Coleman, B. "GATT to Rule Against German Aid to Airbus." *The Wall Street Journal*, January 16, 1992, p. 5.
3. Core, O. C. "Airbus Arrives." *Seattle Times*, July 21, 1992, pp. C1–C3.
4. Davis, B., and Ingersoll, B. "Cloudy Issue." *The Wall Street Journal*, March 8, 1993, p. A1.
5. Dertouzos, M. L.; R. K. Lester; and R. M. Solow. *Made in America*. Cambridge, MA: MIT Press, 1989.
6. "Dissecting Airbus." *The Economist*, February 16, 1991, pp. 51–52.

7. "The Jumbo War." *The Economist,* June 15, 1991, pp. 65–66.
8. Klepper, G. "Entry into the Market for Large Transport Aircraft." *European Economic Review* 34 (1990), pp. 775–803.
9. Lane, P. "Study Complains of Alleged Subsidies." *Seattle Times,* December 4, 1991, p. G2.
10. Stroud, M. "Worries over a Technology Shift Follow McDonnell-Taiwan Accord." *Investor's Business Daily,* November 21, 1991, p. 36.
11. Toy, S., et al. "Zoom! Airbus Comes on Strong." *Business Week,* April 22, 1991, pp. 48–50.

ACTIVE-MATRIX LIQUID CRYSTAL DISPLAYS (A): 1990–91 TRADE DISPUTE

❧ INTRODUCTION

The active-matrix liquid crystal display screen (AM-LCD) is seen as a technology of the future. These flat display screens offer several advantages over the monochromatic, passive-matrix liquid crystal display screens (PM-LCD) used in laptop computer and digital watches. Compared to PM-LCDs, AM-LCDs are light, use little electricity, do not emit radiation, are easy on the eyes, and respond quickly to electrical inputs. These features make high-quality color, text, graphic, and video possible when the screens are integrated into laptop computers. In addition to computer displays, the screens are also critical components in camcorders, medical instruments, high-definition television, auto dashboards, aerospace instruments, factory control devices, and instrumentation for the military. Although production is just getting off the ground—sales were $250 million worldwide in 1990—forecasts suggest worldwide sales of $1 billion in 1994 and $10 billion plus by 2000.

❧ THE MARKET

The technology was pioneered in the United States during the 1960s. In recent years, however, the Japanese have emerged as the major producers of AM-LCDs and now account for 95 percent of worldwide production. Sharp, NEC, and Toshiba dominate the market. Unlike their major U.S. competitors, these Japanese firms made massive investments in AM-LCD research and production facilities during the 1980s. Sharp reportedly spent more than $1 billion on developing the technology during the 1980s and planned to spend $640 million more in the 1991–95 period.

Although a number of small U.S. companies are involved in this business, they tend to focus on highly specialized niches (e.g., supplying the Defense Department) and have made investments only to support their limited production. With the exception of IBM, which has a joint venture with Toshiba in Japan to manufacture AM-LCDs, no major U.S. company has a presence in the industry, and no U.S. company is capable of mass production. There are a number of reasons for this. First, the massive capital expenditures required to produce AM-LCD screens have deterred many U.S. firms, as have the high risks involved. The risks are judged to be particularly acute, given the Japanese lead in the technology and the long payback period for any investments. (Japanese executives regard five or six years of losses as the cost of entering this business.) Few American companies are willing to invest in an industry where Japanese companies are already well ahead. In addition the production process is particularly difficult to master, since even the smallest contaminant in the production process (such as dust) can damage a

Source: Charles W. L. Hill.

display. It is estimated that 80 percent of AM-LCDs coming off Japanese production lines are defective and must be scrapped. Thus the combination of high capital costs, high risks, and a difficult production process have deterred many major U.S. firms from entering the market.

⚘ THE IMPOSITION OF ANTIDUMPING DUTIES

Against this background, in July 1990 a group of small U.S. manufacturers of AM-LCDs filed an antidumping action with the U.S. Department of Commerce. They claimed the Japanese suppliers of AM-LCDs were selling their screens below market value and at less than half of their production cost in the United States. The International Trade Commission (ITC), a branch of the Department of Commerce, investigated the charges. In August 1991 the ITC reported the Japanese producers had been selling AM-LCDs below cost and imposed a 62.67 percent duty on AM-LCDs imported from Japan in an effort to shelter small U.S. manufacturers from unfair foreign competition. The ITC acknowledged the Japanese competition was killing small U.S. companies, but it warned that the duties would not guarantee the U.S. industry's success. U.S. success would require significant investments by U.S. firms; investments the government, with its long-standing opposition to industrial policy, was not prepared to subsidize.

The decision to impose an antidumping tariff on AM-LCD screens imported from Japan follows a 1987 U.S. government decision to impose a 100 percent tariff on laptop computers imported from Japan. Both these tariffs are country specific; they target imports from only Japan.

⚘ THE RESPONSE OF U.S. COMPUTER MAKERS

The response by American computer manufacturers to the imposition of duties took the Department of Commerce by surprise. Most U.S. manufacturers of laptop computers were already importing LCD screens from Japanese suppliers. IBM, for example, was importing screens made in Japan by its joint venture with Toshiba. AM-LCD screens are the most costly component for laptops, accounting for 50 percent of their total cost. Thus the duty increased the cost of manufacturing a laptop computer in the United States by about 30 percent. Not surprisingly U.S. computer companies felt this placed them at a significant competitive disadvantage vis-à-vis companies that manufactured laptops in other countries.

The response of U.S. computer manufacturers was twofold. First, they lodged formal protests with the U.S. government for imposing the duties and filed appeals with the Court of International Trade for a reversal of the decision. IBM, Apple, Compaq, and Tandy all argued that the government's decision to protect small AM-LCD makers via antidumping duties was possible only at their expense. Second, they began to move their assembly of laptop computers out of the United States. Apple abandoned its plans to manufacture its new "notebook" computers in Colorado and decided to move production to Ireland; Compaq announced plans to produce laptops in Scotland. These countries do not levy tariffs on imports of AM-LCDs from Japan and the United States does not levy tariffs on imports of finished laptops from these countries. By pursuing such a strategy, Apple and Compaq could maintain their competitive cost structure, but only at the cost of lost jobs in the United States.

⚘ THE JAPANESE REACTION

Some analysts believe that behind the antidumping duty was a cynical attempt by the Commerce Department to encourage Japanese manufacturers to move their production of AM-LCDs to the United States, which would benefit the United States with job creation and technology transfer. If this is true, the Commerce Department badly miscalculated. At present few if any Japanese companies would seem to have any intention of switching AM-LCD production to the United States. Mass production of AM-LCDs has barely begun in Japan, and it will be years before the capital costs of their investments are recouped, so additional investments in the United States are unlikely. Instead seven Japanese manufacturers, including Sharp, Toshiba, and Hitachi, have joined the U.S. computer manufacturers in lodging appeals with the Court of International Trade. They have charged that the decision to impose duties was illogical because there were virtually no U.S. manufacturers capable of producing AM-LCDs commercially. They also note that the charge of dumping is misplaced. While it is true that no Japanese manufacturers are currently making profits on AM-LCDs, they contend this is due to the enormous capital expenditure required to start production. They argue that production costs will decline and profits will follow once the production process is perfected, output builds, and scale economies are realized. Japan's Ministry of International Trade and Industry is also investigating the possibility the Department of Commerce's decision violates the General Agreement on Tariffs and Trade (GATT).

❧ CAN THE U.S. INDUSTRY BE SAVED?

Many people believe the decision to impose antidumping duties came too late to save the U.S. LCD industry. They point out that Japanese companies have been investing heavily in AM-LCD technology for years now and U.S. companies lack the capacity to sell commercially. Instead U.S. manufacturers sell most of their screens to the Pentagon. It is believed that a minimum investment of $300 million would be required to set up a commercial manufacturing operation—a figure that is probably beyond the reach of most U.S. firms currently in the industry. In addition U.S. firms would have to support five to six years of losses to enter the market and would have to solve the substantial production problems that currently bedevil AM-LCD production in Japan, the world capital of precision manufacturing.

While all this seems unlikely, some government experts remain convinced that the United States is still capable of catching up with Japan. Having toured AM-LCD plants in Japan, these experts believe U.S. companies can obtain enough government and private funds not only to reproduce AM-LCD technology, but also to improve on the manufacturing processes currently in use. Against this background, the U.S. Air Force has proposed to fund AM-LCD production. The Air Force is interested because it uses large numbers of AM-LCD screens for cockpit instrumentation and flight-simulation devices. The U.S. Army also needs the screens for its battle tanks, and the U.S. Navy uses them in its shipboard command centers. The Pentagon says the AM-LCD project meets its criteria for the "selective production" program. This program allows the Pentagon to commit funds for purchasing critical defense materials from selected contractors when projects meet certain standards. Firms obtaining contracts for AM-LCD production would be expected to find commercial buyers for the screens to keep their manufacturing cost effective and to avoid high-priced products. A Pentagon commitment to AM-LCD production may be enough to encourage other U.S. investors to finance AM-LCD production to cultivate a customer base for the screens.

CASE DISCUSSION QUESTIONS

1. Evaluate the Commerce Department's decision to impose duties on Japanese-manufactured AM-LCDs. Has this decision helped or harmed U.S. industry? What is the likely impact on the U.S. consumer?

2. What, if anything, could the U.S. government do to keep U.S. computer manufacturers from moving their manufacturing operations offshore? Should the government take such action?

3. What criteria should the U.S. government apply in targeting industries for antidumping protection?

4. If you were the CEO of a small U.S. firm interested in AM-LCD manufacturing, what factors would be important in your decision to enter the AM-LCD market? Under what conditions might you enter the market?

5. Should the U.S. government urge the Pentagon to support production of AM-LCDs? Explain the reasoning behind your answer.

SOURCES

1. Department of Commerce, International Trade Administration. "High Information Content of Flat Panel Displays and Display Glass Therefor from Japan: Anti-Dumping Duty Orders," September 4, 1992.

2. "Flat Out in Japan." *The Economist*, February 1, 1992, pp. 79–80.

3. "Flat Screens Come to Life." *Far Eastern Economic Review*, August 15, 1991, p. 58.

4. "Imported Japanese Flat Panel Displays Injure U.S. Industry, ITC Says." *International Trade Reporter*, August 21, 1991.

5. Johnson, R. "Flat Out for Profits." *Far Eastern Economic Review*, April 19, 1990.

6. "LCD Makers Appeal against U.S. Anti-Dumping Ruling." Kyodo News Service, October 9, 1991.

7. Magnusson, P. "Did Washington Lose Sight of the Big Picture?" *Business Week*, December 2, 1991.

8. Nomura, H. "IBM, Apple Fight LCD Screen Tariffs: U.S. Decision Forcing Assembly Offshore." *Nikkei Weekly*, October 26, 1992.

9. Tanzer, A. "The New Improved Color Computer." *Forbes*, July 23, 1990, pp. 276–80.

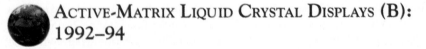

ACTIVE-MATRIX LIQUID CRYSTAL DISPLAYS (B): 1992–94

❧ INTRODUCTION

In response to complaints of dumping filed with the Department of Commerce by four small U.S. firms, including most notably OSI Optical Imaging Systems, in August 1991 the U.S. International Trade Commission (ITC) imposed a 62.67 percent duty on active-matrix liquid crystal display screens (AM-LCDs) imported into the United States from Japan. AM-LCD screens are the flat panel color screens used in laptop and notebook computers. The imposition of duties was designed to help fledgling U.S. AM-LCD producers, who were having trouble competing against the market leaders in this industry, NEC, Sharp, and Toshiba. However, the imposition of duties gave rise to vigorous protests from a number of U.S. manufacturers of laptop and notebook computers—including Apple, Compaq, and IBM—all of which purchased their AM-LCD screens from Japanese companies. These computer companies complained that with the limited capacity available for producing AM-LCD screens in the United States, they would still be forced to buy from Japanese companies, which would raise their unit costs by about 30 percent. This would make them uncompetitive. In response to the imposition of duties, Apple and Compaq announced they would move their production of laptop and notebook computers offshore. The feelings of the computer industry were summed up by a spokesman for

Source: Charles W. L. Hill.

the Tandy Corp., who noted, "By trying to protect a couple of small companies in the U.S. that manufacture these displays, it's almost certain that the next generation of these notebook PCs are going to be built offshore."

❧ FURTHER DEVELOPMENTS

In early 1992 a number of U.S. computer companies and the three main Japanese producers of AM-LCD screens filed a motion with the U.S. Court of International Trade requesting that the 62.67 percent tariff on imports of AM-LCD screens be lifted. The motion claimed the tariff had materially damaged U.S. computer companies while having no beneficial effect on the U.S. AM-LCD industry. The computer industry motion received further support in the fall of 1992 when OSI Optical Imaging Systems, the only U.S.-based volume producer of AM-LCD screens, filed a request with the Commerce Department that the duty be lifted. According to OSI, the penalties had become "counterproductive" and would hurt U.S. computer companies. OSI sells predominately smaller sized screens to the military market, and it indicated it has no plans to gear up production to produce screens for computer makers. OSI also pointed out that the three other firms that filed the original dumping petition along with OSI—UCE, Planar Systems, and Advanced Display Manufacturers of America—*do not* make AM-LCD displays and therefore have no standing in the case.

On January 10, 1993, the Court of International Trade upheld the protests of the U.S. computer companies and their Japanese suppliers and sent the case back to the International Trade Commission with a recommendation that the tariff be lifted. However, the ITC, which is a branch of the U.S. Commerce Department, indicated it would seek additional comments before making a final decision.

On March 2, 1993, the ITC ruled it would maintain the 62.67 tariff on AM-LCD screens. The six-member ITC was split down the middle on the issue, with a 3 to 3 vote. According to the ITC's rules, a tied vote upholds past decisions. The ruling was greeted with vigorous protests from both the Japanese and U.S. computer companies. An official at Japan's Ministry of International Trade and Industry stated, "The decision is extremely unfair. There could be no case of dumping damaging the U.S. industry, since there are no manufacturers in the U.S. that make such high-definition screens for computers." In the same vein, a spokesman for Apple Computer noted, "This is an Alice in Wonderland decision. It defies logic." Meanwhile, OSI reaffirmed its position that it had no intention of gearing up to supply the computer market with AM-LCD screens.

Caught in the awkward position of fostering one high-technology industry at the expense of another, the Commerce Department decided to take another look at the situation. On June 21, 1993, the Commerce Department announced it had decided to revoke immediately the import duties on AM-LCD screens. In making this decision, the Commerce Department brushed aside the views of several companies that were conducting research on AM-LCD screens and had hoped to enter the market. These companies, which lacked legal standing in the case because they were not actually producers of AM-LCDs, included Standish Industries and Planar Systems. They had argued that their ability to raise capital would be jeopardized if the tariffs were lifted and that the growth of the U.S. flat panel industry would be stifled.

❧ EMERGING INDUSTRIAL POLICY

Despite revoking the tariff, the U.S. government indicated it remained committed to building the AM-LCD industry in the United States. This commitment by the government was driven in part by a realization that the flat panel display industry is becoming a huge business. In 1991 forecasts suggested that $1 billion worth of flat panel displays would be sold in 1994, but the actual figure was closer to $4 billion.

Current forecasts suggest the flat panel display market may be worth $15 billion by the end of the century, and yet of the 60 largest firms in this industry as of 1993, only 3 were American, and all were small.

In late June 1993 the government announced it would increase government grants for research into flat panel technology. In June 1993 the Pentagon's Advanced Research Projects Agency handed out $25 million in research grants to U.S. Display, a consortium of 10 U.S. high-technology companies. Modeled after Sematech, the government-aided consortium of semiconductor manufacturers established in 1989, the new group hopes to develop the equipment and know-how required for high-volume production of flat panel display screens. The government indicated it would award as much as $75 million more for additional flat panel research in the following months.

The Pentagon was reported to be considering a special request for $180 million in research funding from a group of firms led by AT&T and Xerox. The funds would be used to build a prototype of a commercial AM-LCD factory, which is expected to cost about $400 million. In seeking support, Xerox noted there is now a window of opportunity opening in the AM-LCD industry. Xerox has developed a flat panel technology that increases by more than six times the number of pixels (tiny points of light) that can be used to draw an image on a flat panel display screen. A spokesman for Xerox noted it might be possible to leapfrog Japanese manufacturing technology, and "do some things that the Japanese didn't get right the first time."

These initial moves by the U.S. government were followed in April 1994 by an announcement that the Clinton administration plans to provide about $1 billion over the next five years for the development and manufacture of flat panel displays. Of this, some $500 million is to be given in the form of grants to U.S. companies, or groups of companies, to establish up to four flat panel display plants in the United States. The proposal also calls for expanding existing flat panel display programs funded by the Department of Defense from a current commitment of $68 million to $500 million over the next five years.

This plan was greeted with a mixed reception. Those firms already undertaking research in this area, such as Xerox and AT&T, responded favorably to the announcement. They pointed out that the industry is characterized by very high barriers to entry and high risks; it costs about $300 million to set up one large-scale flat panel display plant, and the complexities of the production process mean that yields of more than 30 percent are difficult to attain (i.e., 70 percent of the output from such a factory has to be scrapped due to defects). Although demand for flat panel display screens outstrips supply, and although the market is expected to triple between 1994 and 2000, many U.S. firms claim that without government help the high costs and risks of participating in this business will deter entry.

However, critics note that the Clinton administration may be going down a dangerous road. Historically government subsidies in the United States have been limited to military technologies, but the government now seems to have signaled its intent to subsidize the start-up costs of *commercial* operations. One danger here is that such subsidies might encourage other governments to adopt similar subsidies in areas where they are trying to compete with U.S. companies. Traditionally the United States has always criticized governments that subsidize commercial businesses (as it criticized the government backers of the European Airbus consortium), but its bargaining position may be weakened considerably if it too goes down this road.

Another potential problem is that the government's approach assumes it is possible for bureaucrats to pick winners and losers, and allocate their subsidies accordingly. Skeptics question the ability of government to make such decisions. In response the administration has announced that all grant applications will be subject to review by private-sector experts, and that recipients will have to provide at least half the funds for manufacturing ventures.

CASE DISCUSSION QUESTIONS

1. Do you think the Commerce Department was correct to revoke the 62.67 percent tariff on imports of flat panel displays from Japan?

2. Does it make sense for the U.S. government to subsidize the development of technology and establishment of manufacturing facilities by U.S. firms in the flat panel display industry?

3. Assuming the government aggressively subsidizes U.S. companies in this area, what do you think might be the reaction from the governments of other countries where there are firms active in this industry?

4. Do you think it is possible for the government, by drawing on the advice of private-sector experts, to pick winners and losers in this field?

SOURCES

1. Andrews, E. "Duties Ended on Computer Flat Screens." *New York Times,* June 23, 1993, p. 1.

2. Kamiya, A. "ITC Issues Split Ruling." Japan Economic *Newswire,* March 3, 1993.

3. Kehoe, L. "U.S. to Plug Holes in Flat Panel Industry." *Financial Times,* April 4, 1994, p. 3.

4. Lazzareschi, C. "Clinton Comes to Aid of U.S. Screen Makers." *Los Angeles Times,* June 24, 1993, p. 1.

5. Nakamoto, M. "Japan Rejects LCD Ruling." *Financial Times,* March 4, 1993, p. 6.

6. Robertson, J. "Trade Court Ruling Questions Flat Panel Duty." *Electronic News,* January 11, 1993, p. 2.

7. Robertson, J. "Active Matrix LCD Duties Lifted." *Electronic News,* January 25, 1993, p. 5.

CHAPTER NINE

THE FOREIGN EXCHANGE MARKET

JAPAN AIR LINES CRASHES ON THE FOREIGN EXCHANGE MARKET

One of the world's largest airlines, Japan Air Lines (JAL), is also one of the best customers of Boeing, the world's biggest manufacturer of commercial airplanes. Every year JAL needs to raise about $800 million to purchase aircraft from Boeing. Boeing aircraft are priced in U.S. dollars, with prices ranging from about $35 million for a 737 to $160 million for a top of the line 747-400. JAL places orders for an aircraft two to six years before the plane is needed. Although JAL normally pays Boeing a 10 percent deposit when ordering an aircraft, the bulk of the payment is made when the aircraft is delivered.

The long lag between placing an order and making a final payment presents a difficult conundrum for JAL. Most of JAL's revenues are in Japanese yen, not U.S. dollars. Accordingly, when purchasing Boeing aircraft JAL must change its yen into dollars to pay Boeing. The conundrum is that in the interval between placing an order and making final payment, the value of the Japanese yen against the U.S. dollar may change. This can increase or decrease the cost of an aircraft when calculated in yen. Consider an order placed in 1985 for a 747 aircraft that was to be delivered in 1990. In 1985 the dollar value of this order was $100 million. The prevailing exchange rate in 1985 was $1 = ¥240 (i.e., one dollar was worth 240 yen), so the price of the 747 in yen was ¥2.4 billion. By 1990 when final payment was due, however, the dollar-yen exchange rate might have changed. One possibility

is that the yen might have declined in value against the dollar. For example, JAL might have feared that by 1990 the dollar-yen exchange rate would be $1 = ¥300. If this had come to pass, the price of the 747 in yen would have gone from ¥2.4 billion to ¥3.0 billion, an increase of 25 percent. Another (more favorable) scenario is that the yen might have risen in value against the dollar to $1 = ¥200. If this had occurred, the yen price of the 747 would have fallen 16.7 percent to ¥2.0 billion.

In 1985 JAL has no way of knowing what the value of the yen will be against the dollar by 1990. However, JAL can enter into a contract with foreign exchange traders in 1985 to purchase dollars in 1990 based on the assessment of those traders as to what they think the dollar-yen exchange rate will be in 1990. This is called entering into a *forward exchange contract.* The advantage of entering into a forward exchange contract is that JAL knows in 1985 what it will have to pay for the 747 in 1990. So, for example, if the value of the yen is expected to increase against the dollar between 1985 and 1990, foreign exchange traders might offer a forward exchange contract that allows JAL to purchase dollars at a rate of $1 = ¥185 in 1990, instead of the $1 = ¥240 rate that prevailed in 1985. At

this forward exchange rate, the 747 would cost only ¥1.85 billion, a 23 percent savings over the yen price implied by the 1985 exchange rate.

JAL was confronted with just this scenario in 1985. At that time JAL entered into a 10-year forward exchange contract with a total value of about $3.6 billion. This contract gave JAL the right to buy U.S. dollars from a consortium of foreign exchange traders at various points during the next 10 years for an average exchange rate of $1 = ¥185. To JAL this looked like a great deal given the 1985 exchange rate of $1 = ¥240. However, by September 1994 when the bulk of the contract had been executed it no longer looked like a good deal.

To everyone's surprise, the value of the yen had surged against the dollar. By 1992 the exchange rate stood at $1 = ¥120, and by 1994 it was $1 = ¥99. Unfortunately, JAL could not take advantage of this more favorable exchange rate. The airline was bound by the terms of the contract to purchase dollars at the contract rate of $1 = ¥185, a rate that by 1994 looked outrageously expensive. This misjudgment cost JAL dearly. In 1994 JAL was paying 86 percent more than it needed to for each Boeing aircraft bought with dollars purchased via the forward exchange contract! In October 1994 JAL admitted publicly that in its most recent financial year the loss from this misjudgment amounted to $450 million, or ¥45 billion. Furthermore, foreign exchange traders speculated that JAL had probably lost ¥155 billion ($1.5 billion) on this contract since 1988.

Sources: W. Dawkins, "JAL to Disclose Huge Currency Hedge Loss," *Financial Times*, October 4, 1994, p. 19; and W. Dawkins, "Tokyo to Lift Veil on Currency Risks," *Financial Times*, October 5, 1994, p. 23.

❧ INTRODUCTION

This chapter has three main objectives. The first is to explain how the foreign exchange market works. The second is to examine the forces that determine exchange rates and to discuss the degree to which it is possible to predict future exchange rate movements. The third objective is to map the implications for international business of exchange rate movements and the foreign exchange market. This chapter is the first of three that deal with the international monetary system and its relationship to international business. In Chapter 10 we will explore the institutional structure of the international monetary system. The institutional structure is the context within which the foreign exchange market functions. As we shall see, changes in the institutional structure of the international monetary system can exert a profound influence on the development of foreign exchange markets. In Chapter 11 we will look at the recent evolution of global capital markets and discuss the implications of this development for international businesses.

The **foreign exchange market** is a market for converting the currency of one country into that of another country. An **exchange rate** is simply the rate at which one currency is converted into another. We saw in the opening case how JAL used the foreign exchange market to convert Japanese yen into U.S. dollars. Without the foreign exchange market, international trade and international investment on the scale that we see today would be impossible; companies would have to resort to barter. The foreign exchange market is the lubricant that enables companies based in countries that use different currencies to trade with each other.

We know from earlier chapters that international trade and investment have their risks. As the opening case illustrates, some of these risks exist because future exchange rates cannot be perfectly predicted. The rate at which one currency is converted into another typically changes over time. One function of the foreign exchange market is to provide some insurance against the risks that arise from changes in exchange rates, commonly referred to as foreign exchange risk. Although the foreign exchange market offers some insurance against foreign exchange risk, it cannot provide complete insurance. JAL's loss of $1.5 billion on foreign exchange transactions is an extreme example of what can happen, but it is not at all unusual for international businesses to suffer losses because of unpredicted changes in exchange rates.

Currency fluctuations can make seemingly profitable trade and investment deals unprofitable, and vice versa. The opening case contains an example of this as it relates to trade. For an example that deals with investment, consider the case of Mexico. Between 1976 and 1987, the value of the Mexican peso dropped from 22/U.S. dollar to 1,500/U.S. dollar. As a result, a U.S. company with an investment in Mexico that yielded an income of 100 million pesos per year would have seen the dollar value of that income shrink from $4.55 million in 1976 to $66,666 by 1987!

In addition to altering the value of trade deals and foreign investments, currency movements can also open or shut export opportunities and alter the attractiveness of imports. In 1984, for example, the U.S. dollar was trading at an all-time high against most other currencies. At that time one dollar could buy one British pound or 250 Japanese yen, compared to 0.55 of a British pound and about 85 yen in early 1995. In the 1984 U.S. presidential campaign, President Reagan boasted about how good the strong dollar was for the United States. Many U.S. companies did not see it that way. Companies such as Caterpillar that earned their living by exporting to other countries were being priced out of foreign markets by the strong dollar. In 1980 when the dollar-to-pound exchange rate was $1 = £0.63, a $100,000 Caterpillar earthmover cost a British buyer £63,000. In 1984, with the exchange rate at $1 = £0.99, it cost close to £99,000—a 60 percent increase in four years! At that exchange rate Caterpillar's products were overpriced in comparison to those of its foreign competitors, such as Japan's Komatsu. At the same time, the strong dollar reduced the price of the earthmovers Komatsu imported into the United States, which allowed the Japanese company to take U.S. market share away from Caterpillar.

While the existence of foreign exchange markets is a necessary precondition for large-scale international trade and investment, the movement of exchange rates over time introduces many risks into international trade and investment. Some of these risks can be insured against by using instruments offered by the foreign exchange market, such as the forward exchange contracts discussed in the opening case; others cannot be.

In this chapter we will examine these issues. We begin by looking at the functions and the form of the foreign exchange market. This includes distinguishing among spot exchanges, forward exchanges, and currency swaps. Then we will consider the factors that determine exchange rates. We will also look at how foreign trade is conducted when a country's currency cannot be exchanged for other currencies; that is, when its currency is not convertible. The chapter closes with a discussion of these things in terms of their implications for business.

❦ THE FUNCTIONS OF THE FOREIGN EXCHANGE MARKET

The foreign exchange market serves two main functions. The first is to convert the currency of one country into the currency of another. The second is to provide some insurance against **foreign exchange risk,** by which we mean the adverse consequences of unpredictable changes in exchange rates. We consider each function in turn.[1]

Currency Conversion

Each country has a currency in which the prices of goods and services are quoted. In the United States it is the dollar ($); in Great Britain, the pound (£); in France, the French franc (FFr); in Germany, the deutsche mark (DM); in Japan, the yen (¥); and so on. In general, within the borders of a country one must use the national currency. A U.S. tourist cannot walk into a store in Edinburgh, Scotland, and use U.S. dollars to buy a bottle of Scotch whiskey. Dollars are not recognized as legal tender in Scotland; the tourist must use British pounds. Fortunately the tourist can go to a bank and exchange her dollars for pounds. Then she can buy the whiskey.

When a tourist exchanges one currency into another, she is participating in the **foreign exchange market.** The **exchange rate** is the rate at which the market converts one currency into another. For example, an exchange rate of $1 = ¥85 specifies that one U.S. dollar has the equivalent value of 85 Japanese yen. The exchange rate allows us to compare the relative prices of goods and services in different countries. Our U.S. tourist in Edinburgh may find that she must pay £25 for the bottle of Scotch whiskey, knowing the same bottle costs $40 in the United States. Is this a good deal? Imagine the current dollar/pound exchange rate is $1 = £0.50. Our intrepid tourist takes out her calculator and converts £25 into dollars. (The calculation is 25/0.50.) She finds that the bottle of Scotch costs the equivalent of $50. She is surprised that a bottle of Scotch whiskey could cost less in the United States than in Scotland. (This is true; alcohol is taxed heavily in Great Britain.)

Tourists are minor participants in the foreign exchange market; companies engaged in international trade and investment are major ones. There are four main uses of foreign exchange markets to international businesses. First, the payments a company receives for its exports, the income it receives from foreign investments, or the income it receives from licensing agreements with foreign firms may be in foreign currencies. To use those funds in its home country, the company must convert them to its home country's currency. Consider the Scotch distillery that exports its whiskey to the United States. The distillery is paid in dollars, but since those dollars cannot be spent in Great Britain, they must be converted into British pounds.

Second, international businesses use foreign exchange markets when they must pay a foreign company for its products or services in its country's currency. For example, our friend Michael runs a company called NST, a large British travel service for

---

[1]For a good general introduction to the foreign exchange market, see R. Weisweiller, *How the Foreign Exchange Market Works* (New York: New York Institute of Finance, 1990). A detailed description of the economics of foreign exchange markets can be found in P. R. Krugman and M. Obstfeld, *International Economics: Theory and Policy* (New York: Harper Collins, 1994).

MANAGEMENT
FOCUS
George Soros—
The Man Who Can
Move Currency
Markets

George Soros, a 65-year-old Hungarian-born financier, is the principle partner of the Quantum Group, which controls a series of hedge funds with assets of about $12 billion. A hedge fund is an investment fund that not only buys financial assets (such as stocks, bonds, and currencies) but also sells them short. Short selling occurs when an investor places a speculative bet that the value of a financial asset will decline, and profits from that decline.

A common variant of short selling occurs when an investor borrows stock from his broker and sells that stock. The short seller has to ultimately pay back that stock to his broker. However, he hopes that in the intervening period the value of the stock will decline so the cost of repurchasing the stock to pay back the broker is significantly less than the income he received from the initial sale of the stock. For example, imagine that a short seller borrows 100 shares of IBM stock and sells it

in the market at $150 per share, yielding a total income of $15,000. In one year the short seller has to give the 100 units of IBM stock back to his broker. In the intervening period the value of the IBM stock falls to $50. Consequently, it now costs the short seller only $5,000 to re-purchase the 100 units of IBM stock for his broker. The difference between the initial sales price ($150) and the repurchase price ($50) represents the short seller's profit, which in this case is $100 per unit of stock for a total profit of $10,000. Short selling was originally developed as a means of reducing risk (of hedging), but it is often used for speculation.

Along with other hedge funds, Soros's Quantum fund often takes a short position in currencies that he expects to decline in value. For example, if Soros expects the British pound to decline against the U.S. dollar he may borrow £1 billion from a currency trader and immediately

---

school groups. Each year Michael's company arranges vacations for thousands of British schoolchildren and their teachers in France. French hotel proprietors demand payment in francs, so Michael must convert large sums of money from pounds into francs to pay them.

Third, international businesses use foreign exchange markets when they have spare cash they wish to invest for short terms in money markets. For example, consider a U.S. company that has $10 million it wants to invest for three months. The best interest rate it can earn on these funds in the United States may be 8 percent. Investing in a French money market account, however, it may be able to earn 12 percent. Thus the company may change its $10 million into francs and invest it in France. Note, however, that the rate of return it earns on this investment depends not only on the French interest rate, but also on the changes in the value of the franc against the dollar in the intervening period.

Finally, **currency speculation** is another use of foreign exchange markets. **Currency speculation** typically involves the short-term movement of funds from one currency to another in the hopes of profiting from shifts in exchange rates. Consider again the U.S. company with $10 million to invest for three months. Suppose the company suspects the U.S. dollar is overvalued against the French franc. That is, the company expects the value of the dollar to depreciate against that of the franc. Imagine the current dollar/franc exchange rate is $1 = FFr6. The company exchanges its $10 million into francs, receiving FFr60 million. Over the next three months the value of the dollar depreciates until $1 = FFr5. Now the company exchanges its FFr60 million back into dollars and finds it has $12 million.

sell them for U.S. dollars. Soros will then hope that the value of the pound will decline against the dollar, so when he has to repay the £1 billion it will cost him considerably less (in U.S. dollars) than he received from the initial sale.

Since the 1970s Soros has consistently earned huge returns by making such speculative bets. His most spectacular triumph came in September 1992. At that time he believed the British pound was likely to decline in value against major currencies, particularly the deutsche mark. The prevailing exchange rate was £1 = DM2.80. The British government was obliged by a European Union agreement on monetary policy to try to keep the pound above DM2.77. Soros doubted the British could do this, so he shorted the pound, borrowing billions of pounds (using the $12 billion assets of the Quantum Fund as collateral) and immediately selling them for deutsche marks. His

simultaneous sale of pounds and purchase of marks was so large that it helped drive down the value of the pound against the mark. Other currency traders, seeing Soros's market moves and knowing his reputation for making successful currency bets, jumped on the bandwagon and started to sell pounds short and buy deutsche marks. The resulting *bandwagon effect* put enormous pressure on the pound. The British Central Bank, at the request of the British government, spent about £20 billion on September 16 to try to prop up the value of the pound against the deutsche mark (by selling marks and buying pounds), but to no avail. The pound continued to fall and on September 17 the British government gave up on the attempt and let the pound decline (it actually fell to £1 = DM2.00). As a consequence of this bet, Soros made a $1 billion profit in four weeks!

Like all currency speculators, however, George Soros has had his

losses. Most notably in February 1994 he bet the Japanese yen would decline in value against the U.S. dollar and promptly shorted the yen. However, the yen defied the expectations of Soros and continued to rise, costing his Quantum fund $600 million. Similarly a series of incorrect bets in 1987 resulted in losses of over $800 million for Quantum. Despite such defeats, however, Soros's Quantum fund has earned an average annual rate of return of over 40 percent since 1970. Meanwhile Soros has gained a reputation for being able to move currency markets by his actions. This is the result not so much of the money that Soros puts into play, but of the bandwagon effect that results when other speculators follow his lead.

Sources: P. Harverson, "Billion Dollar Man the Money Markets Fear," *Financial Times*, September 30, 1994, p. 10; "A Quantum Dive," *The Economist*, March 15, 1994, pp. 83–84; B. J. Javetski, "Europe's Money Mess," *Business Week*, September 28, 1992, pp. 30–31; and "Meltdown," *The Economist*, September 19, 1992, p. 69.

The company has made a $2 million profit on currency speculation in three months on an initial investment of $10 million.

One of the most famous currency speculators is George Soros, whose Quantum Group of "hedge funds" controls about $12 billion in assets. The activities of Soros, who has been spectacularly successful, are profiled in the above "Management Focus." In general, however, companies should beware of speculation for it is by definition a very risky business. The problem with speculation is that the company cannot know for sure what will happen to exchange rates. While a speculator may profit handsomely if his speculation about future currency movements turns out to be correct, he can also lose vast amounts of money if it turns out to be wrong. For example, in 1991 Clifford Hatch, the finance director of the British food and drink company, Allied-Lyons, bet large amounts of the company's funds on the speculation that the British pound would rise in value against the U.S. dollar. Over the previous three years Hatch had made over $25 million for Allied-Lyons by placing similar currency bets. His 1991 bet, however, went spectacularly wrong when instead of increasing in value, the British pound plummeted in value against the U.S. dollar. In February 1991 one pound bought $2; by April it bought less than $1.75. The total loss to Allied-Lyons from this speculation was a staggering $269 million, more than the company was to earn from all its food and drink activities during 1991![2]

---

[2]C. Forman, "Allied-Lyons to Post $269 Million Loss from Foreign Exchange as Dollar Soars," *The Wall Street Journal*, March 20, 1991, p. A17.

**Insuring against
Foreign Exchange Risk**

A second function of the foreign exchange market is to provide insurance to protect against the possible adverse consequences of unpredictable changes in exchange rates (foreign exchange risk). To explain how the market performs this function, we must first distinguish among spot exchange rates, forward exchange rates, and currency swaps.

Spot exchange rates

When two parties agree to exchange currency and execute the deal immediately, the transaction is referred to as a spot exchange. Exchange rates governing such "on the spot" trades are referred to as spot exchange rates. **The spot exchange rate** is the rate at which a foreign exchange dealer converts one currency into another currency on a particular day. Thus when our U.S. tourist in Edinburgh goes to a bank to convert her dollars into pounds, the exchange rate is the spot rate for that day.

Although it is necessary to use a spot rate to execute a transaction immediately, it may not be the most attractive rate. Exchange rates can change constantly. The value of a currency is determined by the interaction between the demand and supply of that currency relative to the demand and supply of other currencies. For example, if lots of people want U.S. dollars and dollars are in short supply, and few people want French francs and francs are in plentiful supply, the spot exchange rate for converting dollars into francs will change. The dollar is likely to appreciate against the franc (or conversely the franc will depreciate against the dollar). Imagine the spot exchange rate is $1 = FFr5 when the market opens. As the day progresses, dealers demand more dollars and fewer francs. By the end of the day the spot exchange rate might be $1 = FFr5.3. The dollar has appreciated, and the franc has depreciated.

Forward exchange rates

The fact that spot exchange rates change daily as determined by the relative demand and supply for different currencies can be problematic for an international business. One example was given in the opening case; here is another. A U.S. company that imports laptop computers from Japan knows that in 30 days it must pay yen to a Japanese supplier when a shipment arrives. The company will pay the Japanese supplier ¥200,000 for each laptop computer, and the current dollar/yen spot exchange rate is $1 = ¥120. At this rate, each computer costs the importer $1,667 (i.e., 1,667 = 200,000/120). The importer knows she can sell the computers the day they arrive for $2,000 each, which yields a gross profit of $333 on each computer ($2,000 − $1,667). However, the importer will not have the funds to pay the Japanese supplier until the computers have been sold. If over the next 30 days the dollar unexpectedly depreciates against the yen, say to $1 = ¥95, the importer will still have to pay the Japanese company ¥200,000 per computer, but in dollar terms that would be equivalent to $2,105 per computer, which is more than she can sell the computers for. In other words, a depreciation in the value of the dollar against the yen from $1 = ¥120 to $1 = ¥95 would transform a profitable deal into an unprofitable one.

To avoid this risk, the U.S. importer might want to engage in a forward exchange. A **forward exchange** occurs when two parties agree to exchange currency and execute the deal at some specific date in the future. Exchange rates governing such future transactions are referred to as forward exchange rates. For most major currencies, **forward exchange rates** are quoted for 30 days, 90 days, and 180 days into the future. (An example of exchange rate quotations appears in Table 9.1.) In some cases, it is possible to get forward exchange rates for several years into the future. In the opening case, for example, we saw how JAL was able to enter into a contract that predicted forward exchange rates up to 10 years in the future. Returning to our example let us assume the 30-day forward exchange rate for converting dollars into yen is $1 = ¥110. The importer enters into a

TABLE 9.1

Foreign Exchange Quotations

CURRENCY TRADING

EXCHANGE RATES

Thursday, January 25, 1996

The New York foreign exchange selling rates below apply to trading among banks in amounts of $1 million and more, as quoted at 3 p.m. Eastern time by Dow Jones Telerate Inc. and other sources. Retail transactions provide fewer units of foreign currency per dollar.

Country	U.S. $ equiv. Thu	Wed	Currency per U.S. $ Thu	Wed
Argentina (Peso)	1.0007	1.0007	.9993	.9993
Australia (Dollar)	.7358	.7360	1.3591	1.3587
Austria (Schilling)	.09533	.09603	10.490	10.413
Bahrain (Dinar)	2.6532	2.6532	.3769	.3769
Belgium (Franc)	.03296	.03282	30.340	30.470
Brazil (Real)	1.0288	1.0288	.9720	.9720
Britain (Pound)	1.5080	1.5109	.6631	.6619
30-Day Forward	1.5070	1.5100	.6636	.6623
90-Day Forward	1.5051	1.5081	.6644	.6631
180-Day Forward	1.5023	1.5054	.6656	.6643
Canada (Dollar)	.7250	.7292	1.3793	1.3713
30-Day Forward	.7250	.7291	1.3793	1.3715
90-Day Forward	.7248	.7289	1.3797	1.3719
180-Day Forward	.7245	.7274	1.3803	1.3749
Chile (Peso)	.002430	.002436	411.45	410.45
China (Renminbi)	.1199	.1202	8.3380	8.3163
Colombia (Peso)	.0009744	.0009744	1026.30	1026.30
Czech. Rep. (Koruna)	....	....		
Commercial rate	.03674	.03664	27.219	27.291
Denmark (Krone)	.1751	.1744	5.7100	5.7325
Ecuador (Sucre)				
Floating rate	.0003410	.0003410	2932.50	2932.50
Finland (Markka)	.2189	.2204	4.5693	4.5370
France (Franc)	.1960	.1967	5.1025	5.0845
30-Day Forward	.1960	.1968	5.1024	5.0805
90-Day Forward	.1964	.1971	5.0923	5.0745
180-Day Forward	.1966	.1974	5.0852	5.0670
Germany (Mark)	.6715	.6733	1.4891	1.4852
30-Day Forward	.6715	.6744	1.4891	1.4828
90-Day Forward	.6749	.6767	1.4817	1.4778
180-Day Forward	.6715	.6800	1.4891	1.4706
Greece (Drachma)	.004069	.004083	245.76	244.91
Hong Kong (Dollar)	.1293	.1293	7.7342	7.7322
Hungary (Forint)	.006937	.006937	144.16	144.16
India (Rupee)	.02787	.02791	35.880	35.830
Indonesia (Rupiah)	.0004367	.0004367	2290.00	2290.00
Ireland (Punt)	1.5620	1.5649	.6402	.6390
Israel (Shekel)	.3194	.3194	3.1310	3.1310
Italy (Lira)	.0006256	.0006285	1598.50	1591.00
Japan (Yen)	.009354	.009339	106.91	107.08
30-Day Forward	.009395	.009380	106.45	106.62
90-Day Forward	.009472	.009456	105.57	105.75
180-Day Forward	.009582	.009565	104.36	104.55
Jordan (Dinar)	1.4104	1.4104	.7090	.7090
Kuwait (Dinar)	3.3372	3.3361	.2997	.2997
Lebanon (Pound)	.0006279	.0006279	1592.50	1592.50
Malaysia (Ringgit)	.3907	.3905	2.5598	2.5610
Malta (Lira)	2.7643	2.7567	.3618	.3627
Mexico (Peso)				
Floating rate	.1354	.1352	7.3850	7.3950
Netherland (Guilder)	.5995	.6019	1.6681	1.6615
New Zealand (Dollar)	.6673	.6649	1.4986	1.5040
Norway (Krone)	.1547	.1540	6.4637	6.4925
Pakistan (Rupee)	.02922	.02923	34.220	34.216
Peru (new Sol)	.4292	.4292	2.3300	2.3300
Philippines (Peso)	.03820	.03820	26.180	26.180
Poland (Zloty)	.3937	.3938	2.5400	2.5393
Portugal (Escudo)	.006461	.006502	154.77	153.81
Russia (Ruble) (a)	.0002120	.0002120	4718.00	4716.00
Saudi Arabia (Riyal)	.2667	.2666	3.7500	3.7503
Singapore (Dollar)	.7050	.7037	1.4185	1.4210
Slovak Rep. (Koruna)	.03322	.03322	30.098	30.098
South Africa (Rand)	.2742	.2739	3.6475	3.6512
South Korea (Won)	.001272	.001270	786.10	787.10
Spain (Peseta)	.007951	.007999	125.77	125.02
Sweden (Krona)	.1447	.1457	6.9113	6.8636
Switzerland (Franc)	.8351	.8382	1.1975	1.1931
30-Day Forward	.8378	.8408	1.1936	1.1893
90-Day Forward	.8428	.8460	1.1865	1.1821
180-Day Forward	.8501	.8534	1.1764	1.1718
Taiwan (Dollar)	.03643	.03643	27.450	27.450
Thailand (Baht)	.03948	.03948	25.330	25.330
Turkey (Lira)	.00001619	.00001624	61763.00	61594.50
United Arab (Dirham)	.2724	.2723	3.6710	3.6726
Uruguay (New Peso)				
Financial	.1387	.1387	7.2100	7.2100
Venezuela (Bolivar)	.003448	.003448	290.00	290.00
Brady Rate	.002762	.002762	362.00	362.00
SDR	1.4580	1.4557	.6859	.6870
ECU	1.2389	1.2389		

Special Drawing Rights (SDR) are based on exchange rates for the U.S., German, British, French, and Japanese currencies. Source: International Monetary Fund.

European Currency Unit (ECU) is based on a basket of community currencies.

a-fixing, Moscow Interbank Currency Exchange

Source: The Wall Street Journal, *March 19, 1996.*

30-day forward exchange transaction with a foreign exchange dealer at this rate and is guaranteed that she will have to pay no more than $1,818 for each computer (1,818 = 200,000/110). This guarantees her a profit of $182 per computer ($2,000 − $1,818). Moreover she insures herself against the possibility that an unanticipated change in the dollar/yen exchange rate will turn a profitable deal into an unprofitable one.

In this example the spot exchange rate ($1 = ¥120) and the 30-day forward rate ($1 = ¥110) differ. Such differences are normal; they reflect the expectations of the foreign exchange market about future currency movements. In our example the fact that $1 bought more yen with a spot exchange than with a 30-day forward exchange indicates that foreign exchange dealers expected the dollar to depreciate against the yen in the next 30 days. When this occurs we say the dollar is selling at a *discount* on the 30-day forward market (i.e., it is worth less than on the spot market). The opposite can also occur. If the 30-day forward exchange rate were $1 = ¥130, for example, $1 would buy more yen with a forward exchange than with a spot exchange. In such a case, we say the dollar is selling at a *premium* on the 30-day forward market. This reflects the foreign exchange dealers' expectations that the dollar will appreciate against the yen over the next 30 days.

Currency swaps

The above discussion of spot and forward exchange rates might lead you to conclude that the option to buy forward is very important to companies engaged in international trade—and you would be right. But look at Figure 9.1, which shows the nature of foreign exchange transactions in April 1992 for a sample of U.S. banks

FIGURE 9.1

Foreign Exchange
Transactions, April 1992

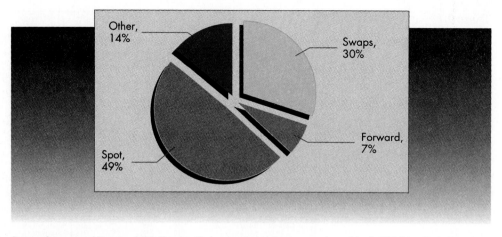

Source: Summary of Results of U.S. Foreign Exchange Market Survey, *conducted April 1992 (New York: Federal Reserve Bank of New York, 1992).*

surveyed by the Federal Reserve Board. The majority (49 percent) of foreign exchange transactions were spot exchanges, followed by swaps (30 percent). Forward exchanges accounted for only 7 percent of all foreign exchange transactions that month. Does this mean forward exchanges are not very important? It does not because swaps are a sophisticated kind of forward exchange.

A **currency swap** is the simultaneous purchase and sale of a given amount of foreign exchange for two different value dates. Swaps are transacted between international businesses and their banks, between banks, and between governments when it is desirable to move out of one currency into another for a limited period without incurring foreign exchange risk. A common kind of swap is spot against forward. Consider a company such as Apple Computer. Apple assembles laptop computers in the United States, the screens for which are made in Japan. Apple also sells some of the finished laptops in Japan. So, like many companies, Apple both buys from and sells to Japan. Imagine Apple needs to change $1 million into yen to pay its supplier of laptop screens today. Apple knows that in 90 days it will be paid ¥120 million by the Japanese importer that buys its finished laptops. It will want to convert these yen into dollars for use in the United States. Let us say today's spot exchange rate is $1 = ¥120 and the 90-day forward exchange rate is $1 = ¥110. Apple sells $1 million to its bank in return for ¥120 million. Now Apple can pay its Japanese supplier. At the same time, Apple enters into a 90-day forward exchange deal with its bank for converting ¥120 million into dollars. Thus in 90 days Apple will receive $1.09 million (¥120 million/110 = $1.09 million). Since the yen is trading at a premium on the 90-day forward market, Apple ends up with more dollars than it started with (although the opposite could also occur). The swap deal is just like a conventional forward deal in one important respect: It enables Apple to insure itself against foreign exchange risk. By engaging in a swap, Apple knows today that the ¥120 million payment it will receive in 90 days will yield $1.09 million.

❧ THE NATURE OF THE FOREIGN EXCHANGE MARKET

So far we have dealt with the foreign exchange market only as an abstract concept. It is now time to look more closely at the nature of this market. The foreign exchange market is not located in any one place. It is a global network of banks, brokers, and foreign exchange dealers connected by electronic communications systems. When companies wish to convert currencies, they typically go through their own banks rather than entering the market directly. In recent years the foreign exchange market has been growing at a rapid pace, reflecting a general growth in the volume of cross-border trade and investment (see Chapter 1). In March 1986, for example,

FIGURE 9.2

Share of Global Foreign
Exchange Trading Accounted
for by London, New York, and
Tokyo

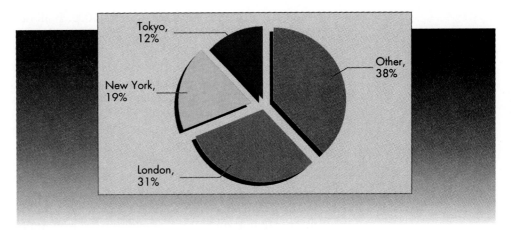

Source: Summary of Results of U.S. Foreign Exchange Market Survey, *conducted April 1992 (New York: Federal Reserve Bank of New York, 1992).*

the average total value of global foreign exchange trading was about $200 billion per day. By April 1989 it had soared to over $650 billion per day, and by 1994 it was over $1,000 billion per day.[3] The most important trading centers are London, New York, and Tokyo. In April 1994, $464 billion was traded through London each day, $244 billion through New York, and $161 billion through Tokyo.[4] Major secondary trading centers include Zurich, Frankfurt, Paris, Hong Kong, Singapore, San Francisco, and Sydney (see Figure 9.2).

London's dominance in the foreign exchange market is due to both history and geography. As the capital of the world's first major industrial trading nation, London had become the world's largest center for international banking by the end of the last century, a position it has retained. Today London also has an advantageous location; its central position between Tokyo to the east and New York to the west has made it the critical link between the Tokyo and New York markets. Because of differences in time zones, London opens as Tokyo closes for the night and is still open for the first few hours of trading in New York.

Two features of the foreign exchange market are of particular note. The first is that the market never sleeps. There are only 3 hours out of every 24 that Tokyo, London, and New York are all shut. During these three hours, trading continues in a number of minor centers, particularly San Francisco and Sydney, Australia.

The second feature of the market is the extent of integration of the various trading centers. Direct telephone lines, fax, and computer linkages between trading centers around the globe have effectively created a single market. The integration of financial centers implies there can be no significant difference in exchange rates quoted in the trading centers. For example, if the dollar/franc exchange rate quoted in London at 3 PM is $1 = FFr5.0, the dollar/franc exchange rate quoted in New York at the same time (10 AM New York time) will be identical. If the New York dollar/franc exchange rate were $1 = FFr5.5, a dealer could make a profit through **arbitrage,** the process of buying a currency low and selling it high. For example, if the prices differed in London and New York as given, a dealer could purchase FFr550,000 for $100,000 in New York and immediately sell them in London for

---

[3]Federal Reserve Bank of New York, *Summary of Results of U.S. Foreign Exchange Market Turnover Survey,* conducted April 1989 (New York: Federal Reserve Bank of New York, 1989); A. Meyerson, "Currency Markets Resisting Power of Central Banks," *New York Times,* September 25, 1992, pp. A1, C15; and W. Glasgall, "Hot Money," *Business Week,* March 20, 1995, pp. 46–50.

[4]Federal Reserve Bank of New York, *Summary of Results of U.S. Foreign Exchange Market Turnover Survey,* conducted April 1992 (New York: Federal Reserve Bank of New York, 1992); R. Chote, "London Keeps Forex Supremacy," *Financial Times,* September 20, 1995, p. 1.

$110,000, making a quick profit of $10,000. If all dealers tried to cash in on the opportunity, however, the demand for francs in New York would result in an appreciation of the franc against the dollar, while the increase in the supply of francs in London would result in their depreciation there. The discrepancy in the New York and London exchange rates would disappear very quickly. Since foreign exchange dealers are continually watching their computer screens for arbitrage opportunities, the few that arise tend to be small, and they disappear in minutes.

Another feature of the foreign exchange market is the important role played by the U.S. dollar. Although a foreign exchange transaction can involve any two currencies, most transactions involve dollars. This is true even when a dealer wants to sell one nondollar currency and buy another. A dealer wishing to sell Dutch guilders for Italian lira, for example, will usually sell the guilders for dollars and then use the dollars to buy lira. Although this may seem a roundabout way of doing things, it is cheaper than trying to find a holder of lira who wants to buy guilders. The advantage of trading through the dollar is a result of the importance of the United States in the world economy. Because of the large volume of international transactions involving dollars, it is not hard to find dealers who wish to trade dollars for guilders or lira. In contrast relatively few transactions require a direct exchange of guilders for lira.

Due to its central role in so many foreign exchange deals, the dollar is a vehicle currency. After the dollar, the most important vehicle currencies are the German mark, the Japanese yen, and the British pound—reflecting the importance of these trading nations in the world economy. The British pound used to be second in importance to the dollar as a vehicle currency, but its importance has diminished in recent years.

✺ ECONOMIC THEORIES OF EXCHANGE RATE DETERMINATION

At the most basic level, exchange rates are determined by the demand and supply of one currency relative to the demand and supply of another. For example, if the demand for dollars outstrips the supply of them and if the supply of deutsche marks is greater than the demand for them, the dollar/mark exchange rate will change. The dollar will appreciate against the mark (or the mark will depreciate against the dollar). However, while differences in relative demand and supply explain the determination of exchange rates, they do so only in a superficial sense. This simple explanation does not tell us what factors underlie the demand for and supply of a currency. Nor does it tell us when the demand for dollars will exceed the supply (and vice versa) or when the supply of German marks will exceed demand for them (and vice versa). Neither does it tell us under what conditions a currency is in demand or under what conditions it is not demanded. In this section we will review economic theory's answers to these questions. This will give us a deeper understanding of how exchange rates are determined.

If we understand how exchange rates are determined, we may be able to forecast exchange rate movements. Since future exchange rate movements influence export opportunities, the profitability of international trade and investment deals, and the price competitiveness of foreign imports, this is valuable information for an international business to have. Unfortunately there is no simple explanation here. The forces that determine exchange rates are complex, and no theoretical consensus exists, even among academic economists who study the phenomenon every day. Nonetheless most economic theories of exchange rate movements seem to agree that three factors have an important impact on future exchange rate movements in a country's currency: the country's price inflation, its interest rate, and its market psychology.[5]

---

[5]For a recent comprehensive review see M. Taylor, "The Economics of Exchange Rates," *Journal of Economic Literature* 33 (1995), pp. 13–47.

Prices and Exchange Rates

To understand how prices are related to exchange rate movements, we first need to discuss an economic proposition known as the law of one price. Then we will discuss the theory of purchasing power parity (PPP), which links changes in the exchange rate between two countries' currencies to changes in the countries' price levels.

The law of one price

The **law of one price** states that in competitive markets free of transportation costs and barriers to trade (such as tariffs), identical products sold in different countries must sell for the same price when their price is expressed in terms of the same currency.[6] For example, if the exchange rate between the dollar and the French franc is $1 = FFr5, a jacket that retails for $50 in New York should retail for FFr250 (50 × 5) in Paris. To see why this must be so, consider what would happen if the jacket cost FFr300 in Paris ($60 in U.S. currency). At this price, it would pay a company to buy jackets in New York and sell them in Paris (an example of arbitrage). Initially the company could make a profit of $10 on each jacket by purchasing them for $50 in New York and selling them for FFr300 in Paris. (Remember we are assuming away transportation costs and trade barriers.) However, the increased demand for jackets in New York would raise their price in New York, and the increased supply of jackets in Paris would lower their price there. This would continue until prices were equalized. Thus prices might equalize when the jacket cost $55 in New York and FFr275 in Paris (assuming no change in the exchange rate of $1 = FFr5).

Purchasing power parity

If the law of one price were true for all goods and services, the purchasing power parity (PPP) exchange rate could be found from any individual set of prices. By comparing the prices of identical products in different currencies, it would be possible to determine the "real" or PPP exchange rate that would exist if markets were efficient. (An **efficient market** has no impediments, such as trade barriers, to the free flow of goods and services.)

A less extreme version of the PPP theory states that given **relatively efficient markets**—markets in which few impediments to international trade and investment exist—the price of a "basket of goods" should be roughly equivalent in each country. To express the PPP theory in symbols, let $P_\$$ be the U.S. dollar price of a basket of particular goods and P_{DM} be the price of the same basket of goods in deutsche marks. The PPP theory predicts that the dollar/DM exchange rate should be equivalent to:

$$\text{\$/DM exchange rate} = P_\$/P_{DM}$$

Thus if a basket of goods costs $200 in the United States and DM600 in Germany, PPP theory predicts that the dollar/DM exchange rate should be $200/DM600 or $0.33 per DM (i.e., $1 = DM3).

The next step in the PPP theory is to argue that the exchange rate will change if relative prices change. For example, imagine there is no price inflation in the United States, while prices in Germany are increasing by 20 percent a year. At the beginning of the year, a basket of goods costs $200 in the United States and DM600 in Germany, so the dollar/DM exchange rate, according to PPP theory, should be $0.33 = DM1. At the end of the year, the basket of goods still costs $200 in the United States, but it costs DM720 in Germany. PPP theory predicts the exchange rate should change as a result. By the end of the year, $0.27 = DM1 (i.e., $1 = DM3.6). Due to the effects of price inflation, the DM has depreciated against the dollar. One dollar should buy more marks at the end of the year than at the beginning.

---

[6]Krugman and Obstfeld, *International Economics*.

FIGURE 9.3   Inflation and the Money Supply

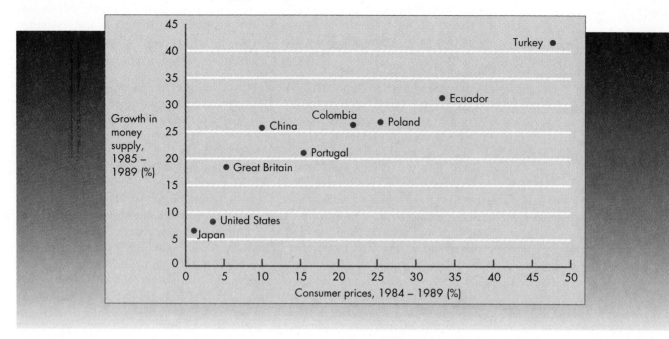

Source: The Economist Book of Vital World Statistics *(New York: Random House, 1990).*

Money supply and price inflation

PPP theory predicts that changes in relative prices will result in a change in exchange rates. Theoretically a country in which price inflation is running wild should expect to see its currency depreciate against that of countries in which inflation rates are lower. We can predict a country's likely inflation rate through the growth rate of a country's money supply.[7]

Inflation is a monetary phenomenon. Inflation occurs when the quantity of money in circulation rises faster than the stock of goods and services; that is, when the money supply increases faster than output increases. The reason for this is relatively straightforward. Imagine what would happen if everyone in the country was suddenly given $10,000 by the government. Many people would rush out to spend their extra money on those things they had always wanted—new cars, new furniture, better clothes, and so on. There would be a surge in demand for goods and services. How would car dealers, department stores, and other providers of goods and services respond to this upsurge in demand? They would do what any sensible businessperson would do—raise prices. The result would be price inflation.

A government increasing the money supply is analogous to giving people more money. An increase in the money supply makes it easier for banks to borrow from the government and for individuals and companies to borrow from banks. The resulting increase in credit causes increases in demand for goods and services. Unless the output of goods and services is growing at a rate similar to that of the money supply, the result will be inflation. This relationship has been observed time after time in country after country. Figure 9.3 shows the relationship between the growth in money supply and the rate of inflation in consumer prices between 1984 and 1989

---

[7]M. Friedman, *Studies in the Quantity Theory of Money* (Chicago: University of Chicago Press, 1956). For an accessible explanation, see M. Friedman and R. Friedman, *Free to Choose* (London: Penguin Books, 1979), chap. 9.

for a sample of countries. Although there is not a perfect one-to-one relationship, it is clear from Figure 9.3 that countries with higher rates of growth in money supply had higher inflation rates.

So now we have a connection between the growth in a country's money supply, price inflation, and exchange rate movements. Put simply, when the growth in a country's money supply is faster than the growth in its output, price inflation is fueled. The PPP theory tells us that a country with a high inflation rate will see a depreciation in its currency exchange rate. A detailed example of how this can play out in practice is given in the next "Country Focus," which describes Bolivia's experience.

Another way of looking at the same phenomenon is that an increase in a country's money supply, which increases the amount of currency available, changes the relative demand and supply conditions in the foreign exchange market. If the U.S. money supply is growing more rapidly than U.S. output, dollars will be relatively more plentiful than the currencies of countries where monetary growth is closer to output growth. As a result of this relative increase in supply of dollars, the dollar will depreciate on the foreign exchange market against the currencies of countries with slower monetary growth.

The only remaining question is, what determines whether the rate of growth in a country's money supply is greater than the rate of growth in output? The answer is government policy. Governments generally have significant control over the money supply. A government can increase the money supply simply by telling the country's central bank to print more money. Governments tend to do this to finance public expenditure (building roads, paying government workers, paying for defense, etc.). A government could finance public expenditure by raising taxes, but since nobody likes paying more taxes and since politicians do not like to be unpopular, they have a natural preference for printing money.

Unfortunately there is no magic money tree. The inevitable result of excessive growth in money supply is price inflation. However, this has not stopped governments around the world from printing money, with predictable results. In short, if an international business is attempting to predict future movements in the value of a country's currency on the foreign exchange market, it should examine that country's policy toward monetary growth. If the government seems committed to controlling the rate of growth in money supply, the country's future inflation rate may be low (even if the current rate is high) and its currency should not depreciate too much on the foreign exchange market. If the country's government seems to lack the political will to control the rate of growth in money supply, the future inflation rate may be high, which is likely to cause its currency to depreciate. Historically many Latin American governments have fallen into this latter category, including Argentina, Bolivia, and Brazil. More recently, there are signs that many of the newly democratic states of Eastern Europe might be making the same mistake.

Empirical tests of PPP theory

PPP theory predicts that changes in relative prices will result in a change in exchange rates. A country in which price inflation is running wild should expect to see its currency depreciate against that of countries with lower inflation rates. This is intuitively appealing, but is it true in practice? There are certainly several good examples of the connection between a country's price inflation and exchange rate position (such as Bolivia; see the "Country Focus"). Some evidence of this connection can be seen in Figure 9.4. This figure compares a country's *total* inflation rate between 1973 and 1993 relative to the U.S. inflation rate against the change in the foreign currency price of U.S. dollars between 1973 and 1993 (an increase in the foreign currency price means there has been a fall in the value of that currency against the dollar). The figure shows that currencies of countries with higher inflation rates than the United States (e.g., Italy and the United Kingdom) depreciated against the U.S. dollar (and vice versa). Price inflation in Italy, for example, was 160 percent greater than

COUNTRY FOCUS
Money Supply Growth, Inflation, and Exchange Rates in Bolivia

In the mid-1980s Bolivia experienced hyperinflation, an explosive and seemingly uncontrollable price inflation in which money loses value very rapidly. Table 9.2 presents data on Bolivia's money supply, inflation rate, and its peso exchange rate with the U.S. dollar during the period of hyperinflation. The exchange rate is actually the "black market" exchange rate, as the Bolivian government prohibited converting the peso to other currencies during the period. The data show that the growth in money supply, the rate of price inflation, and the depreciation of the peso against the dollar all moved in step with each other. This is just what PPP theory and monetary economics predict. Between April 1984 and July 1985, Bolivia's money supply increased by 17,433 percent, prices increased by 22,908 percent, and the value of the peso against the dollar fell by 24,662 percent! In October 1985 the Bolivian government instituted a dramatic stabilization plan, which included the introduction of a new currency and tight control of the money supply, and by 1987 the country's inflation rate was down to 16 percent per annum.

Sources: Juan-Antino Morales, "Inflation Stabilization in Bolivia," in *Inflation Stabilization: The Experience of Israel, Argentina, Brazil, Bolivia, and Mexico,* ed. Michael Bruno et al. (Cambridge, MA: MIT Press, 1988); and *World Book of Vital Statistics* (New York: Random House, 1990).

TABLE 9.2   Macroeconomic Data for Bolivia, April 1984 to October 1985

Month	Money Supply (billions of pesos)	Price Level Relative to 1982 (average = 1)	Exchange Rate (pesos per dollar)
1984			
April	270	21.1	3,576
May	330	31.1	3,512
June	440	32.3	3,342
July	599	34.0	3,570
August	718	39.1	7,038
September	889	53.7	13,685
October	1,194	85.5	15,205
November	1,495	112.4	18,469
December	3,296	180.9	24,515
1985			
January	4,630	305.3	73,016
February	6,455	863.3	141,101
March	9,089	1,078.6	128,137
April	12,885	1,205.7	167,428
May	21,309	1,635.7	272,375
June	27,778	2,919.1	481,756
July	47,341	4,854.6	885,476
August	74,306	8,081.0	1,182,300
September	103,272	12,647.6	1,087,440
October	132,550	12,411.8	1,120,210

Source: Juan-Antino Morales, "Inflation Stabilization in Bolivia," in *Inflation Stabilization: The Experience of Israel, Argentina, Brazil, Bolivia, and Mexico,* ed. Michael Bruno et al. (Cambridge, MA: MIT Press, 1988).

FIGURE 9.4

Exchange Rate Trends and
Inflation Differentials,
1973–93

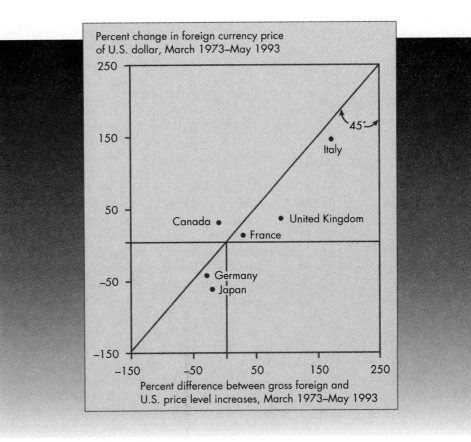

Source: OECD, Main Economic Indicators.

in the United States over the 1973–93 period. Consistent with the predictions of PPP theory, the value of the Italian lira against the dollar declined by about 150 percent over the same period. Similarly, inflation in Germany was about 55 percent less than in the United States over the 1973–93 period, and the value of the deutsche mark against the U.S. dollar increased by about 55 percent over this period.

There has been extensive empirical testing of the PPP theory, and in general, the tests have not shown it to be completely accurate in estimating exchange rate changes.[8] While the PPP theory seems to yield relatively accurate predictions *in the long run*, such as the 20-year period illustrated in Figure 9.4, it does not appear to predict *short-run* movements in exchange rates. PPP theory does not seem to be a good predictor of exchange rate movements for time spans of five years or less. In addition the theory seems to best predict exchange rate changes for countries with very high rates of inflation and underdeveloped capital markets (e.g., Colombia, Poland, Mexico, and Russia). The theory is much less useful for predicting short-term exchange rate movements between the currencies of advanced industrialized nations that have relatively small differentials in inflation rates.

Several factors may explain the failure of PPP theory to predict exchange rates more accurately. PPP theory assumes away transportation costs and barriers to trade and investment. In practice these factors are significant and they tend to create price differentials between countries. As we saw in Chapters 5 and 7, governments routinely intervene in international trade and investment. Such intervention, by violating the assumption of efficient markets, weakens the link between relative price changes and changes in exchange rates predicted by PPP theory.

---

[8]For reviews, see L. H. Officer, "The Purchasing Parity Theory of Exchange Rates: A Review Article," *International Monetary Fund Staff Papers*, March 1976, pp. 1–60; and Taylor, "The Economics of Exchange Rates."

Another factor of some importance is that governments also intervene in the foreign exchange market in attempting to influence the value of their currencies. We will look at why and how they do this in Chapter 10. For now the important thing to note is that governments regularly intervene in the foreign exchange market, and this further weakens the link between price changes and changes in exchange rates.

Perhaps the most important factor explaining the failure of PPP theory to predict short-term movements in foreign exchange rates, however, is the impact of investor psychology on currency purchasing decisions and exchange rate movements. We will discuss this issue in more detail later in this chapter.

Interest Rates and Exchange Rates

Economic theory tells us that interest rates reflect expectations about likely future inflation rates. In countries where inflation is expected to be high, interest rates also will be high, because investors want compensation for the decline in the value of their money. This relationship was first formalized by economist Irving Fisher and is thus referred to as the Fisher effect. The Fisher effect states that a country's "nominal" interest rate (i) is the sum of the required "real" rate of interest (r) and the expected rate of inflation over the period of time for which the funds are to be lent (I). More formally,

$$i = r + I$$

For example, if the real rate of interest in a country is 5 percent and annual inflation is expected to be 10 percent, the nominal interest rate will be 15 percent. As predicted by the Fisher effect, a strong relationship seems to exist between inflation rates and interest rates.[9]

We can take this one step further and consider how it applies in a world of many countries and unrestricted capital flows. When investors are free to transfer capital between countries, real interest rates will be the same in every country. If differences in real interest rates did emerge between countries, arbitrage would soon equalize them. For example, if the real interest rate in Germany was 10 percent and only 6 percent in the United States, it would pay investors to borrow money in the United States and invest it in Germany. The resulting increase in the demand for money in the United States would raise the real interest rate there, while the increase in the supply of foreign money in Germany would lower the real interest rate there. This would continue until the two sets of real interest rates were equalized. (In practice, differences in real interest rates may persist due to government controls on capital flows; investors are not always free to transfer capital between countries.)

It follows from the Fisher effect that if the real interest rate is the same worldwide, any difference in interest rates between countries reflects differing expectations about inflation rates. Thus if the expected rate of inflation in the United States is greater than that in Germany, U.S. nominal interest rates will be greater than German nominal interest rates.

Since we know from PPP theory that there is a link (in theory at least) between inflation and exchange rates, and since interest rates reflect expectations about inflation, it follows that there must also be a link between interest rates and exchange rates. This link is known as the international Fisher effect (IFE). The **international Fisher effect** states that for any two countries, the spot exchange rate should change in an equal amount but in the opposite direction to the difference in nominal interest rates between two countries. Stated more formally,

$$(S_1 - S_2)/S_2 \times 100 = i_\$ - i_{DM}$$

where $i_\$$ and i_{DM} are the respective nominal interest rates in the United States and Germany (for the sake of example), S_1 is the spot exchange rate at the beginning of the period, and S_2 is the spot exchange rate at the end of the period.

---

[9]For a summary of the evidence see the survey by Taylor, "The Economics of Exchange Rates."

If the U.S. nominal interest rate is higher than Germany's, reflecting greater expected inflation rates, the value of the dollar against the deutsche mark should fall by that interest rate differential in the future. So if the interest rate in the United States is 10 percent, and in Germany it is 6 percent, reflecting 4 percent higher expected inflation in the United States, we would expect the value of the dollar to depreciate by 4 percent against the mark.

So do interest rate differentials help predict future currency movements? The evidence is mixed; as in the case of PPP theory. In the long run there does seem to be a relationship between interest rate differentials and subsequent changes in spot exchange rates. However, considerable short-run deviations occur. Like PPP, the international Fisher effect is not a good predictor of short-run changes in spot exchange rates.[10]

Investor Psychology and Bandwagon Effects

As we have noted, empirical evidence suggests that neither PPP theory nor the international Fisher effect are particularly good at explaining *short-term* movements in exchange rates. One reason for this may be the impact of investor psychology on short-run exchange rate movements. There is increasing evidence that various psychological factors, as opposed to macroeconomic fundamentals, play an important role in determining the expectations of market traders as to likely future exchange rates.[11] In turn, expectations have a tendency to become self-filling prophecies.

We discussed a good example of this mechanism in the "Management Focus" on George Soros. When George Soros shorted the British pound in September 1992, many foreign exchange traders, fully aware of Soros's previous successes, jumped on the bandwagon and did likewise, selling British pounds and purchasing German marks. As the *bandwagon effect* built up, with more and more traders selling British pounds and purchasing deutsche marks in expectation of a decline in the pound, so their expectations became a *self-fulfilling prophecy* with massive selling forcing down the value of the pound against the deutsche mark. The pound declined in value not because of any major shift in macroeconomic fundamentals, but because investors moved in a herd in response to a bet placed by a major speculator, George Soros. According to a number of recent studies, such bandwagon effects play a major role in determining *short-run* exchange rate movements.[12] However, by their very nature such bandwagon effects are hard to predict.

Summary

We have seen that relative monetary growth, relative inflation rates, and nominal interest rate differentials are all moderately good predictors of *long-run* changes in exchange rates. They are poor predictors of short-run changes in exchange rates, however, probably because of the impact of psychological factors, investor expectations, and bandwagon effects on short-term currency movements. This information is useful for an international business. Insofar as the long-term profitability of foreign investments, export opportunities, and the price competitiveness of foreign imports are all influenced by long-term movements in exchange rates, international businesses would be well advised to pay attention to countries' differing monetary growth, inflation, and interest rates. On the other hand, international businesses that engage in foreign exchange transactions on a day-to-day basis could benefit by knowing some predictors of short-term foreign exchange rate movements. Unfortunately, short-term exchange rate movements are difficult to predict.

---

[10]R. E. Cumby and M. Obstfeld, "A Note on Exchange Rate Expectations and Nominal Interest Differentials: A Test of the Fisher Hypothesis," *Journal of Finance*, June 1981, pp. 697–703.

[11]Taylor, "The Economics of Exchange Rates."

[12]See H. L. Allen and M. P. Taylor, "Charts, Noise, and Fundamentals in the Foreign Exchange Market," *Economic Journal* 100 (1990), pp. 49–59; and T. Ito, "Foreign Exchange Rate Expectations: Micro Survey Data," *American Economic Review* 80 (1990), pp. 434–49.

⚜ EXCHANGE RATE FORECASTING

A company's need to predict future exchange rate variations raises the issue of whether it is worthwhile for the company to invest in exchange rate forecasting services to aid decision making. Two schools of thought address this issue. The efficient market school argues that forward exchange rates do the best possible job of forecasting future spot exchange rates, and therefore investing in forecasting services would be a waste of money. The other school of thought, the inefficient market school, argues that companies can improve the foreign exchange market's estimate of future exchange rates (as contained in the forward rate) by investing in forecasting services. In other words, this school of thought does not believe the forward exchange rates are the best possible predictors of future spot exchange rates.

The Efficient Market School

Forward exchange rates represent market participants' collective predictions of likely spot exchange rates at specified future dates. If forward exchange rates are the best possible predictor of future spot rates, it would make no sense for companies to spend additional money trying to forecast short-run exchange rate movements. Many economists believe the foreign exchange market is efficient at setting forward rates.[13] An **efficient market** is one in which prices reflect all available information. (If forward rates reflect all available information about likely future changes in exchange rates, it follows that there is no way a company can beat the market by investing in forecasting services).

If the foreign exchange market is efficient, forward exchange rates should be unbiased predictors of future spot rates. This does not mean the predictions will be accurate in any specific situation; it means inaccuracies will not be consistently above or below future spot rates—that they will be random. There have been a large number of empirical tests of the efficient market hypothesis. Although most of the early work seems to confirm the hypothesis (suggesting that companies should not waste their money on forecasting services), more recent studies have challenged it.[14] Most significant, there is increasing evidence that forward rates are not unbiased predictors of future spot rates, and that more accurate predictions of future spot rates can be calculated from publicly available information.[15]

The Inefficient Market School

Citing evidence against the efficient market hypothesis, some economists believe the foreign exchange market is inefficient. **An inefficient market** is one in which prices do not reflect all available information. In an inefficient market, forward exchange rates will not be the best possible predictors of future spot exchange rates.

If this is true, it may be worthwhile for international businesses to invest in forecasting services (as many do). The belief is that professional exchange rate forecasts might be able to provide better predictions of future spot rates than forward exchange rates do. It should be pointed out, however, that the track record of professional forecasting services is not that good. For example, an analysis of the forecasts of 12 major forecasting services over the 1978–82 period concluded the forecasters did not provide better forecasts than the forward exchange rates.[16]

Approaches to Forecasting

Assuming the inefficient market school is correct that the foreign exchange market's estimate of future spot rates can be improved, on what basis should forecasts be prepared? Here again there are two schools of thought. One adheres to fundamental analysis, while the other uses technical analysis.

---

[13]For example, see E. Fama, "Forward Rates as Predictors of Future Spot Rates," *Journal of Financial Economics*, October 1976, pp. 361–77.

[14]R. M. Levich, "The Efficiency of Markets for Foreign Exchange," in *International Finance*, ed. G. D. Gay and R. W. Kold (Richmond, VA: Robert F. Dane, Inc., 1983).

[15]J. Williamson, *The Exchange Rate System* (Washington, DC: Institute for International Economics, 1983).

[16]R. M. Levich, "Currency Forecasters Lose Their Way," *Euromoney*, August 1983, p. 140.

Fundamental analysis

Fundamental analysis draws on economic theory to construct sophisticated econometric models for predicting exchange rate movements. The variables contained in these models typically include those we have discussed, such as relative money supply growth rates, inflation rates, and interest rates. They may also include variables related to countries' balance-of-payments positions.

The logic for including balance-of-payments data in exchange rate forecasts is that if a country is running a deficit on its balance-of-payments current account (it is importing more goods and services than it is exporting), pressures are created that result in the depreciation of its currency on the foreign exchange market. (For background on the balance of payments, see Chapter 7.) Consider what might happen if the United States was running a persistent current-account balance-of-payments deficit. Since the United States would be importing more than it was exporting, people in other countries would be increasing their holdings of U.S. dollars. If these people were willing to hold their dollars, the dollar's exchange rate would not be influenced. However, if these people converted their dollars into other currencies, the supply of dollars in the foreign exchange market would increase (as would demand for the other currencies). This shift in demand and supply conditions would create pressures that could lead to the depreciation of the dollar against other currencies.

The problem with this argument is that it hinges on whether people in other countries are willing to hold dollars. This in turn depends on such factors as U.S. interest rates and inflation rates. So, in a sense, the balance-of-payments position is not a fundamental predictor of future exchange rate movements. For example, during the 1981–85 period, the U.S. dollar appreciated against most major currencies despite a growing balance-of-payments deficit. The reason was that relatively high real interest rates in the United States made the dollar very attractive to foreigners, so they did not convert their dollars into other currencies. Given this, we are back to the argument that the fundamental determinants of exchange rates are monetary growth, inflation rates, and interest rates.

Technical analysis

Technical analysis uses price and volume data to determine past trends, which are expected to continue into the future. This approach does not rely on a consideration of economic fundamentals. Technical analysis is based on the premise that there are analyzable market trends and waves and that previous trends and waves can be used to predict future trends and waves. Since there is no theoretical rationale for this assumption of predictability, many economists compare technical analysis to fortune telling. Despite this skepticism, technical analysis has gained favor in recent years.[17]

❧ CURRENCY CONVERTIBILITY

Until this point we have assumed the currencies of various countries are freely convertible into other currencies. This assumption is invalid. As we shall see, in many countries the ability of residents and nonresidents to convert the local currency into a foreign currency is restricted. The result is that international trade and investment are more difficult in those countries. Many international businesses have used "countertrade" practices to circumvent problems that arise when a currency is not freely convertible.

---

[17]C. Engel and J. D. Hamilton, "Long Swings in the Dollar: Are They in the Data and Do Markets Know It?" *American Economic Review*, September 1990, pp. 689–713.

Convertibility and Government Policy

Due to government restrictions, a significant number of currencies are not freely convertible into other currencies. A country's currency is said to be **freely convertible** when the country's government allows both residents and nonresidents to purchase unlimited amounts of a foreign currency with it. A currency is said to be **externally convertible** when only nonresidents may convert it into a foreign currency without any limitations. A currency is **nonconvertible** when neither residents nor nonresidents are allowed to convert it into a foreign currency.

Free convertibility is the exception rather than the rule. Many countries restrict their residents' ability to convert the domestic currency into a foreign currency (a policy of external convertibility). Restrictions on convertibility for residents range from the relatively minor (such as restricting the amount of foreign currency they may take with them out of the country on trips) to the major (such as restricting domestic businesses' ability to take foreign currency out of the country). External convertibility restrictions can limit domestic companies' ability to invest abroad, but they present few problems for foreign companies wishing to do business in that country. For example, even if the German government placed tight controls on the ability of its residents to convert the mark into U.S. dollars, all U.S. businesses with deposits in German banks may at any time convert all their marks into dollars and take them out of the country. Thus a U.S. company with a subsidiary in Germany is assured it will be able to convert the profits from its German operation into dollars and take them out of the country.

Serious problems arise, however, when a policy of nonconvertibility is in force. This was the practice of the former Soviet Union, and it continued to be the practice in Russia until recently. When strictly applied, nonconvertibility means that although a U.S. company doing business in a country like Russia may be able to generate significant ruble profits, it may not convert those rubles into dollars and take them out of the country. Obviously this is not a desirable situation for international business.

The main reason governments limit convertibility is to preserve their foreign exchange reserves. A country needs an adequate supply of these reserves to service its international debt commitments and to purchase imports. Governments typically impose convertibility restrictions on their currency when they fear that free convertibility will lead to a run on their foreign exchange reserves. This occurs when residents and nonresidents rush to convert their holdings of domestic currency into a foreign currency—a phenomenon generally referred to as capital flight. Capital flight is most likely to occur when the value of the domestic currency is depreciating rapidly because of hyperinflation, or when a country's economic prospects are shaky in other respects. Under such circumstances, both residents and nonresidents tend to believe their money is more likely to hold its value if it is converted into a foreign currency and invested abroad. Not only will a run on foreign exchange reserves limit the country's ability to service its international debt and pay for imports, but it will also lead to a precipitous depreciation in the exchange rate as residents and nonresidents alike unload their holdings of domestic currency on the foreign exchange markets (thereby increasing the market supply of the country's currency). Governments fear that the rise in import prices resulting from currency depreciation will lead to further increases in inflation. This fear provides another rationale for limiting convertibility.

Due to a combination of these reasons, in 1990 more than 80 countries had placed major restrictions on conversions of their currency. Another 32 countries had imposed minor restrictions, and only 31 countries' currencies were considered freely convertible. Countries with major restrictions on currency convertibility include many of the former Communist states of Eastern Europe, most of Africa, China, many of the Middle Eastern countries, and several Latin American nations.[18]

---

[18]*Exchange Agreements and Exchange Restrictions* (Washington, DC: International Monetary Fund, 1990).

Countertrade

A company can deal with the nonconvertibility problem by engaging in counter-trade. Countertrade is discussed in detail in Chapter 15, so we will merely introduce the concept here.

Countertrade refers to a range of barterlike agreements by which goods and services can be traded for other goods and services. Countertrade can make sense when a country's currency is nonconvertible. For example, consider the deal that General Electric struck with the Romanian government in 1984, when that country's currency was nonconvertible. When General Electric won a contract for a $150 million generator project in Romania, it agreed to take payment in the form of Romanian goods that could be sold for $150 million on international markets. In a similar case, the Venezuelan government negotiated a contract with Caterpillar in 1986 under which Venezuela would trade 350,000 tons of iron ore for Caterpillar heavy construction equipment. Caterpillar subsequently traded the iron ore to Romania in exchange for Romanian farm products, which it then sold on international markets for dollars.[19]

How important is countertrade? One estimate is that 20 to 30 percent of world trade in 1985 involved some form of countertrade agreements. Other estimates are that by 1990 more than 40 percent of world trade by volume involved counter-trade.[20] Although these estimates might seem very high—and they are difficult to verify because of the lack of hard data—they are perhaps not that far off, given the large number of countries whose currencies remain nonconvertible. Since counter-trade is apparently so important, we discuss it again in Chapter 15.

IMPLICATIONS FOR BUSINESS

A number of clear implications for business are contained in this chapter. First, it is absolutely critical that international businesses understand the influence of exchange rates on the profitability of trade and investment deals. Adverse changes in exchange rates can make apparently profitable deals unprofitable. The risk introduced into international business transactions by changes in exchange rates is referred to as foreign exchange risk. Means of hedging against foreign exchange risk are available. Most significant, forward exchange rates and currency swaps allow companies to insure against this risk.

International businesses must also understand the forces that determine exchange rates. This is particularly true in light of the increasing evidence that forward exchange rates are not unbiased predictors. If a company wants to know how the value of a particular currency is likely to change over the long term on the foreign exchange market, it should look closely at those economic fundamentals that appear to predict long-run exchange rate movements (i.e., the growth in a country's money supply, its inflation rate, and its nominal interest rates). For example, an international business should be very cautious about trading with or investing in a country with a recent history of rapid growth in its domestic money supply. The upsurge in inflation that is likely to follow such rapid monetary growth could well lead to a sharp drop in the value of the country's currency on the foreign exchange market, which could transform a profitable deal into an unprofitable one. This is not to say an international business should not trade with or invest in such a country. Rather it means an international business should take some precautions before doing so, such as buying currency forward on the foreign exchange market or structuring the deal around a countertrade arrangement.

Complicating this picture is the issue of currency convertibility. Governments' proclivity to restrict currency convertibility suggests the foreign exchange market does not always provide the lubricant necessary to make international trade and investment possible. Given this, international businesses need to explore alternative mechanisms for facilitating international trade and investment that do not involve currency conversion. Countertrade seems the obvious mechanism. We return to the topic of countertrade and discuss it in depth in Chapter 15.

---

[19] J. R. Carter and J. Gagne, "The Do's and Don'ts of International Countertrade," *Sloan Management Review*, Spring 1988, pp. 31–37.

[20] L. W. Tuller, *Going Global: New Opportunities for Growing Companies to Compete in World Markets* (Homewood, IL: Business One Irwin, 1991).

❧ SUMMARY OF CHAPTER

The objectives of this chapter were to explain how the foreign exchange market works, to examine the forces that determine exchange rates, and then to discuss the implications of these factors for international business. Given that changes in exchange rates can dramatically alter the profitability of foreign trade and investment deals, this is an area of major interest to international business. These points have been made in the chapter:

1. One function of the foreign exchange market is to convert the currency of one country into the currency of another.

2. International businesses participate in the foreign exchange market to facilitate international trade and investment, to invest spare cash in short-term money market accounts abroad, and to engage in currency speculation.

3. A second function of the foreign exchange market is to provide insurance against foreign exchange risk.

4. The spot exchange rate is the exchange rate at which a dealer converts one currency into another currency on a particular day.

5. Foreign exchange risk can be reduced by using forward exchange rates. A forward exchange rate is an exchange rate governing future transactions.

6. Foreign exchange risk can also be reduced by engaging in currency swaps. A swap is the simultaneous purchase and sale of a given amount of foreign exchange for two different value dates.

7. The law of one price is that in competitive markets that are free of transportation costs and barriers to trade, identical products sold in different countries must sell for the same price when their price is expressed in the same currency.

8. Purchasing power parity (PPP) theory states the price of a basket of particular goods should be roughly equivalent in each country. PPP theory predicts the exchange rate will change if relative prices change.

9. The rate of change in countries' relative prices depends on their relative inflation rates. A country's inflation rate seems to be a function of the growth in its money supply.

10. The PPP theory of exchange rate changes yields relatively accurate predictions of *long-term* trends in exchange rates but not of *short-term* movements. The failure of PPP theory to predict exchange rate changes more accurately may be due to the existence of transportation costs, barriers to trade and investment, and the impact of psychological factors such as bandwagon effects on market movements and short-run exchange rates.

11. Interest rates reflect expectations about inflation. In countries where inflation is expected to be high, interest rates also will be high.

12. The international Fisher effect (IFE) states that for any two countries, the spot exchange rate should change in an equal amount but in the opposite direction to the difference in nominal interest rates.

13. The most common approach to exchange rate forecasting is fundamental analysis. This relies on variables such as money supply growth, inflation rates, nominal interest rates, and balance-of-payments positions to predict future changes in exchange rates.

14. In many countries, the ability of residents and nonresidents to convert local currency into a foreign currency is restricted by government policy. A government restricts the convertibility of its currency in attempting to protect the country's foreign exchange reserves and to halt any capital flight.

15. Particularly bothersome for international business is a policy on nonconvertibility, which prohibits residents and nonresidents from exchanging local currency for foreign currency. A policy of nonconvertibility makes it very difficult to engage in international trade and investment in the country.

16. One way of coping with the nonconvertibility problem is to engage in countertrade—to trade goods and services for other goods and services.

❧ CRITICAL DISCUSSION QUESTIONS

1. The interest rate on German government securities with one-year maturity is 4 percent, and the expected inflation rate for the coming year is 2 percent. The interest rate on U.S. government securities with one-year maturity is 7 percent, and the expected rate of inflation is 5 percent. The current spot exchange rate for German marks is $1 = DM1.4. Forecast the spot exchange rate one year from today. Explain the logic of your answer.

2. Two countries, France and the United States, produce just one good: beef. Suppose the price of beef in the United States is $2.80 per pound and in France it is FFr3.70 per pound.
   a. According to PPP theory, what should the $/FFr spot exchange rate be?
   b. Suppose the price of beef is expected to rise to $3.10 in the United States, and to FFr4.65 in France. What should the one-year forward $/FFr exchange rate be?
   c. Given your answers to parts *a* and *b*, and given that the current interest rate in the United States is 10 percent, what would you expect the current interest rate to be in France?

3. You manufacture wine goblets. In mid-June you receive an order for 10,000 goblets from Germany. Payment from the customer of DM400,000 is due in mid-December. You expect the deutsche mark to rise from its present rate of $1 = DM1.5 to $1 = DM1.4 by December. You can borrow marks at 6 percent per annum. What should you do?

❧ CLOSING CASE   The Collapse of the Russian Ruble

Between January 1992 and April 1995 the value of the ruble against the U.S. dollar fell from $1 = Rbs125 to $1 = Rbs5130! This dramatic fall occurred at the same time that Russia was implementing an economic reform program designed to transform the country's crumbling centrally planned economy into a dynamic market economy. The reform program involved a number of steps, including the removal of price controls on most goods and services, the gradual dismantling of much of the bureaucratic apparatus that had formally controlled the economy, the privatization of many formerly state-owned enterprises, and the abolition of laws prohibiting private ownership.

One of the first steps to be implemented was the liberalization of price controls on January 1, 1992. Immediately following liberalization, prices surged and inflation was soon running at a *monthly* rate of about 30 percent. For the whole of 1992 the inflation rate in Russia was 3,000 percent. The annual rate for 1993 was approximately 900 percent. The inflation rate moderated during 1994, and by August of that year it was running at a monthly rate of less than 5 percent. At this point price stabilization seemed possible. However, by January 1995 inflation had again surged to 17.8 percent.

Several factors contributed to Russia's high inflation rate. Prices had been held at artificially low levels by state planners during the Communist era. At the same time there was a shortage of many basic goods, so with nothing to spend their money on many Russians simply hoarded rubles. Following the liberalization of price controls the country was suddenly awash in rubles chasing a still limited supply of goods. The result was to rapidly bid up prices.

The inflationary fires that followed price liberalization were stoked by the Russian government. Unwilling to face the social consequences of the massive unemployment that would follow if many state-owned enterprises quickly were privatized, the government continued to subsidize the operations of many money-losing establishments. The result was a surge in the government's budget deficit. In the first quarter of 1992 the budget deficit amounted to 1.5 percent of the country's GDP. By the end of 1992 it had risen to 17 percent of GDP. Unable or unwilling to finance this deficit by raising taxes, the government settled on another solution—it printed money.

With inflation roaring ahead, the ruble tumbled. By the end of 1992 the exchange rate was $1 = Rbs480. By the end of 1993 it was $1 = Rbs1,500. However, the rate of decline in the ruble began to slow markedly in early 1994. One reason for this was that it looked as if the Russian government was starting to bring both the budget deficit and inflation under control. Unfortunately as the year progressed it became increasingly evident that due to vigorous political opposition, the government would not be able to bring down its budget deficit as quickly as had been thought. By September the monthly inflation rate was rising again. October started badly with the ruble sliding more than 10 percent in value against the U.S. dollar in the first 10 days of the month. Then on October 11 the ruble plunged a staggering 21.5 percent against the dollar reaching a value of $1 = Rbs3,926 by the time the foreign exchange market closed!

Many in the Russian government blamed the decline on currency speculation. Some officials even claimed that a cartel of 10 banks had been dumping rubles on the market in a deliberate attempt to drive down its price against the dollar and to destabilize the economy. Despite the announcement of a tough budget plan with tight controls on the money supply, the ruble continued to slide and by April 1995 the exchange rate stood at $1 = Rbs5,120.

However, by mid-1995 inflation was again on the way down. In June 1995 the monthly inflation rate was at a yearly low of 6.7 percent. Moreover, the ruble had recovered to stand at $1 = Rbs4,559 by July 6. On that day the Russian government announced it would intervene in the currency market to keep the ruble in a trading range of Rbs4,300 to Rbs4,900 against the dollar. The Russian government believed it was essential to maintain a relatively stable currency. The government announced the central bank would be able to draw on $10 billion in foreign exchange reserves to defend the ruble against any speculative selling in Russia's relatively small foreign exchange market.

CASE DISCUSSION QUESTIONS

1. What was the root cause of the fall in the external value of the Russian ruble between 1992 and 1995?

2. What must the Russian government do to halt the decline in the value of the ruble?

3. Why do you think it is important for a government to promote a stable currency?

4. Do you think the Russian central bank will be able to defend the ruble against speculative pressure and keep it in the trading range announced July 6, 1995?

Sources: S. Erlanger, *"Russia Will Test a Trading Band for the Ruble,"* New York Times, July 7, 1995, p. 1; C. Freeland, *"Russian to Introduce a Trading Band for Ruble against Dollar,"* Financial Times, July 7, 1995, p. 1; J. Thornhill, *"Russians Bemused by 'Black Tuesday,'"* "Financial Times, October 12, 1994, p. 4; and R. Sikorski, *"Mirage of Numbers,"* The Wall Street Journal, May 18, 1994, p. 14.

CHAPTER TEN

THE INTERNATIONAL MONETARY SYSTEM

THE TUMBLING PESO AND THE AUTO INDUSTRY

In the euphoria that followed the January 1, 1994, implementation of the North American Free Trade Agreement (NAFTA) no industry looked set to gain more than the auto industry. Due to falling trade barriers and booming demand in Mexico, between January and October 1994 U.S. car exports to Mexico increased 500 percent. For all of 1994 Ford shipped 30,000 vehicles to Mexico, up from 6,000 in 1993. The company planned to ship 50,000 in 1995. General Motors and Chrysler also saw their shipments to Mexico surge in 1994 and were planning for even greater increases in 1995. Forecasts suggested the number of vehicles sold in Mexico would rise to 1.2 million by 1999, up from 600,000 in 1994. With this growth in mind, not only had auto companies been exporting more to Mexico, but they had also been investing in Mexican-based production capacity both for serving the Mexican market and for exporting elsewhere. Among the biggest foreign investors were Chrysler, Ford, General Motors, Nissan, Mercedes-Benz, and Volkswagen.

In a few short days in December 1994 the euphoric bubble of the post-NAFTA boom was rudely burst by an unexpected decision on the part of the Mexican government to abandon a system of pegging the value of the peso at 3.5 to the dollar. Instead the government decided to allow the peso to float freely against the dollar. In the weeks that followed this decision, the peso plummeted 40 percent, and by mid-January 1995 it was trading at 5.6 to the dollar.

The peso had been pegged to the dollar since the early 1980s when the International Monetary Fund (IMF) had made it a condition for lending money to the Mexican government to help bail the country out of a 1982

financial crisis. Under the IMF-brokered arrangement the peso had been allowed to trade within a tolerance band of plus or minus 3 percent against the dollar. The band was also permitted to "crawl" down daily, allowing for an annual peso depreciation of about 4 percent against the dollar. The IMF believed the need to maintain the exchange rate within a fairly narrow trading band would force the Mexican government to adopt stringent financial policies to limit the growth in the money supply and contain inflation.

Until the early 1990s it looked as if the IMF policy had worked. However, by 1994 the strains were beginning to show. Since the mid-1980s Mexican producer prices had risen 45 percent more than prices in the United States, and yet there had not been a corresponding adjustment in the exchange rate. Moreover, by late 1994 Mexico was running a $17 billion trade deficit, which amounted to some 6 percent of the country's gross domestic product. Despite these strains, almost right up until the decision to allow the peso to float freely against the dollar, Mexican government officials had been stating

publicly that they would support the value of the peso by adopting appropriate monetary policies and by intervening in the currency markets if necessary. Encouraged by such public statements, investment money poured into Mexico as corporations and mutual fund money managers sought to take advantage of the booming economy.

However, many currency traders concluded the peso would have to be devalued, so they began to dump pesos on the foreign exchange market. The government tried to hold the line by intervening in the market to buy pesos and sell dollars, but it soon found it lacked the foreign currency reserves required to halt the speculative tide. In mid-December 1994 it abruptly changed course and announced a devaluation. Immediately much of the short-term investment money that had flowed into Mexican stocks and bonds over the previous year reversed its course, as foreign investors bailed out of peso-denominated financial assets. This exacerbated the selling off of the peso and contributed to the rapid 40 percent drop in its value.

As with many other industries, the impact on the auto industry was dramatic and immediate. By February 1995 the price of imported autos had risen by 40 percent. There had also been a substantial rise in the price of most autos assembled in Mexico, such as those coming off Ford's Cuautitlan plant, because many of these operations were heavily dependent on parts imported from the United States and Canada. If the price increases weren't enough, in March 1995 the Mexican government introduced an economic austerity plan. One result was to tighten credit and force up interest rates.

Not surprisingly, demand for autos slumped. For the whole of 1995 demand was forecasted to come in anywhere between 30 percent and 50 percent below the levels attained in 1994.

Volkswagen, Nissan, Mercedes-Benz, and Ford were all forced to temporarily close their Mexican factories in January in expectation of the drop in demand. In other developments, Fiat of Italy pulled out of plans to build a new auto factory in Mexico, while Nissan announced plans to cut its 1995 production in Mexico from 210,000 to 180,000 vehicles.

However, while the short-term outlook was grim, in the longer run many auto companies may benefit from the fall in the value of the peso. Although Volkswagen closed its Mexican plant for two weeks in January, it estimated it would be able to ship 175,000 Mexican-made vehicles to the United States in 1995, 25,000 more than in 1994. Similarly, the big three U.S. automakers were

reported to be planning to keep their Mexican plants operating at full capacity in the second half of 1995 by boosting exports to the United States.

Sources: J. Darling and D. Nauss, "Stall in the Fast Lane," *Los Angeles Times*, February 19, 1995, p. 1; "Mexico Drops Efforts to Prop up Peso," *The Wall Street Journal*, December 23, 1994, p. A3; R. Dornbusch; "We Have Salinas to Thank for the Peso Debacle," *Business Week*, January 16, 1995, p. 20; P. Carroll and C. Torres, "Mexico Unveils Program of Harsh Fiscal Medicine," *The Wall Street Journal*, March 10, 1995, pp. A1, A6.

❧ INTRODUCTION

Although we discussed the workings of the foreign exchange market in some depth in Chapter 9, at no point did we mention the international monetary system's role in determining exchange rates. We implicitly assumed currencies were free to float against each other; that is, that a currency's relative value on the foreign exchange market is determined primarily by the impersonal market forces of demand and supply. In turn, we explained, the demand and supply of currencies is influenced by their respective countries' relative inflation rates and interest rates. Only at the end of the chapter in our discussion of currency convertibility did we begin to admit the possibility that the foreign exchange market might not work as we had initially depicted.

Our explanation in Chapter 9 of how exchange rates are determined is oversimplified. Many currencies are *not* free to float against each other. Rather, exchange rates are determined within the context of an international monetary system in which many currencies' ability to float against other currencies is limited by their respective governments or by intergovernmental arrangements. In the opening case, for example, we saw that until December 1994 the value of the Mexican peso was pegged against that of the U.S. dollar. During the early 1990s only 25 of the world's 118 viable currencies were freely floating.[1] The exchange rates of 85 minor currencies were pegged to the exchange rates of particular major currencies—particularly the U.S. dollar and the French franc—or to "baskets" of other currencies. Thus the exchange rates of 25 currencies (including those of Angola, Barbados, Ethiopia, Panama, and Mexico) were pegged to the U.S. dollar's exchange rate. By this means the value of the Mexican peso against major currencies, such as the Japanese yen, was determined by the value of the U.S. dollar against the yen. As the dollar appreciated against the yen in the early 1980s, so did the peso; and as the dollar depreciated against the yen in the 1990s, so did the peso. Other countries have cooperative arrangements that link the values of their currencies. The best known of these is the European Monetary System (EMS) of the European Union (EU).

Against this background, the objective of this chapter is to explain how the international monetary system works and to point out its implications for international business. To understand how the international monetary system works, we must acquire the historical perspective of the system's evolution. We will begin with a discussion of the gold standard and its breakup during the 1930s. Then we will discuss the 1944 Bretton Woods conference, which established the basic framework for the post-World War II international monetary system. The Bretton Woods system called for fixed exchange rates against the U.S. dollar. Under this fixed exchange rate system the value of most currencies in terms of the U.S. dollar was fixed for long periods and allowed to change only under a specific set of circumstances. The Bretton Woods

[1]International Monetary Fund, *International Financial Statistics*, March 1991, p. 22.

conference also created two major international institutions: the International Monetary Fund (IMF) and the World Bank. The IMF, which we encountered in the opening case, was given the task of maintaining order in the international monetary system; the World Bank's was to promote development. Since both of these institutions continue to play a major role in the world economy, we discuss them in some detail.

The Bretton Woods system of fixed exchange rates collapsed in 1973. Since then the world has operated with a managed float system. Under a managed float system some currencies are allowed to float freely, but the majority are either managed in some way by government intervention or pegged to another currency. We will explain the reasons for the failure of the Bretton Woods system as well as the nature of the present managed float system. We will also discuss the European Monetary System (EMS) because of the importance of the European Community in the global economy.

Two decades after the breakdown of the Bretton Woods system, the debate over what kind of exchange rate regime is best for the world continues. Some economists advocate a system in which major currencies are allowed to float against each other. Others argue for a return to a fixed exchange rate regime similar to the one established at Bretton Woods. This debate is intense and important, and we will examine the arguments of both sides.

Finally, we will discuss the implications for international business. The opening case illustrates some implications of exchange rate policy for business practice. Mexico's December 1994 decision to let the peso float freely against the dollar resulted in a 40 percent depreciation in the dollar value of pesos, which undoubtedly hurt companies that were importing cars or car parts from the United States into Mexico. This shows how vulnerable international businesses are to a government's exchange rate policies. At the same time, the case also illustrates how government exchange rate policies can create business opportunities, for in the long run a cheaper peso increases the competitiveness and export potential of Mexican-based auto manufacturing plants.

❧ THE GOLD STANDARD

The gold standard had its origin in the use of gold coins as a medium of exchange, unit of account, and store of value—a practice that stretches back to ancient times. In the days when international trade was limited in volume, payment for goods purchased from another country was typically made in gold or silver. However, as the volume of international trade expanded in the wake of the industrial revolution, a more convenient means of financing international trade was needed. Shipping large quantities of gold and silver around the world to finance international trade seemed impractical. The solution was to arrange for payment in paper currency and for governments to agree to convert the paper currency into gold on demand at a fixed rate.

Nature of the Gold Standard

The practice of pegging currencies to gold and guaranteeing convertibility is known as the gold standard. By 1880 most of the world's major trading nations—including Great Britain, Germany, Japan, and the United States—had adopted the gold standard. Given a common gold standard, the value of any currency in units of any other currency (the exchange rate) was easy to determine.

For example, under the gold standard one U.S. dollar was defined as equivalent to 23.22 grains of "fine" (pure) gold. Thus one could, in theory, demand that the U.S. government convert that one dollar into 23.22 grains of gold. Since there are 480 grains in an ounce, one ounce of gold cost $20.67 (480/23.22). The amount of a currency needed to purchase one ounce of gold was referred to as the gold par value. The British pound was defined as containing 113 grains of fine gold. In other words, one ounce of gold cost £4.25 (480/113). From the gold par values of pounds and dollars, we can calculate what the exchange rate was for converting pounds into dollars; it was £1 = $4.87 (i.e., $20.67/£4.25).

The Strength of the Gold Standard

The great strength claimed for the gold standard was that it contained a powerful mechanism for simultaneously achieving balance-of-trade equilibrium by all countries.[2] A country is said to be in balance-of-trade equilibrium when the income its residents earn from exports is equal to the money its residents pay to people in other countries for imports (i.e., the current account of its balance of payments is in balance).

Suppose there are only two countries in the world, Japan and the United States. Imagine Japan's trade balance is in surplus because it exports more to the United States than it imports from the United States. Japanese exporters are paid in U.S. dollars, which they exchange for Japanese yen at a Japanese bank. In turn the Japanese bank submits the dollars to the U.S. government and demands payment of gold in return. (This is a simplification of what actually would occur, but it will suffice to make our point.)

It follows that under the gold standard, when Japan has a trade surplus there will be a net flow of gold from the United States to Japan. These gold flows automatically reduce the U.S. money supply and swell Japan's money supply. As we saw in Chapter 9, there is a close connection between money supply growth and price inflation. An increase in money supply will raise prices in Japan, while a decrease in the U.S. money supply will push U.S. prices downward. The rise in the price of Japanese goods will decrease demand for these goods, while the fall in the price of U.S. goods will increase demand for these goods. Thus Japan will start to buy more from the United States, and the United States will buy less from Japan, until a balance-of-trade equilibrium is achieved.

This adjustment mechanism seems so simple and attractive that even today, more than half a century after the final collapse of the gold standard, there are people who believe the world should return to a gold standard.

The Period between the Wars, 1918–39

The gold standard worked reasonably well from the 1870s until the start of World War I in 1914, when it was abandoned. During the war several governments financed part of their massive military expenditures by printing money. This resulted in inflation, and by the war's end in 1918, price levels were higher everywhere. The United States returned to the gold standard in 1919, Great Britain in 1925, and France in 1928.

Great Britain returned to the gold standard by pegging the pound to gold at the prewar gold parity level of £4.25 per ounce, despite substantial inflation between 1914 and 1925. This priced British goods out of foreign markets, which pushed the country into a deep depression. When foreign holders of pounds lost confidence in Great Britain's commitment to maintaining its currency's value, they began converting their holdings of pounds into gold. The British government saw that it could not satisfy the demand for gold without seriously depleting its gold reserves, so it suspended convertibility in 1931.

The United States followed suit and left the gold standard in 1933 but returned to it in 1934, raising the dollar price of gold from $20.67 per ounce to $35 per ounce. Since more dollars were needed to buy an ounce of gold than before, the implication was that the dollar was worth less. This effectively amounted to a devaluation of the dollar relative to other currencies. Thus, whereas before the devaluation the pound/dollar exchange rate was £1 = $4.87, after the devaluation it was £1 = $8.24. By reducing the price of U.S. exports and increasing the price of U.S. imports, the government was trying to create employment in the United States by boosting output. However, a number of other countries adopted a similar tactic, and in the cycle of competitive devaluations that soon emerged, no country could win.

---

[2]The argument goes back to 18th century philosopher David Hume. See D. Hume, "On the Balance of Trade," reprinted in *The Gold Standard in Theory and in History*, ed. B. Eichengreen (London: Methuen, 1985).

The net result was the shattering of any remaining confidence in the system. With countries devaluing their currencies at will, one could no longer be certain how much gold a currency could buy. Instead of holding onto another country's currency, people often tried to change it into gold immediately, lest the country devalue its currency in the intervening period. This put pressure on the gold reserves of various countries, forcing them to suspend gold convertibility. As a result, by the start of World War II in 1939, the gold standard was dead.

❧ THE BRETTON WOODS SYSTEM

In 1944, at the height of World War II, representatives from 44 countries met at Bretton Woods, New Hampshire, to design a new international monetary system. With the collapse of the gold standard and the Great Depression of the 1930s fresh in their minds, these statesmen were determined to build an enduring economic order that would facilitate postwar economic growth. There was general consensus that fixed exchange rates were desirable. In addition the conference participants wanted to avoid the senseless competitive devaluations of the 1930s, and they recognized that the gold standard would not assure this. The major problem with the gold standard as previously constituted was that there was no multinational institution that could stop countries from engaging in competitive devaluations.

The agreement reached at Bretton Woods established two multinational institutions—the International Monetary Fund (IMF) and the World Bank. The task of the IMF would be to maintain order in the international monetary system, and that of the World Bank would be to promote general economic development. The Bretton Woods agreement also called for a system of fixed exchange rates that would be policed by the IMF. Under the agreement, all countries were to fix the value of their currency in terms of gold but were not required to exchange their currencies for gold. Only the dollar remained convertible into gold—at a price of $35 per ounce. Each other country decided what it wanted its exchange rate to be vis-à-vis the dollar and then calculated the gold par value of its currency based on that selected dollar exchange rate. All participating countries agreed to try to maintain the value of their currencies within 1 percent of the par value by buying or selling currencies (or gold) as needed. For example, if foreign exchange dealers were selling more of a country's currency than they demanded, the government of that country would intervene in the foreign exchange markets, buying its currency in an attempt to increase demand and maintain its gold par value.

Another aspect of the Bretton Woods agreement was a commitment not to use devaluation as a weapon of competitive trade policy. However, if a currency became too weak to defend, a devaluation of up to 10 percent would be allowed without formal approval by the IMF. Larger devaluations required IMF approval.

The Role of the IMF

The IMF Articles of Agreement were heavily influenced by the inter-war experience of worldwide financial collapse, competitive devaluations, trade wars, high unemployment, hyperinflation in Germany and elsewhere, and general economic disintegration. The aim of the Bretton Woods agreement, of which the IMF was the main custodian, was to try to avoid a repetition of the chaos that occurred between the wars through a combination of discipline and flexibility.

Discipline

A fixed exchange rate regime imposes discipline in two ways. First, the need to maintain a fixed exchange rate puts a brake on the practice of competitive devaluations and brings stability to the world trade environment. Second, a fixed exchange rate regime imposes monetary discipline on countries, thereby curtailing price inflation. For example, consider what would happen under a fixed exchange rate regime if Great Britain rapidly increased its money supply by printing pounds. As explained in Chapter 9, the increase in money supply would lead to price inflation. In turn, given fixed exchange rates, inflation would make British goods uncompetitive in world markets, while the prices of imports would become more attractive in Great Britain. The result would be a widening trade deficit in Great Britain, with the country importing more than it exports. To correct this trade imbalance under a fixed exchange rate regime, Great Britain would be required to restrict the rate of growth in its money supply to bring price inflation back under control. Thus fixed exchange rates are seen as a mechanism for controlling inflation and imposing economic discipline on countries.

Flexibility

Although monetary discipline was a central objective of the Bretton Woods agreement, it was recognized that a rigid policy of fixed exchange rates would be too inflexible. It would probably break down just as the gold standard had. Moreover, in some cases a country's attempts to reduce its money supply growth and correct a persistent balance-of-payments deficit could force the country into recession and create high unemployment. The architects of the Bretton Woods agreement wanted to avoid high unemployment, so they built some limited flexibility into the system. Two major features of the IMF Articles of Agreement fostered this flexibility: IMF lending facilities and adjustable parities.

With regard to lending facilities, the IMF stood ready to lend foreign currencies to members to tide them over during short periods of balance-of-payments deficit, when a rapid tightening of monetary or fiscal policy would harm domestic employment. A pool of gold and currencies contributed by IMF members provided the resources for these lending operations. A persistent balance-of-payments deficit can lead to a depletion of a country's reserves of foreign currency, forcing it to devalue its currency. By providing deficit countries with short-term foreign currency loans, IMF funds would buy countries time in which to bring down their inflation rates and reduce their balance-of-payments deficit. The belief was that such loans would reduce pressures for devaluation and allow for a more orderly and less painful adjustment.

Countries were to be allowed to borrow a limited amount from the IMF without adhering to any specific agreements. However, extensive drawings from IMF funds would require a country to agree to increasingly stringent IMF supervision of its macroeconomic policies. In other words, heavy borrowers from the IMF must agree to conditions concerning monetary and fiscal policy set down by the IMF; these conditions typically include IMF-mandated targets on domestic money supply growth, exchange rate policy, tax policy, government spending, and so on.

The system of adjustable parities allows for the devaluation of a country's currency by more than 10 percent if the IMF agrees the country's balance of payments is in "fundamental disequilibrium." The term *fundamental disequilibrium* was not actually defined in the IMF's Articles of Agreement, but it was intended to apply to countries that have suffered permanent adverse shifts in the demand for their products. Without a devaluation, such a country would experience high unemployment and a persistent trade deficit until the domestic price level had fallen far enough to restore a balance-of-payments equilibrium. The belief was that devaluation could help sidestep a painful adjustment process in such circumstances.

The Role of the World Bank

The official name for the World Bank is the International Bank for Reconstruction and Development (IBRD). When the Bretton Woods participants established the World Bank, the need to reconstruct the war-torn economies of Europe was foremost in their minds. The bank's initial mission was to help finance the building of Europe's economy by providing low-interest loans. As it turned out, the World Bank was overshadowed in this role by the Marshall Plan, under which the United States lent money directly to European nations to help them rebuild. So the bank soon turned its attention to the problem of development and began lending money to the less developed nations of the Third World. In the 1950s the bank concentrated its efforts on public-sector projects. Power station projects, road building, and other transportation investments were much in favor at this time. During the 1960s the bank also began to lend heavily in support of agriculture, education, population control, and urban development.

The bank lends money under two schemes. Under the IBRD scheme, money is raised through bond sales in the international capital market. Borrowers pay what the bank calls a market rate of interest—the bank's cost of funds plus a margin for expenses. This "market" rate is lower than commercial banks' market rate. Under the IBRD scheme the bank offers low-interest loans to risky customers whose credit rating is often poor.

A second scheme is overseen by the International Development Agency (IDA), an arm of the bank created in 1960. Resources to fund IDA loans are raised through subscriptions from wealthy members such as the United States, Japan, and Germany. IDA loans go only to the poorest countries. (In 1991 those were defined as countries with annual incomes per capita of less than $580.) Borrowers have 50 years to repay at an interest rate of 1 percent a year.

✺ THE COLLAPSE OF THE FIXED EXCHANGE RATE SYSTEM

The system of fixed exchange rates established at Bretton Woods worked well until the late 1960s, when it began to show signs of strain. The system finally collapsed in 1973, and since then we have had a managed float system. To understand why the system collapsed, one must appreciate the special role of the U.S. dollar in the system. As the only currency that could be converted into gold, and as the currency that served as the reference point for all others, the dollar occupied a central place in the system. It followed that any pressure on the dollar to devalue could wreak havoc with the system, and that is precisely what occurred.

Most economists trace the breakup of the fixed exchange rate system to the U.S. macroeconomic policy package of 1965–68.[3] To finance both the Vietnam conflict and his welfare programs, President Lyndon Johnson backed an increase in U.S. government spending that was not financed by an increase in taxes. Instead it was financed by an increase in the money supply—which led to a rise in price inflation from less than 4 percent in 1966 to close to 9 percent by 1968 (see Figure 10.1). At the same time the rise in government spending had stimulated the economy. With more money in their pockets, people spent more—particularly on imports—and the U.S. trade balance began to deteriorate rapidly.

The rise in inflation and the worsening of the U.S. foreign trade position gave rise to speculation in the foreign exchange market that the dollar would be devalued. Things came to a head in spring 1971 when U.S. trade figures were released, which showed that for the first time since 1945, the United States was importing more than it was exporting. This set off massive purchases of deutsche marks in the foreign exchange market by speculators who guessed the DM would be revalued against the dollar. On a single day, May 4, 1971, the Bundesbank (Germany's central bank) had to buy $1 billion to hold the dollar/DM exchange rate at its fixed exchange rate given the great demand for DMs. On the morning of May 5, the Bundesbank purchased another $1 billion during the first hour of foreign exchange trading! At that point, the Bundesbank faced the inevitable and allowed its currency to float.

In the weeks following the decision to float the DM, the foreign exchange market became increasingly convinced the dollar would have to be devalued. However, devaluation of the dollar was no easy matter. Under the Bretton Woods provisions, any other country could change its exchange rates against all currencies simply by fixing

---

[3]R. Solomon, *The International Monetary System, 1945–1981* (New York: Harper & Row, 1982).

FIGURE 10.1   U.S. Macroeconomic Data, 1964–72

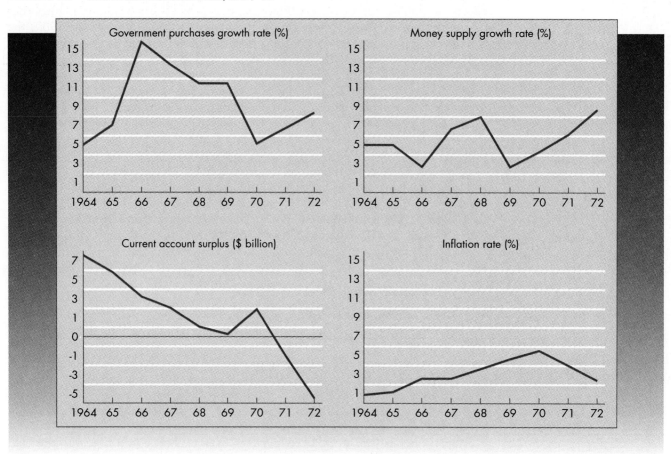

Data: Economic Report of the President, 1985.

its dollar rate at a new level. But as the key currency in the system, the dollar could be devalued only if all countries agreed to simultaneously revalue against the dollar. And many countries did not want this, since it would make their products more expensive relative to U.S. products.

To force the issue, in August 1971 President Richard Nixon announced the dollar was no longer convertible into gold. He also announced a new 10 percent tax on imports would remain in effect until U.S. trading partners agreed to revalue their currencies against the dollar. This brought the trading partners to the bargaining table, and in December 1971 an agreement was reached to devalue the dollar by about 8 percent against foreign currencies. The import tax was then removed.

The problem was not solved, however. The U.S. balance of payments position continued to deteriorate throughout 1972, while the U.S. money supply continued to expand at an inflationary rate (see Figure 10.1). Speculation continued to grow that the dollar was still overvalued and that a second devaluation would be necessary. In anticipation foreign exchange dealers began converting dollars to deutsche marks and other currencies. After a massive wave of speculation in February, which culminated with European central banks spending $3.6 billion on March 1 to try to prevent their currencies from appreciating against the dollar, the foreign exchange market was closed. When the foreign exchange market reopened on March 19, the currencies of Japan and most European countries were floating against the dollar—although many developing countries continued to peg their currency to the dollar, and many still do. At that time the switch to a floating system was viewed as a temporary response to unmanageable speculation in the foreign exchange market. But it is now 25 years since the Bretton Woods system of fixed exchange rates collapsed, and the temporary solution is beginning to look permanent.

It is clear the Bretton Woods system had an Achilles' heel: The system could not work if its key currency, the U.S. dollar, was under speculative attack. The Bretton Woods system could work only as long as the U.S. inflation rate remained low and the United States did not run a balance-of-payments deficit. Once these things occurred, the system soon became strained to the breaking point.

❧ THE FLOATING EXCHANGE RATE REGIME

The floating exchange rate regime that followed the collapse of the fixed exchange rate system was formalized in January 1976 when IMF members met in Jamaica and agreed to the rules for the international monetary system that are in place today. We will discuss the Jamaica agreement before looking at how the floating exchange rate regime has operated.

The Jamaica Agreement

The purpose of the Jamaica meeting was to revise the IMF's Articles of Agreement to reflect the new reality of floating exchange rates. The main elements of the Jamaica agreement included the following:

1. Floating rates were declared acceptable. IMF members were permitted to enter the foreign exchange market to even out "unwarranted" speculative fluctuations.
2. Gold was abandoned as a reserve asset. The IMF returned its gold reserves to members at the current market price, placing the proceeds in a trust fund to help poor nations. IMF members were permitted to sell their own gold reserves at the market price.
3. Total annual IMF quotas—the amount member-countries contribute to the IMF—were increased to $41 billion. Since then they have been increased to $180 billion. Non-oil-exporting, less developed countries were given greater access to IMF funds.

After Jamaica, the IMF continued its role of helping countries cope with macroeconomic and exchange rate problems, albeit within the context of a radically different exchange rate regime. However, as we shall see, the IMF's role has expanded over the past 25 years, and this has led to a debate about the future of the twin pillars of Bretton Woods—the IMF and the World Bank.

Exchange Rates since 1973

Since March 1973 exchange rates have become much more volatile and far less predictable than they were between 1945 and 1973. This volatility has been partly due to a number of unexpected shocks to the world monetary system, including:

1. The oil crisis in 1971, when OPEC quadrupled the price of oil. The harmful effect of this on the U.S. inflation rate and trade position resulted in a further decline in the value of the dollar.
2. The loss of confidence in the dollar that followed the rise of U.S. inflation in 1977 and 1978.
3. The oil crisis of 1979, when OPEC once again increased the price of oil dramatically; this time it was doubled.
4. The unexpected rise in the dollar between 1980 and 1985, despite a worsening balance-of-payments picture.
5. The rapid fall of the U.S. dollar against the Japanese yen and German mark between 1985 and 1987, and against the yen between 1993 and 1995.

FIGURE 10.2
U.S. Dollar Movements,
1970–94

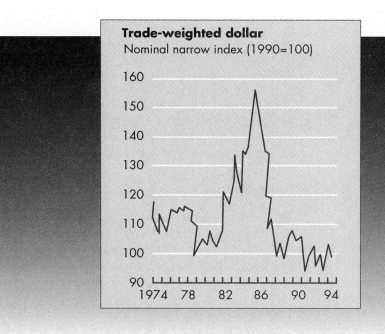

Trade-weighted dollar
Nominal narrow index (1990=100)

Source; Morgan Guaranty, World Financial Markets, various issues.

Figure 10.2 summarizes the volatility of the U.S. dollar in the 1973–94 period. The Morgan Guaranty Index, the basis for Figure 10.2, represents the exchange rate of the U.S. dollar against a weighted basket of the currencies of 15 other industrial countries. As can be seen, the index was as low as 92 (in 1989) and as high as 158 (in 1985) in the 1973–94 period (1990 = 100).

Two of the most interesting phenomena in Figure 10.2 are the rapid rise in the value of the dollar between 1980 and 1985 and its even more rapid fall between 1985 and 1988. These phenomena tell us something about how the international monetary system has operated in recent years.[4]

The rise in the value of the dollar between 1980 and 1985 is particularly interesting because it occurred when the United States was running a large and growing trade deficit, importing substantially more than it exported. Conventional wisdom would suggest that the increased supply of dollars in the foreign exchange market as a result of the deficit should lead to a reduction in the value of the dollar, but it increased in value. Why? A number of favorable factors temporarily overcame the unfavorable effect of a trade deficit. Strong economic growth in the United States attracted heavy inflows of capital from foreign investors seeking high returns on capital assets. Moreover, high real interest rates attracted foreign investors seeking high returns on financial assets. At the same time, political turmoil in other parts of the world, along with relatively slow economic growth in the developed countries of Europe, helped create the view that the United States was a good place to invest. These inflows of capital increased the demand for dollars in the foreign exchange market, which pushed the value of the dollar upward against other currencies.

The fall in the value of the dollar between 1985 and 1988 was caused by a combination of government intervention and market forces. The rise in the dollar, which priced U.S. goods out of foreign markets and made imports relatively cheap, had contributed to a dismal trade picture. In 1985 the United States

---

[4]For an extended discussion of the dollar exchange rate in the 1980s, see B. D. Pauls, "U.S. Exchange Rate Policy: Bretton Woods to the Present," *Federal Reserve Bulletin*, November 1990, pp. 891–908.

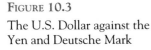

FIGURE 10.3

The U.S. Dollar against the
Yen and Deutsche Mark

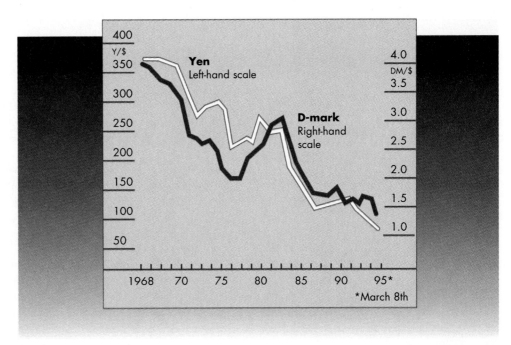

Source: IMF.

posted a record-high trade deficit of over $160 billion. This led to protectionist pressure in the United States. Against this background, in September 1985 the finance ministers and central bank governors of the so-called Group of Five major industrial countries (Great Britain, France, Japan, Germany, and the United States) met at the Plaza Hotel in New York and reached what was later referred to as the Plaza Accord. They announced it would be desirable for most major currencies to appreciate vis-à-vis the U.S. dollar and pledged to intervene in the foreign exchange markets, selling dollars, to encourage this objective. The dollar had already begun to weaken in the summer of 1985, and this announcement further accelerated the decline.

The dollar continued to decline until early 1987. In fact the governments of the Group of Five began to worry that the dollar might decline too far. In response, in February 1987 the finance ministers of the Group of Five met again, in Paris, and reached a new agreement known as the Louvre Accord. They agreed that exchange rates had been realigned sufficiently and pledged to support the stability of exchange rates around their current levels by intervening in the foreign exchange markets when necessary to buy and sell currency. Although the dollar continued to decline for a few months after the Louvre Accord, the rate of decline slowed, and by early 1988 the decline had ended.

Except for a brief speculative flurry around the time of the Persian Gulf War in 1991, the dollar has been relatively stable since then against most major currencies. However, the dollar has continued to slide against the Japanese yen, and to a lesser extent the German mark (see Figure 10.3). According to many observers, the decline in the value of the dollar against these currencies is less a reflection of any inherent weakness in the dollar as it is a confirmation of the unusual strength of these two currencies, and particularly that of the yen.[5] The yen situation is discussed in more detail in the next "Country Focus."

---

[5]S. Hansell, "A Currency Dragged Down by Twin Deficits," *New York Times,* June 23, 1994, p. C3; and "The Dollar's Slide Show," *The Economist,* July 16, 1994, p. 74.

COUNTRY FOCUS
Japan's Soaring Yen

In 1971, before the collapse of the Bretton Woods system of fixed exchange rates, one U.S. dollar purchased 350 Japanese yen. In 1985 the exchange rate was $1 = ¥250; in 1990 it stood at $1 = ¥150; in 1993 it was $1 = ¥125; by March 1995 the exchange rate stood at $1 = ¥85. Much of the decline in the value of the dollar against the yen between 1971 and 1995 can be explained by differences in relative inflation rates. Between 1983 and 1989, for example, inflation in Japan averaged 1.1 percent per annum, whereas U.S. price inflation ran at an average annual rate of 3.6 percent. Similarly, between 1988 and 1993 inflation in Japan ran at an average annual rate of 2 percent, compared to 4.1 percent in the United States.

However, between 1993 and early 1995 the yen appreciated by 50 percent against the dollar. On a purchasing power parity basis, by mid-1995 the yen looked to be overvalued against the dollar by about 30 percent. This overvaluation suggested that differences in U.S. and Japanese inflation rates were not sufficient to explain the rise of the yen during this period.

One explanation for the dramatic rise in the dollar value of the yen between 1993 and 1995 can be found in the recent behavior of Japanese investment institutions (particularly banks and insurance companies). Japan has long run a large trade surplus with the United States. One consequence of this surplus is that many Japanese companies have found themselves holding lots of dollars (earned from the sale of products to U.S. consumers). During the 1980s Japanese financial institutions helped recycle these dollars by purchasing them from Japanese companies and reinvesting them in U.S. stocks and bonds.

So long as Japanese financial institutions reinvested dollars in the

---

Thus we see that in recent history the value of the dollar has been determined by both market forces and government intervention. Under a floating exchange rate regime, market forces have produced a volatile dollar exchange rate. Governments have responded by intervening in the market—buying and selling dollars—in attempting to limit the market's volatility and to correct what they see as overvaluation (in 1985) or potential undervaluation (in 1987) of the dollar. The frequency of government intervention in the foreign exchange markets explains why the current system is variously referred to as a managed float system or a dirty float system.

✺ FIXED VERSUS FLOATING EXCHANGE RATES

The breakdown of the Bretton Woods system has not stopped the debate about the relative merits of fixed versus floating exchange rate regimes. Disappointment with the system of floating rates in recent years has led to renewed debate about the merits of a fixed exchange rate system. In this section we review the arguments for fixed and floating exchange rate regimes.[6] In the next we will discuss the European Monetary System's exchange rate mechanism, which many see as a prototype for a future

---

[6]For a feel for the issues contained in this debate, see P. Krugman, *Has the Adjustment Process Worked?* (Institute for International Economics, 1991); "Time to Tether Currencies," *The Economist*, January 6, 1990, pp. 15–16; P. R. Krugman and M. Obstfeld, *International Economics: Theory and Policy* (New York: Harper Collins, 1994); and J. Shelton, *Money Meltdown* (New York: Free Press, 1994).

United States, as opposed to selling them for yen, the dollar/yen exchange rate was relatively stable. However, in the early 1990s Japan entered its worst recession since 1945. The severity of this recession was compounded by a collapse in Japanese stock and property prices, both of which fell by over 50 percent. This deflation hit Japanese financial institutions hard. Most Japanese financial institutions held many of their assets in the form of Japanese stock and property investments. With stock and property prices plunging, Japanese financial institutions saw their balance sheets deteriorate. Their weak balance sheets reduced the appetite of the financial institutions for risky investments, so they reduced their purchases of U.S. assets and instead increased their investments in Japanese government bonds. In short the financial institutions stopped recycling dollars earned from exports back to the United States. From 1993 onward they changed many of these dollars into yen and reinvested them in Japan. To make matters worse, many financial institutions started liquidating their holdings of U.S. stocks and bonds to increase the funds available for investment in low-risk Japanese government bonds. Thus, after having doubled the value of their U.S. investments in the two years prior to 1989, Japanese financial institutions reduced their foreign assets by 20 percent over the next four years.

The net effect of these developments was to reduce the demand for dollars and increase the demand for yen; hence the appreciation of the yen against the dollar. As the value of the yen accelerated in 1993, so U.S. assets began to look even less attractive (their valuation in yen declined). This only increased the reluctance of Japanese institutions to invest in U.S. stocks and bonds. Thus by 1995 a self-fulfilling bandwagon effect had led to a massive rise in the value of the yen as Japanese investors held back from investing in U.S. assets lest they see the value of those assets reduced by a subsequent appreciation in the value of the yen.

The appreciation in the value of the yen has been a major blow for export-oriented Japanese companies. They have seen prices and profit margins on exports to the U.S. squeezed relentlessly as the yen has climbed to new highs. The situation will persist either until Japanese goods are priced out of foreign markets, at which point Japan's huge trade surplus will disappear, or until Japanese financial institutions start reinvesting in U.S. stocks and bonds.

Sources: S. Brittan, "Tragi-comedy of the Rising Yen," *Financial Times*, March 3, 1994, p. 16; G. Baker, "Stay at Home Investors Drive the Yen's Rise," *Financial Times*, April 21, 1995, p. 5; and "Dial C for Chaos," *The Economist*, March 11, 1995, pp. 69–70.

fixed exchange rate system. We will discuss the case for floating rates before discussing why many commentators are disappointed with the experience under floating exchange rates and yearn for reform to a system of fixed rates.

The Case for Floating Exchange Rates

The case for floating exchange rates has two main elements: monetary policy autonomy and automatic trade balance adjustments.

Monetary Policy Autonomy

It is argued that a floating exchange rate regime gives countries monetary policy autonomy. Under a fixed system, a country's ability to expand or contract its money supply as it sees fit is limited by the need to maintain exchange rate parity. Monetary expansion can lead to inflation, which puts downward pressure on a fixed exchange rate (as predicted by PPP theory; see Chapter 9). Similarly monetary contraction requires high interest rates (to reduce the demand for money). Higher interest rates lead to an inflow of money from abroad, which puts upward pressure on a fixed exchange rate. Thus, to maintain exchange rate parity under a fixed system, countries are limited in their ability to use monetary policy to expand or contract their economies.

Advocates of a floating exchange rate regime argue that removal of the obligation to maintain exchange rate parity would restore monetary control to a government. If a government faced with unemployment wanted to increase its money supply to stimulate domestic demand and reduce unemployment, it could do so unencumbered by the need to maintain its exchange rate. While monetary expansion might lead to inflation, this in turn would lead to a depreciation in the country's currency. If PPP theory is correct, the resulting currency depreciation on the foreign exchange markets should offset the effects of inflation. Put another way, although under a floating exchange rate regime domestic inflation would have an impact on the exchange rate, it should have no impact on the country's businesses' international cost competitiveness due to exchange rate depreciation. The rise in domestic costs should be exactly offset by the fall in the value of the country's currency on the foreign exchange markets. Similarly a government could use monetary policy to contract the economy without worrying about the need to maintain parity.

Trade balance adjustments

Under the Bretton Woods system, if a country developed a permanent deficit in its balance of trade (importing more than it exported) that could not be corrected by domestic policy, this would require the IMF to agree to a currency devaluation. Critics of this system argue that the adjustment mechanism works much more smoothly under a floating exchange rate regime. They argue that if a country is running a trade deficit, the imbalance between the supply and demand of that country's currency in the foreign exchange markets (supply exceeding demand) will lead to depreciation in its exchange rate. By making its exports cheaper and its imports more expensive, an exchange rate depreciation should ultimately correct the trade deficit.

The Case for Fixed Exchange Rates

The case for fixed exchange rates rests on arguments about monetary discipline, speculation, uncertainty, and the lack of connection between the trade balance and exchange rates.

Monetary discipline

We have already discussed the nature of monetary discipline inherent in a fixed exchange rate system when we discussed the form of the Bretton Woods system. The need to maintain a fixed exchange rate parity ensures that governments do not expand their money supplies at inflationary rates. While advocates of floating rates argue that each country should be allowed to choose its own inflation rate (the monetary autonomy argument), advocates of fixed rates argue that governments too often give in to political pressures and expand the monetary supply far too rapidly, causing unacceptably high price inflation. A fixed exchange rate regime would ensure that this does not occur.

Speculation

Critics of a floating exchange rate regime also argue that speculation can cause fluctuations in exchange rates. They point to the dollar's rapid rise and fall during the 1980s, which they claim had nothing to do with comparative inflation rates and the U.S. trade deficit, but everything to do with speculation. They argue that if foreign exchange dealers see a currency depreciating, they tend to sell the currency in the expectation of future depreciation regardless of the currency's longer-term prospects. As more traders jump on the bandwagon, the expectations of depreciation are realized. Such destabilizing speculation tends to accentuate the fluctuations around the exchange rate's long-run value. It can be very damaging to a country's economy by distorting export and import prices. (For example, in 1985 U.S. exports may have been overpriced and imported goods underpriced due to the very high value of the dollar.) Thus advocates of a fixed exchange rate regime argue that such a system will limit the destabilizing effects of speculation.

Uncertainty

Speculation also adds to the uncertainty surrounding future currency movements that characterizes floating exchange rate regimes. The unpredictability of exchange rate movements in the post-Bretton Woods era has made business planning difficult and it makes exporting, importing, and foreign investment risky activities. Given a volatile exchange rate, international businesses do not know how to react to the changes—and often they do not react. Why change plans for exporting, importing, or foreign investment after a 6 percent fall in the dollar this month, when the dollar may rise 6 percent next month? This uncertainty, according to the critics, hinders the growth of international trade and investment. They argue that a fixed exchange rate, by eliminating such uncertainty, promotes the growth of international trade and investment. Advocates of a floating system reply that the forward exchange market does a good job of insuring against the risks associated with exchange rate fluctuations (see Chapter 9). Accordingly the adverse impact of uncertainty on the growth of international trade and investment has been overstated.

Trade balance adjustments
Those in favor of floating exchange rates argue that floating rates help adjust trade imbalances. Critics question the closeness of the link between the exchange rate and the trade balance. They claim trade deficits are determined by the balance between savings and investment in a country, not by the external value of its currency.[7] Moreover, they argue that a depreciation in a currency will lead to inflation (due to the resulting increase in import prices). This inflation will wipe out any apparent gains in cost competitiveness that come from currency depreciation. In other words, a depreciating exchange rate will not boost exports and reduce imports, as advocates of floating rates claim; it will simply boost price inflation. In support of this argument, those who favor fixed rates point out that the 40 percent drop in the value of the dollar between 1985 and 1988 did not seem to correct the U.S. trade deficit. In reply, advocates of a floating exchange rate regime argue that between 1985 and 1992, the U.S. trade deficit fell from over $160 billion to around $70 billion, and they attribute this in part to the decline in the value of the dollar.

Who Is Right?

Today we see a vigorous debate between those who favor a fixed exchange rate regime and those who favor a floating exchange rate regime. Which side is right? At this point we don't know. From a business perspective, this is unfortunate, since as a major player on the international trade and investment scene, business has a large stake in the resolution of the debate. Would international business be better off under a fixed regime, or are flexible rates better? The evidence is not yet in.

We do, however, know that a fixed exchange rate regime modeled along the lines of the Bretton Woods system will not work. Speculation ultimately broke the system—a phenomenon that advocates of fixed rate regimes claim is associated with floating exchange rates! Nevertheless a different kind of fixed exchange rate system might be more enduring and might foster the kind of stability that would facilitate more rapid growth in international trade and investment. In the next section we look at a potential model for such a system, and the problems with such a system, when we discuss the exchange rate mechanism of the European Monetary System.

❧ THE EUROPEAN MONETARY SYSTEM

In our discussion of the European Union (EU) in Chapter 8, we noted that the EU is committed to establishing a single currency by January 1, 1999 (although the feasibility of this is in doubt).[8] A formal commitment to a common currency dates back

---

[7]The argument is made by several prominent economists, particularly Stanford's Robert McKinnon. See R. McKinnon, "An International Standard for Monetary Stabilization," *Policy Analyses in International Economics* 8 (Washington, DC: Institute for International Economics, 1984). The details of this argument are beyond the scope of this book. For a relatively accessible exposition, see P. Krugman, *The Age of Diminished Expectations* (Cambridge, MA: MIT Press, 1990).

[8]In fact for a time the plan was to introduce a common currency by 1997, but in July 1995 this was changed for good until 1999, and many think this date cannot be attained. L. Barber, "EU Leaders Plan 1999 Launch Date of Single Currency," *Financial Times*, June 27, 1995, p. 1.

only to the Treaty of Maastricht in December 1991, but it has been an underlying theme in the EU and a subject of debate for some time. If the EU is ever going to have a common currency, it must first achieve convergence between the inflation rates and interest rates of its 15 member-states. The European Monetary System (EMS) is viewed as a mechanism for attaining this goal.[9] As we will see, however, in late 1992 the EMS was strained to the breaking point by waves of speculative pressure that cast doubt over the future of the system and resulted in its modification.

When the EMS was created in March 1979, it was entrusted with three main objectives:

1. To create a zone of monetary stability in Europe (by reducing exchange rate volatility and converging national interest rates).
2. To control inflation through the imposition of monetary discipline.
3. To coordinate exchange rate policies versus non-EU currencies such as the U.S. dollar and the yen.

To these objectives can now be added paving the way for introduction of a common currency in 1999. Two instruments are being used to achieve these objectives, the European currency unit (ecu) and the exchange rate mechanism (ERM).

The Ecu and the ERM, 1979–92

The ecu is a "basket" of the EU currencies that serves as the unit of account for the EMS. One ecu comprises defined percentages of national currencies. The share of each country's currency in the ecu depends on the country's relative economic weight within the EU. Thus, for example, 30.1 percent of the ecu's value was established by the value of the deutsche mark in 1989, because that was the estimate of Germany's relative strength and size within the EU economy at the time.

Until 1992 the exchange rate mechanism (ERM) worked as follows: Each national currency in the EU was given a "central rate" vis-à-vis the ecu. For example, in September 1989 one ecu was equal to DM2.05853, to FFr6.90404, or to £0.739615. This central rate could be changed only by a commonly agreed realignment (which has occurred 11 times since the inception of the system). From these central rates flowed a series of bilateral rates—the French franc against the Italian lira, the German deutsche mark against the British pound, and so on. For example, the given figures vis-à-vis the ecu indicate the bilateral rate for exchanging deutsche marks into francs was DM1 = FFr2.9586 (i.e., FFr6.90404/DM2.05853). The bilateral rates formed a cat's cradle known as the ERM parity grid, which was the system's operational component. Before 1992 the rule was that a currency must not depart by more than 2.25 percent from its bilateral central rate with another ERM participating currency.

Intervention in the foreign exchange markets was compulsory whenever one currency hit its outer margin of fluctuation relative to another. The central banks of the countries issuing both currencies were supposed to intervene to keep their currencies within the 2.25 percent band. The central bank of the country with the stronger currency was supposed to buy the weaker currency, and vice versa. In practice, however, it tends to be left to the country with the weaker currency to act.

To defend its currency against speculative pressure, each member-state could borrow almost unlimited amounts of foreign currency from other members for up to three months. A second line of defense included loans that could be extended for up to nine months, but the total amount available was limited to a pool of credit—originally about 14 billion ecus—and the size of the member's quota in the pool. Additional funds were available for maturities from two to five years from a second pool of about 11 billion ecus (originally). However, as a condition of using these funds, the borrowing member had to commit itself to correcting the economic policies causing its currency to deviate.

---

[9]N. Colchester and D. Buchan, *Europower* (New York: Random House, 1990); and D. Swann, *The Economics of the Common Market* (London: Penguin Books, 1990).

The Performance of the System, 1979–92	Underlying the ERM are all the standard beliefs about the virtues of fixed rate regimes that we have discussed. EU members believe the system imposes monetary discipline, removes uncertainty, limits speculation, and promotes international trade and investment within the EU. For most of the EMS's existence, its ability to achieve these objectives has been fairly good. When the ERM was first established, wide variations in national interest rates and inflation rates made its prospects seem shaky. For example, in early 1979 inflation was running at 2.7 percent in Germany and 12.1 percent in Italy. By 1992, however, both inflation rates and interest rates had converged somewhat. As this occurred, the need for intervention and realignments declined, and the system appeared to become more stable.

However, there had long been concern within the EU about the dominance of the German deutsche mark within the ERM and about the vulnerability of a fixed system to speculative pressures. Many of these concerns were realized dramatically in September 1992 when two of the major EMS currencies—the British pound and the Italian lira—were hit by waves of speculative pressure. Dealers in the foreign exchange market, believing a realignment of the pound and the lira within the ERM was imminent, started to sell pounds and lira and to purchase deutsche marks. This led to a fall in the value of the pound and the lira against the mark on the foreign exchange markets. Although the central banks of Great Britain and Italy tried to defend their currencies by raising interest rates and buying back pounds and lira, they were unable to keep the values of their currencies within their respective ERM bands. As a consequence, first Great Britain and then Italy pulled out of the ERM, leaving the EMS teetering on the brink of collapse. (For further details on what happened in September 1992, see the case "Chaos in the Currency Markets," which follows Chapter 11.)

The EMS after 1992	The speculative pressures and subsequent withdrawal of Britain and Italy from the ERM led the EU countries to make two major changes to the EMS in August 1993. First, the 2.25 percent fluctuation bands were widened to 15 percent. The idea was to loosen the rigidities in the system and hence reduce the scope for speculation. Second, the EMS no longer obligates the central banks of countries with strong currencies to intervene in the foreign exchange market to purchase weaker currencies. This change essentially recognized what had already occurred. In the crisis of September 1992, for example, the German central bank did not intervene aggressively to help keep the value of the British pound within the prescribed fluctuation bands.[10]

Since 1993 this modified system has again performed fairly well. The biggest strain occurred in March 1995 when speculative pressures again forced devaluations of two EMS currencies, this time the Spanish pesta and Portuguese escudo. Nevertheless this was a relatively minor crisis compared with that of September 1992.[11] However, Britain and Italy have still not reentered the EMS. This has damaged the credibility of the system as a route to monetary union and a single EU currency. In addition the ability of speculative pressures in both 1992 and 1995 to strain the system demonstrates once again a limitation of a fixed exchange rate regime—its vulnerability to breakdown under speculative pressure on the foreign exchange market.

❧ THE IMF AND WORLD BANK AFTER BRETTON WOODS

The collapse of the Bretton Woods system left the IMF with a diminished role in the international monetary system. Recall that the IMF's original function was to provide a pool of money from which members could borrow, short term, to adjust their balance-of-payments position and maintain their exchange rate. Under a floating exchange rate regime, the demand for short-term loans was diminished. A trade

---

[10]M. Wolf, "Ecu May Not Be Dead After All" *Financial Times*, August 1, 1994, p. 13.

[11]P. Norman, "A Test for the ERM and a Warning for the Emu," *Financial Times*, March 7, 1995, p. 2.

deficit would presumably lead to a decline in a country's exchange rate, which in turn would help reduce imports and boost exports. No temporary IMF adjustment loan would be needed. Consistent with this, most industrialized countries developed a tendency to let the foreign exchange market determine exchange rates in response to demand and supply. No major industrial country has borrowed funds from the IMF since the mid-1970s, when Great Britain and Italy did. Moreover since the early 1970s the rapid development of global capital markets has allowed developed countries such as Great Britain and the United States to finance their deficits by borrowing private money, as opposed to drawing on IMF funds.

In response to these changes, the IMF has done what any bureaucracy interested in self-preservation might do; it found a new mission. This new mission was inspired by the OPEC oil price hikes of 1973 and 1979 and the resulting Third World debt crisis.

The Third World Debt Crisis[12]

The OPEC oil price increases in 1973 and 1979 resulted in massive flows of funds from the major oil-importing nations (e.g., Germany, Japan, and the United States) to the oil-producing nations of OPEC. Never slow to spot a profit opportunity, commercial banks quickly stepped in to recycle this money—borrowing from OPEC countries and lending to governments and businesses around the world. Much of the recycled money—too much, as it turned out—ended up in the form of loans to the governments of various Latin American and African nations. These loans were made on the basis of optimistic assessments about these nations' short- and medium-term growth prospects, which did not materialize. Rather, Third World economic growth was choked off in the early 1980s by a combination of factors, including:

- Rising short-term interest rates worldwide (which increased the costs of debt).
- Poor macroeconomic management in a number of Third World countries, in particular, inflationary growth policies.
- Poor use of the funds borrowed by Third World governments (to finance consumption rather than investment).
- A slowdown in the growth rate of the industrialized West, the main markets for Third World products.

The consequence was a Third World debt crisis of massive proportions. At one point it was calculated that commercial banks had over $1 trillion of bad debts on their books, debts that the debtor nations had no hope of repaying. If any major country had defaulted at this time, the shock waves would have shaken the world financial system. Many feared that if this were to occur, the resulting bank failures in the advanced nations would turn the widespread recession of the 1980s into a deep depression.

Against this background, Mexico, long thought to be the most creditworthy of the major Third World debtor countries, announced in 1982 that it could no longer service its $80 billion in international debt without an immediate new loan of $3 billion. Brazil quickly followed, revealing it could not meet the required payments on its borrowed $87 billion. Then Argentina and several dozen other countries of lesser credit standings followed suit. The international monetary system was facing a crisis of enormous dimensions.

From the IMF Solution to the Brady Plan

Into the breach stepped the IMF. Together with several Western governments, particularly that of the United States, the IMF emerged as the key player in resolving the debt crisis. The deal with Mexico involved three elements:

1. Rescheduling of Mexico's old debt.
2. New loans to Mexico from the IMF, the World Bank, and commercial banks.

---

[12]For details see A. J. Schwartz, "International Debt: What's Fact and What's Fiction," *Economic Inquiry* 27 (January 1989), pp. 1–19; and "What Happens to the IMF when a Whole Nation Calls on It?" *The Economist*, December 11, 1982, pp. 69–80.

3. The Mexican government's agreement to abide by a set of IMF-dictated macroeconomic prescriptions for its economy, including tight control over the growth of the money supply and major cuts in government spending.

Orchestrating this agreement required the IMF to persuade approximately 1,600 commercial banks that had already lent money to Mexico to increase the amount of their loans by 8 percent. The IMF's success in pulling this off, first for Mexico and later for other debt-ridden Third World countries, was no small achievement.

However, the IMF's solution to the debt crisis contained a major weakness: It depended on the rapid resumption of growth in the debtor nations. If this occurred, their capacity to repay debt would grow faster than their debt itself, and the crisis would be resolved. By the mid-1980s, it was clear this was not going to happen. The IMF-imposed macroeconomic policies did bring the trade deficits and inflation rates of many debtor nations under control, but it was at the price of sharp contractions in their economic growth rates.

By 1989 it was obvious that the debt problem was not going to be solved merely by rescheduling debt. In April of that year, the IMF endorsed a new approach that had first been proposed by Nicholas Brady, the U.S. Treasury secretary. The Brady Plan, as it became known, stated that debt reduction—as distinguished from debt rescheduling—was a necessary part of the solution and the IMF and World Bank would assume roles in financing it. The essence of the plan was that the IMF, the World Bank, and the Japanese government would each contribute $10 billion to the task of debt reduction. To gain access to these funds, a debtor nation would once again have to submit to a set of imposed conditions for macroeconomic policy management and debt repayment. The first application of the Brady Plan was the Mexican debt reduction of 1989. The deal, which reduced Mexico's 1989 debt of $107 billion by about $15 billion, has been widely regarded as a success.[13]

The Future of the IMF and the World Bank[14]

One consequence of the IMF's involvement in resolving the Third World debt crisis is the blurring of the line between it and the World Bank. Under the original Bretton Woods agreement, the IMF was to provide short-term loans, and the World Bank was to provide long-term loans. Since the 1970s, however, the IMF has been increasingly involved in providing long-term loans to debt-ridden nations. According to one estimate, some 20 of these countries have been continuous users of IMF credit for more than 12 years.

The evolution of the IMF into a long-term lending and development agency looks set to continue. The collapse of communism in Eastern Europe and the subsequent breakup of the Soviet Union has resulted in a flood of applications for IMF membership from the newly democratic nations there, including Russia. No doubt, given the problems associated with transforming their centrally planned economies into market economies, many of these potential new members will be calling on the IMF for long-term loans. As of 1995 both Russia and the Ukraine had become major recipients of IMF loans. The IMF is playing a major role in both countries, helping them to achieve the transformation from state planning to a market economic system.

Not only is the IMF moving closer to the World Bank, but the World Bank has also been moving closer to the IMF since the 1970s. During the 1970s the bank noticed that many of its specific loan projects—such as those for irrigation, energy, and transportation projects—were failing to produce the kind of long-term economic gains for the borrowing countries that the bank's officials had predicted. On closer examination, the bank found that many of its projects were undermined not by

---

[13]For a summary of the arguments for debt reductions, see "And Forgive Us Our Debts: A Survey of the IMF and the World Bank" *The Economist*, October 12, 1991, pp. 23–33; and Krugman, *Diminished Expectations*.

[14]See J. Sachs, "Beyond Bretton Woods: A New Blueprint," *The Economist*, October 1944, pp. 23–27, and M. Wolf, "Bretton Twins at an Awkward Age," *Financial Times*, October 7, 1994, p. 17.

defects in their design but by the broader policy environment of the particular country. The bank found that the returns on its loan projects were much lower in countries where growth was limited by a poor macroeconomic policy. A good project in a bad economy was likely to be a bad project. It was obvious that loan conditions needed to extend beyond the project to the economy as a whole.

The World Bank has devised a new type of loan in response. In addition to providing funds to support specific projects, the bank will now also provide loans for the government of a nation to use as it sees fit in return for promises on macroeconomic policy. This is essentially the same approach as the IMF's in recent years. As we have seen, the IMF has lent money to debtor nations in return for promises about macroeconomic policy. Now the World Bank is doing the same thing.

The convergence between the World Bank and the IMF points to the possibility of a merger between the IMF and the bank sometime in the future. Since these two institutions are now doing each other's jobs, the argument for merging them is compelling. At present though, both institutions are so busy with their new commitments in Eastern Europe that they would not have time for a merger. As one commentator put it, "This is not the time to sap the institutions' energies with grandiose schemes of reform. But a merger makes sense, and in time it will happen."[15]

The evolution of global capital markets has also raised questions about the role of the IMF and the World Bank. In 1944 the global capital market hardly existed. As we shall see in Chapter 11, by 1990 it was channeling immense flows of money around the world every day. Before the emergence of a global capital market there was arguably a strong need for lending institutions such as the World Bank and the IMF to channel funds to poorer nations. Now critics argue that with the exception of emergencies such as a debt crisis, the capital market should perhaps decide which governments are worth lending to and which are not. Put another way, do we need the IMF and the World Bank? There is significant debate over this issue.

IMPLICATIONS FOR BUSINESS

The implications of the material discussed in this chapter for international businesses fall into three main areas: currency management, business strategy, and corporate–government relations.

Currency Management

An obvious implication with regard to currency management is that companies must recognize that the foreign exchange market does not work quite as depicted in Chapter 9. The current system is a managed float system in which government intervention can help drive the foreign exchange market (e.g., as in the cases of the Plaza Accord and the Louvre Accord). Companies engaged in significant foreign exchange activities need to be aware of this and to adjust their foreign exchange transactions accordingly. For example, the currency management unit of Caterpillar Tractor claims it made millions of dollars in the hours following the announcement of the Plaza Accord by selling dollars and buying currencies that it expected to appreciate on the foreign exchange market following government intervention.

A second message contained in this chapter is that under the present system, speculative buying and selling of currencies can create very volatile movements in exchange rates (as exhibited by the rise and fall of the dollar during the 1980s). Moreover, contrary to the predictions of the purchasing power parity theory (see Chapter 9), we have seen that exchange rate movements during the 1980s, at least with regard to the dollar, did not seem to be strongly influenced by relative inflation rates. Insofar as volatile exchange rates increase foreign exchange risk, this is not good news for business. On the other hand, as we saw in Chapter 9, the foreign exchange market has developed a number of instruments, such as the forward market and swaps, that can help to insure against foreign exchange risk. Not surprisingly, use of these instruments has increased markedly since the breakdown of the Bretton Woods system in 1973.

---

[15]"Prelude to Testing Time: A Survey of the IMF and the World Bank," *The Economist*, October 12, 1991, p. 48.

MANAGEMENT FOCUS
Daimler-Benz Suffers from a Strong Mark

In June 1995 the German auto and aerospace company Daimler-Benz, stunned the German business community when it announced it expected to post a severe loss in 1995 of around $720 million. The cause was Germany's strong currency, which had appreciated by 4 percent against a basket of major currencies since the beginning of 1995 and had risen by over 30 percent against the U.S. dollar since late 1994. By mid-1995 the exchange rate against the dollar stood at $1 = DM1.38. Daimler's management reckons it cannot make money with an exchange rate under $1 = DM1.60.

The main problem seemed to be in Daimler's aerospace division, DASA, which accounted for about 20 percent of the group's total sales, although its Mercedes-Benz automobile division was feeling some pain too. DASA receives 74 percent of its income in dollars (airplanes are priced in U.S. dollars), but only 27 percent of its costs are in dollars. This means an appreciation of the mark against the dollar hits DASA particularly hard. The primary reason for DASA's high cost structure is that the bulk of its production is still concentrated in Germany. The Mercedes-Benz division is also suffering from a lack of foreign production. Currently Mercedes-Benz produces only 2 percent of its cars outside of Germany, and yet exports, particularly to the United States, account for 15 percent of Mercedes sales. The strong mark pushed up the price of these exports and made them increasingly uncompetitive.

Daimler's senior managers have concluded that the appreciation of the mark against the dollar is probably permanent. Their strategy for dealing with this problem is to move substantial production outside of Germany and to increase purchasing of foreign components. This will reduce the vulnerability of the company to future exchange rate movements. The Mercedes-Benz division has already made plans for such a move. Mercedes intends to be producing 10 percent of its cars outside of Germany by 2000, mostly in the United States. As for DASA, industry analysts calculate that to become competitive this division will have to cut employment by 20,000 and move substantial productive activities to lower-cost locations outside of Germany.

Sources: P. Gumbel and B. Coleman, "Daimler Warns of Severe 95 Loss Due to Strong Mark, " *New York Times*, June 29, 1995, pp. 1, 10; and M. Wolf, "Daimler-Benz Announces Major Losses," *Financial Times*, June 29, 1995, p. 1.

Business Strategy

The volatility of the present floating exchange rate regime presents a difficult conundrum for international businesses. Exchange rate movements are difficult to predict, yet their movement can have a major impact on the competitive position of a business. An example is given in the above "Management Focus," which details how exchange rate movements have affected the profitability of the German auto and aerospace concern, Daimler-Benz. An increase in the value of the German mark against other major currencies (except the yen) has made Daimler-Benz's German-based production increasingly uncompetitive in world markets.

One response to the uncertainty that arises from a floating exchange rate regime might be to build strategic flexibility. Faced with uncertainty about the future value of currencies, firms can utilize the forward exchange market. However, the forward market is far from perfect as a predictor of future exchange rates (see Chapter 9). Moreover it is difficult if not impossible to get adequate insurance coverage for exchange rate changes that might occur several years in the future. The forward market tends to offer coverage for exchange rate changes a few months—not years—ahead. Given this, it makes sense to pursue strategies that will increase the company's strategic flexibility in the face of unpredictable exchange rate movements.

Maintaining strategic flexibility can take the form of dispersing production to different locations around the globe as a hedge against currency fluctuations (as Daimler-Benz is now trying to do; see the "Management Focus"). Ingersoll-Rand has taken this approach, increasing its overseas capacity and reducing its dependence on U.S. exports in an attempt to protect itself against any future speculative upsurges in the value of the dollar. The move by Japanese automobile companies to expand their productive capacity in the United States and Europe can be seen in the context of the increase in the value of the yen since 1985, which has increased the price of Japanese exports. For the Japanese companies, building production capacity overseas is a hedge against continued appreciation of the yen (as well as against trade barriers).

Another way of building strategic flexibility involves contracting out manufacturing. This allows a company to shift suppliers from country to country in response to shifts in relative costs brought about by exchange rate movements. However, this kind of strategy works only for low-value-added manufacturing (e.g., textiles), in which the individual manufacturers have few if any firm-specific skills that contribute to the value of the product. It is inappropriate in the case of high-value-added manufacturing, in which firm-specific technology and skills add significant value to the product (e.g., the heavy equipment industry) and in which switching costs are correspondingly high. Put another way, in the case of high-value-added manufacturing, switching suppliers will lead to a reduction in the value that is added, which may offset any cost gains arising from exchange rate fluctuations.

The role of the IMF and the World Bank in the present international monetary system also has implications for business strategy. Increasingly the IMF and World Bank are acting as macroeconomic police, insisting that countries coming to them for significant borrowings adopt IMF- or World Bank-mandated macroeconomic policies. These policies typically include anti-inflationary monetary policy and reductions in government spending. In the short run such policies usually result in a sharp contraction of demand. International businesses selling or producing in such countries need to be aware of this and plan accordingly. In the long run the kind of policies imposed by the IMF and World Bank can promote economic growth and an expansion of demand, which create opportunities for international business.

Corporate–Government Relations

As major players in the international trade and investment environment, businesses can influence government policy toward the international monetary system. For example, in 1985 intense government lobbying by U.S. exporters helped convince the U.S. government that intervention in the foreign exchange market was necessary. Similarly, much of the impetus behind establishment of the exchange rate mechanism of the European Monetary System came from European businesspeople, who understood the costs of volatile exchange rates.

With this in mind business can and should use its influence to promote an international monetary system that facilitates the growth of international trade and investment. Whether a fixed or floating regime is optimal is a subject for debate. What does seem probable, however, is that exchange rate volatility such as the world experienced during the 1980s creates an environment less conducive to international trade and investment than one with more stable exchange rates. Therefore it would seem to be in the interests of international business to promote an international monetary system that minimizes volatile exchange rate movements, particularly when those movements are unrelated to long-run economic fundamentals.

❧ SUMMARY OF CHAPTER

The objectives of this chapter were to explain the workings of the international monetary systems and to point out its implications for international business. Specific points we have made include the following:

1. The gold standard is a monetary standard that pegs currencies to gold and guarantees convertibility to gold.

2. It was thought that the gold standard contained an automatic mechanism that contributed to the simultaneous achievement of a balance-of-payments equilibrium by all countries.

3. The gold standard broke down during the 1930s as countries engaged in competitive devaluations.

4. The Bretton Woods system of fixed exchange rates was established in 1944. The U.S. dollar was the central currency of this system; the value of every other currency was pegged to its value. Significant exchange rate devaluations were allowed only with the permission of the IMF.

5. The role of the IMF was to maintain order in the international monetary system to avoid a repetition of the competitive devaluations of the 1930s and to control price inflation by imposing monetary discipline on countries.

6. To build flexibility into the system, the IMF stood ready to lend countries funds to help protect their currency on the foreign exchange market in the face of speculative pressure and to assist countries in correcting a fundamental disequilibrium in their balance-of-payments position.

7. The fixed exchange rate system collapsed in 1973, primarily due to speculative pressure on the dollar following a rise in U.S. inflation and a growing U.S. balance-of-trade deficit.

8. Since 1973 the world has operated with a floating exchange rate regime, and exchange rates have become more volatile and far less predictable. Volatile exchange rate movements have helped reopen the debate over the merits of fixed and floating systems.

9. The case for a floating exchange rate regime claims that such a system gives countries autonomy regarding their monetary policy and that floating exchange rates facilitate smooth adjustment of trade imbalances.

10. The case for a fixed exchange rate regime claims: the need to maintain a fixed exchange rate imposes monetary discipline on a country, floating exchange rate regimes are vulnerable to speculative pressure, the uncertainty that accompanies floating exchange rates hinders the growth of international trade and investment, and far from correcting trade imbalances, depreciating a currency on the foreign exchange market tends to cause price inflation.

11. The objectives of the European Monetary System (EMS) are to create a zone of monetary stability in Europe, control inflation, and coordinate exchange rate policies with non-EU currencies.

12. The ecu is a "basket" of currencies that serves as the unit of account for the EMS. Each national currency in the EMS is given a central rate vis-à-vis the ecu.

13. The collapse of the Bretton Woods system left the IMF and World Bank with diminished roles in the international monetary system. In response, both the IMF and the World Bank have developed into global macroeconomic police. Today they lend money to countries with balance-of-payments, debt, or development problems, extracting promises to adopt specific macroeconomic policies as a condition.

14. The present managed float system of exchange rate determination has increased the importance of currency management in international businesses.

15. The volatility of exchange rates under the present managed float system creates both opportunities and threats. One way of responding to this volatility is for companies to build strategic flexibility by dispersing production to different locations around the globe by contracting out manufacturing (in the case of low-value-added manufacturing) and other means.

❧ CRITICAL DISCUSSION QUESTIONS

1. Why did the gold standard collapse? Is there a case for returning to some type of gold standard? What is it?

2. What opportunities might IMF lending policies to Third World nations create for international businesses? What threats might they create?

3. Do you think it is in the best interests of Western international businesses to have the IMF lend money to the former Communist states of Eastern Europe to help them transform their economies? Why?

4. Debate the relative merits of fixed and floating exchange rate regimes. From the perspective of an international business, what are the most important criteria in a choice between the systems? Which system is more desirable for an international business?

5. Imagine that Canada, the United States, and Mexico decide to adopt a fixed exchange rate system similar to the ERM of the European Monetary System. What would be the likely consequences of such a system for (a) international businesses and (b) the flow of trade and investment among the three countries?

☙ CLOSING CASE   The Fall and Rise of Caterpillar Tractor

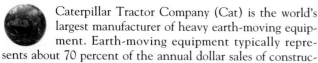

Caterpillar Tractor Company (Cat) is the world's largest manufacturer of heavy earth-moving equipment. Earth-moving equipment typically represents about 70 percent of the annual dollar sales of construction equipment worldwide. In 1980 Cat held 53.3 percent of the global market for earth-moving equipment. Its closest competitor was Komatsu of Japan, with 60 percent of the Japanese market but only 15.2 percent worldwide.

In 1980 Caterpillar was widely considered one of the premier manufacturing and exporting companies in the United States. The company had enjoyed 50 consecutive years of profits and returns on shareholders' equity as high as 27 percent. In 1981 57 percent of its sales were outside the United States, and roughly two-thirds of these orders were filled by exports. Indeed, Cat was the third largest U.S. exporter. Reflecting this underlying strength, in 1981 Cat recorded record pretax profits of $579 million. However, the next three years were disastrous. Caterpillar lost a total of $1 billion and saw its world market share slip to as low as 40 percent in 1985, while Komatsu increased its share to 25 percent. Three factors explain this startling turn of events: the higher productivity of Komatsu, the rise in the value of the dollar, and the Third World debt crisis.

In retrospect Komatsu had been creeping up on Cat for a long time. In the 1960s the company had a minuscule presence outside of Japan. By 1974 it had increased its global market share of heavy earth-moving equipment to 9 percent, and by 1980 it was over 15 percent. Part of Komatsu's growth was due to its superior labor productivity; throughout the 1970s it had been able to price its machines 10 to 15 percent below Caterpillar's. However, Komatsu lacked an extensive dealer network outside of Japan, and Cat's worldwide dealer network and superior aftersale service and support functions were seen as justifying a price premium for Cat machines. For these reasons, many industry observers believed Komatsu would not increase its share much beyond its 1980 level.

What changed the picture was an unprecedented rise in the value of the dollar against most major world currencies. Between 1980 and 1987, the dollar rose an average of 87 percent against the currencies of 10 other industrialized countries. The dollar was driven up by strong economic growth in the United States, which attracted heavy inflows of capital from foreign investors seeking high returns on capital assets. Moreover high real interest rates attracted foreign investors seeking high returns on financial assets. At the same time political turmoil in other parts of the world and relatively slow economic growth in Europe helped create the view that the United States was a good place in which to invest. These inflows of capital increased the demand for dollars in the foreign exchange market, which pushed the value of the dollar upward against other currencies.

Obviously the strong dollar substantially increased the dollar price of Cat's machines. At the same time the dollar price of Komatsu products imported into the United States fell. Due to the shift in the relative values of the dollar and the yen, by 1985 Komatsu was able to price its machines as

much as 40 percent below Caterpillar's prices. In light of this enormous price difference, many consumers chose to forgo Caterpillar's superior aftersale service and support and bought Komatsu machines.

The third factor, the Third World debt crisis, became apparent in 1982. During the early 1970s the oil-exporting nations of OPEC quadrupled the price of oil, which resulted in a massive flow of funds into these nations. Commercial banks borrowed this money from the OPEC countries and lent it to the governments of many Third World Nations to finance massive construction projects—which led to a global boom in demand for heavy earth-moving equipment. Caterpillar benefited richly from this development. By 1982, however, it became apparent that the commercial banks had lent far too much money to risky and unproductive investments, and the governments of several countries (including Mexico, Brazil, and Argentina) threatened to suspend debt payments. At this point the International Monetary Fund stepped in and arranged for new loans to indebted Third World countries, but on the condition that they adopt deflationary macroeconomic policies. For Cat, the party was over; orders for heavy earth-moving equipment dried up almost overnight, and those that were placed went to the lowest bidder—which all too often was Komatsu.

As a result of these factors, Caterpillar was in deep trouble by late 1982. The company responded quickly and between 1982 and 1985 cut costs by more than 20 percent. This was achieved by a 40 percent reduction in work force, the closure of nine plants, and a $1.8 billion investment in flexible manufacturing technologies designed to boost quality and lower cost. At the same time the company launched a campaign of pressing the government to lower the value of the dollar on foreign exchange markets. By 1984 Cat was a leading voice among U.S. exporters in their efforts to get the Reagan administration to intervene in the foreign exchange market.

In the early 1985 things began to go Caterpillar's way. Prompted by Cat and other exporters, representatives of the U.S government met with representatives of Japan, Germany, France, and Great Britain at the Plaza Hotel in New York. In the resulting communiqué—known as the Plaza Accord—the five governments acknowledged that the dollar was overvalued and pledged to take actions that would drive down its price on the foreign exchange market. In practical terms this called for the central bank of each country to intervene in the foreign exchange market, selling dollars and buying other currencies (including its own). The dollar had already begun to fall in early 1985 in response to a string of record U.S. trade deficits. The Plaza Accord accelerated this trend, and over the next three years the dollar fell back to its 1980 level.

The effect for Caterpillar was almost immediate. Like any major exporter, Caterpillar had its own foreign exchange unit. Suspecting that an adjustment in the dollar would come soon, Cat had increased its holdings of foreign currencies in early 1985, using the strong dollar to purchase them. As the dollar fell, the company was able to convert these currencies back into dollars for a healthy profit. In 1985 Cat had pretax profits of $32 million; without foreign exchange gains of $89 million, it would have lost money. In 1986 foreign exchange gains of $100 million accounted for nearly two thirds of its pretax profits of $159 million.

More significant for Cat's long-term position, by 1988 the fall in the dollar against the yen and Caterpillar's cost-cutting efforts had helped to eradicate the 40 percent cost advantage that Komatsu had enjoyed over Caterpillar four years earlier. After trying to hold its prices down, Komatsu had to raise its prices that year by 18 percent, while Cat was able to hold its price increase to 3 percent. With the terms of trade no longer handicapping Caterpillar, the company regained some of its lost market share. By 1989 it reportedly held 47 percent of the world market for heavy earth-moving equipment, up from a low of 40 percent three years earlier, while Komatsu's share had slipped to below 20 percent.

CASE DISCUSSION QUESTIONS

1. To what extent is the competitive position of Caterpillar against Komatsu dependent on the dollar-yen exchange rate?

2. If you were the CEO of Caterpillar Tractor, what actions would you take now to make sure there is no repeat of the early 1980s experience?

3. What potential impact can the actions of the IMF and World Bank have on Caterpillar's business? Is there anything Cat can do to influence the actions of the IMF and World Bank?

4. As the CEO of Caterpillar Tractor, would you prefer a fixed exchange rate regime or a continuation of the current managed float regime? Why?

Sources: R. S. Eckley, "Caterpillar's Ordeal: Foreign Competition in Capital Goods," Business Horizons, March April 1989, pp. 80–86; H. S. Byrne, "Track of the Cat: Caterpillar Is Bulldozing Its Way Back to Higher Profits," Barron's, April 6, 1987, pp. 13, 70–71; R. Henkoff, "This Cat Is Acting Like a Tiger," Fortune, December 19, 1988, pp. 71–76; and "Caterpillar and Komatsu," in Transnational Management: Text, Cases, and Readings in Cross-Border Management, ed. C. A. Bartlett and S. Ghoshal (Homewood, IL: Richard D. Irwin, 1992).

CHAPTER ELEVEN

THE GLOBAL CAPITAL MARKET

BIOMEDEX

Biomedex is a medium-sized Belgian pharmaceutical firm. The company began exploratory biotechnology research in the early 1970s and by the latter half of that decade had developed enzymes that seemed to have industrial applications. Production of a commercially viable biotechnology product would take several years, however. To proceed, Biomedex would need to raise large sums of capital to fund an extensive research and product development phase. The most obvious thing for Biomedex to do would have been to arrange for a new issue of shares on the Belgian stock market. Unfortunately Belgium's stock market was small, lacked liquidity, and was segmented from international markets. It would have been very difficult for Biomedex to successfully float a new equity issue of the size it needed. Even if an equity issue of the required size could have been floated successfully, the rate of return demanded by Belgian stockholders would have made Biomedex's cost of capital significantly higher than its international competitors'. In other words, the limited liquidity and conservative nature of Belgium's capital market would have made it very costly for Biomedex to raise the capital in its own country.

Faced with this dilemma, Biomedex contacted Morgan Grenfell, a London-based commercial bank with major international banking operations. Morgan Grenfell advised Biomedex to issue Eurobonds to foreign investors. In 1979 Morgan Grenfell successfully organized a syndicate to underwrite and sell an issue of convertible Eurobonds that would raise $35 million for Biomedex. Also Morgan Grenfell arranged for

Biomedex to list its shares on the London Stock Exchange to facilitate conversion and gain visibility.

At this time biotechnology was attracting the interest of the U.S. investment community. Stock issues by a number of U.S. start-up firms such as Genentech and Cetus had been oversubscribed. Biomedex, needing additional funds, decided to explore the potential for a U.S. stock offering and listing of its shares on the New York Stock Exchange (NYSE). As a first step, it decided to have its shares quoted on the U.S. over-the-counter market (NASDAQ) to increase its visibility in the U.S. investment community. Having done this, with the assistance of Morgan Grenfell and Goldman Sachs, a major U.S. stockbroker, Biomedex prepared a prospectus for Securities Exchange Commission (SEC) registration of its U.S. stock offering

and listing on the NYSE. To comply with the SEC's regulations, Biomedex had to prepare financial statements consistent with U.S. accounting principles. This was no small task, since its existing accounting systems—tailored to Belgian law— did not supply data in the form required by the SEC.

By June 1981 Biomedex was ready to announce its new share issue, which would increase the number of Biomedex shares outstanding by 20 percent. Immediately following the announcement, Biomedex's shares lost 15 percent of their value on the Belgian stock exchange. This reaction is typical in an illiquid, conservative stock market. Many Belgian investors, worried about the dilution effect of the new share issue, dumped the stock. When the market opened in the United States six hours later, however, Biomedex's shares quickly rose to above their previous value. The demand for Biomedex stock in the United States reflected the U.S. investors' belief that a greater supply of Biomedex stock following the new issue would create a more liquid market for the stock. This attracted many institutional investors that had previously held off buying out of fear they may not be able to subsequently sell the stock without depressing the price. The broader market in Biomedex stock that would exist after the new issue made this less likely, hence the upsurge in U.S. demand for Biomedex stock. As it turned out, the new issue was a huge success, raising an additional $50 million for Biomedex.

Source: Biomedex is a fictitious company. The case is based on information contained in a case on a Danish firm, Nova, that faced similar problems. See A. Stonehill and K. B. Dullum, *Internationalizing the Cost of Capital in Theory and in Practice: The Nova Experience and National Policy Implications* (New York: Wiley, 1983).

❦ INTRODUCTION

Biomedex overcame the limits to its growth imposed by an illiquid, conservative domestic capital market by tapping the international capital market. This kind of financial strategy would not have been possible in the early 1960s when most capital markets were purely domestic. The barriers to the flow of funds across borders made it difficult for companies to raise money through international bond issues or by floating stock on international equity markets. The intervening 30 or so years have seen enormous growth in the international capital market. Due to deregulation of domestic financial markets during the 1980s and the advent of modern communications and data processing technology, such cities as New York, London, and Tokyo have become hubs of an international capital market in which $1 trillion a day flow across national borders.[1]

To get a feel for how dramatic this development has been, consider these statistics:[2]

- In 1980 the stock of "international bank lending" (i.e., cross-border lending plus domestic lending denominated in foreign currency) was $324 billion. By 1991 it had risen to $7.5 trillion.

- In 1982 the total of international bonds outstanding was $259 million; by 1991 it was $1.65 trillion.

- In 1970 U.S. securities transactions with foreigners (purchases and sales of bonds and equities involving a resident and a nonresident) amounted to the equivalent of 3 percent of the U.S. GDP. In 1980 the figure was 9 percent, and in 1990 it was 93 percent. The corresponding figures for West Germany were 3 percent, 8 percent, and 58 percent. For Japan they were 2 percent, 7 percent, and 119 percent. Due to the dominant position of London in the world's financial markets, Great Britain's cross-border securities transactions were equivalent to 368 percent of GDP even in 1985. By 1990 this figure had increased to 690 percent.

- In 1994 companies raised more than $52 billion in equity by issuing shares in countries other than their own. This was five times more than in 1990 and 40 percent more than in 1993. By 1994 individuals and institutions had invested more than $1.3 trillion in stocks outside their home market.

- The flow of capital from the developed to the developing world has accelerated sharply. In 1993 individuals and institutions in developed countries invested $160 billion in developing countries, up from an average of $37 billion a year between 1986 and 1990.

The dramatic rate of growth in the international capital market revealed by these figures has led some to comment that when an economic history of the 20th century is written, the 1980s will not be remembered for the international debt crisis, the dollar's rise and fall, the U.S. budget deficit, or Reaganomics. Rather it will be remembered as the decade in which many of the boundaries between national capital markets dissolved and a truly global capital market emerged.[3] The implications of this transformation in the global financial environment are only starting to become apparent.

---

[1]G. J. Millman, *The Vandals' Crown* (New York: Free Press, 1995).

[2]Data drawn from "Fear of Finance:Survey of the World Economy." *The Economist*, September 19, 1992, pp. 5–9; P. Coggan, "Liberation Movement Lifts Latin America," *Financial Times*, June 23, 1994, p. 5; R. Lapper, "Spreading the World's Wealth," *Financial Times*, January 23, 1995, p. 13; and B. Javetski and W. Glasgall, "Borderless Finance: Fuel for Growth, *Business Week*, November 18, 1994, p. 40–50.

[3]For example, see Javetski and Glasgall, "Borderless Finance."

We have seen the rapid internationalization of the financial services industry to service this global market. Banks that only 20 years ago confined themselves primarily to their domestic markets—banks such as Sumitomo Bank (Japan), Citicorp (United States), Banque Nationale de Paris (France), National Westminster Bank (Great Britain), Deutsche Bank (Germany), and the Union Bank of Switzerland—now have offices in all the world's important financial centers.

In this environment the financial strategy pursued by Biomedex has become common. Nor is international borrowing limited to firms such as Biomedex that are based in countries with illiquid domestic capital markets. As the listed statistics suggest, it is now normal for companies of all nations to raise funds on the international capital market. For example, in 1994 Daimler-Benz, Germany's largest industrial company, raised $300 million by issuing new shares in Singapore.[4] Similarly, in 1989 the Dai-Ichi Kangyo Bank of Japan, then the world's largest bank, helped Dow Chemical, the largest U.S. chemical company, to raise funds in the Japanese credit market by issuing yen-denominated bonds.[5]

In a related development, it is no longer unusual for investors to diversify their portfolios by investing in foreign equity or bond markets. In 1993, for example, cross-border equity investing amounted to about 16 percent of world stock turnover. One transaction out of seven involved a foreign investor, and more than 8 percent of the aggregate value of the world's major stock markets was held by nonresident (foreign) investors.[6]

Against this background, the objective of this chapter is to explain the functions and form of the international capital market and to map out the implications for international business practice. We begin by examining the international capital market, the reasons for its recent growth, and the major players in the market. The international capital market comprises three submarkets: the Eurocurrency market, the international bond market, and the international equity market. We will review each of these in turn. As usual, we close the chapter by pointing out some of the implications of the chapter material for the practice of international business.

❦ THE NATURE OF THE INTERNATIONAL CAPITAL MARKET

Although this section is about the international capital market, we open it by discussing the functions of a generic capital market. Then we will look at the limitations of domestic capital markets, which help explain why an increasing number of companies are using the international capital market to raise funds. Having done this, we will look at the forces responsible for the enormous growth of international capital markets in the past 20 years. Then we will examine the geography of the international capital market and distinguish some of its key players.

The Functions of a Generic Capital Market

A capital market brings together those who want to invest money and those who want to borrow money (see Figure 11.1). Those who want to invest money are corporations with surplus cash, individuals, and nonbank financial institutions (e.g., pension funds, insurance companies). Those who want to borrow money are individuals, companies, and governments. In between these two groups are the market makers. Market makers are the financial service companies that connect investors and borrowers, either directly or indirectly. They include commercial banks (e.g., Citibank, U.S. Bank) and investment banks (e.g., Merrill Lynch, Goldman Sachs).

---

[4]D. Waller, "Daimler in $250m Singapore Placing," *Financial Times*, May 10, 1994, p. 17.

[5]R. J. Maturi, "Foreign Bankers No Longer Bit Players," *Industry Week*, July 17, 1989, pp. 62–63.

[6]Javetski and Glasgall, "Borderless Finance."

FIGURE 11.1   The Main Players in a Generic Capital Market

Commercial banks perform an indirect connection function. They take deposits from corporations and individuals and pay them a rate of interest in return. They then loan that money to borrowers at a higher rate of interest, making a profit from the difference in interest rates. Investment banks perform a direct connection function. They bring investors and borrowers together and charge commissions for doing so. For example, Merrill Lynch may act as a stockbroker for an individual who wants to invest some money. Its personnel will advise her as to the most attractive purchases, buy stock on her behalf, and charge her a fee for the service.

The distinction between debt and equity

Capital market loans to corporations are either equity loans or debt loans. An equity loan is made when a corporation sells stock to investors. The money the corporation receives in return for its stock can be used to purchase plants and equipment, fund R&D projects, pay wages, and so on. A share of stock gives its holder a claim to a firm's profit stream. The corporation honors this claim by paying dividends to the stockholders. The amount of the dividends is determined by management on the basis of how much profit the corporation is making.

A debt loan requires the corporation to repay a predetermined portion of the loan amount (the sum of the principal plus the specified interest) at regular intervals regardless of how much profit it is making. Unlike equity loans, management has no discretion as to the amount it will pay investors. Debt loans include cash loans from banks and funds raised from the sale of corporate bonds to investors. When an investor purchases a corporate bond, she purchases the right to receive a specified fixed stream of income from the corporation for a specified number of years (i.e., until the bond maturity date).

Attractions of the International Capital Market

An international capital market benefits both borrowers and investors. It benefits borrowers by increasing the supply of funds available for borrowing and by lowering the cost of capital. It benefits investors by providing a wider range of investment opportunities than provided by domestic capital markets, thereby allowing investors to build portfolios of international investments that diversify their risks.

The borrower's perspective: a lower cost of capital

In a purely domestic capital market, the pool of investors is limited to residents of the country. This places an upper limit on the supply of funds available to borrowers. In other words, the liquidity of the market is limited. (Biomedex faced this problem in the opening case.) An international capital market, with its much larger pool of investors, provides a larger supply of funds for borrowers to draw on.

Perhaps the most important drawback of the limited liquidity of a purely domestic capital market is that the cost of capital tends to be higher than it is in an international market. The cost of capital is the rate of return borrowers must pay investors (the price of borrowing money). This is the interest rate on debt loans and the dividend yield on equity loans. In a purely domestic market, the limited pool of investors implies that borrowers must pay more to persuade investors to lend them their money. The larger pool of investors in an international market implies that borrowers will be able to pay less.

Figure 11.2   Market Liquidity and the Cost of Capital

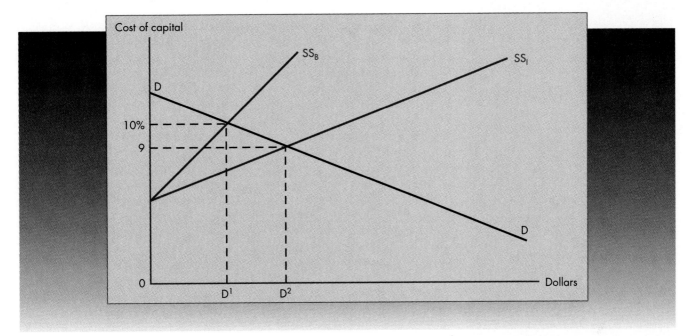

The argument is illustrated in Figure 11.2, using the Biomedex example. The vertical axis in the figure is the cost of capital, and the horizontal axis is the amount of money available at varying interest rates. DD is Biomedex's demand curve for borrowings. Note that Biomedex's demand for funds varies with the cost of capital; the lower the cost of capital, the more money Biomedex will borrow. (Money is just like anything else; the lower its price, the more of it people can afford.) SS_B is the supply curve of funds available in the Belgian capital market, and SS_I represents the funds available in the international capital market. Note that Biomedex can borrow more funds more cheaply on the international capital market. As Figure 11.2 illustrates, the greater pool of resources in the international capital market both lowers the cost of capital and increases the amount Biomedex can borrow. Thus the advantage of an international capital market to borrowers is that it lowers the cost of capital.

You may think that problems of limited liquidity are most often encountered in less developed nations, which naturally tend to have smaller domestic capital markets. To a certain extent this is true. However, in recent years even the very large enterprises based in some of the world's most advanced industrialized nations have begun to aggressively tap the international capital markets in their search for greater liquidity and a lower cost of capital. One example is the German industrial giant Daimler-Benz, which in 1993 and 1994 issued stock in London, New York, and Singapore.[7] A similar example, that of Deutsche Telekom, is profiled in the next "Management Focus."

The investor's perspective: portfolio diversification
From the perspective of an investor, investment opportunities are limited in a purely domestic capital market. By using the international capital market, the investor has a much wider range of investment opportunities. The most significant consequence of this choice is that the investor can diversify her portfolio of holdings internationally, thereby reducing her risk to below what could be achieved by portfolio diversification in a purely domestic capital market.

[7]Waller, "Daimler in $250m Singapore Placing."

MANAGEMENT
FOCUS
Deutsche Telekom
Looks Outside
Germany for
Capital

Based in the world's third largest industrial economy, Deutsche Telekom is one of the world's largest telephone companies. The company is owned by the German government, but plans call for Deutsche Telekom to be privatized by the sale of shares to the general public. The privatization effort is being driven by a realization that state-owned enterprises tend to be inefficient and by the impending deregulation of the European Union telecommunications industry in 1998, which will expose Deutsche Telekom to foreign competition for the first time.

Deutsche Telekom realizes that to become more competitive it needs to undertake massive investments in new telecommunications infrastructure, including fiber optics and wireless, lest it start losing share in its home market to more efficient competitors such as AT&T and British Telecom after 1998. However, financing such investments from state sources would be difficult even under the best of circumstances, and almost impossible in the late 1990s given attempts by the German government to limit its budget deficit. Hence, Deutsche Telekom hopes to finance its investments in capital equipment through the sale of shares to the public.

From a financial perspective the privatization will be anything but easy. Deutsche Telekom is valued at about $60 billion. If it maintained this valuation as a private company, it would dwarf all others listed on the German stock market. However, many analysts doubt there is $60 billion available in Germany for investment in Deutsche Telekom stock. One problem is that there is no tradition of retail stock investing in Germany. Only 1 in 20 German citizens own shares of stock, compared with 1 in every 4 or 5 in the United States and Britain. This

lack of retail interest in stock ownership makes for a relatively illiquid stock market. Nor do banks, the traditional investors in company stocks in Germany, seem enthused about underwriting such a massive privatization effort. A further problem is that a wave of privatizations is sweeping throughout Germany and the rest of Europe. This means Deutsche Telekom will have to compete with many other state-owned enterprises for the attention of investors. Given these factors, probably the only way that Deutsche Telekom could raise $60 billion through the German capital market would be by promising investors a dividend yield that would raise the company's cost of capital above levels that could be serviced profitably.

Managers at Deutsche Telekom have concluded they have no choice but to privatize the company in stages and to sell a substantial proportion of Deutsche Telekom stock to foreign investors. The company plans to sell about 20 percent of its equity to investors in 1996 and another 20 percent before 2000, with the rest being sold early in the next century. Of the 40 percent to be sold by 2000, initially 35 percent was to be sold to foreign investors, primarily by obtaining listings on the London and New York stock exchanges. However, senior managers at Deutsche Telekom now admit this figure may need to be raised to 45 percent or even 50 percent. The choice of London and New York reflects the fact that they are home to the world's largest capital markets and are able to attract funds from investors all over the world.

Sources: S. Ascarelli, "Privatization is Worrying Duetsche Telekom," *The Wall Street Journal,* February 3, 1995, p. A1; "Plunging into Foreign Markets," *The Economist,* September 17, 1994, pp. 86–87; and A. Raghavan and M. R. Sesit, "Financing Boom: Foreign Firms Raise More and More Money in the U.S. Market," *The Wall Street Journal,* October 5, 1993, p. A1.

Consider an investor who buys stock in a biotech firm, such as Biomedex, that has not yet produced a new product. Imagine the price of the stock is very volatile—investors are buying and selling the stock in large numbers in response to information about the firm's prospects. Such stocks are risky investments; the investor may win big if the firm produces a marketable product, but the investor may also lose all her money if the firm fails to come up with a product that sells. The investor can guard against the risk associated with holding this stock by buying other firms' stocks, particularly those weakly or negatively correlated with the biotech stock. The investment strategy here is that of acquiring a diversified portfolio of stock holdings. By holding a variety of stocks, the losses incurred when some stocks fail to live up to their promises are offset by the gains enjoyed when other stocks exceed their promise.

Due to this effect, as an investor increases the number of stocks in her portfolio, the portfolio's risk declines. At first this decline is rapid. Soon, however, the rate of decline falls off and asymptotically approaches the systematic risk of the market. **Systematic risk** refers to movements in a stock portfolio's value that are attributable to macroeconomic forces affecting all firms in an economy, rather than factors specific to an individual firm. The systematic risk is the level of nondiversifiable risk in an economy. Figure 11.3(a) illustrates this relationship for the United States. It suggests that a fully diversified U.S. portfolio is only about 27 percent as risky as a typical individual stock.

By diversifying her portfolio internationally, an investor can reduce the level of risk even further. Because the movement in stock market prices across countries is not strongly correlated. For example, between 1973 and 1982 the correlation of returns for all U.S. stocks was 0.439. However, for all U.S. and British stocks it was only 0.279, while for all U.S. and German stocks it was only 0.170.[8] Among other things, the lower international correlations reflect countries' differing macroeconomic policies and conditions. The implication is that by diversifying a portfolio to include non-U.S. stocks, a U.S. investor can reduce the level of risk still further.

Figure 11.3(b) illustrates the relationship found between international diversification and risk by a now classic study.[9] According to the figure, a fully diversified portfolio that contains stocks from many countries is less than half as risky as a fully diversified portfolio that contains only U.S. stocks. A fully diversified portfolio of international stocks is only about 12 percent as risky as a typical individual stock, whereas a fully diversified portfolio of U.S. stocks is about 27 percent as risky as a typical individual stock. More recent studies have generally confirmed the relationship summarized in Figure 11.3(b). For example, a 1994 study of portfolio diversification in Europe found that a diversified portfolio of stocks held within a single country was on average about 38 percent as risky as a typical individual stock, whereas a portfolio of stocks that was diversified across 12 European countries was only 18 percent as risky as a typical individual stock.[10] Such data suggest that the case for investing internationally as a means of diversifying risk seems to be strong.

The risk-reducing effects of international portfolio diversification would be even greater were it not for the volatile exchange rates associated with the current floating exchange rate regime. Floating exchange rates introduce an additional element of risk into investing in foreign assets. As we have said repeatedly, adverse exchange rate movements can transform otherwise profitable investments into unprofitable investments. The uncertainty engendered by volatile exchange rates may be slowing the otherwise fairly rapid growth of the international capital market.

---

[8]For evidence see C. Eun and B. Resnick, "Estimating the Correlation Structure of International Share Prices," *Journal of Finance*, December 1984, pp. 1314–25.

[9]B. Solnik, "Why Not Diversify Internationally Rather than Domestically," *Financial Analysts Journal*, July 1974, p. 17.

[10]S. L. Heston and K. G. Rouwenhorst, "Does Industrial Structure Explain the Benefits of Internation Diversification?" *Journal of Financial Economics* 36, pp. 3–27.

FIGURE 11.3   Risk Reduction through Portfolio Diversification

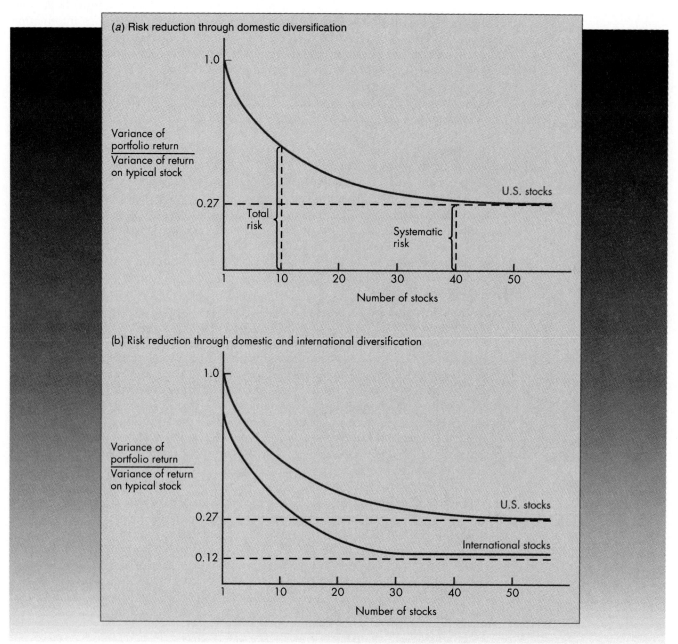

Source: B. Solnik, "Why Not Diversify Internationally Rather than Domestically?" Financial Analysis Journal, *July 1974, p. 17.*

❧ GROWTH OF THE INTERNATIONAL CAPITAL MARKET

Given that an international capital market benefits both investors and borrowers by allowing investors to diversify their risk and borrowers to lower their cost of capital, it may seem surprising that the international capital market did not emerge until the 1960s and did not really come to life until the 1980s. Before the 1960s the world was divided into a series of relatively isolated, or segmented, domestic capital markets. What changed to allow the international capital market to bloom in the 1980s? There seem to be two answers—advances in information technology and deregulation by governments.

❧ **MAP 11.1**   Trading Hours of the World's Major Financial Centers

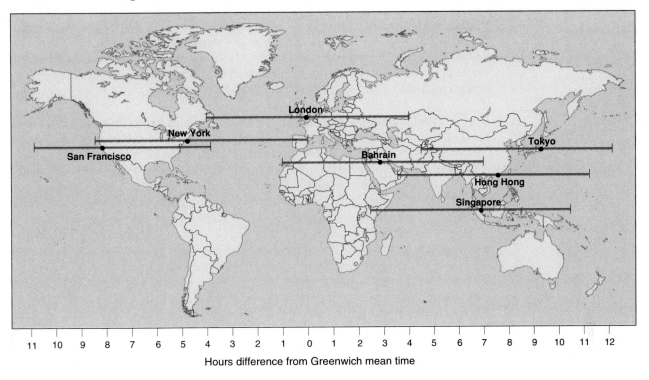

Hours difference from Greenwich mean time

Information Technology

Financial services is an information-intensive industry. It draws on large volumes of information about markets, risks, exchange rates, interest rates, creditworthiness, and so on. It uses this information to make decisions about what to invest where, how much to charge borrowers, how much interest to pay to depositors, and the value and riskiness of a range of financial assets including corporate bonds, stocks, government securities, and currencies.

As a consequence, the financial services industry has been revolutionized more than any other industry by advances in information technology since the 1960s. The growth of international communications technology has facilitated instantaneous communication between any two points on the globe. At the same time rapid advances in data processing capabilities have allowed market makers to absorb and process large volumes of information from around the world. According to one study, a consequence of these technological developments is that the real cost of recording, transmitting, and processing information has fallen by 95 percent since 1964.[11]

Such developments have facilitated the emergence of an integrated international capital market. It is now technologically possible for financial services companies to engage in 24-hour-a-day trading, whether it be in stocks, bonds, foreign exchange, or any other financial asset. Map 11.1 shows how the trading hours of the world's major financial centers overlap. Due to advances in communications and data processing technology, the international capital market never sleeps. San Francisco closes one hour before Tokyo opens but trading continues in New Zealand during this period.

---

[11]T. F. Huertas, "U.S. Multinational Banking: History and Prospects," in *Banks as Multinationals*, ed. G. Jones (London: Routledge, 1990).

The integration facilitated by technology has a dark side.[12] "Shocks" that occur in one financial center now spread around the globe very quickly. The collapse of U.S. stock prices on the notorious Black Monday of October 19, 1987, immediately triggered similar collapses in all the world's major stock markets, wiping billions of dollars off the value of corporate stocks worldwide. However, most market participants would argue that the benefits of an integrated global capital market far outweigh any potential costs.

Deregulation

In country after country, financial services have probably been the most tightly regulated of all industries. Governments around the world have traditionally kept other countries' financial service firms from entering their capital markets. In some cases they have also restricted the overseas expansion of their domestic financial services firms. In addition many countries' laws have segmented the domestic financial services industry. In the United States, for example, commercial banks were prohibited by law from performing the functions of investment banks, and vice versa.

Many of these restrictions have been crumbling since the late 1970s. In part this has been a response to the development of the Eurocurrency market, which from the beginning was outside of national control. (This is explained later in the chapter.) It has also been a response to pressure from financial services companies, which have long wanted to operate in a less-regulated environment. Increasing acceptance of the free market ideology associated with an individualistic political philosophy also has a lot to do with the global trend toward the deregulation of financial markets (see Chapter 2). Whatever the reason, deregulation in a number of key countries around the world has facilitated the growth of the international capital market.

The trend began in the United States in the late 1970s and early 80s with a series of changes that allowed foreign banks to enter the U.S. capital market and domestic banks to expand their operations overseas. In Great Britain, the so-called Big Bang of October 1986 removed barriers that had existed between banks and stockbrokers and allowed foreign financial service companies to enter the British stock market. Restrictions on the entry of foreign securities houses have been relaxed (though not removed) in Japan, and Japanese banks are now allowed to open international banking facilities. In France the "Little Bang" of 1987 is gradually opening the French stock market to outsiders and to foreign and domestic banks. And in Germany, foreign banks are now allowed to lend and manage foreign DM issues, subject to reciprocity agreements.[13] All of this has allowed financial service companies to transform themselves from primarily domestic companies into international operations with major offices around the world—a prerequisite for the development of a truly international capital market.

Impediments to Globalization

Despite the clear shift toward a more international capital market in recent years, some observers claim we do not yet have a truly global capital market. Harvard economist Martin Feldstein, for example, has recently argued that most of the capital that moves internationally is pursuing temporary gains and shifts in and out of countries as quickly as conditions change.[14] He distinguishes between this short-term capital, or "hot money," and "patient money" that would support long-term cross-border capital flows. According to Feldstein, patient money is still relatively rare, primarily because although capital is free to move internationally, its owners and managers prefer to keep most of it at home. Feldstein supports his arguments with statistics that demonstrate that although $1 trillion in short-term capital commitments flow across international borders every day, "When the dust settles most

[12]Millman, *The Vandals' Crown.*

[13]P. Dicken, *Global Shift: The Internationalization of Economic Activity* (London: The Guilford Press, 1992).

[14]Martin Feldstein, "Global Capital Flows: Too Little, Not Too Much," *The Economist,* June 24, 1995, pp. 72–73.

of the savings done in each country stays in that country."[15] Patient money, in other words, is still relatively scarce. As an illustration of his argument, Feldstein claims Mexico's recent economic problems were the result of too much hot money flowing in and out of the country and too little patient money. This example is reviewed in detail in the next "Country Focus."

A major reason for the continuing segmentation of national capital markets from each other may be a lack of information about investment opportunities in other countries. Despite recent advances in information technology, it is still difficult for an investor to get access to the same quantity and quality of information about foreign investment opportunities that is available about domestic investment opportunities. This information gap is exacerbated by adherence to different accounting conventions in different countries, which makes the direct comparison of cross-border investment opportunities difficult for all but the most sophisticated investor (see Chapter 19 for details). For example, German accounting principles are very different from those found in the United States and can present quite a different picture of the health of a company. Thus, when the Germany company Daimler-Benz translated its German financial accounts into U.S.-style accounts in 1993—as it had to do to be listed on the New York Stock Exchange—it found that while it had made a profit of $97 million under German rules, under U.S. rules it had lost $548 million (see the closing case for more details)![16]

Given the problems created by differences in the quantity and quality of information, many investors have yet to venture into cross-border investing and national capital markets still remain relatively segmented from each other. This has been changing, however, and in all probability will continue to change as those who own and manage capital become more sophisticated about the evaluation of cross-border investments and as interest in such investments generates an improvement in the quantity and quality of relevant information.

Geography of the International Capital Market

Map 11.2 presents a hierarchy of the world's 25 largest financial centers.[17] The larger the size of the dot on the map, the more important the city is as a center for international financial transactions. As can be seen, there are three tiers: tier 1 contains London and New York; tier 2, Tokyo, Amsterdam, Paris, Zurich, and Frankfurt; and tier 3, the remaining cities. Tokyo placed in the second tier in the study, although the global financial system is increasingly geared around the New York-London-Tokyo axis. Tokyo's importance rests primarily on the strength of the Japanese economy. Tokyo is distinguished from New York and London in that a relatively small number of foreign financial service companies operate there. In 1985 there were only 76 foreign banking institutions in Tokyo, in contrast to well over 400 in London and about 350 in New York.[18]

London, New York, and (to a lesser extent) Tokyo can be seen as the nerve centers of the international capital market. This is not to say the other centers are unimportant; but none of the second-tier centers has the scale or scope of operations found in the big three centers. The third-tier cities serve mainly as regional financial centers. The third-tier center most likely to grow would seem to be Hong Kong. If China continues its move toward a free market economy (see Chapter 2), Hong Kong will undoubtedly emerge as the financial linchpin of the Chinese economy, and the city could develop to rival Tokyo for regional dominance in financial services by the early years of the next century.

[15]Feldstein, "Global Capital Flows," p. 73.

[16]D. Duffy and L. Murry, "The Wooing of American Investors," *The Wall Street Journal*, February 25, 1994, p. A14.

[17]H. C. Reed, "Financial Center Hegemony, Interest Rates, and the Global Political Economy," *International Banking and Financial Centers*, ed. Y. S. Park and N. Essayyad (Boston: Kluwer Academic, 1989).

[18]Dicken, *Global Shift*.

COUNTRY
FOCUS
Did the
International
Capital Market Fail
Mexico?

In early 1994, shortly after the passage of the North American Free Trade Agreement (NAFTA), Mexico was widely admired among the international community as a shining example of a developing country with a bright economic future. Since the late 1980s the Mexican government had pursued sound monetary, budget, tax, and trade policies. By historical standards inflation was low, the country was experiencing solid economic growth, and exports were booming. This robust picture attracted plenty of capital from foreign investors; between 1991 and 1993 foreigners invested over $75 billion in the Mexican economy, more than in any other developing nation.

If there was a blot on Mexico's economic report card, it was the country's growing current-account (trade) deficit. Mexican exports were booming, but so were its imports. In the 1989–90 period the current-account deficit was equivalent to about 3 percent of Mexico's GDP. In 1991 it increased to 5 percent, and by 1994 it was running at an annual rate of over 6 percent. Bad as this might seem, it is not unsustainable and should not bring an economy crashing down. The United States has been running a current account deficit for decades with apparently little in the way of ill effects. A current-account deficit will not be a problem for a country so long as foreign investors are prepared to take the money they earn from trade with that country and reinvest it within the country. This has been the case in the United States for years, and during the early 1990s it was occurring in Mexico too. Thus companies such as Ford took the pesos they earned from exports to Mexico and reinvested those funds in productive capacity in Mexico, building auto plants to serve the future needs of the Mexican market and to export elsewhere.

Unfortunately for Mexico, much of the $25 billion annual inflow of capital it received during the early 1990s was not the kind of patient long-term money that Ford was putting into Mexico. Rather, according to economist Martin Feldstein, much of the inflow was short-term capital that could flee if economic conditions, however temporarily, changed for the worst.

❧ THE EUROCURRENCY MARKET

A **Eurocurrency** is any currency banked outside its country of origin. **Eurodollars,** which account for about two-thirds of all Eurocurrencies, are dollars banked outside of the United States. Other important Eurocurrencies include the Euro-yen, the Euro-deutsche mark, the Euro-franc, and the Euro-pound. The term *Eurocurrency* is actually a misnomer, since a Eurocurrency can be created anywhere in the world; the persistent Euro- prefix reflects the European origin of the market. As we shall see, the Eurocurrency market is significant because it is an important, relatively low-cost source of funds for international businesses. From small beginnings, this market has mushroomed. In 1982 Eurocurrency deposits amounted to about $2 trillion (U.S.). By 1988 they amounted to more than $4.5 trillion, and the market looks set to continue growing through the 1990s.

Genesis and Growth of the Market

The Eurocurrency market was born in the mid-1950s when Eastern European holders of dollars, including the former Soviet Union, were afraid to deposit their holdings of dollars in the United States lest they be seized by the U.S. government to settle U.S. residents' claims against business losses resulting from the Communist

This is what seems to have occurred. In February 1994 the U.S. Federal Reserve began to increase U.S. interest rates. This led to a rapid fall in U.S. bond prices. At the same time, the yen began to appreciate sharply against the U.S. dollar. These events resulted in large losses for many managers of short-term capital, such as hedge fund managers and banks, who had been betting on the opposite events unfolding. Many hedge funds had been betting that interest rates would fall, bond prices would rise, and the dollar would appreciate against the yen.

Faced with large losses due to these adverse developments, money managers tried to reduce the riskiness of their portfolios by pulling out of risky situations. About the same time events took a turn for the worse in Mexico. An armed uprising in the southern state of Chiapas, the assassination of the leading candidate in the presidential election campaign, and an accelerating inflation rate all helped produce a feeling that Mexican investments were riskier than had been assumed.

Money managers began to pull many of their short-term investments out of the country.

As hot money flowed outward, the Mexican government realized that it could not continue to count on capital inflows to finance its current-account deficit. The government had assumed the inflow was mainly composed of patient long-term money, but in reality much of it appeared to be short-term hot money. Moreover, as money flowed out of Mexico, so the Mexican government had to commit ever more foreign reserves to defending the value of the peso against the U.S. dollar, which was pegged at 3.5 to the dollar. At this point currency speculators entered the picture and began to bet against the Mexican government by selling pesos short. Events came to a head in December 1994 when the Mexican government was essentially forced by capital flows to abandon its support for the peso. Over the next month the peso lost 40 percent of its value against the dollar, the government was forced to introduce an economic austerity program, and the Mexican economic boom came to an abrupt end.

According to Martin Feldstein what really bought the Mexican economy down was not currency speculation on the foreign exchange market, but a lack of long-term patient money. Mexico, he argued, offered, and still offers, many attractive long-term investment opportunities, but due to the segmented nature of the Mexican capital market most of the capital flowing into the country during the 1991–93 period was not long-term money; it was short-term speculative money, the flow of which could quickly be reversed. If we had a true international capital market, Feldstein argues, Mexico should have been able to finance its current-account deficit from inward capital flows since patient capital would naturally gravitate toward attractive Mexican investment opportunities.

Sources: Martin Feldstein, "Global Capital Flows: Too Little, Not Too Much," *The Economist*, June 24, 1995, pp. 72–73; R. Dornbusch, "We Have Salinas to Thank for the Peso Debacle," *Business Week*, January 16, 1995, p. 20; and P. Carroll and C. Torres, "Mexico Unveils Program of Harsh Fiscal Medicine," *The Wall Street Journal*, March 10, 1995, p. A1, A6. See also Martin Feldstein and Charles Horioka, "Domestic Savings and International Captial Flows," *Economic Journal* 90 (1980), pp. 314–29.

takeover of Eastern Europe. So these countries deposited many of their dollar holdings in Europe, particularly in London. Additional dollar deposits came from various Western European central banks and from companies that earned dollars by exporting to the United States. These two groups deposited their dollars in London banks, rather than U.S. banks, because they were able to earn a higher rate of interest (a fact that will be explained).

The Eurocurrency market received a major push in 1957 when the British government prohibited British banks from lending British pounds to finance non-British trade, a business that had been very profitable for British banks. To not lose the business, British banks began financing the same trade by attracting dollar deposits and lending dollars to companies engaged in international trade and investment. As a consequence of this historical event, London became (and has since remained) the leading center of Eurocurrency trading.

The market received another push in the 1960s when the U.S. government enacted regulations that discouraged U.S. banks from lending to non-U.S. residents. Would-be dollar borrowers outside the United States found it increasingly difficult to borrow dollars in the United States to finance international trade, so they turned to the Eurodollar market to obtain the necessary dollar funds.

✵ **MAP 11.2**   The Hierarchy of International Financial Centers, 1994

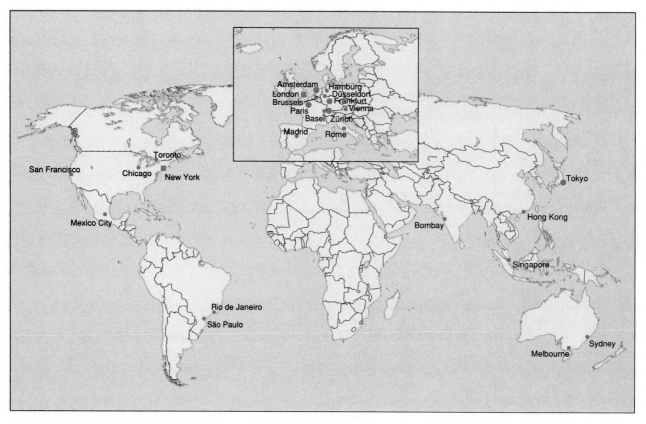

Note: Size of dots (squares) indicates cities' relative importance.

The U.S. government changed its policies in the aftermath of the 1973 collapse of the Bretton Woods system (see Chapter 10), removing an important impetus to the growth of the Eurocurrency market that had existed since the mid-1960s. However, another political event, the oil price increases engineered by OPEC in the 1973–74 and 1979–80 periods, gave the market another big shove. As a result of the oil price increases, the Arab members of OPEC accumulated huge amounts of dollars, oil being priced in dollars. They were afraid to place their money in U.S. banks or their European branches, lest the U.S. government attempt to confiscate them. (Iranian assets in U.S. banks and their European branches had been frozen by President Jimmy Carter in 1979 after the taking of hostages at the U.S. embassy in Tehran; their fear was not unfounded.) Instead these countries deposited their dollars with banks in London, further increasing the supply of Eurodollars.

Although these various political events undoubtedly contributed to the growth of the Eurocurrency market, they alone were not responsible for it. The market grew because it offered real financial advantages—initially to those who wanted to deposit dollars or borrow dollars, and later to those who wanted to deposit and borrow other currencies. We now look at the source of these financial advantages.

Attractions of the Eurocurrency Market

The main factor that makes the Eurocurrency market so attractive to both depositors and borrowers is its lack of government regulation. This allows banks to offer higher interest rates on Eurocurrency deposits than on deposits made in the home currency—making Eurocurrency deposits attractive to those who have cash to deposit. The lack of regulation also allows banks to charge borrowers a lower interest rate for Eurocurrency borrowings than for borrowings in the home currency—making Eurocurrency loans attractive for those who want to borrow money. In other words, the

FIGURE 11.4

Interest Rate Spreads in
Domestic and Eurocurrency
Markets

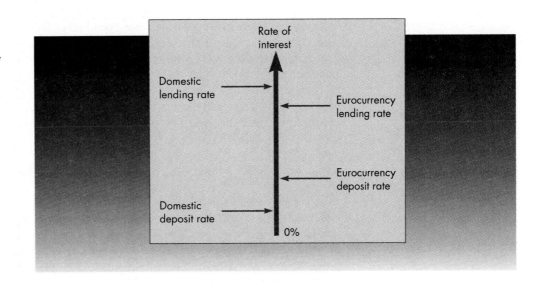

spread between the Eurocurrency deposit rate and the Eurocurrency lending rate is less than the spread between the domestic deposit and lending rates (see Figure 11.4). To understand why this is so, we must examine how government regulations raise the costs of domestic banking.

Domestic currency deposits are regulated in all industrialized countries. Such regulations ensure that banks have enough liquid funds to satisfy demand if large numbers of domestic depositors should suddenly decide to withdraw their money. Most important, all countries operate with certain reserve requirements. For example, each time a U.S. bank accepts a deposit in dollars, it must place some fraction of that deposit in a non-interest-bearing account at a Federal Reserve bank as part of its required reserves. Similarly each time a British bank accepts a deposit in pounds sterling, it must place a certain fraction of that deposit with the Bank of England.

Banks are given much more freedom in their dealings in foreign currencies, however. For example, the British government does not impose reserve requirement restrictions on deposits of foreign currencies within its borders. Nor are the London branches of U.S. banks subject to U.S. reserve requirement regulations, provided those deposits are payable only outside the United States. This gives Eurobanks a competitive advantage.

For example, suppose a bank based in New York faces a 10 percent reserve requirement. According to this requirement, if the bank receives a $100 deposit, it can lend out no more than $90 of that and it must place the remaining $10 in a non-interest-bearing account at a Federal Reserve bank. Suppose the bank has annual operating costs of $1 per $100 of deposits and it charges 10 percent interest on loans. The highest interest the New York bank can offer its depositors and still cover its costs is 8 percent per year. Thus the bank pays the owner of the $100 deposit (0.08) × ($100) = $8, earns (0.10) × ($90) = $9 on the fraction of the deposit it is allowed to lend, and just covers its operating costs.

In contrast a Eurobank can offer a higher interest rate on dollar deposits and still cover its costs. The Eurobank, with no reserve requirements regarding dollar deposits, can lend out all of a $100 deposit. It can earn (0.10) × ($100) = $10 at a loan rate of 10 percent. If the Eurobank has the same operating costs as the New York bank ($1 per $100 deposit), it can pay its depositors an interest rate of 9 percent, a full percentage point higher than that paid by the New York bank, and still cover its costs. That is, it can pay out (0.09) × ($100) = $9 to its depositor, receive $10 from the borrower, and be left with $1 to cover operating costs. Alternatively, the Eurobank might pay the depositor 8.5 percent (which is still above the rate paid by the New York bank), charge borrowers 9.5 percent (still less than the New York bank charges), and cover its operating costs even better. Thus the Eurobank has a competitive advantage vis-à-vis the New York bank in both its deposit rate and its loan rate.

Clearly there are very strong financial motivations for companies to utilize the Eurocurrency market. By doing so they receive a higher interest rate on deposits and can pay less for loans. Given this, the surprising thing is not that the Euromarket has grown so fast in recent years but that it hasn't grown even faster. Why do any depositors hold deposits in their home currency when they could get better yields in the Eurocurrency market?

Drawbacks of the Eurocurrency Market

The Eurocurrency market has two drawbacks. First, when depositors use a regulated banking system, they know the probability of a bank failure that would cause them to lose their deposits is very low. Regulation maintains the liquidity of the banking system. In an unregulated system such as the Eurocurrency market, the probability of a bank failure that would cause depositors to lose their money is greater (although in absolute terms, still low). Thus the lower interest rate received on home country deposits reflects the costs of insuring against bank failure. Some depositors are more comfortable with the security of such a system and are willing to pay the price.

Second, borrowing funds internationally can expose a company to foreign exchange risk. For example, consider a U.S. company that uses the Eurocurrency market to borrow Euro-pounds, perhaps because it can pay a lower interest rate on Euro-pound loans than on dollar loans. Imagine, however, the British pound subsequently appreciates against the dollar. This would increase the dollar cost of repaying the Euro-pound loan and thus the company's cost of capital. Of course (as we saw in Chapter 9) this possibility can be insured against by using the forward exchange market, but the forward exchange market does not offer perfect insurance. Consequently, many companies choose to borrow funds in their domestic currency to avoid foreign exchange risk, even though the Eurocurrency markets may offer more attractive interest rates.

❧ THE INTERNATIONAL BOND MARKET

Bonds are an important means of financing for many companies. The most common kind of bond is a fixed-rate bond. The investor who purchases a **fixed-rate bond** receives a fixed set of cash payoffs. Each year until the bond matures, the investor gets an interest payment and then at maturity he gets back the face value of the bond.

International bonds are of two types: foreign bonds and Eurobonds. **Foreign bonds** are sold outside the borrower's country and are denominated in the currency of the country in which they are issued. Thus when Dow Chemical issues bonds in Japanese yen and sells them in Japan, it is issuing foreign bonds. Many foreign bonds have nicknames; foreign bonds sold in the United States are called Yankee bonds, foreign bonds sold in Japan are Samurai bonds, and foreign bonds sold in Great Britain are bulldogs.

Eurobonds are normally underwritten by an international syndicate of banks and placed in countries other than the one in whose currency the bond is denominated. For example, a bond may be issued by a German corporation, denominated in U.S. dollars, and sold to investors outside the United States by an international syndicate of banks. Eurobonds are routinely issued by multinational corporations, large domestic corporations, sovereign governments, and international institutions. They are usually offered simultaneously in several national capital markets, but not in the capital market of the country, nor to residents of the country, in whose currency they are denominated. Eurobonds account for the lion's share of international bond issues. In 1987, for example, $177.3 billion in Eurobonds were issued, in contrast to only $38.4 billion in foreign bonds.[19]

---

[19]R. C. Smith, "Investment Banks and Merchant Banks," in *The Handbook of International Financial Management*, ed. R. Z. Aliber (Homewood, IL: Dow Jones-Irwin, 1989).

Scale and Scope of the Market

Like the Eurocurrency market, the international bond market grew rapidly during the 1980s. Whereas $177 billion in international bonds were issued in 1987, by 1989 the figure was $258.7 billion. Estimates suggest international bonds accounted for almost 10 percent of all bonds outstanding worldwide by the end of 1988. In addition, by 1988 international bonds accounted for 10.5 percent of all bonds issued in U.S. dollars, 21.3 percent of the bonds issued in British pounds, 14.2 percent of the bonds issued in German marks, 5 percent of the bonds issued in Japanese yen, and 49.2 percent of the bonds issued in Swiss francs.[20]

Attractions of the Eurobond Market

Why has the Eurobond market grown so rapidly in recent years? Three features of the market make it an appealing alternative to most major domestic bond markets:

- An absence of regulatory interference.
- Less-stringent disclosure requirements than in most domestic bond markets.
- A favorable tax status.

Regulatory interference

National governments often impose tight controls on domestic and foreign issuers of bonds denominated in the local currency and sold within their national boundaries. These controls tend to raise the cost of issuing bonds. However, government limitations are generally less stringent for securities denominated in foreign currencies and sold within their market to holders of those foreign currencies. Put another way, Eurobonds fall outside the regulatory domain of any single nation. As such they can often be issued at a lower cost to the issuer.

Disclosure requirements

Eurobond market disclosure requirements tend to be less stringent than those of several national governments. For example, if a firm wishes to issue dollar-denominated bonds within the United States, it must first comply with SEC disclosure requirements. The firm must disclose detailed information about its activities, the salaries and other compensation of its senior executives, stock trades by its senior executives, and the like. In addition the issuing firm must submit financial accounts that conform to U.S. accounting standards. For non-U.S. firms, redoing their accounts to make them consistent with U.S. standards can be very time consuming and expensive. Therefore, many firms have found it cheaper to issue Eurobonds, including those denominated in dollars, than to issue dollar-denominated bonds within the United States.

Favorable tax status

Before 1984 U.S. corporations issuing Eurobonds were required to withhold up to 30 percent of each interest payment to foreigners for U.S. income tax. This did not encourage foreigners to hold bonds issued by U.S. corporations. Similar tax laws were at that time operational in a large number of countries. The effect of these tax laws was to limit market demand for Eurobonds. In 1984 U.S. laws were revised to exempt foreign holders of bonds issued by U.S. corporations from any withholding tax. As a result U.S. corporations found it feasible for the first time to sell Eurobonds directly to foreigners. Repeal of the U.S. laws caused other governments, including those of France, Germany, and Japan, to liberalize their tax laws likewise to avoid outflows of capital from their markets. The consequence was an upsurge in demand for Eurobonds from investors who wanted to take advantage of their tax benefits.

---

[20]C. Pavel and D. McElravey, *Globalization in the Financial Services Industry* (Chicago: Federal Reserve Bank of Chicago, 1990), pp. 3–18.

The Rise of Ecu Bonds   In Chapter 10 we introduced the ecu, the basket of European Union (EU) currencies that serves as the unit of account for the European Monetary System. The EU hopes to establish the ecu as its common currency by 1999. With this goal in mind, governments, corporations, and international institutions have been issuing bonds denominated in ecus. Currently ecu-denominated bonds account for only a small percentage of all bonds issued, but the percentage seems to be growing rapidly. Between 1980 and 1990 the outstanding amount of ecu bonds grew from ecu 250 million to ecu 70 billion. Almost 8 percent of all new international bond issues in 1990 were denominated in ecus, up from 3.8 percent in 1986, and in the first half of 1991, ecu issues accounted for more than 12 percent of all new bond issues. Given the trend toward European integration, the size of this market seems set to grow.[21]

❧ THE INTERNATIONAL EQUITY MARKET

There is no international equity market in the sense that there are international currency and bond markets. Rather many countries have their own domestic equity markets in which corporate stock is traded. The largest of these domestic equity markets are to be found in the United States, Britain, Japan, and Germany. Although each domestic equity market is still dominated by investors who are citizens of that country and companies incorporated in that country, developments are internationalizing the world equity market. Investors are investing heavily in foreign equity markets as a means of diversifying their portfolios. By 1994 individuals and institutions had invested more than $1.3 trillion in stocks outside their home market.[22] Facilitated by deregulation and advances in information technology, this trend seems to be here to stay.

An interesting consequence of the trend toward international equity investment is the internationalization of corporate ownership. Today it is still generally possible to talk about "U.S. corporations," "British corporations," and "Japanese corporations," primarily because the majority of stockholders (owners) of these corporations are of the respective nationality. However, this is changing. Increasingly U.S. citizens are buying stock in companies incorporated abroad, and foreigners are buying stock in companies incorporated in the United States. Looking into the future, Robert Reich has mused about "the coming irrelevance of corporate nationality."[23] If the "stateless corporation" does become a reality, it will be meaningless to talk about "U.S. corporations" or "Japanese corporations."

A second development internationalizing the world equity market is that companies with historic roots in one nation are broadening their stock ownership by listing their stock in the equity markets of other nations. The reasons are primarily financial. Listing stock on a foreign market is often a prelude to issuing stock in that market to raise capital. (Remember that in the opening case Biomedex arranged to get listed on the NASDAQ exchange as a prelude to offering its stock on the NYSE.) The idea is to tap into the liquidity of foreign markets, thereby increasing the funds available for investment and lowering the firm's cost of capital. (The relationship between liquidity and the cost of capital was discussed earlier in the chapter.) As noted in the introduction, in 1994 companies raised more than $52 billion in equity by issuing shares in countries other than their own. This was five times more than in 1990 and 40 percent more than in 1993.[24]

---

[21]T. Corrigan, "European Governments Help Transformation," *Financial Times Survey: International Capital Markets,* July 22, 1991, p. 2.

[22]Javetski and Glasgall, "Borderless Finance."

[23]R. Reich, *The Work of Nations* (New York: Alfred A. Knopf, 1991).

[24]R. Lapper, "Spreading the World's Wealth," *Financial Times,* January 23, 1995, p. 13.

In addition to liquidity and cost-of-capital benefits, firms often list their stock on foreign equity markets to facilitate future acquisitions of foreign companies. Consider Hanson Plc, a large British conglomerate that specializes in acquiring and turning around poorly managed companies. Hanson has long had a New York Stock Exchange listing and a significant proportion of its outstanding shares are traded on the NYSE. This enables Hanson to acquire companies owned by U.S. residents by offering those companies' stockholders Hanson shares in exchange for their shares. The ability to swap shares in making acquisitions relieves Hanson of the pressure to come up with cash each time it wants to acquire a U.S. company. Other reasons for listing a company's stock on a foreign equity market are that the company's stock and stock options can be used to compensate local management and employees; it satisfies the desire for local ownership; and it increases the company's visibility with local employees, customers, suppliers, and bankers.

Data from the late 1980s indicates that at that time, Great Britain had the greatest number of foreign firms listed on its exchange. In 1989 24 percent of the 2,700 or so companies listed on the London exchange were foreign firms. In contrast less than 5 percent of the 1,550 firms listed on the NYSE were non-U.S. enterprises, and only a handful of the 1,450 firms listed on the Tokyo exchange were non-Japanese firms. The relatively small Dutch and Swiss stock markets were the most international. Foreign firms accounted for 50 percent of the approximately 500 listings on the Amsterdam market and 60 percent of the 284 listings on the Zurich exchange in 1989.[25] Since then, however, there has been a surge in the number of foreign firms with listings on U.S. stock exchanges. In the first half of 1994 alone 61 foreign firms gained listings on U.S. exchanges, raising $8.4 billion in new equity capital in the process.[26]

❧ FOREIGN EXCHANGE RISK AND THE COST OF CAPITAL

Until now we have emphasized repeatedly that a firm can borrow funds at a lower cost on the international capital market than on the domestic capital market. However, we have also mentioned that under a floating exchange rate regime, foreign exchange risk clearly complicates this picture. This point needs to be emphasized.

Consider a U.S. company that wants to borrow money for one year to fund U.S. investments. The interest rate on dollar loans from a U.S. bank is 10 percent. Alternatively the firm can borrow deutsche marks on the international market for a year at 6 percent. It may seem that the logical thing to do is to borrow the deutsche marks. However, consider what will occur if the DM appreciates against the dollar by 8 percent during the year. Since the DM loan would have to be repaid in deutsche marks, the appreciation of the DM would increase the dollar cost of the loan by an amount equivalent to the appreciation of the DM. The true cost of capital to the firm would be the 6 percent interest rate on its DM loan plus the increase in the dollar cost of interest and principal on the loan deriving from the appreciation of the DM. The formula for calculating the true cost of capital in such a circumstance is

		Interest on DM loan		Additional interest due to exchange rate change		Additional principal due to exchange rate change		
Cost of capital	=	6%	×	1.08	+	8%	=	14.48%

In other words, as a result of the DM's appreciation, the company's cost of capital would be 14.48 percent, not 6 percent. With the benefit of this hypothetical foresight, it would obviously be less expensive for the company to borrow dollars from a

[25]"One Market or Many," *The Economist*, December 16, 1989, pp. 24–26.

[26]Javetski and Glasgall, "Borderless Finance."

U.S. bank at 10 percent. Of course the U.S. company could insure against such an adverse change in exchange rates by using the forward exchange market (see Chapter 9). However, if the forward exchange market predicts an appreciation of the DM, this would also raise the cost of borrowing DMs.

Perhaps more important, the forward exchange market is not geared to provide coverage for long-term borrowings (see Chapter 9). In addition to their cost, many international businesses have found that borrowing foreign currency over a long term creates considerable exposure to foreign exchange risk. Consider the case of TRW, a U.S. multinational that in October 1969 issued DM-denominated foreign bonds. The bonds were scheduled to reach maturity in October 1989. At the time of issue, the cost of the DM funds was 7.82 percent per annum. The cost of bonds denominated in U.S. dollars at that time was 8.7 percent, so this looked like a good deal. However, over the next few years the Bretton Woods system of fixed exchange rates broke down, and the dollar depreciated against the DM (see Chapter 10). As a result by the time the bonds matured the effective cost of capital for TRW, adjusted for exchange rate changes, was not 7.82 percent per annum, but 14.75 percent per annum! Clearly TRW would have been better off issuing dollar-denominated bonds.[27]

The central message is that when a firm borrows funds from the international capital market, it must weigh the benefits of a lower interest rate against the risks of an increase in the real cost of capital due to adverse exchange rate movements. Although using forward exchange markets may lower foreign exchange risk with short-term borrowings, it cannot remove the risk. Moreover the forward exchange market does not provide adequate coverage for long-term borrowings.

IMPLICATIONS FOR BUSINESS

The implications of the material discussed in this chapter for international business are quite straightforward but no less important for being obvious. The growth of the international capital market has created opportunities for international businesses that wish to borrow and/or invest money. On the borrowing side, by using the international capital market, firms can often borrow funds at a lower cost than is possible in a purely domestic capital market. This conclusion holds no matter what form a firm's borrowings take—equity, bonds, or cash loans. The lower cost of capital on the international market reflects their greater liquidity and the general absence of government regulation. As we have observed, government regulation tends to raise the cost of capital in most domestic capital markets. The international market, being transnational, escapes regulation. Balanced against this, however, is the foreign exchange risk associated with borrowing in a foreign currency.

On the investment side, we have seen how the growth of the international capital market is providing opportunities for firms, institutions, and individuals to better diversify their investments in financial assets to limit risk. By holding a diverse portfolio of stocks and bonds in different nations, an investor can reduce total risk to a lower level than can be achieved in a purely domestic setting. Once again, however, foreign exchange risk is a complicating factor.

As for the future, the trends noted in this chapter seem likely to continue, with the international capital market continuing to increase in both importance and degree of integration over the next decade. Perhaps the most significant development will be the emergence of a unified capital market and common currency within the EU by the end of the decade as that grouping of countries continues toward economic and monetary union. Since Europe's capital markets are currently rather fragmented and relatively introspective (with the major exception of Britain's capital market), such a development could pave the way for even more rapid internationalization of the capital market in the early years of the next century. If this occurs, the implications for business are likely to be positive.

---

[27]D. K. Eiteman, A.I. Stonehill, and M H. Moffett, *Multinational Business Finance* (Reading, MA: Addison-Wesley, 1992).

❦ SUMMARY OF CHAPTER

The objectives of this chapter were to explain the functions and form of the international capital market and to define the implications of this for international business practice. In this chapter we made the following points:

1. The function of a capital market is to bring those who want to invest money together with those who want to borrow money.

2. Relative to a domestic capital market, the international capital market has a greater supply of funds available for borrowing, and this makes for a lower cost of capital for borrowers.

3. Relative to a domestic capital market, the international capital market allows investors to diversify portfolios of holdings internationally, thereby reducing the risk.

4. The growth of the international capital market during the 1970s and 80s can be attributed to advances in information technology and to deregulation of financial services in several major industrialized countries.

5. A Eurocurrency is any currency banked outside its country of origin. The lack of government regulations makes the Eurocurrency market attractive to both depositors and borrowers. Due to the absence of regulation, the spread between the Eurocurrency deposit and lending rates is less than the spread between the domestic deposit and lending rates. This gives Eurobanks a competitive advantage.

6. The international bond market has two classifications: the foreign bond market and the Eurobond market. Foreign bonds are sold outside of the borrower's country and are denominated in the currency of the country in which they are issued. A Eurobond issue is normally underwritten by an international syndicate of banks and placed in countries other than the one in whose currency the bond is denominated. Eurobonds account for the lion's share of international bond issues.

7. The Eurobond market is an attractive way for companies to raise funds due to the absence of regulatory interference, less-stringent disclosure requirements, and Eurobonds' favorable tax status.

8. Foreign investors are investing in other countries' equity markets to reduce risk by diversifying their stock holdings among nations.

9. Many companies are now listing their stock in the equity markets of other nations, primarily as a prelude to issuing stock in those markets to raise additional capital. Other reasons for listing stock in another country's exchange are to facilitate future stock swaps, to enable the company to use its stock and stock options for compensating local holdings' management and employees, to satisfy local ownership desires, and to increase the company's visibility among its local employees, customers, suppliers, and bankers.

10. When borrowing funds from the international capital market, companies must weigh the benefits of a lower interest rate against the risks of greater real costs of capital due to adverse exchange rate movements.

11. One major implication of the international capital market for international business is that companies can often borrow funds at a lower cost of capital in the international capital market than they can in the domestic capital market.

12. The international capital market provides greater opportunities for businesses and individuals to build a truly diversified portfolio of international investments in financial assets, which lowers risk.

❦ CRITICAL DISCUSSION QUESTIONS

1. Why has the international capital market grown so rapidly in recent decades? Do you think this growth will continue throughout the 1990s? Why?

2. A firm based in Mexico has found that its growth is restricted by the limited liquidity of the Mexican capital market. List the firm's options for raising money on the international capital market. Discuss the pros and cons of each option, and make a recommendation. How might your recommended options be affected if the Mexican peso depreciates significantly on the foreign exchange markets over the next two years?

3. Happy Company wants to raise $2 million in U.S. dollars with debt financing. The funds are needed to finance working capital, and the firm will repay them with interest in one year. Happy Company's treasurer is considering three options:

   a. Borrowing U.S. dollars from Security Pacific Bank at 8 percent.
   b. Borrowing British pounds from Midland Bank at 14 percent.
   c. Borrowing Japanese yen from Sanwa bank at 5 percent.

   If Happy borrows foreign currency, it will not cover it; that is, it will simply change foreign currency for dollars at today's spot rate and buy the same foreign currency a year later at the spot rate then in effect. Happy Company estimates that the pound will depreciate by 5 percent relative to the dollar and that the yen will appreciate 3 percent relative to the dollar in the next year. From which bank should Happy Company borrow?

❧ CLOSING CASE   The Internationalization of Daimler-Benz's Ownership

In May 1993 the German industrial conglomerate Daimler-Benz, perhaps best known for its Mercedes-Benz luxury cars, shocked the German business community by announcing it would seek a listing on the New York Stock Exchange (NYSE). The shock was because Daimler had apparently acquiesced to the demand of the U.S. Securities and Exchange Commission (SEC) that foreign firms must abide by U.S. financial reporting standards to be listed on a U.S. exchange. Since 1990 negotiations between the SEC and a number of big German firms seeking NYSE listings had stalled over this issue. Now Daimler had apparently broken ranks and agreed to the SEC demands.

At the heart of the dispute between the SEC and the German companies was the German practice of massaging financial statements by drawing on "hidden reserves" that are not reported on their books. Whenever product demand slackens and operating losses develop, many German companies tap their hidden reserves, which normally take the form of liquid and near liquid investments built up from earlier earnings, to offset the losses and show a modest profit. This practice enables German companies to show steady profits. This use of hidden reserves, however, is an anathema to the SEC, which has steadfastly maintained that the only way Daimler and other German firms can get a NYSE listing is if they first disclose the reserves and their effect on profits.

While the German attitude might sound stubborn, many German companies maintain that U.S. reporting practices emphasize quick profits and short-term thinking. The pressure to show the biggest possible quarterly dividend, they maintain, deprives management of funds for investing in a company's future.

So why did Daimler break ranks? A major factor seems to have been the company's desire to raise capital to finance its international expansion. Daimler plans to move an increasing amount of its automobile and aerospace operations out of Germany. With several major capacity expansion projects already underway in the United States and Southeast Asia, Daimler needs large amounts of capital. Daimler apparently concluded that attempts to raise all this capital in the relatively illiquid German market would increase its cost of capital above the level demanded by international investors. So the company decided to tap into the vast pool of capital that flows through the NYSE, believing this would lower its cost of capital.

A second factor seems to have been a desire by Daimler to broaden its ownership base. In theory, by making its shares more accessible to investors in the United States, greater demand for Daimler stock might drive up the share price. In addition, as it becomes more of a global company, Daimler clearly wants to convey a more international image. By diversifying its ownership base across countries, Daimler can legitimately claim it is no longer just a German company. Company plans call for 30 percent to 35 percent of Daimler's shares to be owned outside of Germany by the year 2000, and possibly more by early next century. Insofar as this helps Daimler to overcome resistance to its entry into foreign markets, this will be good for the company.

Having said this, Daimler's decision was clearly not without some cost. In addition to the hostility from its peer companies in Germany, in September 1993 Daimler found that while it had made a profit of $97 million under German financial disclosure rules, under U.S. rules it had lost $548 million![28] Still, between the announcement in May 1993 and the actual listing of the company's stock on the NYSE in early October 1993, Daimler's shares surged 30 percent, compared to an 11 percent increase in the Dow Jones equity market index for Germany over the same period.

Daimler did not stop with its NYSE listing. In late 1994 the company issued $250 million of new shares through the Singapore stock exchange. The money was to be used to finance the company's capacity expansion plans in the region. The company has also stated it plans to seek additional equity market listings in Madrid, Milan, and Shanghai. In total Daimler-Benz hopes to raise over $2 billion from international share issues by the year 2000. In general capital raised in a particular country or region will be used to finance investments in that region.

CASE DISCUSSION QUESTIONS

1. How might broadening its international ownership base help Daimler-Benz to do business in foreign markets?

2. Daimler seems to be trying to raise capital in regions where it is making major automobile capacity expansion investments, such as Southeast Asia and the United States. Does this strategy make sense? Why?

3. Are other German companies right to be concerned about Daimler's decision? Should Daimler have broken ranks?

4. If ultimately more than 50 percent of Daimler-Benz's equity is owned by investors outside of Germany, and if the company implements its plans for global production, will it still be a German company?

Sources: D. Waller "Daimler in $250 million Singapore Placing," Financial Times, May 10, 1994, p. 17; A. Raghavan and M. R. Sesit, "Financing Boom: Foreign Firms Raise More and More Money in the U.S. Market, The Wall Street Journal, October 5, 1993, p. A1; and G. Whitney and T. Roth, "Daimler May Be Sign of Change for Equities," The Wall Street Journal, March 29, 1993, p. B6.

[28]Duffy and Murry, The Wooing of American Investors."

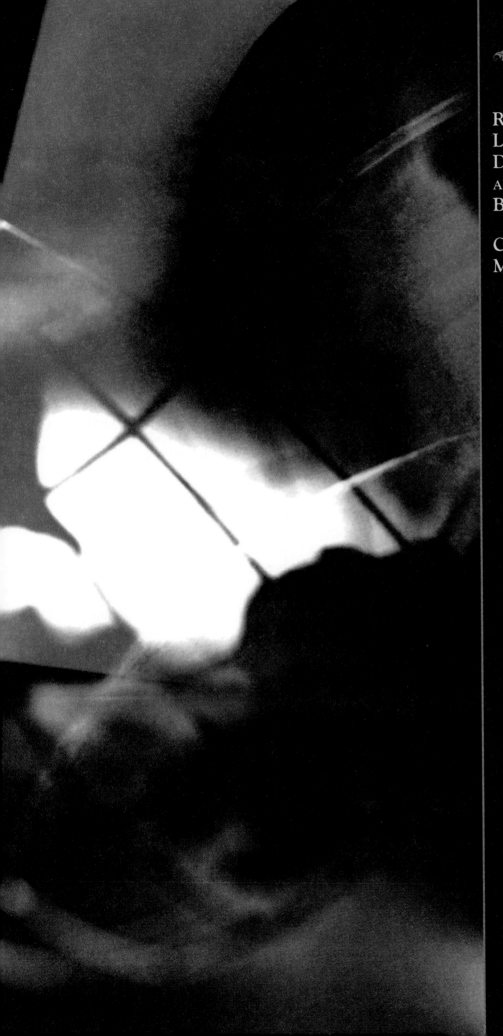

CASES

RISKY BUSINESS: NICK LEESON, GLOBAL DERIVATIVES TRADING, AND THE FALL OF BARINGS BANK

CHAOS IN THE CURRENCY MARKETS

RISKY BUSINESS: NICK LEESON, GLOBAL DERIVATIVES TRADING, AND THE FALL OF BARINGS BANK

> Derivatives need to be well controlled and understood, but we believe we do that here.
> Peter Baring, Chairman,
> Barings Brothers, October 1993.

> I'm sorry.
> Note left by Nick Leeson, February 1995.

❧ INTRODUCTION

In February 1995 the financial world was shaken by the revelation that unauthorized derivatives trading by a 27-year-old Englishman, Nick Leeson, employed at the Singapore office of Britain's oldest bank, Barings Plc, had amassed losses of at least $950 million (the figure was later revised upward to $1.33 billion). The debacle resulted in the collapse of Barings and its purchase, for the princely sum of one pound sterling, by a Dutch bank, International Nederlanden Groep NV (ING). So ended the history of a 233-year-old "aristocratic" bank whose clients at the time of its collapse included Queen Elizabeth II of England.

To many critics, the collapse of Barings offered more proof that the rapid rise of derivatives trading in global financial markets was a dangerous and potentially destabilizing influence in the world economy. Barings joined a growing list of organizations that had lost vast sums of money on derivatives trading, including Metallgesellschaft AG of Germany (lost $1.3 billion), Procter & Gamble (lost $102 million), Kidder Peabody & Co. (lost $350 million), and Orange County of California (lost $1.7 billion). These critics used the collapse of Barings to intensify their calls for tighter regulation of global derivatives trading. But there were those who argued that when employed correctly, derivatives can be used to reduce risk, not increase it. They attributed the losses at Barings to the actions of a rogue financial trader who was engaged in risky speculation and to poor internal management controls at Barings. They argued that the ease with which the world's financial markets absorbed the shock of the Barings collapse is proof that the world financial system is sound and should not be encumbered by unnecessary government regulations.

❧ FINANCIAL DERIVATIVES

A *derivatives transaction* is a contract whose value depends on ("derives from") the value of an underlying asset, reference rate, or index. Derivatives include forward, future, swap, and option transactions that are based on interest rates, currencies, equities, and commodities (for a detailed exposition of the mechanics of forward and swap transactions based on currencies, see Chapter 9). Derivatives have been in use for at least 100 years, although in recent years there has been rapid growth in their popularity. In 1986 derivative contracts with a notional value of about $1 trillion were traded annually. By 1990 this figure had risen to $5 trillion, and by 1994 it approached $20 trillion. This rapid growth in the volume of derivative trading has raised fears that derivatives might destabilize the world financial system.

A major factor leading to the growth of derivatives trading in currencies was the collapse of the Bretton Woods agreement in 1971 and the resulting shift from a fixed to a floating exchange rate regime (see Chapter 10 for details). Under a floating exchange rate regime, exporters and importers hedged (insured against) adverse currency changes by purchasing foreign currency through forward exchanges or by

Source: Charles W. L. Hill.

engaging in currency swaps. During the 1970s and 1980s corporations and traders increasingly turned to derivatives contracts to insure against possibly adverse future changes in a wide range of other assets such as commodities, bonds, or stocks.

For an example of a derivative contract for a commodity, consider a company that knows it will need to purchase one million barrels of oil in six months. Imagine that the current price of oil is $15 per barrel, but the company fears the price might rise substantially over the next six months due to political turmoil in Saudi Arabia, the world's largest oil exporting nation. The company can either wait and bear the risk that the price of oil might rise in six months, or it can enter into a *futures contract* today. Under this contract, it might agree to purchase the price of oil in six months at $16 per barrel. The $1 difference between the price of oil today and the price specified in the contract represents an insurance, or hedge, against a possible rise in the future price of oil. By entering into the contract, the company has reduced its exposure to future rises in oil prices, it has reduced its risk.

Another common form of derivative is a stock option. A stock option is a contract that gives the owner the right to purchase or sell a specific number of shares at a fixed price within a definite time period. For example, imagine that you hold 1,000 shares of Compaq Computer, which is currently trading at $50 per share (the market value of your holding is $50,000). You fear that due to a temporary slowdown in the growth rate of personal computer sales, the price of Compaq might fall in the near future. But you don't want to sell the stock because you like Compaq's long-term prospects. You know that it is by no means a sure thing that sales are slowing, and it is possible that Compaq will continue to do well even if the growth rate of computer sales does slow. Therefore you might take out insurance against the possibility that the stock will fall by purchasing a *put option*. The put option contract might give you the right—but not the obligation—to sell 1,000 shares of Compaq Computer in three months at $50 per share to the *writer of the option*. The put option might cost you $1 per share, or $1,000.

If the price of Compaq shares does not fall, the put option contract might expire worthless in three months. However, if Compaq shares fall to $40 the put option contract will rise to about $10 per share. At this point you can either sell the shares for $50 each to the writer of the put option, or you could sell the option contract for $10,000 (1,000 shares @ $10 per share) and pocket the $9,000 profit while holding onto the shares. Whatever action you choose, although the value of your Compaq shareholding has fallen from $50,000 to $40,000 over the three months, your actual loss is limited to just $1,000—the price of the put option contract. By purchasing a put option contract you have limited your exposure to a fall in the price of Compaq shares.

One can also purchase *call options*. Call options are simply the reverse of put options. They are an option that gives you the right to purchase a certain number of shares *from the option writer* at a fixed price within a specified time period. For example, if you think Compaq's price might rise from $50 to $80 per share, but if you are unwilling to purchase another 1,000 shares for $50,000 at this point, you could enter into a call option contract that gives you the right to purchase 1,000 shares from the call option writer in three months time at $50 per share. Again, the option contract might cost you $1 per share. If the price of shares goes up to $80 you will make a large profit. If the price falls, your loss is limited to the $1,000 cost of the call option contract.

At this point you might be wondering why anyone would want to *write* an option contract. The option writer pockets the price of the option contract if it expires worthless, which happens enough to make the practice worthwhile. To further increase their potential returns, many option writers write "uncovered" or "naked" options. For example, consider a trader who writes a call option that gives the buyer the right to purchase 1,000 shares of Compaq at $50 per share in three months. If the option writer deposited 1,000 shares of Compaq with her stock broker, this would be termed a *covered call*, since if the buyer of the contract exercises his call option to purchase 1,000 shares at $50, the writer (or seller) has enough shares in her account to pay the buyer. An *uncovered call* occurs when the option writer does not deposit enough shares to cover the eventuality that the buyer of the option will exercise his call option. An option writer can write such an uncovered call option in a *margin account*, which is an account where the broker lends the money to the option writer (at an appropriate rate of interest) to cover the cost of meeting the call obligation. Brokers will do this if the option writer can show that she has sufficient funds elsewhere to cover the cost of meeting her potential call obligations and/or servicing any interest payments that must be incurred on funds borrowed to meet call obligations. Writing uncovered calls (or uncovered puts) is a risky strategy, but it does have the great advantage of *leverage*. That is, for a relatively small deposit in a margin account, the option writer can write a relatively large volume of options and potentially earn substantial returns on this relatively small deposit.

Option contracts are not limited to stock equities. They can also be written for many other financial assets. One popular form of options is index options, where the value of an option is linked to the value of a basket of stocks that go to make up a popular stock index, such as the Dow Jones Industrials, the S&P 500, or the Nikkei 225 stock market index.

❧ BARINGS BANK

Although a relatively small player in the investment banking world with about 4,000 employees and assets of $10 billion in 1994, Barings was a widely respected bank that was considered a strong niche player in the emerging markets of Asia, Latin America, and Eastern Europe. Its money management arm managed about $46 billion for a variety of individual and corporate clients, including the Queen of England. The bank was also considered to have a talented corporate-finance team with good connections in British industry.

The bank was established in 1762 by two sons of German immigrants. The bank flourished. Barings was the first bank to reopen trade with America after the Revolutionary War; it helped the American government finance the purchase of Louisiana from France; and it played a major role in financing Britain's wars against Napoleon. For its help in the Napoleonic wars, a grateful British government bestowed five noble titles on the Baring family. The Baring family became prominent members of the British ruling class. The family continued to maintain close ties with the bank, and in 1995 the chairman was Peter Baring.

For most of its 233 years Barings concentrated on the old-fashioned business of investment banking—taking in deposits and lending money to corporations and governments. In a departure from this focus, in 1984 Barings established a securities trading arm, Barings Securities, to take advantage of and profit from the trading opportunities presented by the rapid growth of international financial markets. The trading arm quickly established itself as a profitable operation.

However, a clash of cultures soon began to emerge between the investment banking and securities trading operations of the bank. Part of the problem seems to have been linked to the different backgrounds and attitudes of the personalities involved. The investment banking arm—known as Barings Brothers—was staffed by products of the British establishment, whereas many of the traders came from a different class background. For example, in distinct contrast to the "blue-blooded" investment bankers typified by Peter Baring, Nick Leeson, whose unauthorized trades sunk the bank, was the son of a North London working class family. In this vein, a securities trader who once worked for Barings Securities in Tokyo had the following recollections:

> There was always an uneasy tension between Baring Brothers and Barings Securities. "We're the bankers," they seemed to say, "heirs to a 200-year tradition, and you're the jumped up guys from Liverpool." What seemed to make things worse was that Barings

> Securities was phenomenally profitable for a while. But the attitude persisted: "OK you guys did great for five years, but we've been here for 200. Don't tell us how to run the business." . . . When Peter Baring came to Tokyo to visit the securities department it was like a visit from the Queen.

The British newsmagazine *The Economist* had a similar view of the relationship between Baring Brothers and Baring Securities. According to *The Economist*:

> The old-style bankers who dominated Barings' senior management have long looked down their aristocratic noses at the traders who run the bank's security operations.

Things came to a head in 1992 when tumbling stock prices in Tokyo pushed the normally profitable Barings Securities into a $20 million loss. In an attempt to turn things around, Christopher Heath, the head of Barings Securities, lobbied for more capital to boost proprietary trading (trading on the firm's own account). Andrew Tuckey, the deputy chairman of Barings, objected that this would leave the group too exposed to volatile financial markets. Heath resigned in response, and he was followed by a number of other key directors at Barings Securities. According to one former Barings Securities employee:

> It was effectively a takeover of the securities operation by the (investment) bank. You had the unworkable situation of investment bankers supposedly overseeing investment traders.

Barings employees refer to the period that followed the 1993 coup as "The Turbulence." In Asia it led to a confusing series of personnel moves that ultimately left management dangerously weakened. In Tokyo, for example, the longtime Baring Securities branch manager, Richard Greer, was replaced by Henry Anstey, who was himself soon replaced. Baring Securities in Hong Kong lost a team of seven from its proprietary trading and derivatives desk to the start-up operation, New China Hong Kong Securities. The Hong Kong operation suffered another blow when Willie Phillips, formally head of all security business in Asia outside of Japan, left for Salomon Brothers. Also important was the loss of Richard Johnson, who had headed Barings' derivative operations in Tokyo until he was transferred to London in 1992. Johnson, who left Barings in May 1993, was "the brains of the group," according to a former colleague. "His departure opened a large hole in the region."

As a result of these management changes, in 1995 a former Barings employee observed:

> There has been no continuity of management for the past two years. It was difficult to say who was in charge of what and where from one month to the next. . . . The team that had been built up from the late 1980s (in the Asian securities operations) was scattered to the four winds. . . . The pool of derivatives-based knowledge in the region virtually disappeared."

Another former employee had similar observations:

> You had a situation where the securities side was still at loggerheads with the banking side. On top of that, the derivatives side was little understood by either. . . . Working in derivatives was a little like working in a vacuum. To most of the senior guys on both the securities side and the merchant bank, it was like we were talking a foreign language. They just let us get on with it. We did our own controls and regulated ourselves to all intents and purposes. In hindsight, there wasn't anyone for us to report to.

✎ NICK LEESON'S LITTLE TRADES

It was against this chaotic background in Barings Asian Securities operations that Nick Leeson arrived in Singapore in 1991 to help unravel some backroom trading problems. Within a year Leeson had joined the trading team on the floor of the Singapore International Monetary Exchange (SIME). By day he executed trades in the Nikkei Stock Averages futures contracts under the direction of Barings traders in

Japan. By night he partied in the yuppie bars along the Singapore River. According to a former colleague: "He was your average English guy who likes to go out for a beer after work, and sometimes has a few too many. I wouldn't have said anything negative about him."

Leeson's primary job at Barings was to arbitrage Nikkei index futures contracts that were traded on both the Singapore and Osaka exchanges (trading of Nikkei futures in Singapore began in the 1980s when the Japanese government tried to curtail futures trading in Osaka). Such arbitrage involves buying futures contracts on one market and simultaneously selling them on another. Profits are made by exploiting small price differentials for the same contract between the two exchanges. Since the margins are small, the volumes traded by arbitrageurs tend to be very large. However, the strategy is associated with very little risk.

By all accounts Leeson was a successful arbitrage trader. By September 1994 Leeson was viewed as the senior trader for Barings in Singapore, even though he was only 27 years old. It was at this point that Leeson departed from the low-risk arbitrage strategy and started to speculate on the volatility of the Nikkei 255 Stock Index. Leeson's motives for speculation aren't entirely clear, although maximizing the size of his bonus—which could have easily run into seven figures had his strategy been successful—was certainly a factor. Leeson's strategy involved simultaneously writing uncovered put and call options on Nikkei 255 futures. Known as a straddle strategy, this procedure will make money for the option writer provided the market stays within a relatively narrow trading range. The strategy required Barings to sell the Nikkei 255 index when it crossed 19,500 and to buy it when it fell below 18,500. Leeson's strategy made Barings money so long as the Nikkei stayed within this relatively narrow range. Once the Nikkei went outside this range Barings started to lose large amounts of money—about $70 million for every 1 percent move above or below these limits. The loss was exacerbated by Leeson's aggressive use of leverage (he was writing options from a margin account).

At first the strategy seemed to be working. Traders at other banks reckon that Leeson may have earned as much as $150 million for Barings from this strategy by the end of 1994. However, the strategy started to fall apart when the Kobe earthquake struck January 17, 1995. In response to the economic devastation caused by the earthquake, the Nikkei started to plunge. Worried that the market would fall well below 18,500, Leeson seems to have entered the market and purchased Nikkei futures on a huge scale in an attempt to push the market up above 18,500. This is not an easy thing to do; the Tokyo stock market is the second biggest in the world.

Leeson's position deteriorated further January 23 when the Tokyo stock market plunged 1,000 points to under 17,800. An increasingly desperate Nick Leeson responded to the crisis by drawing on a margin account to continue purchasing Nikkei futures in what was to prove to be a futile attempt to prop up the Nikkei index. By late February 1995 Barings had accumulated index positions that effectively amounted to a $7 billion long bet on the Tokyo stock market. At the height of Leeson's trades, Barings accounted for about half of the open positions in Nikkei 255 futures contracts.

Such financial excess did not go unnoticed either by other traders in Singapore or by executives at Barings Bank in London. However, Barings executives and other traders were all under the impression that Leeson was acting on behalf of a major client, perhaps a big hedge fund. No one could conceive that the positions belonged to Barings. As for the cash required to purchase Nikkei futures, apparently much of this came from an account for a fictitious client that Leeson had set up as early as 1992. Into this account went some of Barings' own cash, along with all the proceeds of Leeson's option sales and some fictitious profits from falsified arbitrage deals. He then used this fictitious account to pay margin calls on his growing futures position. When the account was exhausted, Leeson turned to Barings in London, telling them he was executing trades on behalf of a major client who would settle up in a few days. Barings proved only too willing to send more money to its star trader in Singapore.

Bolstered by the arrival of additional funds from London, Leeson kept up the charade until February 23 when the cash flowing out to cover margin payments exceeded Barings' preset limits. With the Nikkei continuing to decline, Leeson apparently realized he could no longer carry on with the game. He hurriedly faxed a letter to Barings in London tendering his resignation—adding that he was sorry for the trouble he had caused—and along with his wife boarded a plane out of Singapore. The next day shocked Barings' executives informed the Bank of England they were technically bankrupt. The liabilities from Leeson's trades already exceeded $800 million and were growing by the hour as the Nikkei index continued to fall.

❧ AFTERMATH

Over the weekend of February 25 and 26 the stunned management of Barings tried to arrange for a bailout by the Bank of England. The bank tried; over the two-day period several investment banks were summoned to the Bank of England's offices to discuss the possibility of raising enough private money to recapitalize Barings before the Tokyo market reopened Monday morning. However, the attempt failed because of the size of Barings' positions in Japanese derivatives contracts, many of them still open and so liable to incur still bigger losses. No bank was willing to take on these contracts without a large fee—or a guarantee from the Bank of England that it would cover these losses. The Bank of England, which stated later that such a fee might have amounted to $700 million, decided it was not prepared to put the money of British taxpayers at risk.

On March 3 the Dutch financial group ING stepped in and offered to purchase Barings for one pound sterling, in exchange for taking on all Barings' liabilities. With no other offers on the table, Barings directors were obliged to accept the ING offer. In the following weeks ING moved quickly to replace virtually all of Barings' top management, including Chairman Peter Baring, and to start to tighten controls within the group.

As for Nick Leeson, for several day his whereabouts were a mystery. Then on March 3 Leeson was detained by German immigration authorities as he tried to board a plane back to Britain. Leeson was eventually deported back to Singapore, where he faced charges for securities fraud. Among other things, it was alleged that he falsified trading data to create paper profits that were then funneled into accounts attributed to fictitious clients. It was from these accounts that Leeson executed many of his trades in the run up to the collapse of Barings. In December 1995 he was sentenced to a six-and-a-half-year prison sentence.

As for the global financial system, initially there were worries that the revelations about Barings might lead to a loss of confidence in the global financial system, and in the financial position of many of the banks engaged in derivatives trading. But there was no evidence of a negative effect from the Barings collapse. Rather, among the financial community the view soon emerged that the collapse of Barings had little to do with derivatives trading, and much more to do with the lack of internal management controls at Barings. It was this lack of controls that allowed Leeson to speculate using financial instruments that were designed to reduce risk, not increase it. According to the prevailing view among other traders, the problem lay not in the tool Leeson used—derivatives—but in the way Leeson used that tool and the poor monitoring of his activities.

In July 1995 the Bank of England issued a report on the collapse of Barings. The bank also expressed the view that Barings suffered from poor internal management controls. According to the bank's report: "Significant amounts were regularly remitted to BFS without any clear understanding on the part of Barings' management on whose behalf these monies were to be applied, and without any real demur." The Bank of England's report also cited a number of senior managers at Barings, including Andrew Tuckey and Peter Baring, for failing to apply proper controls.

In an interview given to BBC Television's David Frost in September, Nick Leeson, then in a German jail awaiting deportation to Singapore, also gave more insight into the collapse of Barings. According to Leeson, he got away with his trading for so long because of the failure of key executives at Barings' London headquarters to understand the business he was engaged in and to look more closely into his activities.

> The first day that I asked for funding (to meet margin calls) there should have been massive alarm bells ringing. But senior people in London that were arranging these payments didn't understand the basic administration of futures and options. . . . They wanted to believe in the profits being reported, and therefore they weren't willing to question.

CASE DISCUSSION QUESTIONS

1. Why do you think critics are worried that the rapid growth in the use of derivatives might destabilize global financial markets?
2. Do you think derivatives are risky and speculative financial instruments or instruments that can be used to reduce an investor's risk?
3. Does the collapse of Barings expose a fundamental flaw in the global financial system? If so, how might this flaw be fixed?
4. What is your view on the basic causes of the collapse of Barings?

SOURCES

1. Bray, N., and G. Whitney. "Barings Collapse Tied to Wide Cast." *The Wall Street Journal*, July 19, 1995, p. A5.
2. Bray, N. "Leeson Says Losses at Barings Started with Bailout of Errors by Colleagues." *The Wall Street Journal*, September 11, 1995, p. A16.
3. "A Fallen Star." *The Economist*, March 4, 1995, pp. 19–21.
4. Mark, J., and M. Sesit. "Losses at Barings Grow to $1.24 Billion." *The Wall Street Journal*, February 28, 1995, p. A3.
5. Melloan, G. "Leeson's Law." *The Wall Street Journal*, March 6, 1995, p. A15.
6. Nusbaum, D., and J. Reerink. "BoE Report Details Barings' Guiles and Goofs." *Futures*, September 1995, pp. 12–22.
7. "A Royal Mess." *The Wall Street Journal*, February 27, 1995, p. A1.
8. Shale, T. "Why Barings Was Doomed." *Euromoney*, March 1995, pp. 38–41.
9. United Stated General Accounting Office; Report to Congress. *Financial Derivatives*, May 1994, GOA GGD-94-133.
10. Whitney, G. "Dutch Giant Offers to Buy All of Barings." *The Wall Street Journal*, March 3, 1995, p. A3.

CHAOS IN THE CURRENCY MARKETS

Ever since the breakup of the Bretton Woods system of fixed exchange rates in 1971 there has been talk about the possibility of returning to a fixed rate system. Advocates of a fixed exchange rate regime have long maintained that the system has several distinct advantages over the current "managed-float" system. They argue that a fixed exchange rate regime imposes monetary discipline on the nations that participate in it (which, in turn, limits inflation), removes the uncertainty and risk due to fluctuations in exchange rates, limits speculation, and consequently promotes international trade and investment.

In contrast the advocates of floating exchange rates make two points. First, they claim that a floating exchange rate regime gives countries monetary police autonomy. Under a fixed system, a country's ability to expand or contract its money supply is limited by the need to maintain exchange rate parity. Under a floating system, national governments maintain sovereignty over their monetary policy.

Second, these advocates argue that if a country is running a trade deficit, the imbalance between the supply and demand of its currency in the foreign exchange markets will lead to a depreciation of its exchange rate. In turn, by making its exports cheaper and its imports more expensive, an exchange rate depreciation should ultimately correct the trade deficit. Under a fixed regime, in contrast, the adjustment process is nowhere near as smooth, and a formal currency devaluation is required to achieve the same end.

Although this issue has been debated actively in the years since the breakdown of Bretton Woods, it has never been resolved. However, since the early 1980s those who support a return to a fixed rate regime have had a powerful argument on their side: the success of the European Monetary System (EMS), established in 1979. At the heart of the EMS is a system of fixed exchange rates between the currencies of the member-countries of the European Union (EU). This system has been widely credited with closing the inflation rate differentials among the member-countries during the 1980s. Many saw the EMS as paving the way for the eventual establishment of a common currency for the EU. Then in the space of a few days in September 1992, the EMS was exposed to a gale of speculative pressure that nearly shattered the system and renewed concerns about the viability of fixed exchange rate regimes. This case describes what occurred during those few days. We begin with a brief discussion of the EMS. Then we look at the exchange rate crisis and its aftermath.

◈ THE EMS

The EMS is composed of two instruments: the exchange rate mechanism (ERM) and the European currency unit (ecu). The ecu is a basket of the EU currencies that serves as the unit of account for the EMS. The share of each country's currency in the ecu depends on that country's relative economic weight within the EU. In 1989, 30.1 percent of the ecu's value (the largest percentage) was determined by the value of the German deutsche mark, primarily because Germany is viewed as the strongest and largest economy within the EU.

The ERM works as follows: Each national currency in the EU is given a *central rate* vis-à-vis the ecu. For example, in September 1989 one ecu was equal to DM2.05853, FFr6.90404, and £0.739615. This central rate can be changed only by a commonly agreed-on realignment. From these central rates flow a series of *bilateral rates*—the French franc against the Italian lira, the German deutsche mark against the British pound, and so on. For example, the above figures vis-à-vis the ecu indicate that the bilateral rate for exchanging deutsche marks into francs was DM1 = FFR2.9586 (i.e., FFr6.90404/DM2.05853). The bilateral rates form a cat's cradle known as the *ERM parity grid,* the operational part of the system. The rule for most currencies is that they may not depart by more than 2.25 percent from their bilateral ECU-determined rate with another ERM-participating currency. The only exceptions are the Spanish peseta and the British pound, which as recent additions to the ERM are allowed to fluctuate by up to 6 percent against other ERM currencies.

Intervention in the foreign exchange markets is compulsory whenever one currency hits its outer margin of fluctuation relative to another. The central banks of the countries issuing both currencies are supposed to intervene to keep their currencies within the 2.25 percent (or 6 percent) band. The central bank of the country with the stronger currency is supposed to buy the weaker currency, and vice versa. To defend its currency against speculative pressure, each member-state can borrow almost unlimited amounts of foreign currency from other members for up to three months. A second line of defense includes loans that can be extended for up to nine months, but the total amount available is limited to a pool of credit—originally about 14 billion ecus—and the size of the member's quota in the pool. Additional funds are available for two to five years from a second pool of (originally) about 11 billion ecus.

❧ SEPTEMBER 1992

The roots of the European currency crisis of September 1992 can be traced to the fall of the Berlin Wall in 1989 and the subsequent reunification of West and East Germany. In an attempt to reduce the economic pain of reunification on its poorer eastern neighbor, the West German government agreed to a 1-for-1 swap of the East German deutsche mark for the West German deutsche mark after reunification. The Bundesbank, West Germany's (and now Germany's) central bank, objected to this policy, pointing out that a 1-to-2 swap made more sense, but to no avail. The result was a surge in the German money supply after reunification and a subsequent rise in inflation. The government's budget deficit also expanded, adding to the Bundesbank's alarm. In an attempt to control inflation and rein back monetary growth, the Bundesbank began to raise interest rates.

Meanwhile on the other side of the Atlantic, the U.S. economy was mired in its most persistent recession since World War II. After repeated prodding, the U.S. Federal Reserve Board had cut U.S. interest rates several times since late 1991. As a consequence, by August 1992 a significant interest rate differential had opened up between Germany and the United States. For example, on August 25 the interest rate on three-month certificates of deposit was 9.9 percent in Germany and 3.6 percent in the United States. The result? Foreign exchange dealers, financial institutions, and corporations switched their cash balances from dollars to DMs. This drove up the price of DMs relative to the dollar. In April 1992 one dollar bought 1.63 DMs, and by late August it bought only 1.40 DMs.

While the pressure on the dollar was beginning to raise concerns in the United States, its consequences for the EMS were also becoming apparent. The ERM required EU currencies to maintain their value against the DM. Germany's high interest rates were already causing pain in many other EU countries. Great Britain, for example, was suffering its worst recession since 1945 and wanted to cut its interest rates to ease the economic pressure and stimulate domestic demand. However, it had to keep its base rate at 10 percent to match German interest rates and maintain the value of the pound against the DM. Despite these high interest rates, as demand for the DM rose, so did its value on the foreign exchange markets. This began to put pressure on the weaker EU currencies—particularly on the British pound, the Italian lira, and the Spanish peseta. The governments of these countries faced the prospect of having to raise their already high interest rates even further to avoid devaluation within the ERM.

At this point, speculators in the foreign exchange market began to bet on devaluation of several key European currencies against the DM. The basic strategy was simple: buy the currency expected to appreciate (DMs) and sell the ones expected to depreciate. If the speculators bet correctly, they could make large profits in the event of a realignment within the ERM (but losses could also be huge if they bet incorrectly). The first currency to feel the pressure was the Italian lira. Italy had the weakest economy among the major EU countries and a budget deficit amounting to 11.3 percent of its gross domestic product. As foreign exchange dealers dumped the lira, its value plummeted against the DM, forcing the Italian government to raise interest rates to 15 percent. Then, on September 9, the Italian government announced a tough economic package designed to curb the Italian deficit. Foreign exchange dealers were unimpressed, and the pressure on the lira continued.

The continued pressure on the lira prompted a top-level meeting of EU finance ministers and central bankers. Under pressure, the Bundesbank agreed to cut its interest rates on September 14 by one half of a percentage point—the first reduction in five years—in exchange for a 7 percent devaluation in the Italian lira. This was meant to calm the foreign exchange markets and stabilize the ERM, but it did no such thing. Fresh from their victory against the lira, foreign exchange dealers turned their attention to the British pound and the Swedish krona. Although Sweden is not part of the EU, it had linked its currency to the ERM in anticipation of joining the EU sometime during the 1990s. Foreign exchange dealers were undoubtedly encouraged in their belief that further devaluations were likely by statements made by Helmet Schlesinger, Bundesbank president. On September 15, clearly annoyed at being pressured to cut German interest rates, Schlesinger suggested to a German newspaper that the deal of September 14 had not gone far enough toward resolving Europe's currency crisis and that only a broad realignment of EU currencies against the DM would stabilize the EMS. Within minutes this statement was transmitted around the world by wire services. In response the foreign exchange markets were hit by an explosion of speculative pressure.

Attention now concentrated on the British pound. On September 16 the pound was dipping below its permitted floor against the DM of 2.778. To protect the pound, Great Britain's government was forced to raise interest rates, initially from 10 percent to 12 percent, and then later the same day to 15 percent. Moreover, estimates suggest the British government reportedly spent $15 billion to $20 billion, up to half of its total foreign exchange reserves, to support the pound on September 16. All of this was to no avail; the pound remained below its floor in the ERM. That evening, Great Britain admitted defeat. Finance Minister Norman Lamont, who only a few days earlier had stated the pound would not be devalued, announced Great Britain would withdraw from the ERM and the pound would be allowed to float freely. The rise in interest rates from 12 percent to 15 percent was canceled, and a day later rates were cut back to 10 percent.

Also on September 16, the Swedish krona was hit by speculative pressure. Sweden responded by raising its overnight interest rates, first to 30 percent and then to a staggering 500 percent. At least in the short run, this move seemed to scare off speculators—although at enormous cost to Sweden.

On September 17 attention switched once more to the lira. Foreign exchange dealers clearly felt the 7 percent of devaluation of the lira announced on September 14 did not go far enough and that a further devaluation was likely. The Italian government responded to the renewed wave of speculative pressure by following Great Britain's lead and pulling the lira out of the ERM. Although the Italian government announced its intention to get back into the ERM at the first opportunity, many doubted this would be anytime soon.

By this point the EMS was teetering on the brink of collapse. Two of the four largest EU countries, Great Britain and Italy, had quit the ERM. Speculators now turned their attention to the French franc. Although the franc was a much stronger currency than either the pound or the lira, on September 20 France was due to hold a national referendum on the Maastricht Treaty. This treaty would open the way for closer economic and political union within the EU, including the establishment of a common currency by 1999. If the French rejected the treaty, and it looked as if the vote was going to be close, the EMS was likely to be a major victim. The French voted yes, but only by a narrow margin, and speculative pressure increased.

However, the franc was to prove a tougher nut to crack. In marked contrast to its earlier stance with regard to Great Britain and Italy, the German Bundesbank joined forces with the Bank of France to defend the franc against speculative pressure. On September 23 the Bank of France raised interest rates from 10.5 percent to 13 percent. At the same time, central banks and finance ministers from France and Germany issued a rare joint statement stressing that there was no need for a change in the EMS parity between the DM and the franc and stating that France and Germany would fight any speculative pressure. This statement was followed by heavy intervention by both central banks. The Bundesbank openly intervened to support the franc, the first time it had acted this way since the ERM had been instituted in 1979. Estimates suggest that on September 22 and 23 the Bundesbank spent between DM10 billion and DM30 billion ($6.7 billion to $20 billion) defending the franc, while the Bank of France spent more than FFr50 billion ($10 billion). By September

26 the foreign exchange dealers recognized that the franc was not going to go the way of the lira and British pound, and speculative pressure eased. For the time being the EMS and ERM remained intact—but only *just*.

❦ AFTERWORD

Figures released by central banks on September 24 showed that foreign exchange trading had grown by about 50 percent between 1989 and 1992 to an estimated $1 trillion (U.S.) each day. At the same time, the amount of money that the central banks have stockpiled for buying their own currencies when they are weak and carrying out other transactions has grown more slowly. Foreign exchange reserves held by the world's central banks amounted to $1 trillion in 1992, no more than the average daily volume of currency trading. Some economists now doubt that central banks, whatever the size of their reserves, can successfully defend their currencies in the long term.

CASE DISCUSSION QUESTIONS

1. What does the crisis of September 1992 tell you about the relative abilities of currency markets and national governments to influence exchange rates?
2. What does the crisis of September 1992 tell you about the weaknesses of fixed exchange rate regimes?
3. Assess the impact of the events of September 1992 on the EU's ability to establish a common currency by 1999.
4. The crisis of September 1992 occurred because the ERM system was too inflexible. Discuss.
5. If you were an executive for a company that engages in substantial intra-EU trade, how would you react to the events of September 1992?

REFERENCES

Brittan, S. "Anatomy of the UK Defeat." *Financial Times*, September 24, 1992, p. 2.

———, "Devaluation Threat: How 92 Differs," *Financial Times*, September 19, 1992, p. 17.

"France and Germany Unite to Defend Franc." *Financial Times*, September 24, 1992, p. 1.

"A Ghastly Game of Dominoes." *The Economist*, September 19, 1992, pp. 89–90.

Greising, D.; John Templeman; R. Melcher; and Stewart Toy. "The Buck Stops Where?" *Business Week*, September 7, 1992, pp. 26–28.

Javestki, B.; J. Templeman; and R. Melcher. "Europe Money Mess." *Business Week*, September 28, 1992, pp. 30–31.

"Mayhem." *The Economist*, September 19, 1992, pp. 15–16.

"Meltdown," *The Economist*, September 19, 1992, p. 69.

Meyerson, A. "Currency Markets Resisting Power of Central Banks." *New York Times*, September 25, 1992, pp. A1, C15.

Norman, P.; W. Dawkins; and J. Blitz. "French Franc Proves a Tough Nut to Crack." *Financial Times*, September 24, 1992, p. 2.

Sesit, M. R., and D. R. Sease. "Mark Continues to Gain in Uncertain Market." *The Wall Street Journal*, September 18, 1992, pp. C1, C5.

Stephens, P. "Sterling Plummets after U.K. Suspends ERM Membership." *Financial Times*, September 17, 1992, p. 1.

"Tom beyond Repair?" *The Economist*, September 26, 1992, pp. 89–90.

CHAPTER TWELVE

THE STRATEGY OF INTERNATIONAL BUSINESS

IT'S A MAC WORLD

Established in 1955, McDonald's faced a problem by the early 1980s: After three decades of rapid growth, the U.S. fast-food market was beginning to show signs of market saturation. McDonald's response to the slowdown was to expand abroad rapidly. In 1980 28 percent of the chain's new restaurant openings were abroad; in 1986 the figure was 40 percent, in 1990 it was close to 60 percent, and in 1994 it hit 66 percent. Since the early 1980s the firm's foreign revenues and profits have grown at 22 percent per year. By 1994 the firm had 4,700 restaurants in 72 countries outside the United States. Together they generated $3.4 billion (46 percent) of the firm's $7.4 billion in revenues. And McDonald's shows no signs of slowing down. Management notes there is still only one McDonald's restaurant for every 600,000 people in the 72 foreign countries in which it currently does business. This compares to one McDonald's restaurant for every 25,000 people in the United States. The firm's plans call for this foreign expansion to continue at a rapid rate. In England, France, and Germany combined the firm plans to open 500 more restaurants between 1995 and 1997 for a 37 percent gain. During the same period McDonald's is expected to double to 800 the number of its restaurants in the Caribbean, Mexico, Central America, and South America. The firm also plans to enter another 25 to 30 countries by the end of the century.

One key to the firm's successful foreign expansion is detailed planning. When McDonald's enters a foreign country, it does so only after careful preparation. In what is a fairly typical pattern, before McDonald's opened its first Polish restaurant in 1992 the firm spent 18 months establishing essential contacts and getting to know the local culture. Locations, real estate, construction, supply, personnel, legal, and government relations were all worked out in advance. In June 1992 a team of 50 employees from

the United States, Russia, Germany, and Britain went to Poland to help with the opening of the first four resturants. A primary objective was to hire and train local personnel. By mid-1994 all these employees except one had returned to their home country. They were replaced by Polish nationals who had now been brought up to the skill level required to run a McDonald's operation.

Another key to the firm's international strategy is the export of the management skills that spurred its growth in the United States—McDonald's U.S. success was built on a formula of close relations with suppliers, nationwide marketing might, tight control over store-level operating procedures, and a franchising system that encourages entrepreneurial individual franchisees. Although this system has worked flawlessly in the United States, some modifications must be made in other countries. One of the firm's biggest challenges has been to infuse each store with the same gung-ho culture and standardized operating procedures that have been the hallmark of its success in the United

States. To aid in this task, in many countries McDonald's has enlisted the help of large partners through joint-venture arrangements. The partners play a key role in learning and transplanting the organization's values to local employees.

Foreign partners have also played a key role in helping McDonald's adapt its marketing methods and menu to local conditions. Although U.S.-style fast food remains the staple fare on the menu, local products have been added. In Brazil, for example, McDonald's sells a soft drink made from the guarana, an Amazonian berry. Patrons of McDonald's in Malaysia, Singapore, and Thailand savor shakes flavored with durian, a foul-smelling (to U.S. tastes, at least) fruit considered an aphrodisiac by the locals. In addition to their help in product adaptation, these partners can steer the firm away from potentially expensive marketing pitfalls. In Japan, for example, Den Fujita, president of McDonald's in Japan, avoided the suburban locations typical in the United States and stressed urban sites that consumers could walk to.

McDonald's biggest problem, however, has been to replicate its U.S. supply chain in other countries. U.S. suppliers are fiercely loyal to McDonald's; they must be, because their fortunes are closely linked to those of McDonald's. McDonald's maintains very rigorous specifications for all the raw ingredients it uses—the key to its consistency and quality control. Outside the United States, however, McDonald's has found suppliers far less willing to make the investments required to meet its specifications. In Great Britain, for example, McDonald's had problems getting local bakeries to produce the hamburger bun. After experiencing quality problems with two local bakeries, McDonald's built its own bakery to supply its stores there. In a more extreme case, when McDonald's decided to open a store in Russia, it found that local suppliers lacked the capability to produce goods of the quality it demanded. The firm was forced to vertically integrate through the local food industry on a heroic scale, importing potato seeds and bull semen and indirectly managing dairy farms, cattle ranches, and vegetable plots. It also had to construct the world's largest food-processing plant, at a cost of $40 million. The restaurant itself cost only $4.5 million.

Now that it has a successful foreign operation, McDonald's is experiencing benefits that go beyond the immediate financial ones. Increasingly the firm is finding that its foreign franchisees are a source for valuable new ideas. The Dutch operation created a prefabricated modular store that can be moved over a weekend and is now widely used to set up temporary restaurants at big outdoor events. The

Swedes came up with an enhanced meat freezer that is now used firmwide. And satellite stores, or low overhead mini-McDonald's, which are now appearing in hospitals and sports arenas in the United States, were originally invented in Singapore.

Sources: Kathleen Deveny et al., "McWorld?" *Business Week*, October 13, 1986, pp. 78–86; "Slow Food," *The Economist*, February 3, 1990, p. 64; Harlan S. Byrne, "Welcome to McWorld," *Barron's*, August 29, 1994, pp. 25–28; and Andrew E. Serwer, "McDonald's Conquers the World," *Fortune*, October 17, 1994, pp. 103–16.

❧ INTRODUCTION

Our primary concern so far has been with aspects of the larger environment in which international businesses compete. As we have described it in the preceding chapters, this environment has included the different political, economic, and cultural institutions found in different nations, the international trade and investment framework, and the international monetary system. From this point forward our primary focus shifts from the environment to the firm itself, and in particular, to the actions managers can take to compete more effectively as an international business. In this chapter we look at how firms can increase their profitability by expanding their operations in foreign markets, we discuss the different strategies that firms pursue when competing internationally, we consider the pros and cons of these strategies, and we discuss the various factors that impact a firm's choice of strategy. In subsequent chapters we shall build on the framework established here to discuss a variety of topics including the design of organization structures and control systems for international businesses, the use and misuse of strategic alliances, strategies for exporting, and the various manufacturing, marketing, R&D, human resource, accounting, and financial strategies that are pursued by international businesses.

McDonald's, which was profiled in the opening case, gives us a preview of some issues we will be addressing in the current chapter. As described in the case, McDonald's started to expand internationally to continue growing in the face of an increasingly mature and saturated U.S. fast-food market. McDonald's is not alone here; the pursuit of greater profit opportunities has driven many other firms to expand internationally. McDonald's has generated a high profit from its international operations primarily because it has figured out how to transfer the management skills that made it so successful in the United States to other countries where indigenous competitors lack those skills. Before the entry of McDonald's, many countries lacked U.S.-style fast-food outlets. Thus in country after country McDonald's has been the pioneer in the introduction of the fast-food concept, and it has reaped enormous gains from this first-mover position. At the same time, the case describes how another cornerstone of McDonald's success is its willingness to customize the menu being offered on a country-by-country basis so it appeals to national differences in tastes and preferences. Thus McDonald's success is built both on a successful management formula that is applied worldwide and on a willingness to customize aspects of the product offering when it is necessary to success in a given nation. As we shall see, while it is not always required, this combination of a clear central strategic vision and a willingness to customize the firm's product offering on a country-by-country basis is a hallmark of many successful international businesses.

FIGURE 12.1
The Firm as a Value Chain

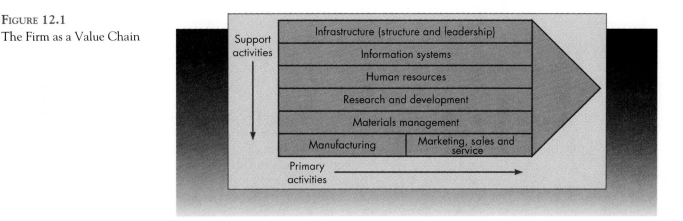

☙ STRATEGY AND THE FIRM

The fundamental purpose of any business firm is to make a profit. A firm makes a profit if the price it can charge for its output is greater than its costs of producing that output. To do this, a firm must produce a product that is valued by consumers. Thus we say that business firms engage in the activity of value creation. The price consumers are prepared to pay for a product indicates the value of the product to consumers.

Firms can increase their profits in two ways: by adding value to a product so consumers are willing to pay more for it, and by lowering the costs of value creation (i.e., the costs of production). A firm adds value to a product when it improves the product's quality, provides a service to the consumer, or customizes the product to consumer needs in such a way that consumers will pay more for it; that is, when the firm *differentiates* the product from that offered by competitors. For example, consumers will pay more for a Mercedes-Benz car than a Hyundai car because they value the superior quality of the Mercedes. Firms lower the costs of value creation when they find ways to perform value creation activities more efficiently. Thus there are two basic strategies for improving a firm's profitability—*a differentiation strategy* and a *low-cost strategy*.[1]

The Firm as a Value Chain

It is useful to think of the firm as a value chain composed of a series of distinct value-creation activities including production, marketing, materials management, R&D, human resources, information systems, and the firm infrastructure. We can categorize these value-creation activities as primary activities and support activities (see Figure 12.1).[2]

Primary activities

The primary activities of a firm have to do with creating the product, marketing and delivering the product to buyers, and providing support and aftersale service to the buyers of the product. Here we consider the activities involved in the physical creation of the product as production and those involved in marketing, delivery, and aftersale service as marketing. Efficient production can reduce the costs of creating value (e.g., by realizing scale economies) and can add value by increasing product quality (e.g., by reducing the number of defective products), which facilitates premium pricing. Efficient marketing also can help the firm reduce its costs of

---

[1]M. E. Porter, *Competitive Strategy* (New York: Free Press, 1980).
[2]M. E. Porter, *Competitve Advantage* (New York: Free Press, 1985).

creating value (e.g., by generating the volume sales necessary to realize scale economies) and can add value by helping the firm customize its product to consumer needs and differentiate its product from competitors' products—both of which facilitate premium pricing.

Support activities

Support activities provide the inputs that allow the primary activities of production and marketing to occur. The materials management function controls the transmission of physical materials through the value chain—from procurement through production and into distribution. The efficiency with which this is carried out can significantly reduce the cost of creating value. In addition an effective materials management function can monitor the quality of inputs into the production process. This results in improved quality of the firm's outputs, which adds value and thus facilitates premium pricing.

The R&D function develops new product and process technologies. Technological developments can reduce production costs and can result in the creation of more useful and more attractive products that can demand a premium price. Thus R&D can affect primary production and marketing activities and, through them, value creation.

An effective human resource function ensures that the firm has an optimal mix of people to perform its primary production and marketing activities, that the staffing requirements of the support activities are met, and that employees are well trained for their tasks and compensated accordingly. The information systems function makes certain that management has the information it needs to maximize the efficiency of its value chain and to exploit information-based competitive advantages in the marketplace. Firm infrastructure—consisting of such factors as organizational structure, general management, planning, finance, and legal and government affairs—embraces all other activities of the firm and establishes the context for them. An efficient infrastructure thus helps both to create value and to reduce the costs of creating value.

The Role of Strategy

A firm's **strategy** can be defined as the actions managers take to attain the goals of the firm. For most firms a principal goal is to be highly profitable. Markets are now extremely competitive due to the liberalization of the world trade and investment environment. In industry after industry many capable competitors confront each other around the globe. To be profitable in such an environment, a firm must pay continual attention to both reducing the costs of value creation and to differentiating its product offering in such a manner that consumers are willing to pay more for the product than it costs to produce it. Thus strategy is often concerned with identifying and taking actions that will *lower the costs* of value creation and/or will *differentiate* the firm's product offering through superior design, quality, service, functionality, and the like.

To fully understand this, consider the case of Swan Optical, which is profiled in the next "Management Focus." A U.S.-based manufacturer of eyeglasses, Swan found its survival threatened by low-cost foreign competitors. To deal with this threat, Swan adopted a strategy intended to lower its cost structure: shifting its production from a high-cost location, the United States, to a low-cost location, Hong Kong. Later Swan adopted a strategy intended to differentiate its basic product so it could charge a premium price. Reasoning that premium pricing in eyewear depended on superior design, its strategy involved investing capital in French, Italian, and Japanese factories that had reputations for superior design. In sum Swan's strategies included some actions intended to reduce its costs of creating value and other actions intended to add value to its product through differentiation.

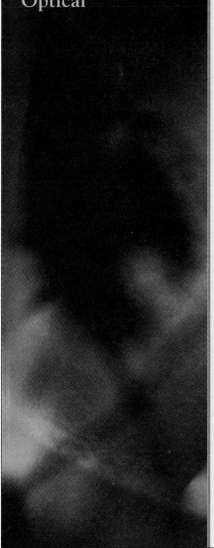

Management Focus
Strategy at Swan Optical

Swan Optical is a manufacturer and distributor of eyewear. Started in the 1960s by Alan Glassman, the firm today generates annual gross revenues of more than $30 million. Not exactly small, but no corporate giant either, Swan Optical is also a multinational firm with production facilities on three continents and customers around the world. Swan began its move toward becoming a multinational in the 1970s. The strong dollar at that time made U.S.-based manufacturing very expensive. Low-priced imports were taking an ever-larger share of the U.S. eyewear market, and Swan realized it could not survive unless it also began to import. Initially the firm bought from independent overseas manufacturers, primarily in Hong Kong. However, the firm became dissatisfied with these suppliers' product quality and delivery. As Swan's volume of imports increased, Glassman decided the best way to guarantee quality and delivery was to set up Swan's own manufacturing operation overseas. Accordingly Swan found a Chinese partner, and together they opened a manufacturing facility in Hong Kong, with Swan being the majority shareholder.

The choice of the Hong Kong location was influenced by its combination of low labor costs, a skilled work force, and tax breaks given by the Hong Kong government. By 1986, however, the increasing industrialization of Hong Kong and a growing labor shortage had pushed up wage rates to the extent that it was no longer a low-cost location. In response Glassman and his Chinese partner moved part of their manufacturing to a plant in mainland China to take advantage of the lower wage rates there. The parts for eyewear frames manufactured at this plant are shipped to the Hong Kong factory for final assembly and then distributed to markets in North and South America. The Hong Kong factory now employs 80 people and the China plant between 300 and 400.

At the same time Swan had begun to look for opportunities to invest in foreign eyewear firms with reputations for fashionable design and high quality. Its objective in this case was not to reduce manufacturing costs but to launch a line of high-quality, "designer" eyewear. Swan did not have the design capability in-house to support such a line, but Glassman knew that certain foreign manufacturers had the capability. As a result, Swan invested in factories in Japan, France, and Italy, taking a minority shareholding in each case. These factories now supply eyewear for Swan's Status Eye division, which markets high-priced designer eyewear.

Source: C. S. Trager, "Enter the Mini-Multinational," *Northeast International Business*, March 1989, pp. 13–14.

❧ Profiting from Global Expansion

Expanding globally allows firms to increase their profitability in ways not available to purely domestic enterprises. Firms that operate internationally are able to:

1. Earn a greater return from their distinctive skills, or core competencies.
2. Realize location economies by dispersing particular value-creation activities to those locations where they can be performed most efficiently.
3. Realize greater experience curve economies, which reduce the costs of value creation.

As we will see, however, a firm's ability to increase its profitability by pursuing these strategies is constrained by the need to customize its product offering, marketing strategy, and business strategy to differing national conditions.

Transferring Core Competencies

The term **core competence** refers to skills within the firm that competitors cannot easily match or imitate.[3] These skills may exist in any of the firm's value-creation activities—production, marketing, R&D, human resources, general management, and so on. Such skills are typically expressed in product offerings that other firms find difficult to match or imitate, and thus the core competencies are the bedrock of a firm's competitive advantage. They enable a firm to reduce the costs of value creation and/or to create value in such a way that premium pricing is possible. For example, Toyota has a core competence in the production of cars. It can produce high-quality, well-designed cars at a lower delivered cost than any other firm in the world. The skills that enable Toyota to do this seem to reside primarily in the firm's production and materials management functions.[4] Similarly McDonald's has a core competence in managing fast-food operations (it seems to be one of the most skilled firms in the world in this industry); Toys R Us has a core competence in managing high-volume, discount toy stores (it is perhaps the most skilled firm in the world in this business); Procter & Gamble has a core competence in developing and marketing name brand consumer products (it is one of the most skilled firms in the world in this business); and so on.

For such firms global expansion is a way of further exploiting the value-creation potential of their skills and product offerings by applying those skills and products in a larger market. The potential for creating value from such a strategy is greatest when the skills and products of the firm are most unique, when the value placed on them by consumers is great, and when there are very few capable competitors with similar skills and/or products in foreign markets. Firms with unique and valuable skills can often realize enormous returns by applying those skills, and the products they produce, to foreign markets where indigenous competitors lack similar skills and products.

For example, as we saw in the opening case, McDonald's has expanded rapidly overseas in recent years. Its skills in managing fast-food operations have proven to be just as valuable in countries as diverse as France, Russia, China, Germany, and Brazil as they have been in the United States. Before McDonald's entry, none of these countries had American-style fast-food chains, so McDonald's brought a unique product as well as unique skills to each country. The lack of indigenous competitors with similar skills and products, and the implied lack of competition, has greatly enhanced the profitability of this strategy for McDonald's.

In earlier eras U.S. firms such as Kellogg, Coca-Cola, H. J. Heinz, and Procter & Gamble expanded overseas to exploit their skills in developing and marketing name brand consumer products. These skills and the resulting products, which were developed in the U.S. market during the 1950s and 60s, yielded enormous returns when applied to European markets, where most indigenous competitors lacked similar marketing skills and products. Their near-monopoly on consumer marketing skills allowed these U.S. firms to dominate many European consumer product markets during the 1960s and 70s. Similarly in the 1970s and 1980s many Japanese firms expanded globally to exploit their skills in production, materials management, and new-product development—skills that many of their indigenous North Americans and European competitors seemed to lack at the time.

---

[3]G. Hamel and C. K. Prahalad, *Competing for the Future* (Boston: Harvard Business School Press, 1989).

[4]J. P. Womack, D. T. Jones, and D. Roos, *The Machine that Changed the World* (New York: Rawson Associates, 1990).

Realizing Location Economies

We know from earlier chapters that countries differ along a whole range of dimensions, including economic, political, legal, and cultural, and that these differences can either raise or lower the costs of doing business in a country. We also know from the theory of international trade that due to differences in factor costs, certain countries have a comparative advantage in the production of certain products. For example, Japan excels in the production of automobiles and consumer electronics. The United States excels in the production of chemicals, pharmaceuticals, biotechnology products, and financial services. Switzerland excels in the production of precision instruments and pharmaceuticals.[5]

What does all this mean for a firm that is trying to survive in a competitive global market? In brief, it means, *trade barriers and transportation costs* permitting, the firm will benefit by basing each value-creation activity it performs at that location where economic, political, and cultural conditions, including relative factor costs, are most conducive to the performance of that activity. Thus if the best designers for a product live in France, a firm should base its design operations in France. If the most productive labor force for assembly operations is in Mexico, assembly operations should be based in Mexico. If the best marketers are in the United States, the marketing strategy should be formulated in the United States. And so on.

Firms that pursue such a strategy can realize what we refer to as location economies. More precisely, we can define **location economies** as the economies that arise from performing a value-creation activity in the optimal location for that activity, wherever in the world that might be (transportation costs and trade barriers permitting). Locating a value-creation activity in the optimal location for that activity can have one of two effects. *Either it can lower the costs of value creation and help the firm to achieve a low-cost position, or it can enable a firm to differentiate its product offering from the offerings of competitors.* Both these considerations were at work in the case of Swan Optical. Swan Optical moved its manufacturing operations out of the United States, first to Hong Kong and then to mainland China, to take advantage of low labor costs, thereby lowering the costs of value creation. At the same time Swan shifted some of its design operations from the United States to France and Italy. Swan reasoned that skilled Italian and French designers could probably help the firm better differentiate its product. In other words Swan thinks the optimal location for performing manufacturing operations is China, whereas the optimal locations for performing design operations are France and Italy. The firm has configured its value chain accordingly. By doing so, Swan hopes to be able to *simultaneously* lower its cost structure and differentiate its product offering. In turn differentiation should allow Swan to charge a premium price for its product offering.

Creating a global web

Generalizing from the Swan example, one result of this kind of thinking is the creation of a **global web** of value-creation activities, with different stages of the value chain being dispersed to those locations around the globe where value added is maximized, or where the costs of value creation are minimized. Consider the case of General Motors' (GM) Pontiac Le Mans cited in Robert Reich's *The Work of Nations*.[6] Marketed primarily in the United States, the car was designed in Germany; key components were manufactured in Japan, Taiwan, and Singapore; the assembly operation was performed in South Korea; and the advertising strategy was formulated in Great Britain. The car was designed in Germany, because GM believed the designers in its German subsidiary had the skills most suited to the job at hand. (They were the most capable of producing a design that added value.) Components were manufactured in Japan, Taiwan, and Singapore, because favorable factor conditions there—relatively

---

[5]M. E. Porter, *The Competitive Advantage of Nations* (New York: Free Press, 1990).
[6]R. B. Reich, *The Work of Nations* (New York: Alfred A. Knopf, 1991).

low-cost, skilled labor—suggested those locations had a comparative advantage in the production of components (which helped reduce the costs of value creation). The car was assembled in South Korea, because GM believed that due to its low labor costs, the costs of assembly could be minimized there (also helping to minimize the costs of value creation). The advertising strategy was formulated in Great Britain because GM believed a particular advertising agency there was the most able to produce an advertising campaign that would help sell the car. (This decision was consistent with GM's desire to maximize the value added.)

In theory a firm that realizes location economies by dispersing each of its value-creation activities to its optimal location should have a competitive advantage vis-á-vis a firm that bases all its value-creation activities at a single location. It should be able to better differentiate its product offering and lower its cost structure than its single-location competitor. In a world where competitive pressures are increasing, such a strategy may well become an imperative for survival (as it seems to have been for Swan Optical).

Some caveats

Introducing transportation costs and trade barriers complicates this picture somewhat. Due to favorable factor endowments, New Zealand may have a comparative advantage for automobile assembly operations, but high transportation costs would make it an uneconomical location for them. A consideration of transportation costs and trade barriers helps explain why many U.S. firms are now shifting their production from Asia to Mexico. Mexico has three distinct advantages over many Asian countries as a location for value-creation activities. First, low labor costs make it a good location for labor-intensive production processes. In recent years wage rates have increased significantly in Japan, Taiwan, and Hong Kong, but they have remained low in Mexico. Second, Mexico's proximity to the large U.S. market reduces transportation costs. This is particularly important in the case of products with high weight-to-value ratios (e.g., automobiles). And third, the North American Free Trade Agreement (see Chapter 8) has removed many trade barriers between Mexico, the United States, and Canada, increasing Mexico's attractiveness as a production site for the North American market. Although value added and the costs of value creation are important, transportation costs and trade barriers also must be considered in location decisions.

Another caveat concerns the importance of assessing political risks when making location decisions. Even if a country looks very attractive as a production location when measured against all the standard criteria, if its government is unstable or totalitarian, the firm might be well advised not to base production there. (Political risk is discussed in Chapter 2.)

Realizing Experience Curve Economies

The **experience curve** refers to the systematic reductions in production costs that have been observed to occur over the life of a product.[7] A number of studies have observed that a product's production costs decline by some characteristic amount each time accumulated output doubles. The relationship was first observed in the aircraft industry, where each time accumulated output of airframes was doubled, unit costs typically declined to 80 percent of their previous level.[8] Thus production cost for the fourth airframe would be 80 percent of production cost for the second airframe, the eighth airframe's production costs 80 percent of the fourth's, the sixteenth's 80 percent of the eighth's, and so on. This experience curve relationship between production costs and output is illustrated in Figure 12.2. Two things explain this: learning effects and economies of scale.

---

[7]G. Hall and S. Howell, "The Experience Curve from an Economist's Perspective," *Strategic Management Journal* 6 (1985), pp. 197–212.
[8]A. A. Alchain, "Reliability of Progress Curves in Airframe Production," *Econometrica* 31 (1963), pp. 693–97.

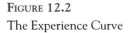

FIGURE 12.2
The Experience Curve

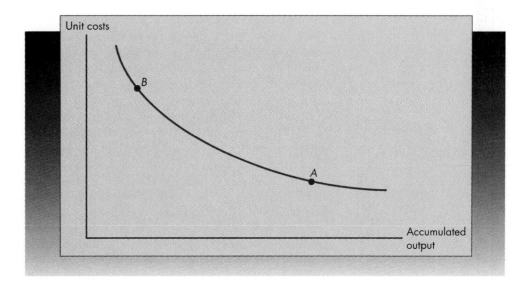

Learning effects

Learning effects refer to cost savings that come from learning by doing. Labor, for example, learns by repetition how to carry out a task such as assembling airframes most efficiently. Labor productivity increases over time as individuals learn the most efficient way to perform particular tasks. Equally important, it has been observed that in new production facilities, management typically learns how to manage the new operation more efficiently over time. Hence production costs eventually decline due to increasing labor productivity and management efficiency.

Learning effects tend to be more significant when a technologically complex task is repeated, since there is more that can be learned about the task. Thus learning effects will be more significant in an assembly process involving 1,000 complex steps than in one of only 100 simple steps. No matter how complex the task, however, learning effects typically die out after a time. It has been suggested they are really important only during the start-up period of a new process and that they cease after two or three years.[9] Any decline in the experience curve after such a point is due to economies of scale.

Economies of scale

The term **economies of scale** refers to the reductions in unit cost achieved by producing a large volume of a product. Economies of scale have a number of sources, the most important of which seems to be the ability to spread fixed costs over a large volume. Fixed costs are the costs required to set up a production facility, develop a new product, and the like, and they can be substantial. For example, establishing a new production line to manufacture semiconductor chips costs about $1 billion. According to one estimate, developing a new drug costs about $250 million and takes about 12 years.[10] The only way to recoup such high fixed costs is to sell the product worldwide, which reduces unit costs by spreading them over a larger volume. Moreover the more rapidly that cumulative sales volume is built up, the more rapidly fixed costs can be amortized, and the more rapidly unit costs fall. Hence, in addition to learning effects, economies of scale underlie the experience curve.

---

[9]Hall and Howell, "The Experience Curve."
[10]J. Main, "How to Go Global—and Why," *Fortune*, August 28, 1989, pp. 70–76.

Strategic significance

The strategic significance of the experience curve is clear. Moving down the experience curve allows a firm to reduce its cost of creating value. The firm that moves down the experience curve most rapidly will have a cost advantage vis-á-vis its competitors. Thus Firm A in Figure 12.2, because it is further down the experience curve, has a clear cost advantage over Firm B.

Many of the underlying sources of experience-based cost economies are plant based. This is true for most learning effects as well as for the economies of scale derived by spreading the fixed costs of building productive capacity over a large output. Thus the key to progressing downward on the experience curve as rapidly as possible is to increase the volume produced by a single plant as rapidly as possible. Since global markets are larger than domestic markets, a firm that serves a global market from a single location is likely to build up accumulated volume more quickly than a firm that serves only its home market or that serves multiple markets from multiple production locations. Thus serving a global market from a single location is consistent with moving down the experience curve and establishing a low-cost position. In addition, to get down the experience curve rapidly, a firm must price and market very aggressively so demand will expand rapidly. It will also need to build sufficient production capacity for serving a global market. And the cost advantages of serving the world market from a single location will be all the more significant if that location is the optimal one for performing the particular value-creation activity.

Once a firm has established a low-cost position, it can act as a barrier to new competition. An established firm that is well down the experience curve, such as Firm A in Figure 12.2, can price so that it is still making a profit while new entrants, which are further up the curve such as Firm B in the figure, are suffering losses.

Matsushita has excelled in the pursuit of such a strategy. Along with Sony and Philips, Matsushita was in the race to develop a commercially viable VCR in the 1970s. Although Matsushita initially lagged behind Philips and Sony, it was able to get its VHS format accepted as the world standard and to reap enormous experience-curve–based cost economies in the process. This cost advantage subsequently constituted a formidable barrier to new competition. Matsushita's strategy was to build global volume as rapidly as possible. To ensure it could accommodate worldwide demand, the firm increased its production capacity 33-fold from 205,000 units in 1977 to 6.8 million units by 1984. By serving the world market from a single location in Japan, Matsushita was able to realize significant learning effects and economies of scale. These allowed Matsushita to drop its prices 50 percent within five years of selling its first VHS-formatted VCR. As a result Matsushita was the world's major VCR producer by 1983, accounting for approximately 45 percent of world production and enjoying a significant cost advantage over its competitors. The next largest firm, Hitachi, accounted for only 11.1 percent of world production in 1983.[11]

❧ PRESSURES FOR COST REDUCTIONS AND LOCAL RESPONSIVENESS

Firms that compete in the global marketplace typically face two types of competitive pressure. They face *pressures for cost reductions* and *pressures to be locally responsive* (see Figure 12.3). These competitive pressures place conflicting demands on a firm. Responding to pressures for cost reductions requires that a firm try to minimize its unit costs. Attaining such a goal may necessitate that a firm base its productive activities at the most favorable low-cost location, wherever in the world that might be. It may also necessitate that a firm offer a standardized product to the global marketplace to ride down the experience curve as quickly as possible. In contrast, responding to pressures to be locally responsive requires that a firm differentiate its product offering and marketing

[11]"Matsushita Electrical Industrial in 1987," In *Transnational Management,* ed C. A. Bartlett and S. Ghoshal (Homewood, IL: Richard D. Irwin, 1992).

Figure 12.3 Pressures for Cost Reduction and Local Responsiveness

ate the diverse demands
references, business prac-
rnment policies. Because
ts can involve significant
ay be to raise costs.
high pressures for cost re-
such as Company B, face
esponsiveness, many firms
gh pressures for cost reduc-
e, dealing with these con-
llenge for a firm, primarily
mainder of this section we
esponsiveness. In the next
hese pressures.

cost reductions. Respond-
wer the costs of value cre-
mal location in the world,
nce curve economies. Pres-
tries producing commodity
factors is difficult and price
for products that serve uni-
erences of consumers in dif-
or conventional commodity
the like. It also tends to be
mple, handheld calculators,
r cost reductions are also in-
-cost locations, where there
erful and face low switching
ralization of the world trade
tating greater international

---

[12]C. K. Prahalad and Yves L. Doz, *The Multinational Mission: Balancing Local Demands and Global Vision* (New York: Free Press, 1987). Prahalad and Doz actually talk about local responsiveness rather than local customization.

Pressures for cost reductions have been intense in the global tire industry in recent years. Tires are essentially a commodity product where meaningful differentiation is difficult and price is the main competitive weapon. The major buyers of tires, automobile firms, are powerful and face low switching costs, so they have been playing tire firms off against each other in an attempt to get lower prices. And the decline in global demand for automobiles in the early 1990s has created a serious excess capacity situation in the tire industry, with as much as 25 percent of world capacity standing idle. The result is a worldwide price war with almost all tire firms suffering heavy losses in the early 1990s. In response to the resulting cost pressures, most tire firms are now trying to rationalize their operations in a manner consistent with attaining a low-cost position. This includes moving production operations to low-cost facilities and offering globally standardized products to try to realize experience curve economies.[13]

Pressures for Local Responsiveness

Pressures for local responsiveness arise from a number of sources including differences in consumer tastes and preferences, differences in infrastructure and traditional practices, differences in distribution channels, and host government demands.

Differences in consumer tastes and preferences

Strong pressures for local responsiveness emerge when consumer tastes and preferences differ significantly between countries—as they may for historic or cultural reasons. In such cases product and/or marketing messages have to be customized to appeal to the tastes and preferences of local consumers. This typically creates pressures for the delegation of production and marketing functions to national subsidiaries.

In the automobile industry, for example, there is a strong demand among North American consumers for pickup trucks. This is particularly true in the South and West where many families have a pickup truck as a second or third car. In contrast, in European countries pickup trucks are seen purely as utility vehicles and are purchased primarily by firms rather than individuals. As a consequence, there is a need to tailor the marketing message to the different nature of demand in North America and Europe.

As a counterpoint, Harvard Business School Professor Theodore Levitt has argued that consumer demands for local customization are on the decline worldwide.[14] According to Levitt, modern communications and transport technologies have created the conditions for a convergence of the tastes and preferences of consumers from different nations. The result is the emergence of enormous global markets for standardized consumer products. Levitt cites worldwide acceptance of McDonald's hamburgers, Coca-Cola, Levi Strauss blue jeans, and Sony television sets, all of which are sold as standardized products, as evidence of the increasing homogeneity of the global marketplace.

Levitt's argument, however, has been characterized as extreme by many commentators. For example, Christopher Bartlett and Sumantra Ghoshal have observed that in the consumer electronics industry consumers reacted to an overdose of standardized global products by showing a renewed preference for products that are differentiated to local conditions.[15] They note that Amstrad, the fast-growing British computer and electronics firm, got its start by recognizing and responding to local consumer needs. Amstrad captured a major share of the British audio market by moving away from the standardized inexpensive music products marketed by global firms such as Sony and Matsushita. Amstrad's product was encased in teak rather than metal cabinets and had a control panel tailor-made to appeal to British consumers' preferences. In response Matsushita had to reverse its earlier bias toward standardized global design and place more emphasis on local customization.

---

[13]"The Tire Industry's Costly Obsession with Size," *The Economist*, June 8, 1993, p. 65–66.
[14]T. Levitt "The Globalization of Markets," *Harvard Business Review*, May–June 1983, p. 92–102.
[15]C. A. Bartlett and S. Ghoshal, *Managing across Borders* (Boston: Harvard Business School Press, 1989).

FIGURE 12.3   Pressures for Cost Reduction and Local Responsiveness

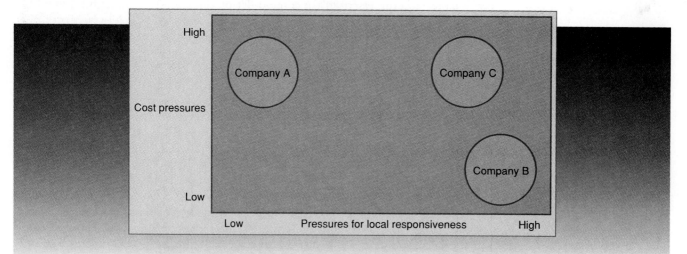

strategy from country to country in an attempt to accommodate the diverse demands that arise from national differences in consumer tastes and preferences, business practices, distribution channels, competitive conditions, and government policies. Because customizing product offerings to different national requirements can involve significant duplication and a lack of product standardization, the result may be to raise costs.

While some firms, such as Company A in Figure 12.3, face high pressures for cost reductions and low pressures for local responsiveness, and others, such as Company B, face low pressures for cost reductions and high pressures for local responsiveness, many firms are in the position of Company C in Figure 12.3. They face high pressures for cost reductions and high pressures for local responsiveness. As we shall see, dealing with these conflicting and contradictory pressures is a difficult strategic challenge for a firm, primarily because being locally responsive tends to raise costs. In the remainder of this section we look at the source of pressures for cost reductions and local responsiveness. In the next section we look at the strategies that firms adopt to deal with these pressures.

Pressures for Cost Reductions

Increasingly international businesses are facing pressures for cost reductions. Responding to pressures for cost reduction requires a firm to try to lower the costs of value creation by mass producing a standardized product at the optimal location in the world, wherever that might be, to try to realize location and experience curve economies. Pressures for cost reductions can be particularly intense in industries producing commodity type products where meaningful differentiation on nonprice factors is difficult and price is the main competitive weapon. This tends to be the case for products that serve universal needs. Universal needs exist when the tastes and preferences of consumers in different nations are similar if not identical. This is the case for conventional commodity products such as bulk chemicals, petroleum, steel, sugar, and the like. It also tends to be the case for many industrial and consumer products (for example, handheld calculators, semiconductor chips, and personal computers). Pressures for cost reductions are also intense in industries where major competitors are based in low-cost locations, where there is persistent excess capacity, and where consumers are powerful and face low switching costs. Many commentators have also argued that the liberalization of the world trade and investment environment in recent decades, by facilitating greater international competition, has generally increased cost pressures.[12]

---

[12]C. K. Prahalad and Yves L. Doz, *The Multinational Mission: Balancing Local Demands and Global Vision* (New York: Free Press, 1987). Prahalad and Doz actually talk about local responsiveness rather than local customization.

Differences in infrastructure and traditional practices

Pressures for local responsiveness emerge when there are differences in infrastructure and/or traditional practices between countries. In such circumstances there can be a need to customize the product to the distinctive infrastructure and practices. This may necessitate delegating manufacturing and production functions to foreign subsidiaries. For example, in North America consumer electrical systems are based on 110 volts, while in some European countries 240-volt systems are standard. Thus domestic electrical appliances have to be customized for this difference in infrastructure. Traditional practices also often vary across nations. For example, in Britain people drive on the left side of the road, thus creating a demand for right-hand drive cars, whereas in neighboring France, people drive on the right-hand side of the road, thus creating a demand for left-hand drive cars. Obviously automobiles have to be customized to take this difference in traditional practices into account.

Differences in distribution channels

A firm's marketing strategies may have to be responsive to differences in distribution channels between countries. This may necessitate the delegation of marketing functions to national subsidiaries. In laundry detergents, for example, five retail chains control 65 percent of the market in Germany, but no chain controls more than 2 percent of the market in neighboring Italy. Thus retail chains have considerable buying power in Germany, but relatively little in Italy. Dealing with these differences requires varying marketing approaches on the part of detergent firms. Similarly in the pharmaceutical industry the British and Japanese distribution systems are radically different from the U.S. system. British and Japanese doctors will not accept or respond favorably to an American-style high-pressure sales force. Thus pharmaceutical firms have to adopt different marketing practices in Britain and Japan compared to the United States (soft sell versus hard sell).

Host government demands

Economic and political demands imposed by host country governments may necessitate a degree of local responsiveness. For example, the politics of health care around the world requires that pharmaceutical firms manufacture in multiple locations. Pharmaceutical firms are subject to local clinical testing, registration procedures, and pricing restrictions, all of which require that the manufacturing and marketing of a drug should meet local requirements. Moreover, since governments and government agencies control a significant proportion of the health care budget in most countries, they can demand a high level of local responsiveness. Threats of protectionism, economic nationalism, and local content rules (which require that a certain percentage of a product should be manufactured locally) all dictate that international businesses manufacture locally. Part of the motivation for Japanese auto firms setting up U.S. production, for example, is to counter the threat of protectionism that is being increasingly voiced by the U.S. Congress.

Implications

Pressures for local responsiveness imply that it may not be possible for a firm to realize the full benefits from experience curve and location economies. For example, it may not be possible to serve the global marketplace from a single low-cost location, producing a globally standardized product and marketing it worldwide to achieve experience curve cost economies. In practice the need to customize the product offering to local conditions may work against the implementation of such a strategy. Automobile firms, for example, have found that Japanese, American, and European consumers demand different kinds of cars, and that this necessitates producing products that are customized for local markets. In response, firms such as Honda, Ford, and Toyota are pursuing a strategy of establishing top-to-bottom

FIGURE 12.4   Four Basic Strategies

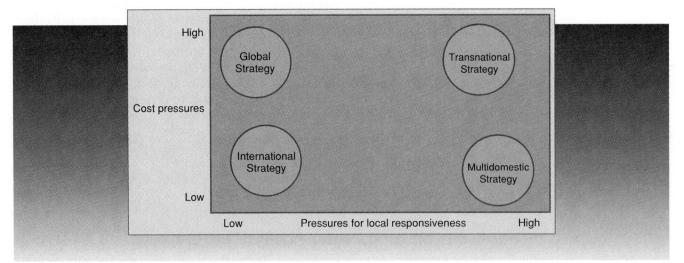

design and production facilities in each of these regions so it can better serve local demands. While such customization brings benefits, it also limits the ability of a firm to realize significant experience curve cost economies and location economies.

In addition pressures for local responsiveness imply it may not be possible to transfer the skills and products associated with a firm's core competencies wholesale from one nation to another. Concessions often have to be made to local conditions. You will recall from the opening case, for example, that McDonald's customizes its product offering (i.e., its menu) to account for national differences in tastes and preferences.

❦ STRATEGIC CHOICE

Firms use four basic strategies to enter and compete in the international environment: an international strategy, a multidomestic strategy, a global strategy, and a transnational strategy.[16] Each of these strategies has its advantages and disadvantages. The appropriateness of each strategy varies with the extent of pressures for cost reductions and local responsiveness. Figure 12.4 illustrates when each of these strategies is most appropriate. In this section we describe each strategy, identify when it is appropriate, and discuss its pros and cons.

International Strategy

Firms that pursue an international strategy try to create value by transferring valuable skills and products to foreign markets where indigenous competitors lack those skills and products. Most international firms have created value by transferring differentiated product offerings developed at home to new markets overseas. Accordingly they tend to centralize product development functions at home (e.g., R&D). However, they also tend to establish manufacturing and marketing functions in each major country in which they do business. But while they may undertake some local customization of product offering and marketing strategy, this tends to be limited. Ultimately, in most international firms the head office retains tight control over marketing and product strategy.

---

[16]This section is based on Bartlett and Ghoshal, *Managing across Borders* .

International firms include the likes of Toys R Us, McDonald's, IBM, Kellogg, and Procter & Gamble. The majority of U.S. firms that expanded abroad in the 1950s and 1960s fall into this category. Consider Procter & Gamble, which is profiled in the next "Management Focus". Procter & Gamble has traditionally had production facilities in all of its major markets outside the United States, including Britain, Germany, and Japan. These facilities, however, manufactured differentiated products that had been developed by the U.S. parent firm and were often marketed using the message developed in the United States. Historically at least, while there has been some local responsiveness at P&G, it has been rather limited.

An international strategy makes sense if a firm has a valuable core competence that indigenous competitors in foreign markets lack, and if the firm faces relatively weak pressures for local responsiveness and cost reductions. In such circumstances, an international strategy can be very profitable. However, when pressures for local responsiveness are high, firms pursuing this strategy lose out to firms that place a greater emphasis on customizing the product offering and market strategy to local conditions. Moreover, due to the duplication of manufacturing facilities, firms that pursue an international strategy tend to suffer from high operating costs. This makes the strategy inappropriate in those industries where cost pressures are high.

Multidomestic Strategy

Firms pursuing a multidomestic strategy orient themselves toward achieving maximum local responsiveness. Like firms pursuing an international strategy, firms pursuing a multidomestic strategy also tend to transfer skills and products developed at home to foreign markets. However, unlike international firms, multidomestic firms extensively customize both their product offering and their marketing strategy to different national conditions. Consistent with this, they also have a tendency to establish a complete set of value-creation activities—including production, marketing, and R&D—in each major national market in which they do business. As a consequence they are generally unable to realize value from experience curve effects and location economies. Accordingly many multidomestic firms have a high cost structure.

A multidomestic strategy makes most sense when there are high pressures for local responsiveness and low pressures for cost reductions. The high cost structure associated with the duplication of production facilities makes this strategy inappropriate in industries where cost pressures are intense. Another weakness associated with this strategy is that many multidomestic firms have developed into decentralized federations in which each national subsidiary functions in a largely autonomous manner. As a result, after a time they begin to lack the ability to transfer the skills and products derived from core competencies to their various national subsidiaries around the world. In a famous case that illustrates the problems this can cause, the ability of Philips NV to establish its V2000 VCR format as the dominant design in the VCR industry during the late 1970s, as opposed to Matsushita's VHS format, was effectively killed by the refusal of its U.S. subsidiary firm to adopt the V2000 format. Instead the subsidiary bought VCRs produced by Matsushita and put its own label on them!

Global Strategy

Firms that pursue a global strategy focus on increasing profitability by reaping the cost reductions that come from experience curve effects and location economies. They are pursuing a low-cost strategy. The production, marketing, and R&D activities of firms pursuing a global strategy are concentrated in a few favorable locations. Global firms tend not to customize their product offering and marketing strategy to local conditions because customization raises costs (it involves shorter production runs and the duplication of functions). Instead global firms prefer to market a standardized product worldwide so they can reap the maximum benefits from the economies of scale that underlie the experience curve. They also tend to use their cost advantage to support aggressive pricing in world markets.

MANAGEMENT FOCUS
Procter & Gamble's International Strategy

Procter & Gamble (P&G), the large U.S. consumer products company, has a well-earned reputation as one of the world's best marketers. With over 80 major brands P&G generates more than $20 billion in revenues worldwide. Together with Unilever, P&G is a dominant global force in laundry detergents, cleaning products, and personal care products. P&G expanded abroad in the post-World War II years by pursuing an international strategy—transferring brands and marketing policies developed in the United States to Western Europe, initially with considerable success. Over the next 30 years this policy resulted in the development of a classic international firm in which new-product development and marketing strategies were pioneered in the United States and only then transferred to other countries. Although some adaptation of marketing policies to accommodate country differences was pursued, this adaptation was fairly minimal.

The first signs that this strategy was flawed began to emerge in the 1970s when P&G suffered a number of major setbacks in Japan. By 1985, after 13 years in Japan, P&G was still losing $40 million a year there. After initially introducing disposable diapers into Japan and at one time commanding an 80 percent share of the market, P&G had seen its share slip to a miserable 8 percent by the early 1980s. In P&G's place, three major Japanese consumer products firms dominated the market. P&G's problem was that its diapers, developed in America, were too bulky for the tastes of Japanese consumers. With this in mind, the Japanese consumer products firm Kao developed a line of trim-fit diapers that appealed more to the tastes of Japanese consumers. Kao supported the introduction of its product with a marketing blitz. The company was quickly rewarded with a 30 percent share of the market. As for P&G, only belatedly did it realize it had to modify its diapers to accommodate the tastes of Japanese consumers. Now the company has increased its share of the Japanese market to 30 percent. Moreover, in an example of global learning, P&G's trim-fit

---

This strategy makes most sense in those cases where there are strong pressures for cost reductions and where demands for local responsiveness are minimal. These conditions prevail in many industrial goods industries. In the semiconductor industry, for example, global standards have emerged that have created enormous demands for standardized global products. Accordingly firms such as Intel, Texas Instruments, and Motorola all pursue a global strategy. However, as we noted earlier, these conditions are not found in many consumer goods markets, where demands for local responsiveness remain high (e.g. audioplayers, automobiles, processed food products). The strategy is inappropriate when demands for local responsiveness are high.

Transnational Strategy   Christopher Bartlett and Sumantra Ghoshal have argued that in today's environment, competitive conditions are so intense that to survive in the global marketplace firms *must exploit experience-based cost economies and location economies, they must transfer distinctive competencies within the firm, and they must do all of this while paying attention to pressures for local responsiveness.*[17] Moreover, they note that in the

---

[17]Bartlett and Ghoshal. *Managing across Borders.*

diapers, originally developed for the Japanese market, have now become a best-seller in the United States.

P&G's experience with disposable diapers in Japan prompted the company to rethink its new-product development and marketing philosophy. The company has now admitted that its U.S.-centered way of doing business will no longer work. Since the late 1980s P&G has been attempting to delegate far more responsibility for new-product development and marketing strategy to its major subsidiary firms in Japan and Europe. The result has been the creation of a company that is more responsive to local differences in consumer tastes and preferences and more willing to admit that good new products can be developed outside the United States.

Despite the apparent changes at P&G, it is still not clear that P&G has achieved the revolution in thinking that is required to alter its long-established practices. P&G's recent venture into the Polish shampoo market illustrates the company still has some way to go. In the summer of 1991 P&G entered the Polish market with its Vidal Sassoon Wash & Go, an all-in-one shampoo and conditioner, which is a best-seller in America and Europe. The product launch was supported by an American-style marketing blitz on a scale never before seen in Poland. At first the campaign seemed to be working as P&G captured more than 30 percent of the market for shampoos in Poland, but in early 1992 sales suddenly plummeted. Then came the rumors—Wash & Go caused dandruff and hair loss—allegations P&G has strenuously denied. Next came the jokes. One doing the rounds in Poland runs as follows, "I washed my car with Wash & Go and the tires went bald." And when President Lech Walesa proposed that he also become prime minister, critics derided the idea as a "two in one solution, just like Wash & Go."

Where did P&G go wrong? The most common theory is that it promoted Wash & Go too hard in a country that has little enthusiasm for brash American-style advertising. A poll by Pentor, a private market research company in Warsaw, found that almost three times more Poles disliked P&G's commercials than liked them. Pentor also argues that the high-profile marketing campaign backfired because years of Communist party propaganda have led Polish consumers to suspect that advertising is simply a way to shift goods that nobody wants. Some also believe that Wash & Go, which was developed for U.S. consumers who shampoo daily, was far too sophisticated for Polish consumers who are less obsessed with personal hygiene. Underlying all these criticisms seems to be the idea that P&G was once again stumbling because it had transferred a product and marketing strategy wholesale from the United States to another country without modification to accommodate the tastes and preferences of local consumers.

Sources: Guy de Jonquieres and C. Bobinski, "Wash and Get into a Lather in Poland," *Financial Times*, May 28, 1989, p. 2; "Perestroika in Soapland, " *The Economist*, June 10, 1989, p. 69–71; "After Early Stumbles P&G Is Making Inroads Overseas," *The Wall Street Journal*, February 6, 1989, p. B1; Bartlett and Ghoshal, *Managing across Borders*.

modern multinational enterprise, distinctive competencies do not just reside in the home country. They can develop in any of the firm's worldwide operations. Thus they maintain the flow of skills and product offerings should not be all one way, from home firm to foreign subsidiary, as in the case of firms pursuing an international strategy. Rather the flow should also be from foreign subsidiary to home country, and from foreign subsidiary to foreign subsidiary—a process they refer to as **global learning** (for an example of such knowledge flows, see the opening case on McDonald's). Bartlett and Ghoshal refer to the strategy pursued by firms that are trying to achieve all these objective simultaneously as a **transnational strategy.**

A transnational strategy makes sense when a firm faces high pressures for cost reductions and high pressures for local responsiveness. Firms that pursue a transnational strategy are trying to simultaneously achieve low cost and differentiation advantages. As attractive as this sounds, in practice the strategy is not easy. Pressures for local responsiveness and cost reductions place conflicting demands on a firm. Being locally responsive raises costs, which obviously makes cost reductions difficult to achieve. How then can a firm effectively pursue a transnational strategy?

FIGURE 12.5

Cost Pressures and Pressures
for Local Responsiveness
Facing Caterpillar

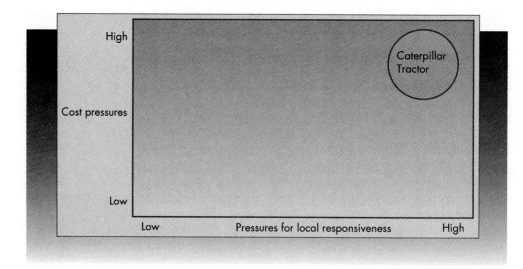

Some clues can be derived from the case of Caterpillar Tractor. The need to compete with low-cost competitors such as Komatsu of Japan has forced Caterpillar to look for greater cost economies. At the same time variation in construction practices and government regulations across countries means Caterpillar has to be responsive to local demands. Therefore, as illustrated in Figure 12.5, Caterpillar confronts significant pressures for cost reductions and for local responsiveness.

To deal with cost pressures Caterpillar redesigned its products to use many identical components and invested in a few large-scale component manufacturing facilities, sited at favorable locations, to fill global demand and realize scale economics. At the same time the firm augments the centralized manufacturing of components with assembly plants in each of its major global markets. At these plants Caterpillar adds local product features, tailoring the finished product to local needs. Thus Caterpillar is able to realize many benefits of global manufacturing while at the same time responding to pressures for local responsiveness by differentiating its product among national markets.[18]

For another example consider Unilever; once a classic multidomestic firm, in recent years Unilever has had to shift toward more of a transnational strategy. A rise in low-cost competition has forced Unilever to look for ways of rationalizing its detergent business. During the 1980s Unilever had 17 different and largely self-contained detergent operations in Europe alone. The duplication, in terms of assets and marketing, was enormous. Moreover, because Unilever was so fragmented it could take as long as four years for the firm to introduce a new product across Europe. Now Unilever is trying to weld its European operation together into a single entity, with detergents being manufactured in a handful of cost-efficient plants and standard packaging and advertising being used across Europe. According to firm estimates, the result could be an annual cost saving of over $200 million. At the same time, however, due to national differences in distribution channels and brand awareness, Unilever recognizes it must still remain locally responsive, even while it tries to realize economies from consolidating production and marketing at the optimal locations.[19]

---

[18]T. Hout, M. E. Porter, and E. Rudden, "How Global Firms Win Out," *Harvard Business Review*, September–October 1982, pp. 98–108.

[19]Guy de Jonquieres, "Unilever Adopts a Clean Sheet Approach." *Financial Times*, October 21, 1991, p. 13.

FIGURE 12.6
The Advantages and
Disadvantages of the Four
Strategies

Strategy	Advantages	Disadvantages
Global	Exploit experience curve effects Exploit location economies	Lack of local responsiveness
International	Transfer distinctive competencies to Foreign Markets	Lack of local responsiveness Inability to realize location economies Failure to exploit experience curve effects
Multidomestic	Customize product offerings and marketing in accordance with local responsiveness	Inability to realize location economies Failure to exploit experience curve effects Failure to transfer distinctive competencies to foreign markets
Transnational	Exploit experience curve effects Exploit location economies Customize product offerings and marketing in accordance with local responsiveness Reap benefits of global learning	Difficult to implement due to organizational problems

Notwithstanding examples such as Caterpillar and Unilever, Bartlett and Ghoshal admit that building an organization that is capable of supporting a transnational strategic posture is complex and difficult. Simultaneously trying to achieve cost efficiencies, global learning, and local responsiveness places contradictory demands on an organization. Exactly how a firm can deal with the dilemmas posed by such difficult organizational issues is a topic we will discuss in more detail in Chapter 13 when we look at the structure of international business. For now it is important to note that the organizational problems associated with pursuing what are essentially conflicting objectives constitute a major impediment to the pursuit of a transnational strategy. Firms that attempt to pursue a transnational strategy can become bogged down in an organizational morass that only leads to inefficiencies.

It might also be noted at this juncture that Bartlett and Ghoshal may be overstating the case for the transnational strategy. They present the transnational strategy as the only viable strategy. While no one doubts that in some industries the firm that can adopt a transnational strategy will have a competitive advantage, in other industries global, multidomestic, and international strategies remain viable. In the global semiconductor industry, for example, pressures for local customization are minimal and competition is purely a cost game, in which case a global strategy, not a transnational strategy, is optimal. This is the case in many industrial goods markets where the product serves universal needs. But the argument can be made that to compete in certain consumer goods markets, such as the consumer electronics industry, a firm has to adopt a transnational strategy.

Summary

The advantages and disadvantages of each of the four strategies discussed above are summarized in Figure 12.6. While a transnational strategy appears to offer the most advantages, implementing such a strategy raises difficult organizational issues. More generally, the appropriateness of each strategy depends on therelative strength of pressures for cost reductions and pressures for local responsiveness.

❧ SUMMARY OF CHAPTER

In this chapter we reviewed the various ways in which firms can profit from global expansion, we reviewed the strategies firms that compete globally can adopt, we discussed the optimal choice of entry mode to serve a foreign market, and we looked at the issue of strategic alliances. The following points have been made in this chapter:

1. For some firms international expansion represents a way of earning greater returns by transferring the skills and product offerings derived from their core competencies to markets where indigenous competitors lack those skills.

2. Due to national differences, it pays a firm to base each value-creation activity it performs at that location where factor conditions are most conducive to the performance of that activity. We refer to this strategy as focusing on the attainment of location economies.

3. By building sales volume more rapidly, international expansion can assist a firm in moving down the experience curve.

4. The best strategy for a firm to pursue may depend on a consideration of the pressures for cost reductions and the pressures for local responsiveness.

5. Pressures for cost reductions are greatest in industries producing commodity-type products where price is the main competitive weapon.

6. Pressures for local responsiveness arise from differences in consumer tastes and preferences, national infrastructure and traditional practices, distribution channels, and from host government demands.

7. Firms pursuing an international strategy transfer the skills and products derived from distinctive competencies to foreign markets, while undertaking some limited local customization.

8. Firms pursuing a multidomestic strategy customize their product offering, marketing strategy, and business strategy to national conditions.

9. Firms pursuing a global strategy focus on reaping the cost reductions that come from experience curve effects and location economies.

10. Many industries are now so competitive that firms must adopt a transnational strategy. This involves a simultaneous focus on reducing costs, transferring skills and products, and local responsiveness. Implementing such a strategy, however, may not be easy.

❧ CRITICAL DISCUSSION QUESTIONS

1. In a world of zero transportation costs, no trade barriers, and nontrivial differences between nations with regard to factor conditions, firms must expand internationally if they are to survive. Discuss.

2. Plot the position of the following firms on Figure 12.3—Procter & Gamble, IBM, Coca-Cola, Dow Chemical, US Steel, McDonald's. In each case justify your answer.

3. Are the following global industries or multidomestic industries: bulk chemicals, pharmaceuticals, branded food products, moviemaking, television manufacture, personal computers, airline travel?

4. Discuss how the need for control over foreign operations varies with the strategy and core competencies of a firm. What are the implications of this for the choice of entry mode?

5. What do you see as the main organizational problems likely to be associated with the implementation of a transnational strategy?

❧ CLOSING CASE Sweden's IKEA

Originally established in the 1940s in Sweden by Ingvar Kamprad, IKEA has grown rapidly in recent years to become one of the world's largest retailers of home furnishings. In its initial push to expand globally, IKEA largely ignored the retailing rule that international success involves tailoring product lines closely to national tastes and preferences. Instead IKEA stuck with the vision, articulated by founder Kamprad, that the company should sell a basic product range that is "typically Swedish" wherever it ventures in the world. The company also remained primarily production oriented; that is, the Swedish management and design group decided what it was going to sell and then presented it to the worldwide public—often with very little research as to what the public actually wanted. Moreover the company emphasized its Swedish roots in its international advertising, even going as far as to insist on a "Swedish" blue and white color scheme for its stores.

Despite breaking some key rules of international retailing, the formula of selling Swedish-designed products in the same manner everywhere seemed to work. Between 1974 and 1994 IKEA expanded from a company with 10 stores, only one of which was outside Scandinavia, and annual revenues of $210 million to a group with 125 stores in 26 countries and sales of close to $5 billion. In 1994 only 11 percent of its sales were generated in Sweden. Of the balance, 29.6 percent came from Germany, 42.5 percent from the rest of Western Europe, and 14.2 percent from North America. IKEA's expansion in North America was its most recent international venture.

The foundation of IKEA's success has been to offer consumers good value for money. IKEA's approach starts with a global network of suppliers, which now numbers 2,700 firms in 67 countries. An IKEA supplier gains long-term contracts, technical advice, and leased equipment from the company. In return IKEA demands an exclusive contract and low prices. IKEA's designers work closely with suppliers to build savings into the products from the outset by designing products that can be produced at a low cost. IKEA displays its enormous range of more than 10,000 products in cheap out-of-town stores. It sells most of its furniture as kits for customers to take home and assemble themselves. The firm reaps huge economies of scale from the size of each store and the big production runs made possible by selling the same products all over the world. This strategy allows IKEA to match its rivals on quality, while undercutting them by up to 30 percent on price and still maintaining a healthy aftertax return on sales of around 7 percent.

This strategy worked well until 1985 when IKEA decided to enter the North American market. Between 1985 and 1990 IKEA opened six stores in North America, but unlike the company's experience across Europe, the stores did not quickly become profitable. Instead, by 1990 it was clear that IKEA's North American operations were in trouble. Part of the problem was an adverse movement in exchange rates. In 1985 the exchange rate was $1 = 8.6 Swedish kronar; by 1990 it was $1=SKr5.8. At this exchange rate many products imported from Sweden did not look inexpensive to American consumers.

But there was more to IKEA's problems than adverse movements in exchange rates. IKEA's unapologetically Swedish products, which had sold so well across Europe, jarred with American tastes and sometimes physiques. Swedish beds were narrow and measured in centimeters. IKEA did not sell the matching bedroom suites that Americans liked. Its kitchen cupboards were too narrow for the large dinner plates needed for pizza. Its glasses were too small for a nation that adds ice to everything. And the drawers in IKEA's bedroom chests were too shallow for American consumers, who tend to store sweaters in them.

In 1990 the company's top management realized that if it was going to succeed in North America, it would have to customize its product offering to North American tastes. The company set about redesigning its product range. The drawers on bedroom chests were designed to be two inches deeper—and sales immediately increased by 30 to 40 percent. IKEA now sells American-style king and queen-sized beds, measured in inches, and it sells them as part of complete bedroom suites. Currently it is redesigning its kitchen furniture and kitchenware to better appeal to American tastes. The company has also boosted the amount of products being sourced locally from 15 percent in 1990 to 45 percent in 1994, a move that makes the company far less vulnerable to adverse movements in exchange rates.

This break with IKEA's traditional strategy has paid off. Between 1990 and 1994 IKEA's North American sales have tripled to $480 million, and the company claims it has been making a profit in North America since early 1993. By 1994 the company had also expanded the number of North American stores to 13, and it plans to have 15 open by the end of 1995.

CASE DISCUSSION QUESTIONS

1. What strategy was IKEA pursuing as it expanded throughout Europe during the 1970s and early 1980s—a multidomestic strategy, a global strategy, or an international strategy?

2. Why do you think this strategy did not work as well in North America as it did in Europe?

3. As of 1995 what strategy is IKEA pursuing? Does this strategy make sense? Can you see any drawbacks with this strategy?

Sources: "Furnishing the World," The Economist, November 19, 1994, pp. 79–80; and H. Carnegy, "Struggle to Save the Soul of IKEA," Financial Times, March 27, 1995, p. 12.

CHAPTER THIRTEEN

THE ORGANIZATION OF INTERNATIONAL BUSINESS

ORGANIZATIONAL CHANGE AT ROYAL DUTCH SHELL

The Anglo Dutch company Royal Dutch Shell is the world's largest nonstate-owned oil company with activities in more than 130 countries and 1994 revenues of over $90 billion. From the 1950s until 1994 Shell operated with a "matrix structure" invented for it by McKinsey, a management consulting firm that specializes in organizational design. Under this matrix structure, the head of each operating company reported to two bosses. One boss was responsible for the geographical region or country in which the operating company was based, while the other was responsible for the business activity the operating company was engaged in (Shell's business activities included oil exploration and production, oil products, chemicals, gas, and coal). Thus, for example, the head of the local Shell chemical company in Australia reported both to the head of Shell Australia and to the head of Shell's entire chemical division, who was based in London. Both bosses had equal influence and status within the organization.

This matrix structure had two very visible consequences at Shell. First, because each operating company had two bosses to satisfy, decision making typically followed a pattern of consensus building, with differences of perspective between country (or regional) heads on the one hand and the heads of business divisions on the other being worked out through debate. Although this process could be slow and cumbersome, it was seen as a good thing in the oil industry where most big decisions are long-term ones that involve substantial capital expenditures and where informed debate between different viewpoints can help to clarify the pros and cons of

issues, rather than hinder decision making. Second, because the decision-making process was slow, it was reserved for only the most important decisions (such as major new capital investments). The result was substantial decentralization by default to the heads of the individual operating companies, who were left to run their own operations. This decentralization helped Shell respond to local differences in government regulations, competitive conditions, and consumer tastes. Thus, for example, the head of Shell's Australian chemical company was given the freedom to determine pricing practices and marketing strategy in the Australian market. Only if she wished to undertake a major capital investment, such as building a new chemical plant, would the consensus-building decision-making system be invoked.

As desirable as this matrix structure seemed to many, in 1995 Shell announced a radical plan to dismantle it. The primary reason given by top management was continuing slack demand for oil and weak oil prices, which had put pressure on Shell's profit margins. Although Shell had traditionally been among the

most profitable oil companies in the world, in the early 1990s its relative performance began to slip as other oil companies, such as Exxon, adapted more rapidly to a world of low oil prices by sharply cutting their overhead costs and consolidating production in efficient scale facilities. Consolidating production at these companies often involved serving the world market from a smaller number of large-scale refining facilities and shutting smaller facilities. In contrast Shell still operated with a large head office, which was required to coordinate Shell's matrix structure, and substantial duplication of oil and chemical refining facilities across operating companies, each of which typically developed the facilities required to serve its own market.

In 1995 Shell's senior management realized that lowering operating costs required a sharp reduction in head office overhead and, where appropriate, the elimination of any unnecessary duplication of facilities across countries. To achieve these goals management decided to reorganize the company along divisional lines. Shell will now operate with five main global product divisions—exploration and production, oil products, chemicals, gas, and coal. Each operating company will report to whichever global division is the most relevant. Thus the head of the Australian chemical operation will now report directly to the head of the global chemical division. The thinking is that this will increase the power of the global chemical division and enable that division to eliminate any unnecessary duplication of facilities. Eventually production may be consolidated in larger facilities that serve an entire region, rather than a single country, thereby enabling Shell to reap greater scale economies.

As for the country (or regional) chiefs, they will remain but their roles and responsibilities will be reduced. Now their primary responsibility will be coordination between operating companies within a country (or region) and relations with the local government. There will be a solid line of reporting and responsibility between the heads of operating companies and the global divisions and only a dotted line between the heads of operating companies and country chiefs. Thus, for example, the ability of the head of Shell Australia to shape the major capital investment decisions of Shell's Australian chemical operation has been substantially reduced as a result of these changes. Furthermore the simplified reporting system has reduced the need for a large head office bureaucracy, and Shell has announced it will trim the work force at its London head office by 1,170, which should help drive down Shell's cost structure.

Sources: "Shell on the Rocks," *The Economist,* June 24, 1995, pp. 57–58; D. Lascelles, "Barons Swept out of Fifedoms," *Financial Times,* March 30, 1995, p. 15; and C. Lorenz, "End of a Corporate Era," *Financial Times,* March 30, 1995, p. 15.

❧ INTRODUCTION

The objective of this chapter is to identify the organizational structures and internal control mechanisms international businesses use to manage and direct their global operations. We will be concerned not just with formal structures and control mechanisms but also with informal structures and control mechanisms such as corporate culture and companywide networks. The basic theme of the chapter is that to succeed, an international business must have appropriate formal and informal organizational structure and control mechanisms. A further theme is that what is "appropriate" is determined by the strategy of the firm. In the language of the last chapter, firms pursuing a global strategy require different structures and control mechanisms than firms pursuing a multidomestic or a transnational strategy. To succeed, a firm's structure and control systems must match its strategy in discriminating ways.

The opening case illustrates this. From the 1960s through the late 1980s the matrix structure utilized by Royal Dutch Shell served the company well. It enabled Shell to respond to national differences in consumer tastes and preferences, government regulations, and competitive conditions while giving the head office control over major strategic decisions and investments. The structure was consistent with the multidomestic strategy Shell was pursuing at the time. However, this structure made sense only so long as the firm did not have to worry about the high overhead costs, slow decision-making processes, and duplication of facilities that were among the consequences of the structure. By the early 1990s increasing cost pressures made it imperative for Shell to look for ways of driving down its cost structure. At this point the matrix structure became a drawback. The environment had become more cost competitive, and Shell had to respond by adopting a global strategy. Implementing this strategy required a change of structure, both to reduce overhead costs and to give the corporate center the power required to minimize operating costs by eliminating any unnecessary duplication of operating facilities across countries and consolidating production in large facilities that could reap scale economies. The structure that Shell chose to adopt, which was based on global product divisions, was consistent with this new emphasis on a global strategy.

Another example of the need for a fit between strategy and structure concerns the recent history of Philips NV. One of the largest industrial companies in the world (with operations in more than 60 countries), this Dutch company has long been a dominant force in the global electronics, consumer appliances, and lighting industries. However, its performance started to slip in the 1970s and by the early 1990s Philips was suffering a string of record financial losses. During the 1970s and 80s, Philips' markets were attacked by Japanese companies such as Matsushita and Sony. These companies were pursuing a global strategy, using their resulting low costs to undercut Philips. To compete on an equal footing with Matsushita and Sony, Philips had to realize experience curve and location economies (see Chapter 12). Unfortunately its attempts to do this were hindered by an organization more suited to a multidomestic strategy.

Most of Philips' foreign subsidiaries were self-contained operations with their own production facilities. Like Shell, Philips desperately needed to consolidate production in a few facilities to realize location and experience curve economies, but it was hindered in its efforts to do so by resistance from its national operations and by the sheer scale of the needed reorganization. As a consequence of this misfit of structure and strategy, Philips suffered a decade of financial trouble. Philips began to get its financial act together in the mid-1990s, primarily because the company changed its organizational structure, moving away from a structure based on national organizations and toward one based on worldwide product divisions. This new structure was much better suited to the global strategy Philips was now trying to pursue, and it allowed the company to start driving down its cost structure.[1]

To come to grips with issues of structure and control in international business, in the next four sections we consider the basic dimensions of structure and control: vertical differentiation, horizontal differentiation, integration, and control systems. Vertical differentiation is the distribution of decision-making authority within a hierarchy (i.e., centralized versus decentralized). Horizontal differentiation is the division of an organization into subunits (e.g., into functions, divisions, or subsidiaries). Integration refers to the body of mechanisms that coordinate and integrate the subunits. These mechanisms are formal and informal. Control systems are the systems top management uses to direct and control subunits, and these also are formal and informal. Throughout these sections we will focus on the implications of the four dimensions for the international firm. Having done this, we will then look at all this material together and attempt to determine the optimal structures and controls for multidomestic, global, international, and transnational firms.

❧ Vertical Differentiation

A firm's vertical differentiation determines where in its hierarchy the decision-making power is concentrated.[2] For example, are production and marketing decisions centralized in the offices of upper-level managers, or are they decentralized to lower-level managers? Where does the responsibility for R&D decisions lie? Are strategic and financial control responsibilities pushed down to operating units, or are they concentrated in the hands of top management? And so on. There are arguments for centralization and other arguments for decentralization. Let us examine them.

Arguments for Centralization

There are four main arguments for centralization. First, centralization can facilitate coordination. For example, consider a firm that has a component-manufacturing operation in Taiwan and an assembly operation in Mexico. There may be a need to coordinate the activities of these two operations to ensure a smooth flow of products from the component operation to the assembly operation. This might be achieved by centralizing production scheduling decisions at the firm's head office. Second, centralization can help ensure that decisions are consistent with organizational objectives. When decisions are decentralized to lower-level managers, those managers may make decisions at variance with top management's goals. Centralization of important decisions minimizes the chance of this occurring.

Third, by concentrating power and authority in one individual or a top-management team, centralization can give top-level managers the means to bring about needed major organizational changes. Fourth, centralization can avoid the duplication of activities that occurs when similar activities are carried on by various subunits within the organization. For example, many international firms centralize their R&D functions at one or two locations to ensure that R&D work is not duplicated. Similarly, production activities may be centralized at key locations for the same reason.

[1]See F. J. Aguilar and M. Y. Yoshino, "The Philips Group: 1987," Harvard Business School Case, 388-050, 1987; and "Philips Fights the Flab," *The Economist*, April 7, 1990, pp. 73–74.

[2]The material in this section draws on John Child, *Organizations* (London: Harper & Row, 1984).

Arguments for Decentralization

There are five main arguments for decentralization. First, top management can become overburdened when decision-making authority is centralized, and this can result in poor decisions. Decentralization gives top management the time to focus on critical issues by delegating more routine issues to lower-level managers. Second, motivational research favors decentralization. Behavioral scientists have long argued that people are willing to give more to their jobs when they have a greater degree of individual freedom and control over their work. Third, decentralization permits greater flexibility—more rapid response to environmental changes—because decisions do not have to be "referred up the hierarchy" unless they are exceptional in nature. Fourth, decentralization can result in better decisions, since decisions are made closer to the spot by individuals who (presumably) have better information than managers several levels up in a hierarchy. Fifth, decentralization can increase control. Decentralization can be used to establish relatively autonomous, self-contained subunits within an organization. Subunit managers can then be held accountable for subunit performance. The more responsibility subunit managers have for decisions that impact subunit performance, the fewer alibis they have for poor performance.

Strategy and Centralization in an International Business

The choice between centralization and decentralization is not absolute. Frequently it makes sense to centralize some decisions and to decentralize others, depending on the type of decision and the firm's strategy. Decisions regarding overall firm strategy, major financial expenditures, financial objectives, and the like are typically centralized at the firm's headquarters. However, operating decisions, such as those relating to production, marketing, R&D, and human resource management, may or may not be centralized depending on the firm's international strategy.

Consider firms pursuing a global strategy. They must decide how to disperse the various value-creation activities around the globe so location and experience economies can be realized. The head office must make the decisions about where to locate R&D, production, marketing, and so on. In addition the globally dispersed web of value-creation activities that facilitates a global strategy must be coordinated. All this creates pressures for centralizing some operating decisions.

In contrast the emphasis on local responsiveness in multidomestic firms creates strong pressures for decentralizing operating decisions to foreign subsidiaries. Thus in the classic multidomestic firm, foreign subsidiaries have autonomy in most production and marketing decisions. International firms tend to maintain centralized control over their core competency and to decentralize other decisions to foreign subsidiaries. This typically centralizes control over R&D and/or marketing in the home country and decentralizes operating decisions to the foreign subsidiaries. Microsoft Corporation, for example, which fits the international mode, currently centralizes its product development activities (where its core competencies lie) at its Redmond, Washington, headquarters and decentralizes marketing activity to various foreign subsidiaries. Thus, while products are developed at home, managers in the various foreign subsidiaries have significant latitude for formulating strategies to market those products in their particular settings.[3]

The situation in transnational firms is more complex. The need to realize location and experience curve economies requires some degree of centralized control over global production centers (as it does in global firms). However, the need for local responsiveness dictates the decentralization of many operating decisions, particularly for marketing, to foreign subsidiaries. Thus in transnational firms, some operating decisions are relatively centralized, while others are relatively decentralized.

---

[3]Allan Cane, "Microsoft Reorganizes to Meet Market Challenges," *Financial Times*, March 16, 1994, p. 1.

FIGURE 13.1   A Typical Functional Structure

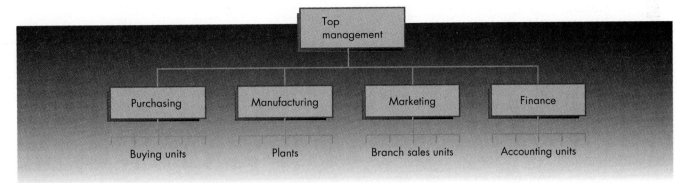

❧ HORIZONTAL DIFFERENTIATION

Horizontal differentiation is basically concerned with how the firm decides to divide itself into subunits.[4] The decision is typically made on the basis of function, type of business, or geographical area. In many firms just one of these predominates, but in others more complex solutions are adopted. This is particularly likely in the case of international firms, where the conflicting demands to organize the company around different products (to realize location and experience curve economies) and different national markets (to remain locally responsive) must be reconciled. One solution to this dilemma is to adopt a matrix structure that divides the organization on the basis of both products and national markets. In this section we look at some ways firms have chosen to divide themselves into subunits.

The Structure of Domestic Firms

Most firms begin with no formal structure and as they grow, the demands of management become too great for one individual to handle. At this point the organization is typically split into functions reflecting the firm's value-creation activities (e.g., finance, production, marketing, R&D). These functions are typically coordinated and controlled by a top-management team (see Figure 13.1). By its very nature decision making in this functional structure tends to be relatively centralized.

Further horizontal differentiation may be required if the firm significantly diversifies its product offering, which takes the firm into different business areas. Take Philips NV as an example. Although the firm started as a lighting company, it now also has activities in consumer electronics (e.g., visual and audio equipment), industrial electronics (integrated circuits and other electronic components), and medical systems (CT scanners). In such circumstances a functional structure can be too clumsy. Problems of coordination and control arise when different business areas are managed within the framework of a functional structure.[5] For one thing, it becomes difficult to identify the profitability of each distinct business area. For another it is difficult to run a functional department, such as production or marketing, if it is supervising the value-creation activities of several business areas.

To solve the problems of coordination and control, at this stage most firms switch to a product division structure (see Figure 13.2). With a product division structure, each division is responsible for a distinct product line (business area). Thus Philips has divisions for lighting, consumer electronics, industrial electronics, and medical systems. Each product division is set up as a self-contained, largely autonomous

---

[4]For more detail see S. M. Davis, "Managing and Organizing Multinational Corporations, 1979," reprinted in C. A. Bartlett and S. Ghoshal, *Transnational Management* (Homewood, IL: Richard D. Irwin, 1992).

[5]A. D. Chandler, *Strategy and Structure: Chapters in the History of the Industrial Enterprise* (Cambridge, MA: MIT Press, 1962).

FIGURE 13.2   A Typical Product Division Structure

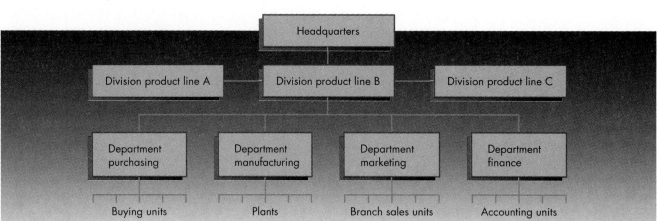

entity with its own functions. The responsibility for operating decisions is typically decentralized to product divisions, which are then held accountable for their performance. Headquarters is responsible for the overall strategic development of the firm and for the financial control of the various divisions.

The International Division

Historically when firms have expanded abroad they have typically grouped all their international activities into an international division. This has tended to be the case for firms organized on the basis of functions and for firms organized on the basis of product divisions. Regardless of the firm's domestic structure, its international division tends to be organized on geography. This is illustrated in Figure 13.3 for a firm whose domestic organization is based on product divisions.

Many manufacturing firms expanded internationally by exporting the product manufactured at home to foreign subsidiaries to sell. Thus, in the firm illustrated in Figure 13.3, the subsidiaries in Countries 1 and 2 would sell the products manufactured by Divisions A, B, and C. In time, however, it might prove viable to manufacture the product in each country, and so production facilities would be added on a country-by-country basis. For firms with a functional structure at home, this might mean replicating the functional structure in every country in which the firm does business. For firms with a divisional structure, this might mean replicating the divisional structure in every country in which the firm does business.

This structure has been widely used; according to a Harvard study, 60 percent of all firms that have expanded internationally have initially adopted it. Nonetheless, it gives rise to problems.[6] The dual structure it creates contains inherent potential for conflict and coordination problems between domestic and foreign operations. The heads of foreign subsidiaries are not given as much voice in the organization as the heads of domestic functions (in the case of functional firms) or divisions (in the case of divisional firms). Rather the head of the international division is presumed to be able to represent the interests of all countries. This effectively relegates each country's manager to the second tier of the firm's hierarchy, which is inconsistent with a strategy of trying to expand internationally and build a true multinational organization.

[6]Davis, "Multinational Corporations."

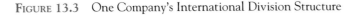

FIGURE 13.3   One Company's International Division Structure

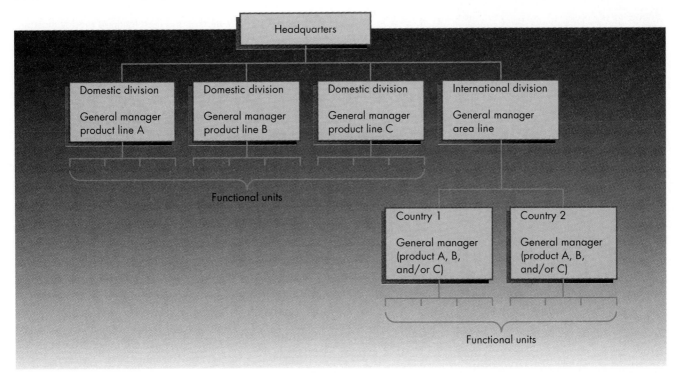

Another problem is the implied lack of coordination between domestic operations and foreign operations, which are isolated from each other in separate parts of the structural hierarchy. Among other things, this can inhibit the worldwide introduction of new products, the transfer of core competencies between domestic and oreign operations, and the consolidation of global production at key locations so as to realize location and experience curve economies. An example of these problems is given in the next "Management Focus," which looks at the experience of Abbott Laboratories with an international division structure.

As a result of such problems, most firms that continue to expand internationally abandon this structure and adopt one of the worldwide structures we discuss next. The two initial choices are a worldwide product division structure, which tends to be adopted by diversified firms that have domestic product divisions, and a worldwide area structure, which tends to be adopted by undiversified firms whose domestic structures are based on functions. These two alternative paths of development are illustrated in Figure 13.4. The model in the figure is referred to as the international structural stages model and it was developed by John Stopford and Louis Wells.[7]

Worldwide Area Structure

A worldwide area structure tends to be favored by firms with a low degree of diversification and a domestic structure based on function (see Figure 13.5). This structure divides the world into areas. An area may be a country (if the market is large enough) or a group of countries. Each area tends to be a self-contained, largely autonomous entity with its own set of value-creation activities (e.g., its own production, marketing, R&D, human resources, and finance functions). Operations authority and strategic decisions relating to each of these activities are typically decentralized to each area, with headquarters retaining authority for the overall strategic direction of the firm and overall financial control.

---

[7]J. M. Stopford and L. T. Wells, *Strategy and Structure of the Multinational Enterprise* (New York: Basic Books, 1972).

MANAGEMENT
FOCUS
The International
Division at Abbott
Laboratories

With annual sales of over $10 billion, Abbott Laboratories is one of the world's largest health care companies. The company first split itself into three divisions—pharmaceuticals, hospital products, and nutritional products—in the 1960s. Each division operated as a profit center, and each was relatively autonomous and self-contained, with its own R&D, manufacturing, and marketing functions. By the late 1960s Abbott's foreign sales were growing rapidly, so the company established an international division to handle all the firm's non-United States operations on geographic rather than product lines.

Alongside these four divisions, however, a new business has grown up that is organized differently. This is Abbott's diagnostics business, which was established in the 1970s, and is now a world leader with global sales of $2.4 billion. Unlike other businesses the diagnostics business is organized on a global basis, operating in foreign countries through its own staff, rather than through the international division. Because of the growth of the diagnostics business, Abbott can compare two different ways of handling global sales—through an international division and through a global product division (which is what the diagnostics business organization amounts to). Perhaps as a result, the company is now debating the best way of organizing international operations.

This debate is being shaped by two changes now occurring in Abbott's environment—changes that are pulling the company in different directions. One change has been a shift toward global product development in the health care industry. In an effort to quickly recapture the costs of developing new products, which for new pharmaceuticals can sometimes run to over $100 million, pharmaceutical companies are trying to introduce new products as rapidly as possible worldwide. Furthermore Abbott has found that developing products first for the U.S.

market and then trying to modify those products for foreign customers is a slow and expensive process. Instead, across all four of the company's businesses, Abbott is trying to build global products and then launch those products simultaneously around the world. This change is pulling Abbott in the direction of adopting global product divisions for all four of its businesses. Only global product divisions would give Abbott the tight control over new-product development and product launch strategy that is deemed necessary.

On the other hand, in both the United States and elsewhere bigger organizations with greater purchasing leverage, such as large hospital groups and health maintenance organizations, are coordinating their buying across a range of product lines. These powerful customers have expressed a preference to have a single contact point at Abbott, and Abbott has recognized that it is becoming increasingly important to develop stronger relations with key customers. The best way of doing this is to have a single marketing organization in each country in which Abbott does business. This organization would sell the products from each of Abbott's four product divisions. In 1994 Abbott established a separate marketing unit in the United States to do just this, while Abbott's international division adopts this approach in each country in which it operates.

Currently Abbott is sticking with the status quo. Not surprisingly executives at Abbott's international division support this move, while the heads of the product divisions favor a shift toward four global product divisions. However, top management seems to have decided there is no perfect solution to the company's organizational problems, and that imperfect as the current structure is, it works too well to contemplate a major change now.

Sources: R. Walters, "Two's Company," *Financial Times*, July 7, 1995, p. 12; and Abbott Laboratories, *1994 Annual Report*.

FIGURE 13.4   The International Structural Stages Model

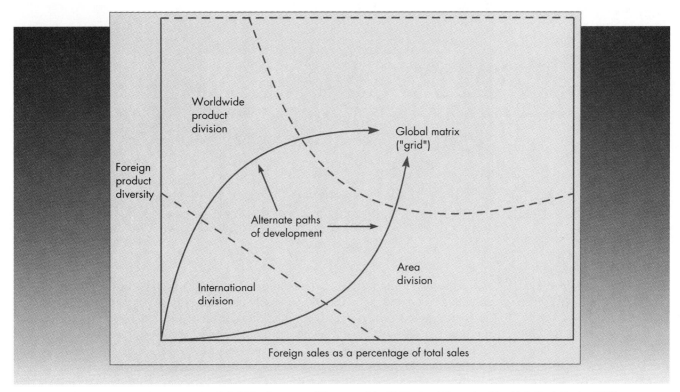

Source: Adapted from John M. Stopford and Louis T. Wells, Strategy and Structure of the Multinational Enterprise (New York: Basic Books, 1972).

FIGURE 13.5   A Worldwide Area Structure

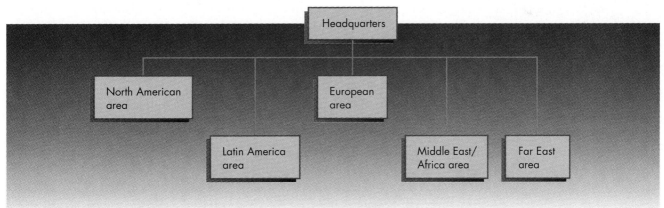

Source: Adapted from John M. Stopford and Louis T. Wells, Strategy and Structure of the Multinational Enterprise (New York: Basic Books, 1972).

The great strength of this structure is that it facilitates local responsiveness. Because decision-making responsibilities are decentralized each area can customize product offerings, marketing strategy, and business strategy to the local conditions. The weakness of the structure is that it encourages fragmentation of the organization into highly autonomous entities. This can make it difficult to transfer core competencies between areas and to undertake the rationalization in value-creation activities required for realizing location and experience curve economies. In other words the structure is consistent with a multidomestic strategy but with little else. Thus firms structured on this basis may encounter significant problems if local responsiveness is less critical than reducing costs or transferring core competencies for establishing a competitive advantage in their industry. For an example of the nature of such problems, see the chapter's closing case on Unilever.

FIGURE 13.6
A Worldwide Product
Division Structure

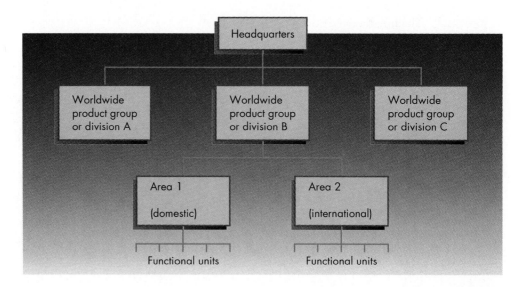

Worldwide Product Division Structure

A worldwide product division structure tends to be adopted by firms that are reasonably diversified and, accordingly, originally had domestic structures based on product divisions. As with the domestic product division structure, the basic idea is that each division is a self-contained, largely autonomous entity with full responsibility for its own value-creation activities. The headquarters retains responsibility for the overall strategic development and financial control of the firm (see Figure 13.6).

Underpinning the organization is a belief that the various value-creation activities of each product division should be coordinated by that division worldwide. Thus the worldwide product division structure is designed to help overcome the problems of coordination that arise with the international division and worldwide area structures (see the "Management Focus" on Abbott Laboratories for a detailed example). The great strength of this structure is that it provides an organizational context in which it is easier to pursue the consolidation of value-creation activities at key locations necessary for realizing location and experience curve economies. It also facilitates the transfer of core competencies within a division's worldwide operations and the simultaneous worldwide introduction of new products. The main problem with the structure is the limited voice it gives to area or country managers, since they are seen as subservient to product division managers. The result can be a lack of local responsiveness, which, as we saw in Chapter 12, can be a fatal flaw.

Global Matrix Structure

Both the worldwide area structure and the worldwide product division structure have strengths and weaknesses. The worldwide area structure facilitates local responsiveness, but it can inhibit the realization of location and experience curve economies and the transfer of core competencies between areas. The worldwide product division structure provides a better framework for pursuing location and experience curve economies and for transferring core competencies, but it is weak in local responsiveness. Other things being equal, this suggests a worldwide area structure is more appropriate if the firm's strategy is multidomestic, whereas a worldwide product division structure is more appropriate for firms pursuing global or international strategies. However, as we saw in Chapter 12, other things are not equal; most important, as Bartlett and Ghoshal have argued, to survive in some industries, firms must adopt a transnational strategy. That is, they must focus simultaneously on realizing location and experience curve economies, on local responsiveness, and on the internal transfer of core competencies (worldwide learning).[8]

---

[8]C. A. Bartlett and S. Ghoshal, *Managing across Borders* (Boston: Harvard Business School Press, 1989).

FIGURE 13.7   A Global Matrix Structure

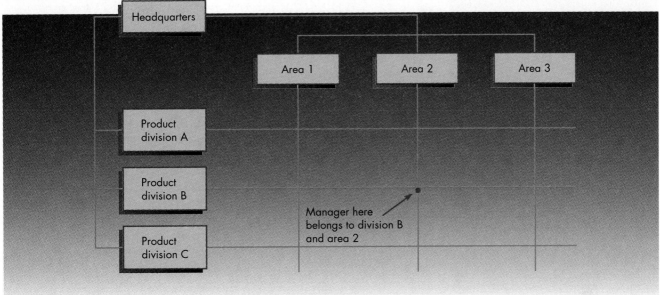

Many firms have attempted to cope with the conflicting demands of a transnational strategy by using a matrix structure. In the classic global matrix structure, horizontal differentiation proceeds along two dimensions: product division and geographical area (see Figure 13.7). The basic philosophy is that responsibility for operating decisions pertaining to a particular product should be shared by the product division and the various areas of the firm. Thus the nature of the product offering, the marketing strategy, and the business strategy to be pursued in Area 1 for the products produced by Division A are determined by consultation between Division A and Area 1 management. It is believed that this dual decision-making responsibility should enable the firm to simultaneously achieve its particular objectives. In most classic matrix structures, the idea of dual responsibility is reinforced by giving product divisions and geographical areas equal status within the organization. Individual managers thus belong to two hierarchies (a divisional hierarchy and an area hierarchy) and have two bosses (a divisional boss and an area boss).

The reality of the global matrix structure is that it often does not work as well as the theory predicts. The matrix often turns out to be clumsy and bureaucratic. It can require so many meetings that it is difficult to get any work done. Too often the need to get an area and a product division to reach a decision slows decision making and produces an inflexible organization unable to respond quickly to market shifts or to innovate. The dual-hierarchy structure can also lead to conflict and perpetual power struggles between the areas and the product divisions, catching many managers in the middle. To make matters worse, it can prove difficult to ascertain accountability in this structure. When all critical decisions are the product of negotiation between divisions and areas, one side can always blame the other when things go wrong. As a manager in one global matrix structure, reflecting on a failed product launch, said to the author, "Had we been able to do things our way, instead of having to accommodate those guys from the product division, this would never have happened." (A manager in the product division expressed similar sentiments.) The result of such finger-pointing can be that accountability is compromised, conflict is enhanced, and headquarters loses control over the organization.

In light of these problems, many transnational firms are now trying to build "flexible" matrix structures based more on firmwide networks and a shared culture and vision than on a rigid hierarchical arrangement. Dow Chemical, which is profiled in

MANAGEMENT FOCUS
Dow Chemical's Matrix Structure

The chemical industry is a global industry in which six major players compete head to head around the world. These companies are Dow Chemical and Du Pont of the United States, Great Britain's ICI, and the German trio of BASF, Hoechst, and Bayer. The barriers to the free flow of chemical products between nations largely disappeared in the 1970s. This, along with the commodity nature of most bulk chemicals and a severe recession in the early 1980s, ushered in a prolonged period of intense price competition. In such an environment the company that wins the competitive race is the one with the lowest costs, and in recent years the clear winner has been Dow Chemical. In 1988 Dow racked up an impressive 33.1 percent return on equity, against second-place ICI's 21.3 percent. Moreover, Dow generated $300,600 of sales per employee in 1988, in contrast with second-place BASF's $183,400.

How did Dow do it? Dow's managers insist that part of the credit must be placed at the feet of its much-maligned "matrix" organization. Dow's organizational matrix has three interacting elements: functions (e.g., R&D, manufacturing, marketing), businesses (e.g., ethylene, plastics, pharmaceuticals), and geography (e.g., Spain, Germany, Brazil). Managers' job titles incorporate all three elements—for example, plastics marketing manager for Spain—and most managers report to at least two bosses. Thus the plastics marketing manager in Spain might report to both the head of the worldwide plastics business and the head of the Spanish operations. The intent of the matrix was to make Dow operations responsive to both local market needs and corporate objectives. Thus the plastics business might be charged with minimizing Dow's global plastics

the above "Management Focus," is arguably one such firm. Within such companies the informal structure plays a greater role than the formal structure. We discuss this issue when we consider informal integrating mechanisms in the next section.

✸ INTEGRATING MECHANISMS

In the previous section we explained that firms divide themselves into subunits. Now we need to examine some means of coordinating those subunits. As we have seen, one way of achieving coordination is through centralization. If the coordination task is complex, however, centralization may not be very effective. The higher-level managers responsible for achieving coordination can soon become overwhelmed by the volume of work required to coordinate the activities of various subunits, particularly if the subunits are large, diverse, and/or geographically dispersed. When this is the case, firms look toward integrating mechanisms, both formal and informal, to help achieve coordination. In this section we introduce the various integrating mechanisms that international businesses can use. Before doing so, however, let us explore the need for coordination in international firms and some impediments to coordination.

Strategy and Coordination in the International Business

The need for coordination between subunits varies systematically with the strategy of the firm. The need for coordination is lowest in multidomestic companies, is higher in international companies, higher still in global companies, and highest of all in the transnational. Multidomestic firms are primarily concerned with local responsiveness. Such firms are likely to operate with a worldwide area structure in

production costs, while the Spanish operation might be charged with determining how best to sell plastics in the Spanish market.

When Dow introduced this structure, the results were less than promising; multiple reporting channels led to confusion and conflict. The large number of bosses made for an unwieldy bureaucracy. The overlapping responsibilities resulted in turf battles and a lack of accountability. Area managers disagreed with managers overseeing business sectors about which plants should be built and where. In short the structure didn't work. Instead of abandoning the structure, however, Dow decided to see if it could be made more flexible.

Dow's decision to keep its matrix structure was prompted by its move into the pharmaceuticals industry. The company realized the pharmaceutical business is very

different from the bulk chemicals business. In bulk chemicals, the big returns come from achieving economies of scale in production. This dictates establishing large plants in key locations from which regional or global markets can be served. In pharmaceuticals, on the other hand, regulatory and marketing requirements for drugs vary so much from country to country that local needs are far more important than reducing manufacturing costs through scale economies. A high degree of local responsiveness is essential for this. Dow realized its pharmaceutical business would never thrive if it were managed by the same priorities as its mainstream chemical operations.

Accordingly, instead of abandoning its matrix, Dow decided to make it more flexible so it could better accommodate the different businesses, each with its own priorities, within a single

management system. A small team of senior executives at headquarters now helps set the priorities for each type of business. After priorities are identified for each business sector, one of the three elements of the matrix—function, business, or geographical area—is given primary authority in decision making. Which element takes the lead varies according to the type of decision and the market or location in which the company is competing. Such flexibility requires that all employees understand what is occurring in the rest of the matrix so they can be coopted into it, rather than acting individually. Although this may seem confusing, Dow claims this flexible system works well and credits much of its recent success to the quality of the decisions it facilitates.

Source: "Dow Draws Its Matrix Again, and Again, and Again," *The Economist*, August 5, 1989, pp. 55–56.

which each area has considerable autonomy and its own set of value-creation functions. Since each area is established as a stand-alone entity, the need for coordination between areas is minimized.

The need for coordination is greater in firms pursuing an international strategy and trying to profit from the transfer of core competencies between the home country and foreign operations. Coordination is necessary to support the transfer of skills and product offerings from home to foreign operations. The need for coordination is greater still in firms trying to profit from location and experience curve economies; that is, in firms pursuing global strategies. Achieving location and experience economies involves dispersing value-creation activities to various locations around the globe. The resulting global web of activities must be coordinated to ensure the smooth flow of inputs into the value chain, the smooth flow of semifinished products through the value chain, and the smooth flow of finished products to markets around the world.

The need for coordination is greatest in transnational firms. Recall that these firms simultaneously pursue location and experience curve economies, local responsiveness, and the multidirectional transfer of core competencies among all the firm's subunits (this is referred to as global learning). As in global companies coordination is required to ensure the smooth flow of products through the global value chain. As in international companies coordination is required for ensuring the transfer of core competencies to subunits. However, the transnational goal of achieving multidirectional transfer of competencies requires much greater coordination than in international firms. In addition transnationals require coordination between foreign subunits and the firm's globally dispersed value-creation activities (e.g., production, R&D, marketing) to ensure that any product offering and marketing strategy is sufficiently customized to local conditions.

Impediments to Coordination

Managers of the various subunits have different orientations, partly because they have different tasks. For example, production managers are typically concerned with production issues such as capacity utilization, cost control, and quality control, whereas marketing managers are concerned with marketing issues such as pricing, promotions, distribution, and market share. These differences can inhibit communication between the managers. Quite simply, these managers often do not even "speak the same language." There may also be a lack of respect between subunits (e.g., marketing managers "looking down on" production managers, and vice versa), which further inhibits the communication required to achieve cooperation and coordination.

Differences in subunits' orientations also arise from their differing goals. For example, worldwide product divisions of a multinational firm may be committed to cost goals that require global production of a standardized product, whereas a foreign subsidiary may be committed to increasing its market share in its country, which will require a nonstandard product. In this case, these different goals can lead to conflict.

Such impediments to coordination are not unusual in any firm, but they can be particularly problematic in the multinational enterprise with its profusion of subunits at home and abroad. Moreover, differences in subunit orientation are often reinforced in multinationals by the separations of time zone, distance, and nationality between managers of the subunits.

For example, as discussed earlier, until recently the Dutch company Philips had an organization comprising worldwide product divisions and largely autonomous national organizations. The company has long had problems getting its product divisions and national organizations to cooperate on such things as new-product introductions. So difficult has this problem proved to be that when Philips developed a VCR format, the V2000 system, it could not get its North American subsidiary to introduce the product. The North American unit adopted the rival VHS format produced by Philip's global competitor, Matsushita. Unilever has experienced a similar problem in its detergents business. Unilever has found that the need to resolve disputes between its many national organizations and its product divisions can extend the time necessary for introducing a new product across Europe to four years. This denies Unilever the first-mover advantage crucial to building a strong market position.[9]

Formal Integrating Mechanisms

The formal mechanisms used to integrate subunits vary in complexity from simple direct contact and liaison roles, to teams, to a matrix structure (see Figure 13.8). In general the greater the need for coordination, the more complex the formal integrating mechanisms need to be.[10]

Direct contact between subunit managers is the simplest integrating mechanism. By this "mechanism," managers of the various subunits simply contact each other whenever they have a common concern. Direct contact may not be effective if the managers have differing orientations that act to impede coordination, as pointed out in the previous subsection.

Liaison roles are a bit more complex. When the volume of contacts between subunits increases, coordination can be improved by giving a person in each subunit responsibility for coordinating with another subunit on a regular basis. The idea is that through these roles, a permanent relationship is established between the people involved, which helps attenuate the impediments to coordination discussed in the previous subsection.

---

[9]Guy de Jonquieres, "Unilever Adopts a Clean Sheet Approach," *Financial Times*, October, 21, 1991, p. 13.
[10]See J. R. Galbraith, *Designing Complex Organizations* (Reading, MA: Addison-Wesley, 1977).

FIGURE 13.8
Formal Integrating
Mechanisms

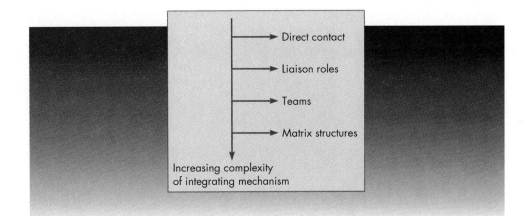

When the need for coordination is greater still, firms tend to use temporary or permanent teams composed of individuals from the subunits that need to achieve coordination. They are typically used to coordinate new-product development and introduction, but they are useful when any aspect of operations or strategy requires the cooperation of two or more subunits. New-product development and introduction teams are typically composed of personnel from R&D, production, and marketing. The resulting coordination aids the development of products that are tailored to consumer needs and that can be produced at a reasonable cost (design for manufacturing).

When the need for integration is very high, firms may institute some kind of matrix structure, in which all roles are viewed as integrating roles. The structure is designed to facilitate maximum integration among subunits. As explained earlier, the most common matrix in multinational firms is based on geographical areas and worldwide product divisions. This achieves a high level of integration between the product divisions and the areas so that, in theory, the firm can pay close attention to both local responsiveness and the pursuit of location and experience curve economies.

In some multinationals the matrix is more complex still, structuring the firm into geographical areas, worldwide product divisions, and functions, all of which report directly to headquarters. Thus, within a company such as Dow Chemical (see "Management Focus") each manager belongs to three hierarchies (e.g., a plastics marketing manager in Spain is a member of the Spanish subsidiary, the plastics product division, and the marketing function). In addition to facilitating local responsiveness and location and experience curve economies, such a matrix fosters the transfer of core competencies within the organization. This occurs because core competencies tend to reside in functions (e.g., R&D, marketing). A structure such as Dow's facilitates the transfer of competencies existing in functions from division to division and from area to area.

However, as discussed earlier, such matrix solutions to the problems of coordination in multinational enterprises can quickly become bogged down in a bureaucratic tangle that creates as many problems as it solves. Matrix structures tend to be bureaucratic, inflexible, and characterized by conflict rather than the hoped-for cooperation. As in the case of Dow Chemical, for such a structure to work it needs to be somewhat flexible and to be supported by informal integrating mechanisms.

Informal Integrating Mechanisms

In attempting to alleviate or avoid the problems associated with formal integrating mechanisms in general, and matrix structures in particular, firms with a high need for integration have been experimenting with two informal integrating mechanisms: management networks and organization culture.[11]

---

[11]See Bartlett and Ghoshal, *Managing across Borders*; and F. V. Guterl, "Goodbye, Old Matrix," *Business Month*, February 1989, pp. 32–38.

FIGURE 13.9

A Simple Management
Network

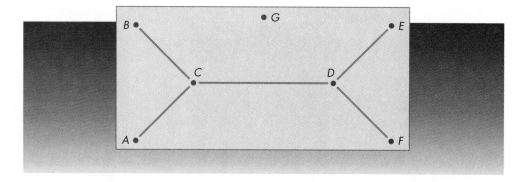

FIGURE 13.9

A Simple Management
Network

Management networks

A management network is a system of informal contacts between managers within an enterprise.[12] For a network to exist, managers at different locations within the organization must be linked to each other at least indirectly. For example, consider Figure 13.9, which shows the simple network relationships between seven managers within a multinational firm. Managers A, B, and C all know each other personally, as do Managers D, E, and F. Although Manager B does not know Manager F personally, they are linked through common acquaintances (Managers C and D). Thus we can say that Managers A through F are all part of the network, and also that Manager G is not.

Imagine Manager B is a marketing manager in Spain and needs to know the solution to a technical problem to better serve an important European customer. Imagine further that Manager F, an R&D manager in the United States, has the solution to Manager B's problem. Manager B mentions her problem to all of her contacts, including Manager C, and asks them if they know of anyone who might be able to provide a solution. Manager C asks Manager D, who tells Manager F, who then calls Manager B with the solution. In this way coordination is achieved informally through the network, rather than by formal integrating mechanisms such as teams or a matrix structure.

For such a network to function effectively, however, it must embrace as many managers within the organization as possible. For example, if Manager G had a problem similar to Manager B's, he would not be able to utilize the informal network to find a solution; he would have to resort to more formal mechanisms. Establishing firmwide networks is difficult, and although network enthusiasts speak of networks as the glue that binds multinational companies together, it is far from clear how successful firms have been at building companywide networks. Two techniques firms have been experimenting with in their efforts to establish firmwide networks are information systems and management development policies.

Firms are using their computer and telecommunications networks to provide the physical foundation for informal information systems networks.[13] Electronic mail, teleconferencing, and high-speed data systems make it much easier for managers scattered over the globe to get to know each other. Without an existing network of personal contacts, however, worldwide information systems are unlikely to meet a firm's need for integration. Firms are using their management development programs to build informal networks. Tactics include rotating managers through various subunits on a regular basis so they build their own informal networks and using management education programs to bring managers of subunits together in a single location so they can become acquainted.

[12]M. S. Granovetter, "The Strength of Weak Ties," *American Journal of Sociology* 78 (1973), pp. 1360–80.

[13]For examples see W. H. Davidow and M. S. Malone, *The Virtual Corporation* (New York: Harper Collins, 1992).

Organization culture

Management networks by themselves may not be sufficient to achieve coordination if subunit managers persist in pursuing subgoals that are at variance with firmwide goals. For a management network to function properly—and for a formal matrix structure to work also—managers must share a strong commitment to the same goals. To appreciate the nature of the problem, consider again the case of Manager B and Manager F. As before, Manager F hears about Manager B's problem through the network. However, solving Manager B's problem would require Manager F to devote considerable time to the task. Insofar as this would divert Manager F away from his own regular tasks, and the pursuit of subgoals that differ from those of Manager B, he may be unwilling to do it. Thus Manager F may not call Manager B, and the informal network would fail to provide a solution to Manager B's problem.

To eliminate this flaw, it is crucial that the organization's managers adhere to a common set of norms and values; that is, that the firm's culture override differing subunit orientations.[14] When this is the case, a manager is willing and able to set aside the interests of his own subunit when doing so benefits the firm as a whole. If Manager B and Manager F are committed to the same organizational norms and value systems, and if these organizational norms and values place the interests of the firm as a whole above the interests of any individual subunit, Manager F should be willing to cooperate with Manager B on solving her subunit's problems.

The critical question then becomes, How can a firm build a common culture? The ability to establish a common vision for the company seems to be critical here.[15] Top management needs to determine the mission of the firm and how this should be reflected in the organization's norms and values. These determinations then need to be disseminated throughout the organization. As with building informal networks, this can be achieved in part through management education programs that "socialize" managers into the firm's norms and value system. Leadership by example is another important tool for building a common culture. Human relations policies also seem to play a critical role. There is a need to select managers who are team players. There is also a need to devise reward and incentive policies that encourage managers to cooperate for the good of the firm. Put simply, Manager F is more likely to cooperate with Manager B if he gets credit for doing so than if he is made to suffer in some way for spending time on problems not directly related to his immediate task.

Summary

The message contained in this section is crucial to understanding the problems of managing the multinational firm. Multinationals need integration—particularly if they are pursuing global, international, or transnational strategies—but it can be difficult to achieve due to the impediments to coordination we discussed. Traditionally firms have tried to achieve coordination by adopting formal integrating mechanisms. These do not always work, however, since they tend to be bureaucratic and do not necessarily address the problems that arise from differing subunit orientations. This is particularly likely with a complex matrix structure, and yet a complex matrix structure is required for simultaneously achieving location and experience curve economies, local responsiveness, and the multidirectional transfer of core competencies within the organization.

The solution to this dilemma seems twofold. First, the firm must try to establish an informal management network that can do much of the work previously undertaken by a formal matrix structure. Second, the firm must build a common culture. Neither of these partial solutions, however, is easy to achieve.

---

[14]W. G. Ouchi, "Markets, Bureaucracies, and Clans," *Administrative Science Quarterly* 25 (1980) pp. 129–44.

[15]J. P. Kotter and J. L. Heskett, *Corporate Culture and Performance* (New York: Free Press, 1992).

❧ CONTROL SYSTEMS

A major task of a firm's leadership is to control the various subunits of the firm—whether they be defined on the basis of function, product division, or geographical area—to ensure their actions are consistent with the firm's overall strategic and financial objectives. Firms achieve this with various control systems. In this section we first review the various types of control systems firms use to control their subunits. Then we will see that appropriate control systems vary according to firms' international strategies.

Types of Control Systems

Four main types of control systems are used in multinational firms: personal controls, bureaucratic controls, output controls, and cultural controls. In most firms all four are used, but their relative emphasis tends to vary with the strategy of the firm.

Personal controls

Personal control is control by personal contact with subordinates. This type of control tends to be most widely used in small firms, where it is seen in the direct supervision of subordinates' actions. However, it also structures the relationships between high-level managers in large multinational enterprises. In fact the CEO may use a great deal of personal control to influence the behavior of his or her immediate subordinates, such as the heads of worldwide product divisions or major geographical areas. In turn these heads may use personal control to influence the behavior of their subordinates, and so on down through the organization. For example, Jack Welch, CEO of General Electric, has regular one-on-one meetings with the heads of all GE's major businesses (most of which are international). He uses these meetings to "probe" the managers about the strategy, structure, and financial performance of their operations. In doing so, he is essentially exercising personal control over these managers and, undoubtedly, over the strategies that they favor.

Bureaucratic controls

Bureaucratic control is control through a system of rules and procedures that direct the actions of subunits. The most important bureaucratic controls in subunits within multinational firms are budgets and capital spending rules. Budgets are essentially a set of rules for allocating a firm's financial resources. A subunit's budget specifies with some precision how much the subunit may spend. By means of such rules, headquarters uses budgets to influence the behavior of subunits. For example, the R&D budget normally specifies how much cash the R&D unit may spend on new-product development. R&D managers know that if they spend too much on one project, they will have less to spend on other projects. Hence they modify their behavior to stay within the budget. Most budgets are set by negotiation between headquarters management and subunit management. Headquarters management can encourage the growth of certain subunits and restrict the growth of others by manipulating their budgets.

Capital spending rules require headquarters management to approve any capital expenditure by a subunit that exceeds a certain amount (at GE, $50,000). A budget allows headquarters to specify the amount a subunit can spend in a given year, and capital spending rules give headquarters additional control—control over how the money is spent. They can be expected to deny approval for capital spending requests that are at variance with overall firm objectives and to approve those that are congruent with firm objectives.

Output controls

Output controls involve setting goals for subunits to achieve; expressing those goals in terms of relatively objective criteria such as profitability, productivity, growth, market share, and quality; and then judging the performance of subunit management by their ability to achieve the goals.[16] The kinds of goals subunits are given depends on their role in the firm. Self-contained product divisions or national subsidiaries are typically given goals for profitability, sales growth, and market share. Functions are more likely to be given goals related to their particular activity. Thus R&D will be given new-product development goals, production will be given productivity and quality goals, marketing will be given market share goals, and so on.

As with budgets, goals are normally established through negotiation between subunits and headquarters. Generally headquarters tries to set goals that are challenging but yet realistic, so subunit managers are forced to look for ways to improve their operations but are not so pressured they will resort to dysfunctional activities to do so (such as short-run profit maximization). Output controls foster a system of "management by exception," in that so long as subunits meet their goals, they are left alone. If a subunit fails to attain its goals, however, headquarters managers are likely to ask some tough questions. If they don't get satisfactory answers, they are likely to intervene proactively in a subunit, replacing its top management and looking for ways to improve its efficiency.

Output controls are typically reinforced by linking management reward and incentive schemes to their attainment. For example, if a worldwide product division achieves its profitability goals, its managers may receive a significant pay bonus. The size of the bonus might reflect the extent to which a subunit exceeds its goal so that subunit management has an incentive to optimize performance.

Cultural controls

We touched on the issue of cultural controls in the previous section when we discussed organization culture as a means of facilitating cooperation. Cultural controls exist when employees "buy into" the norms and value systems of the firm. When this occurs employees tend to control their own behavior, which reduces the need for direct management supervision. In other words, in a firm with a strong culture, self-control can reduce the need for other control systems.

McDonald's is a good example of a firm that actively promotes organizational norms and values. McDonald's refers to its franchisees and suppliers as partners and emphasizes its long-term commitment to them. This commitment is not just a public relations exercise; it is backed up by actions, including a willingness to help suppliers and franchisees improve their operations by providing capital and/or management assistance when needed. In response McDonald's franchisees and suppliers are integrated into the firm's culture and thus become committed to helping McDonald's succeed. One result is that McDonald's can devote less time than would otherwise be necessary to controlling its franchisees and suppliers.

The problem with cultural control is that it is very difficult to build. Substantial investments of time and money are required to cultivate organizationwide norms and value systems. As we saw earlier, this involves defining and clarifying the company mission or vision, disseminating the desired norms and value systems through management education programs, leading by example, and adopting appropriate human relations policies. Even with all these devices in place it may take years more to establish a common, cohesive culture in an organization.

Control Systems and Strategy in the International Business

The key to understanding the relationship between international strategy and control systems is the concept of performance ambiguity.

Performance ambiguity

Performance ambiguity exists when the causes of a subunit's poor performance are ambiguous. This is not uncommon when a subunit's performance is partly dependent on the performance of other subunits; that is, when there is a high degree of

---

[16]C. W. L. Hill., M. E. Hitt, and R. E. Hoskisson, "Cooperative versus Competitive Structures in Related and Unrelated Diversified Firms," *Organization Science* 3 (1992), pp. 501–21.

interdependence between subunits within the organization. Consider the case of a French subsidiary of a U.S. firm that depends on another subsidiary, a manufacturer based in Italy, for the products it sells. The French subsidiary is failing to achieve its sales goals, and the U.S. management asks the managers to explain. They reply that they are receiving poor-quality goods from the Italian subsidiary. So the U.S. management asks the managers of the Italian operation what the problem is. They reply that their product quality is excellent—the best in the industry—and that the French simply don't know how to sell a good product. Who is right? The French or the Italians? Without more information, top management cannot tell. Because they are dependent on the Italians for their product, the French have an alibi for poor performance. It may be that the French are correct or that the Italians are correct. The point, however, is that the U.S. management needs to have more information to determine who is correct. Collecting this information will be expensive and time consuming and it will divert top-management attention away from other issues. In other words, performance ambiguity raises the costs of control.

Consider further how different things would be if the French operation were entirely self-contained, with its own manufacturing, marketing, and R&D facilities. In that case the French operation would lack a convenient alibi for its poor performance; the French managers would stand or fall on their own merits. They could not blame the Italians for their poor sales. The level of performance ambiguity, therefore, is a function of the extent of interdependence of subunits in an organization.

Strategy, interdependence, and ambiguity

Now let us consider the relationship among international strategy, interdependence, and performance ambiguity. In multidomestic firms each national operation is a stand-alone entity and can thus be judged on its own merits. The level of performance ambiguity is low. In an international firm the level of interdependence is somewhat higher. Integration is required to facilitate the transfer of core competencies. Since the success of a foreign operation is partly dependent on the quality of the competency transferred from the home country, performance ambiguity can exist.

In global firms the situation is still more complex. Recall that in a pure global firm the pursuit of location and experience curve economies leads to the development of a global web of value-creation activities. Many of the activities in a global firm are interdependent. A French subsidiary's ability to sell a product depends on how well other operations in other countries perform their value-creation activities. Thus the levels of interdependence and performance ambiguity are high in global companies.

The level of performance ambiguity is highest of all in transnational firms. Transnational firms suffer from the same performance ambiguity problems that global firms do. In addition, since they emphasize the multidirectional transfer of core competencies, they also suffer from the problems characteristic of firms pursuing an international strategy. The extremely high level of integration within transnational firms implies a high degree of joint decision making, and the resulting interdependencies create plenty of alibis for poor performance. There is lots of room for finger-pointing in transnational firms.

Implications for control

The arguments of the previous section, along with the implications for the costs of control, are summarized in Table 13.1. The costs of control might be defined as the time top management must devote to monitoring and evaluating subunits' performance. This will be greater when the amount of performance ambiguity is greater. When performance ambiguity is low, management can use output controls and a system of management by exception; when it is high, they have no such luxury. Output controls do not provide totally unambiguous signals of a subunit's efficiency when the performance of that subunit is dependent on the performance of another subunit within the organization. Thus management must devote time to resolving the problems that arise from performance ambiguity, with a corresponding rise in the costs of control.

TABLE 13.1

Interdependence, Performance Ambiguity, and the Costs of Control for the Four International Business Strategies

Strategy	Interdependence	Performance Ambiguity	Costs of Control
Multidomestic	Low	Low	Low
International	Moderate	Moderate	Moderate
Global	High	High	High
Transnational	Very high	Very high	Very high

Table 13.1 reveals a paradox. We saw in Chapter 12 that a transnational strategy is desirable because it gives a firm more ways to profit from international expansion than do multidomestic, international, and global strategies. But now we see that due to the high level of interdependence, the costs of controlling transnational firms are higher than the costs of controlling firms that pursue other strategies. It follows that unless there is some way of reducing these costs, the higher profitability associated with a transnational strategy could be canceled by the higher costs of control. The same point, although to a lesser extent, can be made with regard to global firms. Although firms pursuing a global strategy can reap the cost benefits of location and experience curve economies, they must cope with a higher level of performance ambiguity, and this raises the costs of control (in comparison with firms pursuing an international or multidomestic strategy).

This is where the issue of control systems comes in. When we survey the control systems that corporations use to control their subunits, we find that irrespective of their strategy, multinational firms all use output and bureaucratic controls. However, in firms pursuing either global or transnational strategies, the usefulness of output controls is limited by substantial performance ambiguities. As a result, these firms place greater emphasis on cultural controls. Cultural control, by encouraging managers to want to assume the organization's norms and value systems, gives managers of interdependent subunits an incentive to look for ways to work out problems that arise between them. The result is a reduction in finger-pointing and, accordingly, in the costs of control. It follows that the development of cultural controls may be a precondition for the successful pursuit of a transnational strategy, and perhaps of a global strategy as well.

❧ SYNTHESIS: STRATEGY AND STRUCTURE

In Chapter 12 we identified four international business strategies: multidomestic, international, global, and transnational strategies. So far in this chapter we have looked at four aspects of organizational structure—vertical differentiation, horizontal differentiation, integration, and control systems—and we have discussed the interrelationships between these dimensions and strategies. Now it is time to synthesize this material. Our synthesis is summarized in Table 13.2.

Multidomestic Firms

Firms pursuing a multidomestic strategy focus on local responsiveness. Referring to Table 13.2, we can see that multidomestic firms tend to operate with worldwide area structures, within which operating decisions are decentralized to functionally self-contained foreign subsidiaries. The need for coordination between subunits (areas) is low, so multidomestic firms operate with few interarea integrating mechanisms, either formal or informal. The lack of interdependence implies that the level of performance ambiguity in multidomestic concerns is low, as (by extension) are the costs of control. Thus headquarters can manage foreign operations by relying primarily on output and bureaucratic controls and a policy of management by exception. The need for cultural controls is low. Were it not for the fact that these firms are unable to profit from the realization of location and experience curve economies, or from the transfer of core competencies, their organizational simplicity would make this a very attractive strategy.

Table 13.2
A Synthesis of Strategy,
Structure, and Control
Systems

Structure and Controls	Strategy			
	Multidomestic	**International**	**Global**	**Transnational**
Vertical differentiation	Decentralized	Core competency centralized; rest decentralized	Some centralized	Mixed centralized and decentralized
Horizontal differentiation	Worldwide area structure	Worldwide product division	Worldwide product division	Informal matrix
Need for coordination	Low	Moderate	High	Very high
Integrating mechanisms	None	Few	Many	Very many
Performance ambiguity	Low	Moderate	High	Very high
Need for cultural controls	Low	Moderate	High	Very high

International Firms

Firms pursuing an international strategy attempt to create value by transferring core competencies from home to foreign subunits. If they are diverse, as most of them are, these firms operate with a worldwide product division structure. Headquarters typically maintains centralized control over the source of the firm's core competency, which is most typically found in the R&D and/or marketing functions of the firm. All other operating decisions are decentralized within the firm to national operations (which in diverse firms report to worldwide product divisions). The need for coordination is moderate in such firms, reflecting the need to transfer core competencies. Thus, although such firms operate with some integrating mechanisms, they are not that extensive. The relatively low level of interdependence that results translates into a relatively low level of performance ambiguity. Thus these firms can generally get by with output and bureaucratic controls. Overall, although the organization of international firms is more complex than that of multidomestic firms, the increase in the level of complexity is not that great.

Global Firms

Firms pursuing a global strategy focus on the realization of location and experience curve economies. If they are diverse, as most of them are, these firms operate with a worldwide product division structure. To coordinate the firm's globally dispersed web of value-creation activities, headquarters typically maintains ultimate control over most operating decisions. In general global firms are more centralized than most multinational enterprises. Reflecting the great need for coordination of the various stages of the firms' globally dispersed value chains, the need for integration in these firms also is high. Thus these firms tend to operate with an array of formal and informal integrating mechanisms. The resulting interdependencies can lead to significant performance ambiguities. As a result, in addition to output and bureaucratic controls, global firms tend to stress cultural controls. On average the organization of global firms is more complex than that of multidomestic and transnational firms.

Transnational Firms

Firms pursuing a transnational strategy focus on the simultaneous attainment of location and experience curve economies, local responsiveness, and global learning (the multidirectional transfer of core competencies). These firms tend to operate with matrix-type structures in which both product divisions and areas have significant influence. The needs to coordinate a globally dispersed value chain and to transfer core competencies create pressures for centralizing some operating decisions (particularly production and R&D). At the same time, the need to be locally responsive creates pressures for decentralizing other operating decisions to national operations (particularly marketing). Consequently these firms tend to mix relatively high degrees of centralization for some operating decisions with relative high degrees of decentralization for other operating decisions.

The need for coordination is particularly high in transnational firms. This is reflected in the use of a wide array of formal and informal integrating mechanisms, including formal matrix structures and informal management networks. The high level of interdependence of subunits implied by such integration can result in significant performance ambiguities, which raise the costs of control. To reduce these, in addition to output and bureaucratic controls, transnational firms need to cultivate cultural controls.

Environment, Strategy, Structure, and Performance

Underlying the scheme outlined in Table 13.2 is the notion that a "fit" between strategy and structure is necessary for a firm to achieve high performance. For a firm to succeed, two conditions must be fulfilled. First, the firm's strategy must be consistent with the environment in which the firm operates. We discussed this issue in Chapter 12 and noted that in some industries a global strategy is most viable, in others an international or transnational strategy may be most viable, and in still others a multidomestic strategy may be most viable (although the number of multidomestic industries is on the decline). Second, the firm's organizational structure and control systems must be consistent with its strategy.

If the strategy does not fit the environment, the firm is likely to experience significant performance problems. If the structure does not fit the strategy, the firm is also likely to experience performance problems. Therefore, to survive, a firm must strive to achieve a *fit* of its environment, its strategy, its organizational structure, and its control systems. We saw the importance of this concept in the opening case. Shell's 1995 switch from a matrix structure to a structure based on global product divisions was founded on the fact that its matrix structure was no longer consistent with the global strategy Shell had to pursue, given the extreme cost pressures in Shell's operating environment.

Philips NV, the Dutch electronics firm, provides us with another illustration of the need for this fit. For reasons rooted in the history of the firm, Philips operated until recently with an organization typical of a multidomestic enterprise. Operating decisions were decentralized to largely autonomous foreign subsidiaries. The problem was that the industry in which Philips competed had been revolutionized by technological change and the emergence of low-cost Japanese competitors who utilized a global strategy. To survive Philips needed to become a transnational. The firm recognized this and tried to adopt a transnational posture, but it did little to change its organizational structure. The firm nominally adopted a matrix structure based on worldwide product divisions and national areas. In reality, however, the national areas continued to dominate the organization, and the product divisions had little more than an advisory role. Moreover Philips lacked the informal management networks and strong unifying culture that transnationals need to succeed. As a result Philips' structure did not fit the strategy the firm had to pursue to survive, and by the early 1990s Philips was losing money. It was only after four years of wrenching change and large losses that Philips was able to tilt the balance of power in its matrix toward the product divisions. By 1995 the fruits of this effort to realign the company's strategy and structure with the demands of its operating environment were beginning to show up in improved financial performance.[17]

---

[17]See Aguilar and Yoshino, "Philips Group"; "Philips Fights Flab," and R. Van de Krol, "Philips Wins Back Old Friends," *Financial Times*, July 14, 1995, p. 14.

🐾 SUMMARY OF CHAPTER

The purpose of this chapter was to identify the organizational structures and internal control mechanisms, both formal and informal, that international businesses use to manage and direct their global operations. A central theme of the chapter was that different strategies require different structures and control systems. To succeed a firm must match its structure and controls to its strategy in discriminating ways. Firms whose structure and controls do not fit their strategic requirements will experience performance problems. More specifically, the following points were made in the chapter:

1. There are four main dimensions of organizational structure: vertical differentiation, horizontal differentiation, integration, and control systems.

2. Vertical differentiation is the centralization versus decentralization of decision-making responsibilities.

3. Operating decisions are generally decentralized in multidomestic firms, somewhat centralized in international firms, and more centralized still in global firms. The situation in transnational firms is more complex.

4. Horizontal differentiation refers to how the firm is divided into subunits.

5. Undiversified domestic firms are typically divided into subunits on the basis of functions. Diversified domestic firms typically adopt a product divisional structure.

6. When firms expand abroad they often begin with an international division. However, this structure rarely serves satisfactorily very long due to its inherent potential for conflict and coordination problems between domestic and foreign operations.

7. Firms then switch to one of two structures: a worldwide area structure (undiversified firms) or a worldwide product division structure (diversified firms).

8. Since neither of these structures achieves a balance between local responsiveness and achievement of location and experience curve economies, many multinationals adopt matrix-type structures. However, global matrix structures have typically failed to work well, primarily due to bureaucratic problems.

9. Firms use integrating mechanisms to help achieve coordination between subunits.

10. The need for coordination (and hence integrating mechanisms) varies systematically with firm strategy. This need is lowest in multidomestic firms, higher in international firms, higher still in global firms, and highest in transnational firms.

11. Integration is inhibited by a number of impediments to coordination, particularly by differing subunit orientations.

12. Integration can be achieved through formal integrating mechanisms. These vary in complexity from direct contact and simple liaison roles, to teams, to a matrix structure. A drawback of formal integrating mechanisms is that they can become bureaucratic.

13. To overcome the bureaucracy associated with formal integrating mechanisms, firms often use informal mechanisms, which include management networks and organization culture.

14. For a network to function effectively, it must embrace as many managers within the organization as possible. Information systems and management development policies (including job rotation and management education programs) can be used to establish firmwide networks.

15. For a network to function properly, subunit managers must be committed to the same goals. One way of achieving this is to foster the development of a common organization culture. Leadership by example, management development programs, and human relations policies are all important in building a common culture.

16. A major task of a firm's headquarters is to control the various subunits of the firm to ensure consistency with strategic goals. Headquarters can achieve this through control systems.

17. There are four main types of controls: personal, bureaucratic, output, and cultural (which foster self-control).

18. The key to understanding the relationship between international strategy and control systems is the concept of performance ambiguity. Performance ambiguity is a function of the degree of interdependence of subunits and it raises the costs of control.

19. The degree of subunit interdependence—and hence performance ambiguity and the costs of control—is a function of the firm's strategy. It is lowest in multidomestic firms, higher in international firms, higher still in global firms, and highest in transnationals.

20. It follows that to reduce the high costs of control, firms with a high degree of interdependence between subunits (e.g., transnationals) must develop cultural controls.

🐾 CRITICAL DISCUSSION QUESTIONS

1. "The choice of strategy for a multinational firm to pursue must depend on a comparison of the benefits of that strategy (in terms of value creation) with the costs of implementing it (as defined by organizational requirements necessary for implementation). On this basis, it may be logical for some firms to pursue a multidomestic strategy, others a global or international strategy, and still others a transnational strategy." Is this statement correct?

2. Discuss this statement: "An understanding of the causes and consequences of performance ambiguity is central to the issue of organizational design in multinational firms."

3. Describe the organizational solutions a transnational firm might adopt to reduce the costs of control.

4. What actions must a firm take to establish a viable organizationwide management network?

❧ CLOSING CASE   Organizational Change at Unilever

 Unilever is a very old multinational with worldwide operations in the detergent and food industries. For decades Unilever managed its worldwide detergents activities in an arm's-length manner. A subsidiary was set up in each major national market and allowed to operate largely autonomously, with each subsidiary carrying out the full range of value-creation activities, including manufacturing, marketing, and R&D. As a result the company had 17 autonomous national operations in Europe alone by the mid-1980s.

In the early 1990s Unilever began to transform its worldwide detergents activities from a loose confederation into a tightly managed business with a global strategy. The shift was prompted by Unilever's realization that its traditional way of doing business was no longer effective in an arena where it had become essential to realize substantial cost economies, to innovate, and to respond quickly to changing market trends.

The point was driven home in the 1980s when the company's archrival, Procter & Gamble, repeatedly stole the lead in bringing new products to market. Within Unilever, "persuading" the 17 European operations to adopt new products could take four to five years. In addition Unilever was handicapped by a high cost structure that was the result of the duplication of manufacturing facilities from country to country and by the company's inability to enjoy the same kind of scale economies as P&G. The company's high costs ruled out its use of competitive pricing.

To change this situation, Unilever established product divisions to coordinate regional operations. In Europe, "Lever Europe" was set up to do this, and the 17 European companies now report directly to Lever Europe. Using its newfound organizational clout, Lever Europe will consolidate the production of detergents in Europe in a few key locations to reduce costs and speed new-product introduction. Implicit in this new approach is a bargain: The 17 companies are relinquishing autonomy in their traditional markets in exchange for opportunities to help develop and execute a unified pan-European strategy.

As a consequence of these changes, manufacturing is now being rationalized, with detergent production for the European market concentrated in a few key locations. The number of European plants manufacturing soap has been cut from 10 to 2, and some new products will be manufactured at only one site. Product sizing and packaging are being harmonized to cut purchasing costs and to pave the way for unified pan-European advertising. By taking these steps, Unilever estimates it may save as much as $400 million a year in its European operations.

Lever Europe is attempting to speed its development of new products and to synchronize the launch of new products throughout Europe. Its efforts seem to be paying off: A concentrated dishwasher detergent introduced in Germany in early 1991 was available across Europe a year later, a distinct improvement.

Nonetheless, history still imposes constraints. Whereas Procter & Gamble's leading laundry detergent carries the same brand name across Europe, Unilever sells its product under a wide variety of names. The company has no plans to change this. Having spent 100 years building these brand names, it believes it would be foolish to scrap them in the interest of pan-European standardization.

CASE DISCUSSION QUESTIONS

1. What strategy was Unilever pursuing before its early 1990s reorganization? What kind of structure did the company have? Were Unilever's strategy and structure consistent with each other? What were the benefits of this strategy and structure? What were the drawbacks?

2. By the 1990s was there still a fit between Unilever's strategy and structure and the operating environment in which it competed? If not, why not?

3. What kind of strategy and structure does Unilever appear to be adopting in the 1990s? Is this appropriate given the environment in which Unilever now competes? What are the benefits of this organizational and strategic shift? What are the costs?

Source: Guy de Jonquieres, "Unilever Adopts a Clean Sheet Approach," Financial Times, October 21, 1991, p. 13; and C. A. Bartlett and S. Ghoshal, Managing across Borders (Boston: Harvard Business School Press, 1989).

CHAPTER FOURTEEN

MODE OF ENTRY AND STRATEGIC ALLIANCES

FUJI-XEROX

Fuji-Xerox is one of the most enduring and reportedly successful alliances between two companies from different countries. Established in 1962, today Fuji-Xerox is structured as a 50/50 joint venture between the Xerox Group, the U.S. maker of photocopiers, and Fuji Photo Film, Japan's largest manufacturer of film products. With 1994 sales of close to $8 billion, Fuji-Xerox provides Xerox with over 20 percent of its worldwide revenues.

A prime motivation for the establishment of the joint venture was that in the early 1960s the Japanese government did not allow foreign companies to set up wholly owned subsidiaries in Japan. The joint venture was originally conceived as a marketing organization to sell xerographic products that would be manufactured by Fuji Photo under license from Xerox. However, when the Japanese government refused to approve the establishment of a joint venture intended solely as a sales company, the joint-venture agreement was revised to give Fuji-Xerox manufacturing rights. Management of the venture was placed in the hands of Japanese managers who were given considerable autonomy to develop their own operations and strategy, subject to oversight by a board of directors that contained representatives from both Xerox and Fuji Photo.

Initially Fuji-Xerox followed the lead of Xerox in manufacturing and selling the large high-volume copiers developed by Xerox in the United States. These machines were sold at a premium price to the high end of the market. However, Fuji-Xerox noticed that in the Japanese market new competitors, such as Canon and Ricoh, were making significant inroads by building small low-volume copiers and focusing on the mid- and low-priced segments of the market. This led to Fuji-Xerox's development of its first "home-grown" copier, the FX2200, which at the time was billed as the world's smallest copier. Introduced in 1973 the FX2200 hit the market just in time to allow Fuji-Xerox to hold its own against a blizzard of new competition in Japan that followed the expiration of many of Xerox's key patents.

About the same time Fuji-Xerox also embarked on a total quality control (TQC) program. The aims of the program were to speed development of new products, reduce waste, improve quality, and lower manufacturing costs. The first fruit of this program was the FX3500. Introduced in 1977, the FX3500 by 1979 had broken the Japanese record for the number of copiers sold in one year. Partly because of the success of the FX3500, in 1980 the company won Japan's prestigious Deming Prize. The success of the FX3500 was all the more notable because at the same time Xerox was canceling a series of programs to develop low- to mid-level copiers and instead reaffirming its commitment to serving the high end of the market. Because of these cancellations Tony Kobayashi, the CEO of Fuji-Xerox, was initially told to stop work on the development of the FX3500. He refused, arguing that the FX3500 was crucial for the survival of Fuji-Xerox in the Japanese market. Given the arm's-length relationship between Xerox and Fuji-Xerox, Kobayashi was able to prevail.

By the early 1980s Fuji-Xerox was number two in the Japanese copier market with a share in the 20 to 22 percent range, just behind that of market leader Canon. In contrast Xerox was running into all sorts of problems in the United States. As Xerox's patents had expired, so a number of companies, including Canon, Ricoh, Kodak, and IBM began to take market share from Xerox. Canon and Ricoh were particularly successful by focusing on that segment of the market that Xerox had ignored—the low end. As a result Xerox's market share in the Americas fell from 35 percent in 1975 to 25 percent in 1980, while its profitability slumped.

In an attempt to recapture share, Xerox began to sell Fuji-Xerox's FX3500 copier in the United States. Not only did the FX3500 help Xerox to halt the rapid decline in its share of the U.S. market, but it also opened Xerox's eyes to the benefits of Fuji-Xerox's TQC program. Xerox found that the reject rate for Fuji-Xerox parts was only a fraction of the reject rate for American-produced parts. Visits to Fuji-Xerox revealed another important truth; quality in manufacturing doesn't increase real costs—it reduces costs by reducing defective products and service costs. These developments forced Xerox to rethink the way it did business.

From being the main provider of products, technology, and management know-how to Fuji-Xerox, Xerox became the willing pupil of Fuji-Xerox in the 1980s. In 1983 Xerox introduced its "Leadership through Quality" program, which was based on Fuji-Xerox's TQC program. Xerox launched a quality training effort with its suppliers and was rewarded when the number of defective parts from suppliers subsequently fell from 25,000 per million in 1983 to 300 per million by 1992.

In 1985 and 1986 Xerox began to focus on its new-product development process. One goal was to design products that, while customized to market conditions in different countries, contained a large number of globally standardized parts. Another goal was to reduce the time it took to design new products and bring them to market. To achieve these goals Xerox set up joint product development teams with Fuji-Xerox. Each team managed the design, component sources, manufacturing,

distribution, and follow-up customer service on a worldwide basis. The use of design teams cut as much as one year from the overall product development cycle and saved millions of dollars.

One consequence of the new approach to product development was the 5100 copier. This was the first product designed jointly by Xerox and Fuji-Xerox for the worldwide market. The 5100 is manufactured in U.S. plants. It was launched in Japan in November 1990 and in the United States the following February. The 5100's global design reportedly reduced the overall time to market and saved the company more than $10 million in development costs.

As a result of the skills and products acquired from Fuji-Xerox, Xerox's position improved markedly during the 1980s. Due to its improved quality, lower costs, shorter product development time, and more appealing product range, Xerox gained market share back from its competitors and boosted its profits and revenues. Xerox's share of the U.S. copier market increased from a low of 10 percent in 1985 to 18 percent in 1991.

Sources: R. Howard, "The CEO as Organizational Architect," *Harvard Business Review*, September–October 1992, pp. 106–23; D. Kearns, "Leadership through Quality," *Academy of Management Executive* 4 (1990), pp. 86–89; K. McQuade and B. Gomes-Casseres, "Xerox and Fuji-Xerox," *Harvard Business School Case #9-391-156*, and E. Terazono and C. Lorenz, " An Angry Young Warrior," *Financial Times*, September 19, 1994, p. 11.

❧ INTRODUCTION

This chapter is concerned with two closely related topics: entry modes and strategic alliances. Entry modes serving foreign markets include exporting, licensing or franchising to host-country firms, joint venturing with a host-country firm, and setting up a wholly owned subsidiary in a host country to serve its market. Each of these options has advantages and disadvantages. The magnitude of the advantages and disadvantages associated with each entry mode are determined by a number of factors, including transport costs, trade barriers, political risks, economic risks, and firm strategy. The optimal entry mode varies depending on these various factors. Thus, whereas some firms may best serve a given market by exporting, other firms may better serve the market by setting up a wholly owned subsidiary or by using some other entry mode.

We touched on the topic of entry modes when we examined foreign direct investment (FDI) in Chapter 6. There we related economic theory to exporting, licensing, and foreign direct investment as means of entering foreign markets. Here we integrate that material with the material we discussed in Chapter 12 on firm strategy to present a comprehensive picture of the factors that determine the optimal entry mode. We consider a wider range of modes in this chapter as well as mixed entry modes. (For example, joint venturing and setting up a wholly owned subsidiary in another country are both FDI, but we did not make a distinction in Chapter 6.)

The second topic of this chapter is that of strategic alliances. **Strategic alliances** are agreements between actual or potential competitors to cooperate. The alliance between Xerox and Fuji Photo profiled in the opening case (Fuji-Xerox) can be viewed as a strategic alliance because Fuji Photo was a potential competitor of Xerox's in the photocopier market. The term *strategic alliance* is often used loosely to embrace a wide range of arrangements between actual or potential competitors including cross-shareholding deals, licensing arrangements, formal joint ventures (as in the Fuji-Xerox case), and informal cooperative arrangements. The motives for entering strategic alliances are varied, but they often include market access; hence the overlap with the topic of entry mode. This was a factor in the formation of the Fuji-Xerox alliance, since the alliance helped Xerox enter the Japanese market. In many respects, the entry modes of licensing, franchising, and joint ventures are strategic alliances. However, strategic alliances tend to involve much more than market access. As seen in the Fuji-Xerox case, strategic alliances can also involve the transfer of technical and managerial know-how between partners and sharing the fixed costs of new-product development.

We will see that strategic alliances have advantages and disadvantages and that a firm must weigh these carefully before deciding whether to ally itself with an actual or potential competitor. Perhaps the biggest danger is that the firm will give away more to its ally than it receives. As we will see, firms can reduce this risk by how they structure their strategic alliances. We will also see how firms can build alliances that benefit both partners, as the Fuji-Xerox alliance seems to be doing.

The rest of this chapter is structured as follows. First, we will review the options available to firms wishing to enter a foreign market, discussing the advantages and disadvantages of each option. Second, we will consider the factors that determine a firm's optimal entry mode. Third, we will look at the advantages and disadvantages of engaging in strategic alliances with competitors. Fourth, we will consider how a firm should select an ally, structure the alliance, and manage it to maximize the advantages and minimize the disadvantages associated with alliances.

✸ Entry Modes

When a firm is considering entering a foreign market, the question arises as to the best means of achieving it. There are basically six ways to enter a foreign market: exporting, turnkey projects, licensing, franchising, joint venturing with a host-country firm, and setting up a wholly owned subsidiary in the host country. Each entry mode has advantages and disadvantages. Managers need to consider these carefully when deciding which entry mode to use.[1]

Exporting

Most manufacturing firms begin their global expansion as exporters and only later switch to another mode for serving a foreign market. We take a close look at the mechanics and processing of exporting in the next chapter. Here we focus on the advantages and disadvantages of exporting as an entry mode.

Advantages
Exporting has two distinct advantages. It avoids the costs of establishing manufacturing operations in the host country, which are often substantial. Exporting also may help a firm achieve experience curve and location economies (see Chapter 12). By manufacturing the product in a centralized location and exporting it to other national markets, the firm may be able to realize substantial scale economies from its global sales volume. This is how Sony came to dominate the global TV market, how Matsushita came to dominate the VCR market, and how many Japanese auto firms made inroads into the U.S. auto market.

Disadvantages
On the other hand, exporting has a number of drawbacks. First, exporting from the firm's home base may not be appropriate if there are lower-cost locations for manufacturing the product abroad (i.e., if the firm can realize location economies by moving production elsewhere). Thus, particularly for firms pursuing global or transnational strategies, it may be preferable to manufacture in a location where the mix of factor conditions is most favorable from a value-creation perspective and to export to the rest of the world from that location. This is not so much an argument against

---

[1]This section draws on two studies: C. W. L. Hill, P. Hwang, and W. C. Kim, "An Eclectic Theory of the Choice of International Entry Mode," *Strategic Management Journal* 11 (1990), pp. 117–28; and C. W. L. Hill and W. C. Kim, "Searching for a Dynamic Theory of the Multinational Enterprise: A Transaction Cost Model," *Strategic Management Journal* 9 (Special Issue on Strategy Content; 1988), pp. 93–104. See also E. Anderson and H. Gatignon, "Modes of Foreign Entry: A Transaction Cost Analysis and Propositions," *Journal of International Business Studies* 17 (1986), pp. 1–26; and F. R. Root, *Entry Strategies for International Markets* (Lexington, MA. D. C. Heath, 1980).

exporting as an argument against exporting from the firm's home country. Many U.S. electronics firms have moved some of their manufacturing to the Far East due to the availability of low-cost, highly skilled labor there. They then export from that location to the rest of the world, including the United States.

A second drawback to exporting is that high transport costs can make exporting uneconomical, particularly for bulk products. One way of getting around this is to manufacture bulk products regionally. This strategy enables the firm to realize some economies from large-scale production and at the same time to limit its transport costs. For example, many multinational chemical firms manufacture their products regionally, serving several countries from one facility.

Another drawback to exporting is that tariff barriers can make it uneconomical. Similarly the threat of tariff barriers by the host-country government can make it very risky. It was an implicit threat by the U.S. Congress to impose tariffs on imported Japanese autos that led to many Japanese auto firms' decisions to set up manufacturing plants in the United States. As a consequence, by 1990 almost 50 percent of all Japanese cars sold in the United States were manufactured locally—up from 0 percent in 1985.

A fourth drawback to exporting arises when a firm delegates its marketing in each country where it does business to a local agent. (This is common for firms that are just beginning to export.) Foreign agents often carry the products of competing firms and so have divided loyalties. In such cases the foreign agent may not do as good a job as the firm would if it managed its marketing itself. There are ways around this problem, however. One way is to set up a wholly owned subsidiary in the country to handle local marketing. Then the firm can exercise tight control over marketing in the country while reaping the cost advantages of manufacturing the product in a single location.

Turnkey Projects

Firms that specialize in the design, construction, and start-up of turnkey plants are common in some industries. In a **turnkey project,** the contractor agrees to handle every detail of the project for a foreign client, including the training of operating personnel. At completion of the contract, the foreign client is handed the "key" to a plant that is ready for full operation—hence the term *turnkey*. This is actually a means of exporting process technology to other countries. In a sense it is just a very specialized kind of exporting. Turnkey projects are most common in the chemical, pharmaceutical, petroleum refining, and metal refining industries, all of which use complex, expensive production-process technologies.

Advantages

The know-how required to assemble and run a technologically complex process, such as refining petroleum or steel, is a valuable asset. The main advantage of turnkey projects is that they are a way of earning great economic returns from that asset. The strategy is particularly useful in cases where FDI is limited by host-government regulations. For example, the governments of many oil-rich countries have set out to build their own petroleum refining industries and, as a step toward that goal, have restricted FDI in their oil and refining sectors. Since many of these countries lacked petroleum refining technology, however, they had to gain it by entering into turnkey projects with foreign firms that had the technology. Such deals are often attractive to the selling firm because they would probably have no other way to earn a return on their valuable know-how in that country.

A turnkey strategy, as opposed to a more conventional type of FDI, may make sense in a country where the political and economic environment is such that a longer-term investment might expose the firm to unacceptable political and/or economic risks (e.g., the risk of nationalization or of economic collapse).

Disadvantages

Three main drawbacks are associated with a turnkey strategy. First, by definition, the firm that enters into a turnkey deal will have no long-term interest in the foreign country. This can be a disadvantage if that country subsequently proves to be a major market for the output of the process that has been exported. One way around this is to take a minority equity interest in the operation set up by the turnkey project.

Second, the firm that enters into a turnkey project with a foreign enterprise may inadvertently create a competitor. For example, many of the Western firms that sold oil refining technology to firms in Saudi Arabia, Kuwait, and other Persian Gulf states now find themselves competing head to head with these firms in the world oil market. Third, and related to the second point, if the firm's process technology is a source of competitive advantage, then selling this technology through a turnkey project is also selling competitive advantage to potential and/or actual competitors.

Licensing

A **licensing agreement** is an arrangement whereby a licensor grants the rights to intangible property to another entity (the licensee) for a specified period of time, and in return, the licensor receives a royalty fee from the licensee.[2] Intangible property includes patents, inventions, formulas, processes, designs, copyrights, and trademarks. For example, in the opening case we saw how Xerox licensed its patented xerographic know-how to Fuji-Xerox. In return Fuji-Xerox paid Xerox a royalty fee equal to 5 percent of the net sales revenue that Fuji-Xerox earned from the sales of photocopiers based on Xerox's patented know-how. In the Fuji-Xerox case the license was originally granted for 10 years, and it has been renegotiated and extended several times since. The licensing agreement between Xerox and Fuji-Xerox also limited Fuji-Xerox's direct sales to the Asian Pacific region (although Fuji-Xerox does supply Xerox with photocopiers that are sold in North America under the Xerox label).[3]

Advantages

In the typical international licensing deal the licensee puts up most of the capital necessary to get the overseas operation going. Thus a primary advantage of licensing is that the firm does not have to bear the development costs and risks associated with opening a foreign market. Licensing is a very attractive option for firms lacking the capital to develop operations overseas. In addition licensing can be attractive when a firm is unwilling to commit substantial financial resources to an unfamiliar or politically volatile foreign market. Licensing is also often used when a firm wishes to participate in a foreign market but is prohibited from doing so by barriers to investment. This was one reason for the formation of the Fuji-Xerox joint venture. Xerox wanted to participate in the Japanese market but was prohibited from setting up a wholly owned subsidiary by the Japanese government. So Xerox set up the joint venture with Fuji and then licensed its know-how to the joint venture. Finally, licensing is frequently used when a firm possesses some intangible property that might have business applications, but when it does not want to develop those applications itself. For example, Bell Laboratories at AT&T originally invented the transistor circuit in the 1950s, but AT&T decided it did not want to produce transistors itself, so it licensed the technology to a number of other companies, such as Texas Instruments. Similarly, Coca-Cola has licensed its famous trademark to clothing manufacturers, who have incorporated the design into their clothing.

Disadvantages

Licensing has three serious drawbacks. First, it does not give a firm the tight control over manufacturing, marketing, and strategy that is required for realizing experience curve and location economies (as global and transnational firms must do; see

---

[2]For a general discussion of licensing, see F. J. Contractor, "The Role of Licensing in International Strategy," *Columbia Journal of World Business*, Winter 1982, pp. 73–83.

[3]See E. Terazono and C. Lorenz, "An Angry Young Warrior," *Financial Times*, September 19, 1994, p. 11; and K. McQuade and B. Gomes-Casseres, "Xerox and Fuji-Xerox," Harvard Business School Case #9-391-156.

Chapter 12). Licensing typically involves each licensee setting up its own manufacturing operations. This severely limits the firm's ability to realize experience curve and location economies by manufacturing its product in a centralized location. Thus, when these economies are important, licensing may not be the best way to expand overseas.

Second, competing in a global market may require a firm to coordinate strategic moves across countries by using profits earned in one country to support competitive attacks in another (again, see Chapter 12). By its very nature licensing severely limits a firm's ability to do this. A licensee is unlikely to allow a multinational firm to use its profits (beyond those due in the form of royalty payments) to support a different licensee operating in another country.

A third problem with licensing is one that we first encountered in Chapter 6 when we reviewed the economic theory of FDI. This is the risk associated with licensing technological know-how to foreign companies. Technological know-how constitutes the basis of many multinational firms' competitive advantage. Most firms wish to maintain control over how their know-how is used, and a firm can quickly lose control over its technology by licensing it. Many firms have made the mistake of thinking they could maintain control over their know-how within the framework of a licensing agreement. RCA Corporation, for example, once licensed its color TV technology to a number of Japanese firms including Matsushita and Sony. The Japanese firms quickly assimilated the technology, improved upon it, and used it to enter the U.S. market. Now the Japanese firms have a bigger share of the U.S. market than the RCA brand. Similar concerns surfaced over the 1989 decision by Congress to allow Japanese firms to produce the advanced FSX fighter plane under license from McDonnell Douglas. Critics of the decision fear the Japanese will use the FSX technology to support the development of a commercial airline industry that will compete with Boeing and McDonnell Douglas in the global marketplace.

On the other hand, there are ways of reducing the risks of this occurring. One way is by entering into a cross-licensing agreement with a foreign firm. Under a **cross-licensing agreement,** a firm might license some valuable intangible property to a foreign partner, but in addition to a royalty payment, the firm might also request that the foreign partner license some of its valuable know-how to the firm. Such agreements are reckoned to reduce the risks associated with licensing technological know-how, since the licensee realizes that if it violates the spirit of a licensing contract (by using the knowledge obtained to compete directly with the licensor), the licensor can do the same to it. Cross-licensing agreements enable firms to hold each other "hostage," which thereby reduces the probability that they will behave opportunistically toward each other.[4] Such cross-licensing agreements are increasingly common in high-technology industries. For example, the U.S. biotechnology firm Amgen has licensed one of its key drugs, Nuprogene, to Kirin, the Japanese pharmaceutical company. The license gives Kirin the right to sell Nuprogene in Japan. In return Amgen receives a royalty payment, and in addition through a licensing agreement it gained the right to sell certain Kirin products in the United States.

Another way of reducing the risk associated with licensing is to follow the Fuji-Xerox model and link an agreement to license know-how with the formation of a joint venture in which the licensor and licensee take an important equity stake. Such an approach aligns the interests of licensor and licensee, since both have a stake in ensuring that the venture is successful. Thus the risk that Fuji Photo might appropriate Xerox's technological know-how, and then compete directly against Xerox in the global photocopier market, was substantially reduced by establishing a joint venture in which both Xerox and Fuji Photo had an important stake.

[4]O. E. Williamson, *The Economic Institutions of Capitalism* (New York: Free Press, 1985).

Franchising

In many respects, franchising is similar to licensing, although franchising tends to involve longer-term commitments than licensing. **Franchising** is basically a specialized form of licensing in which the franchisor not only sells intangible property to the franchisee (normally a trademark), but also insists the franchisee agree to abide by strict rules as to how it does business. The franchisor will also often assist the franchisee to run his business on an ongoing basis. As with licensing the franchisor typically receives a royalty payment that amounts to some percentage of the franchisee's revenues. Whereas licensing is pursued primarily by manufacturing firms, franchising is employed primarily by service firms.[5] McDonald's provides us with a good example of a firm that has grown by using a franchising strategy. McDonald's has set down strict rules as to how franchisees should operate a restaurant. These rules extended to control over the menu, cooking methods, staffing policies, and the design and location of a restaurant. McDonald's also organizes the supply chain for its franchisees and provides management training and financial assistance for franchisees.[6]

Advantages

The advantages of franchising as an entry mode are very similar to those of licensing. The firm is relieved of many of the costs and risks of opening a foreign market on its own. Instead the franchisee typically assumes those costs and risks. This creates a good incentive for the franchisee to build up a profitable operation as quickly as possible. Thus, using a franchising strategy, a service firm can build a global presence quickly and at a relatively low cost and risk, as McDonald's has.

Disadvantages

The disadvantages, though present, are less pronounced than in the case of licensing. Since franchising is often used by service companies, there is no reason to consider the need for coordination of manufacturing to achieve experience curve and location economies. On the other hand franchising may inhibit the firm's ability to take profits out of one country to support competitive attacks in another.

A more significant disadvantage of franchising is quality control. The foundation of franchising arrangements is that the firm's brand name conveys a message to consumers about the quality of the firm's product. Thus a business traveler checking in at a Hilton International hotel in Hong Kong can reasonably expect the same quality of room, food, and service that she would receive in New York. The Hilton name is supposed to guarantee consistent product quality. This presents a problem in that foreign franchisees may not be as concerned about quality as they are supposed to be, and the result of poor quality can extend beyond lost sales in a particular foreign market to a decline in the firm's worldwide reputation. For example, if the business traveler has a bad experience at the Hilton in Hong Kong, she may never go to another Hilton hotel and may urge her colleagues to do likewise. The geographical distance of the firm from its foreign franchisees, however, can make poor quality difficult for the franchisor to detect. In addition the sheer number of franchisees—in the case of McDonald's, tens of thousands—can make quality control difficult. Due to these factors, quality problems may persist.

One way around this disadvantage is to set up a subsidiary in each country or region in which the firm expands. The subsidiary might be wholly owned by the company or be a joint venture with a foreign company. In either case the subsidiary assumes the rights and obligations to establish franchises throughout the particular country or region. McDonald's, for example, establishes a master franchisee in many

[5]J. H. Dunning and M. McQueen, "The Eclectic Theory of International Production: A Case Study of the International Hotel Industry," *Managerial and Decision Economics* 2 (1981), pp. 197–210.

[6]Andrew E. Serwer, "McDonald's Conquers the World," *Fortune*, October 17, 1994, pp. 103–16.

countries. Typically this master franchisee is a joint venture between McDonald's and a local firm. The combination of proximity and the smaller number of franchises to oversee reduces the quality control challenge. In addition, because the subsidiary (or master franchisee) is at least partly owned by the firm, the firm can place its own managers in the subsidiary to help ensure it is doing a good job of monitoring the franchises in that country or region. This organizational arrangement has proven very satisfactory in practice, and in addition to McDonald's, it has been used by Kentucky Fried Chicken, Hilton International, and others to expand their international operations.

Joint Ventures

A **joint venture** entails establishing a firm that is jointly owned by two or more otherwise independent firms. Fuji-Xerox, for example, was set up as a joint venture between Xerox and Fuji Photo (see opening case). Establishing a joint venture with a foreign firm has long been a popular mode for entering a new market. The most typical joint venture is a 50/50 arrangement, in which there are two parties, each of which holds a 50 percent ownership stake (as is the case with the Fuji-Xerox joint venture) and contributes a team of managers to share operating control. Some firms, however, have sought joint ventures in which they have a majority share and thus tighter control.[7] For a description of how one company, the bicycle manufacturer Schwinn, used a joint venture to enter a foreign market, see the "Management Focus."

Advantages

Joint ventures have a number of advantages. First, a firm is able to benefit from a local partner's knowledge of the host country's competitive conditions, culture, language, political systems, and business systems. Thus, for many U.S. firms, joint ventures have involved the U.S. company providing technological know-how and products, and the local partner providing the marketing expertise and the local knowledge necessary for competing in that country. This was the case both with the Fuji-Xerox joint venture and with the Schwinn-Csepel joint venture profiled in the "Management Focus." Second, when the development costs and/or risks of opening a foreign market are high, a firm might gain by sharing these costs and/or risks with a local partner. Third, in many countries political considerations make joint ventures the only feasible entry mode. This was a consideration in establishment of the Fuji-Xerox and Schwinn-Csepel ventures. Furthermore, research suggests that joint ventures with local partners face a low risk of being subject to nationalization or other forms of government interference.[8] This appears to be because local equity partners, who may have some influence on host-government policy, have a vested interest in speaking out against nationalization or government interference.

Disadvantages

Despite these advantages, there are two major disadvantages with joint ventures. First, just as with licensing, a firm that enters into a joint venture risks giving control of its technology to its partner. The joint venture between Boeing and a consortium of Japanese firms to build the 767 airliner raised fears that Boeing was unwittingly giving away its commercial airline technology to the Japanese. However, joint-venture agreements can be constructed to minimize this risk. One option is to hold majority ownership in the venture. This allows the dominant partner to exercise greater control over its technology. The drawback with this is that it can be difficult to find a foreign partner who is willing to settle for minority ownership.

A second disadvantage is that a joint venture does not give a firm the tight control over subsidiaries that it might need to realize experience curve or location

---

[7]For an excellent review of the literature of joint ventures, see B. Kogut, "Joint Ventures: Theoretical and Empirical Perspectives," *Strategic Management Journal* 9 (1988), pp. 319–32.

[8]D. G. Bradley, "Managing against Expropriation," *Harvard Business Review*, July–August 1977, pp. 78–90.

MANAGEMENT FOCUS
Schwinn Enters the Hungarian Market

Joint ventures with host-country firms have many features that make them an attractive means of entering a foreign market, but they also have pitfalls. Consider the case of Schwinn, the U.S. bicycle manufacturer, which set up a joint venture with the Csepel Bicycle Works of Hungary in 1989 to manufacture bicycles for sale in Eastern Europe. Schwinn chose to work with Csepel because the Hungarian enterprise had a good reputation and access to relatively inexpensive, skilled labor.

The joint venture, Schwinn-Csepel, was capitalized at $2.1 million, with Schwinn contributing 51 percent and Csepel 49 percent. Negotiations over the structure of the venture proved to be time consuming and tedious—they took well over a year—because there were no uniform procedures for setting up joint ventures in Hungary. Joint-venture laws changed several times during the negotiations, and they have changed several times since. Nobody—lawyers, government officials, company officials—could keep track of what had to be done to conform to Hungary's confused and rapidly changing joint-venture laws.

Since the venture was formally incorporated in June 1989, further regulatory changes have played havoc with its plans. The joint-venture agreement called for Schwinn to import component parts from the United States, assemble bicycles in Hungary, and then sell them throughout Eastern Europe. However, just as Schwinn-Csepel was starting production, the budget-conscious Hungarian government changed import taxes. Import taxes on component parts were levied that included a 15 percent import duty, a 25 percent value-added tax (VAT), and a 2 percent handling charge.

With nearly 300 different component parts coming in each day and no computers in the customs office, Schwinn-Csepel had to establish a five-person department to calculate import taxes. Moreover, although the VAT on re-exported bikes is refunded, six months may pass before this occurs. In effect Schwinn-Csepel is making an interest-free loan to the Hungarian government that amounts to millions of dollars.

The venture has also been plagued by unanticipated productivity problems. Productivity is significantly lower than at Schwinn's North American plants; the percentage of defects is higher; and workers are apathetic. Worse still, the venture inherited a management problem. Many of the managers of the former Csepel Bicycle Works, although not all ex-Communists, are products of the old Communist system. Traditions of secrecy and favoritism and a lack of attention to productivity and profitability have persisted.

Despite these problems, the venture is beginning to make inroads. The venture sold about 250,000 bicycles in 1991, half of those in Hungary. The company has built a dealer network of 55 shops, whose owners guarantee servicing and spare parts—unheard of in the old days of Communist rule. There is no other Western competition, and competing bicycles built by other Eastern European firms are poorly built and relatively expensive. Consequently, Schwinn-Csepel's U.S. managers still believe their venture will succeed, but they warn other firms contemplating similar moves into the Eastern European market that they should expect the unexpected.

Source: "A Bicycle Made by Two," *The Economist*, June 8, 1991, p. 73.

economies. Nor does it give a firm the tight control over a foreign subsidiary that it might need for engaging in coordinated global attacks against its rivals. Consider the entry of Texas Instruments (TI) into the Japanese semiconductor market. When TI established semiconductor facilities in Japan, it did so for the dual purpose of checking Japanese manufacturers' market share and limiting their cash available for invading TI's global market. In other words TI was engaging in global strategic coordination. To implement this strategy, TI's subsidiary in Japan had to be prepared to take instructions from corporate headquarters regarding competitive strategy. The strategy also required the Japanese subsidiary to run at a loss if necessary. Few if any potential joint-venture partners would have been willing to accept such conditions, since it would have necessitated a willingness to accept a negative return on their investment. Thus, to implement this strategy, TI set up a wholly owned subsidiary in Japan.

A third disadvantage with joint ventures is that the shared ownership arrangement can lead to conflicts and battles for control between the investing firms if their goals and objectives change over time, or if they take different views as to what the strategy of the venture should be. This has apparently not been a problem with the Fuji-Xerox joint venture. According to Tony Kobayashi, the CEO of Fuji-Xerox, a primary reason for this is that both Xerox and Fuji Photo adopted a very arm's-length relationship with Fuji-Xerox, giving the venture's management considerable freedom to determine strategy.[9] However, conflicts of interest that can ultimately result in the dissolution of a venture have apparently been a serious problem in many other joint ventures.[10]

Wholly Owned Subsidiaries

In a **wholly owned subsidiary,** the firm owns 100 percent of the stock. Establishing a wholly owned subsidiary in a foreign market can be done two ways. The firm can either set up a new operation in that country or it can acquire an established firm and use that firm to promote its products in the country's market.

Advantages

There are three clear advantages of wholly owned subsidiaries. First, when a firm's competitive advantage is based on technological competence, a wholly owned subsidiary will often be the preferred entry mode, since it reduces the risk of losing control over that competence. (See Chapter 6 for more details.) For this reason many high-tech firms prefer this entry mode for overseas expansion (e.g., firms in the semiconductor, electronics, and pharmaceutical industries). Second, a wholly owned subsidiary gives a firm the kind of tight control over operations in different countries that is necessary for engaging in global strategic coordination (i.e., using profits from one country to support competitive attacks in another). Third, a wholly owned subsidiary may be required if a firm is trying to realize location and experience curve economies (as firms pursuing global and transnational strategies try to do). As we saw in Chapter 12, when cost pressures are intense, it may pay a firm to configure its value chain in such a way that the value added at each stage is maximized. Thus a national subsidiary may specialize in manufacturing only part of the product line or certain components of the end product, exchanging parts and products with other subsidiaries in the firm's global system. Establishing such a global production system requires a high degree of control over the operations of each affiliate. The various operations must be prepared to accept centrally determined decisions as to how they will produce, how much they will produce, and how their output will be priced for transfer to the next operation. Since licensees or joint-venture partners are unlikely to accept such a subservient role, establishment of wholly owned subsidiaries may be necessary.

---

[9]Speech given by Tony Kobayashi at the University of Washington Business School, October 1992.
[10]H. W. Lane and P. W. Beamish, "Cross-Cultural Cooperative Behavior in Joint Ventures in LDCs," *Management International Review* 30 (1990), pp. 87–102.

TABLE 14.1

Advantages and
Disadvantages of
Entry Modes

Entry Mode	Advantage	Disadvantage
Exporting	Ability to realize location and experience curve economies	High transport costs Trade barriers Problems with local marketing agents
Turnkey contracts	Ability to earn returns from process technology skills in countries where FDI is restricted	Creating efficient competitors Lack of long-term market presence
Licensing	Low development costs and risks	Lack of control over technology Inability to realize location and experience curve economies Inability to engage in global strategic coordination
Franchising	Low development costs and risks	Lack of control over quality Inability to engage in global strategic coordination
Joint ventures	Access to local partner's knowledge Sharing development costs and risks Politically acceptable	Lack of control over technology Inability to engage in global strategic coordination Inability to realize location and experience economies
Wholly owned subsidiaries	Protection of technology Ability to engage in global strategic coordination Ability to realize location and experience economies	High costs and risks

Disadvantages

On the other hand, establishing a wholly owned subsidiary is generally the most costly method of serving a foreign market. Firms doing this must bear the full costs and risks of setting up overseas operations. The risks associated with learning to do business in a new culture are less if the firm acquires an established host-country enterprise. However, acquisitions raise a whole set of additional problems, including those associated with trying to marry divergent corporate cultures. These problems may more than offset any benefits derived by acquiring an established operation.[11]

❦ SELECTING AN ENTRY MODE

As the preceding discussion demonstrated, there are advantages and disadvantages associated with all the entry modes; they are summarized in Table 14.1. Due to these advantages and disadvantages, trade-offs are inevitable when selecting an entry mode. For example, when considering entry into an unfamiliar country with a track record for nationalizing foreign-owned enterprises, a firm might favor a joint venture with a local enterprise. Its rationale might be that the local partner will help it establish operations in an unfamiliar environment and will speak out against nationalization should the possibility arise. However, if the firm's core competence is based on proprietary technology, entering a joint venture might risk losing control of that technology to the joint-venture partner, in which case the strategy may seem very unattractive. Despite the existence of such trade-offs, it is possible to make some generalizations about the optimal choice of entry mode. That is what we do in this section.[12]

---

[11]For a review of the kinds of problems encountered when making acquisitions, see Chapter 9 in C. W. L. Hill and G. R. Jones, *Strategic Management Theory* (Boston: Houghton-Mifflin, 1995).

[12]This section draws on Hill, Hwang, and Kim, "Eclectic Theory of the Choice of International Entry Mode."

Core Competencies and Entry Mode

We saw in Chapter 12 that firms often expand internationally to earn greater returns from their core competencies—transferring the skills and products derived from their core competencies to foreign markets where indigenous competitors lack those skills. We say such firms are pursuing an international strategy. The optimal entry mode for these firms depends to some degree on the nature of their core competencies. In particular, a distinction can be drawn between firms whose core competency is in technological know-how and those whose core competency is in management know-how.

Technological know-how

As was initially observed in Chapter 6, if a firm's competitive advantage (its core competence) is based on control over proprietary technological know-how, licensing and joint-venture arrangements should be avoided if possible so that the risk of losing control over that technology is minimized. Thus, if a high-tech firm sets up operations in a foreign country to profit from a core competency in technological know-how, it will probably do so through a wholly owned subsidiary.

This rule should not be viewed as hard and fast, however. One exception is when a licensing or joint-venture arrangement can be structured so as to reduce the risks of a firm's technological know-how being expropriated by licensees or joint-venture partners. We will see how this might be achieved later in the chapter when we examine the structuring of strategic alliances. Another exception exists when a firm perceives its technological advantage to be only transitory, when it expects rapid imitation of its core technology by competitors. In such a case the firm might want to license its technology as rapidly as possible to foreign firms to gain global acceptance for its technology before the imitation occurs.[13] Such a strategy has some advantages. By licensing its technology to competitors, the firm may deter them from developing their own, possibly superior, technology. Further, by licensing its technology, the firm may be able to establish its technology as the dominant design in the industry (as Matsushita did with its VHS format for VCRs). This may ensure a steady stream of royalty payments. Such situations apart, however, the attractions of licensing are probably outweighed by the risks of losing control over technology, and thus licensing should be avoided.

Management know-how

The competitive advantage of many service firms is based on management know-how (e.g., McDonald's, Hilton International). For such firms the risk of losing control over their management skills to franchisees or joint-venture partners is not that great. These firms' valuable asset is their brand name, and brand names are generally well protected by international laws pertaining to trademarks. Given this, many of the issues arising in the case of technological know-how are of less concern here. As a result many service firms favor a combination of franchising and subsidiaries to control the franchises within particular countries or regions. The subsidiaries may be wholly owned or joint ventures, but most service firms have found that joint ventures with local partners work best for the controlling subsidiaries. A joint venture is often politically more acceptable and brings a degree of local knowledge to the subsidiary.

Pressures for Cost Reductions and Entry Mode

The greater the pressures for cost reductions are, the more likely a firm will want to pursue some combination of exporting and wholly owned subsidiaries. By manufacturing in those locations where factor conditions are optimal and then exporting to the rest of the world, a firm may be able to realize substantial location and experience curve economies. The firm might then want to export the finished product to marketing subsidiaries based in various countries. These subsidiaries will typically be

---

[13]C. W. L. Hill, "Strategies for Exploiting Technological Innovations: When and When Not to License," *Organization Science* 3 (1992), pp. 428–41.

wholly owned and have the responsibility for overseeing distribution in their particular countries. Setting up wholly owned marketing subsidiaries is preferable to joint-venture arrangements and to using foreign marketing agents because it gives the firm the tight control over marketing that might be required for coordinating a globally dispersed value chain. It also gives the firm the ability to use the profits generated in one market to improve its competitive position in another market. Firms pursuing global or transnational strategies tend to prefer establishing wholly owned subsidiaries.

❧ STRATEGIC ALLIANCES

The term **strategic alliances** refers to cooperative agreements between potential or actual competitors. In this section we are concerned specifically with strategic alliances between firms from different countries. Strategic alliances run the range from formal joint ventures, in which two or more firms have equity stakes (e.g., Fuji-Xerox), to short-term contractual agreements in which two companies agree to cooperate on a particular task (such as developing a new product). Collaboration between competitors is fashionable; the 1980s and early 1990s have seen a virtual explosion in the number of strategic alliances. Examples include:

- A cooperative arrangement between Boeing and a consortium of Japanese companies to produce the 767 wide-bodied commercial jet.
- An alliance between General Electric and Snecma of France to build a family of low-thrust commercial aircraft engines.
- An agreement between Siemens and Philips to develop new semiconductor technology.
- An agreement between ICL, the British computer company, and Fujitsu of Japan to develop a new generation of mainframe computers capable of competing with IBM's products.
- An alliance between Eastman Kodak and Canon of Japan under which Canon manufactures a line of medium-volume copiers for sale under Kodak's name.
- An agreement between Texas Instruments and Kobe Steel, Inc., of Japan to make logic semiconductors in Japan.
- An agreement between Motorola and Toshiba to pool their technological know-how in the manufacture of microprocessors.

The Advantages of Strategic Alliances

Firms ally themselves with actual or potential competitors for various strategic purposes.[14] First, as noted earlier in the chapter, strategic alliances may facilitate entry into a foreign market. For example, Motorola initially found it very difficult to gain access to the Japanese cellular telephone market. In the mid-1980s the firm complained loudly about formal and informal Japanese trade barriers. The turning point for Motorola came in 1987 when it allied itself with Toshiba to build microprocessors. As part of the deal Toshiba provided Motorola with marketing help, including some of its best managers. This helped Motorola in the political game of securing government approval to enter the Japanese market and getting radio frequencies assigned for its mobile communications systems. Motorola no longer complains about Japan's trade barriers. Although privately the company admits they still exist, with Toshiba's help Motorola has become skilled at getting around them.[15]

---

[14]See K. Ohmae, "The Global Logic of Strategic Alliances," *Harvard Business Review*, March–April 1989, pp. 143–54; G. Hamel, Y. L. Doz, and C. K. Prahalad, "Collaborate with Your Competitors and Win!" *Harvard Business Review*, January–February 1989, pp. 133–39; and W. Burgers, C. W. L. Hill, and W. C. Kim, "Alliances in the Global Auto Industry," *Strategic Management Journal* 14 (1993), pp. 419–32.

[15]Asia Beckons," *The Economist*, May 30, 1992, pp. 63–64.

Firms also make strategic alliances because it allows them to share the fixed costs (and associated risks) of developing new products or processes. Motorola's alliance with Toshiba also was partly motivated by a desire to share the high fixed costs of setting up an operation to manufacture microprocessors. The microprocessor business is so capital intensive—Motorola and Toshiba each contributed close to $1 billion to set up their facility—that few firms can afford the costs and risks by themselves. Similarly the alliance between Boeing and a number of Japanese companies to build the 767 was motivated by Boeing's desire to share the estimated $2 billion investment required to develop the aircraft.

Third, an alliance is a way to bring together complementary skills and assets that neither company could easily develop on its own. An example is the alliance between France's Thomson and Japan's JVC to manufacture videocassette recorders. JVC and Thomson are trading core competencies; Thomson needs product technology and manufacturing skills, while JVC needs to learn how to succeed in the fragmented European market. Both sides believe there is an equitable chance for gain. Similarly in 1990 AT&T struck a deal with NEC Corporation of Japan to trade technological skills. AT&T will give NEC some of its computer-aided design technology and NEC will give AT&T access to the technology underlying its advanced logic computer chips. Such trading of core competencies seems to underlie many of the most successful strategic alliances.

Fourth, it can make sense to form an alliance that will help the firm establish technological standards for the industry that will benefit the firm. For example, in 1992 Philips NV allied with its global competitor Matsushita to manufacture and market the digital compact cassette (DCC) system Philips had developed. Philips' motive was that this linking with Matsushita would help it establish the DCC system as a new technological standard in the recording and consumer electronics industries. The issue is important because Sony has developed a competing "minicompact disc" technology that it hopes to establish as the new technical standard. Since the two technologies do very similar things, there is probably room for only one new standard. The technology that becomes the new standard will be the one that succeeds. The loser will probably have to write off investments in the billions of dollars. Philips sees its alliance with Matsushita as a tactic for winning the race.[16]

The Disadvantages of Strategic Alliances

The advantages we have discussed can be very significant. Despite this, some commentators have criticized strategic alliances on the grounds that they give competitors a low-cost route to new technology and markets. For example, Robert Reich and Eric Mankin have argued that strategic alliances between U.S. and Japanese firms are part of an implicit Japanese strategy to keep higher-paying, higher value-added jobs in Japan while gaining the project engineering and production process skills that underlie the competitive success of many U.S. companies.[17] They argue that Japanese successes in the machine tool and semiconductor industries were largely built on U.S. technology acquired through various strategic alliances. And they argue that, increasingly, U.S. managers are aiding the Japanese in achieving their goals by entering alliances that channel new inventions to Japan and provide a U.S. sales and distribution network for the resulting products. Although such deals may generate short-term profits, Reich and Mankin argue, in the long run the result is to "hollow out" U.S. firms, leaving them with no competitive advantage in the global marketplace.

---

[16]P. M. Reilly, "Sony's Digital Audio Format Pulls ahead of Philips's," *The Wall Street Journal*, August 6, 1993, p. B1.

[17]R. B. Reich and E. D. Mankin, "Joint Ventures with Japan Give Away Our Future," *Harvard Business Review*, March–April 1986, pp. 78–90.

Reich and Mankin have a point. Alliances do have risks. Unless a firm is careful, it can give away more than it receives. On the other hand, there are so many examples of apparently successful alliances between firms, including alliances between U.S. and Japanese firms, that their position seems more than a little extreme. It is difficult to see how the Motorola-Toshiba alliance, or the Fuji-Xerox alliance, fit Reich and Mankin's thesis. In these cases both partners seem to have gained from the alliance. Since Reich and Mankin undoubtedly have a point, the question becomes, Why do some alliances benefit both firms while others benefit one firm and hurt the other? The next section provides an answer to this question.

❧ MAKING ALLIANCES WORK

The failure rate for international strategic alliances seems to be quite high. For example, one recent study of 49 international strategic alliances found that two-thirds run into serious managerial and financial troubles within two years of their formation, and that although many of these problems are ultimately solved, 33 percent are rated as failures by the parties involved.[18] The next "Management Focus" provides us with a detailed look at one strategic alliance that failed—that between General Motors and the Korean Daewoo Group to build cars (the Daewoo Motor Company). More generally, below we argue that the success of an alliance seems to be a function of three main factors: partner selection, alliance structure, and the manner in which the alliance is managed. We will look at each of these issues in turn.

Partner Selection

One of the keys to making a strategic alliance work is to select the right kind of ally. A good ally, or partner, has three principal characteristics. First, a good partner helps the firm achieve its strategic goals—whether they be market access, sharing the costs and risks of new-product development, or gaining access to critical core competencies. The partner must have capabilities that the firm lacks and that it values. Second, a good partner shares the firm's vision for the purpose of the alliance. If two firms approach an alliance with radically different agendas, the chances are great that the relationship will not be harmonious, will not flourish, and will end in divorce. This seems to have been the case with the alliance between GM and Daewoo (see the "Management Focus"). GM's agenda was to use Daewoo Motor as a source of cheap labor to produce cars for the Korean and U.S. markets, whereas Daewoo wanted to use GM's know-how and distribution systems to grow Daewoo's business not just in Korea and the United States, but also in Europe. Different perceptions over the strategic role of the venture ultimately helped contribute to the dissolution of the alliance.

Third, a good partner is unlikely to try to opportunistically exploit the alliance for its own ends; that is, to expropriate the firm's technological know-how while giving away little in return. Firms with reputations for fair play to maintain probably make the best allies. For example, IBM is involved in so many strategic alliances that it would not pay the company to trample roughshod over individual alliance partners. Such action would tarnish IBM's hard-won reputation of being a good ally and would make it more difficult for IBM to attract alliance partners in the future. Since IBM attaches great importance to its alliances, it is unlikely to engage in the kind of opportunistic behavior that Reich and Mankin highlight. Similarly their reputations make it less likely (but by no means impossible) that such Japanese firms as Sony, Toshiba, and Fuji, which have histories of alliances with non-Japanese firms, would opportunistically exploit an alliance partner.

[18]J. Bleeke and D. Ernst, "The Way to Win in Cross-Border Alliances," *Harvard Business Review*, November–December 1991, pp. 127–35.

MANAGEMENT FOCUS
Anatomy of a Failed Alliance— General Motors and the Daewoo Group

In June 1984 General Motors and the Daewoo Group of Korea signed an agreement that called for each to invest $100 million in a Korean-based 50/50 joint venture, Daewoo Motor Company, that would manufacture a subcompact car, the Pontiac LeMans, based on GM's popular German-designed Opel Kadett (Opel is a wholly owned German subsidiary of GM). Much of the day-to-day management of the alliance was to be placed in the hands of Daewoo executives, with managerial and technical advice being provided by a limited number of GM executives. At the time many hailed the alliance as a smart move for both companies. GM doubted that a small car could be built profitably in the United States because of high labor costs, and it saw enormous advantages in this marriage of German technology and Korean cheap labor. At the time Roger Smith, GM's chairman, told Korean reporters that GM's

North American operation would probably end up importing 80,000 to 100,000 cars a year from Daewoo Motors. As for the Daewoo Group, it saw itself getting access to the superior engineering skills of GM and an entrée into the world's largest car market—the United States.

Eight years of financial losses later the joint venture collapsed in a blizzard of mutual recriminations between Daewoo and General Motors. From the perspective of GM, things started to go seriously wrong in 1987, just as the first LeMans was rolling off Daewoo's production line. Korea had lurched toward democracy, and workers throughout the country demanded better wages. Daewoo Motor was hit by a series of bitter strikes that repeatedly halted LeMans production. To calm the labor troubles, Daewoo Motor more than doubled workers' wages. Suddenly it was cheaper to build Opels in Germany than Korea

To select a partner with these three characteristics, a firm needs to conduct some comprehensive research on potential alliance candidates. To increase the probability of selecting a good partner, the firm should:

1. Collect as much pertinent, publicly available information on potential allies as possible.

2. Collect data from informed third parties. These include firms that have had alliances with the potential partners, investment bankers who have had dealings with them, and some of their former employees.

3. Get to know the potential partner as well as possible before committing to an alliance. This should include face-to-face meetings between senior managers (and perhaps middle-level managers) to ensure that the chemistry is right.

Alliance Structure

Having selected a partner, the alliance should be structured so the firm's risks of giving too much away to the partner are reduced to an acceptable level. Figure 14.1 depicts the four safeguards against opportunism by alliance partners that we discuss here. (Opportunism includes the "theft" of technology and/or markets that Reich and Mankin describe.) First, alliances can be designed to make it difficult (if not impossible) to transfer technology not meant to be transferred. The design, development, manufacture, and service of a product manufactured by an alliance can be structured so as to "wall off" sensitive technologies to prevent their leakage to the

(German wages were still higher, but German productivity was also much higher, which translated into lower labor costs).

Equally problematic was the poor quality of the cars rolling off the Daewoo production line. Electrical systems often crashed on the LeMans, and the braking system had a tendency to fail after just a few thousand miles. The LeMans soon gained a reputation for poor quality, and U.S. sales plummeted to 37,000 vehicles in 1991, down 86 percent from their 1988 high. Hurt by the LeMans reputation as a lemon, Daewoo's share of the rapidly growing Korean car market also slumped from a high of 21.4 percent in 1987 to 12.3 percent in 1991.

But if General Motors was disappointed in Daewoo, that was nothing compared to Daewoo's frustration with GM. Daewoo Group Chairman Kim WooChoong complained publicly that GM executives were arrogant and

treated him shabbily. Mr. Kim was angry that GM tried to prohibit him from expanding the market for Daewoo's cars. In late 1988 Mr. Kim negotiated a deal to sell 7,000 Daewoo Motor's cars in Eastern Europe. GM executives immediately tried to kill the deal, telling Mr. Kim that Europe was the territory of GM's German subsidiary, Opel. Daewoo ultimately agreed to limit the sale to 3,000 cars and never sell again in Eastern Europe. To make matters worse, when Daewoo developed a new sedan car and asked GM to sell it in the United States, GM said no. By this point Mr. Kim's frustrations at having his expansion plans in Eastern Europe and the United States held back by GM were clear to all. Moreover Daewoo management believed the poor sales of the LeMans in the United States were not due to quality problems, but to the poor marketing efforts of GM.

Things came to a head in 1991 when Daewoo asked GM to agree to

expand the manufacturing facilities of the joint venture. The plan called for each partner to put in another $100 million and for Daewoo Motor to double its output. GM management refused on the grounds that increasing output would not help Daewoo Motor unless the venture could first improve its product quality. The matter festered until late 1991 when GM management delivered a blunt proposal to Daewoo—either GM would buy out Daewoo's stake, or Daewoo would buy out GM's stake in the joint venture. Much to GM's surprise, Daewoo agreed to buy out GM's stake. The divorce was completed in November 1992 with an agreement by Daewoo to pay GM $170 million over three years for its 50 percent stake in Daewoo Motor Company.

Sources: D. Darlin, "Daewoo Will Pay GM $170 Million for Venture Stake," *The Wall Street Journal*, November 11, 1992, p. A6; and D. Darlin and J. B. White, "Failed Marriage," *The Wall Street Journal*, January 16, 1992, p. A1.

---

other participant. In the alliance between General Electric and Snecma to build commercial aircraft engines, for example, GE reduced the risk of excess transfer by walling off certain sections of the production process. The modularization effectively cut off the transfer of what GE regarded as key competitive technology, while permitting Snecma access to final assembly. Similarly in the alliance between Boeing and the Japanese to build the 767, Boeing walled off research, design, and marketing functions considered central to its competitive position, while allowing the Japanese to share in production technology. Boeing also walled off new technologies not required for 767 production.[19]

Second, contractual safeguards can be written into an alliance agreement to guard against the risk of opportunism by a partner. For example, TRW, Inc., has three strategic alliances with large Japanese auto component suppliers to produce seat belts, engine valves, and steering gears for sale to Japanese-owned auto assembly plants in the United States. TRW has clauses in each of its alliance contracts that bar the Japanese firms from competing with TRW to supply U.S.-owned auto companies with component parts. By doing this TRW protects itself against the possibility that the Japanese companies are entering into the alliances merely to gain access to the North American market to compete with TRW in its home market.

---

[19]W. Roehl and J. F. Truitt, "Stormy Open Marriages Are Better," *Columbia Journal of World Business*, Summer 1987, pp. 87–95.

Figure 14.1
Structuring Alliances to
Reduce Opportunism

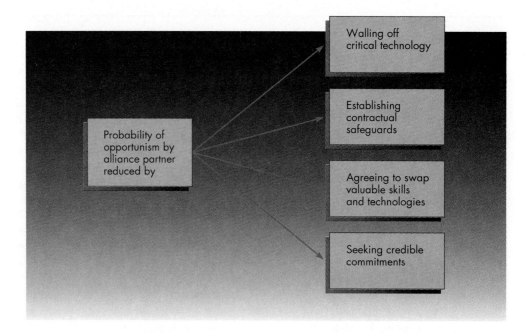

Figure 14.1
Structuring Alliances to
Reduce Opportunism

Third, both parties to an alliance can agree in advance to swap skills and technologies that the other covets, thereby ensuring a chance for equitable gain. Cross-licensing agreements are one way to achieve this goal. In the alliance between Motorola and Toshiba, Motorola has licensed some of its microprocessor technology to Toshiba, and in return Toshiba has licensed some of its memory chip technology to Motorola.

Fourth, the risk of opportunism by an alliance partner can be reduced if the firm extracts a significant credible commitment from its partner in advance. The long-term alliance between Xerox and Fuji to build photocopiers for the Asian market perhaps best illustrates this. Rather than enter into an informal agreement or some kind of licensing arrangement (which Fuji Photo initially wanted), Xerox insisted that Fuji invest in a 50/50 joint venture to serve Japan and East Asia. This venture constituted such a significant investment in people, equipment, and facilities that Fuji Photo was committed from the outset to making the alliance work in order to earn a return on its investment. By agreeing to the joint venture, Fuji essentially made a credible commitment to the alliance. Given this Xerox felt secure in transferring its photocopier technology to Fuji (see the opening case for details).[20]

Managing the Alliance

Once a partner has been selected and an appropriate alliance structure has been agreed on, the task facing the firm is to maximize its benefits from the alliance. As in all international business deals, an important factor is sensitivity to cultural differences (see Chapter 3). Many differences in management style are attributable to cultural differences, and managers need to make allowances for these in dealing with their partner. Beyond this maximizing the benefits from an alliance seems to involve building trust between partners and learning from partners.

Building trust
Part of the trick of managing an alliance successfully seems to be to build interpersonal relationships between the firms' managers. This is one lesson that can be drawn from the successful strategic alliance between Ford and Mazda (described in detail in the closing case). Ford and Mazda have set up a framework of meetings

---

[20]McQuade and Gomes-Casseres, "Xerox and Fuji-Xerox."

within which their managers not only discuss matters pertaining to the alliance, but also get to know each other better through "nonwork" time provided in the meetings. The belief is that the resulting friendships help build trust and facilitate harmonious relations between the two firms. Personal relationships foster an informal management network between the two firms. (Chapter 13 discusses informal management networks.) This network can then be used to help solve problems arising in more formal contexts (such as in joint committee meetings between personnel from the two firms).

Learning from partners

After a five-year study of 15 strategic alliances between major multinationals, Gary Hamel, Yves Doz, and C. K. Prahalad concluded that a major determinant of how much a company gains from an alliance is its ability to learn from its alliance partner.[21] They focused on a number of alliances between Japanese companies and Western (European or American) partners. In every case in which a Japanese company emerged from an alliance stronger than its Western partner, the Japanese company had made a greater effort to learn. Few Western companies studied seemed to want to learn from their Japanese partners. They tended to regard the alliance purely as a cost-sharing or risk-sharing device, rather than as an opportunity to learn how a potential competitor does business.

Consider the alliance between General Motors and Toyota to build the Chevrolet Nova constituted in 1985 and still operating today. This alliance is structured as a formal joint venture, called New United Motor Manufacturing, Inc., and each party has a 50 percent equity stake. The venture owns an auto plant in Fremont, California. According to one of the Japanese managers, Toyota quickly achieved most of its objectives from the alliance: "We learned about U.S. supply and transportation. And we got the confidence to manage U.S. workers."[22] All that knowledge was then quickly transferred to Georgetown, Kentucky, where Toyota opened a plant of its own in 1988. On the other hand, it may be that all GM got was a new product, the Chevrolet Nova. Some GM managers complained that the knowledge they gained through the alliance with Toyota has never been put to good use inside GM. They believe they should have been kept together as a team to educate GM's engineers and workers about the Japanese system. Instead they have been dispersed to various GM subsidiaries.

To maximize the learning benefits of an alliance, a firm must try to learn from its partner and then apply the knowledge within its own organization. It has been suggested that all operating employees should be well briefed on the partner's strengths and weaknesses and should understand how acquiring particular skills will bolster their firm's competitive position. Hamel, Doz, and Prahalad note that this is already standard practice among Japanese companies. For example, they made this observation:

> We accompanied a Japanese development engineer on a tour through a partner's factory. This engineer dutifully took notes on plant layout, the number of production stages, the rate at which the line was running, and the number of employees. He recorded all this despite the fact that he had no manufacturing responsibility in his own company, and that the alliance did not encompass joint manufacturing. Such dedication greatly enhances learning.[23]

For such learning to be of value, it must be diffused throughout the organization (as was seemingly not the case at GM following the GM–Toyota joint venture). To achieve this the managers involved in the alliance should be explicitly used to educate their colleagues about the skills of the alliance partner.

---

[21]Hamel, Doz, and Prahalad, "Collaborate with Competitors."

[22]B. Wysocki, "Cross-Border Alliances Become Favorite Way to Crack New Markets," *The Wall Street Journal*, March 4, 1990, p. A1.

[23]Hamel, Doz, and Prahalad, "Collaborate with Competitors," p. 138.

❧ SUMMARY OF CHAPTER

This chapter has been concerned with two related topics: the optimal choice of entry mode to serve a foreign market and the issue of strategic alliances. The two topics are related in that several entry modes (e.g., licensing and joint ventures) are strategic alliances. Most strategic alliances, however, involve more than just issues of market access. The following points have been made in this chapter:

1. There are six ways of entering a foreign market: exporting, turnkey projects, licensing, franchising, joint venturing, and setting up a wholly owned subsidiary.

2. Exporting has the advantages of facilitating the realization of experience curve economies and of avoiding the costs of setting up manufacturing operations in another country. Disadvantages include high transport costs and trade barriers and problems with local marketing agents. The latter can be overcome if the firm sets up a wholly owned marketing subsidiary in the host country.

3. Turnkey projects allow firms to export their process know-how to countries where FDI might be prohibited, thereby enabling the firm to earn a greater return from this asset. The disadvantage is that the firm may create efficient global competitors in the process.

4. The main advantage of licensing is that the licensee bears the costs and risks of opening a foreign market. Disadvantages include the risk of losing technological know-how to the licensee and a lack of tight control over licensees.

5. The main advantage of franchising is that the franchisee bears the costs and risks of opening a foreign market. Disadvantages center on problems of quality control of distant franchisees.

6. Joint ventures have the advantages of sharing the costs and risks of opening a foreign market and of gaining local knowledge and political influence. Disadvantages include the risk of losing control over technology and a lack of tight control.

7. The advantages of wholly owned subsidiaries include tight control over operations and techno-

logical know-how. The main disadvantage is that the firm must bear all the costs and risks of opening a foreign market.

8. The optimal choice of entry mode depends on the strategy of the firm.

9. When technological know-how constitutes a firm's core competence, wholly owned subsidiaries are preferred, since they best control technology.

10. When management know-how constitutes a firm's core competence, foreign franchises controlled by joint ventures seem to be optimal. This gives the firm the cost and risk benefits associated with franchising, while enabling it to monitor and control franchisee quality effectively.

11. When the firm is pursuing a global or transnational strategy, the need for tight control over operations to realize location and experience curve economies suggests wholly owned subsidiaries as the best entry mode.

12. Strategic alliances are cooperative agreements between actual or potential competitors.

13. The advantage of alliances are that they facilitate entry into foreign markets, enable partners to share the fixed costs and risks associated with new products and processes, facilitate the transfer of complementary skills between companies, and can help firms establish technical standards.

14. The disadvantage of a strategic alliance is that the firm risks giving away technological know-how and market access to its alliance partner in return for very little.

15. The disadvantages associated with alliances can be reduced if the firm selects partners carefully, paying close attention to the issue of reputation, and structures the alliance so as to avoid unintended transfers of know-how.

16. Two of the keys to making alliances work seem to be (i) building trust and informal communications networks between partners and (ii) taking proactive steps to learn from alliance partners.

❧ CRITICAL DISCUSSION QUESTIONS

1. Licensing proprietary technology to foreign competitors is the best way to give up a firm's competitive advantage. Discuss.

2. What kind of companies stand to gain the most from entering into strategic alliances with potential competitors? Why?

3. Discuss how the need for control over foreign operations varies with firms' strategies and core competencies. What are the implications for the choice of entry mode?

4. A small Canadian firm that has developed some valuable new medical products using its unique biotechnology know-how is trying to decide how

best to serve the European Community market. Its choices are
   a. Manufacture the product at home and let foreign sales agents handle marketing.
   b. Manufacture the products at home and set up a wholly owned subsidiary in Europe to handle marketing.
   c. Enter into a strategic alliance with a large European pharmaceutical firm. The product would be manufactured in Europe by the 50/50 joint venture and marketed by the European firm.

The cost of investment in manufacturing facilities will be a major one for the Canadian firm, but it is not outside its reach. If these are the firm's only options, which one would you advise it to choose? Why?

❦ CLOSING CASE   The Ford–Mazda Alliance

 During the 1980s the global auto industry was swept by a wave of strategic alliances between competitors. The number of alliances among the 23 largest competitors increased from 10 in 1978 to 52 in 1988. By 1990 almost all the world's carmakers were linked to at least one other company in this web of alliances. One factor responsible for this trend is the growing cost of developing a new car—it can be as much as $2 billion. By entering into alliances, auto companies can share the fixed costs of new-product development and, at the same time, gain access to new markets and to manufacturing and technological know-how.

One of the most successful and enduring of these alliances is the one between Ford and Mazda. Ford and Mazda began to cooperate in 1971 when Ford started purchasing Mazda trucks for sale in Asia. That same year Henry Ford II approached Mazda about buying a stake in the company but was rebuffed. Then came the oil crisis of 1973. At that time Mazda was using a gas-hungry rotary engine in most of its cars, and its sales slumped. Throughout the 1970s Mazda struggled to recover. Reeling under a string of financial losses, Mazda approached Ford in 1977 to see if the U.S. company was still interested in a relationship. Ford was not, but the two companies kept talking. Then in 1979 the second oil crisis hit, and Ford saw Mazda as an attractive partner because Mazda was manufacturing the type of small, fuel-efficient cars that were likely to sell well in a high-oil-price environment. Ford purchased a 25 percent stake in the Japanese company for $130 million. In 1991 this stake earned Ford dividends of $14.3 million. However, the benefits of the alliance far exceed this return on Ford's initial investment.

For Ford some benefits of the alliance have been in the form of sales in Japan. Ford is now the most popular foreign nameplate in Japan; the company sells more than 72,000 cars and trucks a year through a dealer network it owns jointly with Mazda. Ford also benefits from access to Mazda's manufacturing and engineering skills and by being able to share the costs of developing new models with Mazda. When Ford built an assembly plant in Hermosillo, Mexico, in the mid-1980s, it used Mazda's superefficient Hofu (Japan) factory as the blueprint. The Hermosillo plant has become one of Ford's top-ranking plants for quality and productivity and is now serving as a model in the renovation of many of Ford's older European and U.S. facilities. As for new-product development, Ford and Mazda have worked together on 10 new models, usually with Ford doing most of the styling and Mazda making many key engineering contributions. For Ford these cars include the Escort, the Mercury Tracer, the Festiva, the Probe, the Mercury Capri, and the Explorer. The Ford-aided Mazda models are the MX-6, the 323, the Protege, and the Navajo.

From Mazda's perspective, in addition to the initial injection of cash, the benefits of the alliance include access to the North American market through Ford's dealer network, access to Ford styling and marketing skills, and a partner with whom to share the costs of developing new models.

Both partners view the alliance as a success, but it has not been all smooth sailing. Differences in national and corporate cultures have often stood in the path of harmonious relationships and communications. To reduce the possibility of conflicts arising out of misunderstandings, Ford and Mazda have held a series of meetings between the two companies' top and middle-level managers. The purposes of those meetings have been to coordinate activities and also to help facilitate the growth of enduring interpersonal relationships between Ford and Mazda managers.

Nevertheless at times the competitive squabbles have been fierce. Ford wanted Mazda's rotary engine for use in a sports car, but Mazda refused to share the design. On another occasion Ford refused to let Mazda copy an innovative window design in one of its models. More recently Mazda wanted access to the design of the four-door Ford Explorer, which Mazda intended to use as a blueprint for a four-door Navajo, but Ford refused. Mazda too likes to keep certain models for itself. For example, Mazda refuses to allow Ford to produce its own version of Mazda's best-selling sports car, the Miata. Over the years, however, disagreements and conflict have become increasingly rare. Initially the top management at Mazda and Ford were continually having to arbitrate disagreements between their middle managers. The need for such arbitration is less common now, and the companies are able to assist each other in many ways. For example, seeing how Mazda benefited from many small ideas contributed by its workers, Ford instituted a similar employee suggestion program. At its Hermosillo plant, Ford followed Mazda's practice of building a stamping plant nearby. This facilitated the introduction of a just-in-time inventory system and helped Ford boost quality control.

The ideas have also flowed the other way. Ford gave Mazda access to some sophisticated computer programs for measuring noise and vibrations and some electronic systems for helping control engine emissions. Mazda also hopes to profit from Ford's marketing know-how. While working together on the Navajo/Explorer, Mazda got a close look at the customer surveys Ford had collected on the old Bronco II, the Explorer's predecessor. The surveys showed Ford engineers which components and vehicle systems are most important to consumers. Mazda came away so impressed that it adopted Ford's system wholesale.

CASE DISCUSSION QUESTIONS

1. What are the main strategic benefits of the Ford–Mazda alliance?

2. What risk is Ford running by entering into this alliance with Mazda? What risk is Mazda running?

3. Compare the Ford–Mazda alliance with the alliance between General Motors and Daewoo that was profiled in the "Management Focus" in this chapter. Why do you think the Ford–Mazda alliance has worked so well, while the GM–Daewoo alliance failed?

Sources: J. B. Treece, K. Miller, and R. A. Melcher, "The Partners," Business Week, February 10, 1992, pp. 102–7; C. Rapoport, "Mazda's Bold New Global Strategy," Fortune, December 17, 1990, pp. 109–13; Car Industry Joint Ventures: Spot the Difference," The Economist, February 24, 1990, p. 74; and J. P. Womack, D. T. Jones, and D. Roos, The Machine that Changed the World (New York: Rawson Associates, 1990).

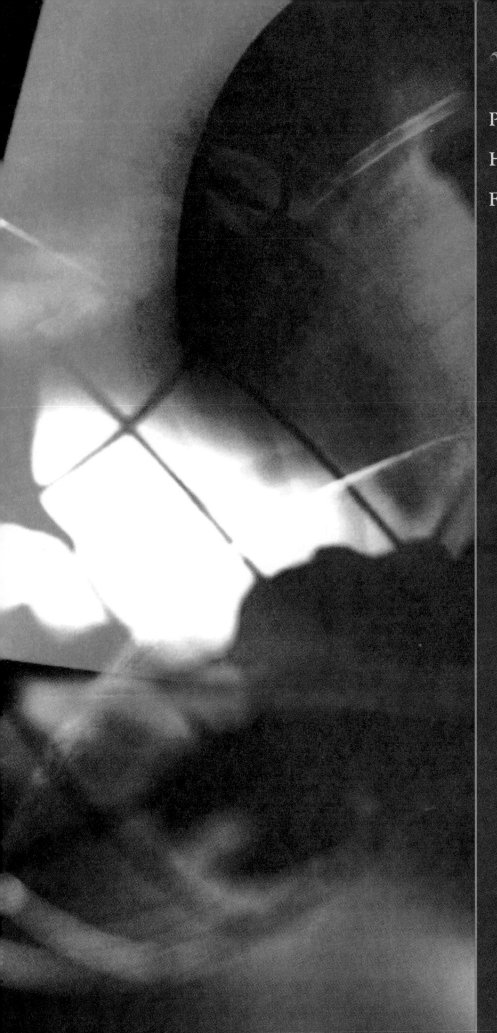

PHILIPS NV

Established in 1891, the Dutch company Philips NV is one of the world's largest electronics enterprises. Its businesses are grouped into four main divisions: lighting, consumer electronics, professional products (computers, telecommunications, and medical equipment), and components (including chips). In each of these areas it ranks alongside the likes of Matsushita, General Electric, Sony, and Siemens as a global competitor. By the late 1980s the company had several hundred subsidiaries in 60 countries, operated manufacturing plants in more than 40 countries, employed approximately 300,000 people, and manufactured thousands of products. Despite this global reach, however, Philips was a company in deep trouble by 1990. After a decade of deteriorating performance, Philips lost $2.2 billion on revenues of $28 billion that year. A major reason for this seems to have been Philips' inability to adapt to the changing competitive conditions in the global electronics industry during the 1970s and 80s.

❧ TRADITIONAL ORGANIZATION

To trace the roots of Philips' current troubles, we must go back to World War II. Until World War II the foreign activities of Philips had been managed from its head office in Eindhoven, the Netherlands. However, the Netherlands were occupied by Germany during the war, and cut off from their home base, Philips' various national organizations began to operate independently. In essence each major national organization developed into a self-contained company with its own manufacturing, marketing, and R&D functions.

Following the war, top management believed the company could be most successfully rebuilt through its national organizations. There were several reasons for this. First, high trade barriers made it logical that self-contained national organizations should be established in each major national market. Second, it was felt that strong national organizations allowed Philips to be responsive to local demands in each country in which it competed. And third, given the substantial autonomy that the various national organizations had gained during the war, top management felt that reestablishing centralized control might prove difficult and yield few benefits.

At the same time, top management felt the need for some centralized control over product policy and R&D to achieve some coordination among the national organizations. Its response was to create a number of worldwide product divisions (of which there were 14 by the mid-1980s). In theory, basic R&D and product development policy were the responsibility of the product divisions, whereas the national organizations were responsible for day-to-day operations in their particular countries. Product strategy in a given country was meant to be determined jointly by consultation between the responsible national organization and the product divisions. The national organizations implemented strategy.

Another feature of Philips' organization was duumvirate leadership. In most national organizations, top-management responsibilities and authority were shared by two managers—one responsible for "commercial affairs" and the other for "technical activities." This form of management had its origins with the company's founders, Anton and Gerard Philips. Anton was a salesman, and Gerard an engineer. Throughout the company there seemed to be vigorous informal competition between technical managers and sales managers, each attempting to outperform the other. As Anton once noted,

> The technical management and the sales management competed to outperform each other. Production tried to produce so much that sales would not be able to get rid of it; sales tried to sell so much that the factory would not be able to keep up.[1]

Source: Charles W. L. Hill.
[1] *The Phillips Group: 1987,* Harvard Business School case 388-050.

The top decision-making and policy-making body in the company was a 10-person board of management. Although the board members shared general management responsibility, they typically maintained a special interest in one of the functional areas of the company (e.g., R&D, manufacturing, marketing). Traditionally, most of the members of this board were Dutchmen who had come up through the Eindhoven bureaucracy, although most had extensive foreign postings, typically as a top manager of one of the company's national organizations.

❧ ENVIRONMENTAL CHANGE

From the 1960s onward a number of significant changes occurred in Philips' competitive environment that would profoundly affect the company. First, due to the efforts of the General Agreement on Tariffs and Trade (GATT), trade barriers fell worldwide. In addition, in Philips' home base, Europe, the emergence of the European Economic Community, of which the Netherlands was an early member, led to a further reduction in trade barriers between the countries of Western Europe.

Second, during the 1960s and 70s a number of new competitors emerged in Japan. Taking advantage of GATT's success in lowering trade barriers, the Japanese companies produced most of their output at home and exported it to the rest of the world. The resulting economies of scale allowed them to reduce unit costs to below those achieved by Western competitors (such as Philips) that manufactured in multiple locations. This significantly increased competitive pressures in most of the business areas in which Philips competed.

Third, due to technological changes, the costs of R&D and manufacturing increased rapidly. The introduction of transistors and then integrated circuits called for significant capital expenditures in production facilities—many of them running into hundreds of millions of dollars. To realize scale economies, substantial levels of output had to be achieved. Moreover the pace of technological change was declining, and product life cycles were shortening. This gave companies in the electronics industry less time to recoup their capital investments before the next generation of products came along.

Finally, as the world moved from a series of fragmented national markets toward a single global market, uniform global standards for electronic equipment began to emerge. This showed itself most clearly in the videocassette recorder business, where three standards initially battled for dominance: the Betamax standard produced by Sony, the VHS standard produced by Matsushita, and Philip's V2000 standard. Ultimately the VHS standard was most widely accepted by consumers, and the others were abandoned. For Philips and Sony, both of which had invested substantially in their own standard, this was a significant defeat. Philips' attempt to establish its V2000 format as an industry standard was effectively killed by the decision of its own North American national organization, over Eindhoven's objections, to manufacture according to the VHS standard.

❧ ORGANIZATIONAL AND STRATEGIC RESPONSES

By the early 1980s Philips realized that if it was to survive, it was going to have to radically restructure its business. Its high cost structure was due to the amount of duplication across national organizations, particularly in the area of manufacturing. Moreover, as the V2000 incident demonstrated, the company's attempts to compete effectively were being hindered by the strength and autonomy of its national organizations.

The first attempt at change came in 1982, when Wisse Dekker was appointed CEO. Dekker quickly pushed for manufacturing rationalization, creating international production centers that served a number of national organizations, and closing many small, inefficient plants. He also pushed Philips to enter into more collaborative alliances with other electronics firms to share the costs and risks of developing new products. In addition, Dekker accelerated the movement away from dual leadership in national organizations (commercial and technical), replacing it with a single general membership. Furthermore Dekker tried to "tilt" Philips' matrix away from national organizations by creating a corporate council where the heads of product divisions would join the heads of the national organizations to discuss issues of importance to both. At the same time, he gave the product divisions more responsibility to determine companywide research and manufacturing activities.

In 1986 Dekker was succeeded by Cor van de Klugt. One of van de Klugt's first actions was to specify that profitability would be the central criteria for evaluating performance in the firm. The product divisions were given primary responsibility for achieving profits. This was followed in late 1986 by his termination of the American Trust, the "subcorporation" that had been given control of North American operations during World War II and still held it as of 1986. By terminating the trust, van de Klugt in theory reestablished Eindhoven's control over its North American subsidiaries. Then in May 1987 van de Klugt announced a major restructuring. He designated four production divisions—lighting, consumer electronics, components, and telecommunications and data systems—as "core divisions," the implication being that the other activities would be sold. At the same time he reduced the size of the management board. Its policy-making responsibility was devolved to a new group management committee comprising the remaining board members plus the heads of the core product divisions. No heads of national organizations were appointed to this body, thereby further tilting power away from the national organizations and toward the product divisions.

Despite these changes, Philips' competitive position continued to deteriorate. Many outside observers attributed this to the huge head office bureaucracy at Eindhoven (comprising more than 3,000 employees in 1989). They argued that although van de Klugt had changed the organizational chart, much of the change was superficial. Real power, they argued, still lay with the Eindhoven bureaucracy and their allies in the national organizations. They pointed out that Philips' work force had declined by less than 10 percent since 1986, far from the 30 percent reduction many analysts were calling for.

Alarmed by a 1989 loss of $1.06 billion, the board forced van de Klugt to resign in May 1990. He was replaced by Jan Timmer. Timmer quickly announced he would cut Philips' worldwide work force by 10,000 to 283,000 and launch a $1.4 billion restructuring. Investors were unimpressed—many of them thinking the company should cut four or five times as many jobs—and reacted by knocking down the share price by 7 percent. Since then, however, Timmer has made some progress. In mid-1991 he sold Philips' minicomputer division—which at the time was losing $1 million per day—to Digital Equipment. He also announced plans to reduce costs by $1.2 billion by cutting the work force by 55,000. In addition he entered into a strategic alliance with Matsushita, the Japanese electronic giant, to manufacture and market the digital compact cassette (DCC). Developed by Philips and scheduled for introduction in late 1992, the DCC reproduces the sound of a compact disc on a tape. The DCC's great selling point is that users will be able to play their old analog tape cassettes on the new system. The DCC's chief rival is Sony's portable compact disc system, the "mini-disc." Many observers expect a replay of the classic battle between the VHS and Betamax videorecorder standards in the coming battle between the DCC and the mini-disc. If the DCC wins, it could be the remaking of Philips.

CASE DISCUSSION QUESTIONS

1. What were the drawbacks of Philips' post-World War II organization?
2. What international strategy was Philips pursuing in the 1960s? What strategy *should* it have been pursuing?
3. Why did Dekker and van de Klugt try to tilt Philips' matrix away from the national organizations and toward the product divisions?
4. Identify the forces opposed to change at Philips.
5. Was it a good move for Philips to ally itself with Matsushita to manufacture and market the DCC? Wouldn't it have been better to go it alone?

REFERENCES

Aguilar, F. J., and M. Y. Yoshino. *The Philips Group: 1987*. Harvard Business School case 388–050.

Bartlett, C. A., and S. Ghoshal. *Managing across Borders: The Transnational Solution*. Boston, MA: Harvard Business School Press, 1989.

Kapstein, J., and J. Levine, "A Would-Be World Beater Takes a Beating." *Business Week,* July 16, 1990, pp. 41–42.

Levine, J. "Philips' Big Gamble," *Business Week,* August 5, 1991, pp. 34–36.

"Philips Fights the Flab." *The Economist.* April 7, 1992, pp. 73–74.

HONDA MOTOR COMPANY

Established in 1948 to manufacture motorcycles, Honda Motor Company has grown into a corporation with $25 billion annual sales worldwide. It is now the 10th-largest automobile company in the world. In 1990 Honda held a 4 percent share of the global market for automobiles. Despite its success, Honda has always been viewed as something of a newcomer in Japan; unlike the other major Japanese automobile companies, it was not established until after World War II. Hence it lacked the extensive contacts with other companies that Nissan and Toyota, which were associated with Japan's prewar *zaibatsu* (business groups), enjoyed. Honda did not enter the automobile business itself until the 1960s, and then it was over the objections of Japan's powerful Ministry of Trade and Industry (MITI). MITI did not want to see another competitor in what it perceived to be an already very competitive domestic automobile market. Consequently MITI tried hard to dissuade Honda from entering the business but to no avail. However, MITI's resistance meant that among other things, Honda had little official support for setting up an export network.

Another problem confronting Honda was the strong competition it faced at home. Marketing muscle and control over distribution systems are very important in Japan. As an upstart outside, Honda found it difficult to break into the well-established distribution system. Most auto dealers in Japan have an exclusive arrangement with a single automobile company. Few dealers were willing to carry Honda cars lest they bring down the wrath of their existing supplier—Toyota, Nissan, or one of the other established automobile companies. Thus the only way for Honda to build a distribution network in Japan was to buy land and build new outlets, which proved costly, particularly in urban Japan where land is very expensive. Honda realized its growth potential in Japan was limited, so it turned its attention overseas. So successful was this strategy that by 1990 more than 60 percent of its total sales were made outside Japan. In addition to its Japanese facilities, Honda had 77 manufacturing plants in 40 countries outside of Japan by that time.

❧ HONDA'S INTERNATIONAL EXPANSION

Honda's initial expansion overseas was in motorcycle sales, not automobiles. Honda first expanded into nearby Asian markets and then in the 1960s into the United States and Europe. In 1962 Honda established a facility to manufacture mopeds in Belgium for sale in the European market. This was the first major direct investment by a Japanese company in manufacturing facilities in an advanced industrialized nation. The Belgian experience was to provide many valuable lessons for Honda.

A number of factors underlay Honda's decision to manufacture mopeds in Belgium: the European market was very large (accounting for 85 percent of the world's non-Japanese motorcycle ownership in 1960); Honda was confident it could manage

Source: Charles W. L. Hill and Maria Gonzalez.

Honda's North American
Automobile Plants, 1991

Location	Opened	Annual Capacity
Marysville, Ohio	1982	360,000
Alliston, Ontario	1987	80,000
East Liberty, Ohio	1989	150,000

European employees; and Honda believed it had a good product that would sell well in Europe. It took more than a decade for the Belgian venture to show a profit. Among the many problems Honda encountered were these:

- Its mopeds did not match the needs of Europeans, so demand was low.
- It had put too much distinctive design and technology into the moped, and thus local manufactures were unable to supply parts of the right specifications.
- A series of misunderstandings between management and labor led to a rash of industrial disputes.

After this experience, Honda concluded that if it was going to establish manufacturing facilities overseas, it needed to localize the product so it was consistent with local demand and supply conditions, and it needed to develop a much better understanding of the local management practices and social conditions.

In the mid-1970s Honda began to think seriously about further major investments in industrialized countries. By this time, the company had made significant inroads into the U.S. automobile and motorcycle markets by exporting from Japan, so the United States seemed the natural choice. In addition Honda saw the establishment of U.S. manufacturing facilities as a hedge against a rise in the value of the yen and any future trade disputes between Japan and the United States. (As it turned out, in the early 1980s the Japanese automobile companies agreed to abide by voluntary restraints on imports into the United States.)

Honda's first major U.S. investment was a motorcycle plant in Ohio, where production began in 1979. Over the next decade this was followed by the establishment of two automobile plants and an engine plant, all in Ohio. During this period Honda also established an automobile plant in Ontario, Canada, and by 1991, Honda had the capacity to produce close to 600,000 cars a year in North America. By 1992 Honda had invested more than $3 billion in U.S. manufacturing facilities and had created more than 11,000 jobs in the Ohio region and 3,000 elsewhere in the United States. Of the 659,659 cars that Honda sold in the United States in 1991, 401,195 were built in North America. In 1990 its North American-manufactured cars helped Honda overtake Chrysler and become the number three passenger car company in the United States with a market share of 9.22 percent. In 1991 the Honda Accord, which is manufactured in Ohio, was the best-selling passenger car model in North America. Honda claims its American-built cars have a domestic content of 75 percent; that is, three quarters of the sticker price goes for U.S. labor, components, and other costs. In 1987 Honda began exporting Accords and Acuras from Ohio to Japan, and by 1991, 14,500 U.S.-built Hondas were sent to Japan. (GM exported 5,600 autos to Japan that year, and Ford only 1,100 autos.) Overall, in 1991 Honda of America exported 27,000 vehicles to 10 countries, including Japan, Israel, and 6 European nations. Honda's plans called for the company to export 40,000 cars per year from the United States by the end of 1992. In addition to car exports, Honda's Marysville plant exported 24 percent of the 55,000 motorcycles it produced in 1991.

Aside from its North American operations, Honda has made substantial investments in Europe in recent years—most notably in Great Britain, where it was building a facility with the capacity to produce 100,000 autos per year. This was scheduled to open in 1994. Like Toyota and Nissan, which are also building facilities there, Honda views Great Britain as a convenient site from which to serve the European Community market.

❧ HONDA'S STRATEGY

Localization

Honda claims its strategy for operating overseas consists of four target concepts: localization of products, profit, production, and management.

Localization of products means developing, manufacturing, and marketing products best suited to the demands of local consumers. Honda sees subtle but important differences between countries in the way a product is used and what consumers expect of it. To localize products so they appeal to local consumers' tastes and preferences, Honda has invested in R&D centers in North America, Europe, and Southeast Asia. These centers do not just customize products designed in Japan; they take the lead in designing products for their local markets. For example, the Acura was designed in the United States for sale in the U.S. markets. Similarly the Honda Accord Wagon was designed, developed, and engineered in California and Ohio and is being built exclusively in the United States.

Localization of profits means reinvesting profits earned in a country *in* that country. This is clearly seen in the case of Honda's North American operations, with profits being used to finance the expansion of North American-based production capacity. It is not clear, however, if the company has pursued this practice elsewhere.

Localization of production means establishing significant production centers in each major market (country or region) where Honda does business. Honda stresses that when it talks about local production, it does not mean "screwdriver plants" that simply assemble parts manufactured in another country. Rather, Honda claims, it strives to increase the ratio of local content in its locally manufactured cars over time. In part the rationale for localizing production is to provide some protection against currency fluctuations and trade barriers.

Localization of management means a number of things. First, it means local people should play a major role in the management of foreign subsidiaries. In the United States, for example, Honda's operations are headed by an American. Second, it means local managers and employees should have a good understanding of Honda's corporate philosophy. And third, it means managers dispatched from Honda's head office (in Japan) should become part of the local community by understanding local culture and ways of thinking.

Policies for Manufacturing outside Japan

When establishing manufacturing facilities outside Japan, Honda attaches particular importance to three policies. The first policy is to establish good human relations between the management and the work force. Management encourages employees to communicate problems directly to them. The management staff wear the same white work clothing and eat in the same cafeteria as other employees do. The second policy is to maintain and promote harmony with the local community by getting involved in local activities and helping to build the local community infrastructure. The third policy is to give top priority to maintaining high product quality. This calls for designing products that are easy to assemble, transferring the best production equipment and quality-control practices from its Japanese plants to its foreign operations, and building a strong commitment to quality control among all employees. To achieve the last goal Honda engages in substantial on-the-job training in production techniques, product design, quality control and the like.

❧ EMERGING TRADE TENSIONS

Despite its substantial investments in Ohio, Honda has run headlong into a potentially serious dispute with the U.S. Customs Service. In 1992 Customs researchers argued that Honda was overstating the local content of the cars it built in Ohio. At the heart of the dispute lies the claim that Honda cars are mostly a collection of Japanese parts handled by Americans but designed, engineered, and fabricated in Japan. Take Honda's Civic as an example. Honda claims that its Civics, built in Ohio, have 75 percent U.S. content. However, a study by the

What Went into a 1989
Honda Civic?

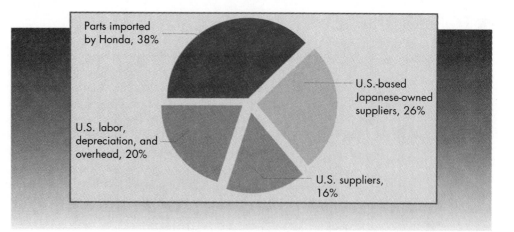

University of Michigan concluded that only 16 percent of the 1989 Civic parts were made by U.S.-owned suppliers based in the United States. Adding 20 percent to this figure for local labor costs, depreciation, and overhead suggests that, in total, only 36 percent of the content of the Civics is "local content." However, the University of Michigan does not regard parts produced in the United States by Japanese-owned suppliers as local content. If these are added to the calculation of local content, then the Civic might be argued to have 62 percent U.S. content—considerably more than the 36 percent claimed by the University of Michigan study, but still less than the 75 percent claimed by Honda.

The U.S. Customs Service has also criticized Honda for overstating the U.S. content of the engines produced at its Anna, Ohio, plant. According to Customs, 58 percent of the parts that go into these engines are imported by Honda (primarily from Japan), 37 percent are produced by Japanese-owned U.S.-based suppliers, and 5 percent are produced by U.S.-owned U.S.-based suppliers. On this basis, according to Customs, at most only 42 percent of the Anna engines can be considered U.S. content, and 5 percent would be a better figure. Yet when Honda ships engines to its assembly plant in Alliston, Ontario, the company claims the U.S. content of the engines is more than 50 percent. According to the North American Free Trade Agreement, parts with more than 50 percent local content are reclassified as 100 percent North American when they cross the border. The engines are then placed into cars assembled in Ontario, which are then shipped back into the United States for resale. On the basis of the classification of the engine as 100 percent North American, Honda claims the cars shipped from Canada are 75 percent North American. As such, they escape the imposition of import duties. It is this 75 percent figure, established on the basis of misleading statements about the U.S. content of Anna engines, that the Customs Service is challenging. According to Customs, Honda owes $20 million in import duties on cars shipped from Ontario to the United States since 1986.

Honda's response is to point out that the U.S. Customs Service is ignoring the input of local labor, depreciation, and overhead in the Anna engines. When this is added in, the total figure for U.S. content is over 50 percent. Honda also points out that U.S. Customs has not yet adopted rules for calculating local origin—a point the Customs Service acknowledges. Thus, according to Honda, there is nothing to say that they can't count labor inputs and parts supplied by U.S.-based Japanese suppliers as being of U.S. origin. Moreover, Honda notes it is ironic that the Customs Service has chosen to focus on an engine it is producing in Ohio at a time when Chrysler, GM, and Ford are all importing small engines for their cars. Honda is the only automaker that manufactures a small fuel-efficient engine in the United States. Honda also argues that it spent $2.9 billion purchasing parts from more than 240 American parts suppliers in 1992, and that its plans are to purchase $5 billion of parts per year from American suppliers by 1995.

CASE DISCUSSION QUESTIONS

1. In terms of the strategies discussed in Chapter 12, what kind of strategy is Honda pursuing? What are the benefits of its strategy? What are the costs?

2. What is the reasoning behind Honda's decision to establish production facilities in the United States?

3. Honda's Ohio plants are reportedly among the most efficient in the United States. How do you think Honda has achieved this in such a short time?

4. Is the Honda Civic an American car? Is it more or less "American" than the Pontiac Le Mans, which, although designed in the United States, is built by Daewoo Motors of Korea, largely of parts manufactured in Southeast Asia?

5. Should parts produced in the United States by Japanese-owned supplies by counted as "U.S. content"?

6. Does Honda's presence in Ohio benefit the U.S. economy?

7. Do you think the Customs Service was correct to focus attention on Honda?

REFERENCES

Honda in America. Company publication, Honda of American, Ohio. 1992.

Ingrassia, P., and C. Chandler. "Japan's Car Makers Now See Advantages in Restraining Growth." *The Wall Street Journal*, January 7, 1992, pp. 1, 6.

Magnusson, P.; J. B. Treece; and W. C. Symonds. "Honda: Is It an American Car?" *Business Week*, November 18, 1991, pp. 105–12.

Mair, A.; R. Florida; and M. Kenney. "The New Geography of Automobile Production: Japanese Transplants in North America." *Economic Geography* 64, pp. 352–73.

Patterson, G. A. "Domestic? Car Firms Play Games with the Categories." *The Wall Street Journal*, November 11, 1991, p. A1.

Reich, R. "The Myth of Made in the USA." *The Wall Street Journal*, July 5, 1991, p. A6.

Sugiura, H. "How Honda Localizes Its Global Strategy." *Sloan Management Review*, Fall 1990, pp. 77–82.

"Taking Root and Blooming." *The Economist*, April 15, 1992, p. 79.

Toy, S.; N. Gross; and J. B. Treece. "The Americanization of Honda." *Business Week*, April 25, 1992, pp. 90–96.

Whitlock, S. N. "Of Honda and the Japanese Presence in America." *Business Week*, December 16, 1991, p. 7.

FORD 2000

❧ INTRODUCTION

Newly named CEO of Ford Alex Trotman made a proclamation in November 1993: "The top priority is to keep doing what we've been doing."[1] No one really believed him. Trotman had made a career of doing the unexpected. When top management refused him a transfer from Britain in 1969, he bought his own ticket to Dearborn, Michigan, and talked his way into a job at headquarters, alias the Glass House. At 61, Trotman holds a master's degree in business although he never attended college. He has spent years working his way up through Ford's management, primarily on the production side in Europe.

The skeptics were right. It did not take long for Trotman to shake things up. Three weeks after being named chairman, Trotman attended a meeting of senior managers at Ford's London office. The subject of the meeting was to review the success of

---

Source: Charles W. L. Hill and Maureen Kibelsted.
[1]J. B. Treece, "Ford: Alex Trotman's Daring Strategy," *Business Week*, April 3, 1995, pp. 94–104.

consolidating the development of power trains, the main components of engines and transmissions. Trotman asked the managers if it was possible to expand this idea to the entire company, not just engines and transmissions. Could Ford tear down its highly segmented regional structure and create one global system? Trotman gave a team of senior managers six weeks to determine if such an idea was feasible.

❧ The Rationale for Restructuring

There were several motivating factors behind the need for restructuring. Under the previous system, there was massive duplication of processes in both North America and Europe. According to the company, this raised annual costs by at least $3 billion.[2] Furthermore, Ford's average new-car development time was much longer than its competitors, approximately six years as compared to Toyota's three. Its competitors have more profits per car and higher pretax margins. Trotman also saw the need to refocus the company in order to efficiently enter emerging markets in China, Russia, and Latin America.

Thus Ford 2000 was born. With the ultimate goal to become "the best automaker in the world," Trotman announced the most massive reorganization of the company in its 91-year history on April 1, 1994. The specific directives include:

- Be faster and more efficient developing new models.
- Expand the range of products and fill in gaps.
- Match the Japanese cost advantage and improve profitability.
- Reduce the time it takes to make a vehicle.
- Follow Toyota's lead of selling the same model around the world.[3]

The finer points of Ford 2000 were hammered out by a team of 150 executives. Led by Bob Transou, who engineered the more efficient power train process, the team devised ways for the company to streamline itself. The team itself was a direct contrast to Ford's old corporate culture. It was housed in a war room, a large open area filled with small desks and cubicles, with no private offices. The idea was to put all the decision makers in one place and force them to hash out decisions on the spot, rather than waste months passing around memos. All the team members had delegated their other responsibilities so they could dedicate their efforts to planning the reorganization. Everyone worked in their shirtsleeves, so it was impossible to distinguish vice presidents from underlings. This informal atmosphere was not an accident. Transou "wanted people to leave their corporate credentials at the door."[4]

The team had the blessing of top management but it still had some history to overcome. Ford's last attempt at building a global car, the Mondeo, which eventually became the Ford Contour, the Mercury Mystique, and the Mondeo, took almost seven years to develop and cost $6 billion. Industry analysts doubt that Ford will ever recoup these development costs through sales. The team's challenge was to incorporate the lessons learned from the Mondeo into its new reorganization plan. The underlying objective was to lay the groundwork for a decade's worth of products all built from a common design and with great economies of scale.

❧ Ford 2000

Ford 2000's initial imperative was to consolidate the North American and European operations. On January 1, 1995, the first part of Ford 2000 was implemented. Ford of Europe and Ford North America merged to form Ford Automotive Operations

---

[2]K. Done, "Ford Maps Out a Global Ambition," *Financial Times,* April 3, 1995, p. 9.

[3]A. Chamberlain, "Major Shakeup at Ford," *Toronto Star,* April 21, 1994, p. C1.

[4]D. Sedgwick, "Ford's Redesigners," *Detroit News,* June 26, 1994, p. 1.

(FAO). (To give a frame of reference for the scale of this merger, Ford of Europe and Ford North America combine to be a $94 billion business. The Nabisco-RJR Reynolds merger was approximately $24 billion.) The new organization will be divided into five vehicle program centers. Each vehicle program center (VPC) will be responsible for the development, manufacture, marketing, and profitability of their specific Ford vehicles, no matter where they are sold.

The vehicle program centers will be divided into small and medium-sized front-wheel-drive cars, large front-wheel-drive cars, rear-wheel-drive cars, light trucks, and commercial trucks. Europe will keep control of the development of small and medium cars because of their obvious expertise. Dearborn in the United States will handle the rest. Although Europe gets only one out of the five new VPCs, the European center does have responsibility for developing vehicles in market segments that hold the biggest potential to gain from Ford's global strategy and are expected to account for around 50% of world cars sales by next decade.

Each VPC will have the capability to alter its product to suit regional markets. The formidable task of each VPC will be to make everything under the hood the same, and everything that has to do with taste and local regulations different, and to do this in a cost-efficient manner. As Trotman puts it, "Even with under the skin components that may be identical, the design and feel of our vehicles can be made very different to suit local tastes."[5]

Ford believes the new organization will be successful, particularly with quicker adaptation to shifting customer demands. New-product time cycles are targeted to be uniformly under three years by 2000. Plant changeovers for new "global" models produced at various locations around the world are scheduled to follow each other in weeks, not months.[6] Extensive investment in computers and videoconferencing technology has been made to facilitate the process. Ford, with the help a consulting firm called Logica, has created its own worldwide integrated purchasing system (WIPS). All of Ford's purchasing activities, which represent over 100,000 separate parts worth $40 billion, are on the workload management system.[7]

❧ ORGANIZATION STRUCTURE

What will the new Ford look like? The new Ford will be a matrix organization (see Figure 1). Most employees will report to two or more managers, one within a vehicle center team and one within a functional discipline such as finance or manufacturing. Instead of being temporarily assigned to work on a new Taurus, a brake engineer will now be permanently assigned to a team to help develop a specific car for individual countries. Career development will be the responsibility of the functional managers while performance evaluation will be the duty of the vehicle program team leader. By shifting the performance evaluation to the vehicle team leader, Ford wants to change the loyalties of its employees from their functional area to the car they are helping to build. This goal has been further reinforced by the co-location of people with their vehicle program teams.

Ford has learned lessons from other failed matrix organizations and has built in safeguards. They include:

- Making doubly sure that objectives are agreed on precisely between the vehicle centers and the functional side of the organization.
- Specifying clearly the respective roles and responsibilities of individuals toward each side of the matrix.
- Changing appraisal and reward systems accordingly.

[5]Done, "Ford Maps Out a Global Ambition."

[6]E. Heinrich, "Ford Takes Historic Gamble," *Financial Post*, August 27, 1994, p. 8.

[7]Logica Assists Ford Motor Company," *Business Wire*, May 9, 1995.

FIGURE 1   Ford's New Global Matrix Structure

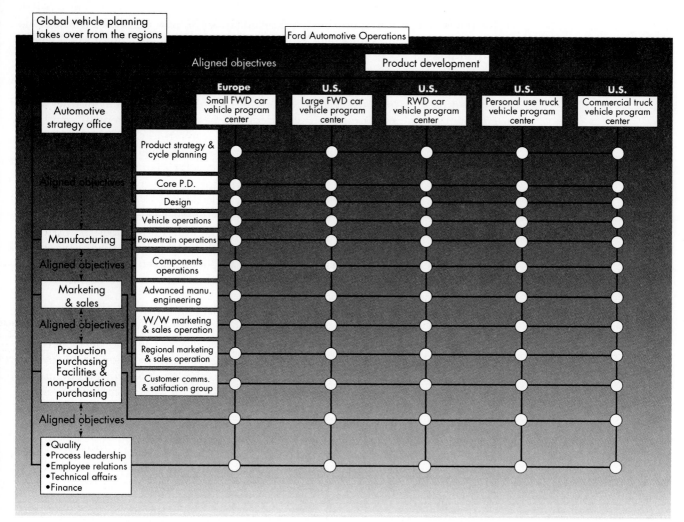

Source: The Ford Motor Company.

- Appointing only senior executives who have shown they can work collaboratively.
- Training everyone involved in the art of developing a cooperative matrix perspective, which largely replaces the need for policing.
- Introducing much more intensive and open communication.[8]

Transou hopes to make the matrix system work by ensuring that accountability is introduced into the structure. "You need accountability," says Transou. "Those that have not succeeded with matrix management did not understand that. Without accountability it is always someone else's fault. There are excuses. There are no excuses in Ford 2000, it is very clear where responsibility is."[9]

Above the VPCs, decision making will be centralized through the creation of a global profit center for all automotive operations. Ed Hogenlocker, president of FAO, says, "By centralizing decision making, we can take the broadest possible view of market opportunities, and we can develop products to serve multiple markets, vastly increasing the return on every product development dollar."[10]

[8]C. Lorenz, "Ford's Global Matrix Gamble," *Financial Times*, December 16, 1994, p. 14.
[9]Done, "Ford Maps Out a Global Ambition."
[10]Lorenz, "Ford's Global Matrix Gamble."

Ford is attempting to change not only how it does business, but also its corporate culture. The Ford 2000 program will trim the layers of management from 10 to 7 to destroy the delaying bureaucracy and facilitate the matrix system. Ford has offered early retirement to a relatively small number of senior officials, including executives, managers, and professionals, approximately 15 percent of the top 2,500. But it is not planning to get by with fewer managers. "It'll be a leaner, hopefully much more efficient, faster, more nimble company than it is today and the management structure will reflect and cause it," Trotman said.[11]

Trotman is conducting this reorganization in a very disciplined and principled manner in order to maximize the probability for success. He is getting the entire company involved in the process. Although the team headed by Transou is doing much of the planning, it is getting hundreds of other employees in on the act. The principle is simple: Get the people who will have to live with the changes involved in making the changes.[12]

Ford is making a great effort to keep all its employees and the public informed of what the changes will be and keep the reorganization efforts out in the open. Its public relations department publishes a weekly faxed newspaper, runs an electronic bulletin board, and broadcasts a weekly in-house television show to keep everyone informed of the latest developments. It has also held numerous employee meetings.

Ford expects confusion in its employees and is attempting to manage it. Hundreds of careers will be sidetracked as Ford attempts to flatten its hierarchy. In addition Ford of Europe, which was once an autonomous unit, will lose a significant amount of control once decisions are moved to Dearborn. There is a notable fear by some European employees that FAO may ultimately stand for "For Americans Only." To ease these fears, members of the reorganization team are making presentations to explain how the new organization will work.

🐾 CONCLUSION

Trotman set an eight-month schedule for revamping Ford. Most multinationals in other industries have taken a decade to shift their organizations gradually to global structures. To some observers, Ford has chosen a strange time to conduct a reorganization. Ford reported record earnings of $5.3 billion for fiscal year 1994 on top of record revenues of $128 billion. Trotman has defended this criticism by saying that concentrating on change and improvement is a lot easier when times are good. "Now it the right time for such a change. The tools are there—computers and communications—and we have a strong balance sheet. If you make big changes when times are difficult, expediency often takes precedence."[13]

If Ford pulls this off, the benefits could be tremendous. Ford anticipates savings of between $2 and $3 billion a year (latest reports bump this figure up to $5 billion).[14] The reconstruction will also create a more efficient Ford with fewer, global suppliers. Ford estimates that by cutting suppliers of everything but auto parts from 50,000 today to 5,000 by 1997, it will save $1 billion a year.[15]

Ultimately, the new Ford will have the flexibility to forcefully enter new emerging markets. But there are some real dangers involved. Ford can potentially make itself too global by producing cars that cannot be cost effectively altered to meet local tastes. Can the global cars be kept affordable?

---

[11]J. Szczensy, "Ford Exec Ranks to Be Halved," *Oakland Press*, October 15, 1994, p. 20.

[12]D. Sedgwick, "Fixing Ford," *Detroit News*, September 18, 1994, p. D1.

[13]"The World Car," *The Economist*, July 23, 1994, p. 69.

[14]C. Lorenz, "Ford Drives to Win World Leadership," *Sunday Times*, January 1, 1995.

[15]Treece, "Ford: Alex Trotman's Daring Strategy."

CASE DISCUSSION QUESTIONS

1. What other possible obstacles might Ford encounter as it becomes a global organization?

2. How important will the new matrix system be in the success or failure of Ford 2000?

3. What is Trotman forgetting in Ford's restructuring?

4. What other efficiencies might also be a by-product of Ford 2000?

5. How successful do you think this program will be in preparing Ford to enter emerging markets? What will be the key factors for success in entering these markets?

CHAPTER FIFTEEN

EXPORTING, IMPORTING, AND COUNTERTRADE

A SMALL COMPANY GOES GLOBAL

Artais Weather Check, Inc., is a small Ohio company with 1994 sales of just $5.5 million; it is also a company that is riding the back of a boom in exports for its main product—an automated weather observation system, or AWOS, for small airports. Artais' AWOS system records runway conditions such as wind speed, direction, and temperature and converts the data into a voice message that pilots can listen to. Only three other companies besides Artais have been certified by the U.S. Federal Aviation Administration to produce the equipment, and Artais dominates the market with a share of over 80 percent.

However, the market for automated weather observation systems is extremely small. Although there are 18,000 public and private airports in the country, the largest have round-the-clock human weather watchers, while most of the smaller airports cannot afford the $45,000 to $60,000 required to install an AWOS. Thus by 1993 only 400 U.S. airports had purchased automatic weather observation systems, and the prospects for growth in the United States seem to be limited to sales of about 75 systems per year nationwide.

To continue to grow the company's revenues, Artais has increasingly looked toward export sales. From slow beginnings in the late 1980s, Artais' exports have surged to account for close to two-thirds of the company's total revenues. However, to get foreign orders Artais has had to deal with frustrations it never encountered at home. The first problem it came up against was name recognition. Although Artais is well known within the United States, the company found it had almost no name recognition overseas. Another problem involves subsidized competition; according to Artais, in some foreign markets its main competitors are subsidized by their governments in an attempt to protect jobs. Artais has also found that it needs to customize its products for foreign markets. To sell in Egypt, for example, its system had to be re-programmed to relay weather information in Arabic as well as English. Customers also require that a cache of spare parts be located close by, and that Artais employees install the equipment and provide on-site training, all of which raises Artais' costs of doing business.

Political factors have also had a major impact on the outcome of some deals. For example, after working hard to secure a deal in Romania, Artais saw the deal fall through at the last moment. Instead the sale went to a German competitor. According to some locals, the Romanian government, eager to improve trading relations with the European Union, gave the job to Artais' German competitor in an attempt to curry favor with the trading bloc's most powerful member.

Despite problems such as these, Artais has sold systems to airports in Taiwan, China, Ecuador, Saudi Arabia, and Egypt. Moreover Artais has found that such overseas contracts can be more lucrative than its domestic sales because of all the extras such as spare parts, installation fees, and training. So far the value of the foreign contracts have ranged from $200,000 to $2 million, compared with $45,000 to $60,000 in the United States. Artais can now see the day when almost all its revenues will be generated by sales outside of the United States.

Source: S. N. Mehta, "Enterprise: Artais Finds that Smallness Isn't a Handicap in Global Market," *The Wall Street Journal*, June 23, 1994, p. B2.

~ INTRODUCTION

In the previous chapter we reviewed exporting from a strategic perspective. We considered exporting as just one of a range of strategic options for profiting from international expansion. In this chapter we are more concerned with the "nuts and bolts" of exporting (and importing). We take the choice of strategy as a given and look instead at "how to export."

As we can see from the opening case, exporting is not an activity just for large multinational enterprises; many small firms such as Artais have benefited significantly from exporting activities. Artais is merely part of a much wider story of the discovery by small and medium-sized enterprises of the money-making opportunities of exporting. In the United States, for example, 49 percent of companies with annual revenues of less than $100 million said they exported products in 1993, up from 36 percent of such companies in 1990.[1] However, the United States is still some way behind a number of other countries in this regard. In Germany, for example, companies with less than 500 employees account for about 30 percent of that nation's exports. In the United States the comparable figure is 10 percent.[2]

All the evidence suggests the volume of export activity in the world economy, by firms of all sizes, is likely to increase in the foreseeable future. One reason for this is that exporting has become easier over the years. The gradual decline in trade barriers under the umbrella of GATT and now the WTO (see Chapter 5), along with regional economic agreements such as the European Union and the North American Free Trade Agreement (see Chapter 8), have significantly increased export opportunities. At the same time the advent of modern communications and transportation technologies have alleviated the logistical problems associated with exporting. Firms are increasingly using fax machines, international 800 telephone numbers, and international air express services to reduce the costs of exporting. As a consequence it is no longer unusual to find small companies like Artais that are thriving as exporters.

Nevertheless exporting remains a difficult challenge for many firms. Whereas large multinational enterprises have long been conversant with the steps that must be taken to export successfully, smaller enterprises can find the process intimidating. Among other things the firm wishing to export must identify foreign market opportunities, avoid a host of unanticipated problems that are often associated with doing business in a foreign market, familiarize itself with the mechanics of export and import financing, learn where it can get financing and export credit insurance, and learn how it should deal with foreign exchange risk. The whole process is made all the more problematic by currencies that are not freely convertible. As a result there is the problem of arranging payment for exports to countries with weak currencies. This brings us to the complex topic of countertrade, by which payment for exports is received in goods and services rather than money. In this chapter we will discuss all these issues with the exception of foreign exchange risk, which was covered in Chapter 9. We open the chapter by considering the promise and pitfalls of exporting.

~ THE PROMISE AND PITFALLS OF EXPORTING

The great promise of exporting is that for most firms in most industries there are huge revenue and profit opportunities to be found in foreign markets. The case of Artais is instructive here. Artais is a company with a very solid competitive position in the United States, including an 80 percent share of the U.S. market for automated weather observing systems, but that alone was insufficient to guarantee continued strong growth in revenues and profits. The company found that the opportu-

---

[1]Data from the consulting firm BDO Seidman. Reported in S. N. Mehta, "Enterprise: Small Companies Look to Cultivate Foreign Business," *The Wall Street Journal*, July 7, 1994, p. B2.
[2]W. J. Holstein, "Why Johann Can Export, but Johnny Can't," *Business Week*, November 4, 1991, pp. 64–65.

nities for growth in foreign markets can more than make up for any lack of opportunities in the United States. What is true for Artais is also true for a large number of other enterprises of all sizes based in many other countries. The international market is normally so much larger than the firm's domestic market, that exporting is nearly always a way of increasing the revenue and profit base of a company.

Despite the obvious opportunities associated with exporting, studies have shown that while many large firms tend to be *proactive* about seeking opportunities for profitable exporting, systematically scanning foreign markets to see where the opportunities lie for leveraging their technology, products, and marketing skills in foreign countries, many medium-sized and small firms are very *reactive*.[3] Typically such reactive firms do not even consider exporting until their domestic market is saturated and the emergence of excess productive capacity at home forces them to look for growth opportunities in foreign markets. Furthermore many small and medium-sized firms tend to wait for the world to come to them, rather than going out into the world to seek opportunities. And even when the world does come to them, they may not respond. An example is MMO Music Group, which makes sing-along tapes for karaoke machines. Foreign sales accounted for about 15 percent of MMO's 1993 revenues of $8 million, but the firm's CEO admits this figure would probably have been much higher had he paid attention to building international sales during the 1980s. At that time unanswered faxes and phone messages from Asia and Europe piled up while he was trying to manage the burgeoning domestic side of the business. By the time MMO turned its attention to foreign markets, other competitors had stepped into the breach and MMO found it tough going to build export volume.[4]

MMO's experience is common and it suggests a need for firms to become more proactive about seeking export opportunities. One reason more firms are not proactive, however, is that they are unfamiliar with foreign market opportunities; they simply do not know how big the opportunities are or where they might lie. Simple ignorance of the potential opportunities is a huge barrier to exporting.[5] Moreover many would-be exporters are often intimidated by the complexities and mechanics of exporting to countries where business practices, language, culture, legal systems, and currency are all very different from those in the home market.

To make matters worse, many neophyte exporters have run into significant problems when first trying to do business abroad, and this has soured them on future exporting ventures. Common pitfalls include poor market analysis, a poor understanding of competitive conditions in the foreign market, a failure to customize the product offering to the needs of foreign customers, lack of an effective distribution program, and a poorly executed promotional campaign in the foreign market.[6] There is also a tendency for neophyte exporters to underestimate the time and expertise needed to cultivate business in foreign countries.[7] Few realize the amount of management resources that have to be dedicated to this activity. Many foreign customers require face-to-face negotiations on their home turf. An exporter may have to spend months learning about a country's trade regulations, business practices, and more before a deal can be closed.

Moreover exporters often face voluminous paperwork, complex formalities, and many potential delays and errors. According to a recent United Nations report on trade and development, a typical international trade transaction may involve 30 parties, 60 original documents, and 360 document copies, all of which have to be

[3]S. T. Cavusgil, "Global Dimensions of Marketing," in P. E. Murphy and B. M. Enis, *Marketing* (Glenview, IL: Scott, Foresman, 1985), pp. 577–99.

[4]Mehta, "Enterprise: Small Companies."

[5]W. Pavord and R. Bogart, "The Dynamics of the Decision to Export," *Akron Business and Economic Review*. 1975, pp. 6–11.

[6]A. O. Ogbuehi and T. A. Longfellow, "Perceptions of U.S. Manufacturing Companies Concerning Exporting," *Journal of Small Business Management*. October 1994, pp. 37–59.

[7]R. W. Haigh, "Thinking of Exporting?" *Columbia Journal of World Business* 29 (December 1994), pp. 66–86.

checked, transmitted, reentered into various information systems, processed, and filed. The United Nations has calculated that the time involved in preparing documentation, along with the costs of common errors in paperwork, often amounts to 10 percent of the final value of goods exported.[8]

⚜ IMPROVING EXPORT PERFORMANCE

There are a number of ways in which inexperienced exporters can gain information about foreign market opportunities and avoid some common pitfalls that tend to discourage and frustrate neophyte exporters. In this section we look at some information sources that exporters can utilize to increase their knowledge of foreign market opportunities, we consider the pros and cons of utilizing export management companies (EMCs) to assist in the export process, and we review various exporting strategies that can be adopted to increase the probability of successful exporting. We begin, however, with a look at how several nations try to assist domestic firms in the export process.

An International Comparison

One big impediment to exporting is the simple lack of knowledge of the opportunities available. Often there are many markets for a firm's product, but because they are in countries separated from the firm's home base by culture, language, distance, and time, the firm does not know of them. Identifying export opportunities is made all the more complex by the fact that 180 countries with widely differing cultures compose the world of potential opportunities. Faced with such complexity and diversity, it is perhaps not surprising that firms sometimes hesitate to proactively seek export opportunities.

The way to overcome ignorance is to collect information. In Germany, one of the world's most successful exporting nations, trade associations, government agencies, and commercial banks perform information-gathering functions, helping small firms identify export opportunities (the German system is profiled in depth in the next "Country Focus"). A similar function is provided by the Japanese Ministry of International Trade and Industry (MITI), which is always on the lookout for export opportunities. In addition many Japanese firms are affiliated in some way with the *sogo shosha*, Japan's great trading houses. The sogo shosha have offices all over the world, and they proactively, continuously seek export opportunities for their affiliated companies large and small.[9] The great advantage of German and Japanese firms is that they can draw on the large reservoirs of experience, skills, information, and other resources of their respective export-oriented institutions.

Unlike their German and Japanese competitors, many U.S. firms are relatively blind when they seek export opportunities; they are information disadvantaged. In part this difference reflects historical differences. Both Germany and Japan have long made their living as trading nations, whereas until recently the United States has been a relatively self-contained continental economy in which international trade played a minor role. This is changing; both imports and exports now play a much greater role in the U.S. economy than they did 20 years ago. As yet, however, the United States has not evolved an institutional structure for promoting exports similar to that of either Germany or Japan.

Information Sources

Despite institutional disadvantages, U.S. firms can increase their awareness of export opportunities. The most comprehensive source of information is probably the U.S. Department of Commerce and its district offices all over the country. Within that

[8]F. Williams, "The Quest for More Efficient Commerce," *Financial Times*. October 13, 1994, p. 7.
[9]M. Y. Yoshino and T. B. Lifson, *The Invisible Link* (Cambridge, MA: MIT Press, 1986).

department are two organizations dedicated to providing businesses with intelligence and assistance for attacking foreign markets: the International Trade Administration and the United States and Foreign Commercial Service Agency.

Among other things, these agencies provide the potential exporter with a "best prospects" list, which gives the names and addresses of potential distributors in foreign markets along with businesses they are in, the products they handle, and their contact person. In addition the Department of Commerce has assembled a "comparison shopping service" for 14 countries that are major markets for U.S. exports. For a small fee a firm can receive a customized market research survey on a product of its choice. This survey provides information on marketability, the competition, comparative prices, distribution channels, and names of potential sales representatives. Each study is conducted on-site by an officer of the U.S. Department of Commerce.

The Department of Commerce also organizes trade events that help potential exporters make foreign contacts and explore export opportunities. The department organizes exhibitions at international trade fairs, which are held regularly in major cities worldwide. The department also has a "matchmaker" program, in which department representatives accompany groups of U.S. businesspeople abroad to meet with qualified agents, distributors, and customers.

In addition to the Department of Commerce, nearly every state and many large cities maintain active trade commissions whose purpose is to promote exports. Most of these provide business counseling services, information-gathering service, technical assistance, and financing service. Unfortunately, many have fallen victim to budget cuts or to turf battles for political and financial support with other export agencies.

A number of private organizations are also beginning to gear up to provide more assistance to would-be exporters. Commercial banks and major accounting firms are more willing to assist small firms in starting export operations than they were a decade ago. In addition large multinationals that have been successful in the global arena are typically more than willing to discuss opportunities overseas with the owners or managers of small firms.[10]

Utilizing Export Management Companies

One way for first-time exporters to identify the opportunities associated with exporting, and to avoid many of the associated pitfalls, is to hire an **export management company** (EMC). EMCs are export specialists who act as the export marketing department or international department for their client firms. EMCs normally accept two types of export assignments. In one they start exporting operations for a firm, with the understanding that the firm will take over operations after they are well established. In another, start-up services are performed with the understanding that the EMC will have continuing responsibility for selling the firm's products. Many EMCs specialize in serving firms in particular industries and in focusing on particular areas of the world. Thus one EMC may specialize in selling agricultural products in the Asian market, while another may focus on exporting electronics products to Eastern Europe.

In theory the advantage of EMCs is that they are experienced specialists who can help the neophyte exporter to identify opportunities and avoid common pitfalls. A good EMC will have a network of contacts in potential markets, will have multilingual employees, will have a good knowledge of different business mores, and will be fully conversant with the ins and outs of the exporting process and with local business regulations. However, studies have revealed there is a large variation in the quality of EMCs.[11] While some perform their functions very well, others appear to add little value to the exporting company. Therefore it is important for an exporter to carefully review a number of EMCs and check references from an EMC's past clients before deciding on a particular EMC. One drawback of overrelying on EMCs is that the company fails to develop its own exporting capabilities in-house.

---

[10]L. W. Tuller, *Going Global* (Homewood, IL: Business One Irwin, 1991).

[11]R. W. Haigh, "Thinking of Exporting?"

COUNTRY FOCUS
The German Export Machine

The German economy is only about one-quarter the size of the U.S. economy and roughly half the size of Japan's, and yet Germany regularly tops both the United States and Japan as the world's biggest exporter. In 1990, for example, Germany racked up $421 billion of exports, while the United States had $394 billion, and Japan $286 billion. A striking thing about Germany's export machine is the role played by small firms—referred to in Germany as the *Mittelstand*. Whereas firms with fewer than 500 employees account for only about 10 percent of U.S. and Japanese exports, the figure is closer to 30 percent for Germany.

Two factors help explain the success of Germany's small-firm sector in the export market: Germany's export infrastructure and the export orientation of small German firms. With regard to infrastructure, Germany's export network is perhaps second to none. German embassies, banks, trade associations, and chambers of commerce in dozens of countries serve as foreign eyes and ears for small businesses. They systematically funnel details of export opportunities to small German firms via newsletters, databases, and trade associations. Once an opportunity has been identified, trade associations, export trading companies, and banks all offer small firms extensive assistance with translation services and the documentation required to export. For example, industry associations provide standard contracts in many languages and translation and legal assistance with foreign contracts at no charge to members. They also allow German firms to use their foreign offices and secretarial services free when negotiating deals. For financing export deals, German firms can turn to a banking system that is well attuned to their needs. Specialized banks and Mittelstand departments of large banks provide export financing and arrange for credit and political-risk insurance.

This is in stark contrast to the U.S. export infrastructure; it is characterized by a lack of coordination among dozens of competing and often poorly staffed federal, state, and local agencies. Consider Benton Corporation, a Pittsburgh manufacturer of

Exporting Strategy

In addition to utilizing EMCs, a firm can reduce the risks associated with exporting if it is careful about its choice of exporting strategy. Here a few guidelines can help firms to improve their odds of success. For example, one of the most successful exporting firms in the world, the Minnesota Mining & Manufacturing Company (3M), has built its export success on three main principles—enter on a small scale to reduce risks, add additional product lines once the exporting operation starts to become successful, and hire locals to promote the firm's products (3M's export strategy is profiled in the next "Management Focus").

The probability of exporting successfully can be increased dramatically by taking a handful of simple strategic steps. First, particularly for the neophyte exporter, it helps to hire an EMC, or at least an experienced export consultant, to help with the identification of opportunities and navigate through the tangled web of paperwork and regulations so often involved in exporting. Second, it often makes sense to initially focus on one market, or a handful of markets. The idea here is to learn about what is required to succeed in those markets, before moving on to other markets. In contrast the firm that enters many different markets

navigational testing devices with revenues of about $4 million per year. Ron Ekas, Benton's international marketing manager, sought information as to how to export the firm's products and was given a list of potential distributors by the Pittsburgh office of the U.S. Department of Commerce. His subsequent quest for working capital to finance an export deal took him from Duquesne University to the Small Business Administration, from the Pennsylvania Commerce Department to the Export-Import Bank, and back again. Ekas says he "got right in the middle of a big loop. Everyone sent me to other places to look for help."

The U.S. infrastructure has suffered from poor funding. The state of Illinois, which once boasted one of the country's most successful export agencies, cut funding for its export agencies by 22 percent in 1992 because of state budget problems. Similarly government funding of the 18 federal agencies that help promote U.S. exports has not kept pace with inflation in recent years.

Perhaps more important than infrastructure in explaining Germany's success, however, is the export orientation of German firms. Unlike the United States, with its largely self-contained, continental economy, Germany sits at the center of the patchwork of countries that make up Europe. Proximity to these foreign markets fosters an awareness of export opportunities. This orientation is further strengthened by the movement of the European Union toward closer economic integration. At the same time small German firms have become adept at global niche marketing, at customizing their products to the needs of foreign customers, and at staying on the cutting edge of technology.

For example, consider Wilhelm Zuleeg, a German textile firm with annual revenues of $18 million. This firm competes profitably in an industry dominated by low-cost Asian imports and managed to increase its exports from 0 percent to 25 percent of revenues in three years. The explanation for this success can be seen in Zuleeg's technological prowess; its state-of-the-art computer-controlled factory churns out textile products with a minimum of labor input. The largely automated factory has only 85 employees—compared to several hundred in a more traditionally run enterprise.

An example of global niche marketing is provided by the Munich firm Panther, which makes computer-controlled camera operator's chairs for use in the film industry. These chairs give photographers the ability to program the chair's movement. Started in 1987, the firm had 50 percent of the European market and 10 percent of the U.S. market by 1991.

As a final example, consider G. W. Barth, a Ludwigsburg-based manufacturer of cocoa bean roasting machinery that employs just 65 people. During the 1980s Barth invested $1.8 million on complex new technology designed to boost the yields and fine-tune the temperature controls of its machinery. This small company had captured 70 percent of the global market for such machines by 1991, up from 25 percent in 1981.

Sources: W. J. Holstein and K. Kelly, "Little Companies, Big Exports," *Business Week*, April 13, 1992, pp. 70–72; W. J. Holstein, "Why Johann Can Export, but Johnny Can't," *Business Week*, November 4, 1991, pp. 64–65; G. E. Schares et al., "Think Small," *Business Week*, November 4, 1991, pp. 58–65; and R. A. Mosbacher, "Opening Export Doors for Smaller Firms," *Seattle Times*. July 24, 1991, p. A7.

at once runs the risk of spreading its limited management resources too thinly. The result of such a "shotgun approach" to exporting may be a failure to become established in any one market. Third, as with 3M, it often makes sense to enter a foreign market on a fairly small scale to reduce the costs of any subsequent failure. Most importantly, entering on a small scale gives the firm the time and opportunity to learn about the foreign country before making significant capital commitments to that market. Fourth, the exporter needs to recognize the time and managerial commitment involved in building export sales and should hire additional personnel to oversee this activity lest the existing management of the firm be stretched too thin. Fifth, in many countries it is important to devote a lot of attention to building strong and enduring relationships with local distributors and/or customers. Sixth, as 3M often does, it is important to hire local personnel to help the firm establish itself in a foreign market. After all, local people are likely to have a much greater sense of how to do business in a given country than a manager from an exporting firm that has previously never set foot in that country.

MANAGEMENT FOCUS
Exporting Strategy at 3M

The Minnesota Mining & Manufacturing Company (3M), which makes over 40,000 products including tapes, sandpaper, medical products, and the ever present Post-it Notes, is one of the world's great multinational operations. In 1994 almost half of the firm's $15 billion in revenues were generated outside of the United States. Although the bulk of these revenues came from foreign-based operations, 3M remains a major exporter with $1.5 billion of exports in 1994. Moreover 3M often uses its exports to establish an initial presence in a foreign market, only building foreign production facilities once sales volume rises to a level where local production is justified.

3M's export strategy is built around some very simple principles. One is known as "FIDO," which stands for First In (to a new market) Defeats Others. The essence of FIDO is to gain an advantage over other exporters by getting into a market first and learning about that country, and how to sell there, before others do. A second principle is "make a little, sell a little"—which is the idea of entering on a small scale with a very modest investment and pushing one basic product, such as reflective sheeting for traffic signs in the Soviet Union, or scouring pads in Hungary. Once 3M believes it has learned enough about the market to reduce the risks of failure to reasonable levels, it adds additional products.

A third principle at 3M is to hire local employees to sell the firm's products. 3M normally sets up a local sales subsidiary to handle its export activities in a country. It then staffs this subsidiary with local hires. Its reasoning is that foreign nationals are likely to have a much better idea of how to sell in their own country than American expatriates. As a result of the implementation of this principle, just 160 of 3M's 39,500 foreign employees are U.S. expatriates.

Another common practice at 3M is to formulate global strategic plans for the export—and eventual overseas production—of its products. Within the context of these plans, 3M gives local managers considerable autonomy to find the best way to sell the product within their particular country. Thus when 3M first exported its Post-it Notes in 1981 it planned to "sample the daylights' out of the product, but it also told local managers to find the best way of doing this. Local managers hired office cleaning crews to distribute samples in Britain and Germany, in Italy office products distributors were used to pass out free samples, while in Malaysia local managers employed young women to go from office to office handing out samples of the product. In typical 3M fashion, when the volume of Post-it Notes was sufficient to justify it, exports from the United States were replaced by local production. Thus by 1984 3M found it worthwhile to set up production facilities in France to produce Post-it Notes for the European market.

Sources: R. L. Rose, "Success Abroad," *The Wall Street Journal*, March 29, 1991, p. A1; and T. Eiben, "U.S. Exporters Keep on Rolling," *Fortune*, June 14, 1994, pp. 128–31.

Finally, it is important for the exporter to keep the option of local production in mind. Once exports build up to a sufficient volume to justify cost-efficient local production, the exporting firm should consider establishing production facilities in the foreign market. The advantage of such "localization" is that it helps foster good relations with the foreign country and can lead to greater market acceptance. Exporting is often not an end in itself, but merely a step on the road toward the establishment of foreign production (again, 3M provides us with an example of this philosophy).

FIGURE 15.1
Preference of the
U.S. Exporter

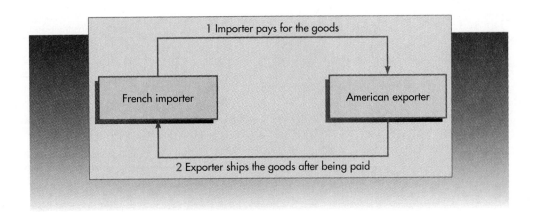

❧ EXPORT AND IMPORT FINANCING

Mechanisms for financing exports and imports have evolved over the centuries in response to a problem that can be particularly acute in international trade: the lack of trust that exists when one must put faith in a stranger. In this section we examine the financial devices that have evolved to cope with this problem in the context of international trade: the letter of credit, the draft (or bill of exchange), and the bill of lading. Then we will trace the 14 steps of a typical export–import transaction.

Lack of Trust

Firms engaged in international trade have to trust someone they may have never seen, who lives in a different country, who speaks a different language, who abides by (or does not abide by) a different legal system, and who could be very difficult to track down if he or she defaults on an obligation. Consider, for example, a U.S. firm exporting to a distributor in France. The U.S. businessman might be concerned that if he ships the products to France before he receives payment for them from the French businesswoman, she might take delivery of the products and not pay him for them. Conversely the French importer might worry that if she pays for the products before they are shipped, the U.S. firm might keep the money and never ship the products or might ship defective products. Neither party to the exchange completely trusts the other. This lack of trust is exacerbated by the distance between the two parties—in space, language, and culture—and by the problems of using an underdeveloped international legal system to enforce contractual obligations.

Due to the (quite reasonable) lack of trust between the two parties, each has preferences as to how the transaction should be configured. To make sure he is paid, the manager of the U.S. firm would prefer the French distributor to pay for the products before he ships them (see Figure 15.1). Alternatively, to ensure she receives the products, the French distributor would prefer not to pay for them until they arrive (see Figure 15.2). Thus each party has a different set of preferences. Unless there is some way of establishing trust between the parties, the transaction might never occur.

The problem is solved by using a third party trusted by both—normally a reputable bank—to act as an intermediary. What happens can be summarized as follows (see Figure 15.3). First, the French importer obtains the bank's promise to pay on her behalf, knowing the U.S. exporter will trust the bank. This promise is known as a letter of credit. Having seen the letter of credit, the U.S. exporter now ships the products to France. Title to the products is given, in due course, to the bank in the form of a document called a bill of lading. In return the U.S. exporter tells the bank to pay for the products, which the bank does. The document for requesting this payment is referred to as a draft. The bank, having paid for the products, now passes the title on to the French importer, whom the bank trusts. At that time or later, depending on their agreement, the importer reimburses the bank. In the remainder of this section we will examine how this system works in more detail.

FIGURE 15.2
Preference of the
French Importer

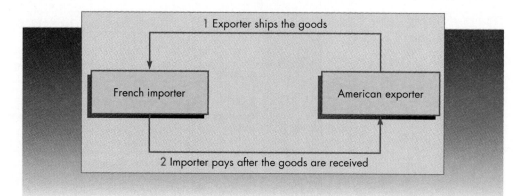

FIGURE 15.3   The Use of a Third Party

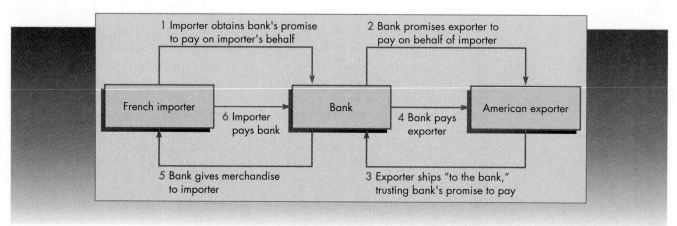

Letter of Credit

A letter of credit, abbreviated as L/C, stands at the center of international commercial transactions. Issued by a bank at the request of an importer, the letter of credit states the bank will pay a specified sum of money to a beneficiary, normally the exporter, on presentation of particular, specified documents.

Consider again the example of the U.S. exporter and the French importer. The French importer applies to her local bank, let's say the Bank of Paris, for the issuance of a letter of credit. The Bank of Paris then undertakes a credit check of the importer. If the Bank of Paris is satisfied with her creditworthiness, it will issue a letter of credit. However, the Bank of Paris might require a cash deposit or some other form of collateral from her first. In addition the Bank of Paris will charge the importer a fee for this service. Typically this amounts to between 0.5 percent and 2 percent of the value of the letter of credit, depending on the importer's creditworthiness and the size of the transaction. (As a rule the larger the transaction, the lower the percentage.)

Let us assume the Bank of Paris is satisfied with the French importer's creditworthiness and agrees to issue a letter of credit. The letter states the Bank of Paris will pay the U.S. exporter for the merchandise so long as it is shipped in accordance with certain specified instructions and conditions. At this point the letter of credit becomes a financial contract between the Bank of Paris and the U.S. exporter. The Bank of Paris then sends the letter of credit to the U.S. exporter's bank, let's say the Bank of New York. The Bank of New York tells the exporter it has received a letter of credit and he can ship the merchandise. After the exporter has shipped the merchandise, he draws a draft against the Bank of Paris in accordance with the terms of the letter of credit, attaches the required documents, and presents the draft to his own bank, the Bank of New York, for payment. The Bank of New York then forwards the letter of credit and associated documents to the Bank of Paris. If all the terms and conditions contained in the letter of credit have been complied with, the Bank of Paris will honor the draft and will send payment to the Bank of New York. When the Bank of New York receives the funds, it will pay the U.S. exporter.

As for the Bank of Paris, once it has transferred the funds to the Bank of New York, it will collect payment from the French importer. Alternatively the Bank of Paris may allow the importer some time to resell the merchandise before requiring payment. This is not unusual, particularly when the importer is a distributor and not the final consumer of the merchandise, since it helps the importer's cash flow position. The Bank of Paris will treat such an extension of the payment period as a loan to the importer and will charge an appropriate rate of interest.

The great advantage of this system is that both the French importer and the U.S. exporter are likely to trust reputable banks, even if they do not trust each other. Once the U.S. exporter has seen a letter of credit, he knows he is guaranteed payment and will ship the merchandise. Moreover an exporter may find that having a letter of credit will facilitate obtaining pre-export financing. For example, having seen the letter of credit, the Bank of New York might be willing to lend the exporter funds to process and prepare the merchandise for shipping to France. This loan may not have to be repaid until the exporter has received his payment for the merchandise. As for the French importer, the great advantage of the letter of credit arrangement is that she does not have to pay out funds for the merchandise until the documents have arrived and unless all conditions stated in the letter of credit have been satisfied. The drawback for the importer is the fee she must pay the Bank of Paris for the letter of credit. In addition, since the letter of credit is a financial liability against her, it may reduce her ability to borrow funds for other purposes.

Draft

A draft, sometimes referred to as a bill of exchange, is the instrument normally used in international commerce to effect payment. A draft is simply an order written by an exporter instructing an importer, or an importer's agent, to pay a specified amount of money at a specified time. In the example of the U.S. exporter and the French importer, the exporter writes a draft that instructs the Bank of Paris, the French importer's agent, to pay for the merchandise shipped to France. The person or business initiating the draft is known as the maker (in this case, the U.S. exporter). The party to whom the draft is presented is known as the drawee (in this case, the Bank of Paris).

International practice is to use drafts to settle trade transactions. This differs from domestic practice in which a seller usually ships merchandise on an open account, followed by a commercial invoice that specifies the amount due and the terms of payment. In domestic transactions the buyer can often obtain possession of the merchandise without signing a formal document acknowledging his or her obligation to pay. In contrast, due to the lack of trust in international transactions, payment or a formal promise to pay is required before the buyer can obtain the merchandise.

Drafts fall into two categories, sight drafts and time drafts. A sight draft is payable on presentation to the drawee. A time draft allows for a delay in payment, normally 30, 60, 90, or 120 days. It is presented to the drawee, who signifies acceptance of it by writing or stamping a notice of acceptance on its face. Once accepted the time draft becomes a promise to pay by the accepting party. When a time draft is drawn on and accepted by a bank, it is called a banker's acceptance. When it is drawn on and accepted by a business firm, it is called a trade acceptance.

Time drafts are negotiable instruments; that is, once the draft is stamped with an acceptance, the maker can sell the draft to an investor at a discount from its face value. Going back to our example, imagine the agreement between the U.S. exporter and the French importer calls for the exporter to present the Bank of Paris (through the Bank of New York) with a time draft requiring payment 120 days after presentation. The Bank of Paris stamps the time draft with an acceptance. Imagine further that the draft is for $100,000.

Figure 15.4   A Typical International Trade Transaction

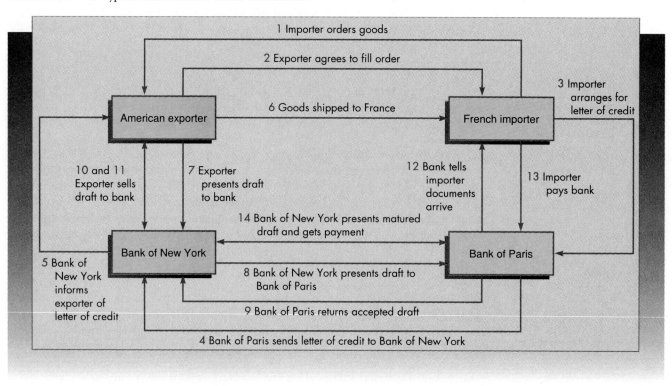

The exporter can either hold onto the accepted time draft and receive $100,000 in 120 days or he can sell it to an investor, let's say the Bank of New York, for a discount from the face value. If the prevailing discount rate is 7 percent, the exporter could receive $96,500 by selling it immediately (7 percent per annum discount rate for 120 days for $100,000 equals $3,500, and $100,000 − $3,500 = $96,500). The Bank of New York would then collect the full $100,000 from the Bank of Paris in 120 days. The exporter might choose to sell the accepted time draft immediately if he needed the funds to finance merchandise in transit and/or to cover cash flow shortfalls.

Bill of Lading

The third key document for financing international trade is the bill of lading. The bill of lading is issued to the exporter by the common carrier transporting the merchandise. It serves three purposes: it is a receipt, a contract, and a document of title. As a receipt the bill of lading indicates that the carrier has received the merchandise described on the face of the document. As a contract it specifies that the carrier is obligated to provide a transportation service in return for a certain charge. As a document of title it can be used to obtain payment or a written promise of payment before the merchandise is released to the importer. The bill of lading can also function as collateral against which funds may be advanced to the exporter by its local bank before or during shipment and before final payment by the importer.

A Typical International Trade Transaction

Now that we have reviewed all the elements of an international trade transaction, let us see how the whole process works in a typical case, sticking with the example of the U.S. exporter and the French importer. The typical transaction involves 14 distinct steps (see Figure 15.4). The steps are enumerated here.

1. The French importer places an order with the U.S. exporter and asks the American if he would be willing to ship under a letter of credit.

2. The U.S. exporter agrees to ship under a letter of credit and specifies relevant information such as prices and delivery terms.

3. The French importer applies to the Bank of Paris for a letter of credit to be issued in favor of the U.S. exporter for the merchandise the importer wishes to buy.

4. The Bank of Paris issues a letter of credit and sends it to the U.S. exporter's bank, the Bank of New York.

5. The Bank of New York advises the U.S. exporter of the opening of a letter of credit in his favor.

6. The U.S. exporter ships the goods to the French importer on a common carrier. An official of the carrier gives the exporter a bill of lading.

7. The U.S. exporter presents a 90-day time draft drawn on the Bank of Paris in accordance with its letter of credit and the bill of lading to the Bank of New York. The U.S. exporter endorses the bill of lading so title to the goods is transferred to the Bank of New York.

8. The Bank of New York sends the draft and bill of lading to the Bank of Paris. The Bank of Paris accepts the draft, taking possession of the documents and promising to pay the now-accepted draft in 90 days.

9. The Bank of Paris returns the accepted draft to the Bank of New York.

10. The Bank of New York tells the U.S. exporter that it has received the accepted bank draft, which is payable in 90 days.

11. The exporter sells the draft to the Bank of New York at a discount from its face value and receives the discounted cash value of the draft in return.

12. The Bank of Paris notifies the French importer of the arrival of the documents. She agrees to pay the Bank of Paris in 90 days. The Bank of Paris releases the documents so the importer can take possession of the shipment.

13. In 90 days the Bank of Paris receives the importer's payment, so it has funds to pay the maturing draft.

14. In 90 days the holder of the matured acceptance (in this case, the Bank of New York) presents it to the Bank of Paris for payment. The Bank of Paris pays.

❧ Export Assistance

Prospective U.S. exporters can draw on two forms of government-backed assistance to help finance their export programs. They can get financing aid from the Export-Import Bank and export credit insurance from the Foreign Credit Insurance Association.

Export-Import Bank

The Export-Import Bank, often referred to as Eximbank, is an independent agency of the U.S. government. Its mission is to provide financing aid that will facilitate exports, imports, and the exchange of commodities between the United States and other countries. Eximbank pursues this mission with various loan and loan-guarantee programs.

Eximbank guarantees repayment of medium- and long-term loans U.S. commercial banks make to foreign borrowers for purchasing U.S. exports. The Eximbank guarantee makes the commercial banks more willing to lend cash to foreign enterprises.

Eximbank also has a direct lending operation under which it lends dollars to foreign borrowers for use in purchasing U.S. exports. In some cases it grants loans that commercial banks would not if it sees a potential benefit to the United States in doing so. The foreign borrowers use the loans to pay U.S. suppliers and repay the loan to Eximbank with interest.

Export Credit Insurance

For reasons outlined earlier, exporters clearly prefer to get letters of credit from importers. However, at times an exporter who insists on a letter of credit is likely to lose an order to one who does not require a letter of credit. Thus, particularly when the importer is in a strong bargaining position and able to play competing suppliers off against each other, an exporter may have to forgo a letter of credit.[12] Obviously the lack of a letter of credit exposes the exporter to the risk that the foreign importer will default on payment. The exporter can insure against this possibility by buying export credit insurance. If the customer defaults the insurance firm will cover a major portion of the loss.

In the United States export credit insurance is provided by the Foreign Credit Insurance Association (FCIA), an association of private commercial institutions operating under the guidance of the Export-Import Bank. The FCIA provides coverage against commercial risks and political risks. Losses due to commercial risk result from the buyer's insolvency or payment default. Political losses arise from actions of governments that are beyond the control of either buyer or seller.

⚬ COUNTERTRADE

We first encountered the topic of countertrade in Chapter 9 in our discussion of currency convertibility. There we noted that many currencies are not freely convertible into other currencies, primarily due to government restrictions. The main reason a government restricts the convertibility of its currency is to preserve its foreign exchange reserves so they can service international debt commitments and purchase crucial imports. In the early 1990s more than 80 countries had major restrictions on the ability of residents and nonresidents to convert domestic currency into foreign currency, while another 30-plus countries had limited convertibility restrictions.[13]

This is obviously problematic for exporters. Nonconvertibility implies the exporter may not be able to be paid in his or her home currency, and few exporters would desire payment in a currency that is not convertible. Countertrade is increasingly the solution of choice for problems posed by nonconvertibility. Countertrade denotes a whole range of barterlike agreements; its principle is to trade goods and services for other goods and services when they cannot be traded for money. Some specific examples of countertrade are:

- Saudi Arabia agreed to buy 10 747 jets from Boeing with payment in crude oil, discounted at 10 percent below posted world oil prices.
- General Electric won a contract for a $150 million electric generator project in Romania by agreeing to market $150 million of Romanian products in areas to which Romania did not have access.
- The Venezuelan government negotiated a contract with Caterpillar Tractor under which Venezuela would trade 350,000 tons of iron ore for Caterpillar earth-moving equipment.
- Albania offered such items as spring water, tomato juice, and chrome ore in exchange for a $60 million fertilizer and methanol complex.
- Philip Morris ships cigarettes to Russia, for which it receives chemicals that can be used to make fertilizer. Philip Morris ships the chemicals to China, and in return, China ships glassware to North America for retail sale by Philip Morris.[14]

The Growth of Countertrade

In the modern era countertrade arose in the 1960s as a way for the Soviet Union and the Communist states of Eastern Europe, whose currencies were generally nonconvertible, to purchase imports. During the 1980s the technique grew in popularity among many developing nations that lacked the foreign exchange reserves required to purchase necessary imports. Today, reflecting their own shortages of

---

[12]For a review of the conditions under which a buyer has power over a supplier, see M. E. Porter, *Competitive Strategy* (New York: Free Press, 1980).

[13]*Exchange Agreements and Exchange Restrictions* (Washington, DC: International Monetary Fund, 1989).

[14]J. R. Carter and J. Gagne, "The Do's and Don'ts of International Countertrade," *Sloan Management Review*, Spring 1988, pp. 31–37.

Figure 15.5   Countertrade as Share of World Trade Value

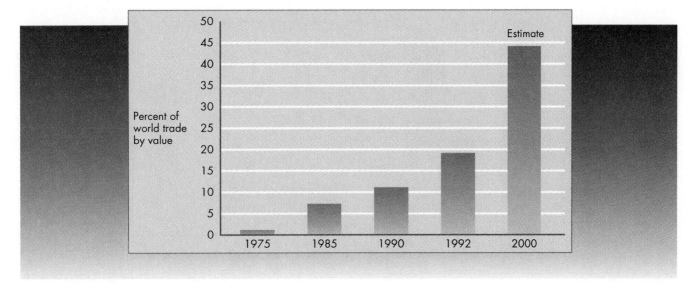

Source: G. Platt, "Worldwide Cash, Credit Crunch Lifts Countertrade," Journal of Commerce, *April 21, 1992, pp. 1A, 2A.*

foreign exchange reserves, many of the successor states to the Soviet Union and the Eastern European Communist nations are engaging in countertrade to purchase their imports. As a result, according to some estimates, more than 20 percent of world trade by value in 1992 was in the form of countertrade, up from only 2 percent in 1975 (see Figure 15.5). Moreover, because of a lack of hard currency and foreign exchange reserves in many developing nations, some commentators predict that by the year 2000, countertrade's share of world trade could rise to as much as 40 to 50 percent—although many others argue that this figure is an exaggeration. In any event current estimates by the American Countertrade Association suggest that countertrade accounts for 20 percent of all U.S. export deals by value.[15]

Given the importance of countertrade as a means of financing world trade, it is apparent that prospective exporters will have to engage in this technique from time to time to gain access to international markets. Many developing and Third World nations may have no other way of doing business.[16]

Types of Countertrade

With its roots in the simple trading of goods and services for other goods and services, countertrade has evolved into a diverse set of activities that can be categorized as five distinct types of trading arrangements: barter, counterpurchase, offset, switch trading, and compensation or buyback.[17] The popularity of each of these arrangements as indicated in a survey of multinational corporations is summarized in Figure 15.6. Many countertrade deals involve not just one arrangement, but elements of two or more. We will consider each arrangement in turn.

Barter

Barter is the direct exchange of goods and/or services between two parties without a cash transaction. Although barter is the simplest arrangement, in practice it is not common. Its problems are twofold. First, if goods are not exchanged simultaneously,

---

[15]G. Platt, "Worldwide Cash, Credit Crunch Lifts Countertrade," *Journal of Commerce,* April 21, 1992, pp. 1A, 2A; and S. Neumeier, "Why Countertrade Is Getting Hotter," *Fortune,* June 29, 1992, p. 25.

[16]J. R. Carter and J. Gagne, "The Do's and Don'ts of International Countertrade," *Sloan Management Review,* Spring 1988, pp. 31–37.

[17]For details, see Carter and Gagne, "Do's and Don'ts"; and J. F. Hennart, "Some Empirical Dimensions of Countertrade," *Journal of International Business Studies,* 1990, pp. 240–60.

FIGURE 15.6 Countertrade Practice

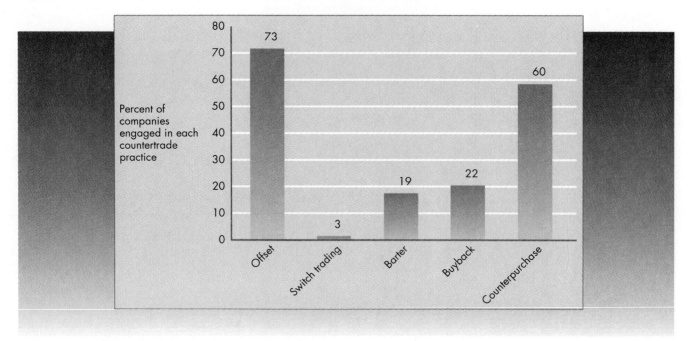

Source: J. R. Carter and J. Gagne, "The Do's and Don'ts of International Countertrade," Sloan Management Review, *Spring 1988, pp. 31–37, Table 2.*

one party ends up financing the other for a time. Second, firms engaged in barter run the risk of having to accept goods they do not want, cannot use, or have difficulty reselling at a reasonable price. For these reasons, barter is viewed as the most restrictive countertrade arrangement. It is primarily used for one-time-only deals in transactions with trading partners who are not creditworthy or trustworthy.

Counterpurchase

Counterpurchase is a reciprocal buying agreement. It occurs when a firm agrees to purchase a certain amount of materials back from a country to which a sale is made. Suppose a U.S. firm sells some products to China. China pays the U.S. firm in dollars, but in exchange, the U.S. firm agrees to spend some of its proceeds from the sale on textiles produced by China. Thus, although China must draw on its foreign exchange reserves to pay the U.S. firm, it knows it will receive some of those dollars back from the U.S. firm due to the counterpurchase agreement. In a recent counterpurchase agreement, Rolls-Royce sold jet parts to Finland. As part of the deal, Rolls-Royce agreed to use some of the proceeds from the sale to purchase Finnish-manufactured TV sets it would then sell in Great Britain.

Offset

Offset is similar to counterpurchase insofar as one party agrees to purchase goods and services with a specified percentage of the proceeds from the original sale. The difference is that this party can fulfill the obligation with any firm in the country to which the sale is being made. From an exporter's perspective this is more attractive than a straight counterpurchase agreement, since it gives the exporter greater flexibility to choose the goods it wishes to purchase.

Switch trading

Switch trading refers to the use of a specialized third-party trading house in a countertrade arrangement. When a firm enters into a counterpurchase or offset agreement with a country, it often ends up with what are called counterpurchase credits, which can be used to purchase goods from that country. Switch trading occurs when a third-party trading house buys the firm's counterpurchase credits and sells them to another firm that can make better use of them. For example, a U.S. firm concludes a counterpurchase agreement with Poland for which it receives some number of counterpurchase credits for purchasing Polish goods. The U.S. firm cannot use and does not want any Polish goods, however, so it sells the credits to a third-party trading house at a discount. The trading house finds a firm that can use the credits and sells them at a profit.

In one example of switch trading, Poland and Greece had a counterpurchase agreement that called for Poland to buy the same U.S.-dollar value of goods from Greece that it sold to Greece. However, Poland could not find enough Greek goods that it required, so it ended up with a dollar-denominated counterpurchase balance in Greece that it was unwilling to use. A switch trader bought the right to 250,000 counterpurchase dollars from Poland for $225,000 and sold them to a European sultana (grape) merchant for $235,000, who used them to purchase sultanas from Greece.

Compensation or buybacks

A buyback occurs when a firm builds a plant in a country—or supplies technology, equipment, training, or other services to the country—and agrees to take a certain percentage of the plant's output as partial payment for the contract. For example, Occidental Petroleum negotiated a deal with the former Soviet Union under which Occidental would build several ammonia plants in the Soviet Union and as partial payment receive ammonia over a 20-year period.

The Pros and Cons of Countertrade

The main attraction of countertrade is that it can give a firm a way to finance an export deal when other means are not available. Given the problems that many developing and Third World nations have in raising the foreign exchange necessary to pay for imports, countertrade may be the only option available when doing business in these countries. Moreover, even when countertrade is not the only option for structuring an export transaction, many countries prefer countertrade to cash deals. Thus if a firm is unwilling to enter into a countertrade agreement, it may lose an export opportunity to a competitor that is willing to make a countertrade agreement. Countertrade allows U.S. firms to remain competitive with large Japanese and European trading companies, which for historical reasons are the masters of countertrade.

The drawbacks of countertrade agreements are fairly substantial. Other things being equal, all firms would prefer to be paid in hard currency. Countertrade contracts may involve the exchange of unusable or poor-quality goods that the firm cannot dispose of profitably. For example, a few years ago one U.S. firm got burned when 50 percent of the television sets it received in a countertrade agreement with Hungary were defective and could not be sold. In addition, even if the goods it receives are of high quality, the firm still needs to dispose of them profitably. To do this countertrade requires the firm to invest in an in-house trading department dedicated to arranging and managing countertrade deals. This in itself can be expensive and time consuming.

Given these drawbacks, the option of countertrade is most attractive to large, diverse, multinational enterprises that can use their worldwide network of contacts to dispose of goods acquired in countertrading. The masters of countertrade are Japan's giant trading firms, the *sogo shosha*, which use their vast networks of affiliated companies to profitably dispose of goods acquired through countertrade agreements. The trading firm of Mitsui & Company, for example, has about 120 affiliated companies in almost every sector of the manufacturing and service industries. As a result, if one of Mitsui's affiliates receives goods in a countertrade agreement that it cannot itself consume, Mitsui & Company will normally be able to find another affiliate that can profitably use them. The opportunity available to firms affiliated with trading houses such as Mitsui to access a network of similarly affiliated companies greatly increases their ability to enter into countertrade agreements. As a result firms affiliated with one of Japan's sogo shosha often have a competitive advantage in countries where countertrade agreements are preferred. In addition Western firms that are large, diverse, and have a global reach (e.g., General Electric and Philip Morris) have a similar profit advantage from countertrade agreements. On the other hand, unless there is no alternative, small and medium-sized exporters should probably try to avoid countertrade deals if possible, since they lack the worldwide network of operations that may be required to profitably utilize or dispose of goods acquired through them.[18]

✺ SUMMARY OF CHAPTER

In this chapter we have examined the steps firms must take to establish themselves as exporters. The specific points we have made include the following:

1. One of the biggest impediments to exporting is ignorance of foreign market opportunities.

2. Neophyte exporters often become discouraged or frustrated with the exporting process because they encounter many problems, delays, and pitfalls.

3. The way to overcome ignorance is to gather information. In the United States a number of institutions, most important of which is the U.S. Department of Commerce, can help firms gather information and in the matchmaking process. Export management companies can also help an exporter to identify export opportunities.

4. Many of the pitfalls associated with exporting can be avoided if a company hires an experienced export management company, or export consultant, and if it adopts the appropriate export strategy.

5. Firms engaged in international trade must do business with people they cannot trust, people who may be very difficult to track down if they default on an obligation. Due to the lack of trust, each party to an international transaction has a different set of preferences regarding the configuration of the transaction.

6. The problems arising from lack of trust between exporters and importers can be solved by using a third party that is trusted by both—normally a reputable bank.

7. A letter of credit is issued by a bank at the request of an importer. It states the bank promises to pay a beneficiary, normally the exporter, on presentation of documents specified in the letter.

8. A draft is the instrument normally used in international commerce to effect payment. It is an order written by an exporter instructing an importer, or an importer's agent, to pay a specified amount of money at a specified time.

9. Drafts are either sight drafts or time drafts. Time drafts are negotiable instruments.

10. A bill of lading is issued to the exporter by the common carrier transporting the merchandise. It serves as a receipt, a contract, and a document of title.

11. U.S. exporters can draw on two types of government-backed assistance to help finance their exports: loans from the Export-Import Bank and export credit insurance from the FCIA.

12. Countertrade includes a whole range of barterlike agreements. It is primarily used when a firm exports to a country whose currency is not freely convertible and who may lack the foreign exchange reserves required to purchase the imports.

13. The main attraction of countertrade is that it gives a firm a way to finance an export deal when other means are not available. A firm that insists on being paid in hard currency may be at a competitive disadvantage vis-à-vis one that is willing to engage in countertrade.

14. The main disadvantage of countertrade is that the firm may receive unusable or poor-quality goods that cannot be disposed of profitably.

✺ CRITICAL DISCUSSION QUESTIONS

1. A firm based in Washington state wants to export a shipload of finished lumber to the Philippines. The would-be importer cannot get sufficient credit from domestic sources to pay for the shipment but insists that the finished lumber can quickly be resold in the Philippines for a profit. Outline the steps the exporter should take to effect this export to the Philippines.

2. You are the assistant to the CEO of a small textile firm that manufactures high-quality, premium priced, stylish clothing. The CEO has decided to see what the opportunities are for exporting and has asked you for advice as to the steps the company should take. What advice would you give to the CEO?

---

[18]D. J. Lecraw, "The Management of Countertrade: Factors Influencing Success," *Journal of International Business Studies*, Spring 1989, pp. 41–59.

3. An alternative to using a letter of credit is export credit insurance. What are the advantages and disadvantages of using export credit insurance rather than a letter of credit for exporting (*a*) a luxury yacht from California to Canada, and (*b*) machine tools from New York to the Ukrainian Republic?

4. How do you explain the growing popularity of countertrade? Under what scenarios might its popularity increase still further by the year 2000? Under what scenarios might its popularity decline by the year 2000?

❧ CLOSING CASE   Downey's Soup

Downey's is an Irish tavern in Philadelphia created over 20 years ago by Jack Downey. Over the years, the restaurant's fortunes have wavered, but the strength of some favorite menu items has helped it survive economic downturns. In particular, the lobster bisque soup has met with increasing popularity but Downey's efforts to market it have been very sporadic. Never did Downey imagine that his lobster bisque would someday be the cause of an international trade dispute.

Unbeknown to Downey, the Japanese have a strong penchant for lobster. When the Philadelphia office of the Japanese External Trade Organization (Jetro) asked Downey to serve his lobster bisque at a mini-trade show in 1991, he began to think about mass production of his soups. The Japanese loved the lobster bisque. They gave Downey a strong impression that the soup would sell very well in Japan. At that time Downey did not have a formal product line but that seemed to be only a minor obstacle.

After the trade show, Michael Fisher, executive vice president for the newly formed Downey Foods, Inc., was sent on an all-expenses-paid 10-day marketing trip to Japan by Jetro. (Jetro sponsors approximately 60 Americans for similar trips each year.) Although interest expressed by the food brokers and buyers he met seemed to be more polite than enthusiastic, he did get an initial order of 1,000 cases of the lobster bisque. The only condition placed by the buyer was to have the salt content reduced to comply with local Japanese tastes. Both Jetro and Fisher considered this initial order the beginning of a rich export relationship with Japan.

Fisher contracted with a food processor in Virginia, adapted the recipe for the new salt content, and shipped the soup to Japan in short order. Visions of expanded sales in Japan were quickly dashed as the cases of soup were detained at customs. Samples were sent to a government laboratory and eventually denied entry for containing polysorbate, an emulsifying and anti-foaming agent used by food processors. Though it is considered harmless in the United States, polysorbate is not on Jetro's list of 347 approved food additives.

Fisher and Downey did not give up. They reformulated the soup to improve the taste and comply with Jetro's additive regulations. They had the soup tested and certified by a Japanese-approved lab, the Oregon Department of Agriculture's Export Service Center, to meet all Japanese standards. Then, in the fall of 1993, they sent another 1,000 cases to Japan.

But the soup was denied entry again. Japanese officials said the expiration date on the Oregon tests had passed, so they retested the cans. Traces of polysorbate were found. A sample from that shipment was sent back to Oregon, and it passed. Two identical cans of soup were sent back to Japan and tested. They failed. Back in Oregon, a sample of the same shipment was tested again and no traces of polysorbate were found.

Japanese officials refused to allow the soup into Japan anyway. By this time Downey had been paid $20,000 that it could not afford to give back. "It stunned the customer," says Fisher. "But it stunned me a lot more. I was counting on dozens of reorders."

Fisher filed appeals with the U.S. Embassy in Tokyo to no avail. "It became a bureaucratic/political issue," says Fisher. "There was a face-saving problem. The Japanese had rejected the soup twice. There was no way they could reverse the decision."

The final irony came when a New York-based Japanese trader sent a few cases of Downey's regular (no reduced salt content) lobster bisque to Japan. This shipment sailed through customs without a problem.

Where was Jetro when Downey's soups were stalled in customs? Fisher thought he had everything covered. He followed the advice of Jetro, adjusted the soups to meet Japanese palates, and had them tested to meet Japanese food standards. Apparently Jetro failed to inform Fisher of the apparent need for a local partner to sell and distribute in Japan. Most food companies have trouble getting into Japan, whether large or small. Agricultural products are one of the most difficult things to get into the Japanese market.

Jetro's agricultural specialist, Tatsuya Kajishima, contradicts this claim that Japan is hostile to food imports by stating the following statistic: 30 percent of Japan's food imports come from the United States. Further, Japan is the fourth largest importer of America's soups to the tune of $6.5 million worth of soup purchased in 1993. Most of these sales came from Campbell's.

Although this venture was not particularly profitable for Downey Foods, Inc., the company has been able to redirect its research and development efforts to build its domestic product line. Through its local broker, Santucci Associates, Downey Foods attracted the attention of Liberty Richter Inc., a national distributor of gourmet and imported food items.

CASE DISCUSSION QUESTIONS

1. Did Downey Foods' export opportunity occur as a result of proactive action by Downey, or was its strategy reactive?

2. Why did Downey experience frustrations when trying to export to Japan? What actions might Downey take to improve its prospects of succeeding in the Japanese market?

3. You have been hired by Downey Foods to develop an exporting strategy for the firm. What steps do you think Downey should take to increase the volume of its exports?

Source: Case written by Mureen Kibelsted and Charles Hill from original research by Mureen Kibelsted.

CHAPTER SIXTEEN

GLOBAL MANUFACTURING AND MATERIALS MANAGEMENT

GLOBAL MANUFACTURING AND LOGISTICS AT TIMBERLAND

Timberland, a New Hampshire-based manufacturer of rugged, high-quality shoes is one of the world's fastest growing companies. From small beginnings in the late 1970s, Timberland has grown into a global business with sales of over $450 million. The company's global expansion began in 1979 when an Italian distributor walked into the then small U.S. outfit and expressed an interest in shoe #100-81, a hand-sewn moccasin with a lug sole. The Italian thought the shoe would sell well in Italy—the land of high-style Gucci shoes. He was right; Timberland quickly became a phenomenon in Italy where Timberland shoes often sold for a 60 percent premium over prices in the United States. Other countries followed, and by the mid-1990s Timberland was generating 50 percent of its sales from 50 foreign countries, including Italy, Germany, France, Britain, and Japan.

Ignored during this rapid growth phase, however, was any attempt to build a tightly managed and coordinated global manufacturing and logistics system. As a result, by the early 1990s Timberland found itself confronted with an extremely complex global manufacturing and logistics network. To take advantage of lower wage costs outside the United States, the company had established manufacturing facilities in Singapore and Spain as well as the United States. Moreover, Timberland had also found it cost efficient to source footwear and apparel from independent suppliers based in dozens of other low-wage countries in Asia, Europe, and Latin America. At the same time

Timberland's distribution network had grown to serve consumers in more than 50 countries. To complicate things further, the average shipment of footwear to retailers was for less than 12 pairs of each type of shoe, which made for an enormous volume of individual shipments to track.

By the early 1990s Timberland found that its logistics system was breaking down under the strains imposed by rapid volume growth, a globally dispersed supply and distribution chain, and a large volume of individual shipments. The company simply lacked the information systems required to coordinate and control its dispersed production and distribution network. The consequences included high costs, poor delivery, and inaccurate billing. There were no common information systems linking suppliers, Timberland, and retailers. Nor was there any attempt to consolidate shipments from different regions of the world to realize shipping economies. For example, products were shipped from six countries in Southeast Asia to the United States and Europe, as opposed to being consolidated at one location and then shipped.

In 1993 Timberland decided to reorganize its global logistics system.

The plan Timberland came up with was to streamline its logistics information pipeline first and then its cargo pipeline. The information challenge was to come up with a system that would enable Timberland to track a product from the factory to its final destination. The problem was that the various links in the supply chain, which included manufacturers, warehouses, shippers, and retailers, did not share common data links and so were not sharing any information. As Timberland's director of distribution explains it: "At every link in the chain, you can make a decision about cargo that would make it flow better, but only if you have the information about the product and the ability to communicate with that location in real time to direct the product." For example, when a product leaves the factory, Timberland can in theory direct a freight forwarder to send the product by air, or alternatively by ocean carrier, depending on the urgency of the shipment. When a shipment lands in, say, Los Angeles, it can be shipped to a distribution center or shipped directly to a customer, again depending on need. These kinds of choices, however, can be made only if Timberland has the requisite information systems. Until 1994 the company lacked such systems.

The company is currently developing the required information systems in conjunction with ACS, a freight forwarder, and The Rockport Group, a software house. To simplify its system at the level of physical distribution, and to make implementation of its information systems easier, Timberland is also moving rapidly toward consolidated regional warehousing. Timberland currently has separate warehouses in a dozen Asian countries, several in the United States, and three in

Europe. Under the new system now being developed, sources in Asia will feed into one warehouse. The company will also have single continental distribution centers in North America and Europe. By centralizing its warehousing at three locations, the company will be able to keep better track of where the product is located so it can be routed quickly and flexibly to where it is needed. The result should be a dramatic improvement in Timberland's ability to deliver products to customers exactly when they need them, as opposed to delivering products too late or too soon. Moreover, by consolidating warehousing, Timberland should be able to realize substantial cost savings from reduced warehousing costs and from shipping economies. Timberland will now have the ability to consolidate shipments from a region into one single transoceanic shipment, which should enable the company to negotiate much better shipping rates.

Sources: P. Buxbaum, "Timberland's New Spin on Global Logistics," *Distribution*, May 1994, pp. 33–36; A. E. Serwer, "Will Timberland Grow Up?" *Fortune*, May 29, 1995, p. 24; and M. Tedeschi, "Timberland Vows to Get on the Ball," *Footwear News*, May 22, 1995, p. 2.

❧ INTRODUCTION

In the opening case Timberland is described as having to deal with a number of issues that many other firms competing in today's global economy have also had to deal with. Over the years Timberland has had to decide where in the world to locate its manufacturing activities, how much manufacturing to perform in-house and how much to outsource to foreign suppliers, and how best to organize and control the resulting supply chain to minimize costs and increase its ability to serve customers in a timely and cost-effective manner. Timberland's decisions have resulted in the creation of a globally dispersed supply chain. Timberland now has to coordinate and control this complex global web of activities to deliver its product to customers who are distributed across 50 nations.

In this chapter we take a detailed look at the problems Timberland and firms like it are facing, and at the various solutions that can be adopted. More specifically we will be concerned with answering three central questions:

- Where in the world should productive activities be located?
- How much production should be performed in-house, and how much should be outsourced to foreign suppliers?
- How best to coordinate a globally dispersed supply chain?

The Timberland case points toward some of the answers to these questions. For example, the case tells us that Timberland's decision to establish foreign manufacturing establishments, and to out-source significant amounts of manufacturing to independent producers in foreign countries, was based on a consideration of relative wage costs. Manufacturing shoes is a labor-intensive activity, and a company such as Timberland can save money by manufacturing in low-wage countries. In this regard Timberland is no different from other large shoe firms, such as the athletic shoe companies Nike and Reebok, which also outsource most of their manufacturing activities to independent suppliers based in low-wage countries.[1] We also learn from the case that coordinating a globally dispersed supply chain required Timberland to develop sophisticated electronic information systems that joined the links in the chain. As we shall see later in this chapter, Timberland is again no different from many other global enterprises in this regard; many companies have found they need to develop sophisticated information systems to manage their global logistics.

To further explore these issues, in this chapter we shall examine each of the three questions posed above. We begin, however, by reviewing how the information covered in this chapter fits into the "big picture" of global strategy that we introduced in Chapter 12.

---

[1]"Nike to Make Shoes in Mexico," *The Wall Street Journal*. January 6, 1995, p. A6.

❧ STRATEGY, MANUFACTURING, AND MATERIALS MANAGEMENT

In Chapter 12 we introduced the concept of the value chain and discussed a number of value-creation activities, including production, marketing, materials management, R&D, human resources, and information systems. In this chapter we focus on two of these activities—production and materials management—and attempt to clarify how they might be performed internationally to (1) lower the costs of value creation and (2) add value by better serving customer needs. We will discuss the contributions of information technology to these activities. In the two chapters that follow we will look at other value-creation activities in this international context (marketing, R&D, and human resource management).

In Chapter 12 we defined *production* as "the activities involved in creating a product." We used the term *production* to denote both service and manufacturing activities, since one can produce a service or produce a physical product. In this chapter we focus more on manufacturing than on service activities, so we will use the term *manufacturing* rather than production. As for *materials management*, recall that we defined it as "the activity that controls the transmission of physical materials through the value chain, from procurement through production and into distribution." Materials management includes **logistics,** which refers to the procurement and physical transmission of material through the supply chain, from suppliers to customers. Manufacturing and materials management are closely linked, since a firm's ability to perform its manufacturing function efficiently depends on a continuous supply of high-quality material inputs, for which materials management is responsible.

The manufacturing and materials management functions of an international firm have a number of important strategic objectives.[2] Two important objectives that are shared by both manufacturing and materials management are to *lower costs* and to *simultaneously increase product quality* by eliminating defective products from both the supply chain and the manufacturing process.[3]

These two objectives are not independent of each other. As illustrated in Figure 16.1, the firm that improves its quality control will also reduce its costs of value creation. Improved quality control reduces costs in three ways:

1. Productivity increases, because time is not wasted manufacturing poor-quality products that cannot be sold. This saving leads to a direct reduction in unit costs.

2. Increased product quality means lower rework and scrap costs.

3. Greater product quality means lower warranty and rework costs.

The effect is to lower the costs of value creation by reducing both manufacturing and service costs.

The main management technique that companies are utilizing to boost their product quality is **total quality management** (TQM). TQM is a management philosophy that takes as its central focus the need to improve the quality of a company's products and services. The TQM concept was developed by a number of American consultants such as W. Edwards Deming, Joseph Juran, and A. V. Feigenbaum.[4] Deming has identified a number of steps that should be part of any TQM program. Deming argues that management should embrace the philosophy that mistakes, defects, and poor-quality materials are not acceptable and should be eliminated. He suggests that the quality of supervision should be improved by allowing more time

---

[2]B. C. Arntzen, G. G. Brown, T. P. Harrison, and L. L. Trafton, "Global Supply Chain Management at Digital Equipment Corporation," *Interfaces* 25 (1995), pp. 69–93.

[3]D. A. Garvin, "What Does Product Quality Really Mean," *Sloan Management Review* 26 (Fall 1984), pp. 25–44.

[4]For general background information, see: "How to Build Quality," *The Economist*, September 23 1989, pp. 91–92; A. Gabor, *The Man Who Discovered Quality* (New York: Penguin, 1990); and P. B. Crosby, *Quality is Free* (New York: Mentor, 1980).

FIGURE 16.1   The Relationship between Quality and Costs

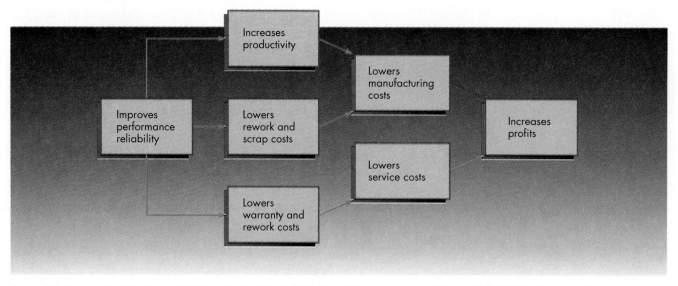

Source:Adapted from David A. Garvin, "What Does Product Quality Really Mean?" Sloan Management Review *26 (Fall 1984), Figure 1, p. 37.*

for supervisors to work with employees and by providing them with the tools they need to do the job. He recommends that management should create an environment in which employees will not fear reporting problems or recommending improvements. He believes work standards should be defined not only as numbers or quotas, but also should include some notion of quality to promote the production of defect-free output. He argues that management has the responsibility to train employees in new skills to keep pace with changes in the workplace. And he believes that achieving better quality requires the commitment of everyone in the company.

Apart from the rise of TQM, the growth of international standards has in some cases focused greater attention on the importance of product quality. In Europe, for example, the European Union requires that the quality of a firm's manufacturing processes and products be certified under a quality standard known as **ISO 9000** before the firm is allowed access to the European Union marketplace. Although the ISO 9000 certification process has proved to be somewhat bureaucratic and costly for many firms, it does focus management attention on the need to improve the quality of products and processes.[5]

In addition to the objectives of lowering costs and improving quality, two other objectives have particular importance in international businesses. First, manufacturing and materials management must be able to accommodate demands for local responsiveness. As we saw in Chapter 12, demands for local responsiveness arise from national differences in consumer tastes and preferences, infrastructure, distribution channels, and host-government demands. Demands for local responsiveness create pressures to decentralize manufacturing activities to the major national or regional markets in which the firm does business.

Second, manufacturing and materials management must be able to respond quickly to shifts in customer demand. In recent years time-based competition has grown more important.[6] In other words, when consumer demand is prone to large and unpredictable shifts, the firm that can adapt most quickly to these shifts will

---

[5]M. Saunders, "U.S. Firms Doing Business in Europe Have Options in Registering for ISO 9000 Quality Standards," *Business America,* June 14, 1993, p. 7.

[6]G. Stalk and T. M. Hout, *Competing Against Time* (New York: Free Press, 1990).

gain an advantage. As we shall see, both manufacturing and materials management play critical roles here. This issue surfaced in the opening case. Timberland's new logistics information system should enable it to respond to consumer needs in a more timely manner by ensuring that products arrive at retailers just when they are needed, and not too late or too soon (which would mean the retailer would have to bear the costs of storing the inventory until it was needed).

❧ Where to Manufacture

A key decision facing an international firm is *where to locate its manufacturing activities* to achieve the twin goals of minimizing costs and improving product quality. For the firm that considers international production to be a feasible option, a number of factors must be considered. These factors can be grouped under three broad headings: country factors, technological factors, and product factors.[7]

Country Factors

We reviewed country-specific factors in some detail earlier in the book and we will not dwell on them here. Suffice it to say that political economy, culture, and relative factor costs differ from country to country. In Chapter 4, for example, we saw that due to differences in factor costs, certain countries have a comparative advantage for producing certain products. In Chapters 2 and 3 we saw how differences in political economy and national culture influence the benefits, costs, and risks of doing business in a country. It follows that, other things being equal, a firm should locate its various manufacturing activities in those locations where the economic, political, and cultural conditions, including relative factor costs, are more conducive to the performance of those activities. In Chapter 12 we referred to the benefits derived from such a strategy as location economies. We argued that one result of the strategy is the creation of a global web of value-creation activities.

Of course other things are not equal. Other country factors that impinge on location decisions include formal and informal trade barriers (see Chapter 6) and rules and regulations regarding foreign direct investment (see Chapter 7). Thus, for example, although relative factor costs may make a country look attractive as a location for performing a manufacturing activity, regulations prohibiting foreign direct investment may eliminate this option. Similarly, a consideration of factor costs might suggest that a firm should source production of a certain component part from a particular country, but trade barriers could make this uneconomical.

Another country factor is expected future movements in its currency's exchange rate (see Chapters 9 and 10). Adverse changes in exchange rates can quickly alter a country's attractiveness as a manufacturing base. Currency appreciation can transform a low-cost location into a high-cost location. Many Japanese corporations have grappled with this problem in recent years. The relatively low value of the yen on foreign exchange markets between 1950 and 1980 helped strengthen Japan's position as a low-cost location for manufacturing. Since the early 1980s, however, the yen's appreciation against the dollar has increased the dollar cost of products exported from Japan, making Japan less attractive as a manufacturing location. In response many Japanese firms have been moving their manufacturing offshore to lower-cost locations in East Asia.

Technological Factors

The technology we are concerned with in this subsection is manufacturing technology—the technology that performs specific manufacturing activities. The type of technology a firm uses in its manufacturing can be pivotal in location decisions. For example, due to technological constraints, in some cases it is feasible to perform certain manufacturing activities in only one location and serve the world market

---

[7]M. A. Cohen and H. L. Lee, "Resource Deployment Analysis of Global Manufacturing and Distribution Networks," *Journal of Manufacturing and Operations Management* 2 (1989), pp. 81–104.

FIGURE 16.2
A Typical Unit Cost Curve

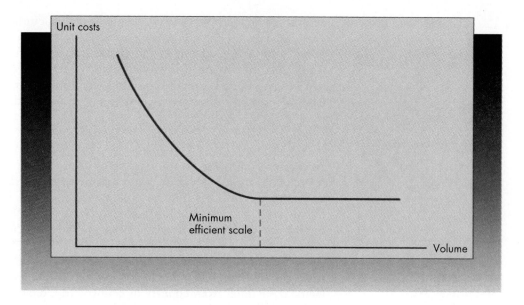

from there. In other cases the technology may make it feasible to perform an activity in multiple locations. Three characteristics of a manufacturing technology are of interest here: the level of its fixed costs, its minimum efficient scale, and its flexibility.

Fixed costs

As we noted in Chapter 12, in some cases the fixed costs of setting up a manufacturing plant are so high that a firm must serve the world market from a single location or from a very few locations. For example, it can cost as much as $1 billion to set up a plant to manufacture semiconductor chips. Given this, serving the world market from a single plant sited at a single (optimal) location makes sense.

A relatively low level of fixed costs can make it economical to perform a particular activity in several locations at once. One advantage of this is that the firm can better accommodate demands for local responsiveness. Manufacturing in multiple locations may also help the firm avoid the risks of becoming too dependent on any one location. Being too dependent on one location is particularly risky in a world of floating exchange rates.

Minimum efficient scale

The concept of economies of scale tells us that as plant output expands, unit costs decrease. The reasons for this relationship include the greater utilization of capital equipment and the productivity gains that come with greater specialization of employees within the plant.[8] In general, however, it is well known that beyond a certain level of output, few additional scale economies are available. Thus the "unit cost curve" declines with output until a certain output level is reached, at which point further increases in output realize little reduction in unit costs. The level of output at which most plant-level scale economies are exhausted is referred to as the minimum efficient scale of output. This is the scale of output a plant must operate at to realize all major plant-level scale economies (see Figure 16.2).

In the present context the implications of this concept are as follows: the larger the minimum efficient scale of a plant, the greater the argument for centralizing production in a single location or a limited number of locations. Alternatively

---

[8]For a review of the technical arguments, see D. A. Hay and D. J. Morris, *Industrial Economics: Theory and Evidence* (Oxford: Oxford University Press, 1979). See also C. W. L. Hill and G. R. Jones, *Strategic Management: An Integrated Approach* (Boston: Houghton Mifflin, 1995).

when the minimum efficient scale of production is relatively low, it may be economical to manufacture a product at several locations. As in the case of low fixed costs, the advantages are allowing the firm to better accommodate demands for local responsiveness or to hedge against currency risk by manufacturing the same product in several locations.

Flexible manufacturing (lean production)

Central to the concept of economies of scale is the idea that the best way to achieve high efficiency, and hence low unit costs, is through the mass production of a standardized output. The trade-off implicit in this idea is one between unit costs and product variety. Put simply, producing greater product variety from a factory implies shorter production runs, which in turn implies an inability to realize economies of scale. The result is that increasing product variety makes it difficult for a company to increase its manufacturing efficiency, and thus reduce its unit costs. According to this logic, the way to increase efficiency and drive down unit costs is to limit product variety and produce a standardized product in large volumes.

This view of manufacturing efficiency has been challenged by the recent rise of flexible manufacturing technologies. The term *flexible manufacturing technology*—or **lean production** as it is often called—covers a range of manufacturing technologies that are designed to (1) reduce set-up times for complex equipment, (2) increase the utilization of individual machines through better scheduling, and (3) improve quality control at all stages of the manufacturing process.[9] Flexible manufacturing technologies allow the company to produce a wider variety of end products at a unit cost that at one time could be achieved only through the mass production of a standardized output. Recent research suggests that the adoption of flexible manufacturing technologies may increase efficiency and lower unit costs relative to what can be achieved by the mass production of a standardized output.[10]

Flexible manufacturing technologies vary in their sophistication and complexity. One famous example of a flexible manufacturing technology, Toyota's production system, is relatively unsophisticated, but it has been credited with making Toyota the most efficient auto company in the global industry. Toyota's flexible manufacturing system was developed by one of the company's engineers, Ohno Taiichi. After working in Toyota for five years and visiting Ford's U.S. plants, Ohno became convinced that the mass production philosophy for making cars was flawed. He saw numerous problems with the mass production system including the following. First, long production runs created massive inventories that had to be stored in large warehouses. This was expensive, both because of the cost of warehousing and because inventories tied up capital in unproductive uses. Second, if the initial machine settings were wrong, long production runs resulted in the production of a large number of defects (i.e., waste). And third, the mass production system was unable to accommodate consumer preferences for product diversity.

Ohno looked for ways to make shorter production runs economical. He developed a number of techniques designed to reduce set-up times for production equipment (a major source of fixed costs). By using a system of levers and pulleys he reduced the time required to change dies on stamping equipment from a full day in 1950 to three minutes by 1971! This made small production runs economical, which in turn allowed Toyota to respond better to consumer demands for product diversity. Small production runs also eliminated the need to hold large inventories, thereby reducing warehousing costs. Furthermore small product runs and the lack of inventory meant

[9]See P. Nemetz and L. Fry, "Flexible Manufacturing Organizations: Implications for Strategy Formulation," *Academy of Management Review* 13 (1988) pp. 627–638; N. Greenwood, *Implementing Flexible Manufacturing Systems* (New York: Halstead Press, 1986); and J. P. Womack, D. T. Jones, and D. Roos, *The Machine That Changed the World* (New York: Rawson Associates, 1990).

[10]Womack, Jones, and Roos, *The Machine That Changed the World*.

that defective parts were produced only in small numbers and entered the assembly process immediately. This reduced waste and helped in tracing defects back to their source and fixing the problem. In sum Ohno's innovations enabled Toyota to produce a more diverse product range at a lower unit cost than was possible with conventional mass production.[11]

Flexible machine cells are another common flexible manufacturing technology. A flexible machine cell is a grouping of various types of machinery, a common materials handler, and a centralized cell controller (computer). Each cell normally contains four to six machines capable of performing a variety of operations. The typical cell is dedicated to the production of a family of parts or products. The settings on machines are computer controlled. This allows each cell to switch quickly between the production of different parts or products.

Improved capacity utilization and reductions in work in progress and waste are major efficiency benefits of flexible machine cells. Improved capacity utilization arises from the reduction in set-up times and from the computer-controlled coordination of production flow between machines (which eliminates bottlenecks). The tight coordination between machines also reduces work in progress (e.g., stockpiles of partly finished products). Reductions in waste arise from the ability of computer-controlled machinery to identify how to transform inputs into outputs while producing a minimum of unusable waste material. As a consequence of all these factors, while a freestanding machine might be in use 50 percent of the time, the same machines when grouped into a cell can be used more than 80 percent of the time and produce the same end product with half the waste. This increases efficiency and results in lower costs.

The efficiency benefits of installing flexible manufacturing technology can be dramatic. For example, following the introduction of a flexible manufacturing systems, General Electric's locomotive operations reduced the time it took to produce locomotive motor frames from 16 days to 16 hours. Similarly, after it introduced a flexible manufacturing system, Fireplace Manufacturers Inc., one of the country's largest fireplace businesses, reduced scrap left over from the manufacturing process by 60 percent, increased inventory turnover threefold, and increased labor productivity by more than 30 percent.[12]

As these examples make clear, the adoption of flexible manufacturing technologies can help improve the efficiency of a company. Moreover, not only do flexible manufacturing technologies allow companies to lower costs, but they also enable companies to customize products to the unique demands of small consumer groups—and to do so at a cost that at one time could be achieved only by mass producing a standardized output. Thus they help a company to increase its customer responsiveness. Most important for an international business, flexible manufacturing technologies can help the firm customize products for different national markets. The importance of this advantage cannot be overstated. When flexible manufacturing technologies are available, a firm can manufacture products customized to various national markets at a single factory sited at the optimal location. Moreover it can do this without absorbing a significant cost penalty. Thus the idea that manufacturing facilities must be established in each major national market in which the firm does business to provide products that satisfy the specific consumer tastes and preferences (part of the rationale for a multidomestic strategy) is becoming outdated (see Chapter 12).

---

[11]M. A. Cusumano, *The Japanese Automobile Industry* (Cambridge, MA: Harvard University Press, 1989); Taiichi Ohno, *Toyota Production System* (Cambridge, MA: Productivity Press, 1885); and Womack, Jones, and Roos, *The Machine That Changed the World*.

[12]J. D. Goldhar, and D. Lei, "The Shape of 21st Century Global Manufacturing," *Journal of Business Strategy*, March/April 1991, pp. 37–41; "Factories That Turn Nuts into Bolts" *U.S. News and World Reports*. July 14, pp. 44–45; and J. Kotkin, "The Great American Revival," *Inc.* February 1988, pp. 52–63.

Summary

Pulling all this material together, we see that a number of technological factors support the economic arguments for concentrating manufacturing facilities in a few choice locations, or even in a single location. Most important, other things being equal, when

- Fixed costs are substantial,
- The minimum efficient scale of production is high, and/or
- Flexible manufacturing technologies are available,

the arguments for concentrating production at a few choice locations are strong. This is true even when substantial differences in consumer tastes and preferences exist between national markets, since flexible manufacturing technologies allow the firm to customize products to national differences at a single facility.

Alternatively, when

- Fixed costs are low,
- The minimum efficient scale of production is low, and
- Flexible manufacturing technologies are not available,

the arguments for concentrating production at one or a few locations are not as compelling. In such cases it may make more sense to manufacture in each major market in which the firm is active if this helps the firm better respond to local demands. However, this holds only if the increased local responsiveness more than offsets the cost disadvantages of not concentrating manufacturing. With the advent of flexible manufacturing technologies, such a strategy is becoming less and less attractive. In sum, technological factors are making it feasible, and indeed necessary, for firms to concentrate their manufacturing facilities at optimal locations. Trade barriers and transportation costs are probably the major brakes on this trend.

Product Factors

Two product features affect location decisions. The first is the product's *value-to-weight* ratio because of its influence on transportation costs. Many electronic components have high value-to-weight ratios; they are expensive and they do not weigh very much. Thus even if they are shipped halfway around the world, their transportation costs account for a very small percentage of total costs. Given this, other things being equal, there is great pressure to manufacture these products in the optimal location and to serve the world market from there. The opposite holds for products with low value-to-weight ratios. Refined sugar, certain bulk chemicals, paints, and petroleum products all have low value-to-weight ratios; they are relatively inexpensive products that weigh a lot. Accordingly, when they are shipped long distances, transportation costs account for a large percentage of total costs. Thus, other things being equal, there is great pressure to manufacture these products in multiple locations close to major markets to reduce transportation costs.

The other product feature that can influence location decisions is whether the product serves **universal needs,** needs that are the same all over the world. Examples include many industrial products (e.g., industrial electronics, steel, bulk chemicals) and modern consumer products (e.g., handheld calculators and personal computers). Since there are few national differences in consumer taste and preference for such products, the need for local responsiveness is reduced. This increases the attractiveness of concentrating manufacturing at an optimal location.

Table 16.1
Location Strategy and
Manufacturing

	Favored Manufacturing Strategy	
	Concentrated	**Decentralized**
Country factors		
Differences in political economy	Substantial	Few
Differences in culture	Substantial	Few
Differences in factor costs	Substantial	Few
Trade barriers	Few	Many
Technological factors		
Fixed costs	High	Low
Minimum efficient scale	High	Low
Flexible manufacturing technology	Available	Not available
Product factors		
Value-to-weight ratio	High	Low
Serves universal needs	Yes	No

Locating Manufacturing Facilities

In sum, there are two basic strategies for locating manufacturing facilities: concentrating them in the optimal location and serving the world market from there, and decentralizing them in various regional or national locations that are close to major markets. The appropriate strategic choice is determined by the various country, technological, and product factors we have discussed in this section. They are summarized in Table 16.1. As can be seen, concentration of manufacturing makes most sense when:

1. Differences between countries in factor costs, political economy, and culture have a substantial impact on the costs of manufacturing in various countries.
2. Trade barriers are low.
3. Important exchange rates are expected to remain relatively stable.
4. The production technology has high fixed costs, a high minimum efficient scale, or a flexible manufacturing technology exists.
5. The product's value-to-weight ratio is high.
6. The product serves universal needs.

Alternatively decentralization of manufacturing is appropriate when:

1. Differences between countries in factor costs, political economy, and culture do not have a substantial impact on the costs of manufacturing in various countries.
2. Trade barriers are high.
3. Volatility in important exchange rates is expected.
4. The production technology has low fixed costs, low minimum efficient scale, and flexible manufacturing technology is not available.
5. The product's value-to-weight ratio is low.
6. The product does not serve universal needs (that is, significant differences in consumer tastes and preferences exist between nations).

In practice location decisions are seldom clear cut. For example, it is not unusual for differences in factor costs, technological factors, and product factors to point toward concentrated manufacturing while at the same time a combination of trade barriers and volatile exchange rates points toward decentralized manufacturing. This is probably the case in the world automobile industry. Although the availability of flexible manufacturing and cars' relatively high value-to-weight ratios suggest concentrated manufacturing, the combination of formal and informal trade barriers and the uncertainties of the world's current floating exchange rate regime (see Chapter 10) have inhibited firms' ability to pursue this strategy.

⚜ M AP **16.1**

The Ford Fiesta Production
Network in Europe

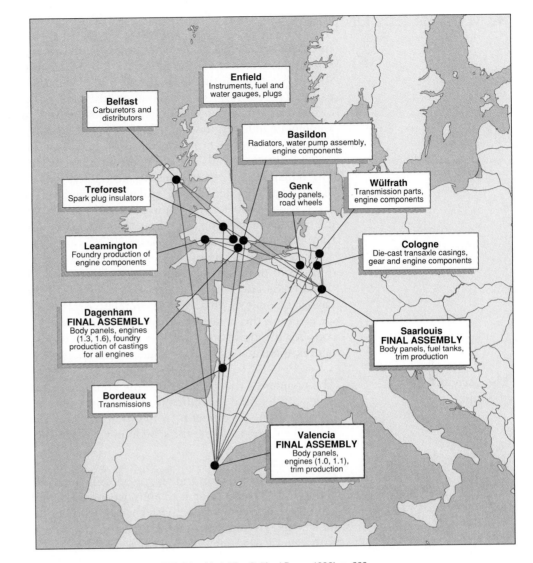

Source: Peter Dicken, Global Shift (New York: The Guilford Press, 1992), p. 300.

For these reasons, Honda is establishing "top-to-bottom" manufacturing operations in its three major markets: Japan, North America, and Western Europe. Honda is able to treat Western Europe as a single market because of the European Community's success in removing trade barriers and stabilizing exchange rates in the member-countries.

Another auto firm that treats Western Europe as a single market is Ford. Map 16.1 shows how Ford of Europe dispersed the various manufacturing activities for its Fiesta to different locations in Western Europe. (This figure shows only the geographical pattern of the network within Ford itself; independent component suppliers are not shown.) Some components are single-sourced to take advantage of economies of scale. For example, all carburetors are supplied by the Belfast plant; all transmissions are built at Bordeaux; Basildon supplies radiator assemblies; Treforest makes spark plugs. At the same time, final assembly operations are performed at three locations: Dagenham in Great Britain, Saarlouis in Germany, and Valencia in Spain. Ford reasons that it can better customize the product to local needs by doing this. Also it can make up for shortfalls of production at one location by shipping cars from one of the other locations. In any event the result is a complex network of cross-border flows of finished vehicles and components. Presumably Ford locates the various activities in particular locations because it believes these are the most favorable locations for performing those activities.

❧ MAKE-OR-BUY DECISIONS

International businesses also face **sourcing decisions,** decisions about whether they should make or buy the component parts that go into their final product. That is, should the firm vertically integrate into the manufacture of its own component parts, or should it outsource them, or buy them from independent suppliers? Make-or-buy decisions are important factors of many firms' manufacturing strategies. In the automobile industry, for example, the typical car contains more than 10,000 components, so automobile firms constantly face make-or-buy decisions. Ford of Europe, for example, produces only about 45 percent of the value of the Fiesta in its own plants. The remaining 55 percent, mainly accounted for by component parts, comes from independent suppliers. In the athletic shoe industry the make-or-buy issue has been taken to an extreme with companies such as Nike and Reebok having no involvement in manufacturing; all production has been outsourced, primarily to manufacturers based in low-wage countries.

Make-or-buy decisions pose plenty of problems for purely domestic businesses but even more problems for international businesses. These decisions in the international arena are complicated by the volatility of countries' political economies, exchange rate movements, changes in relative factor costs, and the like. In this section we examine the arguments for making components and for buying them, and we consider the trade-offs involved in these decisions. Then we discuss strategic alliances as an alternative to manufacturing component parts within the company.

The Advantages of Make

The arguments that support making component parts in-house—vertical integration—are fourfold. Specifically vertical integration may be associated with lower costs, facilitate investments in highly specialized assets, protect proprietary product technology, and facilitate the scheduling of adjacent processes.

Lower costs

It may pay a firm to continue manufacturing a product or component part in-house, as opposed to outsourcing it to an independent manufacturer, if the firm is more efficient at that production activity than any other enterprise. The Boeing Company, for example, recently undertook a very detailed review of its make-or-buy decisions with regard to commercial jet aircraft (for details see the next "Management Focus"). As part of that review process, it decided that although it would outsource the production of some component parts to other enterprises, it would keep the production of aircraft wings in-house. Part of its rationale was that Boeing has a core competence in the production of wings, and that it is more efficient at this activity than any other comparable enterprise in the world. Therefore it makes little sense for Boeing to outsource this particular activity.

Facilitating specialized investments

We first encountered the concept of specialized assets in Chapter 6 when we looked at the economic theory of vertical foreign direct investment. A variation of that concept explains why firms might want to make their own components rather than buy them.[13] The argument is that when one firm must invest in specialized assets to supply another, mutual dependency is created. In such circumstances each party fears the other will abuse the relationship by seeking more favorable terms.

Imagine Ford of Europe has developed a new high-performance, high-quality, and uniquely designed carburetor. The carburetor's increased fuel efficiency will help sell Ford cars. Ford must decide whether to make the carburetor in-house or to contract out the manufacturing to an independent supplier. Manufacturing these uniquely designed carburetors requires investments in equipment that can be used

---

[13]The material in this section is based primarily on the transaction cost literature of vertical integration; for example, O. E. Williamson, *The Economic Institutions of Capitalism* (New York: The Free Press, 1985).

only for this purpose; it cannot be used to make carburetors for any other auto firm. Thus investment in this equipment constitutes an investment in specialized assets.

Let us first examine this situation from the perspective of an independent supplier who has been asked by Ford to make this investment. The supplier might reason that once it has made the investment it will become dependent on Ford for business, since Ford is the only possible customer for the output of this equipment. The supplier perceives this as putting Ford in a strong bargaining position and worries that once the specialized investment has been made, Ford might use this fact to squeeze down prices for the carburetors. Given this risk, the supplier declines to make the investment in specialized equipment.

Now take the position of Ford. Ford might reason that if it contracts out production of these carburetors to an independent supplier, it might become too dependent on that supplier for a vital input. Since specialized equipment is required to produce the carburetors, Ford cannot easily switch its orders to other suppliers who lack that equipment. (It would face high switching costs.) Ford perceives this as increasing the bargaining power of the supplier and worries that the supplier might use its bargaining strength to demand higher prices.

Thus the mutual dependency that outsourcing would create in this case makes Ford nervous, and it scares away potential suppliers. The problem here is lack of trust. Neither party completely trusts the other to play fair. As a result Ford might reason that the only safe way to get the new carburetors is to manufacture them itself. It may be unable to persuade any independent supplier to manufacture them. Thus Ford decides to make rather than buy.

In general we can predict that when substantial investments in specialized assets are required to manufacture a component, the firm will prefer to make the component internally rather than contract it out to a supplier. A growing amount of empirical evidence supports this prediction.[14]

Proprietary product technology protection

Proprietary product technology is technology unique to a firm. If it enables the firm to produce a product containing superior features, proprietary technology can give the firm competitive advantage. Obviously the firm would not want this technology to fall into the hands of competitors. If the firm contracts out the manufacture of components containing proprietary technology, it runs the risk that those suppliers will expropriate the technology for their own use or that they will sell it to the firm's competitors. Thus, to maintain control over its technology, the firm might prefer to make such component parts in-house. An example of a firm that has made such decisions is given in the next "Management Focus," which looks at make-or-buy decisions at Boeing. While Boeing has decided to outsource a number of important components that go toward the production of an aircraft, it has explicitly decided not to outsource the manufacture of wings and cockpits, in part because it believes that doing so would give away key technology to potential competitors.

Improved scheduling

The weakest argument for vertical integration is that production cost savings result from it because it makes planning, coordination, and scheduling of adjacent processes easier.[15] This is particularly important in firms with just-in-time inventory systems (which we discuss later in the chapter). In the 1920s, for example, Ford profited from tight coordination and scheduling made possible by backward vertical integration into steel foundries, iron ore shipping, and mining. Deliveries at Ford's foundries on the Great Lakes were coordinated so well that ore was turned into engine blocks within 24 hours. This substantially reduced Ford's production costs by eliminating the need to hold excessive ore inventories.

---

[14]For a review of the evidence, see O. E. Williamson, *The Economic Institutions of Capitalism* (New York: The Free Press, 1985).
[15]A. D. Chandler, *The Visible Hand* (Cambridge, MA: Harvard University Press, 1977).

MANAGEMENT FOCUS
Make-or-Buy Decisions at the Boeing Company

The Boeing Company is the world's largest manufacturer of commercial jet aircraft with a 60 percent share of the global market. Despite its large market share, in recent years Boeing has found it tough-going competitively. The company's problems are twofold. First, Boeing faces a very aggressive competitor in Europe's Airbus Industrie. The dogfight between Boeing and Airbus for market share has enabled major airlines to play the two companies off against each other in an attempt to bargain down the price for commercial jet aircraft. Second, the world's major airlines have been through some very rough years recently, with many airlines racking up massive financial losses. As a result many now lack the financial resources required to purchase new aircraft. Instead they are holding onto their used aircraft for much longer than has typically been the case. Thus, while the typical service life of a Boeing 737 was

once reckoned to be about 15 years, many airlines are now making the aircraft last as long as 25 years. This translates into lower orders for new aircraft. In 1994 Boeing and Airbus gained orders for 150 new aircraft, down from nearly 700 orders in 1989 at the peak of the last order boom. Confronted with this new reality, Boeing has concluded that the only way it can persuade cash-starved airlines to replace their used airlines with new aircraft is if it is very aggressive with regard to pricing.

Thus Boeing has recently had to face up to the fact that its ability to raise prices for commercial jet aircraft, which was once quite strong, has now been severely limited. Falling prices might now be the norm. If prices are going to come under pressure, the only way Boeing can continue to make a profit is if it also drives down its cost structure. With this in mind, in 1993 Boeing undertook a companywide review of its make-or-buy decisions. The

For international businesses that source worldwide, scheduling problems can be exacerbated by the time and distance between the firm and its suppliers. This is true whether the firms use their own subunits as suppliers or independent suppliers. Ownership is not the issue here. As we saw in the opening case, Timberland may achieve tight scheduling with its globally dispersed parts suppliers without vertical integration. Thus, although this argument for vertical integration is often made, it is not compelling.

The Advantages of Buy

Buying component parts from independent suppliers gives the firm greater flexibility, it can help drive down the firm's cost structure, and it may help the firm to capture orders from international customers.

Strategic flexibility

The great advantage of buying component parts from independent suppliers is that the firm can maintain its flexibility, switching orders between suppliers as circumstances dictate. This is particularly important in the international context, where changes in exchange rates and trade barriers can alter the attractiveness of supply sources over time. One year Hong Kong might be the lowest-cost source for a particular component, and the next year Mexico may be.

Sourcing component parts from independent suppliers can also be advantageous when the optimal location for manufacturing a product is beset by political risks. Under such circumstances foreign direct investment to establish a component

objective was to identify activities that could be outsourced to subcontractors, both in the United States and abroad, to drive down production costs.

When making these decision, Boeing applied a number of criteria. First, Boeing looked at the *basic economics* of the outsourcing decision. The central issue here was whether an activity could be performed more cost-effectively by an outside manufacturer or by Boeing. Second, Boeing considered the *strategic risk* associated with outsourcing an activity. Boeing decided it would not outsource any activity that it deemed to be part of its long-term competitive advantage. For example, the company decided not to outsource the production of wings, because it believed that doing so might give away valuable technology to potential competitors. Third, Boeing looked at the *operational risk* associated with outsourcing an activity. The basic

objective here was to make sure Boeing did not become too dependent on a single outside supplier for critical components. Boeing's philosophy is to hedge operational risk by purchasing from two or more suppliers. Finally, Boeing considered whether it made sense to outsource certain activities to a supplier in a given country to help secure orders for commercial jet aircraft from that country. This practice is known as *offsetting,* and it is common not only in this industry, but also in many other industries. For example, Boeing has decided to outsource the production of certain components to China. This decision was influenced by the fact that current forecasts suggest the Chinese will purchase over $100 billion worth of commercial jets over the next 20 years. Boeing's hope is that pushing some subcontracting work China's way will help gain a larger share of this market than its global competitor, Airbus.

One of the first decisions to come out of this process was a decision to outsource the production of insulation blankets for 737 and 757 aircraft to suppliers in Mexico. Insulation blankets are wrapped around the inside of the fuselage of an aircraft to keep the interior warm at high altitudes. Boeing has traditionally made these blankets in-house, but it found it could save $50 million per year by outsourcing production to a Mexican supplier. In total Boeing reckons that outsourcing will cut its cost structure by $600 million per year between 1994 and 1997. By the time the outsourcing is complete, the amount of an aircraft that Boeing builds will have been reduced from 52 percent to 48 percent.

Sources: Interviews by Charles Hill of Bob Dryden, executive vice president for the Boeing Commercial Aerospace Group, and Larry Clarkson, vice president of strategic planning at Boeing. See also C. W. L. Hill, "The Boeing Corporation," in C. W. L. Hill and G. R. Jones, *Strategic Management: An Integrated Approach* (Boston: Houghton Mifflin, 1995).

manufacturing operation in that country would expose the firm to political risks. The firm can avoid many of these risks by buying from an independent supplier in that country, thereby maintaining the flexibility to switch sourcing to another country if a war, revolution, or other political change alters that country's attractiveness as a supply source.

It should be noted, however, that maintaining strategic flexibility has its downside. If a supplier perceives the firm will change suppliers in response to changes in exchange rates, trade barriers, or general political circumstances, that supplier might not be willing to make specialized investments in plant and equipment that would ultimately benefit the firm.

Lower costs

Although vertical integration is often undertaken to lower costs, it may have the opposite effect and raise costs. When this is the case, outsourcing may be associated with lowering the firm's cost structure. How then might vertical integration raise a firm's costs? One potential source of higher costs arises because vertical integration into the manufacture of component parts increases an organization's scope, and the resulting increase in organizational complexity can raise a firm's cost structure. There are three reasons for this.

First, the greater the number of subunits in an organization, the greater are the problems of coordinating and controlling those units. Coordinating and controlling subunits requires top management to effectively process large amounts of information about subunit activities. The greater the number of subunits, the more information top management must process and the harder it is for them to do this well. Theoretically when the firm becomes involved in too many activities, headquarters management will be unable to effectively control all of them, and the resulting inefficiencies will more than offset any advantages derived from vertical integration.[16] This problem can be particularly serious in an international business, where the problem of controlling subunits is exacerbated by distance and differences in time, language, and culture.

Second, the firm that vertically integrates into component part manufacture may find that because its internal suppliers have a captive customer in the firm, they will lack an incentive to reduce costs. The fact that they do not have to compete for orders with other suppliers may result in high operating costs. The managers of the supply operation may be tempted to pass on any cost increases to other parts of the firm in the form of higher transfer prices, rather than looking for ways to reduce those costs.

Third, vertically integrated firms have to determine appropriate prices for goods transferred to subunits within the firm. This is a challenge in any firm, but it is even more complex in international businesses. Different tax regimes, exchange rate movements, and headquarter's ignorance about local conditions all increase the complexity of transfer pricing decisions in the international business. This complexity enhances internal suppliers' ability to manipulate transfer prices to their advantage, passing cost increases downstream rather than looking for ways to reduce costs.

The firm that buys its components from independent suppliers can avoid all these problems and the associated costs. The firm that sources from independent suppliers has fewer subunits to control. The incentive problems that occur with internal suppliers do not arise when independent suppliers are used. Independent suppliers know they must continue to be efficient if they are to win business from the firm. Moreover, since independent suppliers' prices are set by market forces, the transfer pricing problem does not exist. In sum the bureaucratic inefficiencies and resulting costs that can arise when firms vertically integrate backward and manufacture their own components are avoided by buying component parts from independent suppliers.

Offsets

Another reason for outsourcing some manufacturing to independent suppliers based in other countries is that it may help the firm capture more orders from that country. As noted in the "Management Focus" on Boeing, the practice of offsets is common in the commercial aerospace industry. For example, before Air India places a large order with Boeing, the Indian government might request Boeing to push some subcontracting work the way of Indian manufacturers. This kind of quid pro quo is not unusual in international business, and it affects far more than just the aerospace industry. In another example, representatives of the U.S. government have repeatedly urged Japanese automobile companies to purchase more component parts from U.S. suppliers to partially *offset* the large volume of automobile exports from Japan to the United States.

Trade-offs

It is clear that trade-offs are involved in make-or-buy decisions. The benefits of manufacturing components in-house seem to be greatest when highly specialized assets are involved, when vertical integration is necessary for protecting proprietary technology, or when the firm is simply more efficient than external suppliers at performing a particular activity.

---

[16]For a review of these arguments, see C. W. L. Hill and R. E. Hoskisson, "Strategy and Structure in the Multiproduct Firm," *Academy of Management Review* 12 (1987), pp. 331–41.

When these conditions are not present, the risk of strategic inflexibility and organizational problems suggest it may be better to contract out component part manufacturing to independent suppliers. Since issues of strategic flexibility and organizational control loom even larger for international businesses than purely domestic ones, it follows that an international business should be particularly wary of vertical integration into component part manufacture. In addition we should not forget that some outsourcing in the form of *offsets* may help a firm gain larger orders in the future.

Strategic Alliances with Suppliers

Several international businesses have tried to reap some of the benefits of vertical integration without the associated organizational problems by entering into strategic alliances with key suppliers. For example, in recent years we have seen an alliance between Kodak and Canon, under which Canon builds photocopiers for sale by Kodak; an alliance between Apple and Sony, under which Sony builds laptop computers for Apple; and an alliance between IBM and Epson, under which Epson provides key component parts for IBM's PROPRINTER. By these alliances, Kodak, Apple, and IBM have committed themselves to long-term relationships with these suppliers, encouraging the suppliers to undertake specialized investments. Strategic alliances are a way to build trust between the firm and its suppliers. Trust is built when a firm makes a credible commitment to continue purchasing from a supplier on reasonable terms. For example, the firm may invest money in a supplier, perhaps by taking a minority shareholding, to signal its intention to build a productive, mutually beneficial long-term relationship.

This kind of arrangement between the firm and its parts suppliers was pioneered in Japan by large auto companies such as Toyota. Many of the Japanese automakers have cooperative relationships with their suppliers that go back for decades. In these relationships the auto companies and their suppliers collaborate on ways to increase value added by, for example, implementing just-in-time inventory systems or cooperating in the design of component parts to improve quality and reduce assembly costs. These relationships have been formalized when the auto firms acquired minority shareholdings in many of their key suppliers to symbolize their desire for long-term cooperative relationships with them. At the same time, the relationship between the firm and each key supplier remains market mediated and terminable if the supplier fails to perform up to standard.

By pursuing such a strategy, the Japanese automakers have captured many benefits of vertical integration, particularly those arising from investments in specialized assets, without suffering the organizational problems that come with formal vertical integration. The parts suppliers also benefit from these relationships, since they grow with the firm they supply and they share in its success. As a result of these strategies, Toyota manufactures only 27 percent of its component parts in-house, compared to 48 percent at Ford and 68 percent at GM. Of these three firms, Toyota appears to spend the least on component parts, suggesting it has captured many of the benefits that induced Ford and GM to vertically integrate while avoiding organizational inefficiencies. For example, in 1985 U.S. manufacturers spent an average of $3,350 on parts, materials, and services for small cars, whereas the average Japanese company spent $2,750, a cost saving of $600 that was achieved mainly through more efficient vendor relations.[17]

In general the trends toward just-in-time systems (JIT), computer-aided design (CAD), and computer-aided manufacturing (CAM) seem to have increased pressures for firms to establish long-term relationships with their suppliers. JIT, CAD, and CAM systems all rely on close links between firms and their suppliers supported by substantial specialized investment in equipment and information systems hardware. To get a supplier to agree to adopt such systems, a firm must make some kind of credible commitment to an enduring relationship with the supplier. In other words it must build trust with the supplier. It can do this within the framework of a strategic alliance.

---

[17]C. W. L. Hill, "Cooperation, Opportunism, and the Invisible Hand," *Academy of Management Review* 15 (1990, pp. 500–13).

MANAGEMENT FOCUS
Materials Management at Bose

Bose Corporation manufactures some of the world's best high-fidelity speakers. The Massachusetts corporation annually generates about $300 million in revenues. Its worldwide esteem is evidenced by the fact that Bose speakers are best-sellers in Japan, the world leader in consumer electronics. Bose's core competence is its electronic engineering skills, but the company attributes much of its business success to tightly coordinated materials management.

Bose purchases most of its electronic and nonelectronic components from independent suppliers scattered around North America, the Far East, and Europe. Roughly 50 percent of its purchases are from foreign suppliers, the majority of them in the Far East. Bose attempts to coordinate this globally dispersed supply chain so material holding and transportation costs are minimized. This requires component parts to arrive at Bose's Massachusetts assembly plant just in time to enter the production process. But Bose must remain responsive to customer demands, which requires the company to respond quickly to an increase in customer demand for certain speakers. If it does not, it can lose a big order to competitors. Since Bose does not want to hold extensive inventories at its Massachusetts plant, this need for responsiveness requires Bose's globally dispersed supply chain to respond rapidly to increased demand for component parts.

Responsibility for coordinating the supply chain to meet both objectives—minimizing transportation and inventory holding costs and yet responding quickly to customer demands—falls on Bose's materials

One final word. Alliances are not all good. Like formal vertical integration, a firm that enters into long-term alliances may limit its strategic flexibility by the commitments it makes to its alliance partners. Moreover, as we saw in Chapter 14 when we considered alliances between competitors, a firm that allies itself with another firm risks giving away key technological know-how to a potential competitor.

❧ COORDINATING A GLOBAL MANUFACTURING SYSTEM

We have been discussing aspects of manufacturing strategy. Now it is time to turn our attention to the topic of materials management. **Materials management,** which encompasses *logistics*, embraces the activities necessary to get materials to a manufacturing facility, through the manufacturing process, and out through a distribution system to the end user.[18] The twin objectives of materials management are to achieve this at the lowest possible cost and in a way that best serves customer needs, thereby lowering the costs of value creation and helping the firm establish a competitive advantage through superior customer service.

The potential for reducing costs through more efficient materials management is enormous. For the typical manufacturing enterprise, material costs account for between 50 and 70 percent of revenues depending on the industry. Even a small reduction in these costs can have a substantial impact on firm profitability. According to one estimate, for a firm with revenues of $1 million, a return on investment rate of 5

---

[18]See R. Narasimhan and J. R. Carter, "Organization, Communication and Coordination of International Sourcing," *International Marketing Review* 7 (1990), pp. 6–20; and B. C. Arntzen, G. G. Brown, T. P. Harrison, and L. L. Trafton, "Global Supply Chain Management at Digital Equipment Corporation," *Interfaces* 25 (1995), pp. 69–93.

management function. This function achieves coordination by means of a sophisticated logistics operation. Most of Bose's imports from the Far East come via ships to the West Coast and then across North America to its Massachusetts plant via train. Most of the company's exports also move by ocean freight, but Bose does not hesitate to use air freight when goods are needed in a hurry. To control this supply chain, Bose has a long-standing relationship with W. N. Procter, a Boston-based freight forwarder and customs broker. Procter handles customs clearance and shipping from suppliers to Bose. Procter provides Bose up-to-the-minute electronic data interchange (EDI) capabilities, which gives it the ability to track parts as they move through its global supply chain. Whenever a shipment leaves a sup-

plier, it is entered in this "ProcterLink" system. Bose is then able to fine-tune its production scheduling so supplies enter the production process just-in-time. ProcterLink is more than a simple tracking system, however. The EDI system also allows Bose to run simulations that allow its logistics managers to examine a variety of factors, such as the effect of duties on the cost of goods sold.

Procter provides several other services to Bose, such as selecting overseas agents who can help move goods out of the Far East. Procter's well-established network of overseas contacts is especially useful when shipments must be expedited through foreign customs. Procter is electronically linked to the U.S. customs system, which allows it to clear freight electronically as much as five days before a ship arrives at a U.S. port or hours be-

fore an international air freight shipment arrives. This can get goods to Bose's manufacturing plant several days sooner.

Just how well this system can work was demonstrated recently when a Japanese customer doubled its order for Bose speakers. Bose needed to gear up its manufacturing immediately, but many of the essential components were far from Massachusetts. Using ProcterLink, Bose located the needed parts in its supply chain, pulled them out of the normal delivery chain, and airfreighted them to the manufacturing line to satisfy the accelerated schedule. As a result Bose was able to fill the doubled order for its Japanese customer.

Sources: P. Bradley, "Global Sourcing Takes Split-Second Timing," *Purchasing*, July 20, 1989, pp. 52–58; and S. Greenblat, "Continuous Improvement in Supply Chain Management," *Chief Executive US* 86 (June 1993), pp. 40–44.

---

percent, and materials costs that are 50 percent of sales revenues, a $15,000 increase in total profits could be achieved either by increasing sales revenues 30 percent or by reducing materials costs by 3 percent.[19] In a saturated market it would be much easier to reduce materials costs by 3 percent than to increase sales revenues by 30 percent.

The materials management task is a major undertaking in a firm with a globally dispersed manufacturing system and global markets. Consider the example of Bose Corporation, which is presented in the above "Management Focus." Bose purchases component parts from suppliers scattered over North America, Europe, and the Far East. It assembles its high-fidelity speakers in Massachusetts and ships them to customers the world over. Bose's materials management function must coordinate the flow of component parts so they arrive at the assembly plant just in time to enter the production system. Then it must oversee the timely distribution of finished speakers to customers around the globe. These tasks are complicated by the vast distances involved and by the fact that component parts and finished products are shipped across national borders, where they must pass customs. Moreover, as explained in the "Management Focus," from time to time Bose must interrupt the normal supply chain to accelerate the delivery of key components to respond to sudden upsurges in demand for Bose's products.

In the remainder of this section we will see how firms such as Bose can manage materials efficiently. First, we will look at the just-in-time inventory system's role in influencing the performance of the materials management function. Then we will discuss the role of organization and information technology in facilitating an efficient materials management function.

---

[19]H. F. Busch, "Integrated Materials Management," *IJPD & MM* 18 (1990), pp. 28–39.

The Power of Just-in-Time

Pioneered by Japanese firms during the 1950s and 60s, just-in-time inventory systems now play a major role in most manufacturing firms. The basic philosophy behind just-in-time (JIT) systems is to economize on inventory holding costs by having materials arrive at a manufacturing plant just in time to enter the production process, and not before. The major cost saving comes from speeding up inventory turnover; this reduces inventory holding costs, such as warehousing and storage costs. For example, Ford's switch to JIT systems in the early 1980s reportedly brought the firm a huge onetime savings of $3 billion. Minimal inventory now turns over nine times a year at Ford instead of the former six, which reduced carrying costs by a third almost immediately.

In addition to the cost benefits, JIT systems can also help firms improve product quality. Under a JIT system, parts enter the manufacturing process immediately; they are not warehoused. This allows defective inputs to be spotted right away. The problem can then be traced to the supply source and fixed before more defective parts are produced. Under a more traditional system, warehousing parts for months before they are used allows a large number of defective parts to be produced by a supplier before a problem is recognized.

The drawback of a JIT system is that it leaves a firm without a buffer stock of inventory. Although buffer stocks are expensive to store, they can help tide a firm over during shortages brought about by disruption among suppliers (such as a labor dispute in a key supplier). Buffer stocks can also help a firm respond quickly to increases in demand. However, there are ways around these limitations. To reduce the risks associated with depending on one supplier for an important input, some firms source these inputs from several suppliers. As for responding quickly to increases in consumer demand, the experience of Bose Corporation shows that it is possible to do this while maintaining a JIT system—even if it involves shipping component parts by air express rather than overland or by ship (see "Management Focus").

The Role of Organization

As the number and dispersion of domestic and foreign markets and sources grow, the number and complexity of organizational linkages increase correspondingly. In a full-fledged multinational enterprise, the challenge of managing the costs associated with purchases, currency exchange, inbound and outbound transportation, production, inventory, communication, expediting, tariffs and duties, and overall administration is massive. This is due to the number and complexity of organizational linkages that need to be managed. Figure 16.3 shows the linkages that might exist for a firm that sources, manufactures, and sells internationally. Each linkage represents a flow of materials, capital, information, decisions, and people. Given the complexity, the question is, How best can the firm be organized to achieve tight coordination of the various stages of the value-creation process?

A major requirement seems to be to legitimize materials management by separating it out as a function and giving it equal weight, in organizational terms, with other, more traditional functions such as manufacturing, marketing, and R&D. According to materials management specialists, the idea behind establishing a separate materials management function is that purchasing, production, and distribution are not separate activities but three aspects of one basic task: controlling the flow of materials and products from sources of supply through manufacturing and distribution into the hands of customers.

Despite the apparent cost and quality control advantages of having a separate materials management function, not all firms actually operate with such a function.[20] Those that do not include many firms in which purchasing costs, inventories, and customer service levels are important, interdependent aspects of establishing competitive advantage. Such firms typically operate with a traditional organizational

---

[20]J. G. Miller and P. Gilmour, "Materials Managers: Who Needs Them?" *Harvard Business Review*, July–August 1979, pp. 57–67.

FIGURE 16.3   Potential Materials Management Linkages

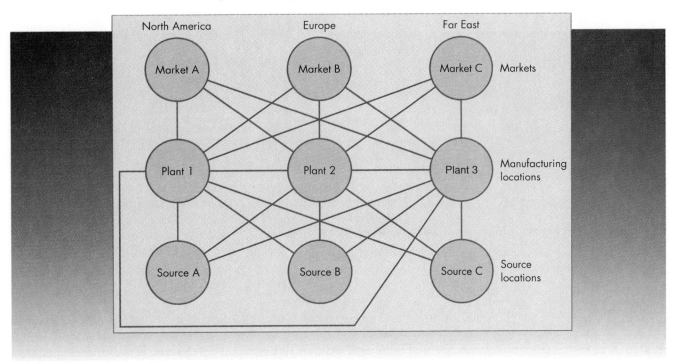

FIGURE 16.4A   Traditional Organizational Structure

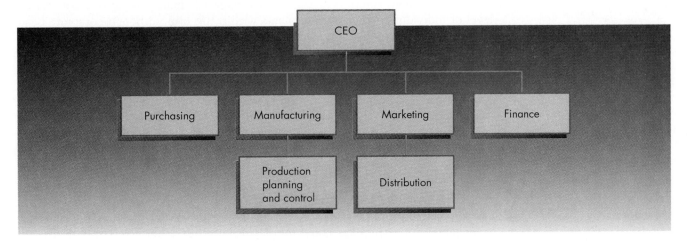

structure similar to the one in Figure 16.4A. In such an organization, purchasing, production planning and control, and distribution are not integrated. Indeed, planning and control are part of the manufacturing function, whereas distribution is part of the marketing function. Such companies will be unable to establish materials management as a major strength and consequently may face higher costs. Figure 16.4B shows the structure of a typical organization in which materials management is a separate function. Note that purchasing, planning and control, and distribution are integrated within the materials management function. Such an arrangement allows the firm to transform materials management into an important strength.

Having established the legitimacy of materials management, the next question is, How best can its influence be structured in a multinational enterprise? In practice

FIGURE 16.4B   Organization Structure with Materials Management as Separate Function

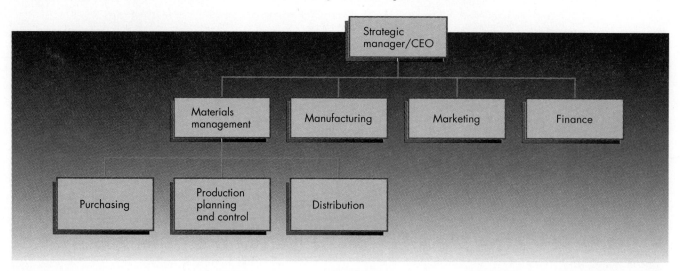

authority is either centralized or decentralized.[21] Under a centralized solution most materials management decisions are made at the corporate level, which can ensure efficiency and adherence to overall corporate objectives. This is the case at Bose Corporation, for example. In large, complex organizations with many manufacturing plants, however, a centralized materials management function may soon become overloaded and unable to perform its task effectively. In such cases a decentralized solution is needed.

A decentralized solution delegates most materials management decisions to the level of individual manufacturing plants within the firm, although corporate headquarters retains responsibility for overseeing the function. The great advantage of decentralizing is that it allows plant-level materials management groups to develop the knowledge and skills needed for interacting with foreign suppliers that are important to their particular plant. This can lead to better decision making. The disadvantage is that a lack of coordination between plants can result in less than optimal global sourcing. It can also lead to duplication of materials management efforts across plants. These disadvantages can be attenuated, however, if the firm has information systems that enable headquarters to facilitate coordination of the various plant-level materials management groups.

The Role of Information Technology

As we saw in the "Management Focus" on Bose Corporation and the opening case on Timberland, information systems play a crucial role in modern materials management. By tracking component parts as they make their way across the globe toward an assembly plant, information systems enable a firm to optimize its production scheduling according to when components are expected to arrive. By locating component parts in the supply chain precisely, good information systems allow the firm to accelerate production when needed by pulling key components out of the regular supply chain and having them air expressed to the manufacturing plant.

Firms are increasingly using electronic data interchange (EDI) to help coordinate the flow of materials into manufacturing, through manufacturing, and out to customers. At a minimum EDI systems require computer linkages between a firm,

---

[21]Narasimhan and Carter, "Organization, Communication and Coordination of International Sourcing."

its suppliers, and its shippers. Sometimes customers also are integrated into the system. These electronic linkages are then used to place orders with suppliers, to register parts leaving a supplier, to track them as they travel toward a manufacturing plant, and to register their arrival. Suppliers typically use an EDI link to send invoices to the purchasing firm. One consequence of an EDI system is that suppliers, shippers, and the purchasing firm are able to communicate with each other in "real time" (with no time delay), which vastly increases the flexibility and responsiveness of the whole supply system. The second consequence is that much of the paperwork between suppliers, shippers, and the purchasing firm is eliminated. Furthermore good EDI systems can help a firm decentralize materials management decisions to the plant level. It does this by giving corporate-level managers the information they need for coordinating and controlling decentralized materials management groups.

❧ SUMMARY OF CHAPTER

This chapter has explained how efficient manufacturing and materials management functions can help improve an international business's competitive position by lowering the costs of value-creation and by performing value creation activities in such ways that customer service is enhanced and value added maximized. We looked closely at three issues central to international manufacturing and materials management: where to manufacture, what to make and what to buy, and how to coordinate a globally dispersed manufacturing and supply system. The following points were made in the chapter:

1. The choice of an optimal manufacturing location must consider country factors, technological factors, and product factors.

2. Country factors include the influence of factor costs, political economy, and national culture on manufacturing costs.

3. Technological factors include the fixed costs of setting up manufacturing facilities, the minimum efficient scale of production, and the availability of flexible manufacturing technologies.

4. Product factors include the value-to-weight ratio of the product and whether the product serves universal needs.

5. Location strategies either concentrate or decentralize manufacturing. The choice should be made in light of country, technological, and product factors. All location decisions involve trade-offs.

6. A key issue in many international businesses is determining which component parts should be manufactured in-house and which should be outsourced to independent suppliers.

7. The advantages of making components in-house are that it facilitates investments in specialized assets and helps the firm protect its proprietary technology. It may improve scheduling between adjacent stages in the value chain also. In-house production also makes sense if the firm is an efficient low-cost producer of a technology.

8. The advantages of buying components from independent suppliers are that it facilitates strategic flexibility and helps the firm avoid the organizational problems associated with extensive vertical integration. Outsourcing might also be employed as part of an "offset" policy, which is designed to win more orders for the firm from a country by pushing some subcontracting work to that country.

9. Several firms have tried to attain the benefits of vertical integration and avoid its associated organizational problems by entering into long-term strategic alliances with key suppliers.

10. Although alliances with suppliers can give a firm the benefits of vertical integration without dispensing with the benefits of a market relationship, alliances have drawbacks. The firm that enters into a strategic alliance may find its strategic flexibility limited by commitments to alliance partners.

11. Materials management encompasses all the activities that move materials to a manufacturing facility, through the manufacturing process, and out through a distribution system to the end user. The materials management function is complicated in an international business by distance, time, exchange rates, custom barriers, and other things.

12. Just-in-time systems generate major cost savings from reduced warehousing and inventory holding costs. In addition JIT systems help the firm spot defective parts and remove them from the manufacturing process, thereby improving product quality.

13. For a firm to establish a good materials management function, it needs to legitimize materials management within the organization. It can do this by giving materials management equal footing with other functions in the firm.

14. Information technology, particularly electronic data interchange, plays a major role in materials management. EDI facilitates the tracking of inputs, allows the firm to optimize its production schedule, allows the firm and its suppliers to communicate in real time, and eliminates the flow of paperwork between a firm and its suppliers.

❦ CRITICAL DISCUSSION QUESTIONS

1. An electronics firm is considering how best to supply the world market for microprocessors used in consumer and industrial electronic products. A manufacturing plant costs approximately $500 million to construct and requires a highly skilled work force. The total value of the world market for this product over the next 10 years is estimated to be $10 to $15 billion. The tariffs prevailing in this industry are currently low. What kind of manufacturing strategy do you think the firm should adopt—concentrated or decentralized? What kind of location(s) should the firm favor for its plant(s)?

2. A chemical firm is considering how best to supply the world market for sulfuric acid. A manufacturing plant costs approximately $20 million to construct and requires a moderately skilled work force. The total value of the world market for this product over the next 10 years is estimated to be $20 to $30 billion. The tariffs prevailing in this industry are moderate. Should the firm favor concentrated manufacturing or decentralized manufacturing? What kind of location(s) should the firm seek for its plant(s)?

3. A firm must decide whether to make a component part in-house or to contract it out to an independent supplier. Manufacturing the part requires a nonrecoverable investment in specialized assets. The most efficient suppliers are located in countries with currencies that many foreign exchange analysts expect to appreciate substantially over the next decade. What are the pros and cons of (a) manufacturing the component in-house and (b) outsourcing manufacture to an independent supplier? Which option would you recommend? Why?

4. Explain how an efficient materials management function can help an international business compete more effectively in the global marketplace.

❦ CLOSING CASE   The Development of a Global Supply Chain at Digital Equipment

Digital Equipment Corporation (DEC), one of the world's largest computer companies, made its name in the 1970s and early 1980s by pioneering the global market for midrange computers (between mainframes and desktop computers). Like IBM, the company was highly vertically integrated, making almost every major component that went into a DEC computer. This vertical integration strategy was driven by DEC's desire to keep its proprietary computer technology in-house. This in-house supply chain included 33 plants in 13 countries, with service, repair, and distribution supplied by 30 facilities around the globe. By 1991 DEC served more than one quarter of a million customer sites, with over half of its $14 billion revenues coming from 81 countries outside the United States. By this time DEC was also a company in deep financial trouble. From having been one of the most profitable companies in America during much of the 1970s and 1980s, DEC found itself looking at a $3 billion loss for 1991.

DEC's problem was that the computer market had moved rapidly away from it. Demand for midrange computers was slumping as customers switched to companywide networks of computer workstations and personal computers linked by central computer servers. Moreover the new computer industry of the 1990s was based on an open standards philosophy, in which computer companies such as Compaq and Dell Computer purchased component parts "off the shelf" from independent manufacturers and assembled and marketed the final product. The key feature of the new open standards environment was that unlike the closed standards environment once championed by DEC and IBM, technical standards were published, allowing any company to build a product that matched the standard—whether that be a component part or a complete computer. In this new world DEC's mas-

sive vertical integration, once viewed as a way of keeping proprietary technology in-house, was now seen as a high-cost albatross around the company's neck. DEC realized it needed to move to an open standards model, and it needed to get into the personal computer, workstation, and computer networking business if it was to have any hope of stemming its huge losses.

The announcement of this strategic shift by DEC CEO Robert Palmer in 1991 was followed by a top-to-bottom review of DEC's global manufacturing and logistics network. DEC's systems had been designed to consolidate and deliver a moderate number of complex orders for large computer systems. Now it needed to reengineer its systems to deliver a huge number of desktop personal computers and workstations rapidly and reliably. DEC also needed to drive down its cost structure and recognized that this would involve substantial outsourcing of activities that had historically been performed in-house.

As part of this review process, DEC closely looked at its global manufacturing supply chain. The study recommended an 18-month plan to restructure its manufacturing and logistics capabilities. The objectives were to reduce costs, reduce assets, and improve customer services. The number of plants was to be reduced from 33 to 12, partly due to the consolidation of certain activities in fewer plants and partly due to much greater outsourcing of component manufacturing to independent suppliers. Moreover, following an evaluation of relative labor costs, tax rates, export and import duties, and currency risk, some manufacturing was moved to new locations. For example, a semiconductor facility in Germany was closed while production was transferred to Queensferry in Scotland, primarily because labor costs were significantly lower at the Queensferry site.

The plan also called for three major customer regions—Pacific Rim, Americas, and Europe—to be served by plants within their own regions. Each region was set up as a relatively self-contained entity. These changes allowed the company to streamline its global logistics network. There were now far fewer points to ship between, which drove down shipping costs, and the volume of shipping between regions was reduced significantly by the policy that each region become a self-contained entity.

By the spring of 1994 some of the early results were becoming apparent. DEC's annual manufacturing costs had fallen by $167 million and were expected to fall by another $160 million by mid-1995. Similarly annual logistics costs had been reduced by $200 million relative to their 1991 level. By the time the plan is fully implemented, annual manufacturing costs should have fallen by $500 million and annual logistics costs by $300 million, and DEC will have reduced its asset base—largely due to plant closures—by over $400 million.

CASE DISCUSSION QUESTIONS

1. What change occurred in DEC's operating environment during the 1980s that transformed its high level of vertical integration from a source of competitive strength into a source of high costs?

2. Why does it make sense for DEC to outsource more activities in the computer industry of the 1990s?

3. How was DEC able to reduce its annual logistics costs? What was the main source of cost saving?

Source: B. C. Arntzen, G. G. Brown, T. P. Harrison, and L. L. Trafton, "Global Supply Chain Management at Digital Equipment Corporation," Interfaces 25 (1995), pp. 69–93.

CHAPTER SEVENTEEN

GLOBAL MARKETING AND R&D

MTV AND THE GLOBALIZATION OF TEEN CULTURE

In a world where there are still major differences between the tastes, preferences, and purchasing habits of consumers in different countries, no one group is more homogenous in its tastes and preferences than those in their teens and early 20s. Whether they live in Los Angeles or London, Tokyo or Prague, Rio de Janeiro or Sydney, young adults the world over wear Levi's and Doc Martin's, dance to the Red Hot Chili Peppers, drink Coke or Pepsi, and eat at McDonald's. Increasingly, they also watch MTV, the music channel owned by Viacom.

MTV has been singled out by many observers as a major cause of the global homogenization of teen culture and also as a major beneficiary. Both charges are probably true. Introduced in the United States in the late 1970s, MTV is now a global marketing phenomenon broadcasting in over 80 countries. By mid-1995 the channel reached an impressive 59.7 million households in the United States and Canada, but it is outside of North America that most of the recent growth has occurred. MTV Europe, which was established in 1987, is now received by over 60 million households across the continent. In Asia over 21 million households receive MTV Asia, and the number is growing exponentially. And in Central and South America, where MTV launched its service in 1994, 15 million households received the channel by mid-1995 (see Map 17.1).

MTV is keenly aware of the concerns and interest of those in their teens and early 20s, and its global program strategy reflects this. As in the United States, its international services transmit news and socially conscious programming that are of interest to their target audience the world over, such as features on global warming, the destruction of the rain forests, and AIDS. The guts of MTV, however, is its music programming. Initially MTV's music programming was dominated by U.S. and British artists, with MTV broadcasting Anglo-American music to the rest of the world. It was thanks to MTV that grunge rock became a global phenomenon, and teens from Italy to Japan came to know Seattle not as the home of Boeing or Microsoft, but as the birthplace of grunge. Increasingly, however, MTV is championing little-known artists from other parts of the world, and it has shown that it has the power to make them international stars. MTV Europe helped discover the Swedish pop group Ace of Base in 1992. Its global programming of the group's single and video, *All That She Wants*, gave them a top 10 hit in Britain, Germany, Italy, and the United States. Thanks to MTV Asia, one of the best-selling albums of 1993 in India was by Cheb Khalad singing in his native Algerian. In Japan the Swedish "gothic rock" guitarist Yngwie Malmsteen has become a huge star, in part due to promotion by MTV Japan. And for heavily anticipated new albums by big international stars, MTV stages what it calls "planetary premiers," airing a new video in 24 hours in all 80 plus countries that it covers.

This worldwide marketing reach has made MTV a premier conduit for many companies hoping to profit from the globalization of teen culture. MTV's roster of 200 major advertisers includes Levi Strauss, Procter & Gamble, Johnson & Johnson, Apple Computer, and Pepsi Cola. According to Donald Holdsworth, head of sales and marketing for Pepsi-Cola International, "MTV not only has broad global coverage, it's also targeted exactly at that segment we want to reach: teenagers." MTV President Tom Freston argues that marketing to those in their teens and early 20s through global communications media such as MTV is becoming increasingly important for many global consumer products companies. He sees music as the most global of communications medium: "You could argue that this is a business even more global than movies, because music is more pervasive than any other form of culture." Due to this pervasiveness, MTV is a natural communications conduit for advertisers trying to build a global brand. Today it is still difficult to sell the same products to 35-year-olds in different countries. They prefer traditional food and fashion. In part that's because they never bonded with international brands as teenagers. But MTV's Freston believes that due to media such as MTV this generation is different; they are becoming more homogenized in their tastes and preferences.

Sources: S. Tully, "Teens: The Most Global Market of All," *Fortune*, May 16, 1994, pp. 90–97; M. Robichaux, "Leave it to Beavis," *The Wall Street Journal*, February 8, 1995, p. A1; A. Rawthorn, "MTV Makes the Big Record Groups Dance to Its Tune," *Financial Times*, July 7, 1995, p. 17; and M. Cox, "Global Entertainment: We Are the World," *The Wall Street Journal*, March 26, 1993, p. 17.

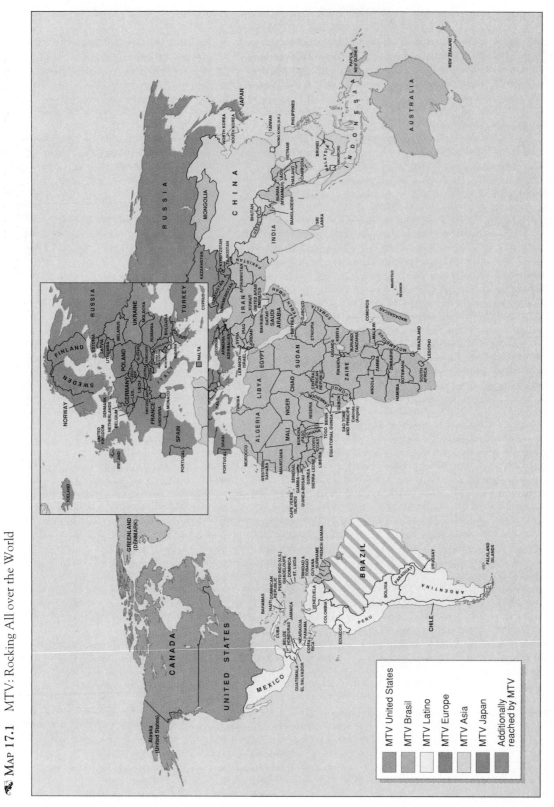

MAP 17.1 MTV: Rocking All over the World

Legend:
- MTV United States
- MTV Brasil
- MTV Latino
- MTV Europe
- MTV Asia
- MTV Japan
- Additionally reached by MTV

Source: Industry estimates

❧ Introduction

In the previous chapter we looked at the roles of global manufacturing and materials management in an international business. In this chapter we continue our focus on specific business functions by examining the roles of marketing and research and development (R&D) in an international business. Our focus is on how marketing and R&D can be performed so they will reduce the costs of value creation and add value by better serving customer needs.

In Chapter 12 we spoke of the tension existing in most international businesses between the needs to reduce costs and at the same time to respond to local conditions, which tends to raise costs. This tension has been a persistent theme in most chapters since then, and it continues to be in this chapter. A global marketing strategy, which views the world's consumers as similar in their tastes and preferences, is consistent with the mass production of a standardized output. By mass producing a standardized output, the firm can realize substantial unit cost reductions from experience curve and other scale economies. On the other hand ignoring country differences in consumer tastes and preferences can lead to failure. Thus an international business's marketing function needs to determine when product standardization is appropriate and when it is not. Similarly the firm's R&D function needs to develop globally standardized products when appropriate as well as products customized to local requirements when they are needed.

We are considering marketing and R&D within the same chapter because of their close relationship. A critical aspect of the marketing function is identifying gaps in the market so that new products can be developed to fill those gaps. Developing new products requires R&D; thus the linkage between marketing and R&D. Specifically new products should be developed with market needs in mind, and only marketing can define those needs for R&D personnel. Moreover only marketing can tell R&D whether to produce globally standardized or locally customized products. Consistent with this, academic research has long maintained that a major factor of success for new-product introductions is the closeness of the relationship between marketing and R&D. The closer the linkage, the greater the success rate.[1]

The opening case illustrates some issues we will be debating in this chapter. On the one hand, the international success of MTV is a testament to the global convergence of tastes and preferences among those in their teens and early 20s in different countries. Moreover, as the case notes, MTV may be able to further this trend through its ability to promote a global teen culture. On the other hand, it is easy to overstate the importance of such globalization. Although there is no doubt that music is, as MTV President Freston notes, the most pervasive and global form of culture, the case also alludes to the fact that important differences still exist between the tastes and preferences of teens in different nations. MTV may have helped to turn Yngwie Malmsteen into a big star in Japan, but there is no sign that this Swedish master of "gothic rock" is going to break into the U.S. market anytime soon, to say nothing of India's favorite Algerian rock star, Cheb Khaled. Even in one of the most global of industries—the music industry—and even among the most homogenous group in the world—teenagers—product standardization has its limits and national differences in tastes and preferences are still of major importance.

With this as background, in this chapter we examine the roles of marketing and R&D in international businesses. We begin by reviewing the debate on the globalization of markets. Then we discuss the four elements that constitute a firm's marketing mix: product attributes, distribution strategy, communication strategy, and pricing strategy. The marketing mix is the set of choices the firm offers to its targeted

---

[1]See R. W. Ruekert and O. C. Walker, "Interactions between Marketing and R&D Departments in Implementing Different Business-Level Strategies," *Strategic Management Journal* 8 (1987), pp. 233–48, and K. B. Clark and S .C. Wheelwright, *Managing New Product and Process Development* (New York: Free Press, 1993).

market(s). Many firms vary their marketing mix from country to country depending on differences in national culture, economic development, product standards, distribution channels, and so on. The chapter closes with a look at new-product development in an international business and at the implications of this for the organization of the firm's R&D function.

❧ The Globalization of Markets?

In a now-famous *Harvard Business Review* article, Theodore Levitt waxed lyrically about the globalization of world markets.[2] Levitt's arguments are worth quoting at some length, since they have become something of a lightning rod for the debate about the extent of globalization. According to Levitt:

> A powerful force drives the world toward a converging commonalty, and that force is technology. It has proletarianized communication, transport, and travel. The result is a new commercial reality—the emergence of global markets for standardized consumer products on a previously unimagined scale of magnitude.
>
> Gone are accustomed differences in national or regional preferences. . . . The globalization of markets is at hand. With that, the multinational commercial world nears its end, and so does the multinational corporation. The multinational corporation operates in a number of countries and adjusts its products and practices to each—at high relative costs. The global corporation operates with resolute consistency—at low relative cost—as if the entire world were a single entity; it sells the same thing in the same way everywhere.
>
> Commercially, nothing confirms this as much as the success of McDonald's from the Champs Elysees to the Ginza, of Coca-Cola in Bahrain and Pepsi-Cola in Moscow, and of rock music, Greek salad, Hollywood movies, Revlon cosmetics, Sony television, and Levi's jeans everywhere.
>
> Ancient differences in national tastes or modes of doing business disappear. The commonalty of preference leads inescapably to the standardization of products, manufacturing, and the institutions of trade and commerce.

This is eloquent and evocative writing, but is Levitt correct? The rise of global media such as MTV (see the opening case) and CNN and the ability of such media to help shape a global culture would seem to lend weight to Levitt's argument. If Levitt is correct, his argument clearly has major implications for the marketing strategies pursued by international business. However, the current consensus among academics seems to be that Levitt overstates his case.[3] Although Levitt may have a point when it comes to many basic industrial products, such as steel, bulk chemicals, and semiconductor chips, globalization seems to be the exception rather than the rule in most consumer goods markets and many industrial markets. Even a firm such as McDonald's, which Levitt holds up as the archetypal example of a consumer products firm that sells a standardized product worldwide, modifies its menu from country to country in light of local consumer preferences.[4] And as we saw in the opening case, although MTV may help to sell teen music across borders, there are still important differences between the tastes and preferences of teens in different nations, which is why the music of Algerian Cheb Khalad sells in India, but not Great Britain or the United States.

On the other hand, Levitt is probably correct to assert that modern transportation and communications technologies, such as MTV, are facilitating a convergence of the tastes and preferences of consumers in the more advanced countries

---

[2]T. Levitt, "The Globalization of Markets," *Harvard Business Review*, May–June 1983, pp. 92–102.

[3]For example, see S. P. Douglas and Y. Wind, "The Myth of Globalization," *Columbia Journal of World Business*, Winter 1987, pp. 19–29; and C. A. Bartlett and S. Ghoshal, *Managing across Borders: The Transnational Solution* (Boston: Harvard Business School Press, 1989).

[4]"Slow Food," *The Economist*, February 3, 1990, p. 64.

of the world. The popularity of sushi in Los Angeles, hamburgers in Tokyo, and grunge rock almost everywhere certainly supports this. In the long run such technological forces may lead to the evolution of a global culture. At present, however, the continuing persistence of cultural and economic differences between nations acts as a major brake on any trend toward global consumer tastes and preferences. In addition trade barriers and differences in product and technical standards also constrain a firm's ability to sell a standardized product to a global market. We discuss the sources of these differences in the next section when we look at how products must be altered from country to country. For now note that these differences are so substantial that Levitt's globally standardized markets seem a long way off in many industries.

❧ PRODUCT ATTRIBUTES

A product can be viewed as a bundle of attributes.[5] For example, the attributes that make up a car include power, design, quality, performance, fuel consumption, and comfort; the attributes of a hamburger include taste, texture, and size; a hotel's attributes include atmosphere, quality, comfort, and service. Products sell well when their attributes match consumer needs (and when their prices are appropriate). BMW cars sell well to people who have high needs for luxury, quality, and performance, precisely because BMW builds those attributes into its cars. If consumer needs were the same the world over, a firm could simply sell the same product worldwide. Actually, however, consumer needs vary from country to country depending on culture and the level of economic development. In addition a firm's ability to sell the same product worldwide is further constrained by countries' differing product standards. In this section we review each of these issues and discuss how they influence product attributes.

Cultural Differences

We discussed the topic of countries' cultural differences in Chapter 3. There we pointed out that countries differ along a whole range of dimensions, including social structure, language, religion, and education. And as alluded to in Chapter 2, these differences have important implications for marketing strategy. For example, "hamburgers" do not sell well in Islamic countries, where the consumption of ham is forbidden by Islamic law. The most important aspect of countries' cultural differences is probably the impact of tradition. Tradition is particularly important in foodstuffs and beverages. For example, reflecting differences in traditional eating habits, the Findus frozen food division of Nestlé, the Swiss food giant, markets fish cakes and fish fingers in Great Britain, but beef bourguignon and coq au vin in France, and vitèllo con funghi and braviola in Italy. In addition to its normal range of products, Coca-Cola in Japan markets "Georgia," a cold coffee in a can, and "Aquarius," a tonic drink, products that appeal to traditional Japanese tastes.

For historical and idiosyncratic reasons, a whole range of other cultural differences exist between countries. For example, scent preferences differ from one country to another. S. C. Johnson & Son, a manufacturer of waxes and polishes, encountered resistance to its lemon-scented Pledge furniture polish among older consumers in Japan. Careful market research revealed the polish smelled similar to latrine disinfectant used widely in Japan in the 1940s. Sales rose sharply after the scent was adjusted.[6]

---

[5]This approach was originally developed in K. Lancaster, "A New Approach to Demand Theory," *Journal of Political Economy* 74 (1965), pp. 132–57.

[6]V. R. Alden, "Who Says You Can't Crack Japanese Markets?" *Harvard Business Review*, January–February 1987, pp. 52–56.

At the same time, there is some evidence of the trends Levitt talked about. Tastes and preferences are becoming more cosmopolitan. Coffee is gaining ground against tea in Japan and Great Britain, while American-style frozen dinners have become popular in Europe (with some fine-tuning to local tastes). Taking advantage of these trends, Nestlé has found that it can market its instant coffee, spaghetti bolognese, and Lean Cuisine frozen dinners in essentially the same manner in both North America and Western Europe. However, there is no market for Lean Cuisine dinners in most of the rest of the world, and there may never be. The diet-conscious Asian is difficult to find. Although some cultural convergence has occurred, particularly among the advanced industrial nations of North America and Western Europe, Levitt's global culture is still a long way off.

Economic Differences

Just as important as differences in culture are differences in the level of economic development. We discussed the extent of country differences in economic development in Chapter 2. Consumer behavior is influenced by the level of economic development of a country. Firms based in highly developed countries such as the United States tend to build a lot of extra performance attributes into their products. These extra attributes are not usually demanded by consumers in less-developed nations, where the preference is for more basic products. Thus cars sold in less-developed nations typically lack many of the features found in the West, such as air-conditioning, power steering, power windows, radios, and cassette players. At the same time, for most consumer durables, product reliability may be a more important attribute in less-developed nations, where such a purchase may account for a major proportion of a consumer's income, than it is in advanced nations.

The other side of the coin is that, contrary to Levitt's suggestions, consumers in the most developed countries are often not willing to sacrifice their preferred attributes for lower prices. Consumers in the most advanced countries often shun globally standardized products that have been developed with the lowest common denominator in mind. They are willing to pay more for products that have additional features and attributes customized to their tastes and preferences. For example, demand for top-of-the-line four-wheel-drive sports utility vehicles, such as Chrysler's Jeep, Ford's Explorer, and Toyota's Land Cruiser, is almost totally restricted to the United States. This is due to a combination of factors, including the high income level of U.S. consumers, the country's vast distances, the relatively low cost of gasoline, and the culturally grounded "outdoor" theme of American life.

Product and Technical Standards

Notwithstanding the forces that are creating some convergence of consumer tastes and preferences (at least among advanced, industrialized nations), Levitt's vision of global markets may still be a long way off due to national differences in product and technological standards.

Differing product standards mandated by governments can rule out mass production and marketing of a standardized product. For example, Caterpillar, the U.S. construction equipment firm, manufactures backhoe-loaders for all of Europe in Great Britain. These tractor-type machines have a bucket in front and a digger at the back. Several special parts must be built into backhoe-loaders that will be sold in Germany: a separate brake attached to the rear axle, a special locking mechanism on the backhoe operating valve, specially positioned valves in the steering system, and a lock on the bucket for traveling. These extras account for 5 percent of the total cost of the product in Germany.[7] Interestingly enough, the European Union (EU) is trying to harmonize such divergent product standards among its member-nations. If the EU is successful, the need to customize products will be reduced, at least within the boundaries of the EU.

---

[7]A. Rawthorn, "A Bumpy Ride over Europe's Traditions," *Financial Times*, October 31, 1988, p. 5.

FIGURE 17.1
A Typical Distribution
System

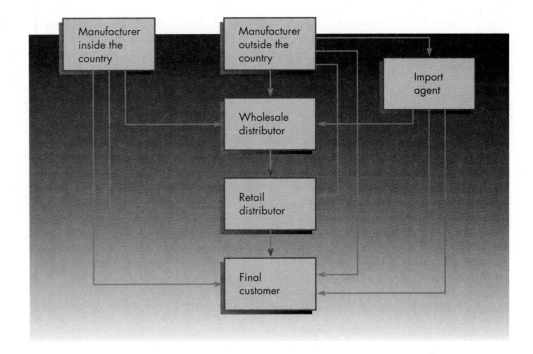

Differences in technical standards also constrain the globalization of markets. Some of these differences result from idiosyncratic decisions made at particular points in history, rather than government actions. Their long-term effects are nonetheless profound. For example, video equipment manufactured for sale in the United States will not play videotapes recorded on equipment manufactured for sale in Great Britain, Germany, and France (and vice versa). Different technical standards for frequency of television signals emerged in the 1950s that require television and video equipment to be customized to countries' prevailing standards. RCA stumbled in the 1970s when it failed to account for this in its marketing of TVs in Asia. Although several Asian countries had adopted the U.S. standard, Singapore, Hong Kong, and Malaysia had adopted the British standard. The result: people who bought RCA TVs in those countries could receive a picture but no sound![8]

❧ DISTRIBUTION STRATEGY

A critical element of a firm's marketing mix is its distribution strategy, the means it chooses for delivering the product to the consumer. The way the product is delivered is determined by the firm's entry strategy, which we discussed in Chapter 14. In this section we examine a typical distribution system, discuss how its structure varies between countries, and look at how appropriate distribution strategies vary from country to country.

A Typical Distribution System

Figure 17.1 illustrates a typical distribution system consisting of a channel that includes a wholesale distributor and a retailer. If the firm manufactures its product in the particular country, it can sell directly to the consumer, to the retailer, or to the wholesaler. The same options are available to a firm that manufactures outside the country. Alternatively this firm may decide to sell to an import agent, who then deals with the wholesale distributor, the retailer, or the consumer. The factors that determine the firm's choice of channel are considered later in this section.

---

[8]"RCA's New Vista: The Bottom Line," *Business Week*, July 4, 1987, p. 44.

Differences between Countries

The main differences between countries' distribution systems are threefold: retail concentration, channel length, and channel exclusivity.

Retail concentration

In some countries the retail system is very concentrated, whereas in other countries it is fragmented. In a concentrated system, a few retailers supply most of the market. A fragmented system is one in which there are many retailers, no one of which has a major share of the market. In Germany, for example, four retail chains control 65 percent of the market for food products. In neighboring Italy retail distribution is fragmented, with no chain controlling more than 2 percent of the market.

Many of the differences in concentration are rooted in history and tradition. In the United States the importance of the automobile and the relative youth of many urban settlements has resulted in a retail system centered around large stores or shopping malls to which people can drive. This has facilitated the concentration of the system. Japan's much greater population density, together with the large number of urban centers that grew up before the advent of the automobile, has resulted in a more fragmented retail system of many small stores that serve local neighborhoods and to which people frequently walk. In addition the Japanese legal system protects small retailers. By law small retailers can block establishment of a large retail outlet by petitioning their local government.

There is a tendency for greater retail concentration in developed countries. Three factors that contribute to this are the increases in car ownership, number of households with refrigerators and freezers, and number of two-income households that accompany development. All these factors have changed shopping habits and facilitated the growth of large retail establishments sited away from traditional shopping areas.

Channel length

Channel length refers to the number of intermediaries between the producer (or manufacturer) and the consumer. If the producer sells directly to the consumer, the channel is very short. If the producer sells through an import agent, a wholesaler, and a retailer, a long channel exists. The choice of a short or long channel is primarily a strategic decision for the producing firm. However, putting this aside for the moment (we will return to this subject later), it should be noted that some countries have longer distribution channels than others. The most important determinant of channel length is the degree to which the retail system is fragmented. Fragmented retail systems tend to promote the growth of wholesalers to serve retailers, which lengthens channels.

The reason for this is simple economics. The more fragmented the retail system, the more expensive it is for a firm to make contact with each individual retailer. Imagine, for example, a firm that sells toothpaste in a country where there are 50,000 small retailers. To sell directly to the retailers, the firm would have to build a huge sales force. This would be very expensive, particularly since each sales call would yield a very small order. Imagine, however, that there are 50 wholesalers in the country that supply retailers not only with toothpaste but also with all other personal care and household products. Since these wholesalers carry a wide range of products, they get bigger orders with each sales call. Thus it becomes worthwhile for them to deal directly with the retailers. Accordingly it makes economic sense for the firm to sell to the wholesalers and the wholesalers to deal with the retailers.

As a result of such factors, countries with fragmented retail systems also tend to have long channels of distribution. The classic example is Japan, where there are often two or three layers of wholesalers between the firm and retail outlets. In contrast, in countries such as Great Britain, Germany, and the United States where the retail system is far more concentrated, channels are much shorter. When the retail sector is very concentrated it makes sense for the firm to deal directly with retailers, cutting out wholesalers. A relatively small sales force is required to deal with a concentrated retail sector, and the orders generated from each sales call can be large. Such circumstances tend to prevail in the United States, where large food companies sell directly to supermarkets rather than going through wholesale distributors.

Channel exclusivity

An exclusive distribution channel is one that is difficult for outsiders to access. For example, it is often difficult for a new firm to get access to shelf space in U.S. supermarkets. This occurs because retailers tend to prefer to carry the products of long-established manufacturers of foodstuffs with national reputations rather than gamble on the products of unknown firms. How exclusive a distribution system is varies between countries. Japan's system is often held up as an example of a very exclusive system. In Japan relationships between manufacturers, wholesalers, and retailers often go back decades. Many of these relationships are based on the understanding that distributors will not carry the products of competing firms. In return the distributors are guaranteed an attractive markup by the manufacturer. As many U.S. and European manufacturers have learned, the close ties that result from this arrangement can make access to the Japanese market very difficult.

Choosing a Distribution Strategy

A choice of distribution strategy determines which channel the firm will use to reach potential consumers. Should the firm try to sell directly to the consumer or should it go through retailers; should it go through a wholesaler; should it use an import agent? The optimal strategy is determined by the relative costs and benefits of each alternative. In turn the relative costs and benefits of each alternative vary from country to country depending on the three factors we have just discussed: retail concentration, channel length, and channel exclusivity.

Since each intermediary in a channel adds its own markup to the products, there is generally a critical linkage between channel length, the final selling price, and the firm's profit margin. The longer a channel, the greater is the aggregate markup, and the higher the price consumers are charged for the final product. To ensure that prices do not get too high due to markups by multiple intermediaries, a firm might be forced to operate with lower profit margins. Thus, if price is an important competitive weapon, and if the firm does not want to see its profit margins squeezed, other things being equal, the firm would prefer to use a shorter channel.

However, the benefits of using a longer channel often outweigh these drawbacks. As we have seen, one benefit of using a longer channel is that it economizes on selling costs when the retail sector is very fragmented. Thus it makes sense for an international business to use longer channels in countries where the retail sector is fragmented and shorter channels in countries where the retail sector is concentrated.

Another benefit of using a longer channel is market access—the ability to enter an exclusive channel. Import agents may have long-term relationships with wholesalers, retailers, and/or important consumers and thus be better able to win orders and get access to a distribution system than the firm on its own. Similarly wholesalers may have long-standing relationships with retailers and, therefore, be better able to persuade them to carry the firm's product than the firm itself would.

Import agents are not limited to independent trading houses; any firm with a strong local reputation could serve just as well. For example, to break down channel exclusivity and gain greater access to the Japanese market, in 1991 and 1992 Apple Computer signed distribution agreements with five large Japanese firms: business equipment giant Brother Industries, stationery leader Kokuyo, Mitsubishi, Sharp, and Minolta. These firms are using their own long-established distribution relationships with consumers, retailers, and wholesalers to push Apple Macintosh computers through the Japanese distribution system. As a result

Apple's share of the Japanese market increased from less than 1 percent in 1988 to 6 percent in 1991, and it was projected to reach 13 percent by 1994.[9]

If such an arrangement is not possible, the firm might want to consider other, less traditional alternatives to gaining market access. Frustrated by channel exclusivity in Japan, some foreign manufacturers of consumer goods have attempted to sell directly to Japanese consumers using direct mail and catalogs. REI, a Northwest retailer of outdoor clothing and equipment, had trouble persuading Japanese wholesalers and retailers to carry its products. So instead it began a direct-mail campaign in Japan that is proving very successful.

✥ COMMUNICATION STRATEGY

Another critical element in the marketing mix is communicating the attributes of the product to prospective customers. A number of communications channels are available to a firm; they include direct selling, sales promotion, direct marketing, and advertising. A firm's communications strategy is partly defined by its choice of channel. Some firms rely primarily on direct selling, others on point-of-sale promotions or direct marketing, others on mass advertising; still others use several channels simultaneously to communicate their message to prospective customers. In this section we will look first at the barriers to international communication. Then we will survey the various factors that determine which communications strategy is most appropriate in a particular country. After that we will discuss global advertising.

Barriers to International Communications

International communication occurs whenever a firm uses a marketing message to sell its products in another country. The effectiveness of a firm's international communication can be jeopardized by three potentially critical variables: cultural barriers, source effects, and noise levels.

Cultural barriers

Cultural barriers can make it difficult to communicate messages across cultures. We have discussed some sources and consequences of cultural differences between nations in Chapter 3 and in the previous section of this chapter. Due to cultural differences, a message that means one thing in one country may mean something quite different in another. For example, when Procter & Gamble promoted its Camay soap in Japan in 1983 it ran into unexpected trouble. In a TV commercial a Japanese man walked into the bathroom while his wife was bathing. The woman began telling her husband all about her new beauty soap, but the husband, stroking her shoulder, hinted that suds were not on his mind. This ad had been very popular in Europe, but it flopped in Japan because it is considered very bad manners there for a man to intrude on his wife.[10] Benetton, the Italian clothing manufacturer and retailer, is another firm that has run into cultural problems with its advertising. The company launched a worldwide advertising campaign in 1989 with the theme "United Colors of Benetton," which had won awards in France. One of its ads featured a black woman breast-feeding a white baby, and another one showed a black man and a white man handcuffed together. Benetton was surprised when the ads were attacked by U.S. civil rights groups for promoting white racial domination. Benetton had to withdraw its ads and it fired its advertising agency, Eldorado of France.

The best way for a firm to overcome cultural barriers is to develop cross-cultural literacy (see Chapter 3). In addition it should employ some local input in developing its marketing message; for example, it could use a local advertising agency. Alternatively, if the firm uses direct selling rather than advertising to communicate its

---

[9]N. Gross and K. Rebello, "Apple? Japan Can't Say No," *Business Week,* June 29, 1992, pp. 32–33.

[10]"After Early Stumbles P&G Is Making Inroads Overseas," *The Wall Street Journal,* February 6, 1989, p. B1.

message, it would be well advised to develop a local sales force whenever possible. Cultural differences limit a firm's ability to use the same marketing message the world over. What works well in one country may be offensive in another.

Source effects

Source effects occur when the receiver of the message (the potential consumer in this case) evaluates the message based on the status or image of the sender. Source effects can be damaging for an international business when potential consumers in a target country have a bias against foreign firms. For example, a wave of "Japan bashing" swept the United States in 1992. Worried that U.S. consumers might view their advertisements negatively, Honda responded by creating advertisements that emphasized the U.S.-content of its cars to show how "American" the company had become. Many international businesses try to counter negative source effects by deemphasizing their foreign origins. When British Petroleum acquired Mobil Oil's extensive network of U.S. gas stations, it changed its name to BP, thereby diverting attention away from the fact that one of the biggest operators of gas stations in the United States is a British firm.

Source effects are not always negative; they can be positive. French wine, Italian clothes, and German luxury cars benefit from nearly universal positive source effects. Far from downplaying their national origins, in such cases it may pay a firm to emphasize its foreign origins. In Japan, for example, there is currently a boom in demand for high-quality foreign goods, particularly those from Europe. It has become an index of chic to carry a Gucci handbag, sport a Rolex watch, drink expensive French wine, and drive a BMW.

Noise levels

Noise tends to reduce the probability of effective communication. In this context noise refers to the amount of other messages competing for a potential consumer's attention, and this too varies across countries. In highly developed countries such as the United States, noise from firms competing for the attention of target consumers is extremely high. In contrast fewer firms vie for the attention of prospective customers in developing countries, and the noise level is lower.

Push versus Pull Strategies

The main decision with regard to communications strategy is the choice between a push strategy and a pull strategy. A push strategy emphasizes personal selling rather than mass media advertising in the promotional mix. Although very effective as a promotional tool, personal selling requires intensive use of a sales force and is thus relatively costly. A pull strategy depends more on mass media advertising to communicate the marketing message to potential consumers.

Although some firms employ only a pull strategy and others only a push strategy, still other firms combine direct selling with mass advertising to maximize communication effectiveness. Factors that determine the relative attractiveness of push and pull strategies include product type relative to consumer sophistication, channel length, and media availability.

Product type and consumer sophistication

A pull strategy is generally favored by firms in consumer goods industries that are trying to sell to a large segment of the market. For such firms mass communication has cost advantages, and direct selling is rarely used. In contrast a push strategy is favored by firms that sell industrial products or other complex products. One of the great strengths of direct selling is that it allows the firm to educate potential consumers about the features of the product. This may not be necessary in advanced nations where a complex product has been in use for some time, where the product's attributes are well understood, and where consumers are sophisticated. However, customer education may be very important when consumers have less sophistication toward the product, which can be the case in developing nations, or in more advanced nations when a complex product is being introduced.

Channel length

The longer the distribution channel, the more intermediaries there are that must be persuaded to carry the product for it to reach the consumer. This can lead to inertia in the channel, which can make entry very difficult. Moreover, using direct selling to push a product through many layers of a distribution channel can be very expensive. In such circumstances a firm may try to pull its product through the channels by using mass advertising to create consumer demand—the theory being that once demand is created, intermediaries will feel obliged to carry the product.

Whereas U.S. distribution channels are relatively short, in other countries they can be quite long. As discussed earlier, in Japan products often pass through two, three, or even four wholesalers before they reach the final retail outlet. This can make it difficult for foreign firms to break into the Japanese market. Not only must the foreigner persuade a Japanese retailer to carry her product, but she may also have to persuade every intermediary in the chain to carry the product. Mass advertising may be one way to break down channel resistance in such circumstances.

Media availability

A pull strategy relies on access to advertising media. In the United States a large number of media are available, including print media (newspapers and magazines) and electronic media (television and radio). The rise of cable television in the United States has facilitated extremely focused advertising targeted at particular segments of the market (e.g., MTV for teens and young adults, Lifetime for women, ESPN for sports enthusiasts). With a few exceptions such as Canada and Japan, this level of media sophistication is not found outside the United States. Even many advanced nations have far fewer electronic media available for advertising. In Scandinavia, for example, no commercial television or radio stations existed in 1987; all electronic media were state owned and carried no commercials. In many developing nations the situation is even more restrictive, since mass media of all types are typically more limited. A firm's ability to use a pull strategy is limited in some countries by media availability. In such circumstances a push strategy is more attractive.

Media availability is limited by law in some cases. Few countries allow advertisements for tobacco and alcohol products on television and radio, though they are usually permitted in print media. When the leading Japanese whiskey distiller, Suntory, entered the U.S. market, it had to do so without television, its preferred medium. The firm spends about $50 million annually on television advertising in Japan.

The push-pull mix

The optimal mix between push and pull strategies depends on product type and consumer sophistication, channel length, and media sophistication. Push strategies tend to be emphasized:

- For industrial products and/or complex new products.
- When distribution channels are short.
- When few print or electronic media are available.

Pull strategies tend to be emphasized:

- For consumer goods.
- When distribution channels are long.
- When sufficient print and electronic media are available to carry the marketing message.

Global Advertising

In recent years, largely inspired by the work of visionaries such as Theodore Levitt, there has been a great deal of discussion about the pros and cons of standardizing advertising worldwide. One of the most successful standardized campaigns has been Philip Morris's promotion of Marlboro cigarettes. The campaign was instituted in the 1950s, when the brand was repositioned, to assure smokers that the flavor would be unchanged by the addition of a filter. The campaign theme of "Come to where the flavor is. Come to Marlboro country" was a worldwide success. Marlboro built on this when it introduced "the Marlboro man," a rugged cowboy smoking his Marlboro while riding his horse through the great outdoors. This ad proved successful in almost every major market around the world, and it helped propel Marlboro to the top of the world market share table.

For standardized advertising

The support for global advertising is threefold. First, it has significant economic advantages. Standardized advertising lowers the costs of value creation by spreading the fixed costs of developing the advertisements over a large number of countries. For example, in the early 1980s Levi Strauss paid an advertising agency $550,000 to produce a series of TV commercials. By reusing this series in many countries, rather than developing a series for each country, the company enjoyed significant cost savings. Over a 20-year period Coca-Cola's advertising agency, McCann-Erickson, claims to have saved Coca-Cola $90 million by using certain elements of its campaign globally.

Second, there is the concern that creative talent is scarce and hence that one large effort to develop a campaign will produce better results than 40 or 50 smaller efforts.

A third justification for a standardized approach is that many brand names are global. With the substantial amount of international travel today and the considerable overlap in media across national borders, many international firms want to project a single image to avoid confusion caused by local campaigns that conflict with each other. This is particularly important in regions such as Western Europe, where travel across borders is as common as travel across state lines in the United States.

Against standardized advertising

There are two main arguments against globally standardized advertising. First, as we have seen repeatedly in this chapter and in Chapter 3, cultural differences between nations are such that a message that works in one nation can fail miserably in another. For a detailed example of this phenomena, see the case of Polaroid which is reviewed in the next "Management Focus." Due to cultural diversity, it is extremely difficult to develop a single advertising theme that is effective worldwide. Messages directed at the culture of a given country may be more effective than global messages.

Second, country differences in advertising regulations may effectively block the implementation of standardized advertising. For example, Kellogg could not use a television commercial it produced in Great Britain to promote its cornflakes in many other European countries. A reference to the iron and vitamin content of its cornflakes was not permissible in the Netherlands, where claims relating to health and medical benefits are outlawed. A child wearing a Kellogg T-shirt had to be edited out of the commercial before it could be used in France, since French law forbids the use of children in product endorsements. Furthermore, the key line, "Kellogg's makes their cornflakes the best they have ever been," was disallowed in Germany because of a prohibition against competitive claims.[11] American Express recently ran afoul of regulatory authorities in Germany when it launched a promotional scheme that had

---

[11]"Advertising in a Single Market," *The Economist*, March 24, 1990, p. 64.

MANAGEMENT FOCUS
Global Advertising at Polaroid

Polaroid introduced its SX-70 instant camera in Europe in the mid-1970s with the same marketing strategy, TV commercials, and print ads it had used in North America. Polaroid's headquarters believed the camera served a universal need—the pleasure of instant photography—and the communication strategy should thus be the same the world over. The television commercials featured testimonials of personalities well known in the United States. Few of these personalities were known in Europe, however, and managers of Polaroid's European operations pointed this out to headquarters. Unperturbed by these concerns, headquarters' management set strict guidelines to discourage deviation from the global plan. Nonetheless, the European personnel were proved correct. The testimonials by "unknown" personalities left consumers cold. The commercials never achieved much impact in raising awareness of Polaroid's instant camera. Even though the camera later became successful in Europe, local management believes the misguided introductory campaign did not help its performance.

The lesson was remembered a decade later when Polaroid's European management launched a pan-European program to reposition Polaroid's instant photography from the "party camera" platform to a serious, "utilitarian" platform. This time headquarters did not assume it had the answers. Instead it looked for inspiration in the various advertising practices of its European subsidiaries, and it found it in the strategy of one of its smallest subsidiaries in Switzerland. With considerable success, the Swiss subsidiary had promoted the functional uses of instant photography as a means of communicating with family and friends. A task force was set up to test this concept in other markets. The tests showed that the Swiss strategy was transferable and that it produced the desired impact. Thus was born Europe's "Learn to Speak Polaroid" campaign, one of the firm's most successful advertising efforts. Ultimately, non-European subsidiaries, including those in Japan and Australia, like the strategy so much that they adopted it.

What made this campaign different than the SX-70 campaign a decade earlier was the decentralized decision making. Instead of headquarters imposing on Europe an advertising campaign developed in the United States, the European subsidiaries developed their own campaign. Equally important, even after the pan-European program was adapted, European managers had the freedom to adapt the campaign to local tastes and needs. For example, where tests showed that the "Learn to Speak Polaroid" tag did not convey the intended meaning in the local language, the subsidiary was free to change it. By adopting this approach Polaroid was able to reap some of the benefits of standardized advertisements, while at the same time customizing its message to local conditions when that proved to be necessary.

Source: Kamran Kashani, "Beware the Pitfalls of Global Marketing," *Harvard Business Review*, September–October 1989, pp. 91–98.

proved very successful in other countries. The scheme advertised the offer of "bonus points" every time an American Express cardholder used his or her card. According to the advertisements, these "bonus points" could be used toward air travel with three airlines and hotel accommodations. American Express soon found itself charged with violating Germany's competition law, which prevents an offer of free gifts in connection with the sale of goods, and the firm had to withdraw the advertisements at considerable cost.[12]

---

[12]D. Waller, "Charged Up over Competition Law," *Financial Times*, June 23, 1994, p. 14.

Dealing with country differences

Given the arguments for and against the feasibility of globally standardized advertising, the question arises as to whether it might be possible to capture some of the benefits of global standardization while recognizing differences in countries' cultural and legal environments. Some firms have been experimenting with this. A firm may select some features for all of its advertising campaigns and localize other features. By doing so it may be able to save on some costs and build international brand recognition and yet customize its advertisements to different cultures.

This is what Polaroid did with the "Learn to Speak Polaroid" campaign (see the "Management Focus" for details). Pepsi-Cola used a similar approach in its 1986 advertising campaign. The company wanted to use modern music to connect its products with local markets. Pepsi hired popular U.S. singer Tina Turner and rock stars from six countries to team up in singing and performing the Pepsi-Cola theme song in a big rock concert. In the commercials the local rock stars appear with Tina Turner. Except for the footage of the local stars, all the commercials are identical. For other countries, local rock stars are spliced into the footage so they appear to be on the stage with Tina Turner. By shooting the commercials all at once, Pepsi saved on production costs. The campaign was extended to 30 countries, which relieved the local subsidiaries or bottlers of having to develop their own campaigns.[13]

❦ PRICING STRATEGY

International pricing strategy is an important component of the overall international marketing mix. In this section we look at three aspects of international pricing strategy. First, we examine the case for pursuing price discrimination, charging different prices for the same product in different countries. Second, we look at what might be called strategic pricing. Third, we briefly review some of the regulatory factors, such as government-mandated price controls and antidumping regulations, that limit a firm's ability to charge the prices it would prefer in a country.

Price Discrimination

In an international context price discrimination exists whenever consumers in different countries are charged different prices for the same product. Price discrimination involves charging whatever the market will bear; in a competitive market, prices may have to be lower than in a market where the firm has a monopoly. Price discrimination can help a company maximize its profits. It makes economic sense to charge different prices in different countries.

Two conditions are necessary for profitable price discrimination. First, the firm must be able to keep its national markets separate. If it cannot do this, individuals or businesses may undercut its attempt at price discrimination by engaging in arbitrage. Arbitrage occurs when an individual or business capitalizes on a price differential for a firm's product between two countries by purchasing the product in the country where prices are lower and reselling it in the country where prices are higher. For example, many automobile firms have long practiced price discrimination in Europe. At one point a Ford Escort cost $2,000 more in Germany than it did in Belgium. This policy broke down when car dealers bought Escorts in Belgium and drove them to Germany, where they sold them at a profit for slightly less than Ford was selling Escorts in Germany. To protect the market share of its German auto dealers, Ford had to bring its German prices into line with those being charged in Belgium. In other words Ford could not keep these markets separate.

Interestingly enough, however, Ford still practices price discrimination between Great Britain and Belgium. A Ford car can cost up to $3,000 more in Great Britain than in Belgium. In this case arbitrage has not been able to equalize the price, because right-hand-drive cars are sold in Great Britain and left-hand-drive cars in the rest of Europe. Because there is no market for left-hand-drive cars in Great Britain, Ford has been able to keep the markets separate.

---

[13]J. Lumbin, "Advertising: Tina Turner Helps Pepsi's Global Effort," *New York Times*, March 10, 1986, p. D13.

Figure 17.2
Elastic and Inelastic
Demand Curves

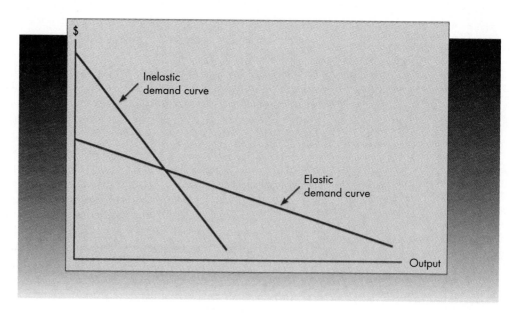

The second necessary condition for profitable price discrimination is different price elasticities of demand in different countries. The price elasticity of demand is a measure of the responsiveness of demand for a product to changes in price. Demand is said to be elastic when a small change in price produces a large change in demand; it is said to be inelastic when a large change in price produces only a small change in demand. Elastic and inelastic demand curves are illustrated in Figure 17.2. As a general rule, for reasons that will be explained shortly, a firm can charge a higher price in a country where demand is inelastic.

The determinants of demand elasticity

The elasticity of demand for a product in a given country is determined by a number of factors, of which income level and competitive conditions are perhaps the two most important. With regard to income levels, price elasticity tends to be greater (more elastic) in countries with low income levels. The reason for this is that consumers with limited incomes tend to be very price conscious; they have less to spend, so they look much more closely at price. Thus price elasticities for products such as television sets are greater in countries such as India, where a television set is still a luxury item, than in the United States, where it is considered a necessity.

With regard to competitive conditions in general the more competitors there are, the greater consumers' bargaining power will be and the more likely consumers will be to buy from the firm that charges the lowest price. Thus a large number of competitors causes high elasticity of demand. In such circumstances if a firm raises its prices above those of its competitors, consumers will switch to the competitors' products. The opposite is true when a firm faces few competitors. When competitors are limited, consumers' bargaining power is weaker and price is less important as a competitive weapon. Thus a firm may charge a higher price for its product in a country where competition is limited than in a country where competition is intense.

Profit maximizing under price discrimination

For those readers with some grasp of economic logic, we can offer a more formal presentation of the above argument. (Readers unfamiliar with basic economic terminology may want to skip this subsection.) Figure 17.3 shows the situation facing a firm that sells the same product in only two countries, Japan and the United States. The Japanese market is very competitive, so the firm faces an elastic demand curve (D_J) and marginal revenue curve (MR_J). The U.S. market is not competitive, so there the

FIGURE 17.3   Price Discrimination

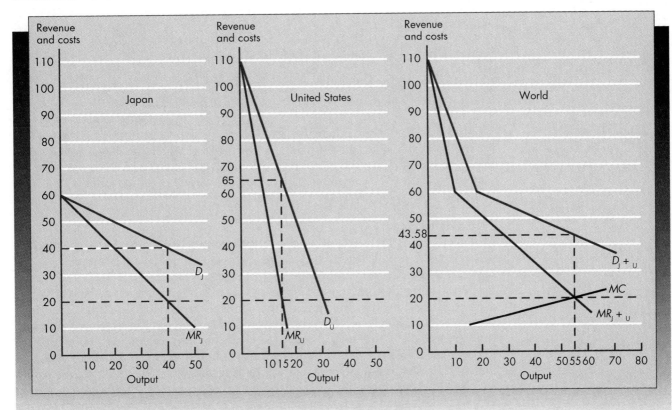

firm faces an inelastic demand curve (D_U) and marginal revenue curve (MR_U). Also shown in the figure are the firm's total demand curve (D_{J+U}), total marginal revenue curve (MR_{J+U}), and marginal cost curve (MC). The total demand curve is simply the summation of the demand facing the firm in Japan and the United States, as is the total marginal revenue curve.

To maximize profits, the firm must produce at the output where $MR = MC$. In Figure 17.3 this implies an output of 55 units. If the firm does not practice price discrimination, it will charge a price of $43.58 to sell an output of 55 units. Thus, without price discrimination the firm's total revenues are

$$\$43.58 \times 55 = \$2,396.90.$$

Now look what happens when the firm decides to engage in price discrimination. It will still produce 55 units, since that is where $MR = MC$. However, the firm must now allocate this output between the two countries to take advantage of the difference in demand elasticity. Proper allocation of output between Japan and the United States can be determined graphically by drawing a line through their respective graphs at $20 to indicate that $20 is the marginal cost in each country (see Figure 17.3). To maximize profits in each country, prices are now set in each country at that level where the marginal revenue for that country equals marginal costs. In Japan this is a price of $40, and the firm sells 40 units. In the United States the optimal price is $65, and it sells 15 units. Thus, reflecting the different competitive conditions, the price charged in the United States is over 50 percent more than the price charged in Japan. More important look at what happens to total revenues. With price discrimination, the firm earns revenues of

$$\$40 \times 40 \text{ units} = \$1,600$$

in Japan and

$$\$65 \times 15 \text{ units} = \$975$$

in the United States. By engaging in price discrimination, the firm can thus earn total revenues of

$$\$1,600 + \$975 = \$2,575,$$

which is $178.10 more than the $2,396.90 it earned before. Price discrimination pays!

Strategic Pricing

The concept of strategic pricing has two aspects, which we will refer to as predatory pricing and experience curve pricing. Both predatory pricing and experience curve pricing can result in problems with antidumping regulations. Once we have reviewed predatory and experience curve pricing, we will look at antidumping rules and other regulatory policies.

Predatory pricing

Predatory pricing is the use of price as a competitive weapon to drive weaker competitors out of a national market. Once the competitors have left the market, the firm can raise prices and enjoy high profits. For such a pricing strategy to work, the firm must normally have a profitable position in another national market, which it can use to subsidize aggressive pricing in the market it is trying to monopolize. Many Japanese firms have been accused of pursuing this strategy. The argument runs like this: Because the Japanese market is protected from foreign competition by high informal trade barriers, Japanese firms can charge high prices and earn high profits at home. They then use these profits to subsidize aggressive pricing overseas, the aim of which is to drive competitors out of those markets. Once this has occurred, so it is claimed, the Japanese firms then raise prices. For example, Matsushita has been accused of using this strategy to enter the U.S. TV market. As one of the major TV producers in Japan, Matsushita was able to earn high profits at home. It then used these profits to subsidize the losses it made in the United States during its early years there, when it priced low to increase its market penetration. Ultimately Matsushita became the world's largest manufacturer of TVs.[14]

Experience curve pricing

We first encountered the experience curve in Chapter 12. There we saw that as a firm builds up its accumulated production volume over time, so unit costs fall due to experience effects. Learning effects and economies of scale underlie the experience curve. Price comes into the picture, since aggressive pricing (along with aggressive promotion and advertising) is a way to build up accumulated sales volume rapidly and thus move down the experience curve. Firms further down the experience curve have a cost advantage vis-à-vis firms further up the curve.

Many firms pursuing an experience curve pricing strategy on an international scale price low worldwide in attempting to build global sales volume as rapidly as possible, even if this means taking large losses initially. Such a firm believes that several years in the future, when it has moved down the experience curve, it will be making substantial profits and, moreover, have a cost advantage over its less-aggressive competitors.

Regulatory Influences on Prices

Firms' abilities to engage in either price discrimination or strategic pricing may be limited by national or international regulations. Most important, a firm's freedom to set its own prices is constrained by antidumping regulations and competition policy.

---

[14]These allegations were made on a PBS "Frontline" documentary telecast in the United States in May 1992.

Antidumping regulations

Both predatory pricing and experience curve pricing can run afoul of antidumping regulations. Dumping occurs whenever a firm sells a product for a price that is less than the cost of producing it. Most regulations, however, define dumping more vaguely. For example, a country is allowed to bring antidumping actions against an importer under Article 6 of GATT so long as two criteria are met: sales at "less than fair value" and "material injury to a domestic industry." The problem with this terminology is that it does not indicate what is a fair value. The ambiguity has led some to argue that selling abroad at prices below those in the country of origin, as opposed to below cost, is dumping.

It was such logic that led the Bush administration to place a 25 percent duty on imports of Japanese light trucks in 1988. The Japanese manufacturers protested that they were not selling below cost. Admitting that their prices were lower in the United States than in Japan, they argued that this simply reflected the intensely competitive nature of the U.S. market (i.e., different price elasticities). In a similar example, the European Commission found Japanese exporters of dot matrix printers to be in violation of dumping regulations. To correct what they saw as dumping, the EU placed a 47 percent import duty on imports of dot matrix printers from Japan. According to EU rules, this import duty must be passed on to European consumers as a price increase.[15]

From the perspective of an international business, the important point is that antidumping rules set a floor under export prices and limit firms' ability to pursue strategic pricing. The rather vague terminology used in most antidumping actions suggests that a firm's ability to engage in price discrimination also may be challenged under antidumping legislation.

Competition policy

Most industrialized nations have regulations designed to promote competition and to restrict monopoly practices. These regulations can be used to limit the prices a firm can charge in a given country. For example, during the 1960s and 70s the Swiss pharmaceutical manufacturer Hoffmann-LaRoche had a monopoly on the supply of Valium and Librium tranquilizers. In 1973 the company was investigated by the British Monopolies and Mergers Commission, which is responsible for promoting fair competition in Great Britain. The commission found that Hoffmann-LaRoche was overcharging for its tranquilizers and ordered the company to reduce its prices 35 to 40 percent. Hoffmann-LaRoche maintained unsuccessfully that it was merely engaging in price discrimination. Similar actions were later brought against Hoffmann-LaRoche by the German cartel office and by the Dutch and Danish governments.[16]

❧ CONFIGURING THE MARKETING MIX

What we have seen so far in this chapter is that there are many reasons a firm might want to vary aspects of its marketing mix from country to country to take into account local differences in culture, economic conditions, competitive conditions, product and technical standards, distribution systems, government regulations, and the like. Such differences may require some variation in product attributes, distribution strategy, communications strategy, and pricing strategy. As a result of the cumulative effect of these factors, it is very rare to find a firm operating in an industry where it can adopt the same marketing mix worldwide, irrespective of the country it is operating in.

---

[15]"Printers Reflect Pattern of Trade Rows," *Financial Times*, December 20, 1988, p. 3.

[16]J. F. Pickering, *Industrial Structure and Market Conduct* (London: Martin Robertson, 1974).

For example, financial services is often thought of as an industry where global standardization of the marketing mix is the norm. However, while a financial services company such as American Express may sell the same basic charge card service worldwide, utilize the same basic fee structure for that product, and adopt the same basic global advertising message ("never leave home without it"), differences in national regulations still mean it has to vary aspects of its communications strategy from country to country (as pointed out earlier, the promotional strategy it had developed in the United States was illegal in Germany). While McDonald's is often thought of as the quintessential example of a firm that sells the same basic standardized product worldwide, we have already alluded to the fact that it varies one important aspect of its marketing mix—its menu—from country to country. McDonald's also varies its distribution strategy from country to country. In Canada and the United States most McDonald's are located in areas that are easily accessible by car, whereas in more densely populated and less automobile reliant societies of the world, such as Japan and Great Britain, location decisions are driven by the accessibility of a restaurant to pedestrian traffic, not cars. Because countries typically still do differ along one or more of the dimensions discussed above, some customization of the marketing mix is normal.

By the same token, however, there are often significant opportunities for standardization along one or more elements of the marketing mix. Firms may find that it is possible and desirable to standardize their global advertising message and/or core product attributes to realize substantial cost economies. At the same time they may find it desirable to customize their distribution and pricing strategy on a country-by-country basis to take advantage of local differences. In reality the "customization versus standardization" debate is not an all or nothing issue; it frequently makes sense to standardize some aspects of the marketing mix across countries, and customize others, depending on conditions prevailing in various national marketplaces. An explicit example, that of Castrol Oil, is given in the next "Management Focus." Castrol sells a standardized product worldwide, lubricating oil, and yet it varies other aspects of its marketing mix from country to country, depending on economic conditions, competitive conditions, and distribution systems. The reader should recognize that decisions about what to customize, and what to standardize, should be driven by a detailed examination of the costs and benefits of doing so for each element in the marketing mix.

❧ NEW-PRODUCT DEVELOPMENT

Firms that successfully develop and market new products can earn enormous returns. Some examples are:

- Xerox's 20-year domination of the photocopier market.
- Du Pont's steady stream of inventions such as cellophane, nylon, Freon (used in all air-conditioners), and Teflon.
- Sony's development of the Walkman and compact disc.
- Bausch & Lomb's development of contact lenses.
- Matsushita's development of the videocassette recorder.
- Intel's pioneering work with microprocessors.

In the late 20th century competition is as much about technological innovation as anything else. The pace of technological change has accelerated since the industrial revolution in the 18th century, and it continues to do so today. The result has been a dramatic shortening of product life cycles. Technological innovation is both creative and destructive.[17] An innovation can make established products obsolete

---

[17]The phrase was first used by economist Joseph Schumpeter in *Capitalism, Socialism, and Democracy* (New York: Harper Brothers, 1942).

MANAGEMENT FOCUS
Castrol Oil

Castrol Oil is the lubricants division of the British chemical, oil, and gas concern, Burmah Castrol. In Europe and in the United States, where Castrol now has a 15 percent share of the DIY lubricants market, Castrol targets motorists who want to cosset their engine by paying a bit more for the liquid engineering of Castrol's high margin GTX brand, rather than a standard lubricant. This differentiated positioning strategy is supported by sponsoring Formula 1 racing and the Indy Car Series in the United States, and by heavy spending on television and in automobile magazines in both Europe and the United States.

Some of Castrol's most notable successes in recent years, however, have not been in Europe or the United States, rather they have been in the developing nations of Asia where Castrol reaps only one-sixth of its sales, but over one-quarter of its operating profits. Take Vietnam as an example; here automobiles are still relatively rare, so Castrol has targeted the vast army of motorcycle owners. Castrol's strategy is to target people who want to take care of their new motorcycles. The long-term goal is to build brand loyalty, so that when automobile ownership becomes common in Vietnam, as Castrol believes it ultimately will, former motorcycle owners will stick with Castrol when they trade up to cars. This strategy has already worked in Thailand. Castrol has held the leading share of the motorcycle market in Thailand since the early 1980s, and it now holds the leading share in that country's rapidly growing automobile market.

Unlike its practice in more developed countries, in Vietnam Castrol's communications strategy does not focus on television and glossy print media (since there is

relatively little of either in Vietnam). Rather, Castrol focuses on building consumer awareness through extensive use of billboards, car stickers, and some 4,000 signboards at Vietnam's ubiquitous roadside garages and motorcycle cleaning shops. Castrol also developed a unique slogan that has a rhythmic quality in Vietnamese *"Dau nhot tot nhat"* ("best quality lubricants"). This rhythmic slogan sticks in consumer's minds. Castrol's own researchers say the slogan is now recognized by a remarkable 99 percent of people in Ho Chi Minh City.

As elsewhere, Castrol has adopted a premium pricing strategy in Vietnam, which is consistent with the company's attempt to build a global brand image of high quality. Castrol oil costs about $1.5 per liter in Vietnam, about three times as much as the cheaper oil imported from countries such as Taiwan and Thailand. Despite the high price of its product, Castrol claims it is gaining share in Vietnam as its branding strategy wins converts.

Castrol has had to tailor its distribution strategy to Vietnam's unique conditions. In most countries where it operates, Castrol divides the country into regions and has a single distributor in each region. In Vietnam, however, Castrol will often have two distinct distributors in a region—one to deal with state-owned customers, of which there are many in this still nominally Communist country, and one to deal with private customers. Castrol acknowledges the system is costly but says it is the only way to operate in a country where there is still some tension between state and private entities.

Sources: V. Mallet, "Climbing the Slippery Slope," *Financial Times*, July 28, 1994, p. 7; and A. Bolger, "Growth by Successful Targeting," *Financial Times*, June 21, 1994, p. 27.

overnight. At the same time an innovation can make a host of new products possible. Witness recent changes in the electronics industry. For 40 years before the early 1950s, vacuum valves were a major component in radios and then in record players and early computers. The advent of transistors destroyed the market for vacuum valves, but at the same time it created new opportunities connected with transistors. Transistors took up far less space than vacuum valves, creating a trend toward miniaturization that continues today. The transistor held its position as the major component in the electronics industry for just a decade. In the 1970s microprocessors were developed, and the market for transistors declined rapidly. At the same time, however, the microprocessor created yet another set of new-product opportunities—handheld calculators (which destroyed the market for slide rules), compact disc players (which destroyed the market for analog record players), personal computers (which destroyed the market for typewriters), to name a few.

This process of "creative destruction" unleashed by technological change makes it critical that a firm stay on the leading edge of technology, lest it lose out to a competitor's innovations. As we explain in the next subsection, this not only creates a need for the firm to invest in R&D, but it also requires the firm to establish R&D activities at those locations around the globe where expertise is concentrated. Moreover, as we shall see, leading-edge technology on its own is not enough to guarantee a firm's survival. The firm must also apply that technology in developing products that satisfy consumer needs. To do that the firm needs to build close links between marketing and R&D. This is difficult enough for the domestic firm, but it is even more problematic for the international business competing in an industry where consumer tastes and preferences differ from country to country. With all this in mind, we now move on to examine the issues of locating R&D activities and building links between R&D and marketing.

The Location of R&D

By and large, ideas for new products are stimulated by the interactions of scientific research, demand conditions, and competitive conditions. Other things being equal, the rate of new-product development seems to be greater in countries where:

- More money is spent on basic and applied research and development.
- Demand is strong.
- Consumers are affluent.
- Competition is intense.[18]

Basic and applied research and development discovers new technologies and then commercializes them. Strong demand and affluent consumers create a potential market for new products. Intense competition between firms stimulates innovation as the firms try to beat their competitors and reap potentially enormous first-mover advantages that result from successful innovation.

For most of the post-World War II period, the country that ranked highest on these criteria was the United States. The United States devoted a greater proportion of its gross domestic product (GDP) to R&D than any other country did. Its scientific establishment was the largest and most active in the world. U.S. consumers were the most affluent in the world, the market was large, and competition among U.S. firms was brisk. Due to these factors, the United States was the lead market, the market where most new products were developed and introduced. Accordingly it was the best location for R&D activities; it was where the action was.

---

[18]See D. C. Mowery and N. Rosenberg, *Technology and the Pursuit of Economic Growth* (Cambridge, U.K.: Cambridge University Press, 1989); and M. E. Porter, *The Competitive Advantage of Nation* (New York: The Free Press, 1990).

Since the late 1970s things have been changing fast. The U.S. monopoly on new-product development has disappeared. Although U.S. firms are still at the leading edge of many new technologies, Japanese and European firms are also strong players. When the Japanese government's Economic Planning Agency surveyed 110 critical leading-edge technologies in 1991, it concluded U.S. firms dominated 43 of them; Japanese firms, 33; and European firms, the remaining 34.[19] Both Japan and Germany are now devoting a greater proportion of their GDP to nondefense R&D than is the United States. In 1990 Japan spent 3 percent of its GDP on nondefense R&D; Germany, 2.7 percent; and the United States, 1.8 percent.[20] In addition, both Japan and the European Community are large, affluent markets, and the wealth gap between them and the United States is closing.

It is no longer appropriate to consider the United States the lead market. It is questionable if any country is. To succeed today it is often necessary to simultaneously introduce new products in all major industrialized markets. Since leading-edge research is now carried out in many locations around the world, the argument for centralizing R&D activity in the United States is now much weaker than it was two decades ago. (It used to be argued that centralized R&D eliminated duplication.) Much leading-edge research is now occurring in Japan and Europe, and it makes sense for many firms to disperse their R&D activities to those locations. Such dispersion allows a firm to stay close to the center of leading-edge activity to gather scientific and competitive information and to draw on local scientific resources. This may result in some duplication of R&D activities, but the cost disadvantages of duplication are outweighed by the advantages of dispersion.

For example, to expose themselves to the research and new-product development work now being done in Japan, many U.S. firms have recently set up satellite R&D centers in Japan. Kodak's $65 million R&D center in Japan employs approximately 200 people. The company hired about 100 professional Japanese researchers and directed the lab to concentrate on electronic imaging technology. A few of the U.S. firms that have established R&D facilities in Japan are Corning, Texas Instruments, IBM, Digital Equipment, Procter & Gamble, Upjohn, Pfizer, Du Pont, and Monsanto.[21] The National Science Foundation (NSF) has documented a sharp increase in the proportion of total R&D spending by U.S. firms that is now made abroad. According to NSF data, between 1985 and 1993 the amount of funds committed to foreign R&D soared ninefold, while R&D spending in the United States remained essentially flat.[22] At the same time, to internationalize their own research and gain access to U.S. research talent, the NSF reports that many European and Japanese firms have begun to make heavy investments in U.S.-based research facilities.

Linking R&D and Marketing

Although a firm that is successful at developing new products may earn enormous returns, new-product development is a very risky business with a high failure rate. One estimate suggests 80 to 88 percent of all research and development projects either fail to produce a marketable product or produce a product that fails to earn an economic return in the marketplace.[23] Another study found that 45 percent of new products introduced into the marketplace did not meet their profitability goals.[24] Despite this high failure rate, some firms seem consistently better than others at successfully introducing new products. Firms such as 3M, Sony, and Matsushita have

[19]"Can America Compete?" *The Economist*, January 18, 1992, pp. 65–66.
[20]C. Farrell, "Industrial Policy," *Business Week*, April 6, 1992, pp. 70–75.
[21]"When the Corporate Lab Goes to Japan," *New York Times*, April 28, 1991, sec. 3, p. 1.
[22]D. Shapley, "Globalization Prompts Exodus," *Financial Times*, March 17, 1994, p. 10.
[23]E. Mansfield, "How Economists See R&D," *Harvard Business Review*, November–December 1981, pp. 98–106.
[24]A. L. Page, "New Product Development Practices Survey: Performance and Best Practices," PDMA 15th Annual International Conference, Boston, October 16, 1991.

well-earned reputations for successful innovation. One reason for these firms' success seems to be that they build close links between their R&D activities and their marketing functions to ensure new products are tailored to consumer needs.[25] Many new products fail because they are not adequately commercialized. For example, many of the early personal computers failed to sell because the user needed to be a computer programmer to use them; their technology had not been commercialized. Steve Jobs of Apple Computer realized that if the technology could be made "user friendly," the market for it would be enormous.

The need to adequately commercialize new technologies poses special problems in the international business, since commercialization may require different versions of a new product to be produced for different countries. To do this the firm must build close links between its R&D centers and its various country operations. This may require R&D centers in North America, Asia, and Europe that are closely linked by formal and informal integrating mechanisms with marketing operations in each country in their regions. (Chapter 13 discusses formal and informal integrating mechanisms.) The imperative of linking R&D and local marketing has been identified by the NSF as one of the main factors leading U.S. firms to shift R&D activities overseas. The NSF has found that as U.S. firms moved their manufacturing overseas in the 1980s and early 1990s, so their R&D activities followed.[26]

❧ SUMMARY OF CHAPTER

This chapter has discussed the marketing and R&D functions in international business. A persistent theme of the chapter is the tension that exists between the need to reduce costs and the need to be responsive to local conditions, which raises costs. The following points have been made.

1. Theodore Levitt has argued that, due to the advent of modern communications and transport technologies, consumer tastes and preferences are becoming global, which is creating global markets for standardized consumer products. However, this position is regarded as extreme by many commentators, who argue that substantial differences still exist between countries.

2. A product can be viewed as a bundle of attributes. Product attributes need to be varied from country to country to satisfy different consumer tastes and preferences.

3. Country differences in consumer tastes and preferences are due to differences in culture and economic development. In addition differences in product and technical standards may require the firm to customize product attributes from country to country.

4. A distribution strategy decision is an attempt to define the optimal channel for delivering a product to the consumer.

5. Significant country differences exist in distribution systems. In some countries the retail system is concentrated; in others it is fragmented. In some countries channel length is short; in others it is long. Access to some countries' distribution channels is difficult to achieve.

6. A critical element in the marketing mix is communication strategy, which defines the process the firm will use in communicating the attributes of its product to prospective customers.

7. Barriers to international communication include cultural differences, source effects, and noise levels.

8. A communication strategy is either a push strategy or a pull strategy. A push strategy emphasizes personal selling, whereas a pull strategy emphasizes mass media advertising. Whether a push strategy or a pull strategy is optimal depends on the type of product, consumer sophistication, channel length, and media availability.

9. A globally standardized advertising campaign, which uses the same marketing message all over the world, has economic advantages, but it fails to account for differences in culture and the various governments' advertising regulations.

10. Price discrimination exists when consumers in different countries are charged different prices for the same product. Price discrimination can help a firm maximize its profits. For price discrimination to be effective, the national markets must be separate and their price elasticities of demand must differ.

11. Predatory pricing is the use of profit gained in one market to support aggressive pricing in another market for the purpose of driving competitors out of that market.

---

[25]K. B. Clark and S. C. Wheelwright, *Managing New Product and Process Development* (New York: Free Press, 1993).
[26]Shapley, "Globalization Prompts Exodus."

12. Experience curve pricing is the use of aggressive pricing for the purpose of building accumulated volume as rapidly as possible to move the firm down the experience curve rapidly.

13. New-product development is a high-risk, potentially high-return activity. To build up a competency in new-product development, an international business must do two things: (*i*) disperse R&D activities to those countries where new products are being pioneered and (*ii*) integrate R&D with marketing.

❧ CRITICAL DISCUSSION QUESTIONS

1. Imagine you are the marketing manager for a U.S. manufacturer of disposable diapers. Your firm is considering entering the European market, concentrating on the major EU countries. Your CEO believes the advertising message that has been effective in the United States will suffice in Europe. Outline some possible objections to this.

2. By the end of this century we will have seen the emergence of enormous global markets for standardized consumer products. Do you agree with this statement? Justify your answer.

3. You are the marketing manager of a food products company that is considering entering the South Korean market. The retail system in South Korea tends to be very fragmented. Moreover retailers and wholesalers tend to have long-term ties with South Korean food companies, which makes access to distribution channels difficult. What distribution strategy would you advise the company to pursue? Why?

4. Price discrimination is indistinguishable from dumping. Discuss the accuracy of this statement.

❧ CLOSING CASE   Procter & Gamble

Procter & Gamble (P&G), the large U.S. consumer products company, has a well-earned reputation as one of the world's best marketers. With its 80-plus major brands, P&G generates more than $20 billion in annual revenues worldwide. Along with Unilever, P&G is a dominant global force in laundry detergents, cleaning products, and personal care products. P&G expanded abroad in the post–World War II years by exporting its brands and marketing policies to Western Europe, initially with considerable success. Over the next 30 years this policy of developing new products and marketing strategies in the United States and then transferring them to other countries became well entrenched. Although some adaptation of marketing policies to accommodate country differences was pursued, this adaptation was fairly minimal.

The first signs that this policy was no longer effective emerged in the 1970s, when P&G suffered a number of major setbacks in Japan. By 1985, after 13 years in Japan, P&G was still losing $40 million a year there. It had introduced disposable diapers in Japan and at one time had commanded an 80 percent share of the market, but yet by the early 1980s it held a miserable 8 percent. Three large Japanese consumer products companies were dominating the market. P&G's problem was that its diapers, developed in the United States, were too bulky for the tastes of Japanese consumers. With this in mind, Kao, a Japanese company, had developed a line of trim-fit diapers that appealed more to Japanese tastes. Kao introduced its product with a marketing blitz and was quickly rewarded with a 30 percent share of the market. As for P&G, it realized it would have to modify its diapers if it were to compete in Japan. So it did, and the company now has a 30 percent share of the Japanese market. And P&G's trim-fit diapers have become a best-seller in the United States.

P&G had a similar experience in marketing education in the Japanese laundry detergent market. In the early 1980s P&G introduced its Cheer laundry detergent in Japan. Developed in the United States, Cheer was promoted in Japan with the U.S. marketing message—Cheer works in all temperatures and produces lots of rich suds. The problem was that many Japanese consumers wash their clothes in cold tap water, which made the claim of working in all temperatures irrelevant. Moreover many Japanese add fabric softeners to their water, which reduces detergents' sudsing action, so Cheer did not make suds as advertised. After a disastrous launch, P&G knew it had to adapt its marketing message. Cheer is now promoted as a product that works effectively in cold water with fabric softeners added, and it is one of P&G's best-selling products in Japan.

P&G's experience with disposable diapers and laundry detergents in Japan forced the company to rethink its product development and marketing philosophy. The company now admits that its U.S.-centered way of doing business no longer works. Since the late 1980s P&G has been delegating more responsibility for new-product development and marketing to its major subsidiaries in Japan and Europe. The company is more responsive to local differences in consumer tastes and preferences and more willing to admit that good new products can be developed outside the United States.

Despite the apparent changes at P&G, it is still not clear that P&G has achieved the revolution in thinking required to alter its long-standing practices. Its recent venture into the Polish shampoo market seems to illustrate that the company still has a way to go. In summer 1991 P&G entered the Polish market with its Vidal Sassoon Wash & Go, an "all-in-one" shampoo and conditioner that is a best-seller in the United States and Europe. The product launch was supported by a U.S.-style marketing blitz on a scale never before seen in Poland. At first the campaign seemed to be effective as P&G captured more than 30 percent of the shampoo market, but early in 1992 sales suddenly plummeted. Then came the rumors—Wash & Go causes dandruff and hair loss—allegations P&G has strenuously denied. Next came the jokes. One doing the rounds in Poland is "I washed my car with Wash & Go, and the tires went bald." And when President Lech Walesa proposed about that time that he also be named prime minister, critics derided the idea as a "two-in-one solution, just like Wash & Go."

Where did P&G go wrong? The most common theory is that it promoted Wash & Go too hard in a country that has little enthusiasm for brash U.S.-style advertising. A poll by Pentor, a private market research company in Warsaw, found that almost three times more Poles disliked P&G's commercials than liked them. Pentor also argues that the high-profile marketing campaign backfired because years of Communist party propaganda have led Polish consumers to suspect that advertising is simply a way to move goods nobody wants. Some also believe Wash & Go, which was developed for U.S. consumers who shampoo daily, was far too sophisticated for Polish consumers who are less obsessed with personal hygiene. Underlying all these criticisms is the idea that P&G once again stumbled because it transferred a product and marketing strategy wholesale from the United States to another country without modifying it to the tastes and preferences of local consumers.

CASE DISCUSSION QUESTIONS

1. What was the root cause of P&G's marketing failures in Japan and Poland?

2. What strategic and organizational actions do you think P&G should take to increase its sensitivity to national differences and their impact on the marketing mix?

3. How might P&G improve its ability to leverage products and marketing strategies developed in one part of the world, and apply them to markets elsewhere?

Sources: Guy de Jonquieres and C. Bobinski, "Wash and Get into a Lather in Poland," Financial Times, May 28, 1992, p. 2; "Perestroika in Soapland," The Economist, June 10, 1989, pp. 69–71; "After Early Stumbles P&G Is Making Inroads Overseas," The Wall Street Journal, February 6, 1989, p. B1; and C. A. Bartlett and S. Ghoshal, Managing across Borders: The Transnational Solution (Boston: Harvard Business School Press, 1989).

CHAPTER EIGHTEEN

GLOBAL HUMAN RESOURCE MANAGEMENT

GLOBAL HUMAN RESOURCE MANAGEMENT AT COCA-COLA

The Coca-Cola Company is perhaps one of the most successful multinational enterprises of our time. With operations in close to 200 countries and nearly 80 percent of its operating income being derived from businesses outside the United States, Coca-Cola is typically perceived as the quintessential global corporation. Coca-Cola, however, likes to think of itself as a "multilocal" company that just happens to be headquartered in Atlanta, but which could be headquartered anywhere, and which presents the Coca-Cola brand with a "local face" in every country where it does business. The philosophy is perhaps best summarized by the phrase "think globally, act locally," which captures the essence of Coca-Cola's cross-border management mentality. A dominant theme at Coca-Cola is to grant different national businesses the freedom to conduct operations in a manner appropriate to the market in which they are competing. At the same time the company tries to establish a common mind-set that all its employees share.

Coca-Cola manages its global operations through 25 operating divisions that are organized under six regional groups: North America, the European Union, the Pacific Region, the North East Europe/Middle East Group, Africa, and Latin America. Within Coca-Cola it is the corporate human resources management (HRM) function that is charged with providing the glue that binds these various divisions and groups into the Coca-Cola family. The corporate HRM function achieves this in two main ways; first, by propagating a common human resources philosophy within

the company, and second, by developing a group of internationally minded midlevel executives for future senior management responsibility.

With regard to HRM philosophy, the corporate HRM group sees its mission as one of developing and providing the underlying philosophy around which local businesses can develop their own human resource practices. For example, rather than have a standard salary *policy* for all its national operations, Coca-Cola has a common salary *philosophy*, which is for its total compensation package to be competitive with the best companies in their local market. Twice a year the corporate HRM group also conducts two-week HRM orientation sessions for the human resource staff from each of its 25 operating divisions. One purpose of these sessions is to give an overview of the company's HRM philosophy and to talk about how different local businesses can translate that philosophy into human resource policies in their own particular area. Coca-Cola has found that information sharing is one of the great benefits of bringing HRM professionals together. For example, tools that have been

developed in Brazil to deal with a specific HRM problem might also be useful in Australia. The sessions provide a medium through which HRM professionals can communicate and learn from each other, which facilitates the rapid transfer of innovative and valuable HRM tools from region to region.

As much as possible Coca-Cola tries to staff its local operations with local personnel. To quote one senior executive: "We strive to have a limited number of international people in the field because generally local people are better equipped to do business at their home locations." However, there's still a need for expatriates in the system for two main reasons. One is to fill a need for a specific set of skills that might not exist at a particular location. For example, when Coca-Cola started operations in Eastern Europe it had to bring in an expatriate from Chicago, who was of Polish descent, to fill the position of finance manager. The second reason for utilizing expatriates is to improve the employee's own skill base. Most importantly Coca-Cola believes that because it is a global company, before anyone takes on serious senior management responsibility they should have international exposure.

Currently the corporate HRM group has about 500 high-level managers that are involved in what it calls its "global service program." Coca-Cola characterizes these managers as people who have knowledge of their particular field, plus knowledge of the company, and who can do two things in an international location—add value by the expertise they bring to each assignment, and enhance their contribution to the company by having international experience. Of the 500 participants in the program, about 200 move each year. To ease the costs of transfer for these employees, Coca-Cola gives those in its global service program a U.S.-based compensation package. In other words, they are paid according to U.S. benchmarks, as opposed to the benchmark prevailing wherever they are currently located. Thus an Indian manager in this program who is currently working in Britain will be paid according to U.S. salary benchmarks—and not those prevailing in either India or Britain. One of the ultimate goals of this program is to build a cadre of internationally minded high-level managers from which the future senior managers of Coca-Cola will be drawn.

Sources: D. A. Amfuso, "HR Unites the World of Coca-Cola," *Personnel Journal*, November 1994, pp. 112–20; and S. Foley, "Internationalizing the Cola Wars," Harvard Business School Case # 9-794-146.

INTRODUCTION

Continuing our survey of specific functions within an international business, this chapter examines international human resource management (HRM). **Human resource management** refers to the activities an organization carries out to utilize its human resource effectively.[1] These activities include determining the firm's human resource strategy, staffing, performance evaluation, management development, compensation, and labor relations. As the opening case on Coca-Cola makes clear, none of these activities is performed in a vacuum; all are related to the strategy of the firm, for, as we will see, HRM has an important strategic component.[2] Most importantly, through its influence on the character, development, quality, and productivity of the firm's human resources, the HRM function can help the firm achieve its primary strategic goals of reducing the costs of value creation and adding value by better serving customer needs.

The strategic role of HRM is complex enough in a purely domestic firm, but it is more complex in an international business, where staffing, management development, performance evaluation, and compensation activities are complicated by profound differences in labor markets, culture, legal systems, economic systems, and the like (see Chapters 2 and 3). For example,

- Compensation practices may have to vary from country to country depending on prevailing management customs.
- Labor laws may prohibit union organization in one country and mandate it in another.
- Equal employment legislation may be strongly pursued in one country and not in another.

Moreover, if it is to build a cadre of international managers, the HRM function must deal with a host of issues related to expatriate managers. (An **expatriate manager** is a citizen of one country who is working abroad in one of the firm's subsidiaries.)

In the opening case we saw how Coca-Cola deals with some of these issues. Coca-Cola copes with differences between countries by articulating a common HRM *philosophy*, but by letting each national operation translate this philosophy into specific *policies* that are best suited to the particular operating environment. Coca-Cola also tries to build a cadre of internationally minded executives through its global service program, which involves the HRM function identifying and managing the career development of a key group of executives from which future senior management will be selected. Finally, and perhaps most importantly, Coca-Cola sees the HRM function as a vital link in the implementation of its strategic goal of thinking globally and acting locally.

In this chapter we will look closely at the role of HRM in an international business. We begin by briefly discussing the strategic role of HRM. Then we turn our attention

---

[1] P. J. Dowling and R. S. Schuler, *International Dimensions of Human Resource Management* (Boston: PSW-Kent, 1990).

[2] J. Millman, M. A. von Glinow, and M. Nathan, "Organizational Life Cycles and Strategic International Human Resource Management in Multinational Companies," *Academy of Management Review* 16 (1991), pp. 318–39.

TABLE 18.1

Strategy, Structure, and
Control Systems

Structure and Controls	International Strategy			
	Multidomestic	**International**	**Global**	**Transnational**
Centralization of operating decisions	Decentralized	Core competency centralized. Rest decentralized	Some centralized	Mixed centralized and decentralized Informal matrix
Horizontal differentiation	Worldwide area structure	Worldwide product division	Worldwide product division	Informal matrix
Need for coordination	Low	Moderate	High	Very High
Integrating mechanisms	None	Few	Many	Very many
Performance ambiguity	Low	Moderate	High	Very high
Need for cultural controls	Low	Moderate	High	Very High

to four major tasks of the HRM function—staffing policy, management training and development, performance appraisal, and compensation policy. Throughout these sections we will point out the strategic implications of each of these tasks. The chapter closes with a look at international labor relations and the relationship between the firm's management of labor relations and its overall strategy.

❧ THE STRATEGIC ROLE OF INTERNATIONAL HRM

In Chapter 12 we examined four strategies pursued by international businesses—the multidomestic, the international, the global, and the transnational. Multidomestic firms try to create value by emphasizing local responsiveness; international firms, by transferring core competencies overseas; global firms, by realizing experience curve and location economies; and transnational firms, by doing all these things simultaneously. In Chapter 13 we discussed the organizational requirements for implementing each of these strategies. Table 18.1, identical to Table 13.2, summarizes the relationships among international strategies, structures, and controls.

None of the structures or controls summarized in Table 18.1 mean much if the human resources that support them are not appropriate. Without the right kind of people in place, organizational structure is just a hollow shell. In Chapter 13 we explained that formal and informal structure and controls must be congruent with a firm's strategy for the firm to succeed. Now we will show that success also requires HRM policies to be congruent with the firm's strategy and with its formal and informal structure and controls. For example, a transnational strategy imposes very different requirements for staffing, management development, and compensation practices than a multidomestic strategy does.

As noted in the introduction, the opening case alluded to the relationship between strategy, structure, and HRM. Like many other consumer products firms, Coca-Cola is trying to become a transnational organization (in some ways "think globally, act locally" is a good definition of a transnational strategy). As indicated in Table 18.1, firms pursuing a transnational strategy need to build a strong corporate culture and an informal management network for transmitting information within the organization. Through its employee selection, management development, performance appraisal, and compensation policies, the HRM function can help develop these things. For example, Coca-Cola's global service program, by creating a cadre of international managers with experience in various nations, should help to establish an informal management network. In addition management development programs can build a corporate culture that supports strategic goals. In short HRM has a critical role to play in implementing strategy. In each section that follows we will review the strategic role of HRM in some detail.

🐟 STAFFING POLICY

Staffing policy is concerned with the selection of employees for particular jobs. At one level this involves selecting individuals who have the skills required to do particular jobs. At another level staffing policy can be a tool for developing and promoting corporate culture.[3] By corporate culture we mean the organization's norms and value systems. We first encountered the concept in Chapter 13 when we discussed the use of "cultural controls" in businesses, noting that strong cultural controls help the firm pursue its strategy. We noted that firms pursuing transnational and global strategies have high needs for a strong unifying culture, whereas the need is somewhat lower for firms pursuing an international strategy and lowest of all for firms pursuing a multidomestic strategy (see Table 18.1).

Thus in firms pursuing transnational and global strategies, we might expect the HRM function to pay significant attention to selecting individuals who not only have the skills required to perform particular jobs but who also "fit" the prevailing culture of the firm. General Electric, for example, which is positioned toward the transnational end of the strategic spectrum, is not just concerned with hiring people who have the skills required for performing particular jobs; it also wants to hire individuals whose behavioral styles, beliefs, and value systems are consistent with those of GE. This is true whether an American is being hired, an Italian, a German, or an Australian and whether the hiring is for a U.S. operation or a foreign operation. The belief is that if employees are predisposed toward the organization's norms and value systems by their personality type, the firm, which has a significant need for integration, will experience fewer problems with performance ambiguity.

By the same token, the need for integration is substantially lower in a multidomestic firm. As a result there is less performance ambiguity there and not the same need for cultural controls. In theory this means the HRM function can pay less attention to building a unified corporate culture. In multidomestic firms the culture can be allowed to vary from national operation to national operation. (Although given the questionable viability of a multidomestic strategy in today's world, this might not be the best policy to pursue. Chapter 12 discusses the viability of this strategy.)

Types of Staffing Policy

Research has identified three types of staffing policies in international businesses: the ethnocentric approach, the polycentric approach, and the geocentric approach.[4] We will review each policy and link it to the strategy pursued by the firm. The most attractive staffing policy is probably the geocentric approach, although there are several impediments to adopting it.

The ethnocentric approach
An **ethnocentric** staffing policy is one in which all key management positions are filled by parent-country nationals. This practice was very widespread at one time. Firms such as Procter & Gamble, Philips NV, and Matsushita originally followed it. In the Dutch firm Philips, for example, all important positions in most foreign subsidiaries were at one time held by Dutch nationals who were referred to by their non-Dutch colleagues as the Dutch Mafia. In many Japanese firms today, such as Toyota and Matsushita, key positions in international operations are still often held by Japanese nationals.

---

[3] E. H. Schein, *Organizational Culture and Leadership* (San Francisco: Jossey-Bass, 1985).

[4] H. V. Perlmutter, "The Tortuous Evolution of the Multinational Corporation," *Columbia Journal of World Business* 4, (1969), pp. 9–18; D. A. Heenan and H. V. Perlmutter, *Multinational Organizational Development* (Reading, MA: Addison-Wesley, 1979); and D. A. Ondrack, "International Human Resources Management in European and North American Firms," *International Studies of Management and Organization* 15 (1985), pp. 6–32.

Firms pursue an ethnocentric staffing policy for three reasons. First, the firm may believe there is a lack of qualified individuals in the host country to fill senior management positions. This argument is heard most often when the firm has operations in less developed countries. Second, the firm may see an ethnocentric staffing policy as the best way to maintain a unified corporate culture. Many Japanese firms, for example, prefer their foreign operations to be headed by expatriate Japanese managers because these managers will have been socialized into the firm's culture while employed in Japan.[5] Until recently Procter & Gamble preferred to staff important management positions in its foreign subsidiaries with U.S. nationals who had been socialized into P&G's corporate culture by years of employment in its U.S. operations. Such reasoning tends to predominate when a firm places a high value on its corporate culture.

Third, if the firm is trying to create value by transferring core competencies to a foreign operation, as firms pursuing an international strategy are, it may believe that the best way to do this is to transfer parent-country nationals who have knowledge of that competency to the foreign operation. Imagine what might occur if a firm tried to transfer a core competency in marketing to a foreign subsidiary without supporting the transfer with a corresponding transfer of home-country marketing management personnel. The transfer would probably fail to produce the anticipated benefits, because the knowledge underlying a core competency cannot easily be articulated and written down. Such knowledge often has a significant tacit dimension; it is acquired through experience over time. Just like the great tennis player who cannot instruct others how to become great tennis players simply by writing a handbook, the firm that has a core competency in marketing, or anything else, cannot just write a handbook that tells a foreign subsidiary how to build the firm's core competency anew in a foreign setting. It must also transfer management personnel to the foreign operation so they can show foreign managers how to become good marketers, for example. In large part the need to transfer managers overseas arises because the knowledge that underlies the firm's core competency resides in the heads of its domestic managers. They have acquired this knowledge through years of experience, not by reading a handbook. Thus, if a firm is to transfer a core competency to a foreign subsidiary, it must also transfer the appropriate managers.

Despite this rationale for pursuing an ethnocentric staffing policy, the policy is now on the wane in most international businesses. There are two reasons for this. First, an ethnocentric staffing policy limits advancement opportunities for host-country nationals. This can lead to resentment, lower productivity, and increased turnover among that group. Resentment can be greater still if, as often occurs, expatriate managers are paid significantly more than home-country nationals.

Second, an ethnocentric policy can lead to cultural myopia, the firm's failure to understand host-country cultural differences that require different approaches to marketing and management. The adaptation of expatriate managers can take a long time, during which they may make major mistakes. For example, expatriate managers may fail to appreciate how product attributes, distribution strategy, communications strategy, and pricing strategy should be adapted to host-country conditions. The result may be some costly blunders. The closing case to Chapter 17 described how this occurred at Procter & Gamble on a number of occasions. In response, P&G is now hiring more host-country nationals for senior management positions in its foreign operations.

[5] S. Beechler and J. Z. Yang, "The Transfer of Japanese Style Management to American Subsidiaries," *Journal of International Business Studies* 25 (1994), pp. 467–91.

The polycentric approach

A **polycentric** staffing policy requires host-country nationals to be recruited to manage subsidiaries, while parent-country nationals occupy key positions at corporate headquarters. In many respects a polycentric approach is a response to the shortcomings of an ethnocentric approach. One advantage of adopting a polycentric approach is that the firm is less likely to suffer from cultural myopia. Host-country managers are unlikely to make the mistakes arising from cultural misunderstandings that expatriate managers are vulnerable to. A second advantage is that a polycentric approach may be less expensive to implement. Expatriate managers can be very expensive to maintain. Insofar as host-country nationals do not require the same level of expenditures, using them can reduce the costs of value creation.

However, a polycentric approach also has its drawbacks. Host-country nationals have limited opportunities to gain experience outside their own country and thus cannot progress beyond senior positions in their own subsidiary. As in the case of an ethnocentric policy, this may cause resentment. Perhaps the major drawback with a polycentric approach, however, is the gap that can form between host-country managers and parent-country managers. Language barriers, national loyalties, and a range of cultural differences may isolate the corporate headquarters staff from the various foreign subsidiaries. The lack of management transfers from home to host countries, and vice versa, can exacerbate this isolation and lead to a lack of integration between corporate headquarters and foreign subsidiaries. The result can be a federation of largely independent national units with only nominal links to the corporate headquarters. Within such a federation, the coordination required to transfer core competencies or to pursue experience curve and location economies may be difficult to achieve. Thus, although a polycentric approach may be effective for firms pursuing a multidomestic strategy, it is inappropriate for other strategies.

Moreover the federation that may result from a polycentric approach can be a force for inertia within the firm. For example, after decades of pursuing a polycentric staffing policy, food and detergents giant Unilever found that shifting from a multidomestic strategic posture to a transnational posture was very difficult. The reason: Unilever's foreign subsidiaries had evolved into quasi-autonomous operations, each with its own strong national identity. These "little kingdoms" objected strenuously to corporate headquarters' attempts to limit their autonomy and to rationalize global manufacturing.[6]

The geocentric approach

A **geocentric** staffing policy seeks the best people for key jobs throughout the organization, regardless of nationality. There are a number of advantages to this policy. First, it enables the firm to make the best use of its human resources. Second, and perhaps more important, a geocentric policy enables the firm to build a cadre of international executives who feel at home working in a number of different cultures. The creation of such a cadre may be a critical first step toward building a strong unifying corporate culture and an informal management network, both of which are required for global and transnational strategies (see Table 18.1).[7] Put another way, firms pursuing a geocentric staffing policy may be better able to create value from the pursuit of experience curve and location economies and from the multidirectional transfer of core competencies than firms pursuing other staffing policies. In addition the multinational composition of the management team that results from geocentric staffing tends to reduce cultural myopia and to enhance local responsiveness. Thus, other things being equal, a geocentric staffing policy seems the most attractive.

---

[6]C. A. Bartlett, and S. Ghoshal, *Managing Across Borders: The Transnational Solution* (Boston: Harvard Business School Press, 1989).

[7]S. J. Kobrin, "Geocentric Mindset and Multinational Strategy," *Journal of International Business Studies* 25 (1994), pp. 493–511.

TABLE 18.2

Comparison of Staffing
Approaches

Staffing Approach	Strategic Appropriateness	Advantages	Disadvantages
Ethnocentric	International	Overcomes lack of qualified managers in host nation Unified culture Helps transfer core competencies	Produces resentment in host country Can lead to cultural myopia
Polycentric	Multidomestic	Alleviates cultural myopia Inexpensive to implement	Limits career mobility Isolates headquarters from foreign subsidiaries
Geocentric	Global and transnational	Uses human resources efficiently Helps build strong culture and informal management network	National immigration policies may limit implementation Expensive

However, despite this, a number of problems limit the firm's ability to pursue a geocentric policy. One problem is that many countries want foreign subsidiaries to employ their citizens. To achieve this goal, they use immigration laws to require the employment of host-country nationals if they are available in adequate numbers and have the necessary skills. Most countries (including the United States) require firms to provide extensive documentation if they wish to hire a foreign national instead of a local national. This documentation can be time consuming, expensive, and at times futile. A further problem is that a geocentric staffing policy can be very expensive to implement. There are increased training costs, relocation costs involved in transferring managers from country to country, and the need for a compensation structure with a standardized international base pay level that may be higher than national levels in many countries. In addition the higher pay enjoyed by managers placed on an international "fast track" may be a source of resentment within a firm.

Summary

The advantages and disadvantages of the three approaches to staffing policy are summarized in Table 18.2. Broadly speaking, an ethnocentric approach is compatible with an international strategy, a polycentric approach is compatible with a multidomestic strategy, and a geocentric approach is compatible with both global and transnational strategies. (See Chapter 12 for details of the strategies.)

Finally, it should be noted that while the staffing policy typology described here is well known and widely used among both practitioners and scholars of international businesses, recently some critics have claimed that the typology is too simplistic and it may obscure the internal differentiation of management practices within international businesses. The critics claim that within some international businesses, staffing policies vary significantly from national subsidiary to national subsidiary so that while some are managed on an ethnocentric basis, others are managed in a polycentric or geocentric manner.[8] Other critics note that the staffing policy adopted by a firm is primarily driven by its geographic scope, as opposed to its strategic orientation, with firms that have a very broad geographic scope being the most likely to have a geocentric mind-set.[9] Thus Coca-Cola, which is involved in around 200 countries, is by this argument more likely to have a geocentric mind-set than a firm that is involved in only three countries.

[8]P. M. Rosenzweig and N. Nohria, "Influences on Human Resource Management Practices in Multinational Corporations," *Journal of International Business Studies* 25 (1994), pp. 229–51.
[9]Kobrin, "Geocentric Mindset and Multinational Strategy."

TABLE 18.3

Expatriate Failure Rates

Recall Rate Percent	Percent of Companies
U.S. multinationals	
20–40%	7%
10–20	69
<10	24
European multinationals	
11–15%	3%
6–10	38
<5	59
Japanese multinationals	
11–19%	14%
6–10	10
<5	76

Source: Data from R. L. Tung. "Selection and Training Procedures of U.S., European, and Japanese Multinationals," California Management Review *25 (1982), pp. 57–71.*

The Expatriate Problem

Two of the three staffing policies we have discussed—the ethnocentric and the geocentric—rely on extensive use of expatriate managers. With an ethnocentric policy, the expatriates are all home-country nationals who are transferred abroad. With a geocentric approach, the expatriates need not be home-country nationals; the firm does not base transfer decisions on nationality. A prominent issue in the international staffing literature is **expatriate failure**—the premature return of an expatriate manager to his or her home country.[10] Here we briefly review the evidence on expatriate failure before discussing a number of ways in which the expatriate failure rate can be minimized.

Expatriate failure rates

Expatriate failure represents a failure of the firm's selection policies to identify individuals who will not thrive abroad. The costs of expatriate failure are high. One estimate is that the average cost per failure to the parent firms can be as high as three times the expatriate's annual domestic salary plus the cost of relocation (which is affected by currency exchange rates and location of assignment).[11] Other research suggests that between 16 and 40 percent of all American employees sent abroad return from their assignments early, and each premature return costs over $100,000. In addition approximately 30 to 50 percent of American expatriates, whose average compensation package runs to $250,000 per annum, stay at their international assignments but are considered ineffective or marginally effective by their firms.[12] In one study, R. L. Tung surveyed a number of U.S., European, and Japanese multinationals.[13] Her results, summarized in Table 18.3., suggest that 76 percent of U.S. multinationals experience expatriate failure rates of 10 percent or more, with 7 percent of U.S. multinationals experiencing a failure rate of more than 20 percent. Tung's work also suggests that U.S.-based multinationals experience a much higher expatriate failure rate than either European or Japanese multinationals.

Tung asked her sample of multinational managers to indicate reasons for expatriate failure. For U.S. multinationals, the reasons, in descending order of importance, were

1. Inability of spouse to adjust.
2. Manager's inability to adjust.
3. Other family problems.
4. Manager's personal or emotional maturity.
5. Inability to cope with larger overseas responsibility.

---

[10]J. S. Black, M. Mendenhall, and G. Oddou, "Towards a Comprehensive Model of International Adjustment, "*Academy of Management Review* 16 (1991), pp. 291–317.

[11]M. G. Harvey, "The Multinational Corporation's Expatriate Problem: An Application of Murphy's Law," *Business Horizons* 26 (1983), pp. 71–78.

[12]Black, Mendenhall, and Oddou, "Towards a Comprehensive Model of International Adjustment."

[13]R. L. Tung, "Selection and Training Procedures of U.S., European, and Japanese Multinationals," *California Management Review* 25 (1982), pp. 57–71.

Managers of European firms gave only one reason consistently to explain expatriate failure: the inability of the manager's spouse to adjust to a new environment. For the Japanese firms, the reasons for failure, in descending order of importance, were

1. Inability to cope with larger overseas responsibility.
2. Difficulties with new environment.
3. Personal or emotional problems.
4. Lack of technical competence.
5. Inability of spouse to adjust.

Perhaps the most striking difference between these lists is that "inability of spouse to adjust" was the number one reason for expatriate failure among U.S. and European multinationals but only the number five reason among Japanese multinationals. Tung comments that this difference is not surprising, given the role and status to which Japanese society traditionally relegates the wife and the fact that most of the Japanese expatriate managers in the study were men.

Since Tung's study a number of other studies have confirmed that the inability of a spouse to adjust, the inability of the manager to adjust, or other family problems remain major reasons for continuing high levels of expatriate failure. One recent study, by International Orientation Resources, an HRM consulting firm, found that 60 percent of expatriate failures occur due to these three reasons.[14] The inability of expatriate managers to adjust to foreign postings seems to be caused by a lack of cultural skills on the part of the manager being transferred. According to one HRM consulting firm, this is because the expatriate selection process at many firms is fundamentally flawed. To quote: "Expatriate assignments rarely fail because the person cannot accommodate to the technical demands of the job. Typically, the expatriate selections are made by line managers based on technical competence. They fail because of family and personal issues and lack of cultural skills that haven't been part of the selection process."[15]

The failure of spouses to adjust to a foreign posting seems to be related to a number of factors. Often spouses find themselves in a foreign country without the familiar network of family and friends. Language differences make it difficult for them to make new friends. While this may not be too great a problem for the manager, who can make friends at work, it can be difficult for the spouse who might feel trapped at home. The problem is often exacerbated by immigration regulations prohibiting the spouse from taking employment.

Expatriate selection

One way of reducing expatriate failure rates is through improved selection procedures for screening out inappropriate candidates in advance. In a review of the research on this issue, Mendenhall and Oddou state that a major problem in many firms is that HRM managers tend to fall into the trap of equating domestic performance with overseas performance potential, selecting candidates for foreign postings accordingly.[16] Domestic performance and overseas performance potential are not the same thing. An executive who performs well in a domestic setting may not be able to adapt to managing in a different cultural setting. From their review of the research, Mendenhall and Oddou identified four dimensions that seem to predict success in a foreign posting: self-orientation, others-orientation, perceptual ability, and cultural toughness.

[14]C. M. Salomon, "Success Abroad Depends upon More Than Job Skills, "*Personnel Journal*, April 1994, pp. 51–58.

[15]Quote in Salomon, "Success Abroad Depends upon More Than Job Skills.

[16]M. Mendenhall and G. Oddou, "The Dimensions of Expatriate Acculturation: A Review, "*Academy of Management Review* 10 (1985), pp. 39–47.

1. *Self-orientation.* The attributes of this dimension strengthen the expatriate's self-esteem, self-confidence, and mental well-being. Expatriates with high self-esteem, self-confidence, and mental well-being were more likely to succeed in foreign postings. Mendenhall and Oddou concluded that such individuals were able to adapt their interests in food, sport, and music; had interests outside of work that could be pursued (e.g., hobbies); and were technically competent.

2. *Others-orientation.* The attributes of this dimension enhance the expatriate's ability to interact effectively with host-country nationals. The more effectively the expatriate interacts with host-country nationals, the more likely he or she is to succeed. Two factors seem to be particularly important here: relationship development and willingness to communicate. Relationship development refers to the ability to develop long-lasting friendships with host-country nationals. Willingness to communicate refers to the expatriate's willingness to use the host-country language. Although language fluency helps here, an expatriate need not be fluent to show willingness to communicate. Making the effort to use the language is what is important. Such gestures tend to be rewarded with greater cooperation by host-country nationals.

3. *Perceptual ability.* This is the ability to understand why people of other countries behave in the way they do; that is, the ability to empathize with them. This dimension seems critical for managing host-country nationals. Expatriate managers who lack this ability tend to treat foreign nationals as if they were home-country nationals. As a result they may experience significant management problems and considerable frustration. As one expatriate executive from Hewlett-Packard observed, "It took me six months to accept the fact that my staff meetings would start 30 minutes late, and that it would bother no one but me." According to Mendenhall and Oddou, well-adjusted expatriates tend to be nonjudgmental and nonevaluative in interpreting the behavior of host-country nationals and willing to be flexible in their management style, adjusting it as cultural conditions warrant.

4. *Cultural toughness.* This dimension refers to the fact that how well an expatriate adjusts to a particular posting tends to be related to the country of assignment. Some countries are much tougher postings than others because their cultures are more unfamiliar and uncomfortable. For example, many Americans regard Great Britain as a relatively easy foreign posting, and for good reason—U.S. and British cultures have much in common. On the other hand many Americans find postings in non-Western cultures, such as India, Southeast Asia, and the Middle East, to be much tougher.[17] The reasons are many, including poor health care and housing standards, inhospitable climate, a lack of Western entertainment, and language difficulties. It is also important to stress that many cultures are extremely male dominated and thus may be particularly difficult postings for female Western managers.

Mendenhall and Oddou note that standard psychological tests can be used to assess the first three of these dimensions, whereas a comparison of cultures can give managers a feeling for the fourth dimension. Their basic point is that in addition to domestic performance, these four dimensions should be given weight when selecting a manager for foreign posting. There is evidence, however, that current practice does not conform to Mendenhall and Oddou's recommendations. Tung's research, for example, showed that only 5 percent of the firms in her sample used formal procedures and psychological tests to assess the personality traits and relational abilities of potential expatriates.[18] Recent work by International Orientation Resources suggests that when selecting employees for foreign assignments, only 10 percent of

---

[17]I. Torbiorin, *Living Abroad: Personal Adjustment and Personnel Policy in the Overseas Setting* (New York: John Wiley & Sons, 1982.)

[18]R. L. Tung, "Selection and Training of Personnel for Overseas Assignments, *Columbia Journal of World Business* 16 (1981), pp. 68–78.

the 50 Fortune 500 firms they surveyed tested for important psychological traits such as cultural sensitivity, interpersonal skills, adaptability, and flexibility. Instead 90 percent of the time employees were selected on the basis of their technical expertise, not their cross-cultural fluency.[19]

One factor that Mendenhall and Oddou do not address is the problem of expatriate failure due to a spouse's inability to adjust. According to a number of other researchers, a review of the family situation should be a part of the expatriate selection process.[20] Yet a recent survey by Windam International, another international HRM management consulting firm, found that spouses were included in preselection interviews for foreign postings only 21 percent of the time, and that only half of them ever receive any cross-cultural training.[21]

❧ TRAINING AND MANAGEMENT DEVELOPMENT

Selection is just the first step in matching a manager with a job. The next step is training the manager to do the specific job. For example, an intensive training program might be used to give expatriate managers the skills required for success in a foreign posting. In contrast management development is a much broader concept. It is intended to develop the manager's skills over his or her career with the firm. Thus, as part of a management development program, over a number of years a manager might be sent on several foreign postings to build up her cross-cultural sensitivity and experience. At the same time, along with a group of other managers in the firm, she might attend management education programs at regular intervals.

Historically most international businesses have been more concerned with training than with management development. They tended to focus their training efforts on preparing home-country nationals for foreign postings. Recently, however, the shift toward greater global competition and the rise of transnational firms have brought about changes in this. It is increasingly common for firms to provide general management development programs in addition to training for particular posts. In many international businesses, the explicit purpose of these management development programs is strategic. The belief is management development is a tool that can be used to help the firm achieve its strategic goals.

With this distinction between training and management development in mind, in this section we first examine the types of training managers receive for foreign postings. Then we discuss the connection between management development and strategy in the international business.

Training for Expatriate Managers

Earlier in the chapter we saw that the two most common reasons for expatriate failure were the inability of a manager's spouse to adjust to a foreign environment and the manager's own inability to adjust to a foreign environment. Training can help the manager and his or her spouse cope with both of these problems. Cultural training, language training, and practical training all seem to reduce expatriate failure. We discuss each of these kinds of training here.[22] First, however, we should note that despite the usefulness of these kinds of training, evidence suggests that many managers receive no training before they are sent on foreign postings. One study found that only about 30 percent of managers sent on one- to five-year expatriate assignments received training before their departure.[23]

[19]Salomon, "Success Abroad Depends upon More Than Job Skills."

[20]S. Ronen, "Training and International Assignee," in *Training and Career Development*, ed. I. Goldstein (San Francisco: Jossey-Bass, 1985); and Tung, "Selection and Training of Personnel for Overseas Assignments."

[21]Salomon, "Success Abroad Depends upon More Than Job Skills."

[22]Dowling and Schuler, *International Dimensions of Human Resource Management.*

[23]Ibid.

Cultural training

Cultural training seeks to foster an appreciation for the host country's culture. The belief is that understanding a host country's culture will help the manager empathize with the culture, which will enhance her effectiveness in dealing with host-country nationals. It has been suggested that expatriates should receive training in the host country's culture, history, politics, economy, religion, and social and business practices.[24] It is also advisable to arrange for a familiarization trip to the host country before the formal transfer, since this seems to ease culture shock. Given the problems related to spouse adaptation, it is important that the spouse, and perhaps the whole family, be included in cultural training programs.

Language training

English is the language of world business; it is quite possible to conduct business all over the world using only English. For example, in ABB, a Swiss electrical equipment giant, the company's top 13 managers hold frequent meetings in different countries. Since they share no common first language, they speak only English, a foreign tongue to all but one.[25] Despite the prevalence of English, however, an exclusive reliance on English diminishes an expatriate manager's ability to interact with host-country nationals. As noted earlier in the chapter, a willingness to communicate in the language of the host country, even if the expatriate is far from fluent in the language, can help build rapport with local employees and improve the manager's effectiveness. Despite this, J. C. Baker's study of 74 executives of U.S. multinationals found that only 23 believed knowledge of foreign languages was necessary for conducting business abroad.[26] Those firms that did offer foreign language training for expatriates believed it improved their employees' effectiveness and enabled them to relate more easily to a foreign culture, which in turn fostered a better image of the firm in the host country.

Practical training

Practical training is aimed at helping the expatriate manager and her family ease themselves into day-to-day life in the host country. The sooner a day-to-day routine is established, the better are the prospects that the expatriate and her family will adapt successfully. One of the most critical needs is for a support network of friends for the expatriate. Where an expatriate community exists, firms often devote considerable effort to ensuring the new expatriate family is quickly integrated into that group. The expatriate community can be a useful source of support and information and can be invaluable in helping the family adapt to a foreign culture.

Repatriation of Expatriates

A largely overlooked but critically important issue in the training and development of expatriate managers is to prepare them for reentry into their home-country organization. Repatriation should be seen as the final link in an integrated, circular process that connects good selection and cross-cultural training of expatriate managers with completion of their term abroad and reintegration into their national organization. However, instead of having employees come home to share their knowledge and encourage other high-performing managers to take the same international career track, expatriates all too often face an entirely different scenario.[27]

---

[24]G. Baliga and J. C. Baker, "Multinational Corporate Policies for Expatriate Managers: Selection, Training, and Evaluation," *Advanced Management Journal*, Autumn 1985, pp. 31–38.

[25]C. Rapoport, "A Tough Swede Invades the U.S.," *Fortune*, June 20, 1992, pp. 67–70.

[26]J. C. Baker, "Foreign Language and Departure Training in U.S. Multinational Firms," *Personnel Administrator*, July 1984, pp. 68–70.

[27]J. S. Black and M. E. Mendenhall, *Global Assignments: Successfully Expatriating and Repatriating International Managers* (San Francisco: Jossey-Bass, 1992).

Often when they return home after a stint abroad—during which time they have typically been autonomous, well-compensated, and celebrated as a big fish in a little pond—they face an organization that doesn't know what they have done for the last few years, doesn't know how to use their new knowledge, and worse still doesn't particularly care. In the worst cases reentering employees have to scrounge for jobs, or firms will create standby positions that don't use the expatriates' skills and capabilities and fail to make the most of the business investment the firm has made in that individual.

Recent research illustrates the extent of this problem. According to one study of repatriated employees, 60 to 70 percent didn't know what their position would be when they returned home. Moreover, 60 percent said their organizations were vague about repatriation, about their new roles, and about their future career progression within the company, while 77 percent of those surveyed actually took jobs at a lower level in their home organization than in their international assignments.[28] It is small wonder then that 10 percent of returning expatriates leave their firm within a year of arriving home, while 14 percent leave within three years.[29]

The key to solving this problem is good human resource planning. Just as the HRM function needs to develop good selection and training programs for its expatriates, so it also needs to develop good programs for reintegrating expatriates back into work life within their home-country organization once their foreign assignment is over, and for utilizing the knowledge they acquired while abroad. For an example of the kind of program that might be used, read the next "Management Focus," which looks at the repatriation program developed at Monsanto.

Management Development and Strategy

Management development programs are designed to increase the overall skill levels of managers through a mix of ongoing management education and rotations of managers through a number of jobs within the firm to give them varied experiences. Put another way, management development programs are attempts to improve the overall productivity and quality of the firm's management resources.

Increasingly international businesses are using management development as a strategic tool. This is particularly true in firms pursuing a transnational strategy, as increasing numbers are. As we have seen, in such firms there are needs for a strong unifying corporate culture and for informal management networks to assist in coordination and control (see Table 18.2). In addition, transnational firm managers need to be able to detect pressures for local responsiveness, and that requires them to understand the culture of a host country.

In the first instance management development programs help build a unifying corporate culture by socializing new managers into the norms and value systems of the firm. In-house company training programs and intense interaction during off-site training can foster esprit de corps—shared experiences, informal networks, perhaps a company language or jargon—as well as develop technical competencies. These training events often include songs, picnics, and sporting events that promote feelings of togetherness. These rites of integration may include "initiation rites" wherein personal culture is stripped, company uniforms are donned (e.g., T-shirts bearing the company logo), and humiliation is inflicted (e.g., a pie in the face). The aim of all these activities is to strengthen a manager's identification with the company.[30]

Bringing managers together in one location for extended periods and rotating them through different jobs in several countries helps the firm build an informal management network. (Chapter 13 explained the importance of such networks in transnational firms.) Consider the Swedish telecommunications company L. M. Ericsson.

[28]Ibid.

[29]Figures from Global Reallocation Trend Survey undertaken by the National Foreign Trade Council. Cited in C. M. Salomon, "Success Abroad Depends upon More Than Job Skills.

[30]S. C. Schneider, "National v. Corporate Culture: Implications for Human Resource Management," *Human Resource Management* 27 (Summer 1988), pp. 231–46.

Monsanto is a global agricultural, chemical, and pharmaceutical company with revenues in excess of $10 billion and 30,000 employees. At any one time the company will have 100 mid- and higher-level managers who are on extended postings abroad. Two-thirds of these are Americans who are being posted overseas, while the remainder are foreign nationals being employed in the United States. At Monsanto the process of managing expatriates and their repatriation begins with a rigorous selection process and intensive cross-cultural training, both for the managers and for their families. As at many other global companies, the idea is to build an internationally minded cadre of highly capable managers who will lead the organization in the future.

One of the strongest features of this program is that employees and their sending and receiving managers, or sponsors, develop an agreement about their understanding of this assignment and how it will fit into the firm's business objectives. The focus is on why they are sending assignees abroad to do the job, and what their contribution to Monsanto will be when they return home. As part of this process, sponsoring managers are expected to be explicit about the kind of job opportunities the expatriate will have once she returns home.

Once they do arrive back in their home country, expatriate managers meet with cross-cultural trainers during debriefing sessions. They are also given the opportunity to showcase their experience to their peers, subordinates, and superiors, in special information exchange sessions.

However, Monsanto's repatriation program focuses on more than just business—it also attends to the family's reentry. Monsanto has found that difficulties with repatriation often have more to do with personal and family-related issues, than with work-related issues. But the personal matters obviously affect an employee's job performance, so it is important for the company to pay attention to such issues.

This is why Monsanto offers returning employees an opportunity to work through personal difficulties. Approximately three months after they return home, expatriates meet for three hours at work with several colleagues of their choice. The debriefing session is a conversation aided by a trained facilitator who has an outline to help the expatriate cover all the important aspects of the repatriation. An important purpose of the debriefing is to allow the employee to share important experiences and to enlighten managers, colleagues, and friends about his or her expertise so that others within the organization can use some of the global knowledge.

According to one participant, "It sounds silly, but it's such a hectic time in the family's life you don't have time to sit down and take stock of what's happening. You're going through the move, transitioning to a new job, a new house, the children may be going to a new school. This is a kind of oasis; a time to talk and put your feelings on the table." And apparently it works, for since the program was introduced in 1992 the attrition rate among returning expatriates has dropped sharply.

Source: C. M. Solomon, "Repatriation: Up, Down, or Out?" *Personnel Journal*, January 1995, pp. 28–34.

Interunit cooperation is extremely important in Ericsson, particularly for transferring know-how and core competencies from the parent to foreign subsidiaries, from foreign subsidiaries to the parent, and between foreign subsidiaries. To facilitate cooperation, Ericsson has a long-standing policy of transferring large numbers of people back and forth between headquarters and subsidiaries. Ericsson sends a team of 50 to 100 engineers and managers from one unit to another for a year or two. This process establishes a network of interpersonal contacts. This policy is effective for both solidifying a common culture in the company and coordinating the company's globally dispersed operations.[31]

❧ Performance Appraisal

A particularly thorny issue in many international businesses is how best to evaluate its expatriate managers' performance.[32] In this section we look at this issue and consider some guidelines for appraising expatriate performance.

Performance Appraisal Problems

The intrusion of unintentional bias makes it difficult to evaluate the performance of expatriate managers objectively. In most cases two groups evaluate the performance of expatriate managers, host-nation managers and home-office managers, and both are subject to bias. The host-nation managers may be biased by their own cultural frame of reference and set of expectations. For example, Oddou and Mendenhall report the case of a U.S. manager who introduced participative decision making while working in an Indian subsidiary.[33] The manager subsequently received a negative evaluation from host-country managers. Due to the strong social stratification that exists in India, managers are seen as experts who should not have to ask subordinates for details. The local employees apparently viewed the U.S. manager's attempt at participatory management as an indication that he was incompetent and did not know his job. This negatively affected his host-country manager's evaluation of his performance.

Home-country managers' appraisals may be biased by distance and, in some cases, by their own lack of experience working abroad. Home-office management is often not aware of what is going on in a foreign operation. Accordingly they tend to rely on "hard" data in evaluating an expatriate's performance, data such as the subunit's productivity, profitability, or market share. The problem with using such criteria is that they may reflect factors outside the expatriate manager's control (e.g., adverse changes in exchange rates, economic downturns). Moreover, hard data do not take into account many less-visible "soft" variables that are also important, such as an expatriate's ability to develop cross-cultural awareness and to work productively with local managers.

Due to such biases, many expatriate managers appear to feel that headquarters management evaluates them unfairly and does not fully appreciate the value of their skills and experience. This could be one reason many expatriates believe a foreign posting does not benefit their careers. In one study of personnel managers in U.S. multinationals, 56 percent of the managers surveyed stated that a foreign assignment is either detrimental or immaterial to one's career.[34]

---

[31]Bartlett and Ghoshal, *Managing across Borders*.

[32]G. Oddou and M. Mendenhall, "Expatriate Performance Appraisal: Problems and Solutions," in *International Human Resource Management*, ed. Mendenhall and Oddou (Boston: PWS-Kent, 1991); Dowling and Schuler, *International Dimensions*; R. S. Schuler and G. W. Florkowski, "International Human Resource Management," in: *Handbook for International Management Research*, ed. B. J. Punnett and O. Shenkar (Oxford: Blackwell, 1996).

[34]"Expatriates Often See Little Benefit to Careers in Foreign Stints, Indifference at Home, "*The Wall Street Journal*, December 11, 1989, p. B1.

FIGURE 18.1   Compensation of General Managers of $30 Million Firms in Selected Countries (in $000)

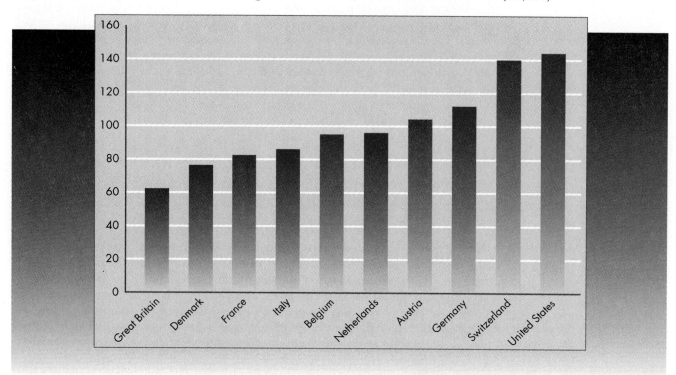

Source: Data from G. Oddou and M. Mendenhall, "Expatriate Performance Appraisal: Problems and Solutions," International Human Resource Management, ed. M. Mendenhall and G. Oddou (Boston: PSW-Kent, 1991).

Guidelines for Performance Appraisal

Several things can reduce bias in the performance appraisal process.[35] First, most expatriates appear to believe more weight should be given to an on-site manager's appraisal than to an off-site manager's appraisal. Due to proximity an on-site manager is more likely to be able to evaluate the soft variables that are important aspects of an expatriate's performance. The evaluation may be especially valid when the on-site manager is of the same nationality as the expatriate, since cultural bias should be alleviated.

In practice, however, home-office managers often write performance evaluations after receiving input from on-site managers. When this is the case, most experts recommend that a former expatriate who served in the same location should be involved in the appraisal process to help reduce bias. Finally, when the policy is for foreign on-site managers to write performance evaluations, home-office managers should probably be consulted before an on-site manager completes a formal termination evaluation. This makes sense because it gives the home-office manager the opportunity to balance what could be a very hostile evaluation based on a cultural misunderstanding.

⚘ COMPENSATION

Two issues are raised in every discussion of compensation practices in an international business. One is how compensation should be adjusted to reflect national differences in economic circumstances and compensation practices. The other issue is how expatriate managers should be paid. In this section we consider each issue in turn.

National Differences in Compensation

Substantial differences exist in the compensation of executives at the same level in various countries. Figure 18.1 compares the gross pay of general managers of $30 million companies in the United States and nine European countries. U.S. executives

---

[35]Oddou and Mendenhall, "Expatriate Performance"; and Schuler and Florkowski, "International Human Resource Management."

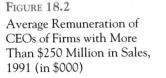

FIGURE 18.2

Average Remuneration of CEOs of Firms with More Than $250 Million in Sales, 1991 (in $000)

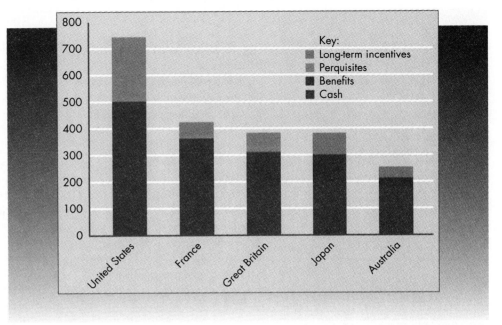

Source: Data estimates from Towers Perrin.

are paid significantly more than executives in most other countries except for Switzerland. The average U.S. executive is paid twice as much as his or her British counterpart. Figure 18.2 compares the average 1991 remuneration for CEOs of firms with sales in excess of $250 million in 5 countries. Again the United States is at the top of the list. In 1991 the average U.S. CEO received more than $750,000 in total compensation, compared with about $400,000 for the average British and Japanese CEO and under $300,000 for the average Australian CEO. More recent data for 1994 indicate these pay differentials have persisted. For example, in 1994 the average European CEO of firms with sales in excess of $250 million was paid $398,7121, while the average U.S. CEO was paid $819,428.[36] Notice, however, that much of the difference between U.S. CEOs and the other CEOs is that the U.S. CEOs receive a substantial proportion of their pay in the form of long-term incentives such as stock options. This reflects the belief, which has gained wider currency in the United States than elsewhere, that performance-related bonuses motivate managers to do a better job.

These differences in compensation practices raise a perplexing question for an international business: Should the firm pay executives in different countries according to the prevailing standards in each country, or should it equalize pay on a global basis? The problem does not really arise in firms pursuing ethnocentric or polycentric staffing policies. In ethnocentric firms the issue can be reduced to that of how much home-country expatriates should be paid (which we will consider later). As for polycentric firms, the lack of managers' mobility among national operations implies that pay can and should be kept country-specific. There would seem to be no point in paying executives in Great Britain the same as U.S. executives if they never work side by side.

However, this problem is very real in firms with geocentric staffing policies. Recall that a geocentric staffing policy is consistent with a transnational strategy. One aspect of this policy, from the HRM perspective, is the need for a cadre of international managers. By definition this cadre may comprise managers of many different nationalities. Should all members of such a cadre be paid the same salary and the same incentive pay? For a U.S.-based firm this would mean raising the compensation of foreign nationals to U.S. levels, which, given the high pay rates prevailing in the

---

[36]Data from Towers Perrin, cited in J. Flynn, "Continental Divide over Executive Pay," *Business Week*, July 3, 1995, pp. 40–41.

MANAGEMENT FOCUS
Executive Pay Policies for Global Managers

A recent survey of human resource professionals in 45 large U.S. multinational companies undertaken by Organizational Resources Consulting, an international HRM consulting firm, found that all 45 companies viewed differing pay levels and perks as their biggest problem when trying to develop an international work force. In contrast only 60 percent of these companies stated that cultural differences and repatriation processes were serious problems. The root of the problem is cost; expatriate pay packages that are based on American salaries and needs are increasingly seen as too expensive. In an attempt to deal with this issue, many international businesses are trying to develop special pay schemes for their cadre of internationally mobile managers.

At Hewlett-Packard (HP) about 600 people a year are transferred across national borders. Although most of these transferees are on short-term (one-to-two-year) assignments, up to 25 percent are on indefinite assignments. HP ties the pay of short-term transferees to pay scales in their home country, but longer-term HP transferees are quickly switched to the pay scale of their host country and paid according to prevailing local standards. For employees moving from high-pay countries such as Germany to lower-pay countries, such as Britain, HP offers temporary bridging payments to ease the adjustment process.

The Minnesota Mining and Manufacturing Co. has a different type of program for longer-term

United States, could be very expensive. If the firm does not equalize pay, it could cause considerable resentment among foreign nationals who are members of the international cadre and work side by side with U.S. nationals. If a firm is serious about building an international cadre, it may have to pay its international executives the same basic salary irrespective of their country of origin or assignment. The next "Management Focus" contains several examples of how some international businesses have tried to deal with this problem.

Expatriate Pay

The most common approach to expatriate pay is the balance sheet approach. This approach equalizes purchasing power across countries so employees can enjoy the same living standard in their foreign posting that they enjoyed at home. The approach also provides financial incentives to offset qualitative differences between assignment locations.[37] Figure 18.3 shows a typical balance sheet. Note that home-country outlays for the employee are designated as income taxes, housing expenses, expenditures for goods and services (food, clothing, entertainment, etc.), and reserves (savings, pension contributions, etc.) The balance sheet approach attempts to provide expatriates with the same standard of living in their host countries as they enjoy at home plus a financial inducement (i.e., premium, incentive) for accepting an overseas assignment.

The components of the typical expatriate compensation package are a base salary, a foreign service premium, allowances of various types, tax differentials, and benefits. We shall briefly review each of these components.[38] For now

---

[37]C. Reynolds, "Compensation of Overseas Personnel," in *Handbook of Human Resource Administration*, ed. J. J. Famularo (New York: McGraw-Hill, 1986).

[38]M. Helms, "International Executive Compensation Practices," in *International Human Resource Management*, ed. M. Mendenhall and G. Oddou (Boston: PWS-Kent, 1991).

expatriates. The company developed the program because it has drastically altered its international organization. In Europe, for example, 3M used to organize its operations on a country-by-country basis. Now, however, 3M has established Europeanwide divisions. As a result many 3M executives who might have spent their entire career in one country are now being asked to move, perhaps permanently, to another country.

The 3M program compares net salaries in both the old and new country by subtracting the major costs, such as taxes and housing, from gross pay. The transferred executive then gets whichever pay packet is highest. Thus when 3M transfers a German executive to France, the German remains on her home-country pay

scale. But a British employee transferred to Germany, where salaries are higher, can expect to be switched to the German pay scale. However, although the policy does consider local housing costs, it doesn't compensate for higher housing costs through a special payment scheme, the way many traditional expatriate pay policies did. The reason being that any housing subsidy that resulted could last for the rest of an executive's career following a transfer—and this would be a very expensive proposition.

The large oil company Phillips Petroleum has adopted yet another policy. At Phillips the policy used to be that when a third country national, such as a British citizen, was transferred abroad (for example, from Britain to Kuwait), he would be paid

in U.S. dollars so his salary would be raised to a level equivalent to that of someone in the United States doing a similar job. This, however, turned out to be a very expensive policy given the generally high level of pay prevailing in the United States. Thus now Phillips has a "third country nationals program." Under this program the transferred employee is given generous housing allowances and educational assistance for his children. However, his salary is now pegged to the level prevailing in his home country, and not that in the United States, or the country to which the employee is being transferred.

Sources: A. Bennett, "Executive Pay: What's an Expatriate?" *The Wall Street Journal*, April 21, 1994, p. A5; and Flynn, "Continental Divide over Executive Pay," *Business Week*, July 3, 1995, pp. 40–41

note that an expatriate's total compensation package may amount to three times what he or she would cost the firm in a home-country posting. Because of the high cost of expatriates, many firms have reduced their use of them in recent years. However, their ability to do so is often limited by their desire to build a cadre of international managers. Thus a firm's ability to reduce its use of expatriates may be limited, particularly if it is pursuing an ethnocentric or geocentric staffing policy.

Base salary
An expatriate's base salary is normally in the same range as the base salary for a similar position in the home country. The base salary is normally paid in either the home-country currency or in the local currency.

Foreign service premium
A foreign service premium is extra pay the expatriate receives for working outside his or her country of origin. It is offered as an inducement to accept foreign postings. It compensates the expatriate for having to live in an unfamiliar country isolated from family and friends, having to deal with a new culture and language, and having to adapt new work habits and practices. Many firms pay foreign service premiums as a percentage of base salary ranging from 10 to 30 percent after taxes.

Allowances
Four types of allowances are often included in an expatriate's compensation package: hardship allowances, housing allowances, cost-of-living allowances, and education allowances. A hardship allowance is paid when the expatriate is being sent

FIGURE 18.3

A Typical Balance Sheet

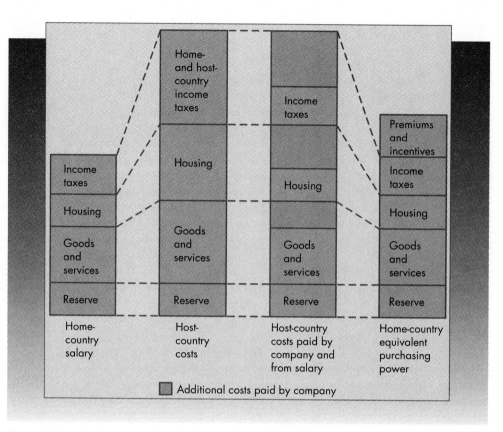

Source: C. Reynolds, "Compensation of Overseas Personnel," in Handbook of Human Resource Administration, 2nd ed., ed. J. J. Famularo (New York: McGraw-Hill, 1986), p. 51.

to a difficult location. A difficult location is usually defined as one where such basic amenities as health care, schools, and retail stores are grossly deficient by the standards of the expatriate's home country. A housing allowance is normally given to ensure that the expatriate can afford the same quality of housing in the foreign country as at home. In locations where housing is very expensive (e.g., London, Tokyo), this allowance can be as much as 10 to 30 percent of the expatriate's total compensation package. A cost-of-living allowance ensures that the expatriate will enjoy the same standard of living in the foreign posting as at home. An education allowance ensures that an expatriate's children receive adequate schooling (by home-country standards). Host-country public schools are sometimes not suitable for an expatriate's children, in which case they must attend a private school.

Taxation

Unless a host country has a reciprocal tax treaty with the expatriate's home country, the expatriate may have to pay income tax to both the home- and host-country governments. When a reciprocal tax treaty is not in force, the firm typically pays the expatriate's income tax in the host country. In addition firms normally make up the difference when a higher income tax rate in a host country reduces an expatriate's take-home pay.

Benefits

Many firms also ensure that their expatriates receive the same level of medical and pension benefits abroad that they received at home. This can be very costly for the firm, since many benefits that are tax deductible for the firm in the home country (e.g., medical and pension benefits) may not be deductible out of the country.

✤ INTERNATIONAL LABOR RELATIONS

The HRM function of an international business is typically responsible for international labor relations. From a strategic perspective, the key issue in international labor relations is the degree to which organized labor is able to limit the choices of an international business. A firm's ability to integrate and consolidate its global operations to realize experience curve and location economies can be limited by organized labor. Put another way, a firm's ability to pursue a transnational or global strategy can be significantly constrained by the actions of labor unions. Prahalad and Doz give the example of General Motors, which bought peace with labor unions by agreeing not to integrate and consolidate operations in the most efficient manner.[39] In the early 1980s General Motors made substantial investments in Germany—matching its new investments in Austria and Spain—at the demand of the German metal workers' unions.

One task of the HRM function is to foster harmony and minimize conflict between the firm and organized labor. With this in mind, this section is divided into three parts. First, we review the concerns of organized labor about multinational enterprises. Second, we look at how organized labor has tried to deal with these concerns. And third, we look at how international businesses manage their labor relations to minimize labor disputes.

The Concerns of Organized Labor

Labor in general is typically most concerned about pay, job security, and working conditions, and labor unions try to get better pay, greater job security, and better working conditions for their members through collective bargaining with management. The union's bargaining power is derived largely from its ability to threaten to disrupt production, either by a strike or some other form of work protest (e.g., refusing to work overtime). This threat is credible, however, only insofar as management has no alternative but to employ union labor.

A principal concern of domestic unions about multinational firms is that the multinational can counter their bargaining power with the power to move production to another country. Ford, for example, very clearly threatened British unions with a plan to move manufacturing to Continental Europe unless British workers abandoned work rules that limited productivity, showed restraint in negotiating for wage increases, and curtailed strikes and other work disruptions.[40]

Another concern of organized labor is that an international business will keep highly skilled tasks in its home country and farm out only low-skilled tasks to foreign plants. Unions feel that if their members perform only low-skilled tasks, those tasks could just as well be performed by workers in yet another country. Such a practice makes it relatively easy for an international business to switch production from one location to another as economic conditions warrant. Consequently the bargaining power of organized labor is once more reduced.

A final union concern arises when an international business attempts to import employment practices and contractual agreements from its home country. When these practices are alien to those in the host country, organized labor fears the change will reduce its influence and power. This concern has surfaced in response to Japanese multinationals that have been trying to export their style of labor relations to other countries. For example, much to the annoyance of the United Auto Workers (UAW), most Japanese auto plants in the United States are not unionized. As a result union influence in the auto industry is on the decline.

---

[39]C. K. Prahalad and Y. L. Doz, *The Multinational Mission* (New York: The Free Press, 1987).
[40]Ibid.

The Strategy of Organized Labor

Organized labor has responded to the increased bargaining power of multinational corporations by taking three actions: (1) trying to establish international labor organizations, (2) lobbying for national legislation to restrict multinationals, and (3) trying to achieve international regulations on multinationals through such organizations as the United Nations. None of these efforts has been very successful.

In the 1960s organized labor began to establish a number of international trade secretariats (ITSs) to provide worldwide links for national unions in particular industries. Their long-term goal was to be able to bargain transnationally with multinational firms. Organized labor believed that by coordinating union action across countries through an ITS, it could effectively counter the power of a multinational corporation by threatening to disrupt production on an international scale. For example, Ford's threat to move production from Great Britain to other European locations would not have been credible if the unions in various European countries had united to oppose it.

In practice, however, the ITSs have had virtually no real success. Although national unions may want to cooperate, they also compete with each other to attract investment from international businesses, and hence jobs for their members. For example, in attempting to gain new jobs for their members, national unions in the auto industry often court auto firms that are seeking locations for new plants. One reason Nissan chose to build its European production facilities in Great Britain rather than Spain was that the British unions agreed to greater concessions than the Spanish unions did. As a result of such competition between national unions, cooperation is difficult to establish.

A further impediment to cooperation has been the wide variation in union structure across countries. Trade unions developed independently in each country. The structure and ideology of unions tend to vary significantly from country to country, as does the nature of collective bargaining. For example, in Great Britain, France, and Italy many unions are controlled by left-wing socialists, who view collective bargaining through the lens of "class conflict." Most union leaders in Germany, the Netherlands, Scandinavia, and Switzerland are far more moderate politically. The ideological gap between union leaders in different countries has made cooperation difficult, since divergent ideologies are reflected in radically different views about the role of a union in society and the stance unions should take toward multinationals.

Organized labor has also met with only limited success in its efforts to get national and international bodies to regulate multinationals. Such international organizations as the International Labor Organization (ILO) and the Organization for Economic Cooperation and Development (OECD) have adopted codes of conduct for multinational firms to follow in labor relations. However, these guidelines are not as far-reaching as many unions would like; moreover, they do not provide any enforcement mechanisms. Many researchers report that such guidelines are of only limited effectiveness.[41]

Approaches to Labor Relations

International businesses differ markedly in their approaches to international labor relations. Perhaps the main difference is the degree to which labor relations activities are centralized or decentralized in the firms. Historically most international businesses have decentralized international labor relations activities to their foreign subsidiaries, since labor laws, union power, and the nature of collective bargaining varied so much from country to country. It made sense to decentralize the labor relations function to local managers. The belief was that there was no way central management could effectively handle the complexity of simultaneously managing labor relations in a number of different environments.

---

[41]Schuler and Florkowski, "International Human Resource Management."

Although this logic still holds, there is now a trend toward greater centralized control over international labor relations in international businesses. This trend reflects international firms' attempts to rationalize their global operations. The general rise in competitive pressure in industry after industry has made it more important for firms to control their costs. Since labor costs account for such a large percentage of total costs, many firms are now using the threat to move production to another country in their negotiations with unions to change work rules and limit wage increases (as Ford did in Europe). Because such a move would involve major new investments and plant closures, this bargaining tactic requires the input of headquarters management. Thus the level of centralized input into labor relations is increasing.

In addition there is growing realization that the way work is organized within a plant can be a major source of competitive advantage. Much of the competitive advantage of Japanese automakers, for example, has been attributed to the use of self-managing teams, job rotation, cross-training, and the like in their Japanese plants.[42] To replicate their domestic performance in foreign plants, the Japanese firms have tried to replicate their work practices there. This often brings them into direct conflict with traditional work practices in those countries, as sanctioned by the local labor unions, so the Japanese firms have often made their foreign investments contingent on the local union accepting a radical change in work practices. The headquarters of many Japanese firms bargains directly with local unions to get union agreement to changes in work rules before committing to an investment. For example, before Nissan decided to invest in northern England, it got a commitment from British unions to agree to a change in traditional work practices. By its very nature, pursuing such a strategy requires centralized control over the labor relations function.

❧ Summary of Chapter

This chapter has focused on human resource management in international businesses. HRM activities include human resource strategy, staffing, performance evaluation, management development, compensation, and labor relations. None of these activities is performed in a vacuum; all must be appropriate to the firm's strategy. The following points were made in the chapter:

1. Firm success requires HRM policies to be congruent with the firm's strategy and with its formal and informal structure and controls.

2. Staffing policy is concerned with selecting employees who have the skills required to perform particular jobs. Staffing policy can be a tool for developing and promoting a corporate culture.

3. An ethnocentric approach to staffing policy fills all key management positions in an international business with parent-country nationals. The policy is congruent with an international strategy. A drawback is that ethnocentric staffing can result in cultural myopia.

4. A polycentric staffing policy uses host-country nationals to manage foreign subsidiaries and parent-country nationals for the key positions at corporate

headquarters. This approach can minimize the dangers of cultural myopia, but it can create a gap between home- and host-country operations. The policy is best suited to a multidomestic strategy.

5. A geocentric staffing policy seeks the best people for key jobs throughout the organization, regardless of their nationality. This approach is consistent with building a strong unifying culture and informal management network and is thus well suited to both global and transnational strategies. Immigration policies of national governments may limit a firm's ability to pursue this policy.

6. A prominent issue in the international staffing literature is expatriate failure, defined as the premature return of an expatriate manager to his or her home country. The costs of expatriate failure can be substantial.

7. Expatriate failure can be reduced by selection procedures that screen out inappropriate candidates. The most successful expatriates seem to be those who have high self-esteem and self-confidence, get along well with others, are willing to attempt to communicate in a foreign language, and can empathize with people of other cultures.

---

[42]See J. P. Womack, D. T. Jones, and D. Roos, *The Machine that Changed the World* (New York: Rawson Associates, 1990).

8. Training can lower the probability of expatriate failure. It should include cultural training, language training, and practical training, and it should be provided to both the expatriate manager and the spouse.

9. Management development programs attempt to increase the overall skill levels of managers through a mix of ongoing management education and rotation of managers through different jobs within the firm to give them varied experiences. Management development is often used as a strategic tool to build a strong unifying culture and informal management network, both of which support transnational and global strategies.

10. It can be difficult to evaluate the performance of expatriate managers objectively due to the intrusion of unintentional bias. A number of steps can be taken to reduce this bias.

11. Country differences in compensation practices raise a difficult question for an international business: Should the firm pay executives in different countries according to the standards in each country or equalize pay on a global basis?

12. The most common approach to expatriate pay is the balance sheet approach. This approach aims to equalize purchasing power so employees can enjoy the same living standard in their foreign posting that they had at home.

13. A key issue in international labor relations is the degree to which organized labor is able to limit the choices available to an international business. A firm's ability to pursue a transnational or global strategy can be significantly constrained by the actions of labor unions.

14. A principal concern of organized labor is that the multinational can counter union bargaining power with threats to move production to another country.

15. Organized labor has tried to counter the bargaining power of multinationals by forming international labor organizations. In general these efforts have not borne fruit.

🐟 CRITICAL DISCUSSION QUESTIONS

1. What are the main advantages and disadvantages of the ethnocentric, polycentric, and geocentric approaches to staffing policy? When is each approach appropriate?

2. Research evidence suggests that many expatriate employees encounter many problems that limit both their effectiveness in a foreign posting and their contribution to the company when they return home. What are the main causes and consequences of these problems, and how might a firm reduce the occurrence of such problems?

3. What is the link between an international business's strategy and its human resource management policies, particularly with regard to the use of expatriate employees and their pay scale?

4. In what ways can organized labor constrain the strategic choices of an international business? How can an international business limit these constraints?

🐟 CLOSING CASE   Global HRM at Colgate-Palmolive, Inc.

Colgate-Palmolive, the $6 billion a year personal products giant, earns nearly two thirds of its revenues outside the United States. For years Colgate succeeded, as many U.S. multinationals have, by developing products at home and then "throwing them over the wall" to foreign subsidiaries. Each major foreign subsidiary was responsible for local manufacturing and marketing. Senior management positions in these subsidiaries were typically held by Americans, and practically all of the company's U.S.-based managers were U.S. citizens.

In the early 1980s Colgate realized that if it was going to succeed in the rapidly changing international business environment, it would have to develop more of a transnational orientation. Its competitors, such as Procter & Gamble, Unilever, and Kao, were trying to become transnational companies, and Colgate needed to follow suit. One of the most important aspects of becoming a transnational is developing an international cadre of executive managers who are as at home working in one culture as in another and who have the ability to rise above their ethnocentric perspectives.

As a first step toward building such a cadre, Colgate began recruiting college graduates in 1987 and putting them through an intensive international training program. The typical recruit holds an M.B.A. from a U.S. university, speaks at least one foreign language, has lived outside the United States, and has strong computer skills and business experience. Over one quarter of the participants are foreign nationals.

The trainees spend 24 months in a U.S. program. During three-month stints, they learn global business development secrets of, for example, Colgate toothpaste, compiling a guide for introducing a new product or revamping an existing one in various national markets. Participants also receive additional language instruction and take international business trips. When they have completed the program, the participants become associate product managers in the United States or abroad. Unlike most U.S. companies, Colgate does not send foreign-born trainees to their native countries for their initial jobs. Instead it is more likely that a French national will remain in the United States, a U.S.

national will be sent to Germany, and a British national will go to Spain. The foreigners receive the same generous expatriate compensation packages the Americans do, even if they are assigned to their home country. One problem that has emerged is that this extra pay can create resentment among locally hired managers of foreign subsidiaries. Colgate is trying to resolve this problem by urging its foreign subsidiaries to send their brightest young managers to the training program.

In addition to the management training program, Colgate has taken a number of other steps to develop its international cadre of managers. In Europe, for example, the company is trying to develop "Euromanagers," managers who have experience working in several European countries. This is a departure from the established practice of having managers spend most (if not all) of their working

careers in their home country. Also Colgate now tries to ensure that project teams contain managers from several countries.

CASE DISCUSSION QUESTIONS

1. What is the relationship between HRM and strategy at Colgate-Palmolive?

2. How could Colgate-Palmolive's international training program improve its economic performance?

3. What potential problem and pitfalls do you see with Colgate-Palmolive's international training program?

Sources: J. S. Lublin, "Managing Globally: Younger Managers Learn Global Skills," The Wall Street Journal, March 31, 1992, p. B1; B. Hagerty, "Companies in Europe Seeking Executives Who Can Cross Borders in a Single Bound," The Wall Street Journal, January 25, 1991, p. B1; and C. M. Salomon, "Global Operations Demand that HR Re-think Diversity," Personnel Journal 73 (1994), pp. 40–50.

CHAPTER NINETEEN

ACCOUNTING IN THE INTERNATIONAL BUSINESS

THE ADOPTION OF INTERNATIONAL ACCOUNTING STANDARDS IN GERMANY

In 1995 a number of major German firms indicated they soon would adopt international accounting standards that will reveal far more about their financial performance. This decision represents a major shift away from inscrutable German accounting standards that often hid as much about a company's financial performance as they revealed. The change was driven by the recognition that German capital markets are too narrow and illiquid to satisfy the future funding requirements of many major German companies. Increasingly major German corporations are realizing that to raise capital internationally, it is in their best interests to get a listing on the New York Stock Exchange (NYSE) as a prelude to issuing equity and raising debt through the New York market.

Historically German firms have almost never resorted to international capital markets to raise additional equity. Their view was that bank debt was adequate. However, in recent years the German market for debt has become quite expensive, while the possibility of raising additional equity in Germany has been limited by the relatively small and illiquid nature of the German equity market. The move among German firms to raise equity on international capital markets began in the early 1990s when a number of major German firms, including Daimler-Benz, Siemens, and Volkswagen, applied to the U.S. Securities and Exchange Commission (SEC) for a listing. The SEC, however, was not particularly responsive. In the SEC's view German accounting standards were not comparable to those in the United States and did not provide sufficient information to investors on a company's

performance. Among the SEC's objections was the German practice of not disclosing the size of a company's financial reserves and pension fund commitments, as well as the more liberal policy for writing down goodwill in Germany, which tended to overstate a firm's financial performance relative to what would be reported under U.S. accounting rules.

After the initial rebuff from the SEC, this group of firms fell apart quite rapidly. Most were shocked, however, when Daimler-Benz announced in 1993 that it had reached a unilateral agreement with the SEC and would soon have a listing on the NYSE. To achieve this Daimler-Benz had to agree to issue two sets of accounts, one that adhered to German standards and another that adhered to U.S. Generally Accepted Accounting Principles (GAAP). When Daimler-Benz reported its 1994 financial result, the impact of using different accounting standards was laid bare for all too see. Under German rules, Daimler-Benz reported a profit of over $100 million, whereas under U.S. GAAP the company reported a $1 billion loss!

Although no other German firm has yet to follow the lead of Daimler-Benz, several have moved a considerable

way toward the SEC's position by announcing they are willing to adopt international accounting standards. International accounting standards were devised by a London-based committee of leading accountants beginning in 1987, the International Accounting Standards Committee (IASC), in an attempt to bring consistency to rules that change from country to country. The international standards are more forthcoming about financial performance than the German rules. However, they still fall some way short of the U.S. GAAP, primarily because they allow for a looser treatment of goodwill. In March 1995 the pharmaceutical company Schering AG became the first German firm to shift completely to international standards. It was quickly followed by Bayer AG. Other German firms that are considering taking similar action include Hoechst AG, BASF, and Siemens.

At this point the planned privatization of Germany's state-owned telecommunications provider, Deutsche Telekom, is emerging as a key event propelling Germany and German firms toward accepting more open international and SEC-approved accounting principles. For years the German Ministry of Justice, which oversees corporate legal matters, was strongly opposed to any shift in German accounting principles. But the government recently acknowledged the Deutsche Telekom equity issue planned for 1996 is too big to be absorbed by the German equity market. Many now believe the SEC will eventually allow international standards, perhaps with some modifications. If that occurs many large German firms may decide to adopt the modified international standards and seek a listing on the NYSE.

Sources: P. Gumbel and G. Steinmetz, "German Firms Shift to More Open Accounting," *The Wall Street Journal*, March 15, 1995, p. C1; "Daimler-Benz: A Capital Suggestion," *The Economist*, April 9, 1994, p. 69; and L. Berton, "All Accountants May Soon Speak the Same Language," *The Wall Street Journal*, August 29, 1995, p. A15.

FIGURE 19.1
Accounting Information
and Capital Flows

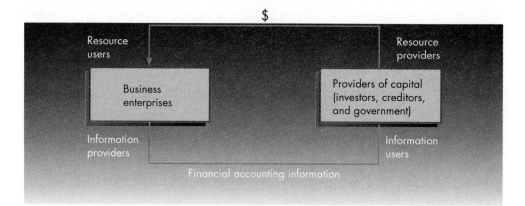

❧ INTRODUCTION

Accounting has often been referred to as "the language of business."[1] This language finds expression in profit and loss statements, balance sheets, budgets, investment analysis, and tax analysis. Accounting information is the means by which firms communicate their financial position to the providers of capital—investors, creditors, and government. It enables the providers of capital to assess the value of their investments, or the security of their loans, and to make decisions about future resource allocations (see Figure 19.1). Accounting information is also the means by which firms report their income to the government, so the government can assess how much tax the firm owes. It is also the means by which the firm can evaluate its performance, control its internal expenditures, and plan for future expenditures and income. Thus it is no exaggeration to say that a good accounting function is critical to the smooth running of the firm.

International businesses are confronted with a number of accounting problems that do not confront purely domestic businesses. The opening case draws attention to one of these problems—the lack of consistency in the accounting standards of different countries. We begin this chapter by looking at the source of these country differences. Then we shift our attention to the attempts currently under way to establish international accounting and auditing standards—the International Accounting Standards Committee (IASC) referred to in the case.

Then we will examine the problems arising when an international business with operations in more than one country must produce consolidated financial statements. These firms face special problems because, for example, the accounts for their operations in France will be in francs, in Italy they will be in lira, and in Japan they will be in yen. If the firm is based in the United States, it will have to decide what basis to use for translating all these accounts into U.S. dollars. The last issue we discuss in the chapter is that of control in an international business. We touched on the issue of control in Chapter 13 in rather abstract terms. Here we look at control from an accounting perspective.

❧ COUNTRY DIFFERENCES IN ACCOUNTING STANDARDS

Accounting is shaped by the environment in which it operates. Just as different countries have different political systems, economic systems, and cultures, so they also have different accounting systems.[2] In each country the accounting system has evolved in response to the demands for accounting information in that country.

---

[1]G. G. Mueller, H. Gernon, and G. Meek, *Accounting: An International Perspective* (Homewood, IL: Richard D. Irwin, 1991).

[2]S. J. Gary, "Towards a Theory of Cultural Influence on the Development of Accounting Systems Internationally," *Abacus* 3 (1988), pp. 1–15; and R. S. Wallace, O. Gernon, and H. Gernon, "Frameworks for International Comparative Financial Accounting," *Journal of Accounting Literature* 10 (1991), pp. 209–64.

An example of differences in accounting conventions concerns employee disclosures. In many European countries government regulations require firms to publish detailed information about their training and employment policies, whereas there is no such requirement in the United States. Another example relates to the treatment of goodwill. A firm's goodwill is any advantage, such as a well-regarded trademark or brand name (e.g., the Coca-Cola brand name and trademark) that should enable a firm to earn higher profits than its competitors. When one company acquires another in a takeover, the value of the goodwill in the acquired firm is calculated as the excess paid for a firm above its book value, which is often a substantial sum. Under accounting rules prevailing in many countries, acquiring firms are allowed to deduct the value of goodwill from the amount of *equity* or *net worth* reported on their balance sheet. In contrast, in the United States goodwill has to be deducted from the *profits* of the acquiring firm over a period that can be as long as 40 years (although firms typically write down goodwill much more rapidly than this). The effect of this different convention is that if we take two equally profitable firms, one German and one American, both of which make comparable acquisitions of firms that have identical goodwill, after the acquisition the American firm will report a significantly lower profit rate than the German firm, primarily because of differences in accounting conventions relating to the treatment of goodwill.[3]

Despite attempts to harmonize accounting standards by developing internationally acceptable accounting conventions (more on this later) a myriad of differences between national accounting systems still remain. A recent study tried to quantify the extent of these differences by comparing various accounting measures and profitability ratios across a sample of 22 developed nations, including Australia, Britain, France, Germany, Hong Kong, Japan, Spain, and South Korea.[4] The study found that among the 22 countries there were 76 differences in the way cost of goods sold was assessed, 65 differences in the assessment of return on assets, 54 differences in the measurement of research and development expenses as a percentage of sales, and 20 differences in the calculation of net profit margin. These differences make it very difficult to compare the financial performance of firms based in different nations.

Although many factors can influence the development of a country's accounting system, there appear to be five main variables:[5]

1. The relationship between business and the providers of capital.
2. Political and economic ties with other countries.
3. The level of inflation.
4. The level of a country's economic development
5. The prevailing culture in a country.

(See Figure 19.2.) We will review each of these variables in turn.

Relationship between Business and Providers of Capital

There are three main external sources of capital for business enterprises—individual investors, banks, and government. In most advanced countries all three sources are of some importance. In the United States, for example, business firms can raise capital by selling shares and bonds to individual investors through the stock market and the bond market. They can also borrow capital from banks and, in rather limited cases (particularly to support investments in defense-related R&D) from the government. The importance of each source of capital varies from country to country. In

---

[3]K. M. Dunne and G. A. Ndubizu, "International Acquisition Accounting Method and Corporate Multinationalism," *Journal of International Business Studies* 26 (1995), pp. 361–77.

[4]W. A. Wallace and J. Walsh, "Apples to Apples: Profits Abroad," *Financial Executive*, May–June 1995, pp. 28–31.

[5]Wallace, Gernon, and Gernon, "Frameworks for International Comparative Financial Accounting."

FIGURE 19.2

Determinants of National
Accounting Standards

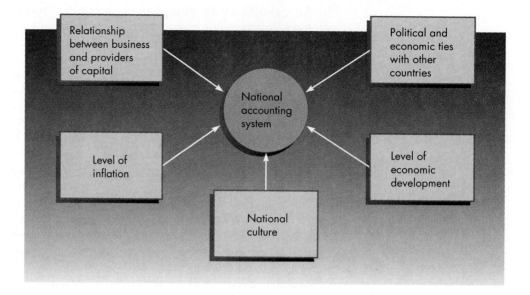

some countries, such as the United States, individual investors are the major source of capital; in others banks play a greater role; in still others the government is the major provider of capital. A country's accounting system tends to reflect the relative importance of these three constituencies as providers of capital.

Consider the case of the United States and Great Britain. Both countries have well-developed stock and bond markets in which firms can raise capital by selling stocks and bonds to individual investors. Most individual investors purchase only a very small proportion of a firm's total outstanding stocks or bonds. As such they have no desire to be involved in the day-to-day management of the firms in which they invest. They leave that task to professional managers. The problem with this arrangement is that due to their lack of contact with the management of the firms in which they invest, individual investors may lack the information required to assess how well their investments are performing. And because of their small stake in firms, individual investors generally lack the ability to get information on demand from management. The financial accounting system in both Great Britain and the United States evolved to cope with this problem. In both countries the financial accounting system is oriented toward providing individual investors with the information they need for making decisions about purchasing or selling corporate stocks and bonds.

In contrast, in countries such as Switzerland, Germany, and Japan, a few large banks satisfy most of the capital needs of business enterprises. Individual investors play a relatively minor role. In these countries the role of the banks is so important that a bank's officers often have seats on the boards of firms to which it lends capital. In such circumstances the information needs of the capital providers are satisfied in a relatively straightforward way—through personal contacts, direct visits, and information provided at board meetings. Consequently, although government regulations in these countries mandate some public disclosure of a firm's financial position, and so firms still prepare financial reports, the reports tend to contain less information than those of British or U.S. firms. Since banks are the major providers of capital, financial accounting practices are oriented toward protecting a bank's investment. Thus assets are valued conservatively and liabilities are overvalued (in contrast to U.S. practice) to provide a cushion for the bank in the event of default.

In still other countries the national government has historically been an important provider of capital, and this has influenced accounting practices. This is the case in France and Sweden, where the national government has often stepped in to lend to or invest in firms whose activities are deemed in the national interest. In these countries financial accounting practices tend to be oriented toward the needs of government planners.

Political and Economic Ties with Other Countries

Similarities in the accounting systems of countries are sometimes due to the countries' close political and/or economic ties. For example, the U.S. system has influenced accounting practices in Canada and Mexico, and since the passage of NAFTA the accounting systems in these three countries seem set to converge on a common set of norms. U.S.-style accounting systems are also used in the Philippines, which was once a U.S. protectorate. Another significant force in accounting worldwide has been the British system. The vast majority of former colonies of the British empire have accounting practices modeled on Great Britain's. Similarly the European Union has been attempting to harmonize accounting practices in its member-countries. At present the accounting systems of EU members such as Great Britain, Germany, and France are quite different, but they may all converge on some norm eventually.

Inflation Accounting

In many countries, including Germany, Japan, and the United States, accounting is based on the **historic cost** principle. This principle assumes the currency unit used to report financial results is not losing its value due to inflation. Firms record sales, purchases, and the like at the original transaction price and make no adjustments in the amounts later. The historic cost principle affects accounting most significantly in the area of asset valuation. If inflation is high, the historic cost principle yields an underestimate of a firm's assets. One result of this is that depreciation charges based on these underestimates can be inadequate for replacing assets when they wear out or become obsolete.

The appropriateness of this principle varies inversely with the level of inflation in a country. The high level of price inflation in many industrialized countries during the 1970s created a need for accounting methods that adjust for the effects of inflation. A number of industrialized countries adopted new practices. One of the most far-reaching approaches was adopted in Great Britain in 1980. Called **current cost** accounting, it adjusts all items in a financial statement—assets, liabilities, costs, and revenues—to factor out the effects of inflation. The method uses a general price index to convert historic figures into current values. The standard was not made compulsory, however, and once Great Britain's inflation rate fell in the 1980s, most firms stopped providing the data.

Level of Development

Developed nations tend to have sophisticated business systems comprising large, complex organizations, whose accounting problems are far more difficult than those of small organizations. Developed nations also tend to have sophisticated capital markets in which business organizations raise funds from investors and banks. These providers of capital require that the organizations they invest in and lend to provide comprehensive reports of their financial activities. The work forces of developed nations tend to be highly educated and skilled, and they can thus be trained to perform complex accounting functions. For all these reasons, accounting in developed countries tends to be far more sophisticated than it is in less developed countries, where the accounting standards may be fairly primitive.

Culture

Recently a number of academic accountants have argued that the culture of a country has an important impact upon the nature of its accounting system.[6] Using the cultural typologies developed by Hofstede,[7] which we reviewed in Chapter 3, researcher have found that the extent to which a culture is characterized by *uncertainty avoidance* seems to have a discernible impact upon accounting systems.[8] You will recall that *uncertainty avoidance* refers to the extent to which different cultures

[6]Gary, "Towards a Theory of Cultural Influence" and S. B Salter and F. Niswander, "Cultural Influences on the Development of Accounting Systems Internationally," *Journal of International Business Studies* 26 (1995), pp. 379–97.
[7]G. Hofstede, *Culture's Consequences: International Differences in Work Related Values* (Beverly Hills, CA: Sage Publications, 1980).
[8]Salter and Niswander, "Cultural Influences."

socialized their members into accepting ambiguous situations and tolerating uncertainty. Members of high uncertainty avoidance cultures placed a premium on job security, career patterns, retirement benefits, and so on. They also had a strong need for rules and regulations; the manager was expected to issue clear instructions, and subordinates' initiatives were tightly controlled. Lower uncertainty avoidance cultures were characterized by a greater readiness to take risks and less emotional resistance to change. According to Hofstede countries such as Great Britain, the United States, and Sweden are characterized by low uncertainty avoidance, whereas countries such as Japan, Mexico, and Greece have higher uncertainty avoidance. Research results suggest that countries with low uncertainty avoidance cultures tend to have strong independent auditing professions that audit a firm's accounts to make sure they comply with generally accepted accounting regulations.[9]

Accounting Clusters

Due to the combined impact of the variables we have discussed, very few countries have identical accounting systems. Notable similarities between nations do exist, however, and three groups of countries with similar standards can be identified (see Map 19.1).[10] One group might be called the British-American-Dutch group. Great Britain, the United States, and the Netherlands are the trendsetters in this group. All these countries have large, well-developed stock and bond markets where firms raise capital from investors. Thus these countries' accounting systems are tailored to providing information to individual investors. A second group might be called the Europe-Japan group. Firms in these countries have very close ties to banks, which supply a large proportion of their capital needs. So their accounting practices are geared to the needs of banks. A third group might be the South American group. The countries in this group have all experienced persistent and rapid inflation. Consequently they have adopted inflation accounting principles.

❧ NATIONAL AND INTERNATIONAL STANDARDS

The diverse accounting practices discussed in the previous section have been enshrined in national accounting and auditing standards. Accounting standards are rules for preparing financial statements; they define what is useful accounting information. Auditing standards specify the rules for performing an audit—the technical process by which an independent person (the auditor) gathers evidence for determining if a set of financial accounts conforms to required accounting standards and if it is also reliable.

Consequences of the Lack of Comparability

As alluded to earlier, an unfortunate result of national differences in accounting and auditing standards is the general lack of comparability of financial reports from one country to another. For example, consider the following:

- Dutch standards favor the use of current values for replacement assets; Japanese law generally prohibits revaluation and prescribes historic cost.
- Capitalization of financial leases is required practice in Great Britain, but it is not practiced in France.
- Whereas research and development costs must be written off in the year they are incurred in the United States, in Spain they may be deferred as an asset and need not be amortized as long as benefits that will cover them are expected to arise in the future.
- German accountants treat depreciation as a liability, whereas British companies deduct it from assets.

---

[9]Ibid.

[10]Mueller, Gernon, and Meek, *Accounting: An International Perspective.*

MAP 19.1 Accounting Clusters

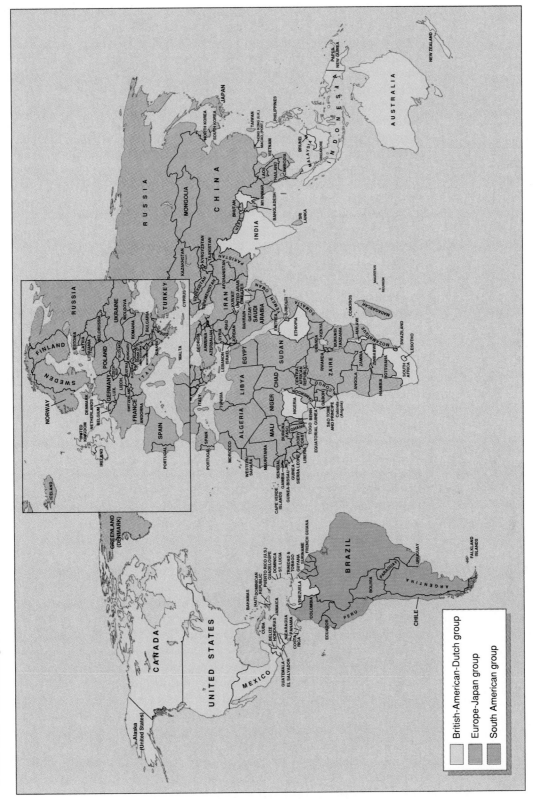

British-American-Dutch group

Europe-Japan group

South American group

Such differences would not matter much if transnational financial reporting was limited; that is, if there was little need for a firm headquartered in one country to report its financial results to citizens of another country. However, as you might recall from Chapter 11, one of the striking developments of the last two decades has been the development of global capital markets. As a result of this, we have seen the growth of both transnational financing and transnational investment.

Transnational financing occurs when a firm based in one country enters another country's capital market to raise capital from the sale of stocks or bonds. A Danish firm raising capital by selling stock through the London Stock Exchange is an example of transnational financing. As we saw in the opening case, a number of large German firms are seeking to increase their use of transnational financing by gaining listings, and ultimately issuing stock, on the New York Stock Exchange. Transnational investment occurs when an investor based in one country enters the capital market of another nation to invest in the stocks or bonds of a firm based in that country. An investor based in Great Britain buying General Motors stock through the New York Stock Exchange would be an example of transnational investment.

The rapid expansion of transnational financing and investment in recent years has been accompanied by a corresponding growth in transnational financial reporting. For example, in addition to its Danish financial reports, the Danish firm raising capital in London must issue financial reports that serve the needs of its British investors. Similarly the U.S. firm with a large number of British investors might wish to issue reports that serve the needs of those investors. However, the lack of comparability between accounting standards in different nations can lead to a lot of confusion. For example, the Danish firm that issues two sets of financial reports, one set prepared under Danish standards and the other under British standards, may find that its financial position looks significantly different in the two reports, and its investors may have difficulty identifying the firm's true worth. Some examples of the confusion that can arise from this lack of comparability appear in the next "Management Focus."

In addition to the problems this lack of comparability gives investors, it can give the firm some major headaches. The firm may have to explain to its investors why its financial position looks so different in the two accountings. An international business may find it extremely difficult to assess the financial positions of important foreign customers, suppliers, and competitors due to the lack of comparability in their financial statements.

International Standards

In light of the problems we have been discussing, substantial efforts have been made in recent years to harmonize accounting standards across countries. Perhaps the most significant body pushing for this is the International Accounting Standards Committee (IASC). The IASC is composed of representatives of 106 professional accounting groups in 79 countries. Governed by a 14-member board of representatives from 13 countries plus a representative from the International Federation of Financial Analysts, the IASC is responsible for formulating international accounting standards. Other areas of interest to the accounting profession worldwide—including auditing, ethical, educational, and public-sector standards—are handled by the International Federation of Accountants (IFA), which has the same membership.

The IASC was begun in 1973 as an outgrowth of an effort by Canada, the United States, and Great Britain to develop international accounting standards. The IFA was established in 1977, when it was determined that the IASC did not have the expertise to deal with broader professional issues. The two organizations work closely, but they are operated and funded separately.

By the mid-1990s the IASC had issued over 30 international accounting standards.[11] To issue a new standard, 75 percent of the 14 members of the board must

---

[11]P. D. Fleming, "The Growing Importance of International Accounting Standards," *Journal of Accountancy*, September 1991, pp. 101–6; and "Bean Counters, Unite!" *The Economist*, June 10, 1995, pp. 67–68.

MANAGEMENT FOCUS
Examples of the Consequences of Different Accounting Standards

In 1989 U.S.-based SmithKline Beecham (SKB) merged with the British company Beecham. After the merger SKB had quotations on both the London and New York stock exchanges, so it had to prepare financial reports in accordance with both U.S. and British standards. SKB's postmerger earnings, properly prepared in accordance with British accounting standards, were 130 million pounds sterling—quite a bit more than the 87 million pounds sterling reported in SKB's statement prepared in accordance with U.S. accounting standards. The difference resulted primarily from the income statement effects of different asset bases arising from treating the merger as a pooling of assets for British purposes and as a purchase of assets for U.S. purposes. Even more confusing, the differences resulted in a shareholders' equity of 3.5 billion sterling in the United States, but a negative 300 million sterling in Great Britain! Not surprisingly, after these figures were released, SKB's stock was trading 17 percent lower on the London Stock Exchange than on the New York Stock Exchange!

Another example is that of Telefonica, Spain's largest industrial company. In the mid-1980s Telefonica was the first company in the world to float a multicountry stock offering simultaneously. In 1990 it reported net income under U.S. accounting standards of 176 billion pesetas, more than twice the 76 billion pesetas it reported under Spanish accounting standards. The difference was mainly due to an "add-back" of the incremental depreciation on assets carried at historic cost in the United States but reflecting more recent market value in the Spanish report. The effect of this difference on shareholders' equity was in the opposite direction; the equity reported in the U.S. accounts was 15 percent less than the equity reported in the Spanish accounts.

A final example is more hypothetical in nature, but just as revealing. Two college professors set up a computer model to evaluate the reported net profits of an imaginary company with gross operating profits of $1.5 million. This imaginary company operated in three different countries—the United States, Britain, and Australia. The professors found that holding all else equal (such as national differences in interest rates on the firm's debt), when different accounting standards were applied, the firm made a net profit of $34,600 in the United States, $260,600 in Britain, and $240,600 in Australia.

Sources: S. F. O'Malley, "Accounting across Borders," *Financial Executive*, March/April 1992, pp. 28–31; and L. Berton, "All Accountants May Soon Speak the Same Language," *The Wall Street Journal*, August 29, 1995, p. A15.

agree. It can be difficult to get such agreement, particularly since members come from different cultures and legal systems. To get around this problem, most IASC statements provide two acceptable alternatives. Arthur Wyatt, chairman of the IASC, says, "It's not much of a standard if you have two alternatives, but it's better than having six. If you can get agreement on two alternatives, you can capture the 11 required votes and eliminate some of the less used practices."[12]

Another hindrance to the development of international accounting standards is that compliance with the IASC standards is voluntary; the IASC has no power to enforce its standards. Despite this support for the IASC and recognition of its standards is growing around the world. Increasingly the IASC is regarded as an effective

---

[12]Fleming, "The Growing Importance of International Accounting Standards."

voice for defining acceptable worldwide accounting principles. Japan, for example, began requiring financial statements to be prepared on a consolidated basis after the IASC issued its initial standards on the topic.

The impact of the IASC standards has probably been least noticeable in the United States. This is because most of the standards issued by the IASC have been consistent with opinions already articulated by the U.S. Financial Accounting Standards Board (FASB). The FASB is the principal body that writes the generally accepted accounting principles by which the financial statements of U.S. firms must be prepared. Some of the IASC standards have had a significant impact on practices in many other countries because they eliminated a commonly used alternative.

Another body that promises to have substantial influence on the harmonization of accounting standards, at least within Europe, is the European Union. In accordance with its plans for closer economic and political union, the EU is attempting to harmonize the accounting principles of its 15 member-countries. The EU does this by issuing directives, EU laws that the member-states are obligated to incorporate into their own national laws. Since EU directives have the power of law, we might assume the EU has a better chance of achieving harmonization than the IASC does. In practice, however, the EU is experiencing some implementation difficulties. These difficulties arise from the wide variation in accounting practices among EU member-countries. Accounting practices in Great Britain, for example, are closer to those of the United States than to those of France or Germany. Despite these difficulties, developments in the EU should be watched closely, since if the EU is successful in achieving harmonization (in all probability, it eventually will be) the accounting principles adopted in the EU could be a major influence on future IASC pronouncements.

In a move that indicates the trend toward adoption of acceptable international accounting standards is accelerating, in August 1995 the IASC announced its intention to develop accounting standards by mid-1999 for firms seeking stock listings in global markets to raise cross-border capital. Around the same time the U.S. FASB joined forces with accounting standard setters in Canada, Mexico, and Chile to explore areas in which the four countries can harmonize their accounting standards (Canada, Mexico, and the United States are members of NAFTA, and Chile may well join by the end of the century). The U.S. Securities and Exchange Commission also seems to be dropping some of its objections to international standards, which could accelerate their adoption. In 1994, for the first time, the SEC accepted three international accounting standards on cash flow data, the effects of hyperinflation, and business combinations for cross-border filings.[13] A taste of what is to come if increasing numbers of international firms do jump on the bandwagon and adopt IASC principles can be found in the next "Management Focus," which details the impact of adopting these standards on Ciba, the Swiss pharmaceuticals and chemicals group.

❧ MULTINATIONAL CONSOLIDATION AND CURRENCY TRANSLATION

A consolidated financial statement combines the separate financial statements of two or more companies to yield a single set of financial statements as if the individual companies were really one. Most multinational firms are composed of a parent company and a number of subsidiary companies located in various other countries. Typically, such firms issue consolidated financial statements, which merge the accounts of all the companies, rather than issuing individual financial statements for the parent company and each subsidiary. In this section we examine the consolidated financial statements and then move on to look at the related issue of foreign currency translation.

---

[13]L. Berton, "All Accountants May Soon Speak the Same Language," *The Wall Street Journal*, August 29, 1995, p. A15.

MANAGEMENT FOCUS
Ciba Joins the International Accounting Club

Switzerland does not have a history of very detailed accounting rules. As a result published financial statements by major Swiss firms such as Ciba, Roche, and Nestlé often obscured as much as they revealed. The standard set of accounts from a Swiss firm was viewed as being very unusual and difficult for international investors to understand and described as being more like a statistical summary than the result of an integrated accounting system.

Swiss firms began to move toward adoption of IASC accounting principles in the early 1990s. The catalyst was increasing interest by foreign investors in the stock of major Swiss corporations. By the early 1990s up to 40 percent of the stock of many of these firms was owned by foreign investors. As a group these investors were demanding more detailed financial statements that were comparable to those issued by other multinational enterprises.

One of the first firms to respond to these pressures was Ciba, Switzerland's largest pharmaceuticals and chemicals firm and a major multinational enterprise with operations around the globe. In 1993 the company announced that its 1994 financial statements would be in accordance with IASC guidelines. At the same time it restated its 1992 results in line with IASC guidelines. The effect was to increase post-tax profits by 18 percent while raising inventories, cash, and marketable securities. Ciba's decision was motivated by a desire to appease foreign stockholders, who in 1994 held over one third of Ciba's stock, and to position itself for the possibility of listings on the London and New York stock markets.

Ciba decided not simply to focus on external financial reporting by international standards, but also to use the same systems internally. As a result its internal accounting systems have gone through a complete overhaul so that internal reporting can be based on the same criteria as external reporting. Ciba set up a small international team to develop and implement its new system. While there were some problems with the development of the system, including a figure thrown up by the system on the insurance value of fixed assets that was off by $690 million, the new system is now running smoothly, and it seems to have produced a number of major benefits.

The change has resulted in large savings for Ciba, including tighter cash management, more efficient capital investment, a different approach to acquisitions, and more rigid asset management, which has reportedly reduced the value of inventories by 6 percent. Another major advantage of the new system is that it has enabled Ciba to benchmark its performance for the first time against some of its global competitors.

One of the largest differences between the new and old systems is a move from the arguably more informative current cost accounting method, which Ciba has used for over 25 years and which regularly updates asset values to account for the impact of inflation, to historic cost accounting under international standards. However, Ciba'a management is the first to admit that this drawback is not serious given the low inflation rate in Switzerland and given the offsetting gains produced by the switch to a new system.

Sources: A. Jack, "Swiss Group moves from Night to Day," *Financial Times*, March 30, 1994, p. 22; and L. Berton, " All Accountants May Soon Speak the Same Language," *The Wall Street Journal*, August 29, 1995, p. A15.

Consolidated Financial Statements

Many firms find it advantageous to organize themselves as a set of separate legal entities (companies). For example, a firm may separately incorporate the various components of its business to limit its total legal liability or to take advantage of corporate tax regulations. Multinationals are often required by the countries in which they do business to set up a separate company in each country. Thus the typical multinational comprises a parent company and a number of subsidiary companies located in different countries, most of which are wholly owned by the parent. The point, however, is that although the subsidiaries may be separate legal entities, they are not separate economic entities. Economically all the companies in a corporate group are interdependent. For example, if the French subsidiary of a U.S. parent company experiences substantial financial losses that suck up corporate funds, the cash available for investment in that subsidiary, the U.S. parent company, and other subsidiary companies will be limited. Thus the purpose of consolidated financial statements is to provide accounting information about a group of companies that recognizes their economic interdependence.

Transactions among the members of a corporate family are not included in consolidated financial statements; only assets, liabilities, revenues, and expenses with external third parties are shown. By law, however, separate legal entities are required to keep their own accounting records and to prepare their own financial statements. Thus transactions with other members of a corporate group must be identified in the separate statements so they can be excluded when the consolidated statements are prepared. The process involves adding up the individual assets, liabilities, revenues, and expenses reported on the separate financial statements and then eliminating the intragroup ones. For example, consider these items selected from the individual financial statements of a parent company and one of its foreign subsidiaries:

	Parent	Foreign Subsidiary
Cash	1,000	250
Receivables	3,000*	900
Payables	300	500*
Revenues	7,000†	5,000
Expenses	2,000	3,000†

*Subsidiary owes parent $300.
†Subsidiary pays parent $1,000 in royalties for products licensed from parent.

The $300 receivable that the parent includes on its financial statements and the $300 payable that the subsidiary includes on its statements represent an intragroup item. These items cancel each other out and thus are not included in consolidated financial statements. Similarly the $1,000 the subsidiary owes the parent in royalty payments is an intragroup item that will not appear in the consolidated accounts. The adjustments are as follows:

			Eliminations		
	Parent	Subsidiary	Debit	Credit	Consolidated
Cash	$1,000	$250			$1,250
Receivables	3,000*	900		$ 300	3,600
Payables	300	500*	$ 300		500
Revenues	7,000†	5,000		1,000	11,000
Expenses	2,000	3,000†	1,000		4,000

*Subsidiary owes parent $300.
†Subsidiary pays parent $1,000 in royalties for products licensed from parent.

Thus, for example, while simply adding the two sets of accounts would suggest that the group of companies has revenues of $12,000 and receivables of $3,900, once intragroup transactions are removed from the picture, these figures drop to $11,000 and $3,600, respectively.

Preparing consolidated financial statements is becoming the norm for multinational firms. Investors realize that without consolidated financial statements, a multinational firm could conceal losses in an unconsolidated subsidiary, thereby hiding the economic status of the entire group. For example, the parent company in our illustration could increase its profit merely by charging the subsidiary company higher royalty fees. Since this has no affect on the group's overall profits, such a practice amounts to little more than window dressing—it may make the parent company look good. If the parent does not issue a consolidated financial statement, however, the true economic status of the group is obscured by such a practice. With this in mind, the IASC has issued two standards requiring firms to prepare consolidated financial statements, and in most industrialized countries this is now required.

Currency Translation

Foreign subsidiaries of multinational firms normally keep their accounting records and prepare their financial statements in the currency of the country in which they are located. Thus the Japanese subsidiary of a U.S. firm will prepare its accounts in yen, a French subsidiary in francs, an Italian subsidiary in lira, and so on. When a multinational prepares consolidated accounts, it must convert all these financial statements into the currency of its home country. As we saw in Chapter 9, however, the problem is that exchange rates vary, often on a day-to-day basis, in response to changes in economic circumstances. This raises the difficult question of what exchange rate should be used when translating financial statement currencies. There are two main methods used to do this, the current rate method and the temporal method.

The Current Rate Method

Under the current rate method, the exchange rate at the balance sheet date is used to translate the financial statements of a foreign subsidiary into the home currency of the multinational firm. Although this may seem a logical choice, it is incompatible with the historic cost principle, which, as we saw earlier in the chapter, is a generally accepted accounting principle in many countries, including the United States. For an example of why this is so, consider the case of a U.S. firm that invests $100,000 in a French subsidiary. Assume the exchange rate at the time is $1 = FFr5. The subsidiary converts the $100,000 into francs, which gives it FFr500,000. It then purchases some land with this money. The dollar subsequently depreciates against the franc, so that by year-end, $1 = FFr4. If this exchange rate is used to convert the value of the land back into U.S. dollars for the purpose of preparing consolidated accounts, the land will be valued at $125,000. The piece of land would appear to have increased in value by $25,000, although in reality the increase would be simply a function of an exchange rate change. Thus the consolidated accounts would present a somewhat misleading picture.

The Temporal Method

One way to avoid this problem is to use the temporal method to translate the accounts of a foreign subsidiary. The temporal method translates assets valued in a foreign currency into the home-country currency using the exchange rate that exists when the assets are purchased. Referring to our example, the exchange rate of $1 = FFr5, the rate on the day the French subsidiary purchased the land, would be used to convert the value of the land back into U.S. dollars at year-end. However, although the temporal method will ensure the dollar value of the land does not fluctuate due to exchange rate changes, it brings with it a serious problem of its own. Since the various assets of a foreign subsidiary will in all probability be acquired at different times, and since exchange rates seldom remain stable for long, different exchange rates will probably have to be used to translate those foreign assets into the multinational's home currency. Consequently the multinational's balance sheet may not balance!

Consider the case of a U.S. firm that on January 1, 1994, invests $100,000 in a new Japanese subsidiary. The exchange rate at that time is $1 = ¥100. The initial investment is therefore ¥10 million, and the Japanese subsidiary's balance sheet looks like this on January 1, 1994:

	Yen	Exchange Rate	U.S. Dollars
Cash	10,000,000	($1 = ¥100)	100,000
Owners' equity	10,000,000	($1 = ¥100)	100,000

Assume that on January 31, when the exchange rate is $1 = ¥95, the Japanese subsidiary invests ¥5 million in a factory (i.e., fixed assets). Then on February 15, when the exchange rate is $1 = ¥ 90, the subsidiary purchases ¥5 million of inventory. The balance sheet of the subsidiary will look like this on March 1, 1994:

	Yen	Exchange Rate	U.S. Dollars
Fixed assets	5,000,000	($1 = ¥95)	52,632
Inventory	5,000,000	($1 = ¥90)	55,556
Total	10,000,000		108,187
Owners' equity	10,000,000	($1 = ¥100)	100,000

Although the balance sheet balances in yen, it does not balance when the temporal method is used to translate the yen-denominated balance sheet figures back into dollars. In translation the balance sheet debits exceed the credits by $8,187. How to cope with the gap between debits and credits is an issue of some debate within the accounting profession. It is probably safe to say that no satisfactory solution has yet been adopted. The practice currently used in the United States is explained next.

Current U.S. Practice

U.S.-based multinational firms must follow the requirements of Statement 52, "Foreign Currency Translation," issued by the U.S. Financial Accounting Standards Board in 1981. Under Statement 52, a foreign subsidiary is classified either as a self-sustaining, autonomous subsidiary or as integral to the activities of the parent company. (A link can be made here with the material on strategy discussed in Chapter 12. Firms pursuing multidomestic and international strategies are most likely to have self-sustaining subsidiaries, whereas firms pursuing global and transnational strategies, by the very nature of those strategies, are most likely to have integral subsidiaries.) According to Statement 52, the local currency of a self-sustaining foreign subsidiary is to be its functional currency. The balance sheet for such subsidiaries is translated into the home currency using the exchange rate in effect at the end of the firm's financial year, whereas the income statement is translated using the average exchange rate for the firm's financial year. On the other hand the functional currency of an integral subsidiary is to be U.S. dollars. The financial statements of such subsidiaries are translated at various historic rates using the temporal method (as we did in the example), and the dangling debit or credit increases or decreases consolidated earnings for the period.

🐚 ACCOUNTING ASPECTS OF CONTROL SYSTEMS

One of the principal roles of any corporate headquarters is to control subunits within the organization to ensure they achieve the best possible performance. In the typical firm the control process is annual and involves three main steps:

1. Head office and subunit management jointly determine subunit goals for the coming year.
2. Throughout the year the head office monitors subunit performance against the agreed goals.
3. If a subunit fails to achieve its goals, the head office intervenes in the subunit to learn why the shortfall occurred, taking corrective action when appropriate.

TABLE 19.1

TABLE 19.1

Importance of Financial
Criteria Used to Evaluate
Performance of Foreign
Subsidiaries and Their
Managers*

Item	Subsidiary	Manager
Return on investment (ROI)	1.9	2.2
Return on equity (ROE)	3.0	3.0
Return on assets (ROA)	2.3	2.3
Return on sales (ROS)	2.1	2.1
Residual income	3.4	3.3
Budget compared to actual sales	1.9	1.7
Budget compared to actual profit	1.5	1.3
Budget compared to actual ROI	2.3	2.4
Budget compared to actual ROA	2.7	2.5
Budget compared to actual ROE	3.1	3.0

*Importance of criteria ranked on a scale from: 1 = very important to 5 = unimportant.
Source: F. Choi and I. Czechowicz, "Assessing Foreign Subsidiary Performance: A Multinational Comparison,"
Management International Review 4 (1983), p. 16.

The accounting function plays a critical role in this process. Most of the goals for subunits are expressed in financial terms and are embodied in the subunit's budget for the coming year. The budget is thus the main instrument of financial control. The budget is typically prepared by the subunit, but it must be approved by headquarters management. During the approval process, headquarters and subunit managements debate the goals that should be incorporated in the budget. One function of headquarters management is to ensure a subunit's budget contains challenging but realistic performance goals. Once a budget is agreed to, accounting information systems are then used to collect data throughout the year so a subunit's performance can be evaluated against the goals contained in its budget.

In most international businesses, many of the firm's subunits are foreign subsidiaries. The performance goals for the coming year are thus set by negotiation between corporate management and the managers of foreign subsidiaries. According to one survey of control practices within multinational enterprises, the most important criterion for evaluating the performance of a foreign subsidiary is the subsidiary's actual profits compared to budgeted profits (see Table 19.1).[14] This is closely followed by a subsidiary's actual sales compared to budgeted sales and its return on investment. The same criteria were also found useful in evaluating the performance of the subsidiary managers (see Table 19.1). We will discuss this point later in this section. First, however, we will examine two factors that can seriously complicate the control process in an international business: exchange rate changes and transfer pricing practices.

Exchange Rate Changes and Control Systems

Most international businesses require all budgets and performance data within the firm to be expressed in the "corporate currency," which is normally the home currency. Thus the French subsidiary of a U.S. multinational would probably submit for approval a budget prepared in U.S. dollars, rather than French francs, and performance data throughout the year would be reported to headquarters in U.S. dollars. This practice facilitates comparisons between subsidiaries in different countries, and it makes things easier for headquarters management. However, it also allows exchange rate changes during the year to introduce substantial distortions into the control process. For example, the French subsidiary may fail to achieve the profit goals contained in its budget not because of any inherent performance problems, but merely because of a decline in the value of the franc against the dollar. The opposite can occur, also, and a foreign subsidiary will look better than it actually is.

---

[14]F. Choi and I. Czechowicz, "Assessing Foreign Subsidiary Performance: A Multinational Comparison," *Management International Review* 4 (1983), pp. 14–25.

Figure 19.3   Possible Combinations of Exchanges Rates in the Control Process

		Rate used to translate actual performance for comparison with budget		
		Initial (I)	Projected (P)	Ending (E)
Rate used for translating budget	Initial (I)	(II) Budget at initial Actual at initial	(IP) Budget at intial Actual at projected	(IE) Budget at initial Actual at ending
	Projected (P)	Budget at projected Actual at initial	(PP) Budget at projected Actual at projected	(PE) Budget at projected Actual at ending
	Ending (E)	Budget at ending Actual at initial	Budget at ending Actual at projected	(EE) Budget at ending Actual at ending

The Lessard-Lorange Model

According to research by Donald Lessard and Peter Lorange, a number of methods are available to international businesses for dealing with this problem.[15] Lessard and Lorange point out three exchange rates that can be used in the budget-setting process and in the subsequent tracking of performance to translate foreign currencies into the corporate currency:

- The **initial rate,** the spot exchange rate when the budget is adopted.
- The **projected rate,** the spot exchange rate forecasted for the end of the budget period (i.e., the forward rate).
- The **ending rate,** the spot exchange rate when the budget and performance are being compared.

These three exchange rates imply nine possible combinations (see Figure 19.3). Lessard and Lorange ruled out four of the nine combinations as illogical and unreasonable; they are shaded in Figure 19.3. For example, it would make no sense to use the ending rate to translate the budget and the initial rate to translate actual performance data. Any of the remaining five combinations might be used for the budget-setting and performance evaluation process.

With three of these five combinations—II, PP, and EE—the same exchange rate is used for translating both budget figures and performance figures into the corporate currency. All three combinations have the advantage that a change in the exchange rate during the year does not distort the control process. This is not true for the other two combinations, IE and PE. In those cases, exchange rate changes can introduce distortions. The potential for distortion is greater with IE; the ending spot exchange rate used to evaluate performance against the budget may be quite different from the initial spot exchange rate used to translate the budget. The distortion is less serious in the case of PE, since the projected exchange rate takes into account future exchange rate movements.

---

[15]D. Lessard and P. Lorange, "Currency Changes and Management Control: Resolving the Centralization/Decentralization Dilemma," *Accounting Review*, July 1977, pp. 628–37.

Of the five combinations, Lessard and Lorange recommend that firms use the projected spot exchange rate to translate both the budget and performance figures into the corporate currency, combination PP. The projected rate in such cases will typically be the forward exchange rate as determined by the foreign exchange market (see Chapter 9 for the definition of forward rate) or some company-generated forecast of future spot rates, which Lessard and Lorange refer to as the **internal forward rate.** The internal forward rate may differ from the forward rate quoted by the foreign exchange market if the firm wishes to bias its business in favor of, or against, the particular foreign currency.

Transfer Pricing and Control Systems

In Chapter 12 we reviewed the various strategies that international businesses pursue. We saw that two of these strategies, the global strategy and the transnational strategy, give rise to a globally dispersed web of productive activities. Firms pursuing these strategies disperse each value-creation activity to its optimal location in the world. Thus a product might be designed in one country, some of its components manufactured in a second country, other components manufactured in a third country, all assembled in a fourth country, and then sold worldwide.

The volume of intrafirm transactions in such firms is very high. Such firms are continually shipping component parts and finished goods between subsidiaries in different countries. This poses a very important question: How should goods and services transferred between subsidiary companies in a multinational firm be priced? The price at which such goods and services are transferred is referred to as the **transfer price.**

The choice of transfer price can critically affect the performance of two subsidiaries that exchange goods or services. Consider this example: A French manufacturing subsidiary of a U.S. multinational imports a major component from Brazil. It incorporates this part into a product that it sells in France for the equivalent of $230 per unit. The product costs $200 to manufacture, of which $100 goes to the Brazilian subsidiary to pay for the component part. The remaining $100 covers costs incurred in France. Thus the French subsidiary earns $30 profit per unit.

Now look at what happens if corporate headquarters decides to increase transfer prices by 20 percent ($20 per unit). The French subsidiary's profits will fall by two thirds from $30 per unit to $10 per unit. Thus the performance of the French subsidiary is wholly dependent on the transfer price for the component part imported from Brazil, and the transfer price is controlled by corporate headquarters. Clearly then, when setting budgets and reviewing a subsidiary's performance, corporate headquarters must keep in mind the distorting effect of transfer prices.

	Before Change in Transfer Price	After 20 Percent Increase in Transfer Price
Revenues per unit	$230	$230
Cost of component per unit	100	120
Other costs per unit	100	100
Profit per unit	$ 30	$ 10

How should transfer prices be determined? We discuss this issue in detail in the next chapter. We will see there that international businesses often manipulate transfer prices to minimize their worldwide tax liability, minimize import duties, and avoid government restrictions on capital flows. For now, however, it is enough to note that the transfer price must be considered when setting budgets and evaluating a subsidiary's performance.

Separation of Subsidiary and Manager Performance

Table 19.1 suggests that in many international businesses, the same quantitative criteria are used to assess the performance of both a foreign subsidiary and its managers. Many accountants, however, argue that although it is perfectly legitimate to compare subsidiaries against each other on the basis of return on investment (ROI) or other indicators of profitability, it may not be appropriate to use these for comparing and evaluating the managers of different subsidiaries. Foreign subsidiaries do not operate in uniform environments; their environments have widely different economic, political, and social conditions, all of which influence the costs of doing business in a country and hence the subsidiaries' profitability. Thus the manager of a subsidiary in an adverse environment that has an ROI of 5 percent may actually be doing a better job than the manager of a subsidiary in a benign environment that has an ROI of 20 percent. Although the firm might want to pull out of a country where its ROI is only 5 percent, it may also want to recognize the manager's achievement of any profits at all in such an adverse environment.

Accordingly it has been suggested that the evaluation of a subsidiary should be kept separate from the evaluation of its manager.[16] The manager's evaluation should involve a degree of subjectivity that considers how hostile or benign the country's environment is for that business. Managers should be evaluated in local currency terms after making allowances for those items over which they have no control (e.g., interest rates, tax rates, inflation rates, transfer prices, exchange rates).

❧ SUMMARY OF CHAPTER

The central focus of this chapter has been on financial accounting within the multinational firm. We have explained why accounting practices and standards differ from country to country and have surveyed the efforts now under way to harmonize countries' accounting practices. We have discussed the rationale behind consolidated accounts and have looked at the problem of currency translation. We have reviewed several issues related to the use of accounting-based control systems within international businesses. More specifically, the following points have been made:

1. Accounting is the language of business, the means by which firms communicate their financial position to the providers of capital and to governments (for tax purposes). It is also the means by which firms evaluate their own performance, control their expenditures, and plan for the future.

2. Accounting is shaped by the environment in which it operates. Each country's accounting system has evolved in response to local demands for accounting information.

3. Five main factors seem to influence the type of accounting system a country has: (*i*) the relationship between business and the providers of capital, (*ii*) political and economic ties with other countries, (*iii*) the level of inflation, (*iv*) the level of a country's development, and (*v*) the prevailing culture in a country.

4. National differences in accounting and auditing standards have resulted in a general lack of comparability in countries' financial reports.

5. This lack of comparability has become a problem as transnational financing and transnational investment have grown rapidly in recent decades (a consequence of the globalization of capital markets). Due to the lack of comparability, a firm may have to explain to investors why its financial position looks very different on financial reports that are based on different accounting practices.

6. The most significant push for harmonization of accounting standards across countries has come from the International Accounting Standards Committee (IASC). So far the IASC's success, while noteworthy, has been limited.

7. Consolidated financial statements provide financial accounting information about a group of companies that recognizes the companies' economic interdependence.

8. Transactions among the members of a corporate family are not included on consolidated financial statements; only assets, liabilities, revenues, and expenses generated with external third parties are shown.

9. Foreign subsidiaries of a multinational firm normally keep their accounting records and prepare their financial statements in the currency of the country in which they are located. When the multinational prepares its consolidated accounts, these financial statements must be translated into the currency of its home country.

10. Under the current rate translation method, the exchange rate at the balance sheet date is used to translate the financial statements of a foreign subsidiary into the home currency. This has the drawback of being incompatible with the historic cost principle.

11. Under the temporal method, assets valued in a foreign currency are translated into the home currency using the exchange rate that existed when the assets were purchased. A problem with this approach is that the multinational's balance sheet may not balance.

12. In most international businesses, the annual budget is the main instrument by which headquarters controls foreign subsidiaries. Throughout the year headquarters compares a subsidiary's performance against the financial goals incorporated in its budget, intervening selectively in its operations when shortfalls occur.

---

[16]Mueller et al., *Accounting.*

13. Most international businesses require all budgets and performance data within the firm to be expressed in the corporate currency. This enhances comparability, but it leads to distortions in the control process if the relevant exchange rates change between the time a foreign subsidiary's budget is set and the time its performance is evaluated.

14. According to the Lessard-Lorange model, the best way to deal with this problem is to use a projected spot exchange rate to translate both budget figures and performance figures into the corporate currency.

15. Transfer prices also can introduce significant distortions into the control process and this must be considered when setting budgets and evaluating a subsidiary's performance.

16. Foreign subsidiaries do not operate in uniform environments, and some environments are much tougher than others. Accordingly it has been suggested that the evaluation of a subsidiary should be kept separate from the evaluation of the subsidiary manager.

❧ CRITICAL DISCUSSION QUESTIONS

1. Why do the accounting systems of different countries differ? Why do these differences matter?

2. Why are transactions among members of a corporate family not included in consolidated financial statements?

3. The following are selected amounts from the separate financial statements of a parent company (unconsolidated) and one of its subsidiaries.

	Parent	**Subsidiary**
Cash	$180	$80
Receivables	380	200
Accounts payable	245	110
Retained earnings	790	680
Revenues	4,980	3,520
Rent income	0	200
Dividend income	250	0
Expenses	4,160	2,960

Notes: i. Parent owes subsidiary $70.
  ii. Parent owns 100% of subsidiary. During the year subsidiary paid parent a dividend of $250.
  iii. Subsidiary owns the building that parent rents for $200.
  iv. During the year parent sold some inventory to subsidiary for $2,200. It had cost parent $1,500. Subsidiary, in turn, sold the inventory to an unrelated party for $3,200.

Given this,
  a. What is the parent's (unconsolidated) net income?
  b. What is the subsidiary's net income?
  c. What is the consolidated profit on the inventory that the parent originally sold to the subsidiary?
  d. What are the amounts of consolidated cash and receivables?

4. Why might an accounting-based control system provide headquarters management with biased information about the performance of a foreign subsidiary? How can these biases best be corrected?

❧ CLOSING CASE China's Evolving Accounting System

Attracted by its rapid transformation from a socialist planned economy into a market economy, economic growth rates of around 12 percent per annum, and a population in excess of 1.3 billion, over the last 10 years or so China has become a favored site for foreign direct investment by Western firms. Most see China as an emerging economic superpower with an economy that, if current growth projections hold true, will be as large as that of Japan by 2000 and as large as that of the United States before 2010. As such China has become a country that many Western firms believe that they must invest in.

The Chinese government sees foreign direct investment as a primary engine of China's economic growth. To encourage such investment, the government has offered generous tax incentives to foreign firms that invest in China, either on their own or in conjunction with a local enterprise in a joint venture. These tax incentives include a two-year exemption

from corporate income tax following an investment, plus a further three years during which taxes are paid at only 50 percent of the standard tax rate. Such incentives, when coupled with the promise of China's vast internal market, have made the country a prime site for inward investment by Western firms. However, once established in China, many Western firms find themselves struggling to comply with the complex and often obtuse nature of China's rapidly evolving accounting system.

Accounting in China has traditionally been rooted in information gathering and compliance reporting designed to measure the government's production and tax goals. The Chinese system was based on the old Soviet system, which had little to do with the profit concept or accounting systems created to report financial positions or the results of foreign operations. Although the system is now beginning to change quite rapidly, many problems associated with the old system still remain.

One problem that investors encounter is a severe shortage of accountants, financial managers, and auditors in China, especially those experienced with market economy transactions and international accounting practices. As of 1995 there were only 25,000 accountants in China, far short of the hundreds of thousands that will be needed if China continues on its path toward becoming a market economy. Chinese enterprises, including equity and cooperative joint ventures with foreign firms, must be audited by Chinese accounting firms, which are regulated by the state. Traditionally many experienced auditors have audited only state-owned enterprises, working through the local province or city authorities and the state audit bureau to report to the government entity overseeing the audited firm. The new market economy environment has generated a need for accountants schooled in the principles of private-sector accounting, and such individuals are difficult to come by. In response several large international auditing firms have established joint ventures with emerging Chinese accounting and auditing firms to bridge the growing need for international accounting, tax, and securities expertise.

A further problem concerns the somewhat halting evolution of China's emerging accounting standards. Current thinking is that China won't simply adopt the international accounting standards specified by the IASC, and nor will it use the generally accepted accounting principles of any particular country as its model. Rather accounting standards in China are expected to evolve in a rather piecemeal fashion, with the Chinese adopting a few standards as they are studied and deemed appropriate for Chinese circumstances.

In the meantime current Chinese accounting principles, based as they are on the old Soviet model, offer several difficult problems for Western firms. For example, the former Chinese accounting system didn't need to accrue for unrealized losses. In an economy where shortages were the norm, if a state-owned company didn't sell its inventory right away it could store it and use it for some other purpose later. Similarly, accounting principles assumed that the state always paid its debts—eventually. Thus Chinese enterprises don't generally provide for lower-of-cost-or market inventory adjustments, or the creation of allowance for bad debts, both of which are standard practices in the West.

CASE DISCUSSION QUESTIONS

1. What factors have shaped the accounting system currently in use in China?

2. What problems does the accounting system currently in use in China present to foreign investors in joint ventures with Chinese companies?

3. If the evolving Chinese system does not adhere to IASC standards, but instead to standards that the Chinese government deems appropriate to China's "special situation," how might this affect foreign firms with operations in China?

Sources: L. E. Graham and A. H. Carley, "When East Meets West," Financial Executive, July/August 1995, pp. 40–45; and K. Theonnes and A. Yeung, "Playing Favorites," Financial Executive, July/August 1995, pp. 46–51.

CHAPTER TWENTY

FINANCIAL MANAGEMENT IN THE INTERNATIONAL BUSINESS

GLOBAL TREASURY MANAGEMENT AT PROCTER & GAMBLE

With more than 300 brands of paper, detergent, food, health, and cosmetics products sold in over 140 countries, and over 60 percent of its $30 billion in revenues generated outside the United States, Procter & Gamble is the quintessential example of a global consumer products firm. Despite this global spread, until the early 1990s P&G's treasury operations—which embrace investment, financing, money management, and foreign exchange decisions—were quite decentralized. Each major international subsidiary managed its own investments, borrowings, and foreign exchange trades, subject only to outside borrowing limits imposed by the international treasury group at P&G's headquarters in Cincinnati.

Today P&G operates with a much more centralized system in which a global treasury management function at corporate headquarters exercises close oversight over the operations of different regional treasury centers around the world. In part this move was a response to the rise in volume of P&G's international transactions and the resulting increase in foreign exchange exposures. Like many global firms, in recent years P&G has been trying to rationalize its global production system to realize cost economies by concentrating the production of certain products at specific locations, as opposed to producing

those products in every major country in which it does business. As it has moved in this direction, P&G has found that the number and volume of raw materials and finished products being shipped across borders has been growing in leaps and bounds. This has led to a commensurate increase in the size of P&G's foreign exchange exposure, which at any one time now runs into billions of dollars. More than one third of P&G's foreign exchange exposure is now in non-dollar exposures, such as transactions that involve the exchange of deutsche marks into francs, or sterling into lira.

P&G believes that centralizing the overall management of the resulting foreign exchange transactions can help the company realize a number of important gains. First, since its various international subsidiaries often accumulate cash balances in the currency of the country where they are based, P&G is now trading currencies between its subsidiaries. By cutting banks out of the process, P&G saves on transaction costs.

Second, P&G has found that many of its subsidiaries purchase currencies in relatively small lots of say $100,000 a time. By grouping these lots into larger purchases, P&G can generally get a better price from foreign trade dealers. Third, P&G has found that it is possible to pool foreign exchange risks and purchase an "umbrella option" to cover the risks associated with various currency positions, which is cheaper than purchasing options to cover each position.

In addition to managing foreign exchange transactions, P&G's global treasury operation is arranging for many of the firm's subsidiaries to borrow money from other Procter & Gamble entities, instead of from local banks. As a result there has been a marked increase in the volume of intracompany loans within P&G, with subsidiaries that have excess cash lending it to those that need cash and with the global treasury operation acting as a financial intermediary. At the same time P&G has been able to cut the number of local banks it does business with from 450 to around 200. The great advantage of using intracompany loans instead of local banks is that P&G can lower the overall borrowing costs of the organization, which may result in annual savings on interest payments that run into tens if not hundreds of millions of dollars.

Sources: R. C. Stewart, "Balancing on the Global High Wire," *Financial Executive*, September/October 1995, pp. 35–39; and S. Lipin, F. R. Bleakley, and B. D. Granito, "Portfolio Poker," *The Wall Street Journal*, April 14, 1994, p. A1.

◈ INTRODUCTION

As the opening case makes clear, the focus of this chapter is on financial management in the international business. Included within the scope of financial management are three sets of related decisions:

- *Investment decisions*, decisions about what activities to finance.
- *Financing decisions*, decisions about how to finance those activities.
- *Money management decisions*, decisions about how to manage the firm's financial resources most efficiently.

The opening case describes P&G's approach toward these decisions. P&G has found that by managing investing, financing, and money management decisions centrally through its global treasury function—as opposed to letting each subsidiary make its own decisions—considerable cost economies can be realized. These economies help P&G to compete more effectively in the global marketplace.

In an international business, investment, financing, and money management decisions are complicated by the fact that countries have different currencies, tax regimes, regulations concerning the flow of capital across their borders, norms regarding the financing of business activities, levels of economic and political risk, and so on. Financial managers in the international business must consider all these factors when deciding which activities to finance, how best to finance those activities, how best to manage the firm's financial resources, and how best to protect the firm from political and economic risks (including foreign exchange risk).

Good financial management can be an important source of competitive advantage. This is implicit in the opening case, where good financial management helps P&G attain cost economies and lower its overall cost structure. For another example, consider FMC, a Chicago-based producer of chemicals and farm equipment, FMC counts on overseas business for 40 percent of its sales. FMC attributes some of its success overseas to aggressive trading in the forward foreign exchange market. By trading in currency futures, FMC can provide overseas customers with stable long-term prices for three years or more, regardless of what happens to exchange rates in the intervening period. Ralph DelZenero, FMC's foreign exchange specialist, says, "Some of our competitors change their prices on a relatively short-term basis depending on what is happening with their own exchange rate. . . . We want to provide longer-term pricing as a customer service—they can plan their budgets knowing what the numbers will be—and we can hopefully maintain and build our customer base." FMC also offers its customers the option of paying in any of several currencies as a convenience to them and as an attempt to retain them as customers. By adopting this policy, FMC's customers "don't have to deal with the hassle of foreign exchange movements," says DelZenero. "FMC does that for them." By offering customers multicurrency pricing alternatives, FMC implicitly accepts the responsibility of managing foreign exchange risk for its business units that sell overseas. To do this, it has set up what amounts to an in-house bank to manage the operation, monitoring currency rates daily and managing its risks on a portfolio basis. This bank handles more than $1 billion in currency transactions annually, which means the company can often beat the currency prices quoted by commercial banks.[1]

In Chapter 12 we talked about the value chain and pointed out that creating a competitive advantage requires a firm to reduce its costs of value creation and/or add value by improving its customer service. P&G and FMC show how good financial management can help the firm both to reduce the costs of creating value and to add value by improving customer service. By reducing the firm's cost of capital,

---

[1]Lawrence Quinn, "Currency Futures Trading Helps Firms Sharpen Competitive Edge," *Crain's Chicago Business*, March 2, 1992, p. 20.

eliminating foreign exchange losses, minimizing the firm's tax burden, minimizing the firm's exposure to unnecessarily risky activities, and managing the firm's cash flows and reserves in the most efficient manner, the finance function can reduce the costs of creating value. As the FMC example illustrates, good financial management can also enhance customer service and thereby add value.

We begin this chapter by looking at investment decisions in an international business. We will be most concerned here with the issue of capital budgeting, but not with a highly technical exposition of it. Our objective is to identify the range of factors that can complicate capital budgeting decisions in an international business, as opposed to a purely domestic business. We will discuss how such factors as political and economic risk complicate capital budgeting decisions.

Then we turn our attention to financing decisions in an international business, focusing on the financial structure of foreign affiliates—the mix of equity and debt financing. We will see that financial structure norms for firms vary widely from country to country. We will discuss the advantages and disadvantages of localizing the financial structure of a foreign affiliate to make it consistent with the norms of the country in which it is based.

Next we examine money management decisions in an international business. We will look at the objectives of global money management, the various ways businesses can move money across borders, and some techniques for managing the firm's financial resources efficiently.

The chapter closes with a section on managing foreign exchange risk. Foreign exchange risk was discussed in Chapter 9, but there our focus was on how the foreign exchange market works and the forces that determine exchange rate movements. In this chapter we focus on the various tactics and strategies international businesses use to manage their foreign exchange risk.

◈ INVESTMENT DECISIONS

A decision to invest in activities in a given country must consider a large number of economic, political, cultural, and strategic variables. We have been discussing this issue throughout much of this book. We first touched on this issue in Chapters 2 and 3 when we discussed how the political, economic, legal, and cultural environment of a country can influence the benefits, costs, and risks of doing business there and thus its attractiveness as an investment site. We returned to the issue in Chapter 6 with a discussion of the economic theory of foreign direct investment. We identified a number of factors that determine the economic attractiveness of a foreign investment opportunity. Building on this, in Chapter 7 we looked at the political economy of foreign direct investment and we considered the role government intervention can play in foreign investment. In Chapter 12 we pulled much of this material together when we considered how a firm can reduce its costs of value creation and/or increase its value added by investing in productive activities in other countries. And finally we returned to the issue again in Chapter 14 when we considered the various modes for entering foreign markets. Against this background, one role of the financial manager in an international business is to try to quantify the various benefits, costs, and risks that are likely to flow from an investment in a given location. This is done by using capital budgeting techniques.

Capital Budgeting

The purpose of capital budgeting is to quantify the benefits, costs, and risks of an investment. This enables top managers to compare, in a reasonably objective fashion, different investment alternatives within and across countries so they can make informed choices about where the firm should invest its scarce financial resources. Capital budgeting for a foreign project uses the same theoretical framework that domestic capital budgeting uses; that is, the firm must first estimate the cash flows associated with the project over time. In most cases the cash flows will at first be negative, since the firm will be investing heavily in production facilities. After some initial period, however, the cash flows will become positive as investment costs decline and revenues grow. Once the cash flows have been estimated, they must be discounted to determine their net present value using an appropriate discount rate. The most commonly used discount rate is either the firm's cost of capital or some other required rate of return. So long as the net present value of the discounted cash flows is greater than zero, the firm should go ahead with the project.[2]

Although this might sound quite straightforward, in practice capital budgeting is a very complex and imperfect process. Among the factors complicating the process for an international business are these:

1. A distinction must be made between cash flows to the project and cash flows to the parent company.

2. Political and economic risks, including foreign exchange risk, can significantly change the value of a foreign investment.

3. There is a connection between cash flows to the parent and the source of financing that must be recognized.

We look at the first two of these issues in this section. Discussion of the connection between cash flows and the source of financing is postponed until the next section, where we discuss the source of financing.

Project and Parent Cash Flows

A theoretical argument exists for analyzing any foreign project from the perspective of the parent company, since cash flows to the project are not necessarily the same thing as cash flows to the parent company. The project may not be able to remit all its cash flows to the parent for a number of reasons. For example, cash flows may be blocked from repatriation by the host-country government, they may be taxed at an unfavorable rate, or the host government may require a certain percentage of the cash flows generated from the project to be reinvested within the host nation. While none of these restrictions affect the net present value of the project itself, they do affect the net present value of the project to the parent company, since they limit the cash flows that can be remitted to it from the project.

When evaluating a foreign investment opportunity, the parent should be interested in the cash flows it will receive—as opposed to those the project generates—because the cash flows it receives are ultimately the basis for dividends to stockholders, investments elsewhere in the world, repayment of worldwide corporate debt, and so on. Stockholders will not perceive blocked earnings as contributing to the value of the firm, and creditors will not count them when calculating the parent's ability to service its debt.

The problem of blocked earnings is not as serious as it once was. The worldwide move toward greater acceptance of free market economics (first discussed in Chapter 2) has reduced the number of countries in which governments are likely to prohibit the affiliates of foreign multinationals from remitting cash flows to their parent companies. In addition, as we will see later in the chapter, firms have a number of options for circumventing host-government attempts to block the free flow of funds from an affiliate.

Adjusting for Political and Economic Risk

When analyzing a foreign investment opportunity, the company must consider the risks that stem from its foreign location. These risks include, most importantly, political risk and economic risk. We will discuss these before looking at how capital budgeting methods can be adjusted to take risks into account.

---

[2]For details of capital budgeting techniques see R. A. Brealy and S. C. Myers, *Principles of Corporate Finance* (New York: McGraw-Hill, 1988).

Political risk

We initially encountered the concept of **political risk** in Chapter 2. There we defined it as the likelihood that political forces will cause drastic changes in a country's business environment that adversely affect the profit and other goals of a business enterprise. So defined, political risk tends to be greater in countries experiencing social unrest or disorder and countries where the underlying nature of the society makes the likelihood of social unrest high. When political risk is high, there is a high probability that a change will occur in the country's political environment that will endanger foreign firms there.

In extreme cases political change may result in the expropriation of the assets of foreign firms. This occurred to U.S. firms in the aftermath of the Iranian revolution of 1979. Social unrest may also result in economic collapse, which can effectively render worthless a firm's assets. This has occurred to many foreign companies' assets as a result of the bloody war following the breakup of the former Yugoslavia. In less extreme cases political changes may result in increased tax rates, the imposition of exchange controls that limit or block a subsidiary's ability to remit earnings to its parent company, the imposition of price controls, and government interference in existing contracts. The likelihood of any of these events impairs the attractiveness of a foreign investment opportunity.

Many firms devote considerable attention to political risk analysis and to quantifying political risk. For example, Union Carbide, the U.S. multinational chemical giant, has an elaborate procedure for incorporating political risk into its strategic planning and capital budgeting process.[3] *Euromoney* magazine publishes an annual "Country Risk Rating," which incorporates assessments of political and other risks (see Table 20.1 and the associated description). The problem with all attempts to forecast political risk, however, is that they try to predict a future that can only be guessed at—and in many cases the guesses are wrong. For example, few people foresaw the 1979 Iranian revolution, the collapse of communism in Eastern Europe, or the dramatic breakup of the Soviet Union, yet all these events have had a profound impact on the business environments of the countries involved. This is not to say that political risk assessment is without value, but it is more art than science.

Economic risk

Like political risk, we first encountered the concept of **economic risk** in Chapter 2. There we defined it as the likelihood that economic mismanagement will cause drastic changes in a country's business environment that adversely affect the profit and other goals of a particular business enterprise. In practice the biggest problem arising from economic mismanagement seems to be inflation. Historically many governments have fallen into the trap of expanding their domestic money supply in misguided attempts to stimulate economic activity. The result has too often been too much money chasing too few goods, and then price inflation. As we saw in Chapter 9, sooner or later price inflation is reflected in a drop in the value of a country's currency on the foreign exchange market. This can be a serious problem for a foreign firm with assets in that country, since the value of the cash flows it receives from those assets will fall as the country's currency depreciates on the foreign exchange market. The likelihood of this occurring decreases the attractiveness of foreign investment in that country.

There have been many attempts to quantify countries' economic risk and long-term movements in their exchange rates. *Euromoney's* annual "Country Risk Rating" (Table 20.1) incorporates an assessment of economic performance in its calculation of each country's overall level of risk. As we saw in Chapter 9, there have been extensive empirical studies of the relationship between countries' inflation

---

[3]For details see E. G. Roberts, "Country Risk Assessment: The Union Carbide Experience," in *Global Risk Assessment*, Book 3, ed. J. Rogers (Riverside, CA: Global Risk Assessments, 1988).

TABLE 20.1   *Euromoney* Magazine's Country Risk Ratings

Rank Sept 1995	Change– Mar to Sept	Mar 1995	Sept 1991		Total	Economic Perfor- mance	Political Risk	Debt Indica- tors	Debt in Default	Credit Ratings	Access to Bank Finance	Access to Short- Term Finance	Access to Capital Markets	Discount on Forfait- ing
Weighting					100.00	25.00	25.00	10.00	10.00	10.00	5.00	5.00	5.00	5.00
1	+2	3	8	Switzerland	97.83	22.83	25.00	10.00	10.00	10.00	5.00	5.00	5.00	5.00
2	+6	8	13	Singapore	97.36	25.00	23.42	10.00	10.00	9.23	5.00	5.00	5.00	4.71
3	-2	1	2	Luxembourg	97.35	24.29	23.29	10.00	10.00	10.00	5.00	5.00	5.00	4.78
4	+1	5	7	United States	97.16	22.55	24.61	10.00	10.00	10.00	5.00	5.00	5.00	5.00
5	+1	6	14	Netherlands	97.02	22.91	24.33	10.00	10.00	10.00	5.00	5.00	5.00	4.78
6	-4	2	1	Japan	96.73	21.88	24.84	10.00	10.00	10.00	5.00	5.00	5.00	5.00
7	—	7	11	Germany	96.15	21.64	24.51	10.00	10.00	10.00	5.00	5.00	5.00	5.00
8	-4	4	5	France	95.84	22.01	23.83	10.00	10.00	10.00	5.00	5.00	5.00	5.00
9	+1	10	4	United Kingdom	95.70	21.69	24.01	10.00	10.00	10.00	5.00	5.00	5.00	5.00
10	-1	9	6	Austria	95.27	21.49	23.78	10.00	10.00	10.00	5.00	5.00	5.00	5.00
11	+1	12	9	Norway	94.32	21.89	23.00	10.00	10.00	9.74	5.00	5.00	5.00	4.69
12	-1	11	10	Denmark	94.13	22.35	22.85	10.00	10.00	9.23	5.00	5.00	5.00	4.71
13	—	13	20	Belgium	92.22	20.67	22.53	10.00	10.00	9.23	5.00	5.00	5.00	4.78
14	—	14	3	Canada	91.46	19.76	22.98	10.00	10.00	8.72	5.00	5.00	5.00	5.00
15	+1	16	18	Ireland	91.24	21.48	21.31	10.00	10.00	8.72	5.00	5.00	5.00	4.72
16	-1	15	12	Taiwan	90.50	22.79	21.37	10.00	10.00	8.46	5.00	3.75	4.50	4.64
17	—	17	17	Australia	90.46	21.07	21.29	10.00	10.00	8.46	5.00	5.00	5.00	4.64
18	+1	19	16	Finland	89.50	21.45	21.03	10.00	10.00	7.95	5.00	5.00	4.50	4.58
19	-1	18	23	New Zealand	89.09	20.17	20.82	10.00	10.00	8.46	5.00	5.00	5.00	4.64
20	—	20	19	Spain	87.42	18.73	20.51	10.00	10.00	8.46	5.00	5.00	5.00	4.72
21	—	21	15	Sweden	87.11	18.50	21.31	10.00	10.00	8.20	5.00	5.00	4.50	4.59
22	+2	24	24	Hong Kong	86.26	20.90	19.76	10.00	10.00	6.41	5.00	5.00	5.00	4.19
23	+3	26	38	Korea, South	86.12	22.71	20.53	9.66	10.00	7.31	1.32	5.00	5.00	4.58
24	-2	22	21	Italy	85.73	18.73	20.17	10.00	10.00	7.69	5.00	5.00	4.50	4.64
25	—	25	22	Iceland	83.69	19.51	19.00	10.00	10.00	6.15	5.00	5.00	5.00	4.03
26	+1	27	42	Portugal	79.94	18.19	19.34	9.00	10.00	7.44	1.23	5.00	5.00	4.74
27	+3	30	25	Thailand	79.73	21.31	18.59	9.14	10.00	6.15	4.21	2.25	3.50	4.58
28	—	28	30	Malaysia	78.63	22.45	18.59	9.40	10.00	6.92	0.20	2.50	4.00	4.56
29	-6	23	28	Brunei	78.05	19.80	19.18	10.00	10.00	0.00	5.00	5.00	4.50	4.56
30	+3	33	29	Malta	76.90	19.95	18.46	9.73	10.00	6.15	0.00	5.00	3.50	4.10
31	—	31	41	Israel	75.53	16.74	16.12	10.00	10.00	4.62	5.00	4.75	4.00	4.30
32	+2	34	39	Chile	75.32	19.00	16.59	8.89	9.92	4.87	5.00	3.50	3.00	4.55
33	-4	29	43	Cyprus	73.66	18.29	17.52	9.27	10.00	7.69	0.00	3.75	3.00	4.14
34	-2	32	37	United Arab Emirates	73.56	18.14	17.29	10.00	10.00	0.00	5.00	5.00	4.00	4.14
35	+5	40	32	Indonesia	73.32	19.17	16.23	8.46	10.00	3.46	2.93	4.75	4.00	4.32
36	+1	37	26	Kuwait	71.64	16.91	16.36	10.00	10.00	0.00	5.00	4.75	4.50	4.13
37	-1	36	72	Saudi Arabia	71.57	16.41	16.51	10.00	10.00	0.00	5.00	5.00	4.50	4.15
38	+4	42	47	China	71.06	19.35	16.25	9.54	10.00	4.62	0.07	3.00	4.00	4.24
39	—	39	50	Greece	71.05	14.49	16.67	10.00	10.00	3.08	4.00	5.00	3.50	4.32
40	-2	38	33	Bahrain	70.33	16.98	16.02	10.00	10.00	0.00	5.00	3.75	4.50	4.08
41	-6	35	—	Czech Republic	69.30	19.36	15.39	9.49	10.00	4.23	0.35	2.50	3.50	4.46
42	-1	41	48	Qatar	68.07	18.14	16.85	10.00	10.00	0.00	5.00	0.00	4.00	4.08
43	—	43	27	Oman	64.38	16.99	16.64	9.41	10.00	0.00	0.00	3.75	3.50	4.08
44	+6	50	35	Hungary	63.79	15.83	14.69	8.24	10.00	2.31	2.48	2.50	3.50	4.25
45	+6	51	46	India	63.61	17.43	14.02	8.91	9.95	2.69	0.51	2.25	3.50	4.34
46	-1	45	44	South Africa	63.56	16.54	15.39	9.70	10.00	0.00	0.00	2.50	5.00	4.37
47	+7	54	64	Tunisia	61.95	15.03	14.56	8.83	10.00	3.08	0.23	3.50	2.50	4.21
48	-4	44	—	Bermuda	61.01	17.42	18.72	0.00	10.00	8.85	0.00	0.00	2.00	4.03
49	-1	48	34	Colombia	60.91	16.07	12.69	8.94	9.85	2.69	0.33	3.50	2.50	4.33
50	-3	47	102	Slovenia	60.49	17.31	12.38	9.71	10.00	0.00	0.68	3.25	3.00	4.16
51	+2	53	54	Slovak Republic	60.08	15.21	13.89	9.46	10.00	2.69	0.00	2.50	2.50	3.83
52	-3	49	62	Botswana	58.33	15.31	15.45	9.75	10.00	0.00	0.00	3.50	1.00	3.32
53	+7	60	75	Philippines	58.09	16.39	12.46	8.67	8.36	1.54	1.35	1.75	3.50	4.08
54	+25	79	59	Mauritius	58.03	18.02	17.29	9.54	10.00	0.00	0.95	2.00	0.00	0.22
55	+2	57	36	Turkey	57.71	13.80	12.59	8.69	10.00	0.77	2.95	3.25	2.00	3.66
56	-10	46	40	Bahamas	57.52	18.45	16.85	0.00	10.00	0.00	5.00	5.00	2.00	0.22
57	-5	52	61	Mexico	57.06	12.81	11.63	8.82	9.86	1.54	2.65	3.50	2.50	3.74
58	—	58	89	Brazil	53.83	13.95	10.88	9.17	9.00	0.00	1.80	2.50	2.50	4.03
59	+2	61	49	Uruguay	52.53	13.24	11.97	8.21	8.92	2.31	0.23	2.50	1.50	3.66
60	+34	94	—	Macao	52.26	19.20	15.84	0.00	0.00	0.00	0.00	0.00	3.50	0.22
61	-5	56	67	Argentina	52.14	14.38	10.25	8.54	6.39	0.77	1.49	4.25	2.50	3.57
62	-3	59	78	Morocco	52.11	14.54	11.32	8.31	9.32	0.00	0.57	2.00	2.00	4.05

TABLE 20.1   *(continued)*

Rank Sept 1995	Change– Mar to Sept	Mar 1995	Sept 1991		Total	Economic Perfor- mance	Political Risk	Debt Indica- tors	Debt in Default	Credit Ratings	Access to Bank Finance	Access to Short- Term Finance	Access to Capital Markets	Discount on Forfait- ing
Weighting					100.00	25.00	25.00	10.00	10.00	10.00	5.00	5.00	5.00	5.00
63	–8	55	51	Barbados	50.89	10.32	13.73	9.33	10.00	1.54	0.00	4.75	1.00	0.22
64	+4	68	65	Romania	50.41	12.19	11.27	9.68	10.00	0.00	0.47	1.25	2.00	3.55
65	–1	64	—	Lebanon	49.99	12.34	10.90	9.66	9.33	0.00	0.00	2.00	2.00	3.75
66	–3	63	58	Zimbabwe	49.41	11.49	11.01	8.31	10.00	0.00	1.05	2.25	2.00	3.30
67	+28	95	52	Fiji	49.28	11.22	14.20	9.67	10.00	0.00	1.46	2.50	0.00	0.22
68	–6	62	—	Trinidad & Tobago	49.22	12.22	12.05	8.78	9.13	1.54	0.00	3.50	2.00	0.00
69	+5	74	—	Vietnam	49.21	13.52	10.93	7.42	10.00	0.00	0.00	0.50	3.00	3.85
70	+7	77	74	Ghana	48.99	14.43	10.15	8.56	9.91	0.00	0.13	1.00	1.50	3.31
71	–6	65	77	Sri Lanka	48.54	12.44	11.01	9.02	10.00	0.00	0.00	1.25	1.50	3.33
72	–1	71	80	Poland	48.42	14.87	11.79	9.16	0.00	2.69	0.24	2.50	3.00	4.17
73	+2	75	56	Pakistan	48.35	11.49	9.16	8.85	10.00	0.00	0.09	2.25	3.00	3.51
74	–5	69	63	Jordan	47.57	12.39	9.97	7.95	7.57	0.00	0.00	3.25	2.50	3.95
75	–5	70	60	Papua New Guinea	47.36	9.91	12.15	8.45	10.00	0.00	2.85	2.50	1.50	0.00
76	–10	66	—	Estonia	46.14	15.46	6.75	9.96	10.00	0.00	0.00	0.00	2.00	1.97
77	–4	73	69	Egypt	45.86	10.81	11.40	8.42	7.27	0.00	0.12	2.50	1.50	3.86
78	+2	80	97	Bangladesh	45.25	10.92	9.84	9.05	10.00	0.00	0.00	1.25	1.00	3.19
79	–12	67	35	Venezuela	45.17	10.44	10.25	8.72	10.00	1.54	0.50	2.50	1.00	0.22
80	+3	83	45	Belize	44.15	8.43	12.98	9.41	9.60	0.00	0.00	2.50	1.00	0.22
81	–9	72	57	Paraguay	44.14	10.96	10.36	9.41	10.00	0.00	0.19	2.50	0.50	0.22
82	+17	99	—	Myanmar	43.30	11.04	7.37	9.61	10.00	0.00	0.00	1.25	1.00	3.02
83	+8	91	76	Gabon	42.35	13.18	6.93	8.93	9.80	0.00	0.00	3.50	0.00	0.00
84	+1	85	90	Panama	42.09	10.32	10.15	8.53	9.62	0.00	0.00	1.25	2.00	0.22
85	+1	86	99	Guatemala	42.07	10.54	8.31	9.37	8.51	0.00	0.62	3.50	1.00	0.22
86	–4	82	—	Seychelles	41.49	11.02	11.03	9.44	10.00	0.00	0.00	0.00	0.00	0.00
87	–9	78	—	Ecuador	41.45	8.99	9.01	8.18	9.72	0.00	1.34	2.50	1.50	0.22
88	–4	84	115	El Salvador	41.32	10.54	8.96	9.37	8.98	0.00	0.00	2.25	1.00	0.22
89	+4	93	101	Peru	41.10	10.33	8.15	7.87	6.84	0.00	0.17	2.00	2.00	3.74
90	—	90	122	Bulgaria	40.78	9.54	7.53	8.38	9.40	0.00	0.00	1.75	1.50	2.69
91	–15	76	83	Costa Rica	40.68	9.60	9.61	8.97	9.25	0.00	0.03	2.50	0.50	0.22
92	–4	88	—	Swaziland	40.03	11.91	8.46	9.65	10.00	0.00	0.00	0.00	0.00	0.00
93	–12	81	103	Kenya	39.90	9.11	7.68	7.73	10.00	0.00	1.40	3.25	0.50	0.22
94	+3	97	—	Nepal	39.67	7.15	9.42	8.93	10.00	0.00	0.00	1.25	0.00	2.92
95	+9	104	—	Burkina Faso	39.23	12.05	7.11	9.38	9.43	0.00	0.00	1.25	0.00	0.00
96	+4	100	—	Cote d'Ivoire	39.12	8.40	7.68	6.34	9.50	0.00	2.70	3.50	1.00	0.00
97	–8	89	96	Jamaica	38.99	9.61	8.41	8.08	8.97	0.00	0.19	2.50	1.00	0.22
98	–2	96	79	Bolivia	38.90	9.58	8.83	7.63	9.15	0.00	0.00	2.50	1.00	0.22
99	+6	105	—	Solomon Islands	38.66	7.15	10.28	9.47	10.00	0.00	0.00	1.75	0.00	0.22
100	+3	103	73	Lesotho	38.60	10.05	7.42	9.40	10.00	0.00	0.00	0.00	1.50	0.22
101	–9	92	81	Iran	38.08	9.94	8.36	9.75	7.04	0.00	0.00	1.75	1.00	0.24
102	–15	87	85	Dominican Republic	37.76	9.94	7.87	9.03	8.18	0.00	0.00	2.25	0.50	0.00
103	+17	120	—	Tonga	37.53	7.53	10.38	9.62	10.00	Credit	0.00	0.00	0.00	Discount
104	+5	109	—	Mali	36.86	12.05	6.49	8.68	9.64	0.00	0.00	0.00	0.00	0.00
105	–4	101	92	Honduras	36.81	9.04	6.54	7.75	9.18	0.00	0.58	2.50	1.00	0.22
106	+17	123	—	Malawi	35.99	8.19	6.15	8.40	10.00	0.00	0.00	2.25	1.00	0.00
107	–5	102	—	Algeria	35.55	6.29	7.53	7.49	10.00	0.00	0.00	3.25	1.00	0.00
108	+21	129	—	Kazakhstan	34.97	10.39	8.75	9.97	2.38	0.00	0.00	0.00	2.00	1.49
109	+1	110	88	The Gambia	34.93	9.68	6.07	8.43	10.00	0.00	0.00	0.75	0.00	0.00
110	–12	98	82	Senegal	34.89	7.93	5.97	9.00	9.72	0.00	0.02	1.25	1.00	0.00
111	+0	111	71	Vanuatu	32.90	0.00	12.64	9.01	10.00	0.00	0.00	1.25	0.00	0.00
112	+12	124	—	Guinea	32.75	9.04	3.76	8.59	9.35	0.00	0.00	1.00	1.00	0.00
113	—	113	109	Central African Republic	32.64	6.02	6.33	9.03	10.00	0.00	0.00	1.25	0.00	0.00
114	+12	126	—	Madagascar	32.26	8.58	4.62	7.97	9.84	0.00	0.00	0.75	0.50	0.00
115	+7	122	70	Cameroon	31.69	5.77	4.88	8.64	8.86	0.00	0.79	2.25	0.50	0.00
116	–10	106	87	Latvia	31.09	12.15	5.19	0.00	10.00	0.00	0.00	0.00	2.00	1.74
117	+8	125	95	Croatia	31.03	12.07	5.32	0.00	10.00	0.00	0.00	1.25	0.50	1.88
118	–10	108	117	Lithuania	30.99	10.50	6.83	0.00	10.00	0.00	0.00	0.00	2.00	1.66
119	–2	117	126	Chad	30.70	4.52	5.84	9.09	10.00	0.00	0.00	1.25	0.00	0.00
120	+11	131	—	Western Samoa	30.68	0.00	12.31	8.38	10.00	0.00	0.00	0.00	0.00	0.00
121	–2	119	—	Maldives	30.68	0.00	11.27	9.19	10.00	0.00	0.00	0.00	0.00	0.22

Continued

TABLE 20.1 (continued)

Rank Sept 1995	Change– Mar to Sept	Mar 1995	Sept 1991		Total	Economic Performance	Political Risk	Debt Indicators	Debt in Default	Credit Ratings	Access to Bank Finance	Access to Short-Term Finance	Access to Capital Markets	Discount on Forfaiting
Weighting					100.00	25.00	25.00	10.00	10.00	10.00	5.00	5.00	5.00	5.00
122	+18	140	—	Armenia	30.55	10.84	1.95	9.96	7.80	0.00	0.00	0.00	0.00	0.00
123	−9	114	119	Cambodia	30.49	3.77	5.69	9.54	10.00	0.00	0.00	0.50	1.00	0.00
124	+10	134	94	Grenada	30.40	3.01	7.79	9.10	10.00	0.00	0.00	0.00	0.50	0.00
125	−13	112	86	Nigeria	30.33	7.04	4.00	8.11	8.43	0.00	0.00	2.25	0.50	0.00
126	+6	132	112	Yemen	30.25	3.97	4.85	9.18	10.00	0.00	0.00	2.25	0.00	0.00
127	−6	121	106	Niger	30.19	6.02	4.85	8.34	9.73	0.00	0.00	1.25	0.00	0.00
128	−13	115	—	Benin	29.82	4.44	6.59	9.03	9.01	0.00	0.00	0.75	0.00	0.00
129	−1	128	—	St Vincent & the Grenadines	29.44	0.00	9.92	9.52	10.00	0.00	0.00	0.00	0.00	0.00
130	—	130	93	St Lucia	29.30	0.00	9.61	9.70	10.00	0.00	0.00	0.00	0.00	0.00
131	+6	137	—	Bhutan	28.84	0.00	7.63	9.46	10.00	0.00	0.00	1.75	0.00	0.00
132	−25	107	68	Syria	28.84	9.49	6.88	0.00	10.00	0.00	0.00	1.75	0.50	0.22
133	−15	118	—	Dominica	28.62	0.00	8.77	9.35	10.00	0.00	0.00	0.00	0.50	0.00
134	+1	135	—	Belarus	28.56	8.03	3.04	10.00	5.99	0.00	0.00	0.00	1.50	0.00
135	+3	138	110	Zambia	28.54	5.91	3.97	6.43	9.72	0.00	0.04	0.75	1.50	0.22
136	+11	147	—	Turkmenistan	28.30	13.25	4.54	0.00	10.00	0.00	0.00	0.00	0.50	0.00
137	−10	127	—	Togo	28.26	5.27	5.19	8.57	9.23	0.00	0.00	0.00	0.00	0.00
138	+7	145	—	Ukraine	28.01	7.05	3.74	9.99	2.95	0.00	0.04	2.25	2.00	0.00
139	+3	142	—	Mongolia	27.96	0.00	8.44	9.52	10.00	0.00	0.00	0.00	0.00	0.00
140	−7	133	—	Tanzania	27.57	6.78	4.70	5.95	9.64	0.00	0.00	0.50	0.00	0.00
141	+16	157	—	Moldova	27.47	7.98	2.60	9.97	6.92	0.00	0.00	0.00	0.00	0.00
142	−1	141	108	Russia	27.40	9.68	5.48	0.00	8.26	0.00	0.00	0.50	1.00	2.49
143	+18	161	—	Uzhbekistan	27.40	10.84	5.63	0.00	5.65	0.00	0.00	0.00	2.00	3.27
144	+10	154	—	Cape Verde	27.04	3.01	4.67	9.36	10.00	0.00	0.00	0.00	0.00	0.00
145	−2	143	91	Namibia	26.41	14.31	10.38	0.00	0.00	0.00	0.00	0.00	1.50	0.22
146	+5	151	105	Mauritania	26.00	6.02	4.52	6.39	9.06	0.00	0.00	0.00	0.00	0.00
147	+13	160	—	Laos	25.35	3.01	6.44	8.00	3.65	0.00	0.00	3.25	1.00	0.00
148	+14	162	—	New Caledonia	25.29	8.73	11.55	0.00	0.00	0.00	0.00	5.00	0.00	0.00
149	+3	152	—	Albania	24.92	7.23	4.44	0.00	10.00	0.00	0.00	1.75	1.50	0.00
150	−11	139	128	Uganda	24.74	3.77	3.84	6.16	9.50	0.00	0.00	1.25	0.00	0.22
151	+15	166	—	Georgia	24.64	6.02	4.83	9.73	3.55	0.00	0.00	0.00	0.50	0.00
152	−16	136	125	Ethiopia	24.35	2.56	3.30	8.43	9.32	0.00	0.00	0.75	0.00	0.00
153	+5	158	—	Djibouti	24.33	0.00	4.93	9.39	10.00	0.00	0.00	0.00	0.00	0.00
154	+13	167	—	Comoros	23.89	0.00	4.93	9.10	9.85	0.00	0.00	0.00	0.00	0.00
155	−11	144	—	FYR Macedonia	23.87	11.30	1.30	0.00	10.00	0.00	0.00	0.00	0.00	1.27
156	+15	171	114	Burundi	23.22	2.26	3.25	7.72	10.00	0.00	0.00	0.00	0.00	0.00
157	−7	150	—	Congo	22.84	2.56	3.12	6.74	9.67	0.00	0.00	0.75	0.00	0.00
158	+10	168	—	Equatorial Guinea	21.81	0.00	4.00	7.82	10.00	0.00	0.00	0.00	0.00	0.00
159	—	159	116	Sudan	21.66	2.56	2.02	6.57	10.00	0.00	0.00	0.50	0.00	0.00
160	−5	155	127	Sierra Leone	21.61	1.81	3.43	7.09	8.79	0.00	0.00	0.50	0.00	0.00
161	+8	169	—	Kyrgyzstan	21.58	11.75	3.45	0.00	4.88	0.00	0.00	0.00	1.50	0.00
162	+10	172	107	Guinea-Bissau	20.87	0.00	5.04	6.24	9.59	0.00	0.00	0.00	0.00	0.00
163	−14	149	120	Rwanda	20.45	0.00	1.30	9.16	10.00	0.00	0.00	0.00	0.00	0.00
164	−8	156	—	Mozambique	20.37	3.61	3.25	4.41	8.24	0.00	0.36	0.50	0.00	0.00
165	−12	153	—	Haiti	19.85	3.84	3.76	0.00	10.00	0.00	0.00	2.25	0.00	0.00
166	−18	148	98	Libya	19.38	9.44	9.11	0.00	0.00	0.00	0.00	0.83	0.00	0.00
167	+6	173	—	Angola	18.70	5.25	2.96	0.00	10.00	0.00	0.00	0.50	0.00	0.00
168	+9	177	124	Somalia	18.08	6.02	1.56	0.00	10.00	0.00	0.00	0.50	0.00	0.00
169	−5	164	104	Guyana	16.53	0.00	3.95	1.34	8.99	0.00	0.00	1.75	0.50	0.00
170	−5	165	—	Nicaragua	16.36	2.26	3.89	0.00	7.95	0.00	0.00	1.75	0.50	0.00
171	−1	170	—	Liberia	15.87	1.81	3.06	0.00	10.00	0.00	0.00	0.00	1.00	0.00
172	+2	174	—	Zaire	14.68	1.96	2.00	0.00	10.00	0.00	0.00	0.50	0.00	0.22
173	+7	180	—	Sao Tome and Principe	14.17	0.00	4.34	0.00	9.83	0.00	0.00	0.00	0.00	0.00
174	+10	184	113	Antigua & Barbuda	11.50	0.00	9.50	0.00	0.00	0.00	0.00	0.00	2.00	0.00
175	+4	179	129	Azerbaijan	11.48	8.89	2.60	0.00	0.00	0.00	0.00	0.00	0.00	0.00
176	+2	178	130	Tajikistan	10.13	0.00	3.89	0.00	5.73	0.00	0.00	0.00	0.50	0.00
177	+6	183	118	Cuba	7.81	2.59	3.48	0.00	0.00	0.00	0.00	1.75	0.00	0.00
178	−3	175	—	Surinam	7.27	0.00	7.27	0.00	0.00	0.00	0.00	0.00	0.00	0.00
179	+8	187	—	Korea, North	6.05	1.78	2.52	0.00	0.00	0.00	0.00	1.75	0.00	0.00
180	+5	185	—	Iraq	5.84	2.33	2.26	0.00	0.00	0.00	0.00	1.25	0.00	0.00
181	+5	186	123	Afghanistan	4.38	0.00	3.63	0.00	0.00	0.00	0.00	0.75	0.00	0.00

Table 20.1 (concluded)

Euromoney Risk Assessment

Euromoney's assessment of country risk makes use of three categories. These are analytical indicators 40%, credit indicators 20%, and market indicators 40%. These offer a broad but sensitive evaluation of the relative risks faced by exposure in these countries.

Analytical Indicators

This is made up of political risk 20%, economic risk 10%, and economic indicators 10%. Political risk is a measure of stability and the potential fallout from any instability. The economic indicators consist of three key ratios: the debt-service-to-export ratio as a measure of liquidity, and balance-of-payments-to-GDP and external-debt-to-GDP as measures of solvency. As these are historical, the prospective view of economic performance to 1993 is used to gauge economic risk.

Credit Indicators

This is made up of payment record 15% and ease of rescheduling 5%. Ease of rescheduling indicates a country's general creditworthiness in the face of temporary liquidity problems.

Market Indicators

These consist of access to bond markets (FRN, straight, and Yankee) 15%, availability of short-term finance 10%, and access to and discount available on forfeiting 15%. Bond market access is fine-tuned by considering access to syndicated loans, credit ratings, and secondary market spreads. The attitudes of the market to countries will incorporate analytical and credit indicators, but its favor can be crucial to sustaining a country's economy as well as maintaining liquidity for its sovereign debt in the secondary markets.

Methodology

The *Euromoney* country risk assessment uses nine categories that fall into three broad groups: analytical indicators, credit indicators and market indicators. The weighted scores are calculated as follows: the highest score in each category receives the full mark for the weighting; the lowest receives zero. In between, figures are calculated according to the formula: Final score = weighting/(maximum score − minimum score) × (score − minimum score). The country risk ranking shows only the final scores after weighting.

The categories are:

- **Economic data** (25% weighting). Taken from the *Euromoney* global economic projections 1995–96. Each country scores the average of the evaluations for 1995 and 1996.
- **Political risk** (25%). *Euromoney* polled risk analysts, risk insurance brokers and bank credit officers. They were asked to give each country a score of between zero and 10. A score of 10 indicates no risk of nonpayment; zero indicates that there is no chance of payments being made. Countries were scored in comparison both with each other and with previous years. Country risk was defined as the risk of nonpayment or nonservicing of payment for goods or services, loans, trade-related finance and dividends. and the nonrepatriation of capital. This category does not reflect the creditworthiness of individual counterparties in any country.
- **Debt indicators** (10%). Scores are calculated using the following ratios from the *World Bank World Debt Tables 1994–95*: debt service to exports (A); current-account balance to GNP (B); external debt to GNP (C). Figures are the latest available, mostly for 1993. Scores are calculated by the formula: C + (A × 2) − (B × 10). The lower the score, the better.

   Because of the lack of consistent economic data for OECD and rich oil-producing countries, these score full points with the exception of Turkey, Portugal and Mexico which report debt figures to the IMF. Developing countries that do not report debt data to the World Bank score zero. Successor states of countries that have split take the former country's figures.
- **Debt in default or rescheduled** (10%). A score of between zero and 10 based on the amount of debt in default or that has been rescheduled over the past three years. Zero equals no nonpayments; 10, all in default or rescheduled. Scores are based on the *World Bank World Debt Tables* and *Euromoney* estimates for countries which do not report under the debtor reporting system (DRS).
- **Credit ratings** (10%). The average of sovereign ratings from Moody's, Standard & Poor's and IBCA. Countries without credit ratings or that are rated lower than BB − score zero.
- **Access to bank finance** (5%). Calculated from disbursements of private, long-term, unguaranteed loans as a percentage of GNP. OECD countries which do not report under the debtor reporting system (DRS) score 10. Source: *World Bank World Debt Tables*.
- **Access to short-term finance** (5%). Members of OECD consensus group I score 10, members of group II score five, members of group III score nothing. Coverage from US Exim Bank and NCM UK is worth between zero and 10, depending on the level of coverage available.
- **Access to international bond and syndicated loan markets** (5%). Reflects *Euromoney*'s analysis of how easily the country might tap the markets now, based largely on issues since January 1994. A score of 10 means no problem whatsoever; eight, no problem on 95% of occasions; six, usually no problem; four, possible (depending on conditions); two, just possible in some circumstances; zero, impossible.
- **Access to and discount on forfaiting** (5%). Reflects the average maximum tenor available and the forfaiting spread over riskless countries such as the US. The score equals the average maximum tenor minus the spread. Countries for which forfaiting is not available score nothing. Data were supplied by Morgan Grenfell Trade Finance, West Merchant Bank, the London Forfaiting Company, Standard Bank and ING Capital.

rates and their currencies' exchange rates. These studies show that in the long run there is a relationship between a country's relative inflation rates and changes in its currency's exchange rates. However, the relationship is not as close as theory would predict; it is not reliable in the short-run and is not totally reliable in the long run. So, as with political risk, any attempts to quantify economic risk must be tempered with healthy skepticism.

Risk and capital budgeting

In analyzing a foreign investment opportunity, the additional risk that stems from its location can be handled in at least two ways. The first method is to treat all risk as a single problem by increasing the discount rate applicable to foreign projects in countries where political and economic risks are perceived as high. Thus, for example, a firm might apply a 6 percent discount rate to potential investments in Great Britain, the United States, and Germany, reflecting those countries' economic and political stability, and it might use a 10 percent discount rate for potential investments in Russia, reflecting the political and economic turmoil in that country. The higher the discount rate, the higher the projected net cash flows must be for an investment to have a positive net present value.

Adjusting discount rates to reflect a location's riskiness seems to be fairly widely practiced. For example, a study of large U.S. multinationals found that 49 percent of them routinely added a premium percentage for risk to the discount rate they used in evaluating potential foreign investment projects.[4] However, critics of this method argue that it penalizes early cash flows too heavily and does not penalize distant cash flows enough.[5] They point out that if political or economic collapse were expected in the near future, the investment would not occur anyway. (This is borne out today in the case of Russia; Western companies are not investing there because they perceive imminent danger of political and economic collapse.) So for any investment being considered seriously, the political and economic risk being assessed is not of the immediate-possibility type but rather risk that is some distance in the future. Accordingly it can be argued that rather than using a higher discount rate to evaluate such risky projects—which penalizes early cash flows too heavily—it is better to revise future cash flows from the project downward to reflect the possibility of adverse political or economic changes sometime in the future. Put another way, rather than revising the discount rate upward to reflect higher risk, advocates of this approach argue that future cash flows several years out should be revised downward to reflect higher risk. Surveys of actual practice within multinationals suggest that the practice of revising future cash flows downward is almost as popular as that of revising the discount rate upward.[6]

❧ FINANCING DECISIONS

When considering its options for financing a foreign investment, an international business must consider two factors. The first is how the foreign investment will be financed. If external financing is required, the firm must decide whether to borrow from sources in the host country or from sources elsewhere. The second factor that must be considered is how the financial structure of the foreign affiliate should be configured.

Source of Financing

If the firm is going to seek external financing for a project, it will want to borrow funds from the lowest-cost source of capital available. As we saw in Chapter 11, firms increasingly are turning to the global capital market to finance their investments. By virtue of its size and liquidity, the global capital market's cost of capital is

---

[4]J. C. Backer and L. J. Beardsley, "Multinational Companies' Use of Risk Evaluation and Profit Measurement for Capital Budgeting Decisions," *Journal of Business Finance*, Spring 1973, pp. 34–43.

[5]For example, see D. K. Eiteman, A. I. Stonehill, and M. H. Moffett, *Multinational Business Finance* (Reading, MA: Addison-Wesley, 1992).

[6]M. Stanley and S. Block, "An Empirical Study of Management and Financial Variables Influencing Capital Budgeting Decisions for Multinational Corporations in the 1980s," *Management International Review* 23 (1983), pp. 61–71.

typically lower than in many domestic capital markets, particularly those that are small and relatively illiquid. Thus, for example, a U.S. firm making an investment in Denmark may finance the investment by borrowing through the London-based Eurobond market rather than the Danish capital market.

In practice, however, host-country government restrictions may rule out this option. The governments of many countries require, or at least prefer, foreign multinationals to finance projects in their country by local debt financing or local sales of equity. In countries where liquidity is limited, this effectively raises the cost of capital used to finance a project. Thus, with regard to capital budgeting decisions, the discount rate must be adjusted upward to reflect this. However, this is not the only possibility. In Chapter 8 we saw that some governments court foreign investment by offering foreign firms low-interest loans. Obviously this lowers the cost of capital. Accordingly, with regard to capital budgeting decisions, the discount rate should be revised downward in such cases.

In addition to the impact of host-government policies on the cost of capital and financing decisions, the firm may wish to consider local debt financing for investments in countries where the local currency is expected to depreciate on the foreign exchange market. The amount of local currency required to meet interest payments and retire principal on local debt obligations is not affected when a country's currency depreciates. However, if foreign debt obligations must be served, the amount of local currency required to do this will increase as the currency depreciates, and this effectively raises the cost of capital. (We looked at this issue first in Chapter 11 when we considered foreign exchange risk and the cost of capital.) Thus, although the initial cost of capital may be greater with local borrowing, it may be better to borrow locally if the local currency is expected to depreciate on the foreign exchange market.

Financial Structure

There is a quite striking difference in the financial structures of firms based in different countries. By financial structure we mean the mix of debt and equity used to finance a business. It is well known, for example, that Japanese firms rely far more on debt financing than do most U.S. firms. Table 20.2 reproduces the results of a study comparing debt ratios for 677 firms in nine industries in 23 countries.[7] As can be seen, there is wide variation in the average debt ratios of firms based in different countries. The average debt ratio of firms based in Italy, for example, is more than double that of firms based in Singapore.

It is not altogether clear why the financial structure of firms should vary so much across countries. One possible explanation is that different tax regimes determine the relative attractiveness of debt and equity in a country. For example, if dividends are taxed highly, a preference for debt financing over equity financing would be expected. However, according to recent empirical research, country differences in financial structure do not seem related in any systematic way to country differences in tax structure.[8] Another possibility is that these country differences may reflect deep-seated cultural norms.[9] This explanation may be valid, although the mechanism by which culture influences capital structure has not yet been explained.

The interesting question for the international business is whether it should conform to local capital structure norms. For example, should a U.S. firm investing in Italy adopt the higher debt ratio typical of Italian firms for its Italian subsidiary, or should it stick with its more conservative practice? There are few good arguments for conforming to local norms. One advantage claimed for conforming to host-country

---

[7]W. S. Sekely and J. M. Collins, "Cultural Influences on International Capital Structure," *Journal of International Business Studies* 1988 (Spring), pp. 87–100.

[8]J. Collins and W. S. Sekely, "The Relationship of Headquarters, Country, and Industry Classification to Financial Structure," *Financial Structure*, Autumn 1983, pp. 45–51; and J. Rutterford, "An International Perspective on the Capital Structure Puzzle," *Midland Corporate Finance Journal*, Fall 1985, p. 72.

[9]Sekely and Collins, "Cultural Influences."

TABLE 20.2   Debt Ratios for Selected Industrial Countries

	Alcoholic Beverages	Auto-mobiles	Chemicals	Electrical	Foods	Iron & Steel	Nonferrous Metals	Paper	Textiles	Country Mean
Singapore		.22		.57	.28	.28	.38			.34
Malaysia	.20	.60	.41		.30	.38	.30	.77	.69	.37
Argentina		.42		.44	.35	.32				.38
Australia	.29	.50	.52	.51	.45	.53	.34	.48	.54	.46
Chile			.33	.28	.70	.48	.50	.47		.46
Mexico	.18		.47	.57	.59	.53	.47	.47		.47
South Africa	.59	.50	.51		.46	.53	.32	.42	.69	.50
Brazil		.66	.48	.53	.57	.61		.37		.54
United Kingdom	.45	.73	.50	.60	.55	.51	.57	.56	.52	.55
United States	.51	.58	.55	.54	.56	.54	.58	.58	.50	.55
Benelux	.41	.62	.60	.51	.64	.61	.49	.65	.54	.56
Canada	.55		.45	.52		.69	.61	.68		.58
India	.08	.75	.55			.49	.69	.74	.48	.60
Switzerland				.63	.54	.64				.60
Germany		.57	.56	.66	.49	.60	.70	.70	.65	.62
Denmark	.66		.47	.74	.69	.52	.61	.74		.63
Spain		.59	.64	.45	.66	.82	.70	.85	.43	.64
Sweden	.79	.75	.67	.67	.63	.67	.64	.61	.60	.68
France	.56	.67	.72	.72	.78	.73	.67	.74	.74	.71
Finland	.40	.82	.71	.73	.77	.73	.72	.76	.82	.72
Pakistan		.87	.87				.71	.66	.70	.72
Norway			.76	.67	.79	.62		.82	.75	.74
Italy		.49	.65	.79	.85	.87	.86	.77	.83	.76
Industry mean	.49	.58	.56	.59	.62	.61	.58	.63	.70	

Note: Debt ratio *is defined as total debt divided by total assets at book value.*

Source: W. S. Sekely and J. M. Collins, *"Cultural Influences on International Capital Structure,"* Journal of International Business Studies *19 (1988), p. 91.*

debt norms is that management can more easily evaluate its return on equity relative to local competitors in the same industry. However, this seems a rather weak rationale for what is an important decision. Another point often made is that conforming to higher host-country debt norms can improve the image of foreign affiliates that have been operating with too little debt and thus appear insensitive to local monetary policy. Just how important this point is, however, has not been established. In general the best recommendation is that an international business should adopt a financial structure for each foreign affiliate that minimizes its cost of capital, irrespective of whether that structure is consistent with local practice.

❧ GLOBAL MONEY MANAGEMENT: THE EFFICIENCY OBJECTIVE

Money management decisions attempt to manage the firm's global cash resources—its working capital—most efficiently. A principal objective of global money management is to utilize the firm's global cash resources as efficiently as possible. Essentially this involves minimizing cash balances and reducing transaction costs.

Minimizing Cash Balances

For any given period a firm must hold certain cash balances. This is necessary for serving any accounts and notes payable during that period and as a contingency against unexpected demands on cash. Of course, the firm does not sit on its cash reserves. It typically invests them in money market accounts so it can earn interest on them. However, it must be able to withdraw its money from those accounts freely. Such accounts typically offer a relatively low rate of interest. The firm could earn a higher rate of interest if it could invest its cash resources in longer-term financial instruments (e.g., six-month certificates of deposit). The problem with longer-term instruments, however, is that the firm cannot withdraw its money before the instruments mature without suffering a financial penalty.

Thus the firm faces a dilemma. If it invests its cash balances in money market accounts (or the equivalent), it will have unlimited liquidity but earn a relatively low rate of interest. If it invests its cash in longer-term financial instruments (certificates of deposit, bonds, etc.), it will earn a higher rate of interest, but liquidity will be limited. In an ideal world the firm would have minimal liquid cash balances. We will see later in the chapter that by centrally managing its total global cash reserves through a centralized depository (as opposed to letting each affiliate manage its own cash reserves), an international business can reduce the amount of funds it must hold in liquid accounts and thereby increase its rate of return on its cash reserves.

Reducing Transaction Costs

Transaction costs are the cost of exchange. Every time a firm changes cash from one currency into another currency it must bear a transaction cost, the commission fee it pays to foreign exchange dealers for performing the transaction. Most banks also charge a **transfer fee** for moving cash from one location to another; this is another transaction cost. Since many international businesses have subsidiaries in different countries around the globe that are continually trading with each other, the commission and transfer fees arising from intrafirm transactions can be quite substantial. As we will see later in the chapter, a technique called multilateral netting can be used to reduce the number of transactions between the firm's subsidiaries, thereby reducing the total transactions costs arising from foreign exchange dealings and transfer fees.

❧ GLOBAL MONEY MANAGEMENT: THE TAX OBJECTIVE

Different countries have different tax regimes. Figure 20.1 shows top corporate income tax rates for countries that are members of the Organization of Economic Cooperation and Development (OECD).[10] The top tax rate varies from a high of 60 percent in Germany to a low of 25 percent in Finland. The picture is actually much more complex than the one presented in Figure 20.1. For example, in Germany and Japan the tax rate is lower on income distributed to stockholders as dividends (36 and 35 percent, respectively), whereas in France the tax on profits distributed to stockholders is higher (42 percent).

Many nations follow the worldwide principle that they have the right to tax income earned outside their boundaries by entities based in their country.[11] Thus, for example, the U.S. government can tax the earnings of the German subsidiary of an enterprise incorporated in the United States. The worldwide principle results in double taxation when the income of a foreign subsidiary is taxed both by the host-country government and by the parent company's home government. However, double taxation is to some extent mitigated by tax credits, tax treaties, and the deferral principle.

A **tax credit** allows an entity to reduce the taxes paid to the home government by the amount of taxes paid to the foreign government. A **tax treaty** between two countries is an agreement specifying what items of income will be taxed by the authorities of the country where the income is earned. For example, a tax treaty between the United States and Germany may specify that a U.S. firm need not pay tax in Germany on any earnings from its German subsidiary that are remitted to the United States in the form of dividends. A **deferral principle** specifies that parent companies are not taxed on foreign source income until they actually receive a dividend.

[10]S. C. Ruchelman, "Cross-Border Targets," *Financial Times*, February 24, 1995, p. 10.
[11]"Taxing Questions," *The Economist*, May 22, 1993, p. 73.

FIGURE 20.1
OECD Corporate
Income Tax Rates

Country	Top tax rate (%)
Australia	33
Austria	34
Belgium	40.17
Canada	44.3
Denmark	34
Finland	25
France	33.33
Germany	58.95/46.13
Greece	40
Iceland	33
Ireland	40
Italy	52.2
Japan	51.6
Luxembourg	40.29
Mexico	34
Netherlands	35
New Zealand	33
Norway	28
Portugal	39.6
Spain	35
Sweden	28
Switzerland	28.5
Turkey	42.8
UK	33
US	40

Source: Organization of Economic Cooperation and Development.

For the international business with activities in many countries, the various tax regimes and the myriad of tax treaties existing between countries have important implications for how the firm should structure its internal payments system among the foreign subsidiaries and the parent company. As we will see in the next section, the firm can use such devices as transfer prices and fronting loans to minimize its global tax liability. In addition the form in which income is remitted from a foreign subsidiary to the parent company (e.g., royalty payments versus dividend payments) can be structured to minimize the firm's global tax liability.

Some firms use **tax havens** such as the Bahamas and Bermuda to minimize their tax liability. A tax haven is a country with an exceptionally low, or even no, income tax and thus can be used by international businesses to avoid or defer income taxes. They do this by establishing a 100 percent-owned, nonoperating subsidiary in the tax haven. The tax haven subsidiary will own the common stock of the operating foreign subsidiaries. This allows all transfers of funds from foreign operating subsidiaries to the parent company to be funneled through the tax haven subsidiary. By this means the tax levied on foreign source income by a firm's home government, which might normally be paid when a dividend is declared by a foreign subsidiary, can be deferred under the deferral principle until the tax haven subsidiary pays the dividend to the parent. In theory this dividend payment can be postponed indefinitely if foreign operations continue to grow and require new internal financing from the tax haven affiliate. For U.S-based enterprises, however, U.S. regulations tax U.S. shareholders on the overseas income of the firm when it is earned, regardless of when the parent company in the United States receives it. This regulation eliminates U.S.-based firms' ability to use tax haven subsidiaries to avoid tax liabilities in the manner just described.

❧ Moving Money across Borders: Attaining Efficiencies and Reducing Taxes

Pursuing the objectives of utilizing the firm's cash resources most efficiently and minimizing the firm's global tax liability requires the firm to be able to transfer funds from one location to another around the globe. International businesses use a number of techniques to transfer liquid funds across borders. These include dividend remittances, royalty payments and fees, transfer prices, and fronting loans. Some firms rely on more than one of these techniques to transfer funds across borders, a practice known as **unbundling.** By using a mix of techniques to transfer liquid funds from a foreign subsidiary to the parent company, unbundling allows an international business to recover funds from its foreign subsidiaries without piquing host-country sensitivities with large "dividend drains."

Before we consider the various means for moving liquid funds from location to location, we must point out that a firm's ability to select a particular policy is severely limited when a foreign subsidiary is partly owned either by a local joint-venture partner or by local stockholders. Serving the legitimate demands of the local co-owners of a foreign subsidiary may limit the firm's ability to impose the kind of dividend policy, royalty payment schedule, or transfer pricing policy that would be optimal for the parent company.

Dividend Remittances

Payment of dividends is probably the most common method by which firms transfer funds from foreign subsidiaries to the parent company. Typically the dividend policy varies with each subsidiary depending on such factors as tax regulations, foreign exchange risk, the age of the subsidiary, and the extent of local equity participation. For example, the higher the rate of tax levied on dividends by the host-country government, the less attractive this option becomes relative to other options for transferring liquid funds. With regard to foreign exchange risk, firms sometimes require foreign subsidiaries based in "high-risk" countries to speed the transfer of funds to the parent through accelerated dividend payments. This is basically a way of moving corporate funds out of a country whose currency is expected to depreciate significantly. The age of a foreign subsidiary influences dividend policy in that older subsidiaries tend to remit a higher proportion of their earnings in dividends to the parent, presumably because a subsidiary has fewer capital investment needs as it matures. Local equity participation is a factor because local co-owners' demands for dividends must be recognized.

Royalty Payments and Fees

Royalties represent the remuneration paid to the owners of technology, patents, or trade names for the use of that technology or the right to manufacture and/or sell products under those patents or trade names. It is common for a parent company to charge its foreign subsidiaries royalties for the technology, patents, or trade names it has transferred to them. Royalties may be levied as a fixed monetary amount per unit of the product the subsidiary sells or as a percentage of a subsidiary's gross revenues.

A fee is compensation for professional services or expertise supplied to a foreign subsidiary by the parent company or another subsidiary. Fees are sometimes differentiated into "management fees" for general expertise and advice and "technical assistance fees" for guidance in technical matters. Fees are usually levied as fixed charges for the particular services provided.

Royalties and fees have certain tax advantages over dividends, particularly when the corporate tax rate is higher in the host country than in the parent's home country. Royalties and fees are often tax deductible locally (because they are viewed as an expense), so arranging for payment in royalties and fees will reduce the foreign subsidiary's tax liability. If the foreign subsidiary compensates the parent company by dividend payments, local income taxes must be paid before the dividend distribution, and withholding taxes must be paid on the dividend itself. Although the parent can often take a tax credit for the local withholding and income taxes it has paid, part of the benefit can be lost if the subsidiary's combined tax rate is higher than the parent's.

Transfer Prices

In any international business there are normally a large number of transfers of goods and services between the parent company and foreign subsidiaries and between foreign subsidiaries. This is particularly likely in firms pursuing global and transnational strategies, since these firms are likely to have dispersed their value-creation activities to various optimal locations around the globe (see Chapter 12). As noted in Chapter 19, the price at which goods and services are transferred between entities within the firm is referred to as the **transfer price.**[12]

Transfer prices can be used to position funds within an international business. For example, funds can be moved out of a particular country by setting high transfer prices for goods and services supplied to a subsidiary in that country and by setting low transfer prices for the goods and services sourced from that subsidiary. Conversely funds can be positioned in a country by the opposite policy: setting low transfer prices for goods and services supplied to a subsidiary in that country and setting high transfer prices for the goods and services sourced from that subsidiary. This movement of funds can be between the firm's different subsidiaries or between the parent company and a subsidiary.

Benefits of manipulating transfer prices

At least four gains can be derived by manipulating transfer prices.

1. The firm can reduce its tax liabilities by using transfer prices to shift earnings from a high-tax country to a low-tax one.

2. The firm can use transfer prices to move funds out of a country where a significant currency devaluation is expected, thereby reducing its exposure to foreign exchange risk.

3. The firm can use transfer prices to move funds from a subsidiary to the parent company (or a tax haven) when financial transfers in the form of dividends are restricted or blocked by host-country government policies.

4. The firm can use transfer prices to reduce the import duties it must pay when an ad valorem tariff is in force, a tariff assessed as a percentage of value. In this case low transfer prices on goods or services being imported into the country are required. Since this lowers the value of the goods or services, it lowers the tariff.

Problems with transfer pricing

It must also be recognized that significant problems are associated with pursuing a transfer pricing policy. Few governments are favorably disposed to it.[13] When transfer prices are used to reduce a firm's tax liabilities or import duties, most governments feel they are being cheated of their legitimate income. When transfer prices are manipulated to circumvent government restrictions on capital flows (e.g., dividend remittances), governments perceive this as breaking the spirit, if not the letter, of the law. A number of governments have passed fairly restrictive legislation that seriously limits international businesses' ability to manipulate transfer prices in the manner just described. The United States, for example, has strict regulations governing transfer pricing practices. According to Section 482 of the Internal Revenue Code, the Internal Revenue Service (IRS) can reallocate gross income, deductions, credits, or allowances between related corporations to prevent tax evasion or to reflect more clearly a proper allocation of income. Under the IRS guidelines and subsequent judicial interpretation, the burden of proof is on the taxpayer to show that the IRS has been arbitrary or unreasonable in reallocating income. The correct transfer price, according to the IRS guidelines, is an arm's-length price—the price that would prevail

---

[12]Stephen Crow and E. Sauls, "Setting the Right Transfer Price," *Management Accounting*, December 1994, pp. 41–47.

[13]J. Kelly, "Administrators Prepare for a More Efficient Future," *Financial Times Survey: World Taxation*. February 24, 1995, p. 9.

MANAGEMENT FOCUS
Transfer Pricing Violations

According to testimony given at hearings held by the House Ways and Means Oversight Subcommittee in July 1990, foreign-based multinationals, through elaborate transfer pricing schemes, underpaid the U.S. government by as much as $35 billion during the 1980s. Japanese companies were cited as the principal offenders, followed by German, Canadian, and British companies. Toyota, Toshiba, Sony, Mitsubishi, Fugi Bank, and Siemens were among the foreign multinationals cited for abusing the U.S. tax code. Yamaha, the Japanese motorcycle manufacturer, for example, paid just $123 in U.S. taxes one year, and the IRS claimed it should have paid more than $27 million!

Some of the schemes foreign-based multinationals are using to pay little or no taxes include charging U.S. subsidiaries for inflated or nonexistent freight, insurance, interest, and other expenses. In one example a Japanese multinational was accused of double-billing its U.S. subsidiary for insurance on motorcycle inventory. In another case U.S. officials testified that a foreign automaker charged its U.S. subsidiary $15 interest per vehicle even though interest payments were not required under the distribution agreement.

In response foreign multinationals argue that they have done nothing wrong. It will take years of litigation to determine whether the United States has a case. But one thing is clear: Multinationals' use of transfer pricing policies has come under increasing scrutiny in the United States and elsewhere. As foreign multinationals face scrutiny in the United States, so other countries seem likely to scrutinize U.S. multinationals more closely in response. Numerous officials testified at the hearings that Congress should be aware that U.S. companies routinely engage in similar transfer pricing schemes in other countries. According to Lawrence Gibbs, a former IRS commissioner and international tax lawyer, the countries in which U.S. multinationals do the most business—Canada, Japan, Germany, and Great Britain—all have higher corporate tax rates than the United States, and that gives U.S. multinationals a lot of incentive to use transfer prices improperly. Echoing the theme, a Treasury Department official noted that many of the measures proposed to limit transfer pricing abuses by foreign multinationals in the United States open the door to retaliation against U.S. multinationals.

Source: E. Neumann, "Washington Escalates the Transfer Pricing War," *Business International Money Report*, July 23, 1990, pp. 277–79.

between unrelated firms transacting in a market setting. Such a strict interpretation of what is a correct transfer price theoretically limits a firm's ability to manipulate transfer prices to achieve the benefits we have discussed. In reality, however, there is a feeling that transfer pricing is still widely practiced, a feeling that seems to be borne out by the data contained in the above "Management Focus."

A further problem associated with transfer pricing is related to management incentives and performance evaluation.[14] The practice is inconsistent with a policy of treating each subsidiary in the firm as a profit center. When transfer prices are manipulated by the firm and, as a result, deviate significantly from the arm's-length price, the performance of each subsidiary may depend as much on transfer prices as it does on other pertinent factors, such as management effort. Thus a subsidiary told to charge a high transfer price for a good supplied to another subsidiary will appear to

---

[14]Crow and Sauls, "Setting the Right Transfer Price."

be doing better than it actually is, while the subsidiary purchasing the good will appear to be doing worse. Unless this is explicitly recognized when performance is being evaluated, serious distortions in management incentive systems can occur. In this case, for example, managers in the selling subsidiary may be able to use high transfer prices to mask inefficiencies, whereas managers in the purchasing subsidiary may become disheartened by the effect of high transfer prices on their subsidiary's profitability.

Despite these problems, research suggests that many international businesses do not use arm's-length pricing but instead use some cost-based system for pricing transfers among their subunits (typically cost plus some standard markup). A survey of 164 U.S. multinational firms found that 35 percent of the firms used market-based prices, 15 percent used negotiated prices, and 65 percent used a cost-based pricing method. (The figures add up to more than 100 percent because some companies use more than one method.)[15] This is significant, since only market and negotiated prices could reasonably be interpreted as arm's-length prices. This does not imply the remaining 65 percent of firms manipulate transfer prices. Nevertheless the opportunity for price manipulation is much greater with cost-based transfer pricing methods.

An important ethical dimension to the transfer pricing debate must be noted. Although a firm may be able to manipulate transfer prices to avoid tax liabilities or circumvent government restrictions on capital flows across borders, this does not mean the firm should do so. Since the practice often violates at least the spirit, if not the letter, of the law in many countries, the ethics of engaging in transfer pricing are often dubious at best.

Fronting Loans

A fronting loan is a loan between a parent and its subsidiary channeled through a financial intermediary, usually a large international bank. In a direct intrafirm loan, the parent company lends cash directly to the foreign subsidiary, and the subsidiary repays it later. In a fronting loan the parent company deposits funds in an international bank, and the bank then lends the same amount to the foreign subsidiary. Thus a U.S. firm might deposit $100,000 in a London bank. The London bank might then lend that $100,000 to a subsidiary of the firm in India. From the bank's view the loan is risk free, since it has 100 percent collateral in the form of the parent's deposit. In effect the bank "fronts" for the parent, hence the name. The bank makes a profit by paying the parent company a slightly lower interest rate on its deposit than it charges the foreign subsidiary on the borrowed funds.

Firms use fronting loans for two reasons. First, fronting loans can circumvent host-country government restrictions on the remittance of funds from a foreign subsidiary to the parent company. Whereas a host government may restrict a foreign subsidiary from repaying a loan to its parent in order (for example) to preserve the country's foreign exchange reserves, it is less likely to restrict a foreign subsidiary's ability to repay a loan to a large international bank. To stop payment to an international bank would hurt the country's credit image, whereas halting payment to the parent company would probably have a minimal impact on its image. International businesses sometimes use fronting loans when they want to lend funds to a subsidiary based in a country with a fairly high probability of political turmoil that might lead to restrictions on capital flows (i.e., where the level of political risk is high).

The second reason for using a fronting loan is that it can provide tax advantages. For example, a tax haven (Bermuda) subsidiary that is 100 percent owned by the parent company deposits $1 million in a London-based international bank at 8 percent interest. The bank lends the $1 million to a foreign operating subsidiary at 9 percent interest. The country where the foreign operating subsidiary is based taxes corporate income at 50 percent (see Figure 20.2).

[15]M. F. Al-Eryani, P. Alam, and S. Akhter, "Transfer Pricing Determinants of U.S. Multinationals," *Journal of International Business Studies*, 1990, pp. 409–25.

FIGURE 20.2   An Example of the Tax Aspects of a Fronting Loan

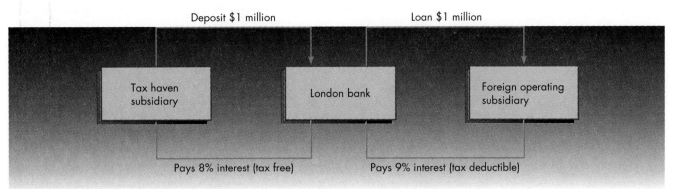

Under this arrangement, interest payments net of income tax will be as follows:

1. The foreign operating subsidiary pays $90,000 interest to the London bank. Deducting these interest payments from its taxable income results in a net aftertax cost of $45,000 to the foreign operating subsidiary.

2. The London bank receives the $90,000. It retains $10,000 of this for its services and pays $80,000 interest on the deposit to the Bermuda subsidiary.

3. The Bermuda subsidiary thus receives $80,000 interest on its deposit, tax free.

The net result is that $80,000 in cash has been moved from the foreign operating subsidiary to the tax haven subsidiary. Because the foreign operating subsidiary's aftertax cost of borrowing is only $45,000, the parent company has been able to move an additional $35,000 out of the country by using this arrangement. If the tax haven subsidiary had made a direct loan to the foreign operating subsidiary, the host government may well have disallowed the interest charge as a tax-deductible expense by ruling that it was in reality a dividend to the parent disguised as an interest payment.

⚜ TECHNIQUES FOR GLOBAL MONEY MANAGEMENT

We have now discussed the objectives of global money management and the various methods international businesses use to move money across borders. We now look at two money management techniques firms use in attempting to manage their global cash resources in the most efficient manner: centralized depositories and multilateral netting.

Centralized Depositories

Every business needs to hold some cash balances for servicing accounts that might be paid and for insuring against unanticipated negative variation from its projected cash flows. The critical issue for an international business is whether each of its foreign subsidiaries should hold its own cash balances or whether cash balances should be held at some centralized depository. In general firms prefer to hold cash balances at a centralized depository for three reasons.

First, by pooling cash reserves centrally the firm is able to deposit larger amounts. Recall that cash balances are typically deposited in liquid accounts, such as overnight money market accounts. Since interest rates on such deposits normally increase with the size of the deposit, by pooling cash centrally the firm should be able to earn a higher interest rate than it would if each subsidiary managed its own cash balances.

Second, if the centralized depository is located in a major financial center (e.g., London, New York, or Tokyo), it should have access to information about good short-term investment opportunities that the typical foreign subsidiary would lack. The financial experts at a centralized depository should be able to develop investment skills and know-how that managers in the typical foreign subsidiary would lack. Thus the firm should be able to make better investment decisions if it pools its cash reserves at a centralized depository.

Third, by pooling its cash reserves, the firm can reduce the total size of the cash pool it must hold in highly liquid accounts, which enables the firm to invest a larger amount of cash reserves in longer-term, less liquid financial instruments that earn a higher interest rate. To understand why, consider an example. (Although this explanation seems technical, it requires only a basic grasp of statistics.) A U.S. firm has three foreign subsidiaries—one in Spain, one in Italy, and one in Germany. Each subsidiary maintains a cash balance that includes an amount for dealing with its day-to-day needs plus a precautionary amount for dealing with unanticipated cash demands. The firm's policy is that the total required cash balance is equal to three standard deviations of the expected day-to-day-needs amount. The three-standard-deviation requirement reflects the firm's estimate that, in practice, there is a 99.87 percent probability that the subsidiary will have sufficient cash to deal with both day-to-day and unanticipated cash demands. Cash needs are assumed to be normally distributed in each country and independent of each other (e.g., cash needs in Germany do not affect cash needs in Italy).

The individual subsidiaries' day-to-day cash needs and the precautionary cash balances they should hold are as follows (in millions of dollars):

	Day-to-Day Cash Needs (A)	One Standard Deviation (B)	Required Cash Balance (A + 3B)
Spain	$10	$1	$13
Italy	6	2	12
Germany	12	3	21
Total	$28	$6	$46

Thus the Spanish subsidiary estimates that it must hold $10 million to serve its day-to-day needs. The standard deviation of this is $1 million, so it is to hold an additional $3 million as a precautionary amount. This gives a total required cash balance of $13 million. The total of the required cash balances for all three subsidiaries is $46 million.

Now consider what might occur if the firm decided to maintain all three cash balances at a centralized depository in London. Since variances are additive when probability distributions are independent of each other, the standard deviation of the combined precautionary account would be

Standard deviation of combined precautionary account

$$= \sqrt{\$R1,000,000^2 + 2,000,000^2 + 3,000,000^2}$$
$$= \sqrt{14,000,000}$$
$$= \$3,741,657$$

If the firm used a centralized depository, it would need to hold $28 million for day-to-day needs plus (3 × $3,741,657) as a precautionary amount, or a total cash balance of $39,224,972. In other words, the firm's total required cash balance would be reduced from $46 million to $39,224,972, a saving of $6,775,028. This is cash that could be invested in less liquid, higher-interest accounts or in tangible assets. The saving arises simply due to the statistical effects of summing the three independent, normal probability distributions.

It must be remembered, however, that a firm's ability to establish a centralized depository that can serve short-term cash needs might be limited by government-imposed restrictions on capital flows across borders (e.g., controls put in place to protect a country's foreign exchange reserves). Also the transaction costs of moving money into and out of different currencies can limit the advantages of such a system. Despite this many firms hold at least their subsidiaries' precautionary cash reserves at a centralized depository, having each subsidiary hold its own day-to-day-needs cash balance in many cases. The globalization of the world capital market and the general removal of barriers to the free flow of cash across borders (particularly among advanced industrialized countries) are two trends likely to increase the use of centralized depositories.

Multilateral Netting

Multilateral netting allows a multinational firm to reduce the transaction costs that arise when a large number of transactions occur between its subsidiaries in the normal course of business. These transaction costs are the commissions paid to foreign exchange dealers for foreign exchange transactions and the fees charged by banks for transferring cash between locations. The volume of such transactions is likely to be particularly high in a firm that has a globally dispersed web of interdependent value-creation activities. Netting reduces transaction costs by reducing the number of transactions that occur.

Multilateral netting is an extension of **bilateral netting.** Under bilateral netting, if a French subsidiary owes a Mexican subsidiary $6 million and the Mexican subsidiary simultaneously owes the French subsidiary $4 million, a bilateral settlement will be made with a single payment of $2 million from the French subsidiary to the Mexican subsidiary, the remaining debt being canceled out.

Under **multilateral netting,** this simple concept is extended to the transactions between multiple subsidiaries within an international business. Consider, for example, a firm that wants to establish multilateral netting among four European subsidiaries based in Germany, France, Spain, and Italy. These subsidiaries all trade with each other, so at the end of each month a large volume of cash transactions must be settled. Figure 20.3A shows how the payment schedule might look at the end of a given month. Figure 20.3B is a payment matrix that summarizes the obligations among the subsidiaries. Note that $43 million needs to flow among the subsidiaries. If the transaction costs (foreign exchange commissions plus transfer fees) amount to 1 percent of the total funds to be transferred, this will cost the parent firm $430,000. However, this amount can be significantly reduced by multilateral netting. Using the payment matrix (Figure 20.3B), the firm can determine the payments that need to be made among its subsidiaries to settle these obligations. Figure 20.3C shows the results. By multilateral netting, the transactions depicted in Figure 20.3A are reduced to just three; the German subsidiary pays $3 million to the Italian subsidiary, and the French subsidiary pays $1 million to the Spanish subsidiary and $1 million to the Italian subsidiary. The total funds that flow among the subsidiaries are therefore reduced from $43 million to just $5 million, and the transaction costs are reduced from $430,000 to $50,000, a saving of $380,000 achieved through multilateral netting.

◆ MANAGING FOREIGN EXCHANGE RISK

The nature of foreign exchange risk was discussed in Chapter 9. There we described how changes in exchange rates alter the profitability of trade and investment deals, how forward exchange rates and currency swaps enable firms to insure themselves to some degree against foreign exchange risk, and how relative inflation rates determine exchange rate movements. It is now time to revisit this topic. This time, however, our perspective is different. In this section we focus on the various strategies international businesses use to manage their foreign exchange risk. Buying forward, the strategy most discussed in Chapter 9, is just one of these. We will examine the types of foreign exchange exposure, the tactics and strategies firms adopt in attempting to minimize their exposure to foreign exchange risk, and things firms can do to develop policies for managing foreign exchange risk.

FIGURE 20.3A
Cash Flows before
Multilateral Netting

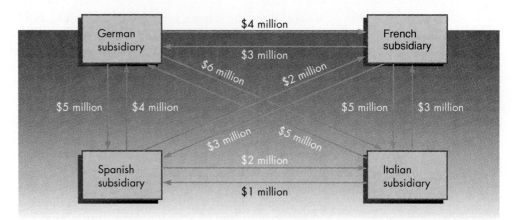

FIGURE 20.3B
Calculation of Net Receipts
(all amount in millions)

Receiving Subsidiary	Paying Subsidiary				Total Receipts	Net Receipts* (payments)
	Germany	**France**	**Spain**	**Italy**		
Germany	—	$ 3	$4	$5	$12	($3)
France	$ 4	—	2	3	9	(2)
Spain	5	3	—	1	9	1
Italy	6	5	2	—	13	4
Total payments	$15	$11	$8	$9		

*Net receipts = Total payments – Total receipts.

FIGURE 20.3C
Cash Flows after
Multilateral Netting

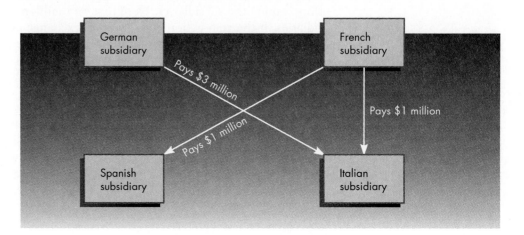

Types of Foreign Exchange Exposure

When we speak of **foreign exchange exposure,** we are referring to the risk that future changes in a country's exchange rate will hurt the firm. As we saw in Chapter 9, changes in foreign exchange values often affect the profitability of international trade and investment deals. Foreign exchange exposure is normally broken down into three categories: transaction exposure, translation exposure, and economic exposure. Each of those is explained here.

Transaction Exposure

Transaction exposure is typically defined as the extent to which the income from individual transactions is affected by fluctuations in foreign exchange values. Such exposure includes obligations for the purchase or sale of goods and services at previously agreed prices and the borrowing or lending of funds in foreign currencies. Consider this example of transaction exposure: A U.S. company has just contracted to import laptop computers from Japan. When the shipment arrives in 30 days, the company must pay the Japanese supplier ¥200,000 for each computer. The dollar/yen spot exchange rate today is $1 = ¥120. At this rate, each laptop computer would cost the importer $1,667 (i.e., 200,000/120 = 1,667). The importer knows it can sell each computer for $2,000 on the day they arrive, so as the exchange rate stands, the U.S. company looks set to make a gross profit of $333 on every computer it sells (2,000 − 1,667). If the dollar depreciates against the yen over the next 30 days, say to $1 = ¥95, the U.S. company will still have to pay the Japanese company ¥200,000 per computer, but in dollar terms that would be $2,105 per laptop computer, more than the computers could be sold for. A depreciation in the value of the dollar against the yen from $1 = ¥120 to $1 = ¥95 would transform this profitable transaction into an unprofitable one.

Translation exposure

Translation exposure is the impact of currency exchange rate changes on the reported consolidated results and balance sheet of a company. This issue was discussed in some detail in Chapter 19 when we looked at currency translation practices. Translation exposure is basically concerned with the present measurement of past events. The resulting accounting gains or losses are said to be unrealized—they are "paper" gains and losses—but this is not to say they are unimportant. For example, consider a U.S. firm with a subsidiary in Mexico. If the value of the Mexican peso depreciates significantly against the dollar, as it did during the early 1980s, this can substantially reduce the dollar value of the Mexican subsidiary's equity. This would reduce the total dollar value of the firm's equity reported in its consolidated balance sheet. This would raise the apparent leverage of the firm (its debt ratio), which could increase the firm's cost of borrowing and restrict its access to the capital market. Thus translation exposure can have a very negative impact on a firm.

Economic exposure

Economic exposure is the extent to which a firm's future international business earning power is affected by changes in exchange rates. Economic exposure is concerned with the long-run effect of changes in exchange rates on future prices, sales, and costs. This is distinct from transaction exposure, which is concerned with the effect of changes in exchange rates on individual transactions—most of which are short-term affairs that will be executed within a few weeks or months. As an example of economic exposure, consider the effect of the wide swings in the value of the dollar on many U.S. firms' international competitiveness during the 1980s. The rapid rise in the value of the dollar on the foreign exchange market in the early 1980s hurt the price competitiveness of many U.S. producers in world markets. U.S. manufacturers that relied heavily on exports (such as Caterpillar Tractor) saw their export volume and world market share plunge. The reverse phenomenon has occurred since the mid-1980s, when the dollar has declined against most major currencies. The fall in the value of the dollar since 1985 has increased the price competitiveness of U.S. manufacturers in world markets and helped produce an export boom in the United States.

Tactics and Strategies for Reducing Foreign Exchange Risk

A number of strategies and tactics can help firms reduce their foreign exchange exposure. The tactics, which include buying forward and the use of leading and lagging, are best suited to alleviating transaction exposure and translation exposure. The strategies, which involve strategic decisions about the configuration of a firm's assets across countries, are best suited to reducing economic exposure.

Reducing transaction and translation exposure

A number of tactics are available to help firms minimize their transaction and translation exposure. These tactics primarily protect short-term cash flows from adverse changes in exchange rates. We discussed two of these tactics in Chapter 9, buying forward and using currency swaps. We will not discuss these two tactics here, except to note they are important sources of insurance against the short-term effects of foreign exchange exposure. (For details, go back to Chapter 9.)

In addition to buying forward and using swaps, firms can adopt other tactics to minimize their foreign exchange exposure. One commonly used one is leading and lagging payables and receivables—that is, collecting and paying early or late depending on expected exchange rate movements. A **lead strategy** involves attempting to collect foreign currency receivables early when a foreign currency is expected to depreciate and paying foreign currency payables before they are due when a currency is expected to appreciate. A **lag strategy** involves delaying collection of foreign currency receivables if that currency is expected to appreciate and delaying payables if the currency is expected to depreciate. Put another way, leading and lagging involves accelerating payments from weak-currency to strong-currency countries, and delaying inflows from strong-currency to weak-currency countries.

Lead and lag strategies can be difficult to implement, however. The firm must be in a position to exercise some control over payment terms if it is to use the tactic. Firms do not always have this kind of bargaining power, particularly when they are dealing with important customers who are in a position to dictate payment terms. Moreover, because lead and lag strategies can put pressure on a weak currency, many governments impose limits on leads and lags. For example, some countries set 180 days as a limit for receiving payments for exports or making payments for imports.

Several other tactics that can reduce transaction and translation exposure have already been discussed in this chapter.

- Transfer prices can be manipulated to move funds out of a country whose currency is expected to depreciate.
- Local debt financing can provide a hedge against foreign exchange risk.
- It may make sense to accelerate dividend payments from subsidiaries based in countries with weak currencies.
- Capital budgeting techniques can be adjusted to deflect the negative impact of adverse exchange rate movements on the current net value of a foreign investment.

Reducing economic exposure

Reducing economic exposure requires strategic choices that go beyond the realm of financial management. The key to reducing economic exposure is to distribute the firm's productive assets to various locations around the globe so the firm's long-term financial well-being is not severely affected by adverse changes in exchange rates. The post-1985 trend by Japanese automakers to establish productive capacity in North America and Western Europe can partly be seen as a strategy for reducing economic exposure (it is also a strategy for reducing trade tensions). Before 1985 most Japanese automobile companies concentrated their productive assets in Japan. However, the rise in the value of the yen on the foreign exchange market has transformed Japan from a low-cost to a high-cost manufacturing location over the past 10 years. Japanese auto firms have moved many of their productive assets overseas in an attempt to ensure the prices of their cars will not be unduly affected by further rises in the value of the yen. In general, reducing economic exposure necessitates that the firm ensure its assets are not too concentrated in countries where likely rises in currency values will lead to damaging increases in the foreign prices of the goods and services they produce. An example of how one company, Black & Decker, has pursued strategies for reducing its economic exposure is given in the next "Management Focus."

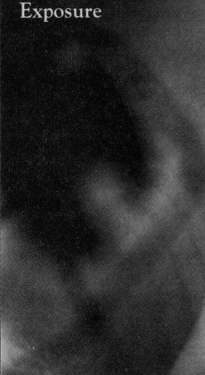

MANAGEMENT FOCUS
How Black & Decker Hedges against Economic Exposure

Black & Decker is one of the few multinationals known to actively manage its economic risk. The key to Black & Decker's strategy is flexible sourcing. In response to foreign exchange movements, Black & Decker can move production from one location to another to effect the most competitive pricing.

Black & Decker manufactures in more than a dozen locations around the world; these include major countries in Europe, Australia, Brazil, Mexico, and Japan. More than 50 percent of the company's productive assets are based outside North America. Although each of Black & Decker's factories focuses on one or two products to achieve economies of scale, there is considerable overlap. The company runs its factories on average at no more than 80 percent capacity. As a consequence, most of the company's factories have the capability to switch rapidly from producing one product to producing another or to add a product. This allows what is produced at a given factory to be changed in response to foreign

exchange movements. For example, as the dollar depreciated during the latter half of the 1980s, the amount of imports into the United States from overseas subsidiaries was reduced, and the amount of exports from U.S. subsidiaries to other locations was increased.

According to the company, the ability to move production of a product in response to changes in foreign exchange movements is a competitive advantage. Black & Decker enjoys a much better long-term competitive position than one of its most significant competitors in the power tool business, Japan's Makita Electric Works, Ltd. This is because 90 percent of Makita's operations are located in Japan, and it exports heavily to the United States. Although Makita may benefit when the yen is depreciating, its margins are vulnerable during periods of yen strength. Black & Decker is not so vulnerable to appreciations in the value of the dollar.

Source: S. Arterian, "How Black & Decker Defines Exposure," *Business International Money Report*, December 18, 1989, pp. 404, 405, 409.

Developing Policies for Managing Foreign Exchange Exposure

The firm needs to develop a mechanism for ensuring it maintains an appropriate mix of tactics and strategies for minimizing its foreign exchange exposure. Although there is no universal agreement among firms as to the components of this mechanism, a number of common themes stand out.[16] First, central control of exposure is needed to protect resources efficiently and ensure that each subunit adopts the correct mix of tactics and strategies. Toward this end many companies have set up in-house foreign exchange centers. Although such centers may not be able to execute all foreign exchange deals—particularly in large, complex multinationals where myriad transactions may be pursued simultaneously—they should at the very least set guidelines for the firm's subsidiaries to follow.

Second, there is a need to distinguish between transaction and translation exposure and economic exposure. Too many companies seem to focus on reducing their transaction and translation exposure and pay scant attention to economic

---

[16]For details on how various firms manage their foreign exchange exposure, see the articles contained in the special foreign exchange issue of *Business International Money Report*, December 18, 1989, pp. 401–12.

exposure, which may have more profound long-term implications for the firm's well-being.[17] Firms need to develop strategies for dealing with economic exposure (see the "Management Focus").

Third, the need to forecast future exchange rate movements cannot be overstated, though, as we saw in Chapter 9, this is a tricky business. No model comes close to perfectly predicting future movements in foreign exchange rates. The best that can be said is that in the short run, forward exchange rates provide reasonable predictions of exchange rate movements, whereas in the long run, fundamental economic factors—particularly relative inflation rates—should be watched, because they influence exchange rate movements. Some firms attempt to forecast exchange rate movements in-house; others rely on the attempts of outside forecasters. The most important thing to recognize, however, is that all such forecasts are imperfect attempts to predict the future.

Fourth, firms need to establish good reporting systems so the central finance function (or in-house foreign exchange center) can monitor the firm's exposure positions on a regular basis. Such reporting systems should enable the firm to identify any exposed accounts, the exposed position by currency of each account, and the time periods covered.

Finally, on the basis of the information it receives from exchange rate forecasts and its own regular reporting systems, the firm should produce monthly foreign exchange exposure reports. These reports should identify how cash flows and balance sheet elements might be affected by forecasted changes in exchange rates. The reports can then be used by management as a basis for adopting tactics and strategies to hedge against undue foreign exchange risks.

Unfortunately, there is plenty of evidence that some of the largest and most sophisticated firms don't take such precautionary steps and so expose themselves to very large foreign exchange risks. For example, in 1990 the treasury department of the British food company Allied Lyons apparently entered the forward foreign exchange market, not so much to hedge against future currency movements as to try to profit from placing large speculative bets that currencies would move one way or another. Unfortunately for Allied Lyons, their treasury department made the incorrect speculative bets and it incurred losses of $240 million. Similarly Showa Shell Sekiyu, the Royal Dutch Shell group's Japanese affiliate, revealed in February 1993 that its treasury department had incurred some $1 billion in unrealized foreign exchange losses.[18]

❦ SUMMARY OF CHAPTER

This chapter has been concerned with financial management in the international business. We have discussed how investment decisions, financing decisions, and money management decisions are complicated by the fact that different countries have different currencies, different tax regimes, different levels of political and economic risk, and so on. Financial managers must account for all these factors when deciding which activities to finance, how best to finance those activities, how best to manage the firm's financial resources, and how best to protect the firm from political and economic risks (including foreign exchange risk). The following points have been made:

1. When using capital budgeting techniques to evaluate a potential foreign project, a distinction must be made between cash flows to the project and cash flows to the parent. The two will not be the same

thing when a host-country government blocks the repatriation of cash flows from a foreign investment.

2. When using capital budgeting techniques to evaluate a potential foreign project, the firm needs to recognize the specific risks arising from its foreign location. These include political risks and economic risks (including foreign exchange risk).

3. Political and economic risks can be incorporated into the capital budgeting process either by using a higher discount rate to evaluate risky projects or by forecasting lower cash flows for such projects.

4. The cost of capital is typically lower in the global capital market than in domestic markets. Consequently, other things being equal, firms prefer to finance their investments by borrowing from the global capital market.

---

[17]Ibid.

[18]T. Corrigan, "Corporate Treasury Management," *Financial Times*, November 2, 1993 p. 31.

5. Borrowing from the global capital market may be restricted by host-government regulations or demands. In such cases the discount rate used in capital budgeting must be revised upward to reflect this.

6. The firm may want to consider local debt financing for investments in countries where the local currency is expected to depreciate.

7. The principal objectives of global money management are to utilize the firm's cash resources in the most efficient manner and to minimize the firm's global tax liabilities.

8. Firms use a number of techniques to transfer liquid funds across borders, including dividend remittances, royalty payments and fees, transfer prices, and fronting loans.

9. Dividend remittances are the most common method used for transferring funds across borders, but royalty payments and fees have certain tax advantages over dividend remittances.

10. The manipulation of transfer prices is sometimes used by firms to move funds out of a country to minimize tax liabilities, hedge against foreign exchange risk, circumvent government restrictions on capital flows, and reduce tariff payments.

11. However, manipulating transfer prices in this manner runs counter to government regulations in many countries, may distort incentive systems within the firm, and has ethically dubious foundations.

12. Fronting loans involves channeling funds from a parent company to a foreign subsidiary through a third party, normally an international bank. Fronting loans can circumvent host-government restrictions on the remittance of funds and provide certain tax advantages.

13. By holding cash at a centralized depository, the firm may be able to invest its cash reserves more efficiently. It can reduce the total size of the cash pool that it needs to hold in highly liquid accounts, thereby freeing cash for investment in higher-interest-bearing (less liquid) accounts or in tangible assets.

14. Multilateral netting reduces the transaction costs arising when a large number of transactions occur between a firm's subsidiaries in the normal course of business.

15. The three types of exposure to foreign exchange risk are transaction exposure, translation exposure, and economic exposure.

16. Tactics that insure against transaction and translation exposure include buying forward, using currency swaps, leading and lagging payables and receivables, manipulating transfer prices, using local debt financing, accelerating dividend payments, and adjusting capital budgeting to reflect foreign exchange exposure.

17. Reducing a firm's economic exposure requires strategic choices about how the firm's productive assets are distributed around the globe.

18. To manage foreign exchange exposure effectively, the firm must exercise centralized oversight over its foreign exchange hedging activities, recognize the difference between transaction exposure and economic exposure, forecast future exchange rate movements, establish good reporting systems within the firm to monitor exposure positions, and produce regular foreign exchange exposure reports that can be used as a basis for action.

❧ CRITICAL DISCUSSION QUESTIONS

1. How can the finance function of an international business improve the firm's competitive position in the global marketplace?

2. What actions can a firm take to minimize its global tax liability? On ethical grounds, can such actions be justified?

3. You are the CFO of a U.S. firm whose wholly owned subsidiary in Mexico manufactures component parts for your U.S. assembly operations. The subsidiary has been financed by bank borrowings in the United States. You have just been told by one of your analysts that the Mexican peso is expected to depreciate by 30 percent against the U.S. dollar on the foreign exchange markets over the next year. What actions, if any, should you take?

4. You are the CFO of a Canadian firm that is considering building a $10 million factory in Russia to produce milk. The investment is expected to produce net cash flows of $3 million each year for the next 10 years, after which the investment will have to close due to technological obsolescence. Scrap values will be zero. The cost of capital will be 6 percent if financing is arranged through the Eurobond market. However, you have an option to finance the project by borrowing funds from a Russian bank at 12 percent. Analysts tell you that due to high inflation in Russia, the Russian ruble is expected to depreciate against the Canadian dollar. Analysts rate probability of violent revolution occurring in Russia within the next 10 years as high. How would you incorporate these factors into your evaluation of the investment opportunity? What would you recommend the firm do?

❧ CLOSING CASE   Motorola's Global Cash Management System

A multinational corporation with operating companies in more than 80 countries and sales in excess of $23 billion, Motorola is one of the world's leading providers of wireless communications equipment, semiconductors, and advanced electronics systems and services. Separate Motorola companies act autonomously and trade with each other on an arm's-length basis, often across national borders. Historically each operating company managed its own payments with other Motorola subsidiaries, and with independent suppliers, and executed its own foreign exchange dealings. By the mid-1990s, however, Motorola had built a global cash management system that not only managed transactions between Motorola operating companies, but also between Motorola companies and key suppliers.

The evolution of Motorola's global cash management system dates to 1976 when the company decided to develop a foreign currency netting system for transactions between Motorola companies. The objective of this system was to achieve cost savings by reducing both cash flows and the amount of foreign exchange deals required to execute cross-border payments. Under this system once every week all foreign currency transactions between Motorola companies are managed with a single payment or invoice from a London-based treasury management center to each Motorola company. Figures C.1, C.2, and C.3 show how this system reduces organizational complexity, while the following table gives a numerical example using the exchange rates detailed in Figure C.3.

FIGURE C.1
Prenetting Information Flows

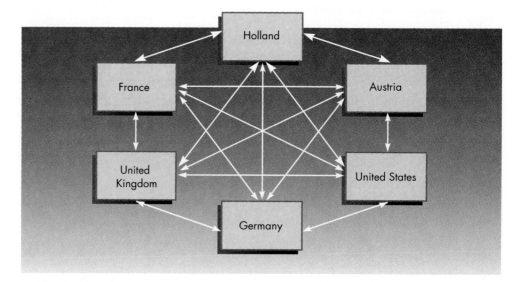

FIGURE C.2
Postnetting Information Flows

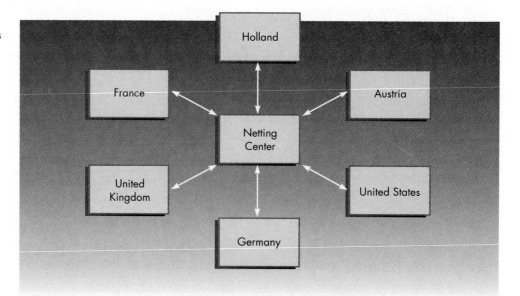

FIGURE C.3

Schematic Model of
Currency Netting

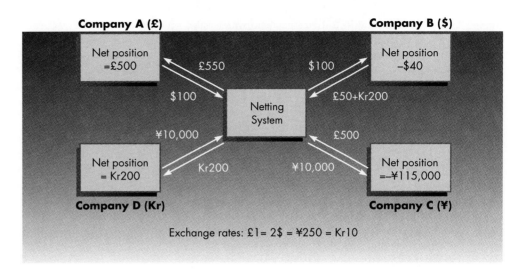

Using the table, the net payments for each operating company can be easily calculated. Specifically,

Company A (£550 – £50 = £500)
Company B ($100 – $140 = –$40)
Company C (¥10,000 – ¥125,000 = –¥115,000)
Company D (Kr200 – Kr400 = –Kr200)

Accounts Receivable

Accounts Payable	Company A (£)	Company B ($)	Company C (¥)	Company D (Kr)	Total Payable
Company A	0	$100	0	0	
Company B	£50	0	0	Kr200	$140
Company C	£500	0	0	0	¥125,000
Company D	0	0	¥10,000	0	Kr400
Total Receivable	£550	$100	¥10,000	Kr200	

Before netting, the total amount of cash flows was the sum of all payments, which in dollar terms amounted to $1,320. The netted cash for each company is the sum of its payables less the sum of its receivables. Therefore in local currency company A will receive £500, B will pay $40, C will pay ¥115,000, and D will pay Kr200. The netted cash flow in dollars is now $1,000. The center receives three different types of currencies, makes one payment to company A, and has a neutral cash position.

The benefits of this system are a reduction in cash flows and in the volume of foreign exchange dealings. Moving from localized treasury management to one centralized system realized an estimated annual financial saving from lower transaction costs (bank fees and foreign exchange commissions) of around $6.5 million for Motorola. However, this figure does not include administrative gains from more streamlined operations, which while more difficult to quantify, are also probably quite substantial.

Motorola's success at implementing this system is attributed to a number of factors. First, senior management had the foresight to become committed to this initiative at a very early stage. Management saw the system, and the information technology systems required to support it, as a source of

strategic advantage. This was helpful in overcoming the normal resistance of operating managers to changes that take away some of their autonomy. Second, Motorola had already made substantial investments in building an information technology backbone to share manufacturing and logistics data between operating companies. Once this system had been built, it could easily be extended to incorporate the data required for global treasury management. Third, Motorola took a gradual approach to implementing the system, which helped the company to perfect it before implementing it organizationwide. In the first instance, a few sites were chosen as prototypes. After these sites had been integrated into the system, and any operating difficulties had been overcome, the inclusion of other sites proceeded smoothly. The number of participating Motorola entities rose from 38 in 1983 to 106 by the early 1990s.

Once the internal cash management system was working smoothly at Motorola, the company moved to extended the system to embrace key suppliers and customers. Extending the system was in principle relatively straightforward. Each week the Motorola netting center collects data from each Motorola entity detailing payments that have to be made to suppliers. The global treasury function executes the required foreign exchange transactions, initiates payment orders, and advises Motorola companies of their net positions. After netting incoming payments with outgoing payments and combining common currencies, an approximate foreign exchange position is reached in which surplus currencies are sold and deficit currencies are purchased. The transaction value is approximately $100 million per week.

As for payments, these are all handled by Citibank, perhaps the world's most multinational bank, which uses its own global information systems network to transfer funds between the various entities involved in the Motorola system, whether they are Motorola companies or independent vendors. Making this system work requires close electronic links between Motorola and Citibank, compatible information systems, a shared vision as to the purpose of the system, and ongoing cooperation between Motorola and Citibank to improve and manage the global flow of money.

As a result of this system, in 1991 the net cash flow between Motorola operating companies was $2.4 billion, a reduction of $2.38 billion from the value of payments settled in 1991. Moreover, without netting Motorola would have had to engage in foreign exchange transactions valued at $4.3 billion. With netting, foreign exchange transactions were reduced to about $1.3 billion, which equates to annual direct savings in transaction costs of around $6.5 million.

CASE DISCUSSION QUESTIONS

1. What are the strategic benefits to Motorola of the global cash management system described in this case?

2. How important is the relationship between Citibank and Motorola to the development, implementation, and smooth functioning of this system?

3. What factors helped Motorola implement this system in a company where treasury operations had been decentralized to various national operations?

Sources: C. P. Holland, G. Lockett, J-M Richard, I. Blackman, "The Evolution of a Global Cash Management System," Sloan Management Review, Fall 1994, pp. 37–47; and B. Ettorre, "How Motorola Closes its Books in Two Days," Management Review, March 1995, pp. 84–89.

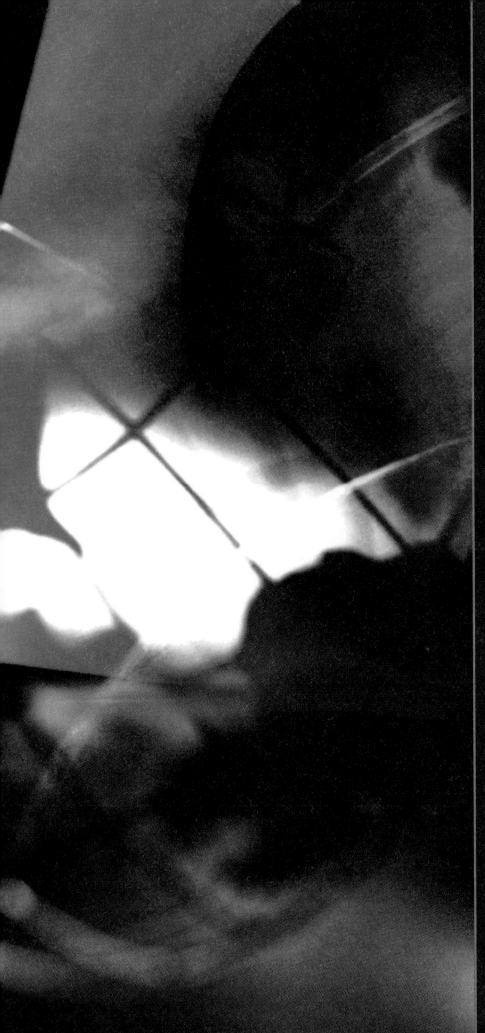

THE GLOBALIZATION OF XEROX CORPORATION

METALFABRIKEN BRAZIL

THE GLOBALIZATION OF XEROX CORPORATION

In March 1960 Xerox Corporation shipped its first 914 series copiers, beginning one of the most successful new-product introductions in history. Its photocopiers were protected from imitation by a wall of patents. Safe behind this wall, Xerox dominated the industry for the next 15 years. By the late 1970s Xerox was a multinational company with three main legs:

- The parent company, Xerox Corporation, designed and produced products in the United States for the North American market.
- Rank-Xerox, a 51 percent-owned Xerox company, developed and manufactured products for the European market.
- Fuji-Xerox, a 50/50 joint venture between Xerox and Fuji, developed and manufactured products for the Japanese and Asian market.

Each Xerox company controlled its own suppliers, manufacturing plants, and distribution channels. Each was, in effect, a self-contained entity.

By 1980, however, Xerox was facing problems. Its patents had expired, and many new competitors were entering its markets. Most significant, the Japanese companies Canon and Ricoh had emerged as significant global competitors. Although Xerox still dominated the copier market, both Canon and Ricoh were selling high-quality copiers at a price approximately equivalent to Xerox's cost for producing comparable products. Moreover, Xerox's market share had fallen by half, and its return on assets had slumped to 8 percent.

Xerox learned firsthand how far it had fallen behind when it began to produce and market a copier in the United States that had been designed by its Japanese affiliate, Fuji-Xerox. Xerox discovered that the reject rate for Fuji-Xerox parts was only a fraction of that of U.S.-produced parts. Visits to Fuji-Xerox revealed another important truth: Quality in manufacturing does not increase real costs; it reduces costs by reducing defective products and service costs.

These developments forced Xerox to fundamentally rethink the way it did business. In 1982 Xerox launched the first of a series of initiatives that over the next decade were to transform its operations. Xerox became the first major U.S. company to win back market share from the Japanese. In 1989 it won the prestigious Malcolm Baldrige Award for quality, and by 1991 its return on assets had increased to 14 percent. The changes underlying this turnaround are detailed in the remainder of this case.

✺ MANAGING SUPPLY SOURCES

In 1981 Xerox had more than 5,000 individual suppliers worldwide. After reviewing Fuji-Xerox's management of suppliers, Xerox realized that if it consolidated its supply base, it could probably achieve three goals:

1. Simplifying the purchasing process would cut overhead in the purchasing area.
2. Having a single supplier produce a particular part for all of Xerox's worldwide operations would allow the supplier to achieve economies of scale in production. The resulting cost savings would be passed on to Xerox in the form of lower prices.
3. Cutting down the number of suppliers would make it easier for Xerox to work with its suppliers to improve the quality of component parts.

Source: Charles W. L. Hill.

As a first step, in 1982 Xerox created multifunctional, multinational "commodity teams." These teams included buyers, engineers, cost experts, and quality control personnel from more than a dozen of its operating companies. Their first task was to reduce Xerox's supplier base from more than 5,000 to less than 500. The teams reduced it to 325 suppliers. In several cases the company decided to use a single supplier for a component. For example, the lamps for Xerox's copiers now come from a single supplier with plants in Asia, Europe, and the United States. Because the consolidation of suppliers simplified the purchasing process, overhead rates fell from 9 percent of total costs for materials in 1982 to about 3 percent by 1992.

Once the supplier base had been consolidated, Xerox launched a quality training effort with its suppliers. Xerox told them that its quality goal was to reduce the number of defective parts coming from them to below 1,000 defects per million. At the time, some suppliers' defect rates were as high as 25,000 per million parts. To implement this policy, Xerox took five steps:

1. Formally established a sole source policy whereby it would deal with only one supplier for a particular part around the world.

2. Entered into long-term (three to five years) contracts with its sole source suppliers, thus reinforcing the notion that it was in a supplier's best interest to work closely with Xerox.

3. Adopted a continuous supplier involvement program that involves suppliers in the design of new products.

4. Established multilevel communications with suppliers. In the past Xerox engineers were prohibited from talking to suppliers for fear they might discuss costs. Now engineers are required to talk with suppliers.

5. Minimized its use of competitive bidding. Xerox now establishes "target costs" for component parts based on its knowledge of what a part should cost to produce. The target cost is then the basis for negotiations with preferred suppliers. In the past, competitive bidding practices had tended to undermine efforts to work with selected suppliers on designs. A supplier that contributed to a design might be left out in the cold if a "garage shop down the street" submitted a slightly lower bid.

As a result of these steps, the company soon met its quality goal of 1,000 defects per million parts. By 1992 its defect rate on parts from suppliers was below 300 per million. Moreover, overall material-related costs were down about 50 percent from the 1980 level—reflecting not only more-concentrated purchases, but also improved designs, new technology, and internal efficiencies, all of which were generated by working more closely with suppliers.

❧ CHANGES WITHIN XEROX

At the same time Xerox was reorganizing its worldwide supplier relations, it was also reorganizing its operations. Borrowing heavily from Fuji-Xerox, the first step was to organize its plant workers into "Quality of Worklife" circles. After training the workers in interpersonal skills, group dynamics, and problem-solving techniques, the worklife circles were asked to evaluate situations ranging from working conditions to production problems, and to come up with recommendations for improvement.

Building on this, Xerox introduced its "Leadership through Quality" program in 1983. The Quality of Worklife circles were merged into "Business Area Work Groups," with membership of these groups including both management and lower-level employees. The Business Area Work Groups were established throughout the hierarchy—from top management down to the factory floor—with each group's membership comprising adjacent levels in the hierarchy, and each group received training in quality improvement programs. Emphasis was on identifying quality shortfalls and the problems that caused them, determining the root causes of the problems, and then developing and implementing solutions for the problems. The training program began with the top-tier groups and then cascaded throughout the organization, gradually spreading worldwide to some 100,000 employees.

Also in 1983 Xerox adopted "competitive benchmarking," a process of measuring the company against the products, services, and practices of some of the most efficient global companies. For example, Xerox benchmarked L. L. Bean for distribution procedures, Deere and Company for central computer operations, Proctor & Gamble for marketing, and Florida Power and Light for its quality improvement process. Approximately 240 functional areas are now benchmarked against comparable areas in other companies.

In 1985 and 1986 Xerox began to focus on its new-produce development process. One goal was to design products that are customized to local market conditions but also contain a large number of globally standardized parts. Another goal was to reduce the time needed to design new products and get them to the market. To achieve these goals, Xerox established multifunctional, multinational new-product development teams. Each team was to manage the design, component sourcing, manufacturing, distribution, and after-sale customer service for its assigned new product on a worldwide basis. For example, one team designed a new product with a universal power supplier and multi-language displays to eliminate the cost of reengineering for new markets at a later date. In general the use of design teams cut as much as a year from the overall product development cycle and saved millions of dollars.

One consequence of the new approach to product development was the 5100 copier, the first product jointly designed by Xerox and Fuji-Xerox for the world market and manufactured in U.S. plants. It was launched in Japan in November 1990 and in the United States the following February. The 5100's global design reportedly reduced the overall time to market and saved the company more than $10 million in development costs.

In 1988 Xerox created a multinational task force to review its progress toward global integration. This task force identified three levels of integration and used them as a basis for restructuring various operations at all facilities. All Xerox plants were required to:

1. Adopt global standards for basic processes that apply to all operations (e.g., use standard databases for materials management).

2. Maintain common business processes but, where necessary, tailor them to local needs (e.g., just-in-time programs).

3. Set site-specific processes for only those systems that must conform to local needs (e.g., government reporting requirements).

In 1989 Xerox calculated that it could eliminate $1 billion in inventory and $200 million in inventory-related costs by linking worldwide customer orders more closely with production. The company implemented a multinational program called "central logistics and assets management," the aid of which is to achieve tight integration between individual customer orders and plant production levels and thereby reduce the need for excessive inventory.

❧ CONCLUSION

As a result of these steps, Xerox's competitive position improved markedly during the 1980s. Due to its improved quality, lower costs, and shorter product development time, Xerox was able to regain market share from its Japanese competitors and to boost its profits and revenues. Xerox's share of the U.S. copier market increased from a low of 10 percent in 1985 to 18 percent in 1981.

CASE DISCUSSION QUESTIONS

1. What strategy was Xerox pursuing in 1979? In 1989?

2. From what source did Xerox receive guidance in transforming its organization in the 1980s? What does this reveal about the advantages of a multinational firm?

3. To what extent did taking a global, rather than local, perspective help Xerox improve its competitive position?

4. Evaluate the roles of global manufacturing, materials management, and R&D in Xerox's improved performance during the 1980s.

REFERENCES

Howard, R. "The CEO as Organizational Architect." *Harvard Business Review*, September–October 1992, pp. 106–23.

Kearns, D. "Leadership through Quality." *Academy of Management Executive* 4, no. 3 (1990), pp. 86–89.

McGrath, M. E., and R. W. Hoole, "Manufacturing's New Economies of Scale." *Harvard Business Review*, May–June 1992, pp. 94–102.

Rohan, T. "In Search of Speed." *Industry Week*, September 3, 1990, pp. 78–82.

Sheridan, J. "America's Best Plants." *Industry Week*, October 15, 1990, pp. 27–40.

———. "Suppliers: Partners in Prosperity," *Industry Week*, March 19, 1990, pp. 12–19.

METALFABRIKEN BRAZIL

For the first time in Brazil's history, direct foreign investment in the country turned negative in 1986 amid rumors of tighter rules on dividend remittances. There had seemed to be some light emerging in 1984 and 1985 as Brazil began to trade its way out of the massive foreign debt dilemma bequeathed to it by the preceding decade of high oil prices. In 1986, however, the gloom deepened as the country's trade surplus fell below its interest obligation, and external debt climbed over US $100 billion. As a consequence of outside pressure on Brazil to set its house in order, 1987 saw GDP growth slow substantially from the 8 percent level of the previous years, and inflation and devaluation began to accelerate yet again (see Tables 1 and 2 for details).

✺ MFK IN BRAZIL

Simon Kirsch, who had served as general manager of MFK Brazil since its inception in 1975, felt that the deterioration in the country's economic condition warranted a review of the company's operating strategy. He was reluctant to consider any fundamental strategic change because the company's Brazilian operations had been remarkably successful and profitable despite rapid domestic inflation. Recent years, however, had shown sales and profits declining in hard currency terms (see Tables 3 and 4). Success was achieved mainly by exploiting parent-company technology in Brazil and by exporting intermittently elsewhere in Latin America. In practice MFK Brazil produced the parent company's line of specialized automatic lathes, importing key components and attachments from the parent company in Germany. The more advanced the model, the more dependent the Brazilian operation was on imported components. However, because of worsening foreign exchange problems in Brazil, the government in 1985 had imposed a 25 percent tax

Source: This case was prepared by Professor Harold Crookell for illustrative classroom purposes. Copyright © 1988. The University of Western Ontario.

TABLE 1
Brazil's Balance of Payments
(in millions of U.S. dollars)

	1973	1982	1984	1986
Balance of trade	182	800	13,100	8,400
Exports	6,198	20,200	27,000	22,400
Imports	–6,018	–19,400	–13,900	–14,000
(of which oil)	—	—	(6,900)	(3,000)
Other current items	–1,472	–17,100	–12,600	–12,400
Inflows	900	3,300	3,300	3,000
Outflows	–2,372	–20,400	–15,900	–15,400
(of which interest)	—	(12,600)	(10,200)	(9,100)
Current account balance	–1,290	–16,300	500	–4,000
Net capital movement	3,680	7,900	6,100	–1,000
Direct investment	820	2,500	1,100	–100
Long–term financing	4,760	12,500	13,600	12,500
Amorizations	–1,900	–7,000	–7,800	–13,200
Other	—	–100	–800	–200
Errors and omissions	–63	–400	400	200
Balance of payments	2,327	–8,800	7,000	–4,800
Reserves	6,389	3,900	11,500	5,800
External debt	12,218	80,800 E	92,400	101,000
Debt coefficient	1.0	3.8	3.0	4.25

Source: Economist, *Intelligence Unit, Country Profile 1987–88 and quarterly report, January–March 1988.*

TABLE 2
Selected Economic
Indicators of Brazil

	1983	1984	1985	1986
GDP at market prices (billions of cruzados)	118	388	1,046	3,688
Real GDP growth (%)	–2.5	5.7	8.3	8.2
Consumer price inflation (%)	142	197	256	67
Exchange rate (average) (cruzado per U.S. dollar)	0.6	1.85	6.20	13.61
Exchange rate (average) (German marks per U.S. dollar)	2.55	2.85	2.94	2.17
Trade surplus with major trading partners in billions US$				
United States				2,670
Japan				630
United Kingdom				277
France				143
West Germany				–176

Source: Economist, *Intelligence Unit, Country Profile 1987–88 and quarterly report, January–March 1988.*

in cruzados on foreign exchange purchases to pay for imports. At the same time, export incentives were introduced that offset the foreign exchange tax. Any Brazilian firm that increased its exports over base year 1985 received a 25 percent rebate in cruzados of the value of the increase in its exports.

✺ MFK PRODUCT LINE

MFK was a small, German-based producer of specialized automatic lathes with worldwide sales in 1986 of DM 870 million from four factories located in Germany, Switzerland, India, and Brazil. The company's success in world markets stemmed from its policy of inhouse design and development of a unique and innovative product line. MFK lathes were basically cheaper than their competitors' and offered comparable performance although for a more limited range of common applications. Over the past decade the range of applications had been broadened gradually by the development of more sophisticated machines built on the same basic principle as the original MFK innovation and by the development of special attachments. The company had also developed a group of highly trained technical specialists both to maintain product standards in the factories and to help company sales reps sell the more complex machines to increasingly sophisticated industrial users.

TABLE 3

Income Statements for Selected Years (in millions of cruzados and marks)

	1984		1985		1986	
	0.65 Cruz	1.00 Marks	2.1 Cruz	1.00 Marks	6.3* Cruz	1.00 Marks
Sales	82.2	126.5	251.5	119.8	708.3	112.4
Cost of Sales†	52.3	80.5	175.0	83.3	520.5	82.6
Gross profit	29.9	46.0	76.5	36.5	187.8	29.8
Selling and administrative	13.9	21.4	42.5	20.3	113.3	18.0
Profit before tax	16.0	24.6	34.0	16.2	74.5	11.8
Monetary correction on working capital‡	8.0	12.3	24.0	11.4	44.5	7.1
Income tax (30%)	2.4	3.7	3.0	1.4	9.0	1.4
Profit after tax	13.6	20.9	31.0	14.8	65.5	10.4
Dividends to Germany (before withholding tax)	6.4	9.8	15.5	7.4	32.5	5.2

*In the fall of 1987, the exchange rate was about 37.5 cruzados to 1 DM.

† Includes 25% foreign exchange tax, on imports of Cr 40 min. in 1985 (partial year) and Cr 158 min. in 1986.

‡ Part of the loss in value of working capital due to inflation is allowed as a tax deduction in Brazil.

TABLE 4

Balance Sheets for Selected Years (in millions of cruzados and marks)

	1984		1985		1986	
	Cruz	Mark	Cruz	Mark	Cruz	Mark
Current assets						
Cash	3.1	4.8	12.5	5.9	28.8	4.6
Accounts receivable	12.1	18.7	39.5	18.8	125.5	19.9
Inventories	8.5	13.1	24.8	11.8	76.4	12.1
Current liabilities						
Short–term debt	(2.1)	(3.2)	(6.0)	(2.9)	(17.4)	2.8
Accounts payable	(6.5)	(10.0)	(20.0)	(9.5)	(57.5)	9.1
Net working capital	15.2	23.4	50.8	24.2	155.8	24.7
Fixed assets (net)	12.5	19.2	24.5	11.7	60.5	9.6
Long-term debt	(3.0)	(4.6)	(7.5)	(3.6)	(24.3)	(3.8)
Equity and retained earnings	24.7	38.0	67.8	32.3	192.0	30.5
Registered capital	40.0		156.0		275.0	

When production began in Brazil in 1976, the factory was not much more than an assembly plant for the basic MFK lathe—the X20 model, capable of machining barstock between 15 and 25 mm in diameter. Components were imported from Germany. However, to qualify for government incentive grants at the time—a time when MFK Brazil was short of funds because of the unanticipated working capital demands of high inflation—Kirsch moved quickly to increase the level of local content in Brazilian-made X20s. He was able to move quickly because of the help he received from parent-company technical specialists. These specialists were always in short supply, but faced with the alternative of investing more capital in Brazil, the parent company agreed to extending specialist support, even though it meant a decline in component exports per unit sold. The hope from Germany's standpoint was that more X20s would be sold in Brazil than would otherwise be possible, and that the smaller volume of exports per unit sold would be offset by higher sales.

In 1978 MFK Brazil began assembly of the X50 lathe—for barstock between 40 and 60 mm—again largely on the basis of imported components and gradual "localization." In 1980 the parent company completed a major R&D project that resulted in a new, more advanced product line capable of closer tolerance work. The company decided to introduce the new line (AX20 and AX50) in addition to the existing line to see how different kinds of customers would react to the choice. Kirsch was not eager to get into production of the new machines in Brazil at first,

TABLE 5   Price and Cost Data by Model

	Factory Price* (Cr.000s)		Factory Cost (Cr. 000s)		Number Sold		Imports as Percent of Factory Cost		Total Value† of Imports (Cr.000s)	
	1984	1986	1984	1986	1984	1986	1984	1986	1984	1986
X20	29.0	205	21.3	149	690	790	14	11	2,057	12,948
X50	45.2	317	29.5	230	195	230	18	18	1,035	9,522
AX20	60.3	442	41.7	330	170	255	48	44	3,402	37,026
AX50	69.5	536	47.7	410	385	405	42	31	7,713	51,475
Total					1440	1680			14,207	110,971

*Price relates to the basic machine without attachments. Attachments constitute about 20 percent of total sales.
† These values represent imports of component parts only and include tariff and transportation costs paid in cruzados. All attachments were also imported.

but demand for them—especially by foreign subsidiaries in Brazil—was stronger than expected. As a result, AX50s were imported in 1980 and AX20s the following year, and as sales grew, assembly and gradual "localization" of production began. By 1987 MFK Brazil was producing, with varying degrees of local content, the X20, X50, and AX20, and AX50 machines. Table 5 shows the factory price and cost of each of these machines, together with the number sold and the level of import content. The sale of a machine usually involved selected attachments to increase its versatility, and the attachments were all imported from Germany because of their complexity.

❧ MARKETING IN BRAZIL

Automatic lathes were not easy to sell. The sales force had to be trained not only to understand the technical capacity of the machines it sold, but also more importantly, to recognize potential applications by studying a customer's production processes. The more sophisticated the machine, the wider its range of applications and hence the more skill required to sell it. Furthermore, the possible range of attachments in a sale added further to the machine's versatility. The MFK sales force was, therefore, supported (and trained) by a strong technical group in the factory, which in turn was supported and trained by parent-company technical specialists. The incentive to sell more sophisticated machines rather than to concentrate on simpler applications stemmed from the higher prices of the former and, hence, by application of the same commission rate, a higher net commission on each sale.

As a rule, the salespeople would identify the potential sale and bring the necessary information back to the technical group for quotation. The quoted price depended on which attachments were added to the basic machine, which in turn depended on the tasks the machine had to perform.

Frequently, technical support staff would have to accompany salespeople to the customers' factories to determine more precisely what attachments were really needed. This was especially true with newer salespeople. All models of the basic machine were subject to Brazilian price controls, but the attachments were not. In general the Price Review Board would allow price increases equivalent to documented cost increases, even if the cost increases were due largely to higher priced imports. The main problem with the system was that it consumed a lot of management time and involved a considerable time gap between cost increases and compensating price increases. As a result, there had been a gradual narrowing of profit margins on basic machines, which Kirsch had tried to offset by increasing the margins on attachments.

Customer financing was another major marketing problem in Brazil. The government-subsidized financing scheme, operating by FINAME, permitted credit-worthy customers to finance purchases of industrial equipment through the banking system at reduced interest rates. This was part of a Brazilian program to promote productivity and modernization. All MFK machines qualified under the scheme except the AX20, which failed because its import content was too high. Attachments sold with machines qualified as long as the machine qualified.

❧ SALES FORCE

There were 24 field salespeople in the organization in 1987, four operating out of Rio and the rest out of Sao Paulo. Over 80 percent of the company's customers (and potential customers) were in the Sao Paulo region, where much of Brazil's industry and settled. Regions outside of Rio and Sao Paulo were serviced through independent Brazilian distributors. The distribution of Brazilian sales by region in 1986 was a follows:

Domestic Brazil Sales of MFK Lathes, 1986

Region	Number of Customers	Number of Machines Sold
Sao Paulo	1,490	1,135
Rio	164	170
Other	166	110
Total	1,820	1,415

In early 1987, Mr Kirsch found it necessary to split Sao Paula into five regions rather than three as had previously been the case and to increase the Sao Paulo sales force from 12 to 20. Two conditions prompted this move. First, the economic boom was slowing down due to inflationary problems brought by the country's foreign exchange problems. And, second, the salespeople, because of the commission system, were earning salaries over 50 percent higher than the technical specialists who supported them. The new sales territories, of course, did not please the existing salespeople, but Kirsch wanted them to dig a little deeper for sales rather than skimming their territories, and he wanted them to invest more time with key customers and sell more attachments to them.

❧ EXPORTING FROM BRAZIL

Kirsch was strongly committed to exporting from Brazil whenever market conditions in the rest of Latin America permitted it. He felt exports, especially of the X20, had made a major contribution to scale economies in the Brazilian factory, and export prices were not subject to Brazilian price controls. There were, however, subject to competitive pressure, particularly from an Argentine competitor who had virtually copied the X20 and X50 machines in the late 1970s. Over the years, an implicit understanding had evolved that he would not sell his version of the X20 in Brazil and MFK would not sell its X50 in Argentina. Shortly thereafter Kirsch began importing AX50s to reduce the Argentinian's share of the top end of the X50 market in Brazil. In third markets in Latin America the two firms competed actively. Data on MFK Brazil's exports appear in Table 6.

One of the company's biggest export problems was the instability of Latin American markets. Despite efforts over many years, the area was still struggling to make free trade a reality. The major economies—Argentina, Brazil, and Mexico—all had major economic problems of their own, but were nevertheless still trying to reduce trade impediments within Latin America. Of the 11 nations that signed the 1980 Montevideo Treaty (ALADI), three (Bolivia, Ecuador, and Paraguay) were classified

TABLE 6   Exports by Model and Country 1984 and 1986 (in millions of cruzados)

	X20		X50		AX20		AX50		Total	
Argentina	1.3	14.4	—	1.0	1.0	6.0	1.2	5.5	3.5	26.9
Mexico	4.5	18.6	0.8	5.5	—	1.0	—	1.5	5.3	26.6
Chile	2.5	17.5	0.4	2.5	—	—	—	—	2.9	20.0
Colombia	1.0	9.5	0.3	—	—	—	—	—	1.3	9.5
Peru	—	6.5	—	1.0	—	—	—	—	—	7.5
Venezuela	1.2	10.0	1.0	5.0	—	—	—	—	2.2	15.0
Total	10.5	76.5	2.5	15.0	1.0	7.0	1.2	7.0	15.2	105.5

TABLE 7

Prices and Costs in Germany by Model (in thousands of German Marks)

	Factory Prices		Factory Cost		Number Produced	
	1984	1986	1984	1986	1984	1986
X20	22.5	24.0	18.0	19.0	4,190	4,085
X50	33.5	35.0	25.7	27.0	3,275	2,915
AX20	44.0	46.5	33.0	35.0	3,850	3,615
AX50	54.0	57.0	40.0	42.5	3,595	3,420
Total					14,910	14,035

as least developed and were given special trade concessions. The other five intermediate economies belonged to Chile, Columbia, Peru, Uruguay, and Venezuela. MFK's parent company also exported to Latin America and had developed an informal understanding with Kirsch that the markets should go to whoever could supply them at the lower cost. For the most part, Germany had lower production costs than Brazil (see Table 7) but faced approximately 25 percent higher tariffs to enter ALADI markets and an even bigger differential in relation to Argentina. In 1986 Brazil and Argentina, concerned at the slow pace of multilateral negotiations, signed their own version of a freer trade agreement. As a result, Brazilian goods had an even greater advantage than German goods entering Argentina.

❧ THE MANAGEMENT MEETING

Kirsch decided to call a meeting of his key executives in the fall of 1987 to discuss whether conditions in Brazil called for fundamental change in MFK's competitive strategy. Attending the meeting were José DaSilva and Philppe Garcia, in charge of marketing and finance, respectively, and Manfred Schmidt and Rolf Kruger, in charge of production and technical support.

Kirsch: So with inflation on the move again and Brazil's debt problems worsening by the week, I'm afraid we may be in for more import controls and perhaps some tightening of Brazil's dividend rules on foreign investment. How do those dividend rules work again, Philippe?

Garcia: You can pay foreign dividends up to 12 percent of registered capital at a 25 percent rate of withholding tax. Anything higher than 12 percent faces a higher rate of tax, up to 60 percent.

Kruger: How can you operate a business on a system like that? Inflation is going through the roof, and they allow you 12 percent on your original investment—then they take a quarter of it for tax. It's not worth the effort.

Garcia: Registered capital allows for inflation and reinvested profits. It's not that bad. And the 12 percent is after withholding tax. It's 16 percent gross.

Kruger: Well, why didn't we send a bigger dividend to Germany in 1986? It sounds like we could have.

Garcia: We probably could have, in retrospect, but we needed to keep more money on hand to meet the new foreign exchange tax, and the strength of the German mark had made the tax even higher.

Kruger: This country is just one stupid rule after another. People spend all their time chasing their shadows instead of getting on . . .

Schmidt: Come on, Rolf. Don't get so worked up. Brazil didn't create high oil prices and high interest rates. If you ask me, this country is paying a hell of a price for other people's greed and mistakes.

Kruger: And its own!

Kirsch: What we have to decide is whether we can continue to do business on the strategy we have used so far. We import a lot more than we export and one of the rumors I've heard is that foreign-owned firms like us are going to have to earn their own foreign exchange needs.

DaSilva: The government's latest regulations are clearly intended to push foreign firms to import less and export more. Why don't we try to do that? Mount an export marketing effort throughout Latin America and speed up the local manufacture of imported components.

Kruger: That's it! Build a stronger business in Brazil at the expense of Germany. Great idea! And how do you propose to manage it?

DaSilva: Brazil's problems are serious. We have to do something to become more independent of imports. Manfred, couldn't the factory produce a lot of the components we now import? And why not launch an export drive?

Schmidt: We could do a little more in our own factory, but to make a real dent in imports will require some new equipment and training of our people.

Kruger: And who will have to do it? More technical specialists from Germany! And how long will that take? About 25 years, the speed people learn around here.

Schmidt: That's uncalled for, Rolf. We've got some first-class people on the shop floor. They could pick up the training fast enough.

Kruger: You've been in Brazil too long, Manfred. I think you've gone native. Look, I spent several weeks earlier this year visiting our agents in Argentina, Mexico, Chile, Peru, and Colombia. You know why our exports are not that great? They don't have the technical know-how to help their customers. I went personally to show customers what our machines can do and made all kinds of sales. Why do you think our exports are mainly X20s? Because they are the easiest to sell. It's simple, if we want to increase exports, we have to provide much stronger technical support in other Latin American countries. And where do you suppose the technical support is going to come from? And why do you suppose Germany has not already provided it to increase its own exports? Because there are better places to put it, that's why!

DaSilva: Another reason our X20 exports are stronger is our Argentinian competitor. He had done a good job of . . .

Kruger: He's not worth powder to blow him to hell. Forget him. Let's stay with the real problem. We need three things: technicians, technicians, and technicians.

Kirsch: Look, José is right about one thing. Brazil is in foreign exchange trouble and we are part of the problem. What's more we have to increase our sales of attachments in Brazil because that's where the big profit is, and all the attachments are imported and require a lot of skill to sell. Maybe we just have to pick away at training as fast as we can. Reduce our imports and increase our exports gradually. We just have to get more technical support from Germany. But how can we convince them of that?

Garcia: I could prepare a very persuasive presentation on Brazil's economic problems and the risk they put us in.

Kruger: They'll cry all the way to the Bundesbank! Try money instead. Not cruzados. Real money.

Schmidt: Stuff it, Rolf!

Garcia: Actually there is a way we could get more foreign exchange to Germany.

Kirsch: You mean raise the dividend to the full 12 percent allowed.

Garcia: Yes, but more than that. The 12 percent allowance is based over a three-year average, and dividends in 1985 and 1986 were below the limit. We could declare a dividend in 1987 high enough to bring the entire three years up to 12 percent net of withholding tax. Mind you, we may have to borrow to do it, and interest rates are going through the roof, but it could be done.

Kirsch: That's really useful, Philippe. Maybe we have something to bargain with if we present it right.

Kruger: But look at what you're doing. You are going to build a bigger, stronger Brazilian company with more assets and more profit just as the country is going to blow up. Everything will be trapped here. What good is that to the company?

Schmidt: Do you have a better idea?

Kruger: Ja wohl.

Schmidt: I don't think I want to hear it.

Kruger: Why not stop manufacturing everything in Brazil but the X20? Import the other models from Germany. Take our technical expertise out of the factory and put it to work marketing and exporting. Get Germany to let Brazil be a major global supplier of X20s. Exports go up, manufacturing costs come down, and the investment exposure in Brazil is reduced, too. Presto, the perfect solution!

Schmidt: I knew I didn't want to hear it. Do you realize, Rolf, that would destroy in one stroke five years of accumulated training and skill-building? Once you wipe out technical capability like that, it's lost forever.

DaSilva: The factory would become quite remote from the sales force. I can see it from Germany's point of view, but it is not good for Brazil.

Kirsch: I don't know whether that's the kind of business I'd enjoy presiding over, Rolf. But it's certainly an idea worth thinking about. In fact, it's been a very useful meeting, indeed. I just wish I knew what to do.

GLOSSARY

A

absolute advantage   A country has an absolute advantage in the production of a product when it is more efficient than any other country at producing it.

administrative trade policies   Administrative policies, typically adopted by government bureaucracies, that can be used to restrict imports or boost exports.

ad valorem tariff   A tariff levied as proportion of the value of an imported good.

Andean Pact   A 1969 agreement between Bolivia, Chile, Ecuador, Colombia, and Peru to establish a customs union.

antidumping regulations   Regulations designed to restrict the sale of goods for less than their fair market price.

arbitrage   The purchase of securities in one market for immediate resale in another to profit from a price discrepancy.

ASEAN (Association of South East Asian Nations)   Formed in 1967, an attempt to establish free trade area between Brunei, Indonesia, Malaysia, the Philippines, Singapore, and Thailand.

B

balance of payments accounts   National accounts that track both payments to and receipts from foreigners.

barriers to entry   Factors that make it difficult or costly for firms to enter an industry or market.

barter   The direct exchange of goods or services between two parties without a cash transaction.

bill of exchange   An order written by an exporter instructing an importer, or an importer's agent, to pay a specified amount of money at a specified time.

bill of lading (or draft)   A document issued to an exporter by a common carrier transporting merchandise. It serves as a receipt, a contract, and a document of title.

Bretton Woods   A 1944 conference in which representatives of 40 countries met to design a new international monetary system.

bureaucratic controls   Achieving control through the establishment of a system of rules and procedures.

C

capital account   In the balance of payments, records transactions involving the purchase or sale of assets.

CARICOM   An association of English-speaking Caribbean states that are attempting to establish a customs union.

caste system   A system of social stratification in which social position is determined by the family into which a person is born, and change in that position is usually not possible during an individual's lifetime.

centralized depository   The practice of centralizing corporate cash balances in a single depository.

channel length   The number of intermediaries that a product has to go through before it reaches the final consumer.

civil law system   A system of law based on a very detailed set of written laws and codes.

class consciousness   A tendency for individuals to perceive themselves in term of their class background.

class system   A system of social stratification in which social status is determined by the family into which a person is born and subsequent socioeconomic achievements. Mobility between classes is possible.

collectivism   An emphasis on collective goals as opposed to individual goals.

COMECON   Now-defunct economic association of Eastern European communist states headed by the former USSR.

command economy   An economic system where the allocation of resources, including determination of what goods and services should be produced, and in what quantity, is planned by the government.

common law system   A system of law based on tradition, precedent, and custom. When law courts interpret common law, they do so with regard to these characteristics.

common market   A group of countries committed to (1) removing all barriers to the free flow of goods, services, and factors of production between each other and (2) the pursuit of a common external trade policy.

communist totalitarianism   A version of collectivism advocating that socialism can only be achieved through a totalitarian dictatorship.

Communists   Those who believe socialism can only be achieved through revolution and totalitarian dictatorship.

comparative advantage   The theory that countries should specialize in the production of goods and services they can produce most efficiently. A country is said to have a comparative advantage in the production of such goods and services.

competition policy   Regulations designed to promote competition and restrict monopoly practices.

controlling interest   A firm has a controlling interest in another business entity when it owns more than 50 percent of that entity's voting stock.

core competence   Firm skills that competitors cannot easily match or imitate.

counterpurchase   A reciprocal buying agreement.

countertrade   The trade of goods and services for other goods and services.

cross-cultural literacy   Understanding how the culture of a country affects the way business is practiced.

cultural controls   Achieving control by persuading subordinates to identify with the norms and value systems of the organization (self-control).

culture   The complex whole that includes knowledge, belief, art, morals, law, custom, and other capabilities acquired by man as a member of society.

currency translation   Converting the financial statements of foreign subsidiaries into the currency of the home country.

current account   In the balance of payments, records transactions involving the export or import of goods and services.

current account deficit   The current account of the balance of payments is in deficit when a country imports more goods and services than it exports.

current account surplus   The current account of the balance of payments is in surplus when a country exports more goods and services than it imports.

current rate method   Using the exchange rate at the balance sheet date to translate the financial statements of a foreign subsidiary into the home currency.

customs union   A group of countries committed to (1) removing all barriers to the free flow of goods and services between each other and (2) the pursuit of a common external trade policy.

D

deferral principle   Parent companies are not taxed on the income of a foreign subsidiary until they actually receive a dividend from that subsidiary.

diminishing returns   Applied to international trade theory, the more of a good that a country produces, the greater the units of resources required to produce each additional item.

draft   See bill of lading.

drawee   The party to whom a bill of lading is presented.

E

economic risk   The likelihood that events, including economic mismanagement, will cause drastic changes in a country's business environment that adversely affect the profit and other goals of a particular business enterprise.

economic union   A group of countries committed to (1) removing all barriers to the free flow of goods, services, and factors of production between each other, (2) the adoption of a common currency, (3) the harmonization of tax rates, and (4) the pursuit of a common external trade policy.

economies of scale   Cost advantages associated with large-scale production.

ecu   A basket of EU currencies that serves as the unit of account for the EMS.

efficient market   A market where prices reflect all available information.

ethnocentric staffing   A staffing approach within the MNE in which all key management positions are filled by parent-country nationals.

Eurobonds   A bond placed in countries other than the one in whose currency the bond is denominated.

Eurocurrency   Any currency banked outside of its country of origin.

Eurodollar   Dollar banked outside of the United States.

European Free Trade Association (EFTA)   A free trade association including Norway, Iceland, and Switzerland.

European Monetary System (EMS)   EU system designed to create a zone of monetary stability in Europe, control inflation, and coordinate exchange rate policies of EU countries.

European Union (EU)   An economic group of 15 European nations: Austria, Belgium, Great Britain, Denmark, Finland, France, Germany, Greece, the Netherlands, Ireland, Italy, Luxembourg, Portugal, Spain and Sweden. Established as a customs union, it is now moving toward economic union. (Formerly the European Community.)

exchange rate   The rate at which one currency is converted into another.

exchange rate mechanism (ERM)   Mechanism for aligning the exchange rates of EU currencies against each other.

exclusive channels   A distribution channel that outsiders find difficult to access.

expatriate manager   A national of one country appointed to a management position in another country.

experience curve   Systematic production cost reductions that occur over the life of a product.

experience curve pricing   Aggressive pricing designed to increase volume and help the firm realize experience curve economies.

Export-Import Bank (Eximbank)   Agency of the U.S. government whose mission is to provide aid in financing and facilitate exports and imports.

exporting   Sale of products produced in one country to residents of another country.

externally convertible currency   Nonresidents can convert their holdings of domestic currency into foreign currency, but the ability of residents to convert the currency is in some way limited.

F

factor endowments   A country's endowment with resources such as land, labor, and capital.

factors of production   Inputs into the productive process of a firm, including labor, management, land, capital, and technological know-how.

Financial Accounting Standards Board (FASB)   The body that writes the generally accepted accounting principles by which the financial statements of U.S. firms must be prepared.

financial structure   Mix of debt and equity used to finance a business.

Fisher effect   Nominal interest rates (i) in each country equal the required real rate of interest (r) and the expected rate of inflation over the period of time for which the funds are to be lent (I). That is, i = r + I.

first-mover advantages   Advantages accruing to the first to enter a market.

fixed exchange rates   A system under which the exchange rate for converting one currency into another is fixed.

fixed-rate bond   Offers a fixed set of cash payoffs each year until maturity, when the investor also receives the face value of the bond in cash.

flexible manufacturing technologies   Manufacturing technologies designed to improve job scheduling, reduce setup time, and improve quality control.

floating exchange rates   A system under which the exchange rate for converting one currency into another is continuously adjusted depending on the laws of supply and demand.

flow of foreign direct investment   The amount of foreign direct investment undertaken over a given time period (normally one year).

folkways   Routine conventions of everyday life.

foreign bonds   Bonds sold outside the borrower's country and denominated in the currency of the country in which they are issued.

foreign direct investment (FDI)   Direct investment in business operations in a foreign country.

foriegn exchange market   A market for converting the currency of one country into that of another country.

foreign exchange risk   The risk that changes in exchange rates will adversely affect the profitability of a business deal.

foreign portfolio investment (FPI)   Investments by individuals, firms, or public bodies (e.g., national and local governments) in foreign financial instruments (e.g., government bonds, foreign stocks).

forward exchange   When two parties agree to exchange currency and execute a deal at some specific date in the future.

forward exchange rate   The exchange rates governing forward exchange transactions.

free trade   The absence of barriers to the free flow of goods and services between countries.

free trade area   A group of countries committed to removing all barriers to the free flow of goods and services between each other, but pursuing independent external trade policies.

freely convertible currency   A country's currency is freely convertible when the government of that country allows both residents and nonresidents to purchase unlimited amounts of foreign currency with the domestic currency.

fronting loans   A loan between a parent company and a foreign subsidiary that is channeled through a financial intermediary.

G

gains from trade   The economic gains to a country from engaging in international trade.

General Agreement on Tariffs and Trade (GATT)   International treaty that committed signatories to lowering barriers to the free flow of goods across national borders led to the WTO.

geocentric staffing   A staffing policy where the best people are sought for key jobs throughout an MNE, regardless of nationality.

global matrix structure   Horizontal differentiation proceeds along two dimensions: product divisions and areas.

global strategy   Strategy focusing on increasing profitability by reaping the cost reductions from experience curve and location economies.

globalization of markets   Moving away from an economic system in which national markets are distinct entities, isolated by trade barriers and barriers of distance, time, and culture, and toward a system in which national markets are merging into one global market.

globalization of production   Trend by individual firms to disperse parts of their productive processes to different locations around the globe to take advantage of differences in cost and quality of factors of production.

gold par value   The amount of currency needed to purchase one ounce of gold.

gross domestic product (GDP)   The market value of a country's output attributable to factors of production located in the country's territory.

gross national product (GNP)   The market value of all the final goods and services produced by a national economy.

H

Heckscher-Ohlin Theory Countries will export those goods that make intensive use of locally abundant factors of production and import goods that make intensive use of locally scarce factors of production.

historic cost principle Accounting principle founded on the assumption that the currency unit used to report financial results is not losing its value due to inflation.

home county The source country for foreign direct investment.

horizontal differentiation The division of the firm into subunits.

horizontal foreign direct investment Foreign direct investment in the same industry abroad as a firm operates in at home.

host country Recipient country of inward investment by a foreign firm.

human development index An attempt by the United Nations to assess the impact of a number of factors on the quality of human life in a county.

I

import quota A direct restriction on the quantity of a good that can be imported into a country.

individualism An emphasis on the importance of guaranteeing individual freedom and self-expression.

infant industry argument New industries in developing countries must be temporarily protected from international competition to help them reach a position where they can compete on world markets with the firms of developed nations.

integrating mechanisms Mechanisms for achieving coordination between subunits within an organization.

intellectual property Products of the mind, ideas (e.g., books, music, computer software, designs, technological know-how). Intellectual property can be protected by patents, copyright, and trademarks.

International Accounting Standards Committee (IASC) Organization of representatives of 106 professional accounting organizations from 79 countries that is attempting to harmonize accounting standards across countries.

international division Division responsible for a firm's international activities.

International Fisher Effect For any two countries, the spot exchange rate should change in an equal amount but in the opposite direction to the difference in nominal interest rates between countries.

International Monetary Fund (IMF) International institution set up to maintain order in the international monetary system.

international strategy Trying to create value by transferring core competencies to foreign markets where indigenous competitors lack those competencies.

J

joint venture A cooperative undertaking between two or more firms.

just-in-time (JIT) Logistics systems designed to deliver parts to a production process as they are needed, not before.

L

lag strategy Delaying the collection of foreign currency receivables if that currency is expected to appreciate, and delaying payables if that currency is expected to depreciate.

law of one price In competitive markets free of transportation cost and barriers to trade, identical products sold in different countries must sell for the same price when their price is expressed in terms of the same currency.

lead market Market where new products are first introduced.

lead strategy Collecting foreign currency receivables early when a foreign currency is expected to depreciate, and paying foreign currency payables before they are due when a currency is expected to appreciate.

lean production systems Flexible manufacturing technologies pioneered at Toyota and now used in much of the automobile industry.

learning effects Cost savings from learning by doing.

legal risk The likelihood that a trading partner will opportunistically break a contract or expropriate intellectual property rights.

Leontief Paradox The empirical finding that, in contrast to the predictions of the Heckscher-Ohlin theory, U.S. exports are less capital intensive than U.S. imports.

letter of credit Issued by a bank, indicating that the bank will make payments under specific circumstances.

licensing Occurs when a firm (the licensor) licenses the right to produce its product, use its production processes, or use its brand name or trademark to another firm (the licensee). In return for giving the licensee these rights the licensor collects a royalty fee on every unit the licensee sells.

local content requirement A requirement that some specific fraction of a good be produced domestically.

location economies Cost advantages from performing a value creation activity at the optimal location for that activity.

M

Maastricht Treaty   Treaty agreed to in 1991, but not ratified until January 1, 1994, that committed the 12 member-states of the European Community to a closer economic and political union.

maker   Person or business initiating a bill of lading (draft).

managed-float system   An exchange rate system in which some currencies are allowed to float freely, but the majority are managed in some way by government intervention.

management networks   A network of informal contract between individual managers.

market economy   The allocation of resources is determined by the invisible hand of the price system.

market imperfections   Imperfections in the operation of the market mechanism.

market makers   Financial service companies that connect investors and borrowers, either directly or indirectly.

market power   Ability of a firm to exercise control over industry prices or output.

mercantilism   An economic philosophy advocating that countries should simultaneously encourage exports and discourage imports.

MERCOSUR   Pact between Argentina, Brazil, Paraguay, and Uruguay to establish a free trade area.

minimum efficient scale   The level of output at which most plant-level scale economies are exhausted.

MITI   Japan's Ministry of International Trade and Industry.

mixed economy   Certain sectors of the economy are left to private ownership and free market mechanisms, while other sectors have significant government ownership and government planning.

mores   Norms seen as central to a functioning of a society and to its social life.

multilateral netting   A technique used to reduce the number of transactions between subsidiaries of the firm, thereby reducing the total transaction costs arising from foreign exchange dealings and transfer fees.

multinational enterprise (MNE)   A firm that owns business operations in more than one country.

multidomestic strategy   Emphasizing the need to be responsive to the unique conditions prevailing in different national markets.

N

new trade theory   The observed pattern of trade in the world economy may be due in part to the ability of firms in a given market to capture first-mover advantages.

nonconvertible currency   A currency is not convertible when both residents and nonresidents are prohibited from converting their holdings of that currency into another currency.

norms   Social rules and guidelines that prescribe appropriate behavior in particular situations.

North American Free Trade Agreement (NAFTA)   Free trade area between Canada, Mexico, and the United States.

O

oligopoly   An industry composed of a limited number of large firms.

output controls   Achieving control by setting goals for subordinates, expressing these goals in terms of objective criteria, and then judging performance by a subordinate's ability to meet these goals.

P

performance ambiguity   Occurs when the causes of good or bad performance are not clearly identifiable.

personal controls   Achieving control by personal contact with subordinates.

political economy   The study of how political factors influence the functioning of an economic system.

political risk   The likelihood that political forces will cause drastic changes in a country's business environment that adversely affect the profit and other goals of a particular business enterprise.

polycentric staffing   A staffing policy in an MNE in which host-country nationals are recruited to manage subsidiaries in their own country, while parent-country nationals occupy key positions at corporate headquarters.

positive sum game   A situation in which all countries can benefit even if some benefit more than others.

predatory pricing   Reducing prices below fair market value as a competitive weapon to drive weaker competitors out of the market ("fair" being cost plus some reasonable profit margin).

price discrimination   The practice of charging different prices for the same product in different markets.

price elasticity of demand   A measure of how responsive demand for a product is to changes in price.

product life-cycle theory   The optimal location in the world to produce a product changes as the market for the product matures.

pull strategy   A marketing strategy emphasizing mass media advertising as opposed to personal selling.

purchasing power parity (PPP)   An adjustment in gross domestic product per capita to reflect differences in the cost of living.

push strategy   A marketing strategy emphasizing personal selling rather than mass media advertising.

R

representative democracy   A political system in which citizens periodically elect individuals to represent them in government.

right wing totalitarianism   A political system in which political power is monopolized by a party, group, or individual that generally permits individual economic freedom but restricts individual political freedom, including free speech, often on the grounds that it would lead to a rise of communism.

S

sight draft   A draft payable on presentation to the drawee.

Single European Act   A 1987 act, adopted by members of the European Community, that committed member-countries to establishing an economic union.

Smoot-Hawley Tariff   Enacted in 1930 by the U.S. Congress, this tariff erected a wall of barriers against imports into the United States.

Social Democrats   Those committed to achieving socialism by democratic means.

social mobility   The extent to which individuals can move out of the social strata into which they are born.

social structure   The basic social organization of a society.

socialism   A political philosophy advocating substantial public involvement, through government ownership, in the means of production and distribution.

sogo shosha   Japanese trading companies; a key part of the *keiretsu*, the large Japanese industrial groups.

specialized asset   An asset designed to perform a specific task, whose value is significantly reduced in its next-best use.

specific tariff   Tariff levied as a fixed charge for each unit of a good imported.

spot exchange rate   The exchange rate at which a foreign exchange dealer will convert one currency into another on that particular day.

stock of foreign direct investment   The total accumulated value of foreign-owned assets at a given point in time.

strategic alliances   Cooperative agreements between two or more firms.

strategic trade policy   Government policy aimed at improving the competitive position of a domestic industry and/or domestic firm in the world market.

Structural Impediments Initiative   A 1990 agreement between the United States and Japan aimed at trying to decrease nontariff barriers restricting imports into Japan.

subsidy   Government financial assistance to a domestic producer.

swaps   The simultaneous purchase and sale of a given amount of foreign exchange for two different value dates.

systematic risk   Movements in a stock portfolio's value that are attributable to macroeconomic forces affecting all firms in an economy, rather than factors specific to an individual firm (unsystematic risk).

T

tax haven   A country with exceptionally low, or even no, income taxes.

tax treaty   An agreement specifying what items of income will be taxed by the authorities of the country where the income is earned.

temporal method   Translating assets valued in a foreign currency into the home currency using the exchange rate that existed when the assets were originally purchased.

theocratic totalitarianism   A political system in which political power is monopolized by a party, group, or individual that governs according to religious principles.

time-based competition   Competing on the basis of speed in responding to customer demands and developing new products.

time draft   A promise to pay by the accepting party at some future date.

trade creation   Trade created due to regional economic integration; occurs when high-cost domestic producers are replaced by low-cost foreign producers in a free trade area.

trade deficit   See current account deficit.

trade diversion   Trade diverted due to regional economic integration; occurs when low-cost foreign suppliers outside a free trade area are replaced by higher-cost foreign suppliers in a free trade area.

trade surplus   See current account surplus.

transaction costs   The costs of exchange.

transaction exposure   The extent to which income from individual transactions is affected by fluctuations in foreign exchange values.

transfer price   The price at which goods and services are transferred between subsidiary companies of a corporation.

translation exposure   The extent to which the reported consolidated results and balance sheets of a corporation are affected by fluctuations in foreign exchange values.

transnational corporation   A firm that tries to simultaneously realize gains from experience curve economies, location economies, and global learning, while remaining locally responsive.

transnational financial reporting   The need for a firm headquartered in one country to report its results to citizens of another country.

Treaty of Rome   The 1957 treaty that established the European Community.

tribal totalitarianism   A political system in which a party, group, or individual that represents the interests of a particular tribe (ethnic group) monopolizes political power.

turnkey project   A project in which a firm agrees to set up an operating plant for a foreign client and hand over the "key" when the plant is fully operational.

U

unbundling   Relying on more than one financial technique to transfer funds across borders.

V

value creation   Performing activities that increase the value of goods or services to consumers.

values   Abstract ideas about what a society believes to be good, right, and desirable.

vehicle currency   A currency that plays a central role in the foreign exchange market (e.g., the U.S. dollar and Japanese yen).

vertical differentiation   The centralization and decentralization of decision-making responsibilities.

vertical foreign direct investment   Foreign direct investment in an industry abroad that provides inputs into a firm's domestic operations, or foreign direct investment into an industry abroad that sells the outputs of a firm's domestic operations.

vertical integration   Extension of a firm's activities into adjacent stages of productions (i.e., those providing the firm's inputs or those that purchase the firm's outputs).

voluntary export restraint   (VER) A quota on trade imposed from the exporting country's side, instead of the importer's; usually imposed at the request of the importing country's government.

W

wholly owned subsidiary   A subsidiary in which the firm owns 100 percent of the stock.

World Bank   International institution set up to promote general economic development in the world's poorer nations.

World Trade Organization (WTO)   The organization that succeeded the General Agreement on Tariffs and Trade (GATT) as a result of the successful completion of the Uraguay round of GATT negotiations.

worldwide area structure   Organizational structure under which the world is divided into areas.

worldwide product division structure   Organizational structure based on product divisions that have worldwide responsibility.

Z

zero sum game   A situation in which an economic gain by one country results in an economic loss by another.

Index